Handbook of BRICS and Emerging Economies

Handbook of BRICS and Emerging Economies

Edited by

P.B. Anand

Shailaja Fennell

Flavio Comim

OXFORD
UNIVERSITY PRESS

OXFORD
UNIVERSITY PRESS

Great Clarendon Street, Oxford, OX2 6DP,
United Kingdom

Oxford University Press is a department of the University of Oxford.
It furthers the University's objective of excellence in research, scholarship, and education by publishing worldwide. Oxford is a registered trade mark of Oxford University Press in the UK and in certain other countries

First Edition published in 2021

Impression: 1

Published in the United States of America by Oxford University Press
198 Madison Avenue, New York, NY 10016, United States of America

British Library Cataloguing in Publication Data

Data available

Library of Congress Control Number: 2018957102

ISBN 978–0–19–882753–5

Printed and bound by
CPI Group (UK) Ltd, Croydon, CR0 4YY

To our respective families for their immense support and to our children who will see the world much better than we could.

PREFACE

Then there was the pandemic. Covid19 brought to a halt many things we have taken for granted. The global economy which was growing albeit sluggishly until 2019 is estimated to contract significantly in 2020 and the impact on the global economy is estimated to be deeper than that of the 2008 Financial Crisis. Recovery could be prolonged. The BRICS and emerging economies played a crucial role in powering the global recovery after the 2008 crisis as they themselves were less seriously affected than the G7 countries. However, even as the curve is being flattened in the UK and European countries, the rate of infections is still increasing significantly in the USA and in India, Brazil, South Africa, and Mexico.

The pandemic appears to have exacerbated underlying structural inequalities in some societies but there have also been many unlikely high performers that appear to have taken stringent measures early on while ditherers appear to have paid a high price in terms of the extent of infections and consequent mortality. Leadership and trust appear to be ever more valuable at this moment. Countries have been primarily focused on domestic responses in implementing various public health measures such as lockdowns, restrictions on public gatherings and events, international travel restrictions, quarantine, requirements for using face coverings, and so on. International cooperation has been strained. Trust and confidence in global governance institutions have been traded for scoring of political points in domestic electoral competition. While liberal democracies struggled hard to impose restrictions on freedoms of people as a last resort, authoritarian regimes and partial democracies appear to have been able to impose such restrictions with much ease and greater efficacy. Freedoms, equality and justice can be casualties in any crisis and the Covid19 pandemic is no exception.

It is our long-term interest in issues of freedoms, equality, justice, and sustainability that brought us together in the first place. In some ways, the three of us are grateful to Professor Amartya Sen (with all usual disclaimers) in that we met each other at the International Conference on Justice and Poverty organized by Flavio Comim at St Edmund's College in Cambridge in 2001. We collaborated on various workshops on the capability approach for several years and produced special issues of journals and worked on human development reports before embarking on this book.

This book is about hope. The experiences of the BRICS and other emerging economies are worthy of study not merely for the economic success potential they have but in all their dimensions including some positive and some negative elements. We firmly believe these shall remain relevant and useful as the international community of nations works together to build an alternative and a more sustainable path to post-pandemic recovery. When we embarked on this journey several years ago, our overarching argument was that there is a need to understand BRICS and emerging economies better if we want to build a more just and sustainable world. Our aim is to present a wide variety of perspectives and discuss a wider range of issues than were prevalent in books on BRICS or emerging economies. This aim enabled us to bring together a very wide range of experts from different disciplines and geographic contexts. We organized several panels at the annual conferences of learned societies including the Human Development and Capability Association, the Development Studies Association and convened workshops at Bradford and Cambridge. One of us also presented some findings at the meeting of the Africa All Party Parliamentary Group's hearing on the role of China in Africa. The book started with the aim of being a handbook—so we were sure it might have upwards of thirty chapters chapters—but the book grew as we became aware of interesting work of relevance which we felt we must include. One of us has worked on water resources and the journey of this book metaphorically resembles the flow of a river on its journey from high mountains as a stream to a wider, deeper river by the time of its confluence with the ocean.

A very large project of this kind would not have reached its climax without the help of numerous people. We begin with our most grateful to thanks to our fellow practitioners and our students who have been the main source of inspiration and encouragement in our long, complicated journey during which self-doubt can often creep up. While journals are no doubt very important for being arbiters of the peer-review process so fundamental to the progress of scientific thinking, we do believe that books are important contributors to structured learning and in-depth argumentation. It is our hope that practitioners, analysts as well as future generations of our students shall find books including this one to be an important source of comprehensive and systematic examination of the topic at hand.

We are very grateful to OUP Commissioning Editor Adam Swallow for the numerous discussions and support during the inception and early stages of this book. Katie Bishop helped us towards the final stages. Our huge thanks and enormous appreciation to the amazing copy-editor Pat Baxter for her meticulous reading of every single line of this book. We are also grateful to project managers who managed the production including Kumar Anbazhagan, S. Lakshmanan and especially Deva Thomas who oversaw the final stage of the production to completion.

We are grateful to all the contributors for their hard work in writing the initial versions of the chapters, responding to comments from the peer reviewers and their enormous patience and swift responses (most of the time) during the copy-editing stage of the book. We would like to thank Martin Daunton, John Weiss, Richard Jolly, Deepak Nayyar, and Raj Kumar for their support to of this project. We are also grateful to Des Gasper, Kaushik Basu, Shantanayan Devarajan, Amartya Sen, Meghnad Desai, Elaine Unterhalter, R. Sudarsan, Anita Patil-Deshmukh, Jaya Krishnakumar, Mozammel Huq, Emma Mawdsley, Yacob Mulugetta, Enrica Chiappero-Martinetti, Pasquale Demuro, Tim Scott, and many others whose encouragement and support has been pivotal to our work. We are grateful to the University of Bradford and University of Cambridge for various small research grants which enabled us to organize the workshops and conference panels mentioned earlier.

This is a handbook—so we have moved away from the tradition of listing chapters and what each of them contains. The reader can move through the book in any sequence and we hope that they will discover many different viewpoints within the book. We hope that the various insights discussed in this book continue to inform discussions and debates on development thinking towards the Sustainable Development Goals and beyond.

PBA
SF
FC

CONTENTS

LIST OF FIGURES

LIST OF TABLES AND BOXES

Tables

Boxes

LIST OF CONTRIBUTORS

Kamiljon Akramov is a Research Fellow at the International Food Policy Research Institute (IFPRI), where he conducts research on foreign aid, economic growth, agricultural development, and food and nutrition security in developing and transition countries. He is the author of *Foreign Aid Allocation, Governance and Economic Growth* (University of Pennsylvania Press, 2012). He received an MA in Development Economics from the Center for Development Economics at Williams College, Massachusetts, and a PhD in Economic Policy Analysis with concentration on International Development from the Pardee RAND Graduate School in Santa Monica, CA.

P.B. Anand is Professor of Public Policy and Sustainable Development and Head of Peace Studies and International Development at the University of Bradford where he has been teaching since 1998. He is a member of the Council of the Development Studies Association and a Fellow of the Human Development and Capability Association. He previously worked in a development bank in India and managed an executive education programme portfolio at Bradford for the staff of China Development Bank (2007–13) and the Aga Khan Foundation (2013–15). He was the principal author and team leader of the Mongolia Human Development Report 2011 and contributed to other UNDP studies on climate change, extractive economies, and sustainable development. His previous works include his book *Scarcity, Entitlements and the Economics of Water in Developing Countries* (2007) and several papers on applying the capability approach to issues related to access to water and sustainability. With Flavio Comim and Shailaja Fennell, he edited *New Frontiers of the Capability Approach* (Cambridge University Press, 2018).

Rashmi Umesh Arora is a Senior Lecturer in Development Economics at the University of Bradford. She previously worked as Research Fellow in the Department of Accounting, Finance and Economics, Griffith Business School, Griffith University, Australia. In 2007 she was a Postdoctoral Research Fellow at the Centre for Asia Pacific Social Transformation Studies, University of Wollongong, Australia. She has also worked as Assistant Adviser and Research Officer in the Reserve Bank of India (India's central bank) in its economic policy department for several years. Her current teaching and research areas are finance for development, economic growth, and developing economies. She has published in several well-known international journals including *World Development, Applied Economics, Journal of Developing Areas,* and *Third World Quarterly* among others.

Suresh Chandra Babu is the head of Capacity Strengthening Program and Senior Research Fellow at IFPRI, where he has been involved in institutional and human capacity strengthening for higher education and research in many countries such as South Asia and sub-Saharan Africa, including Ghana, Nigeria, Mozambique, Ethiopia, Kenya, Uganda, and South Africa for the past twenty-five years. He was educated at Iowa State University, Ames, Iowa (MS Economics and PhD Economics), and has published over sixty peer-reviewed journal articles and authored or edited fourteen books and research monographs.

Felipe A. Bellé is currently a Master of Science student in Applied Economics at the Universidade Federal do Rio Grande do Sul (UFRGS) (Porto Alegre, Brazil). He received his BS degree in Economics from the same university. His undergraduate thesis focused on the dysfunctionalities of education, and he worked for two years as a research assistant on a project on human development and education, addressing topics such as violence, education, and global data. His current research interest is focused on human development, education (cognitive and non-cognitive aspects), and theories of justice.

Luana P. Betti holds a Masters degree in Applied Economics at the UFRGS (Porto Alegre, Brazil), and she has a bachelor's degree in Economics from the same university. She studied part of her degree at the Universidade Nova de Lisboa (Lisbon, Portugal). She is a specialist in the evaluation of the economic impact of projects and public policies by Fundação Itaú Social (São Paulo, Brazil). Currently, Luana is the Urban Economics Specialist at the Cities Program of the World Resources Institute (WRI) Brazil.

Prabir C. Bhattacharya has published extensively in the areas of development economics, financial economics, demography, and gender studies. He is well known for his work on models of economic development and growth. He is currently the editor-in-chief of the *Journal of Interdisciplinary Economics*, having previously been editor-in-chief of *Progress in Development Studies*.

Mario Biggeri is Associate Professor in Development Economics at the Department of Economics and Management, University of Florence; Academic Director of the BA in Economic Development; International Socio-Sanitary Cooperation and Conflict Management; and Scientific Director of the research centre ARCO (Action Research for CO-Development). His research interests include local and industrial development, small and medium-sized enterprises (SMEs) and clusters, sustainable human development, international cooperation, social innovation, child well-being, persons with disabilities well-being, and impact evaluation.

Florence Bonnet is currently Senior Economist at the International Labour Organization (ILO). She is a quantitative analyst, working on issues of informality, social protection, and socio-economic security. She is currently responsible for national diagnostics of the informal economy. And she has been responsible for the statistics of the ILO's Social Protection and Research Departments. She has authored and contributed to a number of ILO's flagship reports, principally the World Employment and Social Outlooks and the World Social Protection Reports

Pádraig Carmody teaches Geography at Trinity College, University of Dublin (TCD) where he completed his undergraduate and masters work. At TCD he directs the Masters in Development Practice. His research centres on the political economy of globalization in Africa and he has published in journals such as *European Journal of Development Research*, *Review of African Political Economy*, *Economic Geography*, and *World Development*.

Saradamoyee Chatterjee is an Affiliated Lecturer in the Centre of Development Studies, University of Cambridge and a Bye-Fellow in Lucy Cavendish College, University of Cambridge. She is a Director of Studies in Land Economy in Lucy Cavendish College. She taught at the

Department of Land Economy and Department of Sociology, University of Cambridge. Before coming to Cambridge she received her PhD from the University of Delhi, India. Her first association with the University of Cambridge was as a postdoctoral researcher in the Von Hügel Institute, St Edmund's College. Her areas of interest and expertise are human and organ trafficking and other gender- and development-related issues.

David A. Clark is an Affiliated Lecturer at the Centre of Development Studies, University of Cambridge; and Senior Research Fellow at ARCO, University of Florence. He has worked extensively on poverty, inequality, and well-being from a capability perspective. His books include *Visions of Development: A Study of Human Values* (2002), *The Elgar Companion to Development Studies* (2006), *Adaptation, Poverty and Development: The Dynamics of Subjective Well-Being* (2012), and *The Capability Approach, Empowerment and Participation: Concepts, Methods and Applications* (2019).

Flavio Comim is a Development Economist and an Associate Professor of Economics at the IQS School of Management, Ramon Llull University in Spain and an Affiliated Lecturer at Land Economy University of Cambridge. He has worked for the United Nations Development Programme (UNDP) and has been a consultant for UNESCO, WHO, UNEP (UN Environment Programme), and ILO in several development projects. He has co-edited several books, including *The Capability Approach: Concepts, Measures and Applications* (2008) with Mozaffar Qizilbash and Sabina Alkire; *Capabilities and Happiness* with Luigino Bruni and Maurizio Pugno (2008); *Capabilities, Gender, Equality* (2014), with Martha Nussbaum; and *New Frontiers of Human Development* with Shailaja Fennell and P.B. Anand (2018).

Aline K. Dalcin is a PhD candidate in Applied Economics at UFRGS (Porto Alegre, Brazil). She holds a Masters degree in Applied Economics (2016) and a Bachelor's degree in International Relations (2013) from the same institution. Her research focuses on applied microeconomics, especially in the fields of economics of education and public policy. She also performs consultancies to institutions.

Martin Daunton was Professor of Economic History at the University of Cambridge from 1997 to 2015, and was previously Astor Professor of British History at University College, London (UCL). He has written extensively on British economic history since 1700, and particularly on economic policy and Britain's position in the world economy. He is currently completing a book on the economic government of the world since the World Monetary and Economic Conference of 1933.

Sabino da Silva Porto Jr is Doctor in Economics and Professor in the Postgraduate Programme in Economics (PPGE-UFRGS). He is Professor of Macroeconomics and Game Theory. He is interested in applied research in the areas of personal and regional income distribution and in the economics of education.

Catalina Droppelmann Roepke is currently the Executive Director of the Centre of Social Studies on Justice and Society at the Pontificia Universidad Católica in Chile. She has worked for over fourteen years researching on justice and crime at the national and international level. She developed her career in diverse settings: working in academia, think-tanks, and leading consultancies to international organizations. Catalina holds a BA in Psychology from the University of Valparaíso, an MPhil in Criminological Research, and is PhD(c) in Criminology at the University of Cambridge. Her interests are on youth crime, alternatives to incarceration, social exclusion, desistance from crime, and access to justice.

Shailaja Fennell is Reader in Regional Transformation and Economic Security at the Department of Land Economy and Centre of Development Studies, University of Cambridge. Her research interests are centred on the intersections between the sub-fields of institutional reform and collective action, food production, and rural development, and gender norms and gender gaps in development interventions; she has undertaken more than two decades of research in both Asian and African countries, and has a particular focus on comparative regional research to examine how the lives of rural and urban informal communities have been affected by the nature and directives of development policy.

Bernardo Frederes Krämer Alcalde has been a PhD student in Applied Economics at Programa de Pós Graduação em Economia in UFRGS since 2016, where he also completed his undergraduate and MSc studies. He is author and co-author of papers in Computer Science and in Informatics in Education. His research interests span Computational Economics, Game Theory, and Economics of Education.

Yan Gao is Assistant Professor at the Institute of New Rural Development and School of Agriculture and Biology at Shanghai Jiao Tong University where she has been teaching since she attained her PhD in Land Economy from the University of Cambridge. Her current research interests include rural–urban migration and rural development, as well as Guangxi and the recent collective ownership reform in rural China. Her articles include 'What is Absent from the Current Monitoring: Idleness of Rural Industrial Land in Suburban Shanghai?', *Habitat International* 49 (2015): 138–47; 'The Role of Tunqin Guanxi in Building Rural Resilience in North China: A Case from Qinggang', *The China Quarterly* 229 (2017): 44–63.

Giorgina Garibotto is Master in Human Development at the Latin American Faculty of Social Sciences (FLACSO), Argentina; and Sociologist and Specialist in Sociodemographic Analysis applied to management. She is a university Professor at FLACSO Argentina. Since 2005, she has been working at the Ministry of Social Development in the design, implementation, and evaluation of policies for early childhood, childhood, and adolescence. Currently she is Chief of Knowledge Management at the direction of Uruguay Crece Contigo (Uruguay Grows with You).

Stefanie Garry is an Economic Affairs Officer at the United Nations Conference on Trade and Development (UNCTAD). She works in the Office of the Director for the Division for Africa, Least Developed Countries and Special Programmes (ALDC). She previously served as an Economic Affairs Officer in the Economic Commission for Latin America and the Caribbean (ECLAC-Mexico), where she coordinated value chain studies in El Salvador and Costa Rica. Prior to joining ECLAC, she served as a Technical Officer at the ILO in Geneva. She holds a BA from the George Washington University in Washington DC, and an MSc in Economic Development Planning from Columbia University in New York.

Javier González is an economist specializing in education, inequality, social mobility, innovation, and social development. He is Director of SUMMA and Affiliate Professor at the Centre of Development Studies, University of Cambridge, where he teaches Institutional Economics and Political Economy of Development. He is also a researcher at the Millennium Science Initiative in Social Sciences 'Higher Education in Chile', housed at the Pontificia Universidad Católica de Chile and financed by the Ministry of Economy of Chile. He is also a member of several advisory boards and co-editor of UNESCO's 2020 Latin America's Education Monitoring Report on Inclusion. He has been a senior consultant for UNESCO, the World Bank and the Inter-American Development Bank (IADB), as well as a Cabinet Advisor for several government bodies in Chile. He holds a PhD and MPhil in Economic and Social Development from the University of Cambridge, and a BA and MA in Economics from the Pontificia Universidad Católica de Chile.

Degol Hailu is an Economist currently working as a Senior Advisor for UNDP. He earned his PhD from the School of Oriental and African Studies (SOAS), University of London. He has published widely on issues ranging from macroeconomics to industrialization and natural resource management.

Tadashi Hirai is an Affiliated Lecturer in Development Studies at the University of Cambridge. His previous publications include *The Creation of the Human Development Approach* (2017) and papers on applying the human development and capability approach to issues related to positive psychology.

Paul Jackson is Professor of African Politics, University of Birmingham, and Research Fellow in the Centre for African Studies, University of the Free State. He has published widely on peace-building, including 'Securing Sierra Leone, 1997–2013: Defence, Diplomacy and Development in Action' (Royal United Services Institute 2016) and *The Elgar Handbook of Security and Development* (Edward Elgar 2015).

Richard Jolly is Honorary Professor and Research Associate of the Institute of Development Studies at the University of Sussex, where he was Director from 1972 to 1981. He served as an Assistant Secretary General of the UN, from 1982 to 1995 as Deputy Executive of UNICEF, and from 1995 to 2000 as Special Coordinator of UNDP's *Human Development Report.* After leaving the UN, he was Co-Director of the UN Intellectual History Project and senior author of the final volume, *UN Ideas That Changed the World* (Indiana University Press, 2009). He has written or edited many books and articles on development and was knighted by the Queen in 2001 for his work in international development.

Aashish Kalra is a business professional and a pioneering equity investor in technology, infrastructure, real estate, energy, logistics, and hospitality. He currently serves as Chair of Cambridge Technology Enterprises and Cambridge Innovations. Since his appointment, he has been credited with transforming the organization into a leading global technology company, transforming organizations into 'AI-first' leaders, and working with selective Fortune 500 companies—a move that has seen the company's revenues triple since 2015. He is a socially conscious investor and has often lent support to new companies with finance, strategic recruitment, planning, and partnerships, while also serving on their boards of directors. He has often been quoted in leading Indian and international media and was featured in the 'Young Turks' programme on the Consumer News and Business Channel (CNBC).

Thomas H. Kang is Assistant Professor at Escola Superior de Propaganda e Marketing in Porto Alegre, Brazil. He holds a Masters in Economics from the Universidade de São Paulo and is currently a PhD candidate in Economics at UFRGS. He has worked in close collaboration with the World Council of Churches as a member of consultative and decision-making bodies. His main research interests include political economy of education, economic history, and development ethics.

Haider A. Khan is John Evans Distinguished University Professor at the Joseph Korbel School of International Studies, University of Denver. He has been chief international adviser to Arab Trade and Human Development in Cairo, and a senior economic adviser to the Secretary General of UNCTAD in Geneva, President of the Asian Development Bank, UNDP, and to other governments. He has published twenty-five books and over two hundred articles in professional journals spanning several areas of Global Political Economy and Security. He has received many international awards, and is also an award-winning poet, translator, and literary, music, and art critic. His critical works are on a wide range of specific global writers, artists, and topics, as well as many modern and postmodern Japanese poets. His poems have been anthologized widely.

Chinpihoi Kipgen is a Researcher at UNDP. She completed her postgraduate studies at Columbia University, New York. Her area of expertise includes econometrics and data visualization.

Nikolay Kolev joined University of Hull Business School as a PhD Management student in 2013. He holds with distinction an Msc in International Business from Hull University Business School. His interests cover international business, outward foreign direct investment (OFDI) of emerging economy companies including China, Russia, Brazil, the energy sector, and institutional theory.

Alice Krozer holds a PhD in Development Studies from the University of Cambridge, and is currently a postdoctoral researcher at the Colegio de México's Inequalities Seminar. Her research focuses on inequality, discrimination, privilege, and perceptions. She has worked as a consultant for the UN Economic Commission of Latin America and the Caribbean (ECLAC-Mexico), Oxfam, and various public sector dependencies in Mexico.

Xiaoyang Li has a PhD in Management from the College of Economics and Management of Southwest University in China, and is the Deputy Dean of Westa College of the university. She is the communication evaluation expert of the Natural Science Foundation of China, and procurement evaluation expert of China's Ministry of Finance. Her current research focus is on the issue of migrant workers in China. Sponsored by China Scholarship Council, Li worked with Dr Shailaja Fennell at the University of Cambridge for one year as visiting scholar. She has published more than ten papers on migrant workers' research.

Lucy McMahon works as a data analyst for a young people's charity and as a teacher and choreographer at a dance school. Previously she worked as a Lecturer in Human Rights at the

School of Advanced Study, University of London, and has conducted research projects in China, India, Brazil, and Cuba. Her PhD research (at the Centre of Development Studies at the University of Cambridge) explored the politics of the 2013–14 protest movement in Brazil.

Moazam Mahmood is currently Professor in Economics at the Lahore School of Economics and Visiting Professor at the Capital University of Economics and Business in Beijing. He was formerly Director of Research at the ILO, and responsible for producing its annual flagship titles, the *World Employment and Social Outlook* and the *Global Employment Trends* reports. He is a macroeconomist, having worked on global and regional economic crises over the past two decades.

Dan Meng is a PhD in Development Studies at the University of Cambridge, a Raymond and Helen Kwok Research Scholar, and a Consultant for the Asian Development Bank and the World Bank, with research interests comprising subjective well-being, the capability approach, and inclusive human development issues occurring during rural–urban migration especially in China. Her publications include 'An Analysis of the Lack of Correlation between Subjective Wellbeing and Objective Indicators for Human Development in China', *Journal of Cambridge Studies* 8/1 (2013): 48–72; and *Mobility and Aspiration: Policies for Securing Capabilities Regarding Migrant Children Education in China from 2005 to 2015*, HDCA 2015 Conference, Washington DC.

Deepanshu Mohan is Assistant Professor of Economics and Director, Centre for New Economics Studies at O.P. Jindal Global University. He is a Visiting Professor to the Department of Economics, Carleton University, Ottawa, Canada and currently works in areas of comparative development studies, political economy, and economic history.

Juan Carlos Moreno-Brid (PhD Cantab) has been Full Professor of the Faculty of Economics of the National Autonomous University of Mexico (UNAM) since 2015, after a long career as Research Coordinator and Associate Director of the Economic Commission of Latin America and the Caribbean (ECLAC-Mexico). He has written extensively on the development economics of Latin America, and in particular Mexico.

Deepak Nayyar is Emeritus Professor of Economics at Jawaharlal Nehru University, New Delhi, and an Honorary Fellow of Balliol College, Oxford. He was Distinguished University Professor of Economics at the New School for Social Research, New York. Previously, he taught at the University of Oxford, the University of Sussex, and the Indian Institute of Management, Calcutta. He served as Vice-Chancellor of the University of Delhi, and as Chief Economic Adviser to the Government of India. He has published widely in academic journals. His books include *Catch Up: Developing Countries in the World Economy* (Oxford University Press 2013).

Miguel Niño-Zarazúa is a Research Fellow at the World Institute for Development Economics Research of the United Nations University (UNU-WIDER) in Helsinki, Finland. He has published extensively in economics and development studies journals and edited several special issues and a book on the *Politics of Social Protection in Eastern and Southern Africa* (Oxford University Press, 2019). Miguel is Associate Editor and Member of the Editorial Advisory Board of the *Journal of International Development* and serves as member of the scientific panel of the Swedish Research Council for the Social Sciences. He holds a PhD in Economics from the University of Sheffield, UK.

Franklin Obeng-Odoom is with Development Studies at the University of Helsinki, where he is Associate Professor of Sustainability Science. A Helsinki Institute of Sustainability Science Professor, he leads the Global South theme. His research interests are centred on the political economy of development, cities, and natural resources. His books in these areas include *Reconstructing Urban Economics: Towards a Political Economy of the Built Environment* (Zed Books 2016).

Kenia Parsons has a PhD in Social Policy from the London School of Economics and Political Science and an MPhil in Development Studies from Cambridge University. Her research interests include social protection, transfers, conditionalities, welfare, and work policies in both developing and developed countries. She has worked for governments, non-governmental organizations (NGOs), international organizations, and multilateral development banks in Latin America, Africa, and Oceania.

Izete Pengo Bagolin is a Doctor in Economics and a Professor at Pontifícia Universidade Católica do Rio Grande do Sul (PUCRS) Business School in Brazil. She works in the field of Development, teaching economic development and poverty and human development. Her research interests are in poverty, inequality, capability and the human development approach, and education.

David Potts is an economist and now a Visiting Researcher at the University of Bradford having retired from full-time work in January 2019. He is the editor of *Tanzanian Development: A Comparative Perspective* (James Currey, 2019) and has worked in a number of developing countries including short-term assignments in six sub-Saharan African countries and a six-year assignment for the Food and Agriculture Organization (FAO) as joint head of the Project Preparation Unit in the Tanzanian Ministry of Agriculture.

C. Raj Kumar is the Founding Vice-Chancellor of O.P. Jindal Global University (JGU), Sonipat, India; Founding Dean of the Jindal Global Law School; and Director of the International Institute for Higher Education Research & Capacity Building (IIHEd) at JGU. He is a Rhodes Scholar and also holds academic qualifications from Harvard University, University of Hong Kong, University of Delhi, and Loyola College, India. He is an accomplished legal scholar and works in the fields of human rights and development, comparative constitutional law, terrorism and national security, corruption and governance, law and disaster management, legal education, and higher education. He has held consultancy assignments with UNU-WIDER, UNDP, and the UN Office of the High Commissioner for Human Rights.

Vinode Ramgopal is currently Chair of Magellan Global Inc. He was formerly Head of Lehman Brothers Global Privatization and Sovereign Advisory business. He is a graduate of the London School of Economics and Merton College, Oxford.

Fábio A. Rasche Jr is currently a Masters student in Applied Economics at the Universidade Federal do Rio Grande do Sul (Porto Alegre, Brazil). He received his BS degree in Economics from the same university. His undergraduate thesis focused on gender inequality in labour markets and education. His current research interest is focused on human development, education, and impact evaluation.

Vsevolod Samokhvalov obtained a BA in International Relations (Odessa, Ukraine), MA in South-East European Studies (Athens), and PhD in International Relations (Cambridge). He worked in 2002–06 as a Research Fellow at the International Center for Black Sea Studies and the European Union Institute for Security Studies; in 2006–07 at the BBC Ukraine; in 2007–08 as a Eurasian Affairs analyst for *New Europe* weekly. He is currently Lecturer in the Centre for International Relations Studies at the University of Liege and Visiting Professor in the College of Europe. He has written extensively on political developments in the post-Soviet space, Russia–EU relations in the Balkans, and the Black Sea region.

Vibhor Saxena's field of specialization is development economics. His research interests are based on a broad range of issues of the Global South: energy, inequality, poverty, microfinance, gender, and demography. His research is focused on applied econometrics and he has employed several large datasets (unit level and aggregated) in his research. He is currently working on energy issues and son preference in India.

Richard Sidebottom is an Affiliated Lecturer at the Centre of Development Studies. His current research focus is on agricultural value chains (millets and cotton), rural entrepreneurship, and capacity building including work for the Global Challenges Research Fund (GCRF), funded Cambridge University-wide TIGR2ESS project (Transforming India's Green Revolution by Research and Empowerment for Sustainable food Supplies). He holds academic qualifications from Cambridge, London Business School, and the University of Oxford and has over twenty years' experience in financial markets. His research interests include the political economy of development and markets, innovation in agricultural commodity chains, and the expansion of livelihood opportunities for youth and women through skills training and entrepreneurship.

Cassandra Sweet is a political economist with expertise in international development. Her research focuses on the effectiveness of institutions in delivering outcomes in sectors including health, education, and innovation. She is the author of myriad studies in leading global editorial houses and journals including *World Development*, *Economics and Politics*, and *Globalization and Health*. She currently works as a consultant to international agencies and as Visiting Professor of Politics at Bard College. Her applied policy work spans projects for the World Bank, the World Health Organization, the UN's Economic Commission on Latin America, and local NGOs throughout Latin America.

Sunil Tankha's research spans the design and implementation of what could broadly be termed reform strategies. In particular, he analyses how the distribution of risks and pay-offs in reform designs affect their performance and sustainability, and how institutions influence how resources are channelled and distributed in these processes, thus setting the stage for politics and conflicts. He is also keenly interested in how political rhetoric is used to form coalitions of diverse stakeholders in support of and in opposition to specific reform designs. His work in this area was originally based on large energy and water infrastructure reforms, and he has recently extended this to climate change and sustainable development initiatives. He has conducted field-based research throughout the developing world, in particular in Brazil and India. His publications have appeared, among others, in the *Journal of Latin American Studies, Global Policy, Energy Policy,* and *Water Policy*. He received his PhD from the Massachusetts Institute of Technology (MIT) and currently teaches at the Institute of Social Studies of Erasmus University, Rotterdam, in the Netherlands.

Utku Teksoz is an economist and policy advisor at the United Nations, which he joined in 2009. Since then, he has worked on a wide range of issues, including global economic governance, green growth, and sustainable development, and served as Sherpa/Finance Deputy Assistant for the United Nations during preparations for various G20 summits. His current work is focused on Africa. Prior to joining the UN, he worked at the Credit Suisse European Economics team and at the Office of the Chief Economist of the European Bank for Reconstruction and Development (EBRD). While at EBRD, he was part of the team that designed and implemented the first household survey in transition countries in 2006. He has also held appointments as a visiting lecturer at the University of Greenwich Business School and Regent's College. He has graduate and undergraduate degrees in Economics and Economic History from Bogazici University in Istanbul and a PhD in Economics with honours from the University of Munich (LMU).

Nicolás Trajtenberg is a Lecturer in Criminology at the School of Social Sciences, Cardiff University. His main areas of interest are cross-cultural criminology, rational and irrational mechanisms in violence, risk factors of offline and online youth violence, prisons and punitiveness.

Olga Ulybina is a Marie Curie postdoctoral researcher at Tampere University, Finland. She has wide expertise in transnational sociology, international development, global governance, and public policy analysis. She received her doctorate in International Development and Institutional Economics at the University of Cambridge, UK. She carried out research at the UN Economic Commission for Europe (UNECE) in Geneva, Cambridge Central Asia Forum, and as an ASK Prize Research Fellow at the WZB Berlin Social Science Center. She focused on natural resource management and child welfare, mostly in the ex-Soviet region. She has also had engagements within the public sector, ranging from environment and social care to education and local government.

Terry van Gevelt is an Assistant Professor in Environmental Sustainability with joint appointments at the Department of Politics and Public Administration and the Department of Civil Engineering at the University of Hong Kong. Previously, he held teaching and research positions at the Department of Land Economy and the Centre of Development Studies at the University of Cambridge.

John Weiss is Emeritus Professor of Development Economics at the University of Bradford, UK, specializing in project analysis, industrialization, and industrial policy. He has written extensively on these issues including several textbooks, for example (with Steve Curry) *Project Analysis in Developing Countries* (2000) and the *Economics of Industrial Development* (2011). He is joint editor (with Michael Tribe) of the *Routledge Handbook on Industry and Development* (2016).

He has been a consultant to many international organizations including most recently the Asian Development Bank and the United Nations Industrial Development Organization.

Yue Xu joined Cardiff University as Lecturer in International Business and Management in November, 2016. She has also acted as Concurrent Visiting Scholar of Wolfson College, University of Cambridge (2012–18). Previously, she worked as Lecturer and Programme Leader of MSc in International Business in the Hull University Business School. There, she accumulated rich experience and innovative methods in teaching and supervising executive MBA students both in the UK and in Asia (Hong Kong and Singapore). After she completed her MBA in Financial Studies at Nottingham University Business School, she joined the MRes and PhD programme of the Cranfield School of Management with full scholarship. She earned her doctoral degree based on her investigation of the regulatory impact on entry strategies of multinational banks in China.

Daiane Zanon is currently an MSc student in Applied Economics at UFRGS (Porto Alegre, Brazil). She received her BS degree in Economics from the same university. She is a specialist in the evaluation of public policies and social projects by Fundação Itaú Social (São Paulo, Brazil). Her research interests include human development, economics of education, and labour economics.

Part I
Introduction

1 BRICS and emerging economies

An assessment

P.B. Anand, Flavio Comim, and Shailaja Fennell

Introduction: from an acronym to an 'arranged marriage'

This book is about human development and what we can learn from the individual and collective experiences of Brazil, Russia, India, China, and South Africa (BRICS) and many other so-called 'emerging markets and developing countries' (EMDCs) or emerging economies. Together the five BRICS countries alone account for 3.11 billion people or 42 per cent of world population and 22 per cent of world economy (gross national income). If we include other emerging economies as well then the case is even more overwhelming. Studying the BRICS and emerging economies (or we could call these BRICSEE which sounds like 'BRISCy' as our teenage daughters would have called such a group of countries) can help us understand many profound issues and challenges for human well-being and prosperity. The challenges faced by these countries are enormous, their successes where they have occurred are inspiring, and the project of development remains far from complete. As Professor Robert Lucas (2002: 21) wrote about the challenges of economic growth: 'Once one starts to think about them, it is hard to think about anything else.'

It is by now customary that a book about BRICS starts with a mention of Jim O'Neill (2001) and the coining of the acronym BRICs in 2001 to mean Brazil, Russia, India, and China (hence BRICs with a small 's') and that G7 should really inlude some of these countries. Much has been discussed since 2001. A search on the Web of Science with the key word BRICS produced 817 results—more than a half of these in the years 2015 and 2016 (see Figure 1.1).

As with any concept, it appears that with BRICS too there are three distinct phases. Phase 1 (approximately from 2001 to 2008) focused on BRICS and emerging economies as the next drivers of growth, hence we can call this the 'growth phase'. During this period, BRICS were discussed a lot more among and by those in the financial services than in academia. Phase 2 can be thought of as the years between 2008 and 2014 when there have been calls for closer and critical reflections even as BRICS began to emerge as

P.B. Anand, Flavio Comim, and Shailaja Fennell, *BRICS and emerging economies: An assessment* In: *Handbook of BRICS and Emerging Economies.* Edited by: P.B. Anand, Shailaja Fennell, and Flavio Comim, Oxford University Press (2021).
DOI: 10.1093/oso/9780198827535.003.0001

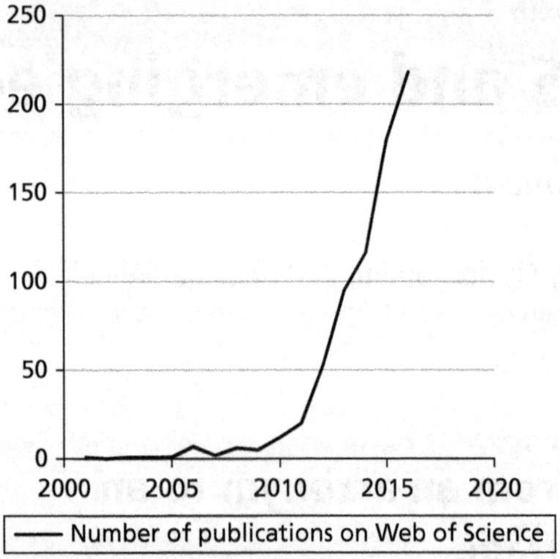

Figure 1.1 Growth in research on BRICS

Source: Produced by authors based on Web of Knowledge (n.d.). Available at https://login.webofknowledge.com, accessed 3 November 2018.

Table 1.1 Most and least popular areas of enquiry on BRICS within 817 articles published between 2001 and 2016

Most frequent	Number of articles	Least frequent	Number of articles
Economics	171	Demography	1
International relations	161	Philosophy	1
Political science	91	Humanities and multidisciplinary	1
Business finance	63	Ethics	2
Planning development	62	History	3
Management	58	Social issues	4

Source: Computed by the authors based on the Web of Knowledge (n.d.). Available at https://login.webofknowledge.com, accessed 3 November 2018.

a club and become institutionalized. *The Economist* (in 2008) and *Foreign Policy* (2012) had already proclaimed doubts about BRICS. There have been several conferences and think-tanks focused on the implications of BRICS for global governance especially during this phase. Currently, we appear to be in Phase 3 which is under way. However, the predominant lenses or angles of analysis appear to be economics, international relations, political science, and business discipline perspectives (see Table 1.1).

Our motivation for this book is to take a wider and multidisciplinary perspective on BRICS and emerging economies covering a range of issues including history, ethics, human rights and security issues, race, gender and intersectionality dimensions, and global and regional governance dimensions in addition to the usual economic and financial perspectives. Critics of neoliberalism in particular and capitalism in general are deeply dissatisfied with the current modes of production and distribution and in that perspective, focusing on BRICS or emerging economies is not useful because they are just part of a global phenomenon of processes of exploitation and expropriation of wealth—perhaps semi-peripheral countries in a Wallerstein world occupying the space between the core and the periphery (see Altinbas 2014; Bond and Garcia 2015). While we acknowledge this perspective, we feel that ideology-based discussions do not offer pragmatic and policy-relevant insights. Another important criticism can be that BRICS are another example of an opportunistic group of countries coming together without any common set of values or principles. Jacobs and van Rossem (2014: S63) note that 'The BRIC countries occupy vastly different power positions in the global system and attain these positions by drawing on different power sources.' Other critics include Krugman (2013) who does not think Russia—basically a 'petro-economy'—should be included in this group.

Our motivation for a book on BRICS and emerging economies is to understand intrinsic and extrinsic reasons for the 'emergence' of these countries, their challenges, and what we can learn from these to inform theories of development in general and also about the political economy of global governance and about the slow and very limited change in existing international organizations that leads to the emergence of alternative global and regional economic groupings and the dynamics that shape this.

The extrinsic reasons for studying BRICS and emerging economies is to acknowledge that while the economic lens has been important, we do need other lenses to understand the full nature of human development. The social and demographic dimensions of BRICS and emerging economies present many puzzles but do include some specific successes too. The number of people living in extreme poverty as defined by an income threshold of US$1.90 per day has fallen significantly worldwide but the record of China in reducing extreme poverty has been the largest contributor to this.

The environmental dimensions attract much attention especially in relation to climate change and the urgent need for economies to decarbonize their growth. Many believe that the shaking of hands between President Obama and Xu Jinping was crucial to the Paris climate change accord (the Paris Agreement). Commitments by China and India have made the deal possible, though for some critics the deal is not strong enough and both countries got away rather lightly.

The natural resources dimensions of BRICS have always been important. Russia is currently natural resource dependent. Other BRICS countries and especially China and India are not only important consumers of global natural resources but they are also important and significant contributors. Many of the emerging economies including Mexico, Chile, Turkey, Indonesia, and Argentina are also significant natural resource extractors.

The rise of BRICS has also provided a variety of national narratives on human security. These national constructions in the BRICKSy countries emerge from their own historical experiences that include colonial and imperial encounters, national movements for independence, and the political and social rights that emerged from such nation building moments. International non-governmental organizations (NGOs) and agencies have often been critical of these different national perspectives on citizenship, yet these different pathways are a natural response to the manner in which both capitalism and globalization have impacted on these countries.

From the point of view of the evolution of global or international organizations there are also important BRICSEE dimensions or angles. The United Nations and the Bretton Woods institutions, namely the World Bank and the International Monetary Fund (IMF) have an institutional inertia. Observation by Rosenstein-Rodan (1984: 219) continues to be relevant: 'Today we have competence, finance, and no democracy in the international banks—and democracy and no finance in the United Nations.' This has been an important reason for the emergence of other forums for international cooperation. Though much has been discussed on the South–South Cooperation (SSC), each of the BRICS countries has its own economic and political reasons to both be part of the South–South club and for going it alone.

A random collection of countries chosen for analytical reasons poses practical questions. Usually regional blocs emerge due to geographic proximity, contiguity, and historical and cultural proximities. However, BRICS countries have very little by way of language or common historical past. Brazil, South Africa, and India have had a colonial past but they have been colonized by different 'masters' and hence the colonial institutions they inherited are very different. Russia (as the Soviet Union from 1945 until 1992 and as the Russian Federation since 1992) and China (since 1971) have been permanent members of the United Nations Security Council while others, especially India, have aspirations for permanent membership. Throughout the 1950s, while China was still isolated from international forums, India used to consider it a moral obligation to stand up for China. However, this stance changed after the 1962 Sino-Indian war. Ever since, both nations have been circumspect about each other. BRICS's contributions to global institutions have been significant but variable. China shares a border with Russia and India but this contiguity has not previously fostered regional cooperation. Therefore, creating a common institution from a diverse group of countries that have very little in common is much like an arranged marriage.

What started as a clever analyst's acronym has by now become formalized with an annual meeting of the heads of government, several regular ministerial meetings, and the creation of multiple forums for cooperation. Though there have been a few special issues of journals and a few books, and many of them do include some profound insights into not merely the economic but also political, social, and environmental dimensions of BRICS, the overwhelming lens through which BRICS are seen has remained an economic one. No doubt the economic argument originally put forward by Jim O'Neill in 2001 and subsequently further examined in a Goldman Sachs book published in 2007 remains an important one. What happens in BRICS can have a very significant impact on global economic growth. However, our motivation is that 'BRICSEE' countries deserve attention not merely for their economic size or performance but mostly as evidence of the power of development in transforming societies and individuals.

BRICS in the global economy

Economic growth and development are complex historical and social processes. Though we may use certain models or theories to explain specific aspects, often such models are abstract views of the reality. Based on the works of Rosentein Rodan, W. Arthur Lewis, Robert Solow, Paul Roemer, Elhanan Helpman, and many others, we know that a number of factors including investment in the factors of production and productivity-enhancing technology, education, economies of agglomeration, together with a growth-enhancing developmental state can work together to create the conditions for a sustained period of growth and development. Growth is not identical to development but only an essential prerequisite for it. In the following sections, while we attempt to examine the 'emergence' of BRICS taking one aspect or 'stylized fact' at a time, it should be remembered that each such discussion provides only a partial and incomplete picture. While we know this, it is still important to consider each of those stylized facts. We will follow this with a brief discussion of the combination of factors.

UNDERSTANDING THE 'EMERGENCE' OF BRICS

In 2001 when the term BRICs was being coined, together these countries constituted around 8 per cent of world income. In some quarters, these were being presented as the new kids on the block. Of course, China and India are cradles of civilization. Angus Maddison (2007) estimates that for nearly seventeen centuries—China until 1820 and India until 1600—each had GDP larger than that of twelve countries of Europe put together. Since 1820 with the 'industrial revolution' and a number of other factors, Europe's GDP raced ahead. Notwithstanding the so-called 'divergence' (see Parthasarathi 2011), BRICSEE countries are hardly new kids on the block. This is evident from world income data going back to 1960.

Even when gross national income (GNI) is measured in current prices without purchasing power parity (PPP) adjustment, already by 1960 China, India, and Brazil were figuring in the top thirteen economies and they have continued to do so throughout the period 1960 to 2015 (see Table 1.2).

China's opening of the economy with the reforms initiated by Deng Xiaoping in 1979 contributed to foreign investment growth; but further reforms especially in 1994 in setting up a financial architecture and subsequent entry into the World Trade Organization (WTO) by China in 2001 constitute two further milestones in the transformation of China's economy (see Knight and Ding 2012; Lin 2012). In the case of India, ever since independence, the 'commanding heights' of the economy were occupied by the state. This seems to have been in line with the thinking that infrastructure and social overhead capital must be provided before industrial growth can take off. However, due to a severe

Table 1.2 World's top thirty economies 1960–2015

	1960	1970	1980	1990	2000	2010	2015
1	United States*	United States	United States	United States	United States	United States	United States
2	France*	Germany*	Japan	Japan	Japan	China	China
3	China*	Japan	Germany	Germany	Germany	Japan	Japan
4	Japan*	France	France	France	United Kingdom	Germany	Germany
5	Italy*	United Kingdom*	United Kingdom	Italy	France	France	United Kingdom
6	Canada*	Italy	Italy	United Kingdom	China	United Kingdom	France
7	India*	China	Canada	Canada	Italy	Brazil	India
8	Australia*	Canada	Spain	Spain	Canada	Italy	Italy
9	Brazil*	India	Brazil	Russian Federation*	Mexico	India	Brazil
10	Sweden	Brazil	Netherlands	Brazil	Brazil	Canada	Canada
11	Mexico*	Australia	China	China	Spain	Russian Federation	Korea, Rep.
12	Netherlands	Spain	Mexico	India	Korea, Rep.	Spain	Russian Federation
13	Spain	Netherlands	India	Netherlands	India	Australia	Australia
14	Belgium	Sweden	Saudi Arabia*	Australia	Netherlands	Korea, Rep.	Spain
15	Switzerland	Mexico	Australia	Korea, Rep.	Australia	Mexico	Mexico
16	Venezuela, RB	Argentina*	Sweden	Switzerland	Switzerland	Netherlands	Turkey
17	South Africa*	Belgium	Belgium	Sweden	Argentina	Turkey	Indonesia
18	Philippines	Switzerland	Switzerland	Mexico	Turkey	Indonesia	Netherlands
19	Austria	South Africa	Austria	Belgium	Sweden	Switzerland	Switzerland
20	Finland	Turkey*	South Africa	Iraq	Russian Federation	Saudi Arabia	Saudi Arabia
21	Norway	Denmark	Argentina	Austria	Belgium	Sweden	Argentina
22	Greece	Austria	Denmark	Turkey	Austria	Belgium	Sweden
23	Nigeria	Greece	Indonesia*	Finland	Saudi Arabia	Iran, Islamic Rep.	Nigeria
24	Chile	Norway	Turkey	Argentina	Hong Kong SAR, China	Poland	Poland
25	Colombia	Venezuela, RB	Venezuela, RB	Denmark	Poland	Norway	Belgium
26	Korea, Rep.*	Nigeria	Korea, Rep.	Iran, Islamic Rep.	Norway	Argentina	Norway
27	Pakistan	Finland	Norway	Saudi Arabia	Denmark	Austria	Thailand
28	Congo, Dem. Rep.	Iran, Islamic Rep.	Nigeria	Norway	Indonesia	Venezuela, RB	Austria
29	Algeria	Pakistan	Greece	South Africa	South Africa	South Africa	United Arab Emirates
30	Portugal	Korea, Rep.	Iraq	Indonesia	Greece	Nigeria	Philippines
New entrants to global 30	—	6	3	1	3	0	2
Present G20 members*	12	4	2	1			

Note: * Denotes current members of the G20 group of countries when they first appeared in global-30 list of countries.

Source: Authors' summary based on GNI at current prices from World Development Indicators (World Bank various years).

balance of payments crisis that led to a major set of reforms being introduced in 1991 it appears that this has been a watershed in India's economic policy (Joshi and Little 1996; Joshi 2017).

With regard to Brazil, Brainard and Martinez-Diaz (2009: 2) note that '...between 1947 and 1962, the country grew at an average rate of 6 per cent annually and was seen as one of the brightest stars in the world economy'. They note that a few years later between 1968 and 1973 Brazil's economic growth reached more than 10 per cent. As with most countries in Latin America, in the wake of international debt during the 1980s, Brazil's growth faltered and Brazil experienced hyperinflation towards the end of the 1980s and early 1990s.

Data for the Russian Federation are available from 1990 and in that year it was the ninth largest economy. This position has since slightly dropped, to twentieth place in 2000, but then bounced back to eleventh place in 2010 and twelfth in 2015. If we look at the top thirty economies in terms of size from 1960 for every decade, namely 1960, 1970, 1980, 1990, 2000, 2010, and the most recent year with complete data 2015 we have a matrix of 30 rows and 7 columns (210 cells). Just thirty-five countries occupy 186 of these possible 210 cells with only 24 of the 210 cells being occupied by nine other countries. This analysis suggests that there is very little change in the top thirty economies of the world over a period of fifty-five years. In fact, the United States, India, Brazil, and Nigeria are in the same rank among the global thirty in 2015 as they were in 1960. The top ten economies in 1970 remain the top ten economies in 2015 though relative placements changed, with Japan and China moving up slightly and Germany, France, Italy, and Canada moving down slightly. In addition, when we look at the current membership of the G20 group of countries, we can see that nineteen of these countries were already part of the global top thirty economies by 1980. This analysis suggests that we need to be cautious when using concepts such as 'rising powers' or 'emerging economies'. These are no doubt important descriptors. However, most of the emerging economies are hardly new kids on the block.

SHARE OF BRICS IN GLOBAL ECONOMIC GROWTH

In the World Development Indicators, GNI adjusted for PPP has been available only since 1990. In that year BRICS share of world economy was 16 per cent. By the time of Jim O'Neill's coining of the term BRICs in 2001, this share had increased to 18 per cent. By 2016, this had increased to 31 per cent. In contrast, the G7 countries, namely the United States of America (USA), Germany, Japan, France, United Kingdom, Italy, and Canada together formed 48 per cent of world economy in purchasing power terms in 1990; but this has declined, rather slowly at first, declining to 42 per cent by 2004; since then the decline has been faster—to 32 per cent by 2016. Thus, in purchasing power terms, in 2016 the five BRICS countries held more or less the same share of the world economy as the G7 countries (Figure 1.2)

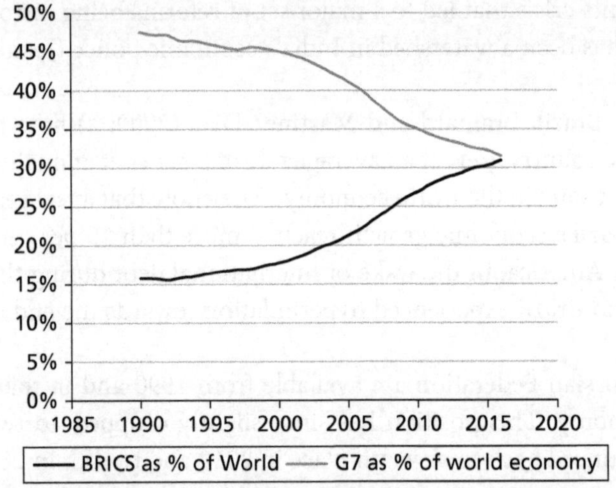

Figure 1.2 Share of BRICS and G7 countries in world economy in purchasing power terms
Source: Authors' calculation based on World Development Indicators (World Bank various years).

A graph such as the one in Figure 1.2 may look like a perfect example of the zero-sum game thinking where the rise of one group means the decline of another (Mohan 2016: 280). In fact, without BRICS it is possible to argue that the global economic recovery post-2008 contraction would have been more expensive, longer lasting, and may have had a greater and longer time impact on the world's poorest people. In 2014, for the first time in recent history, China became the world's largest economy in PPP terms, overtaking the USA. India became the world's third largest economy overtaking Japan in 2010 (Figure 1.3).

The rise of BRICS is even better captured by their contribution to growth in the global economy between 1990 and 2016 (Figure 1.4). After the 2008 financial crisis, while there was a contraction in the G7 economies, growth in BRICS economies has been an important contributor to the recovery. Thus in 1991, 15 per cent of global economic growth came from the BRICS economies while 42 per cent came from the G7 economies. The position had been reversed by 2016 when BRICS contributed to 47 per cent of the global economic growth while G7 economies contributed 14 per cent of global growth.

BRICS countries have always been among the top ten economies but their recent growth episode has propelled them to be the prime movers of the global economic growth engine. The research question of interest is what is their secret and how did they do it? The economic growth of BRICS differs in a significant way from that of the East Asian miracle of the 1980s, that of Japan and the four East Asian economies of Hong Kong, Taiwan, Singapore, and the Republic of Korea. When these economies industrialized, their per capita GDP started to grow significantly and there is clear convergence towards the levels of per capita income in the G7 countries. While the aggregate national income of BRICS countries especially China has been growing significantly, the growth in

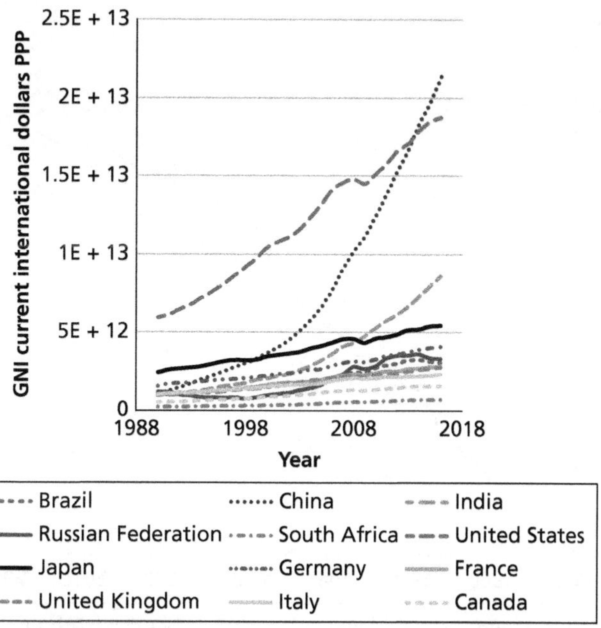

Figure 1.3 GNI of BRICS and G7 countries in current US$ in purchasing power terms

Source: Authors' calculation based on World Development Indicators (World Bank various years).

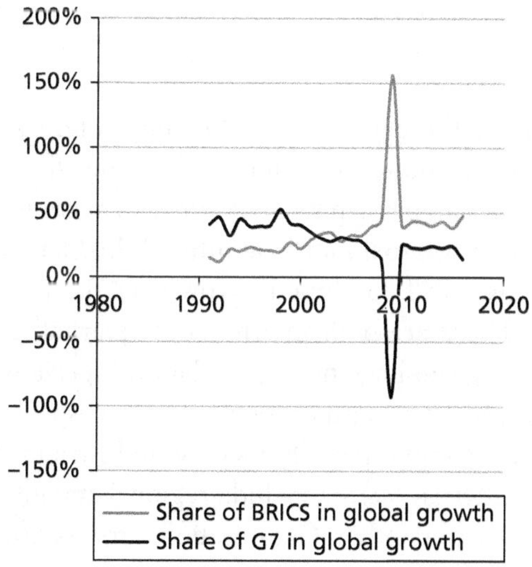

Figure 1.4 Contribution of BRICS and G7 economies to global economic growth

Source: Based on World Development Indicators data (World Bank various years).

per capita GDP still has a long way to go to catch up with G7 economies (Figure 1.5). This is especially so because inequality in BRICS tends to be much greater than it is in many of the G7 countries and thus the average GNI or GDP per capita does not fully capture the unequal distribution (examined in a subsequent section, Economic Inequality).

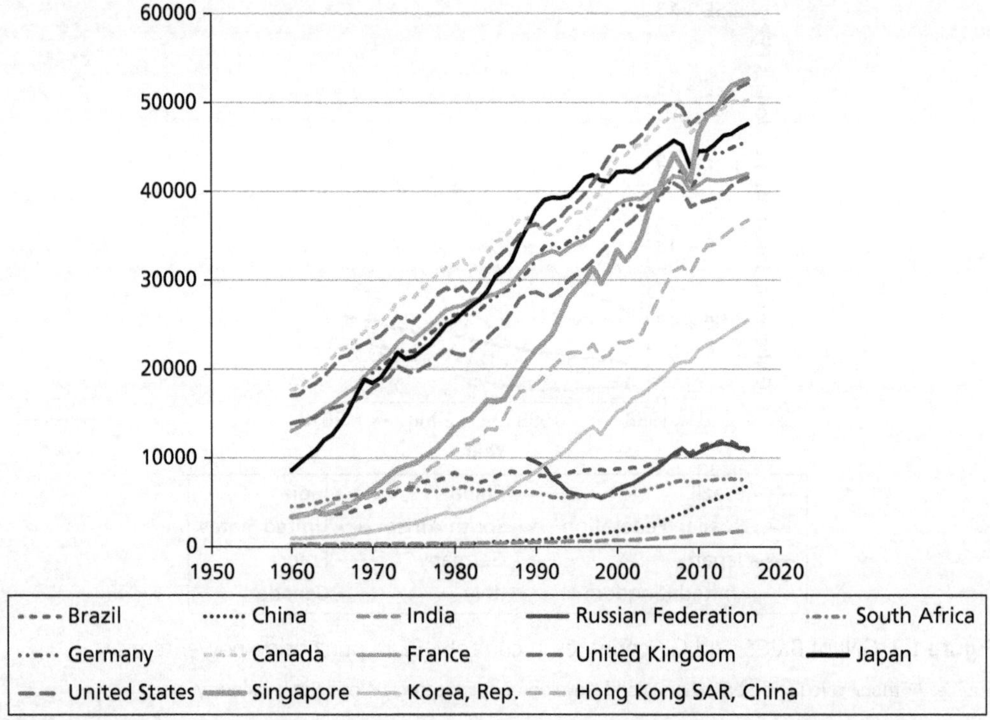

Figure 1.5 Real GDP per capita (constant 2010 US$)—G7, BRICS, and the Asian tigers

Source: World Development Indicators (World Bank various years).

Thus, while in terms of the aggregate size of the economy BRICS are significant contributors to the global economy with almost the same share of the global income growth as the G7 economies, in per capita GDP terms an average person in BRICS today has a real income that is approximately a fifth of his/her counterpart in the G7 economies. Whether BRICS will continue to grow over the next two to three decades is a different question. There are both internal and external factors—internal factors include demographic change and ageing of population especially for Brazil and China; education and the urbanization pattern of the population especially for India; an ability to diversify their economies and especially increase industrialization (for Brazil, India, and South Africa). The external factors include regional stability, cooperation of other nations especially the G7, and other Organisation for Economic Co-operation and Development (OECD) economies.

UNDERSTANDING WHETHER INTERNATIONAL AID PLAYED A ROLE

Official development assistance (ODA) can be an important source of scarce foreign currency and can tide countries over, especially when they are facing hardship due for example to natural disasters, humanitarian emergencies, or recovery from conflict.

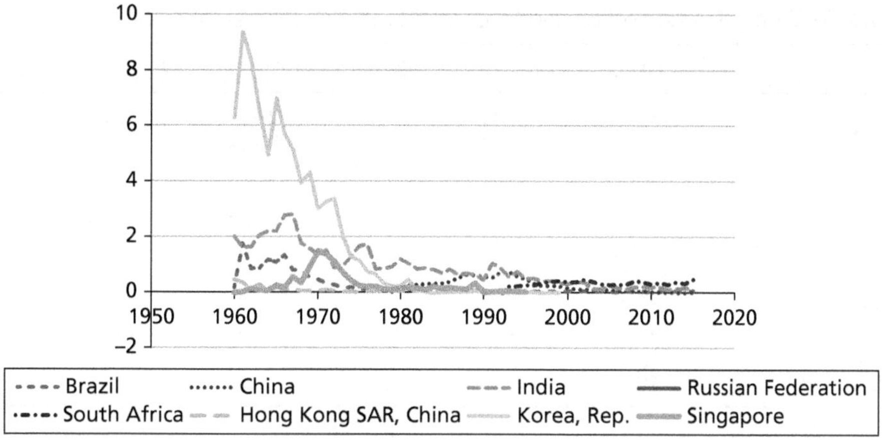

Figure 1.6 Net ODA received as % of GNI

Source: World Development Indicators (World Bank various years).

BRICS countries especially India and China have been aid recipients for a very long time. Hence it is pertinent to ask whether aid played the pivotal role in helping these countries transform into the powerhouses of today. We can examine this by looking at the share of ODA in GNI. As a share of its GNI, India was most aid dependent in the 1960s. Due to the drought of 1966 caused by a complete failure of the 1965 monsoon, India depended on aid for food import. Thus, in 1967, for India the amount of net ODA received formed the highest ever share of GNI at about 2.7 per cent. In comparison, the Republic of Korea received a much greater share of its GNI as net ODA throughout the 1960s and until 1972. Data for China are available only from 1979 onwards. Russia had been receiving ODA since 1990 and South Africa only from 1993 (after the ending of apartheid). Since 1992, for each of the BRICS countries, ODA formed less than 1 per cent of their respective GNI (Figure 1.6). By the time O'Neill coined BRICs in 2001, each of these countries received less than 0.5 per cent of their GNI in the form of aid.

When we look at the total amount of aid received in 2013 at constant prices, in the 1960s, BRICS accounted for nearly 20 per cent of global ODA and official aid (Table 1.3). This came down to around 5 per cent for the first decade of the current millennium and has formed around 3 per cent for the second decade so far.

Russia received around 20 billion dollars of aid in the 1990s. Net ODA and aid received by China peaked in the 1990s but came down quickly in the first decade of the twenty-first century. Since 2010, China has been a net aid contributor. India has its own aid programme even as it continued to receive aid in the period 2010–15. This raised many critical comments in the popular press, especially in 2011. Thus overall while aid has been an important contributor to each of BRICS countries especially during the years of their acute need, the fact that aid has formed less than 1 per cent of their national incomes especially during the last twenty-five years suggests that aid cannot explain the 'emergence' of BRICS. If aid was the sole factor, then that cannot explain South Africa's trajectory.

Table 1.3 Total net ODA and official aid (in constant 2013 US$) received by BRICS countries

	1960–69	1970–79	1980–89	1990–99	2000–09	2010–15
Brazil	13,725	5,643	3,959	2,194	2,920	5,902
China	–	44	19,206	33,214	17,277	(1,550)
India	67,787	47,412	42,770	25,021	18,459	16,498
Russian Federation	–	–	–	20,336	9,065	–
South Africa	–	–	–	4,384	8,831	7,603
Hong Kong SAR, China	210	115	395	187	30	–
Korea, Rep.	15,211	10,507	1,178	(411)	(900)	–
Singapore	294	1,057	631	104	30	–
World	**413,996**	**604,847**	**799,977**	**881,965**	**1,119,800**	**895,855**
BRICS total	81,512	53,099	65,935	85,149	56,552	28,454
BRICS asWorld %	19.7%	8.8%	8.2%	9.7%	5.1%	3.2%

Source: Based on World Development Indicators (World Bank various years).

While BRICS nations have been engaged in providing development assistance to other countries for quite some time, this process has become more formalized and structured since 2000. Through the Forum on China Africa Cooperation (FOCAC) summits, China has been committing a significant amount of development assistance in various forms including through infrastructure projects, concessional loans, and technical assistance especially in Africa. Since BRICS countries do not provide data in the same format as the OECD countries, it is difficult to assess whether and how much aid BRICS have been providing. Using an alternative dataset such as AidData 2.0, gives some idea but this remains a partial picture. Annual gross disbursements during 2010–14 from BRICS amounted to more than US$5 billion (Asmus et al. 2017). This represents slightly more than Italy's aid but is significantly smaller than almost any of the other G7 members. China is by far the biggest contributor to aid from BRICS. Both China and India provide much of their aid in the form of lines of credit which may not strictly qualify as aid. Also, both China and India provide grants and also other forms of development assistance including training, investment in infrastructure and services, and other forms of economic cooperation. Analysis based on AidData 2.0 does not suggest that China is more likely than OECD Development Assistance Committee (DAC) donors to be giving assistance to natural resource rich countries or dictatorships (Anand 2014; Royal African Society 2014). Mohan (2015: 281) argues that 'China impacts on African development in multiple ways that go well beyond the Western focus on aid' due to inter-elite brokerage which can '...bypass domestic channels of debate and accountability and so tends to undermine good governance'. Others argue that the behaviour of these donors is different from traditional donors and within the group there are differences in that while all five BRICS countries are cautious and opaque in their approach to assistance and peacebuilding, there are some differences for instance in terms of support for democratic institutions and grassroots institutions mainly from India, Brazil, and South Africa (IBSA) (see for example, Richmond and Tellidis 2014). From an analysis of India's aid activity over 2008 to 2010, Fuchs and Vadlamannati (2013) found that political self-interest dominated India's aid allocation. The overall volume of aid from BRICS is still small compared to development assistance from OECD–DAC. However, there is some evidence to suggest that the increasing presence of 'new donors' such as BRICS results in fewer conditions being attached to World Bank loans (Hernandez 2017). In that sense, these new donors seem to be influencing overall development assistance architecture both directly with their aid and indirectly by affecting the behaviour of traditional donors.

BRICS AND INTERNATIONAL TRADE

Historically, international trade has been an important source of growth for many countries. Has this also been the case for BRICS? Trade as a share of GDP in 2015 for the G7 economies is in the range of 28 per cent (USA in 2015) to 85 per cent (Germany). For the East Asian tiger economies, this is in the range of 83 per cent (Republic of Korea) to 389 per cent (Hong Kong). In comparison, for BRICS, it is in the range of 26 per cent (Brazil) to 61 per cent (South Africa). In 1970, the share of trade in GDP was fairly low for Brazil (14 per cent), China (5 per cent), and India (7.7 per cent). Only South Africa among BRICS had a much higher level of trade even in the 1960s and had remained above 40 per cent throughout the period from 1961 to 2015 except for the three years 1991–93.

In this section we mainly examine this by looking at exports. The share of exports in GDP for BRICS nations has steadily increased over the last fifty-five years (see Figure 1.7). While exports already constituted nearly 30 per cent of GDP for South Africa even in 1960, this proportion remained more or less at the same level in 2016 and indeed for many of the years in between. For China, India, and Brazil the share of exports in GDP remained well below 10 per cent until 1980. The gradual opening up of China pushed up the share of Chinese exports to GDP ratio in the 1980s but the real growth in exports from China took place in the 1990s. The share of exports to GDP in China increased from 14 per cent in 1990 to 21 per cent in 2000 to reach a peak of 37 per cent in 2007 before declining significantly to 24 per cent in 2009. Since then, it has remained in the mid- to low twenties. India's exports did not take off until the late 1990s but the magnitude is smaller than that of China's: 6 per cent in 1980, 7 per cent in 1990, and 13 per cent in the year 2000. In India's case the share of exports in GDP continued to grow after the 2008 financial crisis to reach its peak of 25 per cent in 2013; since then this share has been declining, reaching 19 per cent in 2016. In comparison, it appears that Brazil has not been a big exporter. The share of exports to GDP for Brazil are: 7 per cent in 1960, 7 per cent in 1970, 9 per cent in 1980, 8 per cent in 1990, 10 per cent in 2000, reaching its peak of 16 per cent in 2004, declining to 10 per cent in 2010, and remaining in that range with 12 per cent in 2016. Russia's sudden opening up in the early 1990s appears to have led to the 'gold rush' of 1992, an anomalous year—followed by wild fluctuations in the next decade—that may have been the year that made the first wave of

Russian billionaires, though Triesman (2016) argues that most of Russia's billionaires of 2015 were actually those who made their wealth in finance—and more diversified trade than merely profiting from the privatization of state assets—or mainly in the oil sector. It is clear that BRICS did not respond in an identical fashion to the financial crisis and the flow from individual BRICS countries had a significant effect on growth rates and employment in the Eurozone and OECD (Fennell et al. 2013).

In contrast, the three East Asian tiger economies have a much higher share of exports to GDP ratio. Even in 1960, Singapore's exports were 162 per cent of its GDP while Hong Kong's exports were 83 per cent of its GDP. Korea on the other hand started from a very low base of 4 per cent in 1960 and increased its share of exports in GDP slowly at first to reach 11 per cent in 1970, 28 per cent in 1980, and 34 per cent in 1986; but declining to

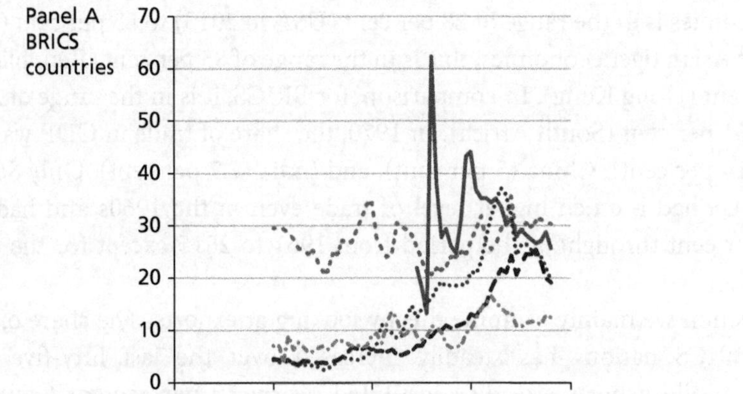

Figure 1.7 Exports as % of GDP for BRICS economies and the three East Asian tiger economies of Hong Kong, Singapore, and South Korea

Source: Based on World Development Indicators (World Bank various years).

25 per cent in 1990. They rose again to reach a peak of 40 per cent in 1998, declining slightly to 35 per cent in 2000; they went up again in the years between 2000 and 2010 to reach 49 per cent by 2010, then reaching a peak of 56 per cent in 2012 before coming down again to 42 per cent in 2016. As Chang (2003: 258) finds, small countries tend to have a much higher share of exports and thus the experience of East Asian tiger economies may not be appropriate for the very large economies of BRICS. Also, import substituting industrialization may require a certain scale and a large enough domestic economy as in the case of BRICS. The story is not merely that China's exports increased very significantly. China's share of the world's creative goods exports increased from 15.3 per cent in 2002 to 33.1 per cent in 2015 (based on United Nations Conference on Trade and Development Stats database [UNCTAD 2017a]). Among other BRICS, this indicator is very small (less than 1 per cent) for Brazil, Russia, and South Africa. India's global share of creative goods exports had increased from 1.6 per cent to 3.3 per cent by 2015.

While international trade by BRICS was increasing, intra-BRICS trade remains a small part of this. Singh (2016) finds that the share of BRICS trade in world trade increased from 7.33 per cent in 2001 to 17.25 per cent in 2015 (more than doubling). However, the share of intra-BRICS trade of their overall trade increased slightly from 6 per cent in 2001 to 12 per cent in 2015—still a very small share of their overall trade. The potential for increasing intra-BRICS trade is noted (EX-IM Bank of India 2016).

Globalization and trade are controversial and ideological policy issues. At a theoretical level, openness to international trade can promote competition, encourage innovation, and benefit consumers. However, the reality is quite complex. A criticism of the neoliberalism exemplified by the so-called Washington Consensus (Williamson 1990) is that such policies encouraged countries to open up trade without the necessary institutional mechanisms for redistribution, participatory governance, and social protections and thus contributed to increasing inequality. While the growth and success of the East Asian tigers, namely Hong Kong, Singapore, Taiwan, and South Korea, has been predominantly linked to their ability to increase their trade and shift from low value to high value exports, trade can only be a part of an overall growth strategy. In fact, critics such as Chang (2002, 2003) suggest that one can reach incorrect recommendations based on the time period chosen for analysing the link between openness to trade and growth. Such critics argue that the present G7 nations, namely richer members of OECD, pursued protectionist policies for a fairly long time before opening up for international trade; but developing countries were encouraged to open up their trade well before institutional development took place. Since 2015, due to the impact of the 2008 financial crisis, the pursuit of policies of austerity, the contraction of public services in most of the G7 countries, have contributed to the polarization of views about globalization. The evidence of a link between trade and reducing poverty is mixed. From an analysis of thirty African countries for the period 1981 to 2010, Le Goff and Singh (2013: 12) found that '. . . more openness results in a reduction in poverty when the financial sector is deeper, education levels are higher, and governance is stronger'. Osakwe and Poretti (2015) argue that for trade to reduce poverty 'the nature of economic transformation matters' and that such transformation has to be inclusive. Based on selected case studies of Asia, Africa, and Latin America they identify several key policies for social inclusion.

PRODUCTIVITY AND INNOVATION IN BRICS

Structural change is about the transformation of economy from low productivity to high productivity equilibrium. However, as Rosenstein-Rodan (1984: 208) reminded us, the 'pursuit curve' i.e. 'the dynamic path towards dynamic equilibrium, not merely the conditions which must be satisfied at the point of equilibrium' is important. The BRICS countries are at different stages in their 'pursuit curve'. The total factor productivity at constant prices with base year 2011 poses some interesting issues (see the three panels in Figure 1.8). Among the G7 economies, Japan and Italy saw a dramatic rise in their total factor productivity in the 1960s. Among the Asian tiger economies, we see a steep increase in the 1960s for Singapore while Korea's is a steady increase in productivity much like that of G7 economies such as Germany and France. Among the BRICS economies, Brazil and South Africa had much higher productivity in the 1960s, which then fell sharply in the 1980s. India and China on the other hand have been steadily increasing their productivity. Among these fourteen economies, only six countries had their total productivity in 2014 higher than it was in 2011. For all other countries total factor productivity in 2014 was lower than in 2011. The six countries were: Japan, USA, UK, China, India, and Russia.

Data presented in the World Development Report 2013 (World Bank 2013) capture the phenomenal growth in productivity per worker in China in both secondary and tertiary sectors between 1995 and 2010 (see Table 1.4).

In South Africa, data are limited to only five years but during this period value added per worker increased only in the primary sector. In Russia, there appears to be an enormous increase in value added per worker mainly in the tertiary sector.

A few studies have noted the importance of productivity aspects especially in relation to the multinational enterprises (MNEs) from BRICS when they compete with MNEs in OECD countries (Sanfilippo 2015) and that innovation is leading to improvement in labour productivity in BRICS (Kurt and Kurt 2015). The economic sanctions imposed by the European Union (EU) on 31 July 2014 (Council regulation 833/2014) following Russia's annexation of Crimea may contribute to improving productivity in some sectors and decreasing productivity in others. The overall effect of these sanctions on growth and productivity would depend on the relative weights of the sectors affected in one way or another. Current data do not allow us to examine this. However, we can see from EU and BRICS trade data (European Commission 2017) that between 2013 and 2016, EU imports of fuel from BRICS have decreased significantly while all other imports such as machinery and vehicles, for example, continued to increase. It is highly likely that fuel imports to the EU are predominantly from Russia and the sanctions led to a significant reduction in imports from Russia. This in a context when globally in 2015 trade growth

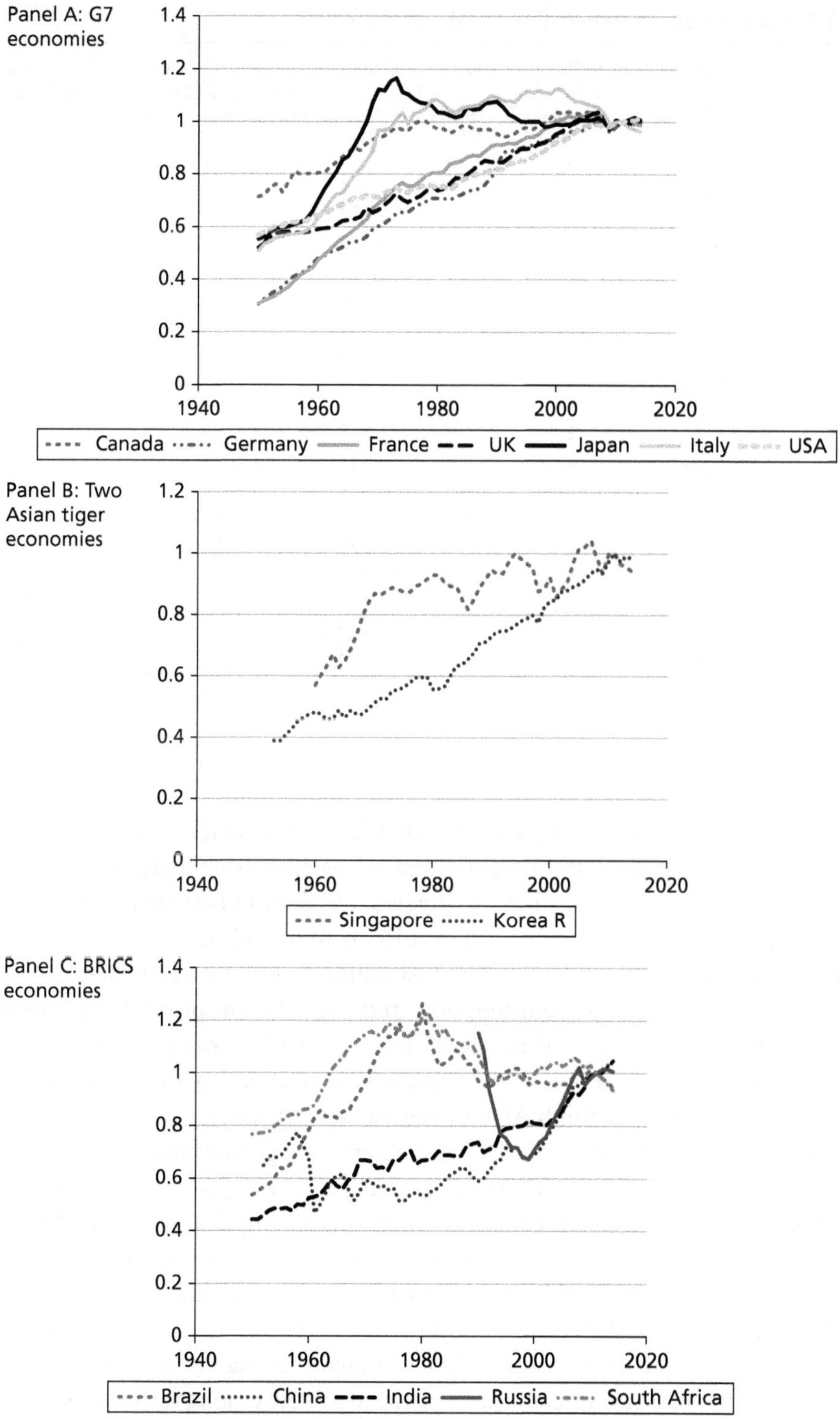

Figure 1.8 Total factor productivity in constant national prices, 2011

Source: Feenstra et al. 2015 (Penn World Tables 9.0).

Table 1.4 Value added per worker (2005 US$ per year)

	Sector	1995	2005	2010	Annual growth rate 1995–2005	Annual growth rate 2005–10
Brazil	Primary	2,764	2,618	5,048	−1%	19%
	Secondary	17,135	13,428	18,599	−2%	8%
	Tertiary	15,379	10,798	16,888	−3%	11%
	Overall	12,450	9,633	15,252	−2%	12%
China	Primary	576	912	1,649	6%	16%
	Secondary	3,077	6,683	10,799	12%	12%
	Tertiary	1,972	4,425	7,788	12%	15%
	Overall	1,500	3,386	6,145	13%	16%
India	Primary	530	620	1,154	2%	17%
	Secondary	1,919	2,733	4,089	4%	10%
	Tertiary	2,395	3,917	6,775	6%	15%
	Overall	1,163	1,846	3,318	6%	16%
Russia	Primary	2,951	5,713	7,744	9%	7%
	Secondary	6,205	13,115	15,498	11%	4%
	Tertiary	5,560	16,253	27,896	19%	14%
	Overall	6,594	11,503	16,536	7%	9%
South Africa	Primary		6,241	10,725		14%
	Secondary		22,418	22,059		0%
	Tertiary		18,468	16,554		−2%
	Overall		18,701	17,639		−1%

Source: World Bank (2013).

has been mainly in energy related goods while trade in all other sectors had seen a contraction (UNCTAD 2017b: 15) suggests the sanctions may have had a significant negative effect on Russia's fuel exports to the EU. However, Russia's overall exports as share of GDP did not decline in 2015 (28 per cent) but declined in 2016 (to around 25 per cent).

Tugcu and Tiwari (2016) used a Granger causality test to see if there is a causal relationship between energy consumption and total factor productivity growth in BRICS. Their analysis suggested no significant causal relationship. However, they do find that non-renewable energy use may have a positive effect on growth in productivity in Brazil (natural gas) and South Africa (coal-based electricity).

Beausang (2012: 98) noted that '…the absence of genuine innovation capability leaves the BRICs with no engine of long-term economic growth'. To examine this argument, we can look at the Global Innovation Index compiled by the World Intellectual Property Organization (Cornell University et al. 2017). These data in Table 1.5 show that China does better than G7 or East Asian tigers in the dimension of knowledge outputs. In all other six dimensions and in terms of overall rank, China alone among BRICS is comparable to the East Asian tiger economies. China's overall rank of 22 puts it closely behind the East Asian economies but ahead of Italy among the G7 economies. All other BRICs are way back in their rankings. Brazil, Russia, India, and South Africa score very poorly on institutions, creative outputs, and infrastructure dimensions. When we dig into these indicators and their components, the only dimension in which India is in the top ten is in the proportion of science and engineering graduates among all graduates. On that score India is within the top ten globally; but merely producing engineering graduates does not lead to innovation. For example, among the G7 economies, the USA ranks eighty-fifth on the proportion of science and engineering graduates out of all graduates but that does not affect the fact that the USA is the world's fourth most innovative economy.

Thus it is clear that innovation was not the driver of economic growth in four of the five BRICS while it appears that in case of China economic growth is associated with China's growing presence as an innovative economy though there are a few aspects especially concerning institutions where China still has some progress to be made.

With regard to productivity, de Vries et al. (2015: 84) reach a different conclusion. After conducting a detailed analysis of structural change in the four BRICs following McMillan and Rodrik (2011) methodology, de Vries et al. note that '... for China, India, and Russia reallocation of labour across sectors is contributing to aggregate productivity growth, whereas in Brazil it is not'. However, the authors note that if we take into account the different contributions from formal and informal sectors, the result is somewhat different. They note that while in Brazil growth in formalization contributed to productivity enhancement, in India the opposite has been happening in the growth of the informal sector since the reforms. However, this is interesting because normally economic reforms such as those initiated in India since 1991 led to dismantling of the so-called 'license raj'. Thus if anything one would have expected fewer reasons for economic activity to hide under the radar by remaining in an unorganized sector. Data available for the years between 2010 and 2016 suggest that the share of the informal sector in non-agricultural wage employment is around 33 per cent for South Africa, between 36 per cent and 40 per cent for Brazil, and around 82 per cent for India (World Development Indicators [World Bank various years]). An earlier study showed that policies such as a minimum wage appear to have had an impact on informal sector wages in Brazil, India, Indonesia, and South Africa where it was argued that while informal sector wages may cluster around a minimum wage, some informal sector workers may continue to be paid well below the legal minimum (Saget 2006). Demographic factors, existing inequalities—and the potential for social security to exacerbate these—and improving access for rural workers are identified as some of the key barriers for improving the coverage of social security in BRICS (ISSA 2017: 168).

SAVINGS AND INVESTMENT

Economic growth can occur in many ways such as by expanding factors of production (mainly labour, if possible capital and until the nineteenth century by expanding land/territory), by improving efficiency through technological advancement, and through innovation. Traditional theories of economic growth suggest capital accumulation,

Table 1.5 Global Innovation Index and components rankings for BRICS, East Asian tigers, and G7 economies compared to number one ranking Switzerland

*	GII	Inst	HC	Infra	MarSoph	BusSoph	KO	CO
Brazil	69	91	50	57	74	43	85	83
China	22	78	25	27	28	9	4	26
India	60	92	64	73	39	55	38	85
Russian Federation	45	73	23	62	60	33	45	62
South Africa	57	54	60	75	21	57	65	78
Singapore	7	1	5	2	4	2	11	32
Hong Kong (China)	16	3	28	4	2	16	25	25
Korea, Rep.	11	35	2	13	14	17	6	15
Canada	18	7	20	18	3	24	19	27
France	15	24	12	12	11	18	20	12
Germany	9	18	10	20	16	15	8	7
Italy	29	38	32	19	36	35	26	33
Japan	14	13	14	9	12	11	12	36
United Kingdom	5	9	6	5	5	13	13	4
USA	4	17	13	21	1	8	7	10
Switzerland	1	8	7	6	7	3	1	3

Notes: * GII—Global innovation index; Inst—institutions; HC—human capital; Infra—Infrastructure; MarSoph—Market sophistication; BusSoph—Business sophistication; KO—knowledge outputs; CO—Creative outputs.
Source: Cornell University et al. (2017).

technological change, investment in human resources, and productivity growth as some of the key drivers of growth.

The gross savings ratio does not give a full picture but it can give a hint of the level of investment. From the three panels in Figure 1.9 it is evident that the level of savings in G7 economies has been consistently decreasing; among BRICS, in China and India it has been increasing significantly especially since 1998. This trend is similar to what the Asian tigers achieved during their growth phase in the 1970s and 1980s.

From the three panels in Figure 1.10, we can see that the gross capital formation follows this trend. As did Germany and Japan after the Second World War, and the East Asian economies did in their growth phase, BRICS—especially China and India—have been investing mainly in infrastructure to power economic growth.

Knight and Ding (2012: 160) noted that China's very high investment has both demand side and supply side factors. As China opened up, especially after entry into the WTO in 2001, the potential for exports grew significantly and the opportunity to make profits attracted investment from the demand side. Savings by both households and firms provided the resources. Knight and Ding note that in in the early 1990s the biggest contribution to savings was from households while this position had changed by 2000 when savings from enterprises became the largest contributor to total savings.

Notwithstanding the general and overall increasing trend of saving and investing, BRICS have a long way to go in terms of their infrastructure quality. For example, the World Economic Forum presents data for 2015 under the so-called twelve pillars of

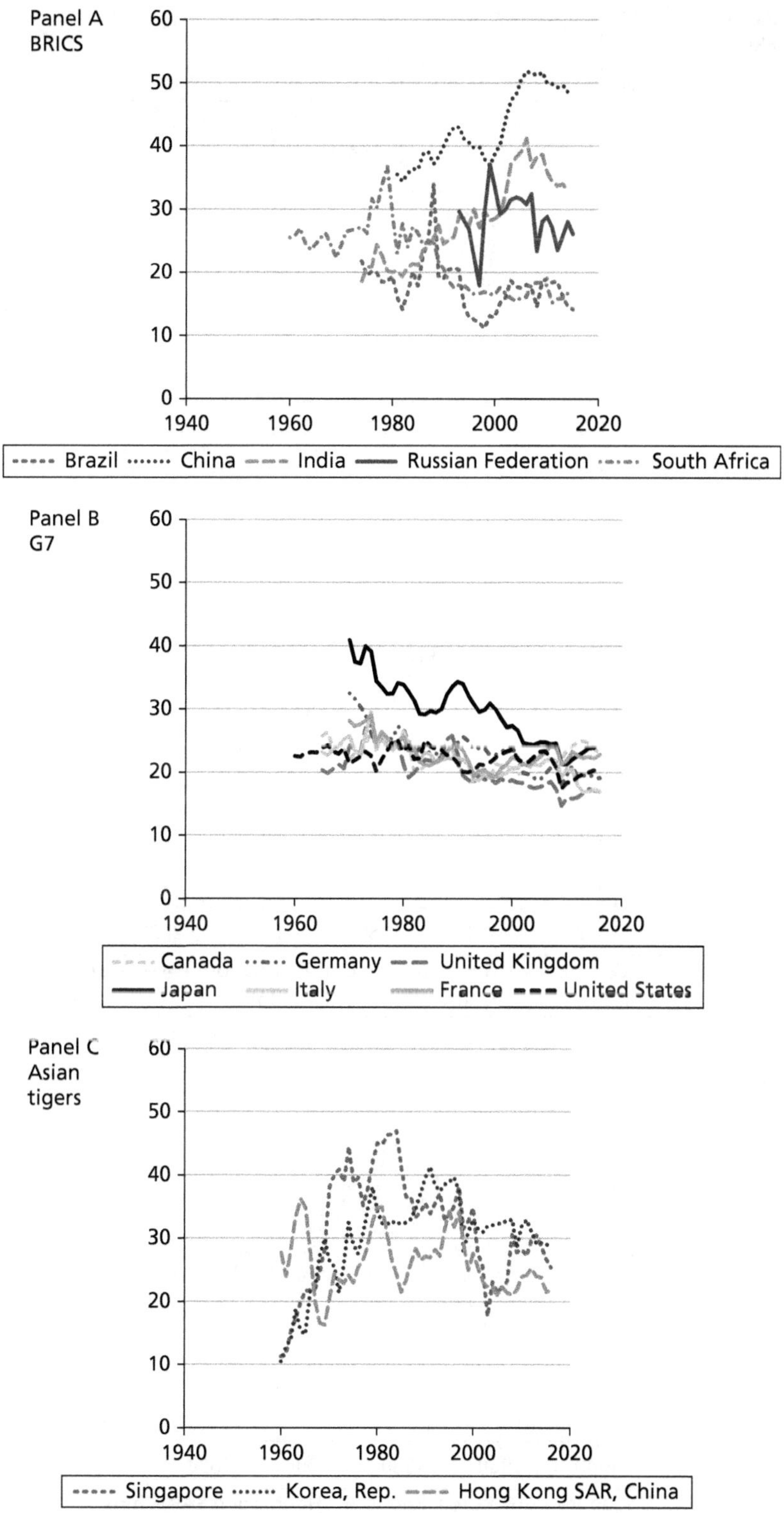

Figure 1.9 Gross savings rate in BRICS, G7, and Asian tigers

Source: World Development Indicators (World Bank various years).

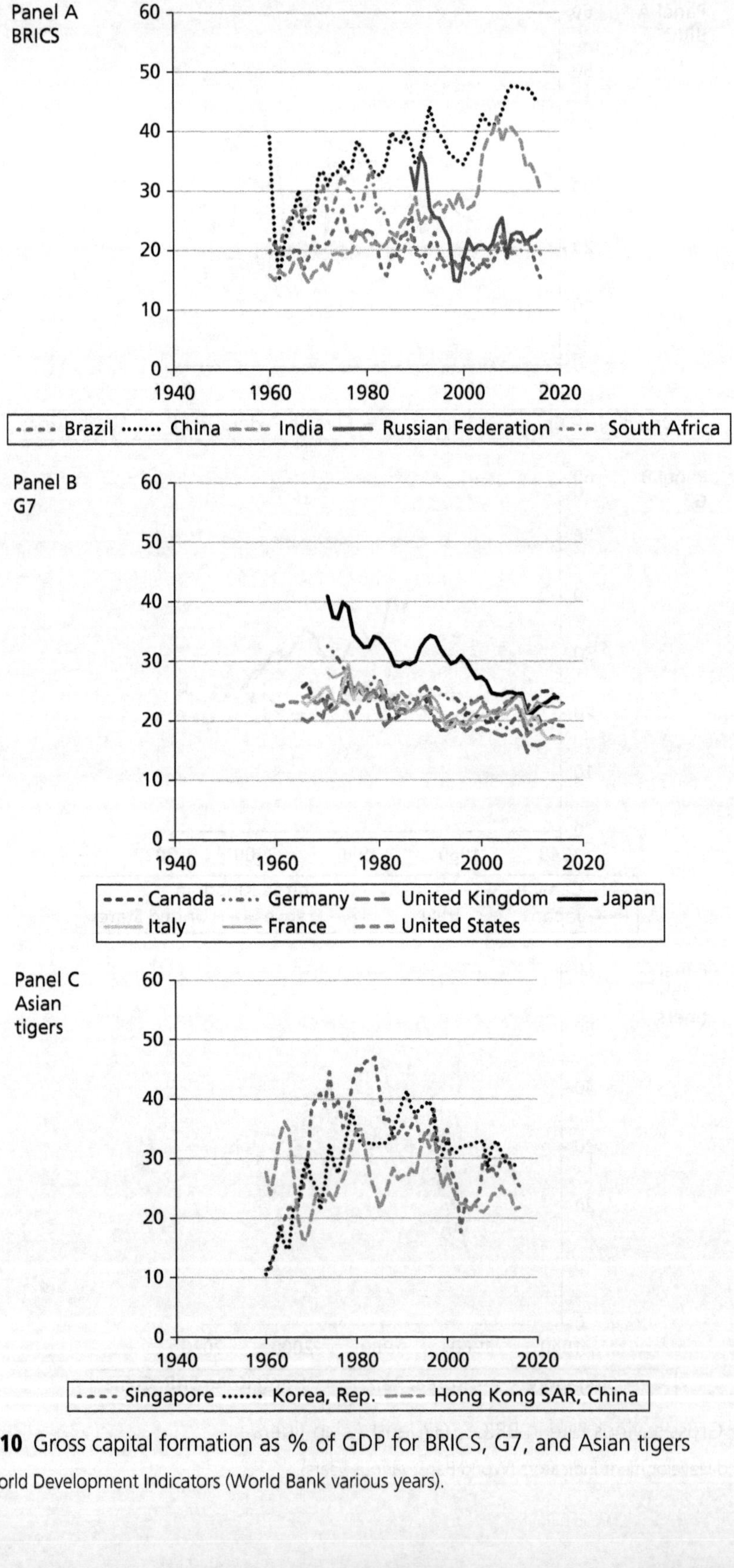

Figure 1.10 Gross capital formation as % of GDP for BRICS, G7, and Asian tigers

Source: World Development Indicators (World Bank various years).

growth and development. The second pillar is called infrastructure quality. Under this, countries are provided a score for components such as the quality of roads and railway infrastructure; quality of ports and airline capacity; quality of electricity supply; and mobile and landline telephone density. The overall infrastructure quality index is constructed from these. Asian tigers perform very well on this, occupying some of the top ranks in 2015. While Switzerland takes the top spot, Hong Kong (at 3) and Singapore (at 4) are not far behind. The Republic of Korea (20) and Taiwan (21) are also not too far off. Four of the G7 countries take ranks within the top 20: Japan (7), France (10), Germany (11), United States (13). Canada (23) and the United Kingdom (24) trail the Asian tigers, and Italy (66) is quite far off. Now consider the positions of BRICS countries: China (51), South Africa (59), Russian Federation (64), India (74), and Brazil (124). This discussion suggests that while BRICS have been saving and investing, the infrastructure gap is still very significant to fully explaining their growth story. In the case of India in particular, Joshi (2017) notes that addressing India's appalling infrastructure deficit should be among policy priorities along with universal income distribution and other ways of reducing inefficiencies.

FOREIGN DIRECT INVESTMENT AND BRICS

Foreign direct investment (FDI) is no doubt an important driver of economic growth. It can bring in technology, organizational, and managerial skills and transform practice in individual sectors. FDI from the G7 countries appears to have taken off in the 1990s but really hit the peak of US$542 billion in 2007 (Figure 1.11) and remained at US$412

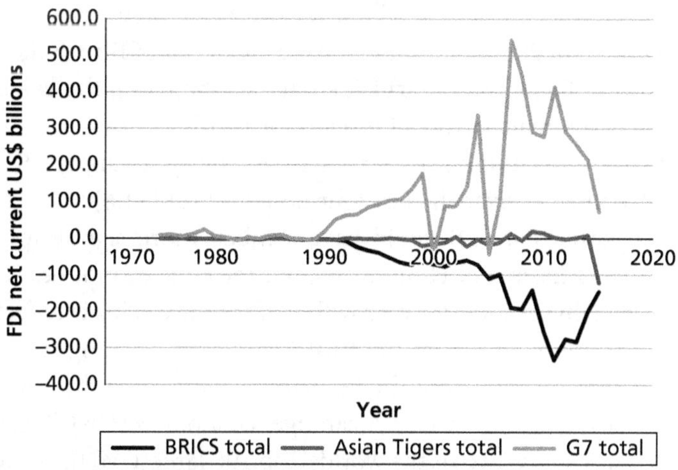

Figure 1.11 FDI net (outflows minus inflows) in current US$ billions for BRICS, three Asian tigers (Singapore, Korea, and Hong Kong), and the G7 countries

Source: World Development Indicators (World Bank various years).

Table 1.6 FDI net outflows and inflows (% of GDP) for BRICS and three Asian tigers

	1975	1985	1995	2005	2015
Brazil FDI out	0.09	0.04	0.18	0.33	0.75
Brazil FDI in	*1.05*	*0.65*	*0.62*	*1.73*	*4.14*
China FDI out	—	0.20	0.27	0.60	1.58
China FDI in	—	*0.54*	*4.88*	*4.55*	*2.19*
India FDI out	—	0.00	0.03	0.33	0.36
India FDI in	*−0.01*	*0.05*	*0.60*	*0.90*	*2.08*
Russian Federation FDI out	—	—	0.15	2.34	1.62
Russian Federation FDI in	—	—	*0.52*	*2.03*	*0.50*
South Africa FDI out	0.33	0.07	1.60	0.35	1.74
South Africa FDI in	*0.49*	*−0.65*	*0.80*	*2.53*	*0.48*
Hong Kong SAR, China FDI out	—	2.69	17.28	18.68	25.38
Hong Kong SAR, China- FDI in	—	—	—	*22.56*	*58.51*
Korea, Rep. FDI out	0.02	0.61	0.70	0.93	1.72
Korea, Rep. FDI in	—	*0.23*	*0.32*	*1.52*	*0.30*
Singapore FDI out	0.67	1.24	8.51	9.85	10.58
Singapore FDI in	*5.18*	*5.47*	*13.12*	*14.20*	*23.78*

Source: World Development Indicators (World Bank various years).

billion in 2008 but then fell to US$290 billion in 2009. Though the East Asian tiger economies receive much inward FDI they are also sources of significant outward FDI. As a result net FDI in these economies is fairly small. At the time of the coining of BRICs by O'Neill in 2001, the net FDI received by BRICS was US$77 billion. This did not significantly increase at all until 2007 when it reached US$189 billion and stayed at around the same level in 2008 but came down to US$142 billion in 2009. However, this bounced to US$253 billion in 2010 reaching the peak of US$333 billion in 2011. Net FDI into BRICS remained above US$200 billion for the next three years before this came down to US$146 billion in 2015. Thus, if FDI were the driver of BRICS then their growth performance before 2009 cannot be explained at all. Therefore, the evidence does not suggest that FDI was the main driver of growth for BRICS.

In fact, both FDI inflows and outflows have been a fairly small part of their GDP for each of the BRICS countries over the last four decades (Table 1.6).

This analysis suggests that FDI could have a much more significant role in small economies such as Singapore and Hong Kong; but for large economies such as BRICS, FDI cannot really explain the long-term growth performance. This is reflected also in the number of non-financial MNEs from the BRICS countries. Among the global top 100 MNEs in 2016, seventy-two are from the G7 nations while only three are from BRICS nations and a further four are from East Asian tiger economies (UNCTAD 2017b). Data for 2005 showed that seventy-two of the worlds' top 100 largest MNEs were from the G7 nations; nine were from the East Asia tiger economies; there were just two MNEs from BRICS (Lenovo from China and Lukoil from the Russian Federation).

Among the top 100 non-financial MNEs from the developing countries in 2015, forty were from BRICS nations; thirty-seven were from the East Asian tiger economies; the remaining ones were from other emerging economies. Of the forty MNEs from BRICS, China had a lion's share of eighteen MNEs; eight were from India; six each were from Brazil and South Africa; and two were from the Russian Federation. These huge 'home grown' MNEs from BRICS cover all areas including energy and mining, telecommunications, computer equipment, software, real estate, finance, and services. Even as BRICS economies began to develop in the early 1990s and opened up markets for foreign investment, domestic stock market capitalization was also significantly increasing. However, Adu et al. (2015: 107) find that BRICS continued to be different from the mature markets in the developed countries. They argue that: '... the underlying structure of the BRICS, particularly their potential for large growth swings, susceptibility to regulatory and political changes may lead their stock returns to deviate significantly' from expectations.

FDI is no doubt an important contributor to growth and may help to bring innovation, promote competition among domestic firms, and help transformation of the economy; but in the case of BRICS, FDI has hardly been the magic bullet.

DEMOGRAPHIC ASPECTS

The theory of demographic transition is contested but if we were to suspend disbelief for a moment, different members of BRICS are at different stages in their demographic transition. The BRICS Report issued by BRICS countries themselves (Ministry of Finance 2012: 161) notes that '... All five countries are abundant in their workforce availability. This is significant in the present context, where, with a few exceptions, most of the Western world has a declining population and a dwindling workforce'. This is borne out by the data presented in Figure 1.12. Population below the age of 15 years now forms nearly 30 per cent in India and South Africa, around 22 per cent in Brazil, and around 17 per cent in China and Russia. In comparison, population below 15 years in the G7 is between 12 per cent in Japan and 17 per cent in the United States.

The wide range of locations of BRICS with regard to the demographic pyramid is important in relation to the size of their labour force and youth population, with Brazil and China having transitioned to low birth rates of 1.9 children per woman, while India is at about 2.5 children per woman (Population Reference Bureau 2014). The 'demographic dividend' defined as the ratio of the productively active population between the ages of 18 and 65 years to the total population also varies hugely across these countries, with China and Russia already in the regime of a rising dependency ratio, while Brazil is likely to join that regime between 2020 and 2025. In the case of India and South Africa, they will continue to enjoy a far more favourable dependency ratio. Of course, achieving a positive dividend does depend on access to quality education and the opportunity to become gainfully employed.

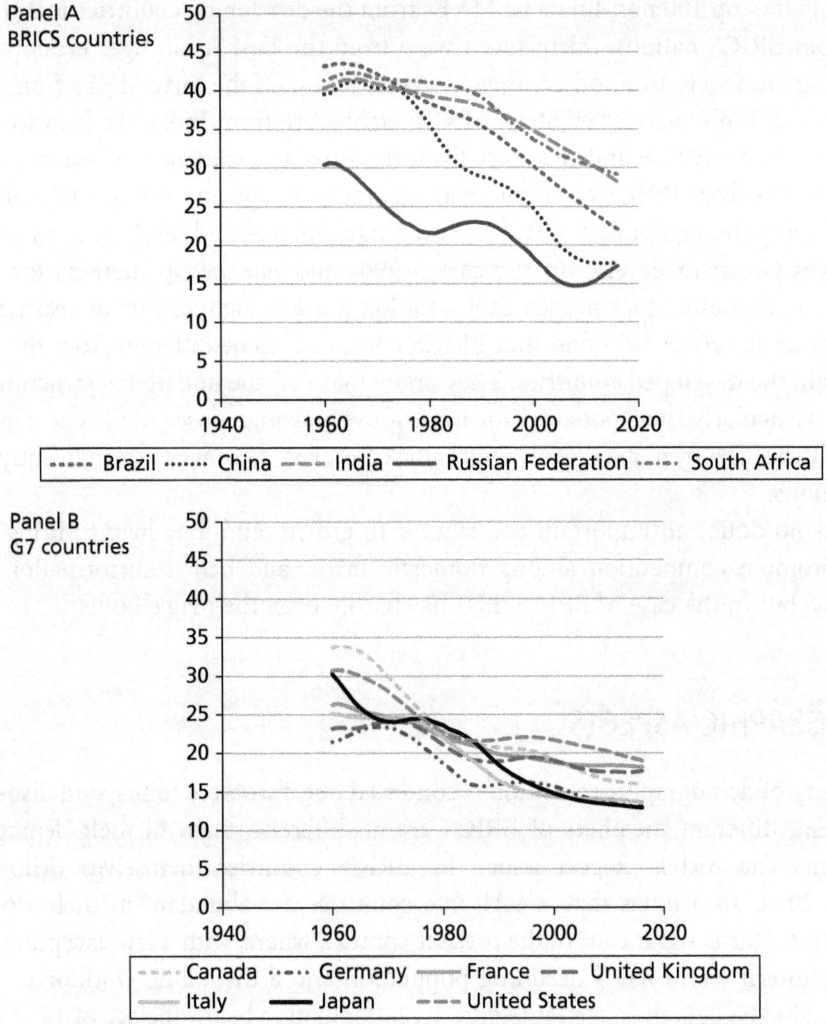

Figure 1.12 Demographic advantage? Population below 15 years of age as % of total population in BRICS and G7 countries

Source: World Development Indicators (World Bank various years).

URBANIZATION IN BRICS

In 2016, BRICS had fourteen of the thirty-one megacities of the world (each with population greater than 10 million) and by 2030 it is estimated that eighteen of the forty-one megacities will be in BRICS (UN 2016). It is clear that cities are an important element of the 'emergence' of BRICS. However, this is a complex story not merely of the megacities but about economic transformation itself.

The great Caribbean economist and Nobel prizewinner Sir Arthur Lewis saw economic development as upheaval and structural transformation from a predominantly

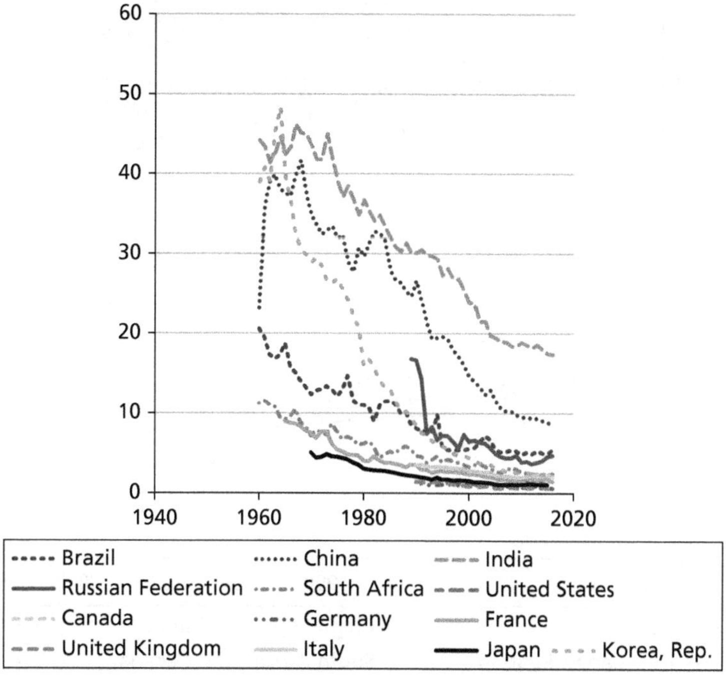

Figure 1.13 Structural change? Share of agriculture value added in GDP for BRICS, G7, and Korea

Source: World Development Indicators (World Bank various years).

agrarian society to an industrialized society as one where productivity growth and surplus generation can create an endless episode of growth when that surplus is reinvested in expanding productive capacity. In a sense all economies have been going through structural change, some rather more slowly than others. The share of agriculture value added in GDP can be an example of an indicator for structural change though there are some complexities. Even in 1960, the share of agriculture in the economies of G7 countries was below 5 per cent and this had decreased to around 1 to 2 per cent by 2016 (Figure 1.13). Measuring the share of agriculture can be complicated in the sense that much of agriculture especially in Brazil has been very high technology- and high investment-intensive. In BRICS we have two distinct groups. In Brazil, Russia, and South Africa, the share of agriculture in GDP had decreased to less than 5 per cent by 2016. China and India had up to 40 per cent of their GDP coming from agriculture in the 1960s but even in those countries this share has been decreasing steadily in India (reaching 17 per cent by 2016) and more dramatically in China (8 per cent in 2016). Among the East Asian tigers, Hong Kong and Singapore had very little by way of agriculture in their GDP even in 1960. The Republic of Korea started off at the same level as China and India in the 1960s but this declined very quickly to around 5 per cent by 1995 and to around 2 per cent by 2016.

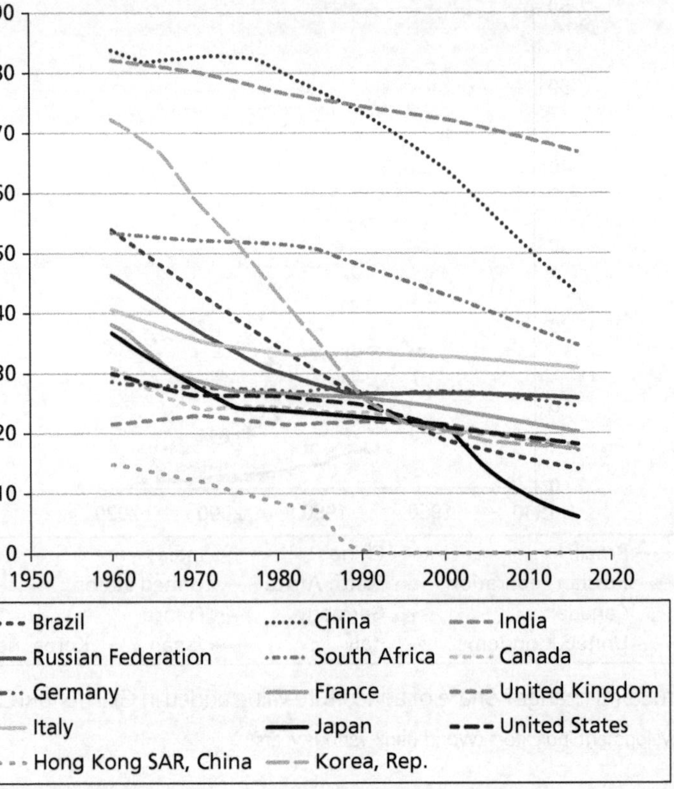

Figure 1.14 Structural change? Share of rural population of total population as % for BRICS, G7, and the Republic of Korea and Hong Kong

Source: World Development Indicators (World Bank various years).

What happened in terms of the structure of the economy is reflected in the demographics too. With structural change of the Arthur Lewis model pattern, you would expect the share of rural population of total population to decline. We can see this clearly in the case of the Republic of Korea most dramatically where the rural population share fell from over 70 per cent in 1960 to less than 10 per cent in 2016 (Figure 1.14). Singapore has been a city economy, so rural population is not relevant but even in the case of Hong Kong by the early 1990s the rural population had more or less disappeared. Thus, believers of the Lewis model pattern of structural change would argue that the East Asian tiger economies appear to be following the textbook case of structural change quite closely. We should add that the Lewis model is an abstract idea where industrialization and urbanization are the main drivers of the economy. There is also the issue that agriculture does not have to be considered as traditional and industry as being the modern sector. In Brazil for example an intensive form of agriculture has more characteristics of industry than of traditional agriculture. In a world dominated by services and digital economies, it is technically possible to achieve structural change and growth in per capita incomes without industrialization or urbanization though it could be somewhat less efficient and much more capital intensive especially in the initial stages.

Among BRICS, Brazil's case in the pre-1990s and China's case post-1990s are also dramatic though China still has over 40 per cent its population in rural areas. India's case is a clear exception. India started off with over 80 per cent of population in rural areas in 1960 and in 2016 slightly more than two-thirds of India's population still lived in rural areas. So what is clearly interesting is that the kind of growth in the aggregate economy in China and India is being achieved while Lewis-type structural transformation appears to be still in progress and far from being completed. Some of this can be a result of economic geography and increasing returns in terms of firms responding to economies of scale and transport costs and thus locating ever closer to their largest domestic markets (Fujita et al. 2009; Krugman, 2008).

This also poses many serious distributional concerns. Are the benefits of economic growth predominantly accruing to the urban and modern part of the economy and are rural households who are dependent on agriculture and traditional sectors being left behind? This question cannot be answered easily. Structural change is not merely about the reallocation of labour from agriculture to industry or the modern sector but from low to high productivity sectors. As Knight and Ding (2012: 146) noted in the case of China, there are dynamic relationships between economic growth, employment, and output and structural change may create growth where labour is being moved from low to high productivity sectors. However, the productivity puzzle includes the so-called 'cost disease' (Baumol 1967) whereby a high productivity sector displaces workers who then have to seek employment in low technology sectors (Imbs 2017.) In BRICS and in many emerging economies, there are layers of modernity and tradition working side by side. There could be people right in the middle of a modern metropolis who are not benefiting from the growth in productivity in the modern sector especially in terms of the digital economy.

As per UN (2014: 12) estimates, 'China has the largest urban population (758 million), followed by India (410 million)'. The report notes that these two countries constitute '. . . 30 per cent of the world's urban population' and that Brazil and Russia together hold another 278 million people. Thus, together, BRICS hold almost 40 per cent of the world's urban population. The report also noted that between 2014 and 2050, the urban population of India is expected to increase by another 404 million people while in China the increase is projected to be 292 million people. An important issue particularly for the urban population concerns housing. Tiwari et al. (2016) highlight the important challenges of housing for each of the BRICS countries and note that in Brazil a sort of over-urbanization led to a very large share of the urban population living in favelas, whereas in South Africa the years of apartheid are still visible in the townships. They note that in the case of India the rural bias of vote share prevented national governments from actively embracing urban housing issues. While this has begun to change in recent years, the policy rhetoric has not yet fully materialized into action.

Electricity consumption is considered a good proxy of urbanization, for example through studies such as those that use satellite imagery and night-time lights to track the urban spatial growth pattern (Angel 2012; World Bank 2015). In four of the BRICS countries (not South Africa), electricity consumption increased significantly. In 1971, in Brazil, China, and India, electricity consumption was fewer than 500 kilowatt hours (kWh) per capita. This increased significantly in China to reach nearly 4,000 kWh; in Brazil to around 2,600 kWh, and in India to around 800 kWh (see Figure 1.15). While these are high compared to their past consumption, they are still way below the levels of consumption of electricity in the G7 economies. In fact, the East Asian economies have a much greater level of electricity consumption per capita than most of the G7 countries. This analysis suggests that in Brazil, China, and India urban growth is likely to continue for some time.

This analysis suggests that even as urban population is expected to grow significantly in BRICS, the urgent need to provide infrastructure and manage the environmental externalities of the projected energy use are very clear. A transition to low-energy intensity or low-carbon urbanization will require vast amounts of investment in so-called 'green energy', in improving public transport, the built environment, comprehensive urban development strategies, land use policies, and urban design. The timing of transition is also important. Making existing cities inclusive and sustainable and developing new cities that deliver on quality of life and sustainability will be crucial for this to happen successfully.

BRICS and the social challenges

EXTREME POVERTY IN BRICS

While BRICS as a group have a way to catch up with the East Asian miracle countries and the G7 economies on per capita income terms, their achievement in absolute numbers in terms of moving people out of poverty especially in China has been unprecedented. In 1990, BRICS had together 1.1 billion people in extreme poverty, mostly in China (756 million) and India (338 million). This number was gradually decreasing until the year 2000 and reduced rapidly after that (Figure 1.16). By 2013, the number of people in extreme poverty in China had come down to 25 million. The number of people still in extreme poverty in the five BRICS together in 2013 was 372 million (with India accounting for 88 per cent of them). As noted by an OECD (2011: 48) study on emerging economies: 'During the two decades to 2008, the fall in the extent of absolute poverty was particularly dramatic for Brazil, China and Indonesia, while India and South Africa, recorded modest reductions.'

Absolute poverty remains significant in India. Even in other BRICS, while the number of those below $1.95 per day has decreased, the number of people just above the poverty line remains significant. Also, poverty is multidimensional. According to the

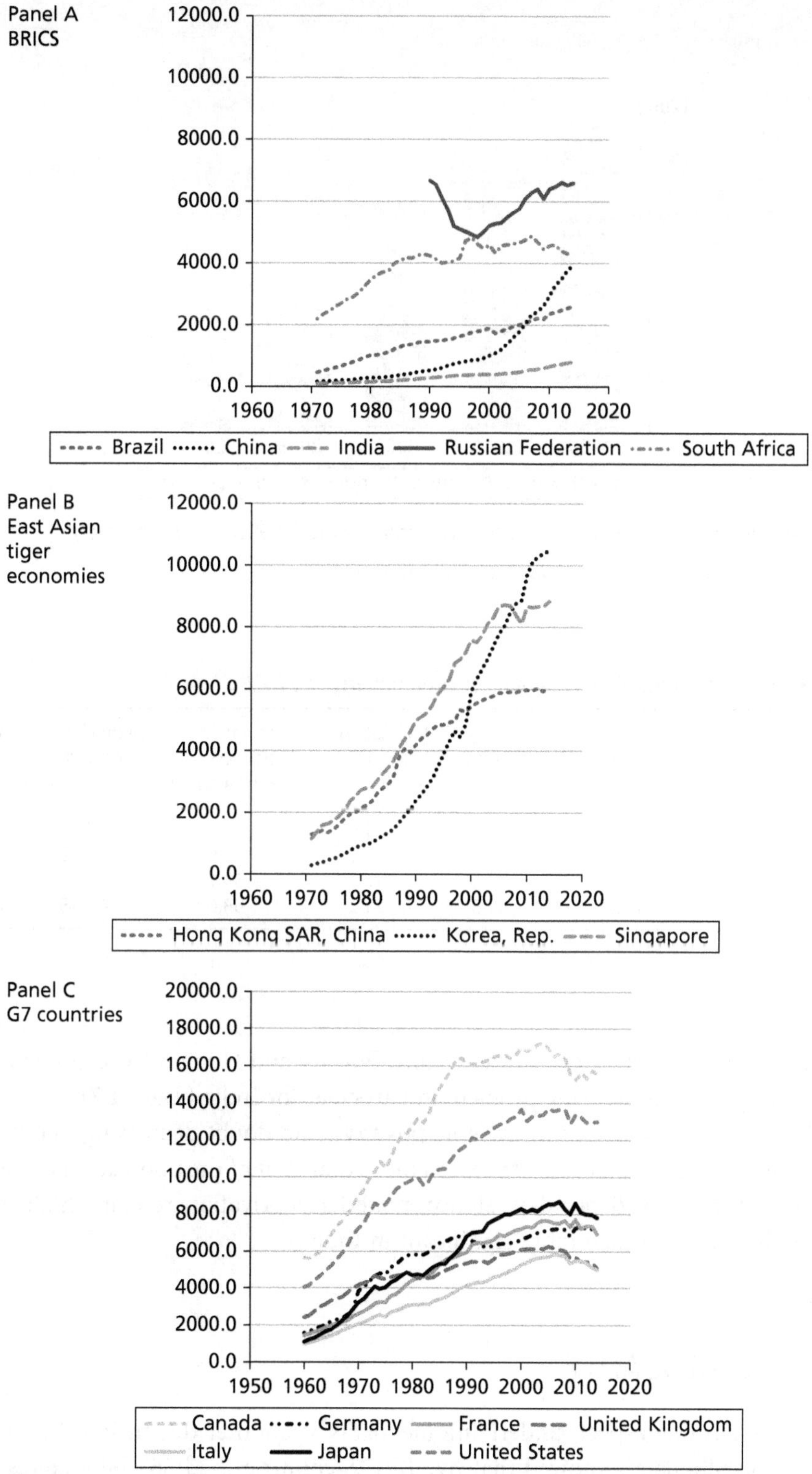

Figure 1.15 Electricity consumption kWh per capita in BRICS, East Asian countries, and G7 countries

Source: World Development Indicators (World Bank various years).

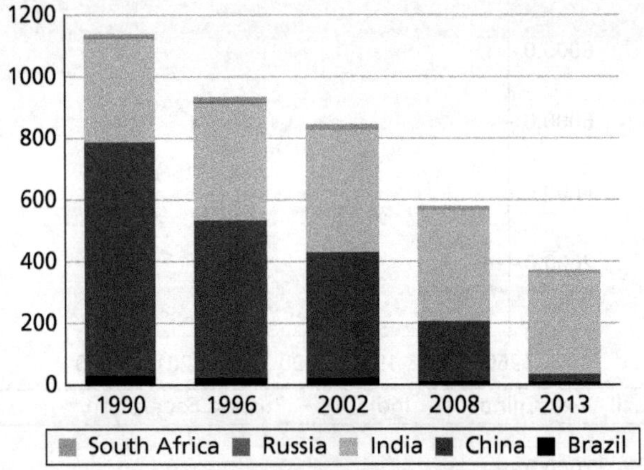

Figure 1.16 Number of persons in extreme poverty in BRICS 1990–2013 (millions)

Source: World Development Indicators (World Bank various years).

Table 1.7 Multidimensional poverty and income poverty in BRICS

	MPI index	Headcount of population in MPI % of population	Intensity of deprivation %	Population below US $1.90 a day %	Population below US $3.10 a day %	Inequality among the poor (0 to 1.0)	Year of survey
China	0.017	4.0	41.3	1.9	11.1	0.043	2014
Brazil	0.021	5.3	40.6	3.7	7.6	0.069	2014
South Africa	0.036	9.2	39.1	16.6	34.7	0.04	2014/15
India	0.191	41.3	46.3	21.2	58.0	0.145	2011/12

Source: Alkire and Robles 2017.

multidimensional poverty index of the Oxford Poverty and Human Development Initiative (OPHI), poverty is an acute problem in particular for India (Table 1.7).

While the number of those in extreme poverty is no doubt decreasing, more than a third of the population in South Africa and more than half of the population in India are living on less than $3.10 per day. Hence, material deprivation remains high in both countries though it is much more significant in India.

ECONOMIC INEQUALITY

While poverty is one aspect, underlying inequality is another dimension. In 2017, the Forbes list of billionaires showed that five BRICS countries had 567 billionaires out of 2,043 billionaires worldwide. Moscow (73 billionaires) and Beijing (54) each had more billionaires than London (50). Similarly, Mumbai (41) and Shanghai (40) each have more billionaires than San Francisco or Singapore or Paris. Triesman's (2016: 238)

Table 1.8 Income share of top 20% of population in BRICS countries

	1993	2006	2008	2011
Brazil	64.3	60.4	58.8	57.6
China			48.5	
India				44
Russian Federation	53.3	47.5	48.5	47
South Africa	64.3	71.1	68.7	68.9

Source: Based on World Development Indicators (World Bank various years).

analysis shows that the number of billionaires is '...most robustly associated with market size (high income, population, and stock market capitalization) and low top marginal income tax rates'.

In terms of income inequality, Brazil and South Africa had a Gini coefficient close to 0.6 in 1993 and this remained more or less at the same level in 2000 and 2001. Since then, social policies (along with labour market reforms and the introduction of a minimum wage) in Brazil appear to have helped in reducing inequality as the Gini coefficient for Brazil has been coming down significantly to reach 0.53 in 2009 and 0.51 in 2015. In the case of Russia also the Gini coefficient has come down from 0.48 in 1993 to 0.37 in 2015. Data for China and India are only available for very few years. Another indicator of inequality is the share of income of the top 20 per cent of the population (Table 1.8). In both Brazil and Russia, the income share of the top 20 per cent of the population has been coming down in the two decades since the early 1990s. In the case of South Africa, however, the trend has been the opposite with the share of the top 20 per cent increasing. For China and India no trend data are available.

Social challenge is not merely in terms of the modern versus traditional sector or urban versus rural sectors. BRICS countries are large countries with numerous cleavages caused by historical, ethnic, geographic, and cultural factors. In contrast to the East Asian tiger economies, BRICS are going through very significant economic and social changes on a much more fragile footing because of these numerous cleavages which can result in one group or community feeling disenfranchised by the development strategy at any given point that political instability, protests, and unrest are never too far away, especially in Brazil, South Africa, and India. The cases of China and Russia are slightly different but even there some of the fragilities are noticeable. How the ruling elite in each of these societies captures and maintains institutions of governance and uses these to negotiate a way forward for a development strategy from time to time is a phenomenally important question. There are forces, encounterss and dialogues within each of these societies between the forces of social justice and those that focus on economic growth. Sometimes, distributional conflicts can trigger violence; and the ability to develop coalitions that can control violence becomes an important element of the institutional development process. There cannot be a trade-off between justice and growth—both are equally important strategic objectives and depending on one's ideology one can see scope for arguments that they should be ethically given equal importance. However, growth and progress sounds hollow if a significant section of the population remains hungry and insecure (in terms of human security, see Ogata and Sen 2003) and does not have access to basic services such as water, sanitation, education, and health care.

Ziesemer (2016) estimated Gini coefficients for education using the Barro and Lee (2010) data at five-year intervals for the period 1950 to 2010. From this data (presented for BRICS and selected countries in Figure 1.17), educational inequality is coming down worldwide. However, it was already comparable to G7 levels in 1950 and this continued throughout the period. In fact in 2010, educational Gini suggests that Russia has more equality than every one of the G7 countries as far as education is concerned. Among the G7, BRICS, and East Asian tiger economies, India has the dubious distinction of having the highest educational inequality.

Health inequality can be measured in various ways, for example through differences in the life expectancy of the richest and the poorest quintiles or deciles of the population. Wilkinson and Pickett (2009) showed that health inequality manifests itself in many forms but is an indicator of underlying economic inequality. The Marmot (2010) review noted that the so-called 'social determinants of health' contributed to the poorer people having a life expectancy of at least seven years shorter than that of richer people within the UK. We do not have similar data for BRICS countries but there are studies which clearly show that there are significant health inequalities in BRICS. Mujica et al. (2014) note that in each of the BRICS countries there are significant health inequalities and these translate into significant differences in the infant mortality rate between the richest and poorest quintiles.

LIFE EXPECTANCY IN BRICS

Life expectancy at birth for the total population in G7 countries in 1960 was between 67 years (Japan) and 71 years (Canada). By 2015, life expectancy in G7 countries increased across the board to 78 years in the USA and to nearly 84 years in Japan (Figure 1.18). Among the East Asia tigers, Hong Kong and Singapore already had G7 levels of life expectancy in 1960 and this had continued to increase, reaching 82 to 84 years by 2015. South Korea in 1960 had life expectancy of 53 years, almost the same level as in Brazil at that time. By 2015, an average Brazilian could expect to live for 75 years, while an average South Korean could expect to live for 82 years, a gap of 7 years achieved over seven decades. Among BRICS, China's progress is comparable in terms of the significant increase in life expectancy. In 1960, Russian life expectancy was 66 years, very close to the then G7 country level. Life expectancy in Brazil (54 years) and South Africa (52 years) were comparable to the Latin American average. Life expectancy in China (44 years) and India (41 years) was comparable to the average for low-income countries. China's life expectancy had overtaken that of Brazil by 1971 (when their life expectancies were around 60 years) and of Russia by 1983. By 2015, China's life expectancy of 76 years was comparable to the G7 level two decades ago. However, social and political changes in

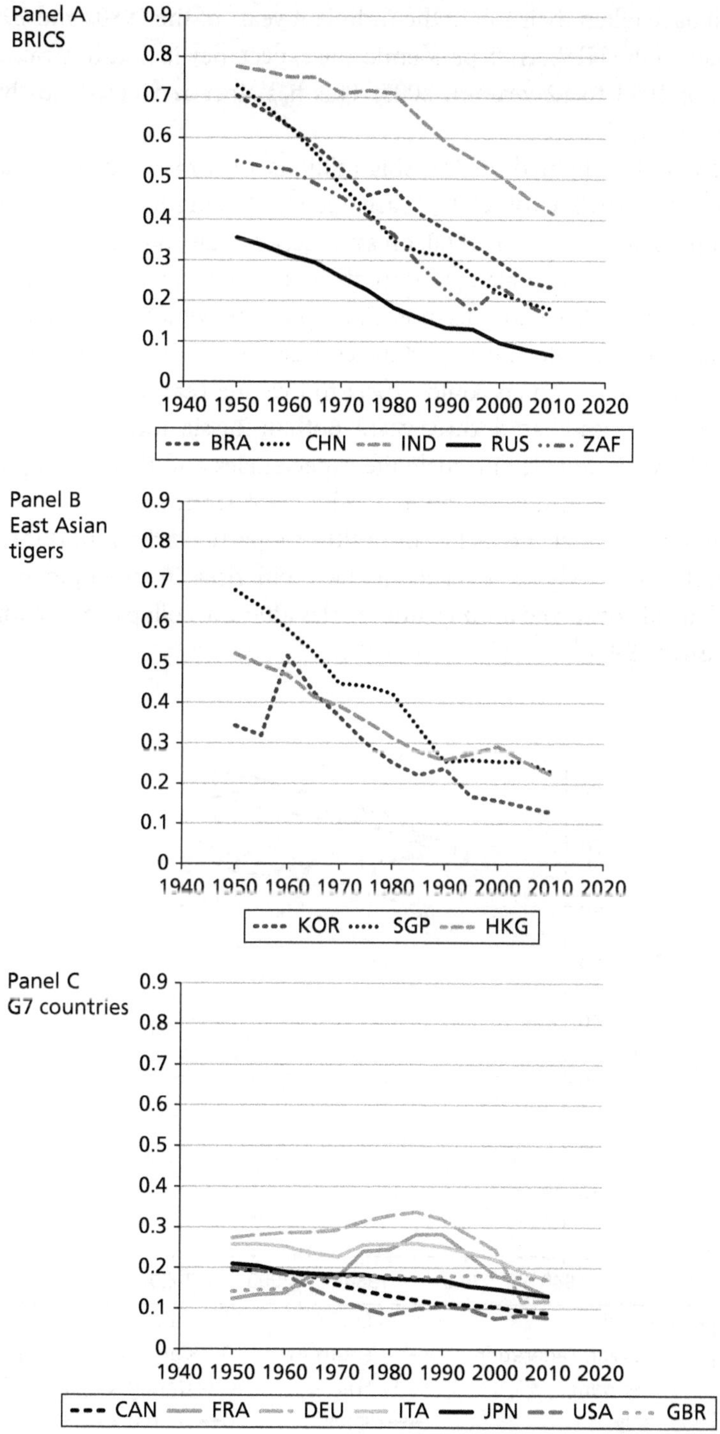

Figure 1.17 Educational Gini

Source: Based on Ziesemer (2016).

Russia seem to have taken their toll in the turbulent years of the 1980s and 1990s. Due to the tragic impact of the HIV/AIDS pandemic, life expectancy in South Africa plummeted from 62 years in 1993 to 52 years in 2005. This has since recovered slowly to slightly below 62 years by 2015.

Amartya Sen has highlighted the 'missing millions' of women due to gender inequalities in societies (Sen 1990; Croll 2001; Klasen 2009). Among BRICS, this is particularly the case for India (Figure 1.19). In 1960, on average, a female in India had 40 years of life expectancy compared to her male counterparts who could expect to live up to 42 years. India alone among BRICS had this notorious position which continued until 1979. Thereafter, male and female life expectancies were more or less the same until the early 1990s when Indian women could expect to live one year longer than Indian men. By 2015, this gap increased had to three years. Both in Russia and South Africa there is a significant gap between female and male life expectancies and this has implications not only for health policies but for economic development strategies as well. As Petrie and Tang (2014) noted: 'Gender inequality in health is a particularly important issue in the Russian Federation—largely as a result of the rapid rises in unemployment, alcohol problems and suicide observed among adult males after the collapse of the former Soviet Union in the early 1990s.'

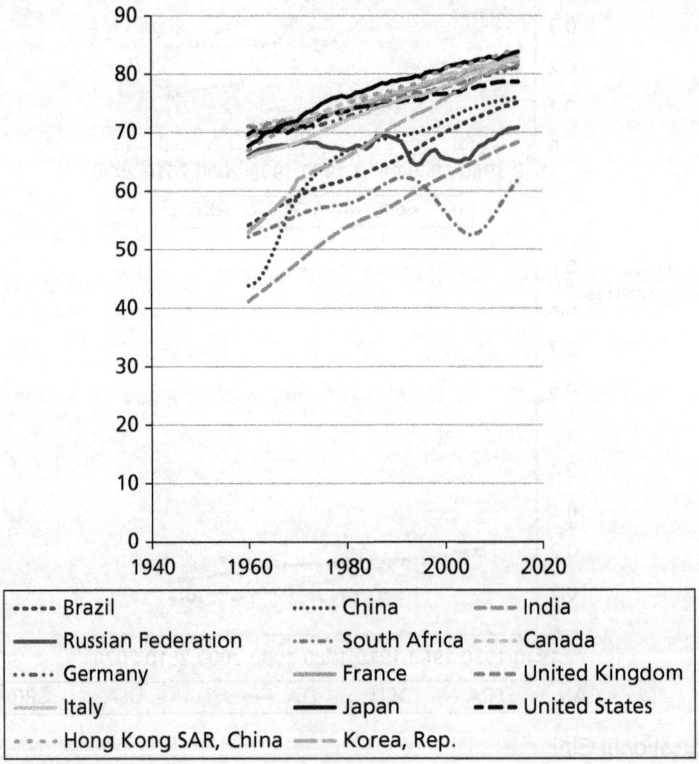

Figure 1.18 Life expectancy at birth (total population) for BRICS, G7, and East Asian tiger economies

Source: World Development Indicators (World Bank various years).

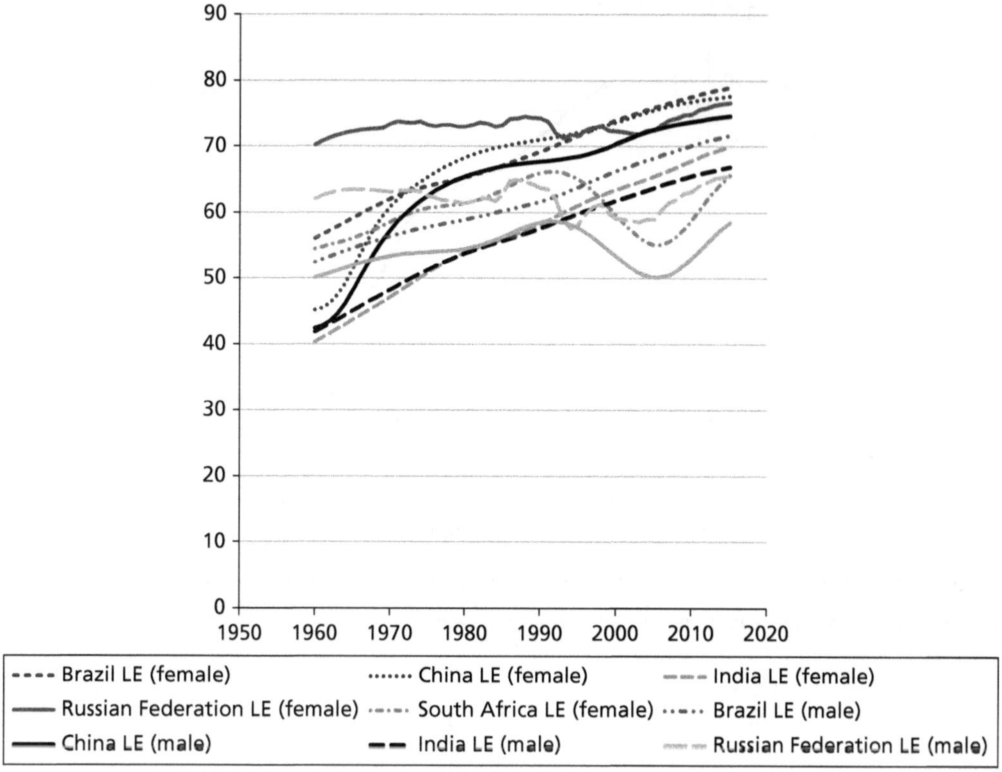

Figure 1.19 Life expectancy at birth for female and male populations in BRICS

Source: World Development Indicators (World Bank various years).

Mortality among children under the age of 5 years (under-5 mortality rate) has improved in all of BRICS but this has not been a smooth journey. For comparison we chose three countries: USA (G7), Republic of Korea (East Asian tigers) and Tanzania (sub-Saharan Africa). India's rate was almost the same as Tanzania's in 1960 and has more or less remained the same by 2015. In this regard, Chen's (2009: 51) observation is noteworthy: 'From 1960 through 2003, India improved in child survival and GDP at a fairly steady, albeit moderate, pace. In contrast, China experienced, with some setbacks, accelerating child survival and slow economic growth in earlier decades, followed by rapid economic growth but more modest gains in child survival in the later decades.' Figure 1.20, based on data from World Development Indicators shows a rather steady decline in the case of India and a plateau in the 1980s in China before continuing to progress with reducing child mortality from the early 1990s. Brazil, Russia, and China have reduced under-5 mortality to below 20 per 1,000 live births. In India and South Africa this rate is still close to 50 per 1,000 live births. The Republic of Korea's case is illustrative of the East Asian tigers, reducing under-5 mortality rapidly. In 1960 when this rate in the USA was 30, in Korea this was around 112. By 1979, both Korea and the

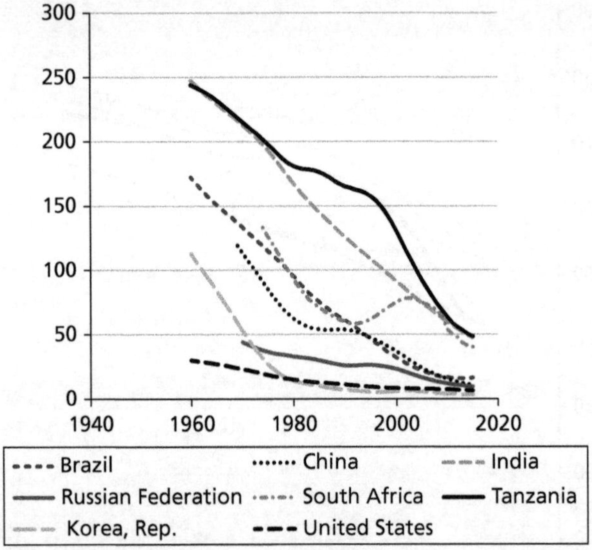

Figure 1.20 Under-5 mortality rate for BRICS, Tanzania, and Republic of Korea

Source: World Development Indicators (World Bank various years).

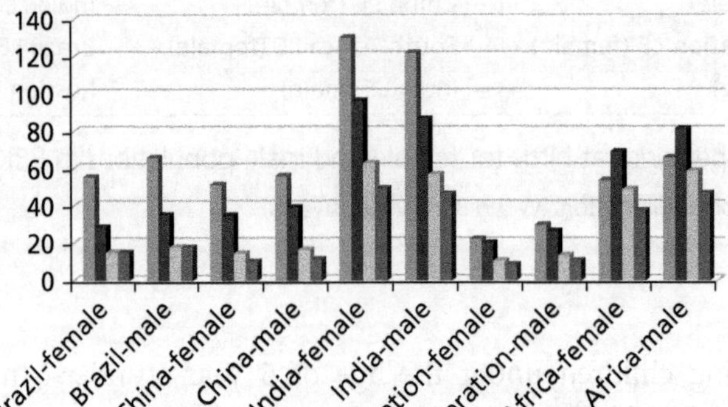

Figure 1.21 Under-5 mortality rate by gender for BRICS countries

Source: World Development Indicators (World Bank various years).

USA had an under-5 mortality rate of around 16 per 1,000 live births. Since 1979, Korea has surpassed the USA rate to reduce the mortality rate to below that in the USA.

When we analyse under-5 mortality rates by gender, we notice that in all BRICS apart from India, female child mortality was lower than male child mprtality in 1990 and by 2015 these had converged (Figure 1.21). In India, the female child under-5 mortality rate was higher than that of male children in 1990 but by 2015 these two rates had gradually converged.

Notwithstanding the variations and the fact that, compared to 1990, by 2011 a greater share of mortality is due to avoidable causes, these mortality figures highlight the underlying structural, institutional, and cultural factors of gender bias which appear to change rather slowly.

BRICS AND LEGITIMACY IN A GLOBAL ORDER

The 2008 global financial crisis raised hopes of the role of BRICS in a global order with the first G20 summit of heads of state called by the then President of the USA, George W. Bush, in 2009. However, no country has arrived on the global stage until it has hosted a global mega-event. Apart from India, the remaining four BRICS countries have already been there by becoming hosts of FIFA World Cup Football (South Africa, Brazil, and now Russia), and the Olympics (China and Brazil with summer games and Russia with the Winter Olympics). India's only claim to this club is its hosting of the XIX Commonwealth Games in 2010 in Delhi; but those games were remembered more for the corruption scandals than the prowess of organizational skills. India continues to have the world's largest number of road traffic accident mortalities.

Mortality can be an indicator of morality in public life and institutionalized inequality. Thus while the usual narrative has been to look at BRICS in terms of their economic might and size in the global economy, many critical voices have been raising questions on each of them and ultimately about the moral legitimacy of a BRICS project. Each of the five nations has its own important critics. For India, the focus is on the still significant level of extreme poverty and its various manifestations including in social metrics such as: the world's largest number of number of illiterate persons; the sex ratio especially in some of India's more populous states; the number of persons without a toilet and thus resorting to open defecation; and various dimensions of gender inequality. India's own engagement in international forums also has been influenced by colonialism, the Kashmir issue and the complexities of security in South Asia, and a general preference for bilateralism over multilateralism (Mukherjee and Malone 2011.)

For China the critics have tended to focus on the monopoly of state power, limited evolution of democratic institutions, limits on independence of media, and ability to express dissent and engage in public deliberation. Others have focused on inter-regional disparities and the fact that the benefits of growth were mainly concentrated in the Southeastern Seaboard region while the landlocked and remote regions did not receive much of the benefit. However, the enormous investment made by China in improving infrastructure has resulted in significantly narrowing down the gap between different provinces. China also has many minorities and ethnic populations though their proportion is small. However, more recently there is recognition that their rights and identities matter and in recent years China's statistical agencies are beginning to collect data by different ethnicities. Though differences continue to exist they are not as dramatic as they are in India and Brazil.

Russia attracts many criticisms, including the trend of increasing human insecurity and the tendency of the Russian state to suppress opposition and dissent. The annexation of Crimea in 2014 and the consequent conflict with Ukraine has led to the imposition of sanctions by the European Union. Allegations have continued to be levelled against Russia of interference in democratic elections in the USA in 2016 and also in Europe. Domestically Russia as the world's largest land area has different kinds of problems. The two major social issues for Russia have been the decline in male life expectancy and the challenges of integrating migrants into its mainstream economic and social institutions.

South Africa's critics point to the limited progress that has been made in wealth redistribution notwithstanding more than two decades of post-apartheid African National Congress (ANC) rule. The legitimacy of that party and its moral claim to govern continue to be challenged on various grounds. In both India and South Africa, human security is becoming an important issue in terms of structural violence against minorities, Dalits, and women in India and violent methods to eliminate opposition in some parts of South Africa. Ever since the notorious and tragic gang rape in India of December 2012, the whole issue of women's rights and security have been under sharper focus and scrutiny even as many rapes continue to get reported almost every month. The depravity in some of these cases makes one question the very meaning of what is meant by development and what is the point of talking about economic growth rates and space science when despicable acts of atrocities and human rights violations can continue to coexist in a country that once produced eminent women at the forefront of literature and scientific pursuits.

The state in each of the BRICS nations can be both fragile and powerful and when it exercises its power the results can be very significant indeed, whether it is in terms of building large dams or nuclear power stations or other infrastructure and displacing millions of people for the development projects to progress. Such displaced persons may eventually be resettled and some of them may even receive the promised benefits but by nature the processes can be complex and time-consuming. If it takes ten to fifteen years before displaced families receive relevant compensation, the accumulated negative externalities and costs incurred by the displaced people in making their claims heard can erode some of the significant gains being made by the growth process. Thus, the growth process continuously creates new haves and have-nots and while some progress is being made in the setting up of compensation processes and institutions to handle the claims, it also appears sometimes that there is limited institutionalized memory. The environmental impacts of BRICS, therefore, should not be seen as an externality here and a regulatory issue there but very much as elements of their growth story itself. Whether and how these countries are able to mediate between different legitimate interests and developmental goals and how despite the time-consuming process that sometimes slows things down very significantly, a broad consensus can be produced and the state institutions play a different kind of mediating role compared to occupying the 'commanding heights of the economy' and by default taking over the lead position in whichever sectors they choose.

This discussion on social and environmental challenges will not be complete without a mention of corruption possibilities and how the state institutions in each of these countries are evolving to address some of the criticisms and indeed put in place organizations to address routinized forms of corruption. However, corruption is not about doing a few things to catch an occasional government servant here or a corrupt policeman there but to distance state institutions from the enormous potential for extracting rents due to monopoly state political power. However, we have to be careful not to fall into the trap of thinking about measures and indicators of corruption. There is a higher-level picture in terms of genuine industrial policy or fiscal policy which advantages certain kinds of industries such as digital and knowledge-intensive industries against the more mundane manufacturing or other dirty parts of the economy. Wealth creation processes of economic growth associated with Schumpeterian creative destruction in different economies may manifest in different forms to deal with the institutional failures in each society, which may be different from another economy or society. Enhancing public agency and deliberative action has been a crucial aspect of all five of BRICS to varying degrees though some critics argue that Russia is different from the other four in this respect.

Putting it all together: seeing BRICS through alternative lenses

In the discussion so far we have looked at various stylized facts and examined issues from a partial or single perspective. We know that though BRICS have only become popular since 2001, their 'emergence' cannot be understood unless we look far enough back—at least to the 1960s. Each BRICS nation faced different kinds of challenges; they opened up their economies rather later than other emerging economies such as the East Asian tiger economies. In the case of Russia and South Africa it took political and social upheavals before those countries 'emerged' though they have been part of the top ten economies for at least four decades. We have also shown that no single factor can explain their emergence and there remain many important challenges, including: significant inequalities and finding ways to reducing such inequalities through social policies; reducing poverty and improving the quality of life of the bottom half of the population (especially an issue for India); the challenges of increasing productivity and promoting innovation (on which China does better than the other four); managing the urbanization process which is under way and making it more inclusive; improving the quality of life for everyone; and continuing to increase quality life expectancy.

A number of alternative theoretical lenses can be used. Classical works on economic growth, including from W. Arthur Lewis (1955) and Rostow (1960) to Rodrik (2009) do not see economic growth in a narrow sense as merely an increase in per capita GDP but as the engine of transformation in improving living standards for all. The policies discussed throughout Barro and Sala-i-Martin (2004) resonate with those identified by Stern et al. (2005: 128) who argue that the goal of a development strategy should be: '...to enable poor people to participate in the processes of growth and to be key drivers of those processes'. Following Sen (1979, 1992, 2009) with regard to development, the fundamental question is about informational space in which inter-person comparisons should be conducted and that development should be ultimately about enhancing capabilities in the form of substantive freedoms. The importance of agency is central to this. Thus it is not about a central planner deciding what public and private goods will most improve the quality of life of people but that people have the agency and are able to actively participate and choose what they would like to be or to do. In that sense, BRICS countries have a long way to go while their record so far on several aspects has been no doubt very impressive. However, a growth fetish can hardly be a development strategy. Merely pursuing growth dogmatically if such growth is contributing to increasing inequality or is not doing anything to reduce inequality will be futile. BRICS countries have shown their ability to create some of the necessary institutions and environments to favour growth. However, for long-term sustainable growth these institutions must be supported by other equality enhancing and equality guaranteeing institutions. While democracies can provide initial conditions for the emergence of such institutions (Aghion et al. 2007), competition for political rents and patronage distribution opportunities can result in the capture of institutions and hijacking them to entrench existing inequalities and create barriers to equality (Gradstein and Konrad 2006; Uslaner 2002, 2008,).

Another alternative lens is to look at institutions to see whether they are emerging to provide stable equilibriums for policies of growth and policies of redistribution to work together and feed each other (Helpman 2004: 141). North's (1990, 2003) original idea of institutions as the norms and rules, and organizations as players has helped in understanding some of the roles that norms and rules play in different societies. For BRICS countries, the combination of formal rules and informal norms poses many challenges especially when these work in opposite directions, sometimes cancelling each other out. Both in the economy and in politics, in BRICS countries the formal and the informal often clash. Where the formal rules are designed with a deep understanding of the barriers of informal norms, and can overcome or counter them in smart ways such that the institutions governing informal norms change and realign them in the same direction as formal rules, friction is reduced and a coalition for growth emerges. Such coalitions may lead to spurts or episodes of growth but short periods of growth are not enough. Unless these growth episodes are sustained over a long period of time, the quality of life of the bottom half of the population cannot be transformed. Within BRICS, the depth and quality of democratic institutions varies significantly. The democratic process can create short-termism and thus prevent long periods of growth and development from prevailing. Brazil, South Africa, and India have a more proclaimed commitment to democracy; but as recent years have shown, political institutions in these countries are vulnerable to capture by particular interests. Both in Brazil and South Africa, the highest offices of the government are under scrutiny for allegations of involvement in bribery and corruption. In India, though the highest offices at present appear not to be directly related to corruption, nevertheless bureaucratic and political corruption are widespread and thrive due to the inefficiency of the state in delivering basic public goods and infrastructure. In Russia and China, democracy operates in limited and context-specific ways with limited overt opposition to hold the government to account. While in Brazil, South Africa, and India demands for freedoms are given more importance than the rule of law, it appears that in China the rule of law is given more importance than freedoms and the citizen voice. In this context, it is tempting to see these countries through the lens of 'limited access orders' (LAOs) as proposed by North et al. (2009). In their view, all societies have to contend with violence and how to control it. They begin by postulating the natural state as that which '...manages the problem of violence by forming a dominant coalition that limits access to valuable resources – land, labour and capital – or access to and control of valuable activities – such as trade, worship and education – to elite groups' (North et al. 2009: 30). Control enables them to create and allocate rents, the process of allocating which may be crucial for stability of the coalition. With the maturity of institutions, states can graduate to become open access orders (OAOs) where both political and economic institutions are truly open to everyone in society irrespective of their status. In a later work (North et al. 2013) they use the expression 'limited access orders' and define three stages of such an LAO—fragile, basic, and mature. In a fragile LAO, '...the dominant coalition can barely maintain itself in the face of internal and external violence' (North et al. 2013: 11). Therefore, in the fragile LAO, access to both economic and political organizations may be limited and may depend more on personal connections and knowing the leaders and powerful elite than on merit or capability. At the next stage, a basic natural state, or LAO, is one where the government may be well established and stable but then government limits entry to others and tries to do everything itself. Therefore, those who are not connected with government may have fewer freedoms in both economic and political spheres. The mature LAO is one where '...the dominant coalition supports a variety of organisations outside the government, as well as within it, but still the LAOs limit access to private organisations that the government allows and supports' (North et al. 2013: 12). In their view, many countries in Latin America, China, India, and South Africa are mature LAOs. They emphasize the point that the spectrum of LAOs is not teleological, meaning it is not as if a society graduates from being a fragile LAO to basic, or basic LAO to mature (North et al. 2013: 12).

For the transition from a basic natural state (or an LAO) to an OAO, they identify three 'door-step conditions'. These are: '(1) Rule of law for elites; (2) Perpetually lived forms of public and private elite organisations including the state itself; (3) Consolidated political control of the military' (2013: 26). Over the last thirty-five years or so, each of BRICS have been trying to develop these door-step conditions, some more so than others. While their success with the first and third of these conditions has been easily seen, the second condition is complex and has many different dimensions and interpretations. North et al. (2013: 13) made a brief mention of Russia when they noted: 'Venezuela, Ecuador and Russia seem to be regressing as they nationalise, inhibit or outlaw once independent organisations'. The lens of the LAO suggests that notwithstanding their economic progress over the last twenty-five years, BRICS remain fragile and the dynamics of state control and allocation of benefits to different stakeholder groups can affect the equilibrium in such a way that any of these countries can move from stable LAO to basic LAO from time to time. This uncertainty could be part of the reason for their lower scores on indexes such as the Doing Business Index (though in the case of China this has been improving significantly). There can be a certain degree of hypocrisy as well on the part of global investors who perhaps care more about political stability and rule of law than voice and agency of the citizens or control of corruption. Dancing on the knife-edge can create tension and unease for each of the members, which can affect the overall ability and confidence of BRICS as a group.

So far we have used the LAO lens to look at the processes within BRICS nations but we can apply a similar lens to analyse what is happening to global governance itself. A proliferation of new multilateral institutions can be seen positively as the next stage of the evolutionary process of global institutions or negatively as evidence of the inability of global institutions to change quickly. In fact Stephen (2017: 498) noted: '... existing institutions face conflicts over positions of leadership and privilege and are more prone to deadlock, while the dimensions of global governance that externalise the liberal social purposes of established powers are facing increased challenges'. He goes on to argue that informal (and thus new) institutions may be ways of adapting global governance to new situations and contexts.

Another alternative lens is to consider whether the emerging economies are taking up moral spaces previously occupied by the 'great powers' or G7 countries through the erosion of their own legitimacy and inability to adequately address issues of historic and continuing injustices. For example, Stuenkel (2013: 612) argues that '... a profound financial crisis among developed countries paired with elative economic stability among emerging powers caused a legitimacy crisis of the international financial order, which led to equally unprecedented cooperation between emerging powers in the context of the BRIC grouping'. As already discussed, many criticisms exist of the limited moral authority of BRICS countries. Brazil may be an exception in this regard, for instance with regard to its leadership on sustainability, green technologies (both in the run up to the Rio+20 summit in 2012 and subsequently in relation to the Sustainable Development Goals [SDGs]). There is also some discussion of Brazil's role in taking a norm leadership with regard to curing electronic espionage, though how far this has been successful remains to be seen (Abdenur and da Silva Gama 2015) but the Covid19 crisis has exposed the lack of norm leadership.

BRICS and summitry

Analysts can come up with sexy acronyms and lump together any countries they choose. What is interesting is that the acronym turned into a formal relationship—an arranged marriage—with the first BRIC summit in 2009 convened by Russia in Ekaterinburg and leaders of the four nations issuing a joint statement (of fewer than 1,000 words stating mainly an intention to cooperate on a wide range of matters). Think of it as more of an engagement by text message than a pre-nuptial agreement.

Somewhat ironically it seems that it took a global financial crisis to bring together the predicted 'economic powerhouses' to formally cooperate. The second summit took place in Brasilia in Brazil in 2010, hosted by the then President Lula, where South Africa's Jacob Zuma was invited as a guest. At 2,440 words the joint statement issued by the leaders of BRIC nations is a bit more detailed with specific calls for action on international trade, poverty, energy, climate change, combating terrorism, and so on. Subsequently, in 2011, South Africa joined as a full member of BRICS and thus the third summit in 2011 in Hainan in China is when all five countries participated and the Sanya declaration (about 2,700 words) was issued. This declaration laid the foundation for formal cooperation, including the regular meetings of sectoral experts and the development of ways of cooperation for their national institutions such as supreme courts, development banks, and statistical organizations; also to cooperate in new areas including in culture, sports, and the 'green economy'.

The fourth summit was held in Delhi in 2012 and the Delhi declaration (4,400 words) is far more detailed than previous statements. The possibility of setting up a development bank was considered in this declaration and finance ministers were tasked with exploring this further. The seventeen-point action plan includes a call for cooperation in a number of areas including in youth affairs, population matters, energy security, and so on.

It is not a surprise that the 'eThekwini declaration' (about the same length as the Delhi declaration) following the fifth summit in Durban 2013 calls for BRICS and Africa partnership. In addition to its eighteen-point action plan, the declaration also mentions new areas of cooperation to include youth policy dialogue, anti-corruption, state-owned enterprises (SOEs), and drug control agencies. There was also a separate statement (another 440 words) on the establishment of the New Development Bank with an initial size of US$100 billion.

By the time of the sixth summit in Fortaleza in Brazil in July 2014, the political challenges in Brazil had already begun to appear. For the critics, the summit is an attempt by the then president to score some domestic points. The summit theme was 'inclusive growth and sustainable solutions'. The declaration (8,400 words) takes stock of what has been achieved in the first round of five previous summits. A number of global issues were mentioned in the statement including the Arab–Israeli conflict, issues of Syria, the need for keeping space off-limits, the placing of weapons, and achieving a global agreement on climate change. Perhaps readers might find para. 58 the most ironic: 'We are committed to combat domestic and foreign bribery, and strengthen international cooperation, including law enforcement cooperation, in accordance with multilaterally established principles and norms, especially the UN Convention Against Corruption.' Notwithstanding this, the fifth summit should also be remembered for the signing of the agreement to set up the New Development Bank (NDB) and the treaty setting up the Contingent Reserve Agreement (CRA) (also of US$100 billion and initially mainly to support BRICs countries in case of need).

In the Ufa Declaration (12,000 words) of the summit in Ufa, Russia, in 2015 notes the successful setting up of the NDB and the CRA. A BRICS working group on Anti-Corruption Cooperation is also established at this summit. Unlike in previous declarations, in Ufa the action plan is not part of the declaration itself but was issued as a separate document (1,140 words). Among other things, the action plan also mentions the BRICS global universities summit, the BRICS universities league, and in areas for possible future cooperation a dialogue on peacekeeping and a BRICS council on regions are mentioned.

The eighth BRICS summit in Goa, India, in October 2016 led to the Goa declaration (7,400 words) and the Goa action plan (1,500 words). The menu of actions increased further and now topics included a BRICS local bodies forum, a film festival, a convention on tourism, a digital conclave, a BRICS Friendship cities conclave, and a BRICS smart cities workshop.

The ninth BRICS summit concluded in Xiamen in China in September 2017 and focused on the theme of a 'Stronger partnership for a brighter future'. The Xiamen declaration (9,440 words) went back to the previous format of including the action plan within the declaration. While BRICS games, film festivals, and friendship cities networks are already happening, areas identified for future cooperation include oceans, remote sensing satellites, and setting up a working group on civil aviation.

We can see the evolution here from the first summit in Ekaterinburg to the ninth summit in Xiamen not merely in the increased length of the declarations, commitment to the United Nations, and the need for reforming the IMF but also on the range of institutional cooperation forums that have proliferated from the initial focus on economic institutions (finance ministers, central banks, and later, customs departments) now covering even parliamentary forums, people to people relationships, cultural and sports forums, university forums, those focused on research and innovation, those related to youth leaders in different fields, and covering many different aspects of global cooperation including on oceans, space, climate change, and others focusing on specific aspects such as tourism, civil aviation, and cities. From their analysis of BRICS summits from Yekaterinburg to eThekwini, Kornegay and Bohler-Muller (2013: 440) noted that some of the so-called 'track-2' channels can become dominated by or 'tie themselves to government-sponsored forums'.

A text analysis of the nine declarations and statements (Tables 1.9 and 1.10) suggests three things: (a) certain words have remained the most popular throughout—including development, international, global, and cooperation; (b) a second set of words reinforces the introspective element of BRICS and the language of 'us' (thus, our BRICS); (c) the third set of words signifies the focus of the summits and how these changed, for example from 'finance' to 'economic', from 'energy' to 'security'.

What we do not see in the top 10 per cent of words are references to sustainability, climate, human rights, ethical development, and aspirations about equality. The word 'including' does make it to the top ten but we need further analysis of the text to see whether much of this usage is in the context of describing lists in sentence form or

Table 1.9 Most popular words in BRICS summit declarations—part 1: 2009–12

Top ten words	Yekaterinburg Statement 2009	Brasilia Joint Statement 2010	Sanya Declaration 2011	New Delhi Declaration 2012
1	International (3.1)	Countries (1.7)	Cooperation (2.4)	Our (1.7)
2	Countries (1.9)	Our (1.7)	BRICS (2.2)	Development (1.7)
3	Development (1.7)	International (1.6)	International (2)	BRICS (1.5)
4	Financial (1.6)	Cooperation (1.3)	Development (1.7)	Global (1.2)
5	Our (1.4)	World (1.2)	Meeting (1.3)	International (0.9)
6	Cooperation (1.4)	Development (1.1)	Countries (1.3)	Meeting (0.9)
7	Energy (1.2)	Economic (1.1)	China (1.3)	Countries (0.9)
8	Global (1)	BRIC (0.9)	Support (1.2)	Cooperation (0.9)
9	Economic (1)	Energy (0.9)	Our (1.1)	Africa (0.6)
10	Among (0.9)	Financial (0.7)	Africa (1)	Support (0.6)

Source: Authors' calculation based on text analysis (figures in brackets are % of all words).

Table 1.10 Most popular words in BRICS summit declarations—part 2: 2013–17

Top ten words	eThenkwini Declaration, Durban 2013	Fortaleza Declaration and action plan 2014	Ufa Declaration and action plan 2015	Goa Declaration and action plan 2016	Xiamen Declaration and action plan 2017
1	Development (2.4)	Our (1.8)	Brics (2.6)	Brics (4.1)	BRICS (5.1)
2	BRICS (1.8)	Brics (1.8)	International (1.6)	Meeting (1.4)	Co-operation (2.8)
3	Our (1.3)	Development (1.5)	Cooperation (1.4)	Development (1.2)	Meeting (1.4)
4	International (1.2)	Cooperation (1.2)	Countries (1.4)	Cooperation (1.2)	Development (1.3)
5	Meeting (1)	International (1.1)	Development (1.3)	International (1.1)	Our (1.1)
6	Africa (0.9)	Sustainable (0.7)	Our (1.3)	Our (1)	International (1)
7	Countries (0.9)	Economic (0.7)	Meeting (0.9)	Countries (1)	Countries (0.9)
8	Cooperation (0.8)	Support (0.6)	Efforts (0.7)	Welcome (0.9)	Security (0.7)
9	Support (0.8)	Meeting (0.6)	Security (0.6)	New (0.8)	Including (0.7)
10	Global (0.8)	Security (0.6)	Economic (0.6)	Including (0.8)	Economic (0.7)

Source: Authors' calculation based on text analysis (figures in brackets are % of all words).

whether some of the occurrences actually refer to including different groups and marginalized people in decision making.

In the Xiamen declaration of 2017 for example, of the nearly 6,000 words considered in the analysis (after omitting one-letter and two-letter words) the most frequent occurrences of phrases are: of BRICS (74), BRICS (47), the BRICS (38), BRICS countries (29), for BRICS (13), and in BRICS (11). Altogether, two-word phrases containing BRICS as one of the parts occur more than 330 times. Then there are pronoun references such as: we will (24 times); we encourage (10 times), we commit (9 times), we call (9), we emphasize (9), we stress (8), we recognize (7), we commend (6), and we support (6). While BRICS business (7), BRICS economic (6), and BRICS trade (6) suggest the importance of economic cooperation, less frequently used word-pairs are: BRICS health (4 times), BRICS research (3), or BRICS science (3).

Other notable expressions include: United Nations (23 times), sustainable development (18 times); human rights (7 times), international law (7), long term (6), social security (4); international peace (4), 'just and' (2).

Text analysis can only reveal part of the documents' intention. However, even from this rather crude analysis it is clear that economic cooperation issues predominate the BRICS summit while a brief mention is made of many 'also ran' issues. Chenoy et al. (2016) find that from the Yekaterinburg 2009 summit to the Fortaleza summit in 2014, commitments on development as a proportion of total commitment varied between 6 per cent and 23 per cent but overall for the period averaged around 10 per cent. This suggests words and actions are more or less going together.

The limited references to global public goods issues such as climate change, sustainability, water, technological innovation, and South-SSC (South–South Co-operation) suggest that BRICS declarations may include an element of subliminal messaging about transforming global governance rather than making active or direct commitments. Commenting on BRICS after the Durban summit, Professor Joseph Nye (2013) commented: 'Three years ago, I wrote that, "BRIC is not likely to become a serious political organization of like-minded states." The BRICS's most recent meeting has given me no reason to revise that assessment.'

From an analysis of the voting pattern by BRICS countries in the General Assembly during the period 2006 to 2014, Hooijmaaijers and Keukeleire (2016) noted that BRICS countries were in full agreement in 56 per cent to 63 per cent of resolutions while they were in partial agreement in a further 27 per cent to 35 per cent of resolutions, and were in disagreement in 6 per cent to 13 per cent of resolutions. What is more interesting is that after a year of more full agreements in 2010 and 2011 sessions, there has been a decreasing trend in full agreements. An example of the point of divergence relates to nuclear weapons and a nuclear non-proliferation treaty with three of BRICS having nuclear capabilities (Russia, China, and India) and two being non-nuclear states (South Africa and Brazil).

Future outlook

Are BRICS playing the role of counterweight to global economic order dominated by the G7 countries? Global governance in terms of ability to influence institutions such as the IMF depends on voting rights. Due to a legitimacy crisis raised by the 2008 financial catastrophe and the ascendance of BRICS and other emerging economies, IMF initiated reforms in 2010 which took several years to be implemented, until finally in January 2016. Since then the combined vote share of BRICS has been 14 per cent (Table 1.11). In

Table 1.11 IMF quota of Special Drawing Rights and voting rights—BRICS and G7 countries

	Millions of SDRs quota	Quota share	Number of votes	Share of votes
Brazil	11,042	2.32	111,885	2.22
China	30,482	6.41	306,294	6.09
India	13,114	2.76	132,609	2.64
Russia	12,904	2.71	130,502	2.59
South Africa	3,052	0.64	31,977	0.64
Total for BRICS	70,594	15	713,267	14
USA	82,994	17.46	831,407	16.52
Canada	11,023	2.32	111,704	2.22
Germany	26,634	5.6	267,809	5.32
France	20,155	4.24	203,016	4.03
UK	20,155	4.24	203,106	4.03
Italy	15,070	3.17	152,165	3.02
Japan	30,820	6.48	309,670	6.15
Total for G7	206,851	44	1,248,301	41

Source: IMF 2016.

comparison, the USA alone controls 16.52 per cent to be able to veto any 'super vote' where a majority of 85 per cent is required.

In fact, together BRICS (even if they were able to vote cohesively) do not have sufficient votes to veto any amendments because their collective vote falls short of the 15 per cent required to block such a super vote. It is possible to argue that the formation of clubs such as the BRICS may be '…indicative of the dissatisfaction of these countries with the current framework of global economic governance' (Mohan and Kapur 2015: 4).

Thompson and de Wet (2017) note from their analysis of an initiative in South Africa that while BRICS statements mention bottom-up and citizen-led collective action, '…the realities of the forms of engagement still resonate with more traditional forms of state led alliance building that are aimed less at transformation than at co-ordinating national self-interest'. Peterson (2015) suggests that a more nuanced and cultural understanding is needed to fully realize the formation of BRICS.

Duggan (2015) uses the role theory within an international relations framework and notes that while BRICS lack a common identity, they all share the same aspiration to be able to set the rules and to change the current system of global governance which is not working to advance their interests. As we noted, this has been an 'arranged marriage' and it could be severely tested in the stress of post-Covid19 recovery challenges.

SINCE BREXIT THEN BRICS IN?

The dynamic can act in both ways in terms of fostering countries to work together or form trade blocs and unions, as well as in the opposite direction as we are currently experiencing in the United Kingdom following the 23 June 2016 BREXIT referendum on whether to leave or remain in the European Union. So it seems really ironic that Jim O'Neill who coined the acronym BRICs (and later N-11 for the next eleven countries, and more recently MINTs for another group of four economies) was a member of David Cameron's government when the decision was made to call the referendum (though he was only a junior minister and cannot be blamed for the then prime minister's decision). The UK's view of BRICS may be changing due to BREXIT and its economic need to have trade deals outside the EU. This is neither the time nor the place to mention that the Goldman Sachs report (O'Neill 2001) which coined BRICs also had two other predictions: one about many countries joining the European Monetary Union taking the total to more than twenty-five countries; and that the G7 could possibly be expanded to become G9 by including Russia and most probably Brazil. It appears that even a brilliant economist can get some predictions right (in foreseeing the emergence of BRICS) but can also occasionally have blind spots on other issues. Though we are using BREXIT as an example, the issue is whether changes internal to the G7 countries will result in seismic shifts or changes in the global economic order and whether BRICS anticipate or respond to such changes. Nye's (2015) comments about the American 'half-hegemony' and the possibility of fostering multilateral institutions and co-opting Brazil, India, and China in such a way that institutions can survive and continue the liberal order even with the decline of America are also relevant to other G7 members and to the world economic order in general.

A BRICSy Future?

While the financial crisis of 2008 may have played a role in the emergence of cooperation among BRICS (as noted in Stuenkel 2013), BRICS remains a parallel multilateral forum while the members maintain their own bilateral channels. Though an NDB has been set up, BRICS maintain their individual development assistance channels. As we saw earlier, they do not appear to vote together in UN forums. There is not much intra-BRICS trade at present, though this is slowly increasing. There is little evidence of financial integration of the stock markets among BRICS and other emerging economies (Sosa and Cabello 2015). Thus, notwithstanding the summitry and pomp, BRICS nations compete with each other in some spheres and cooperate when convenient. On the other hand, the summit declarations are getting longer and more wordy every year; more forms of inter-ministerial and other aspects of cooperation are being set up and exchanges being arranged. So how is this going to go? Would BRICS become a strong and coherent international group standing up for the weak and delivering good when others fail or just remain a temporary phenomenon 'here today, gone tomorrow' in the long evolution of global governance? We cannot answer these questions, but in the following comments we anticipate alternative scenarios.

From Mancur Olson's (1965) logic of collective action and other international relations theories, voluntary cooperation by countries in forming a club such as BRICS depends on: benefits to the group; benefits to the individual countries; costs of participation; and costs of exclusion or enforcement. A relationship between strategic complements is likely to remain stable. Think of a country which needs to import oil and has many arms and defence technological capabilities to export, and another country which has a lot of oil and needs arms. Such a pair would in theory be a pair of strategic complements. Within BRICS countries, Russia and Brazil have energy that they can export while China and to an even greater extent India need energy imports. However, because of the geographic distances and geopolitical considerations, even this strategic complementarity cannot be easily realized.

Would a membership of OECD change the rationale for the existence of the BRICS? Joining OECD can be a long-drawn-out process. While emerging economies such as Mexico, Chile, and Turkey are already members of OECD, it is unlikely that all of BRICS will become members of OECD any time soon. In a previous review of OECD size and membership, the Noboru Report defined four principles for considering membership of any country: like-mindedness, significant player, mutual benefit, and global considerations. Like-mindedness can be interpreted as commitment to '... the values of democracy based on the rule of law and human rights, and adherence to open and transparent market-economy principles' (OECD 2017: 4). While BRICS countries are likely to gain positive scores for the final three of these factors, the main issue may be with regard to 'like-mindedness', especially for Russia and China. Russia had applied to join OECD in 2007 but the Council in its resolution in 2014 postponed the accession process. Consensus of all existing members is essential for admission to OECD. While the possibility of joining the OECD can be closer to democracies, Brazil, South Africa, and India—all of them—have significant issues and challenges.

Several alternative scenarios can be foreseen with regard to the evolution of BRICS in the next phase. Some of these are given below though this list is by no means exhaustive:

Scenario 1: *BRICSTRONG*: In this scenario, BRICS would remain a closed club of the five nations as they continue to develop intra-BRICS trade and alternative global institutions such as the NDB and other multilateral cooperative institutions to address specific issues and challenges. In this scenario, each of the BRICS countries could take the lead on a global challenge or issue and develop new multilateral institutions around their strength. After the Durban summit, Rodrik (2013) commented that '... it is disappointing that they have chosen to focus on infrastructure finance as their first major area of collaboration... What the world needs from the BRICS is not another development bank, but greater leadership on today's great global issues.' One possible future is that these countries develop strong forms of cooperation and solidarity based on a balance of multilateralism and bilateralism. In this scenario institutions such as the NDB flourish further and the five countries may also develop cooperative disaster relief mechanisms and logistics. In this scenario we would expect some weakening of the position of G7 and G20 forums due to domestic political agendas or an inward-looking policy stance in key member states of these forums. We would not go as far as Shahrokhi et al. (2017) in suggesting that these countries should aim for political union, but who knows, anything is possible however inconceivable.

Scenario 2: *BRICS8 or BRICS11*: In this scenario, they could become the emerging economies' (non-OECD members) club in the G20, namely: BRICS plus Argentina, Indonesia, and Saudi Arabia (to form BRICS8); or inviting Republic of Korea, Mexico, and Turkey too to form BRICS11 (which sounds like the title of a Hollywood blockbuster). At the BRICS summit in Xiamen in 2017 five non-members, namely Mexico, Guinea, Egypt, Tajikistan, and Thailand were invited as 'friends'. This suggests that there are possibilities for the club to expand in the future. Essentially, G20 could become two clubs, one of those presently controlling all the global governance institutions (G7) and the other of those who feel they are 'rule takers' and hence would like a greater say. In this scenario, we expect G7 to be weakened but G20 to take its place and BRICS11 countries to become more or less equal in status, such as by hosting the G20 meetings for instance.

Scenario 3: *BRICSTENDED or BRICSEE*: In this scenario, BRICS become a much more open club incorporating many more emerging economies which share the ethos of BRICS that existing global governance institutions do not reflect current economic realities and that they are biased towards G7 countries. This can become a de facto forum for South-SSC especially if the Paris agreement on climate change becomes weakened due to the USA pulling out, for instance.

Scenario 4: *BRITTLE BRICS (BRICBATS?)*: In this scenario, competition among BRICS nations may create friction which is greater than the need for the cooperation which is currently acting as the glue holding these countries together. There are many pressure points that could hinder cooperation. These include the following: (i) competition for natural resources especially oil and gas; (ii) competition for maritime routes especially the South China Sea but also others including Indian Ocean and Atlantic maritime routes; (iii) China's One Belt One Road (or Belt and Road, BAR) Initiative and the discomfort especially for India due to cooperation between China and Pakistan; (iv) the imposition of further sanctions on Russia and other BRICS becoming tainted by association. A weakened BRICS club may continue to exist for some time at status quo at present levels without further deepening of cooperation but mainly as an annual photo opportunity and talking shop with little follow-up action. Also tensions between China and India as seen in Doklam in 2017 and Galwan valley in Ladakh in 2020 can escalate, especially in relation to water resources if China exploits further river flows in the upper Himalayas that feed into the Ganga-Brahmaputra systems (see also Becker 2014: 184). Covid19 is also presently acting as a minor source of tension.

Scenario 5: *From BRICS to BRIS or BICS to IBSA*: In this scenario, while Russia and China do not see the need to be part of the club, either of them may exit or the remaining three 'democracies' may continue cooperation. For example, China's emphasis on the Belt and Road Initiative (BRI) project could lead to China emerging as the undisputed Asian regional power or a strong state. In such a scenario, China would no longer need the cooperation of smaller members of the BRICS club. Similarly, for various reasons, Russia could be isolated or may find it of limited utility to continue being a member of BRICS if relationships with the EU and G7 are fully restored.

Each of these scenarios has important implications not only for BRICS and other emerging economies but also for global economic governance and prosperity. The future will be determined by two things: (a) how much importance BRICS nations give to this 'arranged marriage'; (b) the existence and development of civil society institutions in each of these countries, their ability to hold their respective governments to account and enable them to pursue a cosmopolitan agenda of inclusive pluralism.

Conclusion

We can only hope that from the predominantly economic focus of BRICS in their first ten years, they move to the next stage to promote mutual and global cooperation for ethical economic and sustainable development. Just being another economic bloc may be fine in the short run but BRICS countries and their diplomats must already know that here is an opportunity to make a significant change in transforming global governance architecture. At present, while there are a few glimpses of small changes here and there, it is clear that institutional development on this scale will not take place by itself but needs careful designing and nurturing. If BRICS nations and other emerging economies are able to do this, we shall begin to move in the direction of a fairer and more just global economic order. It is a big if. The post-Covid19 context only enhances the potential for cooperation and impact.

REFERENCES

Abdenur, A. and da Silva Gama, C. (2015). 'Triggering the norms cascade: Brazil's initiatives for curbing electronic espionage', *Global Governance* 21: 455–74.

Adu, G., Alagigede, P., and Karimu, A. (2015). 'Stock return distribution in the BRICS', *Review of Development Finance* 5: 98–109.

Aghion, P., Alesina, A., and Trebbi, F. (2007). 'Democracy, technology and growth'. Working Paper. Cambridge, MA: Harvard University, Department of Economics.

Alkire, S. and Robles, G. (2017). 'Multidimensional poverty index summer 2017: brief methodological note and results'. OPHI Methodological Notes No. 45. Oxford: University of Oxford Poverty and Human Development Initiative.

Altinbas, D. (2014). 'South–South cooperation: a counter-hegemonic movement?', in J. Dargin (ed.) *The Rise of the Global South: Philosophical, Geopolitical and Economic Trends of the 21st Century*. Singapore: World Scientific.

Anand, P.B. (2014). 'Of dragons, tigers and African lions: an analysis of AidDATA 2.0'. Paper presented at the Symposium on New Philanthropy, University of Bradford.

Angel, S. (2012). *Planet of Cities*. Cambridge, MA: Lincoln Institute of Land Policy.

Asmus, G., Fuchs, A., and Muller, A. (2017). 'BRICS and foreign aid'. AID DATA Working Paper No. 43. Williamsburg, VA: College of William and Mary.

Barro, R. and Lee, J. (2010). 'A new dataset of educational attainment in the world, 1950–2010'. NBER Working Paper 15902. Cambridge, MA: NBER.

Barro, R. and Sala-i-Martin, X. (2004). *Economic Growth*. Cambridge, MA: MIT Press.

Baumol, W. (1967). 'Macroeconomics of unbalanced growth: the anatomy of urban crisis', *American Economic Review* 57/3: 415–26.

Beausang, F. (2012). *Globalisation and the BRICs: Why the BRICs Will Not Rule the World For Long*. London: Palgrave.

Becker, U. (2014). 'Prospects and politics: a sketch', in U. Becker (ed.) *The BRICs and Emerging Economies in Comparative Perspective*. London: Routledge.

Bond, P. and Garcia, A. (eds) (2015). *BRICS: An Anti-Capitalist Critique*. London: Pluto Press.

Brainard, L. and Martinez-Diaz, L. (2009). *Brazil as an Economic Superpower? Understanding Brazil's Changing Role in the Global Economy*. Washington, DC: Brookings Institution Press.

Chang, H. (2002). *Kicking Away the Ladder*. London: Anthem Press.

Chang, H. (ed.) (2003). *Rethinking Development Economics*. London: Anthem Press.

Chen, L. (2009). 'India and China: "The art of prolonging life"', in K. Basu and R. Kanbur (eds) *Arguments for a Better World: Essays in Honor of Amartya Sen*, Vol. 2. Oxford: Oxford University Press.

Chenoy, A., Larionova, M., Manning, R., and Constantine, J. (2016). 'Looking across BRICS: an emerging development agenda?', in J. Gu, A. Shankland, and A. Chenoy (eds) *The BRICS in International Development*. London: Palgrave Macmillan.

Cornell University, INSEAD, and WIPO (World Intellectual Property Organization) (2017). *The Global Innovation Index 2017: Innovation Feeding the World*. Ithaca, NY, Fontainbleau, and Geneva: WIPO.

Croll, E. (2001). 'Amartya Sen's 100 million missing women', *Oxford Development Studies* 29/3: 225–44.

de Vries, G., Erumban, A., Timmer, M., Voskoboynikov, I., and Wu, H. (2015). 'Deconstructing the BRIC: structural transformation and aggregate productivity growth', in W. Naude, A. Szimai, and N. Haraguchi (eds) *Structural Change and Industrial Development in the BRICs*. New York: Oxford University Press, chap. 3.

Duggan, N. (2015). 'BRICS and the evolution of a new agenda within global governance', in M. Rewizorski (ed.) *The European Union and the BRICS*. New York: Springer International Publishing.

European Commission. (2017). *BRICS and EU Trade Statistics*. Brussels: Directorate General for Trade of the EC.

Export-Import (EX-IM) Bank of India. (2016). 'Intra BRICS trade: an Indian perspective'. Working Paper No. 56. Mumbai: Export-Import Bank of India.

Feenstra, R., Inklaar, R., and Timmer, M. (2015). 'The next generation of the Penn World Table', *American Economic Review* 105/10: 3150–82.

Fennell, S., Kaur, A., and Singh, A. (2013). 'India and the Eurozone: a commentary on the political economy of adjustment and correction', *Contributions to Political Economy* 32/1: 151–67.

Fuchs, A. and Vadlamannati, K. (2013). 'The needy donor: an empirical analysis of India's aid motives', *World Development* 44: 110–28.

Fujita, M., Krugman, P., and Venables, A. (2009). *The Spatial Economy: Cities, Regions and International Trade.* Cambridge, MA: MIT Press.

Gradstein, M. and Konrad, A. (ed.) (2006). *Institutions and Norms in Economic Development.* Cambridge: MIT Press.

Helpman, E. (2004). *The Mystery of Economic Growth.* Cambridge, MA: Harvard University Press.

Hernandez, D. (2017). 'Are "new" donors challenging World Bank conditionality?', *World Development* 96: 529–49.

Hooijmaaijers, B. and Keukeleire, S. (2016). 'Voting cohesion of the BRICS countries in the UN General Assembly 2006–2014: a BRICS too far?', *Global Governance* 22: 389–407.

Imbs, J. (2017). 'Structural change in the OECD: some facts', in L. Fontagne and A. Harrison (eds) *The Factory-Free Economy: Outsourcing, Securitization, and the Future of Industry.* New York: Oxford University Press.

IMF (International Monetary Fund) (2016). *IMF Members' Quotas and Voting Power, and IMF Board of Governors.* Washington, DC: IMF.

ISSA (International Social Security Association) (2017). *Social Security Coverage Extension in the BRICS: A Comparative Study on the Extension of Coverage in Brazil, the Russian Federation, India, China and South Africa.* Geneva: ISSA.

Jacobs, L. and van Rossem, R. (2014). 'The BRIC phantom: a comparative analysis of the BRICs as a category of rising powers', *Journal of Policy Modelling* 36S: S47–S66.

Joshi, V. (2017). *India's Long Road: The Search for Prosperity.* New York: Oxford University Press.

Joshi, V. and Little, I. (1996). *India's Economic Reforms 1991–2001.* New York: Oxford University Press.

Klasen, S. (2009). 'Missing women: some recent controversies on levels and trends in gender bias in mortality', in K. Basu and R. Kanbur (eds) *Arguments for a Better World: Essays in Honour of Amartya Sen, Volume II – Society, Institutions and Development.* New York: Oxford University Press, chap. 15.

Knight, J. and Ding, S. (2012). *China's Remarkable Economic Growth.* New York: Oxford University Press.

Kornegay, F. and Bohler-Muller, N. (2013). 'Epilogue: eThekwini and beyond', in F. Kornegay and N. Bohler-Muller (eds) *Laying the BRICS of a New Global Order: From Yekaterinburg 2009 to eThekwini 2013.* Pretoria: Africa Institute of South Africa.

Krugman, P. (2008). *The Increasing Returns Revolution in Trade and Geography.* Nobel Prize Lecture. Stockholm: The Nobel Foundation.

Krugman, P. (2013). 'The age of bubbles OP-ED', *New York Times*, 22 August.

Kurt, S. and Kurt, U. (2015). 'Innovation and labour productivity in BRICS countries: panel causality and co-integration', *Procedia-Social and Behavioral Sciences* 195: 1295–302.

Le Goff, M. and Singh, R. (2013). 'Does trade reduce poverty? A view from Africa'. Policy Research Working Paper No. 63. Washington, DC: World Bank.

Lewis, W. (1955). *Theory of Economic Growth.* London: Routledge.

Lin J. (2012). *Demystifying the Chinese Economy.* Cambridge: Cambridge University Press.

Lucas, R. Jr (2002). *Lectures on Economic Growth.* Cambridge, MA: Harvard University Press.

McMillan, M. and Rodrik, D. (2011). 'Globalisation, structural change and productivity growth'. NBER Working Paper No. 17143. Cambridge, MA: NBER.

Maddison, A. (2007). *Contours of the World Economy, 1–2030 AD*. Oxford: Oxford University Press.

Marmot, M. (2010). *Fair Society, Healthy Lives*. London: Department of Health.

Ministry of Finance (2012). *The BRICS Report: A Study of Brazil, Russia, India, China, and South Africa with Special Focus on Synergies and Complementarities*. New York: Oxford University Press.

Mohan, G. (2015). 'China in Africa: impacts and prospects for accountable development', in S. Hickey, K. Sen, and B. Bukenya (eds) *The Politics of Inclusive Development: Interrogating the Evidence*. New York: Oxford University Press.

Mohan, G. (2016). 'Emerging powers in international development: questioning South–South co-operation', in J. Grugel and D. Hammett (eds) *The Palgrave Handbook of International Development*. London: Palgrave Macmillan.

Mohan, R. and Kapur, M. (2015). 'Emerging power and global governance: whither the IMF?' IMF Working Paper No. WP/15/219. Washington, DC: IMF.

Mujica, O., Vazquez, E., Duarte, E., Cortez-Escalante, J., Molina, J., and da Silva Jr, J. (2014). 'Socioeconomic inequalities and mortality trends in BRICS 1990–2010', *Bulletin of the World Health Organisation* 92: 405–12.

Mukherjee, R. and Malone, D. (2011). 'From high ground to high table: the evolution of Indian multilateralism', *Global Governance* 17: 311–29.

North, D. (1990). *Institutions, Institutional Change and Economic Performance*. Cambridge: Cambridge University Press.

North, D. (2003). 'The role of institutions in economic development'. Discussion paper series no. 2003.2. Geneva: United Nations Economic Commission for Europe.

North, D., Walliss, J., and Weingast, B. (2009). *Violence and Social Orders: A Conceptual Framework for Interpreting Recorded Human History*. Cambridge: Cambridge University Press.

North, D., Wallis J., Webb, S., and Weingast, B. (eds) (2013). *In the Shadow of Violence: Politics, Economics and the Problems of Development*. Cambridge: Cambridge University Press.

Nye, J. (2013). 'BRICS without mortar'. *Project Syndicate*, 3 April.

Nye, J. (2015). 'Is the American century over?', *Political Science Quarterly* 130/3: 393–400.

OECD (Organisation for Economic Co-operation and Development) (2011). *Divided We Stand: Why Inequality Keeps Rising*. Paris: OECD.

OECD (Organisation for Economic Co-operation and Development) (2017). *Report of the Chair of the Working Group on the Future Size and Membership of the Organisation to Council: Framework for the Consideration of Prospective Members*. Paris: OECD.

Ogata, S. and Sen, A. (2003). *Human Security Now. Protecting and Empowering People. Report of the Commission on Human Security*. New York: Commission on Human Security.

Olson, M. (1965). *The Logic of Collective Action*. Cambridge, MA: Harvard University Press.

O'Neil, J. (2001). *Building Better Global Economic BRICs*. Global Economics Paper 66. New York: Goldman Sachs.

Osakwe, P. and Poretti, M. (2015). 'Trade and poverty alleviation in Africa: the role of inclusive structural transformation'. Trade and Poverty Paper series No 2. Geneva: UNCTAD.

Parthasarathi, P. (2011). *Why Europe Grew Rich and Asia Did Not: Global Economic Divergence 1600–1850*. Cambridge: Cambridge University Press.

Peterson, D. (2015). 'Transduction and BRICS', *Manuscrito* 38/3: 15–24.

Petrie, D. and Tang, K. (2014). 'Relative health performance in BRICS over the past twenty years: the winners and losers', *Bulletin of the World Health Organization* 92: 396–404.

Population Reference Bureau (2014). *2014 World Population Data Sheet*. New York: United Nations.

Richmond, O. and Tellidis, I. (2014). 'Emerging actors in international peacebuilding and statebuilding: status quo or critical states?', *Global Governance* 20: 563–84.

Rodrik, D. (2009). *One Economics, Many Recipes: Globalization, Institutions, and Economic Growth*. Princeton, NJ: Princeton University Press.

Rodrik, D. (2013). 'What the world needs from the BRICS'. *Project Syndicate*, 10 April.

Rosenstein-Rodan, P. (1984). 'Natura facit saltum: Analysis of the disequilibrium growth process', in G. Meier and D. Seers (eds) *Pioneers in Development*. New York: Oxford University Press.

Rostow, W.W. (1960). *The Stages of Economic Growth: A Non-Communist Manifesto*. Cambridge: Cambridge University Press.

Royal African Society (2014). 'Democracy soup: democracy and development in Africa'. A Discussion Paper by the Africa All Party Parliamentary Group. London: Royal African Society.

Saget, C. (2006). *Wage Fixing in the Informal Economy: Evidence from Brazil, India, Indonesia and South Africa*. Conditions for Work and Employment Series No. 16. Geneva: ILO.

Sanfilippo, M. (2015). 'FDI from emerging markets and the productivity gap—an analysis on affiliates of BRICS EMNEs in Europe', *International Business Review* 24: 665–76.

Sen, A. (1979). *Equality of What?* The Tanner Lectures on Human Values. Stanford, CA: Stanford University Press.

Sen, A. (1990). 'More than 100 million women are missing', *New York Review of Books*, 20 December.

Sen, A. (1992). *Inequality Reexamined*. Oxford: Clarendon Press.

Sen, A. (2009). *The Idea of Justice*. London: Allen Lane.

Shahrokhi, M., Cheng, H., Dandapani, K., Figueiredo, A., Parhizgari, A., and Shachmurove, Y. (2017). 'The evolution and future of the BRICS: unbundling politics from economics', *Global Finance Journal* 32: 1–15.

Singh, K. (2016). 'Intra-BRICS trade intensities: an analytical study', *IOSR Journal of Humanities and Social Sciences* 21/6: 103–14.

Sosa, M. and Cabello, A. (2015). 'Stock market behavior in the emerging G-9 (BRICS+4)', *Problemas del Desarrollo: Revista Latinoamericana de Economia* 46: 181.

Stephen, M. (2017). 'Emerging powers and emerging trends in global governance', *Global Governance* 23: 483–502.

Stern, N., Dethier, J., and Rogers, F. (2005). *Growth and Empowerment: Making Development Happen*. Cambridge, MA: MIT Press.

Stuenkel, O. (2013). 'The financial crisis, contested legitimacy, and the genesis of intra-BRICS co-operation', *Global Governance* 19: 611–30.

Thompson, L. and de Wet, P. (2017). 'BRICS development strategies: exploring the meaning of BRICS "community" and "collective action" in the context of BRICS state-led co-operation in South Africa', *Chinese Political Science Review* 2/1: 101–13.

Tiwari, P., Rao, J., and Day, J. (2016). *Development Paradigms for Urban Housing in BRICS Countries*. London: Palgrave Macmillan.

Triesman, D. (2016). 'Russia's billionaires', *American Economic Review* 106/5: 236–41.

Tugcu, C. and Tiwari, A. (2016). 'Does renewable and/or non-renewable energy consumption matter for total factor productivity (TFP) growth? Evidence from the BRICS', *Renewable and Sustainable Energy Reviews* 65: 610–16.

UNCTAD (United Nations Conference on Trade and Development) (2017a). *Handbook of Statistics*. Geneva: UNCTAD. Available at http://unctadstat.unctad.org/EN/, accessed 21 February 2019.

UNCTAD (United Nations Conference on Trade and Development) (2017b). *Investment and the Digital Economy*. World Investment Report 2017. Vienna: UNCTAD.

United Nations. (2014). *World Urbanisation Prospects: 2014 Revision*. New York: United Nations.

United Nations. (2016). *The World's Cities in 2016: Data Booklet*. New York: United Nations.

Uslaner, E. (2002). *The Moral Foundations of Trust*. Cambridge: Cambridge University Press.

Uslaner, E. (2008). *Corruption, Inequality and the Rule of Law*. Cambridge: Cambridge University Press.

Web of Knowledge (n.d.). Available at https://www.webof knowledge.com/, accessed 21 February 2019.

Wilkinson, R. and Pickett, K. (2009). *The Spirit Level: Why More Equal Societies Almost Always Do Better*. London: Penguin.

Williamson, J. (1990). 'What Washington means by policy reform', in J. Williamson (ed.) *Latin American Adjustment: How Much has Happened?* Washington, DC: Institute for International Economics.

World Bank (2013). *World Development Report: Jobs*. Washington, DC: World Bank.

World Bank (2015). *East Asia's Changing Urban Landscape: Measuring a Decade of Spatial Growth*. Washington DC: World Bank.

World Bank (various years). World Development Indicators. Washington, DC: World Bank. Available at https://datacatalog.worldbank.org/dataset/world-development-indicators, accessed 6 March 2019.

Ziesemer, T.H.W. (2016). 'Gini coefficients of education for 146 countries, 1950–2010'. UNU-MERIT Working Paper No. 44. Maastricht: UNU-MERIT.

Part II

Economic Perspectives, Resources, and Development

2 World Trade Organization and BRICS

A historical perspective

Martin Daunton

Introduction

The World Trade Organization was established at the end of the Uruguay Round of trade talks held between 1986 and 1994—the last round to take place under the auspices of the General Agreement on Tariffs and Trade (GATT). The new body formally commenced on 1 January 1995, replacing and incorporating GATT which was the remnant of the abortive negotiations to create an International Trade Organization (ITO) after the Second World War. After initial exploratory talks in London in 1946, the delegates to the conference on trade and employment met in Geneva to draft a charter for the ITO. They agreed to GATT in 1947, before reconvening in Havana in 1947/8 to finalize the charter. Despite agreement at the conference, the charter was never ratified: the concessions made to the less developed countries to secure support meant that it was unacceptable to politicians back home in the advanced industrial economies, above all in the United States. All that was left was GATT, a contract on trade rules rather than an international institution, whose role was to facilitate rounds of trade talks in order to reduce tariff barriers and to establish rules to prevent the recurrence of trade wars that marred the 1930s (Brown 1952; Diebold 1952; Vernon 1995).

The problem, in the eyes of many developing countries, was that GATT was dominated by the interests of developed industrialized countries, and that its agenda was much narrower than the putative ITO. After the failure of the ITO, the less developed continued to press for a wider agenda through a number of other initiatives and institutions that articulated different and competing programmes for the world economy. At various times, the idea of an international trade organization resurfaced without securing widespread support, with the result that GATT's concern with trade policy remained distinct from wider notions of development. The creation of the World Trade Organization (WTO) at last brought them together, marking a partial return to the wider ambitions of the ITO with the launching of the ninth round of talks held since the formation of

Martin Daunton, *World Trade Organization and BRICS: A historical perspective* In: *Handbook of BRICS and Emerging Economies.* Edited by: P.B. Anand, Shailaja Fennell, and Flavio Comim, Oxford University Press (2021). © Oxford University Press.
DOI: 10.1093/oso/9780198827535.003.0002

GATT—the Doha Development Round. The aim of this chapter is to explain the longer historical background to the creation of the WTO and the Doha Round, explaining developing countries' ambitions for international economic policies held since the Second World War and the role of BRICs in these debates.

Of course, the particular grouping of BRICs made little sense in the post-war trade talks, for Brazil, Russia, India, and China had little in common in terms of their ideologies, economies, or political systems. The Soviet Union had a massive presence in Europe that troubled the advanced capitalist economies—and it offered support or inspiration to nationalist movements in the colonies. The Soviet Union did not participate in the talks leading to GATT, and during the Cold War, the Soviets positioned themselves as allies of the less developed countries, supporting their criticism of GATT and arguing for a wider international trade organization. Nationalist China took part in the talks at Bretton Woods but played little role in later discussions over trade as it faced imminent defeat by Mao's communist forces. India actively engaged in the trade discussions, at the very point that it was emerging from British rule and seeking to implement its approach to economic policy. It played a major part in the discussions, taking over from Australia as the leading advocate of policies designed to assist non-industrial economies. But the lead at trade talks was soon taken by Latin America, with Brazil playing the role of the sensible intermediary between the United States and the more radical countries in Latin America. Any use of the term BRICs is therefore an anachronism, for they were not in any sense a coherent grouping in terms of their politics, ideologies, or economics. But they do illustrate the different visions and tensions over development policies, both between themselves and in relation to the developed world.

The failure of the ITO and survival of GATT

After the war, the American administration—above all, Secretary of State Cordell Hull—wished to return to an open, multilateral world economy that they assumed would lead to economic recovery. This view was not accepted by many other countries. Australia, a primary producing country seriously affected by the depression of the 1930s, argued for the use of international resources to their full extent in order to maintain international demand and employment, and it managed to widen the post-war conference from only trade to include employment. The Australians insisted on an obligation on advanced economies—above all the United States—to maintain high and stable employment so that 'dependent' countries could safely remove protection in the knowledge that there were markets for their commodities. They complained that the American proposals to restore multilateral trade would merely 'fossilize' production and trade on existing lines as if it were natural rather than a product of history (Jenkins 1945: 240–2; NARA 30 Jan 1945, 13 March 1945, 2 July 1945, 30–31 Aug, 2 Sept 1946; Rowse 2000, 2002: Part 5; TNA 4 Oct 1946, 15 Oct 1946; Turnell, 1999).

Leadership soon passed to India which took the argument on employment a stage further, in ways that were even more unacceptable to the industrial economies. They stressed the need for developmental tariffs, quantitative controls, and economic planning by a strong state. Although Gandhi favoured *swadeshi* or self-sufficiency through cottage industries and the village community, the left wing of the Indian National Congress preferred planning, in part following the Soviet march to industrialization through massive capital projects and modern technology, though by democratic means and without collectivization of agriculture. Such a policy would entail controls over imports and exports, a largely closed economy with strict currency regulations, contrary to the American demand for open trade. Furthermore, the result would be 'immediate unemployment in other countries in the industries it was developing'—a threat that alarmed the British government. The Indians were adamant that the charter should allow countries to take action appropriate to their particular stage of development and to their social and political institutions (Government of India Planning Commission, 1952; NARA 1949; TNA 21 Oct 1946, 11 Nov 1946; Zachariah 2005).

When the conference reassembled in Cuba, leadership of the developing countries passed to Latin America. The Cubans argued that members of the ITO 'should be obliged to take every action against conditions detrimental to work-people' (TNA 22 Oct 1946), in particular the exploitation of sweated labour by foreign investors; workers should be guaranteed a 'dignified existence'. Above all, the Latin Americans developed new industries during the war as a result of a reduction in imports from the United States and Europe; after the war, they feared the revival of competition. Consequently, they wanted to retain quantitative restrictions and preferential arrangements to encourage regional economic integration and import, substituting industrialization. The Latin Americans raised a further issue with very serious implications for American business: the treatment of overseas investment. The less developed countries felt that advanced countries had an obligation to provide capital regardless of commercial criteria or political concerns in order to encourage development in accordance with national plans, and profits made from exploiting national resources should go to the nation and not to foreigners (DCER, 4 June 1948, 13 July 1948; NARA March 1948; TNA 28 Oct 1946, 29 Nov 1947).

Such an approach was clearly not acceptable to American interests that feared a continuation of trade warfare, closed markets, industrial inefficiency, and confiscation of investments without adequate compensation. But the American delegation had no alternative except to redraft the charter at Havana to meet the demands of the less developed countries. They gave way on voting rights within the ITO, dropping the weighted voting of the IMF in favour of one member, one vote, in the expectation that it would encourage more members to join, and in the hope that the more inclusive body could still be controlled by the Americans (TNA 12 March 1948). They also gambled on appointing Ramon Beteta, Finance Minister of Mexico, as chairman of the committee for economic development, despite concerns about Mexico's economic policy of 'industry saturation'. When any industry reached a point where expansion would harm labour, capital, or the public, the state could prevent any further growth to maintain a balance of wages, profits, and prices. The choice of Beteta was part of an attempt to divide the Latin Americans, who were split between moderate countries—in particular, Brazil which saw an opportunity to win favour from the United States—and extremists such as the Argentinian economics minister Manuel Molinari who argued that the choice was between capitalism (represented by the ITO), totalitarianism (represented by the Soviets), or a socialized economy as in Peronist Argentina (NARA 3 Dec 1947, 4 Dec 1947, 5 Dec 1947, 9 Dec 1947, 30 Jan 1948, 6 Feb 1948, March 1948; Truman Presidential Library 31 January 1946).

Although the Latin Americans were far from a coherent bloc, and were more concerned with national interest, they could still cause considerable trouble and force the Americans into making concessions. The redrafted Havana Charter included an obligation that each member develop its economic resources, and adopt 'measures appropriate to its political and, economic and social conditions'. A statement was inserted obliging countries to take whatever action was appropriate and feasible to eliminate sub-standard conditions of labour in production for export. New preferences were permitted, and quantitative restrictions (QR) could continue. These were nods in the direction of the demands from Australia, India, and Latin America in order to secure their agreement to the charter. The concessions did not go as far as the less developed countries wished, for the obligations on employment were diluted and there were too few positive obligations to support development. Even so, the ITO, if it had been adopted, would have covered not only trade but also employment, economic development, commodities, investment, and restrictive business practices by international cartels. Revisions to the charter went too far to be acceptable to businessmen or politicians back home on Capitol Hill who saw restrictive, nationalistic measures, socialist attacks on capitalism, and a threat to cartels. It was simply not practical domestic politics (DCER 4 June 1948, 13 July 1948; NARA 9 Feb 1948; TNA 10 March 1948, 12 March 1948, 10 May 1949; Toye 2003; Vernon 1995).

The charter of the ITO faded away without being presented to Congress for ratification. All that was left was the supposedly interim GATT—and a great sense of disappointed hopes both for American disciples of Hull in search of multilateral trade and the underdeveloped countries in search of policies to encourage development. American policy soon changed from Hull's enthusiasm for free trade as the solution to all problems to a more realistic use of Marshall Aid and a European customs' union. Where did this leave the underdeveloped countries?

The road to Bandung

GATT's shortcoming was that it limited the voice of less developed nations and narrowed the agenda from the wider issues of economic development and employment to a concern for trade barriers. Similar limitations appeared in the International Bank for

Reconstruction and Development (IBRD). The original idea of the IBRD emerged from discussions about American policy towards Latin America before the war, when radical New Dealers criticized Hull's free trade policies as inadequate. They wished to help fellow victims of New York financiers and to raise living standards as the basis for political stability. Their ambition was to promote long-run economic development, rejecting tight money policies and supporting large public development loans rather than private investment. After the war, New Dealers had the same ambition for the IBRD; on the other side were cautious Wall Street bankers and fiscal conservatives who felt it should encourage private funds by offering guarantees. The difference of approach was apparent in Colombia in 1949/50. Lauchlin Currie, a New Dealer, argued for a policy of 'balanced growth' based on programme loans, an integrated development plan, and investment in social overhead capital such as health and education. The leaders of the IBRD in Washington favoured specific project loans that were self-financing and liquidating (Alacevich 2009; Helleiner 2014).

Both GATT and the IBRD risked being challenged by less developed countries on the grounds that they maintained the economic status quo, representing the interests of the advanced industrial countries. The less developed countries attempted to reinsert their concerns into the governance of the world economy through the Economic and Social Council of the United Nations (ECOSOC), a body that discussed economic and social questions. Underdeveloped countries were well-represented on ECOSOC, and the question of full employment was discussed in 1949 in the context of a downturn in the American economy. The Australians were eager for the matter to go straight to the General Assembly; the United States was equally eager that the matter remain with ECOSOC, as were the Latin Americans who thought that the Assembly should focus on wider issues of economic development. The outcome was to invite a group of experts to report on the 'national and international measures to achieve and maintain full employment'. The terms of references were a matter of dispute. The Americans agreed when their concern for non-discrimination in trade was added; and underdeveloped nations inserted a commitment to 'a high and stable level of international investment, particularly in under-developed areas of the world' (DAFP 14 Oct 1949). Full employment was of little interest to India, Pakistan, and (nationalist) China who drew attention to underemployment and development. The General Assembly therefore asked ECOSOC to widen its remit from full employment to unemployment and underemployment (DAFP, 9 Aug 1949a, 1949b, 21 Oct 1949, 25 Oct 1949, 10 Nov 1949).

The experts quickly produced a report on *National and International Measures for Full Employment* which was largely the work of Nicholas Kaldor. The report recommended the adoption of Keynesian measures to create domestic full employment, with international measures to prevent the spread of fluctuations around the world by requiring any country whose imports fell below the level needed for full employment to deposit with the IMF a sum equivalent to the deflationary impact. The report took the view that stable exchange rates and free trade could not restore equilibrium in a world of dollar scarcities, and recommended that ECOSOC call a world trade-adjustment conference. It also argued that full employment needed economic development based on planned and stable capital movements between governments, organized by the IBRD as programmatic rather than project loans. The report offered an alternative vision for the IMF and IBRD which they firmly rejected. In any case, interest in full employment was waning for the low level of unemployment in industrial economies meant that the issue was less relevant to them than after the war when they feared the onset of depression in the US would spread to the rest of the world. Meanwhile, the underdeveloped countries turned in a new direction, towards underemployment and economic development (Kindleberger 1955; Toye and Toye 2006).

In 1950, a group of less developed countries at ECOSOC (Brazil, Chile, India, Pakistan, Peru) criticized the report on full employment for neglecting underemployment, and the American representative proposed the appointment of experts to report on the issue, including W. Arthur Lewis who provided much of the intellectual agenda. *Measures for the Economic Development of Under-Developed Countries* appeared in 1951, largely following Lewis's approach. It concentrated on economic development as the route to solving underemployment through industrialization. It emphasized the need for economic, political, social, and legal institutions which would support development—with a political elite committed to a development strategy—and the emergence of governments able to regulate economic activities. Once these preconditions were in place—a highly optimistic assumption—economic development could take place. Lewis believed that underdeveloped countries could utilize the technology of advanced countries, and the marginal productivity of capital would be high because it was scarce relative to labour. In Lewis's opinion, labour was available at a low real cost as a result of underemployment in agriculture where its marginal productivity was low or even negative. Hence labour could be moved from agriculture without any loss of production and employed in industry at a fixed real wage, leading to labour-intensive industrialization for export and the reinvestment of profits. Economic development therefore meant industrialization and long-term structural change rather than Keynesian demand management which might be more appropriate for advanced industrial countries (Lewis 1954; Tignor 2006; Toye and Toye 2006).

The United Nations moved from a concern with managing effective demand and full employment to issues of economic underdevelopment. In 1952, the General Assembly instructed ECOSOC to prepare a plan for a special fund to make grants and low-interest long-term loans to underdeveloped countries 'to finance non-self-liquidating projects which are basic to their economic development'—a way of overcoming the conservative leadership of the IBRD. The American administration was placed in a dilemma: should it refuse to take part in discussions of a plan it was bound to oppose when it came before the Assembly; or should it join discussions to secure the best possible outcome? On balance, it made more sense to participate so as not to appear hostile to the ambitions of the underdeveloped countries. The American line was that assistance should come from the IBRD and private capital flows, but the underdeveloped countries felt that a new international agency was needed, more under their influence and with recognition that the developed world had an obligation to provide non-self-liquidating loans for social and economic overhead capital (FRUS 22 April 1952, 2 May 1952).

In 1953, the plan for the new fund—now with the acronym SUNFED (Special United Nations Fund for Economic Development)—came to ECOSOC. American attitudes started to shift for political reasons. In April 1953, President Eisenhower seized the opportunity provided by the death of Stalin to call for a reduction of armaments, with any savings used to create a 'fund for world aid and reconstruction . . . to help other peoples to develop the undeveloped areas of the world, to stimulate profitable and fair world trade, to assist all peoples to know the blessings of productive freedom'. He was seeking to take the initiative from the Soviets at a vital point of the Cold War (Eisenhower 1953). Obviously, his rhetoric did not sit well with American hostility to SUNFED and another initiative of ECOSOC, the International Finance Corporation, which was intended to make grants or 'fuzzy' loans to underdeveloped countries.

The Americans were in a dilemma. They preferred to rely on the normal forces of free enterprise and competition through tariff reductions, private capital flows, and technical assistance. But they also realized that 'many of the newly sovereign underdeveloped countries consider foreign private capital as a form of colonialism while many of the long independent underdeveloped countries consider it a means of exploitation'. This division fed into Cold War politics, for

> the situation in the Council [ECOSOC] smacks of a naked bid for redistribution of national wealth by the poorer countries of the world. There is always in the background the implication that unless the richer nations, particularly the United States, can provide adequate material assistance the underdeveloped countries must resort to communism and totalitarian means in an effort to lift themselves by their own economic bootstraps. The underdeveloped countries in the Council are not therefore averse to exploiting the cold war for their own benefit.
>
> (FRUS 22 May 1952, 28 Jan 1953, 17 June 1953, 4 Feb 1954, 17 May 1954, 1 June 1954, 1 July 1954, 2 July 1954, 9 Sept 1954, 8 Oct 1954, 2 Nov 1954a, 1954b, 3 Nov 1954, 7 Dec 1954)

John Foster Dulles, the Secretary of State, saw the dangers of a rigid adherence to self-financing loans. 'It might be good banking to put South America through the wringer, but it will come out red' (Kapur et al. 1997: 136). Above all, President Kennedy wished to win back the initiative to the United Nations by announcing the 'Development Decade' of the 1960s.

These tensions over policy took place in the context of the emergence of a stronger voice from the undeveloped countries of the world at the Bandung Conference on Asian and African Countries in April 1955, in the context of struggles against colonialism and the Cold War which allowed developing countries to play the Americans against the Soviets. Politicians in undeveloped countries doubted that the world economy was organized fairly between the interests of industrial and non-industrial countries, and proposed measures to raise as well as stabilize the prices of primary products, and to alter the existing pattern of comparative advantage in the world economy. Rather than international trade offering the benefits of comparative advantage to all participants, they complained that it supplied cheap raw materials to manufacturing countries, leading to exploitation and dependence. The Bandung Conference was initiated by the leaders of five countries—Nehru of India, Sukarno of Indonesia, Tito of Yugoslavia, Nasser of Egypt, and Nkrumah of Ghana—and brought together representatives of a diverse group including Japan, the People's Republic of China, North and South Vietnam, Saudi Arabia, Egypt, Iran, and Iraq (Indonesian Ministry of Foreign Affairs 1955). Whether these countries could hold together as a cohesive bloc was doubtful.

Sukarno had been a leading figure in securing independence after the war against British and American attempts to restore Dutch rule. At Bandung, Sukarno announced that

> we are united... by a common detestation of colonialism in whatever form it appears... We are often told 'Colonialism is dead.'... I say to you, colonialism is not yet dead. How can we say it is dead, so long as vast areas of Asia and Africa are unfree.
>
> And, I beg of you do not think of colonialism only in the classic form which we of Indonesia, and our brothers in different parts of Asia and Africa, knew. Colonialism has also its modern dress, in the form of economic control, intellectual control, actual physical control by a small but alien community within a nation.

He urged the peoples of Africa and Asia—half the population of the world—to unite and show that 'we, the majority are for peace, not for war' (Indonesian Ministry of Foreign Affairs 1955: 19–29). Initially, the Americans backed Sukarno against the threat of Communism, but they soon had doubts as he embarked on a policy of economic nationalism by taking over Dutch companies and turning to both the Soviet Union and China for support. Sukarno played the West and communist powers against each other, accusing them both of spreading neocolonialism and imperialism, but he increasingly moved into the communist orbit in an alliance with China, North Korea, North Vietnam, and Cambodia.

Kwame Nkrumah was the dominant figure in Ghana from its partial self-government in 1951 and independence in 1957. His policy was non-aligned Marxism as explained in *Neo-colonialism: The Last Stage of Imperialism*: 'The essence of neo-colonialism is that the State which is subject to it is, in theory, independent and has all the outward trappings of international sovereignty. In reality, its economic system and this political policy is directed from the outside' (Nkrumah 1965: intro; Rathbone 2004). Hence his policies were designed to lessen Ghana's dependence on foreign capital, to reduce foreign trade, and to industrialize with major schemes such as the Akosombo Dam.

Nehru set out the basis of non-alignment between the advanced Western economies and Communism, a path towards self-sufficiency and freedom in a world divided by the Cold War:

> If I join any of these big groups I lose my identity... If all the world were to be divided up between these two big blocs what would be the result? The inevitable result would be war. Therefore every step that takes place in reducing that area in the world which may be called the *unaligned area is* a dangerous step and leads to war. It reduces that objective, that balance, that outlook which other countries without military might can perhaps exercise.

...Many members present here do not obviously accept the communist ideology, while some of them do. I want positive good for my country and the world. Therefore, are we, the countries of Asia and Africa, devoid of any positive position except being pro-communist or anti-communist?...It is an intolerable thought to me that the great countries of Asia and Africa should come out of bondage into freedom only to degrade themselves or humiliate themselves in this way... (Kahlin 1956: 64–72)

The reality of bringing together such a diverse group of countries was not likely to be easy—indeed, war broke out between some of the countries that attended the Bandung Conference. Nevertheless, the final communiqué confidently reported their 'general desire for economic co-operation...on the basis of mutual interest and respect for national sovereignty'. They supported SUNFED and the International Finance Corporation; they urged action to stabilize international commodity prices and demand; and called on countries to diversify their export trade by processing raw materials. The communiqué denounced colonialism in all its forms, and in particular urged independence for Tunisia, Algeria, and Morocco, and support for Palestine (Indonesian Ministry of Foreign Affairs 1955: 161–9).

The creation of UNCTAD

The countries that met at Bandung largely represented recently independent countries in Asia and Africa rather than Latin America with its longer history of independence. They joined a wider group of countries to take up the issue of development, pressing for a different approach from the Bretton Woods institutions dominated by the advanced industrial countries. The outcome was the creation of the United Nations Conference on Trade and Development (UNCTAD), many of whose ideas came from Latin America which had played a major role at the Havana conference of 1947–8.

The spread of independence gave more underdeveloped countries a voice in the United Nations. By the early 1960s, the original UN membership of fifty-one had more than doubled, and the less developed countries were close to the two-thirds majority needed to pass resolutions, allowing them to express their concerns and challenge the advanced industrial nations. They argued that the IMF, IBRD, and GATT were agencies of the developed 'core', indifferent or hostile to the concerns of the poorer countries of the world. ECOSOC did not reflect the change in the overall membership of the UN which continued with eighteen members more or less equally divided between developed and less developed countries. Reform was blocked by the Soviet Union's insistence that China should have priority in securing a seat. By the time the Soviets changed their position in 1963, the less developed countries preferred to replace ECOSOC with another body that would more adequately reflect their interests. It appeared to the less developed countries that a new approach was needed to deal with the relationship between the majority of poor countries with their large populations, and the minority of rich countries with their smaller populations and dominance of trade and production (Gardner 1968: 101).

Clearly, these issues connected with the Cold War, for the newly independent nations were the battleground between the West and Communism. Both the United States and the Soviets intervened in the Third World for strategic reasons and ideological commitment. In 1956, Khrushchev informed the Communist Party of the Soviet Union that the day had arrived 'when people of the East take an active part in settling the destinies of the whole world... They now have no need to go begging to their former oppressors for modern equipment. They can obtain such equipment in the socialist countries'. In a speech to the UN in 1960, Khrushchev linked the productive possibilities of socialism with national liberation movements, and in 1961 he offered Soviet support to the struggles of colonial peoples in wars of national liberation. Limited American aid gave the Soviets an opportunity to offer large sums to Eqypt, Indonesia, India, and Cuba (Westad 2005: 4–6, 27, 31–2, 40, 68, 71–2, 107–8).

The US had to respond, and President Kennedy's approach was shaped by 'modernization' theory, above all of W.W. Rostow. Traditional society was characterized as inert and inflexible, dominated by agrarian elites without a powerful middle class, a simple economy, subservience to nature, and a sense of fatalism. A modern society was more like America: flexible and adaptable, welcoming change, secular and outward looking, with a complex economy, and a willingness to subjugate the physical world. The theory helped to shape American economic and foreign policy in the 1960s, offering a capitalist alternative to Marx and the Soviet path to modernity and a more constructive post-colonial relationship. Military security was crucial during the stresses of transition which could be exploited by the communists, but was not enough. Aid should be 'unlinked', offered to all non-communist countries without specific political obligations, provided they used the funds effectively to stimulate economic growth, so that societies would be able to increase their military strength and have a direct interest in opposing Communism (Gilman 2003: 175–81; Latham 2000: 43–4). Although it was not practical to remove aid from countries such as Vietnam and Laos facing an immediate communist threat, Rostow argued that funds should be concentrated on countries with the capacity to absorb capital productively such as India, Pakistan, Nigeria, Argentina, Brazil, Colombia, and Venezuela (FRUS 23 February 1961).

Kennedy's public engagement with development started with a speech on 13 March 1961 (Kennedy 1961a) when he announced the Alliance for Progress, a programme for Latin America. The turning point was Operation Pan-America proposed by the President of Brazil, Juscelino Kubitschek, in 1958, to counter uprisings by removing poverty and misery through a large-scale development programme. Raúl Presbisch, an Argentinian economist and former head of the national bank who was now at the Economic Commission for Latin America, saw an opportunity, positioning himself as an ally of America in order to attract support against communist threats in the developing world. He pointed out that the Soviets and Communism were threatening private enterprise, and capitalism had not fully met the challenge. America needed to act, and the only way private enterprise could survive was through improving standards of living and allowing social mobility for the most dynamic members of society. Communism could not be met by 'obsolete nineteenth-century concepts of economic development' but only by America taking bold and imaginative action. In 1960, the Eisenhower administration set up a Social Progress Trust Fund to assist in reforming agriculture, education, health, and housing. Kennedy took the process a step further to a more ambitious programme of modernization. A strong message was needed to counter Communism. A task force was appointed, and reported that the preconditions were already in place in Latin America 'in sharp contrast to most of Africa, which still lacked the preconditions for take-off, and South and Southeast Asia, which would have to overcome ancient cultural obstacles'. In Latin America, the obstacles of a semi-feudal agrarian structure could be overcome through land reform, social welfare, and support for democracy to create a middle-class revolution and a modern technical society. Kennedy announced an Alliance for Progress, 'a vast cooperative effort, unparalleled in magnitude and nobility of purpose, to satisfy the basic needs of the American people for homes, work and land, health and schools'. The Alliance for Progress countered the Cuban revolution with an alternative vision of liberal capitalism that would see the republics of Latin America through the stresses of transition (Kennedy, 1961a; Latham 2000: 77–8, 80–1; Prebisch 1958 [1963]).

The Alliance for Progress dealt with Latin America, and might imply that the United States was creating a trade bloc at the expense of multilateral trade and other developing economies. Kennedy's second major intervention was therefore to widen his ambition by declaring the 1960s a 'development decade' to help 'less-developed nations into self-sustained economic growth'. These new nations faced the threat of Communism, and it was crucial to show that 'economic growth and political democracy can develop hand in hand'. The General Assembly agreed in December 1961, but the Americans were not able to prevent the inclusion of two troublesome items. The first demand came from Iraq: an increasing share of the profit from the exploitation of natural resources by foreign capital should go to the host country. The second demand was a Soviet invitation to ECOSOC to consider the principles of international economic cooperation for the improvement of world economic relations. The Soviets were exploiting the concerns of less developed countries that their voice was not being heard and that the existing structure of multilateral institutions was not ideal. Although the Soviets boycotted the ITO conferences in 1947–8, they introduced a resolution at ECOSOC in 1955 urging the ratification of the charter. In 1956, the Soviets proposed a conference to consider 'the most pressing economic problems connected with the expansion of international cooperation', including the establishment of a world trade organization. The proposal was rejected by the General Assembly but the Soviets returned to the issue in 1958, urging a second UN conference on trade and employment, and the creation of an international trade organization. The Soviets were challenging the international economic institutions associated with the advanced capitalist economies (Cordovez 1967: 255–6; FRUS 16 January 1962; Kennedy 1961b).

The less developed countries felt that GATT's concern with trade barriers and discrimination was largely irrelevant to—or even inconsistent with—their interests in development (Gardner 1964: 688, 1968: 102). They demanded a forum for the comprehensive review of trade and development policy. In 1961, delegates from Latin America and from Africa and Indonesia put forward separate resolutions proposing an international conference on world trade. The Soviets saw an opportunity. In May 1962 Khrushchev denounced the Common Market as a form of neocolonialism, calling for an international trade conference and an increase in the average price of raw materials (Rubinstein 1964: 170–1). In July 1962, a conference on the problems of developing countries was held in Cairo, attended by thirty-six countries. The conference called for strengthening of the economic and social activities of the UN, and for an international economic conference within the framework of the UN to consider trade, commodities, and the economic relations between developing and developed countries (UN ECOSOC 1962). The idea was accepted by the General Assembly and ECOSOC. Although the Americans were not enthusiastic they realized that opposing the idea would confirm Soviet criticism of them and the Common Market.

The first secretary general of UNCTAD was Raúl Prebisch, a charismatic figure who expressed the views of the less developed countries. His views were shaped by the experience of Argentina where he was head of the national bank until 1943. Although he was initially a free trader, he changed his mind with the collapse of the market for beef and wheat as a result of European tariffs between the wars. The price of food exports fell more than the price of imports of manufactures so that debt service was more difficult, and in common with other Latin American economies, Argentina moved to self-sufficiency and import substituting industrialization in the 1930s. In 1949, Hans Singer of the UN economic affairs department argued that the terms of trade between primary producers and advanced industrial countries were systematically skewed against the former and in favour of the latter, and this line was taken up by Prebisch who joined the Economic Commission for Latin America (ECLA) in 1949. ECLA was an initiative of Hernan Santa Cruz of Chile at ECOSOC in 1947. He felt that Latin America was being neglected by the great powers on the grounds that the area escaped wartime devastation. He argued that the charter of the UN obliged it to tackle the problems of undeveloped countries, and that ECLA should deal with the problems of the area (Santa Cruz 1995: 24–5).

In 1950, Prebisch produced a report for ECLA on *The Economic Development of Latin America and its Principal Problems*, drawing on the ideas of Singer to suggest that the fall in primary products relative to manufactures was systemic rather than short term. Prebisch argued that trade benefited exporters of manufactured goods at the expense of primary producers, and that per capita income between the two groups of countries widened as trade grew. Why did the divergence occur? Costs were sticky in industrialized countries because of the power of unions, and technical progress favoured demand for industrial goods over agriculture. In countries with technical progress, labour was better able to retain gains. He stressed the role of the trade cycles as a central element in the growth of capitalist economies: the price of primary products rose faster than industrial prices in booms, whereas in a slump they fell more because of resistance to cutting wages in the centre. By contrast, workers in primary producing countries could not increase wages so much in the boom or maintain them in the slump. Cyclical pressures were passed from the centre to the periphery. It followed that the international division of labour was an 'out-dated schema' and 'industrialization is the only means by which the Latin American countries may fully obtain the advantages of technical progress'. Further, multilateral trade was not fair unless linked with a secular increase in the relative price of primary products, and not merely stabilization. In 1950, Prebisch (1958 [1963]) was moving away from import substituting industrialization, and at UNCTAD he went further in arguing that excessive industrialization could lead to inefficiency and high costs. He turned instead to 'outward looking' industrialization by developed countries opening their markets on preferential terms (Toye and Toye 2004; UN 1950: 5–7).

The first meeting of UNCTAD in Geneva in 1964 was the largest trade conference ever called, with 2,000 delegates from 121 countries. The expectations of the less developed countries ran high. They wanted the conference to recommend steps for developed countries to create a new international division of labour and reduce income disparities. They believed that a transfer of resources from industrial to less developed countries was a matter of right, and that the present organization of trade was rigged against them by the most favoured nation principle and comparative advantage—a serious threat to the entire basis of the liberal multilateral economy advocated by the Americans since the war.

Before any major policy issues could be resolved, the conference had to address the institutional structure for future discussions. There were a number of possible solutions. The Soviets proposed an autonomous ITO, which did not appeal to the advanced industrial countries; or—more surprisingly—to most developing countries who feared a repeat of the failures of Havana. Most favoured the evolution of GATT, provided that it became more representative and modified its policies to assist less developed countries. Prebisch proposed that GATT should work alongside a periodic meeting of UNCTAD, with a standing committee and intellectually independent secretariat with authority to submit proposals within the framework of the UN. Such an approach meant that existing institutions would retain their autonomy while working with the conference on issues of trade and development. It offered the attractions of an ITO without the need for a separate specialized agency which would not be accepted by Congress. The Soviets were placed in a difficult position for they had little to offer to the developing countries. Removing tariffs on imports from developing countries was pointless in a planned economy, and they could not pay the less developed countries in convertible currencies or allow them to escape the rigid bilateralism of Soviet trade. The advanced industrial countries were uneasy about the prospect of constant pressure on GATT, but the conference resolved in favour of reconstituting GATT alongside periodic conferences with a standing committee, the Trade and Development Board. In order to prevent the Soviets from exploiting UNCTAD, and to ensure that developing countries did not dominate, the advanced economies responded by seeking equal representation on the board with conference having only limited power to act independently (Cordovez 1967: 271–9; Gardner 1964: 688; UN 1963).

The solution was to select the members of the Trade and Development Board from four lists of countries: Group A: Africa and Asia, plus Yugoslavia (22 members); B: Western Europe, US, Canada, Japan, Australia, New Zealand, and Cyprus (18); C: Latin America and the Caribbean (9); and D: the socialist countries (6). In theory, each group could work out a common position that would facilitate discussion—but the political and economic interests of the members of each group were not identical, and developing countries adopted a strong line that was rhetorically satisfying and politically unrealistic. The system was not suitable for considering precise concessions, for individual negotiators had little independence and had to refer back to the group. Cross-group concessions and alliances were difficult to achieve. Furthermore, the secretariat was seen as partisan in putting forward controversial views supported by the less developed countries. As a result, the body lacked credibility and was more interested in presenting demands than with actual results. The organizational structure of UNCTAD meant that failure was virtually guaranteed (Cordovez 1967: 281–313, 323–5; Dell 1973; Gardner 1968: 104–6; Walters 1971;Weiss 1986: 5, 59, 98).

The programme for the conference was developed by Prebisch in response to the post-war triumph of 'economic universalism' over the views of the underdeveloped countries. He rejected free trade orthodoxy on the grounds that systemic bias in the world economy reduced the benefits of trade to underdeveloped countries (Toye and Toye 2004: book 5). The bias could be redressed in a number of ways: 'fair and remunerative prices' for the commodities of less developed countries rather than a long-term equilibrium price; a Generalized System of Preferences (GSP) or non-reciprocal, preferential treatment for their manufactures to prevent a repeat of the inward-looking industrialization pursued in Latin America; and compensatory finance to assist countries with a shortfall in export earnings caused by fluctuations in commodity prices. But progress was slow, and in October 1967 ministers from the group of seventy-seven developing countries met in Algiers to review the situation: they were highly critical, and set out an ambitious programme of action, again with scant practical outcome (FRUS 12 Nov 1963; G77 1964, 1967; Kennedy Presidential Library 20 Oct 1963; NARA 6 May 1963).

Continued dissatisfaction with progress led to the creation of a New International Economic Order (NIEO) and the Charter of Economic Rights and Duties of States—an initiative of President Luis Echeverria of Mexico. The NIEO offered a way to overcome divisions between the less developed countries with a longer history of independence in Latin America and poorer, newly independent countries in Africa—a difference that was apparent in the more radical resolutions of the Non-Aligned Movement at Lusaka in 1970, with its stress on neocolonialism, the need for restitution to compensate past victims, and the demand that the exploiters reform the world's economic system (Murphy 1984: 2, 77–9, 85, 91–4, 96, 101, 103, 105–6). In September 1973, a conference of non-aligned countries called for a special session of the General Assembly to study 'problems related to raw materials and development'. The declaration urged steps to reverse the adverse trends in the trade of developing countries, through non-reciprocity and preferential treatment and by extending the GSP to cover the major agricultural commodities. The declaration stressed 'the vital necessity of making every possible effort to consolidate their national independence and reinforce their fighting front by challenging imperialist and neo-colonial exploitation structures and by organising cooperation and solidarity with one another in intercontinental and regional organizations'. They 'reaffirm each country's inalienable right to the full exercise of national sovereignty over its natural resources and all domestic economic activities', and insisted on the right of each state to control its natural resources by means suited to its own situation, including nationalization. They condemned transnational corporations which infringed the sovereignty of developing countries (UN 1973).

The increased militancy of the developing world had been building up for some time, and was now reinforced by the action of the Organization of the Petroleum Exporting Countries (OPEC). In January 1974, the French called for an international energy conference, and President Houari Boumedienne of Algeria, Chairman of the non-aligned movement, argued that it would be more valuable if it covered all raw materials. His proposal for a special session of the General Assembly on raw materials and development attracted sufficient support for it to be called early in 1974. The rise in oil prices did not break the unity of developing countries in the special session, despite the fact that the majority were oil importers. Rather, it united them in showing the power of primary producers, and in demanding an NIEO. Henry Kissinger warned primary producers that they were not insulated from the impact of restricted supplies or higher prices of oil, since a recession in the industrial countries would sharply reduce demand, and higher prices for raw materials would lead to a search for alternatives (Toye and Toye 2005: 169, 170).

Despite Kissinger's warnings, on 1 May 1974 the General Assembly adopted, without a vote, a declaration on the establishment of an NIEO based on:

> equity, sovereign equality, interdependence, common interest and cooperation among all States, irrespective of their economic and social systems which shall correct inequalities and redress existing injustice, make it possible to eliminate the widening gap between the developed and the developing countries and ensure steadily accelerating economic and social development and peace and justice for present and future generations. (Resolution 3201 (S-VI))

Each state was to have:

> full permanent sovereignty . . . over its natural resources and all economic activities. In order to safeguard these resources, each State is entitled to exercise effective control over them and their exploitation with means suitable to its own situation, including the right to nationalization or transfer of ownership to its nationals, this right being an expression of the full permanent sovereignty of the State. (Resolution 3201 (S-VI)

Further, the less developed countries demanded full compensation for the exploitation of their resources by colonial domination, and requested the regulation of transnational corporations. The Charter of Economic Rights and Duties of States followed in December 1974. Developed countries should extend general, non-reciprocal and non-discriminatory preferences to developing countries; and developing countries should extend preferences to each other (UN 1974).

Gamani Corea, a Sri Lankan diplomat and politician, became secretary general of UNCTAD in 1974, and he seized the initiative with a proposal for an integrated programme of commodities. A new international agency should own stocks and manage commodity prices, financed from a central or common fund provided by oil producers. Prices should be 'remunerative to producers and equitable to consumers'—an ambiguous formula. When the G77 countries met in Manila in January–February 1976, they dropped the integrated programme for commodities—in order to secure support from Latin America—in favour of individual commodity agreements backed by a common fund. Despite the endorsement of these proposals at UNCTAD in Nairobi in 1976, and the eventual ratification of the common fund in 1988, nothing of any practical significance emerged. The only success of Prebisch and UNCTAD was the adoption of GSP by GATT as a special waiver in 1971 and an enabling clause in 1979 (Hoekman and Ozden 2005; Toye and Toye 2004: 243–6).

Indeed, the NIEO was in retreat in the early 1980s. In 1981, Mexico had to suspend payments on its international debt. The Mexican moratorium of August 1982 was followed by a much more serious debt crisis in the developing countries, particularly in Latin America. Although the growth rate in industrial countries improved slightly in the 1980s, growth in developing countries fell, and the middle-income developing countries and sub-Saharan Africa contracted. Their policy autonomy was challenged, and aid came with an obligation to follow neoliberal policies (Toye and Toye 2005: 151–2). Solidarity between oil-producing and oil-importing developing countries fractured, for the price of minerals and agricultural commodities fell compared with the surge in oil prices. The failure to set up a common fund meant that less developed countries could not support large buffer stocks. In the absence of cooperation between producers and consumers, some less developed countries looked to collective action on the lines of OPEC, but there were few if any commodities other than oil with sufficient common interest or lack of substitute (ODI 1982).

Attitudes to development were shifting. In India, Indira Gandhi launched a populist programme to end poverty and create employment in the countryside (Bose 1997: 54–6). The policies of the Economic Commission for Latin America and the Caribbean (ECLAC) also underwent a radical change in the mid-1980s. Chile embarked on a neoliberal experiment, and ECLAC was undergoing institutional and ideological change with a new approach to development based on international competitiveness. By 1990, ECLAC's report *Changing Production Patterns with Social Equity* dropped the notion of centre and periphery, and abandoned concern for the terms of trade, and instead stressed international competitiveness and export promotion, with a concern for reforming domestic production rather than the external constraints. But ECLAC had not adopted neoliberalism in its entirety, for it saw the importance of dealing with poverty and creating social equity at the same time as stimulating growth. This 'integrated approach' gave a larger role for the state in industrial, technological, and educational policy, and encouraged development through links between the private sector and public institutions (ECLAC 1990).

A major reason for the change was the experience of economic growth: it was difficult to point to any success for ECLAC's approach compared with the experience in East Asia where economies were open to the rest of the world. Of course, military rule and repression in Brazil, Argentina, Chile, and Uruguay weakened the hold of the left in the 1970s. The economic crisis of the 1980s, with slower growth, widening inequality, debt, and hyperinflation, also forced a reconsideration of policy. Although neoliberal policies managed to control inflation and increase exports, they came at a cost of falling real wages and rising unemployment—so providing the basis for ECLAC's new integrated approach which combined elements of neoliberalism with an attack on poverty, insisting that growth should be combined with equity (Cooper and Packard 1997: 21; ECLAC 1990); Sikkink 1991, 1997).

The Uruguay Round and the creation of the WTO

The Uruguay Round of trade talks started in 1986 and was completed in 1994, running alongside the changing approaches to development and the end of the Cold War. The Soviet Union was given observer status before it collapsed; and talks started for the accession of China. The context changed with the end of colonialism and the Cold War, which blunted the ideological divides of the 1950s, 1960s, and 1970s. The rhetoric was more cautious and muted, with a shift in the politics of GATT and general acceptance of liberal trade and market prices—but it was also clear that it could not long survive with the expansion of the world economy and the growth of more successful emerging economies. Negotiations in GATT were carried out according to the principal supplier principle—the major supplier and consumers of a product negotiated tariff reductions, so excluding developing countries whose major commodities (textiles and agriculture) were not covered by GATT. The role of developing countries was also limited by the way that major players negotiated in the 'green room', though Brazil and India were sometimes invited. Gatt's agenda marginalized development issues, and instead focused on the most favoured nation rule and reciprocity. Of course, these limitations contributed to the success of GATT compared with the much wider ambitions of the ITO—but also contributed to a growing sense of its limitations.

The initiative for the Uruguay Round of trade talks came from the United States, and the creation of a world trade organization was not part of the agenda laid down at Punta del Este in 1986. Rather, the main concern was the advanced economies' realization that GATT's focus on trade was no longer so relevant: they moved from production of industrial goods to a greater interest in non-tariff barriers, trade in services, investment, and protection of intellectual property in high-technology and media. Unlike the ITO, where business interests faced an attack on cartels and the threat of nationalization by less developed countries, this agenda was very much in the interests of large corporations. These issues were of little concern to developing countries, which were more attracted by the East Asian model of export-led growth and wanted to ensure that they could secure some trade-off for allowing the new issues onto the agenda. India and Brazil took a hard line: that GATT should only deal with merchandize trade and not services; other developing countries, including Chile and Mexico and most of Asia, were willing to accept a wider agenda in return for acceptance of their own concerns. The notion of a world trade organization emerged during the process of negotiation.

The more comprehensive agenda led to a realization that greater coordination was needed, both within GATT to create a single, more powerful dispute settlement mechanism, and in relation to the liberalizing policies of the IMF and the World Bank. Negotiations since the first round in Geneva in 1947 led to a host of agreements and a lack of coherence, with legal uncertainty. The proposal for a new organization was put forward in 1990 by a Canadian lawyer who saw the problems of incoherence—and also by the European Union which suggested a multilateral trade organization. The American administration was not convinced, for they had long opposed the idea of an international organization as a recipe for conflict and ineffectiveness, fearing a loss of sovereignty and consequent difficulties in Congress. The developing countries were also suspicious, for the proposal was linked with the widening of the agenda in the interests of the developed world, and a concern that they might lose from the imposition of reciprocity and a stronger dispute resolution mechanism. The outcome was a 'grand bargain': the new issues were added to the agenda, and developing countries secured the inclusion of textiles and agriculture that had not been covered by GATT. The Americans used their opposition as a bargaining weapon in pursuit of a stronger dispute settlement mechanism which was secured on the last day of negotiations. The decision to create the World Trade Organization (WTO) was linked with a much stronger dispute settlement mechanism, the creation of a formal international organization in place of an agreement, and a shift from a pragmatic to a juridical approach. The deals made since the 1940s were 'locked in', and countries had to accept a comprehensive Single Undertaking to become members. How would the emerging or less developed economies be treated in this new body?

The new WTO was closer to GATT than to the putative ITO. It was a limited form of international body compared to the IMF: its secretariat was weak, and most of its activities were driven by members rather than officials or a smaller council. Rather like GATT, it was more of a contract organization concerned with making and enforcing rules, rather than a 'charter' organization that took collective action. The WTO continued the GATT principles of non-discrimination and reciprocity, which threatened the acceptance of special and differentiated treatment under the GSP which was only ever accepted on condition that more successful developing countries such as South Korea and Brazil returned to reciprocity as they became more prosperous. Despite the inclusion of agriculture, developing countries achieved very little. The Cairns group of agricultural exporters was formed in 1986, a wide coalition of both developing and developed countries, including Latin America (Argentina, Brazil, Uruguay, Chile, and Colombia); Asia (Indonesia, Malaysia, Thailand, Philippines; as well as Canada, Australia, and New Zealand). They were able to place agriculture on the agenda, and acted as mediator between the US and EU with their extensive subsidies—but were then largely ignored in the agreement between the US and EU in 1992. Both the Europeans and Americans continued to subsidize their farmers with few gains for the major agricultural exporters. Neither did the WTO cover labour standards or commodity agreements that had been so important in their demands in the 1960s and 1970s, and in the ITO's agenda. Tensions therefore continued, and the WTO was not able to resolve them.

The WTO, unlike the IMF, was based on one member, one vote—a principle that had been adopted for the putative ITO, with alarm on Capitol Hill at the apparent surrender of American influence. Consequently, developing countries had considerable power—if they could use it. But in practice, they did not because of another feature of the WTO that followed the example of GATT: consensus. A decision was only made if no member present at the meeting formally objected which made it more difficult for developing countries to use their numerical superiority and allowed the United States to block anything that they did not like. The requirement to be present was not easily met by developing countries with their smaller delegations, and neither were they able to keep themselves fully informed of the mass of business, in the absence of support from a powerful secretariat. There was a plethora of formal meetings as well as informal political groupings where smaller, powerful groups reached agreement through informal procedures that were opaque. There were few rules in reaching decisions, so leading to improvisation that worked to the advantage of the developed countries. In contrast to this weak system for formulating decisions, the WTO developed a strong legalistic dispute settlement mechanism that enforced the most favoured nation rule and reciprocity, and was more used against the developing countries than by them.

Although the developing countries are now within the WTO rather than on the sidelines in UNCTAD, many of the same issues persist: the WTO remains a rich man's club, and the developing countries retain their established negotiating stance, focusing on redistribution and reluctant to compromise or to agree on issues that are not in conflict. This strategy reflects an understandably low level of trust as a result of the developed world's ability to impose its own agenda, and the difficulty of poorer members to deal with the technicalities of the negotiations needed for a more integrative approach.

These shortcomings were addressed in the Doha Development Agenda of 2001 that was launched after the spectacular failure of the ministerial meeting in Seattle in 1999 as a result both of street protests and the developing countries' criticism of the attempt to include more issues of concern to the developed world. There was a stand-off between developed and developing countries. The developing countries formed various groupings to press their demands, such as the Like-Minded Group that was set up in 1996, including Cuba, Egypt, India, Indonesia, Malaysia, Pakistan, Tanzania, and Uganda. But the powerful developed countries—the so-called Quad—were able to divide and rule, buying off individual members with specific concessions in return for accepting the agenda of the developed countries, leaving India as the sole opponent of the Doha Development Agenda.

Was the inclusion of the word 'development' and the constant reference to the needs of developing countries in the ministerial declaration a piece of public relations rather than anything practical? One success was access to patented drugs for HIV/AIDS, as well as promises for improved market access in non-agricultural goods and differential treatment in agriculture. But these concessions were secured at a high price, and developing countries were disappointed and disillusioned—a state of affairs that led to the formation of the Group of Twenty (G20) in 2003, including the leading BRIC countries—Brazil, China, India. The G20 demanded cuts to EU and US subsidies and greater access to the markets of developed countries, with the continuation of special and differential treatment. At the ministerial meeting at Cancun in 2003, G20 and other coalitions of developing countries resisted divide and rule tactics, and were more able to coordinate their demands. The result was a collapse of negotiations and impasse that continues, with attention turning instead to regional deals. Agreement has proved remarkably difficult: the issues are technically more complex with potentially disruptive domestic impact; developing countries have greater power; there is more stress on issues of fairness than reciprocity; and bilateral and free trade agreements have proliferated, not only in the developed world (such as the North American Free Trade Agreement (NAFTA) but also in Latin America (the Southern Common Market, Mercosur) and Asia (Association of Southeast Asian Nations, ASEAN) (Baldwin 2006; Hoekman and Kostecki 2001; Narlikar 2003, 2005; Odell, 2000, 2006; Tussie 1985; Vernon 1995; Winham, 1998).

Discussion

In the seventy years since the Second World War, the institutions through which the developing world have expressed their views have changed—from the wide-ranging agenda of the putative ITO, to radical demands somewhat peripherally for extending the limits of the Bretton Woods institutions, to involvement within the new WTO where their views have been constrained. The WTO has a narrower remit than the ITO, and has more in common with the GATT from which it evolved. Of course, the ITO was a failure in its attempt to deal with so many topics within a single charter, and GATT was much more successful in dealing with the more limited ambition of restoring multilateral trade. The WTO continues the work of GATT: it is a juridical body that aims to lock in trade agreements and reciprocity. In the aftermath of the Great Recession, it was successful in preventing an outbreak of beggar-my-neighbour trade wars that marked the 1930s. The WTO found that protectionist measures were largely resisted by the G20, and new restrictions imposed between October 2008 and October 2010 amounted to only 1.8 per cent of G20 imports and 1.4 per cent of total world imports so that trade remained more open than it had ever been, despite concerns about currency manipulation and the emergence of preferential trade agreements. The WTO reported in June 2014 that 'The multilateral trading system has acted as an effective backstop against protection' (WTO 2010, 2014).

Daniel Drezner (2014) has argued that the institutions of global governance, for all their faults, provided a set of principles and procedures around which countries could converge, constraining domestic political pressures for protection, unlike in the 1930s when such institutions did not exist. Above all, effective international action was possible because economic power remained highly concentrated and, despite their differences, the leading economies of the world—the US, EU, and China—were committed to an open international economy. The Great Depression had been different, for a weakened Britain could no longer provide leadership; the US lacked the will; Nazi Germany acted as a 'spoiler'; and the Soviet Union was outside the world economy. Drezner claimed that in the Great Recession no one major power acted as a 'spoiler'. Further, the economic ideas underpinning an open global economy were not discredited as in the 1930s by alternative ideologies of Communism, Fascism, or economic nationalism. He was confident that the ideology of an open world economy survived. Indeed, the commitment was reaffirmed by the G20 in September 2009 within its 'Framework for Strong, Sustainable and Balanced Growth', and the meeting of the BRICS in Durban in March 2013 supported 'an open, transparent and rules-based multilateral trading system'. There was, Drezner argues, a marked difference between the state of economic ideas after the Great Recession and in response to the Great Depression. In the 1930s, there were many alternative proposals; by contrast, after 2008 'a strong post-crisis consensus among economists constrained the search for alternative paradigms' (Drezner 2014).

In the aftermath of the vote by Britain to leave the European Union, and the election of Donald Trump in November 2016, these remarks seem complacent, missing the popular discontent against globalization that seemed to threaten jobs and create increased disparities of income and wealth within advanced economies. The international institutions did constrain nationalistic responses to the Great Recession, and globalization did raise millions of people in developing countries from poverty. But the institutions created to deal with the problems of the 1930s failed to evolve to deal with new challenges. The financial crash of the Great Recession indicated a lack of capacity to oversee global financial markets and provide coherent international governance. There is no single body concerned with stabilization of the international financial system in a world of capital mobility, and much of the response to the Great Recession came from a patchwork of 'groups' meeting to decide on action—the G20 or the smaller G7 of the most powerful nations. Indeed, C. Fred Bergsten saw the best hope as a G2 of China and the United States—not as a replacement of the existing institutions of the IMF and WTO, but as a supplement to make them work better by means of prior agreements. Robert Zoellick and Justin Yifu Lin, the President and Chief Economist of the World Bank, agreed that 'without a strong G2 the G20 will disappoint'. The term coined by Niall Ferguson for the G2—Chimerica—aptly captures the chimerical nature of the proposal (Bergsten 2005, 2008, 2009; Ferguson 2008; Wolf 2014: 10; Zoellick and Lin 2009).

Conclusion

The idea that America and China could together provide stability for the world economy has become more improbable since Trump took office, with his cry of 'America first' and his hostility towards multilateral institutions. The question now is whether protectionism will return, with threats to NAFTA and even to the WTO's dispute resolution mechanism. At the G20 meeting of finance ministers in March 2017, the US Secretary of the Treasury refused to commit America to resist all forms of protectionism, in stark contrast with Chinese commitment to globalization and its creation of a new Asian Infrastructure Development Bank as a possible rival to the Washington-based World Bank. The world economy stands at a possible turning point, on a par with other inflection points—the Second World War and the creation of multilateral institutions, the collapse of fixed exchange rates and the oil shock in the early 1970s, and the demise of the Soviet regime and resurgence of China. What will happen in the coming decade is not easy to predict, but an earlier inward turn by the United States at the time of the Great Depression does not offer much comfort. In the early 1970s, one response to American 'benign neglect' of its responsibilities in the international monetary system was to create a zone of stability in Europe around a single market and monetary union. Could the result now be a turn to regional trade zones and a move away from multilateralism? Global governance is at a critical juncture—perhaps presenting an opportunity for China to take a lead. But who is to say that China itself might not experience serious political and economic difficulties?

REFERENCES

Alacevich, M. (2009). *The Political Economy of the World Bank: The Early Years*. Palo Alto and Washington, DC: Stanford University Press and World Bank.

Baldwin, R.G. (2006). 'Failure of the WTO ministerial conference at Cancun: reasons and remedies', *World Economy* 29/6: 677–96.

Bergsten, C.F. (2005). *The United States and the World Economy: Foreign Economic Policy for the Next Decade*. Washington. DC: Institute for International Economics.

Bergsten, C.F. (2008). 'A partnership of equals: how Washington should respond to China's economic challenge', *Foreign Affairs* 84/4: 57–69.

Bergsten, C.F. (2009). 'Two's company', *Foreign Affairs* 88/5: 169.

Bose, S. (1997). 'Instruments and idioms of colonial and national development: India's historical experience in comparative perspective', in F. Cooper and R. Packard (eds) *International Development and the Social Sciences: Essays on the History and Politics of Knowledge*. Berkeley and Los Angeles, CA: University of California Press, 45–63.

Brown, W.A. (1952). *The United States and the Restoration of World Trade: An Analysis and Appraisal of the ITO Charter and the General Agreement on Tariffs and Trade*. Washington, DC, Brookings Institute.

Cooper, F. and Packard, R. (1997). 'Introduction', in F. Cooper and R. Packard (eds) *International Development and the Social Sciences: Essays on the History and Politics of Knowledge*. Berkeley and Los Angeles, CA: University of California Press, 1–41.

Cordovez, R. (1967). 'The making of UNCTAD', *Journal of World Trade Law* 1/3: 243–328.

DAFP (Documents on Australian Foreign Policy) (1948–9 vol 16) (9 August 1949a). Doc. 239, Evatt to Chiffley. Available at https://dfat.gov.au/about-us/publications/historical-documents/Pages/volume-16/239-evatt-to-chifley.aspx, accessed 23 October 2018.

DAFP (Documents on Australian Foreign Policy 1948–9 vol 16) (9 August 1949b). Doc. 240, Australian delegation to Economic and Social Council to Department of External Affairs. Available at https://dfat.gov.au/about-us/publications/historical-documents/Pages/volume-16/240-evatt-to-chifley.aspx, accessed 23 October 2018.

DAFP (Documents on Australian Foreign Policy 1948–9 vol 16) (14 October 1949). Doc. 241, Department of External Affairs to Australian delegation, UN. Available at https://dfat.gov.au/about-us/publications/historical-documents/Pages/volume-16/241-evatt-to-chifley.aspx, accessed 23 October 2018.

DAFP (Documents on Australian Foreign Policy 1948–9 vol 16) (21 October 1949). Doc. 242, Department of External Affairs to Australian delegation, UN. Available at https://dfat.gov.au/about-us/publications/historical-documents/Pages/volume-16/242-evatt-to-chifley.aspx, accessed 23 October 2018.

DAFP (Documents on Australian Foreign Policy 1948–9 vol 16) (25 October 1949). Doc. 244, Australian delegation, UN to Department of External Affairs. Available at https://dfat.gov.au/about-us/publications/historical-documents/Pages/volume-16/244-evatt-to-chifley.aspx, accessed 23 October 2018.

DAFP (Documents on Australian Foreign Policy 1948–9 vol 16) (10 November 1949). Doc. 248, Australian delegation, UN to Department of External Affairs. Available at https://dfat.gov.au/about-us/publications/historical-documents/Pages/volume-16/248-evatt-to-chifley.aspx, accessed 23 October 2018.

DCER (Documents on Canadian External Relations) Volume 14: 4 June 1948: 581, Secretary of State for External Affairs to heads of post abroad. Available at http://epe.lac-bac.gc.ca/100/206/301/faitc-pdf, accessed 23 October 2018.

DCER (Documents on Canadian External Relations) Volume 14: 13 July 1948: 582, Chief delegate, delegation to the United Nations Conference on Trade and Employment to Secretary of State for External Affairs. Available at http://epe.lac-bac.gc.ca/100/206/301/faitc-aecic/history/2013-05-03/www.international.gc.ca/department/history-histoire/dcer/details-en.asp@intRefid=10322, accessed 23 October 2018.

Dell, S. (1973). 'An appraisal of UNCTAD III', *World Development* 1/5: 1–13.

Diebold, W. (1952). *The End of the ITO*. Princeton, NJ: Princeton University Press.

Drezner, D. (2014). *The System Worked: How the World Stopped Another Great Depression*. New York: Oxford University Press.

ECLAC (Economic Commission for Latin America and the Caribbean) (1990). *Changing Production Patterns with Social Equity: The Prime Task of Latin American and Caribbean Development in the 1990s*. Santiago: ECLAC.

Eisenhower, D.D. (1953). 'Address "The chance of peace", delivered before the American Society of Newspaper Editors, 16 April 1953', G. Peters and J. T. Wooley, *The American Presidency Project*. Available at www.presidency.ucsb.edu/ws/index.php?pid=9819&st=&st1=, accessed 12 October 2018.

Ferguson, N. (2008). *The Ascent of Money: A Financial History of the World*. London: Penguin.

FRUS (Foreign Relations of the United States) 1952–4 I (22 April 1952). Memo by Assistant Secretary of State for Economic Affairs (Thorp) and Assistant Secretary of State for UN Affairs (Hickerson) to Secretary of State, 'US role in executing General Assembly decision on International Development Bank'.

FRUS (Foreign Relations of the United States) 1952–4 1 (2 May 1952). Position paper on General Assembly resolution to establish grant fund for economic development. Available at https://history.state.gov/historicaldocuments/frus1952-54v01p1/d71, accessed 23 October 2018.

FRUS (Foreign Relations of the United States) 1952–54 I (22 May 1952). Minutes of the 192nd meeting of the National Advisory Council on International Monetary and Financial Problems Washington, DC: FRUS. Available at https://history.state.gov/historicaldocuments/frus1952-54v01p1/d73, accessed 23 October 2018.

FRUS (Foreign Relations of the United States) 1952–54 I (28 January 1953). Memo by legal counsel for the Technical Co-operation Administration (Glick) to the Deputy Legal Adviser, 'Some major policy issues now under discussion in the Point IV program'. Available at https://history.state.gov/historicaldocuments/frus1952-54v01p1/d77, accessed 23 October 2018.

FRUS (Foreign Relations of the United States) 1952–54 I (17 June 1953). Draft position paper prepared in Department of State: draft position paper concerning the International Finance Corporation. Available at https://history.state.gov/historicaldocuments/frus1952-54v01p1/d81, accessed 23 October 2018.

FRUS (Foreign Relations of the United States) 1952–54 I (4 February 1954). Memo by the Director of the Office of Financial and Development Policy (Corbett) to the Assistant Sec for Economic Affairs (Waugh), the International Finance Corporation. Available at https://history.state.gov/historicaldocuments/frus1952-54v01p1/d85, accessed 23 October 2018.

FRUS (Foreign Relations of the United States) 1952–54 I (17 May 1954). Paper prepared in the Bureau of Economic Affairs, Foreign economic relations of the US. Available at https://history.state.gov/historicaldocuments/frus1952-54v01p1/d22, accessed 23 October 2018.

FRUS (Foreign Relations of the United States) 1952–54 I (1 June 1954). Minutes of the 211th meeting of the NAC on International Monetary and Financial Problems, Washington, DC. Available at https://history.state.gov/historicaldocuments/frus1952-54v01p1/d86, accessed 23 October 2018.

FRUS (Foreign Relations of the United States) 1952–54 I (1 July 1954). Paper prepared by the Staff Committee for the NAC on International Monetary and Financial Problems, 'US position for the 18th session of ECOSOC concerning the International Finance Corporation'. Available at https://history.state.gov/historicaldocuments/frus1952-54v01p1/d88, accessed 23 October 2018.

FRUS (Foreign Relations of the United States) 1952–54 I (2 July 1954). Minutes of the 212th meeting of the NAC on International Monetary and Financial Problems. Available at https://history.state.gov/historicaldocuments/frus1952-54v01p1/d89, accessed 23 October 2018.

FRUS (Foreign Relations of the United States) 1952–54 I (9 September 1954). Memo by the senior adviser to the US delegation to the UN (King), 'A positive US economic program in ECOSOC – is it possible?' Available at https://history.state.gov/historicaldocuments/frus1952-54v01p1/d26, accessed 23 October 2018.

FRUS (Foreign Relations of the United States) 1952–54 I (8 October 1954). The US representative at the UN (Lodge) to Department of State. Available at https://history.state.gov/historicaldocuments/frus1952-54v01p1/d92, accessed 23 October 2018.

FRUS (Foreign Relations of the United States) 1952–54 I (2 November 1954a). Memo by the Assistant Secretary of State for Economic Affairs (Waugh) to the Under-Secretary of State (Hoover), 'US participation in the International Finance Corporation'. Available at https://history.state.gov/historicaldocuments/frus1952-54v01p1/d81, accessed 23 October 2018.

FRUS (Foreign Relations of the United States) 1952–54 I (2 November 1954b). Paper prepared in Treasury: 'US participation in the IFC, an affiliate of the International Bank'. Available at https://history.state.gov/historicaldocuments/frus1952-54v01p1/d94, accessed 23 October 2018.

FRUS (Foreign Relations of the United States) 1952–54 I (3 November 1954). Minutes of the 218th meeting of the NAC on International Monetary and Financial Problems. Available at https://history.state.gov/historicaldocuments/frus1952-54v01p1/d95, accessed 23 October 2018.

FRUS (Foreign Relations of the United States) 1952–54 I (7 December 1954). Memo by the special consultant to the President (Randall) to the President. Available at https://history.state.gov/historicaldocuments/frus1952-54v01p1/d28, accessed 23 October 2018.

FRUS (Foreign Relations of the United States) 1961–63 IX (16 January 1962). Current economic developments: issue 641, 16 Jan 1962: actions on economic items at recent General Assembly; A/RES/1710(XVI), United Nations Development Decade: a programme for international economic cooperation (I). Available at https://history.state.gov/historicaldocuments/frus1961-63v09/d193, accessed 23 October 2018.

FRUS (Foreign Relations of the United States) 1961–63 IX, Current economic developments: issue 641. (16 January 1962). Actions on economic items at recent General Assembly; A/RES/1710(XVI), United Nations Development Decade: a programme for international economic cooperation (I). Available at https:/history.state.gov/historicaldocuments/frus1961-63v09/d193, accessed 23 October 2018.

FRUS (Foreign Relations of the United States) 1961–63 IX. (12 November 1963). Memo from the under-secretary of state (George Ball) to President Kennedy, United Nations Conference. Available at https://history.state.gov/historicaldocuments/frus1961-63v09/d94, accessed 23 October 2018.

G77 (Group of 77) (1964). Joint Declaration of the seventy-seven developing countries made at the conclusion of the United Nations Conference on Trade and Development, Geneva, 15 June 1964. Available at www.g77.org/doc/Joint Declaration.html, accessed 3 October 2018.

G77 (Group of 77) (1967). 'First ministerial meeting of the Group of 77, charter of Algiers, Algiers, 10–25 October 1967', in Mourad Ahmia (ed.) *The Collected Documents of the Group of 77, Volume VI*. New York, Oxford University Press, 22–39.

Gardner, R.N. (1964). 'GATT and the United Nations Conference on Trade and Development', *International Organization* 18/4: 685–704.

Gardner, R.N. (1968). 'The United Nations Conference on Trade and Development', *International Organization* 22/1: 99–130.

Gilman, N. (2003). *Mandarins of the Future: Modernization Theory in Cold War America*. Baltimore, MD and London: Johns Hopkins University Press.

Government of India Planning Commission (1952). *The First Five Year Plan: A Draft Outline*. New Delhi: Government of India.

Harry S. Truman Presidential Library (31 January 1946). RG59 Office files of Clayton, Box 4 folder M(1) 'The Mexican doctrine of industry saturation', Albert E. Pappano.

Helleiner, E. (2014). *Forgotten Foundations of Bretton Woods: International Development and the Making of the Postwar Order.* Ithaca, NY and London: Cornell University Press.

Hoekman. B. and Kostecki, M. (2001). *The Political Economy of the World Trading System: The WTO and Beyond,* 2nd edn. Oxford: Oxford University Press.

Hoekman, B. and Ozden, C. (2005). 'Trade Preferences and Differential Treatment of Developing Countries', World Bank Policy Working Paper 3466.

Indonesian Ministry of Foreign Affairs (1955). *Africa-Asia Speaks from Bandung.* Djakarta: Indonesian Ministry of Foreign Affairs. Available at www.fordham.edu/halsall/mod/1955 sukarno-bandong.html, accessed 12 October 2018.

J.F. Kennedy Presidential Library (20 October 1963). George Ball Papers, Box 8, Folder: trade legislation, 5/63-11/63, telcon, Bundy-Ball, 20 October 1963, 10.30 a.m.

Jenkins, S. (1945). 'Australia plans full employment', *Far Eastern Survey* 14/17: 240–2.

Kahlin, G.M. (1956). *The Asia-Africa Conference.* Ithaca, NY: Cornell University Press.

Kapur, D., Lewis, J.P. and Webb, R. (eds) (1997). *The World Bank: Its First Half Century.* Washington, DC: Brookings Institution Press.

Kennedy, J.F. (1961a). 'Address at a White House Reception for Members of Congress and for the Diplomatic Corps of the Latin American Republics', 13 March 1961 at G. Peters and J.T. Wooley, *The American Presidency Project.* Available at www.presidency.ucsb.edu/ws/?pid=8531, accessed 3 October 2018.

Kennedy, J.F. (1961b). Special message to Congress on foreign aid, 22 March 1961, at G. Peters and J.T. Wooley, *The American Presidency Project.* Available at www.presidency.ucsb.edu/ws/index.php?pid=8545, accessed 3 October 2018.

Kindleberger, C.P. (1955). 'Economists in international organization', *International Organization* 9/3: 338–52.

Latham, M.E. (2000). *Modernization as Ideology: American Social Science and 'Nation Building' in the Kennedy Era.* Chapel Hill, NC and London: University of North Carolina Press.

Lewis, W.A. (1954). 'Economic development with unlimited supplies of labour', *Manchester School* 2/2: 139–91.

Murphy, C. (1984). *The Emergence of the NIEO Ideology.* Boulder, CO: Westview Press.

NARA (National Archives and Records Administration) (30 January 1945). RG43 International trade files, 698 ITO, Box 53, folder: international committee on employment—documents, 'Exchange of notes between Australian and US governments regarding an international conference on employment: Australian note on holding of full employment conference'.

NARA (National Archives and Records Administration) (13 March 1945). RG43 International trade files, 698 ITO, Box 53, folder: international committee on employment—documents, 'US reply to Australian note on full employment conference'.

NARA (National Archives and Records Administration) (2 July 1945). RG43 International trade files, 698 ITO, Box 53, folder: international committee on employment—documents, 'Action taken by the 1945 International Labor Organisation Conference on full employment'.

NARA (National Archives and Records Administration) (30–31 August 2 September 1946). RG43 International trade files, 698 ITO, Box 12, folder: report of discussions of draft charter of ITO, Sydney, 'Report of discussions on draft charter for an ITO held at Commonwealth Bank, Sydney.

NARA (National Archives and Records Administration) (3 December 1947). RG43 International trade files 698 ITO, Box 150, Folder: trade Habana—Latin American countries (misc.), 'Memo of conversation'.

NARA (National Archives and Records Administration) (4 December 1947). RG43 International trade files 698 ITO, Box 150, Folder: trade Habana—Latin American countries (misc.), 'Reaction to Molinari's speech'.

NARA (National Archives and Records Administration) (5 December 1947). RG43 International trade files 698 ITO, Box 150, Folder: trade Habana—Latin American countries (misc.), 'Airgram'.

NARA (National Archives and Records Administration) (9 December 1947). RG43 International trade files 698 ITO, Box 150, Folder: trade Habana—Latin American countries (misc.), 'Nufer to Wilcox, yesterday's meeting of Latin American delegations at the hotel Nacional'.

NARA (National Archives and Records Administration) (30 January 1948). RG43 International trade files 698 ITO, Box 150, Folder: trade Habana—Latin American countries (misc.), 'Nufer to Wilcox, yesterday's meeting of Latin American delegations to discuss the appointment of a conciliatory group'.

NARA (National Archives and Records Administration) (6 February 1948). RG43 International trade files 698 ITO, Box 150, Folder: trade Habana—Latin American countries (misc.), 'Showdown with Latin American delegations', A. Nufer.

NARA (National Archives and Records Administration) (9 February 1948). RG43 698 ITO, Box 6 Folder: charter analysis, 'Memorandum for Mr Wilcox: Changes from suggested Charter – economic development', S.J. Rubin.

NARA (National Archives and Records Administration) (March 1948). RG43 international trade files 698, ITO Box 144, Folder: analysis of Latin American proposals, 'Tactics and behaviour at the UN conference on trade and employment, Habana, 21 November 1947–24 March 1948', J. Robert Schnaetzel.

NARA (National Archives and Records Administration) (1949). RG43 international trade files, 698 ITO, Box 12, Folder: ratification of the Charter—other countries, India and the Havana Charter for an ITO, 'Federation of Indian Chambers of Commerce and Industry'.

NARA (National Archives and Records Administration) (6 May 1963). RG59 Kennedy Round Box 1, Folder: trade staff committee: TEC D-29/63 to TEC D-45/63, 'GATT ministerial meeting, Geneva 1963 – trade preferences for less developed countries TEC D-34/63'.

Narlikar, A. (2003). *International Trade and Developing Countries: Bargaining Coalitions in the GATT and WTO*. London: Routledge.

Narlikar, A. (2005). *The World Trade Organization: A Very Short Introduction*. Oxford: Oxford University Press.

Nkrumah, K. (1965). *Neo-Colonialism: The Last Stage of Imperialism*. London: Thomas Nelson and Sons.

Odell, J. (2000). *Negotiating the World Economy*. Ithaca, NY: Cornell University Press.

Odell, J. (2006). *Negotiating Trade: Developing Countries in the WTO and NAFTA*. Cambridge: Cambridge University Press.

ODI (Overseas Development Institute) (1982). Briefing papers, 'The integrated programme for commodities', No 1, July 1982. Available at www.odi.org/sites/odi.org.uk/files/odi-assets/publications-opinion-files/6666.pdf, accessed 12 October 2018.

Prebisch, R. (1958 [1963]). 'Soviet challenge to American leadership: American's role in helping under-developed countries', April 1958, in Raúl Prebisch, *Discursos, declaraciones y documentos, 1952–63, Volume 2.* Santiago: ECLA, 1963.

Rathbone, R. (2004). 'Nkrumah, Kwame (1909?–1972)', *Oxford Dictionary of National Biography.* Oxford: Oxford University Press, 2004; online edn, January 2011. Available at www.oxforddnb.com/view/article/31504, accessed 12 October 2018.

Resolution adopted by the General Assembly 3201 (S-VI), Declaration on the establishment of a new international economic order, 1 May 1974. Available at www.un-documents.net/s6r3201.htm, accessed 23 October 2018.

Rowse, T. (2000). 'Full employment and the discipline of labour: a chapter in the history of Australia social democracy', *The Drawing Board: An Australian Review of Public Affairs* 1/1: 1–13.

Rowse, T. (2002). *Nugget Coombs: A Reforming Life.* Cambridge: Cambridge University Press.

Rubinstein, A.Z. (1964). *The Soviets in International Organizations: Changing Policy towards Developing Countries, 1953–63.* Princeton, NJ: Princeton University Press.

Santa Cruz, H. (1995). 'The creation of the United Nations and ECLAC'. *Cepal Review* 57: 17–33.

Sikkink, K. (1991). *Ideas and Institutions: Developmentalism in Brazil and Argentina.* Ithaca, NY: Cornell University Press.

Sikkink, K. (1997). 'Development ideas in Latin America: paradigm shift and the Economic Commission for Latin America', in F. Cooper and R. Packard (eds) *International Development and the Social Sciences: Essays on the History and Politics of Knowledge.* Berkeley and Los Angeles, CA: University of California Press, 228–56.

Tignor, R.L. (2006). *W. Arthur Lewis and the Birth of Development Economics.* Princeton, NJ and London: Princeton University Press.

TNA (The National Archive) (15 October 1946). T236/703, 'Preparatory committee on trade and employment: expansion of effective international demand, note by the Australian delegation, UN Economic and Social Council, London, E/FC/T/W.10'.

TNA (The National Archive) (4 October 1946). T236/703. 'Preparatory committee on trade and employment, British Commonwealth talks'.

TNA (The National Archive) (21 October 1946). T236/704. United Nations, Economic and Social Council. 'Preparatory committee of the international conference on trade and employment, Committee I, summary record of meetings, second meeting, first part, 21 October 1946, E/PC/T/CI/4'.

TNA (The National Archive) (22 October 1946). T236/704, 'United Nations, Economic and Social Council, Preparatory committee of the international conference on trade and employment, Committee I, summary record of meetings, second meeting, part two, 21 October 1946, E/PC/T/CI/7'.

TNA (The National Archive) (28 October 1946). T236/704, 'Observations of the Cuban delegation, E/PC/T/C1/10'.

TNA (The National Archive) (11 November 1946). FO317/53050, 'TN(46)60, Trade negotiations committee: Indian industrial development and attitude of India towards United States proposals: note by the India Office'.

TNA (The National Archive) (29 November 1947). BT11/5206, 'Seventh plenary meeting'.

TNA (The National Archive) (10 March 1948). PREM8/1416, 'Havana Trade Conference: Memorandum by the Chancellor of the Exchequer and the President of the Board of Trade, EPC(48)16'.

TNA (The National Archive) (12 March 1948). PREM8/1416, 'CP(48)84, Cabinet, Havana Trade Conference, memorandum by the President of the Board of Trade, H Wilson'.

TNA(The National Archive) (10 May 1949). Prem8/1416, 'CP(49)114, Cabinet, Havana Charter for an International Trade Organization, memorandum by the President of the Board of Trade'.

Toye, R. (2003). 'The Attlee Government, the Imperial Preference System, and the creation of GATT', *English Historical Review* 118/478: 912–39.

Toye, J. and Toye, R. (2004). *The UN and Global Political Economy: Trade, Finance and Development*. Bloomington, IN: Indiana University Press.

Toye, J. and Toye, R. (2005). 'From new era to neo-liberalism: US strategy on trade, finance and development in the United Nations, 1964-82', *Forum for Development Studies* 32/1: 151–80.

Toye, J. and Toye, R. (2006). 'How the UN moved from full employment to economic development', *Commonwealth and Comparative Politics* 44/1: 16–40.

Turnell, S. (1999). 'Monetary reformers, amateur idealists and Keynesian crusaders: Australian economists' international advocacy, 1925–1950'. PhD thesis. Sydney, NSW: Macquarie University. Available at https://trove.nla.gov.au/work/33323736?, accessed 24 November 2018.

Tussie, D. (1985). *The Less Developed Countries and the World Trading System: A Challenge to the GATT*. London: Francis Pinter.

UN (United Nations) (1950). *The Economic Development of Latin America and its Principal Problems*. United Nations E/CN.12/89/rev1, Lake Success. New York: UN Department of Economic Affairs.

UN (United Nations) (1963). 'Report of Experts appointed under Economic and Social Council Resolution 919 (XXXIV)', *Commodity and Trade Problems of Developing Countries: Institutional Arrangements*. Geneva: United Nations.

UN (United Nations) (1973). 'Fourth conference of heads of state or government of non-aligned countries, economic declaration, Algiers, 5–9 September, in UN General Assembly, A/9330. Available at http://cns.miis.edu/nam/documents/Official_Document/4th_Summit_FD_Algiers_Declaration_1973_Whole.pdf, accessed 16 November 2018.

UN (United Nations (1974). Resolution adopted by the General Assembly, 3281 (XXIX), Charter of economic rights and duties of states, 12 December 1974. Available at www.un-documents.net/a29r3281.htm, accessed 3 October 2018.

UN ECOSOC (United Nations Economic and Social Council (1962). Cairo Declaration of developing countries. Available at http://repository.uneca.org/handle/10855/7151?show=full, accessed 3 October 2018.

Vernon, R. (1995). 'The World Trade Organization: a new stage in international trade and development', *Harvard International Law Journal* 36/2: 329–40.

Walters, R.S. (1971). 'International organizations and political communication: the use of UNCTAD by less developed countries', *International Organization* 25/4: 818–35.

Weiss, T.G. (1986). *Multilateral Development Diplomacy in UNCTAD: The Lessons of Group Negotiations, 1964–84*. Basingstoke: Macmillan.

Westad, O.A. (2005). *The Global Cold War: Third World Interventions and the Making of Our Times*. Cambridge: Cambridge University Press.

Winham, G.R. (1998). 'The World Trade Organization: institution building in the multilateral trade system', *World Economy* 21/3: 349–68.

Wolf, M. (2014). *The Shifts and the Shocks: What We've Learned–and Have Still to Learn–from the Financial Crisis*. London: Allen Lane.

WTO (World Trade Organization) (2010). *Report on G20 Trade Measures (May 2010 to October 2010)*. Washington, DC: WTO.

Zachariah, B. (2005). *Developing India: An Intellectual and Social History c.*1930–1950. New Delhi; Oxford University Press.

Zoellick, R.B. and Lin, Justin Yifu (2009). 'Recovery: a job for China and the US', *Washington Post*, 6 March 2009. Available at www.washingtonpost.com/wp-dyn/content/article/2009/03/05/AR2009030502887.html, accessed 23 October 2018.

3 BRICS, emerging markets, and the world economy

Deepak Nayyar

Introduction

This chapter aims to analyse the global economic implications of the rise of BRICS (defined as Brazil, India, China, and South Africa) and emerging markets, which are subsets of countries among developing nations. Their emergence also has considerable political significance in the contemporary world. For the purpose of analysis, BRICS excludes Russia, although it is part of the political formation, because it is a former superpower and a high-income economy located in Europe. Developing countries are made up of Africa, Asia excluding Japan, and Latin America, including the Caribbean. Emerging markets are identified as a larger group of fourteen selected countries from the developing world including the four BRICS. At the outset, it also needs to be said that the focus of this chapter is on BRICS and emerging markets as country groups, situated in the wider context of the global economy, rather than on any particular country within these groups.

The structure of the essay is as follows. The first section outlines the contours of change in the world economy during the second half of the twentieth century, which led to a discernible shift in the balance of economic power during the first decade of the twenty-first century, to set the stage before the play begins. The second section situates BRICS and emerging markets in the wider context of the global economy to sketch a profile of their growing importance in terms of their economic size, reflected in population and income; their engagement with the world economy, reflected in trade, investment, and migration; and their industrialization, reflected in industrial production and manufactured exports. The third section examines the possible impact of rapid economic growth in BRICS on the world economy, industrialized countries, and developing countries, which could be both positive and negative, so that the balance would shape outcomes. The final section considers the factors underlying the evolution of BRICS with reference to the past, to discuss the potential influence of BRICS on international institutions and global governance, which would obviously extend beyond economics into politics.

Deepak Nayyar, *BRICS, emerging markets, and the world economy* In: *Handbook of BRICS and Emerging Economies*. Edited by: P.B. Anand, Shailaja Fennell, and Flavio Comim, Oxford University Press (2021).
DOI: 10.1093/oso/9780198827535.003.0003

Contours of change in the world economy

The world has changed. Soon after the end of the Second World War and the beginning of the post-colonial era, *c.*1950, there were two sharp divides in the world: the East–West divide between communist and capitalist countries and the North–South divide between rich and poor countries. The distinction between East and West vanished with the collapse of Communism in 1990, as capitalism emerged triumphant. The distinction between North and South also became more diffused with the passage of time, as reality changed significantly. In fact, during the second half of the twentieth century and the first decade of the twenty-first century, a short span of six decades, the global economy witnessed a transformation that would have been difficult to imagine six decades ago.

In terms of Maddison PPP (Purchasing Power Parity) statistics, the share of industrialized countries in world GDP declined from 60 per cent in 1950 to 56 per cent in 1980 and 44 per cent in 2008; the share of Eastern Europe and the (former) USSR declined from 13 per cent in 1950 to 12 per cent in 1980 and 6 per cent in 2008; while the share of developing countries in world GDP increased from 27 per cent in 1950 to 32 per cent in 1980 and almost 50 per cent in 2008 (Maddison 2003, 2007; Nayyar 2013). It would seem that this change gathered momentum after 1980. In terms of current prices at market exchange rates, which is more appropriate for such macro comparisons across country groups over time, the share of developing countries in world GDP rose from 22 per cent in 1980 to 33 per cent in 2010, while the corresponding share of industrialized countries fell from 68 per cent to 62 per cent (Table 3.1); the residual share of Eastern Europe and the (former) USSR dropped from 10 per cent to 5 per cent. However, there was no similar transformation in relative per capita incomes. Divergence stopped but the convergence was at best modest. GDP per capita in developing countries as a proportion of that in industrialized countries increased from 15 per cent to 18 per cent in Maddison PPP terms between 1950 and 2008, and from 8 per cent to 9.5 per cent in current prices at market exchange rates between 1980 and 2010 (Nayyar 2013).

The engagement of developing countries with the world economy witnessed a decline during the period from 1950 to 1980, particularly when compared with the past, but revived around 1980 and grew rapidly thereafter (Nayyar 2013). However, this deeper engagement was a matter of choice, in sharp contrast with the compulsion of the past. Their share in world merchandize trade, exports, and imports, fell from 32 per cent in 1950 to 27 per cent in 1980 but rose to 40 per cent in 2010. During the 1990s and 2000s, developing countries' share in the stocks and flows of inward, as well as outward, foreign direct investment (FDI) in the world economy increased at the expense of industrialized countries, although they were more important as countries-of-destination than as countries-of-origin. Movement of people from developing countries to industrialized countries—including guest workers, illegal immigrants, and professional persons—emerged as an increasingly significant form of engagement. Such international migration exercised an important influence on the world economy. For one, it was an important factor

Table 3.1 Share of BRICS, Next-14, developing countries, and industrialized countries in world population and world GDP: 1980–2014

World population

	1980 %	1990 %	2000 %	2010 %	2014 %
Brazil	2.7	2.8	2.8	2.8	2.8
India	15.7	16.3	17.0	17.4	17.8
China	22.1	21.9	20.9	19.7	18.8
South Africa	0.7	0.7	0.7	0.7	0.7
Total BRICS	41.2	41.7	41.4	40.6	40.1
Next-14	51.6	52.3	52.1	51.3	51.0
Developing countries	74.2	77.0	79.2	80.7	81.5
Industrialized countries	17.2	15.3	14.2	13.4	13.0
World	100.0	100.0	100.0	100.0	100.0
World Total (billion)	*4.4*	*5.3*	*6.1*	*6.9*	*7.3*

World GDP in current prices at market exchange rates

	1980	1990	2000	2010	2014
Brazil	1.6	1.8	2.0	3.3	2.8
India	1.5	1.4	1.4	2.6	2.6
China	2.5	1.8	3.6	9.2	13.0
South Africa	0.7	0.5	0.4	0.6	0.5
Total BRICS	6.3	5.5	7.4	15.7	18.9
Next-14	12.3	11.9	15.5	24.0	27.5
Developing countries	21.7	17.5	21.6	32.8	37.7
Industrialized countries	68.4	77.8	76.0	61.9	57.2
World	100.0	100.0	100.0	100.0	100.0
World total US$ billion)	12,043	22,604	32,858	64,401	77,450

Notes:

a) The Next-14 are Argentina, Brazil, Chile, China, Egypt, India, Indonesia, South Korea, Malaysia, Mexico, South Africa, Taiwan, Thailand, and Turkey.

b) The figures for developing countries and industrialized countries do not add up to the world totals. The residual is attributable to Eastern Europe and the former USSR.

Source: United Nations, UN Conference on Trade and Development (UNCTAD) Stat, based on UN National Accounts Statistics and Population Statistics.

underlying productivity increase and economic growth in industrialized countries. For another, remittances from migrants were an important source of external finance in developing countries that eased constraints on growth (Nayyar 2008a).

There was also a significant catch-up in industrialization for the developing world as a whole beginning around 1950 that gathered momentum after 1980. The share of developing countries in world industrial production at current prices rose from just 7 per cent in 1950 (Bairoch 1982) to 18 per cent in 1980 and 42 per cent in 2010. Similarly, their share in world exports of manufactures rose from a mere 6 per cent in 1960 to 12 per cent in 1980 and 40 per cent in 2010 (Nayyar 2013). However, this catch-up in industrialization was most unequal between regions. Asia led the process not only in terms of industrial production and manufactured exports, but also in terms of structural change and trade patterns, while the Latin American performance was modest by comparison, and Africa made almost no progress (Nayyar 2013).

These aggregates, which suggest an impressive transformation, could be deceptive. The catch-up was characterized by uneven development in almost every dimension. Much of it was concentrated in Asia. Latin America stayed roughly where it was. Africa fell further behind. The catch-up was also uneven between countries within regions. There was a high degree of concentration among a few: Argentina, Brazil, Chile, and Mexico in Latin America; China, India, Indonesia, Korea, Malaysia, Taiwan, Thailand, and Turkey in Asia; and Egypt and South Africa in Africa. In fact, the economic significance of these countries, termed as the *Next-14*, in the developing world is overwhelming in terms of their size, reflected in GDP and population; their engagement with the world economy, reflected in trade, investment, and migration; and their industrialization, reflected in industrial production and manufactured exports (Nayyar 2013). There is, of course, enormous diversity among the few, characterized by unequal distribution, in terms of the same attributes that reveal the concentration among them. But that is not all. The distribution of benefits from rapid economic growth underlying the catch-up was also unequal within countries (Nayyar 2013). There was exclusion of regions and of people, not only in countries that lagged behind but also in the Next-14 that led the catch-up process. Economic inequality between regions and among people increased almost everywhere. There was a reduction in the incidence of absolute poverty. Yet, poverty persisted because rapid economic growth was not always transformed into meaningful development, which improved the well-being of ordinary people.

It is clear that the period since 1950 has witnessed a catch-up on the part of developing countries, at least in terms of aggregates, with industrialized countries. This has been associated with a discernible shift in the balance of power in the world economy, which gathered momentum after 1980. Next-14 led this process of catch-up and accounted for a large part of the aggregates in every dimension. This set of countries is perhaps a plausible and tangible first approximation for what are described as emerging economies or emerging markets. Brazil, India, China, and South Africa—the BRICS—are critical as the most important subset of countries in Next-14. Even so, their economic significance in the world must be situated in its wider context. Indeed, the preceding discussion sets the stage for sketching a profile of BRICS and emerging markets in the global economy.

Significance of BRICS and emerging markets

The developing world, made up of Africa, Asia excluding Japan, and Latin America including the Caribbean, is a large and heterogeneous group of countries. For the purpose of analysis, some differentiation, other than geographical, is obviously necessary. Given the transformation in the world economy that gathered momentum after

1980, reflection about its future called for recognition of the economic potential of countries outside North America and Western Europe (Amsden 2001).

The term emerging economies or emerging markets surfaced as a generalized description for these countries. But there was no underlying analytical definition. It is possible to suggest that emerging markets are countries with low GDP per capita and high GDP growth rates. Yet, this is not specific enough to select an appropriate set of countries. And it is no surprise that the term emerging markets means different things to different people. Therefore, it is far better to be specific about such lead countries rather than refer to emerging markets in general. For the purpose of this chapter, then, emerging markets are defined as Next-14, listed above, selected on the basis of criteria and evidence in my recent work (Nayyar 2013). For the purpose of this chapter, again, BRICS include Brazil, India, China, and South Africa, which are developing countries, but not Russia, which is a high-income transition economy that is described by some as an emerging market. It is worth noting that BRICS are the most important, if not leading, subset of Next-14.

The discussion which follows analyses the significance of BRICS and emerging markets (Next-14) in the global economy, with reference to developing countries and industrialized economies as points of comparison. It considers, in turn, trends in population, GDP and growth, engagement with the world economy, and catch-up in industrialization.

POPULATION, OUTPUT, AND GROWTH

Table 3.1 presents evidence on the shares of each of the BRICS, Next-14, developing countries, and industrialized countries, in world population and world GDP (in current prices at market exchange rates), for selected benchmark years during the period 1980 to 2014. It also provides the absolute figures for world totals as a point of reference.

Between 1980 and 2014, the share of industrialized countries in world population fell from 17 per cent to 13 per cent, while their share in world GDP fell from 68 per cent to 57 per cent. In sharp contrast, the share of developing countries in world population rose from 74 per cent to 82 per cent, while their share in world GDP rose from 22 per cent to 38 per cent. Hence, for the developing world, the sharp asymmetry between its shares of world population and world GDP diminished significantly over this period.

Between 1980 and 2014, the share of emerging markets, the Next-14, in world population decreased from 52 per cent to 51 per cent, while their share in world GDP more than doubled from 12 per cent to 28 per cent. Between 1980 and 2014, the share of BRICS in world population decreased from 41 per cent to 40 per cent, while their share in world GDP trebled from 6 per cent to 19 per cent. For both groups, a slight decline in their share of world population was juxtaposed with a large proportionate jump in their share of world GDP, so that the asymmetry between their respective shares diminished far more than it did for developing countries as a whole.

The evidence presented also reveals a striking concentration of population and GDP in a small number of developing countries. Between 1980 and 2014, the share of Next-14 in population of the developing world fell from 70 per cent to 63 per cent, but their share in GDP of the developing world rose from 57 per cent to 73 per cent. Similarly, between 1980 and 2014, the share of BRICS in population of the developing world fell from 55 per cent to 49 per cent, but their share in GDP of the developing world rose from 29 per cent to 50 per cent. Thus, for BRICS, the asymmetry between their shares of population and GDP in the developing world, which was significant in 1980, had vanished by 2014. There was, perhaps, an even greater concentration within BRICS. It is no surprise that China and India together accounted for more than 90 per cent of the BRICS population throughout the period, but the share of China alone in BRICS's GDP rose from 40 per cent in 1980 to 69 per cent in 2014.

Changes in the significance of any subset of countries in the world over time depend upon their economic performance as compared with the rest of the world. It is obvious that differences in GDP growth rates, in real terms, underlie the changing share of country groups in the world economy. It is simple arithmetic that differences in growth rates of GDP and population determine differences in growth rates of GDP per capita, which in turn shape divergence or convergence in per capita incomes between countries.

It is, therefore, worth considering evidence on economic growth across country groups. Table 3.2 sets out growth rates in GDP and GDP per capita for each country in BRICS, the BRICS as a group, the Next-14, developing countries, industrialized countries, and the world economy, during the periods 1981–90, 1991–2000, 2001–08 and 2009–14. The first two periods are decades but the next two periods are not, simply because the financial crisis that surfaced in late 2008 led to a sharp slowdown in growth thereafter. It was a turning point that was followed by the Great Recession (Nayyar 2011). Growth rates for the entire period from 1981 to 2014 are also provided to highlight long-term trends.

GDP growth in developing countries was about the same as in industrialized countries and in the world economy during 1981–90. This was sustained largely by Asia, as economic growth in both Latin America and Africa slumped during the 1980s, later described as the lost decade (Nayyar 2013). However, GDP growth rate in developing countries, as compared with industrialized countries, was 2 per cent per annum higher during 1991–2000 and 4 per cent per annum higher during 2001–08 and 2009–14. Consequently, between 1990 and 2014, the share of developing countries in world GDP rose by 20 percentage points while industrialized countries' share fell by 20 percentage points.

The story about emerging markets is similar but even more striking. For Next-14, real GDP growth per annum was 1.4 per cent higher during 1981–90, 2.6 per cent higher during 1991–2000, 4.4 per cent higher during 2001–09, and 4 per cent higher during 2001–13, than in industrialized countries. For BRICS, real GDP growth per annum was 1.9 per cent higher during 1981–90, 3.7 per cent higher during 1991–2000, 6.1 per cent higher during 2001–08, and 4.8 per cent higher during 2009–14, than in industrialized economies. It is no surprise that, between 1980 and 2014, the share of Next-14 in world GDP increased

Table 3.2 Growth rates in BRICS, Next-14, developing countries, industrialized countries, and the world economy: 1981–2014

GDP					
	1981–90 % p.a	1991–2000 % p.a	2001–08 % p.a	2009–14 % p.a	1981–2014 % p.a
Brazil	3.2	2.8	3.9	2.5	*2.7*
India	5.7	6.1	7.8	5.8	*6.1*
China	9.9	9.9	10.6	8.1	*9.5*
South Africa	1.3	2.4	4.5	3.0	*2.4*
BRICS	5.3	6.4	8.3	6.5	*6.3*
Next-14	4.8	5.3	6.6	5.7	*5.3*
Developing countries	3.7	4.7	6.5	5.4	*4.8*
Industrialized countries	3.4	2.7	2.2	1.7	*2.4*
World	3.5	3.0	3.4	2.9	2.9
GDP per capita					
	1981–90	1991–2000	2001–08	2009–14	1981–2014
Brazil	1.1	1.3	2.8	1.7	*1.2*
India	3.5	4.3	6.3	4.2	*4.4*
China	8.2	9.1	10.0	7.7	*8.6*
South Africa	-1.0	0.5	3.1	1.9	*0.7*
BRICS	3.3	5.1	7.3	5.6	*5.0*
Next-14	2.8	4.0	5.6	4.7	*4.0*
Developing countries	1.5	3.1	5.1	4.0	*3.2*
Industrialized countries	2.8	1.4	1.9	1.3	*1.7*
World	1.7	1.6	2.2	1.7	*1.5*

Notes:
a) The growth rates for each of the countries, country groups, and the world economy have been calculated from data on GDP and GDP per capita in 2005 constant prices at 2005 constant exchange rates.
b) The average annual rates of growth for each of the periods and for the entire period have been calculated by fitting a semi-log linear regression equation LnY = a+ bt and estimating the value of b.
Source: United Nations, UNCTAD Stat, based on UN National Accounts Statistics.

by 15 percentage points, while the share of BRICS in world GDP increased by 12 percentage points. This trend was not interrupted by the financial crisis and the Great Recession that followed in its aftermath, as industrialized countries experienced a sharp slowdown in growth, while emerging markets and BRICS were less affected in terms of impact and showed more resilience in recovery (Nayyar 2011, 2013).

It is worth noting that there were significant differences in growth performance between countries within BRICS. During the entire period, China and India had much higher growth rates than Brazil and South Africa. For China, from 1981 to 2014, GDP growth was 7.1 per cent per annum higher than in industrialized countries and 6.6 per cent per annum higher than in the world economy, so that its share in world GDP rose by 10 percentage points. For India, from 1981 to 2014, GDP growth was 3.7 per cent per annum higher than in industrialized countries and 3.2 per cent per annum higher than in the world economy, but its share in world GDP increased by just over 1 percentage point. For Brazil, between 1981 and 2014, GDP growth per annum was a little higher than in industrialized countries and slightly lower than in the world economy, although its share in world GDP rose by more than 1 percentage point. For South Africa, between 1981 and 2014, GDP growth per annum was the same as in industrialized countries and lower than in the world economy, so that its share in world GDP declined a little.

Until 1990, GDP per capita growth rates in developing countries were distinctly lower than in industrialized countries, essentially because their GDP growth rates were about the same while their population growth rates were high. This situation changed in the 1990s, and was reversed by the turn of the century, as their GDP growth was so much higher than in industrialized countries while their population growth rates slowed down significantly. This change and reversal underlie the end of divergence in per capita incomes *c.*1980 followed by the beginnings of a very modest convergence that is discernible after 1990 and more visible since 2000 (Nayyar 2013).

Emerging markets did much better. Between 1981 and 2014, growth in GDP per capita was 4 per cent per annum for Next-14 and 5 per cent per annum for BRICS, much higher than 1.7 per cent per annum in industrialized countries and 1.5 per cent per annum in the world economy. Thus, emerging markets, Next-14, visibly reduced the wide gap in their per capita incomes relative to industrialized countries (Nayyar 2013). Among BRICS, China was the star performer, with a GDP per capita growth rate of 8.6 per cent per annum during the period 1981–2014, so that its per capita income doubled every eight years and increased by a multiple of eight over thirty-two years. India came next, with a GDP per capita growth rate of 4.4 per cent per annum during the period 1981–2014, so that its per capita income doubled every sixteen years and quadrupled over thirty-two years. Initial levels of per capita income in Brazil and South Africa were much higher. However, during the same period, 1981–2014, growth in GDP per capita was 1.2 per cent per annum for Brazil and 0.7 per cent per annum for South Africa. Consequently, per capita income in BRICS, as a proportion of that in industrialized countries, witnessed a visible convergence in China, a barely discernible convergence in India, a modest divergence in Brazil, and a significant divergence in South Africa (Nayyar 2013).

ENGAGEMENT WITH THE WORLD ECONOMY

The primary channels of engagement with the world economy are international trade, international investment, and international migration (Nayyar 2010).

Table 3.3 outlines the trends in the share of BRICS, Next-14, developing countries, and industrialized countries in world merchandize trade, exports and imports, for selected benchmark years during the period 1980–2014. It shows that, between 1980 and 2014, the share of developing countries rose from 30 per cent to 45 per cent in world exports and from 24 per cent to 42 per cent in world imports, while the share of

Table 3.3 Share of BRICS, Next-14, developing countries, and industrialized countries in world trade: 1980–2014

Merchandize exports

	1980 %	1990 %	2000 %	2010 %	2014 %
Brazil	1.0	0.9	0.9	1.3	1.2
India	0.4	0.5	0.7	1.5	1.7
China	0.9	1.8	3.9	10.3	12.3
South Africa	1.2	0.7	0.5	0.6	0.5
Total BRICS	3.5	3.9	6.0	13.7	15.7
Next-14	9.2	12.1	18.3	25.9	26.4
Developing countries	29.7	24.1	31.9	42.1	44.7
Industrialized countries	63.1	71.2	63.6	50.0	47.6
World	100.0	100.0	100.0	100.0	100.0
World total (US$ billion)	2,050	3,496	6,452	15,302	18,997

Merchandize imports

	1980	1990	2000	2010	2014
Brazil	1.2	0.6	0.9	1.2	1.3
India	0.7	0.7	0.8	2.3	2.4
China	1.0	1.5	3.4	9.1	10.3
South Africa	0.9	0.5	0.4	0.6	0.6
Total BRICS	3.8	3.3	5.5	13.2	14.6
Next-14	9.7	11.5	17.2	25.0	25.5
Developing countries	24.0	22.2	28.8	39.0	42.0
Industrialized countries	68.8	72.7	67.1	53.8	51.3
World	100.0	100.0	100.0	100.0	100.0
World Total (in US$ billion)	2,091	3,609	6,655	15,420	19,007

Notes:

a) The data on exports and imports, from which the percentages are calculated, are in US dollars in current prices at market exchange rates.

b) The figures for developing countries and industrialized countries do not add up to the world totals. The residual is attributable to Eastern Europe and the former USSR.

Source: United Nations, UNCTAD Stat, based on UN International Trade Statistics.

industrialized countries fell from 63 per cent to 48 per cent in world exports and from 69 per cent to 51 per cent in world imports. This substantial increase in the relative importance of developing countries in world trade was distributed in an unequal manner and concentrated in a few countries. Between 1980 and 2014, the share of Next-14 in total developing-country trade increased from three-tenths to three-fifths of exports and from one-fifth to three-fifths of imports. Similarly, from 1980 to 2014, BRICS's share in total trade of the Next-14, increased from fewer than two-fifths to almost three-fifths of both exports and imports. The concentration within BRICS is most striking. During the same period, 1980–2014, China's share in total BRICS trade increased from around a quarter to roughly three-quarters of both exports and imports. Consequently, in 2014, China alone accounted for a quarter of total merchandize exports from, and imports into, developing countries.

Table 3.4 Distribution of inward and outward stocks of FDI in the world economy: 1980–2014

Inward stock					
	1980 %	1990 %	2000 %	2010 %	2014 %
Brazil	2.5	1.8	1.6	3.3	3.1
India	0.1	0.1	0.2	1.0	1.0
China	0.2	1.0	2.6	2.9	4.4
South Africa	2.4	0.4	0.6	0.9	0.6
Total BRICS	5.2	3.3	5.0	8.1	9.1
Next-14	10.6	8.7	10.7	15.4	15.4
Developing countries	42.5	24.7	23.6	32.4	33.7
Industrialized countries	57.5	75.1	74.2	60.6	60.6
World	100.0	100.0	100.0	100.0	100.0
World Total (US$ billion)	698	2,081	7,511	20,371	24,627
Outward stock					
	1980	1990	2000	2010	2014
Brazil	7.0	2.0	0.6	0.9	1.3
India	0.01	0.01	0.02	0.5	0.5
China	0.0	0.2	0.3	1.5	3.0
South Africa	1.0	0.7	0.3	0.4	0.5
Total BRICS	8.01	2.91	1.22	3.3	5.3
Next-14	11.9	5.0	3.3	6.5	9.3
Developing countries	13.0	6.7	11.1	16.4	19.6
Industrialized countries	87.0	93.2	88.6	81.2	77.8
World	100.0	100.0	100.0	100.0	100.0
World Total (in US$ billion)	548	2,093	8,008	21,289	24,602

Notes: The figures for developing countries and industrialized countries do not add up to the world totals. The residual is attributable to Eastern Europe and the former USSR. It is worth noting, however, that this residual is negligible for inward stock figures in 1980 and 1990, and for outward stock figures in 1980, 1990, and 2000, because reporting for Eastern Europe and the former USSR was incomplete. Hence, it is possible that, for these specified years, the share of developing countries in inward and outward stocks of FDI in the world economy is overstated.

Source: UNCTAD FDI Online Database.

Table 3.4 sets out data on the distribution of stocks of FDI in the world economy, inward and outward, with the shares of BRICS, Next-14, developing countries, and industrialized countries, for selected years, during the period 1980–2014. The picture that emerges is rather different. The evidence shows that, between 1980 and 2014, developing countries' share fell from 43 per cent to 34 per cent in inward stocks but rose from 13 per cent to 20 per cent in outward stocks, while industrialized countries' share rose from 58 per cent to 61 per cent in inward stocks but fell from 87 per cent to 78 per cent in outward stocks. There was some concentration but far less than in trade. Between 1980 and 2014, the share of Next-14 in developing countries' inward stock increased from 25 per cent to 45 per cent, while BRICS's share in Next-14 inward stock increased from 48 per cent to 59 per cent. However, between 1980 and 2014, Next-14's

Table 3.5 Remittances in the world economy: distribution across BRICS, Next-14, developing countries, and industrialized countries: 1980–2014

	1980 %	1990 %	2000 %	2010 %	2014 %
Brazil	0.3	0.7	1.3	0.9	0.4
India	6.4	3.0	9.8	12.1	11.9
China	1.3	0.2	4.0	11.2	10.5
South Africa	0.2	0.2	0.3	0.2	0.2
Total above BRICS	8.2	4.1	15.4	24.4	23.0
Next-14	23.2	20.7	30.6	34.6	34.5
Developing countries	46.8	42.0	60.8	68.6	64.7
Industrialized countries	43.8	46.2	33.3	20.0	14.9
World	100.0	100.0	100.0	100.0	100.0
World Total (US$ billion)	43.2	79.6	130.8	453.5	581.6

Notes:
a) The percentages have been calculated from data on remittances in US dollars in current prices at market exchange rates.
b) The figures for developing countries and industrialized countries do not add up to the total for the world economy on account of remittances to Eastern Europe and the former USSR which are not presented in the table.

Source: Nayyar (2013) and United Nations, UNCTAD Stat, based on IMF *Balance of Payments Statistics*, World Bank *Migration and Remittances*, Economist Intelligence Unit, *Country Data*, and national sources. The 2014 figures for Brazil, India, China, and South Africa are from World Bank, *Migration and Remittances*.

share in developing countries' outward stock declined from 92 per cent to 47 per cent, while BRICS's share in Next-14 outward stock declined from 68 per cent to 57 per cent. It is worth noting that, in 2014, the share of China alone in both inward and outward stocks of FDI in developing countries was only around 14 per cent.

Table 3.5 presents available evidence on remittances in the world economy, from migrants to their countries of origin, in BRICS, Next-14, developing countries, and industrialized countries, for selected years, during the period 1980–2014. It shows that, between 1980 and 2014, developing countries' share increased from 47 per cent to 65 per cent, while industrialized countries' share diminished sharply from 44 per cent to 15 per cent. The residual represents remittances to Eastern Europe and the former USSR. The concentration in the distribution was far less than in trade and there was little increase over time. Between 1980 and 2014, Next-14's share in remittances to the developing world remained unchanged at around 50 per cent, while BRICS's share in remittances to Next-14 remained unchanged at about 35 per cent. The concentration within BRICS was high. Over this period, the share of India and China in total remittances to BRICS was more than 95 per cent, essentially because remittances to Brazil and South Africa were low. India was by far the largest recipient of remittances in the developing world. Between 1980 and 2014, its share in total remittances to the developing world increased from 14 per cent to 18 per cent, although its share in remittances to BRICS decreased from 79 per cent to 52 per cent.

Table 3.6 Distribution of manufacturing value added in the world economy: BRICS, Next-14, developing countries, and industrialized countries in: 1990–2014

	1990 %	2000 %	2010 %	2014 %
Brazil	2.2	1.7	2.9	1.8
India	1.1	1.2	2.3	2.7
China	2.6	6.7	18.9	24.0
South Africa	0.5	0.4	0.5	0.3
Total above BRICS	6.4	10.0	24.6	28.8
Next-14	14.0	20.3	35.9	39.4
Developing countries	17.8	24.7	42.0	47.4
Industrialized countries	75.5	72.8	53.1	47.8
World	100.0	100.0	100.0	100.0
World Total(in US$ billion)	4,549	5,715	10,168	12,201

Notes:
a) The percentages have been calculated from data on manufacturing value added in current prices at market exchange rates for each of the countries and country groups.
b) The figures for developing countries and industrialized countries do not add up to the world totals. The residual is attributable to Eastern Europe and the former USSR.
c) For 1990 and 2000, the figures for China are obtained from the UN Industrial Development Organization (UNIDO) *Statistics Data Portal*, as these are not reported in UNCTAD Stat.
d) The figures for 1980 are not presented in this table, as reporting is incomplete for that year, making for a large residual that is not attributable to any of the three country groups in the world economy.
Source: United Nations, UNCTAD Stat, based on UN National Accounts Statistics.

INDUSTRIAL PRODUCTION AND MANUFACTURED EXPORTS

There is also a catch-up in industrialization that is reflected in the rapidly growing significance of developing countries in world manufacturing output and exports.

Table 3.6 outlines changes in the shares of BRICS, Next-14, developing countries, and industrialized countries in world manufacturing value added for selected years from 1990 to 2014. It shows that, between 1990 and 2014, the share of industrialized countries in total manufacturing value added fell sharply from 76 per cent to 48 per cent, while the share of developing countries rose even more, partly at the expense of Eastern Europe and the former USSR, from 18 per cent to 47 per cent. However this industrialization was highly concentrated. Between 1990 and 2014, Next-14's share in developing country manufacturing value added increased from 79 per cent to 83 per cent, while BRICS's share in Next-14 manufacturing value added increased from 46 per cent to 73 per cent. It is worth noting that, between 1990 and 2014, the share of China alone in manufacturing value added increased from 40 per cent to 83 per cent of BRICS, from 19 per cent to 61 per cent of Next-14, and from 15 per cent to 50 per cent of developing countries.

Table 3.7 sets out changes in the share of BRICS, Next-14, developing countries, and industrialized countries in world manufactured exports for selected years, during the period 2000–2014. Comparable time-series data are not available for earlier years.

Table 3.7 Manufactured exports from BRICS, Next-14, developing countries, industrialized countries, and the world: 2000–14

	2000 %	2005 %	2010 %	2014 %
Brazil	0.7	0.8	0.7	0.6
India	0.6	0.8	1.2	1.4
China	4.7	9.5	14.8	17.9
South Africa	0.3	0.3	0.3	0.3
Total BRICS	6.3	11.4	17.0	20.2
Next-14	19.8	23.7	30.4	33.5
Developing countries	29.3	33.1	40.2	43.8
Industrialized countries	67.3	61.8	53.8	49.1
World	100	100	100	100
World Total(US$ billion)	4,672	7,362	9,974	12,289

Notes:
a) Manufactured exports are defined as the sum of SITC (Standard international trade classification) 5 (chemicals), SITC 6 (manufactured goods), SITC 7 (machinery and transport equipment), and SITC 8 (miscellaneous manufactured articles) *less* SITC 68 (non-ferrous metals) and SITC 667 (pearls, precious and semi-precious stones).
b) The percentages have been calculated from data on manufactured exports in US dollars in current prices at market exchange rates.
c) The figures for developing countries and industrialized countries do not add up to the world totals. The residual is attributable to Eastern Europe and the former USSR.
Source: United Nations, UNCTAD Stat, based on UN International Trade Statistics.

But this period witnessed significant changes. In just a decade and a half, between 2000 and 2014, the share of industrialized countries in total manufactured exports fell from two-thirds to a half, while developing countries' share rose from fewer than three-tenths to more than two-fifths. Manufactured exports were concentrated among a few developing countries. Between 2000 and 2014, Next-14's share in developing country manufactured exports increased from two-thirds to three-quarters, while the share of BRICS in the Next-14 manufactured exports increased from three-tenths to three-fifths. This concentration was somewhat less than in manufacturing value added. Even so, there was high concentration in China. Between 2000 and 2014, the share of China alone in manufactured exports increased from 76 per cent to 89 per cent of BRICS, from 24 per cent to 53 per cent of Next-14, and from 16 per cent to 40 per cent of developing countries.

In sum, it is clear that aggregates for developing countries as a whole do not reveal the high concentration in BRICS and emerging markets (Next-14), whether in population, income, trade, investment, migration, industrial production, or manufactured exports. This concentration is perhaps the highest in income, in merchandize exports, and in manufacturing value added. Much of it is attributable to economic size and economic performance. In the developing world, the Next-14 countries account for a large proportion. In Next-14, BRICS account for a large proportion. Among BRICS, China accounts for a large proportion. Yet, it needs to be said that the story of BRICS is about more than China, the story of Next-14 is about more than BRICS, and the story of catch-up in the developing world is about more than BRICS and emerging markets (Nayyar 2016).

Possible impact of rapid growth in BRICS

Rapid economic growth in BRICS, if it is sustained at the projected rates, is bound to exercise considerable influence on prospects for the world economy, industrialized countries, and developing countries. This impact could be either positive or negative.

WORLD ECONOMY

Growth in lead economies drives growth elsewhere in the world by providing markets for exports, resources for investment, finances for development, and technologies for productivity (Nayyar 2010). Britain in the nineteenth century and the United States in the twentieth century are classic examples of these transmission mechanisms which worked as engines of growth for the world economy. And, despite its diminished dominance, the United States continues to perform that role.

It is simply not possible, at least yet, to think of BRICS as engines of growth in these four dimensions, except perhaps as markets for exports (Nayyar 2010). However, Brazil, India, and South Africa do not even fit that role despite their large trade deficits, since their share of world GDP is rather small. The economic size of China, reflected in its share of world GDP and world trade, is much larger, but it cannot quite stimulate growth elsewhere even as a market for exports because of its big current account surplus and massive trade surplus (Nayyar 2011). For this reason, contrary to the belief of some who propagated the decoupling hypothesis, BRICS could not drive recovery in the world despite their resilience in the aftermath of the global economic crisis. Even so, in future, implications for the world economy could be positive if, as the old engine of growth slows down, BRICS emerge as complements rather than substitutes that support the growth process. China, which supports but does not yet lead growth in the world economy, obviously has the potential. In time, sustained rapid growth in India, Brazil, and South Africa could provide an impetus to the growth process in their respective regions.

INDUSTRIALIZED COUNTRIES

The impact of rapid economic growth in BRICS on industrialized countries could be either positive or negative. The focus is often on the negative. But there is also a positive.

There are three reasons why the impact may be negative. First, rapid economic growth in BRICS may worsen the terms of trade for industrialized countries. The burgeoning demand in China and India could drive up prices of primary commodities in the world market. At the same time, rising wages in BRICS could drive up prices of labour-intensive manufactured goods in the world market. Both could turn the terms of trade against industrialized countries. However, the consequences would be easy to absorb since the process would be spread over a long period of time and the loss of real income in the industrialized world would be modest (Rowthorn 2008; Nayyar 2010).

Second, for industrialized countries, BRICS could emerge as new destinations that may become a source of competition for investment. This may happen if firms from the industrialized countries, whether the United States or Europe, relocate production in BRICS. But this is not likely to happen on a significant scale, for such investment is not a zero-sum game in an expanding world economy and technological change might even reverse the process.

Third, the economic rise of BRICS may lead to downward pressure on employment levels and real wages in industrialized countries. It needs to be said that this concern is somewhat exaggerated. It is important to recognize that the stagnation in real wages and the high levels of unemployment in industrialized countries are attributable to the nature of technical progress, which is replacing several unskilled workers with a few skilled workers, and the impact of macroeconomic policies which have sought to maintain price stability at the expense of full employment. Of course, the Great Recession has exacerbated the problem, since recovery has been slow, uneven, and fragile. Moreover, recovery in employment has been distinctly slower than recovery in output (Nayyar 2014). Essentially, the source of these problems lies within the industrialized countries and not in their trade with developing countries (Nayyar 1996). And even if the expansion of such trade in manufactured goods with BRICS could exert some downward pressure on employment levels or real wages in industrialized countries, such pressures are bound to diminish with the ageing of industrial societies (Nayyar 2002a, 2008a). Moreover, in the long run, productivity increase in BRICS would be followed, after a time, by a commensurate increase in real wages. This proposition is validated by economic history (Krugman 1994).

It is just as important to recognize that rapid economic growth in BRICS may have a positive impact on industrialized countries (Singh 2007; Rowthorn 2008; Nayyar 2010). First, starting from low levels of income per capita and high-income elasticities of demand, higher incomes associated with rapid growth would create expanding markets for exports from industrialized countries. Second, BRICS as suppliers of cheap manufactured goods could help reduce inflationary pressures in industrialized countries, thereby enabling them to maintain higher levels of output and employment than would otherwise be possible. Third, BRICS could be a source of new technologies in future, which could help extend production possibility frontiers and consumer possibility frontiers in the industrialized economies.

DEVELOPING COUNTRIES

Rapid economic growth in BRICS could have a positive impact on developing countries if it improves terms of trade, provides appropriate technologies, and creates new sources of finance for development, whether investment or aid.

It is clear that, for some time, the positive impact on developing countries has been transmitted through an improvement in their terms of trade (Kaplinsky 2006; Singh 2007; Nayyar 2008b; Rowthorn 2008).

Rapid economic growth in China and India did boost the demand for primary commodities exported by developing countries and probably was a significant factor underlying the boom that began in the early 2000s. The reasons are simple enough. Both China and India have large populations and have sustained high growth rates. Further, in both countries, levels of consumption per capita in most primary commodities are low, while income elasticities of demand for most primary commodities are high. This burgeoning demand almost certainly raised prices of primary commodities in world markets and thereby improved the terms of trade for developing countries. It did also benefit Brazil and South Africa as exporters of primary commodities, reinforcing their growth process. This might have come to an end, for the present, with the collapse in prices of primary commodities, particularly crude oil, which started in 2014. Such busts and booms are inevitable in world commodity markets. In the long run, however, world prices of commodities will be shaped by underlying economic factors.

Apart from the terms-of-trade effect in primary commodities, China already is, while India and Brazil are likely to become, a source of manufactured goods in the world market. Such manufactures, particularly wage goods but also capital goods from China, India, and Brazil, are likely to be cheaper than competing goods from industrialized countries. At the same time, Brazil and South Africa could provide cheaper natural resources-based manufactures. This would also improve the terms of trade for developing countries.

The positive impact of China, India, Brazil, and South Africa on developing countries through the other potential channels of transmission is not as clear. In principle, it is possible that BRICS would develop technologies that are more appropriate for the factor endowments and the economic needs of developing countries. But it is too early to come to a judgement on this matter. Similarly, BRICS are potential sources of finance for development. Their foreign aid programmes, particularly in Africa, constitute a modest beginning but also represent a significant departure from the old world of development assistance from rich countries to poor countries (Toye 2008; Cheru and Obi 2010; Nayyar, 2012). There are contending views on the subject, but the experience is not long enough to make a systematic comparison. Similarly, their contribution in terms of FDI so far is limited. Yet, evidence available suggests that it is not significantly different from the experience with large international firms from industrialized countries.

The emergence of BRICS in the world economy could also have a negative impact on developing countries if they provide developing countries with competition in markets for exports or as destinations for investment.

At this juncture, China is clearly the largest supplier of labour-intensive manufactured goods in the world market. Even if not as large as China, India is also a significant supplier of labour-intensive manufactured goods in the world market. Brazil and South Africa are important suppliers of natural resource-based manufactures. China, India, and Brazil are emerging suppliers of capital goods. There can be little doubt that manufactured exports from BRICS span almost the entire range of manufactured exports in which other developing countries could have a potential comparative advantage. Hence, it is plausible to argue though impossible to prove that, on balance, BRICS possibly have a negative impact on manufactured exports from other developing countries which have to compete with them for export markets in industrialized countries (Kaplinsky and Morris 2008). This might change if and when China and India vacate their space in the international trade matrix, in much the same way as latecomers to industrialization in Asia such as Japan, Korea, Hong Kong, Taiwan, and Singapore vacated their space in the market for simple labour-intensive manufactures for countries that followed in their footsteps. It is not likely, at least in the medium term, because both China and India have large reservoirs of surplus labour at low wages not only in the rural hinterlands but also in the urban informal sectors. Brazil and South Africa may not have such large reservoirs of surplus labour, but given their abundance in primary commodities and natural resources, it is not likely that they would vacate their space in the market for processed products or resource-based manufactures for other developing countries that have similar endowments from nature (Nayyar 2010).

Given that China, India, and Brazil are now among the most attractive destinations for transnational firms seeking to locate production in the developing world, it is once again plausible to suggest—though impossible to prove—that FDI in these economies might be at the expense of developing countries. South Africa may not have the same attraction as a destination, but it may draw FDI that could have gone to developing countries in Africa. At the same time, the share of BRICS in outward FDI in the world economy, as also from developing countries, is disproportionately small, so that firms from BRICS do not compensate with FDI in other developing countries.

The less discernible but more significant negative impact of BRICS, particularly China, on developing countries, lies in implicit barriers to change in the traditional specialization in production (Nayyar 2010). For one, China and India might pre-empt opportunities for other developing countries to industrialize through exports of labour-intensive manufactures, attributable to their surplus labour and low wages which might continue for some time to come. For another, Brazil and South Africa might pre-empt opportunities for other developing countries to industrialize through agro-based or resource-intensive manufactures, attributable to their abundance in primary commodities and natural resources. But this is no more than a plausible hypothesis about possible future developments, which cannot be tested.

The problem has, however, surfaced in one dimension. China's present division of labour with the developing world, reflected in the composition of trade flows, is not different from the old North–South pattern of trade, insofar as Chinese imports from the developing world are largely primary commodities, while Chinese exports to the developing world are largely manufactured goods (IADB 2005; Jenkins et al. 2008). China's trade with countries in Southeast Asia is the exception to this rule. But Chinese trade with, and investment in, Africa confirms even more closely to this caricature neocolonial pattern (Toye 2008; Nayyar 2012). Such traditional patterns of trade, it should be recognized can neither transform the structure of production in developing countries nor make for a new international division of labour. Indeed, such trade can only perpetuate the dependence of developing countries on exports of primary commodities without creating possibilities of increasing value added before export or entering into manufacturing activities characterized by economies of scale. Such path-dependent specialization can only curb the possibilities of structural transformation in developing countries (Nayyar 2012). Trade with China can support industrialization in developing countries only if there is a successful transition from a complementary to a competitive pattern of trade, so that inter-sectoral trade is gradually replaced by intra-sectoral or intra-industry trade.

The global context

It is necessary to recognize that the importance of BRICS in the world would be shaped not only in the sphere of economics but also in the realm of politics. Their emerging significance in the world economy is attributable in part to their share in world population and in world income and in part to their engagement with the world economy through international trade, international investment, and international migration. Even so, in the economic sphere, their potential importance in future far exceeds their actual importance at present. In the realm of politics, however, their importance is more discernible at the present juncture, which is attributable in part to their size and in part to their rise.

It is plausible to argue, though impossible to prove, that this represents the beginnings of a profound change in the balance of economic and political power in the world. The emergence of countries outside North America and Western Europe, not only the powerhouse economies in Asia but also emerging economies in other continents, represents a striking transformation (Nayyar 2013). These emerging markets, Next-14, which have led the catch-up are part of a larger process of change. Hence, the emergence of BRICS as a formation must also be situated in this wider context.

The acronym—BRICS—began life in a much narrower context on a rather modest note to describe a cluster of five countries that experienced rapid economic growth in the 1990s, which gathered momentum in the boom of the early 2000s (O'Neill et al. 2004). But this was no more than an exercise in compound growth rates and linear extrapolation that aspired to predict the future (Nayyar 2008a; Rowthorn, 2008).

The era of change in the world economy gathered momentum from 1980. The catch-up by developing countries, concentrated in the Next-14, even if the focus is often on BRICS possibly because of the perceived rise of China and India, was continuous. It reached a critical threshold in the early 2000s. This was necessary but not quite sufficient. It was the conjuncture that made an enormous difference. The financial crisis that surfaced in the United States in late 2008, and the Great Recession that followed in its aftermath, was the deepest crisis of capitalism since the Great Depression eight decades ago. This eroded the triumph of capitalism that followed the collapse of Communism in 1991 and reinforced the shift in the balance of power somewhat more towards the developing world. The G8 was replaced by the G20. And it is no coincidence that BRICS as a formation surfaced in 2009.

The composition of BRICS in terms of countries was shaped largely by their economic size, potential if not actual income, and their physical size, in terms of geographical space, which explains the inclusion of Brazil, India, and China. But geography and location also made a difference. This is the reason why it was South Africa, in Africa, rather than Indonesia, in Asia, that was included. The same consideration, reinforced by geopolitics, meant that Russia—a high-income, former superpower, transition economy in Europe—became a constituent of BRICS, rather than Mexico which could have been a plausible choice.

It should come as no surprise that there is enormous diversity between, and relatively little coherence (at least so far) among the nations that make up the BRICS formation. Even so, it has surfaced as a strategic alliance of countries, in part as a reflection of the changing balance of economic power in the world, and in part as a countervailing force in a unipolar world that was born after Communism collapsed. In this world, which was dominated by the United States, the European Union was, in effect, an ally of the sole superpower rather than a countervailing force, which was its original raison d'être. The presence of Russia perhaps reflects a strategic effort to strike a balance in a group that has concerns about the overwhelming rise and growing power of China. It is clear that China is a very important factor underlying the emergence of BRICS. But it also needs to be said that, as a political formation, BRICS is about far more than China.

This formation began life on stepping stones of bilateralism and building blocks of plurilateralism. Brazil, India, China, and South Africa have all engaged in a bilateralism that is both intra- and inter-regional. There are intra-regional initiatives led by China and India in Asia, by Brazil in Latin America, and by South Africa in Africa. There are also some inter-regional initiatives on the part of these countries, such as China taking a lead in forging the Asia-Pacific Economic Cooperation (APEC) and India seeking a partnership with the Association of Southeast Asian Nations (ASEAN). Brazil, India, China, and South Africa have also been engaged in some plurilateralism. There are two striking examples. For one, in 2003, India, Brazil, and South Africa constituted a plurilateral group, the G3, or IBSA, attempting to develop a strategic alliance that would foster partnership among them, promote cooperation with developing countries, and articulate a collective voice in international politics. For another, in 2005, Brazil, India, China, and South Africa, together with Mexico, formed the Outreach 5, who were invited to the G8 Summit even before the global economic crisis. There was a hint of discontent about their status as observers, peripheral to deliberations and decisions, so that the Outreach 5 were always seeking a place at the high table with the G8. Similarly, in 2009, Brazil, India, China, and South Africa came together as BASIC at the Summit on Climate Change in Copenhagen, which was an ad hoc coalition shaped by the event.

Soon after, it evolved into a political reality with the first annual summit of BRICS nations in 2010. South Africa was invited as a late entrant in 2010.

From the perspective of the developing world, working together, BRICS may be able to exercise significant influence through multilateralism, whether institutions or rules, in the global context (Nayyar 2002b). The United Nations, the World Bank, the International Monetary Fund (IMF) and the World Trade Organization (WTO) are among the most important multilateral institutions. The structure of these institutions for global governance created soon after the Second World War and characterized by democratic deficits can now be challenged more easily in the existing institutions (Nayyar 2002b; Gray and Murphy 2013).

In the United Nations, China alone is a permanent member of the Security Council with a right to veto. And it is also a member of the P5. But India, Brazil, and South Africa are engaged in knocking at the door, seeking permanent membership of the Security Council, with or without a veto. There can be little doubt that if and when there is an increase in the number of permanent members of the Security Council of the United Nations, apart from Germany and Japan, these three countries would have the strongest claim to permanent membership.

In the Bretton Woods institutions, the World Bank and the IMF, Brazil, India, China, and South Africa are permanent members of the executive boards. Industrialized countries may be the principal shareholders but developing countries are the principal stakeholders (Nayyar 2002b). Given the democratic deficit in these institutions, which is embedded in unequal voting rights, Brazil, India, China, and South Africa together could influence decisions or even reshape rules. So far, however, coordination and cooperation among BRICS nations, which is possible, has not quite surfaced in any systematic manner. It is also not clear whether BRICS as a formation can transform itself from a countervailing economic grouping to a cohesive political alternative (Thakur 2014). This is a debated proposition with contending views on the subject (Gray and Gils 2016). Unfolding outcomes highlight constraints as well as possibilities.

In some domains, it would seem that BRICS have neither articulated a collective voice nor exercised collective influence. There are two obvious examples. They failed to act in cohesion when the President of the World Bank was appointed in 2012, although there were two strong candidates from the developing world. Soon thereafter, each of the BRICS nations infused large doses of capital into the IMF, but simply did not negotiate any changes in its rules that reduced policy space for developing countries as borrowers let alone attempt to reduce the democratic deficit.

Conclusion

The situation in the WTO provides some reason for hope. India and Brazil have been longstanding advocates of developing countries in the WTO. South Africa is also now part of the strategic alliance among developing countries, although China has kept a low profile possibly because of its much later accession. But India and Brazil, along with the United States and the European Union, are members of the *Quad*, which is the principal institutional mechanism for resolving differences and finding solutions. And there is some discernible solidarity among WTO member countries from the developing world forged in part by BRICS.

The BRICS decision, in July 2014, to create the New Development Bank is another promising step in the right direction. This is the first tangible act of real cooperation and collective action on the part of BRICS despite some potential conflicts and genuine concerns. It could be a real alternative if it evolves as an international institution that provides poor countries with finances for development, as partners, on terms that are better than and different from the terms of the IMF and the World Bank. Such competition might even induce some change in the Bretton Woods institutions. The formative years will be critical. There is a danger that it might evolve in much the same way as the World Bank with a democratic deficit and as a window of financial assistance based on patronage and conditions. Hence, it is essential for BRICS to sustain their solidarity of purpose to preserve equality among the founding countries, the lenders, and nurture partnership with the countries to whom it provides resources, the borrowers, so that its structures of governance remain democratic. It is the only way forward that could avert the dangers and help create an international institution for financing development in a spirit of partnership among equals rather than patronage among unequal partners.

Of course, such changes are always slow to begin with but can gather momentum. On balance, it would seem that BRICS have a considerable potential for articulating a collective voice in the world of multilateralism. Coordination and cooperation among them carries significant possibilities for exercising influence on multilateral institutions, which could reshape rules and create policy space for countries that are latecomers to development. Such coordination and cooperation, which is in the realm of the possible, has not quite surfaced. There could be two reasons for the minimal coordination and cooperation so far. For one, in the early stages of change, these countries might not have recognized their potential for exercising collective influence. For another, their relationship with each other may be characterized more by rivalry, economic or political, and less by unity. It is obviously difficult to predict how reality might unfold in times to come. Even so, it is important to recognize that once these countries become major players, there is a danger that they might opt for the pursuit of national interest rather than the spirit of solidarity among developing countries or the logic of collective action.

ACKNOWLEDGEMENTS

The author would like to thank Atul Sanganeria for valuable research assistance.

REFERENCES

Amsden, Alice H. (2001). *The Rise of the Rest: Challenges to the West from Late Industrializing Economies*. New York: Oxford University Press.

Bairoch, Paul (1982). 'International industrialization levels from 1750 to 1980', *Journal of European Economic History* 11: 269–333.

Cheru, Fantu and Obi, Cyril (eds) (2010). *The Rise of China and India in Africa* London: Zed Books.

Gray, Kevin and Gils, Barry (2016). 'South–south cooperation and the rise of the global south', *Third World Quarterly* 37: 557–74.

Gray, Kevin and Murphy, C.N. (2013). 'Rising powers and the future of global governance', *Third World Quarterly* 34: 183–93.

IADB (Inter-American Development Bank) (2005). *The Emergence of China: Opportunities and Challenges for Latin America and the Caribbean*. Washington, DC: IADB.

Jenkins, Rhys, Peters, E.D., and Moreira, M.M. (2008). 'The impact of China on Latin America and the Caribbean', *World Development* 36: 235–53.

Kaplinsky, Raphael (ed.) (2006). 'Asian drivers: opportunities and threats', *IDS Bulletin* 37/1: 1–11.

Kaplinsky, Raphael and Morris, M. (2008). 'Do the Asian drivers undermine export-oriented industrialization in sub-Saharan Africa?', *World Development* 36: 254–73.

Krugman, Paul (1994). 'Competetiveness: a dangerous obsession', *Foreign Affairs* 73: 28–44.

Maddison, Angus (2003). *The World Economy: Historical Statistics* Paris: OECD.

Maddison, Angus (2007). *Contours of the World Economy, 1-2030 AD: Essays in Macroeconomic History*. Oxford: Oxford University Press.

Nayyar, Deepak (1996). 'Free trade: why, when and for whom?', *Banca Nazionale del Lavoro Quarterly Review* 49: 333–50.

Nayyar, Deepak (2002a). 'Cross-border movements of people', in Deepak Nayyar (ed.) *Governing Globalization: Issues and Institutions*. Oxford: Oxford University Press, 144–73.

Nayyar, Deepak (2002b). 'The existing system and the missing institutions', in Deepak Nayyar (ed.) *Governing Globalization: Issues and Institutions* Oxford: Oxford University Press, 356–84.

Nayyar, Deepak (2008a). 'International migration and economic development', in Joseph Stiglitz and Narcis Serra (eds) *The Washington Consensus Reconsidered: Towards a New Global Governance*. Oxford: Oxford University Press, 277–305.

Nayyar, Deepak (2008b). 'The rise of China and India: implications for developing countries', in Philip Arestis and John Eatwell (eds) *Issues in Economic Development and Globalization* London: Palgrave Macmillan, 73–94.

Nayyar, Deepak (2010). 'China, India, Brazil and South Africa in the world economy: engines of growth?', in Amelia Santos-Paulino and Guanghua Wan (eds) *Southern Engines of Global Growth*. Oxford: Oxford University Press, chap. 2.

Nayyar, Deepak (2011). 'The financial crisis, the Great Recession and the developing world', *Global Policy* 2: 20–32.

Nayyar, Deepak (2012). 'The emerging Asian giants and economic development in Africa', in Akbar Noman, Kwesi Botchwey, Howard Stein, and Joseph Stiglitz (eds) *Good Growth and Governance in Africa*. Oxford: Oxford University Press, 536–64.

Nayyar, Deepak (2013). *Catch Up: Developing Countries in the World Economy*. Oxford: Oxford University Press.

Nayyar, Deepak (2014). 'The future still belongs to emerging markets', *Hong Kong Economic Journal Monthly* 445: 16–19.

Nayyar, Deepak (2016). 'BRICS, developing countries and global governance', *Third World Quarterly* 37: 575–91.

O'Neill, J., Lawson, S., Wilson, D., Purushothamn, R., Buchanan, M., and Griffiths, L. (2004). *Growth and Development: The Path to 2050*. London: Goldman Sachs.

Rowthorn, Robert (2008). 'The renaissance of China and India: implications for the advanced economies', in Philip Arestis and John Eatwell (eds) *Issues in Economic Development and Globalization* London: Palgrave Macmillan, 49–72.

Singh, Ajit (2007). 'Globalization, industrial revolutions in India and China and labour markets in advanced countries: implications for national and international economic policy'. ILO Working Paper 81. Geneva: ILO.

Thakur, Ramesh (2014). 'Inequalities and multilateralism: how representative are BRICS?', *Third World Quarterly* 35: 1791–808.

Toye, John (2008). 'China's impact on sub-Saharan African development: trade, aid and politics', in Philip Arestis and John Eatwell (eds) *Issues in Economic Development and Globalization*. London: Palgrave Macmillan, 95–114.

4 Growth, employment, and social protection in BRICS

Moazam Mahmood and Florence Bonnet

Introduction

BRICS have been considered to be the stars of development and catch-up to advanced economies (AEs). The question that this chapter poses is, why? On what grounds? Is it because they have achieved high growth? Or is it because they have managed to make their growth more broad based and inclusive, with good social development? Or a third reason, have they managed the chimera of both good growth and good social development?

This chapter sets out to search for evidence of all three possible growth and social development paths pursued by BRICS. It finds one group of countries, say G1, to be good at growth, with another group of countries G2, not so much. But in looking at social development, *au contraire*, the G1 good growth countries are not all good at social development, and many of the weak growth G2 countries turn out to be much better. The chimera remains a challenge for most of BRICS, for the good growth countries to up their social development—and for the good social development countries to up their growth—because neither is affordable without the other, growth or social development. One country though, possibly has the makings of this chimera, combining both growth and social development—China—but with significant challenges emerging to its growth of late; and more abiding, longer-term challenges persisting in social development.

Much of the literature since O'Neil's (2001) coining of the term BRICS has focused on growth, gaps in GDP with the AEs (Wilson and Purushothaman 2003), and the sources of productivity growth (IMF 2006; Bosworth and Collins 2007; OECD 2010; McMillan and Rodrik 2011; de Vries et al. 2012). Literature that combines growth and social development in BRICS is rarer and illuminating (see, for example, Ghosh et al. 2009; Arnal and Forster 2010; Vandemoortele et al. 2013).

This chapter juxtaposes both growth and social development for BRICS, examining economic development through growth and its composition, and examining social development through employment and social protection.

Moazam Mahmood and Florence Bonnet, *Growth, employment, and social protection in BRICS* In: *Handbook of BRICS and Emerging Economies*.
Edited by: P.B. Anand, Shailaja Fennell, and Flavio Comim, Oxford University Press (2021). © Oxford University Press.
DOI: 10.1093/oso/9780198827535.003.0004

Growth

CHINA AND INDIA

All of BRICS have not had such high growth; China and India have had much higher growth compared to the rest. Neither the long-run trend nor recent episodic GDP growth show all BRICS to be in the high growth category. Figure 4.1 gives GDP per capita growth over the past third of a century, from 1980 to 2013, for BRICS. China and India stand out with GDP per capita growing above 8 per cent per annum and above 4 per cent per annum respectively. These high growth countries, call them G1, contrast with Brazil, Russia, and South Africa, which have all had GDP per capita growth of 1 per cent or less per annum over this period. Call these low growth countries G2.

The long-run trend in GDP per capita growth for BRICS is consistent with trend growth in each decade, given in Table 4.1. In the 1980s, China led with GDP per capita growth of 8.3 per cent per annum, followed by India with growth of 3.3 per cent per annum. Compared to these G1 countries, the G2 countries for which GDP per capita growth data were available, Brazil was stagnant and South Africa was regressing. In the G1 countries in the 1990s, China grew at 9.4 per cent per annum and India at 3.8 per cent per annum. In the G2 countries, Brazil grew at 0.8 per cent per annum, while Russia and South Africa continued regressing. In the first decade of the 2000s, differentials in per capita growth between the G1 and G2 countries narrowed, with China and India ratcheting up their growth to near 10 per cent per annum and 6 per cent per annum respectively, Russia rising to 5 per cent per annum from a low base, and Brazil and South Africa picking up to just over 2 per cent per annum each. In the second decade of the 2000s, differentials between the G1 and G2 countries widened again, despite China and India settling at lower growth paths of 7 per cent and 5 per cent respectively. This was due to all three G2 countries being hit by the end of the commodities super cycle, with

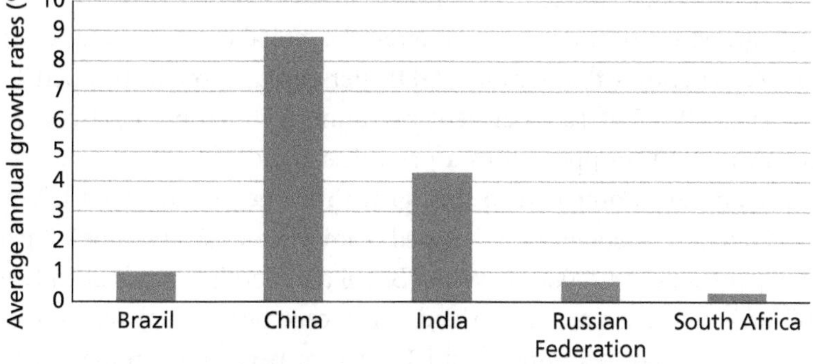

Figure 4.1 GDP per capita average annual growth rates, 1980–2013

Note: The average annual growth rate of Russian Federa on is calculated between1989 and 2013.
Source: ILO calculations based on World Bank, World Development Indicators, 2016.

Table 4.1 GDP per capita annual growth rates, period average (% per annum)

	1980–89	1990–99	2000–11	2012–14
Advanced economies	2.6	1.8	0.8	0.5
Developing countries	1.6	3.2	5.0	2.3
Brazil	0.1	0.8	2.4	0.7
China	8.3	9.4	9.7	7.1
India	3.3	3.8	5.9	5.2
Russian Federation[1]	......	−5.2	5.0	1.1
South Africa	−0.8	−0.6	2.2	0.4

[1] Data missing for: Russian Federation (1980–89).

Source: ILO Research Department calculation based on World Development Indicators, World Bank (various years).

Table 4.2 GDP per capita annual growth rates, before and after the economic crisis (% per annum)

	2000–07	2008–12
Advanced economies	1.5	−0.1
Developing countries	4.9	4.4
Brazil	2.2	1.8
China	10.1	8.6
India	5.9	5.7
Russian Federation	7.2	0.7
South Africa	3.0	0.7

Source: ILO Research Department calculation based on World Development Indicators, World Bank (various years).

Brazil going through its worst recession, and all three countries, Brazil, Russia, and South Africa, barely growing at 1 per cent per annum or less.

The G1 high growth countries also weathered the global financial crisis better in terms of growth. Table 4.2 shows that China's GDP per capita growth dropped from a pre-crisis trend over 2000–07 of 10.1 per cent per annum to 8.6 per cent per annum over 2008–12. India's growth dropped from a pre-crisis trend of 5.9 per cent per annum to 5.7 per cent per annum. Compared to this, growth in the G2 countries tanked with the crisis. Russia's GDP per capita growth dropped from a pre-crisis trend of 7.2 per cent over 2000–07 to 0.7 per cent over 2008–12. While Brazil and South Africa's already low growth over 2000–07 of 2 per cent per annum and 3 per cent per annum respectively dropped further to under 2 per cent per annum and 1 per cent per annum respectively. And over 2012–14, these trends have exacerbated, as Table 4.1 illustrtaes, with all BRICS falling a notch in their GDP growth per capita, except Russia nudging up to 1 per cent per annum.

HIGH GROWTH AND LOW GROWTH RATES

High growth rates have been based on significant productive transformation of the economy, especially industry and manufacturing. Lower growth rates have been led by services and agriculture. High growth in the G1 countries, China, and India has been led in the long run by industry—especially manufacturing and services. Low growth in the G2 countries, Brazil, Russia, and South Africa has been led by services, and agriculture in the case of Brazil. Table 4.3 shows that Chinese growth in the 1990s and the 2000s was led by industry and manufacturing, these sectors having the highest growth rates, followed by services. Agricultural growth rates have remained low, decreasing on trend.

Indian growth over the 1980s, 1990s, and 2000s has been led by both industry and manufacturing, but also by services with equally high growth rates. Agricultural growth rates have remained low. In contrast to the G1 high growth countries, low growth in the G2 countries over the period of the 1980s, 1990s, and 2000s has been led in Brazil by agriculture with the highest growth rates, followed by services. Industry and manufacturing growth have been low, increasing on trend by the early 2000s but then slumping again by 2012–14. Russia regressed over the 1990s, and the pick-up in growth in the 2000s was led by services, followed by industry. Agricultural growth has been unstable in

Table 4.3 Growth rates by sector, period annual averages (% per annum)

		Developing countries	Brazil[1]	Russian Federation[2]	India	China[3]	South Africa
Agriculture	1980–89	3.6	3.2	......	3.3	6.1	2.9
	1990–99	2.8	3.2	–5.0	3.1	4.0	0.3
	2000–11	3.5	4.0	2.7	3.2	4.2	1.6
	2012–14	3.3	4.1	–2.0	2.4	3.8	3.5
Industry(including manufacturing)	1980–89	3.5	1.3	......	6.0	10.2	0.9
	1990–99	5.8	1.4	–7.9	5.5	14.0	0.3
	2000–11	6.8	2.7	3.8	7.7	11.3	2.3
	2012–14	2.8	0.8	0.1	5.2	7.9	0.8
Manufacturing	1980–89	4.7	......	......	6.4	10.1	1.7
	1990–99	7.0	1.0	......	5.8	13.1	0.6
	2000–11	7.2	2.2	......	7.7	10.8	2.5
	2012–14	1.5	–0.9	......	6.0	......	0.4
Services	1980–89	3.7	2.8	......	6.6	13.4	2.0
	1990–99	4.9	3.9	–5.1	7.6	11.1	2.3
	2000–11	6.4	3.6	5.5	9.1	11.0	3.8
	2012–14	2.8	1.4	2.4	9.8	8.3	2.3

[1] Data missing for: manufacturing sector of Brazil (1980–89).

[2] Data missing for Russian Federation: agriculture, industry and services sector (1980–89); and manufacturing sector (1980–2004, 2006–11).

[3] The period (2000–11) average annual growth of the manufacturing sector of China is calculated between 2000 and 2010.

Source: ILO Research Department calculation based on World Development Indicators, World Bank (various years).

the long run, recovering in the 2000s from the earlier involution, but slumping again by 2012–14. South Africa too regressed over the 1980s and 1990s.

The pick-up in growth in the 2000s was led by services with the highest growth rates, followed by industry and manufacturing. Agricultural growth rates have picked up on trend in the 2000s. The crisis hit industry and manufacturing, more so in the low growth countries. For high growth G1 countries, Table 4.4 shows that in both China and India, industrial growth dropped from highs of 8 per cent to 11 per cent over 2000–07, and by barely 1 percentage point over 2008–11. Manufacturing growth in China dropped from near 12 per cent, by 3 percentage points over this period. Manufacturing growth in India dropped from 8 per cent by 1 percentage point over this period.

For low growth G2 countries, Table 4.4 shows that industry, and particularly manufacturing, collapsed with the crisis. In Russia, industrial growth went from 6 per cent to negative over this period. In South Africa, industrial and manufacturing growth went from near 4 per cent each to stagnation over this period. In Brazil, industry and manufacturing went from low growth of 3 per cent over 2000–07 to 2 per cent for industry and 0.2 per cent for manufacturing over 2008–11. Growth in services propped up all BRICS in the crisis, as Table 4.4 shows, except for Russia. Agricultural growth also helped in the crisis, but not in South Africa where agriculture kept stagnating over the whole of the 2000s.

HIGH AND LOW GROWTH DIFFERENCES

The one major structural characteristic that stands out in differentiating between the high growth and low growth countries is the development and trajectory of manufacturing. Services do not provide such an explanation. The long run period over which a structural explanation of growth differences between the high growth G1 countries and the low growth G2 countries, can be sought is 1990 to 2007. There are no data readily available for these structural variables for Russia for the 1980s. And the cyclical impact of the current global crisis on these structural variables also needs to be ironed out.

Table 4.5 gives the sectoral shares in GDP for agriculture, manufacturing, and extractives, which sum up to industry and services. From 1990 to 2007, both high growth G1 countries, China and India maintained a remarkable consistency in their shares in manufacturing, China at 33 per cent of GDP, and India at 16 per cent of GDP. Compared to this, the low growth G2 countries all reduced their share in manufacturing over this period. Brazil's manufacturing share in GDP went from 25 per cent in 1990 to 17 per cent by 2007. Russia's manufacturing share in GDP went from 21 per cent to 18 per cent over this period. And South Africa's manufacturing share in GDP went from 24 per cent to 17 per cent.

None of the other sectors' shares in GDP explains the differences in GDP growth between the high growth G1 countries and the low growth G2 countries as well as manufacturing. Agriculture in any case follows a Lewisian pattern of reducing its share in

Table 4.4 Growth rates by sector, period annual averages, before and after the economic crisis (% per annum)

	GDP		Agriculture		Industry (including manufacturing)		Manufacturing		Services	
	2000–07	2008–11	2000–07	2008–11	2000–07	2008–11	2000–07	2008–11	2000–07	2008–11
Developing countries	6.7	6.2	3.4	3.5	7.1	6.7	7.9	5.8	6.7	6.0
Brazil	3.4	3.3	4.4	2.3	2.9	1.9	3.0	0.2	3.5	3.4
Russian Federation[1]	6.8	0.2	2.5	2.0	5.9	–0.3	……	……	7.4	0.4
India	7.3	8.0	3.3	4.1	8.3	7.2	8.2	7.8	8.7	9.5
China[2]	10.8	9.7	4.0	4.2	11.8	10.8	11.6	8.4	11.8	9.4
South Africa	4.3	1.6	0.6	–0.4	3.5	0.0	3.9	–0.6	4.3	2.4

[1] Data missing for Russian Federation: Manufacturing sector of (1980–2004, 2006–11).

[2] The period (2008–11) average annual growth of the Manufacturing sector of China between 2008 and 2010.

Source: ILO Research Department calculation based on IMF, *World Economic Outlook*, April 2013, IMF (various years[b]); World Development Indicators, World Bank (various years).

Table 4.5 Value added by sector as % of GDP

		Developing countries	Brazil	China	India	Russian Federation[4]	South Africa
Agriculture	1980	15.0	11.0	30.2	35.4	9.7	6.2
	1990	15.0	8.1	27.1	29.0	16.6	4.6
	2000	12.2	5.6	15.1	23.1	6.4	3.3
	2007	9.5	5.6	10.8	18.3	4.4	3.0
	2011	......[1]	5.5	10.0	17.5	4.3	2.5
	2014	......[1]	5.6	9.2	17.0	......	2.5
Industry(excluding manufacturing)	1980	16.8	10.3	8.0	8.1	......	26.7
	1990	16.0	10.8[2]	8.7	10.3	48.4	16.5
	2000	16.0	10.5	13.8	10.7	37.9	12.8
	2007	16.4	10.8	14.4	13.0	18.8	14.3
	2011	......[1]	12.9	46.6	12.3	21.0	16.4
	2014	......[1]	23.4	42.6	30.1	......	29.5
Manufacturing	1980	17.6	33.5	40.2	16.2	......	21.6
	1990	18.9	25.3[2]	32.7	16.2	20.9[5]	23.6
	2000	22.2	17.2	32.1	15.4	17.1[6]	19.0
	2007	23.8	17.0	32.9	16.0	17.6	17.0
	2011	......[1]	14.6	29.6[3]	14.4	16.0	12.8
	2014	......[1]	11.0	......	17.0	......	13.0
Services	1980	49.9	45.2	21.6	40.3	23.8	45.4
	1990	50.2	53.2	31.5	44.5	35.0	55.3
	2000	50.6	66.7	39.0	50.8	55.6	64.9
	2007	51.5	66.6	41.9	52.7	59.1	65.7
	2011	......[1]	67.0	43.4	55.7	58.7	68.3
	2014	......[1]	71.0	48.2	53.0	......	68.0

[1] Aggregate data not available for 'Developing countries' in 2011 and 2014.
[2] Data of industry (excluding manufacturing) sector and manufacturing sector of Brazil (1991).
[3] Data of manufacturing sector of China (2010).
[4] Data for Russian Federation in 1980 is taken from the annual statistical bulletin 'NarodnoyeHozaystvo RSFSR 1990'. The data for the share of manufacturing in total industry production in 1980 is not available. The share for industry including manufacturing is 66.5.
[5] National Accounts Estimates of Main Aggregates, United Nations Statistics Division.
[6] Data of manufacturing sector of Russian Federation (2002).

Source: ILO Research Department calculation based on IMF, *World Economic Outlook*, April 2013, IMF (various years [b]); World Development Indicators 2016, World Bank (various years).

GDP for all of BRICS over 1990 to 2007. Extractives could offer a supplementary explanation in that the G1 countries, China and India both increased these shares in GDP over 1990 to 2007. In contrast, G2 countries either kept their share of extractives in GDP constant over this period, as did Brazil, or decreased it, as did both Russia and South Africa.

The contentious alternative explanation for higher growth is often and increasingly held out to be the services sector. The empirical evidence for BRICS in Table 4.5 does not support this. First of all, all of BRICS increased their extractives shares in GDP over 1990 to 2007. Second, the high growth G1 countries increased their extractives shares by less, ranging from 20 percentage points for China to 12 percentage points for India. Compared to this, the low growth G2 countries increased their extractives shares by more, ranging from 20 percentage points for South Africa to 22 percentage points for

Brazil, and nearly 35 percentage points for Russia. Third, by 2007, the high growth G1 countries had ended up with much lower extractives shares in GDP compared to the low growth G2 countries. China had an extractives share of GDP of 42 per cent by 2007, and India of 52 per cent, compared to two-thirds for Brazil and South Africa and 59 per cent for Russia.

INVESTMENT IN PHYSICAL CAPITAL AND SAVINGS: A FURTHER EXPLANATION

A second explanation of the difference between the high growth and low growth countries emerges in investment in physical capital and savings. Exports do not explain the differential in growth so consistently across BRICS. Table 4.6 and Figure 4.2 decompose GDP growth into its macro-drivers, of consumption, investment, exports, imports, and government expenditure. The macro-driver that explains the difference between the high growth G1 countries and the low growth G2 countries most consistently is investment in physical capital. Investment in the high growth G1 countries increased over time, between 1980 and 2010. In contrast, investment in the low growth G2 countries dropped. So from the high growth G1 countries, in China investment increased from an already high share of GDP of 35 per cent in 1980 to 48 per cent by 2010. Similarly in India, the share of investment more than doubled, from 18 per cent in 1980 to 37 per cent in 2010. In contrast, from the low growth G2 countries, in Brazil the share of investment in GDP dropped from 23 per cent in 1980 to 20 per cent in 2010. Similarly, in both Russia and South Africa the share of investment in GDP dropped from about 30 per cent in 1990 to near 20 per cent in 2010.

An increasingly cited driver of GDP growth, exports, does not consistently explain the differential between the high growth G1 countries and the low growth G2 countries. True, the high growth countries, China and India both increased their export shares in GDP by a factor of more than 3 between 1980 and 2010. However, from among the low growth countries, Russia also more than doubled its export share in GDP between 1990 and 2010 to near 30 per cent, while Brazil maintained its export share in GDP, albeit at a low 10 per cent between 1980 and 2010. South Africa, on the other hand, had reduced its export share in GDP down to a still considerable 27 per cent by 2010.

ENABLING HIGH GROWTH AND INVESTMENT

High growth and investment has been enabled through domestic savings rather than foreign direct investment (FDI), which does not consistently explain them. High growth G1 countries had high and increasing levels of savings over time, enabling their high

Table 4.6 Domestic demand, exports, and imports as % of GDP

	1980	1990	2000	2010
Brazil				
Household consumption expenditure	69.7	59.3	64.3	59.6
Government consumption expenditure	9.2	19.3	19.2	21.1
Gross capital formation	23.3	20.2	18.2	20.2
Exports	9.1	8.2	10.0	10.9
Imports	11.3	7.0	11.7	11.9
China				
Household consumption expenditure	46.3	47.0	46.7	34.7
Government consumption expenditure	14.9	14.1	15.8	13.3
Gross capital formation	35.2	36.1	35.1	48.2
Exports	17.2	14.7	23.3	29.4
Imports	15.7	12.0	20.9	25.6
India				
Household consumption expenditure	74.9	64.6	64.2	56.4
Government consumption expenditure	10.1	11.9	12.6	11.4
Gross capital formation	18.0	24.9	24.1	36.5
Exports	6.0	6.9	12.8	22.0
Imports	9.1	8.3	13.7	26.3
Russian Federation[1]				
Household consumption expenditure		48.9	46.2	50.6
Government consumption expenditure		20.8	15.1	18.7
Gross capital formation		30.1	18.7	22.6
Exports		18.2	44.1	29.2
Imports		17.9	24.0	21.1
South Africa				
Household consumption expenditure	47.8	57.1	63.0	58.7
Government consumption expenditure	14.3	19.7	18.1	21.6
Gross capital formation	29.9	17.7	15.9	19.1
Exports	35.4	24.2	27.9	28.4
Imports	27.3	18.8	24.9	27.7

[1] Data missing for: Russian Federation in 1980.

Source: ILO calculation based on World Development Indicators, World Bank (various years).

investment, while low growth G2 countries had constant or falling levels of savings over time, feeding their falling investment levels.

Table 4.7 shows domestic and foreign sources of funding investment. From the high growth G1 countries, China had increased its savings as a share of GDP from 35 per cent in 1980 to 52 per cent by 2010, while India increased its savings share from 15 per cent to 33 per cent over this period. In contrast, from the low growth G2 countries, Brazil had decreased its savings as a share of GDP from 21 per cent in 1980 to 19 per cent by 2010. Russia kept its savings share constant on trend at 30 per cent between 1990 and 2010, while South Africa had halved its savings share from 38 per cent in 1980 to 19 per cent by 2010.

FDI does not appear to play a significant role in boosting investment, because savings exceeded or approximated investment for all of BRICS, G1, and G2, for pretty much all the benchmark years examined. From the high growth G1 countries, China's savings

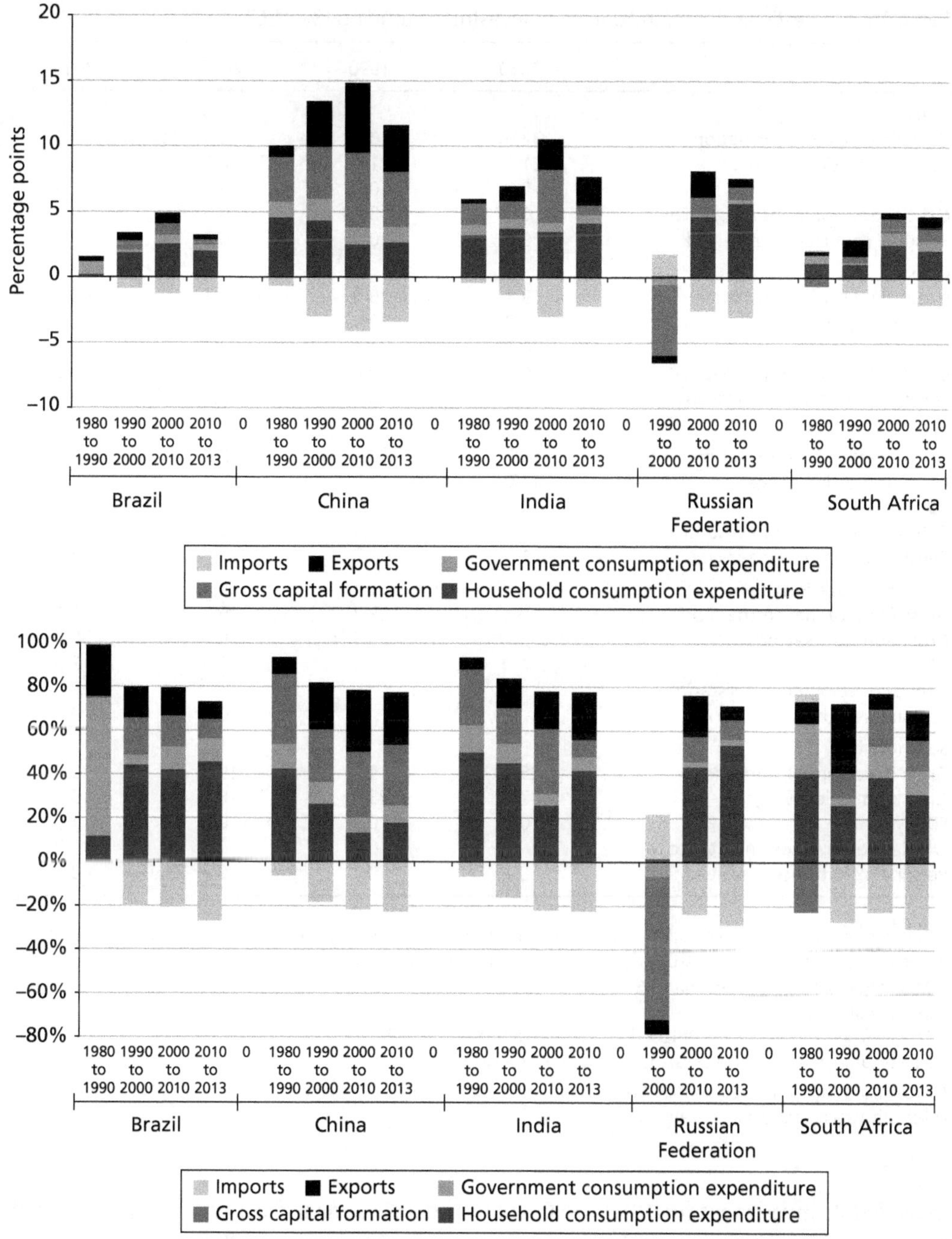

Figure 4.2 Breakdown of economic growth: contribution to average annual GDP growth (%) (1980–2013)

Source: ILO calculations based on IMF, World Economic Outlook, April 2013, and World Development Indicators (World Bank various years).

Table 4.7 Domestic and foreign sources of investment funding (% of GDP)

	1980	1990	2000	2010
Brazil				
Gross fixed capital formation	22.9	20.7	16.8	19.5
Gross domestic savings	21.1	21.4	16.5	19.2
FDI	0.8	0.2	5.1	2.5
Official development assistance	0.0	0.0	0.0	0.0
Personal remittances received	0.0	0.1	0.3	0.1
China				
Gross fixed capital formation	29.1	25.9	34.1	45.7
Gross domestic savings	34.8	39.1	37.5	52.1
FDI	0.2[3]	1.0	3.2	4.6
Official development assistance	0.0	0.6	0.1	0.0
Personal remittances received	……	0.1	0.4	0.6
India				
Gross fixed capital formation	17.9	23.8	22.8	31.7
Gross domestic savings	15.0	23.5	23.3	32.6
FDI	0.0	0.1	0.8	1.6
Official development assistance	1.2	0.4	0.3	0.2
Personal remittances received	1.5	0.7	2.7	3.1
Russian Federation[1]				
Gross fixed capital formation	……	28.7	16.9	21.2
Gross domestic savings	……	30.3	38.7	30.3
FDI	……	0.3[2]	1.0	2.8
Official development assistance	……	……	……	……
Personal remittances received	……	……	0.5	0.3
South Africa[4]				
Gross fixed capital formation	25.9	19.1	15.1	19.3
Gross domestic savings	37.9	23.2	18.9	19.0
FDI	0.0	−0.1	0.7	1.0
Official development assistance	……	0.2[5]	0.4	0.3
Personal remittances received	0.1	0.1	0.3	0.3

[1] Data missing for Russian Federation: Gross fixed capital formation, Gross domestic savings and FDI (1980); Official development assistance (1980–2010), and Personal remittances received (1980–93).
[2] Data of FDI for Russian Federation (1992).
[3] Data of FDI for China (1982).
[4] Data missing for South Africa: Official development assistance (1980–92).
[5] Data of Official development assistance for South Africa (1993).
Source: ILO calculation based on IMF World Economic Outlook (April 2013), IMF (various years [b]; World Development Indicators, World Bank (various years).

exceeded its investment for 1980, 1990, 2000, and 2010. For India, savings approximated investment from 1990 onwards, with a 2 per cent of GDP shortfall in savings in 1980, made up for by official development assistance (ODA). For the G2 countries, it was likewise; Brazil's savings have approximated its investment from 1990 onwards, with a savings shortfall of 2 per cent of GDP in 1980. Russia's savings have consistently exceeded their investment from 1990 onwards, while South Africa's savings too have either exceeded investment or approximated it for each of the benchmark years from 1980 to 2010.

THE MACRO-PRUDENTIAL ENVIRONMENT

The macro-prudential environment explains pick-up in growth over time in each of BRICS, but does not explain the cross country differentials between the high growth and low growth countries. Beginning with Brazil, Table 4.8 shows that its double- and triple-digit hyperinflation of the 1980s and 1990s was tamed into single digits for the 2000s, with its budget deficits falling to about -3 per cent, and a pick-up in growth. China's inflation has always been contained at 3 per cent or under over this whole period, with its budget deficits capped under -3 per cent, and fairly consistently high growth. India's just double-digit inflation in the 1980s and 1990s was tamed in the 2000s, although peaking back up by 2010, with its budget deficits ranging between -7 per cent and -8 per cent. Again its growth picked up in the 2000s. Russia's triple- and double-digit inflation in the 1990s and 2000s has been more structurally caused, and has given way to single-digit inflation by 2010 and a pick-up in growth. Its budgetary balances have wavered between +3 per cent and -3 per cent. And South Africa's double-digit inflation in the 1980s and 1990s has been tamed into single digits for the 2000s, with a pick-up in growth, but with its budget deficits climbing to -5 per cent.

So the macro-prudential environment improved for Brazil, India, Russia, and South Africa, helping growth pick up in each country over the period 1980 to 2010. China had had a more consistently controlled macro-prudential environment over this whole period, along with consistently high double-digit growth. But the macro-prudential environment has not been consistently better for the high growth G1 countries—only for China, but not for India.

Employment

EMPLOYMENT AND SOCIAL PROTECTION

Employment and social protection are the primary mechanisms for participation and inclusion in growth in BRICS. Therefore, ranking BRICS by growth puts China and India in the high growth category, G1, and Brazil, Russia, and South Africa in the low growth category, G2. High growth is seen to be led by high rates of productive transformation, especially manufacturing and services, fuelled by the macro-drivers of high investment and domestic savings. Low growth is seen to be led more by services and agriculture in the case of Brazil, with lower investment and savings.

But the question then arises of growth for whom? Has this pattern of growth across BRICS been broad based and inclusive, or have gains accrued more narrowly to higher income groups? That is, has social development accompanied growth or not?

This chapter considers two broad categories of inclusive growth and social development. One is employment, the second is social protection. The quantum of employment has to be the major macro-mechanism of inclusion and participation in growth of output

Table 4.8 Macro-prudential variables

	1980	1990	2000	2010	2011	2012	2013	2014
Brazil[1]								
General government budget balance (% of GDP)	......	......	−3.4	−2.8	−2.6	−2.8	−3.3	−3.9
General government gross debt (% of GDP)	......	......	66.7	65.0	64.7	68.2	66.2	65.8
Current account balance (% of GDP)	−8.6	−0.8	−3.8	−2.2	−2.1	−2.4	−3.6	−3.5
Inflation rate (compared to previous year)	90.2	2947.7	7.0	5.0	6.6	5.4	6.2	6.3
FDI (% of GDP)	0.8	0.2	5.1	2.5	2.9	3.4	3.6	......
FDI (in billion, constant 2005 US$)	4.2	1.3	39.1	27.3	32.5	38.5	42.0	......
Portfolio investment (% of GDP)	......	......	−0.6[2]	−2.9	−1.4	−0.4	......	......
China[3]								
General government budget balance (% of GDP)	0.2[4]	−0.7	−2.9	−1.2	0.6	0.2	−0.9	−1.0
General government gross debt (% of GDP)	......	20.9[4]	37.4	36.6	36.5	37.4	39.4	40.7
Current account balance (% of GDP)	......	......	1.7	4.0	1.9	2.6	1.9	1.8
Inflation rate (compared to previous year)	......	3.1	0.4	3.3	5.4	2.6	2.6	2.3
FDI (% of GDP)	0.2[4]	1.0	3.2	4.6	4.5	3.6	3.8	......
FDI (in billion, constant 2005 US$)	0.5[4]	5.4	45.4	176.7	190.0	162.3	183.1	......
Portfolio investment (% of GDP)	......	......	0.2[4]	−0.4	−0.3	−0.6	......	......
India[5]								
General government budget balance (% of GDP)	......	−6.5	−7.3	−8.4	−8.0	−7.4	−7.2	−7.2
General government gross debt (% of GDP)	......	75.3	73.6	67.5	66.8	66.6	61.5	60.5
Current account balance (% of GDP)	−1.5	−3.0	−0.6	−2.7	−4.2	−4.7	−1.7	−2.1
Inflation rate (compared to previous year)	11.4	12.8	3.8	9.5	9.5	10.2	9.5	7.8
FDI (% of GDP)	0.0	0.1	0.8	1.6	1.9	1.3	1.5	......
FDI (in billion, constant 2005 US$)	0.1	0.3	4.5	19.9	25.7	17.9	21.9	......
Portfolio investment (% of GDP)	......	......	−1.5[6]	−2.2	−0.1	−1.6	......	......
Russian Federation[7]								
General government budget balance (% of GDP)	......	......	3.3	−3.4	1.5	0.4	−1.3	−0.9
General government gross debt (% of GDP)	......	......	59.9	11.3	11.6	12.7	13.9	15.7
Current account balance (% of GDP)	......	−1.4	18.0	4.4	5.1	3.5	1.6	2.7
Inflation rate (compared to previous year)	......	874.6[8]	20.8	6.9	8.4	5.1	6.8	7.4
FDI (% of GDP)	......	0.3[8]	1.0	2.8	2.9	2.5	3.4	......
FDI (in billion, constant 2005 US$)	......	1.7[8]	5.9	25.7	27.4	24.6	33.5	......

Portfolio investment (% of GDP)	......	......	1.5[8]	0.1	0.8	−0.8	......	......
South Africa[9]								
General government budget balance (% of GDP)	......	......	−1.6	−4.9	−4.0	−4.3	−4.4	−4.9
General government gross debt (% of GDP)	......	......	43.3	35.3	38.8	42.1	45.2	47.9
Current account balance (% of GDP)	4.1	1.4	−0.1	−2.0	−2.3	−5.2	−5.8	−5.7
Inflation rate (compared to previous year)	14.2	14.3	5.4	4.3	5.0	5.7	5.8	6.3
FDI (% of GDP)	0.0	−0.1	0.7	1.0	1.0	1.2	2.3	......
FDI (in billion, constant 2005 US$)	0.0	−0.1	1.5	2.9	3.1	3.7	7.3	......
Portfolio investment (% of GDP)	......	......	−1.9[10]	−2.7	0.3	−1.8	......	......

[1] Data missing for Brazil: General government budget balance (1980–95), General government gross debt (1980–99), and Portfolio investment (1980–2004).

[2] Data of Portfolio investment for Brazil (2005).

[3] Data missing for China: General government gross debt (1980–94), Current account balance (1980–96), Inflation rate (1980–89), and Portfolio investment (1980–2004).

[4] Data for China: General government budget balance (1982), General government gross debt (1995), FDI (1982), and Portfolio investment (2005).

[5] Data missing for India: General government budget balance (1980–88), General government gross debt (1980–90), and Portfolio investment (1980–2004).

[6] Data of Portfolio investment for India (2005).

[7] Data missing for Russian Federation: General government budget balance (1980–97), General government gross debt (1980–98), Current account balance (1980–91), Inflation rate (1980–92), FDI (1980–91), and Portfolio investment (1980–2004).

[8] Data for Russian Federation: Inflation rate (1993), FDI (1992), and Portfolio investment (2005).

[9] Data missing for South Africa: General government budget balance (1980–99), General government gross debt (1980–99), and Portfolio investment (1980–2004).

[10] Data of Portfolio investment for South Africa (2005).

Source: ILO calculation based on IMF World Economic Outlook Database October 2014, IMF (various years [b]; World Development Indicators, World Bank (various years).

and incomes. This is because employment is simply the largest way through which output is produced and incomes earned. After employment, there is evidence from some of BRICS that afforded these data, that social protection, comprising both contributory and non-contributory transfers, may be the next largest contribution to income (ILO 2015a). That is, capital income may come third in contributing to total income. This section examines how well BRICS have done in generating employment, while the following section examines their performance in extending social protection as mechanisms of inclusion and distribution of growth.

STATE OF THE LABOUR MARKET

Among BRICS, the quantum of employment growth is not such a good indicator of the state of the labour market, because it is led by demographics rather than economics. Employment growth turns out not to be a good indicator of economic success or failure in the labour markets of BRICS. This could be for two reasons. One, that employment growth is weakly linked to GDP growth in BRICS. And two, that employment growth is more strongly linked to another variable, demographic growth.

Table 4.9 shows that employment growth is indeed weakly linked to GDP growth. Of the high growth G1 countries, China with the highest GDP growth has had low and falling employment growth over the 1990s and the 2000s, averaging 0.9 per cent per annum over the whole period. India with the second highest GDP growth has had medium but falling employment growth over time, averaging 1.6 per cent per annum over this whole period. Of the low growth G2 countries, Brazil has had high and almost constant employment growth over time, averaging the highest among BRICS at 2.2 per cent per annum over the whole period. Russia has had the lowest employment growth, albeit increasing over time, averaging 0.4 per cent over the whole period. Finally, South Africa has had the highest employment growth in the 1990s, more than halving in the 2000s and averaging 2 per cent per annum over the whole period.

If GDP growth has a weak link to employment growth across BRICS, the reason is a stronger link to demographic growth. Figure 4.3 shows that the underlying trend in employment growth is given by growth of the working age population. China's working age population growth peaked around the millennium, and has fallen since, with its employment growth following that trend. India and South Africa's working age population growths have been decreasing on trend over the whole period of the 1980s and 1990s, with employment growth following suit. Brazil's working age population growth has been near constant over the whole period, as has its employment growth. For Russia, leaving aside its period of involution over the 1990s, its working age population growth has also fallen slightly over the 2000s, along with its employment growth.

If working age population growth gives the broad trend governing employment growth, another demographic variable, labour force growth explains virtually each

Table 4.9 Employment growth rate by gender and age group

Total employment, average annual growth rate (%)			
	1991–2000	2000–13[p]	1991–2013[p]
Advanced economies (AEs)	0.9	0.7	0.8
Developing countries (DCs)	1.8	1.6	1.7
Brazil	2.3	2.1	2.2
China	1.2	0.8	0.9
India	2.0	1.4	1.6
Russian Federation	−0.3	0.8	0.4
South Africa	3.2	1.2	2.0
Youth employment, average annual growth rate (%)			
AEs	−1.0	−1.3	−1.2
DCs	−0.4	0.0	−0.1
Brazil	0.9	0.1	0.4
China	−3.5	−1.1	−2.1
India	1.0	−1.1	−0.2
Russian Federation	−0.2	−2.2	−1.3
South Africa	1.8	−2.1	−0.5
Male employment, average annual growth rate (%)			
AEs	0.6	0.6	0.6
DCs	1.8	1.6	1.7
Brazil	1.6	1.8	1.7
China	1.2	0.9	1.0
India	2.0	1.8	1.8
Russian Federation	−0.3	0.7	0.3
South Africa	1.7	1.3	1.5
Adult employment, average annual growth rate (%)			
AEs	1.2	1.0	1.1
DCs	2.5	1.9	2.2
Brazil	2.8	2.7	2.7
China	2.6	1.1	1.7
India	2.3	1.9	2.1
Russian Federation	−0.3	1.2	0.6
South Africa	3.4	1.6	2.3
Female employment, average annual growth rate (%)			
AEs	1.2	0.9	1.0
DCs	1.9	1.5	1.7
Brazil	3.5	2.7	3.0
China	1.2	0.6	0.8
India	2.1	0.3	1.0
Russian Federation	−0.2	0.9	0.5
South Africa	5.5	1.0	2.8

Notes: p = projection; figures for 2013 are preliminary estimates.

Source: ILO, *Trends Econometric Models*, ILO (various years [a]).

fluctuation in employment growth. Figure 4.3 shows that in the two decades over 1992 to 2013, employment growth literally hugs labour force growth for each of the BRICS.

The reason why employment growth is so closely linked to demographic growth variables such as labour force growth for BRICS is a broader phenomenon of the

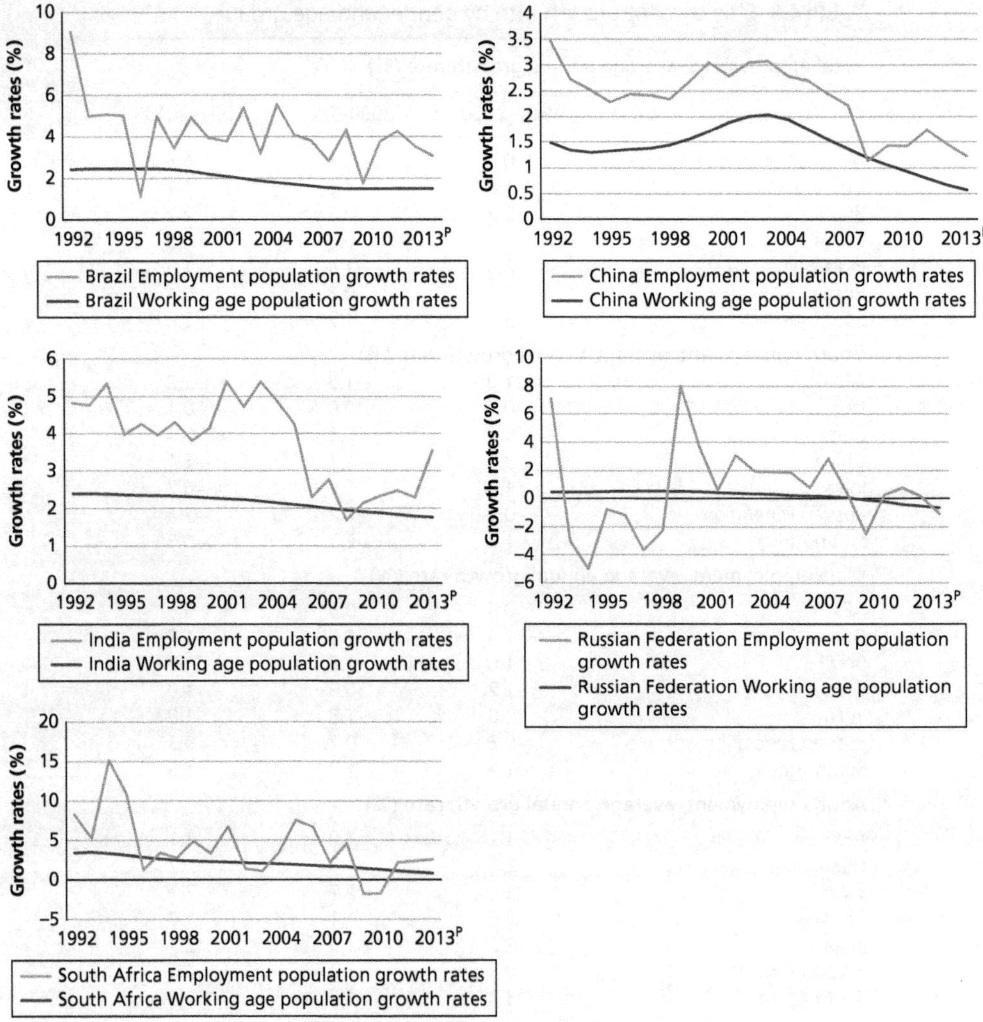

Notes: p = projection; figures for 2013 are preliminary estimates.

Figure 4.3 Employment and working age population growth rates

Source: Trends Econometric Models, ILO (various years [a]).

working poor, seen to be prevalent across most developing countries (ILO 2014a). Developing countries, in contrast to AEs, have very limited to virtually no social protection for the vast majority of the employed population. Hence at low the income levels prevalent for the majority of the employed populations, unemployment, without any significant social protection cover, is not an option. The poor are simply too poor to be able to afford not to work. Hence if employment with better remuneration and working conditions is not possible, the poor still have to work, even in less favourable working conditions; hence the phenomenon characterized and tracked by the ILO as the working poor. And as labour force growth fluctuates (see Figure 4.4), employment growth follows.

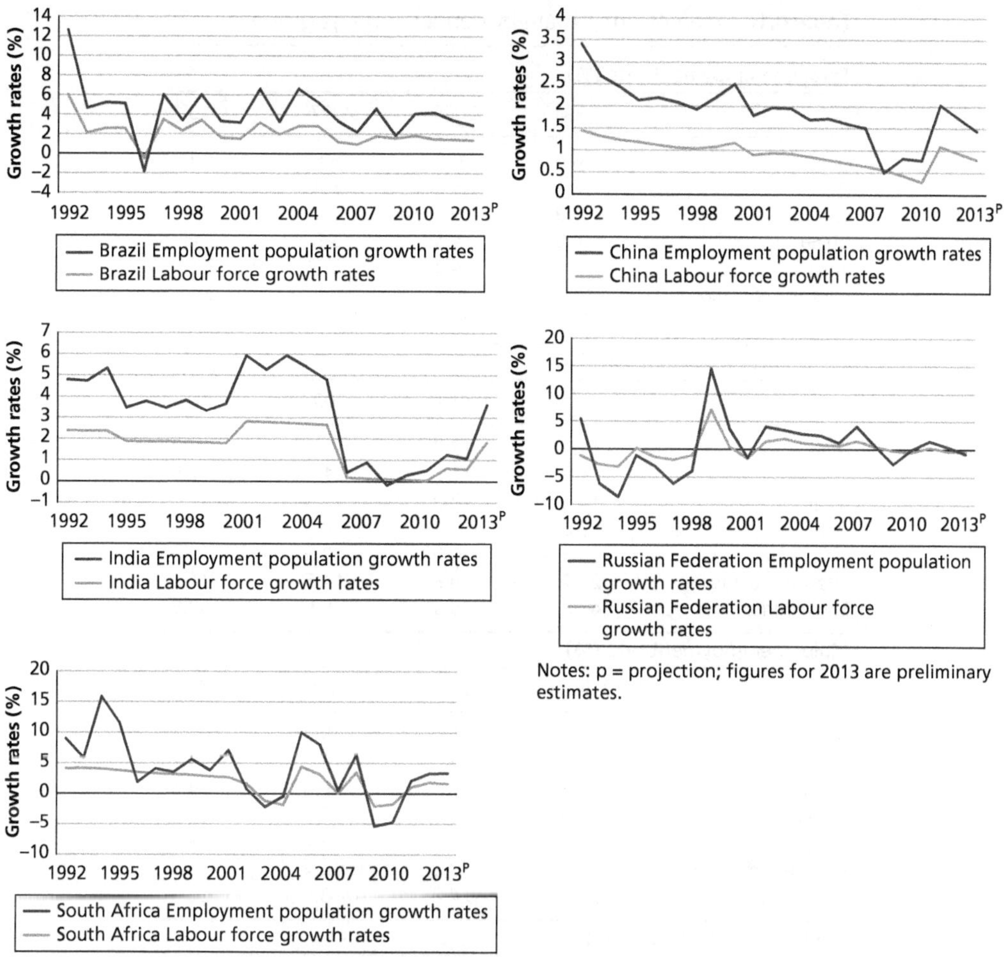

Notes: p = projection; figures for 2013 are preliminary estimates.

Figure 4.4 Employment and labour force growth rates

Source: Trends Econometric Models, ILO (various years [a]).

IS THE UNEMPLOYMENT RATE A GOOD INDICATOR OF THE STATE OF THE LABOUR MARKET?

If the poor in low-income countries cannot afford not to work, then unemployment will tend to be low, and more stable compared to GDP growth. Hence neither will the unemployment rate be a good indicator of labour market slack. Table 4.10 shows there is a relationship between the unemployment rate and GDP growth in BRICS, albeit weak.

There is a broad relationship between the unemployment rate and GDP growth across the high growth G1 countries and the low growth G2 countries. The high growth G1 countries, China and India, also have the lowest unemployment rates among BRICS. While the low growth G2 countries, Brazil, Russia, and South Africa have the highest unemployment rates among BRICS.

Table 4.10 Unemployment rate by gender and age group

Total unemployment rate (%)				
	1991	2000	2007	2013P
AEs	6.9	6.5	5.6	8.1
DCs	6.1	6.3	5.4	5.6
Brazil	6.9	9.5	8.1	5.9
China	4.9	4.5	3.8	4.6
India	4.3	4.3	3.7	3.6
Russian Federation	12.2	10.6	6.0	5.6
South Africa	24.4	26.7	22.3	24.9
Youth unemployment rate (%)				
	1991	2000	2007	2013P
AEs	14.0	13.3	12.5	17.9
DCs	11.6	12.8	11.5	12.5
Brazil	14.2	18.0	16.7	13.6
China	9.0	9.3	8.0	10.1
India	10.6	10.0	8.9	10.6
Russian Federation	23.7	20.8	14.5	14.5
South Africa	47.8	45.3	46.5	53.6
Male unemployment rate (%)				
	1991	2000	2007	2013P
AEs	6.4	6.0	5.3	8.0
DCs	6.0	6.2	5.2	5.3
Brazil	5.3	7.7	6.0	4.5
China	5.5	5.1	4.3	5.2
India	4.0	4.3	3.7	3.5
Russian Federation	12.5	10.8	6.4	5.9
South Africa	21.0	24.8	18.8	22.3
Adult unemployment rate (%)				
	1991	2000	2007	2013P
AEs	5.4	5.4	4.6	6.9
DCs	4.2	4.5	3.8	4.1
Brazil	3.9	6.5	5.5	4.1
China	3.2	3.4	2.8	3.6
India	2.1	2.6	2.4	2.2
Russian Federation	10.3	9.0	4.8	4.7
South Africa	18.3	22.9	17.5	20.5
Female unemployment rate (%)				
	1991	2000	2007	2013P
AEs	7.6	7.1	6.0	8.3
DCs	6.4	6.5	5.8	6.0
Brazil	9.6	12.0	10.9	7.8
China	4.1	3.8	3.1	3.8
India	5.0	4.2	3.8	4.1
Russian Federation	11.8	10.4	5.6	5.2
South Africa	29.9	29.0	26.6	28.0

Notes: p = projection; figures for 2013 are preliminary estimates.

Source: ILO, *Trends Econometric Models*, ILO (various years [a]).

But beyond such a broad brush generalization, the cross-country relationship is weaker. China has had virtually double the GDP growth of India, but their unemployment rates are similar over time. Brazil's growth crept up in the 1990s, while its unemployment rate rose. Russia regressed over the 1990s, while its unemployment rate inched down. South African growth picked up in the 2000s, but its unemployment rate, after inching down, had risen again by 2013.

There are also huge issues in the measurement of unemployment and hence its comparability across countries. For instance China's unemployment rate is based primarily on an urban sample (see Zhang and Mahmood 2007), as is Brazil's (documented in the ILO's *Panorama Laboral* series), while in the remaining BRICS, the unemployment rate is based on both urban and rural samples.

JOB QUALITY AS AN INDICATOR OF INCLUSION IN GROWTH

The original indicator posited above, of inclusion in GDP growth, was taken to be job growth to match GDP growth. However, job growth has been seen to be driven more by the compulsions of the working poor, who cannot afford to be out of work. If the working poor are thus compelled to accept any form of work, even with weak working conditions, then job quality becomes an important, if not primary, indicator of inclusion in GDP growth.

The ILO has estimated two broad indicators of job quality, which it contributes to monitoring the Millennium Development Goals (MDGs) under Indicator 1b. These are vulnerability, and the working poor.

RANKING BRICS BY JOB QUALITY

Vulnerability

Ranking BRICS by job quality changes the rankings based on growth—even where BRICS were better at GDP growth, they have not been better at improving job quality. The data permit definition of four categories or forms of employment—waged employment, self-employment, contributing family workers, and employers. Waged employment has been associated in the literature with generally better working conditions, such as higher productivity, higher incomes, better access to social protection, better working hours, and a more regulated work environment (ILO 2014a). The share of employers in total employment is typically small, between 2 per cent for developing countries and 4 per cent for AEs (see Table 4.11). This shows three main categories of employment: waged, self-(own-account workers and employers), and contributing family workers. With waged employment and employers seen typically as affording better working conditions, its reciprocal of

Table 4.11 Share of employment by status and vulnerable employment (%)

		AEs	DCs	Brazil	China	India	Russian Federation	South Africa
1991	Wage and salaried workers	82.3	32.7	60.5	27.3	15.5	99.2	82.6
	Employers	3.9	2.4	4.0	2.1	2.0	0.1	2.9
	Own-account workers	10.8	35.6	27.8	27.3	62.5	0.6	13.0
	Contributing family workers	3.1	29.3	7.7	43.3	20.0	0.1	1.5
	Vulnerable employment	13.9	64.9	35.5	70.6	82.5	0.7	14.5
2013[P]	Wage and salaried workers	86.3	42.6	69.3	52.7	20.9	92.7	84.2
	Employers	3.6	2.0	4.8	1.2	1.1	1.6	5.6
	Own-account workers	9.0	40.5	21.4	32.6	64.0	5.6	9.4
	Contributing family workers	1.0	14.9	4.5	13.5	13.9	0.1	0.8
	Vulnerable employment	10.0	55.4	25.9	46.1	78.0	5.7	10.1

Relative change in vulnerable employment (%)

	1991	2013[P]	Relative change
Brazil	21,927.1	25,856.5	17.9%
China	443,549.4	356,449.5	−19.6%
India	267,322.3	361,308.3	35.2%
Russian Federation	458.3	4,150.6	805.7%
South Africa	1,370.6	1,480.1	8.0%

Notes: p = projection; figures for 2013 are preliminary estimates.

Source: ILO, *Trends Econometric Models*, ILO (various years [a]).

own-account, and self-employment, and contributing family workers add up to the agreed definition of more vulnerable forms of employment (ILO 2013).

Ranking BRICS by change in vulnerable forms of employment over time changes the rankings based on GDP growth. The rankings by growth put China and India on top (G1), with Brazil, Russia, and South Africa below (G2). Table 4.11 shows that the reduction in the share of vulnerable employment in total employment, between 1991 and 2013, has indeed been the highest for China, with about 35 per cent, keeping it in a G1 ranking by largest improvement in job quality. But India has had the lowest reduction in the share of vulnerable employment, of under 1 per cent, over this period, dropping it down into a G2 ranking through lower improvement in job quality. After China, the next largest reduction in the share of the vulnerable has been in South Africa, with a 30 per cent drop over this period, followed by Brazil with a 27 per cent fall, while Russia actually had an increase in its share of vulnerable employment over this period, albeit from near zero.

This ranking of BRICS by job quality provides a different composition in the group of high change countries, G1, now comprising China, South Africa, and Brazil, while the group of low change countries, G2, now comprises India and Russia.

Working Poor

The working poor are defined as the number of employed people whose per capita budgets fall below the $1.25 poverty line. Table 4.12 shows the change in share of the working poor in total employment between 1991 and 2013. This table again shows that the rankings by GDP growth are changed when ranking by improvements in the share of the working poor. The highest reductions in the share of the working poor over this period have been for Russia, from near zero to zero, followed by China with 91 per cent, Brazil with 76 per cent, India 51 per cent, and South Africa 42 per cent. If we set an arbitrary cut-off between these new G1 and G2 groups of countries, G1 with the largest drop in the working poor now comprises Russia, China, and Brazil, while G2 with a lower fall in the working poor now comprises India and South Africa.

Emergence of a Middle Class

Escaping vulnerability and poverty is an important indicator of job quality, to highlight reduction in distress. The obverse, to indicate improvements in income, can be demonstrated in the rise of the middle class, whose greater purchasing power boosted domestic demand. This rise betokens improvements in micro-welfare for the household, as well as a macro-boost for the economy, by the increase in domestic demand.

Figure 4.5 defines income classes for BRICS, with the per capita per day consumption of the extremely poor falling below a poverty line of $1.25, the moderately poor falling between $1.25 and $2, the near poor falling between $2 and $4, the emerging middle class falling between $4 and $13, and the remainder lying above $13.

Ranking BRICS by the rise of their middle class between 1991 and 2013 again upsets the rankings given by GDP growth. Figure 4.5 shows that China, Brazil, and South Africa have clearly had the largest increase in their middle classes, falling into a new group of G1 countries. Russia has had a smaller rise in its middle class, but a huge rise in its highest class above $13, again putting it into the new G1 group of countries. In contrast, India has had the lowest increase in its middle class, putting it alone in the G2 group.

Investment in Human Capital Upsets Ranking by GDP Growth

An important indicator of job quality is taken to be labour productivity. However, growth of labour productivity is by definition GDP per capita, which ranks BRICS by GDP growth. Hence Figure 4.6 showing labour productivity growth does not add any value to the analysis. Figure 4.7 does add value by decomposing labour productivity into labour productivity due to cross-sectoral transfer of labour, and within sector productivity change, in agriculture, industry, and services. However, here again, the high growth G1 countries will have had the highest amount of cross-sectoral change in productivity, as well as within sector change in productivity in industry and services, since these sectors led the high growth as seen above.

Table 4.12 Working poor

Total US$1.25 (PPP) working poor ('000s)

	1991	2000	2007	2013[p]
Brazil	6,237.1	4,831.9	3,543.2	2,355.6
China	366,742.2	22,7328.9	91,130.0	41,813.7
India	165,667.1	168,016.3	153,215.4	114,517.1
Russian Federation	250.1	469.1	7.7	4.9
South Africa	963.3	1,563.8	1,079.5	865.7

Share of working poor in total employment, US$1.25 (PPP) (%)

	1991	2000	2007	2013[p]
Brazil	10.1	6.4	4.0	2.4
China	58.4	32.4	12.2	5.4
India	51.1	43.3	34.2	24.7
Russian Federation	0.4	0.7	0.0	0.0
South Africa	10.2	12.5	7.5	5.9

Relative change in working poor, total <US$2 (PPP) (%)

	1991	2013[p]	Relative change
Brazil	11,775.1	4,875.9	−58.6%
China	536,365.8	104,986.1	−80.4%
India	273,808.4	288,514.4	5.4%
Russian Federation	2,057.6	22.4	−98.9%
South Africa	1,862.3	2,432.1	30.6%

Total <US$2 (PPP) working poor ('000s)

	1991	2000	2007	2013[p]
Brazil	11,775.1	10,397.4	7,027.0	4,875.9
China	536,365.8	402,791.6	216,690.3	104,986.1
India	273,808.4	304,871.1	317,137.2	288,514.4
Russian Federation	2,057.6	3,113.6	130.5	22.4
South Africa	1,862.3	2,904.5	2,685.7	2,432.1

Share of working poor in total employment, US$2 (PPP) (%)

	1991	2000	2007	2013[p]
Brazil	19.1	13.7	7.9	4.9
China	85.4	57.5	29.0	13.6
India	84.5	78.6	70.7	62.3
Russian Federation	3.1	4.8	0.2	0.0
South Africa	19.7	23.2	18.5	16.7

Notes: p = projection; figures for 2013 are preliminary estimates.

Source: ILO, *Trends Econometric Models*, ILO (various years [a]).

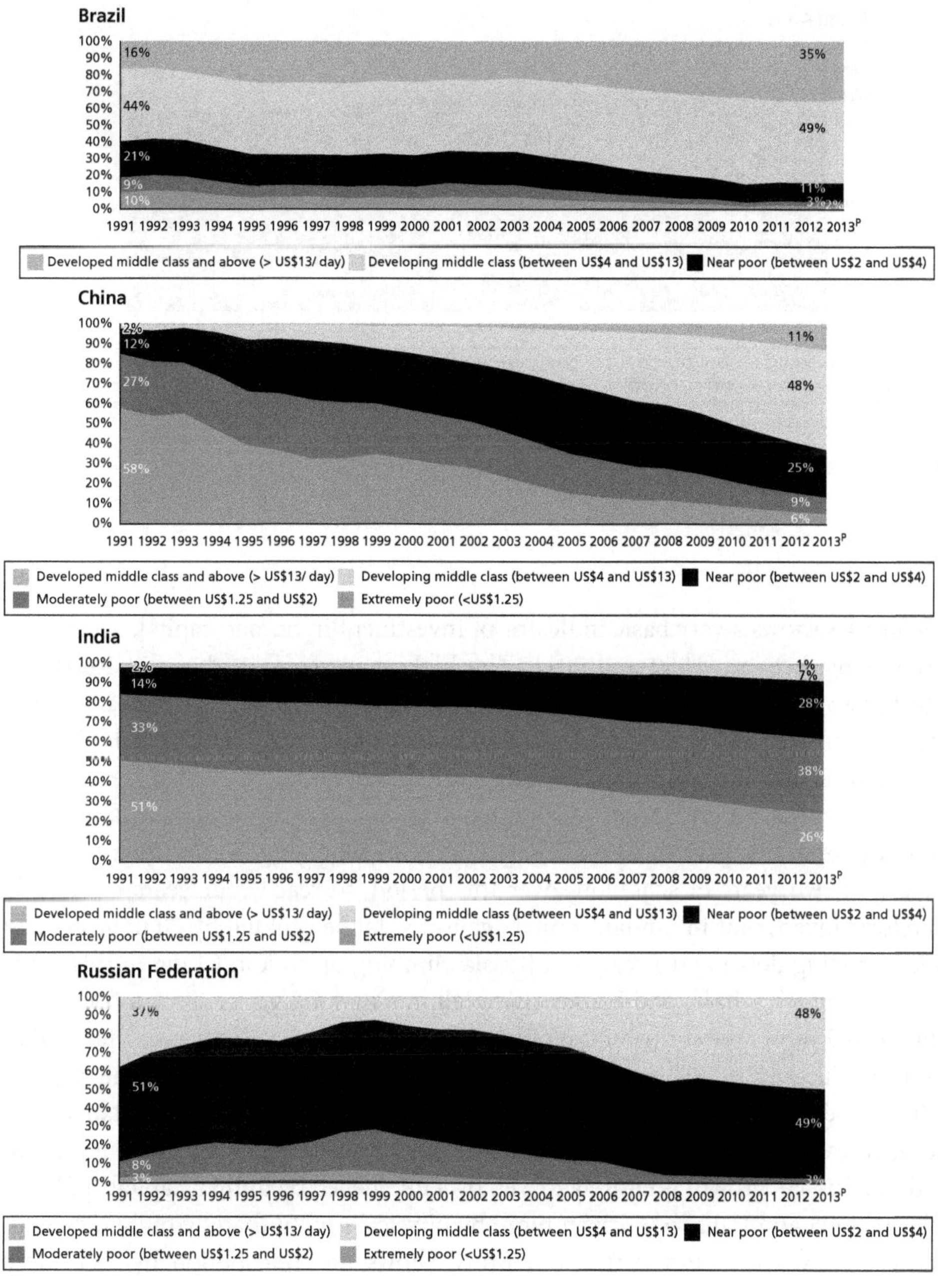

Figure 4.5 Employment by economic class

Source: October 2013 update of the model in S. Kapsos and E. Bourmpoula (2013).

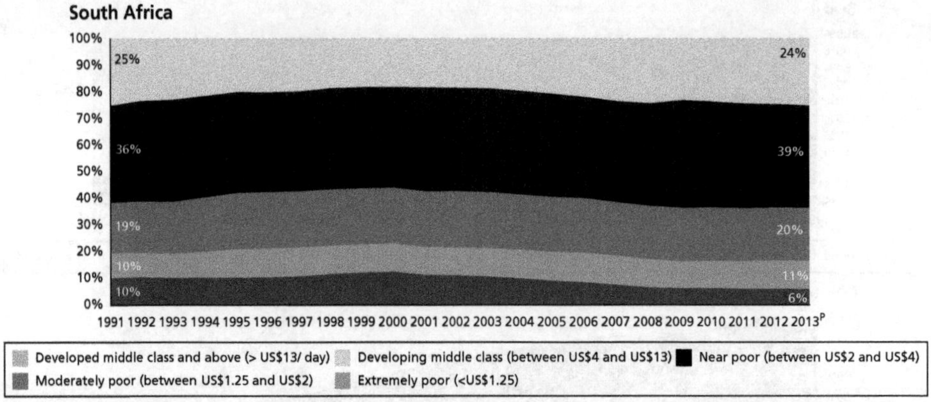

Note: p = projection.

Figure 4.5 Continued

Figure 4.8 shows a very basic indicator of investment in human capital, average years of schooling, between 1980 and 2011. The highest increase has been in Russia, with almost five years of schooling added over this period, and also reaching the highest level of twelve years of schooling. This has been followed by Brazil and China, both with an increase of about four years of schooling over this period, and both to reach close to seven years of schooling. South Africa has had an increase of about three years of schooling, over this period, to reach eight years of schooling, while India has had an increase of two years of schooling over this period, to reach four years of schooling. Therefore, investment in human capital again upsets the ranking by GDP growth, with India dropping down and Brazil and Russia climbing up to join China in this new G1 group of countries. India and South Africa fall in a new G2 group of countries.

Figure 4.9 shows the contribution of labour, physical capital, human capital, and total factor productivity (TFP) to GDP growth between 1991 and 2011. The top panel A shows the absolute contribution to actual growth. Panel B shows the relative contribution of each factor, making it comparable across countries. The result is somewhat startling. Russian growth is entirely driven by TFP, fuelled by human capital. TFP is also high in China and India, but driven more by physical capital than by human capital. In contrast, growth in South Africa and Brazil shows no contribution by TFP, despite significant investment in human capital and being driven by physical capital and labour.

Growth and Job Quality

The puzzle of the inconsistent behaviour of human capital driving technical change in some countries but not in others brings back the argument in full circle, to the dichotomy between two kinds of outcomes achieved by BRICS: growth and social

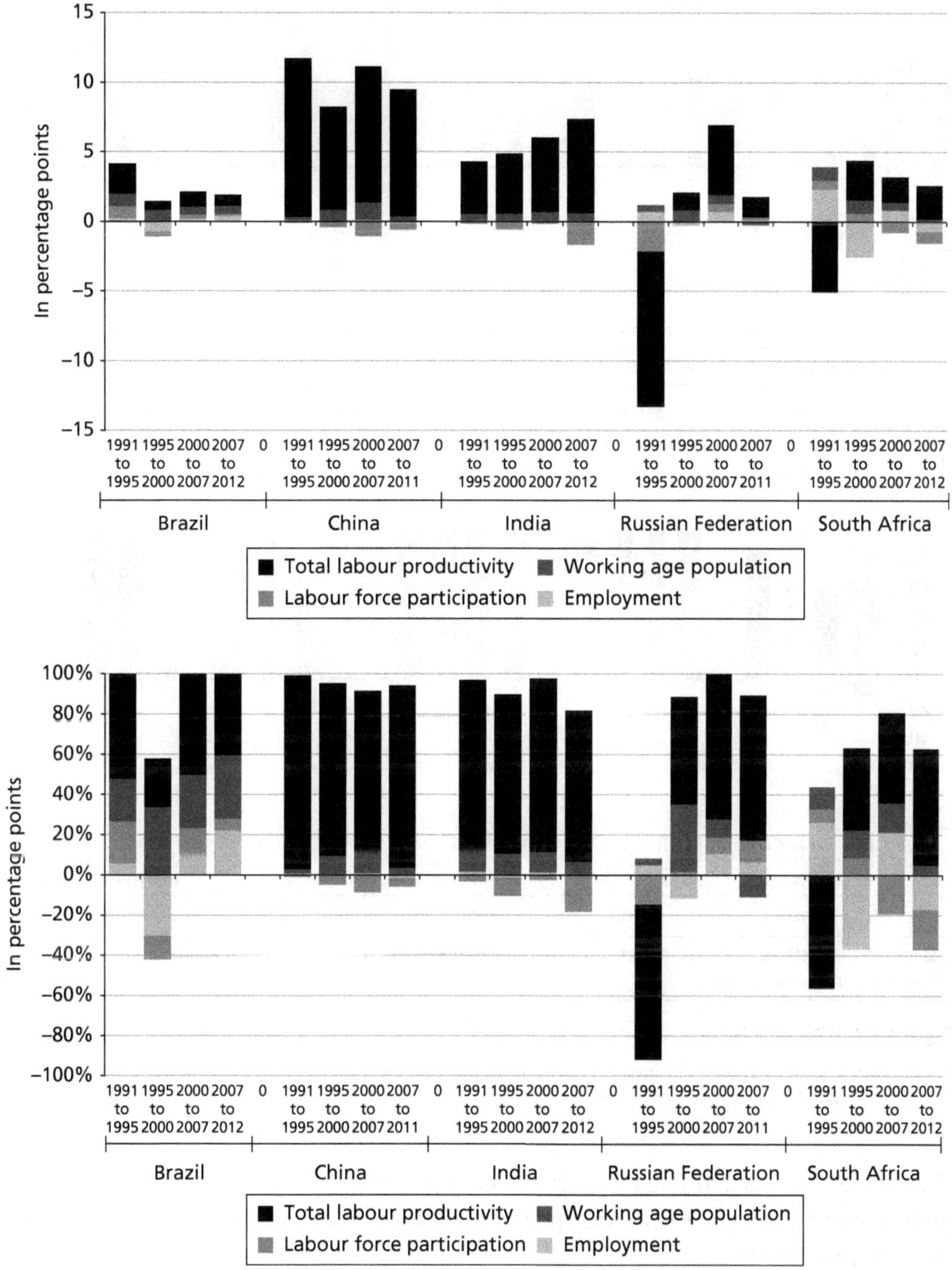

Figure 4.6 Growth breakdown

Source: ILO Research Department, based on World Development Indicators, World Bank (various years); ILO, Trends Econometric Models, ILO (various years [a]).

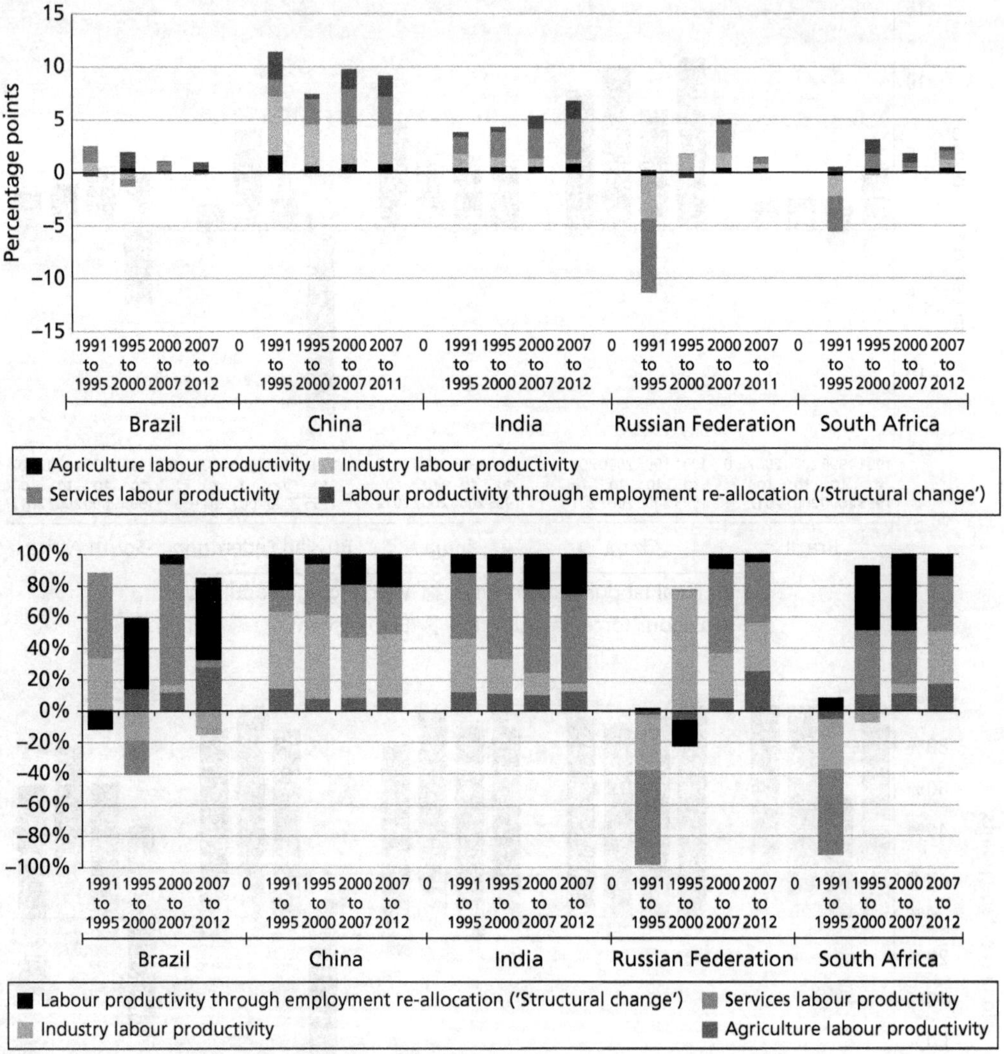

Figure 4.7 Productivity breakdown

Source: ILO Research Department, based on World Development Indicators, World Bank (various years); Trends Econometric Models, ILO (various years [a]).

development. China and India, the G1 group of countries, have had high GDP per capita growth over the past three decades, while Brazil, Russia, and South Africa, the G2 group of countries, have had low GDP growth over this period. But in considering social development, as indicated by job quality, China's outcomes remain high, especially in the reduction of the working poor and the vulnerable, while India drops down from the group of G1 countries into the G2 group; Brazil and Russia climb up into the G1 rankings.

This near dichotomy between growth and social development outcomes in the case of BRICS poses two questions. One is analytical, the other normative. The analytical

Panel A. 1980 and 2007

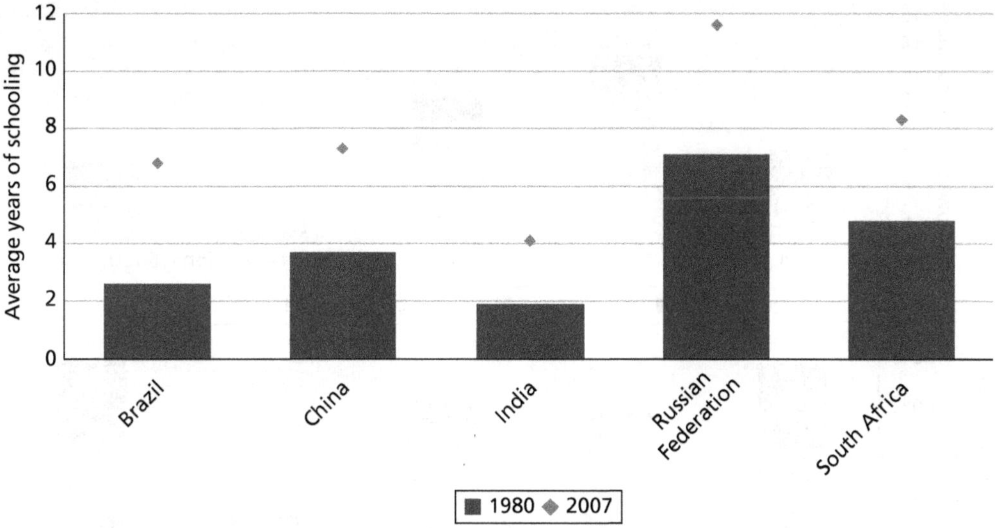

Panel B. 1980 and 2011

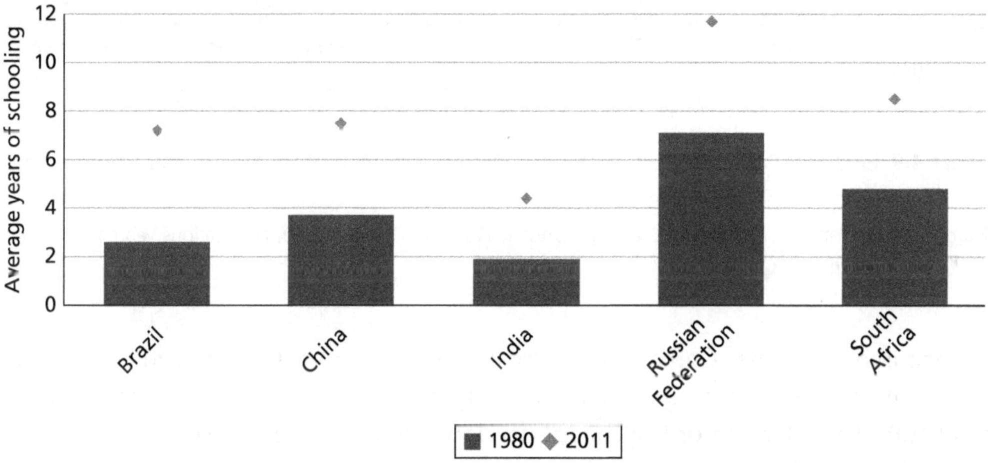

Figure 4.8 Average years of schooling for adults over age 25, 1980 and 2007

Source: Barro-Lee dataset EdStats, World Bank (2000); Human Development Report Office as of 15 October 2012, UNDP (various years).

question is, why has growth not driven social indicators with it for all BRICS except China? Or viewed the other way, why have higher social indicator outcomes, such as job quality, not contributed more towards growth in Brazil, Russia, and South Africa. The normative question is one of a more inclusive policy of balanced growth being more desirable.

But the analytic question is the prior one to be answered in its two parts. First, why has GDP growth not driven social development with it? And the answer is the difference in

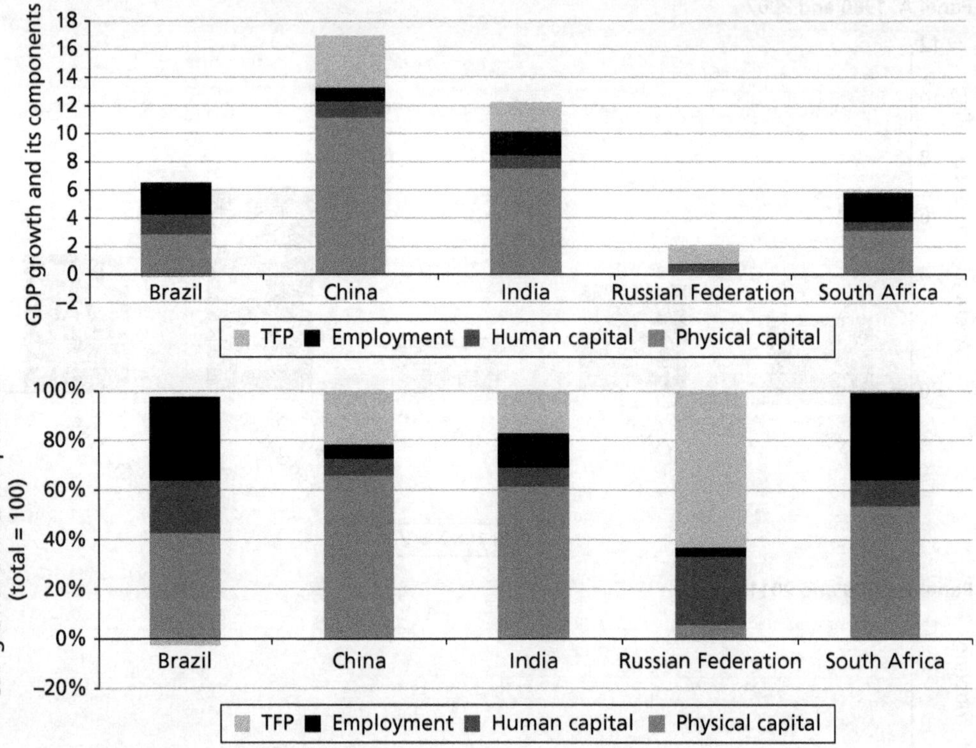

Figure 4.9 Breakdown of output growth into physical capital, human capital, employment, and total factor productivity, 1991–2011

Source: ILO calculations based on IMF, World Economic Outlook, October 2013, IMF (various years [b]); Trends Econometrics Models, ILO (various years [a]).

behaviour of the state. China has chosen to drive up both GDP growth and social development. India has focused more narrowly on GDP growth, just as Brazil, Russia, and South Africa have prioritized social development over GDP growth.

But the second part to the question, why better social outcomes have not made a bigger contribution to GDP growth, is more intractable. The beginnings of an answer can be gleaned by returning to the top panel in Figure 4.9, and comparing Brazil to India. Brazil's GDP growth between 1991 and 2011, of 3 per cent per annum, comprises roughly three equal parts, 1 per cent due to physical capital, 1 per cent due to employment, and 1 per cent due to human capital, with no contribution by TFP. In contrast, India's GDP growth over this period, verging on 7 per cent per annum, has a lower employment contribution compared to Brazil, a slightly lower human capital contribution, but a physical capital contribution more than three times that of Brazil, with this combination adding almost 2 per cent through TFP. Ergo, social development is much needed to contribute to GDP growth, but has to be complemented by investment in physical capital. Contrast China and India—both of whom have a near equal amount of investment in human capital—China's investment in physical capital, double that of India's, doubles its TFP compared to India.

This complementarity between physical capital and human capital allows the normative policy prescription to hold well; that balance between the two is useful for both GDP growth and its inclusion.

Social protection

Ranked by economic growth, BRICS fall into the high growth G1 countries with China and India, and the low growth G2 countries with Brazil, Russia, and South Africa. This ranking reverses considerably if the criteria are social change and level, as indicated above by employment and here by social protection. India falls down the ranking into the G2 countries, while Brazil and Russia climb up into the G1 countries. China manages to stay in the upper ranks of the G1 countries based on its improvements in social protection, if not in terms of its levels of social protection, where Brazil, Russia, and, on some counts, South Africa climb above it.

All BRICS are known for their significant extension of social protection coverage, particularly since the early 2000s, for most of them with remarkable outcomes (see, e.g. Fiszbein and Schady 2009; ILO 2010; ISSA 2013). In India, there are a few specific well-known programmes. In China, Brazil, and South Africa, more comprehensive blocks have been developed as key elements of their national social protection systems. Russia has most recently sought improvement in the efficiency and adaptation of a long-standing established system.

To view social protection in BRICS in perspective, in the early 2010s these countries accounted for 42 per cent of the global population; 28 per cent of the world GDP (in international purchasing power parity [PPP] constant 2011), and just 18 per cent of the world's public expenditure on social protection. In terms of recent change, between 1995 and 2011, social protection expenditure in BRICS has held its own, almost doubling its global share, along with GDP.

This sub-section examines:[1]

(a) rankings of BRICS by social protection, by examining expenditure and coverage;
(b) evolution of social protection systems in BRICS according to the specific features of their labour markets;
(c) impact of social expenditures on poverty and inequality in BRICS.

[1] Due to data availability, trends in social protection covers a shorter period, starting in 1995 for social protection expenditure, 1990 for estimates of legal coverage, and 2000 for indicators of effective coverage.

LEVEL OF PUBLIC INVESTMENT IN SOCIAL PROTECTION

China is under way to reach countries with already relatively high levels of public investment in social protection (Brazil, Russia, and South Africa). In terms of levels and trends in public investment in social protection, there are three main findings:

First, there is a significant disparity in levels of public social protection expenditure per capita. Levels vary widely from 17 US$ (constant) in India, to 236 US$ in China, to 1,196 US$ and to 1,050 US$ in Brazil and Russia. The G1 high growth countries show the lowest levels of social protection per capita (Figure 4.10) and as percentage of GDP (Table 4.13).

Second, all of BRICS significantly increased their level of social protection per capita over the last sixteen years. Growth in per capita expenditure on social protection was faster than GDP growth per capita for all of BRICS, except India.

Third, higher levels of social protection expenditure in G2 countries correspond to higher stages of development of their national social protection systems. This also corresponds to their improvements in job quality seen through their reduction in working poverty and vulnerable employment (see next sub-section). The differences in levels of social protection expenditure result from different choices in terms of mechanisms used to provide social protection that is contributory versus non-contributory, associated levels of benefits, and resulting coverage of their target groups.

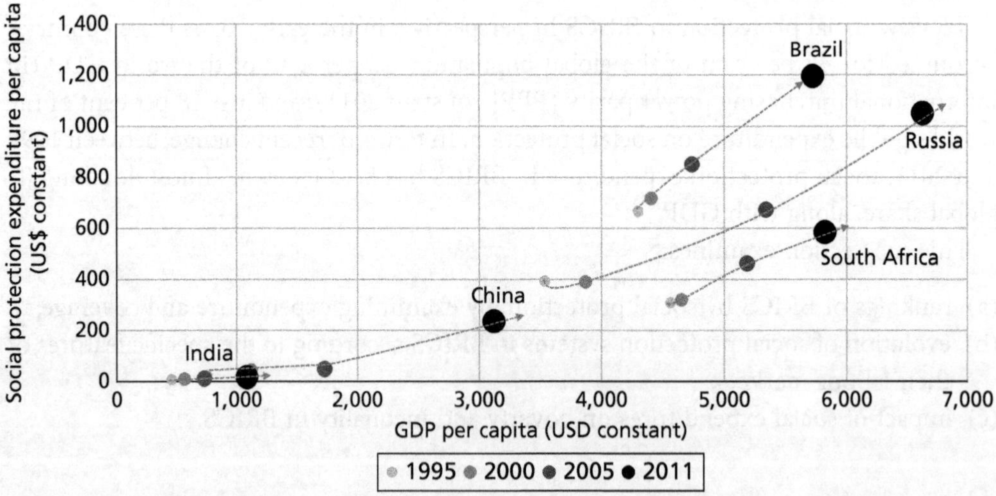

Figure 4.10 GDP per capita and public social protection expenditure per capita (US$ constant; 1995, 2000, 2005, 2011)

Sources: Estimations made at the ILO social protection data based on IMF Government finances statistics, IMF (various years [a]); CEPALStat (various years); World Development Indicators, World Bank (various years).

G1 High Growth Countries

These countries lag behind G2 countries when considering levels of social protection expenditure in constant US$ per capita (Figures 4.10 and 4.11) or as a percentage of GDP (Table 4.13), when the positioning of G1 and G2 countries is opposite to that defined on the basis of per capita growth. It is however not so different from what would be a grouping based on the level of GDP per capita. In 2010, Brazil public spending on social protection represented 21.3 per cent of GDP. This is among BRICS the highest level of public investment, not far from the average level observed in developed economies and the European Union (22.8 per cent). Russia comes second with 15.8 per cent of GDP before South Africa (10 per cent) and then China and India.

Table 4.13 Public social protection expenditure, 1990 to latest available year (% of GDP)

		1995	2000	2005	2006[1]	2007	2008[1]	2009	2010	2011	2012[1]
World	Total	6.01	6.35	6.70		7.36		8.75		8.62	
BRICS	Total	3.77	4.13	3.09		5.10		6.38		6.44	
DCs	Total	3.74	4.19	4.38		5.21		6.34		6.21	
Brazil[2]	**Total**	**15.5**	**16.3**	**18.0**	**19.0**	**19.3**	**19.5**	**21.2**	**21.3**	...	...
	Health	4.5	3.9	4.3	4.5	4.7	4.7	5.2	5.8	...	...
	Non-health	11.0	12.4	13.6	14.5	14.6	14.8	16.0	15.5	...	...
China[3]	**Total**	**3.2**	**3.9**	**2.8**	**5.2**	**5.0**	**5.7**	**6.8**	**6.8**	**7.6**	...
	Health	0.6	0.6	0.7	0.7	0.8	1.0	1.3	1.3	0.9	...
	Non-health	2.6	3.3	2.1	4.6	4.2	4.7	5.6	5.6	6.6	...
India[4]	**Total**	**1.6**	**1.6**	**1.6**	**1.6**	**1.9**	**2.0**	**2.1**	**1.8**	**1.6**	**2.8**
	Health	1.0	1.1	0.9	0.9	1.0	1.0	1.1	1.0	1.2	1.3
	Non-health	0.5	0.5	0.7	0.7	0.9	1.0	1.0	0.8	0.4	1.4
Russian	Total	**11.1**	**10.1**	**12.6**	**12.3**	**12.8**	**13.1**	**16.6**	**17.7**	**15.8**	**15.8**
Federation[5]	Health	2.1	2.0	3.9	4.0	4.1	4.1	5.0	4.5	3.9	3.5
	Non-health	9.0	8.07	8.69	8.2	8.7	9.0	11.7	13.2	11.9	12.3
South Africa[6]	**Total**	**6.8**	**6.88**	**8.92**	**8.9**	**8.9**	**9.1**	**10.2**	**9.8**	**10.0**	...
	Health	3.1	3.2	3.9	4.0	4.0	4.3	4.9	4.8	5.0	...
	Non-health	3.7	3.7	5.1	4.9	4.8	4.8	5.3	5.0	5.0	...

[1] Data missing for a significant number of countries.

[2] ECLAC 1990–2009: total without education; 2010: ILO Social security inquiry. Government expenditure on social protection (including health).

[3] 2000: IMF General Government (cash), 2005–11 IMF General Government Accrual.

[4] IMF 1995–2010: Central and state government expenditure; data available from Government Spending Watch (GSW) for 2011.

[5] IMF: 1995 and 2000: Budgetary central and Local government; 2005–11: General government.

[6] IMF: General government for 1995, 2000–05 and 2008; 2006, 2007 and 2009–11: Budgetary and Extra budgetary central government, social security funds, State and local governments.

Source: IMF Government finances statistics, IMF (various years [b]); CEPALStat (various years); Government spending watch and World Development Indicators, World Bank (various years).

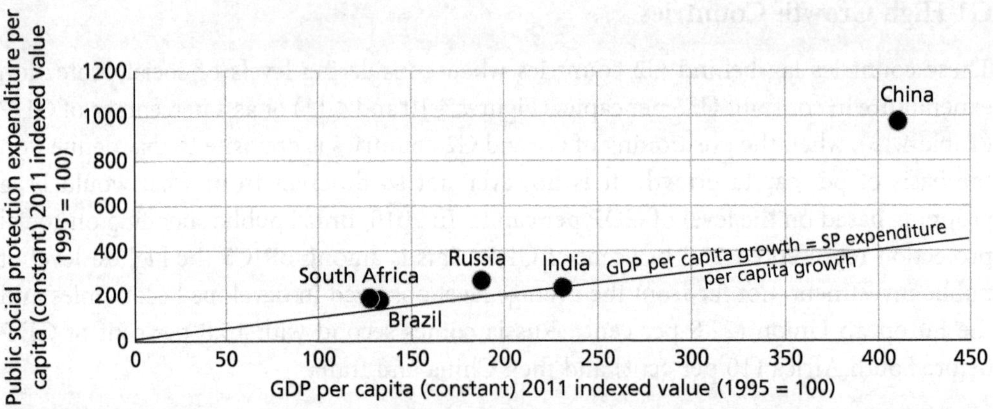

Figure 4.11 Changes in GDP and public social protection expenditure per capita (US$ constant) 2011

Sources: ILO social protection data based on IMF Government finances statistics, IMF (various years [a]; CEPALStat (various years); World Development Indicators, World Bank (various years).

Growth in Social Protection Expenditure

This was faster than GDP growth in all of BRICS except India. BRICS doubled their share of world public spending on social protection between 1995 and 2011 to 17.9 per cent. This was greater than the increase in their share in total world GDP which increased by a factor of 1.6 (Table 4.14). The main contributor to this trend was China, with the combined effect of its large population and the highest increase in public investment in social protection with an annual growth rate of 15.3 per cent from 1995 to 2011 and a per capita expenditure on social protection increased by a factor of nine. Most of this increase happened after 2005. In order to strengthen domestic demand-led growth, China adopted a series of measures after 2008 including increased wages and the expansion of social protection benefits in particular in the areas of pensions[2] and health[3] (ILO 2014b, 2015a). But despite this massive increase, China in 2011 had still not yet reached the 1995 levels of expenditure per capita of Brazil, Russia, and South Africa.

[2] In 2009, China started a process of extension of pension coverage aiming at universal coverage by 2020. The introduction of the rural pension scheme in 2009 and the urban pension scheme for workers otherwise not covered in 2011 were first steps in consolidating the two new pension schemes announced in 2014 (ISSA 2013; ILO 2014b, 2015a). See next sub-section.

[3] In 2003 and 2007, two new social health insurance schemes were established for the rural population and the previously uninsured part of the urban population. Together with other existing health insurance schemes this ensured a total coverage of 1.34 billion people, more than 96 per cent of the population. The adequacy of health insurance benefits was improved to ensure equal and effective access to health care. This took several forms, such as increasing reimbursement rates, extending the range of reimbursable items, raising the cap for reimbursement, introducing insurance for high out-of-pocket payments, reforming the public health sector, and investing more in rural health facilities and urban community-based health centres (ILO 2014b).

Table 4.14 Public social protection expenditure per capita (US$ constant) growth

	Social protection expenditure per capita (US$ constant)				Average annual change in per capita expenditure (US$ constant, % annual change)					Change in social protection expenditure (US$ cst, indexed value 1995)		
	1995	2000	2005	2011	1995–2000	2000–05	2005–11	2000–11	1995–2011	1995–2000	1995–2005	1995–2011
Brazil	665.7	716.5	851.2	1196.2	1.5	3.5	5.8	5.3	3.7	107.6	127.9	179.7
Russia	393.5	389.4	672.1	1050.4	−0.2	11.5	7.7	9.4	6.3	99.0	170.8	267.0
India	7.3	9.3	12.0	17.1	5.0	5.2	6.2	5.7	5.5	127.7	164.6	235.7
China	24.2	44.1	48.1	236.1	12.7	1.7	30.4	16.5	15.3	182.1	198.2	974.1
South Africa	309.2	320.1	462.6	584.2	0.7	7.6	4.0	5.6	4.1	103.5	149.6	188.9

Source: IMF Government finances statistics, IMF (various years [b]); CEPALStat (various years); Government spending watch and World Development Indicators, World Bank (various years).

Differences in Social Protection Spending Levels

Social protection spending levels reflect country differences in their stage in the development of national social protection systems. The overall spending on social protection is the result of three main factors: (i) the scope of social protection measured by the number of social risks or contingencies with statutory provision;[4] (ii) the extent to which the intended target groups are not only legally covered but also effectively reached for a given risk or contingency; (iii) the level of benefits provided.

The majority of developing countries[5] typically provide protection for long-term benefits (old age, disability, and survivors), employment injury, and health but lack protection for unemployment, sickness, maternity (other than labour laws), or family allowances. All of BRICS do provide some benefits for the nine contingencies.

Expenditure on benefits for the elderly is the main component of expenditure in the majority of countries worldwide, especially in countries with already well developed social protection systems (ILO 2014b). This is notably the situation in the Russian Federation (42.6 per cent), China (42.4 per cent), and Brazil (36.5 per cent) (Figure 4.12). Public spending in India and South Africa is dominated by health expenditure (41.2 per cent and 48.4 per cent respectively). In the case of India, this is a result of a limited development of other social protection functions which usually characterized countries in the early stages of development of their national social protection system. In South Africa, social protection systems have been extensively developed through large non-contributory tax-financed programmes providing coverage to a significant number of people from different target groups (elderly, children, and disabled) but at a relatively low level of benefit.

The percentage of GDP spent on benefits for the working age population (unemployment in particular but also maternity, sickness, disability, or employment injury) reflects the degree of development of the national social protection system. Advanced countries typically spent around 3.5 per cent of GDP on benefits for the working age compared to 1.5 per cent for BRICS. Russia and Brazil spent more than 2.5 per cent of GDP while 1.9 per cent was spent in China, 1.6 per cent in South Africa, and just above 0.5 per cent of GDP in India.

A Key Difference

The main difference between types of contributory and non-contributory programmes lies in their financing. Table 4.15 on expenditure and Figure 4.13 on financing sources

[4] The framework of contingencies is specified in the relevant international ILO standards, in particular the Social Security (Minimum Standards) Convention, 1952 (No. 102). Convention No. 102 refers to old age, disability, death of the breadwinner, sickness, employment injury, maternity, family and children, and unemployment.

[5] In 2012, 28 of the 125 developing countries for which information is available had comprehensive social protection systems (ILO 2014a).

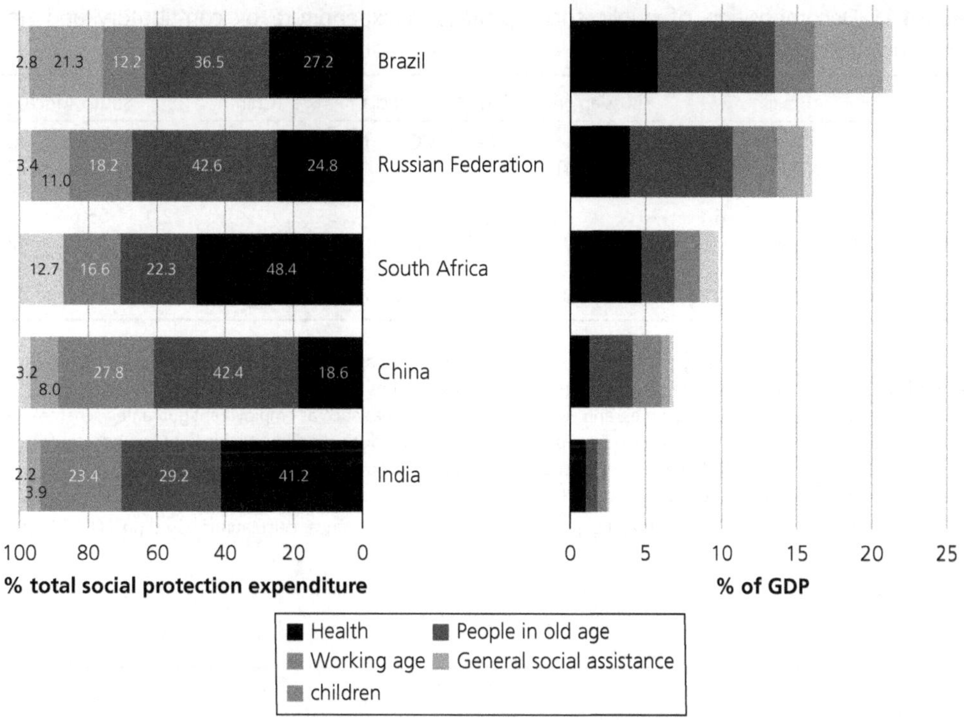

Figure 4.12 Levels and composition of public social protection expenditure

Source: ILO social protection expenditure database, ILO (2014b).

highlight the variety of configurations of social protection systems among BRICS. There is no 'best' configuration but rather options that better fit each country's employment patterns and a choice between Bismarckian and Beveridgean social policies and underlying objectives.[6] Considering the latest year for which data are available, China, Brazil, and Russia spent the most on contributory programmes. In China close to 85 per cent of social protection expenditure was financed through social protection contributions. As part of contributory schemes, the government established in 2002 the New Cooperative Medical Scheme which rapidly expanded to reach 97.5 per cent of the rural population by 2011 (Zhu 2013; ILO 2015a). In 2009 and 2011, the government introduced new contributory (voluntary) state-subsidized pension schemes for the rural and as yet uncovered urban populations. In Brazil, even if relatively high, the share of contributory

[6] Acknowledging the extreme simplification, one can distinguished the main objective of these two approaches as follows: objective of income maintenance and compensation for Bismarckian social policy based on social insurance, with eligibility for earnings-related benefits depending on the contribution record; objective of prevention of poverty for Beveridgean social policy with flat-rate benefits provided universally and financed by taxation.

Table 4.15 Decomposition of public social protection expenditure by contributory and non-contributory schemes (%, several years)

	Brazil			Russian Federation			India		China		South Africa		
	CC	NC-NMT	NC-MT	CC	NC-NMT	NC-MT	CC	NC	CC	NC	CC	NC-NMT	NC-MT
2000	85	8.9	6.1	70	7.5	22.5	...	...	...	...	2.4	55.6	41.9
Mid-2000	82.6	9.9	7.5	64.5	19.9	15.6	...	...	77.8	22.2	4.3	52.9	42.8
2010s	80.8	10	9.3	69.3	19	11.7	11.9	88.9	84.8	15.2	3	55.8	41.2

Notes: CC: Contributory compulsory; NC-NMT: Non-contributory non means-tested (typically universal or categorical tax-financed schemes); NC-MT: Non-contributory means-tested (this includes social assistance programmes targeted at the poor, conditional cash transfer programmes, and self-targeted programmes such as employment guarantee schemes); NC: Non-contributory programmes (China and India). For China and India no distinction is available between non-contributory means-tested and non-means-tested programmes. Real years: 2001 instead of 2000 in Brazil and Russian Federation; 2004 instead of 2000 in South Africa; 2006 instead of 2005 in South Africa.

Source: China and India: ADB (2015); Brazil, Russian Federation, and South Africa, calculations based on ILO (2015c).

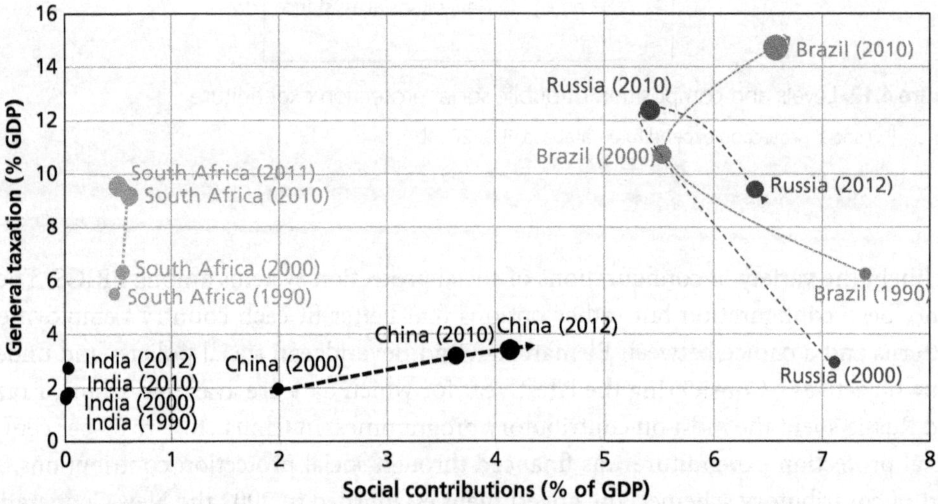

Figure 4.13 Financing social protection: patterns and trends

Source: IMF (2015a)

programmes in total public social protection expenditure has decreased over the last ten years. The gradual increase in the share of non-contributory programmes results from the development of non-contributory programmes since the early 2000s,[7] the

[7] The national programme, Bolsa Escola, in 2001 and Bolsa Família subsequently introduced in 2003, combining and reforming existing programmes and significantly expanding coverage from 5.1 million families under Bolsa Escola to some 14 million families under Bolsa Família by 2014 (ILO 2015a).

consolidation of the Unified Health System (Sistema Único de Saúde, SUS),[8] and the increase in the level of benefit provided by these non-contributory programmes.[9] The Russian Federation is in-between. At the other extreme, South Africa has since the early 1990s strengthened the development of large non-contributory programmes to reach those in informal employment or the unemployed.

Figure 4.13 shows the same pattern from the point of view of financing for social protection. The horizontal axis shows contributory financing, while the vertical axis shows non-contributory financing, usually through taxes. Brazil and Russia reflect the highest level of expenditures and their reliance on social contributions. By contrast, despite significant increases over time, South Africa's social protection remains mainly based on general taxation. The only exceptions are for certain benefits for workers in formal employment.[10]

EXPANDING SOCIAL PROTECTION COVERAGE: LAWS AND PRACTICE

Extension of coverage can be divided into two questions. Who and how many persons are covered by laws and regulations? How many of those legally covered have effective access to their benefits, or to what degree are laws and regulations implemented in practice?[11] In practice, the extension of effective coverage often lags behind that of legal coverage. A gap in effective coverage is thus the result of two gaps—a legal gap and an implementation gap.

Analysis of coverage is relevant if assessed for each social protection contingency. This section has a special focus on old age pension coverage, unemployment benefits, and alternative employment guarantee, maternity, and child protection.

Reduction in Pension Coverage Gaps

In 2013, all of BRICS reached universal or near universal legal pension coverage following different paths in G2 and G1 countries. This is the result of a relative long-

[8] The main objective of the Unified Health System (Sistema Único de Saúde, SUS) is to ensure health care through the public system to all Brazilian citizens. This system promotes equity in terms of the health care of the population, ensuring the delivery of quality services and adequately meeting the needs of people, regardless of their ability to pay.

[9] Including notably the linking payments of Previdência Rural (1991) and of the Benefício de Prestação Continuada (BPC) to the minimum wage (ILO 2015a).

[10] Workmen's compensation fund (employment injury and medical aid), the unemployment insurance fund (unemployment, maternity and illness benefits), and road insurance fund which is also part of the social protection system.

[11] Coverage or coverage gaps can be broken down into legal and implementation coverage gaps, with: total coverage gap = legal coverage gap + implementation coverage gap with: (1) Legal coverage gap = universal coverage – legal coverage; (2) Implementation coverage gap = legal coverage gap – Effective coverage. Implementation coverage gaps occur when, despite being covered by existing laws and regulations, people do not have effective access to their benefits.

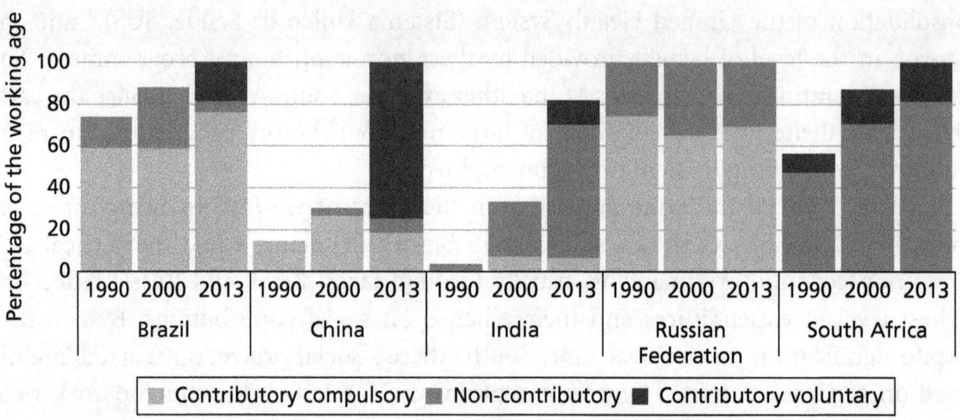

Figure 4.14 Old age pension and survivors' legal coverage: global and regional estimates (2000, 2013)

Source: SSA/ISSA, 2013, 2014a, 2014b, 2014c; ILO, 2015a, 2015b, 2015c; European Commission, 2015; SSA, 1989, 1999; United Nations, Department of Economic and Social Affairs (2015).

standing near universal coverage and gradual extension in Brazil, South Africa, and Russia, and an impressive increase in legal coverage over the last decade in China and in particular in India. BRICS, but China and India in particular, have been at the forefront of a general trend seen since 1990 in many developing countries: of significant progress in addressing gaps in legal coverage for pensions by including new categories of workers within the scope of the legislation (ILO 2015a). In 2013, the proportions of the working age population legally covered for a periodic cash pension benefit ranged from 81.9 per cent in India to 100 per cent in the four other countries (Figure 4.14).

Main differences between BRICS stand in (i) the combination of mechanisms used to provide pension coverage (contributory or not; compulsory or voluntary); (ii) the adequacy of these mechanisms regarding national institutions' capacities and labour market patterns which result in different degrees of implementation of legal coverage; (iii) the contribution of the extension of social protection improved job quality and possibly the formalization process.

The extension in pension legal coverage has been brought about largely by non-contributory mechanisms (South Africa) and legislating voluntary affiliation (China and India).

South Africa, Brazil, and China

South Africa, Brazil, and China adopted legal options that take into account the labour market context resulting in a relatively high degree of effective implementation. In South Africa, close to 80 per cent of the extension in legal pension coverage since 1990 has

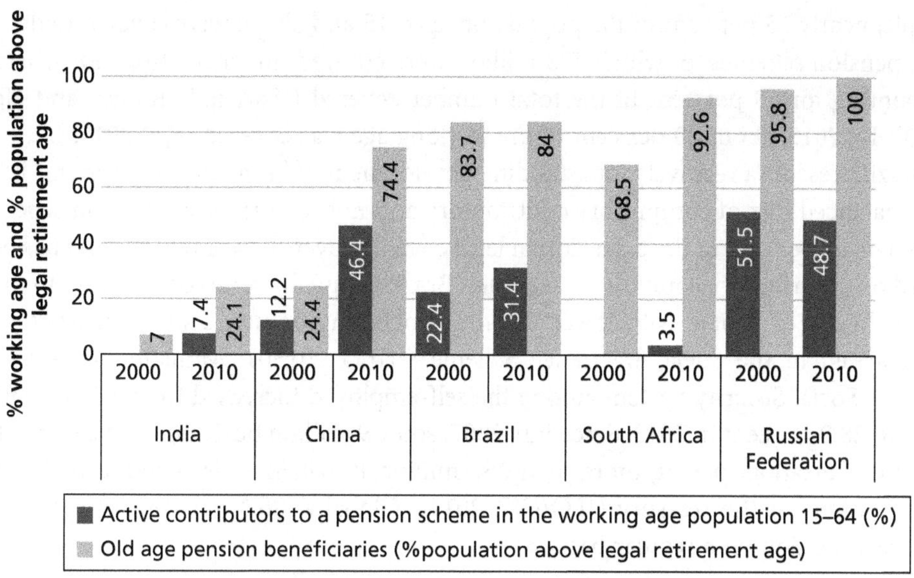

Figure 4.15 Indicators of effective social protection pension coverage (2000, 2013)

Source: Social Protection Database, ILO (various years [d]).

relied on non-contributory mechanisms (Figure 4.15).[12] In effective terms, the means-tested non-contributory old age pension grant expanded significantly to close to 3 million beneficiaries in 2013 (HelpAge International 2015). In 2013, fewer than 10 per cent of the elderly (7.3 per cent) were not covered as a result of implementation gaps.

In China, the universal legal pension coverage achieved in 2011[13] seems to be successfully translated into effective coverage or close to. At the end of 2013, 850 million

[12] South Africa was the first country in Africa to institute a state non-contributory pension. The first parliamentary proposal for an old age grant was made in 1922 and was instituted in 1928. Act No. 22 entitled all 'white' and 'coloured' residents of South Africa aged 65 years and older to receive a pension, subject to an income-based means test. In 1944, black South Africans were first granted the right to claim the pension, albeit at a lower rate than the value transferred to white and coloured residents. Then, with the end of the apartheid government in 1994, the pension was finally equalized across all citizens (CPRC 2007).

[13] In China before 2009, only two institutional mechanisms existed for income security in old age: one for urban workers, based on social insurance principles, and one for civil servants and others of similar status, based on the employer's liability approach. Together, they covered under 250 million people (including pensioners), about 23 per cent of the population aged 15 and above in 2008. In 2009 and 2011, two new old age pension schemes were introduced for the rural population and urban residents otherwise not covered. Participation is voluntary. To encourage people to join, the government adopted a number of measures, including contribution subsidies and the establishment of personal contribution scales for the savings account component and immediate pension payments to the elderly parents of adults registered with a rural pension scheme. The consolidation of the two new pension schemes was announced in 2014 (ISSA 2013; Ringen and Ngok, 2013; ILO 2014b). In January 2015, China's State Council announced pension reforms for civil servants and public sector employees, bringing them under the purview of the urban basic pension insurance scheme, with a view to complete integration of the system (ILO 2014b, 2015a). This unification substantially extends the social question beyond urban workers and points to a notion of unified social citizenship.

people, nearly 75 per cent of the population aged 15 and above were covered under the four pension schemes, of which 498 million were covered under the two new schemes, accounting for 59 per cent of the total number covered (ISSA n.d.; Ringen and Ngok 2013). By 2015, about 80 per cent of the working age was covered (ILO 2015b).

Brazil presents a relatively longstanding development of broad pension systems based on a balanced mix of compulsory contributory and non-contributory pension schemes. In Brazil, 65 per cent of the extension in legal coverage over the last two decades has been based on contributory compulsory schemes. Brazil adopted a series of measures to foster the inclusion of people with lower incomes (including domestic workers, workers in rural areas) in the Social Insurance Scheme[14] (ILO 2015b). Affiliation rates to the General Social Security System among the self-employed increased from 17 per cent in 2005 to 28.2 per cent in 2013. Since July 2007, some 9 million businesses have joined this system of taxation, paying more than 267 million Brazilian reals (US$118 million) in contributions to the treasury (ILO/GIZ 2014). Globally, 86.3 per cent of the elderly receive a pension on a regular basis.

India

In India, the majority of people are legally covered but still lack effective access to their benefits. In India, legal pension coverage jumped from less than 5 per cent in 1990 to 33 per cent in 2000 and more than 80 per cent in 2013. The main reasons are expansion of the means-tested non-contributory Indira Gandhi National Old Age Pension Scheme (IGNOAPS); and voluntary affiliation to the New Pension Scheme (NPS) made available in 2009 to nearly all Indian citizens.[15] Despite changes in legislation and initiatives[16] developed

[14] To this end, the Brazilian National Institute of Social Security defined three categories of workers: employees, individual contributors, and the special insured. The Simplified Social Security Plan established reduced contribution rates for individual contributors from 20 per cent to 11 per cent of the minimum monthly salary for all workers with an income up to 36,000 Brazilian reals per year (US$21,500). Workers who choose the reduced rate have access to all General Social Security System (Regime Geral de Previdência Social) benefits, with the exception of retirement due to contribution time (Durán Valverde et al. 2013). Concerning the 'special insured', the contribution of 2.3 per cent based on the value of production sales allows workers to equate their contributory obligations to their income, usually irregular. Eligibility for pension benefit is subject to 15 years of rural activity.

[15] The National Pension Scheme or New Pension Scheme (NPS) was operationalized on 1 January 2004, originally for state government and public sector employees. Since 1 May 2009, all Indian citizens aged 18–55 have been able to open a National Pension Scheme account on a voluntary basis (ISSA 2013). The non-contributory pension—IGNOAPS—is the most important government direct cash payment scheme, introduced in 1995 for elderly low-income people. On 9 June 2011, central government lowered the eligibility age for IGNOAPS from 65 to 60. It also raised benefits for those aged 80 or older. The government estimates that the lower age limit for IGNOAPS will bring in an additional 7.2 million persons aged 60 to 64. India has about 80 million persons aged 60 or older, with 51 million with incomes below the poverty line (ISSA 2013).

[16] Including the Informal Sector Workers Social Security Scheme launched in 2002 which reached no more than a few thousands workers on a voluntary basis and was closed in 2005. Other schemes such as Rajasthan Vishwakarma Unorganized Sector Workers (Motivational) Contributory Pension Scheme (RVPS) or New Pension System-Lite usually provide only lump sum and are not included as part of this analysis.

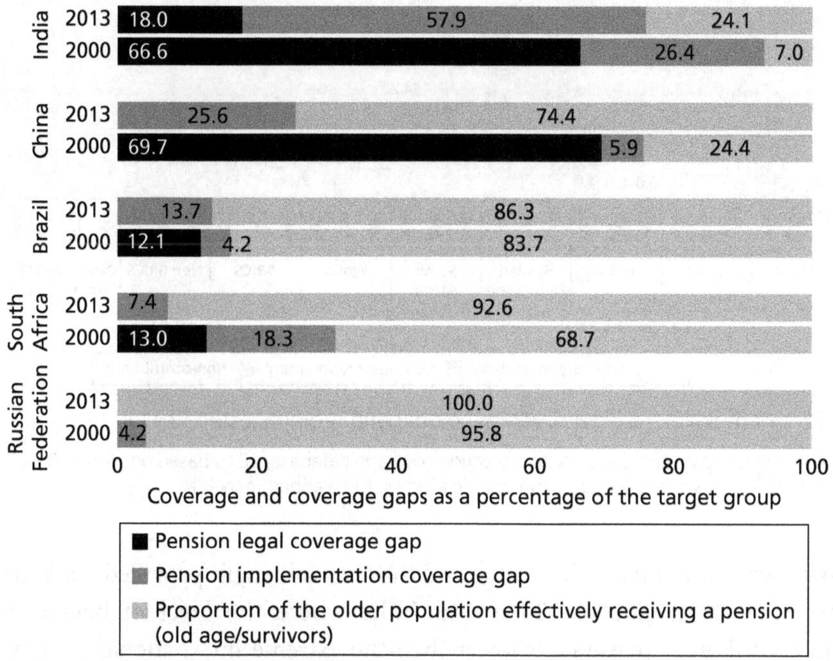

Figure 4.16 Decomposition of pension coverage and gaps (2000, 2013)

Source: Legal and implementation gaps: SSA/ISSA, 2013, 2014a, 2014b, 2014c; ILO, 2015a, 2015b, 2015c; European Commission, 2015; SSA, 1989, 1999; United Nations, Department of Economic and Social Affairs, 2015; Effective coverage: China Statistical Yearbook, NSBC (2015).

over years, today still fewer than a quarter of the elderly receive an old age pension on a regular basis. Close to 58 per cent of the elderly are legally covered but without having effective access to old age benefits (Figure 4.16).

Increased Efficiency in the Russian Federation

In the Russian Federation, universal coverage has been reached in both legal and effective terms. The main issue concerns the levels of benefits now and in the long run.[17]

Ranking by pension coverage would place Russia on top, followed by South Africa, Brazil, China, and India. For systems largely based on general taxation, there is often a

[17] In the Russian Federation, the transition from a centrally planned to an open market economy launched in 1991 resulted in decreasing adequacy of benefits, shrinking coverage and chronic delays in payment of benefits, widespread informalization, and the resulting widespread contribution and tax evasion. Measures adopted since the late 1990s until recently have constantly improved the effectiveness and efficiency of the system. The establishment of an insured person database along with the introduction of a system for individual registration was an important administrative improvement. This reform, which was pioneered by the Pension Fund, was further extended to all branches of social insurance and became an important tool in accounting for insured rights to benefits as well as in combating contribution evasion. The establishment of the National Welfare Fund in 2008 also contributed to the improvement and sustainability of the social security system. In 2010, a new set of measures was launched to further develop the insurance-based pension system by 2020 to enhance its sustainability and adequacy (ISSA 2013).

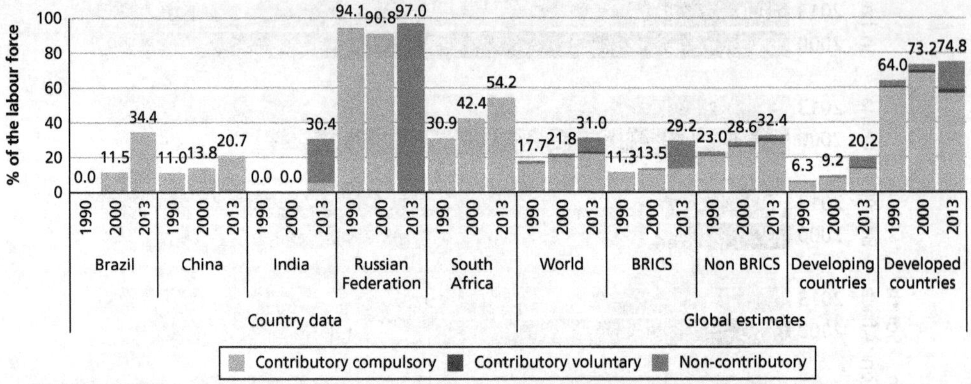

Figure 4.17 Unemployment legal coverage: global and regional estimates

Source: ILO Research department legal social protection coverage database, 2015 based on SSA/ISSA 2013, 2014a, 2014b, 2014c; SSA, 1989, 1999; Trends Econometric Models, ILO (various years [a]).

trade-off between the extent of coverage and the level of benefit provided per beneficiary. This applies in particular to China and India where the level of benefit received from non-contributory pensions is lower than the extreme international poverty line of 1.25 US$PPP a day.[18] By linking the level of benefit to the minimum wage, Brazil insured at least a basic level of income for those who benefit (around US$300 per month) (ILO 2015a).

Other Social Protection Contingencies

Unemployment benefits and alternative solutions adapted to labour market patterns are limited to a happy few. Unemployment protection is still lacking in more than 55 per cent of the countries worldwide but surprisingly exists in BRICS, albeit covering in some cases a minority of the target population. Around 20 per cent of the labour force in China, 30 per cent and 35 per cent in Brazil and India respectively, and 97 per cent in Russia are legally covered by periodic cash benefits for unemployment or alternatively some form of employment guarantee (Figure 4.17). Unemployment protection is limited to urban employees in the case of China but extended to non-standard forms of employment in Brazil and South Africa. These two are among the rare countries to cover domestic workers.[19] One reason for the generally limited development of unemployment protection lies in the relevance of the concept of 'unemployment' in many developing countries where the poor largely have to work. India and South Africa, in this respect, provide at least a basic level of income security, through employment guarantee schemes under India's Mahatma Gandhi National Rural Employment

[18] The Chinese rural and urban non-contributory pensions amount to 55 Yuan (US$9) per month but may be supplemented by local government. In India, the amount is about 200 Rupees, that is, less than US$4 per month (HelpAge International 2015).

[19] In South Africa, in 2003, domestic workers were brought under the Unemployment Insurance Fund, which is also responsible for the payment of maternity benefits.

Table 4.16 Unemployment effective coverage: unemployed receiving periodic unemployment benefits (2000, 2005, 2007–13 (% unemployed)

	2000	2005	2007	2008	2009	2010	2011	2012	2013
World	11.1	14.4	13.7	13.6	14.2	12.1	11.7	11.4	11.2
DCs	4.4	7.7	6.9	6.8	6.6	5.2	5.3	5.1	5.1
AEs	38.1	40.8	40.5	40.8	43.9	38.9	36.8	36.0	35.2
BRICS	6.4	12.8	11.3	11.0	10.7	7.9	7.7	7.7	7.3
Non-BRICS	15.2	15.8	15.8	15.9	17.2	15.6	15.2	14.5	14.4
South Africa	10.0	11.0	10.9	9.7	11.3	14.5	12.8	13.5	15.6
Brazil	...	5.1	6.2	8.0	7.2	7.8	8.0	...	...
China	9.9	20.0	17.1	14.8	14.0	9.2	9.1	9.1	8.5
India [1]	0[2]	0[2]	...	3.0	...	...	...	...	...
Russian Federation	11.8	29.8	28.4	26.2	29.4	24.1	21.3	20.6	18.6

[1] Beneficiaries from the Indian national employment guarantee scheme are not counted. This programme is self-targeted and potentially of interest for all people able to work but with low income and irregular employment. The main target group of this type of programme is composed of working poor, unemployed, and under-employed.

[2] Labour law requires employers to provide a severance payment equal to 15 days' average pay for each year of employment. Labour law requires employers to provide a severance payment equal to 15 days' average pay for each year of employment. Eleven states have instituted temporary unemployment programmes funded by the government (SSA/ISSA 2005).

Source: ILO Research Department based on ILO (2014b) and national sources.

Guarantee Scheme, or other forms of public employment programmes for the working poor, and the underemployed under South Africa's Public Works Programs.[20]

Effective unemployment coverage is significantly lower than legal coverage (Table 4.16). Considering only periodic cash benefits, it ranges from fewer than 10 per cent of the unemployed receiving benefits in India, China, and Brazil to 15.6 per cent and 18.6 per cent in South Africa and Russia.

Maternity protection including health care: the importance of packages going beyond income replacement based on social insurance principles. Worldwide, 34 per cent of countries fully meet the requirements of ILO's Convention No. 183 on the duration of maternity leave (of at least fourteen weeks), amount of cash benefits (not fewer than two-thirds of previous earnings for fourteen weeks), and source of funding (not solely based on employer liability) (ILO 2014c). Among BRICS, three (Brazil, China, Russia) meet all three criteria. India recently moved from employer liability to a social security system and provides at least two-thirds of earnings during maternity leave, but for fewer than fourteen weeks (thirteen weeks) for workers in formal employment. For workers beyond the reach of formal benefits programmes, the Indira Gandhi Matritva Sahyog Yojana

[20] Some public employment programmes, such as India's Mahatma Gandhi National Rural Employment Guarantee Scheme or the Productive Safety Nets Programme in Ethiopia, provide employment or alternatively cash or food transfers for those who are permanently or temporarily unable to work, or for whom work is not available (ILO 2014a, 2014b).

(IGMSY) provides a cash transfer and access to health care.[21] In South Africa, the benefit is up to 60 per cent depending on a worker's level of income (ILO 2014c). China has extended the duration of paid maternity leave in law, meeting requirements of Convention 183.[22] In effective terms, coverage for maternity insurance in China rose from 65 million in 2006 to nearly 139 million in 2011 (ISSA 2013).

If comparing G1 and G2 countries regarding maternity benefits analysed through the extent of legal and effective coverage, again G2 countries come first (Russia, South Africa, and then Brazil), despite significant improvement in China and an innovative approach adopted in India (Figure 4.18).

Child benefits: South Africa and Brazil stand out. Among BRICS, South Africa is the country where expenditure on social protection benefits for children is the highest (12.7 per cent of total public social protection expenditure; 1.2 per cent of GDP). This is above the world average (0.4 per cent of GDP) and not far from average in developed economies and European countries (1.4 per cent). The South African Child Support Grant, although means tested, covers more than half of all children under the age of 18 (10.8 million children in 2012).[23]

The Bolsa Família progamme in Brazil is the largest programme providing child benefit in absolute terms. It reaches around 14 million families and covers about a quarter of Brazil's population—at an annual cost of less than 0.5 per cent of GDP (ILO 2014b). It is estimated that 10 per cent of the change in inequality compared to the 1990s is due to Bolsa Família (Barros et al. 2010).

[21] The Indira Gandhi Matritva Sahyog Yojana (IGMSY) provides a cash transfer programme in 52 pilot districts reaching out to nearly 1.4 million pregnant and lactating mothers, and providing a cash incentive of nearly US$100 in three instalments from the end of the second trimester of pregnancy until the child reaches six months, upon the fulfilment of certain conditions relating to maternal and child health care practices (Fultz and Francis 2013). Due to restricted eligibility criteria related to age, number of births, and poverty restrictions it is estimated that fewer than 1 per cent of women workers are eligible for maternity benefits either contributory or from social assistance (Lingam and Kanchi 2013).

[22] The Social Insurance Law, which took effect on 1 July 1 2011, requires employers to contribute to the maternity insurance fund so as to ensure coverage of their employees by the maternity insurance (Social Insurance Law, art. 53). Female employees are now entitled to ninety-eight days of maternity leave for childbirth, an increase of eight days, paid at 100 per cent of their previous earnings. Since 2003, China has rapidly expanded social security coverage, including maternity and parental benefits, committing to full social security coverage for all workers by 2020. As in the case of pensions, the process is aimed at expanding social security coverage to rural and marginalized communities in order to lower inequality between social groups. Self-employed workers are entitled to contribute to social insurance on a voluntary basis.

[23] Coverage has been significantly extended by gradually increasing the maximum age threshold from six years in 1998 to eighteen years in 2008, and by adjusting the income threshold to inflation (ILO 2014b). In order to facilitate access to the benefit for eligible families, particularly the poorest, the government made efforts to disseminate information about eligibility criteria, simplify the procedure, and reduce the number of documents applicants needed. The grant is considered to have significant impact on children's nutrition, physical development, and education (e.g. Patel et al. 2012, 2013; DSD et al. 2012; Eyal and Woolard 2013).

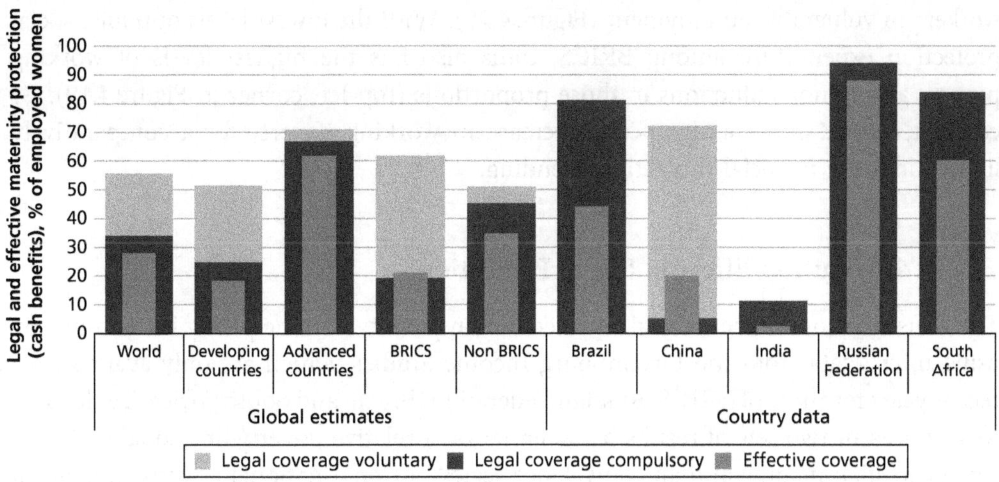

Figure 4.18 Legal coverage for maternity cash benefits: women in employment protected by law for loss of income during maternity, latest available year (%)

Source: ILO social security inquiry, ILO (2014c).

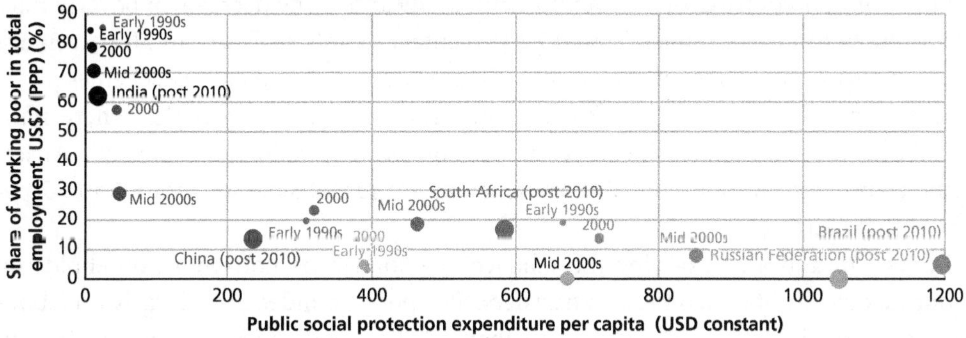

Figure 4.19 Public spending on social protection per capita (early 1990s to post 2010) and working poverty

Source: Public social protection expenditure: IMF Government finances statistics, IMF (various years [a]); CEPALStat (various years); Government spending watch, World Bank (various years). Vulnerable employment: ILO, Trends Econometric Models, October 2013, ILO (various years [a]).

IMPACT OF SOCIAL PROTECTION ON JOB QUALITY, POVERTY, AND INEQUALITY

The Inverse Relationship

In many respects, the differences in social protection 'performances' among BRICS are similar to what was observed earlier for working poverty and employment vulnerability. The figures below show clearly the strong inverse correlation over time between the level of public investment in social protection and the share of working poor (Figure 4.19) or workers in vulnerable employment (Figure 4.20). With the lowest levels of public social protection expenditure among BRICS, India also has the highest levels of working poverty and minor reductions in those proportions (top-left corner in Figure 4.19). By contrast, China shows a significant decrease in working poverty for a comparatively limited increase in social protection spending.

The Redistribution Effect of Social Protection

The redistribution impact of social protection on poverty and inequality is examined by using micro-data from the Luxembourg Income Studies, which are only available for recent years for three of BRICS: Russian Federation, Brazil, and South Africa. Tables 4.17 to 4.19 present two sets of results based either on a relative poverty line equal to 50 per cent of median income and an equivalence scale;[24] or on a national poverty line, or on minimum subsistence income and a per capita basis (Figures 4.21 and 4.22).[25]

Table 4.17 presents poverty rates and Gini coefficients before and after transfers both public and private, and taxes. Public transfers themselves comprise both contributory and non-contributory schemes. In these three countries, public transfers (either contributory or non-contributory) lower poverty significantly. The decrease in poverty rates due to public transfers ranges from 13.2 percentage points in Brazil to 20 percentage points in Russia, to 22 percentage points in South Africa.[26] Contributory schemes play a predominant role in Brazil and Russia, while reversing in South Africa where non-contributory schemes have the bigger impact on poverty reduction. In South Africa, public transfers from non-contributory schemes are responsible for more than 85 per cent in this decrease.

Tables 4.18 and 4.19 examine the reliance of poor versus non-poor households on labour income, capital income, and transfers. The poor do indeed rely largely on labour income in Russia and Brazil but less so than the non-poor, followed by transfers. In South Africa, less than 30 per cent of individuals' income in poor households comes from labour and income from capital is negligible. In the three countries, the poor rely heavily on public transfers: the reliance on public transfers ranges from 32.7 per cent in Russia, to 34.3 per cent in Brazil, and an astonishing 73.4 per cent in South Africa.[27] The corresponding proportions among the non-poor are significantly lower: 26.3 per cent in Russia, 22.8 per cent in Brazil, and 35.2 per cent in South Africa. Again given the nature

[24] The square root of the number of household members.

[25] Whatever the retained option, extreme values have been corrected to remove outliers. These choices have significant consequences on final results, in particular on poverty rates. Results presented in this section might be slightly different from those that can be presented at the national level based on a national absolute poverty line and possibly adapted equivalence scales. 'Poor' should be understood in this section as 'people living (equivalent adult) with less than 50 per cent of the median wage' or 'people living below the national poverty line'.

[26] Calculations based on the relative poverty line of 50 per cent of median equivalised income.

[27] The basis for calculation of the composition of income is the population as a whole including children and the elderly. These proportions refer to the relative poverty line.

Table 4.17 Effects of the secondary distribution of income on poverty and inequality (relative and absolute poverty lines)

			Labour	+ Capital	+ Public transfers			+ Private transfers	-Taxes
					C	NC	Total		
Brazil	2006	Gini	0.577	0.574	0.514	0.558	0.501	0.498	0.487
		Poverty (50% median, equivalence scale)	38.3	35.2	22.4	33.1	20.1	19.6	20.3
		Poverty (national, per capita basis)	53	50	37.4	49	36	35.6	36.8
	2009	Gini	0.565	0.55	0.489	0.535	0.476	0.474	0.461
		Poverty (50% median)	38.8	33.7	20.3	32.1	18.3	18	18.9
		Poverty (national, per capita basis)	44.9	40.1	26.4	39.5	25.6	25.4	26.4
	2011	Gini	0.561	0.547	0.481	0.532	0.468	0.467	0.453
		Poverty (50% median, equivalence scale)	39.7	32.7	19.7	30.9	17.7	17.6	18.1
		Poverty (national, per capita basis)	42.5	35.7	22.4	34.1	20.8	20.6	21.3
Russia	2004	Gini	0.548	0.547	0.438	0.531	0.424	0.409	0.407
		Poverty (50% median; equivalence scale)	43.6	38.4	23.2	36.7	20.9	17.1	15.4
		Poverty (national; per capita basis)	64.9	59.8	49.6	58.6	48	43.6	40.8
	2007	Gini	0.5	0.501	0.404	0.489	0.394	0.38	0.376
		Poverty (50% median; equivalence scale)	44.1	35	23.6	34	22.1	19.3	16.1
		Poverty (national; per capita basis)	58.3	49.1	37.7	48	35.9	32.9	29
	2010	Gini	0.495	0.495	0.382	0.481	0.372	0.364	0.357
		Poverty (50% median; equivalence scale)	41.9	37.3	20.5	35.4	18.6	15.6	13
		Poverty (national; per capita basis)	54.8	50.2	32	48.6	30.3	27	24.1
South Africa	2008	Gini	0.716	0.713	0.606	0.62	0.615	0.604	0.596
		Poverty (50% median)	47	46.5	45	27.5	26.2	23.9	24.2
		Poverty (absolute extreme)	51.3	50.7	49.3	35	34	31.7	32.3
		Poverty (national, per capita basis)	63.2	62.7	61.5	56.7	55.4	54.3	54.9
	2010	Gini	0.736	0.735	0.72	0.633	0.621	0.614	0.611
		Poverty (50% median)	51.6	51.4	48.4	31.9	29.2	27.8	28.6
		Poverty (national food poverty)	55	55.9	53.6	41.6	39.4	38.1	39.1
		Poverty (national, per capita basis)	65.5	65.4	63.5	60.1	57.9	57.1	58.5
Changes (contribution to poverty/gini increase/decrease)									
Brazil	2006	Gini	0.09	−0.003	−0.06	−0.016	−0.057	0.498	−0.011
		Poverty (50% median, equivalence scale)	13	−3.1	−12.8	−2.1	−13	19.6	0.7
		Poverty (national, per capita basis)	15.2	−3	−12.6	−1	−13	35.6	1.2
	2009	Gini	0.104	−0.015	−0.061	−0.015	−0.059	0.474	−0.013
		Poverty (50% median)	19.9	−5.1	−13.4	−1.6	−13.8	18	0.9
		Poverty (national, per capita basis)	13.5	−4.8	−13.7	−0.6	−13.9	25.4	1

(Continued)

Table 4.17 Continued

			Labour	+ Capital	+ Public transfers			+ Private transfers	-Taxes
					C	NC	Total		
	2011	Gini	0.108	−0.014	−0.066	−0.015	−0.064	0.467	−0.014
		Poverty (50% median, equivalence scale)	21.6	−7	−13	−1.8	−13.2	17.6	0.5
		Poverty (national, per capita basis)	21.2	−6.8	−13.3	−1.6	−13.3	20.6	0.7
Russia	2004	Gini	0.141	−0.001	−0.109	−0.016	−0.107	0.409	−0.002
		Poverty (50% median)	28.2	−5.2	−15.2	−1.7	−15.8	17.1	−1.7
		Poverty (national, per capita basis)	24.1	−5.1	−10.2	−1.2	−10.6	43.6	−2.8
	2007	Gini	0.124	0.001	−0.097	−0.012	−0.095	0.38	−0.004
		Poverty (50% median)	28	−9.1	−11.4	−1	−11.9	19.3	−3.2
		Poverty (national, per capita basis)	29.3	−9.2	−11.4	−1.1	−12.1	32.9	−3.9
	2010	Gini	0.138	0	−0.113	−0.014	−0.109	0.364	−0.007
		Poverty (50% median)	28.9	−4.6	−16.8	−1.9	−16.8	15.6	−2.6
		Poverty (national, per capita basis)	30.7	−4.6	−18.2	−1.6	−18.3	27	−2.9
South Africa	2008	Gini	0.12	−0.003	−0.107	−0.093	−0.098	0.604	−0.008
		Poverty (50% median)	22.8	−0.5	−1.5	−19	−20.3	23.9	0.3
		Poverty (absolute extreme)	19	−0.6	−1.4	−15.7	−16.7	31.7	0.6
		Poverty (national, per capita basis)	8.3	−0.5	−1.2	−6	−7.3	54.3	0.6
	2010	Gini	0.125	−0.001	−0.015	−0.102	−0.114	0.614	−0.003
		Poverty (50% median)	23	−0.2	−3	−19.5	−22.2	27.8	0.8
		Poverty (absolute food)	16.9	−0.1	−2.3	−14.3	−16.5	38.1	1
		Poverty (national, per capita basis)	7	−0.1	−1.9	−5.3	−7.5	57.1	1.4

Note: This table should be read as follows: 'labour': poverty rates and Gini coefficient before income from capital or from transfers; 'capital': include income from labour and capital; 'public transfers': include income from labour, capital, and public transfers (either contributory or not). C = Contributory schemes; NC = Non-contributory schemes.

Relative poverty line: the poverty line is defined as 50 per cent of the median equivalized disposable household income. All assessments based on relative poverty lines use the same equivalence scale (square root of the number of household members).

Absolute poverty lines: Brazil assessment uses national urban and rural poverty lines for 2006 (220.6 reals monthly in urban areas, 171.7 reals monthly in rural areas); 2009 (237.8 urban and 188.2 rural) and 2011 (260.7 urban and 206.2 rural). Calculations based on national poverty line are based on a per-capita basis (no equivalence scale).

Russian Federation: national monthly subsistence minimum income equals 5,902 roubles in 2010, 4,005 roubles in 2007, and 2,451 roubles in 2004 (poverty lines for December of each year); calculations on a per capita basis.

South Africa. National absolute poverty lines for 2010: 307 rands per month for food poverty line; 594 rands per month for upper bound poverty line; South Africa 2008: food poverty line of 259 rands monthly; upper bound poverty line of 507 rands monthly; calculations on a per capita basis.

Source: LIS (2015). LIS Cross-National Data Centre, Luxembourg, available at www.lisdatacenter.org/, accessed 18 October 2018.

Table 4.18 Composition of income (people living in poor household and others)

			Labour	Capital	Public transfers			Private transfers	Total
					Contributory	Non-contributory	Total		
Russia (50% median income; equivalence scale)	2010	Poor	56.8	0.9	28.6	4.1	32.7	9.5	100.0
		Non- poor	68.4	0.3	23.9	2.5	26.3	4.9	100.0
		Total	66.9	0.4	24.5	2.7	27.2	5.5	100.0
	2007	Poor	44.1	0.0	42.7	4.9	47.6	8.2	100.0
		Non-poor	72.8	0.5	19.2	2.1	21.3	5.3	100.0
		Total	68.1	0.4	23.1	2.5	25.7	5.7	100.0
	2004	Poor	48.4	0.6	33.1	8.6	41.7	9.3	100.0
		Non- poor	68.0	0.5	22.0	2.9	24.9	6.6	100.0
		Total	65.0	0.5	23.7	3.7	27.5	7.0	100.0
Russia (national; per capita basis)	2010	Poor	65.8	0.6	22.6	3.5	26.1	7.5	100.0
		Non- poor	65.3	0.4	26.2	2.5	28.7	5.6	100.0
		Total	65.4	0.5	25.3	2.8	28.1	6.1	100.0
	2007	Poor	57.5	0.1	31.3	3.9	35.2	7.2	100.0
		Non- poor	67.6	1.1	22.4	2.5	25.0	6.4	100.0
		Total	64.6	0.8	25.1	2.9	28.0	6.6	100.0
	2004	Poor	56.1	0.5	29.6	6.1	35.7	7.7	100.0
		Non- poor	68.3	0.7	22.2	2.2	24.4	6.6	100.0
		Total	63.3	0.6	25.3	3.8	29.0	7.1	100.0
Brazil (50% median; equivalence scale)	2011	Poor	52.1	12.7	12.7	21.7	34.3	0.9	100.0
		Non- poor	74.2	2.7	21.1	1.8	22.8	0.2	100.0
		Total	70.0	4.6	19.5	5.6	25.0	0.3	100.0
	2009	Poor	52.5	11.0	12.4	22.8	35.2	1.3	100.0
		Non poor	74.0	2.8	21.6	1.2	22.8	0.4	100.0
		Total	69.8	4.4	19.8	5.4	25.2	0.6	100.0
	2006	Poor	66.3	1.3	13.2	16.5	29.7	2.7	100.0
		Non- poor	74.1	1.8	21.3	2.2	23.5	0.6	100.0
		Total	72.5	1.7	19.7	5.1	24.7	1.0	100.0
Brazil (national poverty line, per capita basis)	2011	Poor	55.9	12.1	11.4	19.8	31.3	0.7	100.0
		Non- poor	74.1	2.4	21.8	1.4	23.2	0.3	100.0
		Total	70.0	4.6	19.5	5.6	25.0	0.3	100.0
	2009	Poor	59.2	9.8	12.2	17.8	30.0	1.0	100.0
		Non- poor	73.8	2.4	22.6	0.7	23.4	0.4	100.0
		Total	69.8	4.4	19.8	5.4	25.2	0.6	100.0
	2006	Poor	70.1	1.3	15.2	11.6	26.8	1.8	100.0
		Non- poor	74.0	1.9	22.3	1.2	23.5	0.6	100.0
		Total	72.5	1.7	19.7	5.1	24.7	1.0	100.0
South Africa (relative poverty line)	2010	Poor	22.4	0.1	2.1	71.3	73.4	4.2	100.0
		Non- poor	62.0	0.5	4.9	30.4	35.2	2.3	100.0
		Total	52.6	0.4	4.2	40.1	44.3	2.7	100.0
	2008	Poor	28.1	0.3	0.6	59.9	60.6	11.1	100.0
		Non- poor	66.1	1.5	2.8	26.2	29.0	3.4	100.0
		Total	57.9	1.2	2.3	33.5	35.8	5.1	100.0
South Africa (national food poverty line; per capita basis)	2010	Poor	22.1	0.1	2.8	71.2	74.0	3.8	100.0
		Non- poor	69.1	0.5	4.9	23.3	28.3	2.1	100.0
		Total	52.6	0.4	4.2	40.1	44.3	2.7	100.0
	2008	Poor	29.2	0.2	1.1	60.7	61.8	8.8	100.0
		Non- poor	70.3	1.6	2.8	21.8	24.6	3.5	100.0

(Continued)

Table 4.18 Continued

			Labour	Capital	Public transfers			Private transfers	Total
					Contributory	Non-contributory	Total		
		Total	57.9	1.2	2.3	33.5	35.8	5.1	100.0
South Africa (national upper bound poverty line; per capita basis)	2010	Poor	30.7	0.2	2.8	62.9	65.7	3.4	100.0
		Non- poor	80.3	0.7	6.0	11.2	17.2	1.8	100.0
		Total	52.6	0.4	4.2	40.1	44.3	2.7	100.0
	2008	Poor	38.0	0.5	1.0	53.0	53.9	7.5	100.0
		Non- poor	81.1	2.0	3.9	10.8	14.7	2.2	100.0
		Total	57.9	1.2	2.3	33.5	35.8	5.1	100.0

Note: This table should be read as follows: 'labour': poverty rates and Gini coefficient before income from capital or from transfers; 'capital': include income from labour and capital; 'public transfers': include income from labour, capital, and public transfers (either contributory or not). C = Contributory schemes; NC = Non-contributory schemes.

Relative poverty line: the poverty line is defined as 50 per cent of the median equivalized disposable household income. All assessments based on relative poverty lines use the same equivalence scale (square root of the number of household members).

Absolute poverty lines: Brazil assessment uses national urban and rural poverty lines for 2006 (220.6 reals monthly in urban areas, 171.7 reals monthly in rural areas); 2009 (237.8 urban and 188.2 rural) and 2011 (260.7 urban and 206.2 rural). Calculations based on national poverty line are based on a per-capita basis (no equivalence scale).

Russian Federation: national monthly subsistence minimum income equals 5,902 roubles in 2010, 4,005 roubles in 2007, and 2,451 roubles in 2004 (poverty lines for December of each year); calculations on a per capita basis.

South Africa. National absolute poverty lines for 2010: 307 rands per month for food poverty line; 594 rands per month for upper bound poverty line; South Africa 2008: food poverty line of 259 rands monthly; upper bound poverty line of 507 rands monthly; calculations on a per capita basis.

Source: LIS (2015). LIS Cross-National Data Centre, Luxembourg, available at www.lisdatacenter.org/, accessed 18 October 2018.

of the social protection programmes in these countries, the poor rely more on contributory programmes in Brazil and Russia, but more on non-contributory programmes in South Africa.

Table 4.19 shows that the non-poor gain far more benefits from contributory programmes compared to the poor in terms of proportion of beneficiaries and even more in terms of amount of benefit received. The inverse is not true (i.e. more poor than non-poor receive non-contributory benefits) with the exception of Brazil. There, the distribution of non-contributory benefits is, as intended by recent policies, largely for the benefit of those with less than 50 per cent of the national median income. Indeed, 70 per cent of the poor receive non-contributory benefits compared to 25 per cent of the non-poor. Considering the amount of non-contributory benefits received, 35.4 per cent go the poor while they represent less than 20 per cent of the population. In both South Africa and Russia, similar proportions of poor and non-poor receive non-contributory benefits (just more than 12 per cent in Russia and 60 per cent in South Africa). The poor receive however far less in terms of benefit amount. In 2010, close to 30 per cent of the population in South Africa lived under the relative poverty line but they received 9 per cent only of the total amount of public transfers (less than 1 per cent of the amount of benefit provided by contributory schemes and 15 per cent of those from

Table 4.19 Proportion of transfers going to the poor and % of the poor and non-poor receiving public transfers (latest available year)

			% of the poor (or non-poor) receiving benefits			% of total amount going to the poor (or non-poor)			Average level of benefits per beneficiary (poor and non-poor)		
			Public transfers		Private transfers	Public transfers		Private transfers	Public transfers		Private transfers
	Poverty lines		C	NC		C	NC		C	NC	
Russia 2010	50% median income; equiv. scale	Poor	34.8	12.1	19.7	5.6	6.5	5.0	31.282	10.225	13.438
		Non-poor	51.0	12.5	23.1	94.4	93.5	95.0	53.700	21.064	32.215
		Total	48.9	12.5	22.7	100.0	100.0	100.0	51.637	19.705	30.098
	National; per capita basis	Poor	38.2	13.9	10.6	9.0	12.8	9.1	24.602	9 344	24.350
		Non-poor	52.4	12.0	26.5	91.0	87.2	90.9	57.910	23.527	30.829
		Total	48.9	12.5	22.7	100.0	100.0	100.0	51.637	19.705	30.098
Brazil 2011	50% median income; equiv. scale	Poor	29.7	70.4	1.9	2.8	35.4	13.9	1 027	339	891
		Non-poor	56.4	24.7	1.0	97.2	64.6	86.1	4 075	390	2 447
		Total	51.6	32.9	1.1	100.0	100.0	100.0	3 757	370	1 969
	National; per capita basis	Poor	34.4	74.0	1.7	2.8	41.6	11.3	740	322	683
		Non-poor	56.2	21.9	1.0	97.2	58.4	88.7	4 256	414	2 591
		Total	51.6	32.9	1.1	100.0	100.0	100.0	3 757	370	1 969
South Africa 2010	South Africa (50% median income; equiv. scale)	Poor	1.8	59.9	5.5	0.9	15.0	8.6	2 028	1 345	1 222
		Non-poor	8.5	60.5	7.2	99.1	85.0	91.4	18.436	3 020	3 988
		Total	6.6	60.3	6.7	100.0	100.0	100.0	17,126	2 544	3 340
	National food poverty; per capita basis	Poor	3.2	85.2	10.9	2.1	29.3	12.0	1 972	1 351	633
		Non-poor	8.8	44.4	4.0	97.9	70.7	88.0	20,603	4 013	8 056
		Total	6.6	60.3	6.7	100.0	100.0	100.0	17,126	2 544	3 340
	National upper-bound poverty; per capita basis	Poor	3.9	29.0	7.0	4.7	61.3	24.5	2 332	5 541	1 337
		Non-poor	10.5	104.4	6.3	95.3	38.7	75.5	24,842	1 371	6 484
		Total	6.6	60.3	6.7	100.0	100.0	100.0	17,126	2 544	3 340

Note: This table should be read as follows: 'labour': poverty rates and Gini coefficient before income from capital or from transfers; 'capital': include income from labour and capital; 'public transfers': include income from labour, capital, and public transfers (either contributory or not). C = Contributory schemes; NC = Non-contributory schemes.

Relative poverty line: the poverty line is defined as 50 per cent of the median equivalized disposable household income. All assessments based on relative poverty lines use the same equivalence scale (square root of the number of household members).

Absolute poverty lines: Brazil assessment uses national urban and rural poverty lines for 2006 (220.6 reals monthly in urban areas, 171.7 reals monthly in rural areas); 2009 (237.8 urban and 188.2 rural) and 2011 (260.7 urban and 206.2 rural). Calculations based on national poverty line are based on a per-capita basis (no equivalence scale).

Russian Federation: national monthly subsistence minimum income equals 5,902 roubles in 2010, 4,005 roubles in 2007, and 2,451 roubles in 2004 (poverty lines for December of each year); calculations on a per capita basis.

South Africa. National absolute poverty lines for 2010: 307 rands per month for food poverty line; 594 rands per month for upper bound poverty line; South Africa 2008: food poverty line of 259 rands monthly; upper bound poverty line of 507 rands monthly; calculations on a per capita basis.

Source: LIS (2015). LIS Cross-National Data Centre, Luxembourg, available at www.lisdatacenter.org/, accessed 18 October 2018.

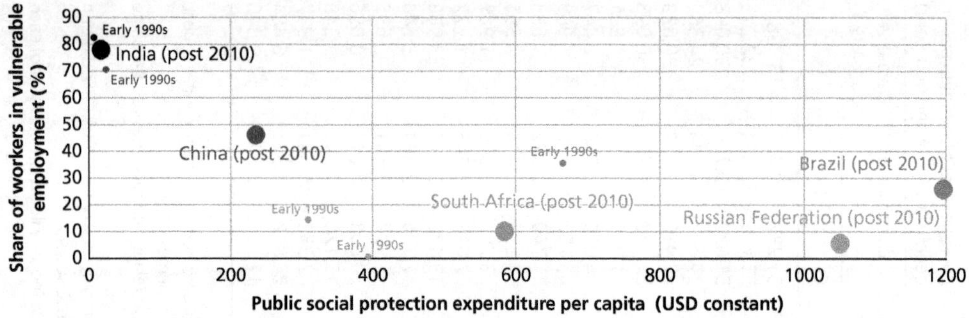

Figure 4.20 Public spending on social protection per capita (early 1990s to post 2010) and employment vulnerability

Source: Public social protection expenditure: IMF Government finances statistics, IMF (various years [a]); CEPALStat (various years); Government spending watch and World Bank (various years). Vulnerable employment: ILO, Trends Econometric Models, October 2013, ILO (various years [a]).

The implementation of large non-contributory pension schemes as in South Africa certainly guarantees at least a regular source of income for eligible people but does not contribute directly to employment formalization. Studies of child grants show that beyond helping the children themselves, the grants also facilitated access to the labour market for unemployed caregivers, especially for women; highlighting indirect impacts on formalization. Measures to facilitate the affiliation of the self-employed to newly developed or existing contributory schemes as mentioned earlier for Brazil enhance direct formalization.

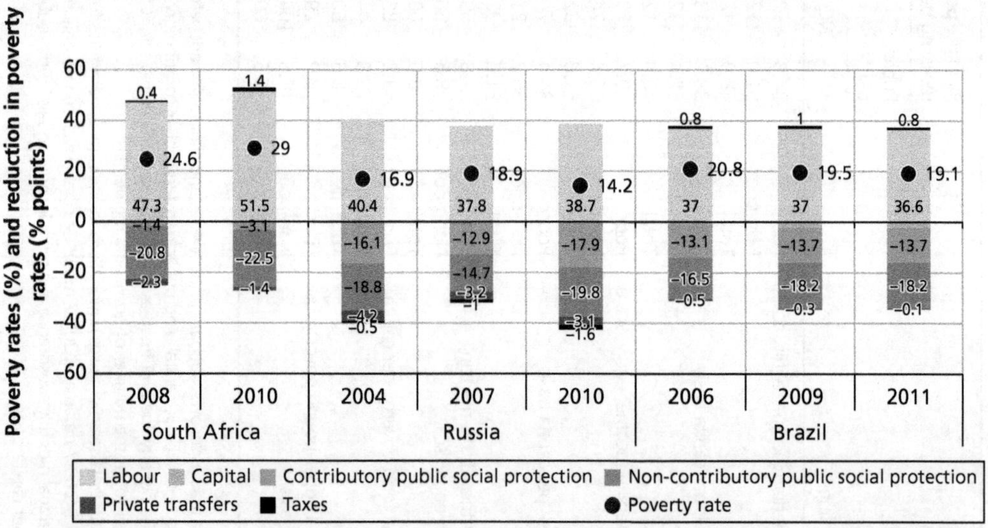

Figure 4.21 Redistribution role of social protection: effects on poverty prevention/reduction

Source: Luxembourg Income Study (LIS) (2015). LIS Cross-National Data Centre in Luxembourg. Available at www.lisdatacenter.org/, accessed 7 October 2018.

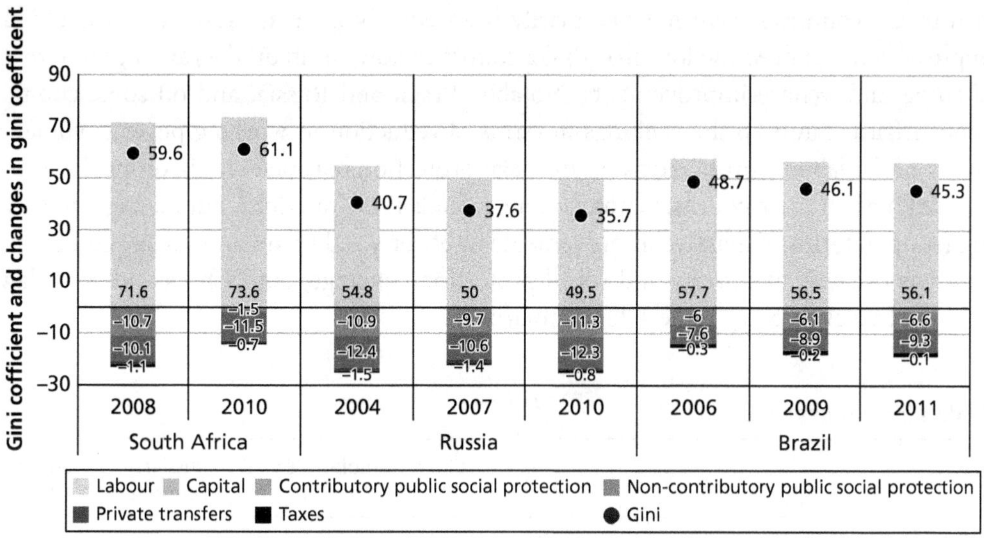

Figure 4.22 Redistribution role of social protection: effects on inequality prevention/reduction

Source: Luxembourg Income Study (LIS). 2015. LIS Cross-National Data Centre in Luxembourg. Available at http://www.lisdatacenter.org/.

non-contributory schemes).[28] In Russia, the poor are nearly 13 per cent of the population but receive less than 6 per cent of the total amount of benefit whether contributory or non-contributory.

Conclusion

BRICS are indeed very deserving of their eponymous reputation, as the stuff of development, as this chapter has attempted to show, in the key areas of economic growth and social development. But they are so collectively. Each of BRICS has not been all things to all people. Ranked by GDP growth, structural transformation of the economy, and macroeconomic drivers, examined over the past third of a century, China and India stand out as a group labelled G1 high flyers. Brazil, Russia, and South Africa rank as a group of G2 low flyers. True, Brazil and Russia with the highest incomes may have had earlier growth spurts, and settled into a low growth trajectory given to high-income countries in the past third of a century. But they do now face huge growth dilemmas.

However, in considering whether this high growth and productive transformation of the economy has been inclusive, with more jobs, better jobs, reduced poverty, more social protection, and resultantly lowered inequality, the ranking reverses. All the high

[28] The situation is similar when considering the national poverty lines. In 2010, 39.1 per cent of the population lived below the food poverty line; they received 12 per cent of the total amount of public transfers (29 per cent of transfers from non-contributory schemes).

growth G1 countries have not necessarily been equally good in terms of these social improvements. Indeed the low growth G2 countries now climb up the rankings in terms of social and welfare improvements. Notably, Brazil and Russia, and on some counts South Africa, climb up the rankings in terms of reduction in working poverty, vulnerability of the labour force, extension in social protection coverage. India drops down in the rankings on these counts. China no longer leads these rankings, but manages to stay higher up in terms of massive improvements in poverty reduction and social protection. In terms of levels of poverty and social protection coverage, both China and India lag behind other BRICS, as Table 4.20 summarizes.

Table 4.20 Synthesis table

	China	India	Brazil	Russian Federation	South Africa
1. Growth					
GDP per capita average annual growth rates, 1980–2013	1	2	3	4	5
GDP per capita annual growth rates (before the crisis)	1	3	5	2	4
GDP per capita annual growth rates (**after** the crisis)	1	2	3	4	5
Industry led (especially manufacturing), growth	1	2	3		4
Value added by sector (% GDP) Manufacturing	1	4	3	2	5
investment in human capital	2	1	3	4	5
Savings	1	2	4	3	5
Score economic growth	0.96	0.68	0.39	0.57	0.07
2. Employment					
Employment growth rate by gender and age group	4	3	1	5	2
Unemployment rate (lowest)	2	1	3	4	5
Vulnerable employment (lowest levels)	4	5	3	1	2
Vulnerable employment (highest decrease)	1	4	2	5	3
Working poverty (lowest levels)	3	5	2	1	4
Working poverty (highest decrease)	2	4	3	1	5
investment in human capital	3	5	2	1	4
Score employment	0.57	0.29	0.68	0.61	0.36
3. Social protection					
Social protection public expenditure (level)	4	5	1	2	3
Social protection public expenditure (growth 1995/2011)	1	3	5	2	4
Pension legal coverage gap (level)	1	2	1	1	1
Pension legal coverage gap (growth)	1	2	4	5	3
Pension effective coverage (level)	4	5	3	1	2
Growth in pension effective coverage	1	2	4	5	3
Unemployment legal coverage	5	3	4	1	2
Unemployment effective coverage	3	5	4	1	2
Maternity protection	4	5	3	1	2
Reach the poor (number)			2	3	1
Reach the poor (amount)			1	3	2
Score social protection	0.48	0.30	0.52	0.68	0.68

Note: Scoring method for each of the three components:
- Define the different elements (and related indicator) for each component;
- Rank countries from 1 to 5;
- Normalized score of each element from 0 to 1 (max value–country value)/(max value–min value);
- Normalized scores by component: Sum scores/number of elements in component (i).

Source: Authors' own compilation based on tabular data shown.

Does this reversal in rankings among BRICS, between growth and social improvements, betoken a dissonance between these two key embodiments of development? On reflection, yes. Neither growth, nor social improvement is a sufficient condition to carry the other. High growth in China for two decades did not lead to a significant improvement in social protection especially in rural areas, until this investment was made in the last decade. Conversely, high levels of investment in human capital, and resulting high levels of TFP, have not helped Russia or Brazil raise their growth rates, because of lack of investment in physical capital. The economic and social can leverage each other, but not without concomitant investment in each—they cannot substitute for each other.

Do BRICS afford such a chimera for development that combines both good growth and good social improvement? Not entirely, but China comes the closest.

APPENDIX 1

Brazil

THE BRAZILIAN MIRACLE (1968–73)

With efforts made to promote exports of industrial products and limit economic liberalization, real output grew at an average 10.8 per cent a year, while per capita GDP climbed an average 7.9 per cent. However, distribution of income became still more skewed as growth accelerated and the economy remained heavily dependent on imported oil. With the oil price rise of 1973 and consequent international recession, export opportunities fell away and the oil import bill rose vertiginously, plunging the external accounts once more into crisis.

THE 'LOST DECADE' (1980S TO EARLY 1990S)

By early 1982, Brazil faced a major external payments crisis, with central bank reserves having fallen sharply from the levels of the late 1970s. Export growth ended as recession in Brazil's major trade partners cut demand (Coes 1995). Brazil had experienced a 4 per cent drop in its GDP, a 211 per cent rise in inflation, and a 12 per cent decline in employment by the end of 1983. Brazil's GDP declined from $296 billion in 1982 to only $226 billion in 1985 (Galano III 1994). From the early 1980s to the early 1990s, the Gini coefficient for the per capita income distribution of the economically active population and the Gini coefficient for per capita household income have both been around 0.60 (Clements 1997). As of 1988, almost half of Brazil's population lived in households where income was lower than US$120 per month. In 1991, the World Bank reported that Brazil is the largest indebted Third World country with approximately US$111 billion of foreign debt (Galano III 1994).

STABILIZATION ATTEMPTS AND FAILURES (1985–93)

During this period, three attempts were implemented to beat inflation by price control but failed. The Cruzado Plan, implemented in 1986, enforced a sophisticated short-term standstill that maintained real income positions and abolished future indexation. However, freezing prices no longer raised eyebrows as the market was well prepared to absorb this situation (Valença 1998). With the Bresser Plan (1987) and the Summer Plan (1989), once again the government froze prices and cut zeros off the face value of the currency; promises to eliminate the budget deficit were made but not kept (Cardoso 1991; Cardoso and Goldfajn 1998).

PLAN FOR THE REAL (1994)

The main elements of the Real Plan included the introduction of a new currency (the real); an initial freeze of public sector prices; the tightening of monetary policy; and the floating of the currency, with a floor specified for its value vis-à-vis the dollar. These policies have enabled Brazil to reduce monthly inflation rates from 45 per cent during the second quarter of 1994 to an average of less than 1 per cent in 1996. The economy grew by 6 per cent in 1994, and by 4.2 and 2.9 per cent in 1995 and 1996, respectively. From 1994 to 1995, per capita labour income increased by roughly 30 per cent for the lowest four deciles of the income distribution, while the top decile's income grew by only 10 per cent. However, there was a very small decline in inequality (Clements 1997).

DEVALUATION OF THE REAL (1998–99)

Russia's 1998 default on its debt sent international investors into a panic. Investors that previously displayed confidence in Brazil's economy suddenly lost faith and expected Brazil's central bank to eventually devalue the real. Between 1996 and 1998, Brazil's reserves dropped by US$24 billion or 40 per cent. The IMF provided a US$41.5 billion loan in 1998 to help Brazil defend its currency, and in January 1999 the central bank decided to devalue the real by 8 per cent. By the end of the month, the real depreciated 66 per cent against the US dollar. During the second quarter of 1999, after a change in the exchange regime, capital outflow diminished, resulting in a slight improvement in foreign reserves from US$32.9 billion to US$40.4 billion (Evangelist and Sathe 2006).

THE LULA ERA—A MORE STABLE VERSION OF THE 'BRAZILIAN MIRACLE' (2003–)

Over the last decade, Brazil has achieved substantial progress in terms of economic and social development without aggravating external fragility and generating macroeconomic instability. GDP per capita grew by 2.85 per cent a year on average between 2004 and 2012 (ILO 2014a). In comparison with the 'Brazilian Miracle' of the 1970s, the achievements of the past decade seem to rest on sounder foundations, social security reforms. In 2003, Brazil introduced the Bolsa Família programme which is now the world's largest conditional cash transfer (CCT) programme (Sanchez-Ancochea and Mattei 2011). It consists of an unconditional transfer to the poorest families and of a conditional part that requires to be granted—that children are enrolled in school and undergo some vaccinations (Neri 2009). The nominal minimum wage almost doubled between 2007 and 2013 while price levels went up by 38 per cent (ILO 2014a). Social protection in Brazil is very extensive, especially when compared to other so-called 'emerging economies' such as China or South Africa (OECD, 2011). Brazil rapidly recovered from the Great Recession of 2008 and obtained an economic growth of over 7 per cent in 2010.

CHALLENGE FOR THE FUTURE

The annual GDP is anticipated to grow through to 2030 by only 2.6 per cent, with productivity growth at 1.8 per cent (EIU 2013). Supply-side constraints, such as a low investment-to-GDP ratio, inadequate infrastructure, and insufficient spending on workforce training and education (IMF 2012; Canuto et al. 2013) need attention if further sustainable growth is to be generated. The dynamism of domestic demand has been driven in part by household indebtedness, which poses potential problems, as episodes of credit boom may be followed by periods of deleveraging. Controlling excessive growth of credit, raising the investment-to-GDP ratio to maintain domestic demand, and reforms to improve the conditions for the operation of manufacturing sector help sustain Brazil's future development (ILO 2014a).

China

ECONOMIC REFORM (1978–)

China started to transform from command economy to market economy in 1978, after suffering from two economic downturns in the Maoist Era, the Great Leap Forward of 1958–76 (causing massive famine and reportedly the deaths of tens of millions) and the Cultural Revolution in 1966–76 (causing political chaos and greatly disrupting the economy). In that period there were large, once-and-for-all, gains in efficiency of resource allocation in agriculture, an explosive expansion of foreign trade, and accelerated absorption of foreign technology through large-scale FDI.

DECOLLECTIVIZATION OF AGRICULTURE

In 1978, peasants regained control of their land and the opportunity to raise their income by their own efforts, with greater access to markets. The relaxation of the price squeeze on agriculture and on labour movement to non-farm activity and the reversion to family farming in the reform period had an extremely favourable impact on productivity performance, which to some extent had a once-and-for-all character (Maddison 2007).

SPECIAL ENTERPRISE ZONES AND INTEGRATION INTO THE WORLD

In 1908 four coastal cities were set as Special Enterprise Zones, which were free trade areas where imported inputs and exports were duty free, where wages were very low by international standards, and where there were substantial tax holidays for new enterprises. With a five-fold devaluation of the yuan between 1980 and 1997, the volume of exports rose by 15 per cent a year from 1978 to 2006 and China's share of world exports rose from 0.8 per cent to 8 per cent. China joined the IMF and the World Bank in 1980, and the Asian Development Bank in 1986. In 1982, it was granted observer status in the General Agreement on Tariffs and Trade (GATT) and began a long battle for membership of the WTO which ended successfully in 2001 (Maddison 2007).

DECENTRALIZATION OF ECONOMIC POLICYMAKING

China adapted a strategy known as 'crossing the river by feeling stones', which encouraged local governments to undertake bold pilot experiments within the broader context of reform priorities (World Bank 2013). The 1994 Fiscal Reform further limited the ability of the central government to conduct macroeconomic or redistributive policies and brought a sharp drop in the tax/GDP ratio, which proved to be successful in protecting the growth centres along the coast and was a key element in providing continuing employment opportunities to migrant workers, leading to a sharp drop in poverty and rapidly increasing living standards (Ahmad et al. 2018).

ENCOURAGEMENT FOR ENTREPRENEURSHIP

Local and provincial governments were allowed to establish and operate various enterprises without interference from the government (Morrison 2014). Local officials and party elites who had been running non-agricultural commune activities became directors and managers of township and village industries. Although these were publicly owned, they could now be run in practice almost as if they were capitalist enterprises. Local officials and party elites earned legal opportunities for greatly increasing their income if they ran the enterprises successfully. Small-scale manufacturing production was encouraged in township and village enterprises. The expanded capitalist sector was able to recruit workers at low wages, with no job security, no social security, and without trade unions to protect their interests. In the reform period, China was able to increase employment nearly twice as fast as population because changes in demographic structure raised the proportion of working-age individuals from 54 per cent to nearly 70 per cent of the population and there were substantial increases in the activity rate of women (Maddison 2007).

STATE-OWNED ENTERPRISE REFORM

According to centrally planned output targets, by 1978 nearly three-quarters of industrial production was produced by centrally controlled state-owned enterprises (SOEs), which were often marked with poor corporate productivity and financial performance (Morrison 2014). Before the mid-1990s, SOE reform was focused on revitalization through providing incentives and increased autonomy to individual enterprises. But these measures were limited in that they neither modified corporate governance nor significantly restructured business. In the mid-1990s, for the first time, measures such as financial support, lay-offs, buy-outs, and action against corporate insolvency were implemented. Restructuring policies were accelerated by Premier Zhu Rongzhi's Three-Year Reform Plan of 1998, which focused on rehabilitating unprofitable SOEs. In 1998, the number of large-scale private companies was only 16.5 per cent compared to the total number of SOEs, but this increased six times by 2006, suggesting that they have absorbed the large number of employees laid off as a result of the SOE restructuring programme. In terms of industrial output, measured by value added and assets, the relative proportions of private and foreign companies to SOEs had also been increasing dramatically (OECD 2009b).

THE GLOBAL RECESSION (2008–09)

The global economic crisis that began in 2008 greatly affected China's economy. China's exports, imports, and FDI inflows declined, GDP growth slowed, and millions of Chinese workers reportedly lost their jobs. The Chinese government responded by implementing a US$586 billion economic stimulus package, loosening monetary policies to increase bank lending, and providing various incentives to boost domestic consumption. Such policies enabled China to effectively weather the effects of the sharp global fall in demand for Chinese products, while several of the world's leading economies experienced negative or stagnant economic growth (Morrison 2014).

CHALLENGE FOR THE FUTURE

The real GDP is anticipated to grow annually through to 2020 at 6.4 per cent, with productivity growth of 7.2 per cent (EIU 2015). The ability of China to maintain a rapidly growing economy in the long run will depend largely on the ability of the Chinese government to implement comprehensive economic reforms that more quickly hasten China's transition to a free market economy; rebalance the Chinese economy by making consumer demand, rather than exporting and fixed investment, the main engine of economic growth; boost productivity and innovation; address growing income disparities; and enhance environmental protection (Morrison 2014).

India

THE FIRST BALANCE OF PAYMENTS CRISIS (1966)

Despite government attempts to obtain a positive trade balance, India has had consistent balance of payments deficits since the 1950s. India's system of severe restrictions on international trade began in 1957 when the government experienced a balance of payments crisis (Johri and Miller 2002). However, during the 1960s, India went through what was known as the 'Three Twos'—death of two prime ministers, two harvest failures, and two wars (Tseng and Cowen 2013). The 1966 devaluation of the rupee was the result of the first major financial crisis the government faced. Following the 1966 devaluation, to stimulate exports, the government initially liberalized its trade restrictions by reducing export subsidization and import tariffs. However, the measures resulted in a backlash against economic liberalization, and quantitative restrictions and export subsidies returned, albeit at lower than pre-1966 levels (Johri and Miller 2002).

THE SECOND BALANCE OF PAYMENTS CRISIS (1991)

Partly because of the gross negligence in macroeconomic management during the second half of the 1980s, the collapse of the Soviet Union, and the surge in oil price during the Gulf War, by the end of the period (1990/91), the current account deficit was about 52 per cent of exports (3.1 per cent of GDP) and the overall fiscal deficit reached 10 per cent of GDP. Between 1988/89 and 1991/92, GPD growth fell from 10 per cent to almost nil (Tseng and Cowen 2013). In July 1991 there was a devaluation of 22 per cent. The exchange rate was unified in March 1993, with an effective devaluation of the rupee of about 50 per cent in nominal terms and 25 per cent in real terms from June 1991–March 1993 (Joshi and Little 1994).

ECONOMIC REFORM (1991)

The 1991 liberalization was an extension of earlier, albeit slower, reform efforts that had begun in the 1970s when India relaxed restrictions on imported capital goods as part of its industrialization plan (Johri and Miller 2002). Prior to the middle of 1991, private investment was not permitted in many key sectors of the economy. Since 1991, major steps in economic reform in five key areas have been taken to liberalize India's investment regime and dismantle the system of controls, including: (1) deregulation of the industrial sector, removing many licensing systems, price controls, and restrictions on companies' expansion, diversification, merger and acquisition; (2) upgrading of infrastructure with efforts to attract private sector investment to provide both financing and technical expertise; (3) reforms of exit policies to reduce labour and property market rigidities; (4) liberalization of the foreign investment regime to improve foreign participation and boost international investment; (5) agricultural reform, removing a series of restrictions such as licensing requirements, barriers to trade, and price distortion.

POST-REFORM DEVELOPMENT

On average, the Indian economy grew at 5.3 per cent per year during the first five years following the reforms, compared to 5.9 per cent during 1986–91 (Nagaraj 2006). Trade liberalization has led to an increasingly open economy; the ratio of exports and imports of goods and non-factor services to GDP rose to more than 23 per cent in 1994/95 from an average of 15 per cent in 1980s (Chopra 1995).

CHALLENGE FOR THE FUTURE

With an annual growth of real GDP anticipated to be 6.4 per cent and productivity growth anticipated to be 7.2 per cent (EIU 2015, cited in Kaye et al. 2015), *The Economist* commented in February 2015 that 'India has a rare opportunity to become the world's most dynamic big economy'. The fast-growing information technology industry will need to move up the value-added chain, while the agricultural sector, which employs nearly 50 per cent of the population, will need investment in order to reduce its reliance on monsoons. Better storage facilities for food grains and perishables, and an improved supply chain could curb consumer price inflation and improve the long-term outlook (EIU 2015).

Russian Federation

COLLAPSE OF THE SOVIET UNION (1991)

The collapse of the Soviet Union in 1991 denoted the end of the era of a command economy, in which production took place in SOEs regulated by a compulsory plan (Harrison 2002). The wage distribution was characterized by unusually low returns to education and human capital and unusually high returns to privileged economic branches and regions, such as defence and heavy industry (Gerber and Hout 2002). During the 1990s, real incomes in Russia remained two-fifths below the level of the 1980s (Harrison 2002).

'SHOCK THERAPY' REFORM FOR MARKET ECONOMY TRANSITION (1992)

In January 1992, the Yeltsin government introduced a package of 'shock therapy' reforms designed to abruptly replace the state socialist economy with market institutions and practices. The January 1992 reforms freed 90 per cent of retail prices overnight; most remaining prices followed in the ensuing months. The Central Bank of Russia's loose monetary policy spurred it on to hyperinflation. A wage-price spiral ensued. Prices increased 1,100 per cent during 1992 (Gerber and Hout 1998). An 'arrears crisis' arose and employers had to curtail output, which led to declines by 18 per cent in 1992, 12 per cent in 1993, 15 per cent in 1994, and 4 per cent in 1995. Unemployment rose from almost zero at the end of 1991 to approximately 7 per cent of the labour force by October 1995. By the end of 1994, 65 per cent of officially registered state and municipal enterprises were transferred to private ownership. However, few new private enterprises opened for business—probably due to barriers posed by criminals and corrupt officials (Åslund 1996).

FINANCIAL CRISIS (1998)

On 13 August 1998, the Russian stock, bond, and currency markets collapsed. Between January and August the stock market lost more than 75 percent of its value. On 17 August the government floated the exchange rate, devalued the rouble, defaulted on its domestic debt, halted payment on rouble-denominated debt, and declared a ninety-day moratorium on payment by commercial banks to foreign creditors. The real GDP saw a decline of 4.9 per cent in 1998 (Chiodo and Owyang 2002). It was considered that the crisis was mainly triggered by the weakness of the Russian economy and exogenous shocks such as the Asian Crisis and the drop in prices of oil and non-ferrous metal. In 1997, on average, real wages were less than half of what they had been in 1991, and only about 40 per cent of the workforce was being paid in full and on time. Tax collection was low, which kept public sector deficit at a high level. In November 1997, after the onset of the East Asian crisis, the rouble came under speculative attack. In December 1997 the prices of oil and non-ferrous metal, up to two-thirds of Russia's hard-currency earnings, began to drop (Chiodo and Owyang 2002).

THE GLOBAL RECESSION (2008–09)

The global crisis put a sudden end to the strong recovery of the Russian economy following its financial crisis of 1998. Collapsing prices of oil and other commodities resulted in a sharp turnaround in the terms of trade, which no longer supported domestic demand. Russian banks and corporations were hit by the drying-up of access to international capital markets. Related to falling oil prices and deterioration in the private capital account, depreciation of the rouble against the dollar greatly increased the burden of foreign currency corporate debt. The real GDP decreased by 6.8 per cent in 2009 (OECD 2009a).

STAGNATION (2014)

Seeing a GDP growth of 0.8 per cent in the first half of 2014, the World Bank commented in September 2014 that Russia's economy was stagnating. Sanctions against Russia limited the country's access to international capital markets and increased the cost of borrowing for households and firms. High uncertainty also triggered massive capital outflows and curtailed the willingness of businesses to invest. Consumers also adjusted to the volatile environment with lower demand as renewed pressure on the rouble and counter-sanctions restricting food imports in August translated into higher inflation. Prospects for the economy and further poverty reduction are limited. Low investment makes it less likely that plentiful well-paying jobs will be created. High inflation, moreover, will slow real income growth and hurt consumption growth, dimming the likelihood of further poverty reduction and limiting the ability of the bottom 40 per cent of the population to share in prosperity (Narayan et al. 2018).

CHALLENGE FOR THE FUTURE

The EIU forecasts Russia's average growth in real GDP as just 1.5 per cent for 2013–30. An unfavourable demographic profile, a difficult business environment, weak institutions, and over-reliance on natural resources will place strong constraints on Russia's long-term growth. Given its strong industrial tradition, Russia's chances of diversifying its economy could be good, but this prospect has receded for the moment following a sharp deterioration in political and economic relations with the West. If the forecast rate of growth over a couple of decades is achieved, it will allow some measure of catch-up with the advanced Western economies.

South Africa

POST-APARTHEID PERIOD (1994–)

Apartheid, the race-based geography and race-based policy in South Africa from 1948 to 1994 resulted in low levels of education, suppressed entrepreneurism, and spatial inequalities among the African population (Verick 2012). Apartheid in South Africa officially came to an end with the democratically held elections in 1994, leaving in its wake a population with vast inequalities across racial groups. Using a poverty line of R322 (South Africa rands at 2000 prices adjusted for provincial cost of living differences), at least 58 per cent of all South Africans and 68 per cent of the African population were in poverty in 1995, while poverty was virtually non-existent for whites (Hoogeveen and Özler 2006). During the post-apartheid period a series of economic policy packages were introduced, including Growth, Employment, and Redistribution (GEAR), the Accelerated and Shared Growth Initiative for South Africa (ASGISA), the New Growth Path, and the National Development Plan. South Africa is advancing; but it is failing to fully achieve its considerable potential (OECD 2013).

INEQUALITY, POVERTY, AND UNEMPLOYMENT IN THE POST-APARTHEID PERIOD

Over the past twenty years, South Africa has not fulfilled its promise on removing poverty, inequality, and unemployment. In 2013, South Africa's Gini coefficient, at around 0.70, was among the highest in the world (OECD 2013). Inequality among households with labour market earnings is also high, as real earnings in the bottom deciles have not risen in the post-apartheid period and have fallen markedly relative to earnings in the top deciles (Hoogeveen and Özler 2006). Inequality has increased over most of the post-apartheid period, and the poverty reduction performance has been lacklustre. Decompositions of inequality by income source show that labour income accounts for 85 per cent of inequality in 2008 and unemployment rates decrease among higher deciles. Much of that is driven by the large number of individuals with no labour income, given the high incidence of unemployment and inactivity. Just over 40 per cent of the working age population is employed. Furthermore, differences among population groups are also striking, with the unemployment rate at 28.5 per cent among Africans compared to 5.5 per cent for whites (OECD 2013).

THE GLOBAL RECESSION (2008–09)

Owing to its strong links with the global economy, South Africa has been hit hard by the Great Recession of 2008–09 (Verick 2010). The country has been in a recession since the fourth quarter of 2008 and a GDP growth of 2009 was -1.7 per cent (Verick 2012). South Africa has so far experienced a relatively weak recovery from the global recession. The impact on the labour market of the recession though was profound. Although in 2008Q4 employment peaked at almost 14. 1 million, the economy lost more than 1 million jobs, and by 2010Q3 employment had plummeted to levels last seen in 2006. Expansion of employment in the South African economy over the 2006–08 period had been completely nullified by the end of 2010 (OECD 2013).

CHALLENGE FOR THE FUTURE

The EIU expects South Africa's growth to average 4.5 per cent a year over 2013–30, with a faster growth of 5.3 per cent a year over 2021–30. South Africa faces a number of long-standing economic problems that still reflect at least in part the lengthy and harmful legacy of apartheid. One is a lack of economic dynamism: convergence towards advanced country per capita income levels has been slower than in most other emerging economies. Educational outcomes are poor on average and extremely uneven, which aggravates the excess supply of unskilled labour as well as worsening income inequality. In addition, the prospects for sustained improvements in well-being are compromised by environmental challenges, notably climate change and water stress. South Africa needs to achieve rapid, inclusive economic growth while at the same time making the transition to a low-carbon economy and managing effectively the country's scarce water resources. Tackling the key problems effectively will require continued skilful management of macroeconomic policies, as part of the process of providing helpful framework conditions for economic activity, but above all improved implementation of structural policies, with education being a particularly critical area (OECD 2013).

ACKNOWLEDGEMENTS

The authors would like to acknowledge research assistance provided by Jiaxin Zhang, Veronika Zhirnova, and Aimal Tanvir.

REFERENCES

ADB (Asian Development Bank) (2015). 'Social protection index'. Available at http://spi.adb.org/spidmz/index.jsp, accessed 5 October 2018.

Ahmad, E., Niu, M., and Xia, K. (eds) (2018). *Fiscal Underpinnings for Sustainable Development in China: Rebalancing in Guangdong*. Singapore: Springer.

Arnal, E. and Forster, M. (2010). 'Growth, employment and inequality in Brazil, China, India and South Africa: an overview', in *Tackling Inequalities in Brazil, China, India and South Africa*. Paris: OECD, 13–55.

Åslund, Anders (1996). 'Reform vs. 'Rent-Seeking' in Russia's economic transformation', *Transition* 26 (January): 12–16.

Barros, R., de Carvalho, M., Franco, S., and Mendonça, R. (2010). 'Markets, the state, and the dynamics of inequality in Brazil', in L.F. López-Calva and N. Lustig (eds) *Declining Inequality in Latin America: A Decade of Progress?* Washington, DC: Brookings Institution Press, 134–74.

Bosworth, B. and Collins, S.M. (2007). 'Accounting for growth: comparing China and India. Working Paper No. 12943. Washington, DC: National Bureau of Economic Research.

Canuto, O. and Cavallari, M. (2013). 'Monetary Policy and Macroprudential Regulation: Whither Emerging Markets.' World Bank Research Paper No. 6310, Washington, DC.

Cardoso, Eliana (1991). 'From Inertia to Megainflation: Brazil in the 1980s'. NBER Working Papers 3585. Cambridge MA: National Bureau of Economic Research.

Cardoso, Eliana and Goldfajn, Ilan (1998). 'Capital flows to Brazil – the endogeneity of capital flows', *IMF Staff Papers* 45/ 1(March): 161–202.

CEPALStat (various years). *Statistics and Indicators*. Available at http://estadisticas.cepal.org/cepalstat/WEB_CEPALSTAT/estadisticasIndicadores.asp?idioma=i, accessed 20 May 2019.

Chiodo, A.J. and Owyang, M.T. (2002). 'A case study of a currency crisis: the Russian default of 1998', *The Federal Reserve Bank of St. Louis Review* 84/6: 7–18. Available at https://doi.org/10.20955/r.84.7-18, accessed 25 May 2019.

Chopra, A., Collyns, C., Hemming, R., Chu, Woosik, Parker, K.E., Fratzscher, O. (1995). 'India: economic reform and growth'. IMF Occasional Paper 134. Washington, DC: International Monetary Fund.

Clements, Benedict (1997). 'The real plan, poverty, and income distribution in Brazil', *Finance & Development* 34/3 (September): 1–3.

Coes, Donald V. (1995). *Macroeconomic Crises, Policies, and Growth in Brazil, 1964-90* (English). World Bank Comparative Macroeconomic Studies. Washington, DC: World Bank. Available at http://documents.worldbank.org/curated/en/299611468769167111/Macroeconomic-crises-policies-and-growth-in-Brazil-1964-90, accessed 21 May 2019.

CPRC (Chronic Poverty Research Centre). (2007). 'The politics behind the non-contributory old age social pensions in Lesotho, Namibia and South Africa. Working Paper No. 83. London: CPRC.

de Vries, J.G., Erumban, A.A., Timmer, M.P., Vokoboynikov, I., and Wu, H.X. (2012). 'Deconstructing the BRICs: Structural transformation and aggregate productivity growth', *Journal of Comparative Economics* 40/2: 211–27.

DSD (Department of Social Development, South Africa), SASSA (South African Social Security Agency), and UNICEF (2012). *The South African Child Support Grant Impact Assessment: Evidence from a Survey of Children, Adolescents and Their Households*. Pretoria: UNICEF. Available at www.unicef.org/southafrica/SAF_resources_csg2012s.pdf, accessed 5 October 2018.

Durán Valverde, F., et al. (2013). *Innovations in Extending Social Insurance Coverage to Independent Workers: Experiences from Brazil, Cape Verde, Colombia, Costa Rica, Ecuador, Philippines, France and Uruguay*. Geneva: ILO.

EIU (Economist Intelligence Unit) (2015). *Prospects and Challenges on China's 'One Belt, One Road': A Risk Assessment Report*. Available at www.eiu.com/public/topical_report.aspx?campaignid=OneBeltOneRoad, accessed 24 May 2019.

European Commission (2015). *Employment, Social Affairs and Inclusion. The 2015 Pension Adequacy Report.* Available at https://ec.europa.eu/social/main.jsp?catId=738&langId=en&pubId=7828&visible=0&, accessed 20 May 2019.

Evangelist, Mike and Sathe, Valerie (2006). 'Brazil's 1998–1999 currency crisis', unpublished manuscript.

Eyal, K. and Woolard, I. (2013). 'School enrolment and the Child Support Grant: evidence from South Africa. Working Paper No. 125. Cape Town: Southern Africa Labour and Development Research Unit. Available at http://opensaldru.uct.ac.za/handle/11090/689, accessed 17 October 2018.

Fiszbein, A., and Schady, N. (2009). *Conditional Cash Transfers: Reducing Present and Future Poverty.* Washington, DC: World Bank. Available at https://openknowledge.worldbank.org/handle/10986/2597, accessed 5 October 2018.

Fultz, E. and Francis, J. (2013). *Cash Transfer Programmes, Poverty Reduction and Empowerment of Women: A Comparative Analysis. Experiences from Brazil, Chile, India, Mexico and South Africa.* Geneva, ILO. Available at www.ilo.org/wcmsp5/groups/public/—dgreports/—gender/documents/publication/wcms_233599.pdf, accessed 5 October 2018.

Galano, Anthony III (1994). 'International Monetary Fund response to the Brazilian debt crisis: whether the effects of conditionality have undermined Brazil's national sovereignty?', *Pace International Law Revue* 6/2: 323. Available at http://digitalcommons.pace.edu/pilr/vol6/iss2/4, accessed 21 May 2019.

Gerber, Theodore P. and Hout, Michael (2002). 'Labour market transition in contemporary Russia', *American Sociological Review* 67: 629–59.

Ghosh, J., Havlik, P., Urban, W., and Riberio, M.P. (2009). 'Models of BRICs' economic development and challenges for EU competitiveness'. Research Report No. 359. Vienna: Vienna Institute for International Economic Studies.

Harrison, Mark (2002). *Accounting for War: Soviet Production, Employment, and the Defence Burden.* Cambridge: Cambridge University Press.

HelpAge International (2015). 'Pension watch: social protection in older age'. Available at www.pension-watch.net/, accessed 5 October 2018.

Hoogeveen J. and Özler B. (2006). 'Not separate not equal: poverty and inequality in post apartheid South Africa, in H. Bhorat and R. Kanbur (eds) *Poverty and Policy in Post Apartheid South Africa.* Cape Town: HSRC Press, chap. 3.

ILO (International Labour Organization) (2010). *Extending Social Security to All: A Guide Through Challenges and Options.* Geneva: ILO.

ILO (International Labour Organization) (2013). 'Report II: Statistics of work, employment and labour underutilization'. Paper presented at the 19th International Conference of Labour Statisticians, Geneva: ILO. Available at www.ilo.org/wcmsp5/groups/public/—dgreports/—stat/documents/publication/wcms_220535.pdf, accessed 5 October 2018.

ILO (International Labour Organization) (2014a). *World of Work 2014: Developing with Jobs.* Geneva: ILO.

ILO (International Labour Organization) (2014b). *World Social Protection Report 2014/15: Social Protection as a Key to Recovery, Inclusive Development and Social Justice.* Geneva: ILO.

ILO (International Labour Organization) (2014c). *Maternity and Paternity at Work: Law and Practice across the World.* Geneva: ILO.

ILO (International Labour Organization) (2015a). *World Employment and Social Protection Report: The Changing Nature of Jobs*. Geneva: ILO.

ILO (International Labour Organization) (2015b). *Social Protection: Building Social Protection Floors and Comprehensive Social Security Systems*. Geneva: ILO.

ILO (International Labour Organization) (2015c). ILO social security inquiry database (ILOSSI)'. Available at www.ilo.org/dyn/ilossi/ssimain.home, accessed 5 October 2018.

ILO (International Labour Organization) (various years [a]). *Trends Econometric Models*. Available at www.ilo.org/empelm/projects/WCMS_114246/lang–en/index.htm, accessed 20 May 2019.

ILO (International Labour Organization) (various years [b] to 2014). *Global Employment Trends*. Geneva: ILO.

ILO (International Labour Organization) (various years [c] 2015 to date). *World Employment Social Outlook: Trends*. Geneva: ILO.

ILO (International Labour Organization) (various years [d]). *Social Protection Database*. Geneva: ILO. Available at www.social-protection.org/gimi/ShowTheme.action?id=10, accessed 20 May 2019.

ILO (International Labour Organization) and GIZ (Deutsche Gesellschaft für Internationale Zusammenarbeit GmbH) (2014). *Enterprise Formalization: Fact or Fiction? A Quest for Case Studies*. Geneva and Eschborn: ILO/GIZ.

IMF (International Monetary Fund) (2006). 'Asia rising: patterns of economic development and growth', *World Economic Outlook, September 2006: Financial Systems and Economic Cycles*. Washington, DC: IMF, chap. 3.

IMF (International Monetary Fund) (2012). *IMF Country Report No. 12/191. Brazil: 2012 Article IV Consultation—Staff Report; Public Information Notice on the Executive Board Discussion; and Statement by the Executive Director for Brazil*. Washington, DC: IMF.

IMF (International Monetary Fund) (various years [a]). *Government Finance Statistics*. Available at https://data.imf.org/?sk=a0867067-d23c-4ebc-ad23-d3b015045405, accessed 20 May 2019.

IMF (International Monetary Fund) (various years [b]). *World Economic Outlook, October 2013*. Available at www.imf.org/en/Publications/WEO/Issues/2016/12/31/World-Economic-Outlook-October-2013-Transition-and-Tensions-40432, accessed 20 May 2019.

ISSA (International Social Security Association) (2013). *Social Security Coverage Extension in the BRICS*. Geneva: ISSA.

ISSA (International Social Security Association) (n.d.). 'Social security country profiles'. Available at www.issa.int/en_GB/country-profiles, accessed 5 October 2018.

Johri, Devika and Miller, Mark (2002). 'Devaluation of the rupee: tale of two years: 1966 and 1991'. Working Paper 28. New Delhi: Center for Civil Society.

Joshi, Vijay and Little, Ian M.D. (1994). *India: Macroeconomics and Political Economy, 1964–1991*. Washington, DC: World Bank.

Kapsos, S. and Bourmpoula, E. (2013). 'Employment and economic class in the developing world'. Research Paper No. 6. Geneva: ILO.

Kaye, C.R., Nye, J.S. Jr, and Ayers, A. (2015). 'Working with a rising India: a joint venture for the New Century'. Task Force Report No. 73. New York: Council on Foreign Relations.

Lingam, L. and Kanchi, A. (2013). *Women's Work, Maternity and Public Policy*. Hyderabad: Tata Institute of Social Sciences.

LIS (Luxembourg Income Study) (2015). LIS Cross-National Data Centre in Luxembourg. Available at www.lisdatacenter.org/, accessed 20 May 2019.

McMillan, M.S. and Rodrik, D. (2011). 'Globalisation, structural change and productivity growth'. Working Paper No. 17143. Washington, DC: National Bureau of Economic Research.

Maddison, Angus (2007) *Chinese Economic Performance in the Long Run, 960–2030 AD*, 2nd rev. edn. Paris: OECD.

Morrison, Wayne (2014). 'China's economic rise'. CRS Report RL33534. Washington, DC: Congressional Research Service of the Library of Congress,

Nagaraj, R. (2006). *Aspects of India's Economic Growth and Reforms.* New Delhi: Academic Foundation.

Narayan, A., van der Weide, R., Cojocaru, A., Lakner, C., Redaelli, S., Mahler, D.G., et al. (2018). *Fair Progress?: Economic Mobility across Generations around the World.* Washington, DC: World Bank.

Neri, Marcelo (2009). 'Income policies, income distribution and the distribution of opportunities', in Lael Brainard and Leonardo Martinez-Diaz (eds) *Brazil as an Economic Superpower? Understanding Brazil's Changing Role in the Global Economy.* Washington, DC: Brookings Institution Press, 221–69.

OECD (Organisation for Economic Co-operation and Development) (2009a). *Economic Outlook 2009/2.* Available at www.oecd-ilibrary.org/economics/oecd-economic-outlook-volume-2009-issue-2_eco_outlook-v2009-2-en, accessed 25 May 2019.

OECD (Organisation for Economic Co-operation and Development) (2009b). *Globalisation and Emerging Economies: Brazil, Russia, India, Indonesia, China and Soth Africa.* Paris: OECD.

OECD (Organisation for Economic Co-operation and Development) (2010). 'Going for growth in Brazil, China, India, Indonesia and South Africa', in *Economic Policy Reforms 2010: Going for Growth.* Paris: OECD, chap. 7.

OECD (Organisation for Economic Co-operation and Development) (2011). *Economic Surverys: Brazil 2011.* Paris: OECD.

OECD (Organisation for Economic Co-operation and Development) (2013). *Economic Surveys: South Africa 2013.* Paris: OECD.

O'Neil, J. (2001). 'Building better global economic BRICS'. Global Economics Paper No. 86. London: Goldman Sachs Economic Research Group.

Patel, L., Hochfeld, T., Moodley, J., and Mutwali, R. (2012). *The Gender Dynamics and Impact of the Child Support Grant in Doornkop, Soweto.* Johannesburg: University of Johannesburg, Centre for Social Development in America. Available at www.childwatch.uio.no/publications/research-reports/gender%20dynamics%20and%20child%20support.pdf, accessed 5 October 2018.

Patel, L., Hochfeld, T., and Moodley, J. (2013). 'Gender and child sensitive social protection in South Africa', *Development Southern Africa* 30/1: 69–83.

Ringen, S., and Ngok, K. (2013). 'What kind of welfare state is emerging in China?' Working Paper No. 2013-2. Geneva: United Nations Research Institute for Social Development.

Sánchez-Ancochea, Diego and Mattei, Lauro (2011). 'Bolsa Família, poverty and inequality: political and economic effects in the short and long run', *Global Social Policy.* Available at https://doi.org/10.1177/1468018111421297, accessed 22 May 2019.

SSA (Social Security Administration of the United States) (1989). *Social Security Programs throughout the World, 1989.* Washington, DC: SSA.

SSA (Social Security Administration of the United States) (1999). *Social Security Programs throughout the World, 1999.* Washington, DC: SSA.

SSA (Social Security Administration of the United States) and ISSA (International Social Security Association) (2005). *Social Security Programs throughout the World: Asia and the Pacific, 2004.* Washington, DC and Geneva: SSA/ISSA.

SSA (Social Security Administration of the United States) and ISSA (International Social Security Association) (2013). *Social Security Programs throughout the World: Asia and the Pacific, 2012.* Washington, DC and Geneva: SSA/ISSA.

SSA (Social Security Administration of the United States) and ISSA (International Social Security Association) (2014a). *Social Security Programs throughout the World: Africa, 2013.* Washington, DC and Geneva: SSA/ISSA.

SSA (Social Security Administration of the United States) and ISSA (International Social Security Association) (2014b). *Social Security Programs throughout the World: The Americas, 2013.* Washington, DC and Geneva: SSA/ISSA.

SSA (Social Security Administration of the United States) and ISSA (International Social Security Association) (2014c). *Social Security Programs throughout the World: Europe, 2014.* Washington, DC and Geneva: SSA/ISSA.

Tseng, W. and Cowen, D. (2013). *India's and China's Recent Experience with Reform and Growth.* London and Washington, DC: Palgrave Macmillan and IMF.

UN Department of Economic and Social Affairs (2015). *World Population Ageing 2015 Report.* Available at www.un.org/en/development/desa/population/publications/pdf/ageing/WPA2015_Report.pdf, accessed 20 May 2019.

UNDP (UN Development Programme) (various years). *Human Development Reports.* Available at http://hdr.undp.org/en/global-reports, accessed 20 May 2019.

Valença, Márcio Moraes (1998). 'The lost decade and the Brazilian Government's response in the 1990s', *Journal of Developing Areas* 33/Fall: 1–52.

Vandemoortele, M., Bird, K., Du Toit, A., Liu, M., Sen, K., and Soares, F.V. (2013). 'Building blocks for equitable growth: lessons from the BRICS'. Working Paper No. 365. London: Overseas Development Institute.

Verick, S. (2010). 'Unravelling the impact of the global financial crisis on the South African labour market'. Employment Working Papers, 68. Geneva: ILO.

Verick, S. (2012). 'High unemployment yet few small firms – the role of centralized bargaining in South Africa'. Department of Economics Working Paper No. 22, Stellenbosch University.

Wilson, D. and Purushothaman, R. (2003). 'Dreaming with BRICS: the path to 2050'. Global Economics Paper No. 99. London: Goldman Sachs Economic Research Group.

World Bank (2000). *EdStats: Barro-Lee Dataset of Educational Statistics.* Available at https://datatopics.worldbank.org/education/wProjection/bpopmodel, accessed 20 May 2019.

World Bank (2013). *East Asia and Pacific Economic Update, October 2013: Rebuilding Buffers and Reinvigourating Growth.* Washington, DC: World Bank.

World Bank (various years). *World Development Indicators*. Available at http://databank.worldbank.org/data/reports.aspx?source=world-development-indicators, accessed 5 October 2018.

Zhang, J. and Mahmood, M. (2007). *Employment, Decent Work and Poverty Reduction in Urban China*. Geneva: International Labour Office. Available at www.ilo.org/wcmsp5/groups/public/—dgreports/—integration/documents/publication/wcms_094089.pdf, accessed 5 October 2018.

Zhu, Y. (2013). 'Current approaches to social protection in China', in J. Midgley and D. Piachaud (eds) *Social Protection, Economic Growth and Social Change*. Cheltenham: Edward Elgar, 44–58.

5 Development banks in BRICS

With a special focus on the Brazilian case

John Weiss

Introduction

Notwithstanding the heterogeneity in economic structure and experience in BRICS, one aspect of commonality appears to be the continued role of publicly owned banks and in particular the important role of a subset of these—development banks. Development banks are those with a mandate to pursue developmental, as opposed to, but often in conjunction with, strictly commercial goals. This mandate can be either specific (for example lending to a particular sector or category of borrower) or general in relation to the promotion of 'development', in either economic or social terms.

There is a long tradition in development studies which argues that at the early stage of development, state ownership of banks can be an important catalyst in mobilizing and allocating savings (Gerschenkron 1962). Experiences both in Europe and North America in the nineteenth century and in Japan and Korea in the early post-1945 period provided evidence in support of this position. In the era of privatizations and a shrinking state in the 1980s this view was challenged, in large part because of the fiscal drain poorly performing state banks were creating. Since then a research literature based on cross-country studies has suggested that state ownership of a banking sector is negatively associated with economic growth and financial depth (la Porta et al. 2002).

The evidence on this negative link is less robust than is sometimes stated and subsequent analyses have found conflicting results, although there is little evidence that state-owned banks positively support financial development in lower middle and low-income economies. Part of the problem is that in such economies weak institutional development is associated with high state ownership, low financial depth and slower growth. Isolating the impact of state ownership alone is difficult and the negative association with growth may be caused by the association with poor institutions, which are the key causal factor. Reworking the original analysis by La Porta et al. (2002) shows that once differences between countries in institutional and financial development are allowed for, universal generalizations on the negative effects of public bank ownership do not hold and that the negative impact is only in countries with very poorly developed financial sectors and very weak institutions (Körner and Schnabel 2011).

John Weiss, *Development banks in BRICS: With a special focus on the Brazilian case* In: *Handbook of BRICS and Emerging Economies*. Edited by: P.B. Anand, Shailaja Fennell, and Flavio Comim, Oxford University Press (2021).
DOI: 10.1093/oso/9780198827535.003.0005

In BRICS, development banks continue to play an important role with at least two—Banco Nacional de Desenvolvimento Econômico e Social (BNDES) from Brazil and the China Development Bank—referred to frequently in the international literature as major financial institutions with an increasingly global outlook. This chapter explores the role of such banks in BRICS in the context of contemporary debates on their role in economic development. A second section provides some statistics on the nature and scale of development banks drawing on a recent detailed survey which reveals a very wide range of characteristics. A third section looks at the economic theory that rationalizes the role of these banks and highlights how they can be used to meet development objectives—investing in and supporting strategic activities, funding small and medium-sized enterprises (SMEs) and small borrowers, linking with and helping to develop financial intermediaries, as well as boosting demand at critical points in the economic cycle. A fourth section reviews the case of BNDES, the Brazilian bank, which has received considerable attention in the literature. A fifth section concludes.

Operations and characteristics of development banks

State-owned banks in general were estimated to have around 22 per cent of all banking system assets in developing countries in 2009. This is a very large reduction relative to 1970 where the comparable figure is put at 67 per cent. This large reduction is due to the wave of privatizations in the 1980s and 1990s. However, the impact of privatization has been very uneven and in a number of large economies including China and India state-owned banks still dominate, taking over half the assets of the banking system in 2010. In others including Brazil and the Russian Federation, as well as Argentina, Indonesia, Korea, Poland, and Turkey they play a significant role accounting for between 20 per cent and 50 per cent (World Bank 2013: 103–4).[1] These figures do not separate development banks from state-owned commercial banks and other state-owned financial institutions. However, development banks tend to be some of the largest state-owned banks and some, such as BNDES and the China Development Bank, are very large.

There is considerable heterogeneity within the category of national development banks, which is revealed by the survey reported in de Luna-Martinez and Vicente (2012). This covered ninety banks in sixty-one countries with data usually referring to 2009.[2] The survey results indicate most development banks are government owned, with many operating through intermediaries. Most target SMEs although they also lend to large public and private sector firms. Roughly half still offer subsidized lending, but

[1] The definition of state-owned banks used in this source is not clear.

[2] Regional coverage is judged to be fairly representative apart from the Middle East and North Africa, where only banks from Egypt and Oman responded to the survey. Banks in a few high-income economies in Europe, as well as Canada, responded.

overall their financial results are not markedly out of line with their national financial sectors. Most are regulated and supervised in the same way as commercial banks.

Financial outcomes need not be a satisfactory indicator of development bank performance because of their non-commercial mandate. However, as noted above, state-owned banks in general have been criticized for their poor financial performance relative to private sector banks.[3] In the case of banks covered in the survey financial performance is uneven, but less weak than is sometimes implied in discussions of development banks. A minority of banks (15 per cent) have serious problems with non-performing loans (NPLs) which are more than 30 per cent of the portfolio. However a majority (55 per cent) have relatively low NPL ratios of below 5 per cent.[4] Second tier banks showed significantly lower NPL ratios with all of these having a ratio below 5 per cent, while only around a quarter (27 per cent) of first tier banks had ratios below 5 per cent.[5] This could imply greater care in credit allocation among the second tier group, but also that as expected first tier banks took greater risks on 'strategic' projects. However, the NPL figures were not high enough to cause widespread financial losses, since only 14 per cent of the banks reported financial losses.

BANKS FROM BRICS

In terms of BRICS, eight development banks are covered in the survey—three from Brazil (BNDES and two regional banks Banco Da Amazonia (BASA) and Banco Do Nordeste DO Brasil); three from India (National Bank for Agriculture and Rural Development (NABARD), Small Industries Development Bank of India, Export-Import Bank of India); the Development Bank of South Africa and the China Development Bank. Of these eight banks by far the largest are the China Development Bank and BNDES. All are government owned, although the two regional banks from Brazil have 10 per cent private capital, and four report their lending is guaranteed by their government. None of the larger banks takes deposits from the public, raises funds through the capital market, and receives funds from governments or international agencies. Six out of the eight lend through other financial institutions and some of these also lend directly to borrowers. The regional banks from Brazil and the small industry bank from India have large branch networks. All but the Development Bank of South Africa report that they lend to SMEs and all but the banks in India and the Development Bank of South Africa report that they lend to individuals and households. All respondents report lending long term with maximum periods ranging from ten to twenty years and some banks also lend

[3] Demirguc-Kunt and Huizinga (1999), for example, provide evidence on relative profitability. De la Torre et al. (2007: 17) cite evidence on macro-costs of development bank recapitalization that came to 6 per cent of GDP in Brazil and as much as 15 per cent in Turkey.

[4] Definitions of NPLs differ across countries so comparative statistics need to be used with caution.

[5] First tier banks lend directly to borrowers, while second tier banks lend through financial intermediaries.

for working capital. The Development Bank of South Africa and NABARD do not finance start-up companies. All report positive returns on assets and equity and NPLs are always below 5 per cent and only close to this in the case of Development Bank of South Africa (4.9 per cent) and Banco Do Nordeste DO Brasil (3.5 per cent). All report that they are subject to the same financial regulations, including capital adequacy ratios, as commercial banks. Table 5.1 summarizes information on the development banks from BRICs from the survey.

Role of development banks

Development banks are typically rationalized in terms of filling gaps in the financial market that commercial banks whether privately or publicly owned cannot fill. For this reason they have been given prominence in recent discussions of industrial policy. The three key roles that have figured in recent policy discussions are:

- lending to or investing long term in strategic or innovative high-risk activities with external benefits;
- contributing to financial inclusion objectives by lending (and possibly providing other financial services) to disadvantaged or low-income borrowers;
- lending counter-cyclically to boost demand in recessions.

The theory underlying the first of these points is illustrated graphically in Figure 5.1. The right-hand segment I shows the demand and supply of loanable funds relating the market interest rate R to the demand Dl and Sl in the market. Demand is based on the marginal productivity of the investment the funds will finance and Dl reflects the private returns to the borrowers. It is downward sloping as more funds are demanded at lower interest rates and the profit maximizing investor will invest up to the point at which R equals the expected return on additional investment. The supply curve for loanable funds is shown as rising with the interest rate up to interest rate R* at which point it bends backwards with the supply of funds falling at rates beyond R*.

The rationale for this backwards bending supply curve stems from the analysis of an imperfect credit market under uncertainty (Stiglitz and Weiss 1981).The supply offer from banks will be based on expected returns from a loan portfolio which is the product of the interest charged and the probability of repayment aggregated over all borrowers. The probability of repayment is likely to be negatively associated with the interest rate due to 'adverse selection' (as the riskier borrowers accept loans at high interest rates) and 'incentive effects' (any individual borrower will tend to make the project more risky to generate a sufficiently high return to pay the higher interest rate). This relation is shown in the left-hand segment II, which has the expected return on loans on the horizontal axis. Beyond R* the increase in the probability of default due to the increased riskiness of the loans outweighs the impact of a high R on expected returns. Hence due to uncertainty in a competitive financial market banks would set R* as the interest rate and not

Table 5.1 Development banks from BRICS

Name of your institution	Development Bank of Southern Africa	Banco Nacional de Desenvolvim ento Econômico e Social (BNDES)	Banco Da Amazonia (BASA)	Banco Do Nordeste DO Brasil	Small Industries Development Bank of India	Export-Import Bank of India (Exim Bank)	National Bank for Agriculture and Rural Development	China Development Bank
Country	South Africa	Brazil	Brazil	Brazil	India	India	India	China People's Rep. of
Total assets US$ mill	6,108	22,2369	1,961	27,957	7,690	10,723	23,194	667,000
Gross loan portfolio $ mill	4,559	163,151	750	19,768	6,864	8,769	19,401	544,493
Number of branches	0	4	210	185	100	17	28	np
Number of staff	680	2,398	2,977	15,178	1,049	232	4,886	6,711
Deposits from the public	no	no	yes	yes	yes	yes	no	no
External borrowing	yes	yes	no	yes	yes	yes	yes	yes
Government guarantees	yes	yes	np	np	yes	no	no	yes
Retailing lending	no	no	np	yes	yes	yes	no	np
Lending for start-ups	no	yes	yes	yes	yes	yes	no	yes
Lending to SMEs	no	yes	yes	yes	yes	yes	yes	yes
Lending working capital	no	np	np	np	yes	yes	yes	yes
Return on Assets %	2.3	2	4.0a	3.4a	3.1	1.1	1.7	0.8
Return on Equity %	5.5	25.5	12.0a	23.8	6.7	12.2	18.9	8.8
NPLs %	4.9	0.2	np	3.5	0.1	0.2	0.3	0.9
Prudential regulation as for commercial banks	no	yes	yes	yes	no	yes	no	yes

Notes: np = data not provided.
a = data for 2008; all other data for 2009.

Source: World Bank Global Financial Development Report website. Available at www.worldbank.org/en/publications/gfdr, accessed 6 December 2018.

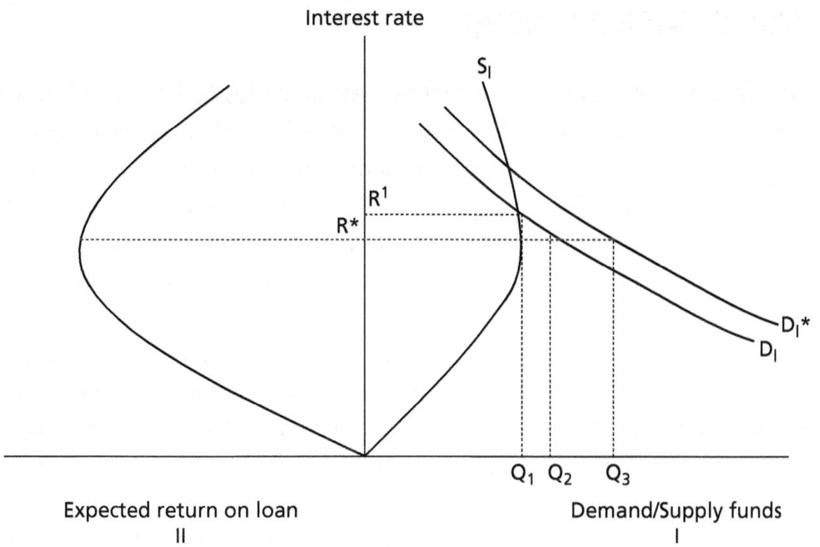

Figure 5.1 Credit market

Source: Author's work.

the market-clearing rate of R^1. There will be an unsatisfied private demand for funds of Q^2Q^1due to the banks' attitude towards risk.

If positive externalities from investment are introduced into the analysis there will be a new demand curve Dl*, which reflects the marginal economic productivity of investment. At an interest rate of R* there will be a second unsatisfied economic demand for funds Q^3Q^2 reflecting the fact that externalities by definition are not taken into account in the borrowing decisions of investors.[6] In total therefore left to themselves commercial banks will undersupply the credit market by the sum of these two credit gaps or the distance Q^3Q^1.

In practice it is not possible to isolate these two gaps but they provide a rationale for a development bank to lend to both high-risk but high-return projects, and to projects which benefit not just the investor, but others in the economy. External benefits are typically innovation and knowledge spillovers—which the innovator or pioneer does not capture in monetary charges—and the benefits from various forms of physical infrastructure, like roads or water systems, which have public good characteristics, so private providers cannot charge fully for these benefits. In principle, it is possible to incorporate the other two objectives of outreach to target groups and counter-cyclical lending into this framework by treating them as a form of external benefit which is incorporated into Dl*.

[6] Dl reflects ex ante perceptions of returns by investors while Dl* can be interpreted as probability weighted outcomes. In theory the optimal level of investment will be determined by the intersection between Dl* and the supply of funds from savers, so the marginal economic productivity of investment equals the social time preference cost of saving.

HIGH-RISK/LONG-TERM LENDING

The role of development banks in stimulating new activities in low- and lower middle-income countries has been stressed in recent discussions of industrial policy (Rodrik 2007; Hausmann et al. 2008). The argument is that innovation creates external benefits as followers can learn from the first-movers and this innovation justifies support and a subsidy, in the sense of a loan at an interest rate that does not reflect the risks involved. By pooling their risk and investing government funds across a wide portfolio development banks can afford to fund some loss-making projects, provided successes outweigh failures. This is an illustration of a development bank both ignoring risks that would dissuade a commercial bank and at the same time supporting an externality-generating activity. Furthermore, as part of a wider industrial policy, this approach suggests that development banks should take a proactive not passive role. This implies researching market opportunities, taking an equity stake in projects, helping to initiate a dialogue between the government and prospective investors, and pointing out to the government bottlenecks to investment that need to be addressed.[7] The more established development banks such as BNDES and Kreditanstalt fur Wiederaufbau [Reconstruction Credit Institute] (KfW) already play an 'intelligence role' as a guide to policymakers in Brazil and Germany, respectively (Crespi et al. 2014: 201–2).

The alternative means of addressing the risk issue is for a development bank not to lend directly but to provide funding to or guarantee lending by other institutions in a second tier role. This has the advantage of drawing on the credit assessment skills and branch networks of the intermediary, but the disadvantage that it leaves final decisions on who receives the funds to the intermediary. Where the aim is to reach a large number of borrowers and the development bank does not have a large branch network, working on a second tier basis seems inevitable. That guarantees have become a popular tool for supporting risk and best practice advice on how to apply these suggests that where private financial intermediary institutions are the recipient, development banks should not offer too high a guarantee coverage ratio of a loan portfolio (for example, no more than 80 per cent of a portfolio of loans to SMEs) to give the intermediary adequate incentive to apply a sound loan assessment. In addition, the guarantee should be priced so that the charge to the intermediary is high enough to ensure the financial viability of the guarantee fund so that it does not become a drain on the development bank's budget, but low enough to attract participation from intermediaries and ultimate borrowers. The counter-argument to these positive roles for development banks is that as these banks have access to relatively low cost government funding a large development bank

[7] For example, in relation to their proposals for industrial policy in South Africa, Hausmann et al. (2008: 11) discuss development banks as 'sources of ideas about high return activities and about the obstacles that need to be addressed to increase chances of success of projects that attempt to realize those ideas. This is particularly useful for strategic projects where the relevant actors will not come knocking at your door'.

presence risks blocking the emergence of a more efficient system of private sector financial intermediation.

FINANCIAL INCLUSION

In theory, due to the market failure caused by lack of information on the part of banks illustrated in Figure 5.1, at interest rate R* there will be some potential borrowers who are indistinguishable from those who receive credit, who could afford to repay at R*, but who do not receive funds. Access to finance has been cited widely as a key constraint on firms in low- and middle-income countries (Ayyagari et al. 2008) and exclusion from financial services is also seen as a major barrier to poverty reduction. Development bank lending is one means of addressing this lack of inclusion. As noted, part of the mandate of many development banks is lending targeted at small firms who would otherwise have difficulty in accessing finance either because of a perceived high risk, a lack of credit history, or lack of collateral. However, the mandate can also be extended to excluded low- income households who do not receive financial services, like savings accounts and insurance, because of the high cost (for example due to the small size of individual transactions or the remoteness of their locations). Development banks can be used to address both these client groups of small firms and poor households.

Microfinance has emerged as a segment of the financial sector geared towards small borrower clients. Microfinance can be delivered by different types of institution, such as non-governmental organizations (NGOs), cooperatives, regulated non-bank financial institutions, and commercial microfinance banks. In addition lending can be on a group or individual basis. In principle a development bank can also offer a microfinance lending window, as well as providing a range of financial services such as deposit and current accounts for small low-income savers. Microfinance is a specialist operation which has proved highly profitable in commercial terms in many places, and development banks deciding to move into this area would need to develop specialist skills. How far it has actually succeeded in reducing poverty among borrowers is the subject of considerable debate, in part because of the difficulty of assessing its true impact.[8]

COUNTER-CYCLICAL LENDING

It has been suggested that since the global financial crisis of 2008–09, there has been a tendency for private sector banks to become less risk averse in the upturn of an economic cycle and more risk averse in the downturn; if valid this means that commercial banks can exacerbate the economic cycle. The recent financial crisis has stimulated interest in the role of state-owned banks, including development banks, in counteracting this

[8] See for example ECG (2010).

tendency (World Bank 2013). Many governments injected capital into their state-owned banks to fill the gap in the credit market left by commercial banks. In some countries this role was taken on by development banks.[9]

Definitive assessments of this type of macro-intervention are not yet available. Part of the difficulty is that the three different roles for development banks highlighted here are potentially contradictory. To lend to high-risk activities or to target special groups of borrowers requires a specialist focus to identify suitable clients who would not be eligible for commercial bank funding. On the other hand, the counter-cyclical role is principally about demand stimulation in the aggregate and requires lending to clients, many (if not most) of whom are the recipients of commercial bank loans. Here the gap that is to be filled is credit in the aggregate not in relation to any specific niche, since lending to niches will not by definition have a significant macro impact.

RISK OF MARKET DISTORTION

The counter-argument to these positive roles for development banks is that as these banks have access to relatively low-cost government funding a large development bank presence risks blocking the emergence of a more efficient system of private sector financial intermediation. In addition, where a significant capital injection to a development bank occurs to support counter-cyclical lending, there is the risk that it is used to support lending expansion beyond the point in the economic cycle where counter-cyclical loans are needed. As commercial bank clients are targeted in counter-cyclical lending there is the risk of the original goal of a development bank becoming blurred with this expansion and of it retaining these clients and moving into more commercially focused activity.[10] The importance of the counter-cyclical role will vary between economies depending on the size of state financial institutions and how far the central bank can encourage commercial banks to lend to stimulate demand, for example through adjustments to the base rate or through direction or 'administrative guidance'. It is likely to be more of a significant role in high-income and upper middle-income emerging economies than for poorer countries.

BNDES Brazil: the model development bank?

BNDES combines many of the features of a development bank highlighted in the previous section and due to its size and influence in Brazil is arguably the most

[9] In Brazil BNDES expanded credit by 70 per cent in real terms from September 2008 to December 2011 and offered credit at rates 7.5 percentage points below the market rate (World Bank 2014).

[10] One suggestion to counter this is for the capital injection to be on terms that require it to be repaid within a period related to the repayment of loans granted during the downturn (Gutierrez et al. 2011:10).

influential development bank in terms of its national impact. In terms of assets it is the third largest development bank after the China Development Bank and KfW of Germany. The bank has always acted as a 'policy bank', as well as with aspects of a 'knowledge bank' and its role and responsibilities have changed in line with changing government objectives and priorities (Tavares de Aruajo 2013). It was established in 1952 specifically to channel funds from US Aid to infrastructure projects, with an initial focus on energy and transport and the construction of a new capital, Brasilia. From the 1970s it started to lend to manufacturing on a large scale in support of the import substitution programme set out in the Second National Development Plan. This meant that—due to the emphasis until then on infrastructure—until the mid-1960s annual funding allocation had shifted from around 90 per cent to the public sector to around 20 per cent by the late 1970s as funds were directed at large private sector firms in manufacturing (Hermann 2010: 196).

In 1982 its mandate was broadened to encompass social goals and an S was added to the acronym of the bank (it had previously been BNDE) to reflect this. An external debt crisis with associated tight fiscal and monetary policy in the 1980s limited the bank's lending activity, and real disbursements fell by 64 per cent between 1979 and 1990 (Hermann 2010: 96). In 1988 a major change was introduced in its funding base with the creation of a Workers Assistance Fund (FAT) financed by a payroll levy on all enterprises with the stipulation that at least 40 per cent of the annual revenue would go to BNDES investments in employment and income generating projects. As discussed below this remains an important source of funding today.

The 1990s saw major moves towards economic liberalization principally under the presidencies of Collor (1990–92) and Cardoso (1995–2002) with a key emphasis on privatization and export growth, and BNDES activity was adjusted to reflect this. Between 1991 and 2001 the cumulative value of privatizations was as much as US$103 billion and the bank played a key role in financing both the restructuring of state enterprises in preparation for their sale and their acquisition by new owners (Hermann 2010: 199). In relation to exports in 1991 the bank began to provide suppliers' credits for capital goods sales to countries in the region and this programme was expanded in 1997 and renamed BNDES-EXIM. Export–import finance rose from around 7 per cent of total disbursements in the mid-1990s to 28 per cent in 2004–06 (Hermann 2010: 201).

The period post-2003 under the presidencies of first Lula da Silva (2003–10) and then Dilma has seen a shift of emphasis with programmes of 'renewed developmentalism' (Hochstetler and Montero 2013). The renewed emphasis on industrial policy and technological change, as well as a more generally interventionist view of policy, saw an enhanced role for BNDES and a doubling of its disbursements as a share of GDP between 2003 and 2010 (Tavares de Aruajo 2013: 10). Three objectives were central to this expanded role. The first was support for the manufacturing sector as part of the new industrial polices set out in three plans starting with the Industrial, Technological and Foreign Trade Policy (PITCE) 2004–07. This support included direct loans to industry, as well as loans for technological innovation, investment in company equity through the BNDES equity arm, and funding for SMEs through the BNDES card.[11] Over 2006–10, of the loans to the productive sector roughly one-third went to plan priority sectors (Ferraz et al. 2013: 151) and lending to the manufacturing industry averaged around 45 per cent of total disbursements over 2004–10 (Tavares de Aruajo 2013: 12).

The second expanded goal was to support the internationalization of the economy. This involved a considerable expansion of the existing trade finance programmes, including credit lines to foreign countries linked to purchases from Brazilian firms and support for foreign investment by Brazilian firms. Export financing rose from US$3.9 billion in 2002 to $11.3 billion in 2010 (which was over 10 per cent of the value of total exports). The bank's statutes were changed to allow support for foreign investment although its initial impact was limited and by 2013 only nineteen such operations, chiefly for overseas acquisitions, had been approved (Tavares de Aruajo 2013: 8).

The third new role was counter-cyclical demand management in the face of the global downturn of 2008–09 and a weakening of domestic investment activity. The key mechanisms were the Investment Maintenance Programme (PSI) and extraordinary programmes for BNDES to support working capital needs.[12] The scale of extra funding made available to BNDES to fund these activities was very large as BNDES expanded credit by 70 per cent in real terms from September 2008 to December 2011. The increase in BNDES disbursements between 2008 and the peak in 2010 was as much as 2.7 per cent of GDP (Tavares de Aruajo 2013: 10).

Since the early 1950s BNDES has been an important source of long-term, low-cost credit whose magnitude has grown over time. However, its relative importance as a source of credit has fluctuated with changes in macroeconomic conditions and policy objectives. For example, its share of capital formation disbursements was around 3 per cent in the mid-1960s, rising to nearly 9 per cent by the later 1970s and falling back to 3 per cent again by 1989. The 'renewed developmentalism' of more recent years saw this share rise to 28 per cent in 2004–06 (Hermann 2010: tab. 5.2). The long-term nature of this funding has been particularly significant, given the focus of commercial banks on the short-term end of the market and in 2011 BNDES provided as much as 72 per cent of all loans with a maturity of three years or more (Colby 2013).

[11] Through BNDES the government launched a new credit line, Cartão, aimed at supplying credit to SMEs while avoiding bureaucratic delays and at the same time encouraging domestic linkages. The credit line is distributed via VISA cards issued by BNDES and by participating commercial banks acting on its behalf. The credit must be spent on approved products (machinery, vehicles, raw materials, and components) supplied by firms registered with BNDES and registration requires a minimum national content of 60 per cent. Loans are for a maximum of four years and are at an interest rate based on the rate for government bonds. Eligible borrowers must be below a minimum size of turnover. The main advantage is seen as speed of processing, since borrowers do not need to undergo credit analysis for each operation (ILO 2011).

[12] Ferraz et al. (2013) explain the different programmes.

Table 5.2 Sources of funding for BNDES 2001–14 (%)

Funding source	2001	2005	2009	2012	2014
National treasury	6	13	37	52	54
FAT/PIA-Pasep	69	70	40	27	26
International loans	18	10	4	3	8
Others	7	7	19	17	12

Source: Tavares de Araujo (2013: graph 8); BNDES (2014).

Real interest rates in Brazil have been high by the standards of other emerging economies principally it appears due to the low domestic savings rate.[13] Commercial banks operate with high interest rate spreads and generate high profits from shorter-term lending. The provision of low-cost credit channelled through BNDES and other development institutions has been the main policy response to this. BNDES is funded by a combination of loans from the National Treasury, compulsory transfers from the Workers Assistance Fund (FAT and PIS-Pasep), its retained earnings (principally from its equity holdings in private companies), international loans, and its issuance of bonds. Historically the compulsory transfers financed by payroll taxes on enterprises have been the most significant source of funding providing 69 per cent of total funds in 2001. Their relative importance fell after 2008 with the major expansion of government funding for the counter-cyclical lending, so that their share in funding was 27 per cent in 2012, when more than half of funding came from the National Treasury; see Table 5.2.

There has been a relatively large subsidy in BNDES lending, since it receives funds from the treasury and the compulsory savings schemes FAT and PIS-Pasep at the long-term interest rate (TJLP) set by the National Monetary Council and always below the government overnight rate for commercial banks (the SELIC). Historically the gap between the two rates has been high although it has come down in recent years as inflationary pressures have been reduced. In 1995 the gap was around 15 percentage points; although it had come down to about 7 percentage points at the end of 2015 this remains a relatively wide margin. The subsidy has been passed on directly to borrowers since the bank has operated with a very low margin estimated at only 1.4 per cent on average on its loans 1996–2009. This margin is well below that charged by commercial banks with some operating with an average margin of around 10 per cent and one with a margin of 15 per cent (Lazzarini et al. 2011: tab. X).

In addition to its financing role BNDES has at times been active in the design and implementation of economic policy. For example, BNDES (then BNDE) played a key coordinating role in the implementation of the first plan with major targets for industrialization, Plan de Metas (1956–61) (Tavares de Aruajo 2013). Its staff produced studies

[13] Segura Ubiergo (2012) examines the causes of high domestic rates of interest in Brazil. He finds these to be 2 percentage points above what would be expected allowing for as many explanatory factors as possible.

that anticipated and possibly influenced later policies, for example on the need for technological upgrading and on the potential for foreign investment by domestic firms (Hochstetler and Montero 2013). Similarly technical inputs from bank staff assisted the preparation of the privatization programme in the 1990s and subsequent national plans such as the Plan Brasil Mayor of the Dilma Rouseff administration. BNDES has ex officio seats on various ministerial-level committees that provide inputs to the design of economic policy (Crespi et al. 2014: 201–2).

With varying emphases at different times BNDES has addressed all three of the idealized roles identified for a development bank and has done so while meeting relatively strict performance targets in terms of its own commercial viability. It had the highest return on equity of the development banks reported in Table 5.1, while passing on most of the subsidy component of the cost of its funds to the final borrower.[14] It has been able to achieve this by an efficient lending operation—its cost to income ratio 1996–2009 was shown to be the lowest of any major bank in Brazil—and by generating income through investments in company equity and in government bonds (Lazzarini et al. 2011).[15] Its staff are recognized for their professionalism and objectivity in dealing with loan applications and there is little evidence of politically connected lending leading to a weakening loan portfolio and undermining the financial position of the bank.

It has without doubt been a major force in the economy, although it is not without its critics. The most profound objection suggests the existence of a large state-owned bank with access to low-cost funds has distorted the financial market in Brazil and blocked the emergence of private financial institutions willing to lend long term (Cull 2013; World Bank 2014). This is a counterfactual argument which implies there would have been an equivalent flow of credit available from private suppliers. There is no empirical evidence in direct support of this assertion and given the high profits and interest spreads in commercial banking in Brazil the counter-argument is that for most of the past fifty years commercial banks would probably have chosen to focus on the highly profitable short-term segment of the market and on relatively high yield safe assets like government bonds, although this may have changed to some extent with the decline in nominal interest rates after 2011.[16] Nonetheless there is recognition in policy circles that such a heavy reliance on BNDES for long-term credit is undesirable and that greater diversification is needed. Some types of BNDES loan now have a mandatory co-financing component and one of BNDES' stated goals is the further development of the capital market

[14] A positive surplus was made in 2013 and 2014, where the rate of return on assets was 1.1 per cent and 1.0 per cent respectively and the rate of return on equity was 16.5 per cent and 13.1 per cent; see BNDES (2014).

[15] The weighted cost of capital for BNDES was estimated to be between 5 and 10 percentage points below the government base rate, the SELIC for the period 2002–09. This meant that parking funds temporarily in government bonds could be relatively profitable.

[16] This implies that while BNDES lending was intended to overcome the problem of high interest rates for investment its own activity may have contributed to keeping them high. Segura Ubiergo (2012) considers this as a possibility but concludes that it is untestable.

in Brazil. In support of this, for example, infrastructure projects supported by the bank are encouraged to issue debentures, which are partially guaranteed by the bank, as a means of encouraging capital market development. BNDES (2014: 23) points out that fourteen such schemes went ahead in 2014 and that on average they represented a 10 per cent financial leverage.

PATTERNS OF LENDING

As would be expected of a bank with a wide mandate, disbursements cover a wide range of activities, although long-run lending to infrastructure and industry dominates (see Table 5.3). Lending for innovation appears relatively low but covers loans only from funds earmarked specifically for this purpose. More general loans could also fund innovative activities and will not be reflected in Table 5.3, although critics have suggested that there might have been an excessive focus on traditional parts of manufacturing like petroleum and food processing, at the expense of newer more technologically dynamic areas (Tavares de Ajauro 2013: 12).[17]

Establishing whether these proportionate allocations should be different requires a detailed assessment of the returns to different types of activity, which to our knowledge has not been done. However, one widely reported claim is that BNDES loans are skewed excessively towards large firms, which often receive repeat loans and which are highly profitable, with the implication that they could have accessed either domestic or

Table 5.3 Pattern of BNDES disbursements 2014

Disbursements 2014		
	Rs billion	%
Infrastructure	69	36.7
Industry	50.1	26.7
Social development	25.9	13.8
Green economy	28.3	15.1
Innovation	5.9	3.1
Export finance	4.4	2.3
Others	4.2	2.3
	187.8	100

Source: BNDES (2014).

[17] In their analysis of loans to firms Hochstetler and Montero (2013: 1494–5) comment that 'the vast majority of BNDES loans in our database (*sic* are to) do no more than what they are doing already. Using the short descriptions that accompany each loan we identified about 16 per cent that involved qualitative change; however, the modernization of equipment, development of new products and the like'.

international commercial sources of funds; in effect, the sort of firms which commercial banks should not be targeting.[18]

Overall in 2014, 31 per cent of disbursements went to what the bank defines as medium, small, and micro-borrowers and 69 per cent to large borrowers although by number the vast majority of loans were small (BNDES 2014).[19] The bank is sensitive to this criticism and BNDES (2014) points out that for industrial loans the share going to large firms is slightly below their estimated share in industrial value added. Similarly it argues that the overall division between large and smaller borrowers is skewed by the fact that roughly one-third of disbursements is in areas—infrastructure, export finance, and public sector finance—where smaller borrowers are not present to any significant degree. Where they are active—as in agriculture and services—they received 82 per cent and 56 per cent of disbursements respectively.

The exact distribution of funds between large and small borrowers is probably less important than are the purposes to which the funds are put and the additionality created by the bank. There have been a few studies which examine the characteristics of firms in receipt of BNDES funds and the extent to which their behaviour is changed as a result. The findings are mixed, with several analyses failing to find an impact on productivity growth.[20] One of the most detailed and widely cited analyses is that of Lazarrini et al. (2011) who construct a database on 286 publicly listed companies 2002–09 and identify those in receipt of BNDES loans or equity. A clear pattern emerges in that BNDES lends to or invests in more profitable and larger firms. However, once specific firm- and industry-level effects are allowed for, BNDES funding appears to have no impact on financial performance. There is some evidence that funding through loans, but not through equity, influences investment positively, although this depends on how the funding variable is specified. The authors argue that the main impact of BNDES lending is through lowering the cost of finance to firms, thus creating a transfer between taxpayers, who fund the credit subsidy, and owners of the enterprises.

This type of evidence while not conclusive is a concern. The role of interest rate subsidies from development banks is justified where it leads to investment that would otherwise not take place or to additional productivity growth and technical change. Where these impacts are not found the justification disappears. Concerns such as this have prompted the recommendation that BNDES focuses on its funding for infrastructure, innovation, and SMEs and scales back lending to large firms (OECD 2013).

[18] Hochstetler and Montero (2013: 1491) refer to a comment in a news magazine describing this lending pattern as equivalent to a 'Bolsa BNDES'; i.e. a BNDES stock exchange. The ten largest loans in their dataset made up 35 per cent of disbursements in 2009–11.

[19] The definition of large used here appears to be enterprises with a revenue above R$ 90 million per year.

[20] One paper reports a positive impact on productivity growth for loans, but only for those where BNDES itself participates in the approval process. Another finds a positive effect on productivity for loans pre-2003, when firms were deemed credit constrained, but no such effect post-2003. Others find no impact. Lazzarini et al. (2011) and Colby (2013) summarize the results of these studies.

In general BNDES has been a success by conventional banking standards and has been an active policy and knowledge bank. Its role as supplier of long-term credit to different types of borrower and for different uses will no doubt need to be adjusted as the economy and the strength of the financial sector evolve. It is not an 'ideal' model—for example it may not have had major success in the type of innovation-focused, venture capital lending advocated for development banks by Hausmann and Rodrik—but nonetheless its record shows that a large well-run development bank can meet a mix of economic and social objectives while remaining financially viable.

Conclusion

Arguably a distinguishing feature of BRICS is the role of relatively large development banks which can address gaps in the financial market at a relatively early stage of development. Interest in such banks has been stimulated both by the revival of interest in an active industrial policy as means of supporting structural change and by the macroeconomic consequences for individual economies of the global financial crisis of 2008–09. BNDES discussed here as a case study reveals some of the features of a successful development bank. Its role has evolved over time and will no doubt need to evolve further in the future. The main criticism that it needs to address is that it has catered too much for large-scale borrowers who are credit-worthy and who could otherwise access funds on commercial terms. As there is inevitably some form of subsidy inherent in development bank lending, a critical question is who will benefit from it and how far it is used to meet social objectives or to stimulate innovation and investment. This is a challenge all development banks struggle with and even a relatively successful bank like BNDES has failed to adequately address the dilemma.

REFERENCES

Ayyagari, M., Demirguc-Kunt, A., and Maksimovic, V (2008). 'How important are financial constraints? The role of finance in the business environment', *World Bank Economic Review* 22/3: 483–516.

BNDES (2014). *Annual Report 2014.* Available at https://www.bndes.gov.br/SiteBNDES/bndes/bndes_en/Institucional/Investor_Relations/Annual_Report/annual_report2014.html, accessed 10 October 2018.

Colby, S. (2013). 'Explaining the BNDES: what it is, what it does and how it works', *CEBRI Artigos* 3, Ano VII. Available at www.cebri.org. accessed 10 October 2018.

Crespi, G., Fernández-Arias, E., and Stein, E. (2014). *Rethinking Productive Development: Sound Policies and Institutions for Economic Transformation.* New York: Inter-American Development Bank and Palgrave Macmillan.

Cull, R. (2013). 'Comments on "Financing Development the case of BNDES"', in J. Stiglitz and J. Y. Lin (eds) *The Industrial Policy Revolution 1; The Role of Government Beyond Ideology*, IEA Conference Vol. 151-1. Basingstoke: Palgrave Macmillan.

de la Torre, A., Gozzi, J.C., and Schmukler, S (2007). 'Innovative experiences in access to finance: market friendly roles for the visible hand?' Policy Research Working Paper 4326. Washington, DC: World Bank.

de Luna-Martinez, J. and Vicente, C. (2012). 'Global survey of development banks'. Policy Research Working Paper 5969. Washington DC: World Bank.

Demirguc-Kunt, A. and Huizinga, H. (1999). 'Determinants of commercial bank interest margins and profitability: some international evidence', *World Bank Economic Review* 13/2: 379–408.

ECG (Evaluation Co-operation Group) (2010). 'making microfinance work: evidence from evaluations'. Paper 2, December. ECG.

Ferraz, J.C., Figueiredo Coelho Leal, C., Silveira Marques, F., and Trindade Miterhof, M. (2013). 'Financing development: the case of BNDES', in J. Stiglitz and J. Y. Lin (eds) *The Industrial Policy Revolution 1; The Role of Government Beyond Ideology*, IEA Conference Vol 151–1. Basingstoke: Palgrave Macmillan.

Gerschenkron, A (1962). *Economic Backwardness in Historical Perspective*. Cambridge, MA: Harvard University Press.

Gutierrez, E., Rudolph, H., Homa, T., and Blanco Beneit, E. (2011). 'Development banks: role and mechanisms to increase their efficiency'. Policy Research Working Paper 5729. Washington, DC: World Bank.

Hausmann, R., Rodrik, D., and Sabel, C. (2008). 'Reconfiguring industrial policy: a framework with an application to South Africa'. CID Working Paper 168. New York: Harvard Centre for International Development.

Hermann, J. (2010). 'Development banks in the financial-liberalization era: the case of BNDES in Brazil', *CEPAL Review* 100 April.

Hochstetler, K. and Montero, A (2013). 'The renewed developmental state: the national development bank and the Brazil model', *Journal of Development Studies* 49/11: 1484–99.

ILO (International Labour Organization) (2011). *Brazil: An Innovative Income-Led Strategy*, Studies on Growth with Equity. Geneva: ILO.

Körner, T. and Schnabel, I. (2011). 'Ownership of banks and economic growth: the role of heterogeneity', *Economics of Transition* 19/3: 407–41.

La Porta, R., Lopez de Silanes, F., and Shleifer, A. (2002). 'Government ownership of banks', *Journal of Finance* 57: 265–301.

Lazzarini, S., Musacchio, A., Bandeira de Mello, R., and Marcon, R. (2011). 'What do development banks do?' Harvard Business School Working Paper 12–047.

OECD (Organisation for Economic Co-operation and Development) (2013). *Economic Survey: Brazil*. Paris: OECD.

Rodrik, D. (2007). 'Normalizing industrial policy', mimeo. Commission on Growth and Development Working Paper No. 3. Washington, DC: World Bank.

Segura Ubiergo, A. (2012). 'The puzzle of Brazil's high interest rates'. IMF Working Paper 12/62. Washington: DC: IMF.

Stiglitz, J. and Weiss, A. (1981). 'Credit rationing in markets with imperfect information', *American Economic Review* 71/3: 393–410.

Tavares de Araujo, J. (2013). 'The BNDES as an instrument of long run economic policy in Brazil'. CINDES Working Paper. Geneva: UNCTAD.

World Bank (2013). *Global Financial Development Report 2013*. Washington, DC: World Bank.

World Bank (2014). *Global Financial Development Report 2014*. Washington, DC: World Bank.

6 Capitalizing the world

Aashish Kalra and Vinode Ramgopal

Introduction

The poor are so for many reasons; but the defining economic characteristic of poverty is the lack of capital and access to it. It is almost a truism. Nearly half the world has no access to savings markets or credit markets (Demirguc-Kunt et al. 2014). Without capital, their productivity is frozen and they have a limited chance of escaping the fate that tomorrow will look a lot like another version of yesterday. This is not a statement to deride the genuine human wealth of poor lives; nor is it contestable that capital is the foundation of modern opportunity. Capital is opportunity in abstraction.

A great mass of the world's poor is in developing countries or emerging markets (EMs) (International Monetary Fund, 2014/2015). Strategies to get capital to the poor in capital-rich societies is often, perhaps too often, focused on the distribution or redistribution of capital that already exists. In capital-poor economies, redistributing what little capital there is can leave everyone poorer. In such societies, the challenge of getting capital to the poor can seem truly hopeless—a task for the Knight of La Mancha. Microfinance is an inspirational call to break the mould, but even two decades after its emergence, it remains a drop in the bucket, marginal by most measures of poverty's scale.

Almost everywhere the governing approach of planners and economists to the challenge of capital deprivation is to urge patience. Build a sound economy, the wisdom goes, and over a generation or two, capital will filter down to the poorest.

The model, the cascade, and the ladder

The most successful method for young or capital-deprived economies to become capital-rich is the Asian Tiger Model (Sarel, 1996). It was pioneered by Japan, adopted by Hong Kong, Malaysia, Korea, Taiwan, and Singapore and taken to a wholly new level by China. Vietnam, Indonesia, the Philippines, and others are the next generation of crouching tigers. Measured by the numbers of individuals it has capitalized, the success of the model is incontrovertible. In a few generations, its application has lifted billions out of poverty and set them firmly on the path to consumption and wealth.

Aashish Kalra and Vinode Ramgopal, *Capitalizing the world* In: *Handbook of BRICS and Emerging Economies*. Edited by: P.B. Anand, Shailaja Fennell, and Flavio Comim, Oxford University Press (2021).
DOI: 10.1093/oso/9780198827535.003.0006

The model relies on the catalysing power of exports to the developed markets. Capital-poor economies must find a way to import capital if they cannot generate it internally, and it would be even better if this 'imported' capital came with a multiplier effect. Many capital-poor economies have relied on the extraction and sale of their commodities to provide 'starter capital' for their economies—but with the exception of the oil-rich economies in OPEC (Organization of the Petroleum Exporting Countries), few commodities have provided a path to sustained capital growth. Basic extraction margins were poor and commodity cycles were extreme. The tigers pioneered strategies to harness the larger and cheaper labour markets of developing countries to clamber up to the bottom rung of the manufacturing ladder. The labour arbitrage or the replacement of expensive labour in developed markets with cheaper labour from developing countries has sustained increasingly sophisticated manufacturing and service industries. They might have begun with umbrellas and pencils, but today the manufacturing bases of the tigers encompass everything. And the labour arbitrage has moved beyond manufacturing. India has pioneered offshore delivery models and brought them to the global service markets.

Profits from exports created liquid, mobile capital in economies starved of it. Mobile capital financed their balance of payments, built their reserves, stabilized their currencies, and most critically, stimulated their domestic economies. Profits and income from export industries fostered domestic spending, cranking up the engines of local consumption. Producing for export led to producing for local demand and carved a niche for 'emerging markets'. At the upper rung of the ladder is the capitalized, consuming economy and it becomes an export market for the lower rung of capital-poor, low-cost labour markets. It takes a generation or two to climb the ladder.

Those who have begun to build their local economies move up rungs of the ladder and pass the baton for the exports of pencils, umbrellas, and textiles to the next generation of climbers.

China is the poster child to those looking to the ladder model as the answer to poverty. In approximately thirty-five years—a mere generation—it has raised its gross domestic product (GDP) per capita from *c.*US$200 in 1980 to over US$8,000 in 2016 (*The Guardian* 2012) and has built the largest middle class in the world. It is poised to transition from being the greatest exporter to being the greatest consumer, perhaps even being the anchor of a global economy for the next generation. Over half a billion people have crossed the poverty line in China during the last two decades (*The Economist* 2013). The scale of this achievement against the extraordinary challenges that beset the country thirty years ago has fired optimism in the poorest of countries. Emaciated cats, everywhere, are thinking they too can grow up to be a tiger.

However, there are good reasons to fear that the conditions, which sustained the model for half a century, may be changing. Automation technologies are advancing. They are doing so, true to Hollywood's sensibilities, at a relentless and accelerating pace. The next wave of intelligent machines may combine sensory, data, and linguistic skills that could leave few jobs secure. The cost of producing and deploying these technologies is shrinking and the capital-earning opportunities for the labour markets in both the developed and developing economies are declining. In some dystopian scenarios, the role of labour in the production of goods and services may be marginalized to the stylistic and decorative. As these technologies advance, the lower rungs of the ladder are disappearing. China itself is turning to greater automation to address its weakening labour arbitrage. The expectation that as it moved up the rungs, it would play its part in the ladder model and outsource less skilled manufacturing to feed the ambitions of hungry, low-cost neighbours is fading. The technological challenge to the labour arbitrage is already here (Rodrik 2015). The great bulk of the world's capital-deprived countries may find the bottom rung of the globalization ladder being lifted beyond their reach.

There is another, equally profound, challenge to the health of the model. Developments in energy, materials, and manufacturing technologies are altering historic factors of production that have underpinned globalization. These technologies are enabling new frameworks for localized manufacturing with competitive economies of scale. The great global supply chains that emerged after the Cold War depended on volume. Volume in turn depended on standardization of product design and assembly so as to maximize input/output efficiencies. Micro-grids, distributed energy, biomaterials, and 3D manufacturing hold out an alternative prospect—smaller-scale manufacturing of highly customized products marketed to smaller geographies. Again, this prospect is both distant and tantalizingly close. It promises the isolation and elimination of what may be the most expensive leg of the current globalization model—the transportation costs associated with the logistics of moving billions of components and products over thousands of miles of land and sea routes whose security is increasingly suspect. It is a vision of 'organic manufacturing' and its development is most likely in the very markets whose demand is the linchpin of the ladder (i.e. the US, Europe, and Japan). If automation is lifting the ladder, the autarchic vision of 'organic manufacturing' will raise it further and possibly even dissolve it.

The third and perhaps the most immediate challenge to the model and its optimists is the reorganization of labour markets in the developed economies. Labour in Europe and the US is increasingly giving political expression to their frustration at the loss of productivity and opportunity from the global labour arbitrage. There is undoubted merit in their argument that the cost of labour in a work environment that has been built over a century of battles to uphold healthcare, environment protection, worker safety, and other social standards cannot compete with those where such burdens and decencies are not in place. The cry of unfair competition is giving way to demands for a less generous and less 'naïve' free trade vision than that which emerged in the full-blooded, almost senseless optimism of the 1990s, those heady spring days of the post-Cold War. Calls for walls and tariffs, International Protection (IP), and the rising wail of xenophobia in Europe, Japan, and the US may well be the most proximate danger to globalization. If Brutus's was the 'unkindest cut of them all', of the three knives thrust at globalization—automation, autarchy, and politics—it is politics that may be the Brutus of the day.

Given the force of these factors, the time to climb the ladder is short. The likelihood is that there are few remaining winners of the lottery. Most of the cats will not grow up to be tigers. If so, what is the option for the hundreds of young economies that will not get their paws on the first rung as the ladder is lifted?

Another charge from La Mancha

Yet, what if we can, in a few years capitalize the poor everywhere and do so sufficiently to get them into the banking and credit world, onto that elusive first rung of their domestic capital ladders? Better yet, what if we can do so with assets they already own but lack individual title to? It would not be redistribution through taxation. It would not be elimination of poverty over centuries. It would be something very different.

In the mid-1990s, the Bolivian President Sanchez de Lozada set out to transform Latin America's poorest country with an initiative labelled Capitalization (Ewing and Goldmark 1994). The plan transferred 50 per cent of equity in all the principal public companies to pension accounts for every Bolivian family. The funds were to be managed by independent, professional fund managers. While shares were deposited in funds in the name of individuals, the individuals could not withdraw or sell them readily; rather the holdings were designed to fund annuities paid out over time. The remaining 50 per cent stake was sold to corporate investors, but instead of proceeds from sales going to the government, they went into the companies themselves to fund their investment and expansion programmes. As the newly capitalized companies grew under the expertise of private management, the value of individual holdings in the newly created mutual funds would also grow and provide a 'currency' for other social goods and services or entry to the savings and credit markets. The Lozada plan was a visionary attempt to return ownership of public sector assets to individuals, to secure economic uplift through direct universal participation in the future monetary benefits arising from the transfer of assets away from state control. It did a second thing; it targeted the bottom of the pyramid. The direct beneficiaries of his plan, not surprisingly, were the poor.

The Bolivian experiment was not sustained. It failed for two core reasons—Bolivian state-owned assets were too impoverished to create a sense of tangible value in the short term and the Lozada government, constitutionally constrained from running for a further term, gave way to successors who plundered and unwound the programme. It was an experiment that received little global attention (Gordon 2010). There have been no subsequent followers.

Yet the capitalization vision is compelling, almost profoundly just. Public sector assets are shared properties, owned by the general public, managed on their behalf by the government. These assets, varying by country, held often at multiple levels of government (national, regional, municipal) are diverse; roads, railways, ports and airports, land, natural resource companies, utilities, industrial holdings, banks, airlines, licenses, concessions, spectrum, databases, IP, etc. It is a storeroom of extraordinary content, an Aladdin's cave of visible and unimaginable prospects. Return 50 per cent of these assets to the individuals who make up the public. It will capitalize the poor and unleash broader economic growth. This is not charity; nor is it taxing the rich for the benefit of the poor. This is transfer of title to individuals of property that they already own.

Public sector restructuring

Even before the end of the Cold War, there had been a dominant and contagious idea on how to restructure national public sectors. It originated with Mrs Thatcher and it is labelled 'privatisation' (Todhunter 2013). It is a simple idea—sell public sector assets to the private sector. Allow, where possible, citizens to buy shares in the privatized assets through the capital markets. Use the proceeds from the sales to reduce taxes or national deficits.

In the aftermath of the Cold War, as people lost faith in socialism and started believing in capitalism, the privatization fever swept across Asia, Eastern Europe, and Latin America in the 1990s. The British model became in vogue among intellectuals. It was adopted in most developing countries, and the British investment banks built a roaring business advising appreciative governments around the world as to its intricacies. Yet, in many ways, Mrs Thatcher had the wrong model for EMs.

The UK setting of large, sophisticated capital markets, a wealthy upper-income society with a tested, diversified, capital-rich private sector industrial base was not the EM norm. Most EMs had underdeveloped industrial and private sector bases. Few had capital markets of note. For many, public ownership of national industries was an icon of sovereignty. Applied to EMs, the Thatcher model stirred a deep sense of injustice. The visible beneficiaries of sales were too often a select few with capital and entrepreneurial cognisance. In too many cases, domestic private sectors lacked the capital means to buy the privatized assets, opening the door for foreign buyers, too often from the former colonial world. The privatization sales created some of the world's wealthiest—Carlos Slim, Mittal, the oligarchs of Russia and Ukraine and South Africa, and more. An enormous value base, hundreds of billions of dollars, was shifted in the process and it is hard to counter the public's grievance that their assets had been sold cheaply and they had been cheated (Marr 2009).

Despite the dominance of the British vision of privatization, there was another model that was tried in the heyday of the post-Cold War euphoria. Bolivia's was not in fact the first effort to transfer public sector assets directly to individuals in a society. This model had been pioneered in Central and Eastern Europe following the collapse of the Soviet Bloc. Poland, Hungary, the Czech Republic, Slovenia, and Russia itself experimented with differing strategies to transfer public sector assets to their citizens. It was called 'mass privatisation' (Pitt-Watson 2013).

There was no single or standard transfer mechanism employed in these once-uniform Communist Bloc nations. The public sectors of the Communist Bloc were, as expected, the most expansive of all economies. They included the great utilities (power, energy, telecoms, etc.), the largest manufacturing and industrial enterprises (pre-war or pre-revolutionary private sectors seized in paroxysms of ideological fervour), and thousands upon thousands of houses, corner shops, commercial buildings, etc. Measured by the sheer number of pieces of property to be transferred, no public sector in the West or in developing countries was comparable.

The challenges to restructuring and privatizing these public sectors were mountainous. There were little or no domestic savings and few natural buyers for most assets. Citizens lacked means to buy basics, much less buildings or shares. Few had more than a rudimentary understanding of financial markets, property ownership, investment metrics, and growth of asset values over time. The infrastructure for a mass sale was lacking. Property registers, legal protections for individual title, a market or auction apparatus—necessities in a sale programme—were underdeveloped or simply missing. And there was pressure to execute the sales as rapidly as possible to ensure there would be no 'going back'. A great deal of property was simply stolen or occupied.

In Russia, the official mass privatization programme was a straightforward distribution of shares in thousands of enterprises to employees in those enterprises (Boycko et al. 1993a). Beneficiaries received their largesse with little education as to its value or meaning, and in desperate economic times were easily persuaded to part with it for token sums. Perceptive, opportunistic, and connected individuals secured empires for peanuts. Over the next decade, Russia, a country in economic crisis and despair, spawned a disproportionate number of billionaires, an oligarchy that partnered with the state for protection and economic direction. The original employee shareholder base had largely vanished.

Further west, in Poland, the Czech Republic, and Hungary, a more nuanced mode of 'mass privatisation' was explored. Governments transferred the largest public assets to their citizens via 'intermediary' mutual funds. The newly minted funds, staffed by investment professionals, would provide the expertise to interact with the management of the privatized companies and preserve shareholder values over time. It would avoid the Russian naïvety. Instead of shares in companies, citizens were granted 'vouchers', which could be converted into 'shares' of the newly created institutional mutual funds; the funds, in turn, used the turned-in vouchers to acquire shares in the privatized companies (Boycko et al. 1993b).

In their use of intermediary fund structures with professional fund managers, these mass privatization programmes of Central Europe were the forerunner of the model that Lozada applied in Bolivia later in the decade. Yet they addressed one half of the challenge. They safeguarded the distributed shareholdings but did little to address the viability and needs of the newly privatized companies. Many of these were to wither for lack of vision, leadership, and capital. The Bolivian capitalization programme incorporated a critical new element into 'mass privatisations' (i.e. the capitalization of the privatized companies alongside the capitalization of the citizens). It was more than a modest refinement; it was the second half of the equation.

The capitalization blueprint

The transfer of the public sector into a direct 50:50 partnership between the individual citizen shareholder and corporate entities that bring management expertise and capital is global in application and almost revolutionary in terms of its impact. It could be a path for the capitalization of the world at a time when technology may be closing traditional channels for the accumulation of capital.

There is arguably no nation in which capitalization does not work. Even where the public assets of a community may seem uninspiring and the effort at first glance would seem to dwarf the reward, the following case can be made—at any one time the public assets of a community are but a fraction of its future and potential asset base. If we need a vivid reminder of the elasticity and unpredictable breadth of the value of the public sector, consider the 'wireless spectrum'. Until the emergence of wireless technologies, it was a moribund, unrecognized asset. Today the spectrum is valued in the billions in poor countries and hundreds of billions in rich ones. We cannot yet fathom what other assets held in common may emerge over the next decades to be of incomparable value. However, if we were to accept that these assets are owned by us individually and not by the state on our behalf, then each of us has a value by virtue of our citizenship that is both tangible and partially quantifiable. Citizenship becomes a financial asset—bankable and leverageable.

As conceived and discussed in the following pages, capitalization can be the largest single wealth distribution and wealth-creation initiative in history. Here are some obvious and less obvious insights in support of this bold statement:

- In almost every country, the transfer of 50 per cent of the public sector will amount to individual distributions that are multiples of per capita GDP. For the majority of the population, especially in developing countries, it can be the first meaningful set of assets they own that is liquid and leverageable.
- The distributions have an unrivalled 'multiplier' effect. They are doorways for hundreds of millions to enter the mainstream financial sector, to access credit, to be banked; they are a boon to microfinance.
- Capitalization unleashes the bottom of the pyramid. The distributions are indiscriminately equal. It has an inverse impact on the poorest.
- With no discrimination between men and women, the bulk of beneficiaries will be women and we have come to know what this means for economic growth.
- The endowment goes beyond the financial. Shared ownership of growing economic assets is a new social bind especially if the transfer comes with the education of a people as to how the assets they own in their own names are valued and can grow in

value, an extraordinary and unrivalled civic education. Countries can emerge with their populace market aware, if not savvy, and a powerful democratic asset in its own right.

- It will be a fillip too to the institutional development of domestic capital markets—the opportunity to launch new funds and to list hundreds of new companies. The economic empowerment of the public is a boon for capital markets.

Implementing capitalization

Capitalization requires visionary politicians and good technocrats. The tasks, while complex, are well within the capabilities of most countries. There are two parts to an implementation plan—capitalizing the public and capitalizing companies whose shares are being distributed. The second safeguards the first for if the assets transferred are poorly managed, the value of individual holdings is, in turn, ineffectual.

Capitalizing companies results in both growth and management. Private sector corporates are invited to develop a growth plan for the company and to fund that growth. As the capital is infused into the company rather than being paid out to its shareholders, the nominal value of the company is immediately increased. This approach, common in private equity investing, is rarely applied to public sector sales. Consider the scenario of a public sector company worth US$100 million where 50 per cent of it is sold for US$50 million; under capitalization, the US$50 million of sale proceeds is added to the balance sheet of the company, increasing the company's nominal value (post-money) from US$100 million to US$150 million (US$100 million of original value plus US$50 million of new cash on the balance sheet). There is an immediate increase in the value of citizen holdings (the value of 50 per cent has grown from US$50 million to US$75 million following the infusion of new capital) and with the execution of the funded growth plan, there should be further value growth. The capitalized company becomes a partner with the capitalized public. Corporates replace the government in managing and funding and the public are both consumers and shareholders.

Capitalizing the public in contrast has few precedents. The technical and administrative preparations required are considerable. There is a need for trustworthy population registers, for the legal and administrative infrastructure to support millions of individual accounts, for investment management machinery to monitor and distribute annuities over time, for robust capital and entrepreneurial markets and, of course, for independent and competent regulatory framework. Some lucky societies have all of these; most lack many. Yet, all of these institutions are essential to modern societies. With the wealth of modern technologies, it is rarely a technical problem to build them. Absence reflects absent political leadership. Is there a more powerful call to galvanize people into action to build these institutions than the prospect of a universal distribution and wealth-creation event? The politician who could not sell this is in the wrong profession.

Capitalizing the BRICS

If capitalization is to be transformative, it must succeed in the BRICS countries. They are both the largest constituents, and the economic leaders, of EMs. They account for three-quarters of the EM population and a great share of the world's poor. Adoption and success of a capitalization plan in any of the BRICS is likely to inspire emulation. Each of the BRICS is actively seeking the mantle of global leadership—what they do is hugely influential across the EM world, and more and more so in the developed world. It could be said, how the BRICS countries go, so goes the twenty-first century.

The BRICS countries are of course a simple club. 'Size' is what matters—population, land mass, and aggregate economic base. What BRICS have in common is that they are the five largest high growth economies in the world; putting them into a single category was a brilliant marketing tool, almost a shock device. It simplified the complexity of the EMs, the multiplicity of countries and voices; it highlighted the scale of the non-OECD world with a rectangle. In aggregate, the 'five' represented the bulk of humanity. If one thought in terms of the extension of the enlightenment project to the rest of the world, the message was almost unavoidable. It was a matter of time, but here was the economic geography of the future.

Below the metrics of size, the BRICS countries exhibit very different social, political, and economic landscapes. The GDP per capita of the five giants is illuminating—in 2016, South Africa's was US$5,700, China's was US$8,000, Brazil's US$9,000, Russia's US$9,000, while India was US$1,700 (World Economic Forum 2016). From the standpoint of a capitalization plan, the scales of national poverty, the internal capital bases, and the financial, social, and political levers in these five giants, all indicate very different starting points. As too does the scale of their public sectors, their conception of the role and place of government, of property, finance, etc. It is tantalizing to sketch a capitalization programme for each of the BRICS, but the confines of this chapter will not permit such extrapolation. Instead, we choose to examine a capitalization plan for one—perhaps the best suited, at this point in its development, for such a plan—India.

Capitalizing India

India did not jump on the privatization bandwagon of the 1990s; its public sector remains vast and relatively intact. China, despite its communist public ideology, has been more aggressive in reducing public sector assets at all levels, federal, state, and municipal. Brazil significantly reduced its state holdings over the past twenty years via conventional sales programmes and Russia implemented a mass privatization programme in the 1990s that sold many of the most valuable of its public sector assets. Inertia and resistance to Thatcherite models has left India with probably the largest traditional public sector restructuring opportunity. It may be as close to a pristine capitalization opportunity as one can find.

There are many execution issues and challenges to an Indian capitalization, but three questions stand above all others.

1. Is it material? Is the Indian public sector valuable enough to make a material difference if distributed to 1.3 billion people?
2. Is it practicable? Does India have the financial infrastructure—registries, trustee, and custodial infrastructure, education foundation, and more to facilitate such a massive shift of title and property ownership? Can we set up accounts for a billion people and safeguard against all the challenges of corruption, deception, and more?
3. Is there political will? If the first two conditions were met, is the political will to effect this change foreseeable or imaginable?

IS IT MATERIAL?

India's public sector accounts for approximately 25 per cent of its estimated US$2.0 trillion GDP. There are giant nationwide enterprises (the Maharatnas, Navratnas, and Miniratnas)[1] and thousands of smaller ones—at the federal, state, and municipal levels. The portfolio encompasses an extraordinary gamut of businesses—most of India's power and transportation infrastructure, much of its underdeveloped mineral resources, hundreds of manufacturing businesses, many of the country's largest banks and insurance companies, some of the world's most valuable land banks; and the list goes on. And when the current registry of companies is exhausted, we can look to the prospective value of future licenses and permits, spectrum sales, and the technology output of India's growing national research establishments. Intuitively, we sense that the aggregate value of these assets is enormous; but how do we validate this?

There are crude, intuitive values that can be attributed to this mass of companies. We can apply a revenue multiple to the US$500 billion (25 per cent of US$2,000 billion) with the multiples some estimate of India's long-term growth. The resulting value could be enormous based on one's level of optimism or alcohol consumption; but this is nothing more than a bar conversation. We could extrapolate from the market capitalizations of the handful of public sector companies listed on the Indian exchanges, but this is also little more than a speculative exercise. India's capital markets are underdeveloped and illiquid, inadequate value pointers. The sole acceptable methodology is really the

[1] Various Indian public sector undertakings (PSUs) have been awarded additional financial autonomy. These companies are public sector companies that have comparative advantages, giving them greater autonomy to compete in the global market so as to support them in their drive to become global giants. Financial autonomy was initially awarded to nine PSUs as Navratna status in 1997. Originally, the term Navaratna meant a talisman composed of nine precious gems. In 2010, the Indian government established the higher Maharatna category, which raises a company's investment ceiling from INR 1,000 crore to INR 5,000 crore. The Maharatna firms can now decide on investments of up to 15 per cent of their net worth in a project while the Navaratna companies could invest up to INR 1,000 crore without explicit government approval. Two categories of 'Miniratnas' afford less extensive financial autonomy.

individual valuation of each company based on its capital, product, and market characteristics—a prosaic, but enormous undertaking.

Yet, the current balance sheets, income statements, and business vision of most of the public sector companies are likely to be poor indicators of their potential. Many are undercapitalized; some may even be overcapitalized. Most, perhaps all are constrained by operating cultures and state bureaucracies. It is precisely this weakness that the capitalization plan addresses. We will know the financial values of these assets and platforms when we have capitalized these companies around business plans developed by corporate partners. Some companies may not survive this scrutiny, but given the scale of India's existing and foreseeable domestic demand, a majority of these operating platforms will find avid suitors within India or abroad. The capitalization of the Indian public sector through this process, the sale of 50 per cent of these assets to finance their growth, almost certainly creates a value base in the trillions. Around 50 per cent of this asset base is likely to be multiple of India's GDP per capita, either at the outset, or soon thereafter.

India's GDP per capita today is approximately US$1,700; even with its huge and rising population, the transfer of 50 per cent of India's capitalized public sector asset base is likely to be a transformative distribution. For the vast majority of Indians who earn materially below the average GDP per capita it is a dramatic change of fortunes—the first meaningful tangible asset that they own, which can be banked and leveraged. The multiplier effect is likely to be extraordinary. It is a boon to India's microfinance platforms; but the assets are also windows and doorways for hundreds of millions to enter the mainstream financial sector. Perhaps more than any other single initiative, a capitalization programme achieves financial inclusion.

IS IT PRACTICABLE?

The scale and complexity of India's social and political landscape—people, geography, linguistic, and regional divides—combined with its legendary bureaucracy and squabbling democracy, is daunting for any sweeping, single nationwide programme. Let us leave aside, for a moment, the challenge of political will and address a preliminary question. Does India have the financial, regulatory, legal, institutional, and educational infrastructure to effect the two parts of the capitalization programme or will it take a generation to secure these tools? It is hard to muster political will for Herculean tasks. Let us take the parts separately.

Capitalizing Companies

India has a deep and wealthy private sector with notable management skills. It has a well-established if yet young equity capital market. There is robust company law and an active domestic mergers and acquisitions (M&A) market. India, despite perceptions of its challenges for foreign investors, is a rising destination for direct investment; most of the globe's leading corporates have domestic subsidiaries. India's diaspora is capital-rich, technologically and managerially adept and there are powerful remittance pulls. In sum, it can be said that the financial, managerial and sale mechanisms are largely in place for capitalizing the Indian public sector.

Let us acknowledge the extraordinary task list and organizational complexity required to effect an Indian capitalization programme. In facing this task list, we have the experience of over two decades of public sector restructuring precedents across the world. An Indian capitalization programme may be unprecedented in terms of scale but in little else. There is a rich world of tools and expertise to ease the travails of strong politicians, great bureaucrats, and the requisite armies of lawyers, accountants, consultants, and investment bankers. Here are some of the tasks and prerequisites that must be met:

- We will need to validate the financial statements and audit the asset bases of India's public sector. It will be a boon to India's army of auditors and accounting firms.
- We will need to model the operational impact on businesses as they shift from public tender laws and public sector employment rules to private sector practices.
- In many cases, there is a need for regulatory or sector reform to end *de jure* and *de facto* monopolistic practices.
- The orchestration, sequencing, and management of this unprecedented sales programme will require judicious handling. This is not a fire sale; not Eastern Europe. It can and should be done with due care to maximize values and safeguard businesses. But it should be done quickly for uncertainty can erode value and allow 'gaming'. It can be done steadily, a multi-year process with batches of companies going through the transition, or it can be done in a series of 'Big Bangs'. There are virtues in either approach.
- Not all public sector companies need be candidates for the distribution programme—some may be too small and better left to more conventional solutions.
- Perhaps most challenging is the potential for multiple uncoordinated processes. Public sector assets at federal, state, and municipal levels will entail multiple independently managed programmes under independent leadership; without centralized oversight, this is an opening for a discordant and fundamentally corrosive dynamic.

Capitalizing the Public

The greater task is the second half of the capitalization equation—distributing 50 per cent of the shares in the capitalized companies to India's populace. Again, the work plan can be conceptually divided into two components:

i. executing the legal, administrative, and distributive framework for transferring holdings to individuals;
ii. safeguarding those holdings after the transfer.

Despite the novelty of the undertaking, and without seeking to understate its enormity, India has a number of building blocks already in place:

- most critically, Aadhaar, its National Identification system nearing fruition whose promise of a unique identity for all Indians is a dreamed-of foundation for a nationwide distribution programme;
- a substantial domestic institutional investment framework that provides both investment management expertise alongside custodial, trustee, and reporting capabilities. India's National Pension System, set up in 2003, offers both a relevant experience and a number of national scalable mechanisms to complement the expansion of private sector platforms;
- last, India's truly extraordinary asset—its mass democracy. Perhaps the single most critical implementation requirement for a successful capitalization programme is a mass education and communication programme, one that informs and educates citizens as to the value of their holdings and on how to safeguard them. Such a programme seems unfathomable in a non-democratic society.

To the extraordinary question of whether one of the world's largest and poorest countries has the institutional framework to execute a massive ownership transfer and distribution, a *prima facie* review of what is there and what could be put in place quickly, suggests that India may be comparatively well placed to meet the institutional, legal, and administrative challenges for a capitalization blueprint. There is further cause for optimism. The technologies available to support a mass-distribution programme are significantly greater than those that were available to the Bolivian or Eastern and Central European programmes. A mass-distribution and mass-investment management programme in India is a boon for the application of a host of financial technologies from mobile to distributed ledger. Capitalization would be a catalyst for India to possess the most advanced financial infrastructure in the world.

There will be many administrative negotiations requiring swift decisions from bureaucrats:

- Does everyone qualify for the distribution or is there an age threshold and if so what should it be? Should we set 18 years or 16 years, given India's youth demographics?
- What about the next generation? How do they participate in this bounty? Inheritance? Or do we keep issuing new shares diluting the original shareholders? Perhaps this may become a tool for family planning if a ceiling for new participants is introduced.
- What constraints should be put on decisions to sell holdings? In Bolivia and Eastern Europe, assets were held in mutual funds and professionally managed for their beneficiaries to provide long-term annuities. If this is replicated, how should this be calibrated to deal with older versus younger recipients of the transfer?
- If holdings cannot be sold can they be used as collateral for loans?
- Will the shareholder base of companies in the programme be equivalent to the half a billion or so participants in the initial population of India, a half a billion plus shares for each company?
- How do we limit the known forms of abuse that will occur—the threats to individuals to hand over their shares, etc.?

Some of these decisions are technical, some less so but all can be solved pragmatically and implemented with the requisite balance of justice and efficacy.

IS THERE POLITICAL WILL?

India appears to have a visionary leader in Narendra Damodardas Modi, possessing the elusive blend of charismatic and technocratic skills to execute transformational strategies. Capitalization is in accordance with a great number of Modi's goals of social empowerment, financial inclusion, a better balance of urban and rural dynamics, accelerated growth rates, and above all a vision of India vaulting to the twenty-first century over the legacy models it missed due to its relative insulation from the global economy, for much of the twentieth century.

If the 'material' and 'practicable' tests are met, let us for a moment imagine the following political statement (emphasis original):

India's public sector is owned by every Indian; it has enormous realisable monetary value; we are returning it to its owners. It will capitalise the base of India's pyramid and the economic growth unleashed will be explosive. We have looked at the lessons of Eastern Europe and other places – and we are giving back the public sector in a way that is customised to India's demographics, state structures, property laws, and sensibilities. We estimate the transfer *to be over $1000 per individual at the outset, and we expect this to grow multifold as India grows. From this day forward, every Indian has an economic share alongside their political voice in shaping our country and its success.*

There are so many ways to sell such a programme; so many constituencies that will benefit. The capitalization endowment goes beyond the financial. Shared ownership of growing economic assets has its own binding social force, another glue to clarify and reinforce the social and street dialogue (Heller 2008). If it learns from the experiences of Eastern Europe and Bolivia, and India's transfer comes with the education of a people as to how the assets they own in their own names are valued and can grow in value, it would be an extraordinary and unrivalled mass education. No nation has done this to date—but then no nation has economically empowered its base as contemplated here.

Capitalization will be a boon too to the institutional development of India's capital markets—the opportunity to launch new funds to manage transferred holdings and to list hundreds of new companies. Building transparent, liquid, competitive, and deep domestic capital markets is a vital event in India's economic growth. The capital markets of the US and the UK are integral to their competitiveness—perhaps the single most important factor in the continuing economic primacy of these two countries. Recognition of this has come late to EM planners; no EM has yet built the full suite of financial products that yields efficient and competitive pricing of capital to corporates and pension funds. Their impoverished debt markets are often the consequence of the public sector's coercive consumption of savings. The economic empowerment of India's public is a catalyst for liberation of its capital markets.

Yet, great change stirs fear and political opposition. India's capitalization plan will erode the patronage system of its famous political machines; public sector jobs and contracts are important largesse in electoral arithmetic. In India's sprawling, mass political parties there will be powerful forces of opposition and inertia to this shift of control and ownership. Trade union opposition to this plan will certainly be fierce for newly capitalized, commercially driven companies and will almost certainly lead to unemployment. And the prospect of something so large and new will bring out familiar, legitimate, and honest conservative fears—across regions, castes, and religious camps. The old, the cautious, the traditionalists, the Darwinians, the unimaginative, the winners in the current economic equations, and more will form a powerful coalition against capitalization. There are sound arguments and tools to address these constituencies, but winning requires greater passion, conviction, political will, and organization.

This dependency on political will seems almost a determinant. But the will for capitalization is not wholly reliant on the energy and vision of its national leaders. Capitalization can be done at state and municipal levels. It is both a macro- and a 'grassroots' programme. Anyone of India's twenty-nine state leaders can launch the programme using state assets; potentially, any one of its thousands of municipal and village leaders could do the same. It is only at the national level that the full-scale and transformative benefits will be felt; but the catalysts are all over the country.

Potentially the greatest 'will' for this change lies in the hands not of Modi, but in India's massive wave of youth—the 400 million youth wave crashing into its economy over the next decade. It is a powerful and propitious economic wave, which if harnessed—as China did with its youth wave in the 1990s to rise to economic greatness—could make India the second largest economy in the world within the generation. And which if not harnessed will plunge India, in all likelihood, into revolutionary times. This mass of youth is mobile, connected, aspiring, and needy. To meet their needs, India's growth rate must be greater than anything it has achieved in the past and sustained for decades. If the globalization ladder is lifting, there is no evident way to secure such growth. India will need to turn to its own consumption for growth, and capitalization is a powerful tool for unlocking India's consumption while safeguarding its governance. Modi's partner in building a capitalization coalition is India's youth.

Vaulting and leading again

EMs are pursuing a twentieth-century growth model of industrialization and urbanization; hundreds of millions are leaving the countryside for grotesquely burgeoning cities. Billions are being spent on infrastructure and in this narrative of economic growth there is great social upheaval. The environmental wreckage from this economic growth path is a global nightmare.

While EMs pursue this older path of industrial urbanization, a post-industrial schematic is emerging in Europe, the US, and Japan, of distributed living powered by distributed technologies—greater mobility and options on how we live and work—cheaper, smaller, and less environmentally destructive technologies. It promises to restore manufacturing to local habitats and economic vitality outside the giant cities. This postmodern economy looks to a landscape of localized service industries of which finance may be its most critical, and financial empowerment a fundamental requirement. Few EMs are confronting these issues today, locked as they are in the clutches of yesterday's models.

EMs have been economic followers from birth—but there is an extraordinary opportunity to 'vault', to take advantage of the fact that they are unburdened of legacies that inhibit the adoption of next-generation technologies. They can leap over the second industrial revolution directly to the third and fourth. It happened in telecommunications. It can also happen in power, finance, and manufacturing.

The institutional authority of states in both the developed and developing world is eroding. Social media allows for new tools of mobilization and organization; wealth is concentrating, labour is devaluing; the globalization ladder is being lifted; battles between Social Democrats and Social Darwinists are growing in intensity; political amity almost everywhere seems in decline. In the developed countries, the tools of government—taxation, monetary authority, media control, etc.—are fraying. 'Failed states', states where large parts are beyond the control of the centres, are multiplying across the developing world; their numbers will grow as the ladder is lifted.

Conclusion

Capitalization is a powerful mechanism to rebuild institutional authority. It capitalizes the bottom of the pyramid in a bold singular act. It takes a few generations out of the long wait for trickle-down capital. It enables distributed economy. Challenging as the capitalization vision is, the social, environmental, and sheer economic challenges for India of trekking to the twenty-first century via the second industrial revolution, are probably greater.

India led the break-up of the colonial world, finding theories and weapons in the depths of its civil society. It influenced the post-colonial world of independent states with the failed economic vision of Third World Socialism. The capitalization vision is an opportunity to lead again. It changes the dynamics of development—everywhere.

REFERENCES

Boycko, M., Shleifer, A., and Vishny, R.W. (1993a). *Privatizing Russia.* Brooking Papers on Economic Activity. Cambridge, MA: MIT Press.

Boycko, M., Shleifer, A., and Vishny, R.W. (1993b). *Voucher Privatization.* Chicago, IL: University of Chicago Press.

Demirguc-Kunt, A., Klapper, L., Singer, D. and Van Oudheusden, P. (2014). 'The Global Findex Database 2014: Measuring financial inclusion around the world'. Policy Research Working Paper 7255. Washington, DC: World Bank.

The Economist (2013). 'Towards the end of poverty'. June 2013. Available at www.economist.com/news/leaders/21578665-nearly-1-billion-people-have-been-taken-out-extreme-poverty-20-years-world-should-aim, accessed 15 July 2017.

Ewing, Andrew and Goldmark, Susan (1994). 'Privatization by capitalization—the case of Bolivia: a popular participation recipe for cash-starved SOEs'. Public policy for the private sector; FPD note no. 31. Washington, DC: World Bank.

Gordon, G. (2010). 'Bolivia Briefing Series: Gas and Oil Nationalization. President Morales' Decree, June 2006'. Available at https://democracyctr.org/archive/gas-in-bolivia/gas-and-oil-nationalization/, accessed 12 January 2020.

The Guardian (2012). 'China GDP: how it has changed since 1980'. March 2012. Available at www.theguardian.com/news/datablog/2012/mar/23/china-gdp-since-1980, accessed 15 July 2017.

Heller, M.B. (2008). *Corporate Governance Lessons from Transition Economy Reforms.* Princeton, NJ: Princeton University Press.

IMF (International Monetary Fund) (2014/2015). *Global Monitoring Report 2014/2015.* Washington, DC: World Bank Group.

Marr, A. (2009). *A History of Modern Britain.* London: Macmillan.

Pitt-Watson, C.S. (2013). *Privatization and Transition in Russia in the Early 1990s.* Oxford: Routledge.

Rodrik, D. (2015). 'Premature deindustrialization'. Economics Working Papers. Princeton, NJ: Institute for Advanced Study, School of Social Science.

Sarel, M. (1996). 'Growth in East Asia – What We Can and What We Cannot Infer', Economic Issues no. 1. Washington, DC: International Monetary Fund.

Todhunter, C. (2013). *Britain's De-industrialization and Privatization: The Economic and Social Legacy of Margaret Thatcher, 'The Iron Lady', Global Research*, April 2013. Available at www.globalresearch.ca/britains-de-industralization-and-privatization-the-economic-and-social-legacy-of-margaret-thatcher-the-iron-lady/5329683, accessed 12 January 2020.

World Economic Forum (2016). *The Global Competitiveness Report 2015–16.* Available at http://reports.weforum.org/global-competitiveness-report-2015-2016/, accessed 15 July 2017.

7 Links between financial inclusion and financial stability

A study of BRICS

Rashmi Umesh Arora

Introduction

In recent years financial inclusion has become an important policy goal in developing countries. The definition of financial inclusion is, however, unclear and varies from 'banking the unbanked' to 'branchless banking'. It is also increasingly viewed as a tool of poverty alleviation. Further, it enables the poor to be risk averse and allows investment in their health and education (Arora 2012). Financial inclusion has become all the more important as studies have shown that the poor, despite their low incomes and small amounts of funds available, actively manage and diversify their portfolios into different financial products even though outside the formal financial system (Collins et al. 2009).

The number of people with accounts at financial institutions grew by 700 million between 2011 and 2014, with 62 per cent of the world's population having an account with a financial institution up from 51 per cent in 2011 (World Bank 2014).[1] At the same time the number of unbanked adults declined from 2.5 billion in 2011 to 2 billion in 2014. While the increase in the number of accounts has taken place in almost all regions, it was particularly significant in East Asia and the Pacific, South Asia, Latin America, and the Caribbean each increasing by more than 10 per cent. In the sub-Saharan Africa region around 12 per cent of all adults had a mobile money account. The growth in overall penetration in sub-Saharan Africa was 24 per cent in 2011 and rose to 34 per cent in 2014.

Although several measures have been taken to promote financial inclusion, nonetheless, ill-conceived measures to increase financial inclusion can lead to financial instability (Griffith-Jones and Karwowski 2013).[2] The financial crisis of 2008 has also underscored

[1] The Global Findex database (Demergue-Kunt et al. 2014) compiled by the World Bank covers approximately 150,000 people in 140 countries representing 97 per cent of the world's population. The survey was carried out by Gallup Inc using randomly selected fifteen years and above population.

[2] As in the case of financial inclusion, the definition of financial stability is also not clear. Morgan and Pontines (2014) comment that it is easier to define instability rather than financial stability as it is influenced by multiple dimensions such as different institutions, different products, and markets. Schinasi (2004) noted 'a financial system is in a range of stability whenever it is capable of facilitating (rather than impeding) the

Rashmi Umesh Arora, *Links between financial inclusion and financial stability: A study of BRICS* In: *Handbook of BRICS and Emerging Economies.* Edited by: P.B. Anand, Shailaja Fennell, and Flavio Comim, Oxford University Press (2021).
DOI: 10.1093/oso/9780198827535.003.0007

the importance of financial stability in several respects. For instance, it showed that financial instability can take place despite macroeconomic and price stability and can occur at any stage of a country's economic development. Neither can financial stability be considered as a passive outcome; rather it should be targeted explicitly. Further, it also underscored that financial instability could pose a threat to the global economy. It also showed that the poor are most affected as a result of instability in the financial sector (Khan 2011). The role of promoting financial stability along with financial inclusion has, therefore, assumed increased importance.

While the development impact of financial inclusion has been well acknowledged in the recent literature, macroeconomic impact including the relationship between financial stability and financial inclusion has not been much examined (Hannig and Jansen 2010; CGAP 2012; Han and Melecky 2013; Morgan and Pontines 2014). Such a study is especially missing in the context of BRICS. Our study therefore raises two broad questions and fills a gap in the existing literature: what is the extent of financial inclusion and financial stability in the BRICS economies? What is the nature of the relationship between financial inclusion and financial stability in these countries? BRICS are an interesting group of countries in which to explore these research questions, as financial inclusion strategy has been adopted as an overarching goal of inclusive economic growth and development in all BRICS countries. Financial sector reforms along with other macroeconomic reforms were also introduced in several BRICS economies. The countries were quite resilient during the global financial crisis and were growth drivers of the global economy; however in the recent period their growth rates have somewhat fallen due to a fall in commodity prices and political instability impacting Brazil, rebalancing in China, and infrastructural and structural bottlenecks in India.

The rest of the study is organized as follows. The second section presents an analytical framework for the linkage between financial inclusion and financial stability and produces evidence from the literature. The third section reviews the state of financial inclusion and financial development in BRICS. The fourth section examines issues related to financial inclusion and financial stability. Finally, the study concludes.

Evidence from the literature

ANALYTICAL FRAMEWORK

Although the financial systems of developing countries are evolving and less complex in terms of financial structure and products, their development agenda is considerably complex in terms of the need for targeting multiple development goals. Inclusive

performance of an economy, and of dissipating financial imbalances that arise endogenously or as a result of significant adverse and unanticipated events'.

financial systems have become a major priority goal for developing countries, yet a challenge remains to develop the financial sector without undermining financial stability (Park 2013).

World Bank (2014) reiterates that the twin objectives of the financial system in developing countries are improving access to finance and assuring financial stability. These should be achieved by using appropriate public sector interventions such as building financial infrastructure in partnership with the private sector; promoting or developing financial literacy including in the school curriculum; and enhancing regulatory reforms including enforcement and dispute resolution mechanisms; improving the quality of micro-prudential supervision; strengthening data collection systems; and developing appropriate financial products.

The two objectives of financial inclusion and financial stability are interconnected and together build up resilience to instabilities or crises facing the real economy. The Sustainable Development Goals (SDGs), adopted in 2015, state that universal access to finance is considered as a critical factor in job creation and the promotion of economic growth. Goal 17 of the SDGs aims at 'a revitalized and enhanced global partnership that brings together Governments, civil society, the private sector, the United Nations system and other actors and mobilizes all available resources' (UN 2013). Improving access to finance through strengthening domestic resource mobilization, foreign aid, foreign direct investment (FDI), remittances, and assisting developing countries in attaining long-term debt sustainability are some of the key targets of Goal 17. Regulatory reforms related to the financial sector, therefore, need to consider the sustainable development agenda and the challenges faced by low- and middle-income countries (Park 2013).

Figure 7.1 illustrates in a nutshell the interlinkages and the channels from financial inclusion to financial stability. A two-way relationship exists between financial inclusion and financial stability which could be both positive and negative. The positive relationship is shown in Figure 7.1, wherein increased financial inclusion through the channels of increased savings contributes to financial stability.

The theoretical argument is that increased financial inclusion improves the efficiency and size of the financial system and enhances formalization of the economy, improving transmission of monetary policy. It also smooths consumption and leads to a shift of savings from the informal to the formal sector. The informal financial sector can potentially lead to instability due to unregulated players (Cull et al. 2012). However, it can reach those outside the formal financial system, make financial products more readily accessible, enable increased household savings, provide finance to start-ups and new firms, enable innovation, and lead to reduced inequality thereby fostering social and political stability.

On the other hand, enhanced financial inclusion can lead to increased transactional costs, enhanced risks as financial institutions move into new areas, and can potentially cause financial instability. The negative effect could be through undue access and its impact on financial stability; for instance, an example of the negative impact of increasing financial access on financial stability is that of sub-prime mortgages and their impact

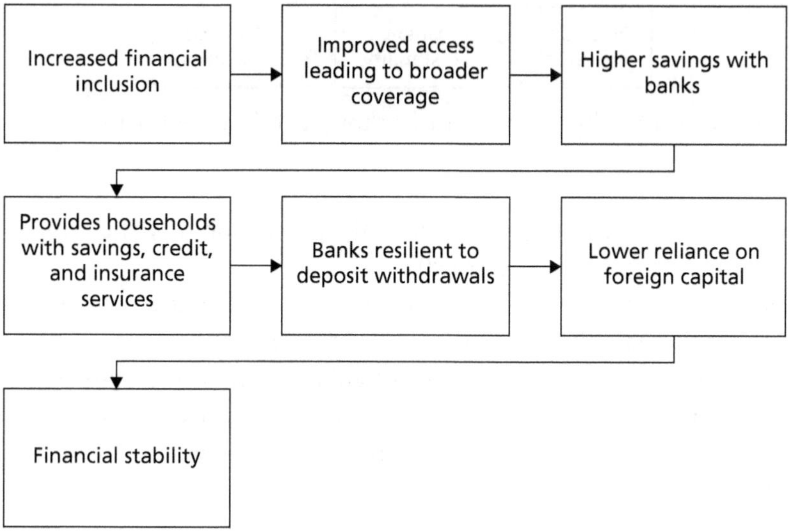

Figure 7.1 Links between financial inclusion and financial stability

Source: Author's work.

on the financial system in the US (see Crotty 2009; Lin and Treichel 2012). Describing the run-up to the 2008 financial crisis, Brunnermeier (2009) in the case of the US reports:

> Mortgage brokers offered teaser rates, no-documentation mortgages, piggyback mortgages (a combination of two mortgages that eliminates the need for a down payment), and NINJA [no income, no job or assets] loans. All these mortgages were granted under the premise that background checks are unnecessary because house prices could only rise, and a borrower could thus always refinance a loan using the increased value of the house. This combination of cheap credit and low lending standards resulted in the housing frenzy that laid the foundations for the crisis.

Increased, unplanned, and irresponsible financial inclusion can lead to an increase in defaults, leading to an extension of non-performing loans and affecting banks' profitability which in turn will act as a disincentive to improving financial access. High non-performing loans could severely jeopardize the financial system as they require higher provisioning and result in less interest income and higher funding costs for the banks. Net non-performing assets also have to be backed by adequate capital, leading to the use of scarce resources. Also banks with high non-performing loans are reluctant to lend, reducing the growth of overall credit and affecting further investments and economic growth. Thus there is a negative relationship between high non-performing loans and bank lending (IMF 2014a).

At the macro-level, the increased extent of financial inclusion achieved solely by opening bank accounts is not going to make a significant difference (and influence financial stability) unless accompanied by other interventions such as education, health, and improved infrastructural facilities (Aduda and Kalunda 2012). An Increase in financial inclusion without addressing gender imbalances would also have less of a

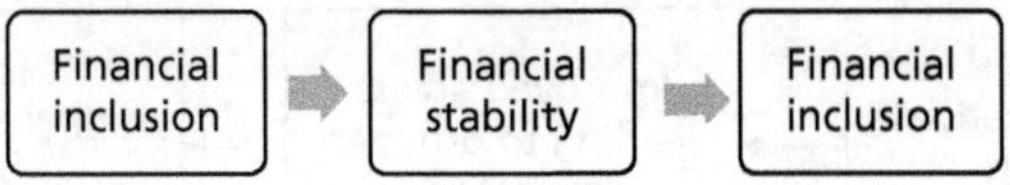

Figure 7.2. Bidirectional link between financial inclusion and financial stability

Source: Author's work.

macroeconomic effect as a large proportion of the population may still remain excluded with potential impact on economic growth.

The relationship between financial inclusion and financial stability could be bidirectional—increased population included in the financial system with the linkages shown in Figure 7.1 leads to greater financial stability; increased stability of the financial sector, which in turn, builds consumer trust, stabilizes inflation and interest rates making financial services more affordable to the poor thus increasing financial inclusion (Figure 7.2).

EMPIRICAL LITERATURE

Literature on the relationship between financial inclusion and financial stability is growing, though still quite limited. Among the few studies, Calice (2013) raises the question of whether financial inclusion and financial stability are complementary or whether they have a substitute relationship; that is, they cannot coexist alongside each other and one of them has to be given up to gain another. In the sub-Saharan African region the increased focus of central banks on promoting financial inclusion is through a five pillar approach—promoting access in rural areas; promoting access to finance; promoting savings; regulation of microfinance; and financial capability and consumer protection. Calice (2013) suggests that in order to reconcile the twin objectives of financial inclusion and financial stability it is essential that the financial products offered are in alignment with the needs of the poor.

Mehrotra and Yetman (2015) note that financial inclusion enables consumption smoothing, as it facilitates increased consumption by households. It may also lead to an increase in savings as households may move their savings from the informal sector or other assets such as gold to the financial sector. This will also strengthen transmission of monetary policy as the number of households increases from the informal to the formal sector. The downside impact of financial inclusion on financial stability could be in terms of increased risks for the banking system; a fall in lending standards as too much lending can take place; limited screening due to the absence of financial history for financially excluded households leading to a fall in credit quality; and increased financial inclusion could lead to unsustainable financial development.

CGAP (2012a) in a review of literature noted that most cross-country studies on financial sector have focused on the depth of the financial sector rather than the breadth (access) of financial services. This it reasoned could be due to easy availability of data on financial depth for most countries. In contrast, a paucity of studies on financial inclusion could be due to the absence of long-term data and absence of any single indicator which could holistically capture financial inclusion. The survey noted that improving financial inclusion adds to the savings pool and boosts financial stability; however, more evidence is required to establish this link. Stability at the microeconomic level (at household or firm level) could add to macroeconomic stability; although this link remains unexplored. In order to achieve responsible financial inclusion and financial stability, the quality and type of financial product is very important. Effective consumer protection is thus crucial to ensuring financial stability. Another micro-link could be the provision of credit to small firms, thus assisting their growth and promoting financial stability. At the macro-level, the links from financial inclusion to financial stability could be through domestic savings and a diversified base of customers leading to social and political stability. The survey further noted that financial exclusion (the reverse of financial inclusion) has strong implications in terms of lost growth opportunities for a large section of the population leading to dysfunctional societies and high poverty and inequality. Recourse to unregulated informal financial services can also lead to financial instability. CGAP (2012a) also pointed to the linkages between financial inclusion, financial integrity, consumer protection, and financial stability.

Noting the importance of financial inclusion, Hannig and Jansen (2010) explored whether increasing financial inclusion is compatible with financial stability. While the authors argue that technology-driven financial inclusion in many developing countries has caused concerns of financial stability yet, in their opinion, financial inclusion has a potentially low-level effect on financial stability due to the constrained financial behaviour of low-income savers and borrowers. They maintained that financial inclusion leads to a diversified and deeper financial system which contributes to financial stability.

In a cross-country analysis Morgan and Pontines (2014) examined the impact of financial inclusion measures on financial stability and noted positive evidence this occurring mainly through the reduction of non-performing loans. The authors empirically test the link between financial inclusion and financial stability using data for the period 2005–11 and employing the technique of a system of generalized method of moments (GMM) dynamic panel estimator. The measures of financial inclusion in their study are small and medium-size enterprise (SME) outstanding loans as a proportion of the total outstanding loans of commercial banks and the number of SME borrowers as a proportion of total borrowers from commercial banks. The measures of financial stability are banks' Z-score (that is, the sum of capital to assets and return on assets divided by the standard deviation of return on assets) and banks' non-performing loans (NPLs) as a proportion of gross loans by banks.[3] The results of the study showed that financial inclusion has a

[3] According to World Bank's Global Findex database, 'Z-score compares the buffer of a country's banking system (capitalization and returns) with the volatility of those returns. It is estimated as (ROA+(equity/assets))/sd(ROA) where sd(ROA) is the standard deviation of ROA. ROA, equity, and assets are country-level aggregate figures'. The higher the Z-score, the more financially sound the banking system is.

positive effect on financial stability and is negatively related to NPLs. The greater number of SMEs also leads to a lower probability of default and also causes lower NPLs. Among the control variables, income significantly influences GDP, that is, high-income countries are less prone to financial instability.

Morgan and Pontines (2014) also find that higher private sector credit relative to GDP leads to a higher possibility of financial instability. They further establish that greater liquidity by banks leads to greater financial stability through lower probability of default by financial institutions. Financial openness in their results was positively related to financial stability. Overall, the study examined the relationship between financial stability and financial inclusion. In alignment with a number of studies which have shown a complementary rather than a substitute relationship, Morgan and Pontines also find that an increased share of lending to SMEs in total bank lending promotes financial stability, mainly through the reduction of NPLs and the lower probability of default. This suggests that an increased level of financial inclusion would positively influence financial stability.

While the objectives of financial stability, financial consumer protection, and financial integrity are generally pursued by the financial regulators, financial inclusion in recent years has been recognized by the G20 countries as a pillar of the global development agenda. In order to reconcile these seemingly contradictory objectives, the global standard setting bodies have been urged to include all of them in their mandates. Together, these objectives have been termed as financial **inclusion**, financial **stability**, financial **integrity**, and consumer **protection** (I-SIP) (see BFA and Russian Microfinance Center 2014) and are considered to be theoretically complementary, although at the policy level there could be a trade-off. Some country-level studies have been conducted using a rapid research exercise incorporating the I-SIP objectives for two of BRICS, South Africa and Russia. CGAP (2012b) in its study on South Africa noted that the country has been able to integrate I-SIP objectives through inter-agency collaboration to identify linkages, potential risks and benefits of defined policy objectives, a clear framework of financial inclusion, consultation, and coordination with the providers. Within South Africa's financial sector mandate, the core priority objectives are financial stability, consumer protection, and market conduct. Using interviews, the study examined the effectiveness of linkages in South Africa. The authors concluded that a balance needs to be maintained between risks and benefits against the costs of regulation and supervision in deciding about the linkages among I-SIP.

Ackah and Asiamah (2014) examined the triangular relationship between financial development, financial inclusion, and financial stability. The authors study the case of Ghana, which has carried out significant financial sector reforms since the early 1980s. The Ghanaian policy framework has underscored the crucial role of the financial sector in inclusiveness. The focus is on increasing the availability of credit, lowering the cost of credit to productive enterprises, and extending the reach of savings, payments, and credit. Although these measures have improved the competitiveness and depth of the financial system, they have also rendered the financial sector risky and vulnerable particularly as a number of foreign banks operate in the country. The authors argue that effective financial regulation is necessary to deal with such risks and macroeconomic challenges.

Khan (2011) argues that financial stability and financial inclusion coexist and mutually complement each other. Financial stability is not sustainable if a large proportion of the population is financially excluded; similarly, financial inclusion is not feasible in a situation of unstable and unsound banks.

Mbutor and Uba (2013) show the impact of financial inclusion on monetary policy in Nigeria between 1980 and 2012. The results show that growing financial inclusion improves the effectiveness of monetary policy.

In an interesting study, Aduda and Kalunda (2012) argue that financial exclusion is more often accompanied with social exclusion and only a holistic approach which involves dealing with the absence of all forms of capital would lead to financial inclusion in a true sense. The study further examines whether financial inclusion and financial stability are substitutes or complementary. An important point which the study argues is that reducing financial exclusion should not be looked at in isolation as this is often the outcome of the absence of several other factors leading to poverty.

World Bank (2014) also found no correlation between the proportion of the population with a bank account and the indicator of financial stability (Z-score). Even considering crisis- and non-crisis-hit countries, the usage of bank accounts was not found to be different. Both panel data and cross-section analysis produced similar results.

Existing studies have examined the financial access and financial stability relationship in the overall context. In looking at the financial access–financial stability relationship the role of public banks is crucial. More recent literature suggests that public banks may lead to financial stability and avoid extreme moral hazard problems associated with the private sector banks, encourage constrained behaviour often accompanied by development objectives, and promote economic growth (Micco and Panizza 2006; Yeyati et al. 2007; Andrianova et al. 2012). Rezende (2015) examines the stability and resilience of Brazil's banking system in the context of the 2007–08 global financial crisis. The study noted that public sector banks enable greater financial access and also promote financial stability. Rezende argued that Brazil needs public banks to promote development. The private banks in the country have failed to provide long-term finance for infrastructure needs.

Financial development in BRICS

BRICS are a heterogeneous group of countries at different stages of development, different political forms of governments, cultures, and beliefs; yet a common feature among them has been their high growth rate in recent years (Makin and Arora 2014). The relative share of BRICS in world output is expected to rise from 5.8 per cent in the 1991–94 period to 21.6 per cent in 2018. The financial sector of BRICS has undergone significant reform over recent years. In the paragraphs below we briefly describe the major characteristics of their financial sectors.

BRAZIL

The Brazilian financial system is fairly well developed. It is headed by the Central Bank of Brazil and includes deposit taking institutions such as commercial banks, universal banks, savings and credit unions. Different supervision entities and regulators exist for banking, insurance, and pensions. The regulating entity for deposit taking institutions is the National Monetary Council. The supervision entity for the stock market is the Securities and Exchange Commission and the operating entities are commodities and futures exchanges and stock exchanges.

Banks are the major financial intermediaries in the country. The banking sector spreads are high in the country with the result that SMEs are crowded out of the credit market (Jorgensen and Apostolou 2013). Some of the reasons for high spreads are: high central bank's official interest rate; compulsory reserve requirements; high taxes on the banking sector; targets for directed lending to priority sectors (OECD 2011). A major role in the Brazilian financial system is played by the Brazilian National Development Bank (BNDES) which provides long-term credit at low interest rates. During the 2008–09 financial crisis BNDES played a major role in reducing the impact of the crisis.

Significant economic reforms have been carried out in the country since the 1990s. Filho et al. (2014) note that the major characteristics of the Brazilian financial system until the mid-2000s were the volatility and scarcity of credit; the high cost of credit (as has also been noted by other studies); and the major role played by the large banks especially the state-owned banks. In recent years, credit to households has increased significantly. This was accompanied by a fall in interest rates and a lift in the regulatory standards; financial stability was thus sustained, despite a sharp increase in home loans. Among the regulatory steps was the stipulation of a high capital adequacy ratio; a rise in the minimum capital threshold for banks; the restructuring of the banking system including non-banking financial institutions; the creation of a deposit insurance fund; and the transfer of payment settlement systems to the banks from the central bank (Filho et al. 2014).

RUSSIA

As in Brazil, banks are the major financial intermediaries in Russia and the major participants in the Russian financial system are (i) the Central Bank of Russia; (ii) state-owned banks; (iii) large private banks; (iv) local private banks; (v) foreign controlled banks. Non-banking institutions account for only 10 per cent of total banking sector assets. State-controlled banks are predominant in retail and corporate banking and altogether hold more than 48 per cent of banking sector assets (BRICS 2012).

The Russian financial system, as in other emerging economies, is gradually evolving in terms of form, instruments, and focus. Until 2007 the focus of the Russian financial system was on assisting and providing finance to SMEs. The core objectives were to diversify the economy, and to develop individual sectors and he infrastructure (Simachev et al. 2013). However, a vigorous and aggressive approach was applied from 2007 onwards and the focus of the government was to support innovation and technological modernization and to attract investment. Prior to 2007 focus was on small projects; this changed to large-scale projects from 2007. This rapid development of the Russian financial system, however has not been accompanied with financial regulation, thus raising potential risks to the economy.

The growth of the Russian banking system can thus be described in terms of three stages—prior to 1987; 1987–91; and 1992–2007. Prior to 1987 the banking sector was very much state led and lending was largely to state-led enterprises. During the period 1987 to 1991, the banking sector underwent significant changes; the emergence of commercial banks; and reform in the existing banks (Gosbanks). From 1992 to 1998 banks continued to provide credit to state-owned enterprises (SOEs), state related programmes, and government debt and did not provide credit to the private sector. Large profits generated by these banks are attributed to political connections and connections with state-run enterprises (Berkowitz et al. 2012). This, coupled with a fall in oil prices and the Asian financial crisis, led to the near collapse of the Russian financial system along with a fall in growth rates, outflow of capital, and closure of a large number of banks. It was in the post-Asian financial crisis that the banking sector recovered and credit to private sector enterprises increased. Also, economic growth improved during this period leading to a rise in per capita incomes.

INDIA

The Indian financial sector is comprised of banks and non-banks. Banks are the major financial intermediaries in India. These are divided into commercial banks; cooperative banks; newly established payments banks; and small finance banks. Among non-banks are development banks (mostly wound up now); insurance companies; non-banking financial institutions; mutual funds; pension funds; and primary dealers (Mohan and Ray 2017). Commercial banks are further divided into four categories: public sector banks (which includes nationalized banks and State Bank of India banks); private sector banks; foreign banks in India;[4] and regional rural banks.

[4] The branch authorization policy introduced in 2005 lays down that foreign banks can open branches/offices in India based on the following criteria: (i) financial soundness of the parent bank; (ii) rating of the parent bank internationally; (iii) India's commitments at the World Trade Organization (WTO); (iv) economic and political relations between the two countries; (v) a consideration that the home country of the bank should not discriminate against Indian banks. The minimum capital requirement is US$25 million required at the time of opening a first branch in India. Requests for subsequent branches are considered only when capital requirement conditions are met. Also, foreign banks, as in the case of Indian banks, are required to submit their branch expansion plans on an annual basis.

Government ownership of public sector banks ranged from 57 per cent to 85 per cent in 2010–11, much above the statutory requirement of 51 per cent. Public sector banks (including regional rural banks) hold the major proportion of banking sector assets at 72.7 per cent. The share of private banks' assets of total banking sector assets increased from 3.5 per cent in 1991 to 20.2 per cent in 2012 and the remainder are held by foreign banks at 7 per cent.

The public sector banks group is dominated by a single large bank, the State Bank of India, followed by its associate banks and nationalized banks.[5] At the time of the country's independence in 1947 all banks were in the private sector; however with the nationalization of larger banks in 1969 and again in 1980, most banking assets moved into the hands of public sector banks. While some private sector banks existed even prior to the reforms, the entry of new ones was largely initiated in 1993 when the norms for private banks were announced and subsequently ten new private banks were set up. Further, in the early 2000s, two large development finance institutions were also converted into banking institutions.

CHINA

Allen et al. (2012) observed that 'although there is no consensus regarding the prospects for China's future economic growth, a prevailing view on China's financial system speculates that it is one of the weakest links in the economy and it will hamper future economic growth'. China's financial sector is largely dominated by the banking sector as in the case of other BRICS as well, and can be grouped into banking, financial markets, and a non-standard financial sector which can be further divided into informal financial institutions and hybrid institutions. The banking sector can be further grouped into policy banks and commercial banks (further into state-owned, partially state-owned, and private and foreign banks). China's banking sector is dominated by large state-owned banks, namely the Big Four banks, implying a high concentration ratio and low degree of competition within the banking sector (Allen et al. 2012; Elliott and Yan 2013).

The regulatory structure of the financial system is organized based on the functions undertaken by the organizations. Thus banks are regulated by the China Banking Regulatory Commission; securities and financial markets by the China Securities Regulatory Commission; and insurance by the China Insurance Regulatory Commission. The Chinese central bank, the People's Bank of China, monitors financial stability; serves as the lender of

[5] The State Bank was earlier known as the Imperial Bank of India (created after the amalgamation of three presidency banks in 1921). Historically, even in 1934 these banks held the highest paid-up capital and deposits. The Imperial Bank of India was converted into the State Bank with the enactment of the State Bank of India Act, 1955. This led to the opening of a large number of bank branches in unbanked areas (RBI Currency and Finance Report 2008).

last resort; and formulates monetary policy. Further the Ministry of Finance is also involved as a shareholder in the major commercial banks (Elliott and Yan 2013).

The three major characteristics of the Chinese financial system are: the high level of savings; the large number of formal bank accounts; and lastly a low level of credit to SMEs resulting in the exclusion of a large number of SMEs from the formal financial system and the gap being filled by the shadow bankers (Fungáčová and Weill 2014). Allen et al. (2012) also noted the existence of a third financing channel besides banks and the capital market which consists of 'informal financial intermediaries, internal financing and trade credits, and coalitions of various forms among firms, investors, and local governments' (Allen et al. 2012). This channel has provided a significant amount of credit to various non-state, non-listed firms, and even the township village enterprises. Another paradox is the high level of private sector credit to GDP, yet the World Bank's Global Findex database found a very low level of provision of credit to households (Hale and Long 2011; Geng and N'Diaye 2012).

Overall, the financial system in China is opaque and evolving rapidly with the ongoing reforms (Elliott and Yan 2013). Elaborating further on the opacity of the Chinese financial sector, Elliott and Yan (2013) note:

> The use of the banking system for government purposes increases opacity in at least two ways. Government leaders often wish to obscure their interventions into the financial system, making that system harder to understand. The interventions also lead non-government participants to seek ways around governmental policy. For example, direct controls on the total amount of lending by banks can be circumvented to some extent by shifting loans onto the books of trust companies and their asset management customers, with an implicit guarantee by the bank. This creates incentives for Chinese banks to obscure the continuing financial risks associated with those loans, comparable to the reliance in the West on Structured Investment Vehicles (SIVs), whose blow-up contributed to the financial crisis.

On the whole, the financial system is characterized by high political interventions; regulatory arbitrage by the banks; implicit guarantees assumed from the central bank; high levels of lending to state-owned corporations resulting in exclusion of small businesses; and the rise of the informal sector as they fill in the void left by formal financial intermediaries.

SOUTH AFRICA

South Africa's financial sector is large, with financial sector assets around 298 per cent of GDP. The South African financial system is well developed, having thirty banks with around 4,000 bank branches, two mutual banks, and a number of foreign bank branches and offices, and non-banking financial institutions. The share of non-banking financial companies is considerably high in the total financial sector assets, of which pension funds account for 110 per cent of GDP, insurance funds 64 per cent of GDP, and unit trusts 42 per cent of GDP. The banking sector is highly concentrated with four banks

(ABSA, FirstRand, Nedbank, and Standard) accounting for around 80 per cent of total banking assets; around 95 per cent of total banking assets are domestic (IMF 2014b).

Although the banks are well capitalized, NPLs have increased significantly in recent years. Domestic deposits are the largest source of funding with 60 per cent of the deposits from non-banking financial companies. Unlike other BRICS, the South African financial sector is highly interconnected as banks are affiliated with insurance companies through holding companies or direct ownership (IMF 2014b). The capital market is also large and comparable to that of developed countries. Some of the issues plaguing the economy are high unemployment, high household debt, a slow growth rate affected by strikes, infrastructural problems, and high inequality. The profitability of South African banks declined as a result of the global financial crisis.

Among the risks, credit risk remains high due to a high level of indebtedness among households and the corporate sector coupled with low growth and a rising interest rate environment. Other risks are of systemic liquidity as high levels of capital inflows can lead to an increase in funding costs for banks, particularly as they are dependent on short-term wholesale funding. Other problems are caused by the high concentration and interconnectedness of the financial system.

Table 7.1 provides an overview of the financial development indicators in BRICS. The indicators cover the depth, efficiency, and stability of the financial system of the five

Table 7.1 Financial structure of BRICS (1994–2011 averages) (%)

Variables	Brazil	China	India	Russia	South Africa
Depth					
Central Bank assets to GDP	12.6	2.9	5.5	4.7	1.6
Deposit money banks assets to GDP	64.8	110.0	47.8	27.0	72.0
Non-bank financial institutions assets to GDP	4.9			2.1	137.3
Financial system deposits/GDP	44.7	37.6	46.9	20.1	52.7
Bank private credit to GDP	35.8	102.5	32.0	20.8	65.4
Private credit by deposit money banks and other Financial institutions to GDP	38.1	102.5	32.0	21.2	1.6
Liquid liabilities/GDP	46.6	132.2	56.7	27.2	50.5
Stock market capitalization/GDP	40.4	45.6	49.8	37.9	184.7
Stock market total value traded/GDP	20.3	60.2	48.5	21.0	66.8
Efficiency					
Bank overhead costs/assets*	5.1	1.2	2.2	7.4	3.7
Net interest margin*	6.4	2.4	3.3	4.2	4.1
Credit to government & state run enterprises to GDP	31.7	8.1	17.0	7.1	7.1
Cost–income ratio of the banks*	63.1	47.1	51.4	90.1	58.0
Stock market turnover ratio	58.7	149.8	117.8	75.2	37.2
Stability					
Return on assets*	1.5	0.7	0.9	1.8	1.3
Bank Z-score*	18.7	15.7	31.6	8.1	16.9
Banks NPLs to gross loans*	4.9	11.7	7.2	6.7	3.4
Regulatory capital to risk weighted assets*	17.3	9.6	12.5	17.2	12.9

Notes: * Data relates to 1998–2011.

Source: Computed by author from Global Findex Database, 2014 (see Demirgue-Kunt et al. 2014).

Table 7.2 Macroeconomic indicators in BRICS

Indicators	Brazil	China	India	Russia	South Africa
CPI 2015 (%)	3.5	1.2	5.8	12.0	5.0
Deviation of CPI	3.5	-2.3	-0.2	7.5	0.5
Commodity exports (%)	52.0	4.0	25.0	68.0	34.0
Commodity related share of corporate sector (%)	20.0	29.0	23.0	53.0	28.0
Private non-financial sector FX debt/GDP (%)	15.1				
Non-financial corporate total debt/GDP (%)	46.9	149.9	47.5	49.2	32.6
Current account deficit (as % of GDP)	-3.7	3.2	-1.3	5.4	-4.6
Reserves/short-term external financing					
Non-resident holdings of domestic government debt (% of total domestic government debt)	20.1	-	-	24.3	36.0
NPLs (%)	2.9	1.1	4.0	6.5	3.4
Loan to deposit ratio (%)	84.3	56.5	86.1	149.9	187.7
Loan absorbing buffers (%)	14.3	11.3	7.9	7.8	10.8

Note: Short-term external financing requirement is defined as short-term debt maturities plus current account deficit. Loss-absorbing buffers is (Tier 1 capital + loan loss reserves – NPL)/(risk-weighted assets).
Source: IMF (2015).

BRICS economies. Table 7.1 presents an interesting picture of the state of the financial system in BRICS economies.

As financial instability can exacerbate macroeconomic instability, it is imperative to have a look at the macroeconomic indicators in BRICS economies. Table 7.2 provides an overview of the key macroeconomic indicators. NPLs as a proportion of total loans varies considerably across the countries, with China recording the lowest in most recent years. Loan absorbing buffers are particularly low in India and Russia. IMF (2015) noted that Tier 1 capital for China, India, and Russia remains low. Loan to deposit ratios are particularly high in Russia and South Africa. Also noteworthy to mention is the high non-financial corporate debt/GDP ratio in China which is potentially risky and could create vulnerabilities.

Financial inclusion in BRICS

Financial inclusion has evolved as a key policy goal of BRICS, although it varies considerably across the countries. The index of outreach (that is, the spread of bank branches and ATMs) of the financial sector developed by Arora (2014) for seventy developed and developing countries showed that India and Brazil ranked fairly high among BRICS. The remaining BRICS (China (63), Russia (61), and South Africa (39)) rank much below in terms of outreach. In the overall financial access index, India ranked 25, Brazil 31, followed by South Africa 45, and China 49.

Table 7.3 reveals varying levels of financial inclusion among BRICS. China certainly performs much better in terms of number of bank accounts in financial institutions than

Table 7.3 Financial inclusion indicators in BRICS (2014)

Indicators	Brazil	China	India	Russia	South Africa
Account (% age 15+)	68.1	78.9	53.1	67.4	70.3
Account at a financial institution, income, poorest 40% (% ages 15+)	58.5	72.0	43.8	61.8	56.5
Account, male (% age 15+)	71.7	81.4	62.8	63.8	70.3
Account, female (% age 15+)	64.8	76.4	43.1	70.2	70.4
ATMs (per 100,000 adults)	117.9	..	8.9	151.8	59.1
Mobile account (% age 15+)	0.9	..	2.4	..	14.4
Mobile account, income, poorest 40% (% ages 15+)	0.8	..	1.0	..	8.0
Outstanding mortgage (% age 15+)	10.5	8.5	3.7	18.4	9.2
Point-of-sale terminals (per 100,000 adults)	..	..	..	..	..
Saved at a financial institution (% age 15+)	12.3	41.2	14.4	15.5	32.7
Credit					
Poverty headcount ratio at US$2 a day (PPP) (% of population)	8.15	18.61			26.2

Source: Global Findex Database, 2014 (see Demirgue-Kunt et al. 2014).

other countries within the group. China has a high level of formal bank accounts which is in fact higher than its level of development, as in terms of per capita income the country lags behind Brazil, Russia, and South Africa although it is ahead of India. In the case of Brazil, branchless banking has made huge strides in the country, enhancing financial inclusion. The banks operate 149,507 banking correspondent agents in every municipality of the country (CGAP 2010; McKay and Pickens 2010). Bill payments (mostly in the urban areas) comprise most of the volumes of transactions (Kumar et al. 2005). This banking model has not only led to increased financial inclusion but has also led to increased profits for the agents as 73 per cent of the agents report an increase in the non-agent business due to increased foot traffic (CGAP 2010).

Figure 7.3 shows that among BRICS in 2014 the proportion of adults with an account at a financial institution ranges from the lowest in India (52.8 per cent) to 79 per cent in China. In India the proportion of adults with accounts at a financial institution, despite years of expanding access to finance through government-stated policies such as nationalization of banks and directed lending, is quite low compared to other BRICS.

The proportion of adults saving at a financial institution was at 41.2 per cent, again highest in China but considerably lower in other BRICS economies—Brazil, India, and Russia (Figure 7.4).

Among the reasons for financial exclusion, common among all BRICS is lack of sufficient income. In China, unlike other BRICS, the cost of documentation, number of documents, and lack of trust were not considered as major barriers for financial exclusion. Rather, the two major reasons in China were lack of income and a family member already having an account. Fungáčová and Weill (2014) concluded that unlike other BRICS, financial exclusion in China is often voluntary, rather than involuntary as in other BRICS. The authors concluded that formal credit is very low in the country and

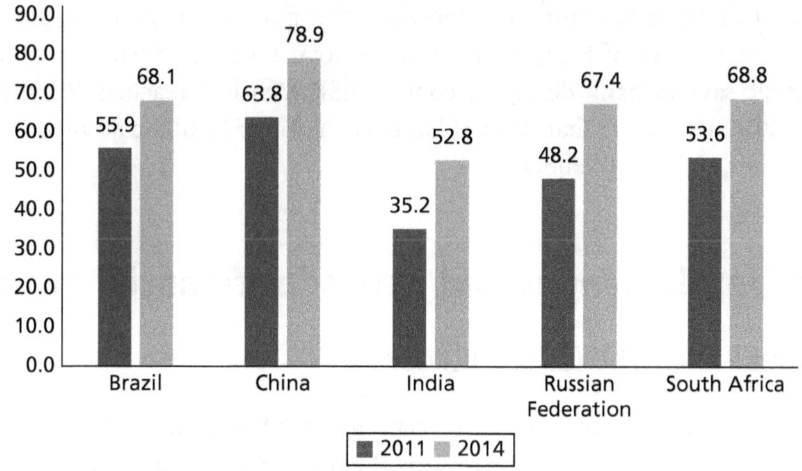

Figure 7.3 Account at a financial institution (% age 15+)

Source: Author's work.

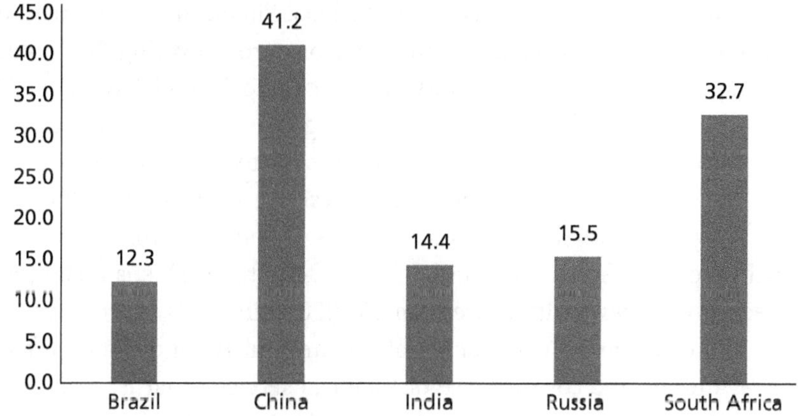

Figure 7.4 Amount saved at financial institution (%)

Source: Author's work.

the gap is filled by informal credit which is beyond the regulatory perimeters, with implications for financial stability. In Russia, in contrast, the trust factor played a major role in financial exclusion.

Strategies to enhance financial inclusion vary from country to country with some focusing on increasing access through financial institutions, agent banking, and business correspondents, while in others, particularly Africa, mobile accounts are more popular. The proportion of the population with mobile money accounts was 14.4 per cent in South Africa contrasting with a very low penetration in Brazil. Financial inclusion has gained a significant place in India's financial sector development strategy since 2010. The financial inclusion strategy is led by a technical group on financial inclusion and financial literacy, under the Financial Stability and Development Council (FSDC) sub-committee, and involving all financial sector regulators and other government and non-government agencies. As at the end of September 2014, the total number of banking outlets was 446,752. Basic savings bank deposit accounts (BSBDAs) had reached 305 million by September 2014. Under Pradhan Mantri Jan Dhan Yojana 51 million accounts had been opened as at the end of September 2014.

Discussion: challenges and issues for financial inclusion

DATA ISSUES ON FINANCIAL INCLUSION

Few studies have rigorously tested the relationship between financial inclusion and financial stability. A major problem in testing the relationship between the two variables is the limited availability of data on financial inclusion in contrast to the long-term data available for most countries on the indicators associated with financial stability. A major source of data on the indicators related to financial development, including financial inclusion and financial stability, is World Bank's Global Financial Development database (GFDD). GFDD is an annual dataset from 1960 onwards covering 203 countries. It captures data on depth, efficiency, stability, and access to financial systems. Although comprehensive in coverage, there are several missing values for a number of countries.

In the case of BRICS, while data on most indicators related to financial stability, depth, and efficiency are available, data on financial access are missing altogether for many indicators or are sparse, with several missing values. Another useful database is World Bank's Global Findex or Global Financial Inclusion database. This is a comprehensive database based on interviews with more than 150,000 individuals (over 15 years of age) covering over 140 countries. It consists of data on around 100 indicators differentiated by gender, age, and income covering use of financial services, that is, savings, borrowings, making payments, and managing risks. A limitation of the database, however, is that it is currently available for only the two years 2011 and 2014. The limited availability coupled with a select group of countries (in our case BRICS) severely limits the number of observations for carrying out a rigorous econometric exercise.

In addition to the World Bank's databases, IMF's Financial Access Survey (FAS) provides data on financial inclusion, indicators of financial access, and usage by households and non-financial corporations. The database contains statistics on forty-seven indicators covering geographic outreach and use of financial services. Among the indicators covered are those related to credit and deposit, availability of ATMs, loans to SMEs, and access to and use of mobile money services. Although this database covering the years 2004–13 on most indicators is a useful resource, yet once again in our case it does not prove to be so useful as there are missing values for several years or others are completely missing—for instance, absence of any data on SMEs for two of the BRICS economies, Brazil and South Africa. In addition to the above databases, Enterprise Surveys is another and is based on surveys conducted by the World Bank and provides data on 130,000 firms in 135 countries. The survey covers a range of topics including access to finance. However, again as in the case of the above databases, there are a considerable number of missing values for each of the economies under our consideration.

RISE OF SHADOW BANKING AND FINANCIAL INCLUSION

Since the financial crisis of 2007–08, increasing attention has been drawn towards the sharp rise of shadow banking in developed, emerging, and developing economies.[6] Shadow banking has been defined as 'credit intermediation involving entities and activities (fully or partially) outside the regular banking system' (FSB 2017). Some other studies have defined it in terms of instruments or markets. Shadow bank entities are either less regulated or not regulated at all; have no explicit access to central bank liquidity support; lack disclosure and information; and are characterized by a sequence of discrete operations (Pozsar et al. 2010). IMF (2014a) noted that shadow banking activities increased significantly in countries which experienced growth in the size of the banking sector. Other key drivers were tighter regulation, the search for higher yields, and the deepening of the financial sector in the emerging economies (IMF 2014a).

The rise of shadow banks has benefited in expanding access to financial services and they are often considered complementary to the traditional banks as they perform functions of 'supporting market liquidity, maturity transformation, and risk sharing' and provide finance to the unbanked, less privileged population or to small companies, for instance microfinance companies and microfinance institutions. Unlike traditional banks, the advantages of shadow banking lie in low transaction costs, quick decision making, customer orientation, and prompt provision of financial services (Sinha 2013). Besides inclusion of the large segments of population in the financial system, shadow banking also bolsters competition and supports innovation (Donnelly 2015). The FSB in its 2014 regional report on shadow banking in Asia observed that:

> OFIs [other financial intermediaries] in emerging and developing economies generally play a role in socio-economic and financial sector development. To a large extent, they have a key financial inclusion role, e.g. to broaden access to financing via provision of basic financial services to individuals and SMEs. . . In some jurisdictions, they also contribute towards development of niche markets and services through the provision of specialized products to promote the development of domestic capital markets, hedging platforms and alternative investment channels (collective investment schemes, mortgage corporations, venture capital) (FSB 2014: 25).

[6] The term 'shadow banking' was first coined by McCulley in 2007 with reference to the US financial sector, where shadow banks (non-banks) were recognized as major players in the run-up to the global economic crisis (Ghosh et al. 2012). Subsequently, in order to regulate the financial sector (including shadow banks), the Financial Stability Board (FSB) was set up as a follow-up to the G20 summit held in 2009. The board was assigned the task of assessing vulnerability in the financial sector and suggesting measures to improve regulation, particularly for shadow banking (FSB 2017).

According to the FSB, in emerging economies shadow banking is growing rapidly and shadow banking assets as a proportion of GDP expanded from 6 per cent in 2002 to 35 per cent in 2012. This growth is driven partially as a natural corollary of economic growth and deepening of the financial sector. Figure 7.5 shows the rise in shadow banking in BRICS economies from 2002 onwards.

Shadow banking in China has grown significantly alongside the country's high growth rates witnessed in recent years and was fifth largest among the countries monitored by FSB (Ghosh et al. 2012; Li 2013). The reasons for strong growth typically in China's case are related to regulatory arbitrage and restrictions on banks. In South Africa, including the assets from money market funds, investment funds, trust companies, finance companies, hedge funds, and bond schemes it is estimated at R2.4 trillion (Donnelly 2015). In Brazil as well, the growth in shadow banking has been driven by growth in mutual funds. In India, non-bank financial sector companies (considered as shadow banks) are often perceived as an important participant in the objective of achieving financial inclusion.

A trend which is clearly visible from Figure 7.6 is the rising share of China from US$5.3 billion in 2002 to US$2,999 billion in 2013, registering the largest increase among the emerging economies including BRICS. In terms of the components of OFIs, finance companies, money market funds, and special finance vehicles (SPVs), finance companies recorded the highest increase over the period 2007–11 in China (33 per cent); Hong Kong (12 per cent); India (25 per cent); and Indonesia (24 per cent). A major potential systemic risk in the emerging economies is the interconnectedness between OFIs and the banking system which could lead to the spilling over of risks. Interconnectedness between the parent institution and other institutions can also lead to systemic risk to the financial sector, particularly banks linked to a shadow banking system and cross-border banking (World Bank 2014).

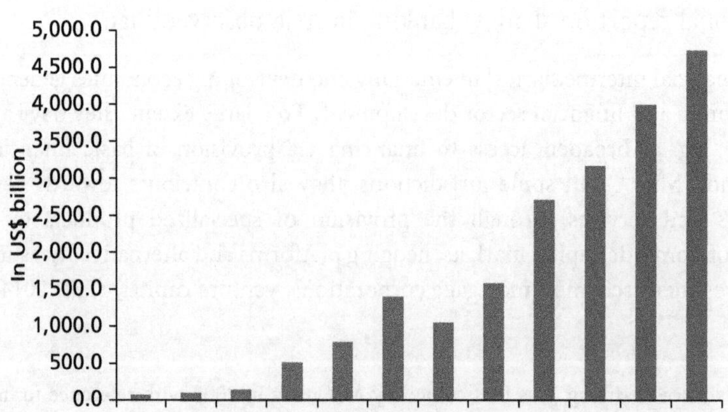

Figure 7.5 Rise in shadow banking (broadly defined) in BRICS

Source: Author's work.

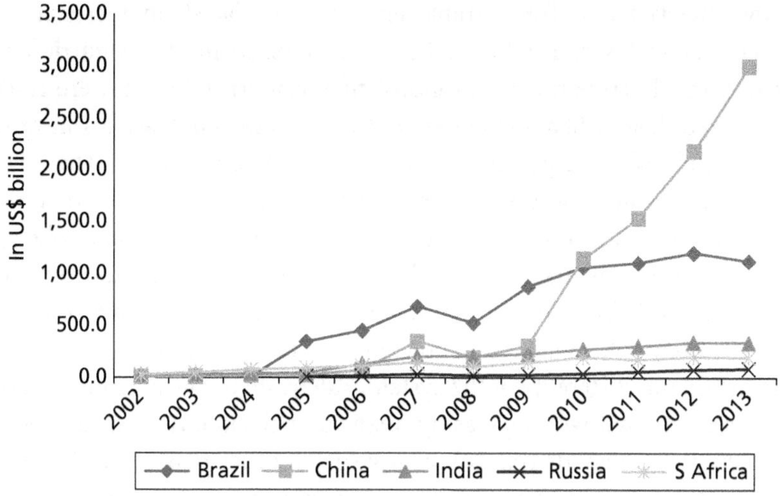

Figure 7.6 Shadow banking in individual BRICS

Source: Author's work.

Shadow banking entails systemic risks and could potentially destabilize the financial system. As IMF (2014a) noted, the challenge remains to contain risks emanating from shadow banking through a macro-prudential regulatory framework, yet to maximize the benefits of an expanding financial system. Henn (2014) noted that although the FSB is monitoring shadow banks and has been able to highlight the problems associated with shadow banking, yet this has not been adequate. Henn (2014) suggests that the FSB should focus on the availability of data on shadow banking, identify risks, and monitor effectively. Also the exposure of small businesses and households to shadow banking must be ascertained and vulnerabilities need to be addressed in the interim.

Conclusion

Financial inclusion has become an important policy objective in recent years in a number of developing and developed countries. Although several measures have been taken to promote financial inclusion, poorly conceived measures to increase financial inclusion can, however, lead to financial instability. A dilemma among policymakers and researchers is how to achieve a balance between the two and how to promote financial inclusion without destabilizing the financial system. Does increasing financial inclusion necessarily lead to financial instability? In this study we examined the extent of financial inclusion and financial stability in the case of a group of emerging economies termed BRICS. BRICS are a heterogeneous group of countries, yet a common unifying factor among them is their high level of growth experienced in recent years. Our study raised two questions: what is the extent of financial inclusion in BRICS? and what is the nature of the relationship between financial inclusion and financial stability.

The study observed that considerable emphasis is placed on increasing financial inclusion yet financial sector reforms have taken place in the countries, including regulatory reforms. Despite the recent global financial crisis BRICS were resilient and did not face direct losses. Shadow banking also in these countries is still much lower compared to the global average, particularly the US, UK, and Europe. There is however no room for complacency and the need is to remain vigilant of the potential risks likely to surface in the case of macroeconomic vulnerabilities. Some of the key policy priorities would be strengthening the databases for both financial inclusion indicators and financial stability. The availability of a good database would help not only researchers and academics but policymakers as well in tracking the progress of financial inclusion and monitoring the financial stability of the system. Adequate financial regulation is another key priority area required with increasing financial inclusion. As considerable financial access has been technology driven in recent years, another policy priority would be to strengthen cyber security systems. Secure and strong security systems would not only make financial transactions safer and promote financial stability, but would also build the trust of the general public in digitization of financial services, thereby further enhancing financial inclusion.

REFERENCES

Ackah, C. and Asiamah, J.P. (2014). 'Financial regulation in Ghana: balancing inclusive growth with financial stability'. Working Paper 410. London: Overseas Development Institute.

Aduda, J. and Kalunda, E. (2012). 'Financial inclusion and financial sector stability with reference to Kenya: a review of literature', *Journal of Applied Finance & Banking* 2(6): 95–120.

Allen, F., Qian, Jun "QJ", Zhang, C., and Zhao, M. (2012). *China's Financial System: Opportunities and Challenges*. Cambridge, MA: National Bureau of Economic Research.

Andrianova, S., Demetriades, P.O., and Shortland, A. (2012). 'Government ownership of banks, institutions and economic growth', *Economica* 79: 449–69.

Arora, R.U. (2012). 'Financial inclusion and human capital in developing Asia: the Australian connection', *Third World Quarterly* 33/1: 177–99.

Arora, R.U. (2014). 'Access to finance: an empirical analysis', European Journal of Development Research 26/5, December: 798–814. doi: 10.1057/ejdr.2013.50.

Berkowitz, D., Mark Hoekstra and Koen Schoors (2012). 'Does finance cause growth? Evidence from the origins of banking in Russia'. BOFIT Discussion Papers 10/2012. Helsinki: BOFIT (Bank of Finland Institute for Economies in Transition).

BFA (Bankable Frontier Associates) and CGAP (Consultative Group to Assit the Poor) (2012). *Financial Inclusion and The Linkages to Stability, Integrity and Protection: Insights from the South African Experience*. Washington, DC: CGAP. Available at www.cgap.org/sites/default/files/I-SIP%20Report_1.pdf, accessed 10 Apr 2015.

BFA (Bankable Frontier Associates) and Russian Microfinance Center (2014). *Final Report: Financial Inclusion and the Linkages to Financial Stability, Integrity and Consumer Protection: Insights from the Russia Experience*. Available at www.microfinancegateway.org/sites/default/files/publication_files/financial_inclusion_and_the_linkages_to_financial_stability_ integrity_and_consumer_protection_insights_from_the_russia_experience.pdf, accessed 20 February 2015.

BRICS (2012). *A Study of Brazil, Russia, India, China, and South Africa with Special Focus on Synergies and Complementarities*. Delhi: Oxford University Press.

Brunnermeier, M.K. (2009). 'Deciphering the liquidity and credit crunch 2007–2008', *Journal of Economic Perspectives* 23: 77–100.

Calice, P. (2013). 'The trade-off between financial inclusion and financial stability', in T. Triki and I. Faye (eds) *Financial Inclusion in Africa*. Abidjan: African Development Bank, 130–8.

CGAP (Consultative Group to Assist the Poor) (2010). *Branchless Banking Agents in Brazil: Building Viable Networks*. Available at www.findevgateway.org/sites/default/files/mfg-en-paper-branchless-banking-agents-in-brazil-building-viable-networks-feb-2010.pdf, accessed 29 November 2018.

CGAP (Consultative Group to Assist the Poor) (2012a). *Financial Inclusion and Stability: What Does Research Show?* Washington, DC: CGAP.

CGAP (Consultative Group to Assist the Poor) (2012b). *Financial Inclusion and the Linkages to Stability, Integrity and Protection: Insights from the South African Experience*. Available at www.cgap.org/sites/default/files/researches/documents/Working-Paper-Insights-from-the-South-African-Experience-Nov-2012_0.pdf, accessed 6 December 2018.

Collins, D. et al. (2009). *Portfolios of the Poor: How the World's Poor Live on $2 a Day*. Princeton, NJ and Oxford: Princeton University Press.

Crotty, J. (2009). 'Structural causes of the global financial crisis: a critical assessment of the "new financial architecture"', *Cambridge Journal of Economics* 33: 563–80.

Cull, R., Demirguc-Kunt, A., and Lyman, T. (2012). 'Financial Inclusion and Stability: What Does Research Say?' *CGAP Brief*. Washington, DC: CGAP.

Demirguc-Kunt, Asli, Klapper, L., Singer, D., and Van Oudheusden, P. (2014). 'The global Findex Database 2014: measuring financial inclusion around the world'. Policy Research Working Paper 7255. Washington, DC: World Bank.

Donnelly, L. (2015). 'Bring shadow banks into the light', *The Mail & Guardian*, 10 July.

Elliott, D.J. and Yan, K. (2013). *The Chinese Financial System: An Introduction and Overview*. Washington, DC: John L. Thornton China Center at Brookings.

Filho, E.T.T., Macahyba, L., and Zeida, R. (2014). *Restructuring Brazil's National Financial System*. Manchester: University of Manchester, International Research Initiative on Brazil and Africa (IRIBA).

FSB (Financial Stability Board) (2014). *Report on Shadow Banking in Asia. Financial Stability Board, Regional Consultative Group for Asia*. Basel: Financial Stability Board.

FSB (Financial Stability Board) (2017). *Global Shadow Banking Monitoring Report 2016*. Basel: Financial Stability Board.

Fungáčová, Z. and Weill, L. (2014). 'Understanding financial inclusion in China'. Working Paper 2014–06. Strasbourg: Cedex, Université de Strasbourg.

Geng, N. and N'Diaye, P. (2012). 'Financial development, corporate investment and savings in China'. IMF Working Paper 12/80. Washington, DC: International Monetary Fund.

Ghosh, S., del Mazo, I.G., and Ötker-Robe, I. (2012). 'Chasing the shadows: how significant is shadow banking in emerging markets?', in *Economic Premise*. Washington, DC: World Bank, 1–7.

Griffith-Jones, S. and Karwowski, E. (2013). 'Finance and growth in sub-Saharan Africa: policy and research challenges'. Paper presented at Africa Task Force Meeting, JICA and the Initiative for Policy Dialogue, June, Yokohama, pp. 139–132. Available at http://jicari.jica.go.jp/publication/assets/WP_JICA_IPD_Africa_Task_Force_Meeting.pdf, accessed 29 November 2018.

Hale G. and Long, C. (2011). 'What are the sources of financing for Chinese firms?', in Yin-Wong Cheung, Vikas Kakkar, and Guonan Ma (eds) *The Evolving Role of Asia in Global Finance*. Bingley: Emerald, chap. 13, 313–39.

Han, R. and Melecky, M. (2013). *Financial Inclusion for Financial Stability: Access to Bank Deposits and the Growth of Deposits in the Global Financial Crisis*. Washington, DC: World Bank.

Hannig, A. and Jansen, S. (2010). *Financial Inclusion and Financial Stability: Current Policy Issues*. Tokyo: Asian Development Bank Institute.

Henn, M. (2014) Brief an Financial Stability Board (FSB) zu Finanzmarktregulierung. (2015). Available at www.weed-online.org/meldungen/7829982.html, accessed 10 July 2015.

IMF (International Monetary Fund) (2014a.) *Global Financial Stability Report: Moving from Liquidity to Growth-Driven Markets*. Washington, DC: IMF.

IMF (International Monetary Fund) (2014b). *South Africa, Financial System Stability Assessment*. IMF Country Report No. 14/340. Washington, DC: IMF.

IMF (International Monetary Fund) (2015). *Global Financial Stability Report*. Washington, DC: IMF.

Jorgensen, Ole H. and Apostolou, A. (2013). 'Brazil's bank spread in international context : from macro to micro drivers'. Policy Research Working Paper Series 6611. Washington, DC: World Bank.

Khan, H.R. (2011). 'Financial inclusion and financial stability: are they two sides of the same coin?' BIS central bankers' speeches. Available at www.bis.org/review/r111229f.pdf, accessed 20 March 2015.

Kumar, A., Beck, T., Campos, C., and Chattopadhyay, S. (2005). 'Assessing financial access in Brazil'. Working Paper No. 50. Washington, DC: World Bank.

Li, C. (2013). *Shadow Banking in China: Expanding Scale, Evolving Structure*. San Francisco, CA: Federal Reserve Bank of San Francisco, Country Analysis Unit, Asia Focus.

Lin, J.Y. and Treichel, V. (2012). 'The crisis in the euro zone: did the Euro contribute to the evolution of the crisis?'. Policy Research Working Paper 6127. Washington, DC: World Bank.

McKay, C. and Pickens, M. (2010). *Branchless Banking 2010: Who's Served? At What Price? What's Next?* (No. 66). Washington, DC: CGAP.

Makin, T. and Arora, R.U. (2014). 'How solid are the BRICS? An economic overview', in Vai Io Lo and Mary Hiscock (eds) *The Rise of the BRICS in the Global Political Economy: Changing Paradigms*. Cheltenham: Edward Elgar, 11–26.

Mbutor, M.O. and Uba, I.A. (2013). 'The impact of financial inclusion on monetary policy in Nigeria', *Journal of Economics and International Finance* 5/8: 318–26.

Mehrotra, A. and Yetman, J. (2015). 'Financial inclusion – issues for central banks', *BIS Quarterly Review* (March): 83–96.

Micco, A. and U. Panizza (2006). 'Bank ownership and lending behavior'. Working paper no. 67. Alexandria: Department of Public Policy and Public Choice (POLIS), Universita del Piemonte Orientale "Amedeo Avogadro".

Mohan, R. and P. Ray (2017). 'Indian financial sector: structure, trends and turns'. IMF Working Paper. Washington, DC: International Monetary Fund.

Morgan, P. and Pontines, V. (2014). 'Financial stability and financial inclusion'. ADBI Working Paper 488. Tokyo: Asian Development Bank Institute.

OECD (Organisation for Economic Co-operation and Development) (2011). *OECD Economic Surveys: Brazil 2011*. Paris: OECD.

Park, C.-Y. (2013). 'The Asian financial system: development and challenges', in M. Kawai and E. S. Prasad (eds) *New Paradigms for Financial Development: Emerging Market Perspectives*. Tokyo and Washington, DC: Asian Development Bank Institute, Brookings Institution Press.

Pozsar, Z., Adrian, T., Ashcraft, A.B., and Boesky, H. (2010). 'Shadow banking', *Federal Reserve Bank of New York Staff Reports*. New York: Federal Reserve Bank of New York.

RBI Currency and Finance Report: RBI (2008). Report on Currency & Finance 2006–08, Vol. 1, Reserve Bank of India, Mumbai.

Rezende, F. (2015). 'Why does Brazil's banking sector need public banks? What should BNDES do?', Working Paper No. 825. Annandale, NY: Levy Economics Institute of Bard College.

Schinasi, G.J. (2004). *Defining Financial Stability*. Washington, DC: International Monetary Fund.

Simachev, Iu, Kuzyk, M., and Ivanov, D. (2013). 'Russian financial development institutions', *Problems of Economic Transition* 56/2: 66–95.

Sinha, A. (2013). *Regulation of Shadow Banking – Issues and Challenges*. Mumbai: Reserve Bank of India.

UN (United Nations) (2013). 'A renewed global partnership for development'. Working Paper. New York: United Nations System Task Team on the Post-2015 UN Development Agenda.

World Bank (2014). *Financial Inclusion: Global Financial Development Report 2014*. Washington, DC: World Bank.

Yeyati, E.L., Micco, A., Panizza, U., Detragiache, E., and Repetto, A. (2007). 'A reappraisal of state-owned banks [with comments]', *Economia* 7: 209–59.

8 Small and medium enterprises and industrial clusters in BRICS countries

Mario Biggeri

Introduction: the relevance of industrial clusters of small and medium enterprises

Nowadays, BRICS countries are key players in the industrial sector (see Chapter 1 of this handbook), and their industrial economic performances are remarkable, but at the same time very diverse in terms of development structures, processes, and outcomes. Indeed, small and medium enterprises (SMEs) and industrial clusters of SMEs are the backbone of the industrial sector in most developed and emerging countries, including BRICS (Arroio and Scerri 2014).

Industrial clusters of SMEs[1] have a prominent role both for SMEs (Markusen 1996) and industrial development and thus represent an important variable in assessing the industrial competitiveness of countries in the global arena (Sepulveda and Amin 2006; Sengenberger 2009).

According to the literature, SME development in local areas depends on their capacity to utilize the benefits of clustering, in particular on spillover effects arising from the creation of positive external economies (Pyke and Sengenberger 1992; Becattini et al. 2003, 2009). Collective efficiency, based on a mix of cooperation and competition, is an essential element for fostering production efficiency and constant innovation (Schmitz 1995), and to compete in world markets (Humphrey 2003). Clustering, as a place-based phenomenon related to geographical, cognitive, organizational, institutional, and social proximity (Boschma 2005), encourages technological upgrading and diffusion through information sharing (such as knowledge, technology and skilled labour) between producers operating close to each other, and between producers, suppliers, traders, and

[1] An industrial cluster is a geographic concentration of interconnected firms in a particular production sector (Porter 1998). The theoretical concept of industrial cluster has evolved in different strands of social science disciplines (Lazzeretti et al. 2014).

Mario Biggeri, *Small and medium enterprises and industrial clusters in BRICS countries* In: *Handbook of BRICS and Emerging Economies.* Edited by: P.B. Anand, Shailaja Fennell, and Flavio Comim, Oxford University Press (2021). © Oxford University Press.
DOI: 10.1093/oso/9780198827535.003.0008

other actors connected to the cluster (Nadvi and Schmitz 1994, 1999). According to Porter (1998), clusters have the potential to affect competition in three ways: (i) by increasing the productivity of the firms in the cluster; (ii) by stimulating new businesses in the field; (iii) by driving innovation[2] in the field. The conditions and features for a successful industrial cluster of SMEs' development are not easily reproduced. This capacity is generated from factors that are often external to SMEs, such as the human and physical infrastructure, and social capital, which in turn are necessary conditions (but not sufficient) for generating positive external economies, as well as long-term growth trajectories. Moreover, development through SMEs can be very limited without timing institutional reforms and public and collective actions and local public goods, requiring local policymakers' intervention to upgrade human capital, institutions, and infrastructure that are external to single enterprises (Becattini 1990; Biggeri et al. 1999). Finally, industrial clusters' evolution itself is influenced by favourable macroeconomic conditions and by national and international competition and economic trends. In other words, industrial clusters—as a form of agglomerated economic activities and industrial organization for firms—are deeply rooted on place-based factors, including resources (human and natural) and institutions, as well as meso- and macro-policies. This means that different typologies of industrial clusters of SMEs are found in each country.

Moreover, as underlined by the extensive literature, they have a relevant role, not only in terms of competitiveness and GDP growth but also in employment creation and poverty reduction (Nadvi and Barrientos 2004), becoming potential drivers for economic and social development at the local level. In the Agenda 2030, Sustainable Development Goal 9 moves in this direction[3] indicating the need to 'build resilient infrastructure, promote inclusive and sustainable industrialization and foster innovation'.

However, when a broader vision of development is taken into account, the overall positive impact of the industrial sector can be questioned and can even become an element of concern.[4] In this regard, the importance of dealing not only with economic competitiveness, but also with social inclusion and environmental protection at the territorial level (i.e. in this case at the cluster level) remains essential (Pike et al. 2007; Biggeri and Ferrannini 2014). In other words, most development outcomes (positive and negative) depend not only on national processes, but also on the performances of local development systems at territorial level, as in the case of industrial clusters (Becattini 2004; Biggeri and Ferrannini 2014). In particular, industrial clusters' development processes and outcomes usually diverge, especially if the analysis moves beyond

[2] Systems of innovation are central and can be defined as a set of different institutions that contribute to the development of innovation and learning capacity, including a series of elements and relations that relate production, absorption, use, and diffusion of knowledge.

[3] With a special focus on small-scale firms, see Target 9.3.

[4] For instance, China and India alone are producing 35 per cent of all global CO2 emissions.

economic growth towards a sustainable human development (SHD) perspective at the local level (Biggeri and Ferrannini 2014). The objective of the human development framework, built mainly on the capability approach (Sen 1999), is 'to create an enabling environment for people to enjoy long, healthy and creative lives' (UNDP 1990: 9). All in all, the SHD perspective has challenged development thinking distinguishing between the means and goals of the development processes and thus questioning the political economy objectives of development in itself (Anand and Sen 2000; Biggeri and Chiappero Martinetti 2010; Chiappero Martinetti and Biggeri 2013; Anand 2014) and of development processes including different forms of participation and empowerment of different settings and communities (Clark et al. 2019). Industrial development is not just economic performance but it can affect the 'good life' of people from different angles, for instance in terms of employment, environment, and inclusion (Mehrotra and Biggeri 2007). In other words, living conditions, multidimensional well-being, and capabilities of people are deeply influenced by the productive industrial performances of their own territories.

The aim of this chapter is to analyse the evolution of industrial clusters of SMEs in BRICS countries in the last two decades. Particular focus is dedicated to the main endogenous and exogenous drivers of change and how these concurred in shaping different outcomes in each country, also in terms of SHD.[5]

The chapter is structured in four sections. After this introduction, in the second section we present very briefly recent industrial outcomes in BRICS countries, including SMEs' setting and development. In the third section, the core of the chapter, the main endogenous and exogenous drivers of change behind the evolution of industrial clusters of SMEs in BRICS countries are analysed. Indeed, different institutions and factors can enhance or shrink the development processes of cluster formation, upgrading or downgrading both in developed and emerging economies. It should be noted that the analysis concentrates the attention on evolutionary processes and it does not intend to be exhaustive in the description of the characteristics of industrial clusters within each country. In the fourth section the final remarks and implications for future research are given.

Industrial outcomes and SME development in BRICS countries

BRICS countries recorded remarkable differences in terms of industrial growth and development outcomes (Table 8.1). Between 2000 and 2014, China and India achieved a

[5] It is important to acknowledge that there is a scarcity of data regarding both SMEs and industrial clusters in most countries, including BRICS. Moreover, the official definitions and classification of both SME and cluster can vary considerably across countries.

Table 8.1 Key development outcomes of the industrial sector in BRICS countries 1990–2015

	Year	Industrial GDP as % of GDP	Industrial export % over total	Industrial technological export % over total industrial export	Unemployment %	CO2 emissions per capita
Brazil	1990	38.69	43.05	6.46	–	1.39
	2000	26.49	48.20	18.73	9.50	1.87
	2015	23.41	38.09	12.31	11.45^	2.46*
China	1990	40.90	77.85	–	–	2.18
	2000	45.43	88.20	18.98	4.50	2.70
	2015	42.72	94.32	25.75	4.61^	7.55*
India	1990	26.49	56.10	3.94	–	0.79
	2000	26.00	54.18	6.26	4.30	1.13
	2015	30.08	70.6	7.52	3.45^	1.59*
Russia	1990	48.35	–	–	–	–
	2000	37.95	21.76	16.07	10.60	10.63
	2015	35.82	20.54	13.76	5.72^	12.47
South Africa	1990	40.10	–	–	–	9.08
	2000	31.89	43.59	7.00	26.7	8.38
	2015	29.47	49.37	5.88	25.92^	8.84*

Note: * 2013 data, ^ 2016 data.

Source: Author's elaborations from World Development Indicators Database (World Bank 2016b). Available at https://datacatalog.worldbank.org/dataset/world-development-indicators, accessed 9 March 2019.

very high increase in industrial GDP growth, i.e. respectively 7.30 per cent and 5.57 per cent per annum, while the other three countries had a limited or even negative score (Russia 0.36 per cent; South Africa -0.15 per cent; Brazil -1.75 per cent), based on the World Development Indicators (World Bank 2016b).

In general, it is clear that China is dominant among BRICS countries in terms of performance, such as the share of the industrial sector over total GDP, the share of industrial exports over total industrial value, and the share of technological export over the total (Table 8.1).

In terms of negative outcomes, BRICS countries are increasing their ecological footprint as the data on CO2 emissions per capita confirm, while in terms of unemployment the worst situation is in South Africa (SA).

The role of manufacturing SMEs in terms of GDP varies greatly among BRICS countries, from 20 per cent of total industrial GDP in Brazil, to 45 per cent in India, and to 58.5 per cent in China (Arroio and Scerri 2014). Moreover, although the presence of SME units is predominant in almost all countries, SMEs face very different situations in terms of absolute numbers of enterprises (see for instance Table 8.2) and in terms of time and procedures to start a business (Table 8.2). Overall, data show an improvement in the last four years especially for Brazil and Russia, although Brazil remains the worst in terms of time to start a business (almost eighty days).

Table 8.2 SME in BRICS countries: business environment, 2012, 2016

	SME (million units %) 2012	Firms using banks to finance investments (% firms)	Total tax rate (% of profit) 2012	Time to start a business (days) 2012	Time to start a business (days) 2016	Procedures for starting a business (number) 2012	Procedures for starting a business (number) 2016	New business density* 2012	New business density* 2016
Brazil	5.37/99%	48.4 (2012)	69.3	122	79.5	13	11	2.16	2.88
Russia	4/97%	30.6 (2012)	54.1	18	9.8	8	4	4.3	4.2
India	26/94%	30.3 (2014)	61.8	28	26	14	13	0.12	0.12
China	42/99.6%	14.7 (2012)	63.7	33	28.9	13	9	...	...
South Africa	2.5	34.8 (2007)	33.3	45	43	6	7	6.5	...

Notes: It is important to bear in mind that these figures do not comprise informal business indicators.
* Number of registrations for 1,000 inhabitants aged between 15 and 64.

Source: Author's elaborations from Arroio and Scerri (2014); Doing Business Report (World Bank 2016a); World Development Indicators (World Bank 2016b). World Bank, Development Economics Data Group and Investment Climate Department of the Financial and Private Sector Development Vice-Presidency.

Table 8.3 SME policies in BRICS

	SME Policies	SME innovation policy	Main support institutions*	Innovation finance	SME gender policies
Brazil	✓	Local productive arrangements	SEBRAE	Innovation funds	✓
Russia	✓	University and industrial parks, innovation centres, industrial growth poles	Rosnauka	Innovation funds	//
India	✓	MSMED Act, 2006; clusters	Ministry of MSME	//	//
China	✓	High-tech zones, incubators, S&T parks, industrial growth poles	Productivity Promotion Center	Innovation funds	//
South Africa	✓	Spatial development initiatives (SDI), clusters, technology stations	South Africa SEDA	Khula Enterprise Finance	✓

Note: * In BRICS, SMEs are supported by a myriad of federal, state, and local institutions. This column draws out the main institution responsible for technical, training, and other non-financial support services.

Source: Arroio and Scerri (2014).

Finally, before entering into the core analysis of the evolution of industrial clusters in BRICS countries, it is relevant to notice (Table 8.3) that policies were implemented for SME development in all BRICS countries. However, as we are going to see in the next section, these policies and the endogenous and exogenous factors are profoundly different among these countries.

The evolution of industrial clusters in BRICS countries

The aim of this section is to examine the main factors influencing clusters evolution in the five BRICS countries and their outcomes in terms of SHD.

SMALL BUSINESS AND INDUSTRIAL CLUSTERS EVOLUTION IN BRAZIL

Today, SMEs represent 99 per cent of total firms, contributing to more than 50 per cent of total formal employment and to almost half of total wages in the Brazilian economy (Arroio 2014). Going beyond official statistics, which point to the existence of over 5 million firms officially established, there are an estimated 20 million small informal business units, involving around 60 million persons (SEBRAE 2005).[6] However, although the idea of clustering started in the 1950s, the formulation and implementation of policies for the promotion of SMEs and clusters are a relatively recent experience in the context of Brazilian industrialization.[7]

Brazil has developed an extensive system to provide business assistance to SMEs: the Brazilian Micro and Small Business Support Service (SEBRAE) implements programmes throughout the country providing assistance to businesses, including access to technology services, and finance and training services (Teixeira 2010; Wilson 2011; Arroio 2014). In addition, several laws and initiatives were launched by the Brazilian government, such as the 'SIMPLES Law' in 1996, the SME Statute in 1999, and the Industrial Survey of Technological Innovation (PINTEC).

New place-based policies for SMEs started from 2000 onwards for those SMEs in the so-called local productive systems (LPS), i.e. any productive agglomeration involving economic, political, and social agents localized in the same area, performing related economic activities and presenting consistent articulation, interaction, cooperation, and learning processes (Teixeira 2010; Arroio 2014). The territorial focus of these extensive programmes implemented by SEBRAE is useful to tailor products and services according to diverse local realities and actors, facilitating not only access to credit and other forms of support, but also the concession of these resources and services by financial and other support agents, contributing to the cohesion, integration, and coordination of initiatives within LPS (Arroio 2014). According to PINTEC, 957 LPS were identified in 2009.

Although Brazil presents very important well-known industrial clusters, the situation is quite differentiated within the country. In general terms, while clusters in the north-east are more incipient, clusters in the south-east regions are more advanced and dominated by manufacturing sectors (e.g. producing jewellery, wood products, ceramics,

[6] These informal businesses have recently proliferated, especially in urban settings, as a result of the economic recession and high unemployment rate in the country in the last decades (Arroio 2014).

[7] In the twentieth century, Brazilian industrialization was based on state support to large firms and import substitution strategy.

footwear, and innovative high-technology clusters in the biotechnology and IT sectors). In addition, the extensive evidence on Latin America applies also to Brazilian clusters, revealing that both the local and the global dimensions matter, and firms often participate in clusters as well as in global value chains (Humphrey 2003; Pietrobelli and Rabellotti 2004; Giuliani et al. 2005; Parrilli and Garcia 2009). For instance, Zavatta (2008) discusses the well-established ICT/ICTE sector clusters in Sao Paulo/Campinas, Rio de Janeiro, and Recife, which represent emerging world-class IT sites with around 8,000–9,000 units and facilities established by several multinational corporations (MNCs).

Along with these world-class IT clusters, there still exist in Brazil 'survival' clusters with a high density of informal activities and 'incipient' clusters, with a low level of joint action (Altenburg and Meyer-Stamer 1999). Cooperation and collective action among local stakeholders can give local small enterprises the opportunity to access markets, overcome constraints, and confront vulnerabilities that they face in local and global markets. The aeronautics cluster demonstrates that in a global competitive environment the challenge of the cluster is thus a challenge for its SMEs. Therefore, the 'opening' is a necessary condition especially for traditional manufacturing clusters, natural resources clusters, and complex products clusters in order to upgrade the technology and scale up in value added in the production chain. However, such openings lead clusters to face increasing global pressures, and often ties with external actors begin to supersede local linkages (Brazil's Sinos Valley is an example; see Schmitz 1999).

All in all, policies for LPS vary from the most rudimentary to more complex and articulated. These involve for instance the design of policies that simply support social capital formation, information flows, and joint activities, to other policies to promote local public goods and foster knowledge flows, mobilizing endogenous resources within local productive and innovative systems. Although not directly using the notion of clusters, Cravo et al. (2015: 2005) show that in Brazil 'the presence of SMEs per se does not generate economic growth directly but through spatial interactions'. In addition, according to Pires et al. (2013) cluster-based development programmes are seen as appropriate tools for reducing regional inequalities within the country, and enterprises that belong to clusters are more correlated with good economic performances and employment generation. As already mentioned, despite these efforts, the increased international competition/pressure—mainly from the new emerging markets and in particular Asian clusters products—and the recent global crisis played a relevant role in triggering the further development of Brazilian clusters especially for more mature sectors (Humphrey 2003: 9).

From an SHD perspective, according to Arroio (2014), 'LPS do not comprise policy objectives per se, but rather are an instrument for social and economic development, providing the means to offer greater economic dynamism to small enterprises, an environment that is favourable to innovation and the development of sustainable social and political governance systems'. Moreover, the interest and participation of new institutional actors in initiatives to promote LPS has contributed to broadening the focus to comprise issues beyond competitiveness, innovation, and sustainable economic development. New contributions have brought to the forefront the interconnection between issues such as social inclusion, employment and wage generation, gender issues in employment and self-employment, and diminution of social and economic disparities (Arroio 2014).

RUSSIAN ECONOMIC TRANSITION AND ITS IMPACT ON SME EVOLUTION

Despite the fact that during the last ten years Russian SMEs have been showing significant growth, the role they play in the economy is still rather limited, as well as the industrial SME organization in the form of clusters.[8] In transition countries such as Russia, SME entrepreneurial dynamism and industrial SME clusters have been discouraged for decades by the planned system. A major aim of the restructuring effort in transition countries was thus to create a new private sector and to replace centrally controlled economy (collective enterprises and state-owned enterprises [SOEs]) with competitive and decentralized market mechanisms for resource allocation. Russia, as in former socialist economies, suffered from the absence of an SME sector 'that represented a huge hole in the size distribution of firms that was also called the "socialist black hole"' (Stiglitz 1999). The goods planned and supplied were not sufficient to meet the potential demands for goods both in quantity and in quality, i.e. light industrial products typically produced by SMEs.

Therefore, the capacity to form a consistent number of industrial SMEs and clusters of SMEs can be considered a symptom of a successful marketization from planned to market-oriented economy.

As widely discussed in the literature (Cornia and Popov 2001), Russia adopted the so-called 'shock therapy' to transition, consisting of the implementation of a series of reforms, such as price liberalization, current account convertibility, opening to trade and capital movements, privatization, and policies of macroeconomic stabilization. Gradualism, on the other hand, consisted of a certain sequencing of policy measures and the persistence of mixed systems. This gradual approach gave time to institutions, economic agents, and social networks at least to adapt to the changes. At the same time, a gradual opening to industrial international competition gave the opportunity to protect the 'new national private' industrial sector. Therefore, while China chose to follow a gradualist approach, satisfying the growing demand domestically protecting its economy, Russia opened to a disruptive international competition following the advice of World Bank, International Monetary Fund (IMF), and World Trade Organization (WTO) rules. In addition, Russia's initial conditions for market-type reforms were not as favourable as in the countries of Central and Eastern Europe. Russia suffered huge

[8] In 2009, the number of SMEs in Russia exceeded 4 million, i.e. about 97 per cent of the total number of enterprises in the country (Sokolov and Rudnik 2014).

distortions at both macro- and micro-levels: high militarization; over-industrialization and underdevelopment of the service sector; big size and excessive specialization of enterprises (in the resource sector); serious macroeconomic instability (e.g. budget deficits, high inflation, growing domestic and foreign indebtedness, and overvalued exchange rates); under-openness of the economy; and a perverse structure of trade among former Soviet Republics and among socialist countries (Cornia and Popov 2001).

Finally, not only did the idea that privatization by itself would have eliminated production and incentives problems and created a self-dynamic system prove to be false (McIntyre 2001), but even the original shock therapy measures were conducted in a careless and incompetent fashion (McIntyre 2001). In other words, privatization was carried out in a way that was totally corrupt and destructive in its economic effects (Ellman 2003), also because the conditions necessary for the development of the SME sector were far from being those described by the neoclassical perfectly competitive model.

Evidence shows that, as central controls were dismantled, small businesses started to emerge, growing from 268,000 by the end of 1991 to 840–890,000 in 1995. This development is however very modest if compared to any other transition economies.

In terms of macroeconomic policy and legislation, different stages in SME development in Russia can be identified in the late 1980s–90s (Radaev 2001). During the first phase (1988–90) there was a push towards political liberalization and the introduction of new legislation for the non-state sector, with SMEs mainly emerging in the production of consumer goods, housing construction, communal services, and catering, despite a virtual absence of institutional support. The second phase (1992–94) was instead characterized by the implementation of the government privatization programme. Despite the fact that SMEs were the first channel through which state-owned resources had been converted into private property, a reduction in SME expansion was registered during this stage. The third phase (1995–97) was characterized by relative economic stabilization, a decline of small-scale privatization, and substantial efforts to build institutions to support SMEs. Finally, the fourth phase (1998–2004) was characterized by the outbreak of the economic and financial crisis, and by the reduction of political and economic support for SMEs, which together negatively affected the SME sector. In addition, the lack of dynamism in the development of SMEs was also related to an unfriendly administrative environment, such as the high costs of preparing the required accounting and taxation documents, lack of financing and infrastructure, badly functioning judiciary system, and organized crime. Finally, by not taking advantage of clustering, SMEs were often not able to be integrated into relevant global value chains.

New policies for SMEs were introduced in the second half of the 2000s: the Federal Law no. 209 in 2007, 'On Development of SMEs in the Russian Federation'; simplified taxation procedures for individual entrepreneurs and SMEs; a more elaborate system for providing financial support to SMEs at all stages of their operations; specialized higher training for SMEs; and mechanisms for regulating the intellectual property issues including its creation, distribution, and use (Sokolov and Rudnik 2014). In addition, the state fostered developing SMEs in the Science and Technology (S&T) sector, while higher education institutions provided support to SMEs via a system of eighty-five industrial parks and about forty business incubators and technological innovation centres (forty nationwide) (Sokolov and Rudnik 2014).

The incipient growth of SMEs has resulted till now in a limited number of SME industrial clusters in Russia, mostly related to natural resources, such as in mining industry, wood-processing, and agrifood clusters. However, also at the cluster level there appear relevant problems affecting their growth. For instance, the main problem of the Arkhangelsk timber products cluster is obsolete infrastructure, together with depletion of forests, paucity of funding, growing transport costs, difficult procedures for getting logging permits, and discrimination by 'natural monopolies'; Krasnodar agrifood cluster, despite a high degree of cooperation, experiences weak equipment manufacturing, lack of skilled labour, insufficient access to credit, inefficient tax administration, and competition from food manufacturers who use low-quality imported raw materials; the Tomsk information and communication technology cluster suffers from lack of collective efficiency and interaction between enterprises (Sokolov and Rudnik 2014). All in all, the current level of development of SMEs and industrial clusters in Russia is slower than in other BRICS countries and several aspects of the business environment need to be addressed by policymakers on a local and national level.

To conclude, it is clear that the previous conditions, institutions, and the shock therapy not only generated the collapse of the system by privatizing and selling the best industries to be suddenly plunged into the global economy, disregarding their weak competitiveness, antiquated technology, low and declining productivity, etc. Also the potential opportunities deriving from the development of a dynamic SME sector and their clusters that could have satisfied increasing internal demand were swept away by the excessively rapid conduction of transition. All in all, transition policies produced dramatic results both in terms of SMEs' economic outcomes, as well as from an SHD perspective, with the economic collapse leading to similar impacts on the standards of living and health, and on the rise of the mortality rate.

INDIA'S INDUSTRIAL CLUSTERS EVOLUTION AND THE ROLE OF THE INFORMAL SECTOR

Despite the fact that India, as global player, is mainly recognized as a service sector economy, recent trends show that the industrial sector and micro, small, and medium enterprises (MSME) industrial clusters are increasing their role and relevance in the Indian economy.

Independent India, led by the National Congress Party, started off by following a path of industrialization close to the Soviet model and relying on import-substituting industrialization with public sector heavy industries (Sen 2008). Thereafter, year after year, industrial policy was constrained and hampered by a system of highly dysfunctional bureaucratic controls (PC 2013) with a 'gradual erosion of state authority and steady advances of the market logic' (Sen 2008: 543). In this regard, the year 1991 can be considered as the turning point in India's official position on economic policies, with the launch of wide-ranging measures to deregulate the economy along 'an irreversible path of TINA (there is no alternative) syndrome' (Sen 2008: 543). Undoubtedly, this path enabled elements of success in the ability of IT industries to compete in world markets, and to create a hub for jobs and newer facilities for communication in the country, as well as in the ability to provide additional sources of foreign exchange earnings. However, this free market approach to economic growth implied the abandonment of any concept of 'industrial policy' altogether (PC 2013).

Recently, the government has been resuming an active role in providing incentives for domestic industrial growth and in relieving constraints on industrial competitiveness, especially through the National Manufacturing Policy introduced in 2011 and the twelfth Five-Year Plan (FYP) (PC 2013). Moreover, if the eleventh FYP had already insisted on inclusive development, the twelfth FYP—in its new industrial strategy approach—adds clearly the importance of 'Making Businesses More Responsible Towards Society', with particular reference to ecologically sustainable industrial growth.

India's manufacturing strategy and plan focus particularly both on the performance of some selected manufacturing sectors in order to achieve large-scale growth, and on a set of thematic 'cross-cutting' issues (PC 2013: 59) that includes at least two with a most clear territorial character:

i) the creation of *National Investment and Manufacturing Zones* (NIMZ), conceived as greenfield townships that will develop to ensure agglomeration economies, superior infrastructure, a lower compliance burden, flexible labour market conditions, and skilled labour;
ii) *Clustering and Agglomeration*, as cluster development becomes a central policy lever within the strategy to build a dynamic manufacturing ecosystem, facilitate technological learning, and boost the development of MSMEs in the same geographical location (PC 2013).[9]

The MSME sector has emerged as a highly vibrant and dynamic sector of the Indian economy over the last few decades. According to PC (2013), in 2009 MSMEs contributed to about 45 per cent of manufacturing output and 45 per cent of total Indian exports (Naser 2013: 153 [from annual report of Ministry of MSME]), employing about 69 million workers in over 29 million units throughout the country. According to the micro,

[9] In previous plans, the MSME manufacturing sector and clustering were just seen mainly as a strategy to absorb labour force rather than a potential strategic sector for the entire economy (Mehrotra et al. 2012). Firms in this sector range from pure household enterprises (very small in size), mixed household enterprises (using both family and non-family labour), to non-household enterprises (employing mostly non-family labour), which are the source of most of the productivity and income growth among small and mid-sized firms in India (Mazumdar and Sarkar 2008).

small, and medium enterprises development (MSMED) Act of 2006, these enterprises operate in different sectors (including the service sector) and can be found both in the organized (formal) and unorganized (informal) sector, as well as in both urban (55 per cent) and rural areas (45 per cent). However, more than 94 per cent of MSMEs are unregistered, mostly operating in the informal/unorganized sector (PC 2013: 89).[10]

For these reasons, the prime minister's task force on MSMEs (of the past government up to June 2016) stated that no discussion on MSMEs in the industrial sector could be completed without full treatment of the unorganized sector (PC 2013: 89), which requires an enabling environment to flourish and integrate with the organized sector, possibly through a cluster-based approach.

According to the twelfth FYP, 'there are around 7,000 clusters in traditional handloom, handicrafts and modern SME industry segments' (PC 2013: 83). The information collected on 5,047 MSME clusters by the Foundation for MSME clusters (FMC) and UNIDO (FMC 2011) enables distinguishing between different cluster typologies:

1) *A manufacturing cluster*, which is a conglomeration of units producing goods for other industrial or consumption purposes in the form of either *industrial clusters*—composed of at least one hundred enterprises of different sizes and/or a minimum turnover of Rs100 million, for a total of 1,157 industrial clusters (for instance, 146 in textiles and garments)—or *micro enterprise clusters*—composed exclusively of micro and mostly own account enterprises (OAEs) and at times only a few small ones.
2) *Traditional industry clusters* producing handicrafts (around 3,000 clusters) and handloom (around 600) products and consisting of micro-enterprises (MEs) and mostly OAEs.
3) *Services clusters* providing a specific service, e.g. tourism, computer software, etc.

Moreover, as expected, spatial differences among the Indian state are quite prominent (Roy 2012). For instance, the states with more than fifty industrial clusters are Andhra Pradesh, Gujarat, Karnataka, Kerala, Madhya Pradesh, Maharashtra, Punjab, Tamil Nadu, and Uttar Pradesh, with the last state showing the largest number (169).

A recent study in forty-six selected poverty-intensive clusters conducted by FMC (2012) identifies the main micro-factors hampering the economic development of existing MEs: lack of market information, market access, and weak marketing skills, together with credit constraints, obsolete technology, weak technical skills, and low availability of adequate raw materials. Widening the perspective to the meso-level (i.e. industrial cluster level), the main issues affecting cluster development and upgrading are related to (i) low technology for enhancing productivity and lack of sufficient labour

[10] The formal manufacturing sector in India is considered to be equivalent to the organized sector, which comprises enterprises that are registered under the Factories Act of 1948 of the Government of India if they employ ten or more workers and use electricity in their operations, or if they employ twenty or more workers without the use of electricity in their operations. The Act also regulates working conditions (e.g. minimum safety, sanitary, health and welfare standards, regulations on hours of work, leave with wages, and holiday provisions) in the formal manufacturing sector (NCEUS 2007).

supply; (ii) infrastructure (especially lack of power); (iii) pollution, especially insufficient capacity of effluent treatment plants; (iv) marketing woes of downturn in global markets. As reported by the Planning Commission (PC 2013: 83–4), the Ministry of MSMEs is pushing the cluster approach[11] as a key strategy for enhancing the productivity and competitiveness as well as capacity building of small enterprises. In particular, the hard interventions will include investment in infrastructure (such as common facilities, common testing centres, roads), while soft interventions will include training, capacity building, skills improvement, marketing inputs, product design and development, and so on, including soft skills for cluster aggregators. However, the current amount allocated for soft interventions is grossly inadequate, and the deficit of trust within clusters crucially needs to be addressed (PC 2013).

Other elements of strong concern comprise the cross-cutting issues of environmental protection and working conditions, which cannot be tackled simply through traditional industrial policies. These require adding the social dimension linked to the Indian institutional structure and complex stratification of the workforce along class and caste lines (Harris-White 2003; Basile 2013). In addition, spatial inequalities and differences within the country substantially affect the Indian economy and society as a whole, with some megacities and districts emerging as areas of high development, while many rural areas are being left behind with little development benefits accruing to them (Mehrotra et al. 2012).

All in all, although the large number of MSMEs are seen as a potential factor for positive change through clustering and upgrading processes, they represent a source of underemployment and social and environmental degradation, leading to a low equilibrium trap (for a SWOT analysis see Venkataramanaiah and Parashar 2007) characterized by low productivity, low wages, and low investment, as well as high pollution and scarce social protection. Although overcoming these issues appears quite difficult, being institutionally sedimented, as well as considering the low reflexivity of institutions in the Indian economy and society (Harris-White 2003), the new industrial policy pillars of the twelfth FYP appear promising as they open up the path of sustainable, human, and inclusive development through MSMEs' clustering processes. In this regard, special attention is devoted by FMC (2011) to promote responsible business through improved infrastructure (e.g. subsidizing hostels for labourers), and to enhance employee social insurance facilities across the country (e.g. supporting new entities or tie-ups with existing hospitals). The area of environmental protection is also analysed by FMC (2011) in terms of opportunities for pollution control with acceptable technologies and approved vendors for sourcing of such technologies.

To conclude, in India overarching industrial cluster policies could assume a relevant role not only for the late industrialization strategy, but also to ensure sustainable, human, and inclusive development across the country. However, this could become a reality only if some of the most binding constraints are tackled and social upgrading opportunities are fostered.

[11] In order to assess the level of intervention required, the Ministry of MSMEs carried out a diagnostic study on clusters.

FROM SCATTERED TO CLUSTERED, FROM COLLECTIVE TO PRIVATE: CHINA'S INDUSTRIAL CLUSTER 'REVOLUTION'

Chinese industrial performances, since the 1978 reforms, have been outstanding compared to any other country in the world, bringing China to be defined as the 'fabric of the world'. In this regard, industrial clusters of township and village enterprises (TVEs) have played a key role in terms of industrial GDP, export, and employment creation (Biggeri et al. 1999).

The extraordinary performance and development of the TVEs sector and TVEs industrial clusters are attributed to many economic, political, and socio-economic factors and their roots can be traced back mainly to the rural institutional and socio-economic reforms implemented by the Chinese government after 1978. Such reforms changed some elements of the Maoist institutional framework that reduced personal incentives and hampered potential economic growth, and led China's transition to a 'market socialist economy' with its own pragmatic, experimental, and gradual style (Biggeri et al. 1999).[12] Agricultural reforms—the cornerstone of the rural economic development strategy—played an important role in removing economic stagnation in rural areas, and in particular in freeing up human and capital resources for the development of the TVEs sector. For instance, the increase in income of farmers and rural dwellers was fundamental to creating the initial demand for SMEs' manufactured products launching a pro-poor economic growth.

In addition, the Maoist system was modified to increase space for local initiatives and to introduce proper incentives, leaving both central and local governments with an impressive array of policy instruments and political capacity. In this regard, the gradual decentralization of the fiscal system, which allowed part of local governments' revenues to be used to facilitate local socio-economic growth, was the major incentive for action. Once in control of their own revenues, local authorities had a greater incentive to develop their administrative areas, to increase their tax income, and to invest in new infrastructure and in new TVEs, thus diversifying community business risk, as well as initiating pragmatic experimental reform programmes. For instance, collective TVEs (usually owned by local governments) could capitalize on the new market opportunities, having readier access to credit, productive inputs, and information, and possessing administrative advantages (Qian 2003). On the other side, community members received direct and indirect benefits from collective TVEs such as job opportunities, job security, pension funds, and communal welfare programmes.

[12] During the Maoist period China, despite its mistakes, achieved important results in economic development as well as in some important social issues. For instance, a base industrial sector was built up with the potential for further development, together with improvement of the agricultural infrastructure, such as building irrigation schemes. The healthcare and education systems were improved or introduced (especially in rural areas) and open to all citizens.

Furthermore, these market oriented enterprises also benefited from the presence of SOEs in heavy industries (e.g. for inputs) and at the same time enjoyed a smaller burden connected to welfare costs, together with a lower labour and land cost than urban enterprises.

Therefore, at the beginning of the reforms most of the new Chinese firms were neither private firms nor SOEs, but local government firms (i.e. run by TV governments) (Biggeri 2001). Although in the 1990s most TVEs were privatized, the performance of collective TVEs was pivotal for newly born SME industrial clusters and China's economic growth. Chinese local governments were so pragmatic that, even without any deep theoretical background on clustering processes, they followed the '*yi zhen yi pin*' policy, with one town or area specializing in one product and named as a 'Specialized Town' i.e. clusters based on both an industrial and territorial specialization.

The year 1984 is considered a turning point for reforms in the rural enterprise sector, since individual private enterprises (with fewer than eight employees) were allowed to exist. In addition, a year later the State Science and Technology Commission began implementing the 'Spark Plan' through technological demonstration centres, in order to overcome the problems of obsolete technologies and the lack of management training in the Chinese TVE sector (Biggeri et al. 1999). Once the institutional reforms took effect in the 1980s, enterprises were given the opportunity to retain profits, thus providing the first stage of an incentive structure. At this stage, central government encouraged a high rate of reinvestment of enterprise earnings through preferential tax treatment (especially for poor areas). In particular, TVEs were required to use after tax profits essentially for two purposes: reinvestment and provision of local public goods. In 1992, 59 per cent of the after tax profits of TVEs were reinvested, and 40 per cent were used for local public expenditure, a slightly higher proportion in each case than in 1985. Therefore, linkages between TVEs and local governments in China ensured avoiding the frequent situation of most developing countries, with low revenues collected by local governments and incapacity to invest in local public goods, especially in rural areas. These incentives were later enhanced when TVEs assumed responsibility for their own profits and losses, and when profit retention for higher administrative-level units was in part replaced by taxation.

From 1988 private TVEs (with more than eight employees) were allowed to register and pay tax. Thereafter, TVEs had to increasingly rely on markets for their inputs and sale of outputs, thus leading to intensification of competition between them. All in all, Chinese reforms gradually created a domestic competitive environment and 100 million new jobs were created in manufacturing.

Since collective TVEs remained poorly managed, in the late 1980s another institutional reform similar to the Household Responsibility System (HRS) in agriculture was introduced following the contract system. In particular, the opportunity to transfer—on the base of a short-/medium-term contract—full or partial management and control of the collective TVEs to an individual or a group of private entrepreneurs was introduced. At this stage, TVEs' development was facilitated indirectly by the Chinese Communist

Party (CCP) policy of 'leaving the land but not the village', which favoured investment on social infrastructure in small-sized towns, and directly by the decentralization and expansion of the Agricultural Bank of China and rural credit cooperatives. Finally, further institutional reforms and specific policies were implemented at the beginning of the 1990s to reinforce incentives for managers of collective TVEs and to reduce interference from local governments.

The development path of TVEs has also been influenced by two interdependent socio-economic features of Chinese economic development during the 1980s and 1990s: strong regional differences (e.g. in natural resources, human capital, and strategic economic location) and the international 'open-door' policy. The former, arising out of comparative advantages linked to initial factor endowments and of the implementation of different policies, were positively capitalized during the Dengist strategy of provincial development, along with agricultural specialization and diversification. The latter, started in 1979 with the opening of the first four 'special economic zones' in coastal areas, aimed at attracting foreign capital and technology in the coastal macro-region, making TVEs internationally competitive exporters of labour-intensive products (Findlay et al. 1994). In addition, joint ventures in the transfer of technology were important in helping rural firms, which had the advantages of cheaper land and labour, in overcoming the constraints of lack of capital, modern technology, and management skills. Moreover, protection of the Chinese economy implemented till 2001 provided Chinese infant industries with the opportunity to satisfy internal demand and protect it from disruptive international competition, opposite to the Russian case.

Although TVE clusters are one of the most captivating examples of industrial clusters development, the non-economic impact of industrial sector growth on the progress of Chinese society has been questioned by several authors, bringing China to the 'cross roads' (Nolan 2004). Chinese industrial clusters revealed their potential dark side on development especially after 1990. Indeed, this 'fabric of the world' has produced wealth and well-being but also rising inequalities, huge internal migration, environmental degradation and pollution, and unsuitable workplaces (Meng et al. 2005; Biggeri 2008). The level of exploitation of workers, especially migrant workers (more than 150 million), has been extremely high, with very limited rights (Chan 2003) and no increase in terms of minimum wages throughout the 1990s (Chan 2003). In particular, what has been 'negatively' impressive in China—from the workers' standpoint of well-being—is the precarious and unsafe workplace, and scarce social protection due to the quasi-absence of workers' unions, especially for temporary migrant workers (Hirsch 2005). For instance, in 2005, 2 million persons decided not to migrate as temporary workers to Guangdong Province. Labour discontent led to a huge upsurge in demonstrations, strikes, and other kinds of protests but also to more rights in some areas.

The over-exploitation of temporary migrant workers and low human development is connected both to the pressure from international markets and to local institutional arrangements on migration (Du et al. 2005; Biggeri 2008). In some Specialized Towns the presence of temporary migrant workers exceeds the local population (Hirsch 2005) and local institutions, and by allowing low income and minimal worker rights, created a vicious circle and negative outcomes to spread from the delocalization of production (i.e. a race to the bottom with high profits for investors) (Biggeri 2008). Therefore, these clusters were characterized on the one side by high collective efficiency with strong technological progress and productivity increase, and on the other side by very low social development with workers to serve as a 'reserve army of labour', in a Marxian sense. The high risk is to see this typology of clusters becoming even more frequent, both in China and in other BRICS and emerging countries, due to the exacerbation of international competition in an ever more connected and unstable global economy.

SOUTH AFRICAN POST-APARTHEID CHALLENGES: POLICIES FOR INDUSTRIAL CLUSTER DEVELOPMENT

In SA, MSMEs are estimated at between 1.6 and 3 million (2012 data) and are considered to play a relevant role in the national economy and in manufacturing, both in terms of employment and income generation (Kesper 2001; Ndabeni 2014). Since the beginning of a new democratic era for SA (1994), small business development has become a key policy focus of the socio-economic transition. Indeed, MSMEs have been considered pivotal in addressing high unemployment, activating domestic competition, tackling inequalities inherited from the apartheid period, contributing to black economic empowerment, and playing a crucial role in people's effort to meet their basic needs (see Republic of South Africa's White Paper, RSA 1995). However, several endogenous and exogenous factors affected the design, implementation, and impact of industrial policies in SA as similarly in many sub-Saharan economies (McCormick 1999).

A first group of factors concerns historical issues and the array of legacy issues dating back to the apartheid period that have been undermining economic and social progress and making the change at least partially 'unfulfilled'. According to the literature, the structural segmentation of the economy and society together with spatial inequalities are among the most significant historical distortions (Ndabeni 2014; Rogerson 2014). In particular, during the apartheid period industrial and business policies were in line with racial discrimination: the black population was simply seen as providing cheap labour for white business establishments and there was little scope for any policy to promote SMEs (Goldman 2003; Ndabeni 2014), leading to the creation of two disconnected and parallel economies: the 'first economy and second economy' (Ndabeni 2014). The first economy is made up of large firms in capital-intensive production for the upper end of the market, while the second economy is composed of small-scale producers largely informally producing labour-intensive goods for the lower end of the market (Ranis and Stewart 1995).

The other endogenous element of concern is about inherited spatial distortions, i.e. the rural–urban dichotomy and provincial disparities. For instance, it has been observed that service providers tend to be located in the prominent provinces of Gauteng, Western Cape, and Kwa-Zulu Natal (Ndabeni 2014).

The second group of factors are exogenous to MSMEs, being linked to the underperformance of the South African economy after its reinsertion into the global economy, and in particular due to the combination of global economic crises and ineffective national macro-/industrial policies. For instance, liberalization policies, China's entry into the WTO, and the contemporary expiry of the Multi-Fibre Arrangement in 2005 led to dramatic consequences for the textile sector. MSMEs facing international competition were thus unable to grow as expected and they even became incapable of exporting due to the pressure of international price products (Kesper 2001). As a consequence, most MSME products were directed to local markets, which were thus saturated by domestic production and imports.

All in all, economic policy between 1994 and 2007 has been overwhelmingly dominated by orthodox economic reforms, without giving enough time to domestic MSMEs to adapt to international fierce competition. In addition, the South African government initially almost entirely neglected the needs of informal enterprises and micro-enterprises, and the role of clustering.

Apart from several policies introduced within the official local economic development strategy,[13] a real shift in relation to industrial policy has emerged only since 2007 (Rogerson 2014). According to the literature (Rogerson 2014; Kaplinsky and Morris 2014; Ndabeni 2014), recognition that the 'one size fits all' approach was not appropriate for local economic development (LED) led to the Industrial Policy Action Plan from the national Department of Economic Development, the National Treasury, and from the Department of Trade and Industry. The plan identifies both key industrial sectors for government support and cluster-type programmes to be promoted with the help of the Small Enterprise Development Agency (SEDA). The activities of this agency were implemented with more sophisticated enterprise support through local business service centres, retail finance intermediaries, and manufacturing advice centres (Rogerson 2014: 311–12). The strategy is based on a proactive and locally driven approach for building a better local business environment by reducing red tape, upgrading the existing infrastructure and network of support for business incubators, and spreading technology stations in order to offer technology support to MSMEs (Ndabeni 2014).

According to Pisa et al. (2015), in SA clustering is a way of building a better local business environment in a manner that is ultimately risk reducing, because it spreads risk, reduces upgrading costs, and brings collectivized efficiency gains. Nonetheless,

[13] According to Rogerson (2014), it is possible to recognize three relevant steps. First, the 1996 constitution recognizes the significance of local governments and Section 152 obliges municipalities to promote the economic development of local communities. Second, in 1998 the White Paper on Local Government established the notion of 'developmental local government'. Third, the Local Government Municipal Systems Act of 2000 made the pursuit of Integrated Development Planning (IDP) a compulsory activity for local governments, and legislated for a number of key local economic development functions and responsibilities.

clustering initiatives have emerged through local purposive actions and despite being rarely the product of national government interventions, precisely because of the need to be sectorially embedded and to establish institutional intimacy with local firms, facilitators, and supporting organizations (Morris and Barnes 2006). In addition, the World Bank has been warning that clusters should neither be government-driven nor subsidized by public funds, and that government should not try to create them from 'scratch' (Morris and Barnes 2006: 2).

For what concerns the informal economy in SA, informal employment in non-agricultural activities is close to 80 per cent, with around 60 per cent of women in employment. According to most research, the informal sector enterprises or activities are characterized by: (i) small-scale operation; (ii) labour-intensive and low-skill demands; (iii) reliance on indigenous resources; (iv) unregulated and often competitive markets with relatively easy entry (Biggeri 2004). These informal activities in SA are not usually clustered and are located in black townships (Goldman 2003). In this regard, it is important to recall that in most countries, including SA, there is a strong heterogeneity within the informal sector with the presence of a dynamic part of and important linkages with the formal sector. Therefore, instead of considering the informal sector as an undifferentiated entity, it is necessary to distinguish a dynamic-advanced component in policymaking. This recognition should lead also to integrated traditional skills development policies with other policy instruments for SHD, such as the provision of credit, access to markets, enterprise development (David and Birch 1992), and empowerment issues (Sender 2003).

Embracing a place-based perspective, there is no 'single recipe' for all clusters,[14] and particularly for those in less favoured regions in SA in terms of human development. However, without specific proactive policies there would be little space for informal manufacturing activities in particular localities to upgrade and contribute to inclusive growth.

Thus, clustering upgrading policies in terms of productivity, social and environmental outcomes are central. Moreover, the informal sector role can go beyond the survival function by enhancing: employment generation (in the labour intensive sector); poverty reduction (job income, income diversification); output creation; internal/domestic trade expansion opportunities; emerging entrepreneurs formation; local human resource development; transformation of savings into local investment; use of appropriate technology in relation to local resources; skills endowment, and so on (Biggeri 2004). These initiatives should be aimed at improving the sector's performance and its capacity to employ more workers and transform what are often marginal and survivalist activities into decent forms of work through an empowerment process (Ndabeni 2014).

[14] For instance, a novelty to be examined is brought by Chinese state sponsored, but privately run, special economic zones, which have been established in six African economies including SA (Kaplinsky and Morris 2014).

Conclusion

Industrial clusters of SMEs are recognized worldwide as an effective means of industrial development. In BRICS countries their performances were substantially different, ranging from outstanding results in terms of industrial GDP growth, employment creation, and export strategy (as in China), to very poor performances (as in Russia where previous institutional settings encountered ineffective transition reforms). The different SME industrial clusters' evolution among BRICS arises from different institutional structures and reforms, different resource endowments (including human, social, and physical capital), and different industrial and macroeconomic policies. In addition, although some main patterns can be delineated in each country, SME industrial cluster development and patterns are also very differentiated within each country, being a product of a mix of contextual and territorial characteristics, and institutional settings' evolution.

As shown, we also learnt that even the very successful economic performances of industrial clusters can hide low social development and environmental degradation.

Therefore, the main policy implication for BRICS and other emerging countries is that separation of the 'economic' from the 'social' discourse in industrial policies, and especially in industrial cluster development strategies, is revealed to be short sighted and represents a myopic look at the effects in terms of social, technological, environmental, as well as economic development.

To conclude, key factors for moving industrial clusters of SMEs towards SHD concern the upgrading of human capital, the triggering of institutional arrangements and networks at local level, as well as the capacity to undertake collective action for the social and economic development of the area; and to respond, via resilience, to external shocks and recession periods. Social progress, however, is usually the result of a conscious coordination/governance among local stakeholders (Dei Ottati 2002). Therefore, it requires genuinely shared objectives, as well as a satisfactory distribution of income and benefits among the parties involved (fundamental for the renewal of the system); and increasing standards of living for the whole local population, which is fundamental to promoting cooperative labour–supplier relations and to obtaining social and environmentally friendly industrial production.

REFERENCES

Altenburg, T. and Meyer-Stamer, J. (1999). 'How to promote clusters: policy experiences from Latin-America', *World Development* 27/9: 1693–713.

Anand, P.B. (2014). 'Capability approach and sustainability: from theory to practice?', in S. Ibrahim and M. Tiwari (eds) *Capability approach – from theory to practice*. London: Palgrave Macmillan, 118–47.

Anand, S. and Sen, A.K. (2000). 'Human development and economic sustainability', *World Development* 28/12: 2029–49.

Arroio, A. (2014). 'Local productive systems and SME development in Brazil', in A. Arroio and M. Scerri (eds) *The Promise of Small and Medium Enterprises*. Oxford: Routledge, 36–75.

Arroio, A. and Scerri, M. (2014). *The Promise of Small and Medium Enterprises*. Oxford: Routledge.

Basile, E. (2013). *Capitalist Development in India's Informal Economy*. London: Routledge.

Becattini, G. (1990). 'The Marshallian industrial district as a socio-economic notion', in F. Pyke, G. Becattini, and W. Sengenberger (eds) *Industrial Districts and Inter-firm Cooperation in Italy*. Geneva: International Institute for Labour Studies, 83–105.

Becattini, G., Bellandi, M., Dei Ottati, G., and Sforzi, F. (eds) (2003). *From Industrial Districts to Local Development: An Itinerary Research*. Cheltenham: Edward Elgar Publishing.

Becattini, G., Bellandi, M., and De Propris, L. (eds) (2009). *A Handbook of Industrial Districts*. Cheltenham: Edward Elgar.

Biggeri, M. (2001). 'The township and village enterprises: the success of SMEs in rural China'. *Quaderni ISESAO*. Milan: Università Bocconi.

Biggeri, M. (2004). 'Growth with development: informal sector and human development in low-income sub-Saharan economies'. Studi e discussioni, no.140. Florence: Dipartimento di Scienze Economiche, Università degli Studi di Firenze.

Biggeri, M. (2008). 'China in perspective: from economic 'miracle' to human development?', in A. Deshpande (ed.) *Globalization and Development: A Handbook of New Perspectives*. New Delhi: Oxford University Press, 232–56.

Biggeri, M. and Chiappero Martinetti, E. (2010). 'Sviluppo umano sostenibile, capability approach e cooperazione internazionale' [Sustainable Human Development, capability approach and international cooperation], in M. Biggeri and G. Canitano (eds) *Temi avanzati di economia e politica della cooperazione internazionale allo sviluppo* [New topics in economics and policy for international development cooperation]. Milan: FrancoAngeli, 37–64.

Biggeri, M. and Ferrannini, A. (2014). *Sustainable Human Development: A New Territorial and People-Centred Perspective*. Basingstoke and New York: Palgrave Macmillan.

Biggeri, M., Gambelli, D., and Phillips, C. (1999). 'Small and medium enterprise theory: evidence for Chinese TVEs', *Journal of International Development* 2/2: 197–219.

Boschma, R. (2005). 'Proximity and innovation: a critical assessment', *Regional Studies* 39/1: 61–74.

Chan, A. (2003). 'Globalisation and China's "race to the bottom" in labour standards', *China Perspectives* 46/2003: 41–50.

Chiappero Martinetti, E. and Biggeri, M. (2013). 'Oltre l'agente rappresentativo e la metrica monetaria: il contributo di Amartya K. Sen' [Beyond the representative agent and the monetary metrics: the contribution by Amartya Sen], in E. Basile, G. Lunghini, and F. Volpi (eds) *Pensare il Capitalismo: nuove prospettive per l'Economia Politica* [Thinking Capitalism: New perspectives for Political Economy]. Milan: FrancoAngeli, 151–66.

Clark, D.A., Biggeri, M., and Frediani, A.A. (eds) (2019). *Sen's Capability Approach, Empowerment and Participation: Concepts, Methods and Applications*. Basingstoke and New York: Palgrave Macmillan.

Cornia, G. and Popov, V. (2001). *Transition and Institutions: The Experience of Late and Gradual Reformers*. Oxford: Oxford University Press.

Cravo, T.A., Becker, B., and Gourlay, A. (2015). 'Regional growth and SMEs in Brazil: a spatial panel approach', *Regional Studies* 49/12: 1995–2016.

David, S. and Birch, S.L. (1992). 'Formalizing the informal sector in a changing South Africa: Small-Scale Manufacturing on the Witwatersrand', *World Development* 20/7: 1029–45.

Dei Ottati, G. (2002). 'Social concertation and local development: the case of industrial districts', *European Planning Studies* 10/4: 449–66.

Du, Y., Park, A., and Wang, S. (2005). 'Migration and rural poverty in China', *Journal of Comparative Economics* 33: 688–709.

Ellman, M. (2003). 'Transition economies', in H.J. Chang (ed.) *Rethinking Development Economics*. London: Anthem Press, 179–98.

Findlay, C., Watson, A., and Wu, Harry X. (eds) (1994). *Rural Enterprises in China*. London: Palgrave Macmillan.

FMC (Foundation for MSME Clusters) (2011). *Report on 'Analysis of Factors for Employment in MSME Clusters*. New Delhi: FMC.

FMC (Foundation for MSME Clusters) (2012). *Micro Enterprise Development: Demand Side Perspective*. New Delhi: FMC.

Giuliani, E., Rabellotti, R., and Van Dijk, M.P. (eds) (2005). *Cluster Facing Competition: The Importance of External Linkages*. Aldershot: Ashgate.

Goldman, T. (2003). 'Organizing in South Africa's informal economy: an overview of four sectoral case studies'. SEED Working Paper No. 60. Geneva: International Labour Office.

Harris-White, B. (2003). *India Working: Essays on Society and Economy*. Cambridge: Cambridge University Press.

Hirsch, G. (2005). *Internal Labour Migration in China: Social and Economic Implications for the Guangdong Province*. Florence: Università degli Studi di Firenze, Tesi di dottorato di Ricerca in Politica ed Economia dei Paesi in Via di Sviluppo.

Humphrey, J. (2003). 'Opportunities for SMEs in developing countries to upgrade in a global economy'. SEED Working Paper No. 43. Geneva: International Labour Office.

Kaplinsky, R. and Morris, M. (2014). *Developing Industrial Clusters and Supply Chains to Support Diversification and Sustainable Development of Exports in Africa: A Composite Report*. Cairo: African Export-Import Bank.

Kesper, A. (2001). 'Failing or not aiming to grow? Manufacturing SMMEs and their contribution to employment growth in South Africa', *Urban Forum* 12/2: 171–203.

Lazzeretti, L., Sedita, S.R., and Caloffi, A. (2014). 'Founders and disseminators of cluster research', *Journal of Economic Geography* 14/1: 21–43.

McCormick, D. (1999). 'African enterprise clusters and industrialisation: theory and reality', *World Development* 27/9: 1531–52.

McIntyre, R. (2001). 'The role of SMEs in transition: growth and enterpreneurship'. Research for Action 49. Helsinki: UNU World Institute for Development Economics Research.

Markusen, A. (1996). 'Sticky places in slippery space: a typology on industrial districts', *Economic Geography* 72/3: 293–313.

Mazumdar, D. and Sarkar, S. (2008). *Globalization, Labour Markets and Inequality in India*. Oxford: Routledge.

Mehrotra, S. and Biggeri, M. (eds) (2007). *Asian Informal Workers: Global Risks, Local Protection*. London and New Delhi: Routledge.

Mehrotra, S., Gandhi, A., Kishore Sahoo, B., and Saha, P. (2012). 'Creating employment in the 12th Five Year Plan', *Economic & Political Weekly* 47/19: 63–73.

Meng, X., Gregory, R., and Wang, Y. (2005). 'Poverty, inequality, and growth in urban China 1986–2000', *Journal of Comparative Economics* 33: 710–29.

Morris, M. and Barnes, J. (2006). *Regional Development and Cluster Management: Lessons from South Africa.* Cape Town: SALDRU (Southern Africa Labour and Development Research Unit). Available at www.saldru.uct.ac.za, accessed 5 November 2018.

Nadvi, K. and Barrientos, S. (2004). *Industrial Clusters and Poverty Reduction. Towards a Methodology for Poverty and Social Impact Assessment of Cluster Development Initiatives.* Vienna: United Nations Industrial Development Organization.

Nadvi, K. and Schmitz, H. (1994). 'Industrial clusters in less developed countries: review of experiences and research agenda'. Institute of Development Studies Discussion Paper no. 339. Brighton: University of Sussex.

Nadvi, K. and Schmitz, H. (eds) (1999). 'Industrial cluster in developing countries', *World Development* Special Issue 27/9.

Naser, A. (2013). 'A critical evaluation of contributions made by the micro, small and medium enterprises in Indian economy', *International Journal of Marketing, Financial Services & Management Research* 2/7: 151–8.

NCEUS (National Commission for Enterprises in the Unorganised Sector) (2007). *Report on Conditions of Work and Promotion of Livelihoods in the Unorganised Sector.* New Delhi: NCEUS, Government of India.

Ndabeni, L.L. (2014). 'National systems of innovation and small enterprise development in South Africa', in A. Arroio and M. Scerri (eds) *The Promise of Small and Medium Enterprises.* Oxford: Routledge, 203–40.

Nolan, P. (2004). *China at the Crossroads.* Cambridge: Polity Press.

Parrilli, M.D. and Garcia, R. (2009). 'Industrial districts in Latin America: The role of local learning for endogenous development', in G. Becattini, M. Bellandi, and L. De Propris (eds) *The Handbook of Industrial Districts.* Northampton, MA, and Cheltenham: Edward Elgar, 585–97.

PC (Planning Commission, Government of India) (2013). *Twelfth Five Year Plan (2012–2017) Faster, More Inclusive and Sustainable Growth.* New Delhi: SAGE Publications.

Pietrobelli, C. and Rabellotti, R. (2004). *Upgrading in Clusters and Value Chains in Latin America: The Role of Policies.* Sustainable Development Department Best Practices Series. Washington, DC: Inter-American Development Bank.

Pike, A., Rodríguez-Pose, A., and Tomaney, J. (2007). 'What kind of local and regional development and for whom?', *Regional Studies* 41/9: 1253–69.

Pires, J.C., Cravo, T., Lodato, S., and Piza, C. (2013). 'Industrial clusters and economic performance in Brazil', IDB Working Paper Series, No. 475. Washington, DC: Inter-American Development Bank.

Pisa, N., Rossouw, R., and Viviers, W. (2015). 'Identifying industrial clusters for regional economic diversification: the case of South Africa's North West Province', *International Business & Economics Research Journal* 14/3: 501–24.

Porter, M. (1998). *The Competitive Advantage of Nations (with a new foreword).* New York: The Free Press.

Pyke, F. and Sengenberger, W. (eds) (1992). *Industrial Districts and Local Economic Regeneration.* Geneva: International Institute of Labour Studies.

Qian, Y. (2003). 'How reform worked in China', in D. Rodrik (ed.) *In Search of Prosperity. Analytical Narratives on Economic Growth.* Princeton, NJ: Princeton University Press, 297–333.

Radaev, V. (2001). 'The development of small entrepreneurship in Russia'. WIDER Discussion Paper n.2001/135. Helsinki: UNU World Institute for Development Economics Research.

Ranis, G., and Stewart, F. (1995). 'V-goods and the role of the urban informal sector in development'. Development Studies Working Paper. Turin: Centro Studi Luca D'Agliano.

Rogerson, C.M. (2014). 'Reframing place-based economic development in South Africa: the example of local economic development', *Bulletin of Geography. Socio-economic Series* 24/2014: 203–18.

Roy, S. (2012). 'Spatial organization of production in India: contesting themes and conflicting evidence', *Journal of Regional Development and Planning* 1/1: 1–16.

RSA (Republic of South Africa) (1995). *White Paper on National Strategy for the Development and Promotion of Small Business in South Africa.* Cape Town: Department of Trade and Industry.

Schmitz, H. (1995). 'Collective efficiency: growth path for small-scale industry', *Journal of Development Studies* 31/4: 529–66.

Schmitz, H. (1999). 'Global competition and local cooperation: success and failure in Sinos Valley, Brazil', *World Development* 27/9: 1627–50.

SEBRAE Brazilian Micro and Small Business Support Service and CNI (Confederação Nacional da Indústria) (2005). *Lei Geral das Micro e Pequenas Empresas: Anteprojeto de Lei — Frente Empresarial pela Lei Geral das Micro e Pequenas Empresas* [General Law of Micro and Small Enterprises: Preliminary Draft Law – Business Front by the General Law of Micro and Small Enterprises]. Brazil: Brazilian Micro and Small Business Support Service.

Sen, A.K. (1999). *Development as Freedom.* Oxford: Oxford University Press.

Sen, S. (2008). 'State, society and the market: Indian economy under economic reforms', in S.R. Hashim, K.S. Chalapati Rao, K.V.K. Ranganathan, and M.R. Murthy (eds) *Indian Industrial Development and Globalisation: Essays in Honour of S.K. Goyal.* Delhi: Academic Foundation, 539–56.

Sender, J. (2003). 'Rural poverty and gender: analytical frameworks and policy proposals', in H.J. Chang (ed.) *Rethinking Development Economics.* London: Anthem Press, chap. 18.

Sengenberger, W. (2009). 'The scope of industrial districts in the third world', in G. Becattini, M. Bellandi, and L. De Propris (eds) *The Handbook of Industrial Districts.* Northampton, MA, and Cheltenham: Edward Elgar, 630–42.

Sepulveda, L. and Amin, A. (2006). 'Decentralizing industrial policies: threat or opportunity in developing countries?', in P. Bianchi and S. Labory (eds) *International Handbook of Industrial Policy.* Cheltenham: Edward Elgar, chap. 8.

Sokolov, A. and Rudnik, P. (2014). 'Innovation in Russian SMEs: growth under transition', in A. Arroio and M. Scerri (eds) *The Promise of Small and Medium Enterprises.* Oxford: Routledge, chap. 3.

Stiglitz, J. (1999). *New Bridges across the Chasm: Institutional Strategies for the Transition Economies.* Washington, DC: World Bank.

Teixeira, F. (2010). 'Políticas de articulação productiva e suas vinculações com a política de desenvolvimento productivo no Brasil' [Productive articulation policies and their linkages with productive development policy in Brazil], in C. Ferraro (ed.) *Clusters y políticas de articulación productiva en América Latina* [Clusters and policies for productive development in Latin America]. Santiago de Chile: Comisión Económica para América Latina y el Caribe (CEPAL), 73–105.

UNDP (United Nations Development Programme) (1990). *Human Development Report 1990—Concept and Measurement of Human Development*. New York: Oxford University Press.

Venkataramanaiah, S. and Parashar, S.P. (2007). 'Enhancing the competitiveness of SMEs through industrial clusters: the Indian experience', *International Journal of Technology Management and Sustainable Development* 6/3: 227–43.

Wilson, P. (2011). 'Industrial policies in Latin America'. Working paper. Helsinki: World Institute for Development Economics Research, 2011/48.

World Bank (2016a). *Doing Business: Measuring Regulatory Quality and Efficiency*. Washington, DC: World Bank.

World Bank (2016b). *World Development Indicators*. Available at https://datacatalog.worldbank.org/dataset/world-development-indicators, accessed 9 March 2019.

Zavatta, R. (2008). *Financing Technology Entrepreneurs & SMES in Developing Countries: Challenges and Opportunities: Brazil Country Study*. Washington, DC: International Bank for Reconstruction and Development/World Bank.

9 Rural–urban migration and its multidimensional impact in China

Dan Meng, Yan Gao, and Xiaoyang Li

Introduction

The last few decades since China's reform and opening-up policy in 1978 have witnessed a quicker than ever growth of migration of labour from rural to urban areas seeking more employment opportunities and better livelihoods. There is a migration population of 6.57 million taking up only 0.66 per cent of China's total population based on the data of China's Third National Census in 1982. The latest results from the National Bureau of Statistics (NBS) survey carried out in China in 2015 suggest that such a migration population has reached 0.27747 billion which accounts for around 20 per cent of the total population (1.37462 billion), with an increase of 3.52 million over the previous year, an annual increase rate of 1.3 per cent. The migrant population size and its increasing rate from 2011 to 2015 can be seen in Figure 9.1 which is drawn from data from the 2016 Report on Migrant Population released by the Chinese National Bureau of Statistics.

According to Figure 9.1, despite a gradual decrease in the growing rate of migrant population from 2010 to 2015, total migrant population size has been increasing steadily from 0.24223 billion people to 0.27747 billion during this time period. Such an unprecedented process of rural–urban migration in China's society has influenced the well-being of large yet still rapidly growing numbers of rural–urban migrant workers, the regional economy of labour outflow and inflow areas, and the development of China's three major industries between which these migrant workers have transferred. In addition, national policies have in so many ways reflected the fact that issues of rural–urban migration in the China context have been at the centre of many economic and social scientific studies in recent years. In this round-up introductory chapter on China's rural–urban migration, we will introduce and summarize the existing literature reviews on this issue, make our own analysis on this basis, and then find possible gaps in the existing research that can be filled by future studies.

This chapter will begin by giving a clearer definition and classification of China's migrant workers, a rather diversified and complex social group in China, and then

Dan Meng, Yan Gao, and Xiaoyang Li, *Rural—urban migration and its multidimensional impact in China* In: *Handbook of BRICS and Emerging Economies*. Edited by: P.B. Anand, Shailaja Fennell, and Flavio Comim, Oxford University Press (2021).
DOI: 10.1093/oso/9780198827535.003.0009

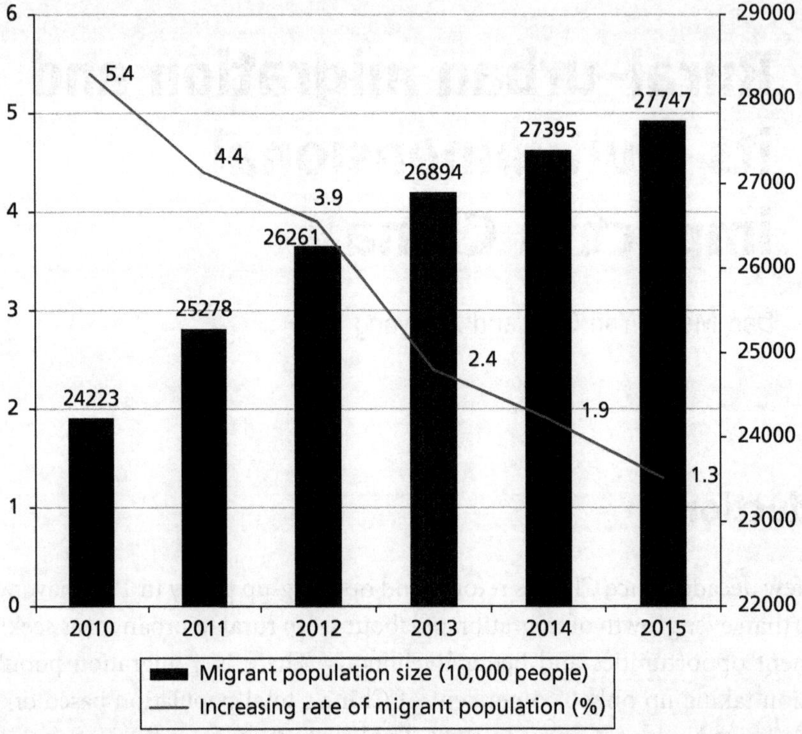

Figure 9.1 Migrant population size and its increasing rate in China, 2011–15

Source: Based on data drawn from NBS (2016).

explore how such a large-scale rural–urban labour flow taking place in this country in the past few decades has influenced (1) the well-being—both objective and subjective—of China's rural–urban migrant workers; (2) the regional economies of the labour outflow and inflow areas; (3) the impact of rural–urban migration on the development of China's primary, secondary, and tertiary industries; (4) China's national policy regarding these third industries and the people engaged in them.

The concept of China's migrant workers

'Migrant workers' in China's context can be seen as an umbrella term comprising two groups of people who are registered as rural residents: one group living in rural areas involved in non-agricultural industries; the other group who have been working not at their registered permanent residence or domicile but in other areas for more than six months (see data released by the Chinese [NBS 2014]). Even though there are many possible classifications of China's migrant workers based on different standards such as age—those born before the 1980s can be categorized as the original or first generation of migrant workers, and those born after as the new or second, or even third generation of migrants—the major ways of categorizing China's migrant workers depend on their work location, work category, or both

CLASSIFICATION OF CHINA'S MIGRANT WORKERS

Based on the classification found in the data released by China's NBS in the past decade, China's rural–urban migrant workers can mostly be divided into two different groups based on their living and working locations. The group transferring from working in agriculture to be occupied in other industries in their home town can be classified as local, or indigenous migrant workers; and the other group, moving out of their original places, as outflowing migrant workers. The outflowing rural–urban migrant workers can be further differentiated by whether they have migrated and made the transition to urban living by themselves or along with their whole family.

Based on the results of the Chinese NBS's sample survey in 2015, there are 1.0863 billion indigenous migrant workers with an increase of 2.89 million over the previous year at an annual growth of 2.7 per cent, and 1.6884 billion outflowing migrant workers with an increase of 0.63 million than in the year 2014 at an annual growth of 0.4 per cent (see data in NBS 2016 [*Report on Migrant Population*]).

We can see more clearly how the number of different types of migrant workers differentiated by their living and working location has grown from 2008 to 2015 in Figure 9.2 which is drawn based on the data from the 2014 and 2016 Report on Migrant Population released by the Chinese NBS.

Another widely used classification of China's rural–urban migrant workers is based on the type of work they do. The results of the Chinese NBS's survey on migrant people released in 2016 show that in 2015, 0.4 per cent of China's migrant workers were working in the primary industry, or in agriculture, which is 0.1 per cent lower than in 2014. A total of 55.1 per cent of migrant workers are engaged in the secondary industry which is 1.5 per cent lower than the previous year, and 44.5 per cent in the tertiary industry which is 1.6 per cent higher than 2014 (see the occupation structure of China's migrant workers in 2014 and 2015 in Table 9.1).

We can also combine the two key elements—their work location and work category—together and classify China's migrant workers based on what type of work they are doing in which location (see Table 9.2).[1]

We can see from Table 9.3 that generally speaking, the majority of China's migrant workers in the eastern and middle areas are occupied in the secondary industry, while those

[1] The eastern areas of China are made up of eleven cities or provinces comprising Beijing, Tianjing, Hebei, Liaoning, Shanghai, Jiangsu, Zhejiang, Fujian, Shandong, Guangdong, and Hainan; the middle areas of eight provinces comprising Shanxi, Jilin, Heilongjiang, Anhui, Jiangxi, Henan, Hubei, and Hunan; and the western areas of twelve provinces or municipalities comprising Inner Mongolia, Guangxi, Chongqing, Sichuan, Guizhou, Yunnan, Tibet, Shanxi, Gansu, Qinghai, Ningxia, and Xinjiang.

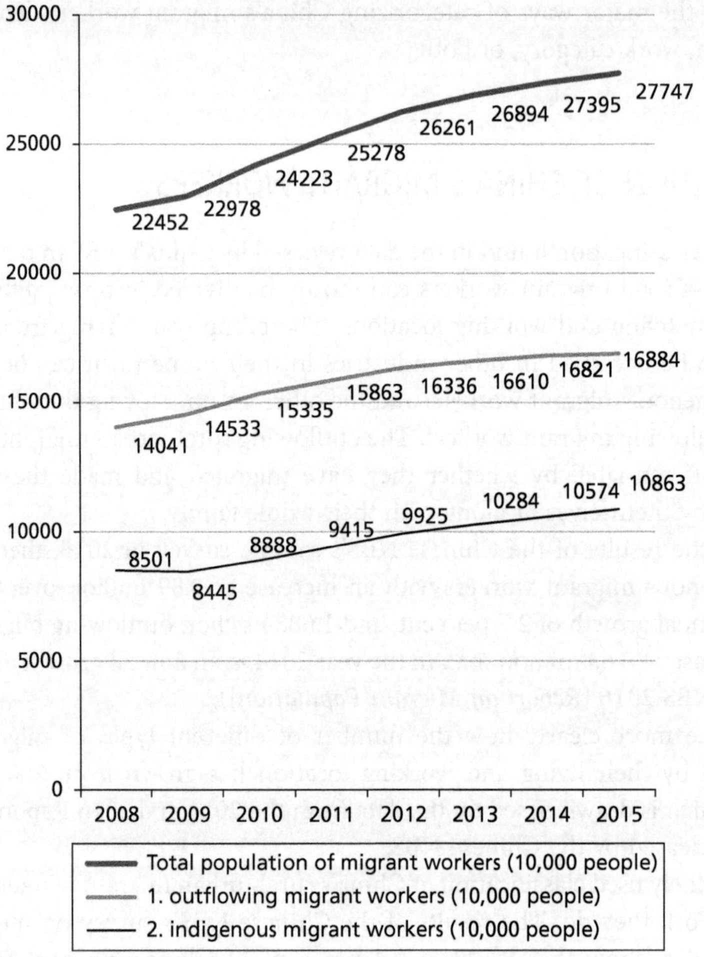

Figure 9.2 Number of different types of migrant worker differentiated by living and working location, 2008–15

Source: Based on data drawn from NBS 2016.

in the western areas are mainly in the tertiary industry. While the proportion of China's migrant workers engaged in the first and second industries in different areas has been consistently steady or slightly decreasing from 2014 to 2015, the proportion of migrant workers engaged in the third industry in these areas has been increasing in the eastern, middle, and western areas at an annual rate of 1 per cent, 1 per cent, and 3.1 per cent respectively over the same time period.

THE FOCUS OF THIS CHAPTER: RURAL–URBAN MIGRANT WORKERS

Of all the different types of migrant workers we have explained so far, our discussion will focus on those who have migrated out of rural areas and made the transition to urban

Table 9.1 Proportion of China's migrant workers occupied in different industries in 2014 and 2015

(%)

Category of occupation	Total migrant workers engaged in this industry in 2014	Total migrant workers engaged in this industry in 2015	The growing or reducing rate of migrant population engaged in this industry from 2014 to 2015
First industry (Agriculture)	0.5	0.4	–0.1
Second industry	56.6	55.1	–1.5
Manufacture	31.3	31.1	–0.2
Construction	22.3	21.1	–1.2
Tertiary industry	42.9	44.5	1.6
Wholesale and retail	11.4	11.9	0.5
Transportation, storage, and post-industry	6.5	6.4	–0.1
Accommodation and catering	6.0	5.8	–0.2
Neighbourhood services, repair, and other services	10.2	10.6	0.4

Source: 2016 Report on Migrant Population released by the Chinese (NBS 2016). Available at www.stats.gov.cn/tjsj/zxfb/201604/t20160428_1349713.html, accessed 6 November 2018.

Table 9.2 Proportion of China's migrant workers based on work location and work category, 2014 and 2015

(%)

Category of occupation	Eastern areas		Middle areas		Western areas	
	2014	2015	2014	2015	2014	2015
First industry (Agriculture)	0.4	0.4	0.4	0.3	0.8	0.7
Second industry (Manufacture and construction)	61.2	60.2	52.5	50.7	47.1	44.1
Third industry (Wholesale and retail; Transportation, storage and post-industry; Accommodation and catering; Neighbourhood services, repair, and other services)	38.4	39.4	47.1	49.0	52.1	55.2

Source: Data extracted from the 2016 Reports on Migrant Population released by the Chinese (NBS 2016). Available at www.stats.gov.cn/tjsj/zxfb/201604/t20160428_1349713.html, accessed 6 November 2018.

Table 9.3 Working time and labour intensity of rural–urban migrant workers

	2012	2013	2014	2015
Annual working time (months)	9.9	9.9	10.0	10.1
Monthly working time (days)	25.3	25.2	25.3	25.2
Daily working time (houses)	8.7	8.8	8.8	8.7
Percentage of rural–urban migrant workers working more than 8 hours per day (%)	39.6	41.0	40.8	39.1
Percentage of rural–urban migrant workers working more than 44 hours per week (%)	84.4	84.7	85.4	85.0

Source: Data extracted from the 2013 and 2016 Reports on Migrant Population released by the Chinese (NBS 2013, 2016). Available at www.stats.gov.cn/tjsj/zxfb/201405/t20140512_551585.html, accessed 6 November 2018; www.stats.gov.cn/tjsj/zxfb/201604/t20160428_1349713.html, accessed 6 November 2018.

employment and living for more than six months, a particular group usually referred to as rural–urban migrant workers. This particular group of migrants had become the majority of China's migrant population by 2013 judging from data released by the Chinese NBS in 2013 suggesting that more than 60 per cent of China's total migrants came from rural areas, and nearly 70 per cent of them have migrated into urban areas (see the 2014 [NBS 2014] *Report on Migrant Population*).

We choose to put this particular group of migrant workers at the centre of this chapter to gain an insight into whether the well-being and/or livelihood—which can be measured both by their objective well-being denoted by income and social welfare they enjoy, and by their subjective well-being denoted by their self-reporting on happiness and life satisfaction—of these migrants has improved compared to their family or friends who remain in rural areas and to their new neighbours or co-workers after they have migrated from rural to urban areas. In addition, their moving between different spatial areas may have influenced the economies both of the areas out of which they have moved and of the areas into which they have migrated in a significant way that is worth investigating. Furthermore, along with their migration from rural to city areas, they have also made a transition from working in the primary industry, agriculture, to occupations in the secondary or tertiary industries. The corresponding effects such transition may have exerted on these different industries will be shown, while China's economic development cannot and should not be dismissed itself. So when these rural–urban migrants have made the transition from rural to urban living, and shifted from working in the primary to the secondary or the tertiary industries, China's policymakers may also have made some corresponding changes to national policies regarding the development of rural and urban areas—in the three major industries—agriculture, manufacture, and services—as well as the people who are living in China's diversified spatial areas and working in these different industries. Research on such policy changes can be very helpful in providing us with a more comprehensive understanding of all the deep influences rural–urban migration may have inflicted on this country and its people. In light of all these, rural–urban migrant workers might be the best entry point for our investigation into all the possible influences of China's rural–urban migration on China's economic development and the livelihood or the well-being of its people.

Influence of China's rural–urban migration

The possible influences of China's rural–urban migration on the well-being or livelihood of these rural-urban migrant workers themselves, the economies of labour workforce outflow and inflow areas, development of the three major industries in China, and China's national policies regarding these industries and the people working in them will be explored in this section.

WELL-BEING OF CHINA'S RURAL–URBAN MIGRANT WORKERS

The concept of well-being can be seen as an umbrella term consisting of a series of factors that contribute to quality of life. According to the UK Office for National Statistics, well-being 'includes both subjective and objective measures'.[2] The quality of an individual's life used mainly to be measured and evaluated in an external and objective way, a way in which their life was judged by others based on objective criteria such as income, wealth, health, education, and so on until the late 1950s when the subjective approach emerged as an important alternative to the objective approach for measuring people's well-being, as social scientists tried to pursue a humanistic scientific agenda by developing indicators of quality of life to examine social change and to advance policymaking (Land 1975: 5–36). A more comprehensive understanding of the well-being of China's rural–urban migration should take into consideration both their objective and subjective well-being.

Objective Well-Being

There is no denying that judging by the objective or more easily calculated economic measures—such as income level, usually regarded as the most important well-being index in the traditional well-being study—the objective well-being of China's rural–urban migrants has improved significantly since they made the transition into urban employment and living (see Figure 9.3 based on data drawn from the 2014 and 2016 Reports on Migrant Population released by the Chinese NBS).

Figure 9.3 illustrates that the average monthly per capita income of outflowing migrant workers, or rural–urban migrant workers, was 2,609 yuan (around US$379) in 2013, nearly double that of rural–urban migrant workers in 2008, with an increase of 319 yuan (around US$46) over the previous year, an annual growth rate of 13.9 per cent. Even though the annual growth rate has been declining between 2013 and 2015, from 13.9 per cent to 7.2 per cent, the absolute monthly per capita income of rural–urban migrant workers has been increasing from 2,609 yuan (around US$379) per person to 3,072 yuan (around US$447) per person over the same time period.

Subjective Well-Being

It has been discovered that among the total population, Chinese rural–urban migrants have reported the lowest mean happiness score (2.3) compared to that of rural residents (2.7) and urban residents (2.5) (Knight and Gunatilaka 2012: 96). It seems that even though China's rural–urban migrants may have experienced a boost in livelihood with a higher income level and accordingly increasing spending power, they are not necessarily

[2] Available at www.ons.gov.uk/ons/index.html, accessed 7 November 2018.

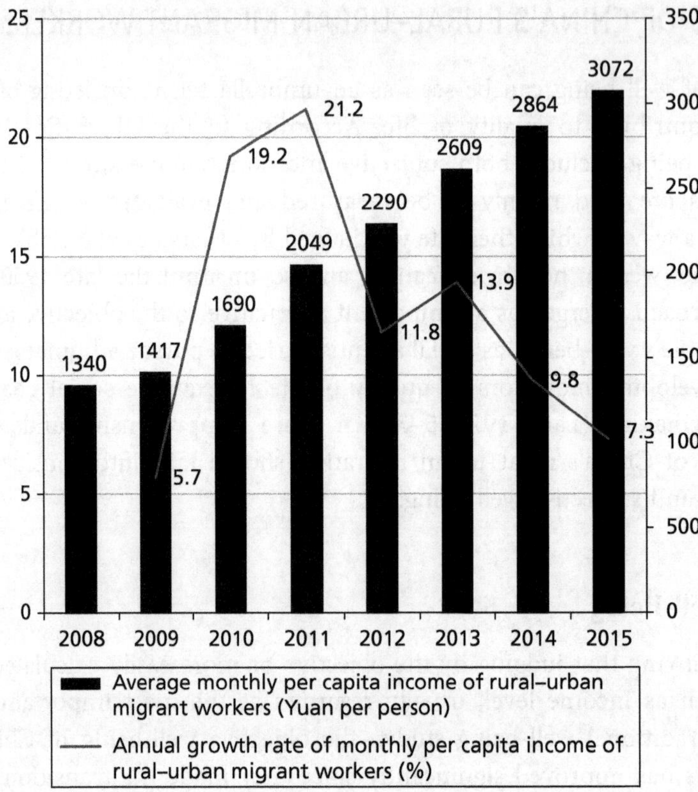

Figure 9.3 Average monthly per capita income of rural–urban migrant workers and annual growth rate, 2008–15

Source: Data drawn from NBS 2014, 2016.

happier or more satisfied with their lives. Or to put it in another way, the objective well-being of China's rural–urban migrants may not be directly proportional to their subjective well-being, and this is a major reason why we shouldn't measure their well-being merely from the lens of objective indicators for well-being that can easily be denoted by their annual or monthly income levels. Possible reasons for why there seems to be a sharp contrast between the significantly improved objective well-being of China's rural–urban migrant workers shown by a much higher average income level on one hand, and a much lower level of subjective well-being denoted by the lowest self-reported happiness scores on the other will be discussed in the next sub-section.

Lack of Correlation between Objective and Subjective Well-Being of China's Rural–Urban Migrant Workers

It will be argued in this sub-section that there are at least three lenses through which we could try to make sense of the lack of correlation between the subjective and objective well-being of China's rural–urban migrants. These are: (1) the relativistic judgement models; (2) adaptation; (3) lack of correlation between increased choices and opportunities, and actual happiness (Kahneman et al. 1999; Hirata 2008: 173).

To begin with, we could understand this lack of correlation between subjective and objective well-being from the lens of the relativistic judgement models such as that suggested by Easterlin who argues that raising income may not necessarily result in raising happiness because people evaluate the adequacy of their income not in absolute terms but in social comparisons with others (Easterlin 1974: 89–125, 1995, 35–47; Veenhoven 2005; Veenhoven and Vergunst 2014: 311–43). A possible explanation is that rural–urban migrant workers tend to feel less satisfied with their lives when they compare themselves with urban residents who are better off in terms of income, welfare benefits they are entitled to enjoy, or social status. In other words, they are less happy because they don't feel like they are able to 'keep up with the Joneses'.

Another possible explanation is that Chinese rural–urban migrants tend to adjust their aspirations upwards after they relocate to urban areas and hence become harder to satisfy. Among all six major forms of adaptation and related phenomena that influence mental reactions (Knight and Gunatilaka 2012: 96), a certain type of adaptation—the hedonic treadmill—is most likely to have affected subjective well-being of Chinese rural–urban migrants (Easterlin 2001: 465–84). In sharp contrast to non-grumbling acceptance or resignation which indicates that people who live in unsatisfying objective conditions may identify themselves as better off than they are or should be—taking Chinese rural residents who reported an overall greater happiness and/or life satisfaction than objectively better off urban residents and rural–urban migrants for example—there is another common form of adaptation that could be seen as the reverse or opposite of non-grumbling resignation: the hedonic treadmill to improved circumstances, which is very likely to be the case of Chinese rural–urban migrants.

Theoretically and empirically speaking, people in the middle of the income ladder—or in other words, people who are on the onward trend of social mobility—often tend to report lower levels of happiness and/or life satisfaction than those who are in the upper or lower bottom of the income ladder due to the hedonic treadmill (Graham and Pettinato 2000). A possible explanation for the lowest mean happiness score of Chinese rural–urban migrants in the middle of the income ladder is that they can be identified as 'frustrated achievers'. Their feelings towards relative deprivation are much stronger than those of rural residents who, unlike rural–urban migrants, rarely get to observe the rich and fancy urban lifestyle personally at such close quarters, or to experience discrimination in terms of access to jobs, wages, and education as well as all kinds of welfare towards housing, healthcare, etc., due to China's residential registration, or *hukou*, system (Meng 2013: 48–72).

There is a third explanation for the lack of correlation between Chinese rural–urban migrant workers' objective and subjective well-being which can be seen as a critique of the capability approach to subjective well-being which focuses mainly on capabilities and freedom of choice instead of on how or whether these capabilities and freedoms can be transformed into an actual happy or happier life. As we can see from the declining subjective well-being of Chinese rural–urban migrants—who, after making the transition to urban employment and living, became economically better off and had more choices and opportunities in life—that capabilities themselves, or an increasing number of capabilities within the capabilities set may not necessarily, let alone automatically, transform into an improvement in subjective well-being. Along with new choices made possible for Chinese rural migrant workers after they moved to urban areas—such as choices to seek better employment opportunities, to enjoy more comprehensive welfare, to send their children to better schools, to obtain an urban *hukou*, and become official urban residents, or to come back to their rural settings, etc.—they did not seem to be leading a happier life than before considering that they reported the greatest decline in happiness as well as the lowest happiness score compared to both urban and rural residents.

It has been argued that 'a larger range of options apparently makes people more likely to feel regret afterwards because the chance of choosing a suboptimal option is greater' (Hirata 2008: 173). It is also been found that there may be a positive correlation between more choices and depression (Schwartz 2000: 80). Schwartz noticed that new choices were usually accompanied by an increase in life expectation (ibid.: 81). From a psychological perspective, it is rather natural that people would feel a sense of frustration and maybe even depression when things did not go as expected. If improved expectations are based on new choices, people are more likely to regret the choices they made when faced with multiple alternatives when the results of their choices couldn't live up to their higher expectations, and to blame themselves for making the allegedly wrong choices, or for not having made better choices.

Last but not least, it has been confirmed by an in-depth PhD research conducted from 2013 to 2016 based on samples drawn from 241 rural residents in the Kangping County in Liaoning Province and 154 rural–urban migrants who had migrated from Kangping to Beijing that it is possible that the subjective well-being of Chinese rural residents is mediated not only by the financial domains of their lives, which can be denoted by income level and wealth, but also by the non-financial domains of their lives (Meng 2013). The robustness of the correlation between all these 395 respondents' self-reported overall happiness scores and their psychological needs for autonomy shown in the data in the subjective well-being survey questionnaire specifically designed for this research can be verified; so can the positive correlation between these 395 respondents' self-reported overall happiness scores and the lack of changes in their daily behaviour (such as sleeping and eating) and possible low moods (such as depression and hopelessness).

THE REGIONAL ECONOMY

We mentioned in the Introduction that a large number of rural residents as workforce had been rushing into city areas so that China's urbanization process has been quicker than ever since its economic reformation in 1978; remarkably, this massive labour migration seems to have been contributing to China's economic growth which can be denoted by, for instance, a rather high average annual GDP growth rate of 9.5 per cent. However, while China's overall economy develops rapidly, at the same time the gap in the regional economy has gradually widened. In 2011, for example, Tianjin's per capita GDP is 85,213 yuan, while Guizhou's GDP per capita is only 16,413 yuan. Such a large gap may not only exert a huge influence on overall economic growth, but may also cause conflict between and within different regions, and even endanger unity and security on a national level (Demurger 2001: 95–117). Speaking from these perspectives, a study of the interactive relationship between labour migration and regional economic growth can be of great importance in researching China's development.

According to the new classical economic theory, mobility or migration of the labour workforce in Chinese society might be very helpful in promoting regional economic growth convergence and balancing economic development; investigation of such a phenomenon can be of great significance for policymakers thinking of coordinating China's regional economic development. Furthermore, a study of the spatial link between China's labour migration and regional economic growth might be of great referential value to studies on labour migration in the framework of spatial economics either in China's environment or in the international context.

Whether the gap in the growth of China's regional economy tends to be divergent or convergent has always been the focus of previous academic debates. On the one hand, according to Karl Gunnar Myrdal's cumulative circular causality theory, such a widening regional economic gap seems to be the result of a cumulative economic effect. On the other hand, J.G. Williamson's inverted 'U' type theory, John Friedman's core periphery theory, and Albert Otto Hirschman's unbalanced growth theory seem to have pointed to a consensus indicating that change in this regional economic gap is a constant process of fluctuation. A great number by far of theoretical and empirical analyses on this fluctuation trend have been made by Chinese as well as by foreign scholars from the lens of divergence and convergence theory. As early as 1991, Barro and Sala-i-Martin had applied the new classical economic model (β convergence model) created by Baumol in 1986 to measure economic convergence in twenty countries (Barro et al. 1991: 107–82). Following this empirical analysis, this model became the standard for measuring regional economic development. Rey and Montuori have summarized three types of regional convergence, and used the convergence to study the US's regional economic convergence from 1929 to 1994, revealing the dynamic mechanism of regional economic convergence from a groundbreaking angle of space (Rey and Montouri 1999: 143–56). Later, Fingleton and Bernard, Fidrmuc, and Kırdar and Saracoğlu have respectively studied the contribution of migration to the regional economic convergence in the EU, Central Europe, and Turkey (Fingleton 2001: 117–47; Fidrmuc 2004: 230–47; Kırdar and Saracoğlu 2008: 545–66).

In China's academic world, Qiang (2001) seems to be the first to bring labour mobility into the convergence test, and to have found that China's regional economic growth convergence can be significantly periodic and regional (Qiang 2001: 70–7). Many efforts have been made to adopt the new classical model to analyse the influence of China's human capital and net population migration on the regional economic growth convergence (Mao and Zhai 2013: 45–56), while much more specific research on the link between migration and regional development can also be found in the China context (Ma 1999: 783–802).

To sum up, many accomplishments have been made so far by both Chinese and foreign scholars within the framework of the regional economic development research. Nevertheless, the majority of scholars in this field tend to investigate the influential factors of regional economic development, spillover effects, and regional economic convergence. There are very few literatures studying the space correlation between migration, population distribution, and regional economic growth in China's urbanization process. Hence, the spatial structure evolution from the lens of time series remains to be investigated. Great effort in using the spatial lag regression model and Moran scatter plot to measure the convergence of China's provincial and regional economic growth, and to analyse how labour mobility or migration is linked to regional economic growth based on the data sample of China's thirty provinces can be seen in a recent paper on which two of this chapter's authors have collaborated (Li et al. forthcoming).

The Economy of Labour Inflow Areas

On the topic of how China's rural–urban migration has affected the economic development of labour inflow areas, the existing literature seems to have been focused on three major effects: output, crowding-out and welfare effects.

To begin with, the output effect usually refers to the phenomenon of (1) a noteworthy increase in supplementing labour into areas to which rural–urban migrant workers have migrated; (2) considerable enhancement in employment productivity in labour inflow areas because other than the fact that many of these rural–urban migrant workers are quite efficient and productive at work themselves, with the inflow of an increasingly growing number of rural–urban migrant workers—usually hard working, strictly disciplined, and willing to work at a relatively low level of pay—seeking for employment opportunities, existing workers in the secondary and tertiary industries in urban areas are also pressured to improve their own labour productivity. And overall labour productivity in various industries in these labour inflow areas can be greatly boosted as a result (Peng 1999: 34–41).

Second, the inflow of a large low-cost labour workforce from rural to urban areas may cause the unsaturated labour market in these areas to become flooded; this is called the crowding-out effect (Banister and R.J. 1991: 3–20). The major reason why these rural–urban migrant workers could cause the crowding-out effect in workforce inflow areas is because they are often willing to work just as hard—or even harder—than the urban workers—and at a lower, sometimes much lower, price. We can take a look at general working time and labour intensity nowadays among rural–urban migrant workers in

Table 9.4 Percentage of rural–urban migrant workers who enjoy such welfare benefits as insurances

(%)

	2008	2009	2010	2011	2012	2013
Pensions insurance	9.8	7.6	9.5	13.9	14.3	15.7
Accident insurance	24.1	21.8	24.1	23.6	24.0	28.5
Medical insurance	13.1	12.2	14.3	16.7	16.9	17.6
Unemployment insurance	3.7	3.9	4.9	8.0	8.4	9.1
Maternity insurance	2.0	2.4	2.9	5.6	6.1	6.6

Source: 2014 Report on Migrant Population released by the Chinese (NBS 2014). Available at www.stats.gov.cn/tjsj/zxfb/201405/t20140512_551585.html, accessed 6 November 2018.

China in Table 9.4 based on data from the 2014 and 2016 Reports on Migrant Population released by the Chinese (see NBS 2014, 2016).

It can be observed from Table 9.4 that by 2015, the average annual working time for rural–urban migrant workers is 10.1 months, with an annual increase of 0.1 months over the previous year. These rural–urban migrant workers work 25.2 days per month on average, with around 8.7 hours per day being spent working. Besides, more than 39.1 per cent of these rural urban migrant workers work more than 8 hours on a daily basis, and more than 85 per cent of them work more than 44 hours on a weekly basis according to data drawn from the 2016 *Report on Migrant Workers* released by the NBS (2016).

In addition, unlike urban workers with urban *hukou* who can enjoy basic welfare benefits such as pension insurance, employers don't often have to provide rural migrant workers with these, hence rural–urban migrant workers become more and more appealing in the eyes of urban employers, especially in the low-skill labour market. But it should be mentioned that despite a much lower percentage of rural–urban migrant workers who can enjoy basic welfare benefits from their employers compared to their urban co-workers, such a percentage has been rising over the years, as seen in Table 9.5 (due to a lack of data on this subject in the 2016 *Report on Migrant Population* released by the Chinese NBS, possible changes in the percentage of rural–urban migrant workers who enjoy social welfare remain unknown).

There is a crowding-out effect caused by the inflow of these rural migrant workers into the highly skilled labour market as well, even though such an effect may not be as obvious as the one which can be observed in the low-skilled labour market. A certain percentage of rural–urban migrant workers are properly educated and can be further trained to be highly skilled workers, thus becoming more competitive in the highly skilled labour market and making it harder for locals to be employed in such a market.

Table 9.5 Percentage of rural–urban migrant workers who have received skills training

(%)

	Received agricultural skills training		Received non-agricultural skills training		Received skills training	
	2012	2013	2012	2013	2012	2013
Total	10.7	9.3	25.6	29.9	30.8	32.7
20 years and under	4.0	5.0	22.3	29.9	24.0	31.0
21–30	6.2	5.5	31.6	34.6	34.0	35.9
31–40	11.0	9.1	26.7	31.8	32.0	34.1
41–50	14.9	12.7	23.1	27.8	30.5	32.1
50 years and above	14.5	12.4	16.9	21.2	25.5	25.9

Source: 2014 Report on Migrant Population released by the Chinese (NBS 2014). Available at www.stats.gov.cn/tjsj/zxfb/201405/t20140512_551585.html, accessed 6 November 2018.

Finally, the welfare effect brought up by many scholars means that these rural–urban migrants usually take up jobs that are either too demanding, difficult, or even dangerous for most of the urban workers who are unwilling to do them, such as back-breaking manual labour in the construction or mining industries; or too troublesome for relatively low revenue in the eyes of urban residents, for example working all night to prepare simple food to sell to residents in the nearby neighbourhood for breakfast every morning. According to Table 9.1, 10.2 per cent of migrant workers were occupied in these neighbourhood services in 2014, and 10.6 per cent in 2015. Even though these jobs—taken by rural–urban migrant workers—may not be so economically rewarding for their hard work, they do make many urban citizens' lives much more comfortable and convenient, and thus the so-called welfare effect on the daily life of urban residents (Kai 1995: 90–5).

Economy of Labour Outflow Areas

The four dominant influences of China's rural–urban migration on the economy of workforce outflow areas that can be found in the existing literature are on shortages, revenue, industrial capital, and the technology spillover effects.

First, there is an obvious shortage of agricultural labour in many rural areas as the original rural residents working in agriculture either turn to secondary or tertiary industries in their home town or migrate to urban areas. Moreover, with an increasingly large number of young people leaving for urban areas hunting for urban employment and living, the remaining workforce in rural areas is usually at an advanced age and relatively less educated so that they can only take on the simplest agricultural activities without using many more sophisticated agricultural production techniques, while much of the originally cultivated land has gradually gone out of agricultural use through neglect and lack of proper protection. And all this deficiency of agricultural labour and waste of land can be labelled 'the shortage effect' (Fleisher and Yang 2004).

Next, the revenue effect refers to the fact that with higher income levels and thus increasing spending power of rural–urban migrants when they have made the transition into urban employment, a large percentage of migrants take a big percentage of their newly earned revenue back to where they are from—to improve the living conditions of their family who remain in these rural areas—either by giving money directly back to their family so that people left in rural areas can afford to invest more in their daily agricultural production, or by purchasing for them all kinds of improvement goods such as large household appliances or even new real estate properties. All this new revenue flowing into the original places from which these rural–urban migrant workers came can be very beneficial to the economic development of these labour outflow areas (Ahlburg 1996: 391–400; Shi and Renwei 1999: 17–26).

Furthermore, the industrial capital effect many scholars have been talking about means that many rural–urban migrant workers may have chosen to return to their home town to establish businesses after they have managed to save up enough seed money and learned the necessary skills and knowledge to start a business after years of hard work in urban areas (Fang 2003: 21–9).

Last but not least, the technology spillover effect on labour outflow areas means that many of the technologies mastered by these rural–urban migrant workers—which have gained them useful economic information during their work in urban areas—could easily be brought back to their original places of work and benefit the economic development of these areas accordingly (Yifu 2000).

THE IMPACT OF RURAL–URBAN MIGRATION ON CHINA'S INDUSTRIES

The impact of rural–urban migration on the development of China's agricultural and non-agricultural industries including the primary (agricultural), secondary (manufacturing), and tertiary (service) industries will be explored in this section.

The Impact of Migration on Manufacturing and Service Industries

The impact of migration on China's industry— especially on manufacturing and services—has been discussed extensively in existing literature,. It is generally believed that migration has helped China ensure a supply of cheap labour so that the country has been able to sustain its economic development, much of it depending on world trade (Lin et al. 2003). Studies show that in Shenzhen, while migrant workers increased from 105 million in 2001 to 140 million in 2007 (Cai and Chan 2009: 513–31), exports grew at annual rates exceeding 20 per cent almost at the same time (Chan 2010: 513–30). According to Kroeber (2010), between 2003 and 2008 around 50 million new positions were created in manufacturing and 39 million in services (Kroeber 2010: 35–46).

This is because—due to the large rural–urban income gap divided institutionally by the dual household registration system—the cost of migrant labour has been very low. For example, it has been found that in China unit labour costs in manufacturing are very low relative to a wide range of countries including the US, EU countries, Japan, Mexico, Korea, and most other newly industrialized countries, being about 25–40 per cent of the US level (Ceglowski and Golub 2007: 597–617). At the same time, however, industries in manufacturing and services are both facing the challenges of less qualified domestic workers. According to another source, hotel managers have unanimously recognized that they had to depend on less qualified migrant employees, resulting in high training costs and turnover rates (Zhang and Wu 2004: 424–8).

It is well acknowledged that migrant workers are a vulnerable group due to various discriminative policies in employment, medical insurance, pensions, and education, leaving the majority of migrant workers unprotected. In many big cities, jobs are closed to migrant workers, so that they are left with the jobs with lowest wages and least formality (Zhao and Howden-Chapman 2010: 363–84). Institutional constraints create difficulties for migrants living in urban areas and these deter or prevent migrant workers from bringing their families with them. In addition to institutional barriers, the decline in fertility is considered to have reduced the supply of young rural labour, the essential pool of labour for China's export industry (Li et al. 2012: 57–74). In recent years, shortages of migrant labour in cities are widely reported following the 2008–09 financial crises, especially in the Pearl River Delta and Yangtze River Delta areas.

Despite all this, the trend of rural–urban migration has continued. According to a government report in 2014 (see the 2014 China Migrant Population Development Report, NBS 2014), China's migrant population had reached 236 million by 2012, or 16.7 per cent of all citizens. It is estimated that the figure might reach 400 million in 2025. Compared with the earlier generation of migrant workers, the new generation moved to the cities at a much younger age. Around 75 per cent of them left their rural areas before their twentieth birthday, and 70 per cent of them expected to settle down in large cities.

The Impact of Migration on Agriculture

With more rural population migrated to towns and cities, village hollowing has become a phenomenon in recent years. During 1996–2008, the rural resident population in China decreased by 135.2 million as a result of out-migration to urban areas (Liu and Chen 2010: 876–88). As a result, current studies have been mostly focused on the vacancy and idleness of rural dwellings (Long et al. 2009: 1203–13; Chen et al. 2010: 727–35), and there has been less research on the impact of migration on agricultural production.

An early study reveals that migration had considerable impact on agriculture on at least two accounts (Croll and Ping 1997: 128–46). The first is the relation between migration remittance and agricultural investment. It was found that migrant remittances to households subsidized the rising costs of agriculture and the payments required for rural services, taxes, and fees, especially in poor and remote rural areas (ibid.). For example, studies found that migration had in the short run reduced production due to labour loss, but was compensated by access to capital through increased remittances with positive effects on yields (Rozelle et al. 1999: 287–91). Others, however, found no association with migration and productivity asset investment (de Brauw 2008; Wang et al. 2014: 413–25).

Second, with profits reducing agriculture has become unattractive so that out-migration has resulted in farmland being left to the least capable in income generation such as older people and women. Studies have shown that there has rarely been true retirement in rural China and decisions about young people's migration are in most cases usually based on whether their parents are healthy enough to work or farm (Pang et al. 2004: 73–94). There is a well-accepted saying in the rural sector in Shanghai that the ages of three farmers today add up to more than 220 years. Therefore, agriculture is facing the challenges of depopulation of rural areas—deskilling as well as rapid ageing of the agricultural population (Croll and Ping 1997: 128–46).

It seems that agricultural production has not been affected by migration, as by 2013 China had realized grain output rises for the tenth consecutive year.[3] However, it is reported that about 2 million hectares of arable land are abandoned from farming each year.[4] What is more important, with the continuous out-migration of the better educated younger generation, agricultural development mostly involving less trained elderly people might pose the biggest obstacle to the state's goal of realizing agricultural modernization alongside industrialization, urbanization, and information technology.

POLICY CHANGES REGARDING INTEGRATION OF THE RURAL POPULATION IN URBAN AREAS

Policy solutions to the current problem of the effect migration workers on industries can generally be divided into urban and rural categories; policy changes in recent years regarding the incorporation of the rural population in urban areas will also be studied in this next sub-section.

Policies Concerning the Urban Sector

From the perspective of the urban sector, it was first proposed in 2005 during the second plenary session of the Central Comprehensive Management Committee that provinces and departments should integrate the problem of population flow into their local

[3] Available at http://www.chinadaily.com.cn/china/2013-11/29/content_17141713.htm, accessed 6 December. 2018.

[4] Available at http://usa.chinadaily.com.cn/china/2011-09/13/content_13678947.htm, accessed 8 November. 2018.

economic and social development plans—depending on their availability of resources and energy—to solve the issues of employment, living, labour security, healthcare, and basic education in order to achieve an equal employment system for urban and rural workers. Until mid-2013, fourteen provinces (autonomous regions, municipal cities) explored the establishment of a unified household registration system, while the other eighteen opened up a channel for the settlement of agricultural populations in cities and towns. Statistics show that from 2010 to 2012, the urban settlement figure for the rural population was estimated to be 25.05 million, or an annual average of 8.35 million.

In July 2014, the State Council on further reform of the household registration system was issued with a requirement to further adjust household registration migration policy, to unify urban and rural household registration systems, to fully implement the resident permit system, and to accelerate the construction of a national population database. The purpose has been to steadily extend existing urban welfare such as compulsory education, employment services, pensions, medical care, housing security, and other basic public services to cover the entire resident population. By 2020, it is expected to establish the new household registration system with a rural population of about 100 million and other resident populations settled in urban areas.

In September 2014, the State Council issued a statement 'on further improving services for migrant workers', indicating that migrant workers had become the majority of industrial workers, an important force in promoting the country's modernization, and had made great contributions to economic and social development. It emphasized that despite various state policies in favour of migrant workers in recent years, settlement, and employment of migrant workers is far from stable. Therefore, four measures were proposed to promote the urbanization of migrant workers, including stabilizing and expanding employment and business setting up for migrant workers; safeguarding the labour interests and social security of migrant workers; promoting the progressive realization of migrant workers' equal access to public services and the town settlement; and to promote the social integration of migrant workers in towns.

By 2020, it is expected that transfer of the total agricultural labour workforce will continue to increase every year; and the provision of vocational training will benefit 20 million migrant workers to significantly improve their overall quality of life. Meanwhile, it is expected that their working conditions will improve, with no wage arrears and stable income growth, as well as full coverage of social insurance. It is also expected that about 100 million migrant workers will be assisted to settle in nearby towns in the mid-western region. Those migrant workers unable to settle will also have access to the urban public services, helping them to gradually integrate into cities and towns, for the realization of urbanization of migrant workers.

Policies Concerning the Rural Sector

Meanwhile, efforts are also being made to solve the problem of farming in rural areas. The basic goal has been to consolidate the previously scattered farmland and realize comparatively large-scale farming. The No.1 Central Document, 2013, known as the most important agricultural policy of the year encouraged land transfer towards large-scale landholders, family farms, and rural cooperatives, to accelerate the establishment of bigger, specialized farming units. The No.1 Central Document, 2014, reinforced the central concept by intensifying rural reforms for the realization of rural modernization, which also highlighted three points: to encourage farmers to transfer land use rights; to support new agricultural management and business entities; and to take family operation as the basis. All these have emphasized the principle that land transfer and moderate-scale operation is the only way for the development of modern agriculture. As emphasized by Premier Li Keqiang during the Central Rural Work Conference held in Beijing in 2015, China will further accelerate agricultural modernization and actively develop various forms of moderate scale operation. To achieve these, it is necessary to guide and regulate the orderly transfer of land use rights for the development of new types of agricultural business entities. The 2016 No.1 Central Document, 2016, stressed the importance of agricultural reforms in terms of production structure, regional distribution, and the cultivation of a new type of professional farmers, the agricultural insurance system, the rural collective property system, etc.

In general, the state aims to accommodate more migrant workers in cities, and to transform farmers in the sending communities into larger landholders for moderate-scale farming to achieve the integrated development of the rural and urban sectors.

Conclusion

After articulating a clearer classification of China's rural–urban migrants, the impacts of this unprecedented rural–urban labour flow witnessed by past decades in China on the well being of these rural urban migrants, the regional economy of labour outflow and inflow areas, the development of China's agricultural and non-agricultural industries between which these migrant workers have transferred, and the relevant national policies that can be distilled in the existing literature on these issues were examined in this chapter.

Conclusions that can be made through the perspectives examined in this chapter so far are as follows:

(a) Improved objective well-being in terms of increased income levels and improved living conditions does not for various reasons seem to have been projected onto an increased subjective well-being level shown in their self-reported happiness and life satisfaction scores.

(b) While China's overall economy has developed rapidly, the gap in terms of regional economy in labour inflow and outflow areas has been widened.

(c) Although rural–urban migration has prompted the development of China's manufacturing and service industries due to a large supply of cheap labour, such a large scale of rural–urban migration has left rural areas with a scarcity of labour (especially the younger, relatively better educated individuals), and the resulting large area of abandoned farmland, reduced agricultural productivity, and bigger obstacles to the state's goal of realizing agricultural modernization.

(d) Responding to the changes brought to both rural and urban sectors by large-scale rural–urban migration, the state has issued and implemented many policies aimed at accommodating the rapidly increasing and large number of migrant workers in cities, and transforming farmers in the labour outflow rural areas into larger landholders for moderate-scale farming to achieve the integrated development of rural and urban sectors.

Many gaps in the existing research are to be filled by future studies: (1) a study of the reasons behind the lack of correlation between increased objective well-being and declining subjective well-being as reported by rural–urban migrants; (2) a study of the interactive relationship between labour migration and regional economic growth in both labour inflow and labour outflow areas; (3) a study of the influences of rural–urban labour migration on the separate as well as the integrated development of China's three major industries including agricultural, manufacturing, and service industries, especially the less studied agricultural industry; (4) future policy approaches to better address the issues raised by the large scale of rural–urban migration in both rural and urban areas in China.

REFERENCES

Ahlburg, D. (1996). 'Remittances and the income distribution in Tonga', *Population Research and Policy Review* 15: 391–400.

Banister, J. and Taylor, R.J. (1991). 'China: surplus labor and migration', *Asia-Pacific Population Journal* 4: 3–20.

Barro, R.J., Sala-I-Martin, X., Blanchard, O.J., and Hall, R.E. (1991). 'Convergence across states and regions', *Brookings Papers on Economic Activity* 22/1: 107–82.

Cai, F. and Chan, K.W. (2009). 'The global economic crisis and unemployment in China', *Eurasian Geography and Economics* 50: 513–31.

Ceglowski, J. and Golub, S. (2007). 'Just how low are China's labour costs?', *The World Economy* 30: 597–617.

Chan, K.W. (2010). 'A China paradox: migrant labor shortage amidst rural labor supply abundance', *Eurasian Geography and Economics* 51: 513–30.

Chen, Y.F., Sun, H., and Liu, S.Y. (2010). 'Reconstruction models of hollowed villages in key agricultural regions of China', *Acta Geographica Sinica* 65: 727–35.

Croll, E.J. and Ping, H. (1997). 'Migration for and against agriculture in eight Chinese villages', *The China Quarterly* 149: 128–46.

de Brauw, A. (2008). 'Migrant labor markets and the welfare of rural households in the developing world: evidence from China'. Policy Research Working Paper. Washington, DC: World Bank.

Demurger, S. (2001). 'Infrastructure development and economic growth: an explanation for regional disparities in China?', *Journal of Comparative Economics* 29: 95–117.

Easterlin, R.A. (1974). 'Does economic growth improve the human lot? Some empirical evidence', *Nations and Households in Economic Growth* 89: 89–125.

Easterlin, R.A. (1995). 'Will raising the incomes of all increase the happiness of all?', *Journal of Economic Behavior & Organization* 27: 35–47.

Easterlin, R.A. (2001). 'Income and happiness: towards a unified theory', *Economic Journal* 111: 465–84.

Fang, C. (2003). 'The Chinese urban development during transition: urban hierarchical structure, its financing capacity and migration policies', *Economic Studies* 2: 21–9.

Fidrmuc, J. (2004). 'Migration and regional adjustment to asymmetric shocks in transition economies', *Journal of Comparative Economics* 32: 230–47.

Fingleton, B. (2001). Equilibrium and economic growth: spatial econometric models and simulations', *Journal of Regional Science* 41: 117–47.

Fleisher, B. and Yang, T. (2004). 'Problems of China's rural labor markets and rural–urban migration'. Paper presented at the International Symposium on China's Rural Economy after WTO: Problems and Strategies, June, Hangzhou, China: Chinese Economists Society and Zhejiang University.

Graham, C. and Pettinato, S. (2000). 'Frustrated achievers: winners, losers and subjective well-being in new market economies'. Center on Social and Economic Dynamics Working Paper Series No. 20. Washington, DC: The Brookings Institution.

Hirata, J. (2008). 'The division of labor between the capability and the happiness perspectives', in L. Bruni, F. Comim, and M. Pugno (eds) *Capabilities and Happiness*. Oxford: Oxford University Press, 160–86.

Kahneman, D., Diener, E. and Schwarz, N. (1999). *Well-being: Foundations of Hedonic Psychology*. New York: Russell Sage.

Kai, T. (1995). 'The investigation, analysis and thinking of how the rural migrant workers have adapted to urban lives', *Social Science Studies* 5: 90–5.

Kirdar, M.G. and Saracoğlu, D.Ş. (2008). 'Migration and regional convergence: an empirical investigation for Turkey', *Papers in Regional Science* 87: 545–66.

Knight, J. and Gunatilaka, R. (2012). 'Aspirations, adaptation and subjective wellbeing of rural-urban migrants in China', in C. David (ed.) *Adaptation, Poverty and Development: The Dynamics of Subjective Wellbeing*. Basingstoke: Palgrave Macmillan, 91–110.

Kroeber, A. (2010). 'The end of surplus labor', *China Economic Quarterly* 1: 35–46.

Land, K.C. (1975). 'Social indicator models: an overview', in K. C. Land and S. Spilerman (eds) *Social Indicator Models*. New York: Russell Sage, 5–36.

Li, H., Li, L., and Wu, B. (2012). 'The end of cheap Chinese labor', *Journal of Economic Perspectives* 26: 57–74.

Li, X.Y., Fennell, S., Huang, Y.X., Meng, D., Peng, Y.L., and Luan, B. (forthcoming). 'The study of spatial interactions between China's labor migration and regional economic development', *Environment and Planning A*.

Lin, J.Y., Cai, F., and Li, Z. (2003). *The China Miracle: Development Strategy and Economic Reform*. Hong Kong: Chinese University Press.

Liu, Y. and Chen, Y. (2010). 'The process and driving forces of rural hollowing in China under rapid urbanization', *Journal of Geographical Sciences* 20: 876–88.

Long, H.L., Li, Y.R., and Liu, Y.S. (2009). 'Analysis of evolutive characteristics and their driving mechanism of hollowing villages in China', *Acta Geographica Sinica* 64: 1203–13.

Ma, Z. (1999). 'Temporary migration and regional development in China', *Environment and Planning A* 31/5: 783–802.

Mao, X.Y. and Zhai, Z.W. (2013). 'The convergence research of population migration and regional economic growth', *Chinese Journal of Population Science* 6: 45–56.

Meng, D. (2013). 'An analysis of the lack of correlation between subjective wellbeing and objective indicators for human development in China', *Journal of Cambridge Studies* 8: 48–72.

NBS (National Bureau of Statistics), China (2013). *Report on Migrant Population*. Available at www.stats.gov.cn/tjsj/zxfb/201405/t20140512_551585.html, accessed 6 November 2018.

NBS (National Bureau of Statistics), China (2014). *Report on Migrant Population*. Available at www.stats.gov.cn/tjsj/zxfb/201405/t20140512_551585.html, accessed 6 November 2018.

NBS (National Bureau of Statistics), China (2016). *Report on Migrant Population*. Available at www.stats.gov.cn/tjsj/zxfb/201604/t20160428_1349713.html, accessed 6 November 2018.

Pang, L., de Brauw, A., and Rozelle, S. (2004). 'Working until you drop: the elderly of rural China', *The China Journal* 52: 73–94.

Peng, W.Q. (1999). 'An evaluation of the migration of the surplus labor in China's agricultural section', *Economic Studies* 4: 34–41.

Qiang, L. (2001). 'The convergence analysis of the economic growth in China', *Economic Research Journal* 5: 70–7.

Rey, S.J. and Montouri, B.D. (1999). 'US regional income convergence: a spatial econometric perspective', *Regional Studies* 33: 143–56.

Rozelle, S., Taylor, J.E., and de Brauw, A. (1999). 'Migration, remittances, and agricultural productivity in China', *American Economic Review* 89/2: 287–91.

Schwartz, B. (2000). 'Self-determination. the tyranny of freedom', *American Psychologist* 55: 80.

Shi, L. and Renwei, Z. (1999). 'Another look into the distribution of Chinese residents' income', *Economic Studies* 4: 17–26.

Veenhoven, R. (2005). 'Average happiness in 90 nations in the early 2000s', in *World Database of Happiness*. Rotterdam: Erasmus University.

Veenhoven, R. and Vergunst, F. (2014). 'The Easterlin illusion: economic growth does go with greater happiness', *International Journal of Happiness and Development* 1: 311–43.

Wang, C., Rada, N., and Qin, L. (2014). 'Impacts of migration on household production choices: evidence from China', *Journal of Development Studies* 50: 413–25.

Yifu, L. (2000). *Another Analysis on Institution, Technology and China's Agricultural Development*. Peking: Peking University Press.

Zhang, H.Q. and Wu, E. (2004). 'Human resources issues facing the hotel and travel industry in China', *International Journal of Contemporary Hospitality Management* 16: 424–8.

Zhao, P. and Howden-Chapman, P. (2010). 'Social inequalities in mobility: the impact of the hukou system on migrants' job accessibility and commuting costs in Beijing', *International Development Planning Review* 32: 363–84.

10 Extractive economies, institutions, and development

Implications for BRICS and emerging economies

P.B. Anand

Introduction

BRICS countries in general and China and India in particular are often seen as mainly natural resource importing countries (see for instance Alden and Alves 2009; Carmody 2011; Carpintero et al. 2016; Dollar 2016). Their impact on mineral exporting countries receives much critical scrutiny. Natural resource export to China is found to be associated with positive growth in African countries (Meyersson et al. 2008) and for all developing countries (Su et al. 2016).

This chapter takes a different perspective and considers BRICS countries as natural resource rich countries. All BRICS countries do have significant domestic natural resources. Natural resource rents contribute around 4 per cent of gross national income in Brazil, China, and India, 6 per cent in South Africa, and some 16 per cent in Russia. However, none of them has yet joined the international initiative called Extractive Industries Transparency Initiative (EITI). The aim of this chapter is to examine some of the key policy issues for development in the context of extractive economies or resource dependent countries using a case study approach. The original contribution of this chapter is to consider BRICS as extractive economies and apply lessons from some of the successful natural resource-based economies taking two cases from countries that joined the EITI and two countries that have not joined but are nevertheless considered to be successful in managing their natural resources. We also use the same framework to examine one of the BRICS countries. For each case study country, we examine data on social and economic indicators of progress to evaluate the extent to which natural resource revenues have impacted on development outcomes. By so doing we raise important issues for BRICS and other natural resource rich emerging economies to use their natural resources for sustainable development.

Natural resources or extractive activities offer enormous potential for doing good. Our estimates based on World Development Indicators suggest that the magnitude of resource rents worldwide in 2015 was approximately US$1.27 trillion (in 2010 constant

P.B. Anand, *Extractive economies, institutions, and development: Implications for BRICS and emerging economies* In: *Handbook of BRICS and Emerging Economies.* Edited by: P.B. Anand, Shailaja Fennell, and Flavio Comim, Oxford University Press (2021).
DOI: 10.1093/oso/9780198827535.003.0010

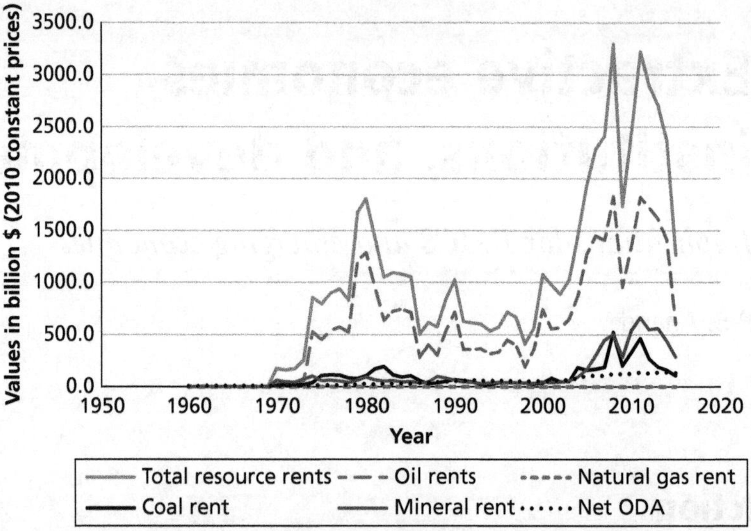

Figure 10.1 Resource rents compared with official development assistance (ODA)
Source: Compiled by author based on World Bank (various years).

prices) (which itself is much lower than the rents in any of the previous five years at above $2.40 trillion). In 2015, the biggest share of rents to the tune of about US$0.59 trillion was from oil economies; gas economies generated rents of about US$0.13 trillion; US$0.108 trillion was from coal; and the mineral economies generated about US$0.28 trillion. In comparison total net aid (Official Development Assistance [ODA]) from OECD countries in 2015 was estimated to be US$131 billion (OECD 2017). This highlights the significance of natural resource rents and the potential positive impact for sustainable development (see Figure 10.1).

FROM RESOURCE CURSE TO RESOURCE BOON

If well managed, natural resources can contribute to sustainable economic growth. Some scholars observed that an abundance of natural resources can actually dampen or reduce economic growth rather than enhancing it—a result termed 'resource curse' (Sachs and Warner 1995, 1997; Auty 2002) or a 'trap' (Collier 2008). An abundance of natural resources can reduce incentives or the need for innovation, crowd out non-resource sectors, reduce competition, create monopolistic firms often under the ownership of the state, distort the functioning of capital and labour markets, and create fiscal and macroeconomic management problems (the so called 'Dutch disease' effects—see Corden and Neary 1982) making the economy vulnerable to fluctuations in world market prices of commodities. Huge revenue flows from natural resources can affect financial governance and accountability, and create opportunities for rent seeking and patronage distribution. Van der Ploeg and Peolhekke (2009) argue that a natural resource curse is actually caused by volatility. Prebisch and Singer noted almost seventy years ago that terms of trade in export favour manufactured goods as opposed to commodities (Prebisch 1950; Singer 1950). As a result, the relative price of commodities falls over the long term. Schumpeter (1939) examined three commodity price cycles over the period 1786–1938 and considered innovation and creative destruction as drivers of prosperity while stagnation led to declining output growth and a fall in prices. Erten and Ocampo (2012) examined the period 1865 to 2009 and observed four super-cycles each with a range of thirty to forty years during which period prices varied by up to 20 to 40 per cent (increase or reduction). They note that with each cycle the mean price for non-oil commodities is getting lower, supporting the Prebisch–Singer thesis; but for oil they find the real price to be increasing over the period of these super-cycles. This suggests that different types of commodities can have different types of effect. In this regard, Woolcock et al. (2001) argued that the resource curse effect depends on the type of natural resource while Oskenbayev et al. (2013) argue with the case of Kazakhstan that it is not the type of resource but the nature of rent-seeking activities that determine resource curse effects.

In many natural resource rich economies, issues related to corruption, poor governance, and in some cases ethnic conflict pose significant challenges to human development (HD). A number of studies discuss some of these issues related to the resource curse and its avoidance (Torvik 2002; Maloney and Lederman 2006; Arezki and van der Ploeg 2007; Humphreys et al. 2007; Hogan and Sturzenegger 2010; Polterovich et al. 2010; van der Ploeg 2010; Deacon, 2011; Bazilian et al. 2013; Papyrakis 2014; Williams and Le Billon 2017). Critical literature reviews on the resource curse include Frankel (2010) and Badeeb et al. (2017).

Brunnschweiler and Bulte (2008) argue that Sachs and Warner (1997) were modelling resource dependence and not abundance. Boyce and Emery (2011) argue that a mere correlation between natural resources and growth is not adequate for concluding that a resource curse exists. While they did find a negative relationship between resource abundance and growth rate, they also find a positive relationship between resource abundance and per capita income. Ross (2012) argues that countries rich in petroleum tend to have less democracy, less economic stability, and greater tendency to civil wars than others not having oil and thus the resource curse effect may be mainly an oil country problem. Alexeev and Conrad (2009) argue that in fact a large endowment of oil or other resources has a positive effect on long-run growth and that oil does not affect the quality of a country's institutions. Jones Luong and Weinthal (2010) include several case studies to argue why oil is not a curse. Obi and Rustad (2011) discuss the politics of violence in the specific case of the Niger Delta and suggest that the 'trap' is not inescapable provided there are the necessary institutions to manage resource allocation problems.

Mehlum et al. (2006) suggest that institutions determine whether the relationship between natural resource abundance and economic growth rate is negative or positive. They re-examined Sachs and Warner's 1997 data by adding institution variables and found that there was no relationship between resource abundance and growth in countries with good institutions. Robinson et al. (2006) also make a similar argument. They focus on political processes and the behaviour of politicians in extracting rents and allocating these. They argue that institutions are key to determining whether politicians use a high discount rate and prefer resource booms or use resources more prudently. A similar institutional argument can be seen with regard to how the silver boom in the sixteenth century was handled by institutions in Spain (Drelichman and Voth 2008). Kolstad and Wiig (2008) examined the role of transparency in fighting corruption in resource rich societies. Their analysis suggests that improving transparency may not be adequate in lifting the resource curse. Menaldo (2016) argues that what is considered as a natural resource curse is essentially an institutions curse. Boschini et al. (2012) find that good-quality institutions can reverse the curse mainly in countries rich in ores and metals. They also observe that within institutions, contracting institutions have no significant effect in reversing the resource curse but property rights institutions do. Based on this they conclude that '. . . it is the direct involvement of governments in the resource sectors that determines the potential reversal of the resource curse, than the government in its role as enabling contracting between private parties in society'.

BRICS AS RESOURCE RICH NATIONS

BRICS nations are among significant natural resource extracting countries. While Brazil, Russia, and South Africa are well-recognized as natural resource abundant economies, popular perceptions of China and India present them mainly as natural resource importing countries and focus on whether they are contributing to a resource curse in Africa and elsewhere. However, total resource rents as a share of GDP have been high in China in the past and have started to become important again since the year 2000 (see Table 10.1).

Data on gross national income (GNI) in constant prices are not available for China except for one year (2010). Therefore, we can calculate the total value of resource rents in China only for that year when at US$379 billion they were far greater than those of Brazil (US$95 billion), Russia (US$205 billion), India (US$53 billion), or South Africa (US$28 billion). United States Geological Survey (USGS) data for these countries

Table 10.1 Total natural resource rents for BRICS countries—selected years

	1970	1980	1990	2000	2010	2015	Average for 2000–15
Brazil	1.56	2.73	2.16	2.45	4.45	2.91	4.07
China	0.82	19.00	8.24	2.47	6.25	1.28	4.45
India	0.67	3.06	3.37	2.48	4.65	1.88	3.69
Russian Federation	—	—	14.12	21.66	13.90	10.31	16.37
South Africa	1.97	15.06	6.03	2.89	7.66	4.20	6.07

Source: World Development Indicators (World Bank various years).

highlight the significance and importance of mineral sectors to BRICS economies. As of 2014, Brazil was the world's largest producer of niobium (with 89 per cent of world production), third largest producer of vermiculite (18 per cent of world production), and ninth largest producer of petroleum (with proven reserves of approximately 16 billion barrels) (Soto-Viruet 2017). As of 2013, China's world rankings were: first for coal, fourth for crude oil, and sixth for natural gas (Xun 2017). India's world rankings for mineral production were: first for garnet and iron oxide pigments, second for cement and natural graphite, third for chromium, lime, nitrogen, and pig iron; fourth for crude steel and iron ore; fifth for aluminium, and sixth for lead, manganese, bromine, and vermiculite (Renaud 2017). While coke and petroleum production contributed together to more than 10 per cent of Russian GDP in 2014, Russia is the leading world producer of numerous minerals (Safirova 2017). South Africa is the world's largest producer of platinum, rhodium, chromite, kyanite, palladium, gold, and many other minerals (Yager 2017).

BRICS also have some features of the governance challenges associated with resource curse and capture. While Russia is for some critics much like a 'petro-state' (Krugman 2013), other BRICS have also faced significant natural resource governance-related corruption scandals. In the case of Petrobras in Brazil, a probe into a money-laundering scheme known as the '*Lava Jato*' or 'car-wash' or '*petrolao*' (big oily) scandal revealed systematic over-pricing of contracts and a web of political connections linking it to the ruling party, Partido dos Trabalhadores (PT). This eventually contributed to the impeachment of Dilma Roussef (though she was not directly implicated) (Watts 2017). Odebrecht, the construction firm involved in this case, settled with a payment of fines of over US$2.5 billion to the Brazilian government. However, uncovered corruption led to further investigations into irregularities concerning beef exports and two giants of Brazil's food industry (Felter 2017). In the so-called 'Coal-gate' scam in India, irregularities in the process of opening up coal mining to private sector participation in 2004 resulted in a significant loss to the exchequer of an amount equivalent to approximately US$30 billion (CAGI 2012). In South Africa, the corruption scandal involving the Gupta brothers also includes irregularities related to allocation of contracts by Escom to Tegeta with regard to the Optimum Coal Mine. The Office of the Public Protector's (2016) report notes several violations in this regard. These examples reveal that natural resource management challenges are as important in BRICS countries as they have been elsewhere.

Mineral resources are often concentrated in remote or interior regions which tend to have a lower Human Development Index (HDI) compared to other more urbanized regions within those countries. For example, in India, states in which mining activities are concentrated (such as Jharkhand, Chattisgarh, and Odissha) have higher levels of poverty and deprivation than non-resource states. In these states in India, much of the mining activity takes place in areas traditionally home to tribal populations with premodern or traditional institutions of collective ownership. The power that the modern corporate form of capitalism can bring to bear in such contexts can be brutal. The kind of local versus global governance conflicts highlighted by Bebbington (2009) in the case of

Peru can take place anywhere. In India, Eynde (2016) finds that the Maoist rebels (Naxalites) are more likely to attack security forces in the event of monsoon failure as the value of mineral resources in the district increases. Managing resources and developing appropriate institutions to avoid or reverse the resource curse effects are important for BRICS and emerging economies.

The next section of the chapter presents an original analysis of resource rents and the HDI. The third section develops in-depth case studies from Norway, Botswana, Chile, Mongolia, and Brazil; while the fourth presents comparative analysis of the case studies with regard to institutions. The fifth section presents an analysis of whether countries that have joined the EITI are systematically better off in terms of governance indicators than those that have not joined. The final section presents the conclusions and three recommendations for BRICS countries.

Natural resources and human development

There has been some work on applying the concepts of entitlements, agency, and the capability approach to natural resources such as water (see Anand 2007a, 2013); but the aim of this chapter is to focus on mineral resources and explore how policies related to managing the mineral resources can contribute to human development. The central argument in Mehlum et al. (2006) is that whether natural resource abundance becomes a 'curse' or not is determined by institutions. In countries with good institutions, resource abundance does not result in a decline in per capita incomes; but in countries with poor institutions this can happen. HDI includes two non-income dimensions representing health (longevity of life) and education. A relationship between mineral rents and HD means extracting one form of wealth (oil or minerals) and investing in another (education and better quality of life for citizens). Causality can be in both directions. The links between extractive rents and HDI are depicted in Figure 10.2.

Causality in the other direction can work in such a way that a higher level of HD means knowledge and capabilities to find extractive economies and also the ability to manage resources prudently. However, possibilities for temptation and diverting resources for personal benefit can exist in any society. A higher level of HDI does not in itself say anything about the quality of government or the quality of institutions that can hold the government to account on mineral wealth.

Much attention has been focused on avoiding the negative macroeconomic effects (through careful management of exchange rate and foreign currency reserves) and consequent fiscal impacts (such as unsustainable increases in public expenditure). Limited attention has been focused on impacts on HD (with studies such as Gylfason 2001 or Constantini and Monni 2008 being more the exceptions than the norm). Pineda and Rodriguez (2010) question the natural resources trap idea and argue that data from 1980 to 2005 show that there exists a positive association between resource abundance and HDI (as an indicator of HD).

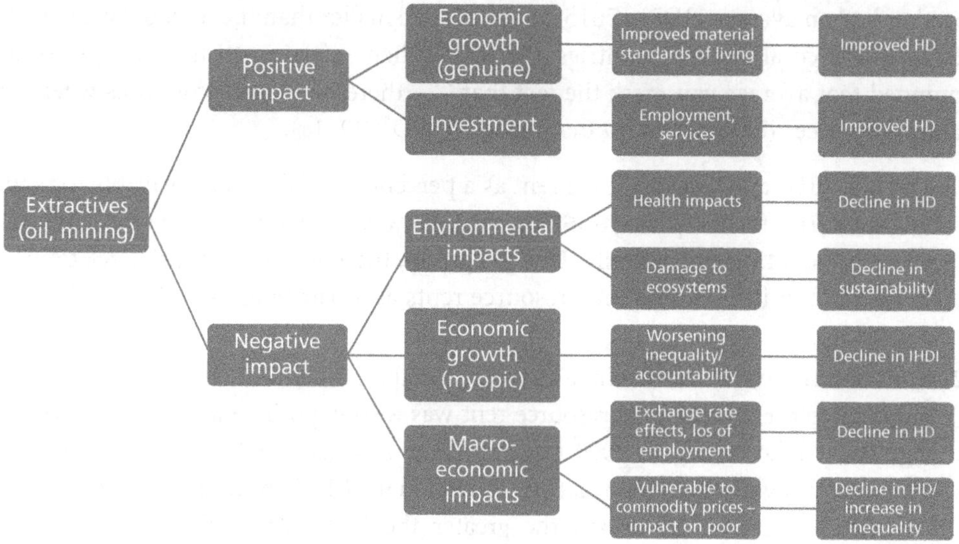

Figure 10.2 Extractives and HD—an outline of the links

Source: Author's compilation.

Table 10.2 Summary statistics of 'resource abundant' and non-resource abundant countries: HDI and total resource rent per cent of GDP—averages

	Year	Number of countries N	Average HDI	Average Resource rents % of GDP
Non-resource abundant	1990	63	0.666	0.559
	2000	76	0.710	0.764
	2010	93	0.744	1.913
	2015	93	0.762	1.233
Resource abundant	1990	80	0.536	12.194
	2000	89	0.562	12.712
	2010	94	0.616	14.461
	2015	91	0.637	9.982

Source: Based on World Bank (various years) and UNDP (2016).

HDI is in itself not a full indicator of HD which is about enhancing substantive freedoms. However, as a starting point, HDI can throw some light on non-income dimensions of well-being. To examine whether extractive economies as a group perform differently with regard to HDI, we analysed data from 1990 to 2015 (see Table 10.2). We divided the countries into two groups with an arbitrary cut-off point of total resource rent of 2 per cent of GDP to make two groups: non-resource abundant countries (rents <2 per cent of GDP) and resource abundant countries (rents ≥2 per cent of GDP). While 2 per cent is an arbitrary cut-off, this produced two sets of countries with approximately equal numbers of countries. We note from Table 10.2 that as a group the non-resource abundant countries already had a higher HDI in 1990 and they maintained this lead throughout the period. Even after twenty-five years, the resource abundant countries together had an average HDI in 2015, which is still smaller than the level of average HDI of non-resource abundant countries in 1990. When referring to the average we are reminded that average can mask the fact that '. . . there are several countries where the natural resources did more harm than good' (UNDP 2011a).

(1) Data for HDI and total resource rent as a percentage of GDP are available for some 187 countries for the period 1990 to 2015. However, in 1990, data are available for (80 + 63 =) 143 countries only. For this group, there is a weak positive relationship between HDI in 1990 and total resource rents as a percentage of GDP in 1990 (see Figure 10.3).

(2) For countries with total resource rents greater than 2 per cent of GDP: The relationship between HDI and total resource rent was weakly positive in 1990; there was no significant relationship in 2000 but it became a negative relationship in 2010 and remained a slightly stronger negative correlation in 2015. This means that even among 'resource dependent' countries, the greater the HDI, the smaller is the share of resource rents in GDP. This can be seen from the four panels in Figure 10.4.

(3) For countries with total resource rents less than 2 per cent of GDP in 1990: The relationship between HDI and total resource rents is always negative in all four time periods and in each case the correctness of fit is much better than for the 'resource dependent' countries above (see the four panels in Figure 10.5).

(4) However, an interesting result emerges when we analyse the average annual growth in HDI and that of total resource rent for the period 2000–15. Here, as a group, resource abundant countries had a weak but positive relationship—both HDI and total resource rents' share in GDP grew. For non-resource abundant countries, the correlation is much weaker and negative (Figure 10.6)

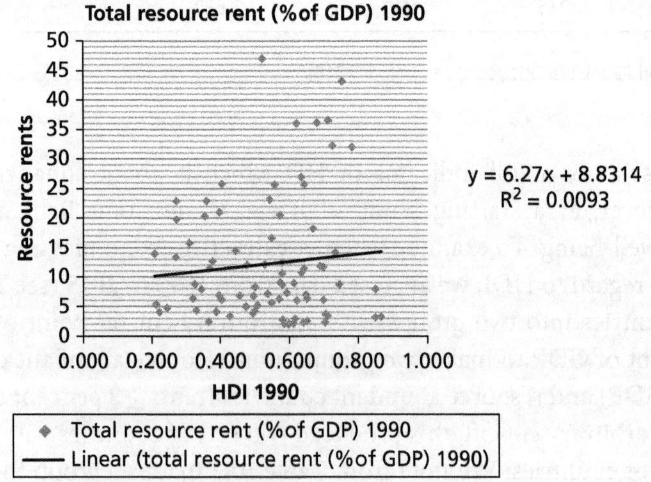

Figure 10.3 HDI and resource rents in 1990

Source: Based on World Bank (various years) and UNDP (2016).

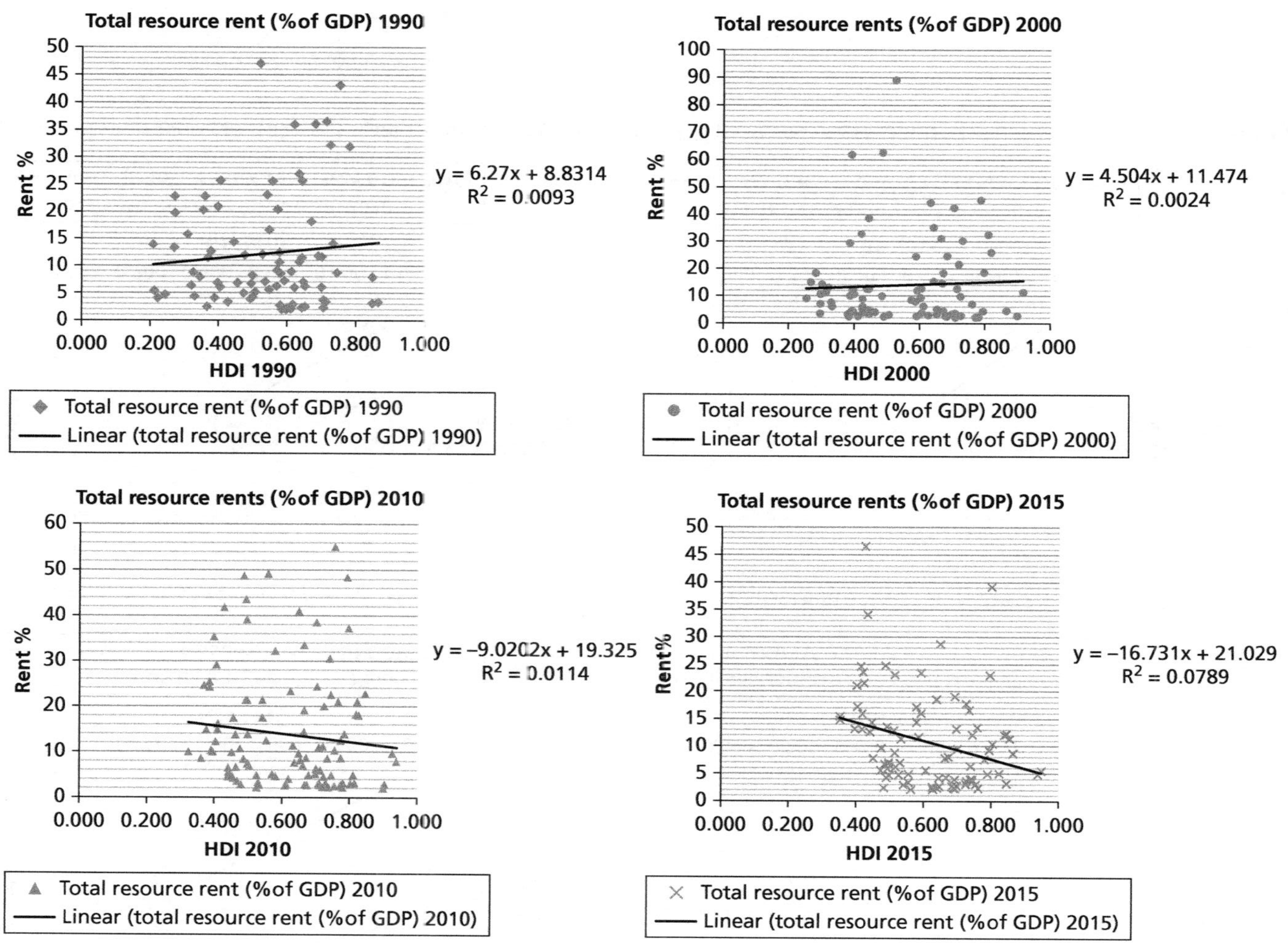

Figure 10.4 Relationship between HDI and total resource rents as % of GDP for years 1990, 2000, 2010, and 2015: resource abundant countries (total rent $\geq 2\%$)

Source: Based on World Bank (various years) and UNDP (2016).

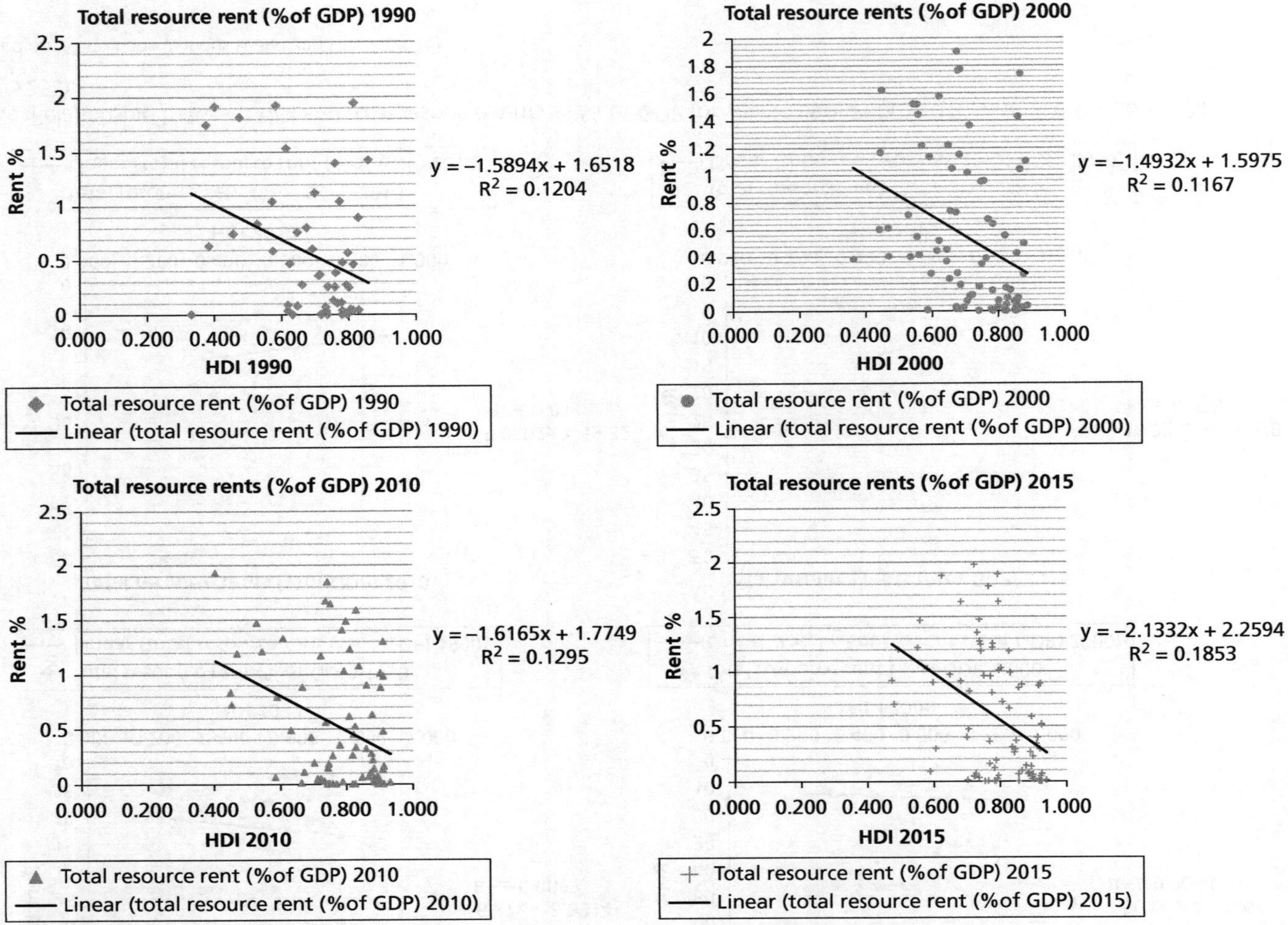

Figure 10.5 Relationship between HDI and total resource rents as % of GDP for years 1990, 2000, 2010, and 2015: non-resource abundant countries (total rent <2%)

Source: Based on World Bank (various years) and UNDP (2016).

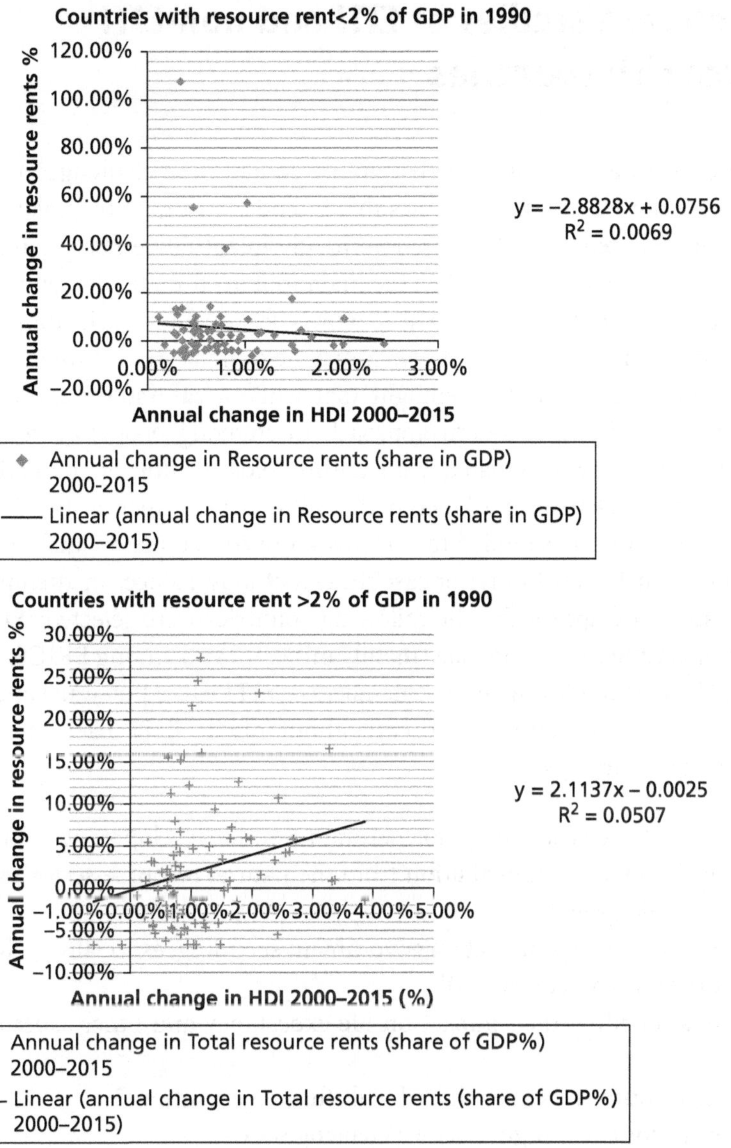

Figure 10.6 Annual rate of change in HDI and total resource rents as % of GDP between years 2000 and 2015

Source: Based on World Bank (various years) and UNDP (2016).

These results highlight that the relationship between natural resource rents and HDI is dynamic and that though HDI for resource abundant countries is much lower, this is growing at a faster rate now along with an increase in the share of total resource rents in GDP. This suggests that resource abundant countries are using the increasing resource rents on improving HDI. These results are preliminary and require further careful work. However, these seem to suggest that HD can be an important element of a multi-pronged strategy in using natural resources for sustainable development.

Selected case studies of EITI and non-EITI resource rich countries

In this section, an attempt is made to capture some of the challenges and successes in selected resource rich countries. Studies that intend to examine the link between natural resources and HD tend to take a predominantly quantitative perspective where cross-country regression analysis is used as the main tool. In this chapter, an attempt is made to take the case study approach which allows for qualitative, historical, and deeper analysis of institutions and context which may be difficult to capture in a cross-country analysis. A number of studies highlight that while a case study approach may have existed for millennia, the modern approach to studying people or cultures in depth through detailed notes originated with anthropologists during the early part of the twentieth century (Denzin and Lincoln 2011; Yin 2014). Much of the literature on the natural resource curse has tended to use cross-country regression analysis methodology with few studies using qualitative or case study methods. Hence, an attempt is made here to take a case study approach. The following countries were selected: Norway (mainly oil); Botswana, Chile, and Mongolia (mainly mineral); and among BRICS, Brazil (mainly oil). Here, Norway and Mongolia are members of EITI while Botswana and Chile appear to have managed their natural resources without joining EITI. Each case study aims to examine the following questions:

(a) What is the historical context for natural resource development in the country?
(b) What is the share or contribution from the natural resource sector to the economy and economic growth?
(c) Do resource revenues impact on government spending, especially spending on social sectors (health and education)?
(d) Does this spending then impact on life expectancy and other aspects of quality of life?
(e) How are resource revenues shared with future generations?
(f) What institutional and governance challenges exist?

While the in-depth case studies deal with questions (a) to (d), the remaining questions are examined in the comparative analysis section, and answered using data from secondary sources and World Bank (various years).

NORWAY

Since its independence from Denmark in 1814, the Norwegian economy grew steadily throughout the nineteenth century mainly through the export of fish, timber, and some textile industry. However, from 1870 to 1915, the Norwegian economy seems to have suffered from a global slowdown and was subsequently affected by the Great Depression during the inter-war years. After the Second World War, aid as part of the Marshall Plan between 1948 and 1952 seems to have helped in recovery (Grytten 2008). However, Norway's boom as a natural resource economy took off mainly after 1969 with the discovery of oil. We can see from Figures 10.7 and 10.8 that oil has played a significant role in the tripling of per capita GDP (constant prices) over four decades as the share of fuel in exports increases from being non-existent in 1968 to over 60 per cent in the last decade.

There has been a corresponding increase in the share of government expenditure in GDP (Figure 10.9). We do not have figures for the share of GDP spent on education and

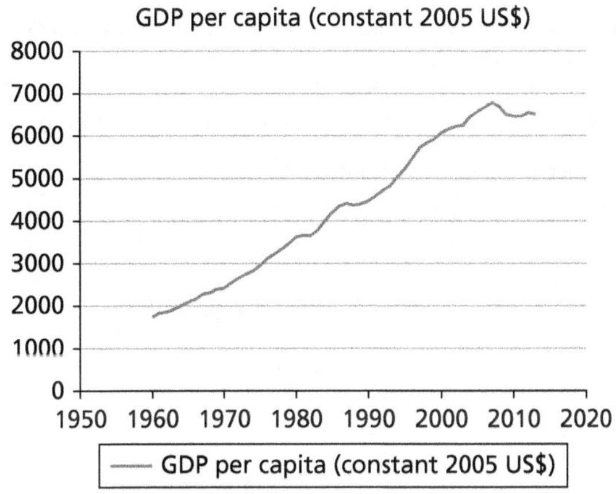

Figure 10.7 Norway's income per capita 1960–2012

Source: Compiled by author based on data from World Bank (various years).

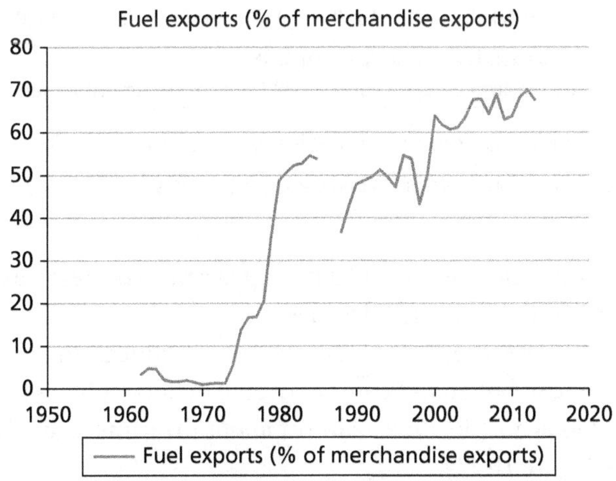

Figure 10.8 Share of fuel in Norway's exports

Source: Compiled by author based on data from World Bank (various years).

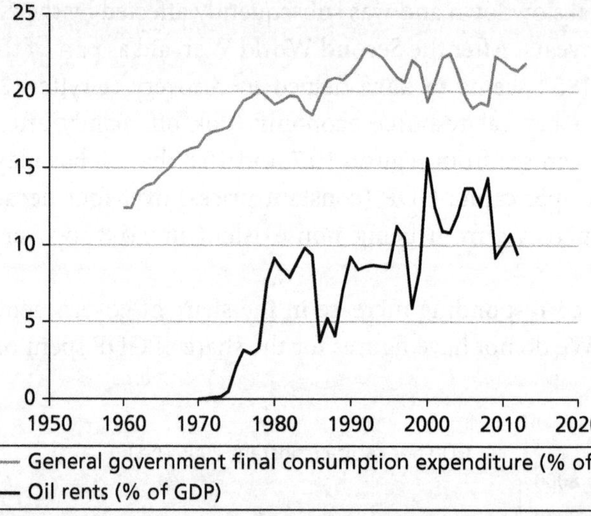

Figure 10.9 Oil rents and government expenditure as a share of Norway's GDP

Source: Compiled by author based on data from World Bank (various years).

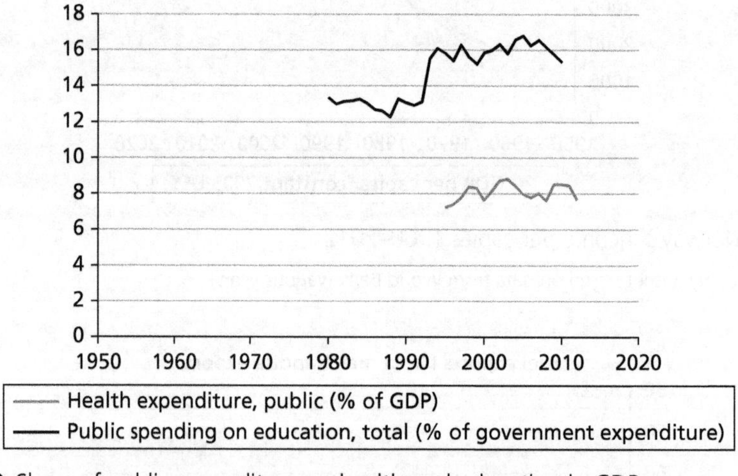

Figure 10.10 Share of public expenditure on health and education in GDP

Source: Compiled by author based on data from World Bank (various years).

health prior to 1980 but from Figure 10.10 it is apparent that these have been sustained significantly throughout the last three decades.

Norway already had near universal enrolment in education even before the oil revenues began to come in but an indicator of overall quality of life is that life expectancy increased from around age 73 in 1968—almost about the same as in Denmark—to over age 81 in 2012 (see Figure 10.11).

In 1969, in Norway sixteen infants born out of one thousand were dying before the age of 5. This mortality rate has fallen to fewer than three infants in 2012. Though this has

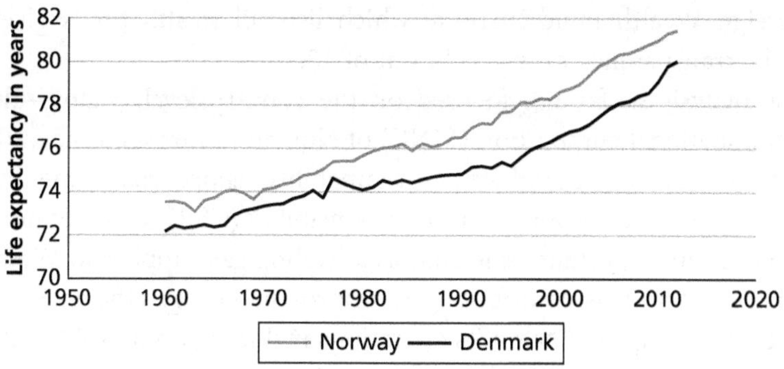

Figure 10.11 Life expectancy at birth in years—Norway and Denmark

Source: Compiled by author based on data from World Bank (various years).

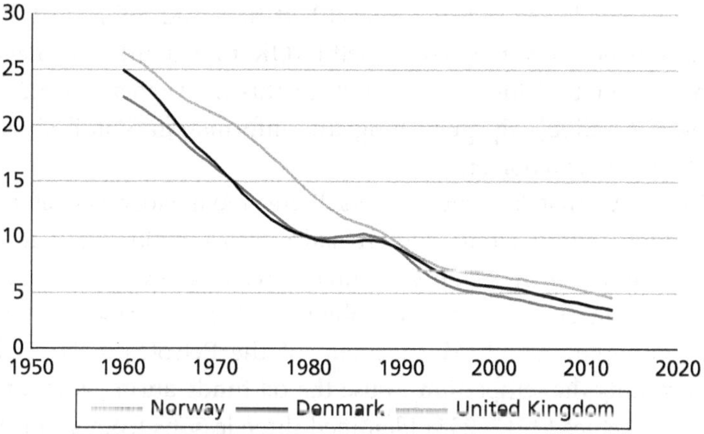

Figure 10.12 Under-5 mortality rate per 1,000 live births—Norway, Denmark, UK

Source: Compiled by author based on data from World Bank (various years).

been reducing in all neighbouring countries, convergence was not achieved until the late 1980s (see Figure 10.12).

Norway had also been unique in setting up the Petroleum Fund or Oil Fund (now called the Government Pension Fund Global) as a sovereign wealth fund by law of parliament in 1990. The fund was set up in 1996 with the transfer of capital from the Ministry of Finance.

Since 1998 Norges Bank Investment Management has had responsibility for managing the fund and submitting reports. Based on these reports (and converting the current figures based on the consumer price index), we calculate the fund's value in constant (2010) prices to have increased from NOK63 billion in 1996 to NOK4,835 billion in 2013.

Since 2004 the fund has been crucial in promoting ethical investment and it is prohibited from investing in certain companies such as those involved in nuclear arms manufacture or in sales of tobacco, or those violating human rights or causing serious environmental degradation.

The Sovereign Wealth Fund Institute which lists all wealth funds gives Norway's pension fund a transparency rating of 10 out of 10.

While the analysis so far has focused on the country level, Statoil—the main oil producing multinational corporation (MNC) of Norway—mirrors some of the commitments; for instance in 2013 it produced a sustainability report broadening the issues that are normally covered in a corporate social responsibility (CSR) report. Statoil recognizes climate change as an important issue; and as a leading gas supplier to Western Europe the company feels that it is contributing to improving energy efficiency. It tries to be transparent by reporting all data on its operations including on oil spills, safety records, and fines. The report notes that: 'transparency is vital to ensuring that the wealth derived from the energy we produce is put to effective and equitable use' (Statoil 2013: 19). In 2013, Statoil had operations in thirty countries but the bulk of its NOK117 billion investments were in: Norway (NOK61 billion); USA (NOK25 billion); Angola (NOK9 billion); UK and Canada (NOK4 billion each). It had paid NOK117 billion in direct taxes, the bulk of which was in Norway itself (NOK107 billion). It had also paid oil in kind equivalent to NOK38 billion—the bulk of this in Angola (NOK21 billion) and Azerbaijan (NOK9 billion). By publishing this information Statoil aims to illustrate transparency to other stakeholders.

Holden (2013) notes that: '. . . when oil was discovered in Norway it already had a long and stable tradition of democratic rule. It had a well-functioning state bureaucracy'. Other factors identified include the government reaping revenues including through taxation, and while taxes are high, the stability and transparency of taxation is also considered an important point. Management of the Petroleum Fund also has been important in avoiding the temptation to use the oil funds during years of declining oil prices. Moses and Letnes (2017: 236) identified three lessons from an in-depth case on Norway. In their view, the first lesson is that '. . . politics matters; . . . the state must determine an appropriate pace of resource development: finding a workable compromise between the short-term interests of the industry and the long-term interests of the community'. In their view, the state should play an important role in managing the institutional architecture needed. In their list, the second lesson concerns the importance of deliberative democracy and the development of trust in institutions through long-term engagement, providing a stable and transparent set of rules of the game and the state acting as an impartial interest holder. The third lesson in their list is '. . . to recognize the dynamism of petroleum management policies'. Thus, while it is important to have a stable and transparent set of rules of the game, these rules must respond to changes in market conditions and technology. In a way, all three of the lessons from Norway's case are inherently connected with the evolution and development of institutions, trust, and transparency.

The case of Norway and my own analysis also indicated that through democratic institutions it is possible to use oil rents to promote social and economic well-being, reduce infant mortality, increase significantly expenditure on education and health, and maintain counter-cyclical policies and promote intergenerational equity by investing a portion of the rents for future generations. There have been debates within Norway on whether the oil fund should be used by the government to meet the unidentified needs of the present generation and whether the Norwegian economy is vulnerable to the recent fall in global oil prices. Notwithstanding these issues, the overall message from the case of Norway appears to be an optimistic one—that with good institutions it should be possible to manage resource rents for lasting HD.

BOTSWANA

At about the same time as Botswana's independence from Britain in 1966, explorations for diamond mining were in progress and in 1967 De Beers geologists located seams containing *elemenite* and *garnet* (indicators of diamondiferous kimberlite) in abundant quantities. In 1968 the De Beers Botswana Mining Company Ltd was formed as a joint venture between the government and De Beers. In real terms, at the time of its independence, Botswana's per capita GDP was below sub-Saharan Africa's average but by the mid-1970s divergence began and Botswana's real income increased by 700 per cent in four decades while the average for sub-Saharan Africa remained more or less stagnant (see Figure 10.13).

By the time of inauguration of the Jwaneng mine in 1982, diamond exports appeared to be already contributing to 70 per cent of Botswana's foreign exchange annually. The 2005 Debswana (2005) Annual Report proclaimed: 'Can you imagine Botswana without diamonds, specifically Debswana? It's difficult, because modern Botswana and Debswana are virtually synonymous given the undeniable contribution the Company has made to underpin the growth of the economy over the years. What makes it even more difficult to imagine is that Debswana is such a strong, profitable company.' Though

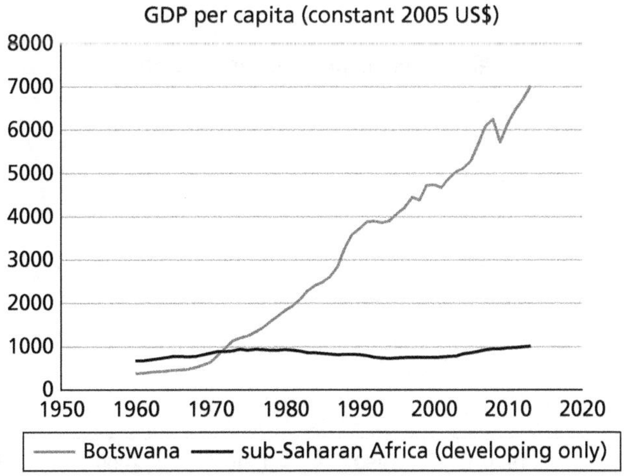

Figure 10.13 Real income of Botswana and sub-Saharan Africa

Source: Compiled by author based on data from World Bank (various years).

diamond exports contribute significantly to mineral revenues, it appears that there have been significant fluctuations in mineral rents due to the impact of global events such as oil price shocks, the collapse of the Soviet Union and the rise of the HIV/AIDS pandemic in Southern Africa (both in the early 1990s), the September 2001 terrorist events in New York and the subsequent downturn in the global economy, and the 2008 financial crisis (see Figure 10.14). An analysis by De Beers indicates that the USA continues to be the world's largest consumer of diamonds although emerging markets such as China and India also have some significant demand (De Beers 2014). However, it is still not entirely clear why resource rents should show such wide fluctuations.

The Government of Botswana set up the Pula Fund as a sovereign wealth fund in 1994 to set aside some of the diamond revenues for future generations. Data for the Pula Fund from various annual reports from the Bank of Botswana and the consumer price index (CPI) data were used to analyse the fund (Figure 10.15) The susceptibility of the fund to global events can also be seen here.

Over the years Botswana's resource wealth appears to have enabled it to increase its spending on health and education though data on health spending are of limited range and even during that period fluctuations year on year are visible (see Figure 10.16).

Though life expectancy at birth has improved from 52 years at the time of independence in 1965 to 63 years by 1989 since then it has begun a downward trend to reach about 50 years by 2000; the slide continued to 46.25 in the year 2008 mainly due to the HIV/AIDS pandemic. In the last few years, the downward slide has stopped though expectancy remains below 47 years.

The under-5-year mortality rate was around 160 per 1,000 live births at the time of independence in 1965 (see Figure 10.17). This had fallen to around forty-five by 1990 but then shot up again in the 1990s to reach eighty-six in the year 2001; it has now come back to around forty-seven per 1,000 live births in 2013. In comparison, Zambia and Swaziland had significant increases in the under-5-year mortality rate in the 1990s and

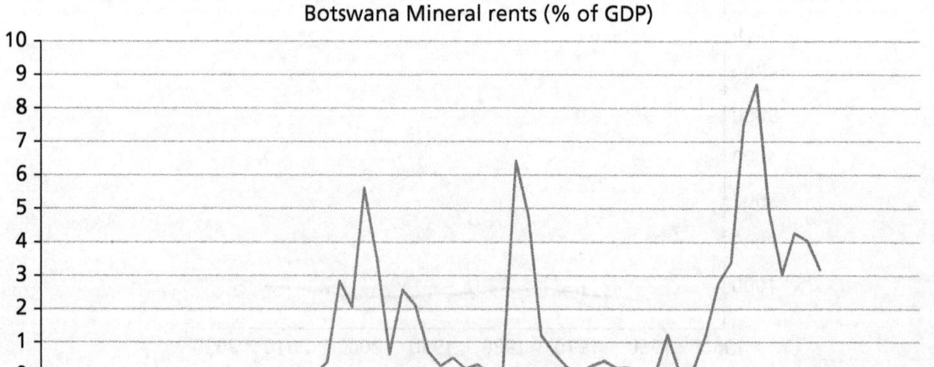

Figure 10.14 Mineral rents as % of Botswana's GDP

Source: Compiled by author based on data from World Bank (various years).

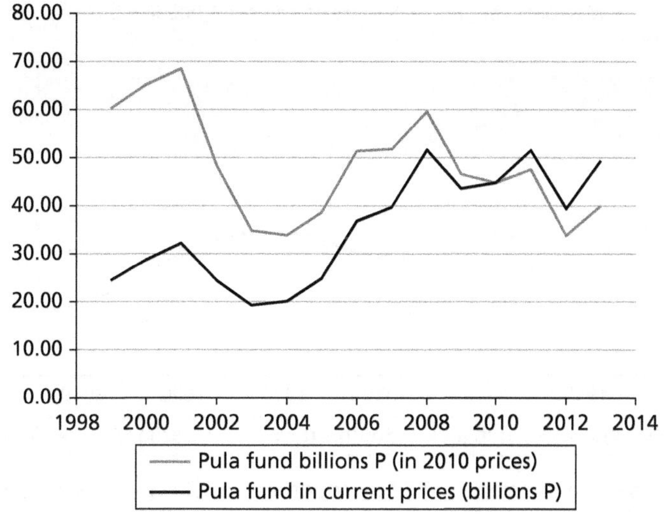

Figure 10.15 Botswana Pula Fund in current and constant prices

Source: Compiled by author based on data from Bank of Botswana annual reports and CPI information from World Bank (various years).

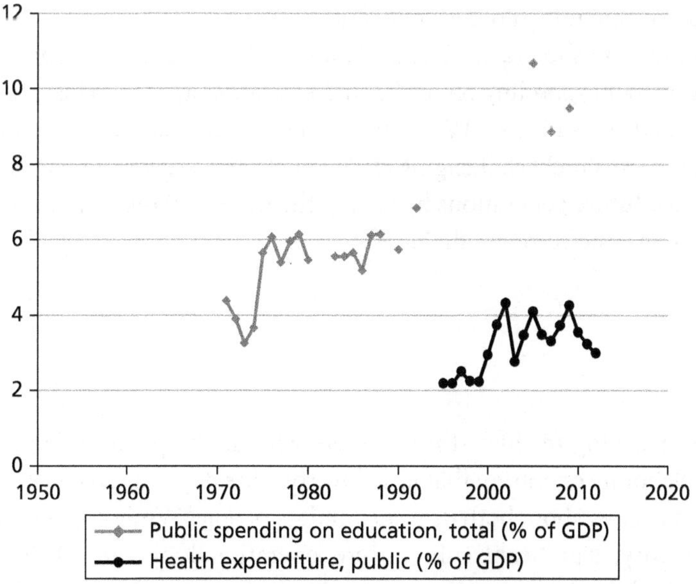

Figure 10.16 Botswana—share of public expenditure on health and education as % of GDP

Source: Compiled by author based on data from World Bank (various years).

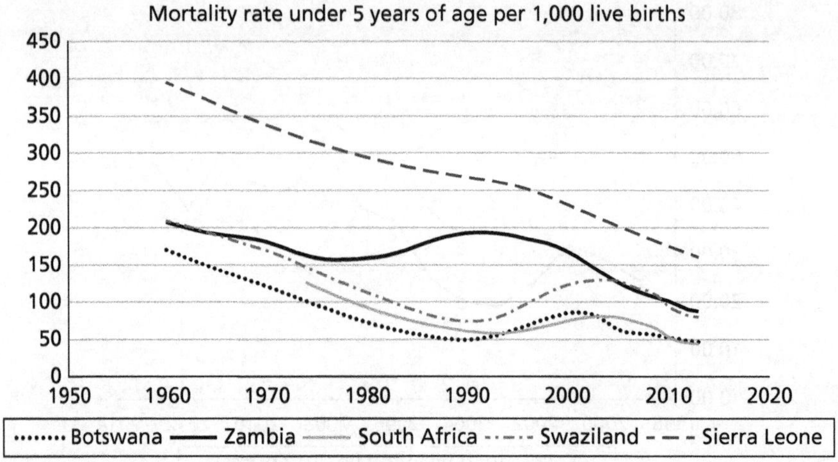

Figure 10.17 Botswana and selected African countries—under-5 mortality rate per 1,000 live births

Source: Compiled by author based on data from World Bank (various years).

2000 respectively. Though both Sierra Leone and Botswana are diamond producing countries, a child born in the former has a four times greater chance of dying before the age of 5 than in Botswana.

The impact of increased educational spending is correlated with educational outcomes especially in terms of primary completion (which had reached 90 per cent by 1980 and has remained in that range ever since) and secondary enrolment which shot up from 20 per cent at the beginning of the 1980s to 80 per cent by the year 2000. Enrolment in tertiary education remains under 10 per cent.

The Botswana case illustrates that sustained policies to use resource revenues for enhanced government spending on health and education appear to have helped it to face the unprecedented crisis of the HIV/AIDS pandemic. The case of the Pula Fund suggests that in spite of an extremely challenging crisis situation, the government was able to meet its obligations for future generations by having the necessary institutions to pre-empt the temptation to consume resource dividends.

CHILE

The successful rescuing of thirty-three miners who got trapped in Copiapo in August 2010 with an elaborate operation that lasted thirty-nine days has given Chile a worldwide reputation that it cares about both its mines and its people. While copper mining in Chile has a long history, significant mines were operational by the 1950s. In 1969, the Government of Chile signed an agreement to acquire a 51 per cent stake in what has been referred to as 'negotiated nationalisation'. In 1971, Congress passed a law effectively nationalizing all copper mines in Chile. Codelco—a fully government-owned mining company—was formed in 1976 and manages the copper mines. According to its 2013 report, it had 19,000 direct employees and created work for another 47,000 workers, produced some 1.7 million tonnes of copper, generated a pre-tax profit of nearly US$4 billion and contributed to the exchequer US$2.9 billion.

GDP per capita (in 2005 prices) doubled from about 3,000 in 1970 to 6,000 in 1996 and continued to increase to reach nearly 9,700 in 2013. However, fluctuations in copper prices appear to have had a significant effect on export performance (Figure 10.18) as well as on mineral rents generated (Figure 10.19 and 10.20).

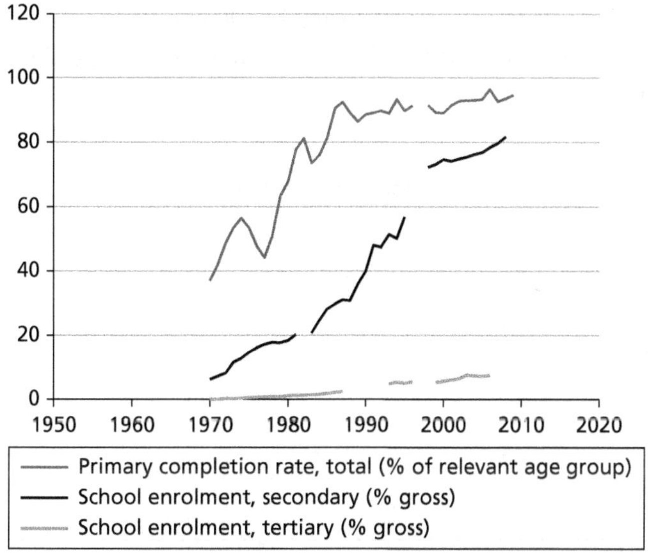

Figure 10.18 School enrolment rates in Botswana

Source: Compiled by author based on data from World Bank (various years).

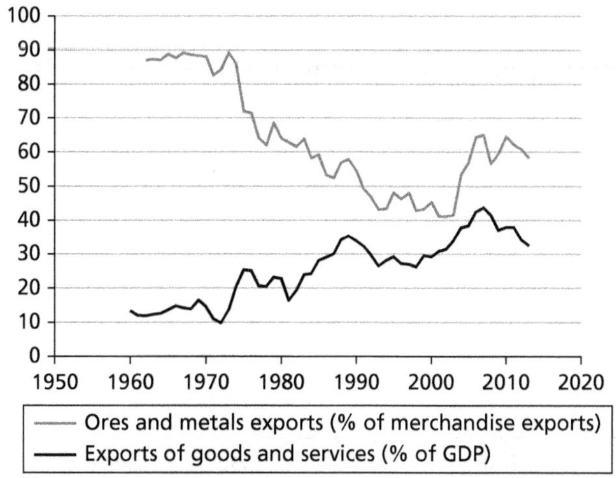

Figure 10.19 Chile—exports as % of GDP

Source: Compiled by author based on data from World Bank (various years).

As a result, there are also wide fluctuations in general government consumption expenditure (Figure 10.21) and in public spending on health and education (Figure 10.22).

In the year 1960, a child born in Chile could have expected to live for fifty-seven years—some eight years fewer than a child born in neighbouring Argentina. Mining revenues must have played a role in narrowing the gap in life expectancy such that by 1982, a child born in Chile would have outlived his/her Argentinian counterpart. The gap widened in the 1990s and 2000s. A child born in Chile today can expect to live some 79.5 years—that is three years longer than his/her Argentinian counterpart (see Figure 10.23).

Even more dramatic is the reduction in the under-5 mortality rate which was around one hundred and fifty per thousand live births in 1960 and reduced to 56.7, surpassing Argentina by 1976, and continued to fall to about eight per thousand live births in 2013 (see Figure 10.24).

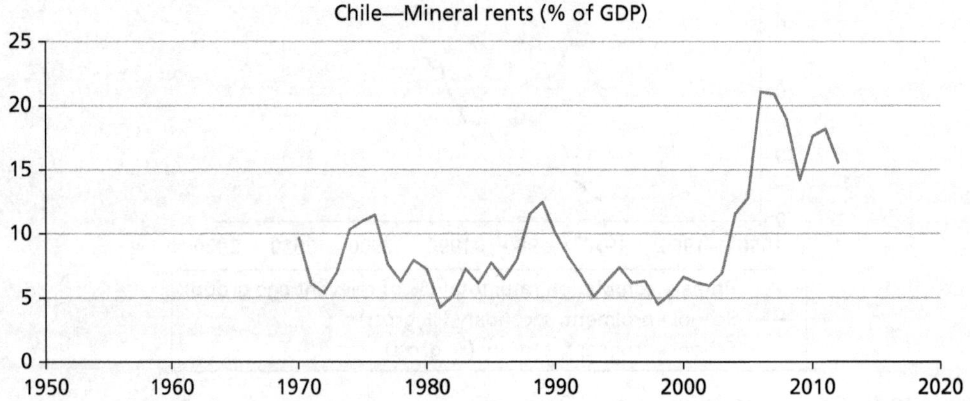

Figure 10.20 Chile—mineral rents as % of GDP

Source: Compiled by author based on data from World Bank (various years).

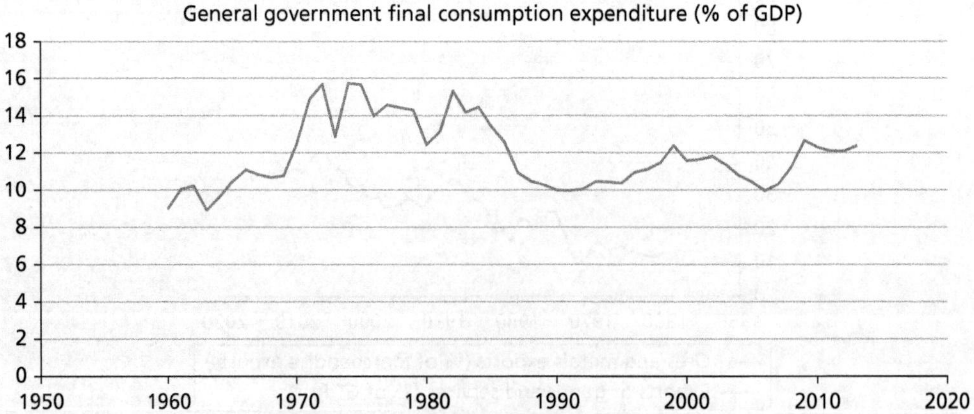

Figure 10.21 Chile—general government consumption as % of GDP

Source: Compiled by author based on data from World Bank (various years).

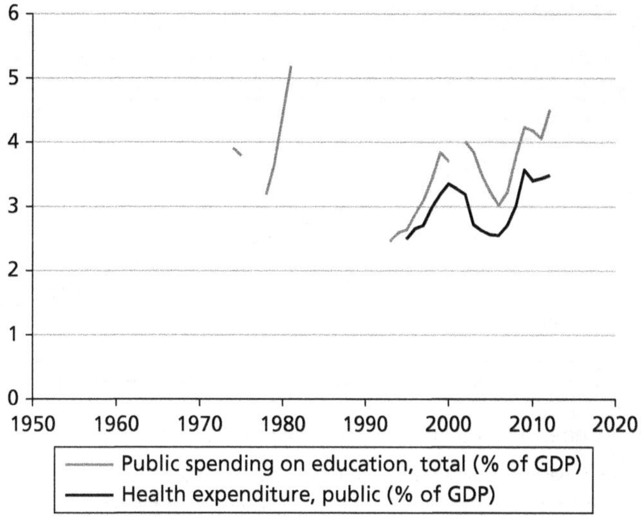

Figure 10.22 Chile—health and education public expenditure as a share of GDP

Source: Compiled by author based on data from World Bank (various years).

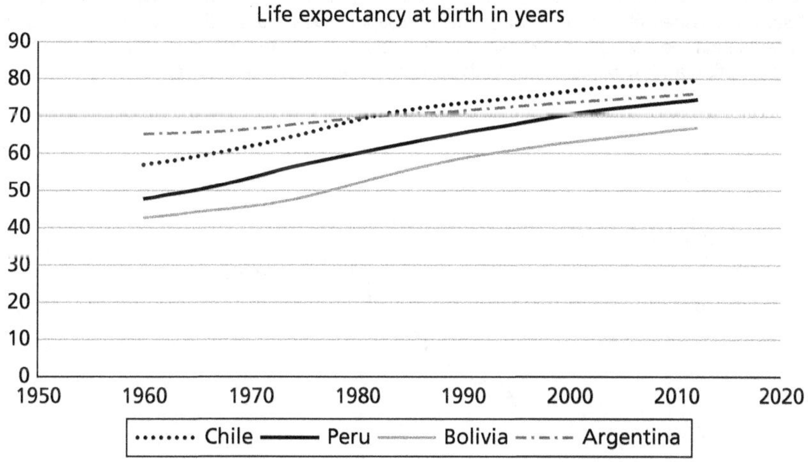

Figure 10.23 Chile—life expectancy at birth

Source: Compiled by author based on data from World Bank (various years).

The share of ores and metals in merchandise exports has been coming down, though between the years 2000 and 2008 the trend reversed in the wake of the commodity price boom and China's demand for copper. However, in recent years, China's demand has been slightly decreasing and there is also increased competition from other copper producers such as Zambia and Mongolia. So the future outlook for Chile is somewhat mixed. Diversification appears to be in progress, though there is still significant dependence on copper. Hopefully, the increasing enrolment in tertiary education can help to improve the productivity and skills of young people entering the labour market and increase opportunities for diversifying the economy (see Figure 10.25).

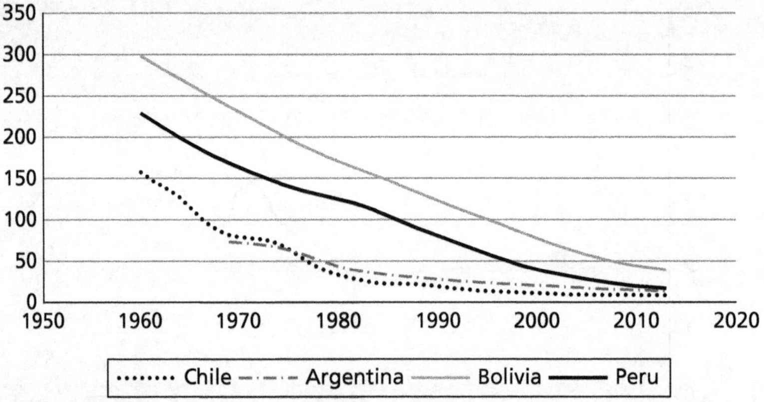

Figure 10.24 Chile—under-5 mortality per 1,000 live births

Source: Compiled by author based on data from World Bank (various years).

While the Chilean case appears to suggest that Chile has used mineral resource rents to increase and sustain public spending on education and health, the picture appears to be somewhat mixed when it comes to creating a wealth fund or investing resource rents for the benefit of future generations. Chile did create a Pension Reserve Fund in 2006 and the Economic and Social Stabilization Fund (ESSF) (transferring some US$2.5 billion from the erstwhile Copper Stabilisation Fund). By 2009, the funds together were valued at US$14.7 billion and this had increased by December 2012 to US$20.8 billion (Government of Chile 2013). Until 2011, funds were permitted to be invested in government securities issued by the USA, Germany, and Japan but since 2012, they were also permitted to be invested in international equity. On the whole, the sovereign wealth funds are a welcome addition to Chile's approach to stabilization and sustainability but this appears to have come rather recently.

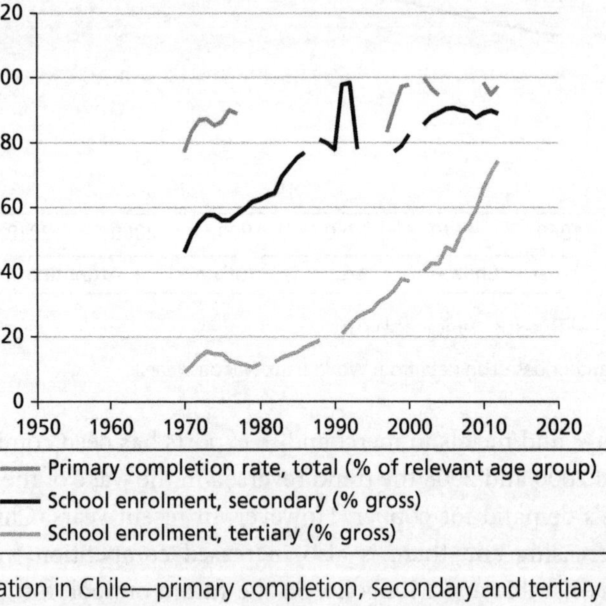

Figure 10.25 Education in Chile—primary completion, secondary and tertiary enrolment

Source: Compiled by author based on data from World Bank (various years).

The case of Chile suggests that it has some institutions such as protection of private property rights, protection for mining workers, capturing benefits for the national economy, and safeguarding some of these for future generations. There has been some significant progress on social aspects in improving health and education but these should be continued; the diversification strategy needs to be pursued further.

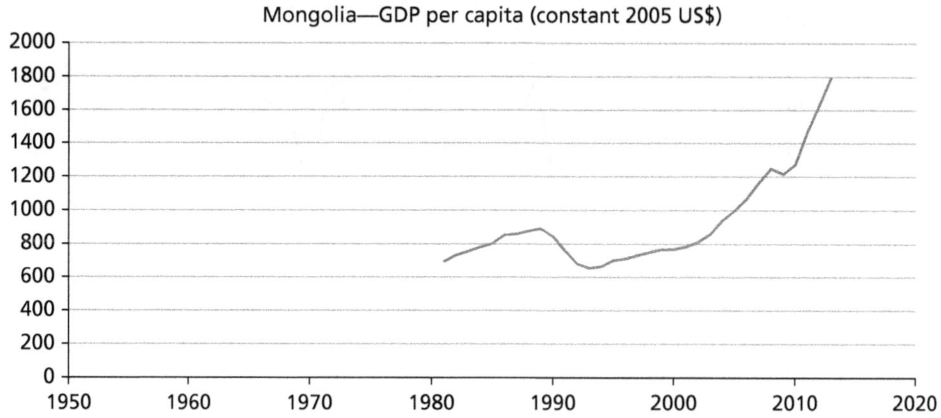

Figure 10.26 Mongolia—real GDP per capita

Source: Compiled by author based on data from World Bank (various years).

Mongolia is a nation where nomadic pastoral herding has always been an important aspect of economy and society. In 1990 the share of agriculture value added in GDP was 12 per cent compared with industry value added of around 40 per cent (Figure 10.27). These figures had more or less reversed with deindustrialization by 1996 when agriculture occupied the primary position in GDP until 2001. Since 2002, industry has taken off along with growth in the mining sector.

The issue of investing in human resources identified by Ffrench-Davis (2005: 245) continues to be relevant even now. Many issues of economic inequality in Chile remain important. (See also Chapter 28 in this volume.)

MONGOLIA

Until 1990, when Mongolia was under a single-party socialist regime, there are limited reliable data on the economy, its performance, and social and well-being indicators. Since the opening up of the economy, in the initial years Mongolia like many transition economies experienced deindustrialization, and real income per capita fell before starting to recover in 1995 (see Figures 10.26 to 10.29).[1]

The Erdenet township was built in the 1970s basically to support the copper mining operations of the Erdenet Mining Corporation in what was then considered to be the world's largest copper deposits. Erdenet continues to be one of the main pillars of mining and mineral exports of Mongolia. However, after 1991 when Mongolia undertook the transition to a multiparty democracy and market economy, the mining sector gradually opened up and other mining projects began to take shape. According to data from the Erdenet Mining Corporation, in 2001, annual throughput of its copper ore mining was about 25 million tonnes which had steadily increased to 29 million tonnes by 2013. The mine produces mainly copper concentrate and molybdenum. The amount of copper ore

[1] For a discussion on Mongolia's HDI and environmental vulnerability issues see UNDP 2011b.

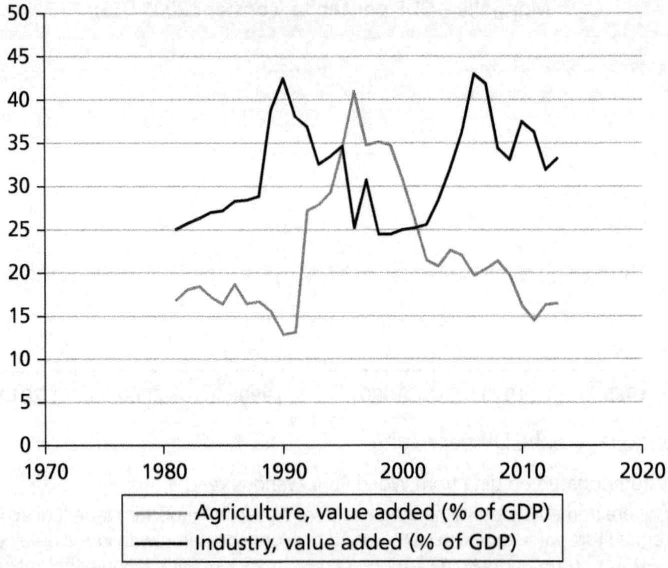

Figure 10.27 Mongolia—share of agriculture and industry value added as % of GDP

Source: Compiled by author based on data from World Bank (various years).

However, agriculture continues to employ nearly 40 per cent of all workers while industry employs around 17 per cent (Figure 10.28). This can create problems in terms of low productivity in agriculture, increasing the rural–urban income gap and inequality.[2]

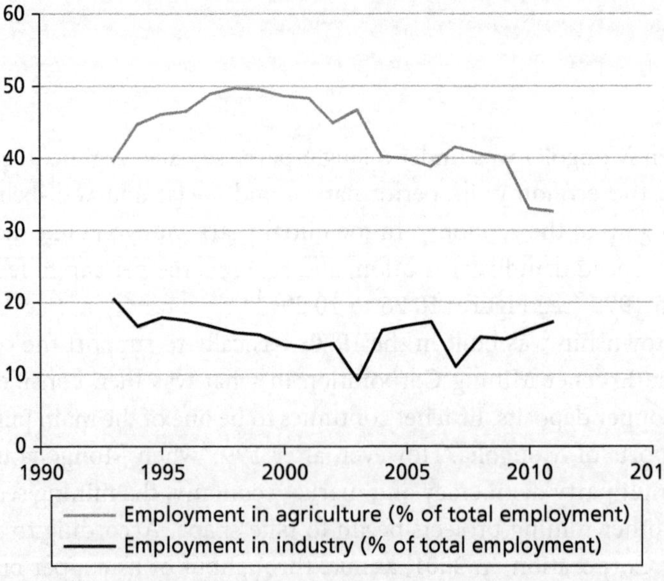

Figure 10.28 Mongolia—share of agriculture and industry in employment

Source: Compiled by author based on data from World Bank (various years).

Since the year 2000, growth in industrial activities appears to have made urban areas more attractive. At the time of transition to a multiparty democracy in the early 1990s, 40 per cent of the population was in rural areas. This had decreased to 30 per cent by 2012 while population in urban areas has increased to 70 per cent (see Figure 10.29).

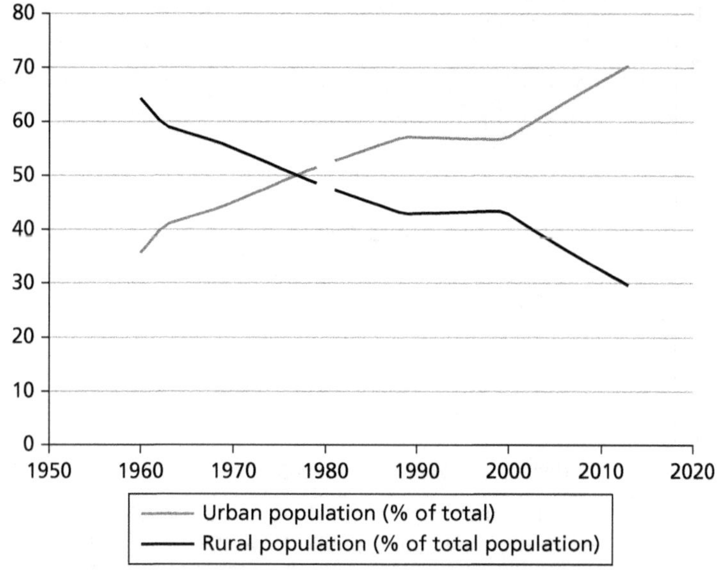

Figure 10.29 Mongolia—share of rural and urban population in total population

Source: Compiled by author based on data from World Bank (various years).

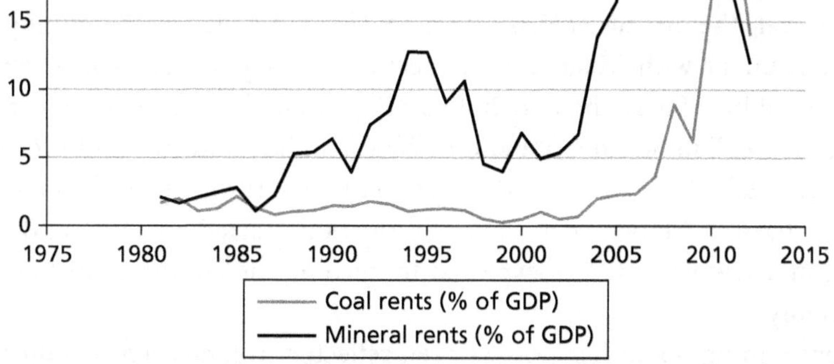

Figure 10.30 Mongolia—share of coal rents and mineral rents as % of GDP

Source: Compiled by author based on data from World Bank (various years).

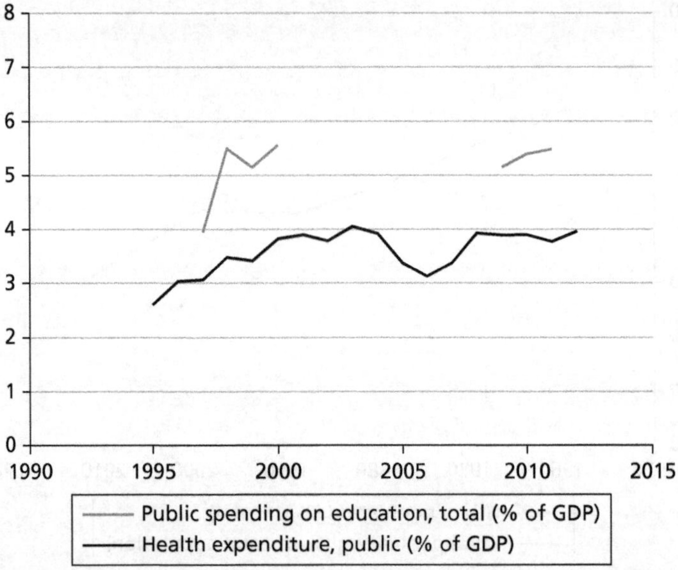

Figure 10.31 Share of public spending on health and education as % of Mongolia's GDP

Source: Compiled by author based on data from World Bank (various years).

processed also increased in the corresponding period from around 22 million tonnes in 2001 to 25 million tonnes in 2013.

Mongolia also has several open pit coal mines and produces and exports a significant share of global coal. It was among the top ten coal producers during 2001–15 and until 2014 it was in second place behind South Africa for the share of coal rents in GDP. The ranks appear to have been swapped, with Mongolia taking the top spot in 2015.

Both coal and mineral mining activities have taken off in a significant manner since 2001, and prior to the 2008 financial crisis, mineral rents were contributing to 30 per cent of GDP (see Figure 10.30).

In 2009, Mongolia signed another major agreement for the Oyu Tolgoi Mining (OT) project. However, the project's origins lie in 1995 when Erdenet (the mining company) signed an agreement with Magma, an American mining corporation which was then acquired by BHP in 1996. In the year 2000 BHP gave Ivanhoe Mining 100 per cent of the rights to acquire OT in South Gobi and in 2006 Ivanhoe and Rio Tinto formed a joint venture which finally led in 2009 to the signing of an agreement for the Government of Mongolia to have a 34 per cent stake. Production started in 2013 and when fully operational in a few years OT is expected to become the largest contributor to Mongolia's economy.

The recent mining boom has not yet been reflected in increased spending on health and education. In fact, prior to the financial crisis of 2008 there was actually a dip in public spending on health (see Figure 10.31).

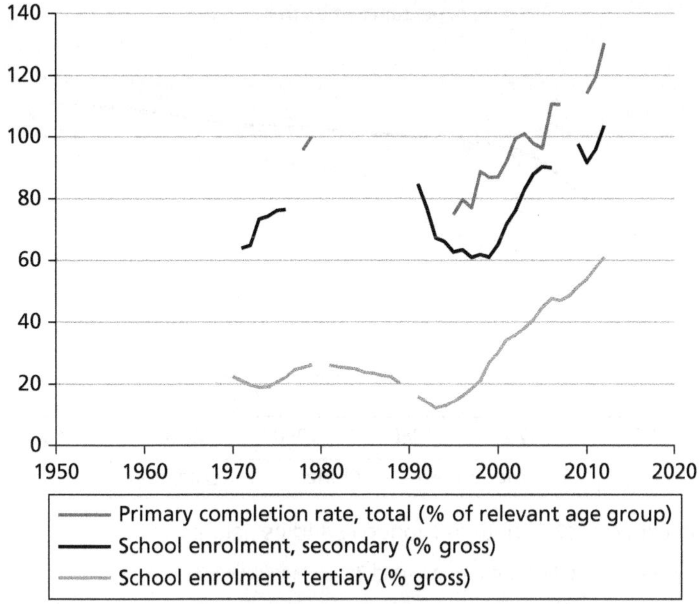

Figure 10.32 Education in Mongolia—primary completion rate, secondary and tertiary enrolment rates

Source: Compiled by author based on data from World Bank (various years).

As with many former socialist economies, Mongolia has had a fairly good system of primary and secondary education and this continued during the 1990s and 2000s (see Figure 10.32).

However, a new phenomenon since the 1990s is the increasing demand for tertiary education. This may have both supply side and demand side factors. On the supply side, declining productivity in agriculture, the so called 'dzud' or winter droughts of 1998 to 2000 and the perceived increase in opportunities in mining and industry sectors may have contributed to a greater proportion of young persons seeking tertiary education. On the demand side, increasing urbanization and industrialization including the mining sector attracts specialist and technical skills; thus the relative wages for such jobs might increase making them attractive (and thus human capital investment worthwhile). During my research, I have noticed that a greater proportion of girls than boys continue into tertiary education. This may be due to inherent gender bias in employment opportunities requiring more girls than boys to invest in human capital to have any chance of succeeding in the employment market. Also, while mining contributes a high share of GDP, its absorptive capacity in terms of sustainable jobs is rather limited. This can create short-term shortages which drive up relative wages in mining and attract talent away from all other sectors; but over the long run this can lead to unemployment issues, over-investment of talent in the mining sector, relative disadvantaging of other

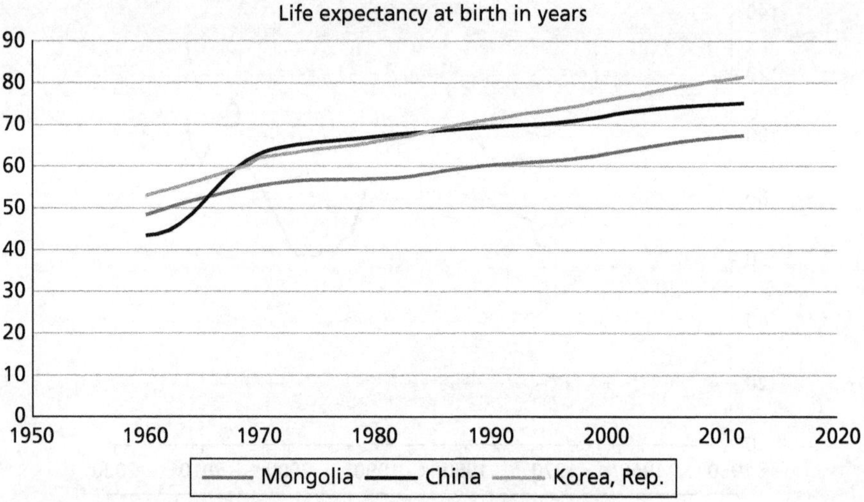

Figure 10.33 Life expectancy at birth in Mongolia and its neighbours

Source: Compiled by author based on data from World Bank (various years).

sectors, and it can create overall structural problems of low efficiency or low productivity in the economy as a whole.

While real GDP per capita tripled between 1990 and 2012, life expectancy at birth increased from 60 years at the beginning of the 1990s to about 67 years by 2012—several years lower than its neighbours in North West Asia, namely China and South Korea (see Figure 10.33).

The under-5 mortality rate is coming down. At the beginning of 1990 this was 107 per 1,000 live births and has since come down to about 31 per 1,000 live births.

The Mongolia case suggests that the very rapid opening up of the mining sector has created a mining-driven boom which has resulted in a tripling of real incomes within a matter of twenty years between 1990 and 2010. As in the case of Chile, Mongolia is also susceptible to commodity prices. While macroeconomic policies appear to be in the right direction in the sense that Mongolia was able to avoid the 'Dutch disease' effects of exchange rate appreciation, the employment aspect of the Dutch disease, i.e. attracting more people towards the high-paying mining sector could be causing some structural changes including migration and deskilling of the agriculture sector. Water productivity (in terms of dollars of GDP per cubic metre of freshwater water) is increasing. However, given that much of Mongolia's fresh water is located in a handful of sources in three provinces, water sources in all other provinces are under pressure both from the increased number of livestock and from increasing water demand due to mining activities. Sustainability of water resources can act as a local constraint in some of the locations with regard to mining activities. Though mineral revenues have increased dramatically, a corresponding dramatic rise in either public expenditures on health and education or in setting up sovereign wealth funds is not yet immediately visible from the statistics.

In terms of institutions, Mongolia has joined the EITI, and the State Great Khural (the Parliament) appears to have an all-party consensus that mineral revenues should not be used for short-term cash transfers but rather be invested for long-term development.

Though protection for private property rights is fairly robust, there are restrictions on ownership of assets by foreign nationals.

BRAZIL

Brazil is an important case both as an extractive economy and as a nation that has been trying to put in place policies for redistribution.

Brazil's resource sector took off in the 1970s with both oil and mineral rents contributing more or less in equal share. At the beginning of 1970s, total resource rents were 3 per cent of GDP and these had increased to about 5 per cent by the end of that decade. However, between 1980 and 1998, the share of resource rents in GDP fell from 5 per cent to below 2 per cent. Between 1998 and 2008, resource rents quadrupled to reach 8 per cent in the year of the global financial crisis. Though this share fell to just under 5 per cent in 2009, it has since climbed back to over 6 per cent in recent years (see Figure 10.34).

Though resource rents were only a small part of the Brazilian economy, two episodes of significant growth in per capita income; namely, the first in the 1970s and the second

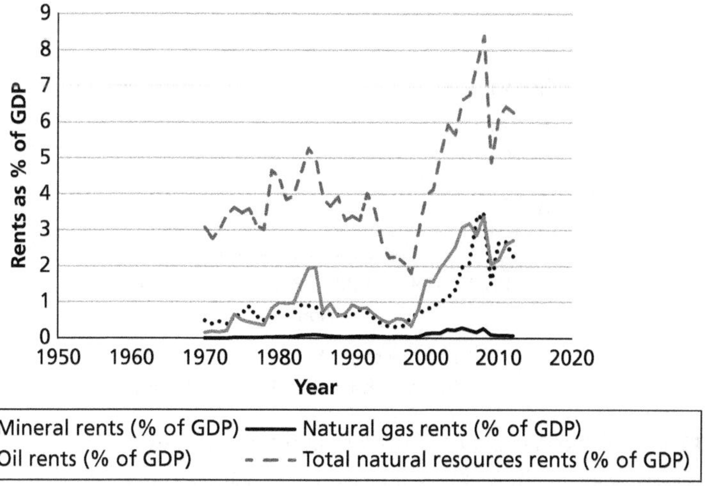

Figure 10.34 Brazil—natural resource rents

Source: Compiled by author based on data from World Bank (various years).

since 1999 appear to correlate to growth periods in resource extraction sectors (see Figure 10.35).

However, Brazil remains a society with significant inequality though there has been some improvement since 2000. The share of income held by the poorest 20 per cent remains well below 4 per cent while the share of income held by the richest 20 per cent—which used to be well above 60 per cent—has come down to around 56 per cent since 2000 (see Figure 10.36).

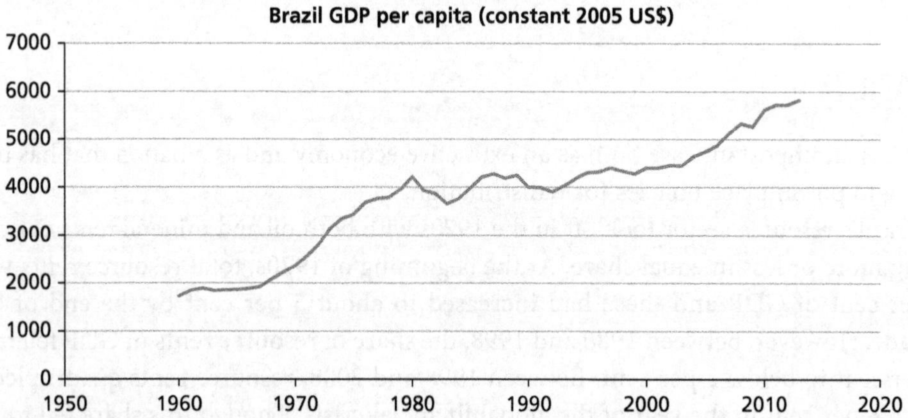

Figure 10.35 Brazil—real GDP per capita

Source: Compiled by author based on data from World Bank (various years).

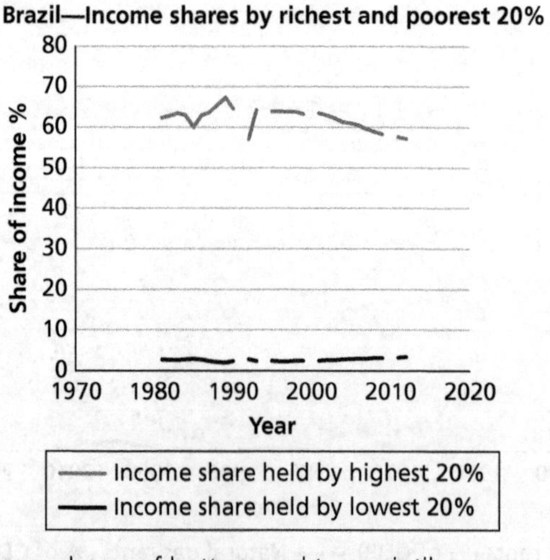

Figure 10.36 Brazil—income shares of bottom and top quintiles

Source: Compiled by author based on data from World Bank (various years).

Data on public expenditure are available only for a few recent years. This suggests that after the 1990s, successive governments steadily increased the share of public expenditure for health and education (see Figures 10.37 and 10.38).

A comparative analysis: governance indicators

Every resource rich economy is unique and thus worthy of selection as a case study. The five cases chosen here represent a range of challenges and also a range of successes in utilizing natural resource revenues in social and economic development. The Norwegian case study highlights the importance of investing in social sectors, making significant reductions in under-5 mortality, and in expanding educational outcomes. The Norwegian case also shows the use of a sovereign wealth fund as a means of building up capital for the benefit of future generations.

The Botswanan case study highlights the importance of political institutions in setting up clear private property protection mechanisms and a transparent tax regime, and resisting the temptation to dip into the wealth fund. The case also highlights the enormity of the challenge posed by HIV/AIDS and raises the question as to what would have been the situation had Botswana not been a resource rich country. Notwithstanding this challenge Botswana has raised real per capita GDP by 700 per cent and improved primary and secondary education enrolment. However, tertiary education enrolment is just picking up.

The Chilean case study indicates a mixed picture in terms of some important measures to ensure mining revenues lead to increased GDP per capita as well as increased government expenditure including on health and education. Some of the outcomes such as life expectancy and educational outcomes have improved significantly. However, tertiary education expansion appears to be taking off and this needs to be pursued to ensure that Chile has a diversification strategy for the sustainability of incomes beyond mining. The setting up of a trust fund appears to be a recent phenomenon; but the trust fund is essential given Chile's dependence on copper which is highly volatile in terms of global commodity prices and this volatility seems to have affected Chile's public expenditure patterns.

The Mongolian case suggests that a rapid boom in mining can deliver some quick short-term gains such as an increase in real GDP per capita. However, such rapid transition can also undermine the stability of the economy, significantly alter the rural economy and its character, and lead to migration and excessive dependence on urban activities. Proper management of this transition requires huge investment in infrastructure creation including in urban infrastructure which can take some time. Though Mongolia is setting up a wealth fund, these are still early days and as yet the impact of mining on health and educational outcomes is not yet fully visible. While the broader consensus of political institutions is important, Mongolia needs to maintain its investments and resist the temptation to use mining revenues for increasing consumption expenditures.

The Brazilian case indicates that addressing inequality through targeted policies can be important, that it can take years of progress to undo past inaction, and that progress can be slow. The Brazilian case study also indicates that sustained investment in social sectors such as health and education will need to continue before there is significant impact in terms of educational outcomes or health indicators.

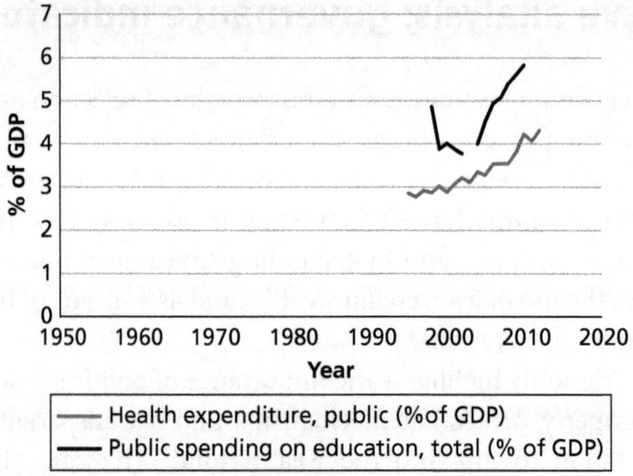

Figure 10.37 Brazil—public expenditure on health and education

Source: Compiled by author based on data from World Bank (various years).

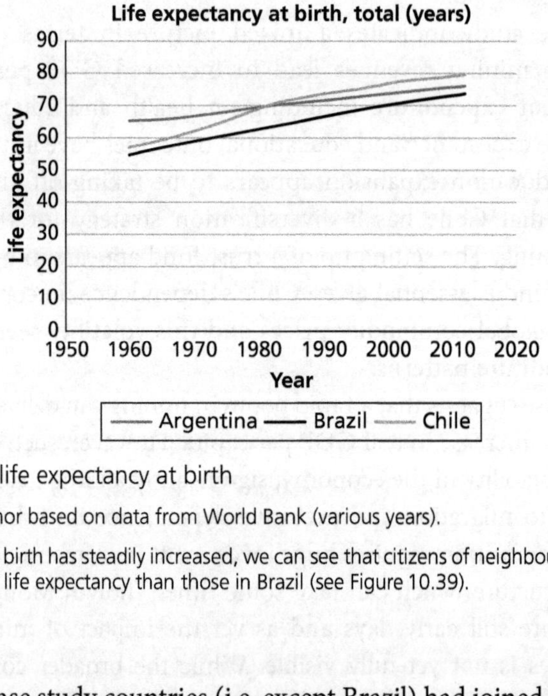

Figure 10.38 Brazil—life expectancy at birth

Source: Compiled by author based on data from World Bank (various years).

Though life expectancy at birth has steadily increased, we can see that citizens of neighbouring Chile and Argentina continue to enjoy greater life expectancy than those in Brazil (see Figure 10.39).

Four of the five case study countries (i.e. except Brazil) had joined EITI and are taking transparency initiatives seriously. Publishing what the government receives from mining is one part of the story. Involving all stakeholders in discussions about how to use such revenues and how to create the necessary institutions to guarantee that benefits from mining accrue to all stakeholders (i.e. equality, fairness, transparency, and intergenerational equity) requires public institutions which can promote and sustain argumentation and debate.

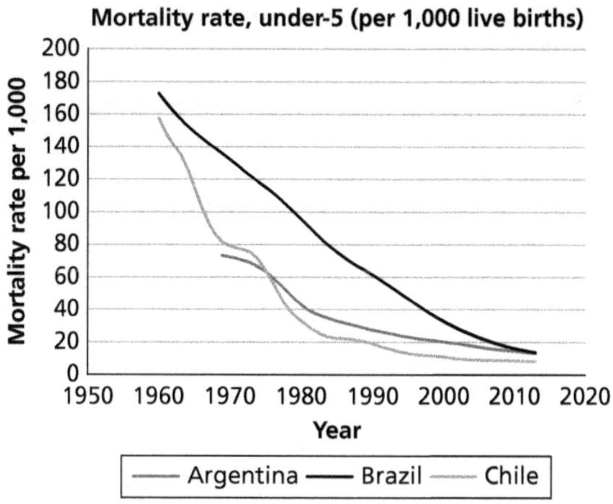

Figure 10.39 Brazil—under-5 mortality rate

Source: Compiled by author based on data from World Bank (various years).

Likewise, the under-5 mortality rate has caught up with Argentina only in the last few years. These social indicators suggest that while progress made by Brazil has been significant, there was delay in accelerating progress on these indicators until the 1990s. Costa and Santos (2013) observed in their study of municipalities in one oil rich state (Rio Grande de Norte) in Brazil that municipalities that benefited most from oil revenues did spend money on education and culture but also that on the whole their municipal administration expenditures were also very high, contravening national law.

Governance indicators are controversial and such indicators can fully capture the truly complex phenomena of the quality of institutions in different societies. However, notwithstanding their limitations such indicators can give a broad picture of relative progress. From the Worldwide Governance Indicators dataset compiled by Kaufman and Kraay (2017) we have six indicators, namely voice and accountability, political stability, government effectiveness, regulatory quality, rule of law, and control of corruption. A comparative summary of the rank order of the five case study countries indicates that Norway and Chile have made substantial progress in most indicators while Botswana has also been making significant progress (see Figure 10.40A).

Among the five case study countries, not surprisingly Norway comes out as being the strongest on voice and accountability while the situation in Mongolia seems to have become more difficult just when the mining boom had started to take place in the early 2000s (see Figure 10.40B).

On political stability, significant fluctuations and an overall lack of improvement in Brazil can be noted (see Figure 10.40C).

With regard to government effectiveness and regulatory quality, Norway and Chile appear to be doing well—both in the top 20 percentile ranks (see Figures 10.40D and 10.40E).

A steady decline in the rule of law and control of corruption in Mongolia is a cause for concern. In the case of Brazil, there has been some improvement in the rule of law since 2005 but the issue of corruption control appears to be fluctuating, with a drop in recent years. Recent political scandals involving former presidents and the role

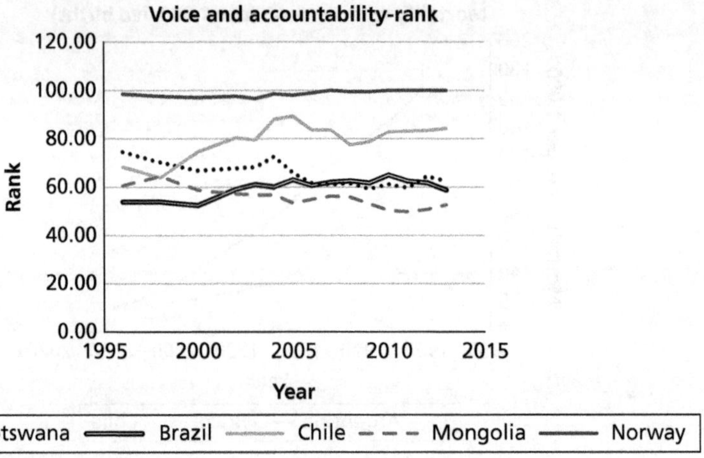

Figure 10.40A Voice and accountability

Source: Author's compilation based on World Bank (various years).

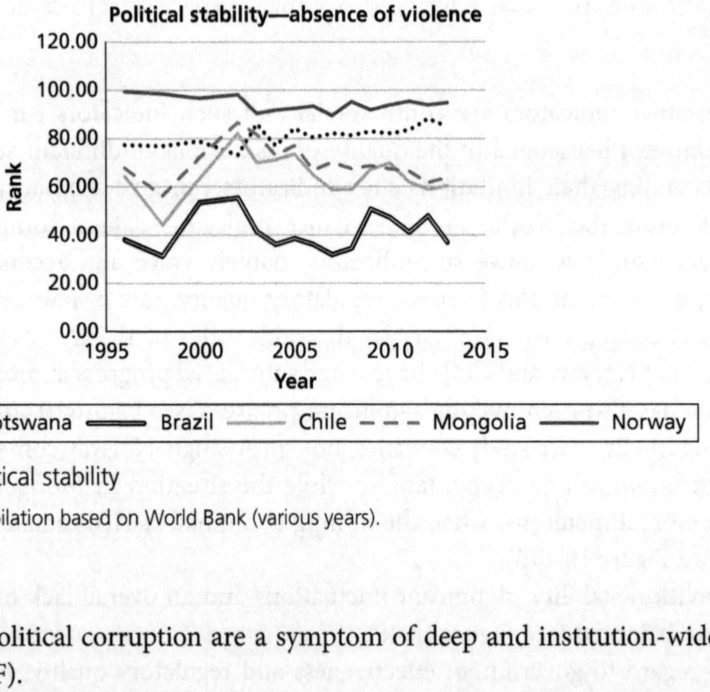

Figure 10.40B Political stability

Source: Author's compilation based on World Bank (various years).

of Petrobras in political corruption are a symptom of deep and institution-wide issues (see Figure 10.40F).

An indicator of sustainability is what is known as the adjusted net savings calculated by the World Bank following the methodology discussed in World Bank (2011). The methodology is based on the Hartwick–Solow rule of sustainable management of a depletable natural resource. The so-called 'weak sustainability' rule suggests that a nation is on a path to sustainability so long as its overall wealth (including natural resources, human-made wealth, and human capital) is not decreasing.

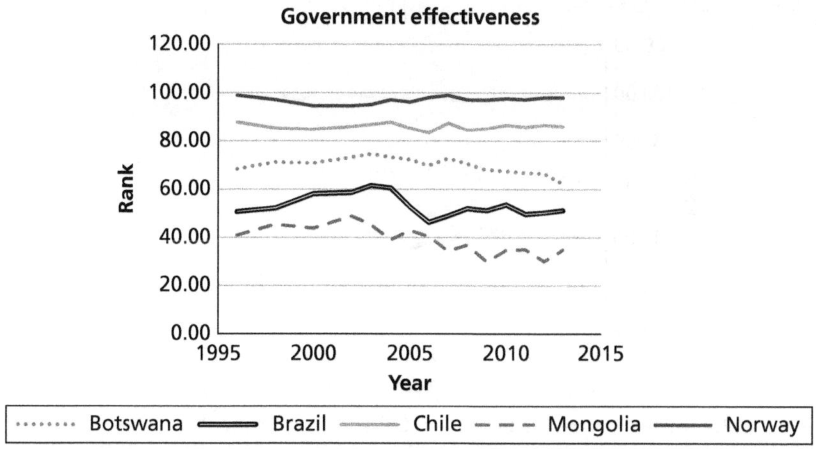

Figure 10.40C Government effectiveness

Source: Author's compilation based on World Bank (various years).

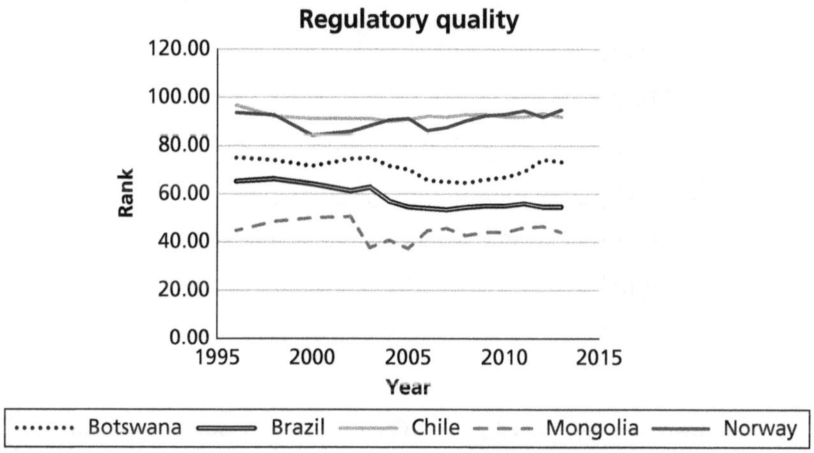

Figure 10.40D Regulatory quality

Source: Author's compilation based on World Bank (various years).

In this approach, adjusted net savings are calculated to take into account any changes to the wealth of the nation—educational investment is considered as a positive change while extraction or depletion of minerals, energy, or forests have a negative impact, as does pollution created during the year (in terms of CO2 damage and particulate matter damage). A nation that does not save enough to compensate for the energy or mineral depletion is considered unsustainable. Figure 10.41 provides a comparison of the four case study countries and appears to show that Botswana has been consistently investing to create adjusted savings of almost 30 per cent. At the beginning of 1990 Norway's adjusted net savings were negligible but this had steadily increased to over 20 per cent by 2012.

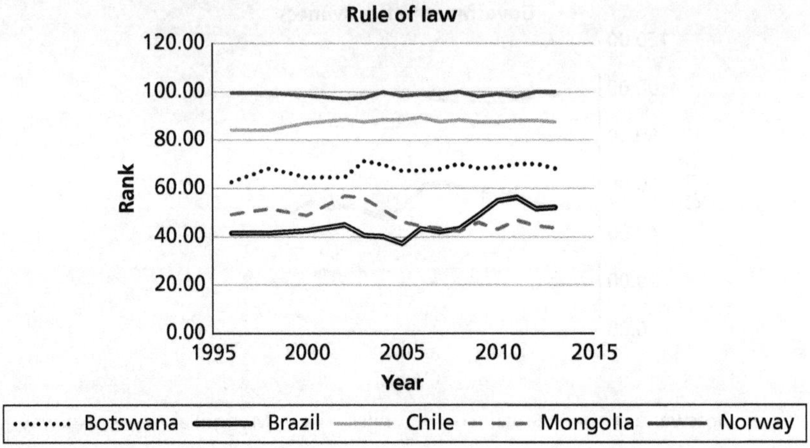

Figure 10.40E Rule of law

Source: Author's compilation based on World Bank (various years).

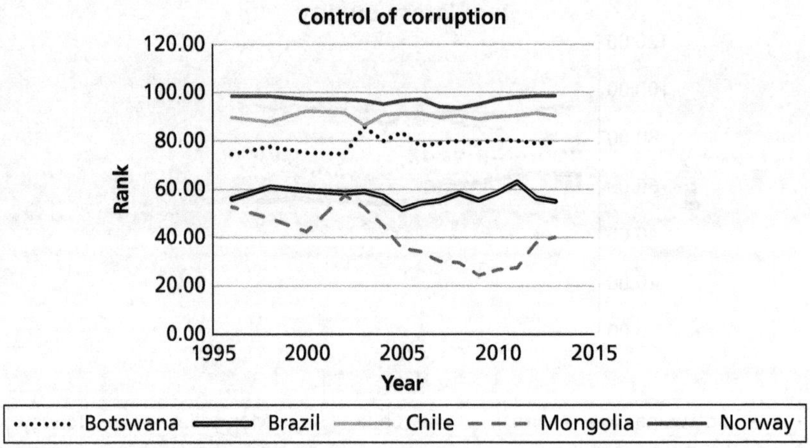

Figure 10.40F Control of corruption

Source: Author's compilation based on World Bank (various years).

Chile's adjusted net savings have been steadily declining and have been negative since 2005. Mongolia started off with negative adjusted net savings which increased to about 10 per cent for most years in the 1990s but then plummeted to close to zero in 2002 and again became negative after the financial crisis of 2008.

Adjusted savings gives a macro-picture and is overly weighted by net savings rates such that energy and mineral depletion and forest and CO2 damage have very low values. Notwithstanding this criticism, adjusted savings as an indicator of sustainability serves a useful purpose here in terms of the need for a consistent approach to saving resource revenues and using these to invest for the benefit of all stakeholders rather than consuming them. Investing in improving basic services including health and educational

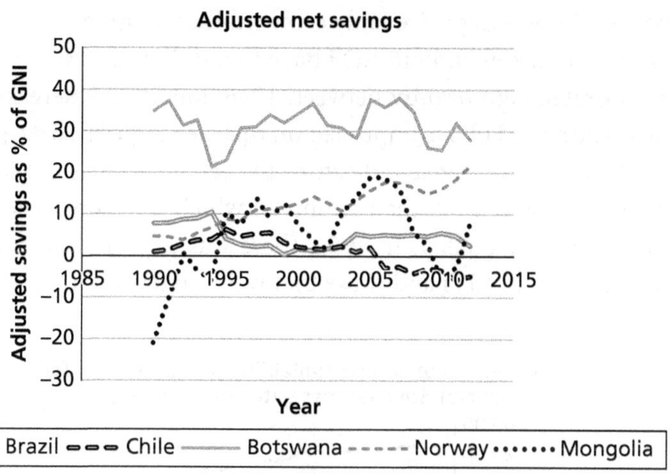

Figure 10.41 Adjusted net savings—Botswana, Chile, Mongolia, Norway

Source: Compiled by author based on data from World Bank (various years).

outcomes will increase adjusted net savings and thus ensure that mineral revenues are used in a sustainable manner.

Extractive Industries Transparency Initiative and governance indicators

EITI is a global initiative aimed at improving the transparency of resource rents in extractive economies. The underlying thesis is that if mineral revenues are transparent then the public can hold the government to account for better use of those resources. In some ways, EITI is similar to 'Publish What You Pay' (PWYP) the main difference being that PWYP focuses on mineral corporate firms while EITI focuses on the government to publish what it receives. EITI is an initiative from a 2005 conference hosted by the UK but subsequently being led mainly by Norway. To the critics of EITI, it is a top heavy initiative that is voluntary for countries to join; even if the information on revenue received from natural resource sectors is published, there is no guarantee that such revenues will be put to good use.

It will be interesting to examine whether joining EITI results in better government performance and reduction in corruption. For this analysis, we look at the fifty-six mineral economies and forty oil economies and divide them into two groups, in each case based on whether the country is one of the forty-eight EITI implementing countries or not and then compare the two averages. This analysis indicated that in most cases countries that have joined EITI are lower ranked than countries that have not. This can be a good thing if it is indicating that EITI has been well-targeted within resource rich countries that most need the transparency improvements. EITI seems to be having a positive impact on improving voice and accountability in mineral rich as well as oil rich countries. Oil rich countries without EITI have found that their voice and accountability rank have deteriorated significantly between 1996 and 2012 whereas oil rich countries who are implementing EITI have improved on this (see Figures 10.42A, 10.42B, 10.42C).

For almost all other governance indicators, the set of countries which has joined EITI on the whole have a lower rank than countries which have not. The only exception is with regard to regulatory quality. In 1996, there was gap of almost ten ranks between countries that did not join EITI and those that went on to join it. This gap had closed by

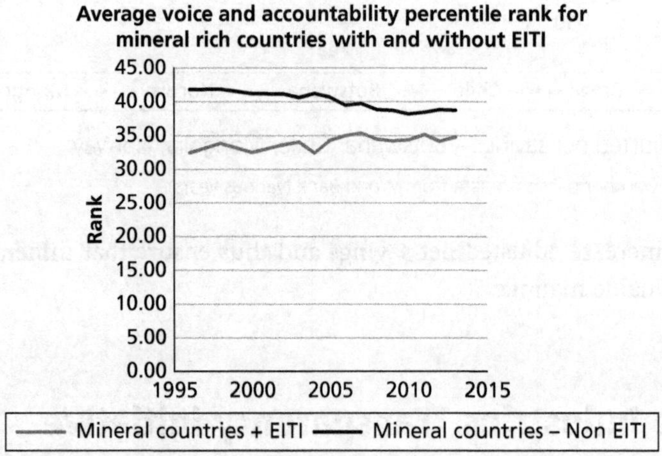

Figure 10.42A Voice and accountability—mineral rich countries with and without EITI

Source: Compiled by author based on data from World Bank (various years).

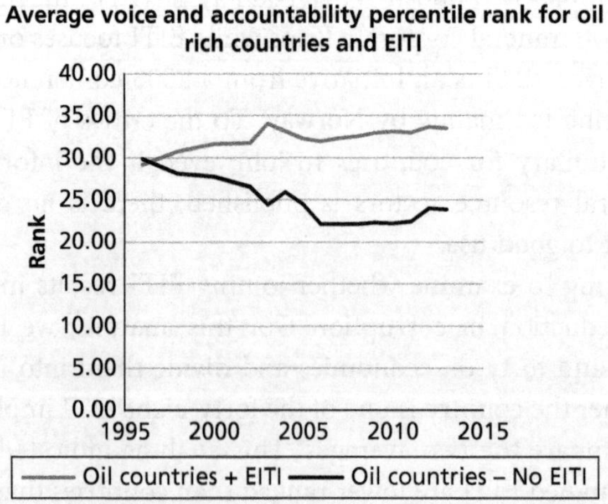

Figure 10.42B Voice and accountability—oil rich countries with and without EITI

Source: Compiled by author based on data from World Bank (various years).

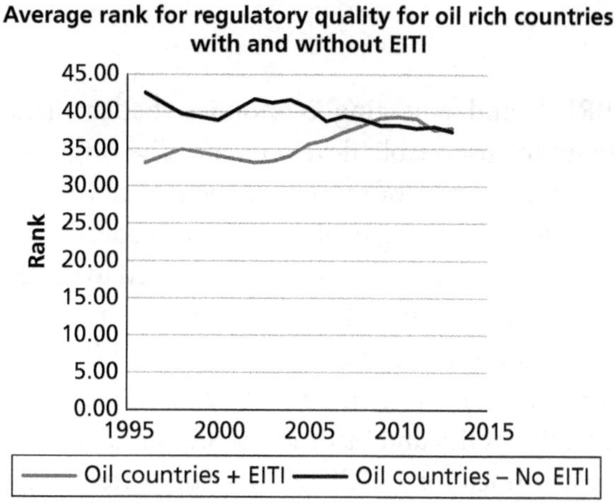

Figure 10.42C Regulatory quality and oil economies with or without EITI

Source: Compiled by author based on data from World Bank (various years).

2008 and since then EITI members do as well as non-members. This analysis suggests that joining EITI is perhaps most effective for oil economies with regard to improving voice and accountability. With regard to mineral countries, the difference between those who joined EITI and those who did not is becoming less significant. While governance reforms in general and transparency in particular are important for all countries including resource rich countries, it appears that joining international initiatives such as EITI may be effective for oil economies. Mineral economies can continue to publish what they receive but more work may be needed in developing civil society institutions that can mediate between diverse groups of stakeholders and facilitate better and sustainable use of the resource revenues. In all cases, adjusted savings can be a good guide to policy. The divergence between resource rents and adjusted savings is worth monitoring and this can be a useful diagnostic device and guide for policy design. Distribution of resource rents equitably between generations requires setting up some kind of trust fund. Allocation within the present generation needs to address issues related to spatial, geographic, and ethnic aspects of who benefits and how. There are implications for China, India, and other emerging economies with large natural resources which are located in economically backward regions. For a number of decades, local populations in provinces or states where natural resources are situated feel alienated from the development process. In China this applies especially to the interior and western provinces while in India this applies to many central and eastern Indian states, including some of the states in the north eastern region. In the case of China, significant infrastructure investment especially in recent years has attempted to close the gap between these inland regions and the more prosperous and urbanized coastal regions. In India, such infrastructure development and more importantly HD improvement in the mineral rich states is still lagging behind.

Conclusion

In the context of BRICS and emerging economies, better management of natural resources can contribute to sustainable development. The original analysis of the relationship between HDI and the level of resource dependence (second section) suggested that resource rich countries tend to lag behind the non-resource dependent countries in HDI. This means naturally resource rich countries will need to design and pursue careful policies with a clear view to advancing HD to overcome the 'resource disadvantage'. The case studies (analysed in the third and fourth sections) indicate that while extractive sectors can play a very important role in driving economic and social change, there is need for caution and careful policy and institutional design to identify what works. Three main messages can be identified for BRICS: (a) develop better macroeconomic management tools for managing natural resource wealth, including through sovereign wealth funds where this is appropriate; (b) create greater transparency of resource revenues either by joining international initiatives such as EITI or by creating a BRICS-wide platform for this purpose and simultaneously create the capacity at local level to use such information; (c) use resource revenues in an accountable and targeted manner for social and sustainable development strategies with a further focus on developing institutions and infrastructure in the remote and backward regions where mining activities are often located for the benefit of local people.

Extractive sectors can generate significant revenue for the government which can be directed towards health, education, and key aspects of inclusive social spending with a view to making a serious dent in poverty and promoting healthy lives. However, this will not happen unless the necessary policy instruments appropriate to the context are carefully designed through a consultative process of voice and accountability. BRICS countries as significantly natural resource rich countries do need to do more to improve the transparency of resource revenues. We do know that international standards mechanisms such as EITI can help in improving the transparency of income generated by natural resource sectors. While BRICS may not be exactly rushing to join EITI mainly for global and domestic political economy reasons, at the very least they should develop the equivalent of an 'EITI–BRICS' standard for better natural resources management. Whether the increased transparency of income translates into a transparent and accountable allocation of such resources to sectors and activities that can have most impact on making development inclusive and sustainable is a moot point. Analysis conducted but not reported in the chapter showed that on many of the development performance indicators such as those relevant to Sustainable Development Goals (SDGs), there is not much systematic difference between countries that have joined EITI and resource rich countries that have not. Our case study countries Botswana and Chile have been improving natural resource wealth management systematically even though they are still outside EITI. However, our analysis also shows that EITI can make a difference in macroeconomic indicators especially with regard to exchange rates.

EITI is having an effect in reducing 'Dutch disease' incidence among extractive economies. However, there is now need to make further progress and either build on EITI (and ensure all big extractive economies, whether emerging or developed economies, become members of EITI) or develop other multilateral instruments to encourage, facilitate, monitor, and use evidence to help extractive economies to achieve inclusive sustainable development. As we saw, the relationship between HD and mineral wealth is complex and dynamic but this needs to be better understood. Joining EITI does not seem to make a difference to mineral economies which continue to perform poorly on many of the governance indicators; but in the case of oil economies, it appears that joining EITI can lead to improvements in governance indicators. Transparency in revenues is important. Such international standards can help in promoting public deliberation on how best to use mineral and oil rents for sustainable development and improving the quality of life of all citizens in an inclusive manner. There is a need for further dialogue on the possible ways in which this can be done.

ACKNOWLEDGEMENTS

Some of the research for this chapter has been made possible by support from the Foreign and Commonwealth Office of the UK, the United Nations Development Programme in Brazil, and the United Nations University/World Institute for Development Economics Research, Helsinki. The author alone remains responsible for the analysis and results presented here and these should not be attributed to the above mentioned organizations.

REFERENCES

Alden, C. and Alves, A. (2009). 'China and Africa's natural resources: The challenges and implications for development and governance'. Occasional paper No. 41. Johannesburg: South African Institute of International Affairs.

Alexeev, M. and Conrad, R. (2009). 'The elusive oil curse', *Review of Economics and Statistics* 91/3: 586–98.

Anand, P.B. (2007a). *Scarcity, Entitlements and the Economics of Water in Developing Countries.* Cheltenham: Edward Elgar.

Anand, P.B. (2013). 'Every drop counts: assessing aid for water and sanitation'. Working Paper 2013/25. Helsinki: United Nations University-World Institute for Development Economics Research (UNU-WIDER).

Arezki, R. and van der Ploeg, F. (2007). 'Can the natural resource curse be turned into a blessing? The role of trade policies and institutions' IMF Working Paper 07/55. Washington, DC: IMF.

Auty, R.M. (2002). *Resource Abundance and Economic Development.* New York: Oxford University Press.

Badeeb, R., Lean, H., and Clark, J. (2017). 'The evolution of the natural resource curse: a critical literature survey', *Resources Policy* 51: 123–34.

Bank of Botswana (various years). *Annual Report.* Gaberone: Bank of Botswana. Available at http://www.bankofbotswana.bw/index.php/content/2009110614058-bank-publications, accessed 30 April 2019.

Bazilian, M., Onyeji, I., Aqrawi, P., Sovacool, B., Ofori, E., Kammen, D., and de Graaf, T. (2013). 'Oil, energy poverty and resource dependence in West Africa', *Journal of Energy and Natural Resources Law* 31/1: 33–53.

Bebbington, A. (2009). 'Please Mr Bebbington don't come here and tell us what to do', *Antipode* 41/1: 191–202.

Boschini, A., Pattersson, J., and Roine, J. (2012). 'The resource curse and its potential reversal', *World Development* 43: 19–41.

Boyce, J. and Emery, J. (2011). 'Is a negative correlation between resource abundance and growth sufficient evidence that there is a "resource curse"?', *Resources Policy* 36/1: 1–3.

Brunnschweiler, C.N. and Bulte, E.H. (2008). 'The resource curse revisited and revised: A tale of paradoxes and red herrings', *Journal of Environmental Economics and Management* 55/3: 248–64.

CAGI (Comptroller and Auditor General of India) (2012). *Report of the Comptroller and Auditor General of India on Allocation of Coal Blocks and Augmentation of Coal Production for the year ended March 2012.* New Delhi: CAGI.

Carmody, P. (2011). *The New Scramble for Africa.* London: Polity Press.

Carpintero, O., Murray, I., and Bellver, J. (2016). 'The new scramble for Africa: BRICS strategies in a multi-polar world', in R. Desai (ed.) *Analytical Gains of Geopolitical Economy.* Research in Political Economy, volume 30B. Bingley: Emerald Publishing, 191–226.

Collier, P. (2008). *The Bottom Billion.* London: Penguin.

Constantini, V. and Monni, S. (2008). 'Environment, human development and economic growth', *Ecological Economics* 64: 867–80.

Corden, M. and Neary, J. (1982). 'Booming sector and deindustrialization in a small open economy', *Economic Journal* 92: 825–48.

Costa, H. and Santos, M. (2013). 'Institutional analysis and the "resource curse" in developing countries', *Energy Policy* 63: 788–95.

De Beers (2014). *The Diamond Insight Report 2014.* London: De Beers Group.

Deacon, R. (2011). *The Political Economy of the Natural Resources Curse.* Breda: Now Publishers.

Debswana (2005). *Annual Review 2005.* Botswana: Debswana.

Denzin, N. and Lincoln, Y. (2011). *Sage Handbook of Qualitative Research.* London and Thousand Oaks, CA: Sage.

Dollar, D. (2016). *China's Engagement with Africa: From Natural Resources to Human Resources.* New York: The John L. Thornton Center, Brookings Institution.

Drelichman, M. and Voth, H. (2008). 'Institutions and resource curse in early modern Spain', in E. Helpman (ed.) *Institutions and Economic Performance.* Cambridge, MA: Harvard University Press, 120–47.

Erten, B. and Ocampo, A. (2012). 'Super-cycles of commodity prices since the mid-nineteenth century'. DESA Working Paper No. 110. Geneva: United Nations.

Eynde, O. (2016). 'Targets of violence: evidence from India's Naxalite conflict', *The Economic Journal* DOI: 10.1111/eco j.12438.

Felter, C. (2017). *Brazil's Corruption Fallout.* New York: Council on Foreign Relations.

Ffrench-Davis, R. (2005). *Economic Reforms in Chile: From Dictatorship to Democracy.* Ann Arbor, MI: University of Michigan Press.

Frankel, J. (2010). 'The natural resource curse: a survey'. NBER Working Paper 15836. Cambridge, MA: National Bureau of Economic Research.

Government of Chile (2013). *Sovereign Wealth Fund Annual Report.* Santiago: Ministry of Finance.

Grytten, O. (2008). 'The economic history of Norway', Economic History Association, *EH.Net Encyclopedia,* edited by Robert Whaples, 16 March. Available at http://eh.net/encyclopedia/the-economic-history-of-norway/, accessed 11 November 2018.

Gylfason, T. (2001).'Natural resources, education and economic development', *European Economic Review* 45/4–6: 847–59.

Hogan, W. and Sturzenegger, F. (2010). *The Natural Resources Trap: Private Investment without Public Commitment.* Cambridge, MA: MIT Press.

Holden, S. (2013). 'Avoiding the resource curse: the case Norway', *Energy Policy* 63: 870–6.

Humphreys, M., Sachs, J., and Stiglitz, J. (eds). (2007). *Escaping the Resource Curse.* New York: Columbia University Press.

Jones Luong, P. and Weinthal, E. (2010). *Oil is Not a Curse: Ownership Structure and Institutions in Soviet Successor States.* Cambridge: Cambridge University Press.

Kaufman, D. and Kraay, A. (2017). *Worldwide Governance Indicators.* New York: World Bank.

Kolstad, I. and Wiig, A. (2008). 'Is transparency the key to reducing corruption in resource rich countries?', *World Development* 37/3: 521–32.

Krugman, P. (2013). 'This age of bubbles', *New York Times,* 23 August 2013. Available at https://economistsview.typepad.com/economistsview/2013/08/paul-krugman-this-age-of-bubbles.html, accessed 19 May 2019.

Maloney, W. and Lederman, D. (2006). *Natural Resources: Neither Curse Nor Destiny.* Washington, DC: World Bank.

Mehlum, H., Moene, K., and Torvik, R.. (2006) 'Institutions and resource curse', *The Economic Journal* 116: 1–20.

Menaldo, V. (2016). *The Institutions Curse: Natural Resources, Politics and Development.* Cambridge: Cambridge University Press.

Meyersson, E., Miquel, G., and Qian, N. (2008). *The Rise of China and the Natural Resource Curse in Africa.* Cambridge, MA: Harvard University.

Moses, J. and Letnes, B. (2017). *Managing Resource Abundance and Wealth: The Norwegian Experience.* New York: Oxford University Press.

Obi, C. and Rustad, S. (eds) (2011). *Oil and Insurgency in the Niger Delta.* London: Zed Books.

OECD (Organisation for Economic Co-operation and Development) (2017) *Development Aid Statistics At a Glance.* Paris: OECD.

Office of the Public Protector (2016). 'State of capture: Report on an investigation into alleged improper and unethical conduct by the President and other state functionaries relating to alleged improper relationships and involvement of the Gupta family in the removal and appointment of Ministers and Directors of State Owned Enterprises resulting in improper and possibly corrupt award of state contracts and benefits to the Gupta family's businesses'. Report number 6 of 2016/17. Report available at www.sahistory.org.za/archive/state-capture-report-public-protector-14-october-2016, accessed 13 January 2020.

Oskenbayev, Y., Yilmaz, M., and Abdulla, K. (2013). 'Resource concentration, institutional quality and the natural resource curse', *Economic Systems* 37/2: 254–70.

Papyrakis, E. (2014). 'A development curse: formal vs informal activities in resource dependent economies', *International Journal of Social Economics* 41: 244–64.

Pineda. J. and Rodriguez, F. (2010). 'Curse or blessing? natural resources and human development'. Human Development Research Paper 2010/04. New York: UNDP.

Polterovich, V., Popov, V., and Tonis, A. (2010). 'Resource abundance: a curse or a blessing?' UN DESA Working Paper 93. Geneva: United Nations.

Prebisch, R. (1950). *The Economic Development of Latin America and Its Principal Problems*. New York: United Nations.

Renaud, K. (2017). *The Mineral Industry of India*, 2014 Minerals Yearbook, Reston, VA: United States Geological Survey.

Robinson, J., Torvik, R., and Verdier, T. (2006). 'Political foundations of the resource curse', *Journal of Development Economics* 79: 447–68.

Ross, M. (2012). *The Oil Curse: How Petroleum Wealth Shapes the Development of Nations*. Princeton, NJ: Princeton University Press.

Sachs, J. and Warner, A. (1995). 'Natural resource abundance and economic growth' NBER Working Paper 5398. Cambridge, MA: NBER.

Sachs, J. and Warner, A. (1997). 'Natural resource abundance and economic growth', HIID Working Paper. Cambridge, MA: Harvard University.

Safirova, E. (2017). *The Mineral Industry of Russia*, 2014 Minerals Yearbook. Reston, VA: United States Geological Survey.

Schumpeter, J. (1939) *Business Cycles: A Theoretical, Historical, and Statistical Analysis of the Capitalist Process*. New York: McGraw Hill Book Company.

Singer, H. (1950). 'The distribution of gains between investing and borrowing countries', in *The Strategy of International Development: Essays in the Economics of Backwardness*. London: Macmillan, 43–57.

Soto-Viruet, Y. (2017). *The Mineral Industry of Brazil*, 2014 Minerals Yearbook Reston, VA: United States Geological Survey.

Statoil (2013). *Sustainability Report*. Available at www.statoil.com/no/InvestorCentre/AnnualReport/AnnualReport2013/Documents/DownloadCentreFiles/01_KeyDownloads/SustainabilityReport.pdf, accessed 11 November 2018.

Su, F., Wei, G., and Tao, R. (2016). 'China and natural resource curse in developing countries: empirical evidence from a cross-country study', *China and World Economy* 24/1: 18–40.

Torvik, R. (2002). 'Natural resources, rent seeking and welfare', *Journal of Development Economics* 67/2: 455–70.

UNDP (United Nations Development Programme) (2011a). 'Managing natural resources for human development in low-income countries. Working Paper 2011-002. New York: UNDP, Regional Bureau for Africa.

UNDP (United Nations Development Programme) (2011b). *From Vulnerability to Sustainability: Mongolia Human Development Report* 2011. Ulaanbaatar: UNDP.

UNDP (United Nations Development Programme) (2016). *Human Development Report 2016: Human Development for Everyone*. New York: UNDP.

van der Ploeg, F. (2010). 'Natural resources: curse or blessing?' CES Infor Working Paper 3125. Las Vegas, NV: Centre for Economic Studies (available from Ideas RePec).

van der Ploeg, F. and Poelhekke, S. (2009). 'Volatility and the natural resource curse', *Oxford Economic Papers* 61: 727–60.

Watts, J. (2017). 'Operation Car Wash: Is this the biggest corruption scandal in history?', Long read in *The Guardian*, Thursday 1 June.

Williams, A. and Le Billon, P. (eds) (2017). *Corruption, Natural Resources and Development: From Resource Curse to Political Ecology*. Cheltenham: Edward Elgar.

Woolcock, M., Pritchett, L., and Isham, J. (2001). 'The social foundations of poor economic growth in resource rich economies', in R. Auty (ed.) *Resource Abundance And Economic Development*. New York: Oxford University Press, chap. 5.

World Bank (2011). *Changing Wealth of Nations: Measuring Sustainable Development in the New Millennium*. Washington, DC: World Bank.

World Bank (various years). *World Development Indicators*. Washington, DC: World Bank. Available at https://datacatalog.worldbank.org/dataset/world-development-indicators, accessed 30 April 2019.

Xun, S. (2017). *The Mineral Industry of China, 2014 Minerals Yearbook*. Reston, VA: United States Geological Survey.

Yager, T. (2017). *The Mineral Industry of South Africa, 2014 Minerals Yearbook*. Reston, VA: United States Geological Survey.

Yin, D. (2014). *Case Study Research*. London: Sage.

11 Diversification as a panacea for commodity price volatility in sub-Saharan Africa

Degol Hailu and Chinpihoi Kipgen

Introduction

Natural resource endowments present opportunities for propelling economic growth and advancing human development. Harnessing these opportunities, however, comes with a unique set of challenges, mainly the management of volatility in income. As a result, many resource dependent countries have seen their economies oscillate with the trends of commodity booms and busts, resulting in pro-cyclical policies.

For instance, the first decade of the 2000s saw dramatic increases in commodity prices.[1] However, since 2011, coal, copper, iron, and oil prices have fallen by 53 per cent, 38 per cent, 67 per cent, and 51 per cent, respectively.[2] Commodity prices are forecasted to remain depressed over the next few years.

This chapter examines the impact of commodity price decline and the response from the fourteen sub-Saharan Africa (SSA) countries (seven that are oil exporters and the other seven mineral exporting countries).

The chapter is organized as follows. The next section highlights the significance of the resource sector in driving growth and human development. The third section examines the response from commodity exporting economies to the collapse of prices. The fourth section discusses how the lack of economic structural change renders resource dependent countries vulnerable to the perils of commodity price volatility, while the fifth section concludes.

[1] Prices temporarily declined during the global financial and economic crisis of 2008/09.
[2] Commodity price data are from IndexMundi (2015).

Degol Hailu and Chinpihoi Kipgen, *Diversification as a panacea for commodity price volatility in sub-Saharan Africa* In: *Handbook of BRICS and Emerging Economies.* Edited by: P.B. Anand, Shailaja Fennell, and Flavio Comim, Oxford University Press (2021).
DOI: 10.1093/oso/9780198827535.003.0011

Table 11.1 Resource dependent countries (2011)

Country	Extractive Revenues (% fiscal revenue)	Extractives Export (% total exports)	EDI*
Angola	81.25	99.78	83.28
Botswana	41.69	90.42	62.04
Cameroon	28.38	45.17	37.47
Chad	43.08	95.09	65.88
DRC	37.79	84.24	56.00
Congo Rep.	79.07	87.75	81.86
Equatorial Guinea	90.74	95.85	91.13
Gabon	55.19	85.15	69.11
Guinea	25.25	88.02	50.65
Mali	19.10	54.82	34.89
Mauritania	31.21	63.25	50.03
Niger	12.46	45.07	27.61
Nigeria	78.23	94.74	81.05
Zambia	25.17	75.56	45.00

Note: *The EDI scores Sudan as having high dependence on the sector, however, it is not included in the analysis, due to data limitations.

Source: Hailu and Kipgen (2017).

Resource driven growth and development

Table 11.1 shows the fourteen countries that we classify as resource driven based on our Extractive Dependence Index (EDI).[3] In these countries, oil, gas, and mineral exports make up more than 46 per cent of total fiscal revenues and 79 per cent of total export earnings. The sector is a dominant source of revenue in countries such as Angola and Equatorial Guinea, accounting for 81 per cent and 91 per cent of total fiscal revenues, respectively.

During the boom years (2001–10), these resource reliant economies saw GDP growing at an average annual rate of 6 per cent compared to 4.5 per cent in the 1990s. Gross national income (GNI) per capita also grew faster, by almost 60 per cent, compared to 39 per cent for the other non-resource dependent SSA countries. Chad, Equatorial Guinea, and Nigeria, for instance, saw GNI per capita more than double.

Resource dependent countries also achieved faster improvements in the Human Development Index (HDI). Between 2001 and 2010, annual HDI growth rates in the resource dependent countries averaged 1.72 per cent. Non-resource dependent SSA countries and all developing countries achieved average annual growth rates of 1.55 per cent and 1.23 per cent, respectively. Among the fourteen resource dependent countries, five are classified as low-income countries and another five are classified as lower middle-income countries. In 2014, their performance on the HDI, averaging 0.40 and 0.54 respectively, however, falls short when compared to the average scores in low-income and lower middle-income countries in general, which are 0.45 and 0.60, respectively.

[3] See Hailu and Kipgen (2017).

Response to commodity price declines

While the extent of the responses to recent price decreases varied, we discern at least six types and we analyse their implications. The policymakers responded by changing output levels, withdrawing from sovereign wealth funds, drawing-down reserves, reducing public expenditure, scaling up domestic resource mobilization, and seeking external borrowing.

THE SUPPLY RESPONSE

Since 2012, several countries have increased their supply of hydrocarbon and minerals to compensate for the fall in prices. Equatorial Guinea boosted oil exports by 13 per cent, but revenues declined by the same percentage. Increased iron ore production in Mauritania contributed to stabilizing export earnings. But, by the end of 2014, the increased production was unable to compensate for declining prices and iron ore export earnings declined by US$253 from the year before. Similarly, the Democratic Republic of Congo (DRC) increased copper production. However, by the end of 2014 the continuing decline in copper prices led to the suspension of major copper projects, including the country's largest Katanga Mine, operated by Glencore. Thus, although increases in production helped some countries avoid immediate declines in earnings, the continued fall in prices cut into profit margins, and the strategy of compensating price declines with higher export volumes became unsustainable.

Others reduced supply in the hope of prices going up. Oil producers, except Equatorial Guinea, were quick to respond to falling oil prices by cutting production to 705 thousand barrels per day, a 10 per cent decline from the average production rates in 2010.

However, between 2011 and 2014, all oil producers saw an average decline in oil revenues by US$7 billion. For example, Angola and Nigeria saw oil revenues decline by US$5 billion and US$26 billion, respectively. Chad, Congo, and Gabon saw oil revenues decline by over US$2 billion. Zambia experienced a fall in revenues by 23 per cent after reducing copper production.

WITHDRAWING FROM SOVEREIGN WEALTH FUNDS

By 2014, six of the fourteen countries established sovereign wealth funds (SWFs), including Angola, Botswana, Equatorial Guinea, Gabon, Mauritania, and Nigeria. The assets range from US$5.7 billion in Botswana's Pula Fund to US$200 million in Equatorial Guinea's Fund for Future Generations (see Table 11.2). However, SWFs in the region as a whole are significantly small compared to those of other resource dependent countries and represent less than 2 per cent of total global SWFs in value (Triki and Faye 2011).

Table 11.2 SWFs in resource dependent countries (latest estimates)

Country	Sovereign wealth	Assets, US$ billion (latest estimate)	Fiscal balance US$ billion (2014)	Fund origin
Angola	Angola Sovereign Fund	US$5	US$8.35*	Petroleum
Botswana	Pula Fund	US$5.7	US$1.2**	Minerals
Equatorial Guinea	Fund for Future Generations	US$0.2	US$1.12*	Petroleum
Gabon	Gabon Sovereign Wealth Fund	US$0.4	US$1.20*	Petroleum
Mauritania	National Fund for Hydrocarbon Reserves	US$0.09	US$0.17*	Petroleum
Nigeria	Nigerian Sovereign Investment Authority	US$1.35	US$11.25*	Petroleum

* Deficit.
** Surplus.

Source: Bauer and Toledano (2013). 'Managing the public trust: How to make natural resource funds work for citizens.'

The main objective of SWFs is to act as stabilization funds and smooth public expenditure. However, regular withdrawals from the funds have been made to balance government budgets.[4] Apart from Botswana, SWFs are not sufficient to finance the fiscal deficits. For instance, Nigeria's Stabilization Fund, a component of the Sovereign Investment Authority, is estimated to be valued at US$0.45 billion, representing less than 1 per cent of fiscal revenues. Nigeria's fiscal deficit in 2016 stood at US$11 billion.

Similarly it is unlikely that Equatorial Guinea's Fund for Future Generations will play a significant role in helping pull the country out of the slump. When the fund was created in 2002, the government pledged to deposit 0.5 per cent of annual oil revenues into the account. With a receipt of about 90 per cent of fiscal revenues from the oil sector, this would have resulted in a cumulative deposit of US$1.26 billion into the fund (between 2006 and 2010). The value of assets in 2016 was 16 per cent of this potential value. Moreover, with a budget deficit of US$1.12 billion, the fund could have provided some cushion. However, in 2016, estimated assets were US$0.2 billion, representing 4 per cent of fiscal revenues.

Angola's Fundo Soberano de Angola has a relatively healthy balance at US$5 billion, representing about 60 per cent of the country's fiscal deficit. The fund can provide a significant cushion for Angola's fiscal shortages. As the name suggests, the main stated objective of SWFs is to promote intergenerational equity. Using the funds to finance government deficits would place the primary objective at risk.

Only Botswana's Pula Fund, which has in the past been used to stabilize government revenue and promote intergenerational equity, secures its position as the highest valued SWF in the region.

Other countries such as Zambia and the DRC do not yet have SWF outlets, which are still in the early stages.

[4] Triki and Faye (2011).

DRAWING-DOWN ON CENTRAL BANK RESERVES

With significant increases in export earnings during the boom years, resource dependent countries accumulated enough reserves to cover almost five months of imports, compared to 3.7 months for non-resource dependent countries in the region. Botswana, for instance, had the highest reserves in SSA, enough to cover almost a year of imports. Congo Rep. accumulated enough reserves to cover seven months of imports. Nigeria, Angola, and Cameroon accumulated reserves that could cover five months of their import bills. On the other hand, Guinea and Chad were able to cover fewer than two months of import bills—much lower than the regional average of four months.

But there is little room left. The decline in commodity prices immediately impacted current account balances, reversing the above positive trends. In Nigeria, the current account surplus of US$14 billion in 2010 had turned into a deficit of US$8.9 billion by the end of 2015. Gabon, Congo Rep., and Angola also saw surplus accounts turn into deficits. By 2015, current account deficits stood at around 8.53 per cent of GDP in the resource dependent countries, compared to a deficit of 2.5 per cent of GDP in non-SSA resource dependent countries.

The oil dependent countries made significant withdrawals from central bank reserves. Nigeria, Angola, Congo Rep., and Equatorial Guinea withdrew US$3.1 billion, US$4.3 billion, US$1.74 billion, and US$969 million, respectively. Mineral dependent countries, including DRC, Niger, and Cameroon withdrew US$76 million, US$221 million, and US $541 million, respectively.

Subsequently, for oil dependent countries, foreign reserves that in the boom period could cover about seven months of import bills were, in 2016, estimated to cover only four months. For mineral dependent countries, foreign exchange reserves that could once cover about 6.5 months of import bills had fallen to five months by the start of 2016. Both Nigeria and Angola had reserves that could cover fewer than four months of imports, respectively. In 2016, Equatorial Guinea and Zambia had reserves covering three months of imports, while DRC had enough to cover only one month.

CUTBACKS IN PUBLIC EXPENDITURE

During the boom years, resource dependent countries experienced significant increases in government revenue. Excluding the 2008/09 financial crisis years, government revenues grew by an average of 8 per cent annually. In 2011, the extractive sector made up 69 per cent of government revenues in oil dependent countries and about 30 per cent of government revenues in mineral dependent countries.

Many governments were quick to spend the windfall revenues. For more than half of the resource dependent countries, increases in average expenditure between 2007 and 2010 exceeded increases in revenue, resulting in fiscal deficits, despite their having maintained healthy fiscal accounts in the first half of the decade. Moreover, gross national savings declined by about 2 per cent of GDP between 2007 and 2010. In particular, savings in oil dependent countries declined by about 6 per cent of GDP.

Since 2011, resource dependent countries have seen fiscal revenues decline by an average of US$5 billion, representing about 4 per cent of GDP. Angola and Nigeria experienced the greatest declines of US$23 billion and US$37 billion representing 21 per cent and 10 per cent of GDP, respectively. In Congo Rep. government revenues declined from 46 per cent of GDP in 2013 to 41 per cent of GDP in 2015, representing a decline of US$2.7 billion.

Excluding Botswana, fiscal deficits by the end of 2015 averaged 7.6 per cent of GDP—a stark reversal from the average surplus of 5 per cent of GDP in 2007. Angola, Guinea, and Congo Rep. experienced the largest fiscal deficits representing 13 per cent, 22 per cent, and 23 per cent of GDP, respectively. Public expenditure declined by 10 per cent in Angola and 6 per cent in Nigeria.

While it is too early to tell which sectors will be impacted most, fiscal expenditure cuts often fall on social sectors including health, education, and social safety nets. Such cuts negate any development gains made during commodity booms. Furthermore, cuts in public expenditure hinder progress towards achievement of the Sustainable Development Goals (SDGs).

DOMESTIC RESOURCE MOBILIZATION EFFORTS

The gap between tax effort and tax capacity, which includes inefficiencies in administration, technical gaps, rent seeking, etc., has been found to be particularly high for resource dependent countries (Fenochietto and Pessino, 2013).

Between 2006 and 2010, average taxes collected by the resource dependent countries stood at 25 per cent of GDP, which is 6 percentage points higher than their average performance in the 1990s. However, the averages hide significant differences in the performance of individual countries. In 2010, Chad collected US$231 worth of taxes per capita, significantly higher than the average of US$82 collected by other low-income SSA countries. Moreover, Chad's improvement in per capita tax collection is impressive in terms of percentage, but as a value, it represents about one-third of the SSA average. On the other spectrum, Equatorial Guinea collected US$5,005.

The general increase in taxes collected during 2000–10 comes mainly from increases in resource taxes such as royalty payments. Thus, the improvement does not necessarily reflect improved tax capacity or a broader tax base. Collecting direct taxes from a few companies that dominate the economy is a relatively easier task than to collect income and sales taxes for instance. The trends signal instead a greater dependence on the extractive sector for fiscal revenues. For example, non-extractive corporate taxes have stagnated in resource dependent countries amounting to about 1.3 per cent of GDP between 2000 and 2010.

The imbalance is especially pronounced for oil dependent countries. In 2010, tax revenues represented 30 per cent of GDP, which is compatible with the OECD average of 33 per cent of GDP. However, resource related taxes represented an average of 73 per cent of total taxes collected, ranging from 94 per cent in Equatorial Guinea to 55 per cent in Gabon. Average non-extractives-related corporate taxes made up just 6 per cent of total tax revenues.

In contrast, although non-resource dependent countries in the region collected a smaller share of tax revenues, they display a more diversified tax base distribution with direct tax, indirect tax, resource tax, and trade tax accounting for 30 per cent, 38 per cent, 6 per cent, and 26 per cent of the total, respectively.

Another challenge is curbing illicit financial flows. In the 1990s, illicit outflows from SSA were estimated at US$95 billion. The boom years in particular saw increases in illicit financial outflows. Between 2003 and 2010, the cumulative amount of illicit outflows totalled US$145 billion, representing 14 per cent of total illicit financial outflows from developing countries. Of the US$145 billion, US$118.3 billion came from oil dependent countries, US$2.5 came from mineral dependent countries, and the remaining US$23.5 billion came from the rest of SSA (Kar and Spaniers 2014).

Between 2003 and 2010, outflows from Nigeria were the highest, at US$112.5 billion, representing 78 per cent of total outflows from SSA and about 11 per cent of total outflows from developing countries. In comparison, outflows from resource dependent countries in Latin America and the Caribbean, for instance, totalled US$39 billion. Currently, illicit financial outflows from SSA are estimated to reach a cumulative total of US$340 billion, of which US$218 billion comes from oil and gas exporters (Kar and Spanjers 2014).

The implications of a highly unbalanced tax base and a significant amount of illicit financial outflows are that there is room for domestic resource mobilization initiatives. But successful implementation requires radical improvements in governance and enhancement of technical capacities. At the same time, international agreements are needed to curb illicit financial flows as well as close loopholes for tax evasion and avoidance.

EXTERNAL BORROWING

In the 1990s, resource dependent countries were highly indebted where average public sector external debt stock represented 85 per cent of GDP, or 385 per cent of exports. Moreover, interest payments on external debt were around US$174 million, representing 2.3 per cent of GDP. During the boom years, significant improvements were made in debt reduction. By 2010, debt stocks had declined by an average of 61 percentage points to 22 per cent of GDP or 84 per cent of exports. For non-resource dependent SSA countries, external debt stocks declined by 58 percentage points and represented 29 per cent of GDP or 114 per cent of exports.

Notable improvements were made by resource dependent countries such as Angola, Congo Rep., and Zambia where external public debt (per cent GDP) in 2010 dropped to 19 per cent, 17 per cent, and 6.5 per cent, respectively from more than 110 per cent of GDP throughout the 1990s. By 2010, Nigeria's public external debt stock, which stood at 1.2 per cent of GDP, representing 18.8 per cent of exports, was the lowest in SSA and a significant reduction from the debt stock that represented 50 per cent of GDP in the 1990s.[5]

However, resource dependent countries are beginning to see a gradual increase in public external debt to GDP. Between 2011 and 2014, debt stocks rose by an average of 4 percentage points. Congo Rep., for instance saw debt stocks increase by about 8 percentage points to 24 per cent of GDP. Similarly, in Cameroon, Gabon, and Zambia, debt stocks to GDP ratios grew from 9 per cent, 14 per cent, and 6.5 per cent in 2010 to 14 per cent, 22 per cent, and 16 per cent in 2014, respectively.

A breakdown of debt shows that borrowing from private creditors has increased significantly in Chad and Zambia making up 22 per cent and 40 per cent of external public debt in 2014, compared to 1.5 per cent and 2.5 per cent in 2010, respectively. Although the composition of debt from private creditors has gradually increased over the years, it is likely that with continued low commodity prices and low projected growth rates, the space to borrow from private sector will become more constrained.

Some countries have turned to multilateral institutions leading to an increase in multilateral debt stock by an average of US$400 million. Multilateral loans to Nigeria increased the most—by US$2 billion between 2011 and 2014. By 2014, average multilateral debt service increased to US$75 million from US$65 million in 2010. By 2016, debt service in resource dependent countries is expected to average 6 per cent of exports. However, if private sector borrowing becomes more constrained and countries resort to multilateral loans with conditionalities attached, it can infringe the freedom of policymakers.

The urgency of structural change

In the long run, the capacity to weather commodity price swings necessitates economic diversification. However, trends in economic diversification have been weak in many resource dependent countries. The extractive sector's contribution to GDP continues to dwarf other sectors. Since the 1990s, the manufacturing share of GDP in resource dependent countries has stagnated at around 7 per cent. In fact, during boom years, the sector had contracted and averaged 6.7 per cent of GDP by 2010. Manufacturing value added (MVA) per capita in resource dependent countries increased from US$63 in the 1990s to US$132 in 2010. In comparison, MVA per capita in other SSA countries

[5] Due to limited data, the analysis does not include Equatorial Guinea.

averaged around US$200 and in resource dependent Latin American countries, it averaged US$1,200.

SDG 9 on industry, innovation, and infrastructure has among its targets the promotion of 'inclusive and sustainable industrialization'. The indicators selected to measure the achievement of target 9.2 on industrialization are: (1) MVA as a proportion of GDP and per capita; (2) manufacturing employment as a proportion of total employment.

To see how far this target will be achieved, which is essentially a diversification target, we have analysed the performance of the seven resource dependent countries that have also prioritized diversification and industrialization in their national development plans and strategies. Their plans and strategies aim to process raw commodities domestically; invest resource revenues to support industrial development in other economic sectors; and share the infrastructure developed for oil, gas, and mining with manufacturing and agricultural sectors.

Equatorial Guinea's national development plan, Horizon 2020 (launched in 2007) and Government of Angola's 2025 Strategy (launched in 2012), for instance, stress the development of other sectors to achieve diversification and industrial development. This is indeed good news.

However, these seven countries do not have positive track records in translating their mineral and hydrocarbon wealth into industrial development. At the height of the commodity boom in the first decade of the 2000s, the seven countries collected significant amounts of resource revenues. Export earnings from oil, gas, and mining increased from an average of US$4.9 billion in 2000 to US$22.9 billion in 2010. However, in the same period, the manufacturing sector's contribution to GDP contracted from 6 per cent to 5 per cent. In Zambia and Mauritania, the manufacturing sector contracted by about 2 per cent or more; while in Equatorial Guinea and Nigeria, it stagnated at less than 1 per cent and 6.5 per cent, respectively. By 2014, per capita MVA in the seven countries remained low at US$193 compared to the African average of US$214 and a global average of US$1,662.

Similarly, there were no significant improvements in the diversification of their export baskets. In fact, the baskets had become more concentrated by the end of the boom period. The average concentration index—which ranges from 0 to 1, with 1 indicating that a country's exports are highly concentrated in a few products—had increased from 0.68 in 1999 to 0.74 by 2011. In fact, countries such as Angola, Cameroon, Congo Rep., Chad, and Zambia saw their export baskets become more concentrated. Non-resource dependent countries diversified their export basket and in 2010 scored 0.39 on the concentration index.

Moreover, manufactured goods represent only about 5 per cent of total exports from resource rich countries. Exports of medium- and high-technology manufactured goods such as chemicals and electrical equipment also stagnated at around 2.5 per cent of total exports. High-technology manufactured goods represent less than 2 per cent of total exports. Comparatively, manufactured exports make up 12 per cent of export baskets in resource dependent Latin American and Caribbean countries. Furthermore, diversification of trade partners was weak with 25 per cent of their exports going to China.

Thus, the commodity bust left many of the resource dependent countries' fiscal space and foreign exchange earnings closely tied to the performance of the extractive sector. Despite the development of several national diversification strategies, including in Nigeria, Angola, and DRC, not much was achieved in economic diversification.

But aspiration to industrialize continues and goes beyond national-level ambitions. In the African Union's Agenda 2063, the wish is to see economies that are 'structurally transformed to create shared growth, decent jobs and economic opportunities for all'. The African Mining Vision (AMV) aspires to see a sector 'that has become a key component of a diversified, vibrant and globally competitive industrializing African economy'.

The articulation of industrialization strategies at the continental and national levels is a worthwhile exercise. But much remains to be done on the formulation and implementation of industrial policies if we are to meet the SDG target to industrialize by 2030.

Conclusion

Resource dependent SSA countries made significant gains in growth when high commodity prices prevailed. They also saw higher growth rates in development outcomes such as the HDI. However, with expenditure accompanying movements in commodity prices, sufficient fiscal buffers, including in the form of SWFs, were not established. As commodity prices plummeted, fiscal accounts deteriorated and led to massive cuts in government expenditure.

The failure to intensify diversification efforts during the boom period also exposed them to commodity price cycles. The current price shock presents yet another opportunity to embark on economic diversification strategies. This is not a novel idea. However, it has not yet been taken seriously in terms of implementation.

REFERENCES

Bauer, A. and Toledano, P. (2013). 'Managing the public trust: how to make natural resource funds work for citizens'. Vale Columbia Center on Sustainable International Investment. Available at https://academiccommons.columbia.edu/catalog/ac:206128, accessed 22 October 2018.

Fenochietto, R. and Pessino, C. (2013). 'Understanding countries' tax effort'. IMF Working Papers, 13 (244). Washington, DC: International Monetary Fund.

Government of Angola (2012). *National Development Plan 2013–2017.* Embassy of the Republic of Angola.

Hailu, D. and Kipgen, C. (2017). 'The Extractives Dependence Index (EDI)', *Resources Policy* 51: 251–64.

IndexMundi (2015). 'Commodity Prices'. Available at www.indexmundi.com/commodities/, accessed 22 October 2018.

Kar, D. and Spanjers, J. (2014). *Illicit Financial Flows from Developing Countries 2003–2012*. Washington, DC: Global Financial Integrity.

Triki, T. and Faye, I. (2011). 'Africa's quest for development: can sovereign wealth funds help?', *Institutional Investors in Global Capital Markets* 12: 263–90.

12 Building BRICS in Africa?

Pádraig Carmody

It is a truism to say that the world is undergoing a fundamental power shift or related shifts. In recent decades the world has witnessed the rise of informational and informationalized capitalism and, partly as a consequence, the global centre of economic dynamism and gravity has shifted east and southwards, as offshoring in all its dimensions has flourished (Urry 2014). Consequent to the growth of their economies emerging powers have dramatically increased their engagement in other parts of the developing world, such as Africa. Africa is also said to be 'rising' (Mahajan 2009), although others dispute this (cf. Taylor 2014a). (See also Chapter 29 in this volume.)

Recent books such as Carmody (2013) and Taylor (2014a) have outlined the nature of BRICS's (Brazil, Russia, India, China, South Africa) individual and collective engagement in Africa. The purpose of this contribution is a slightly different one: to explore whether BRICS's, at times paradoxical, policies of engagement and non-interference are resulting in a transfer of their socio-economic models to the continent.[1] Traditional 'donors' exported their models of 'free market democracy' to the continent through the imposition of structural adjustment programmes and, later, associated governance conditionalities. The 'BRICS model' has often been posited as an alternative to the Western one, but is it in the process of transfer to, and construction in, Africa? In particular this contribution seeks to investigate whether or not the model of rapid, largely state-led, economic growth and authoritarianism, characteristic of China, and also during certain time periods Russia, is being transferred to Africa. Are there 'BRICS' being built in Africa? Before doing this however it is necessary to briefly interrogate the nature of BRICS themselves, and their engagements with Africa.

Nature of BRICS

There is a debate in the literature as to the usefulness of the concept of the BRIC(S) grouping. In part this may be because of the etiology of the term, which was originally

[1] 'Africa' is comprised of fifty-four or fifty-five different states, depending on whether membership at the United Nations or African Union is counted, each with their own histories and institutional structures. Nonetheless there are also commonalities in their histories, in terms of colonialism, for most of them, and legacies of authoritarian rule and resource, agricultural, and export dependence.

Pádraig Carmody, *Building BRICS in Africa?* In: *Handbook of BRICS and Emerging Economies.* Edited by: P.B. Anand, Shailaja Fennell, and Flavio Comim, Oxford University Press (2021). © Oxford University Press.
DOI: 10.1093/oso/9780198827535.003.0012

coined by Jim O'Neill, a Goldman Sachs analyst in 2001, where he used the term to signal a major forthcoming shift in the global centre of economic gravity. It may also reflect an unease that the popularity of the term derives from its intuitive appeal, sounding as it does like bricks, rather than the structural characteristics or growth trajectories of the participating political economies.

As some of BRICS have recently experienced substantial economic problems, other acronyms which claim to better capture the most dynamic emerging economies in the world have emerged, such as MINT (Mexico, Indonesia, Nigeria, Turkey) or CIVETS (Columbia, Indonesia, Vietnam, Egypt, Turkey, and South Africa).[2] However, these other groupings of countries cannot rival the scale and power resources of BRICS countries, with the exception of South Africa, which is by far the smallest in terms of its economy and population size and consequently the least powerful member of the grouping.

There is a variety of perspectives that can be brought to the examination of the BRICS grouping. It is useful to interrogate it as a concept, process, reality, and also as a lens through which broader changes in the global political economy can be observed. While some analysts argue that BRICs arose out of Jim O'Neill's imagination, he identified an important empirical reality and trend, and the four original members of the grouping now regularly appear in the lists of the world's largest economies. However, his identification of the commonalities among BRICs led, in a recursive way, to the 'deepening' of structural idealism (Wendt 1999), as the group formally convened and met for the first time in Yekaterinberg in Russia in 2009. The grouping admitted South Africa as a member in 2010/11 and has gradually been developing new institutions, such as the BRICS development bank and contingency reserve fund in 2014. Thus BRICS are both an empirical reality and an evolving process in the international political economy. They also provide us with a lens through which to view broader shifts in the global political economy, such as 'the rise of the South' (UNDP 2013).[3]

According to the International Monetary Fund (IMF 2014) China is now the world's largest economy in purchasing power parity (PPP) terms and as noted earlier, Brazil, Russia, and India regularly feature in the indices of the world's ten biggest economies, depending on which agency is reporting the statistics. The scale of China's and India's populations is unrivalled globally, and they, along with Russia, are nuclear powers. China and Russia also hold permanent seats, with veto power, on the United Nations Security Council, while Russia is the world's biggest energy exporter. However, their growing economic influence has not been reflected in reforms of global institutions such as the World Bank and IMF, promoting them to create parallel institutions (Stuenkel 2016).

[2] Some of these acronyms are not just plays on words, but evocative of economic processes. For example a civet is a mammal which eats coffee berries; when the berries are excreted they capture a high price as a result of this 'processing'. The implication is, potentially, that the CIVETS countries also serve this value-added function in global production networks.

[3] Although this concept has recently been debunked by Dahi and Demir (2017), who distinguish analytically and empirically between the 'Emerging South' and 'the Rest of the South'.

For example, Belgium continues to have greater weight in voting at the World Bank than Brazil (Spratt 2014), despite having an economy only roughly a fifth the size (IMF 2014). 'Tired of waiting for their weight to be reflected in international financial institutions, the BRICS countries understandably decided to set up their own' (Spratt 2014), although Taylor (2017) argues that in reality the emerging powers are being absorbed into the structures of transnational capitalist hegemony, as this suits their ruling elites' interests.

That is not to say that the BRICS economies have not faced problems, such as slow economic growth for Brazil and Russia in particular in recent years, or labour unrest and conflict in South Africa. However, as a grouping, which is formally constituted, they hold substantial foreign exchange reserves and resources across different power fields. China is the driver of the BRICS grouping as it contributes roughly 60 per cent of the groups' economic output. Its formidable and growing power resources mean that even as other members of the grouping experience economic or geopolitical setbacks, such as sanctions being imposed on Russia as a result of involvement in conflict in Ukraine, the power of the grouping[4] collectively is likely to continue to grow in international affairs. As Jim O'Neill (2014) writes, 'Because of China's huge importance, the weighted average performance of the BRIC growth rate since 2011 is 6.5%. Now this is down from 7.9% the last decade, but higher than the previous two decades... In US$ terms, they are contributing decade to date more than 3 times to the world economy that of the US, and obviously in PPP terms, even more.' Thus the 'rise of the BRICS in Africa' is likely to continue.

In relation to Africa, some countries outside of the BRICS grouping have stronger economic ties than some of the members. For example Turkey's engagement on the continent has been rapidly accelerating and marked (cf. Carmody 2016) and is arguably more important than that of Russia. However, the geography of Turkish engagement is very geographically confined and defined. For example the biggest economies in East Africa—Tanzania and Kenya—are registered as having no Turkish investment as of 2012, whereas Egypt has almost a quarter of a billion dollars' worth and Mauritania US$66 million worth (Turkey 2014). Furthermore there are signs that Russian economic engagement on the continent is set to increase. In September 2014 the Russian foreign minister visited Zimbabwe and announced a US$4.8 billion dollar platinum mining investment (Xinhua 2014). During the announcement he, along with Zimbabwe's President Robert Mugabe, denounced Western sanctions on the two countries and some have speculated that Russia is deepening ties with other 'rogue' states and China to bolster its geopolitical and economic standing (Schoen and Kaylan 2014).

4 Although relations between the group are characterized by 'co-opetition' (Brandenburger and Nalebuff 1997). Furthermore BRICS and the newly announced 'BRICS plus', where it seeks to project itself as representing the broader interests of the developing world, is a way of amplifying Chinese power by embedding it in a multilateral organization.

Conceptualizing BRICS engagement in Africa

It is an oft-cited statistic that China is now Africa's largest single trading partner, with bilateral trade of approximately US$150 billion in 2016. However, others note that Africa's trade with the European Union is still (rapidly reducing) multiples of Chinese trade with the continent. Getting exact statistics on African economies is sometimes easy (Jerven 2013), but they are often unreliable. The scale of Brazilian trade with Africa is much smaller than that of China at around US$27 billion a year. Thus the nature and scale of trade, investment, and aid relations is very different among BRICS depending on whether or not they are primarily commodity or manufactures exporters, the size of their own economies, and their previous histories of engagement (for more detail see Carmody 2013).

Different BRICS have different drivers of engagement; however, all bar Russia are primarily driven by economic imperatives, although the precise dimensions of these vary (see Carmody 2013 for more detail). The foreign economic policies of the different BRICS are substantially shaped by the structure of their own economies. This structures the nature of their engagement and how they embed in the different 'partner' countries in which they and their companies operate. While natural resource access is a primary driver of Chinese engagement, Raphael Kaplinsky (2014) argues that market access is equally important; this contention is borne out by the trade statistics as imports and exports from the continent to China are roughly balanced.

Chinese-driven globalization in Africa has a distinct sectoral composition, spatiality, and temporality. In the literature there is a substantial debate about whether or not China is pursuing neoliberal policies (Harvey 2005; Lim, 2010). There has also been a debate about what exactly constitutes neoliberalism or its ontological status. Some authors prefer to speak of neoliberalization (Peck and Tickell 2002). However, the structure of Chinese engagement in Africa is informed by the nature of state engagement and ownership in that economy.

Given the continued importance of state ownership in the Chinese economy and its highly interventionist economic approach, characterizing it as neoliberal is misplaced, even as it engages in selective neoliberalization. There are also counter-examples, such as the greater difficulty which foreign companies now find in operating in the country. New (informal) restrictions aim to tilt the competitive playing field in favour of domestic companies (*The Economist* 2014). The heavy influence of the state extends to the mode of engagement in Africa.

The two sectors of the Chinese economy that remain most heavily state dominated are the natural resources and financial sectors. As the World Trade Organization (WTO n.d.) notes in a recent trade policy review of China:

> China's energy sector continues to be characterized by a high level of state ownership, regulation, and limited competition. (WTO n.d.: 69)

and

> While financial reforms continue, China's capital market remains heavily dependent on loans provided by state-owned banks, which have lent mainly to SOEs [state-owned enterprises]. Lack of access to external financing through the capital market, particularly for small domestic private companies, continues to result in these companies relying heavily on retained earnings (or funds raised from family and friends). Stringent qualification requirements still apply to foreign-funded banks; these include comparatively high minimum asset requirements on sole or controlling shareholders and high minimum paid-in capital amounts, restrictions on the supply of credit-card services, and restrictions on the business scope of foreign banks branches. (WTO n.d.: 70)

Both of these are critical for continued economic growth in China, as 'dragon's head' natural resource companies, which are sometimes private or provincial government-owned, are encouraged by that country's 'go out' policy to source new reserves and supplies overseas and to grow.

In line with Keynes's dictum that finance should be primarily national, the banking sector remains primarily focused on mobilizing capital for domestic investment, although China is also the world's biggest exporter of financial capital (Fan Lim 2010). There is also still significant state ownership of the vital infrastructure and construction sectors. The sectoral composition of Chinese engagement in Africa, led as it is by state-owned natural resource and infrastructure companies, has also led to a particular step-wise temporality to engagement.

While the 'Angola model' of resource for infrastructure swaps has sometimes been overstated in importance, it is nonetheless an important modality of engagement in Africa (Bräutigam 2009). It has also been controversial, given loan conditionalities which require the contracting of Chinese companies to fulfil infrastructure requirements, often bringing Chinese labour with them. When these contracts are completed some Chinese workers stay on and set up small businesses in trading, as restauranteurs or farmers, for example (French 2014). This deepens and further embeds processes of translocalization and creates markets for other Chinese companies, such as banks. The sectoral composition, temporality, and embeddedness of these processes serves to deepen interdependence between China and the African countries with which it has the most significant engagement. The precise implications of this for African states and their economic policies are explored in the section on building BRICS.

The drivers and modalities of Indian engagement on the continent are different, even if they are heavily influenced by politics or—more accurately—political economy. Whereas Chinese engagement is heavily state-directed and led, facilitated by that country's authoritarianism, in India it is partly that country's political system which also structures the nature of engagement, even if the engagement is primarily private sector-led. In China there is an authoritarian 'social contract' whereby the populace largely seems—for the moment at least—to acquiesce to non-democratic rule in exchange for economic development and political stability. On the other hand India is a vibrant—some might say raucous—democracy (Guha 2007). This means that while there has been population displacement and dispossession in India in relation to the construction of major infrastructure projects, such as the Narmada Dam and special economic zones (SEZs) (Anwar and Carmody 2016), the doctrine of eminent domain cannot be used domestically for the appropriation of large tracts of land for agro-investments. This has resulted in the offshoring of this demand to countries in Africa in particular, given often falling agricultural yields in parts of India, land fragmentation, and other issues (Parenti 2011). Ian Taylor (2014a) also notes India is now setting aside financing for infrastructure and other projects in Africa to facilitate engagement.

As explored elsewhere Brazilian engagement in Africa is driven by a variety of imperatives, but foremost among these is the need to try to sustain, and now reinvigorate, the country's economy. However, one of the biggest Brazilian corporations involved in Africa—the energy firm Petrobras—is scaling back its involvement on the continent to focus more on domestic reserves and resources (Africa Energy Intelligence 2013). The Brazilian economic recession/crisis beginning in 2014 has also reduced other companies' expansion plans.

South African engagement is also driven by combined political and economic imperatives. Whereas apartheid was in part a 'racial fix' to the blockages to capital accumulation in the mining sector, given often deep deposits and low grade ores, the post-apartheid government has sought to use the rest of the continent as a spatial fix to the current contradictions of capital accumulation in that country and generate resources through economic growth for redistribution, thereby stabilizing the class compromise which has underlain that country's post-apartheid transition.

For Russia, while it has economic interests, Africa is primarily a space where 'great power' status can be reasserted. Russian engagement on the continent is somewhat different from that of the other BRICS powers, given its history. Whereas realist and materialist international relations theorists focus on the importance of power and material interests, for Russia, the innate desire of its people to be part of something bigger than themselves, in this case a 'great' nation, is a legacy of Russian and then Soviet power and imperialism.

In Paul Kennedy's (1987) thesis great powers decline because they engage in military overstretch. There are signs that this may be the case for Russia—in Ukraine for example—even as President Obama belittled it as a 'regional power'. For Vladamir Putin making Russia a great power again is a question of will, in the first instance, through the creation of a 'power vertical' and secondarily of political and economic structures, which can be created through agency. As the US has experienced relative decline in the international system, Russia and China are testing the boundaries of the resultant power 'vacuum' (Rachman 2016), conceptualizations of 'interdependent hegemony' notwithstanding (Li 2014).

There has been a variety of impacts of BRICS's engagement in Africa, which can be characterized as economic, political, and social. The primary economic impact, of Chinese demand in particular, was the commodity super-cycle of the first decade of the new millennium and the reversal of the terms of trade between basic manufactures and primary goods. This was at the heart of the African growth revival, although there have been questions raised about the quality of this growth and its often enclavic nature.[5] High commodity prices also helped release the foreign exchange constraint on manufacturing in Africa, even if much of the sector is subject to competitive displacement pressures from more efficient, and subsidized, Chinese production. This has resulted in a somewhat contradictory situation where the manufacturing sector's output is growing, even as its share of GDP contracts (UNCTAD 2012). This has important political implications as natural resource dependence is often associated with poor governance, as governments can rely on rents from the sector, rather than taxes from a more diversified economy. However, in some cases authoritarian developmental states, such as Rwanda and Ethiopia have emerged in Africa in the last two decades, which have been most focused on development of the agricultural sector (Booth and Cammack 2013).[6] As these are 'resource poor' countries this suggests that the extensive nature of agriculture requires a different and more inclusionary, if authoritarian, social contract with the population than that associated with natural resource extraction.

Building brics for a new world order?

According to Ian Taylor (2014b) emerging powers differ substantially from Western countries in their economic model as there is a strong directive role for the state in the economy. As he puts it 'they . . . uphold a broadly statist approach to business that enables private enterprise and mercantile commerce. This state capitalism is increasingly coming to the fore, particularly in the aftermath of the global financial crisis' (2014b: 2).

The West has in recent years undergone a prolonged and painful financial crisis. In contrast, much of Africa has experienced relatively more rapid economic growth. While there are questions about the environmental impact, sustainability, and quality of Africa's economic growth, a substantial part of the explanation for these different growth trajectories lies in the growth of the BRICS economies. These economies are largely responsible for higher African economic growth through increased demand for primary commodities and investment in mining, infrastructure, and other economic sectors. They are also changing the nature of globalization and of the state–society formations with which they interact and influence. Are there brics being built in Africa? Has greater BRICS engagement resulted in the bolstering of authoritarian states and opened up economic policy space?

As noted earlier China is now Africa's largest trading partner and also source of new loans. According to some estimates, in the first decade of the new millennium the Chinese Export–Import Bank lent more than US$60 billion to African countries, which

[5] For a contrary argument on the potential linkage and diversification effects from natural resources see Morris et al. (2012).

[6] Although some have recently disputed the developmental state status of Rwanda (cf. Himbara 2016). The Ethiopian government has recently shifted focus towards manufacturing.

substantially exceeded the loans provided by the World Bank during that period (French 2014). Furthermore, according to the Land Matrix database (2014) the Indian government is the largest lessor and purchaser of land on the continent in a 'new scramble' to produce food and agro-fuels in particular. South African and Brazilian companies are also substantial investors on the continent, and Russia is a major source of arms, although behind the United States in this respect. China was the single biggest supplier of arms to sub-Saharan Africa from 2006 to 2009 (Grimmett 2011). However, much investment from BRICS, and from China in particular, is through state-owned corporations, such as the Chinese Non-Ferrous Metals Corporation. Rather than being driven by quarterly stock market returns these companies have longer time horizons. The fact that these companies' operations are influenced by strategic national planning also gives them a different character from that of Western corporations.

Globalization is often thought to be private sector-led. This is not the case for some of BRICS, where we are seeing a globalization of state power (Carmody et al. 2012). This globalization of state power is also reflected in 'recipient states' of Chinese and other BRICS investment, although there is a substantial debate about the role of African agency in these relations (Mohan and Lampert 2012; Corkin 2013; Carmody and Kragelund 2016). This may create demonstration effects, showing that state-owned corporations can be efficiently run and be developmentally beneficial. In some African countries there are processes of renationalization taking place; in Zambia for example where the government has taken back control of the telephone company and the railroad, although the largely extractive, neoliberal nature of economies in Southern Africa remains largely intact (Carmody 2017a). There is also evidence that African political elites have substantial bargaining power in their relations with BRICS, depending on the issue area.

As noted earlier, in the literature recently there has been a heavy emphasis on the agency of African state elites in their dealings with China for example (Power et al. 2012). Corkin (2013) has shown, for example, how the Angolan state was able to negotiate that its loans from China would be repaid using the advantageous spot price for oil, rather than a lower contracted price. African state elites are acutely aware that the Western (near) monopoly on power and finance has been broken and strategically play off different foreign powers against one another. The dimension of structural power related to high natural resource demand which African state elites are able to leverage are the effects of sunk costs. Once pipelines or oil facilities have been constructed their embeddedness within the juridically sovereign territories of African states confers substantial bargaining power and leverage on political elites. This is a phenomenon which is at play in relation to BRICS investments, but has also been in evidence in relation to the World Bank funded Chad–Cameroon pipeline for example (cf. Carmody 2010). According to Nossiter (2013) 'In Niger, government officials have fought a Chinese oil giant step by step, painfully undoing parts of a contract they call ruinous. In neighbouring Chad, they have been even more forceful, shutting down the Chinese and accusing them of gross environmental negligence.'

The BRICS powers individually (and hence collectively) have policies of 'non-interference' in the domestic politics of their partner or client states, at least in terms of rhetoric. This is very attractive to incumbent African political elites, who tend to stay in power substantially longer than their counterparts in other world regions. The BRICS powers provide alternative sources of trade, investment, loans, aid, and arms from traditional Western 'partners'.

According to Obiarah (2007) 'China provides a powerful development model which urges economic growth before human rights, which has a number of possible effects on African development debates. First, African leaders can use this model to deny political rights to their people and rebuff efforts at building good governance and promoting democracy' (cited in Power et al. 2012: 181). An Angolan academic has noted that Chinese involvement in Africa is 'a good idea' as 'China is the weapon that Africa can use to end western hegemony' (quoted in Corkin 2013: 41). As Patey (2014) notes, human rights pressure on Western oil companies in Sudan which forced their exit paradoxically ended up improving the position of Asian oil companies, who were less susceptible to this, in that country. According to Kurlantzick (2007) China prefers to maintain authoritarian regimes in power, to prevent it becoming increasingly isolated in international affairs.

Whereas Western countries and institutions which they have historically controlled, such as the World Bank and IMF, have often insisted on free market economic and governance reforms, this is not the case for the BRICS powers. However, the rise of BRICS is also altering Western foreign policies in Africa. According to Verhoeven (2014: 58) 'but 2013 [*sic*] Western and Chinese dignitaries are both entertaining privileged ties with the same African elites. Diplomats consider the opposition irrelevant and pay attention almost exclusively to building relations with whoever is in power, a reversal [*sic*] of pre-1989 policies that African leaders have not failed to exploit'. Corkin (2013: 2) notes in relation to Angola that the 'government has effectively managed to harness its relationship with China to bolster its position, both politically and economically'. Thus the power of extant political elites is being solidified by the commodity super-cycle and declining aid dependence, for resource rich countries at least (Peiffer and Englebert 2012). In Equatorial Guinea the ruling party receives aid from the Chinese Communist Party through the embassy in Malabo (Esteban 2010).

The power of traditional donors has certainly declined across much of Africa. Whereas the former Zambian Minister of Finance noted that if they privatized the mining industry on the advice/insistence of the World Bank and IMF in the late 1990s that the government 'would be able to access debt relief, and this was a huge carrot in front of us – like waving medicine in front of a dying woman. We had no option [but to go ahead]' (Action for Southern Africa et al. 2007: 6). By 2011 this had changed, with a civil servant in the Ministry of Finance and National Planning noting that 'At one point in time we had to agree with everything the donors said. Now we can disagree. The donors still act in a very coordinated manner but of late we have often disagreed with their policies' (quoted in Kragelund 2014: 156). This has meant that certain industries such as Zambia Railways and Zamtel, the telecommunications provider, have been taken back into state ownership (Kragelund 2014). Whereas Gillian Hart (2014) sees a dialectical tension between processes of economic denationalization (globalization) and the rhetoric of nationalism in South Africa, in the Zambian case this rhetoric is in the process of being translated into policy, if slowly and incompletely. Consequently there is evidence that there is a tentative shift away from neoliberalism to neo-developmentalism (Godio 2004), at least in parts of the continent. This is partly a result of the policies of non-interference propounded and promulgated by the BRICS powers, and their role modelling.

The nature of economic interactions with China in particular have resulted in deindustrialization across the continent, however, and a greater dependence on resource exports and consequently a diversification of dependency (Taylor 2014a).[7] This is particularly problematic in the context of slowing economic growth in BRICS, which was partly responsible for the price of oil falling to approximately US$30 a barrel in early 2016, with substantial price declines for hard commodities such as copper also registered. Furthermore, the World Bank (2013) predicted substantial primary commodity price falls through 2015, with the exception of timber, although prices for this also declined (World Bank 2017). Falling commodity prices reduce the policy space available to many African states. For example, when the price of copper fell dramatically in 2009 as a result of the global financial crisis, Zambia reversed the windfall taxes it had previously imposed on producers. Thus telling donors to 'go home' may be premature.

Some countries, such as South Africa, have also developed industrial policies (DTI 2014). However, this policy emphasizes the attraction of foreign investment and is compatible with South Africa's maintenance of a 'liberal market economy' (personal communication, Brazilian ambassador to South Africa, Pretoria, August 2014). The Brazilian ambassador noted that his country also structured its economic governance on these lines. However, Brazil is what some might refer to as a social developmental state, which has managed to substantially reduce inequality, in addition to creating 'permanent' jobs.

South Africa, since the end of apartheid, has also instituted substantial social transfers and as a result state transfers now comprise the highest income component for the poorest 30 per cent of the population (de Klerk 2012). These transfers were largely responsible for the proportion of the population living in the four lowest Living Standards Measures falling from 52.6 per cent to 24.4 per cent from 2001 to 2011 (South African Institute of Race Relations cited in de Klerk 2012). Thus South Africa might also be categorized as a social developmental state, even as pre-transfer levels of inequality in that country have risen, although questions remain about the sustainability of this model given South Africa's resource dependence, lack of economic diversification, and ongoing social and labour unrest. Other African countries, such as Rwanda have also

[7] Leather goods and shoe production in the Chinese SEZ in Ethiopia is competitive; but this is not the case for many other products across the continent. For more detail see Dinh (2012).

adopted social policy innovations such as universal health insurance, although these do not appear to have been inspired by BRICS, although some countries have experimented with programmes similar to *Bolsa Familia* in Brazil.

Latent versus actualized policy space

The philosophy of non-interference among BRICs is one of the factors which accounts for the emergence of a new type of geopolitics. The growth of emerging powers and their increasing projection of influence in Africa is reconfiguring global geopolitics, creating a new large-scale region—a 'South Space'—which seeks and increasingly is achieving greater autonomy from the West. This new macro-region is defined by a shared history of colonial exploitation and Western intervention, intensifying flows of trade, investment, and aid, and increasingly 'hard shell' sovereignty, where governments in Africa are often able to resist calls to respect human rights, for example, as in the case of Sudan. At the same time the BRICS powers exercise increasing influence on the continent through aid, diplomacy, and economic investment. For example, countries which trade more with China are more likely to vote the same way as if in the United Nations General Assembly (Flores-Macías and Kreps 2013). This model of 'influence without interference' represents a form of 'dethority' or geo governance the projection of 'national' power across borders (for more detail see Carmody et al. 2012).

The rise of BRICS in Africa has many positive dimensions to it. Chinese and Indian demands for natural resources have dramatically increased their prices, to the benefit of many African economies as these are often their primary exports. Chinese infrastructure for resource swaps, where new roads and railways are paid for in copper, for example, are less susceptible to corruption. Also the fact that BRICS are less prescriptive about economic policy has opened up space for policy experimentation and learning based on developing country rather than Western conditions, through the development of Chinese sponsored SEZs, for example.

The rise of BRICS in Africa is a momentous event for Africa, as the continent's economic relations are reoriented from the West to the East and South. This has many progressive dimensions to it, such as some of those listed above. However, the rhetoric of 'South–South Cooperation' and 'win–win' globalization disguises huge and deepening power inequalities between African countries and China in particular.

As African countries often vote as a bloc at the United Nations, WTO, and other forums such as the International Olympic Committee, Bodomo (2009: 172) argues that 'Africa sometimes wields more power than China in international settings'. However, Adem (2010) argues that while China has not completely shunned multilateralism it prefers bilateralism in its relations with African states, so that it can leverage its power advantages with them. This, however, is not necessarily inimical to African political elites, who benefit from current arrangements.

As has been the case previously political elites in Africa have been very skilful in converting and leveraging international relations to bolster their own regimes and authority. The BRICS powers have generally been happy to help them in this endeavour, as long as they are assured continued access to resources, land, and markets. For example, the Chinese government reportedly helped Robert Mugabe's regime monitor internet traffic and phone calls in advance of the extremely dubious and disturbing election of 2013 there. As levels of Chinese and other BRICS powers' investment in the continent has grown they have necessarily become more embroiled in domestic politics in African countries. According to one Chinese ambassador in Africa 'of course we are increasingly involved in the politics of African countries, we are being pulled in, we have no choice. But do the Africans really want our input? I don't know, it is not clear' (quoted in Verhoeven 2014: 56).

One of the keys to China's economic success has been the development of SEZs (Stein 2012). This model has also been exported to Africa and elsewhere, although there they are developed with Chinese rather than Western or overseas Chinese capital. In Africa these zones are mainly built as investments by SOEs; their main tenants are small and medium-size enterprises (SMEs), accounting for 85 per cent of the businesses in them (Tang and Zhang 2011, cited in Power et al. 2012). According to the Chinese ambassador to Zambia:

> We would also like to introduce mature Chinese enterprises with comparative advantages to Zambia to help address the country's over-reliance on import of consumer and manufactured goods. Therefore, the establishment of the Cooperation Zone can help both Zambia develop and mature Chinese industries redeploy and win more space of development at home (quoted in Southern Weekly 2010 in Braütigam and Tang 2011).

As Braütigam and Tang note however, in contrast to China, none of the African zones has been designed to develop synergies with local technology institutes or universities, even if several of them have been developed by Chinese companies with experience of zone development at home. Also, according to an analysis by Kolstad and Wiig (2011) the dominant motive for Chinese foreign direct investment (FDI) in Africa is resource seeking, although this varies by context (Kragelund and Hampwaye 2012).

According to Cowaloosur (2014: 5):

> Regardless of whether the CSEZA [Chinese Special Economic Zone in Africa] companies are private or state-owned, Chinese government retains the reigns (*sic*) of the CSEZAs through its authority to select the developer, provide the funds and also because the CSEZAs are essentially bilateral state ventures between China and African countries.

Some other authors argue that these are really 'pseudo-economic zones' designed to allow Chinese companies to take advantage of tax breaks, rather than being developmentally beneficial (Michel et al. 2009). While China is strategic about neoliberalization internally, it, along with other BRICS, favours neoliberalism internationally to open up markets for trade, investment, and resources. They have thus been able to leverage the 'new constitutionalism' for the global economy (Gill 2008) provided by the WTO, while being discursively, rhetorically, and with limited practical application, more open to mixed economy approaches in partner countries.

According to Kwan Lee (2009: 666) 'As Chinese capitalism in Africa is poised to become a major story shaping the global economy, the spirit of Bandung, rather than the trite rhetoric of "colonialism," may provide a more relevant, productive and critical lens for observing development in the 21st century.' The shared history of colonial exploitation, with the exception of Russia, certainly shapes the BRICS interactions with Africa, with concrete material effects (Mawdsley 2012). However, self-interest would appear to be the primary motivation in their foreign economic policies. As the Indian consul general to South Africa noted, 'altruism is in short supply in international relations' (personal communication, Randir Jaiswal, Johannesburg, August, 2014).

Conclusion

Some are pessimistic about the future growth of BRICS (Sharma 2012). Hart-Landsberg (2013) notes that US trade deficits have fuelled growth in Latin America and Africa and that the Chinese economy is also dependent on these. Consequently, in the context of the global financial crisis he is pessimistic about the possibility for China to retain rapid economic growth. However, the revival of economic growth in the US and falling energy prices as a result of the 'shale revolution' in the US meant that that country dramatically reduced the amount of oil it imported from Nigeria, for example. As noted earlier China continues to substantially drive economic growth and its economic footprint in Africa is set to continue to expand, even if its cultural or soft power falters (French 2014). Furthermore BRICS already affect global, regional, and local politics, and are set to rise in influence as they more closely coordinate and develop new institutions. They serve as role models for the potential of mixed economy approaches to development and largely avoided the worst effects of the global financial crisis. BRICS are not prescriptive about the economic models of partner countries, favouring a flexeconomy approach (Carmody 2016). However, they do favour 'free trade' (market access) and investment. This largely favours the maintenance of the status quo, rather than a dramatic revision of the dominant resource export assemblage (Carmody and Kragelund 2016). Nonetheless, the revival of African economies may result in future substantial changes to their political economies.

Growing economies in Africa, if they can be sustained over the medium and longer terms hopefully mean the further enlargement of the middle and working classes, who have historically been better at making and keeping states more accountable. However, to date political and politically connected elites have been very effective at capturing the gains of recent economic growth. Dangote Group in Nigeria has a more than 60 per cent profit margin on its cement as a result of an import ban, for example. Nonetheless in Africa, the struggle to ensure a fairer and more beneficial sharing of the results of a rebalancing, and increasingly Eastern-centred, global order has begun, as evidenced by the numerous organizations on the continent seeking justice for those displaced, for example by land grabbing. The future of the continent increasingly hinges on the outcomes of these struggles and the continent's relationship with BRICS powers.

Africa is now comprised of sometimes fast growing, but authoritarian political economies—a model which some BRICS share. Part of what defines BRICS is the size of their economies, with the partial exception of South Africa, although this is once again the largest economy in Africa. Obviously most African economies are unlikely to be able to rival the economic size or political power of the members of the BRICS grouping, at least in the medium term, with the partial exception of Nigeria. BRICS is a diverse group of countries, containing as it does democracies such as Brazil, South Africa, and India and autocracies such as China and perhaps Russia. However, as noted earlier all share the policy of 'non-interference' in other countries' affairs, at least rhetorically. This can be questioned on a number of grounds however. For example, arms sales to incumbent elites represent a form of extreme interference in internal affairs. The rhetorical attachment to 'non-interference' is partly to refute Western accusations of Chinese neocolonialism in Africa (Corkin 2013).

Even the actions of the democratic members of BRICS may further entrench authoritarian regimes in Africa. For example, one of the attractions of Ethiopia for Indian land investors is that it is an authoritarian country. Indian companies are desperate to source land overseas given that the country is losing a foot of groundwater a year—at least in the northern and central parts of the country (Rowden 2013).

While sub-Saharan Africa is characterized by a variety of regime types and variation in levels of conflict and other socio-political indicators, the proportion of countries rated as 'free' by Freedom House declined from 23 per cent to 20 per cent from 2003 to 2013 and the proportion of 'not free' increased from 35 per cent to 41 per cent over that period (Freedom House 2014). This suggests that more rapid economic growth is compatible with increasing authoritarianism, at least in the short term. However, the character of African regimes remains largely neo-patrimonial, given the challenges of rule in unequal and dependent economies. While some argue that developmental patrimonialism is possible (Kelsall 2013), it has not resulted in the structural transformation of African economies. While there is some evidence of neo-developmentalism across the continent, it is limited, and overall the relationship with BRICS can be characterized as one of 'diversifying dependence' (Taylor 2014a). Also much of the policy space which has been achieved as a result of the relative decline of influence of the World Bank and the IMF has been latent rather than actualized because current arrangements often suit African political elites and China and the other BRICS remain substantially committed to the neoliberal principles, at least internationally, as this opens up markets and investment opportunities for their companies. Consequently it would appear that 'brics' or substantially more economically interventionist political economies are not being built in Africa, with the exception of Ethiopia (Carmody 2017b), even as the influence of BRICS continues to grow on the continent.

ACKNOWLEDGMENTS

Thanks to Peter Kragelund for his very helpful and insightful comments.

REFERENCES

Action for Southern Africa, Christian Aid, and SCiAF (2007). 'Undermining development? copper mining in Zambia'. Available at www.actsa.org/Pictures/UpImages/pdf/Undermining%20development%20report.pdf, accessed 16 November 2018.

Adem, S. (2010). 'The paradox of China's policy in Africa', *African and Asian Studies* 9/3: 334–55.

Africa Energy Intelligence (2013). *Petrobras*. Available at www.africaintelligence.com/, accessed 16 November 2018.

Anwar, A. and Carmody, P. (2016). 'Bringing globalization to the countryside: The political economy of special economic zones in India', *Singapore Journal of Tropical Geography* 37/2: 121–38.

Bodomo, A. (2009). 'Africa–China relations: Symmetry, soft power and South Africa', *The China Review* 9/2: 169–78.

Booth, D. and Cammack, D. (2013). *Governance for Development in Africa: Solving Collective Action Problems*. London: Zed.

Brandenburger, A. and Nalebuff, B. (1997). *Co-opetition*. New York: Doubleday.

Braütigam, D. (2009). *The Dragon's Gift: The Real Story of China in Africa*. Oxford: Oxford University Press.

Braütigam, D. and Tang, X. (2011). 'African Shenzhen: China's special economic zones in Africa', *Journal of Modern African Studies* 49/1: 27–54.

Carmody, P. (2010). *Globalization in Africa: Recolonization or Renaissance?* Boulder, CO: Lynne Rienner.

Carmody, P. (2013). *The Rise of the BRICS in Africa: The Geopolitics of South-South Relations*. London: Zed.

Carmody, P. (2016). *The New Scramble for Africa*, 2nd edn. Cambridge: Polity.

Carmody, P. (2017a). 'The geopolitics and economics of BRICS' market and resource access in Southern Africa: aiding development or creating dependency?', *Journal of Southern African Studies* 43/5: 863–77.

Carmody, P. (2017b). 'Assembling effective industrial policy in Africa: An agenda for Action', *Review of African Political Economy* 44/152: 336–45.

Carmody, P. and Kragelund, P. (2016). 'Who is in charge? State power, agency and Sino-African relations', *Cornell International Law Journal* 49: 1–24.

Carmody, P., Hampwaye, G., and Sakala, E. (2012). 'Globalisation and the rise of the state? Chinese geogovernance in Zambia', *New Political Economy* 17/2: 209–29.

Corkin, L. (2013). *Uncovering African Agency: Angola's Management of China's Credit Lines*. Farnham and Burlington, VT: Ashgate.

Cowaloosur, H. (2014). 'Land grab in new garb: Chinese special economic zones in Africa', *African Identities* 12/1: 94–109.

Dahi, O. and Demir, F. (2017). 'South–south and north–south economic exchanges: Does it matter who is exchanging what and with whom?', *Journal of Economic Surveys* DOI: 10.1111/joes.12225.

de Klerk, F.W. (2012). 'South Africa is one of the Most Unequal Societies in the World', *Global Education Magazine*, 17 October, p. 6. Available at www.globaleducationmagazine.com/south-africa-unequal-societies-world/, accessed 22 October 2018.

Dinh, H.T. (2012). *Light Manufacturing in Africa: Targeted Policies to Enhance Private Investment and Create Jobs*. Washington, DC: World Bank.

DTI (Department of Trade and Industry) (South Africa) (2014). *Industrial Policy Action Plan*. Available at www.thedti.gov.za/news2013/ipap_2013-2016.pdf, accessed 22 October 2018.

The Economist (2014). 'China loses its allure: Life is getting tougher for foreign companies. Those that want to stay will have to adjust', 23 January. Available at www.economist.com/news/leaders/21595001-life-getting-tougher-foreign-companies-those-want-stay-will-have-adjust-china, accessed 22 October 2018.

Esteban, M. (2010). 'A silent invasion? African views on the growing Chinese presence in Africa: The case of Equatorial Guinea', *African and Asian Studies* 9/3: 232–51.

Fan Lim, K. (2010). 'On China's growing geo-economic influence and the evolution of variegated capitalism', *Geoforum* 41/5: 677–88.

Flores-Macías, G. and Kreps, S. (2013). 'The foreign policy consequences of trade: China's commercial relations with Africa and Latin America, 1992–2006', *The Journal of Politics* 75/2: 357–71.

Freedom House (2014). *Freedom in the World 2014*. Washington, DC: Freedom House.

French, H. (2014). *China's Second Continent: How a Million Migrants are Building a New Empire in Africa*. New York: Knopf.

Gill, S. (2008). *Power and Resistance in the New World Order*, 2nd edn. Basingstoke and New York: Palgrave Macmillan.

Godio, J. (2004). 'The "Argentine anomaly": From wealth through collapse to neo-developmentalism', *IPG* 2: 128–46.

Grimmett, R. (2011). 'Conventional arms transfers to developing nations.' United States Congressional Research Service. Available at https://fas.org/sgp/crs/weapons/R42017.pdf, accessed 22 October 2018.

Guha, R. (2007). *India after Gandhi: The History of the World's Largest Democracy*. London: Macmillan.

Hart, G. (2014). *Rethinking the South African Crisis: Nationalism, Populism, Hegemony*. Durban: University of Kwa-Zulu Natal and University of Georgia Press.

Hart-Landsberg, M. (2013). *Capitalist Globalization*. New York: Monthly Review Press.

Harvey, D. (2005). *A Brief History of Neoliberalism*. Oxford: Oxford University Press.

Himbara, D. (2016). *Kagame's Economic Mirage*. CreateSpace Independent Publishing Platform.

IMF (International Monetary Fund) (2014). Data and Statistics. Available at www.imf.org/external/data.htm, accessed 22 October 2018.

Jerven, M. (2013). *Poor Numbers: How We Are Misled by African Development Statistics and What to Do About It*. London and Ithaca, NY: Cornell University Press.

Kaplinsky, R. (2014). 'Comments at geopolitics and Chinese megaprojects in Africa', workshop. Brighton: University of Sussex.

Kelsall, T. (2013). *Business Politics and the State in Africa: Challenging the Orthodoxies of Growth and Transformation*. London: Zed.

Kennedy, P. (1987). *The Rise and Fall of the Great Powers: Economic Change and Military Conflict from 1500 to 2000*. New York: Random House.

Kolstad, I. and Wiig, A. (2011). 'Better the devil you know? Chinese foreign direct investment in Africa', *Journal of African Business* 12/1: 31–50.

Kragelund, P. (2014). '"Donors go home": Non-traditional state actors and the creation of development space in Zambia', *Third World Quarterly* 35/1: 145–62.

Kragelund, P. and Hampwaye, G. (2012). 'Seeking markets and resources: State-driven Chinese and Indian investments in China', *International Journal of Technology and Globalisation* 6/4: 352–68.

Kurlantzick, J. (2007). *Charm Offensive: How China's Soft Power is Transforming the World.* New Haven, CT and London: Yale University Press.

Kwan Lee, C. (2009). 'Raw encounters: Chinese managers, African workers and the politics of casualization in Africa's Chinese enclaves', *The China Quarterly* 199: 647–66.

Li, X. (2014). 'Conceptualizing the nexus of "interdependent hegemony" between the existing and the emerging world orders', *Fudan Journal of the Humanities and Social Sciences* 7/3: 343–62.

Mahajan, V. (2009). *Africa Rising: How 900 Million African Consumers Offer More Than You Think.* Upper Saddle River, NJ: Wharton School Pub.

Mawdsley, E. (2012). *From Recipients to Donors: Emerging Powers and the Changing Development Landscape.* London and New York: Zed Books.

Michel, S., Beuret, M., Woods, P., and Valley, R. (2009). *China Safari: On the Trail of China's Expansion in Africa.* New York: Nation Books.

Mohan, G. and Lampert, B. (2012). 'Negotiating China: Reinserting African agency into China–Africa relations', *African Affairs* 112/446: 92–110.

Morris, M., Kaplinksy, R., and Kaplan, D. (2012). *One Thing Leads to Another: Promoting Industrialisation by Making the Most of the Commodity Boom in sub-Saharan Africa.* Self-published.

Nossiter, A. (2013). 'China finds resistance to oil deals in Africa', *New York Times.* Available at www.nytimes.com/2013/09/18/world/africa/china-finds-resistance-to-oil-deals-in-africa.html, accessed 16 November 2018.

Obiarah, N. (2007). 'Who's afraid of China in Africa?', in F. Manji and S. Marks (eds) *African Perspectives on China in Africa.* Oxford: Fahamu, 35–56.

O'Neill, J. (2014). 'Is the BRICS rise over?'. Available at www.bruegel.org/nc/blog/detail/article/1404-is-the-brics-rise-over/, accessed 22 October 2018.

Parenti, C. (2011). *Tropic of Chaos: Climate Change and the New Geography of Violence.* New York: Nation Books.

Patey, L. (2014). *The New Kings of Crude: China, Indian and the Global Struggle for Oil in Sudan and South Sudan.* London: Hurst.

Peck, J. and Tickell, A. (2002). 'Neoliberalizing space', *Antipode* 34/3: 380–404.

Peiffer, C. and Englebert, P. (2012). 'Extraversion, vulnerability to donors, and political liberalization in Africa', *African Affairs* 111/444: 355–78.

Power, M., Mohan, G., and Tan-Mullins, M. (2012). *China's Resource Diplomacy in Africa: Powering Development?* Basingstoke: Palgrave Macmillan.

Rachman, G. (2016). *Easternisation: War and Peace in the Asian Century.* New York: Vintage.

Rowden, R. (2013). 'Indian agricultural companies "land grabbing" in Africa and activists response', in F. Cheru and R. Modi (eds) *Agricultural Development and Food Security in Africa: The Impact of Chinese, Indian and Brazilian Investments.* London: Zed, 107–23.

Schoen, D. and Kaylan, M. (2014). *The Russia-China axis and its Threat to the West.* Available at www.foxnews.com/opinion/2014/09/10/russia-china-axis-and-its-threat-to-west.html, accessed 22 October 2018.

Sharma, R. (2012). 'Broken BRICs: Why the rest stopped rising', *Foreign Affairs* 91/6: 2–7.

Southern Weekly (2010). 'Accusation of "China looting resources" groundless, an interview with the Chinese ambassador to Zambia', 8 April 2010, translated and posted at the website of the Forum on China Africa Cooperation (FOCAC). Available at www.focac.org/eng/jlydh/sjzs/t679463.htm, accessed 8 December 2018

Spratt, S. (2014). 'BRICS Bank: Will it be able to fulfill ambitions of emerging nations?', *Economic Times*, 20 July. Available at http://economictimes.indiatimes.com/news/economy/finance/brics-bank-will-it-be-able-to-fulfil-ambitions-of-emerging-nations/articleshow/38694219.cms, accessed 22 October 2018.

Stein, H. (2012). 'Africa, industrial policy, and export processing zones: lessons from Asia', in A. Noman, K. Botchwey, H. Stein, and J. Stiglitz (eds) *Good Growth and Governance in Africa: Rethinking Development Strategies.* Oxford: Oxford University Press, 322–44.

Stuenkel, O. (2016). *Post-Western World: How Emerging Powers Are Remaking Global Order.* Cambridge: Polity.

Tang, J. and Zhang, C. (2011). 'SMEs play "big role" in Africa' *International Business Journal.* Available at www.fmprc.gov.cn/zflt/eng/zfgx/jmhz/t859358.htm, accessed 16 November 2018.

Taylor, I. (2014a). *Africa Rising? BRICS—Diversifying Dependency.* London: James Currey.

Taylor, I. (2014b). 'Emerging powers, state capitalism and the oil sector in Africa', *Review of African Political Economy* 41/141: 341–57.

Taylor, I. (2017). *Global Governance and Transnationalizing Capitalist Hegemony: The Myth of the 'Emerging Powers'.* London and New York: Routledge.

Turkey, Republic of (2014). Available at www.hazine.gov.tr/default.aspx?nsw=EilDPQez15w=-H7deC+LxBI8=&mid=100&cid=16&nm=36, accessed 15 December 2018.

UNCTAD (United Nations Conference on Trade and Development) (2012). *Economic Development in Africa Report 2012: Structural Transformation and Sustainable Development in Africa.* Geneva: UNCTAD.

UNDP (United Nations Development Programme) (2013). *Human Development Report: The Rise of the South: Human Progress in a Diverse World.* Geneva: UNDP.

Urry, J. (2014). *Offshoring.* Cambridge: Polity.

Verhoeven, H. (2014). 'Is Beijing's non-interference policy history? How Africa is changing China', *Washington Quarterly* 37/2: 55–70.

Wendt, A. (1999). *Social Theory of International Politics.* Cambridge: Cambridge University Press.

World Bank (2013). *Commodity Markets Outlook.* Washington, DC: World Bank. Available at http://documents.worldbank.org/curated/en/127251468340216312/pdf/750590WP0Box370ties2013A0FullReport.pdf, accessed 22 October 2018.

World Bank (2017). *World Bank Commodities Price Forecast* (nominal US dollars). Available at http://pubdocs.worldbank.org/en/926111485188873241/CMO-January-2017-Forecasts.pdf, accessed 22 October 2018.

WTO (World Trade Organization) (n.d.) 'Trade policies by sector'. Available at www.wto.org/english/tratop_e/tpr_e/s230-04_e.doc, accessed 8 December 2018.

Xinhua (2014). 'Zimbabwe, Russia platinum investment to hit 4.8 bln USD'. Available at www.kitco.com/news/2014-09-16/Zimbabwe-Russia-platinum-investment-to-hit-4-8-bln-USD.html, accessed 22 October 2018.

13 All that glitters is not white gold

Richard Sidebottom

Introduction

For the majority of sub-Saharan Africa's (SSA) young population, the 'Africa Rising' narrative has translated as 'jobless growth' (Sumberg et al. 2014: 1). While it may seem axiomatic that engagement with global markets forms part of the remedy to this malaise, it is far from evident that previous development pathways remain open (Collier and Dercon 2009).

This chapter discusses the examples of the cotton, textile, and apparel sector (CTA). These have played a major role in the economic history of each of the BRICS countries and are seen as a conduit through which SSA can generate labour-intensive growth (Uganda 2013; SASTAC 2014; UEMOA 2014). Currently, however, the sector is symptomatic of the continent's development profile: low production yields; small manufacturing presence; and persistence of poverty (Collier and Dercon 2009).

To appreciate the complexities of this paradigm, the chapter endeavours to take a holistic approach that combines the global with the local; supply side with demand side; technical with institutional; and contemporary with historical. Following an overview of global supply and demand from a historical and contemporary perspective, the chapter analyses how these drivers interact with dynamic loci of power that frame shifting rules of the game (North 1990) that govern SSA countries' entrance to the arena.

Global historical perspective

Over 200 years the leadership baton of the CTA sector has passed full circle between Asia, Britain, and the USA (Riello 2013; Sidebottom 2017). The USA is still the world's largest lint exporter and retail market while China is the largest manufacturer (ICAC 2015; ITC 2015). The development of British and European CTA sectors was shaped by the relative strength of the existing wool and linen lobbies but which were ultimately doomed to substitution under changing demand patterns that favoured cotton (Mathias 1969; Yafa 2005).

Richard Sidebottom, *All that glitters is not white gold* In: *Handbook of BRICS and Emerging Economies.* Edited by: P.B. Anand, Shailaja Fennell, and Flavio Comim, Oxford University Press (2021).
DOI: 10.1093/oso/9780198827535.003.0013

Control of trade routes meant that European traders began to dominate textile exports to Africa, where fabric became a medium of exchange for slaves. Dominance of demand markets, exchange and logistics through wide business, and social networks lay behind initial European success, not comparative advantage in manufacturing (Riello 2013; Beckert 2014). Demand was nurtured through a marketing strategy akin to today's 'Fast fashion' high turnover business model (Riello 2013). This created a market for a variety of origins and quality grades which required standardized market exchange protocols (Beckert 2014). These in turn generated quality enforcement requirements through the Liverpool Cotton Brokers' Association (LCBA) in 1841—the predecessor of the Liverpool Cotton Association in 1882 (ICA 2015).

On the supply side, America's plantations became the dominant supplier to European textile manufacturers (Rivoli 2015). This vulnerability of the European supply chain was highlighted during the shortages of the US Civil War and continued thereafter as American farmers switched their supply to the growing domestic textile industry (Beckert 2014). By 1900, major textile manufacturers in Europe, Japan, and Russia were looking to their colonies to supplement American supplies of cotton lint (Wrigley 1959; Fok and Tazi 2004). By the 1920s, the balance of power in the CTA sector had shifted away from the British—to Japanese manufacturers and to American governors of the rules of exchange (Beckert 2014). In the post-war era global shifts (Dicken 2011) have slowly continued but as late as 1980, 38 per cent of spinning remained in Europe, USSR, or USA. Today this is below 10 per cent (Sidebottom 2017).

In 2014 global textile exports of US$783 billion exceeded those of iron and steel (WTO 2015) and retail markets exceeded US$1.5 trillion (Gherzi 2014). SSA countries have hitherto focused upon particular segments—cotton production or the assembly of garments. While each offers potential for low-quality employment, neither captures a high portion of value added or offers significant scope for the creation of quality jobs or skills (Morris and Barnes 2009). Moreover, in the face of competition from man-made fibres, cotton's share of the raw material fibre market is now below 30 per cent (CIRFS 2015)—amounting to only US$30 billion (FAO 2015). The growth of textiles manufacturing is therefore no longer synonymous with a growing demand for cotton production.

Shifting patterns of cotton production

The distribution of cotton production displays elements of continuity, as well as change. Since 1990 there has been market consolidation and geographical redistribution to Asia. The share of the top five producers (China, India, USA, Pakistan, Brazil) has increased from 65 per cent to 77 per cent (Figure 13.1) but the USA remains the single largest exporter and third largest producer. Developed countries still control 20 per cent—despite

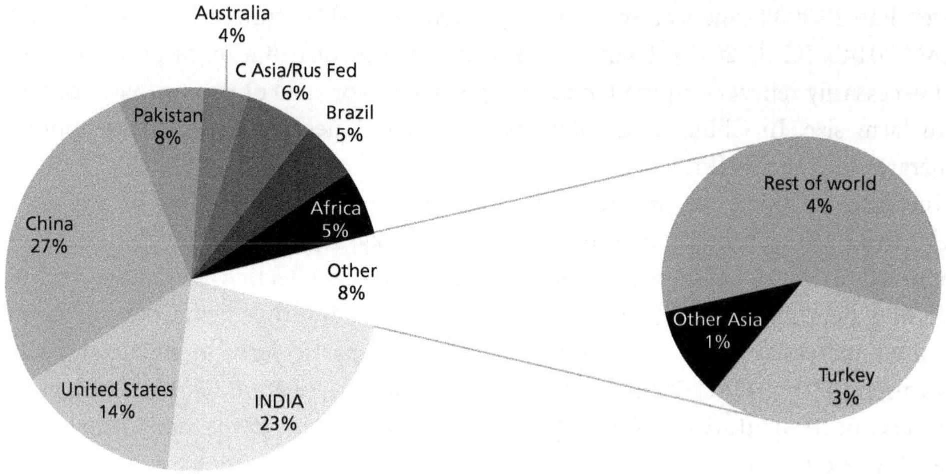

Figure 13.1 Leading cotton producers, 2014

Source: Graph: Sidebottom (2017); Data source: ICAC (2015).

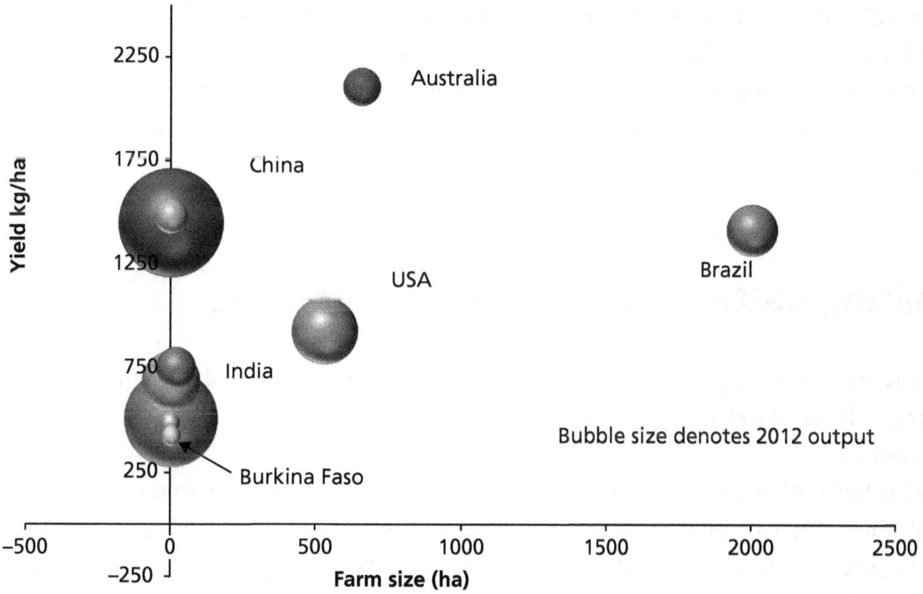

Figure 13.2 Size distribution of cotton production

Source: Graph: Sidebottom (2017); Data sources: FAO (2015); ICAC (2015).

declines in their textile manufacturing sectors. The production share of Central Asia[1] has declined to only 6 per cent, just above that of SSA (ICAC 2015).

Production is bifurcated between countries where smallholders predominate (China, India, Pakistan, SSA) and large-scale operations in Australia, USA, and Brazil—where

[1] Uzbekistan, Turkmenistan, Tajikistan, Kazakhstan, Kyrgyzstan.

fewer than 20,000 farmers account for 23 per cent of world cotton production (ITC 2007; ICAC 2014b; ICAC 2015). Figure 13.2 shows that this distribution of production does not necessarily reflect comparative advantage in terms of yield or productivity correlated with farm size. In China many plots are less than 1 hectare but intensive input use generates high yields (Pray et al. 2001).

Increases in global cotton production have resulted from a tripling of average lint yields from 230 kg/hectare in 1950 to just under 800kg/hectare in 2014. These are due to improved irrigation and production techniques; more effective pesticides; and seed breeding (Townsend 2009; Sidebottom 2017). Yield improvements have frequently required increased water and chemical footprints—particularly in Brazil and China (Townsend 2009; ICAC 2014b)—but the link between irrigation, GM technology, and yields is not straightforward. Indian yields remain 66 per cent lower than China and half the USA (Stone 2011).

After an initial boost from the spread of genetically modified (GM) cotton to 70 per cent of production after the 1990s, yield improvement has slowed and pest and weed resistance are growing (Sidebottom 2017). Institutional, socio-political, and agro-economic contingencies to the success of GM cotton have thus far limited its adoption in SSA (Smale et al. 2009; Schnurr 2012). Despite such innovation, the economics of cotton production are deteriorating. Production costs have doubled from US$0.38 per lb in 2000. Although prices spiked in 2000 and 2011, real lint prices have declined 40 per cent since 1960.

Shifting patterns of raw material demand

In a replay of the eighteenth-century contest between cotton and wool, cotton is now facing a demand paradigm shift due to the growth of man-made fibres (MMF)—mainly polyester.

This has both a global and local dimension. Excess MMF production capacity in Asia continues to drive prices lower. Given that raw fibre accounts for 60 per cent of yarn costs, price (as well as quality) has been a key driver of substitution of polyester for cotton. Though total fibre consumption continues to rise, cotton demand is in *relative* decline (Townsend 2013). Cotton still accounts for 80 per cent of natural fibres but its share of the total 90 million tonne fibre market has halved since 1970 to just 27 per cent (Gherzi 2014).[2]

Due to the heterogeneity of fibre qualities and the complicated nature of logistics, the *location* of lint demand is as important as its magnitude. Most lint is sourced *domestically*. Although India, for example, imports lint that has different quality properties from domestic growths, it is difficult for SSA exporters to sell to spinners where there

[2] Wool by comparison is just 1 per cent (Sidebottom 2017).

is sufficient domestic lint supply of the same known quality. Interviews with spinning mills indicated they would rather buy a local product from known agents than deal anonymously solely on the basis of price. Exchange has a strong relational element (Sidebottom 2017).

Raw material demand has shifted as the spinning industry has relocated to concentrate 87 per cent of its spindles in Asia (Sidebottom 2017). Over the last ten years, all lint exporters have become increasingly reliant upon demand from Chinese spinners who increasingly favour cheap locally produced MMFs (UNCTAD 2015). Although East African cotton goes to South Africa, 90 per cent of West African cotton is sold to Asia (UEMOA 2014). The global consolidation of spinning means that SSA lint exporters are competing with efficient large-scale producers (Brazil and Australia) and with domestic growers in countries with their own integrated production–manufacturing interlinkages (Sidebottom 2017).

Shifting patterns of consumer demand

The cotton market is not only facing external pressures but is also subject to multiple changing internal shifts.

First is the nexus of retail demand. Although most Asian textile manufacturing is currently centred on exports for developed markets, China's apparel market is expected to exceed that of the USA within five years and India's to grow to over US$200 billion (CottonInc 2013, 2014a, 2014b). As Kaplinsky and Farooki (2010) have shown, the shift in the nexus of commodity demand to developing countries poses intriguing questions with regard to quality, sustainability, and sourcing configurations. Unlike previous global cycles in the textile sector, production, manufacturing, and final demand are located in one place. This heterogeneity and dynamism of markets requires SSA exporters to engage with new contexts, relationships, and rules. Previous development models no longer apply (Sidebottom 2017).

The second development is the re-crafting of the non-price rules of the game upon which retailers base their sourcing strategies (Neilson and Pritchard 2009; Aerni 2013). One aspect of this is sustainability transparency. A plethora of market-sponsored 'sustainable initiatives' have appeared in recent years to address growing supply, environmental, and reputational risks and to facilitate the marketing of cotton in its fight against MMFs (Sidebottom 2017).

Their development implications may be quite profound as these standards frame particular innovation pathways as acceptable (Dosi 1988). Some schemes (Cotton made in Africa (CmiA), Fairtrade, and Organic cotton) explicitly limit SSA's *production upgrading* options through the prohibition of GM technology and artificial irrigation. Although the dominant global scheme, the Better Cotton Initiative (BCI), is agnostic with respect to GM technology, like CmiA, it offers training and marketing but no price premium (BCI 2015). Moreover, CmiA has far more extensive coverage in SSA (CmiA 2015). The prohibition of particular modes of intensification in order to gain access to training and markets creates the possibility of a two-speed development path for cotton producers.

There also appear to be limitations to *functional upgrading* (Coe and Yeung 2015). The rationale for Fairtrade and organic schemes is that the provision of a producer price premium (PPP) helps to alleviate poverty. Yet their track record indicates that success may be contingent upon a *pre-existing* minimal threshold of local manufacturing, rather than being a catalyst for it (Organic Exchange 2009). It is also unclear whether BCI or CmiA do much to address the failure to capture more value added in Africa as their traceability models currently rely primarily on spinners located in Asia (CmiA 2015; Sidebottom 2017).

Shifting rules of the game

These private rules nestle inside a web of formal industry or international trade rules governing the exchange of cotton lint, as well as fabric and garments. These rules continue to shape the geography and form of the CTA sector (Fukunishi and Yamagata 2014). Under the umbrella of successive trade incentives, manufacturing in SSA has focused on apparel to try to replicate the Asian strategy of development through 'low value added parts of production' (Morris et al. 2011). In all SSA textile manufacturing countries (except South Africa), apparel accounts for more than 80 per cent of exports (WTO 2015).

Single-stage transformation rules of origin (ROO) for SSA countries under the 1974–95 Multi-Fibre Agreement (MFA) and the 1995–2004 Agreement on Textiles and Clothing (ATC), skewed the nature of textile foreign direct investment (FDI) towards labour-intensive (but low value-added) garments (Staritz and Frederick 2014) and offered no incentives for local functional upgrading (Morris et al. 2011). Once the MFA expired in 2005, firms simply left (Fukunishi and Yamagata 2014).

The introduction of the African Growth and Opportunity Act (AGOA) in 2000 (recently renewed until 2022) provided duty free entry to the USA but is contingent upon agreement to particular governance and market reforms (ITA 2015). As of July, 2015, 39 sub-Saharan African countries were eligible; Swaziland and South Africa temporarily suspended; and the benefits concentrated in Kenya, Lesotho, and Mauritius (AGOA 2015).[3]

Even amongst the latter, there is little evidence that value capture or social upgrading are synonymous with value creation or employment growth—particularly for female and

[3] These three plus South Africa and Madagascar accounted for 95 per cent of SSA apparel exports in 2014 (WTO 2015).

migrant workers (Palpacuer 2008; Staritz 2012; Coe and Yeung 2015). Apparel employment remains low skilled, poorly paid and informal (Mayer and Gereffi 2010; Morris et al. 2011; Bernhardt and Milberg 2011; Goger et al. 2014).

The sub-Saharan Africa experience

These historical, technical, supply, demand, and governance phenomena provide the lens through which the growth and shape of the CTA sector in SSA can be viewed.

While there is evidence of artisanal textile manufacturing before colonialization, large-scale cotton production was largely a derivative of colonial diktat (Bassett 2001; Riello 2013; Clarence-Smith 2014). Prior to independence, the Belgian Congo and British Uganda were Africa's largest single producers, outside Sudan and Egypt (ICAC 2015). Between 1950 and 1970, SSA cotton production tripled and spinning consumption rose from just 6 per cent of production to peak at 46 per cent in the 1980s when structural adjustment programmes (SAPs) prompted deregulation of production and removal of tariff protection for spinners (Meredith 2006).

PRODUCTION—PROCESS INNOVATION

While manufacturing has since stalled, production has doubled. SSA cotton makes up 5 per cent of global production and occupies approximately 2 million farmers on 11 million hectares of land and supports up to 20 million people (Peltzer and Röttger 2013; Bayer 2015; ICAC 2015). Production is mainly in West Africa but there is manufacturing in the South and East. In 2015 the top five producers were all Francophone countries (Burkina Faso, Benin, Côte d'Ivoire, Mali, and Cameroon) and accounted for 64 per cent of the total (ICAC 2015). Production increases mainly result from expanded planting areas, rather than improved yields (ITC 2007). Virtually all of this is rain fed (Estur 2008). The average lint yield of SSA's top nineteen producers remains one-third of the world benchmark (775kg/hectare) and ranges widely—from 126kg in Chad to 561kg in Cameroon (ICAC 2014a; ICAC 2015).[4]

These redistributions have seen a move towards more regulated production regimes in which inputs are centrally coordinated and output prices heavily discounted (Moseley 2008). This regulation has simultaneously been lauded for increases in production and lint quality (Fok and Tazi 2004), yet condemned for hindering farmers' process and functional upgrading opportunities (Staritz and Tröster 2015).

In SSA, Peltzer and Röttger (2013) calculate that farmers allocate 30 per cent of an average 6–7 hectare plot to cotton. This obvious generalization serves to make the point

[4] Excluding South African large-scale farms with yields above 1,500 kg/hectare (Cotton SA 2015).

that in many parts of SSA, the primary constraint to production is often labour—not land. Many Ugandan cotton farmers, for example, grow up to nine other crops in rotation and switch between cash crops dependent upon market prices. SSA cotton farmers use crops as pest traps, cash, or food sources or as risk management tools (Sidebottom 2017). This implies that production innovation that focuses on *land* (but not *labour*) productivity (Lipton 2007) or on only *one* crop is misplaced. It also highlights a key role for commodity traders and non-governmental organizations (NGOs) as intermediaries between actors *within* chains as well as *between* different chains (Coe and Yeung 2015; Sidebottom 2017).

MANUFACTURING—FUNCTIONAL INNOVATION

As well as low value added in production, there is virtually no value added beyond it. Spinning in the South and East has been more successful (especially in Tanzania) but is well below its 1990 peak. Due to a lack of domestic capacity, Francophone growers are dependent upon Chinese and Southeast Asian spinners. Although West Africa has more than forty spinning mills, few are actually *active* and process only 2 per cent of the region's lint (USAID 2006; UEMOA 2014).

East and Southern Africa dominate SSA manufacturing but this is concentrated in low-value apparel in Mauritius, Madagascar, Kenya, and Lesotho. The exception is South Africa where textiles contribute 45 per cent.[5] These five account for more than 84 per cent of SSA textile exports (ICAC 2015; WTO 2015).

These patterns reflect local and historical influences, not simply the exigencies of the global market. While South Africa's textile sector has access to a US$10 billion domestic retail market (Cotton SA 2015), as well as export capacity of US$900 million, Burkina Faso and Uganda managed only US$15 million (WTO 2015). Burkina Faso accounts for 20 per cent of SSA lint exports, yet spins only 2 per cent of its production (USAID 2006; ICAC 2015; WTO 2015).

South African textile employment and cotton production have collapsed and smallholder production is virtually non-existent (Cotton SA 2015; SACTWU 2015). Once the leading cotton producer in SSA, Uganda now sits between these two extremes with both the production and manufacturing sectors testament to repeated failure (Kasekende and Afingi-Ego 2007). Each of these pathways bears the hallmarks of a range of influences, opportunities, choices, and histories (Collier and O'Connell 2008). Through a *combination* of local and global perspective, researchers can enrich our understanding of specific country experiences.

[5] Nigeria, Tanzania, and Côte d'Ivoire also rely more on textiles than apparel, but totals are smaller (WTO 2015).

Local case studies

BURKINA FASO

Burkina Faso is a resource poor, arid, landlocked country classified as one of the world's most underdeveloped countries (HDR 2015; World Bank 2015a). Persistent hunger and political crises kept GDP per capita below independence levels until 1980 and left the economy aid dependent (Grimm and Gunther 2004). Manufacturing exports totalled only US$180million in 2014, of which just US$15 million were textiles (UNCTAD 2015). With the recent discovery of gold deposits, agriculture now accounts for only 34 per cent of GDP but remains the main income source for 80 per cent of the population (World Bank 2015a). Although cotton's direct contribution to GDP declined to 3.5 per cent in 2014 (IMF 2014), it is still grown by 350,000 smallholders, occupies 10 per cent of arable land, and indirectly supports over 10 per cent of the population (ADI 2012; ISAAA 2015; World Bank 2015a).

Colonial era attempts to boost cotton production for export to the French textile industry foundered on a shortage of labour, incentives, and food (Bassett 2008). In the 1930s France's African colonies supplied only 3 per cent of French textile requirements and by independence still less than 10 per cent. In Côte d'Ivoire farmers preferred to intercrop cotton with food crops and sell to local artisans (at a higher price than France paid). Farmers in Upper Volta focused on livestock and food provision (World Bank 1970; Bassett 2001).

After the Second World War, cotton production in French West Africa was placed under the stewardship of the Compagnie Développement des Fibres Textiles (CFDT)[6] and l'Institut de Recherches du Coton et des Textiles Exotiques (IRCT) funded by the French Development Agency and French textile firms (Bassett 2001). Initially CFDT owned the gins and still retains stakes in many of them (World Bank 1970; Estur 2008). Cotton marketing was controlled by Compagnie Cotonnière (COPACO) (a CFDT subsidiary)[7] (Basset 2008). Through the introduction of new hybrid varieties and pesticide use, production and yields increased dramatically (World Bank 1970).

Quality control was exercised through a vertically integrated structure in which CFDT had monopsony buying rights and monopoly input supply rights (Gray 2008). Farmers were guaranteed a pre-harvest floor price from which the cost of inputs and credit would be automatically deducted by the gin. Input, credit, knowledge, and output markets were 'internalised' (World Bank 1970; Dowd-Uribe 2013). Exclusion of local traders prevented side selling to reduce risks in credit provision to farmers but also eliminated price competition. This was a linear technology model that presumed yield improvements

[6] CFDT became Dagris in 2001 and was privatized in 2006. It is owned by Géocoton, part of Advens (Sidebottom 2017).

[7] CFDT received a 6 per cent commission on exports (Bassett 2001).

derived from new seeds and inputs would be sufficient incentive for farmers to grow cotton (Bassett 2001).

Despite World Bank and IMF pressure to reform, the core of this model remains. Production is now distributed across three regional monopsonies whereby two small private gins—Socoma and Faso Coton—operate alongside the dominant state-owned Sofitex (Kaminski et al. 2009). Pre-harvest prices are set by an inter-professional committee (Association Inter-professionnelle du Coton du Burkina Faso [AICB]). This incorporates the state and farmers' union (the Union Nationale des Producteurs de Coton de Burkina) alongside the state and gin companies (Staritz and Tröster 2015); but farmers still receive only 58 per cent of world prices on average and have no choice about seed varieties (Peltzer and Röttger 2013).

This control forms part of a complex governance and ownership structure of interconnected private and state organizations. Sofitex has equity stakes in input provider (Saphyto); cotton oil processor SN-Citec (jointly with Géocoton); and spinning mill Filsah (jointly with the state). Beyond Filsah, there is no added value further along the textile chain or opportunity for farmers to process their own cotton. Burkina Faso has no knitting or weaving capacity outside the artisanal sector (USAID 2006; Sidebottom 2017).

SOUTH AFRICA

Although South Africa is the second largest economy in SSA after Nigeria (World Bank 2015a) and has the largest manufacturing sector which accounts for 15 per cent of GDP (Media Club 2015), it is currently struggling under the weight of structural unemployment, an over-reliance on extractive industries, and social inequality (HDR 2015).

Unlike Burkina Faso and Uganda, South African agriculture contributes just 3 per cent of GDP. Although there are approximately 2 million smallholders,[8] output is dominated by 38,000 large-scale farms (Kotze and Rose 2015). It has a large CTA sector (which provides 14 per cent of manufacturing jobs but virtually no cotton production (Media Club 2015; World Bank 2015b).

This lack of production is partly due to agro-economic circumstances, meaning that only 13 per cent of South African land is suitable for arable farming (Kotze and Rose 2015). Climatic conditions also largely explain why South Africa's textile industry has its origins in woollen, not cotton, fibre. Although cotton farms expanded under apartheid tariff protection (Gouse 2013), it is now cheaper to source cotton from Zambia and Zimbabwe (Sidebottom 2017). South African cotton production now covers fewer than 10,000 hectares and, like the rest of the sector, is bifurcated by scale and water dependence. Having adopted Bt cotton in 1998—ten years prior to Burkina Faso—almost all South African cotton seed is genetically modified (Schnurr 2012).

[8] Official estimates range from 1.3 to 3 million (Kotze and Rose 2015).

Irrigated yields are six times those of rain-fed production but investment in irrigation is beyond the means of smallholders who averaged just 6 per cent of production from 2004–15 (Cotton SA 2015). One of the main smallholder cotton regions—the Makhathini Flats in KwaZulu Natal—has been subject to numerous innovation initiatives but each has foundered on drought, disease, pestilence, or finance (Schnurr 2012). Unlike in Burkina Faso, input markets and gin processing have been completely deregulated since 1997, though the non-profit company Cotton SA continues to coordinate marketing and research (Fok et al. 2007).

Apart from the relative importance of wool, rather than cotton, South Africa's textile industry shows a number of other unique characteristics. The first is that local demand rather than the availability of raw materials has been the foundation for the sector (McDowell 2010). Second is the degree of state involvement (through the Industrial Development Corporation [IDC]) and tariff protection throughout the apartheid era and its re-emergence as a key coordinator in recent industry-wide initiatives—including direct equity and loan financing of spinners (McDowell 2010; Gouse 2013; Sidebottom 2017).

The latter represents a step back from post-1994 withdrawal of the state in order to address the collapse of employment to just 100,000 in the face of Chinese clothing imports (Texfed 2007; Cotton SA 2015) and outsourcing to Lesotho and Swaziland (SACTWU 2015). South Africa is the second largest textile exporter in SSA (after Mauritius) (ITC 2015) but most of the 500 small, family-owned firms target the domestic market (Sidebottom 2017).

UGANDA

Although poverty headcounts have reduced in Uganda its young population remains primarily employed in agriculture (ITC 2014; World Bank 2015a). Successful adherence to IMF programmes has not been coupled with resolution of key infrastructure bottlenecks or competitiveness (Uganda 2013).

Agriculture still accounts for 65 per cent of exports of which coffee is the main component (BOU 2015). Although Uganda historically was a larger cotton producer than either Burkina Faso or South Africa and accounted for 25 per cent of all SSA cotton exports until independence in 1962, cotton is ranked far behind coffee and tea in terms of export earnings (Youé 1978; Baffes 2009). Ugandan cotton is valued for its high quality and homogeneity but production of 20 million tonnes in 2015 is well below target (CDO 2011; ICAC 2015). With more than thirty operators chasing such a small harvest, the ginning sector suffers from chronic overcapacity (Sidebottom 2017).

In 2014 Uganda was a net importer of clothes and finished textiles, while cotton exports during 2009–14 averaged fewer than US$50 million per annum (UNCTAD 2015). Like many SSA government development plans, Uganda's 'Vision 2040' puts the revival of the CTA sector at its heart (Uganda 2009, 2013).

While South Africa's cotton textile industry has been shaped by domestic demand and cotton production limited by climatic circumstances, Uganda's history illustrates the importance of external demand that its Uganda development path be one of production, rather than manufacturing. Its trajectory reflects not only the evolution of other supply side choices (coffee, sesame) but the cycle of demand from Lancashire mills (Onyeiwu 2000).

The introduction of cotton by the British in 1905 resulted from lobbying by UK manufacturers (acting through the British Cotton Growing Association [BCGA]), anxious to diversify supply risks away from the USA (Ehrlich 1957). Cotton remained Uganda's main export until the expansion of coffee in the 1950s (Jamal 1976). Africa was the preferred source over India due to problems of logistics and quality (Ehrlich 1957). The British focused on Uganda due to the *absence* of a domestic textile sector, relative political stability, ample land and labour, and a recently constructed railway to Mombasa (Onyeiwu 2000). Governor Bell wrote in 1907 'no part of our Empire is more promising for cotton' (Bell 1907, cited in Wrigley 1959: 18).

However, as the economy was un-monetized, inducing farmers to grow cotton required coercion (making poll taxes payable in cotton bales or the paying of tribute through growing cotton for the chief) and facilitation (by building roads using coerced labour to transport lint) (Mamdani 1976; Onyeiwu 2000). The key intermediaries were Indian (dukawallah) traders who were skilled labourers brought to Uganda to build the Mombasa railway. They not only bought farmers' cotton but sold them consumer goods, as part of a deliberate government strategy to monetize market exchange (Ehrlich 1957; Wrigley 1959; Nayenga 1981).

Demand side lobbying saw the restriction of ginning competition under the Cotton Ordinance of 1908 in order to prioritize lint quality for UK spinners (Ehrlich 1957; Mamdani 1976). Seed varieties were restricted and seed reuse prohibited (Nayenga 1981). The authorities established a precedent of centralized control of seed inputs and a state-funded research capability that has survived to this day (Sidebottom 2017). In some ways, this structure resembled that of Burkina Faso today. The BCGA offered premiums for quantity and quality; research and free seeds; and credit to farmers and ginners (Onyeiwu 2000).

During the interwar period, colonial authorities faced a constant battle to maintain this control as Indian gins and production extended to remote areas unfrequented by European ginners (Jamal 1976; Nayenga 1981). Although increased competition benefited farmers through higher prices, this was not in BGCA's interest (Okereke 1968; Mamdani 1976). The resulting Cotton Ordinance of 1933 placed further restrictions on ginning competition and once again illustrated the power of demand side actors (Mamdani 1976).

The continuation of low farm gate prices after the Second World War prompted a redistribution of cotton production to more marginal areas while more fertile zones concentrated on more profitable crops (Wrigley 1959; Mamdani 1976). As the British textile sector declined, its hold over the Ugandan cotton chain weakened, especially as coffee developed as an alternative cash crop (Jamal 1976). Policy attention switched to empowering producers through cooperatives' ownership of gins (Okereke 1968) which helped encourage further growth in production before its collapse in the Amin era (Mamdani 1976).

Cotton is currently grown widely (but sparsely) throughout Uganda including in Kasese in the South West; in Mbale in the East; and Gulu in the North (Sidebottom 2017). In 2014 lint output was only 19,000 kg from 74,000 hectares yielding just 250 kg/hectare (ICAC 2015). Farmers frequently switch between cotton and sesame depending upon market prices, so they are unwilling to invest in cotton-specific innovations (Sidebottom 2017).

Market governance is the responsibility of the Cotton Development Organisation (CDO) established in 1994 alongside the Uganda Ginners and Cotton Exporters' Association (UGCEA) (CDO 2011). Under the 1990s liberalization drive, CDO replaced the state Lint Marketing Board but still limits seed choice to just one variety; prohibits replanting; and conducts all cotton research (Locke and Byrne 2008).

Although prices are not fixed as in Burkina Faso, a hybrid scheme differentiates Uganda from the free market model in South Africa. Prices are negotiated between the UGCEA and CDO according to a formula that reflects world prices minus costs of ginning, logistics, and seeds (Sidebottom 2017). However, this system is struggling to generate sufficient cotton production to utilize gin capacity. CDO blames a litany of problems in production (including lack of irrigation; poor soil fertility; and high input costs) on governance (absence of farmer cooperatives); in processing and marketing (high borrowing and energy costs; lint price volatility); and inadequate research. These issues of governance have meant that with the continued risk of side selling, provision of new seeds, spray pumps, subsidized pesticides and training is secured only through a compulsory gin levy (Sidebottom 2017).

Most fundamentally CDO laments the lack of domestic value addition either in textiles or cotton by-products. As in Burkina Faso, most of Uganda's crop is sold unprocessed (CDO 2010, 2015). This is despite a relatively extended history of attempts to foster the development of a CTA sector. Although pre-Second World War ventures were thwarted by the BGCA, the Worthington Development Plan of 1947 saw the construction of the Owens Fall Dam and Nyanza Textile Industries Limited (NYTIL) in Jinja, funded by the state-owned Uganda Development Corporation (UDC) (Jamal 1976; Clarence-Smith 2014). The 1960s also saw the influx of Indian and Japanese capital into textiles manufacturing independently or through joint ventures, such as the United Garment Industry Limited (UGIL) (Mamdani 1976).

However, post-independence textile initiatives supported under the umbrella of an import substitution (IS) industrial policy focused solely on a small domestic market and created no integration between firms or functions (Obwona et al. 2013; Clarence-Smith 2014). Political and economic pressures in the 1970–90 period saw a sector-wide collapse. Although the state has made repeated attempts at revival, manufacturing remains relatively small and focused on the domestic market or state procurement contracts (Sidebottom 2017). Uganda's exports under AGOA remain minimal (ITC 2015).

In 2014 NYTIL was the largest local buyer of Ugandan lint, but following the loss of an army uniforms contract to China, production and employment collapsed. This episode is emblematic of NYTIL's history—bankruptcy, nationalization, resale, investment boom and bust (Sidebottom 2017). Despite a reported US$28 million capital injection by new owners Picfare (Bharat 2007), the company is still lobbying for public procurement, import restrictions, and concessional finance to help it survive (New Vision 2014). A similar tale of woe at the Lira Spinning mill revealed takeover by investors that had neither textile expertise nor sufficient capital and resulted in fraud and bankruptcy, despite a US$1.5 million credit facility from Uganda Development Bank (Sidebottom 2017). The collapse of spinning capacity has meant that local apparel companies, such as Tri-Star Apparel, were dependent upon Asian imports that could take two months to arrive (Ryan 2004). Tri-Star operated a cut, make, and trim (CMT) business model supplying Wal-Mart, JC Penney, and Target under AGOA. Despite state subsidies, loans, free premises, and tax concessions and a US$20 million investment from US company ISIS Pacific Capital in early 2006, Tri-Star ceased trading in 2007 (Sidebottom 2017).

Conclusion

These three case studies show contrasting development histories and distinct comparative advantages. They also illustrate the importance of the interaction between local and global—exercised primarily through the demand side channel.

The global shift away from cotton fibre is putting downward pressure on prices such that without yield enhancement, the economics of cotton farming are becoming untenable. The global shift of manufacturing away from Asia to SSA in search of cheaper labour costs is far from axiomatic. A number of studies (Fernandez-Stark et al. 2011; UNIDO 2011; Fukunishi and Yamagata 2014) find that Southeast Asian wage rates are lower than those of SSA. The nexus of retail demand is also shifting east.

In light of these shifts, a focus on cost and the encouragement of apparel production through trade preferences may reflect a misdiagnosis of the development problem. Sourcing criteria are changing. Lead buyers are looking for consolidated supply networks able to offer speed, inventory management, production flexibility, and risk and quality control as part of a 'manu-servicing' package, not just low cost (Staritz 2012; OECD 2013; McKinsey 2015). These include social and environmental standards compliance which therefore becomes a de facto entry requirement, rather than an aspirational goal (Gereffi and Frederick 2010; Aerni 2013; Tokatli 2013). With a lack of organizational skills, speed, and flexibility to adapt to rapid shifts in demand, as well as energy and infrastructure constraints, the comparative advantage of SSA in apparel (other than at the very low end) is weak (Gereffi and Frederick 2010; OECD 2013).

This lack of organizational capacity implies that criteria governing CTA sector projects may require a broader focus than export revenues or low-quality jobs. Long-term development outcomes are contingent upon *with whom* aspiring SSA manufacturers engage, *on what terms*, and *in what particular markets* (Tokatli 2013; Goger et al. 2014). In Lesotho, Taiwanese firms focus on long low-value runs for the American market. South African firms (targeting their own domestic market) may be more inclined towards upgrading (Morris et al. 2015). Reliance on FDI flows and ephemeral trade preferences does little for capacity building, as exporters receive unconditional rents (Staritz and Frederick 2014; Rivoli 2015).

The potential for other stages viewed in isolation (such as spinning) also seems limited due to energy costs and the absence of regional coordination (UNIDO 2011). Analysing each node separately, however, is part of the problem. China established comparative advantage throughout the *entire* chain across *all* fibres, through coordinated skills provision, spatial clustering (Milberg et al. 2014), access to raw materials, and a large local market (Morris et al. 2011; Lu and Dickson 2015). Textile sector growth in Thailand, Pakistan, Indonesia, and India was led by the textiles sector, not apparel (Yamagata 1998; Staritz 2012; OECD 2013). European manufacturers have maintained a significant presence in the spinning, fabric, industrial textiles, and high-value fashion segments, while contracting CMT to cheaper neighbours in Eastern Europe (Morris et al. 2011, 2015). Germany, Korea, and Taiwan remain among the world's top ten textile exporters (WTO 2015).

While development of the capital-and energy-intensive spinning and weaving stages is more problematic, captures less value, and offers fewer jobs (Morris and Barnes 2009), investment tends to be 'stickier' than in garments (Fukunishi and Yamagata 2014) and acts as a fulcrum for horizontal and vertical linkages (Hirschman 1958).

In SSA, the textile leg of the chain, the nature of regional demand, the type of investors, and the interlinkages with production remain pivotal but largely unexplored research areas. Production, spinning, and fabric and garment making are inextricably linked, yet diagnosis of SSA's structural stasis treats them as unrelated worlds (Sidebottom 2017).

REFERENCES

ADI (Agro-industries Development Initiative) (2012). 'Bt cotton production in Burkina Faso'. Traore, K. and Traore H., INERA-Burkina Faso. Ghana: Paper presented at Accelerated Agribusiness and Agro-industries Development Initiative (3ADI) meeting, June 2012.

Aerni, P. (2013). 'Do private standards encourage or hinder trade and innovation?'. NCCR WP 2013/18, Swiss National Centre of Competence in Research. Available at www.nccr-trade.org/fileadmin/user_upload/nccr-trade.ch/wp3/2013_06_final_Private_Standards_Paper_Philipp.pdf, accessed 23 October 2018.

AGOA (African Growth and Opportunity Act) (2015). AGOA Extension and Enhancement Act of 2015. Available at https://agoa.info/downloads/legal/5660.html, accessed 9 January 2020.

Baffes, J. (2009). 'Cotton sector of Uganda'. Africa Region Working Paper No. 123. Washington, DC: World Bank.

Bassett, T.J. (2001). *The Peasant Cotton Revolution in West Africa: Côte d'Ivoire, 1880–1995.* Cambridge: Cambridge University Press.

Bassett, T.J. (2008). 'Producing poverty: power relations and price formation in the cotton commodity chains of West Africa', in W.G. Moseley and L.C. Gray (eds) *Hanging by a Thread.* Sweden: Nordic Africa Institute, 35–64.

Bayer (Bayer Crop Science) (2015). *Bayer Crop Science.* Available at www.cropscience.bayer.com/en/Products-and-Innovation/Key-Crops/Cotton.aspx#Research&Innovation, accessed 19 November 2018.

BCI (Better Cotton Initiative) (2015). Better Cotton Initiative website. Available at www.bettercotton.org, accessed 23 October 2018.

Beckert, S. (2014). *Empire of Cotton: A New History of Global Capitalism.* UK: Penguin.

Bernhardt, T. and Milberg, W. (2011). 'Economic and social upgrading in global value chains: analysis of horticulture, apparel, tourism and mobile telephones', Working Paper 2011/06, Capturing the Gains, 2011.

Bharat (2007). 'Picfare Group invests $28m in textile division', *BharatTextile*, 20 November. Available at www.bharattextile.com/newsitems/2006679, accessed 23 October 2018.

BOU (Bank of Uganda) (2015). Bank of Uganda website. Available at www.bou.or.ug, accessed 12 September 2015.

CDO (Cotton Development Organisation) (2010). *Cotton Development Organisation, Annual Report 2009–10.* Available at www.cdouga.org/wp-content/uploads/2013/09/Annual-Report2009-2010-.pdf, accessed 9 January 2020.

CDO (Cotton Development Organisation) (2011). 'Cotton from Uganda'. Brochure produced by the International Trade Centre for the Cotton Development Organization in Uganda. Available at www.coton-acp.org/sites/default/files/documents/downloads/final_uganda_brochure_october_2011.pdf, accessed 23 October 2018.

CDO (Cotton Development Organisation) (2015). Cotton Development Organisation website. Available at www.cdouga.org/, accessed 15 December 2015.

CIRFS (2015). European Man-made Fibres Association website. Available at www.cirfs.org/, accessed 23 October 2018.

Clarence-Smith, W.G. (2014). 'The textile industry of Eastern Africa in the longue duree', in E. Akyeampong, R.H. Bates, N. Nunn, and J. Robinson (eds) *Africa's Development in Historical Perspective.* New York: Cambridge University Press, 264–94.

CmiA (Cotton made in Africa) (2015). Website. Available at www.cottonmadeinafrica.org/en/, accessed 23 October 2018.

Coe, N.M. and Wai-Chung Yeung, H. (2015). *Global Production Networks: Theorizing Economic Development in an Inter-connected World.* Oxford: Oxford University Press.

Collier, P. and Dercon, S. (2009). 'African agriculture in 50 years: Smallholders in a rapidly changing world?'. Expert meeting on how to feed the world in 2050. Food and Agriculture Organization of the United Nations Economic and Social Development Department.

Collier, P. and O'Connell, S.A. (2008). 'Opportunities and choices', in B.J. Ndulu, S.A. O'Connell, R.H. Bates, P. Collier, and C. Soludo (eds) *The Political Economy of Economic Growth in Africa 1960–2000.* Cambridge: Cambridge University Press, 76–136.

Cotton SA (2015). Cotton South Africa website materials. Available at www.cottonsa.org.za/, accessed 23 October 2018.

CottonInc (2013). 'Captivating the Indian apparel shopper'. Available at www.lifestylemonitor.com, accessed 7 January 2016.

CottonInc (2014a). 'Global lifestyle monitor Brazil, consumer apparel shopping attitudes and habits'. Available at www.lifestylemonitor.com, accessed 17 December 2015.

CottonInc (2014b). 'Lifestyle monitor: US apparel customers, cotton incorporated supply chain insights'. Available at www.lifestylemonitor.com, accessed 3 January 2016.

Dicken, P. (2011). *Global Shift: Mapping the Changing Contours of the World Economy*. London: SAGE.

Dosi, G. (1988). 'Sources, procedures, and microeconomic effects of innovation', *Journal of Economic Literature* 26/3: 1120–71.

Dowd-Uribe, B. (2013). 'Engineering yields and inequality? How institutions and agro-ecology shape Bt cotton outcomes in Burkina Faso', *Geoforum* 53: 161–71.

Ehrlich, C. (1957). 'Cotton and the Uganda economy 1903–9', *The Uganda Journal* September 1957.

Estur, G. (2008). 'Comparative analysis of organisation and performance of African cotton sectors, quality and marketing of cotton lint in Africa'. Africa Region Working Paper Series No. 121, October 2008.

FAO (Food and Agriculture Organization) (2015). 'Measuring sustainability in cotton farming systems towards a guidance framework'. Joint publication of Food and Agriculture Organization of the United Nations and the International Cotton Advisory Committee, 2015.

Fernandez-Stark, K., Gereffi, G., and Frederick, S. (2011). 'The apparel global value chain: economic upgrading and workforce development, in Gary Gereffi, Karina Fernandez-Stark, and Phil Psilos (eds) *Skills for Upgrading: Workforce Development and Global Value Chains in Developing Countries*. Durham, NC: Duke University Press Center on Globalization, Governance and Competitiveness, 75–131. Available at https://gvcc.duke.edu/wp-content/uploads/Skills-for-Upgrading-Workforce-Development-and-GVC-in-Developing-Countries_FullBook-2.pdf, accessed 25 February 2014.

Fok, M. and Tazi, S. (2004). 'Lessons learnt to overcome the costly and uncertain institutional re-arrangements under the globalisation process: The African cotton case'. Text Associated to a poster presented at the 85th EAAAE Seminar, Florence, Italy, September 8–11. Available at www.researchgate.net/publication/237754669_Lesson_learnt_to_overcome_the_costly_and_uncertain_institutional_rearrangement_under_the_globalization_process_The_African_cot ton_case, accessed 24 October 2018.

Fok, M., Gouse, M., Hofs, J.L., and Kirsten, J. (2007). 'Contextual appraisal of GM cotton diffusion in South Africa', *Life Science International Journal* 1/4: 468–82.

Fukunishi, T. and Yamagata, T. (2014). 'Introduction: The dynamism of the garment industry in low income countries', in T. Fukunishi and T. Yamagata (eds) *The Garment Industry in Low-Income Countries: An Entry Point of Industrialization*. London: Palgrave-Macmillan, 1–37.

Gereffi, G. and Frederick, S. (2010). 'The global apparel value chain, trade and the crisis: Challenges and opportunities for developing countries', in O. Cattaneo, G. Gereffi, and C. Staritz (eds) *Global Value Chains in a Post-crisis World*. Washington, DC: World Bank, 157–208.

Gherzi (2014). 'Prerequisites for textile industry growth'. Gherzi Textile Organisation, Zürich, Switzerland. Available at www.icac.org/getattachment/mtgs/Plenary/73rd-Plenary/Agenda/OS5-Gherzi.pdf, accessed 9 January 2020.

Goger, A., Hull, A., Barrientos, S., Gereffi, G., and Godfrey, S. (2014). 'Capturing the gains in Africa: making the most of global value chain participation'. Centre on Globalization, Governance & Competitiveness at the Social Research Institute, Duke University, February 2014.

Gouse, M. (2013). 'Socio-economic and farm-level effects of genetically modified crops: the case of Bt Crops in South Africa', in J. Falck-Zepeda, G. Gruere, and I. Sithole-Niang (eds) *Genetically Modified Crops in Africa*. Washington DC: International Food Policy Research Institution, 25–42.

Gray, L.C. (2008). 'Cotton production in Burkina Faso: international rhetoric versus local realities', in W.G. Moseley and L.C. Gray (eds) *Hanging by a Thread*. Athens, OH: Ohio University Press, 65–82.

Grimm, M. and Gunther, I. (2004). 'Operationalising pro-poor growth'. A country case study on Burkina Faso, October 2004. Available at http://siteresources.worldbank.org/INTPGI/Resources/342674-1115051237044/oppgburkinafaso.pdf, accessed 24 October 2018.

HDR (Human Development Report) (2015). 'Work for human development'. Available at http://report.hdr.undp.org/, accessed 24 October 2018.

Hirschman, A.O. (1958). *The Strategy of Economic Development*. New Haven, CT: Yale University Press.

ICA (International Cotton Association) (2015). International Cotton Association website. Available at www.ica-ltd.org, accessed 24 October 2018.

ICAC (International Cotton Advisory Committee) (2014a). 'Cotton: Technology transfer/logistics in Africa'. DG's consultative framework mechanism on cotton, Geneva, 20 June, José Sette ICAC.

ICAC (International Cotton Advisory Committee) (2014b). *Cotton Production Practices*. A report by the Technical Information Section of the International Cotton Advisory Committee, Washington, DC, November 2014.

ICAC (International Cotton Advisory Committee) (2015). International Cotton Advisory Committee Cotton database. Available at https://icac.gen10.net/www.ICAC.org, accessed 3 September 2015.

IMF (International Monetary Fund) (2014. *Country Report No. 14/230, Burkina Faso*. Selected Issues, June 2014. Washington, DC: IMF.

ISAAA (International Service for the Acquisition of Agri-Biotech Applications) (2015). Available at www.isaaa.org/resources/publications/biotech_country_facts_and_trends/download/Facts%20and%20Trends%20-%20Burkina%20Faso.pdf, accessed 24 October 2018.

ITA (International Trade Administration) (2015). International Trade Administration website. Available at http://trade.gov/agoa/index.asp, accessed 24 October 2018.

ITC (International Trade Centre) (2007). 'Cotton exporter's guide'. Available at www.intracen.org, accessed 24 October 2018.

ITC (International Trade Centre) (2014). 'ITC by country report: Uganda, International Trade Centre'. Available at www.intracen.org, accessed 24 October 2018.

ITC (International Trade Centre) (2015). 'Trade map'. Trade statistics for international business development. International Trade Centre website. Available at www.trademap.org/, accessed 24 October 2018.

Jamal, V. (1976). 'The role of cotton and coffee in Uganda's economic development. PhD dissertation. Stanford, CA: Stanford University.

Kaminski, J., Headey, D., and Bernard, T. (2009). 'Institutional reform in the Burkinabe cotton sector and its impacts on incomes and food security'. WP 17, London, Africa Power & Politics.

Kaplinksy, R. and Farooki, M. (2010). 'What are the implications for global value chains when the market shifts from the North to the South?'. World Bank Policy Research Working Paper WPS5205, World Bank, Poverty Reduction and Economic Management Network, International Trade Development, February 2010.

Kasekende, L.A. and Afingi-Ego, M. (2007). 'Restarting and sustaining growth in a post-conflict economy: the case of Uganda in the political economy of economic growth in Africa, 1960–2000, Volume 2', in B.J. Ndulu, S.A. O'Connell, J.P. Azam, R.H Bates, A.K. Fosu, J. W. Gunning, and D. Nijinkeu (eds) *Country Case Studies*. Cambridge: Cambridge University Press.

Kotze, I. and Rose, M. (eds) (2015). *Farming Facts and Futures: Reconnecting South Africa's Food Systems to Its Ecosystem*. Cape Town, South Africa: WWF-SA.

Lipton, M. (2007). 'Plant breeding and poverty: can transgenic seeds replicate the "Green Revolution" as a source of gains for the poor?', *Journal of Development Studies* 43/1: 31–62.

Locke, R. and Byrne, K.G. (2008). 'Cotton value chain'. Case study for Northern Uganda, Microreport #91.

Lu, S. and Dickson, M.A. (2015). 'Where is China's textile and apparel industry going?' Available from https://blogs.nottingham.ac.uk/chinapolicyinstitute/2015/07/24/where-is-chinas-textile-and-apparel-industry-going, accessed 30 December 2015.

McDowell, J.C. (2010). 'A history of the South African textile industry: the pioneering phase, 1820–1948'. Natal: University of Kwa-Zulu Natal MA Thesis. Available from http://researchspace.ukzn.ac.za/xmlui/handle/10413/5442, accessed 24 October 2018.

McKinsey (2015). 'Sourcing in a volatile world—The East Africa opportunity'. Apparel, McKinsey & Co, Fashion & Luxury Group. Available from www.mckinsey.com/Sourcing_in_a_volatile_world_The_East_Africa_Opportunity.pdf, accessed 22 September 2015.

Mamdani, M. (1976). *Politics and Class in Uganda*. London: Heineman.

Mathias, P. (1969). *First Industrial Nation: An Economic History of Britain 1700–1814*. London: Methuen.

Mayer, F. and Gereffi, G. (2010). 'Regulation and economic globalization: Prospects and limits of private governance', *Business and Politics* 12/3: 1–25.

Media Club (2015). 'South Africa's economy: Key sectors'. Available at www.mediaclub%20southafrica.com/economy/37-economy/economy-bg/111-sa-economy-key-sectors, accessed 9 January 2020.

Meredith, M. (2006). *The State of Africa: A History of 50 years of Independence*. London: Free Press.

Milberg, W., Jiang, X., and Gereffi, G. (2014). *Industrial Policy in the Era of Vertically Specialized Industrialisation*. Available at www.ilo.org/wcmsp5/groups/public/%97dgreports/%97inst/documents/publication/wcms_315670.pdf, accessed 31 January 2016.

Morris, M. and Barnes, J. (2009). 'Globalisation, the changed global dynamics of the clothing and textile value chains and the impact on Sub-Saharan Africa'. Working paper No. 10, UNIDO Research and Statistics branch, UNIDO, Vienna.

Morris, M, Staritz, C., and Barnes, J. (2011). 'Value chain dynamics, local embeddedness, and upgrading in the clothing sectors of Lesotho and Swaziland', *International Journal of Technological Learning, Innovation and Development* 4/1–3: 96–119.

Morris, M., Plank, L., and Staritz, C. (2015). 'Regionalism, end markets and ownership matter: Shifting dynamics in the apparel export industry in Sub Saharan Africa', *Environment and Planning A* 0/0: 1–22.

Moseley, W.G. (2008). 'Mali's cotton conundrum: commodity production and development on the periphery', in W.G. Moseley and L.C. Gray (eds) *Hanging by a Thread*. Athens, OH: Ohio University Press, 83–102.

Nayenga, P. (1981). 'Commercial cotton growing in Busoga District, Uganda, 1905–1923', *African Economic History* 10: 175–95.

Neilson, J. and Pritchard, B. (2009). *Value Chain Struggles, Institutions and Governance in the Plantation Districts of South India*. Hoboken, NJ: Wiley-Blackwell.

New Vision (2014). 'Textile manufacturers want the national textile policy implemented'. Available at www.newvision.co.ug/new_vision/news/1315501/textile-manufacturers-national-textile-policy-implemented#sthash.RenOlA9f.dpuf, accessed 24 October 2018.

North, D.C. (1990*). Institutions, Institutional Change and Economic Performance*. St Louis, MO: Washington University in St Louis Press.

Obwana, M., Shinyekwa, I., Kiiza, J., and Hisali, E. (2013), 'The evolution of industry in Uganda, Learning to Compete'. Working paper No. 9. Washington, DC: Brookings Institute.

OECD (Organisation for Economic Co-operation and Development) (2013). *Aid for Trade and Value Chains in Textiles and Apparel*. Paris: OECD, WTO, IDE-JETRO.

Okereke, O. (1968). 'The place of marketing co-operatives in the economy of Uganda'. Makerere University, Faculty of Agriculture, Department of Rural Economy and Extension.

Onyeiwu, S. (2000). 'Deceived by African cotton: The British Cotton Growing Association and the demise of the Lancashire textile industry', *African Economic History* 28: 89–121.

Organic Exchange (2009). *Farm and Fibre Report 2009*. Organic Exchange. Available at http://farmhub.textileexchange.org/upload/library/Farm%20and%20fiber%20report/Farm_Fiber%202009%20-%20Executive%20Summary_final.pdf, accessed 30 November 2015.

Palpacuer, F. (2008). 'Bringing the social context back in: governance and wealth distribution in global commodity chains', *Economy & Society* 37/3: 393–419.

Peltzer, R. and Röttger, D. (2013). 'Cotton sector organisation models and their impact on farmer's productivity and income'. Discussion Paper 4/2013, Deutsches Institut für Entwicklungspolitik, Bonn.

Pray, C.E., Ma., D., Huang, J., and Qiao, F. (2001). 'The impact of Bt cotton in China', *World Development* 29/5: 813–25.

Riello, G. (2013). *Cotton: The Fabric that Made the Modern World*. Cambridge: Cambridge University Press.

Rivoli, P. (2015). *The Travels of a T-Shirt in the Global Economy*. Hoboken, NJ: Wiley.

Ryan, O. (2004). 'Ugandan firms struggle despite US deal', BBC News, 4 July. Available at http://news.bbc.co.uk/1/hi/business/3857573.stm, accessed 23 October 2018.

SACTWU (Southern African Clothing and Textile Workers Union) (2015). 'A turnaround for South Africa's textile industry?' Industrial Global Union. Available at www.industriall-union.org/a-turnaround-for-south-africas-textile-industry, accessed 24 October 2018.

SASTAC (South African Sustainable Textile and Apparel Cluster) (2014). 'Presentation to 73rd Plenary of the International Cotton Advisory Committee', November, Thessaloniki. Available at www.icac.org/getattachment/mtgs/Plenary/73rd-Plenary/Agenda/OS1-Schultz-De-Wet.pdf, 16 November 2015.

Schnurr, M. (2012). 'Inventing Makhathini: creating the prototype for the dissemination of genetically modified crops into Africa', *Geoforum* 43/4: 784–92.

Sidebottom, R.I. (2017). 'How do market actors manage the "rules of the game" in the cotton textiles & apparel sector?'. PhD thesis. Cambridge: University of Cambridge.

Smale, M., Zambrano, P., Gruere, G., Falck-Zepeda, J., Matuschke, I., Horna, D. et al. (2009). 'Measuring the economic impacts of transgeneric crops in developing agriculture during the first decade. Approaches, findings and future directions'. Food Policy Review 10, International Food Policy Research Institute.

Staritz, C. (2012). 'Apparel exports—still a path for industrial development? Dynamics in apparel global value chains and implications for low-income countries'. Working Paper No. 34. Austrian Foundation for Development Research (ÖFSE).

Staritz, C. and Frederick, S. (2014). 'Sector case study: Apparel', in T. Farole and D. Winkler (eds) *Making Foreign Direct Investment Work for Sub-Saharan Africa: Local Spillovers and Competitiveness in Global Value Chains*. Washington, DC: World Bank, Chap. 7, 209–44. Available at https://openknowledge.worldbank.org/bitstream/handle/10986/16390/9781464801266.pdf?sequence=1, accessed 24 October 2018.

Staritz, C. and Tröster, B. (2015). 'Cotton-based development in Sub-Saharan Africa? Global commodity chains, national market structure and development outcomes in Burkina Faso, Mozambique and Tanzania'. Working Paper No. 54, Austrian Foundation for Development Research (ÖFSE).

Stone, G.D. (2010). 'The anthropology of genetically modified crops', *Annual Review of Anthropology* 39: 381–400.

Stone, G.D. (2011). 'Field versus farm in Warangal: Bt cotton, higher yields and larger questions', *World Development* 39/3: 387–98.

Sumberg, J., Anyidoho, N.A., Chasukwa, M., Chinsinga, B., Leavy, J., Tadele, G. et al. (2014). 'Young people, agriculture and employment in rural Africa'. WIDER Working Paper 2014/080, United Nations University. Available at www.wider.unu.edu, accessed 23 November 2018.

Texfed (Textile Federation of South Africa) (2007). 'Current trading environment 2007'. Available at www.texfed.co.za/, accessed 24 October 2018.

Tokatli, N. (2013). 'Toward a better understanding of the apparel industry: A critique of the upgrading literature', *Journal of Economic Geography* 13/6: 993–1011.

Townsend, T. (2009). 'Empowering producers—An initiative to improve all cotton production', in K. Buckingham, G. Henley, and L. Yiping (eds) *Certification of Commodities: Opportunities and Challenges for the Rural Poor*. Proceedings of the ICB-CFC International Certification workshop, Beijing, April. Available at www.academia.edu/9028243/Certification_of_Commodities_Opportunities_and_Challenges_for_the_Rural_Poor, accessed 24 October 2018.

Townsend, T. (2013). 'World fibre production'. ICAC Presentation to 1st International Natural Fibre Conference, Guimaraes, Portugal, 9–11 June.

UEMOA (The West African Economic and Monetary Union) (2014). 'The white gold from West Africa conquering the world market'. Available at www.afcot.org/west-african-cotton/the-white-gold-from-africa.html, accessed 24 October 2018.

Uganda (2009). Government of Uganda, National Textile Policy. Available at www.mtic.go.ug/wp-content/uploads/2019/08/National-Textile-Policy.pdf, accessed 9 January 2020.

Uganda (2013). National Planning Authority, Government of Uganda, Uganda Vision 2040. Available at www.gou.go.ug/content/uganda-vision-2040, accessed 9 January 2020.

UNCTAD (United Nations Conference on Trade and Development) (2015). Available at http://unctad.org/en/Pages/Statistics.aspx, accessed 24 October 2018.

UNIDO (United Nations Industrial Development Organizations) (2011). *Feasibility Study for a Cotton Spinning Mill in 11 Sub-Saharan Countries.* Vienna: UNIDO.

USAID (2006). 'Adding value to West African cotton, assessment of cotton-textile apparel value chain'. WATH/ACCRA Technical Report No. 21, West Africa Trade Hub, December, 2006.

World Bank (1970). International Bank for Reconstruction & Development, International Development Association, West Volta Cotton Project, Upper Volta, Report No. PA-58a.

World Bank (2015a). World Bank database. Available at data.worldbank.org, accessed 24 October 2018.

World Bank (2015b). World Bank, South Africa Country overview. Available at www.worldbank.org/en/country/southafrica/overview, accessed 24 October 2018.

Wrigley, C.C. (1959). *Crops and Wealth in Uganda.* East African Studies No. 12. Kampala: East African School of Research.

WTO (World Trade Organization) (2015). World Trade Organization website database. Available at www.wto.org/english/res_e/statis_e/statis_e.htm, accessed 9 January 2020.

Yafa, S. (2005). *Cotton: The Biography of a Revolutionary Fibre.* New York: Penguin.

Yamagata, T. (1998). 'Ineffective protection, weak linkage and poor performance: the Philippine & Thai textile industries', in M. Kagami, J. Humphery, and M. Piore (eds) *Learning, Liberalization and Economic Adjustment.* Tokyo: Institute of Developing Economies, 33–59.

Youé, C.P. (1978). 'Peasants, planters and cotton capitalists: The "dual economy" in colonial Uganda', *Canadian Journal of African Studies* 12/2: 163–84.

Part III

Social Development Challenges and Perspectives

14 Publicness and human development

An illustration from BRICS

Flavio Comim

Introduction

The quest for human development[1] seems to be intrinsically associated with the provision of public goods, from the most tangible ones, such as health and education, to the most intangible such as a public framework of thought (Sen 2009) or the stability of a society's political culture (Nussbaum 2013). Quite often international organizations[2] present in their regular reports a 'parade of failures' of public goods provisions with their respective negative impacts. It is noticeable how they often avoid delving into the causes of these failures. This is a question particularly important for the group of countries known as BRICS because they all face dramatic challenges in the provision of public goods that are directly relevant for over 40 per cent of the world's population.

But why are some countries fair providers of public goods whereas others are much below any minimum standards?[3] More concretely, why do some countries have decent health and education systems, comprehensive welfare programmes, progressive taxation, fair institutions, and a wide range of public goods while others do not?[4] Specific answers

[1] A basic assumption of this chapter is that the capability approach is the main conceptual foundation of the human development perspective. This is substantiated from early contributions by Mahbub ul Haq (1999), Streeten (1995) to recent ones such as the *Human Development Report* (UNDP 2010). The tensions between these two perspectives are not examined here.

[2] We could mention here the most well-known regular reports such as UNDP's *Human Development Reports*, or UNICEF's *The State of the World's Children*, or UNESCO's *Education for All* reports. These are simply some illustrations.

[3] We can find a rich array of distinguished answers to this question in the economic literature such as Mancur Olson's *The Logic of Collective Action* or Elinor Ostrom's *Governing the Commons*. Considering their focus on institutions and the utilitarian basis, there is nothing wrong with their answers. Nevertheless, here we try a different answer within a human development perspective.

[4] We do not assume a complete ordering, neither a full dominance relation between this nor any other set of development issues/variables. In fact, in the last Human Development Report, Japan was the country with the highest life expectancy, Germany with the highest number of average years of study after twenty-five years, Australia had the highest expectancy at school, and Qatar had the highest gross national income (GNI) per capita in the list, whereas Norway was top of the overall ranking.

Flavio Comim, *Publicness and human development: An illustration from BRICS* In: *Handbook of BRICS and Emerging Economies.* Edited by: P.B. Anand, Shailaja Fennell, and Flavio Comim, Oxford University Press (2021).
DOI: 10.1093/oso/9780198827535.003.0014

to the problem of insufficient public goods should be searched in the social history of each particular country (and often for big countries, as in the case of BRICS, in the social history of their particular regions). Whereas different disciplines[5] will look for causes within their particular theories, here we simply explore one possible line of inquiry that follows from recent arguments by Amartya Sen and Martha Nussbaum about the concepts of public reason and public values. We suggest here that thinking about *publicness* can provide a general umbrella to tackle these issues within a human development perspective.

Publicness is far from being a consecrated concept in the human development or capability literature. Instead, it is common to find references to other expressions about 'public' such as 'public reason' or 'public reasoning', 'public values' and 'public goods'. It is important to examine the key concept of 'public reason' in Rawls and how it has been discussed by Sen and Nussbaum. However, a concrete concern of this chapter is how we can think more broadly in terms of publicness from a human development perspective.

Sen and Nussbaum's recent works on capabilities are based on different critiques of John Rawls's conceptions of public reason and reasonableness. Somehow, an assumption about our public values and how we think about the other is essential to talk about the structure of society and how its priorities, including its provision of public goods, are influenced by public values. On a regular basis, the provision of public goods does not work for the poor (World Bank 2004; Drèze and Sen 2013) and part of the problem is that often societies don't care for the voice of the vulnerable. Even when publicness makes its way through politics, if providers don't share this sense of care for the other, problems in the provision of public goods remain (Sen 1997; Comim and Amaral 2013).

In order to make this discussion more concrete, this chapter considers the context of BRICS in terms of the provision of public goods, defining three different levels of publicness. By doing so, it dialogues with what Nussbaum called 'the institutional side of political emotions' in societies that have been going through key economic and societal transformations (Nussbaum 2013). The public sphere of human development is easier to theorize than to see reflected in concrete indicators. For this reason we try to categorize publicness in levels as a strategy for looking for concrete indicators. With these questions and objectives in mind this chapter is divided into three sections: the first examines the issue of public goods and publicness in the promotion of human development and in Rawls; the second section addresses the problem of publicness in Sen's and Nussbaum's writings; and in the third section the chapter concludes with an illustration of public goods and publicness in BRICS.

[5] Economists have for a long time provided theoretical answers to the problem of under-provision of public goods, see for instance Samuelson (1954).

Public goods and human development

Concerns with the provision of public goods have been at centre stage in the history of development policies since the emergence of the 'social development' movement in the 1970s[6] (Arndt 1987; Rist 2008). However, it is interesting to note that after the twilight of the basic needs approach, not much emphasis was given to the notion of public goods and publicness in the new rhetoric put together by the human development paradigm and the capability approach. As Streeten (1995: 22) argued 'Human development is defined as the enlargement of choices, the presentation of options. Happiness cannot be delivered. But opportunities for exercising one's choices can.' While advocates of the new paradigm were very vocal in pointing out the shortcomings of economic growth as a development strategy (Haq 1999), they missed the importance of public goods for human development as if basic capabilities could be achieved without a public strategy, for instance, for better health and education outcomes.

Sen's discussion about public goods in his (1999) *Development as Freedom*, leaving ambiguous the issue of public provision of public goods, offers a good illustration of this lack of assertiveness of human development's advocates about the importance of public goods as a key ingredient of development.[7] Similarly, the argument put forward by Mahbub ul Haq that 'There is no automatic link between income and human lives' (Haq 1999: 14) became a mantra in human development reports at the expense of the concern about how states can deliver public goods.

A new vocabulary was introduced in the first *Human Development Report* in (UNDP) 1990 where references to 'human freedom', 'human choices', 'flourishing lives', 'basic human capabilities' populated a framework centred on proposals for fostering individual opportunities. In fact, none of the fifteen central conclusions and policy messages put forward by that report were dedicated to the importance of public goods and publicness. Quite the opposite—there was a critique of the basic needs approach for focusing on the provision of public goods 'rather than on the issue of human choices' (UNDP 1990: 11). This does not mean that human development denied the need for public goods, but rather that it focused its attention on the promotion of human freedoms vis-à-vis economic growth and not on issues about public goods in shaping human development policies.

It is revealing for instance that in Gasper's (2004) authoritative account of human development, there are no references to the role of the state and the provision of public

[6] An important watershed between the 'development as growth' movement and the 'era of social objectives' was Robert McNamara's (then president of the World Bank) 1972 annual address to the board of governors on the theme of 'Social Equity and Economic Growth' (see Arndt 1987: 97).

[7] He first argues that (1999: 128) 'it can be shown that there may be a good case for the provisioning of public goods, going beyond what the private markets would foster' but after considering the advantages of the public provision of services such as basic education he argues that (1999: 129) 'While these considerations provide good grounds for public expenditure in the areas crucial for economic development and social change, there are contrary arguments that must also be considered in the [1999: 130] same context', referring to budget deficits, inflation, and perverse incentives.

goods in promoting human capabilities.[8] Human development's overwhelming focus on the promotion of individual agency crowded out a more systematic concern with the state and public goods. Recent contributions, such as Ibrahim and Tiwari (2014) provide good examples about how the human development perspective and the capability approach use a language that is almost self-referential where there is no scope for systematic references to the role of public goods and the state.[9]

It is interesting to observe that *prima facie* the category of public goods, despite its importance as the potential 'source' of many 'basic capabilities' does not sit well with the human development perspective for two opposing reasons. On the one hand, this category seems to be too much about 'resources' and too broad to accommodate concepts based on individual advantage such as agency, autonomy, human freedom, and human flourishing, among others. The existence or not of 'group capabilities' (Stewart 2005) or 'social capabilities' (Comim 2008) is part of an ongoing debate that ultimately refers to intrinsic characteristics of societies such as their level of trust, public goods, and cooperation[10] that are ignored as ends in the capability informational space. Therefore, public goods were seen as instrumental, rather than having any intrinsic value.

On the other hand, the category of public goods seemed to be too narrow to articulate the overall challenges brought by public reason and publicness that emerged from the capability literature. Issues about 'open vs closed impartiality' (Sen 2009) or 'political emotions' (Nussbaum 2013) are clearly issues that transcend the mere provision of public goods and refer to moral characteristics embedded in the general structure of societies. It is important to explore the links between public goods and publicness in much more depth, but before trying that, it is relevant to make a (brief) case for the importance of public goods for human development.

International agencies constantly refer to the importance of public goods for development. For instance, in its *World Development Report*, the World Bank (2004) argues that 'growth is not enough' (2004: 35) for achieving Millennium Development Goals (MDGs) and that 'For basic services in education, health, and infrastructure to work for poor people, governments have to be involved' (2004: 180). Similarly, UNIDO (2008: 1) put quite boldly that 'The provision of public goods is a key element of the quality of life and environmental sustainability.' Kaul et al. (1999: 9) expand the scope of public goods

[8] According to Yusuf and Stiglitz (2001: 233), 'Of the major issues of the past half-century, the role of the state has been among the most contentious.'

[9] Hardin explains that economists have contributed to three categories of explanatory theories of the state and according to him the theory of public goods is (1997: 21) 'the best known . . . and the most extensively articulated'.

[10] Sen (2009) argues that groups don't think as individuals and that (2009: 246) 'Ultimately, it is individual valuation on which we would have to draw, while recognizing the profound interdependence of the valuations of individuals who interact with each other.' However, there is an important conceptual difference, raised by Arrow (2012 [1951]: 18) between 'tastes' (based on individual preferences) and 'values' (about general standards of equity) that shows how individuals' judgements about their particular well-being can be different from their judgements about society. So, individuals can think about their individual or social capabilities.

by noting that 'today international, and particularly global, public goods are becoming more central to national and individual well-being'. It is common to find remarks such as that of Paul et al. (2006: 31) that 'The absence or inadequacy of basic services is a major dimension of poverty experienced by poor people across the world'. Drèze and Sen (2013: 33) echoed this principle, arguing that 'well-functioning public services can make a big difference to people's lives'. On the same line, they refer to (2013: 37) 'the solid rock of support of basic public health facilities that has been the basis of almost every successful health transition in the history of the world'.

Woodward and Smith (2003: 8) see public goods as 'goods exhibiting a significant degree of publicness',[11] but for them publicness refers to non-excludability and non-rivalry as in the mainstream analysis of public goods. This does not seem to be the case for the human development perspective that discusses publicness as part of a set of values and moral sentiments that characterize how citizens speak and treat each other.[12] It is important to elaborate on this conceptual difference and Figure 14.1 provides an illustration[13] of how we can better see the relationship between publicness and public goods within a human development perspective.

From a purely utilitarian perspective, the quality in the provision of public goods is related to solutions to collective action problems that can result from self-interested behaviour such as public bureaucracy, interest groups and political business cycles, or problems such as corruption. But from a human development perspective the problem seems to be related to value systems shaped by economic and social inequalities, social norms, political engagement of different social groups, the role of the media, institutionalization of human rights, restraints on democratic governance, taxation regimes, and other issues related to how societies define their public priorities.

In other words, the visible problem of the provision of public goods, so squarely treated under utilitarian ethics mostly as a function of economic features of the goods themselves (within self-interested motivations), becomes within human development a deeper and more complex issue about how publicness can be defined (and built) in each particular society. If public goods don't prominently appear in human development discussions as a separate category it is because the place of publicness within the capability approach is disputed at a different level. The main issue seems to be not how to improve the provision of public goods per se but what are the main reasons and justifications for the provision in the first place. In order to tackle this problem we should initially acknowledge that much of what we call human development theory is built on critiques of John Rawls's work on justice and public reason.

[11] Their emphasis is on the issue of global public goods and how these goods have publicness across national boundaries.

[12] This is not a homogenous view. As discussed below there are important differences about how Rawls, Sen and Nussbaum see publicness and the role of public reason in the promotion of justice.

[13] Iceberg models are often used in systems thinking to highlight the importance of underlying structures that explain complex phenomena.

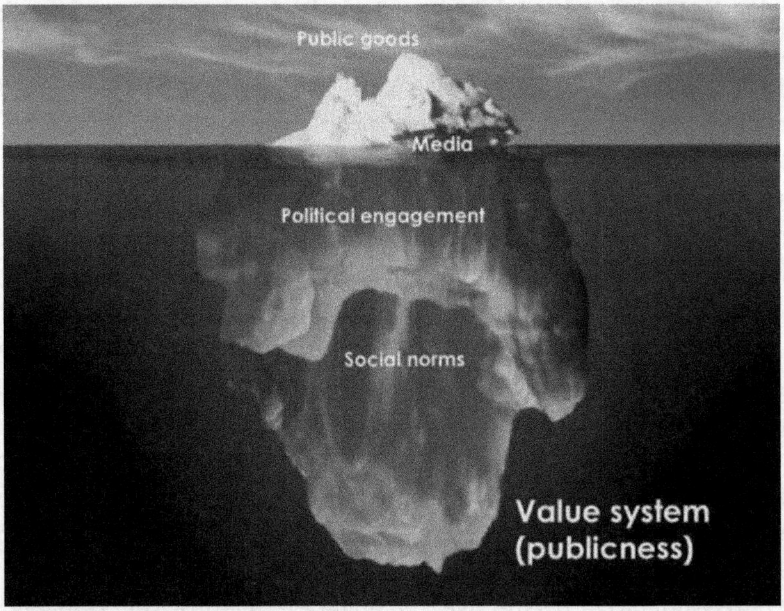

Figure 14.1 Publicness and public goods

Source: Author's work.

One of the theoretical challenges faced by Rawls's later work was to find justification for public agreement on how institutions should work for equality and democracy. As he boldly remarked (2001: 2–3), 'the members of any civilized society need a conception that enables them to understand themselves as members having a certain political status'. One is tempted to replace 'developed' for 'civilized' but it would certainly make more sense to do the reverse. Rawls finds this conception in the notion of reciprocity or mutuality and explains how people with moral powers will support public reason. However, as Newman (2015: xxi) puts it, 'Rawls's psychology is inadequate to his task; he cannot explain how or why citizens would ever become committed to public reason.' Nussbaum (2013: 221) also criticizes Rawls's psychological account as 'highly abstract' because it does not specify how different sentiments (of love and friendship) can lead to a formation of general political principles. The critical issue is about Rawls's motivational account of people's morality and psychology.

The moral psychology that Rawls puts forward is structured around a sequential theory of moral development that starts with the morality of authority, mostly seen in children. In his words (Rawls 1971: 462), 'I assume that the sense of justice is acquired gradually by the younger members of society as they grow up.' This first stage would be followed by the morality of association when people would develop their capacity for fellow feeling and feelings of trust, confidence, and friendly feelings towards others[14] as a

[14] Rawls refers to three psychological laws. As he explains the move from the first to the second (1971: 470), 'Thus once a person's capacity for fellow feeling has been realized by his acquiring attachments in

result of those associations. Finally, people would evolve towards more complex forms of morality beyond friendship ties into a morality of principles. And this would take us to a common allegiance to justice. As he argues (1971: 474), 'We develop a desire to apply and to act upon the principles of justice once we realize how social arrangements answering to them have promoted our good and that of those with whom we are affiliated. In due course we come to appreciate the ideal of just human cooperation.' This morality of principles is important for explaining how individuals could move beyond the promotion of their own good towards notions of right, independently of people's contingencies. Whereas Rawls's theory of moral cognition has been considered as part of the development of individuals' moral grammar (Mikhail 2011), it remains open to the criticism of the 'liberal conundrum'.

On the one hand, if liberalism fully protects individuals' liberty of thought, it might exclude some that advocate unreasonable comprehensive doctrines for society. On the other hand, it if tries to educate or 'nudge' people towards civic virtue, it might undermine individuals' freedom. How can a 'decent society' promote a morality of justice without becoming 'illiberal and dictatorial'?[15] The broader 'problem of political liberalism' as discussed by Rawls (1993) changes the focus of discussion from further elaborations of a psychology of public reason to justification of a political conception of justice. But the problem about how people operate in moral realms and how they share (or not) commitments and beliefs about the importance of reciprocity and publicness in political life does not go away.

What is the relevance of 'the liberal conundrum' to human development? It seems that the main issue about the provision of public goods is ultimately, intimately related to the issues of publicness and public reason. If public reason, as Newman (2015: 11) suggests 'represents a set of dispositions, values, and commitments that guide the way citizens speak with one another' centred on the idea of reciprocity, it constitutes indeed an essential element in understanding how individuals in different societies treat each other with equal moral worth and respect. What we call here publicness is *prima facie* nothing but how individuals care for each other in their narrower or broader societies. It is necessary that we scrutinize this concept to better define its meaning.

Development as publicness

Rawls introduces in *A Theory of Justice* the concept of 'publicity' meaning first (1971: 16) 'a knowledge of the principles that others follow'. This original notion limited to the idea of common knowledge was further expanded on in *Political Liberalism* (1993) to include

accordance with the first psychological law, then as his associates with evident intention live up to their duties and obligations, he develops friendly feelings toward them, together with feelings of trust and confidence. And this principle is a second psychological law.'

[15] Exactly this question is put forward by Nussbaum in her *Political Emotions* (2013: 5).

a level of 'justification' of a public conception of justice that comprises a commonly shared *and* justified point of view.[16] What lies behind this concept is the idea of reciprocity based on people showing mutual respect. This means that in a liberal society individuals do not need to agree with each other's comprehensive doctrines nor that they have to hide their beliefs under a common point of view. Rather, they adjudicate disagreements by openly arguing in favour of their convictions in terms that others could potentially agree. This dimension of 'reasoning together' is essential for Rawls's argument for public reason that justifies the role of mutual respect and cooperation in 'a well-ordered society'.

But the concept of public reason should not be thought of as a broad church. Larmore (2003: 381) notes that 'Political debate rightly shows a greater mix of voices in areas of society other than the circumscribed realm of public reason, and it would be wrong to suppose that Rawls's theory of public reason means to encompass the "public sphere" in this broader sense.' Rawls in his *Justice as Fairness* emphasizes that the idea of public reason should be left to matters of (2001: 91) 'constitutional essentials and questions of basic justice', discarding issues of 'tax legislation', 'environmental legislation', and 'laws regulating property' among others. The basic separation here is between a 'constitutional stage' vis-à-vis a 'legislative stage' in Rawls's model. The main debate is not about public vs non-public reasons but about giving priority to constitutions in capturing publicly based values in society.

If we wish to apply Rawls's concepts of publicity and public reason to the domain of human development, it seems that we need a broader understanding of mutual respect, reciprocity, justification, and shared principles that is not restricted to a constitutional stage. We need a concept, such as publicness, that can include processes in which citizens can arrive at binding decisions at the same time that it can encompass 'background culture' discussions. It is common to find Rawls using the concepts of 'reasonableness' and 'reciprocity' as a way to circumvent the limited scope given to the concept of public reason. But before trying to elaborate on the concept of publicness, it is important that we examine what the founders of the capability approach, Amartya Sen and Martha Nussbaum, wrote about the issue of public reason in Rawls and what are the possible ways forward they see in overcoming its limitations.

A complete survey of what Sen and Nussbaum have said about public reason would go a long way beyond the purpose of this chapter. However, it is important to register some key arguments that can be found in their latest work, such as Sen's *Idea of Justice* (2009) and Nussbaum's (2013) *Political Emotions* against Rawls's theory. For those who might think that Sen bases his theory merely on feelings of injustice, he argues that (2009: viii) 'A sense of injustice could serve as a signal that moves us, but a signal does demand critical examination, and there has to be some scrutiny of the soundness of a conclusion

[16] Rawls introduces the 'full publicity condition' that has three levels, namely (1993: 66–7) public knowledge, general beliefs about human nature and the way social and political institutions work, and full justification.

based mainly on signals'. Sen is concerned with the characteristics of appropriate critical reasoned scrutiny and some irreducibility that can remain in conflicting arguments. Thus, he maintains Rawls's valuational plurality but within a different framework that he calls 'social realisations' or 'realisation-focused'.

Sen gives more emphasis to some key characteristics of public reasoning such as the issues of impartiality[17] and objectivity[18] than to the definition of 'reasonable persons'.[19] By doing so, he seems more concerned with informational issues on how different arguments can survive objective reasoned scrutiny rather than on changing people's moral sentiments. As he puts it (2009: 48) 'To prevent catastrophes caused by human negligence or callous obduracy, we need critical scrutiny, not just goodwill towards others.' Thus, it is clear that Sen's emphasis on public reason is about its aspect of 'good reasoning' without assuming any kind of change in individuals' public emotions (as can be seen in Nussbaum's work).

Sen's interpretation of Rawls's notion of fairness (as a demand for impartiality) frees him from examining the existence or not of reasonable behaviour as a precondition for public reason.[20] Sen criticizes Rawls for not being 'realistic' (2009: 81) in assuming that once institutions are in place individuals would behave reasonably. He concludes this discussion arguing that (2009: 81) 'Demanding more from behaviour today than could be expected to be fulfilled would not be a good way of advancing the cause of justice.' Sen highlights the relevance of a non-mechanical 'framework for public reasoning' that can focus on issues that really matter to people, such as poverty, hunger, illiteracy, medical care, discrimination, torture, etc.

His arguments for using social choice theory as a framework for public reasoning do not depend on any criteria about reasonable values, instead they delve into informational limitations that come with a complete theory of justice, such as Rawls's. Thus, Sen engages with Rawls's earlier version of publicly *shared knowledge* (that is necessary for shared understanding and communication) and his later characteristic of *justification* in *Political Liberalism* but not to the psychological and moral principles that are necessary to produce and give some stability to public reason itself. But if, as Sen argues (2009: 129), 'justice is partly a relation in which ideas of obligation to each other are important'

[17] Sen (2009: 123) focuses on impartial judgements that are necessary to avoid parochial bias in assessments. As he puts it (2009: 123), 'The place of impartiality in the evaluation of social justice and societal arrangements is central to the understanding of justice, seen from this perspective.'

[18] He uses the discipline of social choice and its methodology of ranking of alternatives to talk about how people can arrive at refined values and priorities.

[19] Sen (2009: 43) argues that 'all of us are capable of being reasonable through being open-minded about welcoming information and through reflecting on arguments coming from different quarters, along with undertaking interactive deliberations and debates on how the underlying issues should be seen'.

[20] Sen (2009: 68) argues that 'The unanimous choice of the principles of justice is ground enough, Rawls argues, for their forming a "political conception" of justice that all accept, but that acceptance may still be a far cry from the actual patterns of behavior that emerge in any actual society with those institutions. Since no one has argued more powerfully and more elaborately than John Rawls for the need for "reasonable" behavior by individuals for a society to function well, he is clearly very aware of the difficulty in presuming any kind of spontaneous emergence of universal reasonable behavior on the part of all members of a society.'

how can we think about the ways in which we consider the others without fully addressing how values of reciprocity and recognition of each other's equal moral worth are formed? At Sen's hands this becomes a cognitive challenge about open impartiality and objectivity. There is indeed a key question of 'motivational adequacy' between Rawls's and Sen's frameworks that needs to be scrutinized. Sen considers that one's objectives can go well beyond one's self-interest but he prefers to focus on a pluralism of reasons[21] without settling for any specific motivating moral sentiment.[22] There is nothing irrational in someone being concerned with others, but at the same time for Sen it would be difficult to argue that there is some obligation to do so.

In this sense the criterion of reasonableness is too demanding for Sen. His concern is that the condition of publicity applied to reasonableness could lead to commonality and uniqueness in thinking, which would be unacceptable. Instead, Sen prefers to focus on the issue of responsibility and cooperation, leaving open the possibility of a plural justification of reasonable behaviour (either based on self-interested mutual cooperation or on feelings of responsibility and duty towards others) rather than settling for a particular version. It is for this reason that Sen avoids laying down any blueprint for dealing with informational trade-offs. This does not mean that people should be passive recipients of development programmes, but instead that they should have an active role in exercising their abilities of participation, duty, obligation, reasoning, evaluation, agency,[23] and choice. So, by using the concept of 'agency' Sen builds a framework that has a plurality of motivations (reasonableness can be one of them, but not 'the' one) rather than settling with one specific notion of reasonableness or reciprocity as the bases of individuals' sense of values. The forcefulness of Sen's argument depends on the need for shared human values for achieving certain kinds of public reasoning that are conducive to just arrangements.

Nevertheless, when Sen addresses the issue of the recognition of human rights he considers a broad range of alternatives, such as legislation, media exposure, public debates, and agitation. He argues that sometimes the protection of a human right can be sought (2009: 365) 'through the influence of education and public discussion on civility and social conduct'. Human rights can be different from other freedoms because they should satisfy some 'threshold condition of relevance'. The main mechanism however through which these thresholds can be settled is impartial scrutiny.

[21] For instance, there is an interesting debate about whether our national identity has any role to play in developing our sense of duty and concern towards fellow human beings (see Sen 2009: 142–3 and Nussbaum 2013: 10 who argue that the human mind is particularistic and that there is role for nation states to raise our concern with other human beings).

[22] He acknowledges that 'if one is committed, say, to doing what can be done to remove the misery of others –whether or not one's own welfare is affected by it, and not merely to the extent to which one's own welfare is so influenced –then that *is* a clear departure from self-interested behavior'. This is an old topic in Sen's analysis going back to the days of 'Rational Fools' and his work on 'The Impossibility of the Paretian Liberal'.

[23] Sen's concept of agency, as he explains (2009: 287) 'encompasses all the goals that a person has reasons to adopt'.

Moral sentiments, such as frustration and ire can provide a starting point but they need reasoned scrutiny for understanding with impartiality and objectivity the grounds for the indignation against injustices. Public reason should coexist with non-commensurability and with ways of publicity solving trade-offs. Sen argues that (2009: 395) 'Judgements about justice have to take on board the task of accommodating different kinds of reasons and evaluative concerns.' For him public reason needs judgement, in particular through impartial reasoning that can help people handle their vested interests and preconceptions.

Nussbaum disputes that the ideas of agreement and justifiability can sustain a minimum notion of the good necessary for a theory of justice. In particular, she criticizes Rawls's contractarianism for having a very narrow moral psychology that excludes motivations such as compassion, sympathy, or benevolence (2006: 108, 148, 158). She advocates in her capabilities approach a *shared public conception* of the person[24] in which she proposes to replace Rawls's idea of mutual advantage by an idea of equal[25] human dignity within a 'richer and moralized account of the good' (2006: 163). Her argument is that people's notions of the good should include other people, not because they should feel better when doing charity or because they will have some form of advantage in caring for them. Her point is that respecting each other's dignity is a question of our love of others. As she argues (2006: 222), to create a decent society, 'It can only be out of our attachment to justice and our love of others, our sense that our lives are intertwined with theirs and that we share ends with them.' The dispute here seems to be about what are the 'deepest and most basic of our moral judgments and intuitions', as often Nussbaum refers to it.

This does not imply that people should all have the same values. Quite the opposite; a certain bifurcation between individuals' ethical principles and the principles they endorse is necessary for the political sphere to avoid dictatorial regimes. As she argues (2013: 382–3), 'Political emotions are the real emotions of real people; because people are heterogeneous, having different opinions, histories, and personalities, they can be expected to love, mourn, laugh, and strive for justice in specific and personal ways – particularly if their freedom of expression is protected and valued, as it is here.' The route she chooses is to discuss the 'malleability of the moral sentiments' and how it is possible to cultivate, within the limits of liberalism, individuals' emotional life towards others. So, she engages in a pedagogical discussion that ultimately tries to explain the conditions

[24] The point is about what should count as someone's good. In her words (2006: 158): 'The person leaves the state of nature not because it is more mutually advantageous to make a deal with others, but because she cannot imagine living well without shared ends and a shared life. Living with and toward others, with both benevolence and justice, is part of the shared public conception of the person that all affirm for political purposes.'

[25] She emphasizes the role of equality as a political value in itself. In her words (2006: 295), 'For the capabilities approach, at any rate, equality is important at the very base of the theory; for it is not just human dignity that must be respected, it is equal human dignity.' That applies to those capabilities that are more directly related to human dignity (2006: 381).

that could shape individuals' commitment to public reason (a question much emphasized by Newman 2015).

Nussbaum dedicates an entire book, her *Political Emotions*, to tackle this issue. Her argument is straightforward: decent societies should cultivate public emotions and (2013: 15) 'all of the core emotions that sustain a decent society [which] have their roots in, or are forms of, love'. Whereas a large part of her book offers a comparative analysis between liberal and illiberal ways of pursuing this target, her main thesis is about the importance of public emotions to the justification of principles of justice.[26] The issue, going back to Rawls's account, as she puts it (2013: 9) is that 'Rawls is proposing a society of human beings, not angels, and he knows well that human beings do not automatically pursue the common good.' One might wonder how self-interested people could care for the common good. It is tempting to think about alternatives such as the promotion of 'civic love' for fostering the common good, but she warns us of the risks of imposing feelings of obedience, hierarchy, and homogeneity in promoting civic love.

Thus, she goes back to Mozart, Tagore, and Mill to examine ways in which appropriate moral sentiments of general sympathy, equal respect, toleration, fellow feeling, and deeper emotions, such as compassion and altruism can be promoted. It is true that some violations of core political values, such as racial discrimination, should not be tolerated and laws against them should be coercively enforced, but the focus of her proposals is on educating people and cultivating their emotions within the liberal tradition. She does not seem to agree with Sen's approach that suggests that through impartiality and objectivity people can achieve a sort of reasonable behaviour. The 'justification path' of public reason does not seem sufficient for Nussbaum. She is quite clear about this point when she argues that (2013: 261) 'Rational deduction alone will not tell us whether women are full-fledged human beings, or whether rape really hurts.'[27]

According to Nussbaum, reason or even respect[28] are not enough to connect people, differently from emotions.[29] Only through emotions, she argues, can individuals examine their lives and connect with each other, having a sense of a common fate (2013: 345). The implication of this argument is quite dramatic for human development: development should contain beyond what Rawls and Sen have suggested is a clear set of ideas

[26] She argues that our minds are 'particularistic' and that our emotions depend on the connections we have with people who belong to our 'circle of concern'.

[27] As she also argues (2013: 320), 'The idea is, instead, that the public culture cannot be tepid and passionless, if good principles and institutions are to survive: it must have enough episodes of inclusive love, enough poetry and music, enough access to a spirit of affection and play, that people's attitudes to one another and the nation they inhabit are not mere dead routine.'

[28] The cultivation of public emotions is key for her understanding of a just society. The arguments based on justification don't seem strong enough to produce the bonds that she assumes are necessary for producing justice. When she talks about respect she argues that (2013: 380), 'Respect on its own is cold and inert, insufficient to overcome the bad tendencies that lead human beings to tyrannize over one another.'

[29] This argument has Aristotelian roots. As she argues (2013: 289), 'If people talk without tapping into their emotions, they often don't really understand the depth of the problem, or communicate their full thinking to others.'

about what is good and bad. Her point is that there is nothing illiberal about this explicit morality provided that dissent is protected.

In what follows we explore some empirical implications of the above discussion, trying first to organize in levels the different senses in which we can refer to the connections between the concepts of public goods, publicity, public reason, and public emotions under the general umbrella of publicness. We then search for an illustration with BRICS countries assuming that it is possible to read from their indicators different moral structures of concern and levels of publicness in their respective societies.

Publicness and human development

We need to widen the current definition of human development. In its iconic form, as it appears, already digested by Fukuda-Parr and Kumar (2003: xxi), it is 'an expansion of human capabilities, a widening of choices, an enhancement of freedoms and a fulfilment of human rights'. UNDP (2010: 2) goes on the same route, claiming that 'Human development is the expansion of people's freedom to live long, healthy and creative lives; to advance other goals they have reason to value; and to engage actively in shaping development equitably and sustainably on a shared planet.' As it is, this definition mentioned ad nauseam in human development reports brings the meaning of development half-baked without a proper reflection about the importance of publicness for achieving human development. It would be more precise to say that human development is about treating each other with dignity (this respects everyone's agency and at the same time acknowledges the importance of treating each other well). More specifically this definition implies that individuals are seen as ends in themselves (autonomous individuals) at the same time capable of public reason and public emotions.

At the root of Sen's and Nussbaum's accounts of human development we have to tackle Rawls's distinct concepts of publicity and public reason. These authors provided different answers to the problem of how we can understand public reason. Whereas Rawls's and Sen's answers follow the path of *justification* they differ in how they define impartiality. Nussbaum chooses a broader route disputing the 'soft' right to interfere in the content of individuals' moral sentiments. Sen's theory is flexible enough to accommodate a wide range of moral sentiments but it is against sponsoring a particular theory of the good as its source. The key point is that within this intellectual battlefield references to public reason are too specific to the analytical structure defined by Rawls. For this reason, in searching for more concrete alternatives for understanding the implications of public reason to real societies, we chose to define publicness as a broad notion concerning public values referring to a wide range of moral sentiments that sustain the moral structures of concern displayed by different societies.

It is common to find in the human development and capability literature the use of a wide range of expressions such as 'public access', 'public domain', 'public good', 'public interest',[30] among others that refer to causes or consequences of what could be named publicness. Indeed, there are at least three different levels in which we can understand the broad notion of publicness within a human development perspective. The first, and the most visible level of publicness, is the level of government's actions. Here, we can pay attention to how much of their budget governments allocate to health, education, and other public goods. Not simply the overall level matters but how public goods are distributed among different groups in society. For instance, in education, is government spending only funding education for the rich or is it targeting the poor? It can also be interesting to see how governments warrant or not some rights to people with corresponding legislation. This first level, inspired in the idea of primary goods, can be called the 'Rawlsian level of publicness'.

The second level of publicness follows from the human development caveat that resources are imperfect indicators of human well-being.[31] This is the traditional field of human development statistics, such as the Human Development Index (HDI), that focuses on outcomes, results, and impacts of public goods provisions. Publicness here refers to the results of actions often produced by national governments, but not only. There are many factors influencing these outcomes, not all of them attributable to governments' actions. In small countries, international organizations can have a decisive influence. But wars, the environment, and many other factors can make the exercise of attribution very difficult. Be that as it may, we can look at these outcome statistics as ways of assessing how capabilities are distributed among individuals in a certain society. Because this is the traditional HDI way of assessing human development, we can call this the 'Senian level of publicness'. This is not a perfectly accurate label given that Sen argues as well for participation, public reason, accountability, and democracy as essential elements of publicness, but it is the way inbuilt in the current definition of human development that is centred on the idea of individual freedoms.

Finally, the third level of publicness goes beyond the justification element of public reason focusing on motivational aspects of publicness. This level is quintessentially what can be called 'development as publicness' where the way that people treat each other (and how this is captured by institutions) is what matters. Here, we can look for evidence of publicness in civil society (homicides, traffic accidents, etc) as well as for a wide range of proactive governmental policies, such as the ones of public use of resources, redesign of public spaces, promotion of public culture, etc. Because this level is most closely associated with the work of Martha Nussbaum we call it the 'Nussbaumian level of publicness'. It follows from Nussbaum's (2013) proposal for seeing both motivational and institutional aspects of public emotions. The basic

[30] It could be mentioned, just as an illustration, that these expressions are all used in the articles edited by Wong and Dutfield (2011).

[31] This critique can be found often in Sen's works and before the *Idea of Justice*, this critique was the main objection against Rawls's *Theory of Justice*. It was a direct critique of the use of primary goods for well-being evaluations.

assumption, as Nussbaum summarizes it, is that (2013: 135) 'institutions themselves embody the insight of emotions'. So, we would expect that societies that care for their citizens would develop laws and particular institutions that would give shape to these feelings of care, compassion, and fairness that in their turn would be reflected on public spending and the provision of public goods[32] as well as in civil society's actions.

LEVEL 1—THE RAWLSIAN LEVEL OF PUBLICNESS

Quite often publicness is limited to what governments do. The running of governments is not a trivial matter, not only because of administrative challenges and the history of particular state institutions, but mostly because governments ultimately reflect a balance of power between different groups, producing outcomes that are a result of political priorities. But how important is publicness to the establishment of these priorities? Or, alternatively, how we can read countries' level of publicness based on what governments do?

Table 14.1 focuses on health and education public spending in BRICS. We can see that, as a rule India spends proportionally less in both public goods when compared to

Table 14.1 Level 1 publicness for BRICS countries

	India	South Africa	China	Brazil	Russia
Public expenditure on health, 2013					
As a proportion of total health expenditure (%)	30.04	48.23	55.79	46.03	52.2
As a proportion of GDP (%)	1.40	4.24	3.09	3.83	3.70
Per capita, PPP (constant 2011 international $)	267.41	1,148.37	730.52	1,318.17	1,835.71
Hospital beds (per 1,000 people), 2012	0.7	2.8[a]	3.8[d]	2.3	9.7[a]
Government expenditure on education as a proportion of GDP, 2013 (%)	3.84	6.03	n/a	5.99	3.86[c]
Government expenditure on education, total (% of government expenditure), 2013	14.09	19.13[b]	n/a	15.97	11.5
Government expenditure per student, primary (% of GDP per capita), 2013	9.77	17.62[b]	n/a	20.03	n/a
Government expenditure per student, secondary (% of GDP per capita), 2013	16.8	2089[c]	n/a	21.63	n/a
Government expenditure per student, tertiary (% of GDP per capita), 2013	49.15	37.74 [b]	n/a	29.50	14.25[e]

Notes: a 2005, b 2014, c 2012, d 2011, e 2008.
Source: World Development Indicators (World Bank various years).

[32] When publicness is filtered through institutions it can become more stable. As Nussbaum (2013: 135) argues 'So too with tax and welfare policies: they embody sympathy, but in a way that is more stable and less prone to special pleading than is sympathy in real life.'

other countries in the group. In particular, it is notable how India publicly spends only 1.4 per cent of its GDP on health. Similarly, it also spends much more proportionally on tertiary education than other countries in the group, which can be an indication that it caters to its elites more than to any other social group (this seems to be a common characteristic of BRICS). Sen (2009: 349) extrapolates these results to other areas, arguing that 'The relative weakness of Indian social policies on school education, basic healthcare, child nutrition, essential land reform and gender equity reflects deficiencies of politically engaged public reasoning and social pressure, not just inadequacies in the official thinking of the government.'

Nussbaum is much more up front about the role of the state than Drèze and Sen, when she argues for instance that (2006: 288) 'the state needs to take action if traditionally marginalized groups are to be treated fairly'. The whole question about the level 1 of publicness is about how we can read publicness from how governments allocate their resources. Although resources are imperfect indicators of human well-being they reflect values and priorities about what societies and governments consider more relevant. Table 14.1 suggests how BRICS are not very strong even in the first level of publicness. In any case, this measure is a very rough approximation of how governments reflect a balance of power and political priorities among distinct social groups.

LEVEL 2—THE SENIAN LEVEL OF PUBLICNESS

Publicness is also a matter of efficient and accountable delivery of public goods. In some countries government officials capture public resources, not allowing them to get to those most in need; the list of potential problems includes corruption, paternalism, administrative inefficiency, lack of administrative transparency, lack of accountability, lack of planning, etc. So, in the second level we look for evidence that governments have actually delivered (helped or not by other public initiatives) public goods that have changed the well-being of their populations. Here is the usual battlefield for human development statistics where GDP vs HDI are contrasted against each other and against a wide range of development statistics as illustrated by Table 14.2.

A quick analysis of BRICS numbers shows that there is a difference of more than eighty positions between the highest (Russia) and the lowest (India) HDI in the group and over four times their GDP per capita. However, these differences don't play too much on Russia's advantage in terms of male life expectancy when compared to India's and then in terms of immunization and the Programme for International Student Assessment (PISA) results when compared with China's. The health status of South Africans seems much more dramatic when compared with the other countries in the group, given that it presents the lowest life expectancy at birth for both men and women, and infant and under-5 mortality rates very close to the ones in

Table 14.2 Level 2 publicness for BRICS countries

	India	South Africa	China	Brazil	Russia
GDP per capita, PPP (constant 2011 international $), 2016	6,092	12,446	12,609	15,412	23,293
HDI ranking, 2015	131	119	90	79	49
Life expectancy at birth, 2015					
Male	66.8	58.5	74.6	71.6	65.4
Female	69.9	65	77.7	75.2	76.6
Infant mortality rate, 2016	34.6	34.2	8.5	13.5	6.6
Under-5 mortality rate, 2013	43	43.3	9.9	15.1[a]	7.7
Total fertility rate, 2015	2.35	2.48	1.62	1.74	1.75
Improved sanitation facilities (% of population with access), 2015	39.6	69.6	76.5	86.1	77
Undernourishment among children under-5, 2010–15 (%)					
Underweight	44	9	3	2	n/a
Stunted	38.7	24	9	7.1	n/a
Child immunization rates, 2016 (%)					
DPT	88	66	99	86	97
Measles	88	75	99	96	98
Prevalence of anaemia among children (% of children under 5), 2016	57.3	36.8	21.4	25.1	25.7
Prevalence of anaemia among pregnant women (%), 2016	50.1	28.1	32.4	37.3[a]	24
Mean years of schooling, age 25+, 2013	4.4	9.9	7.5	7.2	11.7
Literacy rate, age 15–24, 2014 (%)					
Male	88.41	98.7	99.7[b]	98.4	99.6[b]
Female	74.36[c]	99.3	99.6[b]	99.2	99.8[b]
Literacy rate, 2014					
Male	75.19[c]	95.4	97.48[b]	91.4	99.73[b]
Female	50.82[c]	93.4	92.71[b]	92	99.65[b]
PISA, 2015					
Mathematics	n/a	n/a	531[d]	377	494
Readings	n/a	n/a	494	407	495
Science	n/a	n/a	518	401	487
Repeaters, primary, total (% of total enrolment), 2013	5.02	n/a	0.15	8.75	0.37
Repeaters, secondary, total (% of total enrolment)	4.63	n/a	0.09	16.25	0.29
Poverty headcount ratio at $2 a day (PPP) (% of population), 2012–15	59.2	26.2	1.9	2	0
Income share held by lowest 20%, 2015	8.5	2.4	5.2	3.6	6.9
Income share held by highest 20%, 2015	42.8	69.9	47.1	56	45.3
Income share held by lowest 10%, 2015	3.7	1.05	2.0	1.1	2.8
Income share held by highest 10%, 2015	28.8	53.8	31.4	40.5	29.7

Notes: Countries are ranked in increasing order of GDP per capita. Poverty data for China is for 2013 and income shares for 2012.

Footnotes: a 2016, b 2010, c 2006, 2012, d data for China refer to students in Beijing-Shanghai-Jiangsu-Guangdong (BSJG).

Source: World Development Indicators (World Bank various years). Mean years of schooling from UNDP 2013; child undernutrition from UNICEF (2014).

Table 14.3 Level 3 publicness for BRICS countries

	India	South Africa	China	Brazil	Russia
Gini index, 2010–15	35.2	63.4	42.2	51.5	41.6
Homicide per 100,000 people, 2012–15	3.50	34.3	1.00	25.2	9.20
Road fatalities per 100,000 people, 2010	18.90	31.90	20.50	22.5	18.60
Road fatalities pedestrians, 2009/10 (%)	8.70	n/a	25.00	23.4	33.40
Number of jailed population per 100,000 people, 2012	30	316	123	275	528
Rule of law, 2015					
Property rights	55.0	50.0	20.0	50.0	20.0
Freedom from corruption	36.0	42.0	40.0	42.0	28.0
Progressivity of the tax structure (%)	37.7	57.5	33.2	32.1	41.3
Tax burden % of GDP, 2015	7.3	25.8	19.4	35.3	28.7

Source: World Development Indicators (World Bank various years); Kundu (2014).

India. It might well be a demographic question given that these countries still have fertility rates above 2.

Now, if one thinks that a key dimension of publicness is protection of the childhood of a country then India is in a very vulnerable position. Its indicators of infant mortality rate, under-5 mortality rate, undernourishment among children below the age of 5, child immunization rate, prevalence of anaemia among children below 5 years of age, and prevalence of anaemia among pregnant women are all the worst in the group. On the one hand, there is a group of administrative factors behind low achievement such as corruption in public administration, prosecutable difficulty, general tolerance of misdeeds, and asymmetric information between the public and the administration. On the other hand, at the centre of Drèze and Sen's critique of India's public social policy is how the Indian government is influenced by corporate and vested interests. As they argue (2013: 268) 'the comparatively small group of the relatively privileged seemed to have created a social universe of their own'. They also criticize India's media for ignoring the needs of the Indian population. This ultimately raises the issue of why some societies are more caring than others. For Sen, public involvement is essential, but it is a question of public scrutiny as a key element in the practice of democracy, not of political emotions[33] on the lines supported by Nussbaum. That is why it is important to examine the third level of publicness.

[33] The closest they get is when they refer to 'caring' vs 'uncaring' societies. But their focus of attention is more on the bias of democracy. For instance, they argue that (Dreze and Sen 2013: 239) 'The growing influence of corporate interests on public policy and democratic institutions does not particularly facilitate the reorientation of policy priorities towards the needs of the underprivileged.' They criticize the media, the existence of vested interests, and the lack of political organization of the poor.

LEVEL 3—THE NUSSBAUMIAN LEVEL OF PUBLICNESS

Rawls's concept of public reason, followed by Sen, is not meant to include the 'public sphere' in its broader sense. Instead, it focuses on matters of constitutional principles. To a large extent Nussbaum is also concerned with her list of capabilities as foundations for constitutional principles. But then she opens an agenda of how governments can proactively think about promoting public emotions (Nussbaum 2006: 222). For her, a decent society should organize its public spheres (e.g. public space, public health, public education, public transport, etc.) that can support people to pursue valuable lives. In addition, as she puts it (2013: 20) a 'government may attempt to influence citizens' psychology directly (for example, through political rhetoric, songs, symbols, and the content and pedagogy of public education), or it may devise institutions that represent the insights of a valuable type of emotion—as a decent tax system, for example, could represent the insights of a duly balanced and appropriately impartial compassion'. She assumes that shared public values can be changed,[34] not only, but mostly, by public education systems,[35] avoiding uniformity or misplaced values.[36]

The institutional nature of public emotions can be seen not merely in the provision of public goods but in how societies reveal their shared values of equal respect, fellow feeling, or even compassion and altruism in their daily affairs. Ultimately, that is what development should be about: people seeing other people not as a means to their self-interested objectives but as ends in themselves. The assumptions of reasonableness in Rawls and open impartiality in Sen do for their theories the work of bringing humanity together without trying to change humanity. Nussbaum goes a step further, arguing that it is important to work on people's motivations and public emotions.

Variables of level 3 publicness can be difficult to find out because they should represent public emotions of equal respect and fellow feeling. Within the government, variables related to the degree of progressivity of countries' tax structure can provide a good illustration about how the tax burden is divided between different social groups. Beyond the operation of governments, it is even more difficult to find variables that reflect how people treat each other, but on very general terms, we could consider variables such as homicide rates, road fatalities (in particular of pedestrians), the number of jailed population, and the level of economic inequality as proxies for variables not regularly compiled.

34 Sen believes that impartiality can be tantamount to 'love of humanity'. Nussbaum thinks that a purely abstract object such as 'humanity' does not have 'enough motivational strength' (2013: 209).

35 The cultivation of public emotion should follow the idiosyncrasies of different societies. As Nussbaum argues (2013: 201), 'Good public emotions do embody general principles, but they clothe them in the garb of concrete narrative history.'

36 Nussbaum (2013: 213) argues that 'The best response we give to this group of objections is that we must be extremely vigilant about the values we encourage people to love and pursue, and we must encourage continued vigilance by the cultivation of a critical public culture, the teaching of history in a critical mode, and the teaching of critical thinking and ethical reasoning in the schools.'

BRICS societies on average have a very high level of economic and social inequality. Homicide levels in South Africa and Brazil suggest that these are societies with lower levels of publicness where people are simply killing each other in a much higher proportion than in other parts of the world. The information on road fatalities, in particular of pedestrians, in its turn suggests that more consideration is given to people in India than in other countries of the group. In fact, India and China seem to have a much lower level of jailed population than Russia, South Africa, and Brazil; but it should be kept in mind the existence of death penalties in China and the difficulties for building new prisons in Brazil. When it comes to the progressivity of the tax structure it is clear that most BRICS (apart from South Africa) have a very low percentage of their tax revenue coming from direct taxes. This can be seen as a privilege for well-off groups and a low degree of publicness in these countries.

It is not the objective of this chapter to provide a comprehensive composite indicator of 'development as publicness', but only to illustrate the issue from a human development perspective. It is thus important to see BRICS countries not simply as 'emerging economies' or in terms of what their governments are doing for the direct provision of public goods but in terms of publicness and the corresponding motivations behind the way that different societies give materiality to their shared values of equal respect and fellow feeling. Just as an illustration, we created a simple index of publicness based on the three levels of publicness. For the first level we chose public expenditure on health as a proportion of GDP (per cent) as a meaningful variable when it comes to the provision side of publicness. Second, for the achievement level, we chose a composite between under-5 mortality rate and expected years of schooling (from HDI tables). We combined both indicators to represent the second level of publicness. Finally, we chose homicides per 100,000 people as a coarse proxy for how people are treating each other. We normalized the variables and aggregated them using an arithmetic average, just to make the procedure simpler. The results are presented, just for motivating a debate about publicness, in the last column of Table 14.4.

The index of publicness suggests a divide of BRICS between two different groups, the first including China, Brazil, and Russia, with a higher level of publicness, and the second with South Africa and India constituting the second group. There are reasons to believe that India and South Africa have lower levels of publicness, despite their democratic achievements. For those who disagree with these results we could ask in the case of India 'if its publicness is so high, why does it invest so little on health, why is its under-5 mortality rate so high, and why is school expectancy so modest?' This rough classification seems to correspond to Drèze and Sen's (2013: 67) comparison of India with other BRICS in which they argue that 'It is, in fact, worth noting that among these four countries [they did not include South Africa], India is the only one that has not (at least not yet) gone through a phase of major expansion of public support or economic redistribution.' Similarly, one might wonder about South Africa what kind of caring society would maintain such high levels of homicides and such high levels of under-5 mortality?

Table 14.4 The index of publicness and other indicators

2013 HDI ranking	GDP pc ranking	Equality ranking (reverse Gini order)	2016 Human Freedom Index/ Cato	2014 Freedom House Index	Index of Publicness
Russia	Russia	Russia	South Africa	South Africa, Brazil	China—0.727
Brazil	China	China	Brazil	South Africa, Brazil	Brazil—0.717
China	Brazil	Brazil	India	India	Russia—0.703
South Africa	South Africa	India	Russia	Russia	South Africa—0.402
India	India	South Africa	China	China	India—0.305

Note: For comparability we used India's Gini coefficient based on income data, of 0.54, as suggested by the 2004–05 Indian Human Development Report (rather than 0.35 based on expenditure data).

Source: Freedom House 2014; Cato Institute 2018.

There is no single answer about these statistics and we would have probably to look for an intersection partial order to try to make sense of these variables with the risk of arriving finally at the conclusion that BRICS are difficult to compare. Thus, the best strategy seems to be a categorization and acknowledgement of their incommensurabilities. In any case the main objective of this discussion was to raise the issue of publicness, trying to consider at the same time concrete ways of seeing it in these societies. They probably pervade different perceptions and institutions in different ways.

Conclusion

Publicness seems an important ingredient to human development. At a micro-level it is about equal respect, fellow feeling, tolerant behaviour that citizens offer to each other. At a macro-level, it is behind governments' priorities and the distributive impact and efficiency of a wide range of public policies. A short investigation into what Rawls said about 'public' pointed out the concept of public reason (in particular in the context of his (1993) *Political Liberalism*) and the assumption of reasonableness. But Rawls defined the public sphere of public reason very narrowly towards the formulation of constitutional principles. Sen's criticism of Rawls's public reason focuses on increasing the justificatory power of that concept, widening it to open forms of impartiality and strengthening its objectivity. Sen acknowledges that individuals can display a wide range of moral sentiments and that self-interest is only one of the possible reasons that people might have to act. Sen's argument undoubtedly strengthens Rawls's wider argument and his notion of public reason but it does not dispute the origin of individuals' motivations, as does Nussbaum's concept of public emotions. Nussbaum's main point is an extension of

Rawls's concern that institutions are shaped by public emotions (this goes back to Rawls's problem of stability), complemented by a historical research that identified in moral philosophy as well as in the arts, different movements for changing individuals' public feelings towards others.

The elements of the Rawls–Sen–Nussbaum debate were translated into a classification to help us think about different levels of publicness. One level is about how governments use their resources. A second level is about the impact they can cause (together with other actors). A third level is more directly about how people treat each other. These levels are obviously interlinked but here the purpose was not to conceptualize their relations but to look for empirical proxies that could convey a concrete sense of publicness in different countries. BRICS provide an illustration that allows us to think about the label of 'emerging economies' vis-à-vis the consequences of publicness in their societies. New resources are not going to be translated into more human development for these countries if distinct interventions for promoting more publicness are not put in place. The standard half-baked definition of human development, limited to the notion of basic freedoms, misses this publicness dimension. Development is freedom but development is publicness too.

REFERENCES

Arndt, H. (1987). *Economic Development: The History of an Idea*. Chicago, IL: Chicago University Press.

Arrow, K. (2012 [1951]). *Social Choice and Individual Values*, 3rd edn. New Haven, CT: Yale University Press.

Cato Institute (2018). *Human Freedom Index*. Available at www.cato.org/human-freedom-index-new, accessed 16 March 2019.

Comim, F. (2008). 'Social capital and the capability approach', in D. Castiglione, J. van Deth, and G. Wolleb (eds) *The Handbook of Social Capital*. Oxford: Oxford University Press, 624–51.

Comim, F. and Amaral, P. (2013). 'The Human Values Index', *Cambridge Journal of Economics* 37/6: 1221–41.

Drèze, J. and Sen, A. (2013). *An Uncertain Glory: India and Its Contradictions*. London: Penguin Books.

Freedom House (2014). *Freedom in the World*. Available at https://freedomhouse.org/report/freedom-world/freedom-world-2014), accessed 16 March 2019.

Fukuda-Parr, S. and Kumar, A.K. (2003). *Readings in Human Development: Concepts, Measures and Policies for a Development Paradigm*. Oxford: Oxford University Press.

Gasper, D. (2004). *The Ethics of Development*. Edinburgh: Edinburgh University Press.

Haq, M. (1999). *Reflections on Human Development*. Delhi: Oxford University Press.

Hardin, R. (1997). 'Economic theories of the state', in D. Mueller (ed.) *Perspectives on Public Choice: A Handbook*. Cambridge: Cambridge University Press, 21–34.

Ibrahim, S. and Tiwari, M. (2014). *The Capability Approach: From Theory to Practice*. Basingstoke: Palgrave Macmillan.

Kaul, I., Grunberg, I., and Stern, M. (1999). *Global Public Goods: International Cooperation in the 21st Century*. Oxford: Oxford University Press and UNDP.

Kundu, P. (2014). *Major Dimensions of Inequalities in India: Taxation*. New Delhi: CBGA.

Larmore, C. (2003). 'Public reason', in S. Freeman (ed.) *The Cambridge Companion to Rawls*. Cambridge: Cambridge University Press, 368–93.

Mikhail, J. (2011). *Elements of Moral Cognition: Rawls' Linguistic Analogy and the Cognitive Science of Moral and Legal Judgment*. Cambridge: Cambridge University Press.

Newman, O. (2015). *Liberalism in Practice: The Psychology and Pedagogy of public Reason*. Cambridge, MA: The MIT Press.

Nussbaum, M. (2006). *Frontiers of Justice: Disability, Nationality, Species Membership*. Cambridge, MA: The Belnak Press of Harvard University Press.

Nussbaum, M. (2013). *Political Emotions: Why Love Matters for Justice*. Cambridge, MA: The Belnap Press of Harvard University Press.

Paul, S., Balakrishnan, S., Thompi, F., Sekhar, S., and Vivekananda, M. (2006). *Who Benefits from India's Public Services? A People's Audit of Five Basic Services*. New Delhi: Academic Foundation.

Rawls, J. (1971). *A Theory of Justice*. Oxford: Oxford University Press.

Rawls, J. (1993). *Political Liberalism*. New York: Columbia University Press.

Rawls, J. (2001). *Justice as Fairness: A Restatement*. Cambridge, MA: The Belknap Press of Harvard University Press.

Rist, G. (2008). *The History of Development: From Western Origins to Global Faith*. London: Zed Books.

Samuelson, P. (1954). 'The pure theory of public expenditure', *The Review of Economics and Statistics* 36/4: 387–9.

Sen, A. (1999). *Inequality Re-Examined*. Oxford: Oxford University Press.

Stewart, F. (2005). 'Groups and capabilities', *Journal of Human Development* 6/2: 185–204.

Streeten, P. (1995). *Thinking about Development*. Cambridge: Cambridge University Press.

UNDP (United Nations Development Programme) (1990). *Human Development Report*. New York: Oxford University Press.

UNDP (United Nations Development Programme) (2010). *Human Development Report—The Real Wealth of Nations: Pathways to Human Development*. New York: Palgrave Macmillan.

UNDP (United Nations Development Programme) (2013). *Human Development Report. The Rise of the South: Human Progress in a Diverse World*. New York: UNDP

UNICEF (United Nations Children's Fund) (2014). *Levels and Trends in Child Mortality*. New York: UNICEF.

UNIDO (United Nations Industrial Development Organization) (2008). *Public Goods for Economic Development*. Vienna: UNIDO.

Wong, T. and Dutfield, G. (2011). *Intellectual Property and Human Development: Current Trends and Future Scenarios*. Cambridge: Cambridge University Press.

Woodward, D. and Smith, R. (2003). 'Global public goods and health: concepts and issues', in R. Smith, R. Beaglehole, D. Woodward, and N. Drager (eds) *Global Public Goods for Health: Health Economic and Public Health Perspectives*. Oxford: Oxford University Press, 3–29.

World Bank (2004). *World Development Report 2004: Making Services Work for Poor People*. Washington, DC: World Bank and Oxford University Press.

World Bank (various years). *World Development Indicators.* Washington, DC: World Bank. Available at https://datacatalog.worldbank.org/dataset/world-development-indicators, accessed 16 March 2019.

Yusuf, S. and Stiglitz, J. (2001). 'Development issues: settled and open', in G. Meier and J. Stiglitz (eds) *Frontiers of Development Economics: The Future in Perspective.* Oxford: Oxford University Press and the World Bank, 227–68.

15 Reason, argument, and agitation

Can South Africa follow in the footsteps of the BRIC countries?

David A. Clark

Introduction

Three-quarters of a century ago Dr Babasaheb R. Ambedkar, the effective author of the Indian constitution, penned the following warning:

> On the 26th January 1950, we are going to enter into a life of contradictions. In politics we will have equality and in social and economic life we will have inequality. In politics we will be recognizing the principle of one man one vote and one vote one value. In our social and economic life, we shall, by reason of our social and economic structure, continue to deny the principle of one man one value . . . We must remove this contradiction at the earliest possible moment or else those who suffer from inequality will blow up the structure of political democracy which this Assembly has so laboriously built up. (Parliament of India 1949)[1]

Half a century on, the same might have been said about South Africa on the eve of the first fully inclusive democratic elections. In the case of India, the worst of Ambedkar's fears did not come to pass. Instead of a potential collapse, the world witnessed the survival and growth of a democratic nation that continues to be 'deeply compromised' by the social and economic inequalities foretold by Ambedkar (Drèze and Sen 2002: 376). Although democratic institutions and ideals have endured in India, there remains considerable room for improvement in both the practice and reach of Indian democracy as Jean Drèze and Amartya Sen's lengthy books on this momentous topic clearly show.

Like India in the post-independence era, South Africa has come a long way since the end of apartheid in 1994. But there are still those who seem to believe that the transition to democracy might not be sustainable. Some critics have pointed to the nature of the political settlement agreed at the time, and the subsequent misuse of economic power

[1] The last sentence of this passage appears to be widely misquoted, including in the official record. I have followed Drèze and Sen's (2002: 376) reiteration, which does not include typos or change the intended meaning.

David A. Clark, *Reason, argument, and agitation: Can South Africa follow in the footsteps of the BRIC countries?* In: *Handbook of BRICS and Emerging Economies.* Edited by: P.B. Anand, Shailaja Fennell, and Flavio Comim, Oxford University Press (2021). © Oxford University Press.
DOI: 10.1093/oso/9780198827535.003.0015

(most notably, Bond 2010, 2016), while others have highlighted the grinding poverty, endemic corruption, and rampant abuse of political power (e.g. Malik 2015). As the headline of an article in *The Telegraph* newspaper put it, in the wake of the revolt against the African National Congress (ANC) during the 2016 municipal elections, 'Despotism or model democracy—South Africa could now go either way' (Blair 2016). If such pessimism turns out to be warranted, South Africa rather than India may fall foul of Ambedkar's warning.

Drèze and Sen point to the linkages between 'democratic' pressures and positive results in democratic and non-democratic countries alike. Their latest book briefly discusses the other BRIC nations (Brazil, Russia, and China) in this regard, but is inexplicably silent about South Africa. Can South Africa follow in the footsteps of the other BRIC countries (particularly 'B' and 'I')? Or might the South African brand of democracy really fall short? Drèze and Sen (2013: xii) find reason to be 'contingently optimistic' about the role of public discussion and agitation in India, despite the compromised nature of Indian democracy. Can similar grounds be found to be cautiously optimistic about South Africa's experiment with democracy?

Democratic freedoms and human capabilities

This chapter takes Sen's writings on democracy and development as its point of departure.[2] A recurring theme in Amartya Sen's writings is that democracy is fundamentally important for development. In fact, Sen has become one of the strongest advocates of this potentially controversial and powerful idea—particularly among the intellectual Left.[3] In response to a question from a Japanese journalist in 1997, Sen (1999a: 2–3) reports that he had no trouble selecting 'the rise of democracy' as the single most important event of the twentieth century (despite being able to choose from events as significant as two world wars, the rise and decline of fascism, the collapse or transformation of communism, and the restructuring of the world economic order). In defence of democracy, Sen argues that it is not an inherently Western idea; in fact, he shows that it has deep roots in many other historical and cultural settings including but by no means limited to India (Sen 2006a, 2009: 322 ff). He also argues that democracy can be regarded as a 'universal value' in the sense 'that people anywhere may have reason to see it as valuable' (Sen 1999a: 12).[4] This argument is not easy to defeat, as the claim

[2] For an overview of the broader literature and other perspectives see Berendsen (2008), and Acemoglu et al. (2019), inter alia. For commentary and criticism of Sen's work in this area, see Gasper (2016) and the essays collected in Clark (2014) as well as some of the work cited (see especially nn. 7 and 14).

[3] Crocker (1995: 182) has observed that 'Sen is trying to (re)claim the concept of freedom for the democratic left . . . ' from right-wing libertarians such as Friedrich Hayek, Robert Nozick, and Milton Friedman.

[4] Sen (1999b) is critical of arguments against political freedom (1999b: 147 ff.), and shows that the poor care about democracy and political rights (151, 152, 223–4).

being made does not require universal consent and actively draws support from the various struggles for democratic freedom in many autocratic parts of the world.[5]

In his extensive writings on economics and philosophy, and in joint work with Jean Drèze on India, Sen has identified several theoretical and empirical linkages between democracy and development.[6] The overarching theme that ties these various contributions together is that democracy is good for development (and vice versa). This logic applies irrespective of whether development is construed in economic or social terms. At this risk of some simplification, I shall attempt to draw together the various strands of Sen's thinking in this area. I also argue that it is possible to distinguish between an ideal theory of democracy (prevalent in most of Sen's writings on this topic) and a more practical account of democracy that emerges most clearly in his books with Drèze on India.

Although Sen distinguishes between different notions of development, he argues that it must ultimately be judged in terms of the quality of people's lives rather than the pace of economic production. More specifically, he argues that development is about expanding the *capabilities* people have reason to value (Sen 1990, 1999b; Clark 2006). A chief advantage of the capability approach is that it places people rather than material things at the centre of development. Like Immanuel Kant, the capability approach recognizes that human beings are not only means (to production), but are also important ends in themselves. It follows that steps should be taken to ensure equitable forms of development and to promote key social achievements, particularly in the areas of health, education, and employment (Sen and Drèze 1999; Sen 1999b). The capability approach also recognizes that people are active agents of change (Sen 1985). As such, they not only participate in, but also have the potential to shape development processes and outcomes. The agency aspect of the capability approach resonates strongly with Sen's emphasis on democratic freedoms.

THE ROLE OF DEMOCRACY

Sen favours a broad interpretation of democracy that looks beyond representative forms of government (Sen 2006b: 14). Although the right to vote and free elections are vital ingredients of democracy, an effective and functional democratic system requires active

[5] This argument anticipates the spirit of the Arab Spring which swept across much of the Middle East and North Africa from 2010 affecting countries such as Tunisia, Egypt, Libya, Yemen, Syria, and Bahrain. The rise of popular protest in the Middle East (like the 1989 Tiananmen Square protests in China), helps to discredit the idea that certain peoples and cultures living under authoritarian rule do not value freedom and democracy.

[6] See for example Sen (1983, 1999a, 1999b, 2002: chs 2 and 8, 2006b, 2009); Nussbaum and Sen (1989); Drèze and Sen (1996, 2002, 2013); Sen and Drèze [1999)]). See also UNDP (2002); Crocker (2008); Mehrotra (2008); Deneulin (2009); Crocker and Robeyns (2010); Biggeri et al. (2011); Clark and Fennell (2014); Clark et al. (2019); and further references cited in *India: Economic Development and Social Opportunity* (Sen and Drèze 1999: n. 23, 194).

participation in governance and the protection of other rights (Sen 1999a: 8–9).[7] Following John Stuart Mill and others democracy in its purest form is defined as 'government by discussion', which involves 'the exercise of public reason' and political forms of participation (Sen 1999b, 2002, 2009: 324 ff). Among the defining features of such a system are free elections, multiparty politics (including an effective opposition and parliament), freedom of speech and information, a free and responsible media, constitutional rights, and an independent judiciary (Sen 1999b; Drèze and Sen, 2013: 12).

According to Sen (1999a, 1999b), democracy plays at least three roles in enriching life and promoting capabilities. First, it has *direct* (or intrinsic) significance, insofar as basic freedoms and rights (including social and political forms of participation) are valuable aspects of life. Second, it has *instrumental* value, in the sense that it enables people to express views, receive a hearing, and press claims for economic and political redress. Third, it has *constructive* importance, in that it helps people to learn from one another (through the exchange of information, knowledge, and argument), and shapes social values and priorities.[8] In addition, Sen (1999b: 154 ff., 180–4, 2006b: 195–6, 2009: 348 ff.) sometimes argues that democracy has a *protective* role to play, in terms of providing the necessary political incentives to uphold rights and prevent economic and social calamities.

A more practical and less ideal account of democracy emerges from Sen's joint work on India with the Belgium born social activist, Jean Drèze. In their latest book, *An Uncertain Glory: India and Its Contradictions*, they call for a proactive form of democracy based on education, agitation and organization (2013: 5). Such efforts should be grounded in public reason, although the expression of reason may involve 'more assertive means of communication' including 'noisy speech', public campaigns, demonstrations, strikes, public interest litigation, and other forms of democratic action (2013: 259–60). Drèze and Sen also argue that public reason does not involve some cultured—or exclusive—form of refined deliberation. Instead, public reason should be viewed as a 'general opportunity' and a vital part of a functional democracy:[9]

> The role of public reasoning does not depend on any credulous assumption that what we tell each other must be invariably well reasoned and persuasive. Rather, it is public reasoning that helps make us understand each other's problems and to see each other's perspectives – and this is absolutely essential to the operation of an electoral democracy. (Drèze and Sen 2013: 260)

Drèze and Sen also recognize that the practice of Indian democracy is crippled by inadequate political institutions, rampant corruption, and blatant forms of inequality, privilege, and power, including submission and resistance to change (2013: 244 ff., 285 ff.).

[7] 'Democracy is a demanding system, and not just a mechanical condition (like majority rule) taken in isolation' (Sen 1999a: 10). Drèze and Sen (2002: esp. 378 ff.) provide some concrete examples and discuss the limitations of focusing on majority rule.

[8] See also Sen (1983: 757–9, 2002, 2006b, 2009); Nussbaum and Sen (1989); Drèze and Sen (2002: 24–5) on the 'functional' roles of democracy.

[9] See also Sen (2006b: xiii).

Many of these themes are perhaps best expressed in Drèze and Sen's earlier book, *India: Participation and Social Opportunity*. In the enlarged version of this book, which covers democracy among other topics in greater depth, they argue that democratic participation requires 'symmetry of political rights', and works best in the absence of serious social and economic inequalities (2013: 9 ff., 28 ff.). Central issues include the 'voicelessness' of the marginalized and disadvantaged, the effectiveness of the media, and the importance of democratic institutions and basic accountability.[10] In this respect, they explicitly call for the need to buttress democratic institutions and democratic ideals with democratic practice (2013: 347 ff.). At one point, they observe that the practice of democracy involves 'a certain amount of "learning by doing"' and constitutes 'a form of political education' (2013: 362–3). A few pages later they invoke John Kenneth Galbraith's concept of 'countervailing power' and argue for 'developing and reinforcing . . . countervailing institutions that . . . give greater "voice" to those who have a stake in the efficient provision of public services' (2013: 371). Such ideas have more in common with critical pedagogy and transformative participation than they do with the ideal theories of public reason entrenched in Sen's own writings (Corbridge 2002; Clark et al. 2019; Patrón 2019).[11]

The functional role of democracy has been illustrated through several powerful examples, the most well-known of which is Sen's (1999b: 16) recurring observation that 'no famine has ever taken place in the history of the world in a functioning democracy'.[12]

> Famines have occurred in ancient kingdoms and contemporary authoritarian societies, in primitive tribal communities and in modern technocratic dictatorships, in colonial economies run by imperialists from the north and in newly independent countries of the south run by despotic national leaders or by intolerant single parties. But they have never materialised in any country that is independent, that goes to elections regularly, that has opposition parties to voice criticism and that permits newspapers to report freely and question the wisdom of government policies without extensive censorship. (1999b: 152–3)

A wealth of evidence consistent with this aphorism is presented in *Poverty and Famines* and *Hunger and Public Action* (reprinted in Sen and Drèze 1999).[13] Another example relates to the 1997 East Asian crisis which took place in countries that lacked the democratic institutions and practices required to scrutinize financial arrangements and hold big business and powerful families to account (Sen 1999b: 258). Following the financial crisis, democracy became a pressing issue in these countries with South Korea

[10] See for example, Drèze and Sen (2002: 28 ff., 300 ff., 2013: 81 ff., 244 ff., 262–9).

[11] It is not my intention to suggest that these ideas do not feature at all in Sen's writings. In *The Idea of Justice*, for example, Sen sometimes acknowledges the role of public agitation in tackling issues such as rights violations (2009: 351) or social inequalities (2009: 366), although his discussion does not move beyond mere recognition.

[12] This declaration can be traced back to Sen's (1982) discussion of the Great Bengal famine in *The New York Review of Books*. See also Sen (1999a: 7–8, 1999b: 51, 2002: 287, 2009: 342); Sen and Drèze (1999: 212, 2002: 133).

[13] For a critique and response see Nolan (1993) and Sen (1993).

electing a new President, Kim Dae Jung, on a platform of democratic reform and social protection (Drèze and Sen 2013: 261).

A final example involves a transformative moment in democratic attention to rape and violence against women in India (2013: 226 ff.). In December 2012, the brutal gang rape of a medical student in Delhi provoked widespread public anger and protest in India as well as international condemnation. Overnight the high incidence of rape and sexual violence in India became a pressing national concern in way that it had not been previously. The media scrambled to reinvent themselves as rape reporting instruments; prejudicial and sexist attitudes were challenged; the police and legal system were criticized for failing to provide women with sufficient protection; and within a week of the attack, there was the prospect of tangible legal reform culminating in a new parliamentary act to protect women from sexual violence (Sen, 2013).

BRICS

In their latest book, Drèze and Sen (2013) briefly reflect on some regional contrasts from within India. They also compare India with other nations, including the other BRIC (Brazil, Russia, and China) countries. The overarching theme of their discussion is that countries and regions with participatory practices and progressive social policies perform comparatively well in terms of basic capabilities.

In terms of Indian contrasts, Kerala and Tamil Nadu feature most prominently. Kerala has a long history of achieving sustained improvements in life expectancy, literacy, and poverty reduction despite initial lags in growth. This is because of proactive government, progressive health and education policies, and widespread public participation in development programmes (among other things). More recently, Tamil Nadu has made similar progress by introducing universal feeding programmes in primary schools and expanding public services and social infrastructure. Crucially, these reforms were the product of organized public pressure and active involvement in democratic politics, rather than the legacy of a benevolent ruling elite. In contrast, less efficient and politically active states (such as Bihar, Madhya Pradesh, and Uttar Pradesh) have achieved relatively little progress.[14]

In comparing India with the other BRIC countries, the most has been written about China.[15] In the 2013 book, they briefly reiterate the government failures associated with the Great Leap Forward and the exploits of the Cultural Revolution. The former culminated in the great famines of 1958–61 (with a death toll of up to 30 million people), while the latter led to the forced movement of people and sustained social terror. The absence of basic freedoms and the remoteness of political leaders from ordinary people not only allowed, but actively fuelled, these socially engineered calamities. In contrast,

[14] Drèze and Sen (2002: 90–4) trace the relatively poor performance of Uttar Pradesh to the lack of political participation and social activism.

[15] See especially Sen and Drèze (1999) and Drèze and Sen (2002: ch. 4).

China's remarkable progress since the 1979 economic reforms owe much to earlier social programmes that laid the foundations for healthcare, education, and access to land. Russia also put in place a comprehensive system of social welfare and public service provision prior to economic reform. Unlike China, however, the economic stresses that followed were more severe and were also exacerbated by western 'non-interventionist' policies. By the time recovery came a decade later, much of Russia's economy and social infrastructure had been degraded.

The latest book on India has more to say about Brazil than Russia or China. Drèze and Sen welcome the change in Brazil's direction from the mid-1980s, which followed two decades of repressive government and limited social progress. They observe that '[t]his change has been largely driven by the flourishing of democracy that followed the promulgation of a democratic constitution in 1988, soon after the end of a long spell of military dictatorships' (Drèze and Sen 2013: 69). The right to health was included in the constitution as a justiciable right, and the new 'Universal Health System' was largely conceived by health activists. They also point to the expansion and reform of the education system (including the introduction of the 'funding equalisation law'), which has dramatically improved access to education and student performance. Popular social welfare programmes including pensions schemes, minimum wage policies, and *Bolsa Família* (conditional cash transfers to families) have also helped to significantly reduce poverty.[16]

Although Drèze and Sen (2013) are enthusiastic about the 'democratic upsurge' in Brazil since the mid-1980s, they have nothing to say about South Africa's extraordinary transition to democracy from the early 1990s. Their focus is on the BRIC countries (Brazil, Russia and China; India's preferred 'peer group'), rather than the BRICS (including South Africa). In *Hunger and Public Action* (reprinted in Sen and Drèze 1999), they briefly argue that South Africa's disappointing performance in life expectancy and infant mortality is due to blatant inequalities in healthcare, education, and the social environment. In later books on India (*Economic Development and Social Opportunity* [reprinted in Sen and Drèze 1999]); and *India: Development and Participation* [Drèze and Sen 2002]), they attribute the high levels of violence found in South Africa to grinding inequality and poverty. But these three books largely predate South Africa's democratic transition. Sen's own work contains sporadic references to South Africa, but is silent on the functional role of democracy in the post-apartheid era.

The South African experience

Initially, the prospects of creating a flourishing democracy in the new South Africa looked promising. Nelson Mandela's national unity government included representatives from

[16] Many of these initiatives have created new forms of participation (such as participatory budgeting at the local level), although this is not discussed in *An Uncertain Glory*. See Pereira (2015) for a discussion.

other political parties—most notably, F.W. de Klerk as one of two deputy presidents. A new flag combined the colours of the former Boer Republics with those of the ANC, and the former national anthem was merged with the liberation hymn ('God Bless Africa') and sung in five different languages. In 1996, the coalition government approved a new constitution and bill of rights that is among 'the most liberal in the world' (Worden 2012: 156). The emphasis was on reconciliation and building a new inclusive democracy for all South Africans.

There is considerable capacity at grassroots level for social and political forms of participation in the new South Africa, as history has witnessed. Many South Africans are unhappy or dissatisfied with the quality of their lives, although their dissonance is tempered by optimism for the future (Helliwell et al. 2017). Although such optimism might be viewed as indicative of adaptive preferences,[17] studies show that ordinary South Africans (including many of the most deprived and disadvantaged people) are generally less happy than their neighbours in poorer African countries (Grant 2015) or contemporaries in the BRIC nations (*The Economist* 2014). More fittingly, studies show that most South Africans are more than capable of articulating a substantially better form of life. An open-ended survey administered by Clark (2002) found that South Africans from a rural village and urban township associated the top ten aspects of a 'good' form of life with jobs, housing, education, income, family, religion, health, food, happiness, and love. A later survey of the 'essentials of life' covering other parts of South Africa produced similar lists, and uncovered meaningful distinctions between perceptions of 'getting by' and 'living well' (Clark and Qizilbash 2008).

The intense form of 'political consciousness' identified by Clark (2002: 103) is prevalent at the bottom of South African society. In the aftermath of the first democratic elections, Møller (1996) showed that South Africans had a long list of development priorities and high expectations for the government's Reconstruction and Development Programme (RDP). As time elapsed, it 'became clear that the RDP was achieving less than had been hoped' (Worden 2012: 157). In 1997, the government replaced it with a new strategy known as GEAR (Growth Employment and Redistribution), which emphasized economic liberalization and integration into the world economy over measures for tackling poverty and inequality directly (May 2000). Living standards and employment prospects faltered (see Van der Byl 2014), and dissatisfaction with basic service delivery grew (Higgs 2011). In the decade following the transition to democracy, ordinary South Africans began to express their frustration with poor service delivery and low-level corruption through strikes and civil unrest (von Holdt et al. 2011; Heller 2015). Local protests across South Africa escalated with many becoming violent (Table 15.1).[18] Reason and argument gave way to aggressive forms of political agitation.

[17] See Clark (2012) for an overview of the literature on adaptive preferences and related concepts.
[18] For a catalogue of local service delivery protests and their causes see Wikipedia (2017a).

Table 15.1 Protests and unrest in South Africa, 2004–16

	Peaceful	Unrest	Total
2004/05	7,382	622	8,004
2005/06	9,809	954	10,763
2006/07	8,703	743	9,446
2007/08	6,431	705	7,136
2008/09	6,125	718	6,843
2009/10	7,913	994	8,907
2010/11	11,680	971	12,651
2011/12	10,832	1,226	12,058
2012/13	10,517	1,882	12,399
2013/14	11,601	1,907	13,508
2014/15	12,451	2,289	14,740
2015/16	11,151	3,542	14,693

Note: Figures from earlier sources have been updated wherever possible to reflect the latest available estimates from the police.

Source: von Holdt et al. (2011: 590), SAPS (2012: 85, 2016: 153).

South Africa's democratic deficit

In South Africa, popular participation and social and political struggle have been mediated by the quality and effectiveness of democratic institutions. Many of these institutions fall short of meeting basic democratic principles.

Although South Africa enjoys a vibrant multiparty system with free elections every five years, a single political party (with deep historical roots in the liberation movement) is effectively assured electoral victory. In the first five fully inclusive general elections, the ANC polled between 62.2 and 69.7 per cent of the vote.[19] Booysen's (2013) focus group discussions show how 'voting for the ANC is part of the culture and identity of most black South Africans' (2013: 51). In contrast, the Democratic Alliance continues to remind many voters of 'white domination under apartheid' despite receiving high praise for including black leaders within its ranks (53). Elections are widely perceived as fair in South Africa (IEC, 2017: 60), although the dominance of the ANC is reinforced by the funding allocated to the main political parties by the Independent Electoral Commission. In 2009, the ANC received three-quarters of the money allocated to political parties,

[19] All the election statistics reported in this chapter are taken from the Electoral Commission of South Africa's official website. Available at http://www.elections.org.za/, accessed 30 October 2018).

although this fell to little more than half in 2014 with opposition parties receiving greater sums for their election campaigns.[20]

Black South Africans remain committed to the ANC to 'defend liberation' but are deeply resentful of corruption. They are also increasingly disillusioned with the 'hollow words' and broken promises of politicians (Booysen 2013: 55–7). Support for the ANC remains strong but has waned. Large numbers of eligible voters did not register to vote ANC in the run-up to the 2014 elections (Pheko 2014). The ANC's share of the vote in the 2014 national election also declined to a record low representing a fall of almost 8 percentage points since the previous election. Meanwhile the Democratic Alliance has steadily increased its share of the vote to around 16 per cent in the 2009 and 2014 national elections, and took control of the Western Cape from the ANC in the 2009 provincial elections. In the 2016 municipal elections, popular support for the ANC fell to the lowest levels witnessed since 1994, as the party lost control of three metropolitan municipalities and shared power in a fourth, while coalition and minority government became far more common at local and district levels.

In the ten years since Jacob Zuma became President of South Africa concern has been expressed about the growth of cronyism and narrowing of democracy. The ANC has become subject to 'Zuma-fication' as those loyal to the president have managed to take control of the organization for mutual advantage.[21] Parliament and other state institutions along with substantial parts of the economy have also become 'Zuma-fied' (see Buys 2015). In his book, *Recovering Democracy in South Africa*, Raymond Suttner (2015: 69–70) recounts how parliament and the speaker flouted their constitutional obligation to hold Zuma to account for refusing to answer questions about personal gain from public spending on his Nkandla estate. Parliament has also failed to remove Zuma for wrongdoing on eight separate occasions, even though the last vote of 'no confidence' in August 2017 was conducted by secret ballot and followed death threats against one of his own MPs for publicly questioning his leadership (BBC 2017b). In a separate incident, reflecting the abuse of executive powers, Zuma has been criticized for disregarding a High Court judgement that required the Sudanese President Umar Al-Bashir to be detained until a South African court could decide whether he should be extradited to the International Criminal Court to face genocide charges (Clarke 2015). Zuma's brand of corruption and chain of personal networks extends to state-owned enterprises (SOEs) and ripples through the economy. Appointment to company boards often takes place for political reasons, and many cases of collusion in the award of government contracts have been uncovered—including lucrative contracts for the construction of the 2010 World Cup football stadiums (Naidoo 2017).

[20] In 2009 the ANC received R61 million of the R88 million allocated to parties in parliament. In 2014, the ANC received R64.9 million of the R114.8 allocated to political parties. The Democratic Alliance received R17 million and the Congress of the People got R9.7 million (Pheko 2014).

[21] In the *Sunday Independent*, Booysen (2014) describes how '[a] faction of the ANC has been waging a precarious game of institutional warfare aimed at keeping themselves and Zuma in power'.

Studies show that 'corruption and greed are seen to have infected the post-Mandela era and particularly the current government' (Booysen 2013: 31). Speaking in 2001, Nelson Mandela himself spoke out against the corruption among black leaders that creates division and undermines reconciliation:

> Little did we suspect that our own people, when they got a chance, would be as corrupt as the apartheid regime. That is one of the things that has really hurt us . . . Nothing in our struggle for liberation entitles an individual to think that he has a right to rob the public.
>
> (Cited in le Roux 2001)

Distrust in the police force and the court system is also high. The police force is viewed 'as perversely corrupt and in cahoots with criminals' while the courts are often regarded as 'inept and incapable of dealing with crime and violence' (Booysen 2013: 31, 40). Concern has also been raised about the disbandment in 2009 of the Scorpions, an independent agency for investigating and prosecuting organized crime and corruption. The government subsequently replaced it with the Hawks, which is widely regarded as a less effective agency that has been politicized by the ANC (Berning and Montesh 2012; Booysen 2013: 41; Poplak 2017). Few people view the courts as corrupt, however. And it is not difficult to find examples of the courts clashing with the executive, striking down legislation, or engaging in introspection (Masinga 2015; Suttner 2015: 74–6).

Some commentators have taken issue with the media or have questioned the quality of open democracy in South Africa. Large sections of the media have been vocal on a range of public interest issues, including HIV/AIDS, the Marikana massacre, and government corruption. Although the media are credited with keeping people informed, extending their voice, and helping to hold the government to account (Booysen 2014: 30, 50), harsh critics have complained that 'the press is shirking its responsibility "to tell it like it is" in the name of justice' (Pheko 2014). Suttner (2015: 31) has called for renewing 'the culture of debate' that existed under apartheid to 'bring politics back into politics'. This may not be easy to accomplish, as supporters of Jacob Zuma have sought to expand their ownership and control of the media (Biz Staff Writers 2017).

Access to information is vital for open debate and active participation in a flourishing democracy. It is also essential for claiming socio-economic rights, uncovering corruption, and holding the government and service providers to account (February and Tapula 2010; ISS 2014; Mandela Foundation 2015). In South Africa, the flow of information is threatened by the controversial Protection of State Information Bill (the so-called 'Secrecy Bill'), which has been approved by parliament but has not yet been signed into law by the president (Krüger 2017). The problem with the Secrecy Bill is that it seems to place excessive controls on the right to information and freedom of expression because almost any restriction could be deemed to be in the national interest. Such legislation is likely to reinforce the culture of secrecy and lack of transparency that pervades all levels of government. The Mandela Foundation (2015) reports that around 60 per cent of requests for information submitted to government departments under the Promotion of Access to Information Act (PAIA) fall into the category of 'muted responses'; that is, they are simply ignored. According to Tilly (2010) non-compliance with the reporting requirements of the PAIA is more prevalent in local government (93 per cent) than national government (43 per cent).

Reason for cautious optimism

The discussion so far suggests that the nature and scope of South African democracy is questionable at best and deeply compromised at worst. Yet on the whole, South African democracy is not discernibly weaker than Indian democracy despite its relatively young age and lamentable setbacks (Figure 15.1). In global terms, both countries are classified as 'flawed democracies' with India ranking just seven places above South Africa in the 2016 democracy index (EIU 2017). Both countries perform relatively well in the overall league table (32nd and 39th place, respectively, out of 167 countries covered) and achieved similar overall scores (7.81 versus 7.41) on a scale of 0 to 10. In contrast, Brazil (another 'flawed democracy') only managed 51st place (with an overall score of 6.90), despite high praise from Drèze and Sen for its democratic transition and surge of social progress.[22]

In terms of political participation, South Africa scores more highly than India and Brazil. In fact, in this dimension, South Africa outperforms every other 'flawed democracy' (except for Israel), and most countries classified as 'full democracies'. In 2016, South Africa was ranked fifth in the world, along with Sweden, Denmark, Ireland, the Netherlands, and Austria (all scoring 8.83). Only four countries received a higher score for political participation: Norway (10.00), Ireland (8.89), New Zealand (8.89), and Israel (also 8.89). It follows that there are strong grounds for being cautiously optimistic about the transformative potential of South African democracy, despite the deplorable handicap in 'political culture' that tempers effective political participation.

Further investigation reveals that it is not necessary to look far to find noteworthy examples of democratic success as well as failure. Three brief examples of democratic institutions, processes, and pressures that have produced meaningful social change are considered in turn. Broadly speaking, these examples encompass institutions and actors at the global, national, and local levels, respectively.

THE HIV/AIDS EPIDEMIC AND ACCESS TO ANTIRETROVIRAL DRUGS

One of the greatest development challenges facing South Africa is the HIV/AIDS epidemic. The proportion of adults living with HIV in South Africa has increased

[22] Russia and China are ranked 134th and 136th in the world respectively (with overall average scores of 3.24 and 3.14). Both countries are classified as 'authoritarian' by the democracy index (EIU 2017).

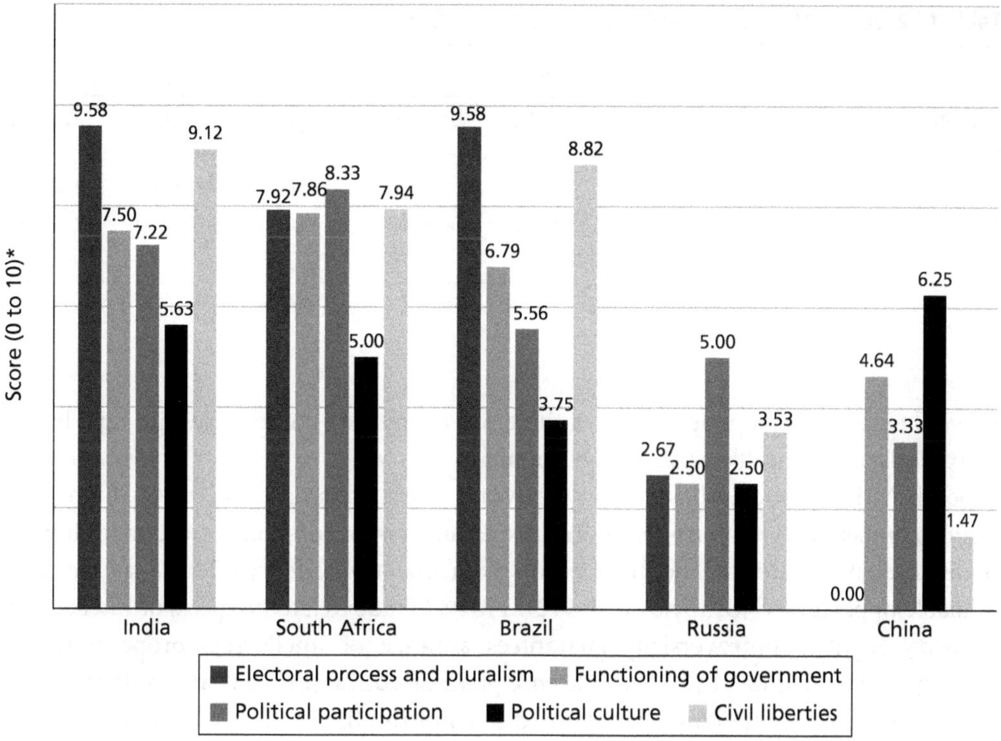

Figure 15.1 Five aspects of autonomy—South Africa and the BRICS nations (2016)

Note: Based on 60 indicators fitted into 5 categories.
Source: Author based on data from EIU (2017).

from around one in twenty people following the 1994 election to one in five people today (Table 15.2). Although the worst of the HIV/AIDS epidemic has passed (with new HIV infection rates and AIDS-related deaths declining from the early and mid/late 2000s), progress in tackling the disease has involved considerable political struggle.

Initially, the post-apartheid governments showed little interest in prioritizing HIV/AIDS, despite including the right to 'public health services' in the new constitution.[23] In fact, just before the 1994 elections, an ominous decision was taken by the transitional government to close the national AIDS Centre at the South African Institute of Medical Research on the grounds of cost.[24] Šehović (2014: 102 ff.) recounts how the incoming post-apartheid government was primarily interested in remaining a sovereign independent state, which meant avoiding dependence on external money from the International Monetary Fund (IMF). The new government also sought to demonstrate capacity to manage the economy and attract foreign investment by adhering to strict neoliberal economic policies, and honouring loans incurred by the Reserve Bank to support its

[23] See DoJ&CD (1996: 27 (1) a).

[24] Interview with Professor Ruben Sher cited in Šehović (2014: 108). Among other things, the AIDS Centre had been responsible for drafting a 'Strategic plan for containment of AIDS in South Africa' (2014: 107).

Table 15.2 South Africa's HIV/AIDS epidemic, 1994–2016

	1994	2000	2005	2010	2016
New HIV infections	340,000	540,000	500,000	380,000	270,000
Prevalence of HIV (% of adults, 15–49)	4.3	14.0	17.3	18.3	18.9
AIDS-related deaths	18,000	130,000	270,000	210,000	110,000
People living with HIV	950,000	3,600,000	5,100,000	6,100,000	7,100,000
ARV coverage (% of people living with HIV)	—	0	2	20	56

Source: UNAIDS (2017); World Bank (2017).

forward exchange rate policy. None of these objectives were compatible with high levels of expenditure on health or social development.

South Africa also scrambled to join the World Trade Organization (WTO), becoming a full member on 1 January 1995. To 'dispel any notion of itself as a developing or underdeveloped state, the South African government acceded to TRIPS at the first available opportunity' (Šehović 2014: 112). TRIPS (Trade Related Aspects of Intellectual Property Rights) controversially guarantees a range of intellectual property rights (Chang 2001), including the right to license pharmaceutical products and restrict access to cheap generic alternatives manufactured in countries like India. This raised the price of antiretroviral (ARV) drugs used in HIV treatment phenomenally, putting them well beyond the reach of almost all South Africans.[25] Like most other developing countries, South Africa also failed to exploit provisions in TRIPS that would have permitted access to vital medication in times of crisis (Wise 2006). Instead, initial attempts to negotiate access to cheap ARVs through the WTO were thwarted by bureaucracy, and the threat of trade sanctions from the United States (Šehović 2014: 64, 84).

The political situation and lack of will to fund expensive ARV drugs encouraged initial post-apartheid administrations to participate in a culture of AIDS denialism. High-ranking members of the government persistently talked down the threat posed by HIV/AIDS. For example, Thabo Mbeki publicly stated that 'personally, I don't know anybody who has died of AIDS', despite unconfirmed reports that some of his colleagues and staff had succumbed to the disease (Murphy 2003). He also suggested, in his opening address to the Thirteenth Annual AIDS conference in Durban, that poverty rather than HIV is the greatest threat to health in Africa (Mbeki 2000). More provocatively still, on at least four separate occasions between July and October 2000, Mbeki infamously disputed the accepted view that HIV is the only virus that leads to AIDS:

> As I listened [to the World Health Organization] and heard the whole story told about our own country, it seemed to me that we could not blame everything on a single virus . . . (Mbeki 2000).

[25] In 1995 the annual cost of triple drug therapy in Africa was around US$12,000 per person (Reich 2005: 329).

> . . . the notion that immune deficiency is only acquired from a single virus cannot be sustained. Once you say immune deficiency is acquired from that virus your response will be antiviral drugs. But if you accept that there can be a variety of reasons, including poverty and the many diseases that afflict Africans, then you can have a more comprehensive treatment response. (Interview with Time 2000)

> A virus cannot cause a syndrome. A virus can cause a disease, and Aids is not a disease, it is a syndrome (response to parliamentary question; BBC 2000).

> [The CIA is part of] a conspiracy to promote the view that HIV causes AIDS. (UPI 2000)

Mbeki has also expressed doubt about the accuracy of AIDS mortality statistics and questioned whether the disease was as fatal as claimed (Šehović 2014: 137). These views were affirmed by others, including the Finance Minister, Trevor Manuel, who denounced the effectiveness of HIV ARV drugs as 'a lot of voodoo', and declared that purchasing them 'would be a waste of very limited resources' (Carroll 2003; Šehović 2014: 106). Ministers also preferred to support cheaper alternatives to expensive ARV drugs. In 1997, the South African government decided to push an 'African cure' called Virodene (Mbeki 1998), developed by a scientist with dubious credentials (Wikipedia 2017b). Meanwhile the longstanding health minister at the time, Manto Tshabalala-Msimang, advocated a diet of beetroot, spinach, and garlic for those suffering from HIV, earning her the nickname of 'Dr Beetroot'. After six years in government, the post-apartheid administration had only allocated R10 per person to the annual national HIV/AIDS budget (Department of Health 2000: 24).

A strong backlash against AIDS denialism followed from the South African media and international press. Mbeki, Tshabalala-Msimang, and others were heavily chastized for misinforming the public and preventing access to ARVs. Headlines such as 'AIDS: The New Apartheid', 'Aids Protesters Accuse Pretoria Ministers of Manslaughter', '"Dr Beetroot" hits back at media over AIDS exhibition', and 'Crimes of the Great Denialist' became regular features in the popular press (McGreal 2000; Carroll 2003; Blandy 2006). Heightened and effective media campaigns were made possible by the growth of specialist health journalists with sufficient knowledge of AIDS to 'counter almost every incorrect government statement' (Malan 2006: 42). Several campaigns with the objective of raising awareness of HIV/AIDS also emerged, including Khomanani, LoveLife, and two television series that targeted adults and teenagers, respectively (see Peltzer et al. 2012).

Medical researchers also reacted against the government's denialist stance by reaffirming the scientific links between HIV and AIDS through the 'Durban Declaration', which collected over 5,000 signatures from local and international experts (Nature 2000). The scientific community and the media were also quick to show that Verodene does not disrupt the progress of HIV, and that the development of the drug contravened accepted scientific practice and medical ethics (Sidley 1997; Staff Reporter 1998). Some scientific activists even filed a lawsuit against the minister of health and a controversial drug supplier for running illegal medical trials in two townships and for providing 'false hope' to people who later died by claiming that multivitamins alone can overcome AIDS (Watson 2006).

The media and scientific community were bolstered by non-governmental organizations (NGOs) and advocacy organizations that formed a 'global-local alliance' (Šehović 2014: 6–7). Foremost among these organizations was the home-grown Treatment Action Campaign (TAC), which has been described as 'probably the world's most effective AIDS group' (Rosenberg 2006). A power struggle between the government and this alliance of non-state actors erupted (Šehović 2014: 94 ff.), that eventually applied enough pressure to change the state's response to HIV/AIDS for the better in several key respects (see Table 15.3).

An early example of an important victory was TAC's legal action in November 2002 that obliged the government to make Nevirapine available to pregnant women to reduce the transmission of HIV between mother and child. By this time, some provinces had already contravened the national government's authority by opting to provide the drug (News24 2002). The court case, however, effectively extended the coverage of Nevirapine to the rest of the country, although roll-out initially stalled after the Medical Control Council deregistered the drug in June 2003 before re-registering it three months later (Šehović 2014: 130). The court case had the bonus of raising awareness of the vertical transmission of HIV, and helping TAC convey the message that 'Nevirapine was effective and the state was being "stubborn"' (Malan 2006: 46). The impact of this message was reflected in the fact that 80 per cent of HIV positive mothers elected to take Nevirapine during the pilot (Malan 2006: 46).

The most well-known example of a victory for a global–local alliance of HIV/AIDS campaigners relates to an attempt to stop South Africa from importing cheap generic versions of ARV drugs from India and Thailand. Although the African market for these drugs was small (consisting of about 1 per cent of global revenues), western manufacturers were concerned that allowing South Africa to import cheap substitutes might set a dangerous precedent and threaten profits elsewhere (*The Economist* 2001; Mathiason 2001; Keeplar 2013). In 1998, a three-year legal action was brought by a consortium of thirty-nine leading pharmaceutical companies including Bristol Myers Squibb, Merck, GlaxoSmithKlein, Hoffman-La Roche, and Boheringer Ingelheim. Mounting public pressure led not only to the case being dropped in 2001, but to significant reputational damage to the companies involved.

In South Africa, TAC fervently campaigned against the pharmaceutical companies, arguing that many had benefited from tax breaks or had patented drugs based on compounds discovered by publicly funded research (*The Economist* 2001). The founder of TAC, Zachie Achmat, even refused to take his own ARV drugs until they became publicly available (Karon 2001; Keeplar 2013).[26] Ordinary South Africans became increasingly vocal and took to the streets to protest patents (Keeplar 2013). Some

[26] In another highly publicized act of defiance, Achmat returned to South Africa with a case of prohibited generic HIV drugs that could be purchased fifty times cheaper in Thailand (Karon 2001).

Table 15.3 Landmarks in the struggle against the South African state for effective action to tackle HIV/AIDS in the era of state sponsored denialism

Sarafina II	1995–96	Pressure from the EU, AIDS activists, and the media ended production of a controversial play (funded by misappropriated money) that contained 'no relevant AIDS prevention message' (Malan 2006: 42).
HIV awareness campaigns	From 1996	Communication campaigns intended to raise awareness of HIV/AIDS began to emerge, including LoveLife in 2002 backed by private money, Khomanani ('caring together') in 2003 sponsored by the state, and the long running television series, *Soul City* (from 1996) and *Soul Buddyz* (from 2000). See Peltzer et al. (2012); SAHO (2017); Soul City Institute (2017).
Virodene P508 'AIDS Cure'	1997–2002	Contrary to the government's position, a media storm showed that Virodene is a toxic substance that does not slow or prevent the development of HIV or reverse AIDS. The media also questioned the efficacy of testing Virodene on military troops stationed in Tanzania, and the alleged financial involvement of the ANC in the development of the drug. The government eventually abandoned Virodene in April 2002 following the release of un-blinded test results for phase 2 trials (Myburgh 2007).
Pharmaceutical-lawsuit	1998–2001	Local and international pressure forced a consortium of thirty-nine pharmaceutical companies to drop a three-year lawsuit against the South African government's attempt to import cheap generic antiretroviral products under a new law known as the Medical and Related Substances Control Act (Swarns 2001).
Nevirapine	2002	In a challenge to the national government's ban, some provinces led by Kwa-Zulu Natal made Nevirapine available as a moral imperative to curb mother-to-child transmission of the virus and reduce child mortality (*News24* 2002; Šehović 2014: 122–3). South Africa's High Court and Constitutional Court both ordered the national government to make Nevirapine available to pregnant women, following campaigns by TAC and others (Butcher 2002; CCSA 2017b).
HAART	2003–04	Cheaper drugs, public pressure, and a looming election prompt the government to commit to universal HAART in September 2003, although progress in implementing the treatment and meeting targets is slow due to financial bottlenecks (Šehović 2014: 131–4).
Dr Beetroot strikes again	2004, 2006	The incumbent health minister, Manto Tshabalala-Msimang, is heavily criticized in the media for advocating a diet of beetroot, spinach, and garlic (among other things) for those suffering from HIV/AIDS (e.g. Walsh 2004; Associated Press 2009).
A new era	2009	In a historic speech to the National Council of Provinces, heralded as the end of 'state supported AIDS denialism' by TAC (2009), Jacob Zuma acknowledges the devastating impact of HIV/AIDS on South Africa and pledged not to lose sight of meeting key strategic targets in tackling the disease (Zuma, 2009).

Source: Compiled by author.

pharmaceutical companies responded by substantially reducing the price of their drugs (Swarns 2001). Meanwhile, TAC activists began to hound the US vice-president on the campaign trail (Karon 2001), and the international media covered the story.[27]

[27] See Cauvin (2001) and Mathiason (2001), among many others.

International pressure on the pharmaceutical companies began to escalate. The Secretary General of the United Nations, Kofi Anann, and Nelson Mandela both called for the pharmaceutical companies to drop their lawsuit against South Africa. The European Union, the World Health Organization (WHO), and France's National AIDS Council publicly supported South Africa's position. Even the United States, a staunch supporter of pharmaceutical companies, indicated that trade sanctions would not be applied if poor countries plagued by AIDS broke American patent laws (Swarns 2001). On 20 April 2001, the pharmaceutical companies dropped the case. One industry analyst, Herman K. Shah, commented that the affair 'had been a public relations disaster for the companies' (Swarns 2001).

In the wake of the abandoned pharmaceutical lawsuit and the Virodene scandal things slowly began to change. In September 2003, the South African government commissioned a comprehensive health plan to tackle HIV (Mbali 2005). The following year the government rolled out Highly Active Antiretroviral Treatment (HAART), although the timing coincided with the election in April 2004 and the subsequent implementation of the plan did not run smoothly (see Šehović 2014: 131–4). More substantial change did not take place until Mbeki left office in 2008, and Jacob Zuma publicly acknowledged the devastating impact of AIDS in a speech the following year heralded by TAC 'as the end of state supported AIDS denialism' (TAC 2009). Cheaper drugs, higher levels of public funding, and greater commitment to tackling the AIDS epidemic began to turn things around.[28] ARV therapy coverage increased dramatically from 2005, and the number of new infections and AIDS-related deaths began to decline (Table 15.2). By 2013, the South African government had procured access to the lowest price ARV drugs anywhere in the world through competitive bidding processes (UNAIDS 2013).

THE ROLE OF THE PUBLIC PROTECTOR AND THE CONSTITUTIONAL COURT

Following the transition to democracy, the Public Protector and the Constitutional Court of South Africa (CCSA) have both played critical roles in supporting and defending democratic institutions, and protecting a range of economic, social, and political rights.

The office of the Public Protector has a mandate to investigate, report on, and remedy misconduct in all spheres of public life independently of government. The office currently has almost 400 remunerated staff, an annual budget in the region of R275 million, and handles up to 38,000 complaints each year.[29] By far the most popular, effective, and fearless Public Protector was Thuli Madonsela, who served from 2009 to 2016 and has been described as 'South Africa's conscience' (Mbanjwa 2009; Chutel 2016b; Enright 2016).

[28] By 2014 the government reported R1.9 billion of expenditure on HIV/AIDS (UNAIDS 2017).
[29] See Public Protector (2014: 5, 2017: 12, 15).

In recent years, the Public Protector has investigated several noteworthy cases of corruption among high ranking politicians, state officials, and the police force. In 2014, Madonsela investigated the President of South Africa himself, Jacob Zuma—the man who appointed her, told her to 'operate without fear or favour or prejudice', and supported and implemented her findings and remedial actions during her first five years in office (Enright 2016). Her investigation focused on R246 million of improvements to Zuma's private Nkandla residence in Kwa-Zulu Natal that included a swimming pool, amphitheatre, visitors' centre, cattle kraal, and chicken run constructed with public money that had no apparent connection with strengthening the president's security. Madonsela's (2014) extensive report uncovered evidence of maladministration and misconduct, found that Zuma 'unduly benefited' (2014: 66), and obliged him to repay the cost of non-security upgrades (2014: 442). Death threats and a smear campaign alleging that Madonsela was a CIA spy followed (Chutel 2016b; Enright, 2016). Two subsequent government reports exonerated the president, one of which concluded that the swimming pool was a fire safety precaution. Zuma and his supporters even suggested that Madonsela's recommendation was not legally binding (Chutel 2016b). The main opposition parties, and, more importantly, the Constitutional Court of South Africa disagreed. In a landmark ruling, Chief Justice Mogoeng Mogoeng ruled that Zuma 'failed to uphold, defend and respect the constitution' when he disregarded Madonsela's directive, and ordered him to personally repay a proportion of the funds spent on renovations (see Mohammed 2016). Six months later, Zuma's office finally issued a statement saying that R7.8 million had been repaid (Chutel 2016a).

Intimidation and threats did not deter Madonsela from investigating allegations of 'state capture' involving President Zuma's personal and business links with the Guptas (a wealthy Indian family with an extensive business empire), during her final days in office. It was alleged that the Guptas could exercise undue political influence, including the appointment of cabinet ministers (Chutel 2016b). Concerns were raised over the award of government contracts to the Guptas as well as the nature of their relationship with prominent ANC politicians (Chutel 2016b; Etheridge 2017). Among other things, it was claimed that the Guptas paid for a house owned by Bongi Ngema-Zuma, one of the president's wives. In 2013, they caused a media storm by landing a chartered plane full of wedding guests at a military base usually reserved for state dignitaries, before receiving a police escort to a luxury holiday resort. Prior to leaving office, Madonsela attempted to release her preliminary findings, but agreed to delay her report following a pending legal action from the president, who argued that more time was required to respond to the report (Chutel 2016b). Her successor, Public Protector Busisiwe Mkhwebane, is regarded as friendlier to the government (Etheridge 2017). In November 2016, Madonsela's long-awaited report on 'state capture' was finally released. As expected, it documents how the Gupta family offered ministerial appointments in return for favours (Tandwa 2017). Political pressure has grown for the release of several other Gupta-related reports (Etheridge 2017).

Table 15.4 Landmark constitutional rulings that protect economic, social, and political rights

S. v. Baloyi (1999)	Recognition that domestic violence is a form of gender inequality, and that the state has a constitutional obligation to provide effective remedies.
Government of the RSA v. Grootboom (2000)	Recognition of the right to adequate housing, including a constitutional right to basic housing for children.
Minister of Health v. TAC (2002)	Promotion of healthcare by requiring the government to make Nevirapine available to treat HIV for mothers and new-born children.
Bhe and Others v. The Magistrate, Khayelitsha and Others; Shibi v. Sithole and Others; South African Human Rights Commission and Another v. President of the Republic of South Africa (2004)	Promotion of gender equality by promoting the rights of women to inherit under the African customary law of intestate succession.
Minister of Home Affairs and Another v. Fourie and Another; Lesbian and Gay Equality Project and Others v. Minister of Home Affairs and Others (2005)	Recognition that same sex couples are constitutionally entitled to the same status, entitlements, and responsibilities as heterosexuals couples.
Occupiers of 51 Olivia Road, Berea Township and 197 Main Street, Johannesburg v. City of Johannesburg and Others (2008)	Attempts to evict tenants must take account of all circumstances, ensure procedural fairness, and 'engage meaningfully' to alleviate homelessness.
Shilubana and Others v. Nwamitwa (2008)	Development of customary law to bring it in line with the constitutional commitment to gender equality, including allowing the appointment of female chiefs.
Leon Joseph and Others v. City of Johannesburg and Others (2009)	Service provider required to afford procedural fairness to tenants (including those without a contract) and provide notice before terminating the electricity supply.
Economic Freedom Fighters v. Speaker of the National Assembly and Others; Democratic Alliance v. Speaker of the National Assembly and Others (2016)	Remedial actions recommended by the Public Prosecutor are legally binding, unless struck down by a court.

Source: Author based on CCSA (2017a); final example from CCSA (2017b).

Other high-profile investigations have focused on corruption in the South African Broadcasting Corporation, financial fraud at the top of the police force, irregularities in the management and award of railway procurement contracts, and excessive spending by cabinet ministers (News Desk 2011; Corruption Watch 2014; Hunter 2015). The Office of the Public Protector has also pursued many low-profile cases that address the concerns and complaints of ordinary South Africans. Some isolated examples relate to the breach of constitutional obligations to assist people being evicted from a hostel, undue delays in the processing of official documents, the improper marking of university exam scripts, non-payment of invoices and salaries, the irregular award of contracts, and issues with service delivery (see Public Protector 2014, 2017; Kasipo and Majola-Kinyunyu 2017).

The Constitutional Court of South Africa has also passed judgement on several cases that strengthen the social and democratic rights of ordinary people (Table 15.4). Among these are landmark judgements that protect rights to housing and public services, advance gender equality and address domestic violence, and facilitate access to ARV drugs. As we have seen, the Constitutional Court has also successfully defended the Office of the Public Protector from the misuse of state power. In the Nkandla case, the Constitutional Court not only ruled that the president must comply with the Public Protector's remedial action, but went on to declare that:

> The Public Protector is . . . one of the most invaluable constitutional gifts to our nation in the fight against corruption, unlawful enrichment, prejudice and impropriety in State affairs and for the betterment of good governance . . . She is the embodiment of a biblical David, that the public is, who fights the most powerful and very well-resourced Goliath, that impropriety and corruption by government officials are . . . Her investigative powers are not supposed to bow down to anybody, not even at the door of the highest chambers of raw state power. (Chief Justice Mogoeng Mogoeng, cited in Munusamy 2016)

The precise work of the Constitutional Court is less well-known than that of the Public Protector. Booysen's (2013: 37) study, however, indicates that South Africans 'have a generally favourable impression' of the Constitutional Court's role, particularly in relation to other parts of the judiciary. In contrast, the work of the Public Protector is widely appreciated, and has considerable demonstration value in stimulating public participation and debate.

LOCAL DEMOCRACY IN ACTION—BOKFONTEIN

A final example draws on Malose Langa's study of Bokfontein in *The Smoke That Calls*—a report that brings together eight separate case studies of local protest and community violence from across South Africa (von Holdt et al. 2011). In the report, Bokfontein is hailed as 'a reminder of what is possible in South Africa' (2011: 4). In contrast to the other communities featured in the report, Bokfontein has managed to address service delivery problems through collective effort and participatory action. Locals and foreigners have also learned to live together and cooperate for mutual advantage, without resorting to destructive forms of xenophobic violence.

Bokfontein is a community in the North West Province settled by local people evicted from nearby farms in 2005. Many lost their jobs at the time and were unable to educate their children. Among those expelled from the farms were foreign nationals from Zimbabwe, Mozambique, and Lesotho. The following year, these settlers were joined by people from a neighbouring community who were evicted by the local municipality following a dispute over housing rights.

Both communities were forced to share a small piece of land and limited water supply, which initially precipitated violent conflict. According to the community, the situation was reversed by an organizational workshop that helped residents to reflect on their 'collective trauma' and work together to 'restore their sense of humanity and dignity' (2011: 109). It also helped nationals and foreigners alike appreciate identity issues, respect cultural diversity, and recognize their common African heritage (114).

The workshop was based on principles of 'participatory action' and 'consciousness raising' (110). It empowered local people to actively identify, manage, and implement their own community-driven development projects which included opportunities for paid employment. A road was constructed, vegetable gardens were cultivated to feed the hungry, and home-based care services were provided for the sick and elderly. A day care centre with a nutrition programme was opened, and the community began to develop a park for leisure purposes. The prospect of paid employment and the establishment of a community policing forum helped curb crime and violence. The community also began to develop water, sanitation, and electricity projects, instead of engaging in violent service delivery protests.

Reason, agency, and self-help prevailed. Community leaders repeatedly tried to negotiate better service delivery with the municipality, but without any success. Yet they remain adamant that violent protest is not the solution; it merely destroys public property, creates a culture of violence, and sets a bad example for their children. Instead, 'they believe in negotiations to solve community problems' (2011: 117), and prefer to channel energy into other more positive endeavours (such as the creation of an income-generating supermarket through the Bokfontein Community Development Forum), which are preferable to waiting for the municipality to initiate positive change in their community.[30]

Conclusion

Amartya Sen has shown that democracy has universal appeal and is not an inherently 'western' concept. The appeal of democracy is not only *intrinsic* to the human condition, but is firmly embedded in the *instrumental* and *constructive* roles of democratic institutions. These institutions help extend voice and criticism, hold politicians and bureaucrats to account, safeguard economic and political rights, and shape social values and priorities.

Several examples of the functional role of democracy have been identified, including Sen's striking observation that famine never occurs in a working democracy. The absence of democratic institutions can contribute to economic and social catastrophe, as witnessed in China during the Great Leap Forward or Cultural Revolution. Democratic pressures can also play meaningful roles in flawed democracies (such as India), and sometimes in non-democratic settings too (consider the mixed results of the Arab Spring).[31] Effective participation is mediated through the quality of state institutions

[30] Media reports indicate that talks with the municipality and peaceful forms of protest have continued but largely to no avail (e.g. Kormorant 2014).

[31] Compare, for example, the stalled revolution in Egypt and subsequent imposition of a government backed by the military with the democratic transition that took place in Tunisia following the wave of political protests that swept across the Middle East from December 2010. The Tunisian protests were

(democratic or otherwise), the prevailing balance of power, the extent of economic and social inequalities, and the capacity—and desire—to organize collectively and express voice (including through the media).

In the twenty-five years since South Africa became a fledgling democracy, the country has continued to endure pervasive and deep-seated social and economic inequalities. As with India, Ambedkar's warning about the threatening effects of such inequalities have not come to pass. Democracy has endured in the new South Africa, even if it has not thrived. Ambedkar may well have placed too much emphasis on the destabilizing effects of inequality. In his critique of parliamentary democracy in Western Europe (dating back to the Second World War), he writes of 'the failure to realise that political democracy cannot succeed where there is no economic or social democracy' (Ambedkar 2002: 62). But he was right to recognize that functional democracy involves more than regular elections and 'the maintenance of a constitutional form of government' (2002: 60, 63). Inclusive forms of governance capable of serving the interests of all people require direct forms of social and political participation (which may well work best in the absence of significant inequalities, as Drèze and Sen argue).

The South African brand of democracy falls short of the ideal. Although the country benefits from a liberal constitution and vibrant multiparty system, the ANC is all but assured electoral victory for historical reasons, effectively turning South Africa into a single party state. The executive and legislator are largely co-opted by the ANC (or ruling faction of the ANC), although the judiciary has not always been so easy to subdue. Corruption and the abuse of economic and political power have escalated. But ordinary people, civil society, and large sections of the media have fought back. In these spheres, democracy has flourished.

South Africans exhibit high levels of political consciousness and have well-defined values and priorities. They are deeply resentful of government corruption and highly critical of poor service delivery. As dissatisfaction has grown, they have not hesitated to voice dissent or take to the streets. In fact, South Africa has rapidly become known as 'the protest capital of the world' (Rodrigues 2010). In these respects, South Africa has embraced 'reason, argument and agitation' more closely than perhaps almost any other country in the world, including India and Brazil (see also Figure 15.1).

South Africa and India have much in common. In both countries, widespread corruption and ineffective democratic instructions have been countered by active participation and the expansion of civil society (see also Heller 2012). Returning to the question posed at the beginning of this chapter, it might now be asked: If these two countries are not so different, shouldn't we expect to find reason to be 'contingently optimistic' about South African democracy as well as Indian democracy? There are many reasons to be sceptical, but there are also some grounds for encouragement and hope.

sparked by Mohamed Bouazizi, a 26-year old poverty-stricken fruit vendor, who set himself on fire after a government official humiliated him and attempted to confiscate his wares for allegedly refusing to pay a bribe (Fahim 2011).

This chapter has considered three concrete examples of participation in South Africa that inspire confidence and focus on actors at the global, national, and local levels. The first example shows how a reluctant government was repeatedly obliged to modify its chaotic response to the HIV/AIDS epidemic through persistent campaigns, demonstrations, and legal actions orchestrated by a local–global alliance of activists led by TAC. This alliance eventually forced the government to abandon its AIDS denialist stance and devote significant sums of money to treating the disease with spectacular results. The second example explores the role of the Public Protector in investigating corruption and state capture at the highest levels. It also considers how the Constitutional Court has defended the Office of the Public Protector from the misuse of state power, and how both institutions have helped to protect and promote a range of human rights. The final example reflects on the practice of local democracy in Bokfontein, which was inspired by a participatory workshop. The workshop provided reconciliation for South African and foreign nationals living in close proximity, and empowered local people to work together on community development projects and collectively address service delivery problems without resorting to violent protest or xenophobia.

In a longer chapter, further examples of democratic pressure contributing to positive change could have been considered. One possible example is the work of the independent Marikana Commission (2015) that investigated the killing of thirty-four striking miners by the police and security services in 2012. Another example is the defeat of Zuma's Traditional Courts Bill (killed by 'popular opposition' at public meetings[32]) which threatened to create a separate legal system in the former homelands depriving many people of access to due process (Malik 2015). It would also be useful to consider cases where democratic institutions have floundered. A case in point relates to South Africa's brief experiment with a national health insurance scheme that was piloted in 2012. The scheme was opposed by private sector service providers, received relatively little support in the media, and was effectively allowed to fail by the government (van Niekerk 2016).[33]

Democracy is very much alive in South Africa even if it is a messy and complicated process tarnished by corruption and power imbalances. At the time of writing, Jacob Zuma has just been replaced as leader of the ANC by Cyril Ramaphosa. Zuma's preferred candidate in the ANC leadership election, ex-wife Nkosazana Dlamini-Zuma, was narrowly defeated despite fears of bribery and intimidation.[34] Ramaphosa campaigned on an anti-corruption ticket and replaced Zuma as President of South Africa in February 2018. His election to the leadership of the ANC provides further grounds for optimism and has been welcomed in the press and by financial markets, although it is worth remembering that the future of democracy in South Africa will depend on far more than the removal of one corrupt leader.

[32] See Gasa (2014).
[33] I am grateful to Elaine Unterhalter for flagging this example.
[34] See Mortimer (2017) and Burke (2017).

ACKNOWLEDGEMENTS

This chapter is dedicated to the late Dudley B. Horner (for many years Deputy Director of the Southern Africa Labour and Development Research Unit at the University of Cape Town). Dudley loved South Africa and he loved democracy. He never lost faith or hope, and he never gave up. In the darkest days of apartheid, he valiantly fought for a free and democratic South Africa for all people, races, and creeds. As chair of the Minimum Wage Board, he redirected his energy to the formation of a more equal and prosperous South Africa. In writing this chapter, I have benefited from extensive discussions with Elaine Uterhalter, Melanie Walker, and David Woolfrey. Prathivadi B. Anand, Shailaja Fennell, and Gay Meeks have provided helpful comments on various drafts, and Pat Baxter has provided valuable editorial support. Any errors or omissions are, of course, my own.

REFERENCES

Acemoglu, D., Naidu, S., Restrepo, P., and Robinson, J. (2019). 'Democracy does cause growth', *Journal of Political Economy*, 127/1: 47–100.

BBC (2017b). 'South Africa Jacob Zuma survives no-confidence vote', 8 August. Available at www.bbc.co.uk/news/world-africa-40869269, accessed 29 October 2018.

Berendsen, B. (ed) (2008). *Democracy and Development*. Amsterdam: KIT Publishers.

Berning, J. and Montesh, M. (2012). 'Countering corruption in South Africa: the rise and fall of the Scorpions and Hawks', *South African Crime Quarterly* 39: 3–10.

Biggeri, M., Ballet, J., and Comim, F. (eds) (2011). *Children and the Capability Approach*. Basingstoke: Palgrave Macmillan.

Biz Staff Writers (2017). 'Revealed! How Gupta brothers taught Independent group's Iqbal Survé a state capture trick or two'. *Biznews Guptaleaks*, 8 June. Available at www.biznews.com/guptaleaks/2017/06/08/iqbal-surve-guptaleaks/, accessed 29 October 2018.

Blair, D. (2016). 'Despotism or model democracy – South Africa could now go either way', *The Telegraph*, 6 August. Available at www.telegraph.co.uk/news/2016/08/06/despotism-or-model-democracy—south-africa-could-now-go-either/, accessed 29 October 2018.

Blandy, F. (2006). '"Dr Beetroot" hits back at media over Aids exhibition', *Mail & Guardian Online*, 16 August. Archived from the original 4 January 2007. Available at https://web.archive.org/web/20070104191247/http://www.mg.co.za/articlepage.aspx?area=%2Fbreaking_news%2Fbreaking_news__national%2F&articleid=280903, accessed 29 October 2018.

Bond, P. (2010). 'South Africa's bubble meets boiling urban social protest', *Monthly Review* 62/2: 17–28.

Bond, P. (2016). 'Why South Africa should undo Mandela's economic deals', *Mail & Guardian*, 12 January. Available at https://mg.co.za/article/2016-01-12-why-south-africa-should-undo-mandelas-economic-deals, accessed 29 October 2018.

Booysen, S. (2013). *Twenty Years of South African Democracy: Citizen Views of Human Rights, Governance and the Political System*. Washington, DC: Freedom House.

Booysen, S. (2014). 'Nkandla – the ANC's house of cards', *Sunday Independent*, 6 April. Available at www.iol.co.za/sundayindependent/nkandla-the-ancs-house-of-cards-1671773, accessed 29 October 2018.

Burke, J. (2017). 'Future of ANC and South Africa at stake as party meets to choose new leader', *The Guardian*, 15 December. Available at www.theguardian.com/world/2017/dec/15/future-of-anc-and-south-africa-at-stake-as-party-meets-to-choose-new-leader, accessed 29 October 2018.

Butcher, T. (2002). 'Judges rule that South Africa must offer Aids drug', *The Telegraph*, 5 April. Available at www.telegraph.co.uk/news/worldnews/africaandindianocean/southafrica/1389941/Judges-rule-that-South-Africa-must-offer-Aids-drug.html, accessed 29 October 2018.

Buys, F. (2015). 'On the Zumafication of South Africa', *Politicsweb*, 25 February. Available at www.politicsweb.co.za/news-and-analysis/on-the-zumafication-of-south-africa, accessed 29 October 2018.

Carroll, R. (2003). 'Aids protesters accuse Pretoria ministers of manslaughter', *The Guardian*, 21 March. Available at www.theguardian.com/world/2003/mar/21/southafrica.aids, accessed 29 October 2018.

Cauvin, H.E. (2001). 'Trial in AIDS drug lawsuit opens in Pretoria', *New York Times*, 6 March. Available at www.nytimes.com/2001/03/06/world/trial-in-aids-drug-lawsuit-opens-in-pretoria.html, accessed 29 October 2018.

CCSA (Constitutional Court of South Africa) (2017a). 'History of the court: Landmark cases', Available at https://collections.concourt.org.za/, accessed 11 February 2019.

CCSA (Constitutional Court of South Africa) (2017b). 'ConCourt Collections [Judgements search engine]'. Available at https://collections.concourt.org.za/, accessed 11 February 2019.

Chang, H.J. (2001). 'Intellectual property rights and economic development: historical lessons and emerging issues', *Journal of Human Development* 2/2: 287–309.

Chutel, L. (2016a). 'South Africa's president finally paid back $540,000 the state used to renovate his private home', *Quartz Africa*, 12 September. Available at https://qz.com/779758/south-africas-jacob-zuma-has-paid-the-state-for-nkandlas-security-with-a-vbs-bank-loan/, accessed 29 October 2018.

Chutel, L. (2016b). 'South Africa's public protector has finished her seven-year masterclass on how to fight corruption', *Quartz Africa*, 15 October. Available at https://qz.com/809753/the-head-of-south-africas-public-protector-thuli-madonsela-ends-her-7-year-term-of-fighting-government-corruption/, accessed 29 October 2018.

Clark, D.A. (2002). *Visions of Development: A Study of Human Values*. Cheltenham: Edward Elgar.

Clark, D.A. (2006). 'The capability approach', in D.A. Clark (ed.) *The Elgar Companion to Development Studies*. Cheltenham: Edward Elgar, 32–45.

Clark, D.A. (ed.) (2012). *Adaptation, Poverty and Development: The Dynamics of Subjective Well-Being*. Basingstoke: Palgrave Macmillan.

Clark, D.A. (ed.) (2014). 'Book symposium on *An Uncertain Glory: India and its Contradictions*', *Journal of Human Development and Capabilities* 15/4: 414–51.

Clark, D.A. and Fennell, S. (2014). 'Democratic freedoms, capabilities and public provision: A defence and some possible extensions', *Journal of Human Development and Capabilities* 15/4: 437–47.

Clark, D.A. and Qizilbash, M. (2008). 'Core poverty, vagueness and adaptation: a new methodology and some results for South Africa', *Journal of Development Studies* 44/4: 519–44.

Clark, D.A., Biggeri, M., and Frediani, A.A. (eds) (2019). *The Capability Approach, Empowerment and Participation: Concepts, Methods and Applications*. Basingstoke: Palgrave Macmillan.

Clarke, J.S. (2015). 'South Africa's failure to arrest Omar al-Bashir "is betrayal of Mandela's ideals"', *The Guardian*, 24 June. Available at www.theguardian.com/global-development-professionals-network/2015/jun/24/south-africas-failure-arrest-al-bashir-not-in-keeping-mandelas-ideals, accessed 29 October 2018.

Corbridge, S. (2002). 'Development as freedom: the spaces of Amartya Sen', *Progress in Development Studies* 2/3: 183–217.

Corruption Watch (2014). 'Time to stop the rot at SABC', 18 February. Available at www.corruptionwatch.org.za/time-to-stop-the-rot-at-the-sabc/, accessed 29 October 2018.

Crocker, D.A. (1995). 'Functioning and capability: the foundation of Sen's and Nussbaum's Development Ethic, part II', in M.C. Nussbaum and J. Glover (eds) *Women, Culture and Human Development*. Oxford: Clarendon Press, 153–98.

Crocker, D.A. (2008). *The Ethics of Global Development: Agency, Capability and Deliberative Democracy*. Cambridge: Cambridge University Press.

Crocker, D. and Robeyns, I. (2010). 'Capability and agency', in C. W. Morris (ed.) *Amartya Sen*. New York: Cambridge University Press, 60–90.

Deneulin, S. (2009). 'Democracy and political participation', in S. Deneulin and L. Shahani (eds) *An Introduction to the Human Development and Capability Approach*. Oxford: Earthscan, 185–206.

Department of Health (2000). *HIV/AIDS & STD Strategic Plan for South Africa*. Department of Health, Republic of South Africa. Available at http://data.unaids.org/topics/nsp-library/nsp-africa/nsp_south_africa_2000-2005_en.pdf, accessed 29 October 2018.

DoJ&CD (Department of Justice and Constitutional Development) (1996). *Constitution of the Republic of South Africa: Chapter 2—Bill of Rights*. Republic of South Africa: DoJ&CD. Available at http://www.justice.gov.za/legislation/constitution/SAConstitution-web-eng-02.pdf, accessed 29 October 2018.

Drèze, J. and Sen, A.K. (eds) (1996). *India: Selected Regional Perspectives*. Oxford: Oxford University Press.

Drèze, J. and Sen, A.K. (2002). *India: Development and Participation* (enlarged edn). Oxford: Oxford University Press.

Drèze, J. and Sen, A.K. (2013). *An Uncertain Glory: India and its Contradictions*. Princeton, NJ: Princeton University Press.

The Economist (2001). 'Drugs, patents and poor people', 17 April. Available at www.economist.com/node/576903, accessed 29 October 2018.

The Economist (2014). 'The wellness of nations: surviving or thriving? How people judge their own well-being', 16 September. Available at www.economist.com/blogs/graphicdetail/2014/09/wellness-nations?fsrc=scn/fb/wl/bl/thrivingorsurviving, accessed 29 October 2018.

EIU (Economist Intelligence Unit) (2017). 'Democracy index 2016: revenge of the "deplorables"'. The Economist Intelligence Unit, 27 January.

Enright, M. (2016). 'Meet Thuli Madonsela—South Africa's conscience', *CBC Radio*, 11 December. Available at www.cbc.ca/radio/thesundayedition/michael-s-book-list-south-africa-s-public-protector-in-the-crossword-diversity-1.3885666/meet-thuli-madonsela-south-africa-s-conscience-1.3887237, accessed 29 October 2018.

Etheridge, J. (2017). 'Public protector must release Gupta reports—DA'. *News24*, 19 June. Available at www.news24.com/SouthAfrica/News/public-protector-must-release-gupta-reports-da-20170619, accessed 29 October 2018.

Fahim, L. (2011). 'Slap to a man's pride set off tumult in Tunisia', *New York Times*, 21 January. Available at www.nytimes.com/2011/01/22/world/africa/22sidi.html?_r=1&pagewanted=2&src=twrhp, accessed 29 October 2018.

February, J. and Tapula, T. (2010). 'Why everyone needs to know', *Sunday Weekend Argos*, 17 October, p. 21.

Gasa, N. (2014). 'Who killed the traditional courts bill?', *Sunday Independent*, 2 March. Available at www.iol.co.za/sundayindependent/who-killed-the-traditional-courts-bill-1654811#.VeiWTHhR6gy, accessed 29 October 2018.

Gasper, D. (2016). 'Human development in India: waiting for inspiration'. Paper presented at the Cambridge Capability Conference, Centre of Development Studies, University of Cambridge, 13–14 June.

Grant, L. (2015). 'Africa: the not-so-happy continent', *Mail & Guardian*, 28 April. Available at https://mg.co.za/article/2015-04-28-africa-the-not-so-happy-continent, accessed 29 October 2018.

Heller, P. (2012). 'Democracy, participatory politics and development: some comparative lessons from Brazil, India and South Africa', *Polity* 44/4: 643–65.

Heller, P. (2015). 'BRICS from below: counterpower movements in Brazil, India and South Africa', *Open Democracy*, 30 April. Available at www.opendemocracy.net/patrick-heller/brics-from-below-counterpower-movements-in-brazil-india-and-south-africa, accessed 29 October 2018.

Helliwell, J., Layard, R., and Sachs, J. (eds) (2017). *The World Happiness Report 2017*. New York: The Earth Institute, Columbia University.

Higgs, N. (2011). 'Half of metro residents unhappy with service provision – TNS', *Politicsweb*, 11 March. Available at www.politicsweb.co.za/news-and-analysis/half-of-metro-residents-unhappy-with-service-provi, accessed 29 October 2018.

Hunter, Q. (2015). 'Maladministration is off the rails at Prasa, finds Madonsela', 25 August. Available at https://mg.co.za/article/2015-08-25-maladministration-is-off-the-rails-at-prasa, accessed 29 October 2018.

IEC (Electoral Commission of South Africa) (2017). *A Vote of Confidence: Election Satisfaction Survey 2016*. Pretoria: Human Science Research Council.

ISS (Institute of Security Studies) (2014). 'Where is open democracy in South Africa today?'. Institute of Security Studies. Available at https://issafrica.org/events/where-is-open-democracy-in-south-africa-today, accessed 29 October 2018.

Karon, T. (2001). 'South African AIDS activist Zackie Achmat', *Time*, 19 April. Available at http://content.time.com/time/nation/article/0,8599,106995,00.html, accessed, 29 October 2018.

Kasipo M. and Majola-Kinyunyu, M-K. (2017). 'Thuli Madonsela: the untold stories of SA's former Public Protector', 3 January. Available at www.cnbcafrica.com/news/southern-africa/2017/01/03/thuli-madonsela-the-untold-stories/, accessed 29 October 2018.

Keeplar, H. (2013). 'The untold AIDS story: how access to antiretroviral drugs was obstructed in Africa'. Available at https://theejbm.wordpress.com/2013/10/01/the-untold-aids-story-how-access-to-antiretroviral-drugs-was-obstructed-in-africa/, accessed 29 October 2018.

Kormorant (2014). 'Bokfontein still left out in the cold', 28 March. Available at https://kormorant.co.za/16106/bokfontein-still-left-out-in-the-cold/, accessed 29 October 2018.

Krüger, F. (2017). 'Why media freedom remains fragile in South Africa', *The Conversation*, 18 October. Available at https://theconversation.com/why-media-freedom-remains-fragile-in-south-africa-85868, accessed 29 October 2018.

le Roux, M. (2001). 'Mandela slams ANC again', *News24 Archives*, 4 March. Available at www.news24.com/SouthAfrica/Politics/Mandela-slams-ANC-again-20010304, accessed 29 October 2018.

McGreal, C. (2000). 'AIDS: South Africa's new apartheid', *The Guardian Online*, 30 November. Available at www.theguardian.com/world/2000/nov/30/aids.chrismcgreal, accessed 29 October 2018.

Madonsela, T. (2014). *Secure in Comfort*. Report No. 25 of 2013/14. Pretoria: Office of the Public Protector.

Malan, M. (2006). 'Exposing AIDS: media's impact in South Africa', *Georgetown Journal of International Affairs* 7/1: 41–9.

Malik, K. (2015). 'What happened to South African democracy', *New York Times*, 22 September. Available at www.nytimes.com/2015/09/23/opinion/what-happened-to-south-african-democracy.html, accessed 29 October 2018.

Mandela Foundation (2015). 'Accessing information is key to open democracy'. Available at www.nelsonmandela.org/content/page/accessing-information-is-key-to-open-democracy, accessed 29 October 2018.

Marikana Commission (2015). *Report on Matters of Public, National and International Concern Arising Out of the Tragic Incidents at the Lonmin Mine in Marikana, in the North West Province*. Available at www.sahrc.org.za/home/21/files/marikana-report-1.pdf, accessed 29 October 2018.

Masinga, L. (2015). 'Judiciary responds to criticism of courts', *IOL*, 8 July. Available at www.iol.co.za/news/crime-courts/judiciary-responds-to-criticism-of-courts-1882462, accessed 29 October 2018.

Mathiason, N. (2001). 'South Africa fights Aids drug apartheid', *The Observer*, 14 January. Available at www.theguardian.com/business/2001/jan/14/aids.theobserver1, accessed 29 October 2018.

May, J. (2000). *Poverty and Inequality in South Africa: Meeting the Challenge*. London: Zed.

Mbali, M. (2005). 'TAC in the history of rights-based, patient driven HIV/AIDS activism in South Africa'. Available at http://hdl.handle.net/2027/spo.4761530.0010.011, accessed 29 October 2018.

Mbanjwa, X. (2009). 'I will not be intimidated – Madonsela', *IOL*, 23 October. Available at www.iol.co.za/news/politics/i-will-not-be-intimidated-madonsela-462448, accessed 29 October 2018.

Mbeki, T. (1998). 'ANC has no financial stake in Virodene', March. Available at https://web.archive.org/web/20070202174845/http://www.anc.org.za:80/ancdocs/history/mbeki/1998/virodene.html, accessed 29 October 2018.

Mbeki, T. (2000). 'Speech at the opening of the 13th International AIDS Conference'. Issued by the Office of the President, 9 July. Available at www.nelsonmandela.org/omalley/index.php/site/q/03lv03445/04lv04206/05lv04302/06lv04303/07lv04312.htm, accessed 29 October 2018.

Mehrotra, S. (2008). 'Democracy, decentralisation and access to basic services: an elaboration on Sen's capability approach', in F. Comim, M. Qizilbash and S. Alkire (eds) *The Capability*

Approach: Concepts, Measures and Applications. Cambridge: Cambridge University Press, 385–420.

Mohammed, O. (2016). 'South Africa's top court says Jacob Zuma's home renovations were unconstitutional', *Quartz Africa*, 31 March. Available at https://qz.com/651549/south-africas-top-court-has-ruled-that-jacob-zumas-home-renovations-were-unconstitutional/, accessed 29 October 2018.

Møller, V. (ed.) (1996). *Perceptions of Development in Kwa-Zulu Natal*. Durban: Social Indicators Press.

Mortimer, C. (2017). 'South Africa ANC election: Cyril Ramaphosa replaces Jacob Zuma as new party leader after tight race', *The Independent*, 18 December. Available at www.independent.co.uk/news/world/africa/south-africa-anc-election-cyril-ramaphosa-party-leader-jacob-zuma-replace-race-nkosazana-dlamini-a8117036.html, accessed 29 October 2018.

Munusamy, R. (2016). 'Nkandla judgment: the mastery of the Concourt vs The Invincibility of Jacob Zuma', *Daily Maverick*, 1 April. Available at www.dailymaverick.co.za/article/2016-04-01-nkandla-judgment-the-mastery-of-the-concourt-vs-the-invincibility-of-jacob-zuma/, accessed 29 October 2018.

Murphy, V. (2003). 'Mbeki stirs up Aids controversy', *BBC News Online*, 26 September. Available at http://news.bbc.co.uk/1/hi/world/africa/3143850.stm, accessed 29 October 2018.

Myburgh, J. (2007). 'The Virodene Affair: The secret history of the ANC's response to the HIV/AIDS epidemic', *Politicsweb*, 21 September. Available at http://politicsweb.co.za/documents/the-virodene-affair, accessed 29 October 2018.

Naidoo, J. (2017). 'Accountants & accountability: Courage is free', *Daily Maverick*, 21 September. Available at www.dailymaverick.co.za/opinionista/2017-09-21-accountants-accountability-courage-is-free/#.WjIotcFLHD4, accessed 29 October 2018.

Nature (2000). 'The Durban Declaration', *Nature* 406: 15–16.

News Desk (2011). 'South African fraud investigators slam country's top police chief', 14 July. Available at www.pri.org/stories/2011-07-14/south-african-fraud-investigators-slam-countrys-top-police-chief, accessed 29 October 2018.

News24 (2002). 'KZN Aids drug move "a surprise"'. *News24* Archive, 22 January. Available at www.news24.com/SouthAfrica/Politics/KZN-Aids-drug-move-a-surprise-20020122, accessed 29 October 2018.

Nolan, P. (1993). 'The causation and prevention of famines: A critique of A.K. Sen', *Journal of Peasant Studies* 21/1: 1–28.

Nussbaum, M.C. and Sen, A.K. (1989). 'Internal criticism and Indian rationalist traditions', in M. Krausz (ed.) *Relativism, Interpretation and Confrontation*. South Bend, IN: University of Notre Dame Press, 299–325.

Parliament of India (1949). 'Government of India Act (Amendment) Bill', *Constituent Assembly of India, vol. XI*, 25 November. Parliament of India Archives. Available at http://164.100.47.194/Loksabha/Debates/cadebatefiles/C25111949.html, accessed 11 February 2019.

Patrón, P. (2019). 'Power and deliberative participation in Sen's capability approach', in D.A. Clark, M. Biggeri, and A.A. Frediani (eds) *The Capability Approach, Empowerment and Participation: Concepts, Methods and Applications*. Basingstoke: Palgrave Macmillan.

Peltzer, K., Parker, W., Mabaso, M., Makonko, E., Zuma, K., and Ramlagan, S. (2012). 'Impact of national HIV and AIDS communication campaigns in South Africa to reduce HIV risk behaviour', *Scientific World Journal* (online) 8. Available at doi:10.1100/2012/384608, accessed 29 October 2018.

Pereira, A.W. (2015). 'Bolsa Família and democracy in Brazil', *Third World Quarterly* 36/9: 1682–99.

Pheko, M. (2014). 'Where is open democracy in South Africa today?', 18 November. Available at https://web.archive.org/web/20150106122039/http://www.eurasiareview.com/18112014-open-democracy-south-africa-today-oped/, accessed 12 February 2019.

Poplak, R. (2017). 'Trainspotter: The end of law, the end of democracy', *The Daily Maverick*, 20 September. Available at www.dailymaverick.co.za/article/2017-09-20-trainspotter-the-end-of-law-the-end-of-democracy/?utm_medium=email&utm_campaign=Afternoon%20Thing%2021%20September%202017%20Chamber%20of%20Commerce&utm_content=Afternoon%20Thing%2021%20September%202017%20Chamber%20of%20Commerce+CID_e5f871ce65510d308e294e0c3db99f65&utm_source=TouchBasePro&utm_term=TRAINSPOTTER%20The%20End%20of%20Law%20The%20End%20of%20Democracy#.WcPU98GWx1x, accessed 29 October 2018.

Public Protector (2014). *Annual Report 2012/13*. Pretoria: Office of the Public Protector.

Public Protector (2017). *Annual Report, 2016/17: Broadening Access: Taking the Services of the Public Protector to the Grassroots*. Pretoria: Office of the Public Protector.

Reich, M.R. (2005). 'Expanding global access to ARVs: The challenges of prices and Patents', in K.H. Mayer and H.F. Pizer (eds) *The AIDS Pandemic: Impact on Science and Society*. New York: Academic Press, New York, 325–50.

Rodrigues, C. (2010). '"Black boers" and other revolutionary songs', 5 April, *Thought Leaders*. Available at http://thoughtleader.co.za/chrisrodrigues/2010/04/05/on-revolutionary-songs/, accessed 29 October 2018.

Rosenberg, E. (2006). 'For People with AIDS, a government with two faces', *New York Times*, 30 August. Available at www.nytimes.com/2006/08/30/opinion/30wed4.html, accessed 29 October 2018.

SAHO (South African History Online) (2017). 'HIV/Aids in South Africa timeline 1940s–2009', *South African History Online*. Available at www.sahistory.org.za/article/hivaids-south-africa-timeline-1940s-2009, accessed 29 October 2018.

SAPS (South African Police Service) (2012). *Annual Report 2011/2012, SAPS Strategic Management*. Pretoria: SAPS.

SAPS (South African Police Service) (2016), *Annual Report 2015/2016, SAPS Strategic Management*. Pretoria: SAPS.

Šehović, A.B. (2014). *HIV/AIDS and the South African State: Sovereignty and the Responsibility to Respond*. Farnham: Ashgate.

Sen, A.K. (1982). 'How is India doing?', *New York Review of Books* 16 December: 41–5.

Sen, A.K. (1983). 'Development: which way now?', *Economic Journal* 93/372: 745–62.

Sen, A.K. (1985). 'Well-being, agency and freedom: the Dewey Lectures', *Journal of Philosophy* 82/4: 169–221.

Sen, A.K. (1990). 'Development as capability expansion', in K. Griffin and J. Knight (eds) *Human Development and the International Development Strategy for the 1990s*. London: Macmillan, 41–58.

Sen, A.K. (1993). 'The causation and prevention of famines: A reply', *Journal of Peasant Studies* 21/1: 29–40.

Sen, A.K. (1999a). 'Democracy as a universal value', *Journal of Democracy* 10/3: 3–17.

Sen, A.K. (1999b). *Development as Freedom*. Oxford: Oxford University Press.

Sen, A.K. (2002). *Rationality and Freedom*. London: Belknap Press.

Sen, A.K. (2006a). 'Democracy isn't "Western"', *Wall Street Journal* (Eastern Edition), 24 (March). Available at www.wsj.com/articles/SB114317114522207183, accessed 12 February 2019.

Sen, A.K. (2006b). *The Argumentative Indian*. London: Penguin.

Sen, A.K. (2009). *The Idea of Justice*. London: Allen Lane.

Sen, A.K. (2013). 'India's women: the mixed truth', *New York Review of Books,* 10 October.

Sen, A.K. and Drèze, J. (1999). *India: Economic Development and Social Opportunity*. New Delhi: Oxford University Press.

Sidley, P. (1997). 'South African research into AIDS "cure" severely criticised', *British Medical Journal* 314/7083: 771.

Soul City Institute (2017). 'Soul City television series'. Available at www.soulcity.org.za/projects/soul-city-series, accessed 30 October 2018.

Staff Reporter (1998). 'The real Verodene scandal', *Mail & Guardian*, 6 March. Available at https://mg.co.za/article/1998-03-06-the-real-virodene-scandal, accessed 30 October 2018.

Suttner, R. (2015). *Recovering Democracy in South Africa*. London: First Forum Press.

Swarns, R.L. (2001). 'Drug makers drop South Africa suit over AIDS medicine', *New York Times,* 20 April. Available at www.nytimes.com/2001/04/20/world/drug-makers-drop-south-africa-suit-over-aids-medicine.html, accessed 30 October 2018.

TAC (Treatment Action Campaign) (2009). 'Landmark speech by President Zuma'. Treatment Action Campaign, 30 October. Available at https://tac.org.za/news/landmark-speech-by-president-zuma-2/, accessed 12 February 2019.

Tandwa, L. (2017). 'State capture better hidden under Mandela, Mbeki – R2K', *News24,* 22 November. Available at www.news24.com/SouthAfrica/News/state-capture-better-hidden-under-mandela-mbeki-r2k-20161122, accessed 30 October 2018.

Tilly, A. (2010). 'Fear and disdain keep the public in the dark', *Business Day*, 27 October: 15.

Time (2000). 'Mbeki – Africa's challenges', *Time Magazine* (South African edition), 11 September. Available at http://content.time.com/time/world/article/0,8599,2039809,00.html, accessed 30 October 2018.

UNAIDS (2013). 'Around 10 million people living with HIV now have access to antiretroviral treatment'. Press Release. Available at www.unaids.org/sites/default/files/web_story/20130630_PR_Treatment_en_0.pdf, accessed 30 October 2018.

UNAIDS (2017). *AIDSinfo*. Available at http://aidsinfo.unaids.org/, accessed 21 December 2017).

UNDP (2002). *Human Development Report 2002: Democracy in a Fragmented World*. New York: Oxford University Press.

UPI (United Press International) (2000). 'Mbeki says CIA had role in HIV/AIDS conspiracy', *United Press International,* 6 October. Available at www.upi.com/Archives/2000/10/06/Mbeki-says-CIA-had-role-in-HIVAIDS-conspiracy/2976970804800/, accessed 30 October 2018.

Van der Byl, C. (2014). 'Twenty years of freedom: South Africa 1994–2004'. Background Paper: Income, Poverty, and Inequality. Pretoria: Planning, Monitoring and Evaluation Department.

van Niekerk, R. (2016). 'PPPs and health care as a public good: an exploration of contestations in South Africa'. Unpublished paper presented at the Public Private Partnership Workshop, University of London.

von Holdt, K., Langa, M., Molapo, S., Mogapi, N., Ngubeni, K., Dlamini, J. et al. (2011). *The Smoke That Calls: Insurgent Citizenship, Collective Violence and the Struggle for a Place in the new South Africa*. Oslo: Norwegian Ministry of Foreign Affairs.

Walsh, D. (2004). 'Beetroot and spinach the cure for Aids, say some in S Africa', *The Irish Times*, 12 March. Available at www.irishtimes.com/news/beetroot-and-spinach-the-cure-for-aids-say-some-in-s-africa-1.1135185, accessed 30 October 2018.

Watson, J. (2006). 'Scientists, activists sue South Africa's AIDS "denialists"', *Nature Medicine* 12/6. doi:10.1038/nm0106-6a.

Wikipedia (2017a). 'Protests in South Africa'. Available at https://en.wikipedia.org/wiki/Protests_in_South_Africa, accessed 30 October 2018.

Wikipedia (2017b). 'Virodene'. Available at https://en.wikipedia.org/wiki/Virodene#cite_note-WSJ-1, accessed 30 October 2018.

Wise, J. (2006). 'Access to AIDS medicine stumbles on trade rules', *Bulletin of the World Health Organization* 84/5: 342–4.

Worden, N. (2012). *The Making of Modern South Africa: Conquest, Apartheid, Democracy*, 5th edn. Chichester: John Wiley and Sons.

World Bank (2017). *World Development Indicators*. Available at http://databank.worldbank.org/data/home.aspx, accessed 30 October 2018.

Zuma, J. (2009). 'Address by the President of the Republic of South Africa, HE Mr Jacob Zuma, to the National Council of Provinces (NCOP)'. National Council of Provinces, Cape Town, 29 October. Available at www.thepresidency.gov.za/speeches/address-president-republic-south-africa,-he-mr-jacob-zuma,-national-council-provinces-ncop, accessed 12 February 2019.

16 Education in BRICS

Aline K. Dalcin, Thomas H. Kang, Daiane Zanon, Felipe A. Bellé, Luana P. Betti, Fábio A. Rasche Jr, and Flavio Comim

Introduction

Education is one of the most challenging development issues for BRICS. Although most of BRICS have experienced remarkable improvements in their educational outcomes in the last decades, they have not reached the level of the educational systems found in developed countries. On the one hand, BRICS have reportedly achieved gross enrolment ratios close to or higher than 100 per cent in primary education. Gender parity was nearly achieved in all these countries and the expansion of other schooling levels is on course (UNESCO 2014). Russia is largely ahead at the tertiary level, but the other BRICS have experienced an enrolment expansion in their tertiary education in recent years (Schwartzman 2015). Enhancing the quality of education at all levels while dealing with demographic changes is a further challenge for BRICS. As these countries together account for more than 40 per cent of the world population and experience meaningful education inequalities, educational policies in BRICS have drastic consequences on global poverty, income, and other forms of inequality and development.

Indeed, an increase in the quantity and quality of education would be crucial for both economic growth and income inequality reduction in those societies. In the long-run growth literature, theoretical models that embody the importance of knowledge became canonical after the influential works of Paul Romer (1986, 1990) and Lucas (1988). On the empirical side, Hanushek and Woessmann (2012) have found convincing evidence of the positive role of human capital on economic growth using educational quality measures as proxies. The labour market approach to education, largely inspired by the seminal works of Mincer (1958, 1974), Schultz (1963), and Becker (1964) have also shed light on labour market-generated inequalities. If the supply of skilled workers increases slowly, inequality soars when growth leads to skill-biased technological change (Goldin and Katz 2008). Some of the BRICS are good examples of cases in which inequality remains high partly as a result of skilled labour scarcity.

In addition to the positive effects of education on economic growth and income distribution, education is expected to be a positive influence on institutions, particularly in developing economies where institutional aspects are still being shaped. That is the case of many if not all BRICS. None of the BRICS is considered a 'full democracy'

Aline K. Dalcin, Thomas H. Kang, Daiane Zanon, Felipe A. Bellé, Luana P. Betti, Fábio A. Rasche Jr, and Flavio Comim, *Education in BRICS*
In: *Handbook of BRICS and Emerging Economies.* Edited by: P.B. Anand, Shailaja Fennell, and Flavio Comim, Oxford University Press (2021).
 DOI: 10.1093/oso/9780198827535.003.0016

according to the Polity IV database (Marshall et al. 2016).[1] Better education promotes public reasoning, enhances political participation and government accountability, facilitates social inclusion and enhances institutions, generates positive effects on women and children's health, and decreases demographic pressure—which would also have positive effects on the environment (Thomas et al. 2000). Many of those features have greater importance in developing countries. The human development/capability approach to well-being has placed a special emphasis on education. Sen (1999) argues that education not only has an instrumental role in human welfare, it is a key intrinsic component of well-being.

There is a large literature trying to answer *why* several developing countries have so many problems in providing quality education for their populations, despite the lack of consensus on where exactly the problem lies. Research on labour markets has demonstrated that private returns to schooling are often positive in both developed and developing countries—and the return rates are higher in the latter (Montenegro and Patrinos 2014). However, demand for schooling is not as strong as expected in developing countries, including some of the BRICS. Some studies suggest that informational problems are one of the main reasons underlying the low demand for education in developing countries (Jensen 2010; Banerjee and Duflo 2011). Indeed, Jensen (2012) and Oster and Steinberg (2013) found that informational problems constrain the demand for education in India. Bursztyn (2016) found that Brazilians prefer government cash transfers over public education spending. Another strand of the literature stresses that governments in many developing countries have undersupplied education for their populations for political economy reasons (Ansell 2010; Kosack 2012). Economic strategies adopted in those countries might have had an enduring influence on educational outcomes. According to Ansell (2010), Brazil and India are examples of countries that relied on a relatively closed strategy of import substituting industrialization (ISI), which in its turn hampered the interest of elites in expanding mass education. More schooling would lead to a depletion of wage premiums that stem from skills scarcity in a relatively closed economy, where there are fewer opportunities to 'export skills' through international markets.

Comparing education systems in BRICS is not a trivial task because it entails taking into account different educational challenges in these countries. However, a first approximation might be attempted by looking at formal schooling and other educational data. The method chosen to make a comparative analysis of education systems in BRICS is cluster analysis. Its basic assumption is to verify the degree of homogeneity among educational systems in BRICS.

Our results suggest that the Russian Federation presents educational outcomes closer to the ones found in developed countries, while India is on the opposite side. Applying different criteria, Brazil, China, and South Africa are at the same intermediate cluster.

[1] Brazil, India, and South Africa are at least considered democracies, but not full democracies. Russia is listed as an anocracy, while China is regarded as an autocratic country (Marshall et al. 2016).

This chapter is divided into four additional parts. Following the Introduction, the second section presents a summary of the historical evolution of education outcomes in each of the BRICS, as well as a description of the educational system of each country. In the third section, we present the methodology of cluster analysis, a well-known tool of multivariate analysis. The fourth section presents the results classifying BRICS countries' education systems within several groups and exploring their main differences. The last section presents our conclusions. The main argument of this chapter is that education systems, despite their historical differences and circumstances, have common elements of differentiation that place these systems at different stages and with specific education agendas to face.

BRICS educational systems

BRICS have several features in common. All these countries have large populations and regional economic leadership, but they are still considered developing countries. They have all experienced fast economic growth in the past decade, though some of them have faced political and economic crises in recent years. In historical terms, all BRICS adopted a strategy of rapid industrialization whose costs were not negligible. Brazil and India adopted a strategy of ISI for decades, while poverty and inequality remained widespread. The former Soviet Union also speculated on a fast industrialization strategy, achieving high rates of growth between the decades of 1920 and 1960 and became a world superpower (Allen 2003). After the economic reforms of the 1970s, China adopted a state-controlled industrialization strategy with an export-oriented approach, in line with the so-called 'East Asian model'. South Africa did not follow an orthodox ISI strategy, but the manufacturing industry increased significantly, while the mining sector kept its prominence in the national economy (Natrass and Seekings 2011). Poverty and inequality defined on race, class, or caste lines is another feature that stands out in all these societies.

Most BRICS have presented historical struggles with their education systems. BRICS seem to have provided limited publicly funded education from the beginning of the twentieth century. Primary school enrolment rates were not larger than 20 per cent around 1910 in these countries, while North America and European educational leaders had already universalized primary education (Lindert 2004; Engerman et al. 2012; Chaudhary et al. 2012). In fact, BRICS's enrolment rates were remarkably low even when compared to other developing countries at the time such as Spain, Chile, Jamaica, and Peru (Chaudhary et al. 2012). Although the comparative historical study of Chaudhary et al. (2012) does not cover South Africa, it seems safe to argue that education in Russia was the most advanced among BRICS at the time. Enrolment rates achieved 19.3 per cent in European Russia around 1910–11, whereas Brazil had achieved 11.9 per cent around 1914–15 and British India and China presented even lower coefficients of 7.8 per cent and 4.0 per cent respectively around 1911–12. The evidence analysed in this chapter suggests the remarkable result that the relative education performance among BRICS countries is not much different a century later. Russian education indicators are closer to the advanced countries and India's are closer to the most backward countries, while the indicators of other three countries are somewhere in between. The results found in the cluster analysis carried out suggest that education systems are better seen as a result of path-dependent processes rather than outcomes of current policies.

It is interesting to note that from a legal perspective education is acknowledged as central within all BRICS (UNESCO 2014). Primary and lower secondary education is compulsory in all countries, despite some variations. Brazil has the longest compulsory track, from pre-primary up to upper secondary level, which comprises fourteen years of schooling. The Russian education system has eleven years of compulsory education (from primary to upper secondary). Indian and Chinese laws require primary and lower secondary levels, which account for eight years of compulsory education. In the South African system, compulsory education takes nine years to be completed. At least this is the theory. In practice, as will be discussed below, the legal framework in place is weakly implemented in several of these countries. Before carrying out a more systematic analysis we proceed to a brief examination of the historical background and analysis of each educational system.

BRAZIL

Brazil did not have national educational policies before the 1930s. It started with the creation of the Ministry of Education and Public Health and the 1934 Constitution which stated that primary education was compulsory. In addition, it determined minimum percentages of expenditure on education for each government level (federal, states, and municipalities). However, the first clear national policy was introduced in the country only in 1961, with the First National Education Regulatory Framework ([*Lei de Diretrizes e Bases da Educação Nacional*] – in Portuguese 1st LDB) after thirteen years of parliamentary and public disputes between progressive and conservative groups over the matter (Kang 2011; Wjuniski 2013). Before that time, in 1950, about half of the population aged 15 years or more was illiterate (Astorga et al. 2005).

The creation of the Ministry of Education and Public Health in the early 1930s marked the organization of national educational policies in Brazil. The 1934 Constitution stated that primary education was compulsory and determined minimum percentages of expenditures on education for each government level (federal, states, and municipalities). In 1961 there was a reconfiguration of the national educational system with the First National Education Regulatory Framework ([Lei de Diretrizes e Bases da Educação Nacional]—in Portuguese—1st LDB), enacted after thirteen years of parliamentary and public disputes between progressive and conservative groups over the matter (Kang, 2011; Wjuniski, 2013).

The Second National Education Regulatory Framework (2nd LDB), sanctioned during the military regime in 1971, led to an extension of compulsory schooling from 4 to 8 years of age. The military government promoted the development of technical skills as the country was under an intense process of industrialization. Three years after the military left power in 1985, a new constitution was enacted in 1988. The new document prioritized the decentralization and expansion of social policies including education. Further changes came with the 1996 Third National Education Regulatory Framework (3rd LDB) and later amendments. As a result, the current Brazilian educational system is divided into six compulsory and non-compulsory levels: pre-school (0–5 years of age), elementary school (primary plus lower secondary, 6–14 years of age), and upper secondary (15–17 years of age) are compulsory levels, while vocational, supplementary, and tertiary education are not considered mandatory.

The Brazilian regulatory framework has always assigned the responsibility of the provision of primary and secondary education to local and sub-national governments, despite the fact that most tax revenues had been increasingly in the hands of the federal government since the 1930s (Kang 2011). According to the current 1988 Constitution, municipalities and sub-national states are responsible for the provision of primary education, while the federal government is responsible for tertiary education. The emphasis on decentralization of social policies after 1988 called attention to the economic disparities between different government levels. To tackle that problem, a national fund was created in 1996 named FUNDEF in Portuguese. The purpose of this fund was to redistribute resources for boosting primary education in the poorest localities ensuring a minimum amount of resources per student. In 2005 FUNDEF represented 63 per cent of the total municipal spending in the elementary school (Haddad et al. 2016). In 2006 FUNDEF was renamed highlighting *Fundo de Manutenção e Desenvolvimento da Educação Básica e de Valorização dos Profissionais da Educação* (FUNDEB), which broadened the scope of the fund for the entire basic education (early childhood, elementary, and upper secondary school). There is evidence that FUNDEF allowed at least small gains in enrolments (Gordon and Vegas 2005; Mello and Hoppe 2005). However, there is little evidence of positive effects on educational quality (Menezes-Filho and Pazello 2007; Haddad et al. 2016).

The last two decades have seen considerable progress in some education variables in Brazil. The average years of schooling for people of 15 years of age and over in Brazil went from 5.6 years in 1995 to 7.9 years in 2010 (Barro and Lee 2013). That was largely a result of the expansion of enrolment in elementary schools that went from 88.4 per cent in 1995 to 98.8 per cent in 2015. School access also increased at pre-primary and secondary school levels. In 2015, the gross enrolment rates at these levels were 92.2 per cent and 99.7 per cent, respectively (UNESCO 2017). At tertiary level, admission for the limited system of public universities, which charge no tuition fees, is highly competitive. The large majority of tertiary education is provided by private institutions regulated by the federal government.[2] Enrolments increased in tertiary education from

[2] Public institutions of tertiary education comprise only 12.5 per cent of the whole system (INEP 2016).

1.9 million in 1995 to 8 million in 2015 (INEP 1997, 2016). This process was supported to a large extent by two federal programmes: the Prouni and the FIES. The former was a programme of scholarships directed to high-performing low-income students from public schools to allow them to attend private universities, while the latter provided subsidized loans to students. Despite the growth of enrolment in tertiary education, the share of Brazilian population between 25- and 34-year-olds in tertiary education is not more than 15 per cent, roughly a third of the OECD average of 41 per cent (OECD 2015).

This progress in enrolment at all schooling levels was not however accompanied by progress in other education indicators in Brazil. For instance, 36.1 per cent of 15-year-old Brazilian students repeated at least one grade (about three times the OECD average of 12.4 per cent) and 8 per cent of them are not in school (approximately four times the OECD average of 2 per cent) (OECD 2015). The performance of Brazilian 15-year-old students in the Programme for International Student Assessment (PISA) has enhanced in all evaluated subjects (mathematics, reading, and science); but about two-thirds of Brazilian participants were still classified as low-performers in 2012 (below the OECD average performance of 23 per cent) (OECD 2015). Data from the Basic Education Evaluation System (SAEB), conducted by the National Institute of Educational Research *Anísio Teixeira* (INEP), shows that the trajectory of the performance in Portuguese and mathematics of secondary students has stagnated since the beginning of the 2000s. In 2015, only 42.9 per cent of fifth-graders had adequate or above-grade performance in mathematics, and 54.7 per cent of those students performed well or above in Portuguese. In high school, this figure was even lower; only 7.3 per cent of young people who finished high school that year had adequate knowledge in mathematics and merely 27.5 per cent had adequate knowledge or above in Portuguese Language.[3] Taking stock, it seems that the recent story of the education system in Brazil was quantity (enrolment expansion) at the expense of quality (poor performance on quality of education indicators).

RUSSIA

For more than seventy years, the prevailing approach to education in the former Soviet Union was tied to a centralized system aligned with the political regime. In addition, pupils had little room for questioning tutors, since classroom didactics was deeply hierarchical (Nikandrov 1995). The development of education was a government priority, and both basic and tertiary education were free of charge and under the responsibility of central government (Zajda 2003; Lukov 2005; Kyui 2016). Compulsory eight-year

[3] The data referring to the definition of adequate performance for each series is based on the methodology adopted by the All for Education movement, which follows a minimum score of SAEB: for the fifth year of elementary school performance acceptable in Portuguese it is a score above 200 points, while in mathematics it is a score above 225 points. For the third grade of high school adequate performance in Portuguese is a score above 300 points and above 350 points in mathematics. For more information, see Todos Pela Educação (2017).

schooling was introduced in 1958, and access to secondary education expanded considerably. As a result, while in 1959 61 per cent of the Russian population aged 15 or over did not finish secondary level, only a fifth did not finish it forty years later (Kyui 2016).

After the introduction of liberalizing policies under Gorbachev from 1985 onwards, the Soviet Union entered a transition period that led to its dismantling in 1991. In the educational sphere, changes occurred gradually. Ideas once considered progressive but that went against previous state ideology started now to find a place in public discussion. Issues such as civil rights, environmental studies, and market economy were covered by some teaching plans (Nikandrov 1995). The impact of transition years, with their institutional and economic consequences, led to a halving of public spending on education in Russia, reaching only 3.6 per cent of GDP in 2003 (OECD 2004; Nikolaev and Chugunov 2012).[4]

Currently the Russian education system is structured in eleven compulsory school years, nine years in general education (primary and lower secondary) and two years in upper secondary education. Children are supposed to start compulsory schooling when they are 6 years of age. They start at primary school, which is comprised of four grades (from 6 to 10 years of age). After primary school, students attend lower secondary school, for five additional years (Nikolaev and Chugunov 2012). After two years of upper secondary education, students take the Unified State Examination (USE), which is used for admission to higher education institutions (UNESCO 2014).

Since the establishment of the Russian Federation in 1993, the government has decentralized education funding. In the current structure, central government finances tertiary education, regional governments are responsible for vocational education, and municipalities take care of pre-primary, primary, and secondary education (Silva et al. 2009). However, this governance structure has increased regional inequalities in terms of expenditure per student in general education, given that the richer parts of the country (especially natural resource abundant regions) provide higher funding for their schools (Nikolaev and Chugunov 2012).

Russia's education system stands out positively among BRICS. While most of the BRICS countries had poorly educated populations with fifteen years of schooling or over in the 1990s, Russians already had ten years of schooling on average in 1990. In 2010, they were achieving almost twelve years of schooling (Barro and Lee 2013). Basic education reached universal access; thus in 2015 gross enrolment rates were 100.5 per cent in primary and 104.5 per cent in secondary. In addition, although pre-primary education is not compulsory in the country, its gross enrolment rate is 87.0 per cent. Another remarkable aspect of Russian education is the high participation of the population in tertiary education. In 2015, the gross enrolment rate at this level was 80.4 per cent (UNESCO 2017).

[4] Historically, public expenditure on education was very high in Russia. In the 1950s it averaged 10 per cent of GDP, declining gradually in the 1960s and 1970s to an average of 7 per cent (Bray and Borevskaya 2001).

Russia also performs better than the rest of the BRICS countries in quality education indicators. In international examinations such as PISA, Russian performance is close to OECD's average in all evaluated subjects (reading, maths, and science) while Brazil appears in the last places. In terms of class size, the country had an average of 19.8 pupils per teacher in primary education in 2014 (UNESCO 2017).

These good results don't mean that we cannot find bottlenecks in Russia's education system. In particular, the high level of inequality in access to quality education among urban and rural students is notable (Pinskaia et al. 2014; Amini and Nivorozhkin 2015). In rural areas of the country, with a large number of small towns and low demographic density, there is a scarcity of medium-sized schools. As a result, we find lower performances of rural students in the USE and hence lower probabilities for them to pursue a higher education degree, with future consequences for them in the labour market (Pinskaia et al. 2014).

Corruption seems to be widespread throughout the school system, involving practices such as bribery and the sale of diplomas, for example (Ismagilov et al. 2016). Among the BRICS countries, Russia has the highest perception that education is affected by corruption, according to the Global Corruption Barometer, produced by Transparency International (2013). Along an index that ranges between 1 and 5, where 1 represents 'not at all corrupt' and 5 represents 'extremely corrupt', the country has an average of 4.1 according to research undertaken in 2013. Taking stock, the story of education in Russia seems to be characterized by an excellent but unequal performance among its students and schools in a context particularly affected by corruption.

INDIA

Historically, traditional education was directed at upper castes in India, a view that remained widespread under the British East India Company. The lack of interest in mass education persisted during the British Raj period (1858–1947). Therefore, mass education was not effectively considered a priority (Naik and Nurullah 1974; Biswas and Agrawal 1986; Lindert 2003; Lall 2005). Around 1910 India's expenditure on primary education represented only 0.2 per cent of the country's GDP per capita, a figure even lower than the one for China (0.3 per cent) and substantially below Brazil (1.8 per cent) and Russia (2.1 per cent). Basic education enrolment rate was only 7.8 per cent, while the United States, England/Wales, and the Prussian Empire had respectively rates of 96.1 per cent, 83.6 per cent, and 71.4 per cent. One possible explanation for this lack of priority in education in India, as suggested by Chaudhary et al. (2012), is that local elites would not benefit from extending primary education in rural areas, leading governments to channel public resources to secondary and tertiary education.

In the 1930s and 1940s, several Indian provinces became more autonomous and approved compulsory education laws, but lack of enforcement and funding led to disappointing results (Lindert 2003). In the first decades after independence in 1947, few effective changes were implemented. While the bias in favour of tertiary education remained, basic education advanced very slowly and unevenly across regions, genders, and castes, in contrast with the pro-education rhetoric of elected Indian governments.[5] As a result, educational indicators remained dismal: literacy rates for 15-year-olds increased from lower levels of 28 per cent in 1960 to a mere 41 per cent in 1980, reaching only 63 per cent in 2010 when most BRICS were near universalization (Drèze and Sen 2013).

The current Indian educational structure was based on the National Policy on Education of 1986, which was modified in 1992. The constitution imposed free and compulsory education for children from 6 to 14 years of age, including basic education. Schooling consisted of ten years of basic education, two years of senior secondary education, and three years of higher education (Govinda and Bandyopadhyay 2008). Indian education institutions are organized into private, government-aided, and public schools. Private schools are the ones with the highest prestige and recognition, while public schools absorb the poorest and are maintained by states or municipalities (Lall 2005). The quality of education varies according to the social extracts and backgrounds of students (Drèze and Sen 2013).

There has been limited progress in closing the education gap between boys and girls, but India remains far from achieving gender equality in education. In the first post-independence census of 1951, only 9 per cent of women and 27 per cent of men were literate (Kingdon 2007). This problem remains in Indian society, with literacy rates of 75 per cent for men and 51 per cent for women in 2010 (Drèze and Sen 2013). This factor is also reflected in the differences in average years of schooling of the population aged 15 years or older: men on average had 7.6 years of schooling in 2010, 2.8 years more than women (Barro and Lee 2013). Many parents believe that girls' education is not necessary since they should only marry and care for the family. Interviews conducted in five states in northern India in 1999 for a Public Report on Basic Education (PROBE) showed that 57 per cent of parents of the sample wanted their children to study as much as possible, but only 28 per cent wanted the same for their daughters (compared to 72 per cent who wanted that for their sons). Moreover, only 1 per cent of parents believed that boys' education was unimportant, while approximately 10 per cent had the same claim for girls (PROBE 1999; Duflo 2012).

Furthermore, neither do inequalities among different Indian states contribute to improving the situation of the less advantaged. States such as Kerala and Himachal Pradesh obtained school attendance rates of 97.7 per cent and 96.2 per cent respectively around 2005–06, while the states of Bihar and Jharkhand reached only 62.2 per cent and 71.7 per cent (Drèze and Sen 2013). The high prevalence of malnutrition and poor health among children and young people, preventing them from attending regular classes also pose a challenge. These demands become even more pronounced in poorer regions and

[5] According to Drèze and Sen (1995), caste-based ideology and anti-colonialism, as well as a distorted view of Gandhi's ideas, acted as further barriers to the expansion of mass education.

states. In addition to the challenge of providing education to a large number of deprived children, poorer states receive lower tax revenues to fund their educational systems. Secondary education in India seems to be a consequence of these difficulties. While most BRICS member countries have gross enrolment ratios of roughly 100 per cent, India had a rate of 74 per cent in 2015 (UNESCO 2017). Kingdon (2007) suggests that low participation at this level results from a combination of education supply shortage, family credit constraints, and gender discrimination. The last point also deprives girls of pursuing a higher education degree.

The fragile infrastructure of public schools is another critical point in India. According to Drèze and Sen (2013), only 91.9 per cent of public schools had drinking water available and only 31.4 per cent had electricity. In Bihar, one of the poorest states, only 72.3 per cent of schools offered lunch. Considering the whole school system, the student–teacher ratio reached 31.5 in 2015 (UNESCO 2017). Also, a supply of good teachers is still a key challenge for the country. In addition to the high student–teacher ratio (close to the South African figures), the country still suffers from high rates of absenteeism. According to Chaudhury et al. (2006), while a quarter of primary school teachers from public schools were absent from school, only about half of teachers were actually teaching when enumerators made unannounced visits to primary schools in the country. As a result, quality of education is a pressing situation for 47 per cent of the fifth grade students who could not read a text and 55 per cent who could not solve simple division sums (Kingdon 2007).

Caste- and gender-based inequalities as well as regional imbalances are structural problems in India concerning both access and quality. Although some progress has been made since the 1980s, they seem comparatively insignificant bearing in mind other Asian countries that have achieved remarkable educational improvements, such as South Korea, China, and Sri Lanka (Pradhan and Singh 2004; Lall 2005).[6] Taking stock, the issues of inequality in India seem to be exacerbated when compared to Brazil and Russia, with much lower results in comparison to other BRICS.

CHINA

After the Communist Party seized power in 1949, education was tightly controlled by central government in China. Educational policy formulations and resource allocation were the sole responsibility of central government. There was a focus on providing primary education for working-class children (both urban and rural). Following the practice of all public policies in China, educational investment was concentrated on

[6] There are several studies comparing the evolution of education in India and China, since both countries had similar educational indicators in the 1940s, as well as the largest populations on earth and millenary traditions. This literature raises several hypotheses to explain how authoritarian China outperformed democratic India in several educational aspects (Drèze and Saran 1995; Rao et al. 2003; Goldman et al. 2008).

urban areas. Typically, provision of educational services in rural areas depended on the economic situation of rural collectives, better known as popular communes (Ngok 2007). Through the *hukou* or household registration system created during this period, population mobility was restricted, eventually restricting students to their local educational system.[7]

Education went through a period of crisis during the Cultural Revolution (1966–76). Although most primary schools continued to operate, almost all secondary and tertiary institutions were completely closed down in 1966. When secondary schools reopened in 1968, they faced the problem of overcrowding, caused by the accumulation of student cohorts and the lack of teachers, since many of them had been removed from their posts for political reasons. This context continued until the 1970s, as new teachers could only be hired on the basis of political credentials. When universities reopened in 1972, admission tests were extinguished, and political orientation became the most important admission criterion. Only in 1977 were admission exams re-established at universities (Deng and Treiman 1997).

Economic reforms under Deng Xiaoping also had consequences for China's education policy. Market-oriented reforms led to decentralization in education. In 1985, the National Conference on Education made basic education the responsibility of local and provincial governments (Tsang 1996). This factor eventually contributed to large disparities in educational development, since the quality of the school depended on local public finance (Kai-Ming 1994; Heckman 2005). In some localities, schools faced extreme problems of access and lack of resources for infrastructure and teachers' salaries. In 2001, central government decided that financial responsibility for primary education would be taken by county governments. The Compulsory Education Law, amended in June 2006, reaffirmed the change. Thus, as we have seen in Brazil and India, decentralization of education provision in China represented a burden on poorer localities.

In terms of educational structure, the Chinese system is one of the largest in the world. In 2015 there were 182 million students attending basic education (UNESCO 2017). With the Compulsory Education Law of 1986, compulsory education was stretched to nine years, with entry at 6 years of age. Educational levels consist of: *primary education*, which lasts for six years (for children between 6 and 12 years of age); and *junior secondary education*, which lasts for another three years and marks the end of compulsory schooling (OECD 2016).

Entry to *senior secondary school* requires students to pass a public examination (*Zhongkao*). Results of the examination allocate students to different school programmes: a three-year vocational training programme, or a four-year senior professional high school. The duration of basic education is twelve years, but education is free of charge only for the compulsory levels. Admission to university is based on another examination (*Gaokao*), but in some cases entrance is allowed without it.

[7] During the planned system (1950–80), a person could only live and work at the location specified on their *hukou* card. The system was relaxed in the early 1990s (Li et al. 2017).

Chinese children aged between 3 and 5 years of age can attend pre-primary school, which is not compulsory. More than half of pre-primary enrolments are in private schools (52.5 per cent in 2015). There was a substantial increase in enrolment at this level: gross enrolment rates in pre-primary education were 83.6 per cent in 2015 compared to only 24.4 per cent in 1995. Gross enrolment rates were 104.2 per cent in 2015 for primary education and 94.3 per cent for secondary education in spite of its significant growth in the last decades (51.2 per cent in 1995). At the same time, 10.6 per cent of secondary pupils attended private schools (UNESCO 2017).

Tertiary education enrolment also expanded from 4.5 per cent in 1995 to 43.4 per cent in 2015. With the implementation of the *Program for Reform and Development of Chinese Education* in 1993, universities became the responsibility of local authorities. Since 1997, universities have charged tuition fees that allowed an expansion of places (Mok 2000). However, minority female and rural areas have not equally benefited from it (Li and Xing 2010).

Average years of study for the population aged 15 and over was 5.3 years in 1980, increasing to almost 8.0 years in 2010 (Barro and Lee 2013). However, education still remains a problem in rural areas. The differences in investment by each region allied to the *hukou* policy, as well as high tuition and accommodation fees, restrict educational opportunities for poor children in senior secondary and tertiary levels (Heckman and Yi 2012).[8] The rural worker has on average four years fewer of schooling when compared to the urban worker (Heckman 2005). By 2015, 44.1 per cent of urban workers aged 25–64 had at least finished secondary education, while only 11.3 per cent of rural workers had the same level of education. Fewer than 40 per cent of children in rural areas attended senior secondary schools between 2007 and 2012. Senior secondary school has a minimum cost of US$160 per year, corresponding to 27 per cent of rural per capita income, too high a cost for families living in rural areas. Another reason for the low attendance rates is that students are required to pass entrance examinations. Only 40 per cent of rural students pass the exams for high school and 10 per cent for entrance exams to universities (Li et al. 2017).

Although the government has a historical trajectory of low public investment as a ratio of GDP (it was 3 per cent in 2007) (Heckman and Yi 2012), the quality of education in China has improved over time. According to the *Global Competitiveness Report*, the country ranks 43 out of a total of 138 countries in the OECD quality of education system. One of the factors in favour of these results is that the student–teacher ratio has declined over the years. While there were 28.9 students for each teacher in primary education in 1970, this figure reached the 16.3 ratio in 2015. In secondary education it is even lower (13.8 in 2015). In general, teachers are respected in China and the profession is popular, especially in large cities. Although they receive moderate wages, they have stable jobs with a right to good benefits (OECD 2016).

[8] Under the *hukou* policy, children of interregional immigrants are allowed to attend school only if their families pay additional fees (Heckman and Yi 2012).

In terms of teacher quality, there is also a rural–urban gap. Scarcity of resources often forces rural schools to hire cheaper and less skilled teachers (Han 2013). As a result, Wang et al. (2017) argue that children of rural migrants are the ones who suffer most from the quality of education. Due to the *hukou* system, children of rural migrants cannot attend urban public schools. They usually attend private migrant schools, which in general have lower quality, fewer trained teachers and larger class size when compared even to schools in rural areas. Thus, despite different historical and geographical contexts, it is interesting to note that Brazil, Russia, India, and China have education systems characterized by deep inequalities, often made concrete through decentralization processes that transferred unbearable financial obligations to the poorest communities. The inequality divides however are more complex, as seen above.

SOUTH AFRICA

The South African educational system has been marked by racial inequality, which was to a large extent inherited from the apartheid regime (1948–94). Under apartheid, different ethnic groups were segregated into separate residential areas and consequently within different educational systems. In addition, the government's educational policy was instrumental in maintaining the regime. To this end, the National Party established in 1953 the Bantu Education Act, which centralized the basic education of the black population in the hands of government, and the Extension of the University Education Act in 1959, which extended the Bantu Education Act to higher education.

After adoption of the Bantu Education Act, the number of black children enrolled in basic education rose from 800,000 in 1953 to 1.8 million in 1963 and to 3.5 million in 1979 (Thompson 2001; Giliomee 2009). The number of black children enrolled in secondary education rose from 46,000 in 1960 to more than one million in 1985. In the period 1975–85 university enrolment increased five times to around 36,000 (Dubow 2014). The same law that led to an increase in access to education served to suppress blacks' education as it limited resources and infrastructure and introduced a biased school curriculum to black children.

Thus, apartheid increased the education gap between white and black children. Schoolteachers for black children received lower wages and were also less prepared than white schoolteachers. Alongside these factors, the government was unable to meet the demand for teachers to cope with the growing number of black school enrolments (Thompson 2001). The pupil–teacher ratio of black-child schools remained in the 50–70 range between 1957 and 1993, while white-child schools never had a number above twenty-five (Fedderke et al. 2000). In 1975, a year before the Soweto uprising, when black students rebelled against apartheid education, average spending on white students was more than fifteen times higher than the average expenditure on black students (Thomas 1996).

With the end of the apartheid regime in 1994, the new democracy faced serious challenges in relation to educational divides. The South African educational system inherited nineteen distinct departments, each maintaining its own structure and applying its own school exams. Moreover, most education indicators were very low: the pass rate of the students enrolled was only 53.4 per cent, the literacy rate of the adult population was below 70 per cent, and only 7.1 per cent of the adult population had higher education. Infrastructure conditions were precarious: in schools, electricity was lacking in 57 per cent, access to water in 40 per cent, and didactic materials in 69 per cent of them. As a reformulation of the system, the nineteen existing departments were unified and the race criterion for enrolment in the different schools was abolished (The Presidency 2014).

Under the current educational system in South Africa, basic education is the joint responsibility of national government and the provinces, while higher education is the responsibility of national government. Basic education consists of the following phases: Early Childhood Development (ECD), General Education and Training (GET), and Further Education and Training (FET). The ECD serves children between 0 and 4 years of age; GET is subdivided into (i) Foundation Phase (grades R to 3), (ii) Intermediate Phase (grades 4 to 6), and (iii) Senior Phase (grades 7 to 9); and FET includes grades 10 to 12. Primary education comprises grades 1 to 7, and secondary education consists of grades 8 to 12. Education is compulsory for children between the ages of 7 and 15 or up to grade 9. At the end of grade 12, students must take an examination to obtain the National Senior Certificate (NSC), a document of completion of basic education used as a form of university entrance (OECD 2008).

South Africa has recently made great strides in quantitative terms: while in 1980 the average number of years of study for the population aged 15 years or older was 5.1; that average increased to 9.7 in 2010, with little difference between men (9.7) and women (9.6) (Barro and Lee 2013). Another advance in the country was in pre-primary education: the gross enrolment rate increased by 49.3 percentage points over the last twenty years, reaching a value of 77.4 per cent in 2014 (UNESCO 2017). This advance can reflect educational policies such as White Paper 5, which was launched in 2001 and aimed at achieving universal access for 5-year-olds in Reception Year (grade R) by the year 2010 (Department of Education, 2001). At primary level, the gross enrolment rate is high (99.7 per cent in 2014). There was a substantial increase in secondary education: the gross enrolment rate rose from 79.6 per cent in 1994 to 98.8 per cent in 2014. Regarding tertiary education, the country presents the worst gross enrolment rate among BRICS, rising from 4.0 per cent in 1970 to 15.0 per cent in 1994 and 19.4 per cent in 2014; Brazil, for example, had a rate of 49.3 per cent in 2014 (UNESCO 2017).

As happens in almost all BRICS, Russia being an exception, quality education in South Africa remains a major challenge. According to the *Global Competitiveness Report*, the country ranks 134th out of a total of 138 in the education system's quality ranking—the worst position of a BRICS. In international tests, South African students perform even more poorly than other countries' students on their continent, although they have higher resources and more educated parents (van der Berg 2007). For example, in the *Trends in International Mathematics and Science Study* (TIMSS), although the South African score increased between 2011 and 2015 for grade 9 students, the country remains at the penultimate place in mathematics and at the last place in sciences.

Similar to the other BRICS, the country has serious issues related to the teaching profession in terms of quality and quantity. First, there is a historical and controversial difference in student–teacher ratios between educational systems (Case and Deaton 1999; Case and Yogo 1999). By 2014, there was an average of 31 pupils per teacher in public schools, while in private schools this number was 15.6 (Department of Basic Education 2016a). Second, in addition to the shortage of teachers, existing teachers do not have on average an adequate qualification. For instance, a study using data from a representative sample of the 2007 Southern and Eastern African Consortium for Monitoring Educational Quality (SACMEQ) found that 79 per cent of grade 6 maths teachers showed levels of content knowledge below the expected level of their students (Venkat and Spaull 2015).

South Africa's government increased its share of spending on education to 6 per cent of GDP in 2014, above the average expenditure of most BRICS (National Treasury 2017; UNESCO 2017). Despite this spending effort, school infrastructure is still far from ideal. It was found that 70.8 per cent of its schools had no library, 58.6 per cent did not have a computer centre, and 81.7 per cent did not have a laboratory (Department of Basic Education 2016b).

A straightforward compilation of basic data about the education systems in BRICS carried out above suggests several similar features such as the high level of inequalities in these systems (on racial, gender, and spatial lines) and their general low standards, apart from Russia, which suffers however from other institutional problems. In what follows, we try a more systematic analysis of available data in order to understand and categorize BRICS countries in relation to other countries of the world.

Methodology and data

Cluster analysis seems a natural choice of technique to understand the place of BRICS's education systems in the world given that it provides a set of multivariate techniques with the purpose of classifying objects (countries) into groups based on the similar characteristics they have. In this technique one would look for similar characteristics within clusters (internal) and heterogeneous features between clusters (external). Differently from all other multivariate techniques, cluster analysis does not estimate the variate empirically because it uses the existing variate of the characteristics to compare objects (Hair et al. 2009).

There are two different procedures of cluster analysis: hierarchical procedures and non-hierarchical procedures. When we use hierarchical procedures, we find $N-1$ clusters solutions, where N is the number of objects (in this chapter, it is the number of countries). For example, if we have five objects, we form a four clusters solution, then a three clusters solution, then a two clusters solution, and then a one cluster solution—or in the opposite sequence (a one cluster solution to a four clusters solution). When we use non-hierarchical procedures, we find only a single cluster solution for a set of cluster seeds (starting points) and for a given number of clusters (Hair et al. 2009).

In this chapter, we use k-means algorithms, which is a set of non-hierarchical clustering algorithms. These algorithms work by grouping objects into a given number of clusters and then iteratively reassigning these objects to clusters until some criterion is met. The criterion is related to maximizing the similarity of objects in a cluster and maximizing the dissimilarity between clusters (Hair et al. 2009). Thus, we minimize the sum of squares from points to the assigned cluster centres, utilizing the Hartigan and Wong (1979) algorithm. Briefly, the main objective of cluster analysis is taxonomy development. In the case of BRICS we are interested in developing a taxonomy that segments countries into groups with similar educational systems and then seeing if all BRICS countries are in the same group. Knowing that multicollinearity can be a problem in using cluster analysis (Hair et al. 2009), we tried to use variables that are not strongly correlated to one another. To do so, we selected, based on the previous analyses of each country, variables to represent the following factors:

- Average years of schooling: the Barro and Lee (2013) data set provides average years of schooling for people aged 15 years and over for many countries in 2010.
- Quality of education: in the *Global Competitiveness Report* (Schwab and Sala-i-Martin 2011, 2012, 2013, 2014, 2015), there is the following question: 'How well does the educational system in your country meet the needs of a competitive economy?' The answer ranges from 1 to 7. Number 1 represents 'not well at all' while number 7 represents 'very well'.
- School enrolment: we used the following data from the World Bank on gross enrolment rates at different levels: (i) total enrolment in pre-primary education, regardless of age, expressed as a percentage of the population of official pre-primary education age; (ii) total enrolment in primary education, regardless of age, expressed as a percentage of the population of official primary education age; (iii) total enrolment in secondary education, regardless of age, expressed as a percentage of the population of official secondary education age; (iv) total enrolment in tertiary education, regardless of age, expressed as a percentage of the total population of the five-year age group following on from leaving secondary school.[9] We used also the following enrolment data: (v) percentage of total enrolment in primary education in private institutions; (vi) percentage of total enrolment in secondary education in private institutions.
- Corruption in education: in the *Global Corruption Barometer* questionnaire (Transparency International 2013), there is the following specific question: 'To what

[9] Gross enrolment rates can exceed 100 per cent due to the inclusion of overaged and underaged students, often a consequence of early or late school entrance and grade repetition.

Table 16.1 Descriptive statistics for cluster variables

	Number of countries	Mean	Standard deviation	Minimum	Maximum
Average years of schooling	70	9.41	2.58	2.74	13.18
Quality of educational system	70	3.80	0.90	1.86	5.98
Enrolment in pre-primary	70	74.88	30.44	1.34	156.98
Enrolment in primary	70	104.58	9.41	81.43	142.29
Enrolment in private primary	70	11.04	15.66	0.09	88.84
Enrolment in secondary	70	91.58	24.34	31.48	135.55
Enrolment in private secondary	70	16.25	18.79	0.17	94.68
Enrolment in tertiary	70	51.29	27.03	0.75	108.97
Corruption in education	70	3.05	0.62	1.42	4.37
Pupil–teacher ratio	70	20.91	12.10	8.59	73.47

Source: Elaborated by the authors.

extent do you perceive education in your country to be affected by corruption?' The answer ranges from 1 to 5. Number 1 represents 'not at all corrupt' while number 5 represents 'extremely corrupt'.

- Pupil–teacher ratio: primary school pupil–teacher ratio is the average number of pupils per teacher in primary education. Pupil–teacher ratio data is available from World Bank open data (2017).

We chose these variables for several reasons: first, because they are available for a large set of countries including BRICS, with different aspects of their educational systems being well represented; second, because of this diversity the variables are not strongly correlated to one another, which is important for statistical reasons; third, a more complete database was put together using the mean value of all variables between 2010 and 2016. Table 16.1 displays the descriptive statistics of these means.

In order to test the validation of the resulting clusters, we replaced the variable of average years of schooling by three other variables: (i) the percentage of the population of 15 years of age and over with no schooling (Barro and Lee 2013); (ii) the percentage of the population of 15 years of age and over with tertiary education (Barro and Lee 2013); (iii) literacy rates among young people (between 15 and 24 years of age) (World Bank 2017). We also replaced the variable of quality of educational system by two other variables: (i) the quality of primary education; (ii) the quality of scientific research institutions (Schwab and Sala-i-Martin 2011, 2012, 2013, 2014, 2015).

Results

Table 16.2 presents the resulting clusters when the given number of clusters is three, just as a first approximation. In the first cluster are all the sub-Saharan countries from the

Table 16.2 Resulting clusters 1

Cluster 1	Cluster 2	Cluster 3
Bangladesh	Albania	Austria
Burundi	Algeria	Belgium
Cameroon	Brazil	Chile
Ghana	Bulgaria	Cyprus
India	China	Czech Republic
Liberia	Colombia	Denmark
Malawi	Croatia	Estonia
Rwanda	Egypt	Finland
Senegal	El Salvador	Germany
Tanzania	Greece	Hungary
Yemen	Indonesia	Iceland
Zimbabwe	Kazakhstan	Ireland
	Kyrgyzstan	Israel
	Mexico	Italy
	Moldova	Japan
	Mongolia	Latvia
	Paraguay	Lithuania
	Peru	Luxembourg
	Romania	Netherlands
	Russia	New Zealand
	Serbia	Norway
	Slovakia	Poland
	South Africa	Portugal
	Sri Lanka	Slovenia
	Thailand	South Korea
	Tunisia	Spain
	Turkey	Switzerland
	Ukraine	United Kingdom
	Uruguay	United States

Source: Elaborated by the authors.

sample, except for South Africa, plus Asian countries such as Yemen, Bangladesh, and, most importantly, India. These countries are characterized by poor educational standards. As shown in Table 16.3, these countries have on average schools with a very high number of pupils per teacher, a worse perception of quality of education and that corruption affects the educational system. They have low access to pre-primary and tertiary education and still fall short of achieving universal access to secondary education. These educational outcomes are reflected in the poor education of the population aged 15 years or older, who on average have 5.2 years of schooling.

In the second cluster, we found three BRICS: Brazil, South Africa, and China. Besides Brazil, other Latin American countries from the sample are also in the second cluster, except for Chile. South Africa is the only sub-Saharan country in this cluster, while all European and Asian countries in this cluster are transition economies (socialist or former socialist), with the exception of Indonesia, Thailand, and Turkey. These countries have in general intermediate educational indicators, with the exception of enrolment in

Table 16.3 Clusters means 1

	1	2	3
Average years of schooling	5.16	9.35	11.24
Quality of educational system	3.49	3.24	4.48
Enrolment in pre-primary	44.42	68.85	93.51
Enrolment in primary	109.68	105.10	101.95
Enrolment in private primary	22.65	7.26	10.01
Enrolment in secondary	45.87	93.17	108.90
Enrolment in private secondary	33.80	9.32	15.92
Enrolment in tertiary	9.73	48.94	70.84
Corruption in education	3.45	3.31	2.64
Pupil–teacher ratio	41.68	20.07	13.16

Source: Elaborated by the authors.

private schools; where they present a smaller portion of enrolments in this type of institution. As shown in Table 16.3, on average, cluster 2 has 7.6 per cent of primary enrolment in private schools (compared to 22.7 per cent for cluster 1 and 10 per cent for cluster 3) and 9.3 per cent for secondary enrolment (compared to 33.8 per cent for cluster 1 and to 15.9 per cent for cluster 3).

Finally, in the last cluster, we found all Western and Central European countries from the sample. The third cluster also includes Slovenia, Hungary, and the Baltic countries. Chile, the United States, Cyprus, Israel, Japan, South Korea, and New Zealand complete the list, characterized by countries with good educational indicators. On average, these countries present universal access to basic education, high rates of access to tertiary and pre-primary education, high quality of education system (represented by the perception of the population), and lower number of students per teacher. Among the clusters, cluster 3 has the adult population (15 years or more) with more years of education; on average, 11.2 years of schooling, as can be seen in Table 16.3.

According to the Elbow method—a method designed to find the estimated optimal number of clusters—seven is the optimal number of clusters for this sample. Therefore, Table 16.4 presents the resulting clusters when the given number of clusters is seven. When we define seven as the number of clusters, the first two resulting clusters contain most of the countries characterized by poor educational indicators—that were in the first cluster when the given number of clusters was three. Now the first cluster contains some sub-Saharan countries such as Burundi, Senegal, and Tanzania, along with Yemen. In the second cluster, we find India and Bangladesh, together with Liberia and Zimbabwe. As shown in Table 16.5, the countries in clusters 1 and 2 have in general low average years of schooling, low quality of educational system, low enrolment rates in pre-primary, secondary, and tertiary education, high gross enrolment rates in primary education

Table 16.4 Resulting clusters 2

Cluster 1	Cluster 2	Cluster 3	
Burundi Cameroon Malawi Rwanda Senegal Tanzania Yemen	Bangladesh India Liberia Zimbabwe	Algeria Brazil China Colombia Egypt El Salvador Ghana Indonesia Mexico Paraguay Peru South Africa Sri Lanka Thailand Tunisia Uruguay	
Cluster 4	**Cluster 5**	**Cluster 6**	**Cluster 7**
Albania Croatia Kazakhstan Kyrgyzstan Moldova Mongolia Russia Serbia Turkey Ukraine	Bulgaria Czech Republic Greece Hungary Israel Italy Japan Latvia Lithuania Poland Portugal Romania Slovakia Slovenia South Korea United States	Belgium Chile Spain	Austria Cyprus Denmark Estonia Finland Germany Iceland Ireland Luxembourg Netherlands New Zealand Norway Switzerland United Kingdom

Source: Elaborated by the authors.

(which might represent the existence of a large amount of overaged students[10]), high primary school pupil–teacher ratios, and perceived corruption in education. What differentiates countries in the first cluster from the second is that: (i) the first group performs poorly on almost all indicators, suggesting that their educational systems are 'incipient'. For example, cluster 1 has an adult population (people aged 15 years or more) with an average of only 4.4 years of schooling and a much higher pupil–teacher ratio (47.5) than the corresponding figures for the second cluster; (ii) countries in the second

[10] This group includes countries with the highest repetition rates. For example, in 2014, Burundi had a 22.9 per cent repetition rate in primary education and Rwanda had 19.2 per cent. Bangladesh had 10.2 per cent in 2010 (UNESCO 2017).

Table 16.5 Clusters means 2

	1	2	3	4	5	6	7
Average years of schooling	4.41	5.99	8.10	10.34	11.30	10.25	11.40
Quality of educational system	3.21	3.90	3.27	3.30	3.70	4.07	5.08
Enrolment in pre-primary	26.28	58.35	70.81	65.31	87.90	105.14	94.02
Enrolment in primary	112.35	105.38	108.13	103.07	101.13	103.51	101.66
Enrolment in private primary	7.07	49.82	12.51	1.89	5.49	48.76	5.04
Enrolment in secondary	39.84	52.96	88.91	94.75	101.44	120.54	111.80
Enrolment in private secondary	15.52	70.18	14.73	3.16	9.55	50.32	12.66
Enrolment in tertiary	6.98	13.45	34.06	60.15	72.23	79.22	67.70
Corruption in education	3.40	3.46	3.08	3.78	2.99	2.73	2.37
Pupil–teacher ratio	47.50	34.10	22.69	19.07	14.14	15.17	12.11

Source: Elaborated by the authors.

cluster have a larger participation in private schools—India, for example, has 34.8 per cent of primary school enrolment in private schools and 50.2 per cent of secondary school enrolment. It seems that when developing countries start developing their education systems they depend greatly on the role of the private sector.

The countries characterized by medium educational indicators (those in the second cluster when the given number of clusters was three) are now divided into two clusters (clusters 3 and 4). The third cluster contains Brazil, China, and South Africa among the BRICS. There are also countries as diverse as, for example, Algeria, Colombia, Ghana, Indonesia, and Uruguay. As shown in Table 16.5, when cluster 3 is compared to clusters 1 and 2, countries present on average an adult population (people aged 15 years or more) more educated, represented by higher average years of schooling (8.1 years of schooling in cluster 3 against 4.4 and 6.0 in clusters 1 and 2, respectively), larger enrolment rates in pre-primary (70.8 per cent against 26.3 per cent and 58.4 per cent), in secondary (88.9 per cent against 39.9 per cent and 53.0 per cent) and in tertiary education (34.1 per cent against 7.0 per cent and 13.5 per cent), as well as a lower pupil–teacher ratio (22.7 against 47.5 and 34.1). The fourth cluster contains not only Russia, but several other countries that also belonged to the socialist bloc, except for Turkey. Compared to the third cluster, these countries have more years of schooling on average, similar enrolment rates in pre-primary education, larger enrolment rates in secondary and in tertiary education, a lower pupil–teacher ratio, larger participation in private schools, and more perceived corruption (Table 16.5). The quality of educational system and total enrolment in primary are on average similar in all these first four clusters. But what differentiates cluster four from the other six clusters is the low participation in private schools in total enrolment. Russia, for example, has approximately 1 per cent of primary and secondary enrolment in private educational institutions (UNESCO 2017).

Finally, the last three clusters are mostly formed by countries characterized by good educational indicators (ones that were in the third cluster when the given number of clusters was three). The fifth cluster contains several countries of the European periphery, as well as Israel, Italy, Japan, South Korea, and the United States. The sixth cluster has only three countries: Belgium, Chile, and Spain. Finally, the last cluster is composed in general of European developed countries and New Zealand. These three clusters have on average better educational indicators, compared to the previous four clusters (Table 16.5). On average, the countries belonging to these three clusters (cluster 5, 6, and 7) achieved, in addition to universal access to basic education, high gross enrolment rates in tertiary and pre-primary education. They also have a lower perception that corruption affects the education system and lower pupil–teacher ratio, reaching an average of 12.11 in cluster 6. Although these last three clusters present similarities in many average indicators, they also have specificities—which determined the separation of the countries in those different clusters. For example, countries in the sixth cluster have much larger participation in private schools, and countries in the last cluster have the best indicator of quality of educational system (far ahead of the second best).

Different education systems develop according to different paths defined by their distinct historical circumstances but the previous cluster analysis suggests that we can categorize education systems according to some common features that they possess. A very tentative scheme is suggested in Figure 16.1. It generalizes some of these features and as such would unavoidably incur some mistakes. However, it brings into perspective the idea that different BRICS countries are in distinct stages of development of their education systems involving certain specific challenges and characteristics.

Thus, in the case of BRICS it is worth mentioning that despite its rapid economic growth in the past decade: (i) there are still quality education challenges that have not been solved for all BRICS, although they are at different stages; (ii) Brazil, China, and South Africa are similar in several educational aspects, while Russia is more advanced and India lags behind. The results did not change considerably when we replaced some variables with other similar variables or when we changed the number of clusters. In the Appendix, we also present the results for the given numbers of clusters of 5, 9, and 11 (Tables 16.6, 16.7, and 16.8).

India stands out for its dismal results. Although the other BRICS countries have gross secondary enrolment rates close to 100 per cent, Indian rates still remain close to

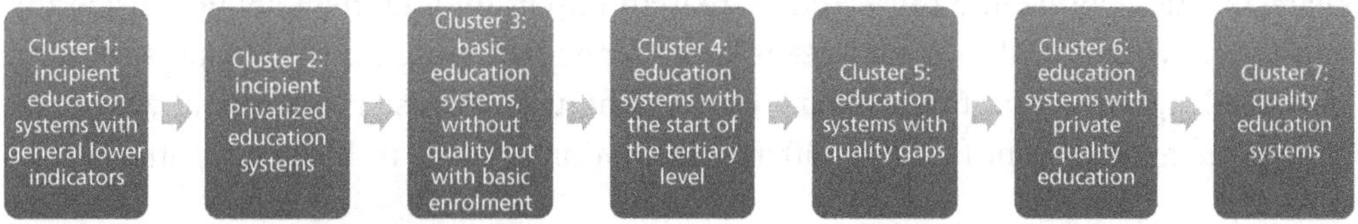

Figure 16.1 Clusters descriptions

Source: Elaborated by the authors.

70 per cent. The population of 15 years of age or more has only 6.2 years of study and 4.8 if we consider only women, generating a difference of 2.8 points when compared to men (7.6) (Barro and Lee 2013). India has 46 per cent of the world's illiterates and a high proportion of out-of-school children and youth (Kingdon 2007). We have already mentioned the problems of widespread teacher absenteeism in public schools and the historical under-provision of schooling in India.

At the other extreme, Russia has a history of high investment in education. In 1990, one year before the end of the Soviet Union, the population over 15 years of age had 9.5 years of education, 4.2 years more than the average of the other BRICS countries in the same period (Barro and Lee 2013).[11] The expansion of secondary education was one of the government's main objectives. In 1959, 61 per cent of the Russian population aged 15 or over did not complete this level of education, while only 20 per cent did not in 1989. In addition, the country inherited an elaborate system of higher education from the Soviet Union, which facilitated the expansion of the higher education system from 1990, leading the country to have a large portion of the population with a tertiary degree, above the OECD average (Kyui 2016). Russia also has a low pupil–teacher ratio: an average of 19.8 pupils per teacher in primary education in 2014 (UNESCO 2017). These indicators justify the clustering of the country among the advanced ones in educational terms.

On the other hand, Brazil, China, and South Africa display several similar educational indicators, which explains why they are located in the same clusters under different criteria. The three countries have a gross enrolment rate of approximately 100 per cent in secondary education. There are some differences though. South Africa presents 9.7 average years of study of the 15-year-old population, a better outcome compared to Brazil (7.9) and China (8.0) (Barro and Lee 2013). On the other hand, the gross enrolment rate in tertiary education is approximately 50 per cent in both Brazil and China, while the South African rate is close to 20 per cent. The same happens with pupil–teacher ratios: Brazil (20.9 in 2014) and China (16.3 in 2015) are ahead of South Africa (33.9 in 2014) (UNESCO 2017).

Conclusion

It seems almost tautological to argue that different education systems have different characteristics, but behind this claim there is an important argument about considering education systems within a long-term, path-dependent perspective that puts forward new challenges as education systems evolve. The use of cluster analysis unveiled not simply the most evident fact that different education systems in BRICS countries are at

[11] In 1990, the average years of study of the 15-year-old population were: 4.7 in Brazil, 3.3 in India, 6 in China, and 6.8 in South Africa (Barro and Lee 2013).

different stages of development, but highlighted some of the characteristics behind these stages. Thus, it is not simply the issue that Russia has better educational outcomes than those found in Brazil, China, and South Africa and that India scores at much lower levels. But, instead, that while India seems to be at start of a kind of 'inverted-U' for the role of the private sector in shaping education systems (when the government does not seem to be able to provide education at all levels), Russia is at the other extreme, facing challenges related to corruption and improving thc quality of its education system. A cluster analysis carried out with eleven groups suggests that Russia has to face several challenges in order to aspire to a quality education system. The challenges related to enrolment and quality but mostly to inequality in the other BRICS countries are remarkable. Thus, BRICS are very diverse and should get together to learn from their historical lessons and the trajectories of their distinct education systems.

APPENDIX

Table 16.6 Resulting clusters 3

Cluster 1	Cluster 2	Cluster 3	Cluster 4	Cluster 5
Burundi	Bangladesh	Algeria	Albania	Austria
Cameroon	Chile	Brazil	Bulgaria	Belgium
Malawi	India	China	Croatia	Cyprus
Rwanda	Liberia	Colombia	Czech Republic	Denmark
Senegal	Zimbabwe	Egypt	Greece	Estonia
Tanzania		El Salvador	Hungary	Finland
Yemen		Ghana	Israel	Germany
		Indonesia	Italy	Iceland
		Kyrgyzstan	Japan	Ireland
		Mexico	Kazakhstan	Luxembourg
		Mongolia	Latvia	Netherlands
		Paraguay	Lithuania	New Zealand
		Peru	Moldova	Norway
		Portugal	Poland	Spain
		South Africa	Romania	Switzerland
		Sri Lanka	Russia	United Kingdom
		Thailand	Serbia	
		Tunisia	Slovakia	
		Turkey	Slovenia	
		Uruguay	South Korea	
			Ukraine	
			United States	

Source: Elaborated by the authors.

Table 16.7 Resulting clusters 4

Cluster 1	Cluster 2	Cluster 3	Cluster 4
Burundi	Bangladesh	Brazil	Algeria
Cameroon	India	China	Egypt
Malawi	Liberia	Colombia	Kyrgyzstan
Rwanda	Zimbabwe	El Salvador	Mongolia
Senegal		Ghana	Turkey
Tanzania		Indonesia	
Yemen		Mexico	
		Paraguay	
		Peru	
		South Africa	
		Thailand	
		Tunisia	
		Uruguay	

Cluster 5	Cluster 6	Cluster 7	Cluster 8	Cluster 9
Cyprus	Albania	Czech Republic	Belgium	Austria
Luxembourg	Bulgaria	Estonia	Chile	Denmark
Sri Lanka	Croatia	Greece		Finland
United Kingdom	Kazakhstan	Hungary		Germany
	Japan	Israel		Iceland
	Moldova	Italy		Ireland
	Romania	Latvia		Netherlands
	Russia	Lithuania		New Zealand
	Serbia	Poland		Norway
	Slovakia	Portugal		Switzerland
	Ukraine	Spain		
		Slovenia		
		South Korea		
		United States		

Source: Elaborated by the authors.

Table 16.8 Resulting clusters 5

Cluster 1	Cluster 2	Cluster 3	Cluster 4	Cluster 5	
Burundi	Cameroon	Bangladesh	Brazil	Algeria	
Malawi	Senegal	India	China	Egypt	
Rwanda	Tanzania	Liberia	Colombia	Kyrgyzstan	
	Yemen	Zimbabwe	El Salvador	Mongolia	
			Ghana	Turkey	
			Indonesia		
			Mexico		
			Paraguay		
			Peru		
			South Africa		
			Tunisia		
Cluster 6	**Cluster 7**	**Cluster 8**	**Cluster 9**	**Cluster 10**	**Cluster 11**
Hungary	Cyprus	Albania	Czech Republic	Belgium	Austria
Israel	Luxembourg	Bulgaria	Greece	Chile	Denmark
Italy	Sri Lanka	Croatia	Latvia		Estonia
Portugal	United Kingdom	Kazakhstan	Lithuania		Finland
Spain		Japan	Poland		Germany
Thailand		Moldova	Slovenia		Iceland
Uruguay		Romania	South Korea		Ireland
		Russia	United States		Netherlands
		Serbia			New Zealand
		Slovakia			Norway
		Ukraine			Switzerland

Source: Elaborated by the authors.

REFERENCES

Allen, R.C. (2003). *Farm to Factory: A Reinterpretation of the Soviet Industrial Revolution.* Princeton, NJ: Princeton University Press.

Amini, C. and Nivorozhkin, E. (2015). 'The urban–rural divide in educational outcomes: evidence from Russia', *International Journal of Educational Development* 44: 118–33.

Ansell, B.W. (2010). *From the Ballot to the Blackboard: The Redistributive Political Economy of Education.* Cambridge: Cambridge University Press.

Astorga, P., Bergés, A.R., and FitzGerald, V. (2005). 'The standard of living in Latin America during the twentieth century', *Economic History Review* 58/4: 765–96.

Banerjee, A.V. and Duflo, E. (2011). *Poor Economics: A Radical Rethinking of the Way to Fight Global Poverty.* New York: Public Affairs.

Barro, R.J. and Lee, J.W. (2013). 'A new data set of educational attainment in the world, 1950–2010', *Journal of Development Economics* 104: 184–98.

Becker, G. (1964). *Human Capital: A Theoretical and Empirical Analysis with Special Reference to Education*. Chicago, IL: University of Chicago Press.

Biswas, A. and Agrawal, S.P. (1986). *Development of Education in India: A Historical Survey of Documents Before and After Independence*. New Delhi: Concept.

Bray, M. and Borevskaya, N. (2001). 'Financing education in transitional societies: lessons from Russia and China', *Comparative Education* 37/3: 345–65.

Bursztyn, L. (2016). 'Poverty and the political economy of public education spending: evidence from Brazil', *Journal of the European Economic Association* 14/5: 1101–28.

Case, A. and Deaton, A. (1999). 'School inputs and educational outcomes in South Africa', *Quarterly Journal of Economics* 114/3: 1047–84.

Case, A. and Yogo, M. (1999). 'Does school quality matter? Returns to education and the characteristics of schools in South Africa'. National Bureau of Economic Research Working Paper No. w7399. New York: NBER.

Chaudhury, N., Hammer, J., Kremer, M., Muralidharan, K., and Rogers, F.H. (2006). 'Missing in action: teacher and health worker absence in developing countries', *Journal of Economic Perspectives* 20/1: 91–116.

Chaudhary, L., Musacchio, A., Nafziger, S., and Yan, S. (2012). 'Big BRICs, weak foundations: the beginning of public elementary education in Brazil, Russia, India, and China', *Explorations in Economic History* 49/2: 221–40.

Deng, Z. and Treiman, D J. (1997). The impact of the cultural revolution on trends in educational attainment in the People's Republic of China', *American Journal of Sociology* 103/2: 391–428.

Department of Basic Education (2016a). *Education Statistic in South Africa 2014*. Pretoria: Department of Basic Education.

Department of Basic Education (2016b). National Infrastructure Management System. Pretoria: Department of Basic Education.

Department of Education (2001). Education White Paper 5 on Early Childhood Education: Meeting the Challenge of Early Childhood Development in South Africa. Pretoria: Department of Education.

Drezè, J. and Saran, M. (1995). 'Primary education and economic development in China and India: overview and two case studies', in K. Busu, P.K. Pattanaik, and K. Suzumura (eds) *Choice, Welfare, and Development: A Festschrift in Honour of Amartya K. Sen*. Oxford: Clarendon Press, 182–241.

Drèze, J. and Sen, A. (1995). *India: Economic Development and Social Opportunity*. Oxford: Oxford University Press.

Drèze, J. and Sen, A. (2013). *An Uncertain Glory: India and its Contradictions*. Princeton, NJ: Princeton University Press.

Dubow, S. (2014). *Apartheid, 1948–1994*. New York: Oxford University Press.

Duflo, E. (2012). 'Women empowerment and economic development', *Journal of Economic Literature* 50/4: 1051–79.

Engerman, S., Mariscal, E., and Sokoloff, K. (2012). 'The evolution of schooling, 1800–1925', in S. Engerman, and K. Sokoloff (eds) *Economic Development in the Americas since 1500: Endowments and Institutions*. Cambridge: Cambridge University Press, 121–67.

Fedderke, J.W., De Kadt, R., and Luiz, J.M. (2000). 'Uneducating South Africa: the failure to address the 1910–1993 legacy', *International Review of Education* 46/3: 257–81.

Giliomee, H. (2009). 'A note on Bantu education, 1953 to 1970', *South African Journal of Economics* 77/1: 190–8.

Goldin, C. and Katz, L. (2008). *The Race between Education and Technology*. Cambridge, MA: Harvard University Press.

Goldman, C.A., Kumar, K.B., and Liu, Y. (2008). *Education and the Asian Surge: A Comparison of the Education Systems in India and China*. Rand Corp Arlington, VA: National Security Research Div.

Gordon, N. and Vegas, E. (2005). 'Educational finance equalization, spending, teacher quality, and student outcomes: the case of Brazil's FUNDEF', in E. Vegas (ed.) *Incentives to Improve Teaching: Lessons from Latin America*. Washington, DC: World Bank, 151–86.

Govinda, R. and Bandyopadhyay, M. (2008). *Access to Elementary Education in India*. Falmer: Consortium for Research on Educational Access, Transitions and Equity (CREATE).

Haddad, M.A., Freguglia, R., and Gomes, C. (2016). 'Public spending and quality of education in Brazil', *Journal of Development Studies* 53/10: 1–18.

Hair, J.F., Black, W.C., Babin, B.J., and Anderson, R.E. (2009). *Multivariate Data Analysis*. New York: Pearson Prentice Hall.

Han, L. (2013). 'Is centralized teacher deployment more equitable? Evidence from rural China', *China Economic Review* 24: 65–76.

Hanushek, E.A. and Woessmann, L. (2012). 'Schooling, educational achievement, and the Latin American growth puzzle', *Journal of Development Economics* 99/2: 497–512.

Hartigan, J.A. and Wong, M.A. (1979). 'Algorithm AS 136: a K-means clustering algorithm', *Applied Statistics* 28/1: 100–8.

Heckman, J.J. (2005). 'China's human capital investment', *China Economic Review* 16/1: 50–70.

Heckman, J.J. and Yi, J. (2012). 'Human capital, economic growth, and inequality in China'. National Bureau of Economic Research, Working Paper No. w18100. Cambridge, CA: NBER.

INEP (Instituto Nacional de Estudos e Pesquisas Educacionais [National Institute for Educational Studies and Research] Anísio Teixeira (1997). *Sinopse estatística da educação superior* [Statistical Synopsis of Higher Education] 1996. Brasília: INEP.

INEP—Instituto Nacional de Estudos e Pesquisas Educacionais [National Institute for Educational Studies and Research] Anísio Teixeira (2016). *Sinopse estatística da educação superior* [Statistical Synopsis of Higher Education] 2015. Brasília: INEP.

Ismagilov, R.F., Salnikov, P.P., Ger, O.E., and Kaizer, A.G. (2016). 'Russian education: a revolution and then a fall', *Russian Education & Society* 58/5–6: 355–87.

Jensen, R. (2010). 'The (perceived) returns to education and the demand for schooling', *Quarterly Journal of Economics* 125/2: 515–48.

Jensen, R. (2012). 'Do labor market opportunities affect young women's work and family decisions? Experimental evidence from India', *Quarterly Journal of Economics* 127/2: 753–92.

Kai-Ming, C. (1994). 'The changing legitimacy in a decentralizing system: the state and education development in China', *International Journal of Educational Development* 14/3: 265–9.

Kang, T.H. (2011). 'Descentralização e financiamento da educação brasileira: uma análise comparative [Decentralization and finance of Brazilian education: a comparative analysis], 1930–1964', *Estudos Econômicos* 41/3: 573–98.

Kingdon, G.G. (2007). 'The progress of school education in India', *Oxford Review of Economic Policy* 23/2: 168–95.

Kosack, S. (2012). *The Education of Nations*. Oxford: Oxford University Press.

Kyui, N. (2016). 'Expansion of higher education, employment and wages: evidence from the Russian Transition', *Labour Economics* 39: 68–87.

Lall, M. (2005). 'The challenges for India's education system'. Briefing Paper ASP BP 05/03. London: Chatham House.

Li, H., Loyalka, P., Rozelle, S., and Wu, B. (2017). 'Human capital and China's future growth', *The Journal of Economic Perspectives* 31/1: 25–47.

Li, S. and Xing, C. (2010). 'China's higher education expansion and its labor market consequences'. IZA Discussion Paper, No. 4974. Beijing: Beijing Normal University.

Lindert, P.H. (2003). 'Voice and growth: was Churchill right?', *Journal of Economic History* 63/2: 315–50.

Lindert, P.H. (2004). *Growing Public: Social Spending and Economic Growth since the Eighteenth Century*. Cambridge: Cambridge University Press.

Lucas, R.E. (1988). 'On the mechanics of economic development', *Journal of Monetary Economics* 22/1: 3–42.

Lukov, V.A. (2005). 'Educational reforms', *Encyclopedia of the Humanities* 3: 217–19.

Marshall, M., Gurr, T., and Jaggers, K. (2016). *Polity IV Project*. Vienna, VA: Center for Systemic Peace.

Mello, L. and Hoppe, M. (2005). 'Education attainment in Brazil: the experience of FUNDEF'. OECD Economics Department Working Papers No. 424. Paris: OECD Publishing.

Menezes-Filho, N. and Pazello, E. (2007). 'Do teachers' wages matter for proficiency? Evidence from a funding reform in Brazil', *Economics of Education Review* 26/6: 660–72.

Mincer, J. (1958). 'Investment in human capital and personal income distribution', *Journal of Political Economy* 66/4: 281–302.

Mincer, J. (1974). *Schooling, Experience, and Earnings*. New York: NBER.

Mok, K.H. (2000). 'Marketizing higher education in post-Mao China', *International Journal of Educational Development* 20/2: 109–26.

Montenegro, C. and Patrinos, H. (2014). 'Comparable estimates of returns to schooling around the world'. Policy Research Working Paper Series 7020. Washington, DC: World Bank.

Naik, J.P. and Nurullah, S. (1974). *A Student's History of Education in India (1800–1973)*. Delhi: Macmillan.

National Treasury (2017). *Budget Review 2017*. Pretoria: National Treasury.

Nattrass, N. and Seekings, J. (2011). 'The economy and poverty in the twentieth century', in R. Ross, A. Mager, and B. Nasson (eds) *The Cambridge History of South Africa*. Cambridge: Cambridge University Press, 518–72.

Ngok, K. (2007). 'Chinese education policy in the context of decentralization and marketization: evolution and implications', *Asia Pacific Education Review* 8/1: 142–57.

Nikolaev, D. and Chugunov, D. (2012). *The Education System in the Russian Federation: Education Brief 2012*. Washington, DC: World Bank.

Nikandrov, N.D. (1995). 'Russian education after perestroika: the search for new values', *International Review of Education* 41/1–2: 47–57.

OECD (Organisation for Economic Co-operation and Development) (2004). *Equity in Education Thematic Review Country Analytical Report—Federation of Russia*. Moscow: OECD.

OECD (Organisation for Economic Co-operation and Development) (2008). *Reviews of National Policies for Education*. South Africa. Paris: OECD.

OECD (Organisation for Economic Co-operation and Development) (2015). *Education Policy Outlook—Brazil.* Available at www.oecd.org/edu/Brazil-country-profile.pdf, accessed 31 October 2018.

OECD (Organisation for Economic Co-operation and Development) (2016). *Education in China: A Snapshot.* Available at www.oecd.org/china/Education-in-China-a-snapshot.pdf, accessed 31 October 2018.

Oster, E. and Steinberg, B M. (2013). 'Do IT service centers promote school enrollment? Evidence from India', *Journal of Development Economics* 104: 123–35.

Pinskaia, M.A., Kosaretskii, S.G., Iiastrebov, G.A., and Grunicheva, I.G. (2014). 'Access to education: an assessment of the situation in Russia', *Russian Education & Society* 56/11: 14–24.

Pradhan, B. and Singh, S. (2004). 'Policy reforms and financing of elementary education in India: a study of the quality of service and outcome'. National Council of Applied Economic Research (NCAER) Working Paper. New Delhi: NCAER.

The Presidency (2014). *Twenty Year Review, South Africa 1994–2014.* Pretoria: The Presidency.

PROBE (Public Report on Basic Education) Team (1999). *Public Report on Basic Education in India.* New Delhi: Oxford University Press.

Rao, N., Cheng, K.M., and Narain, K. (2003). 'Primary schooling in China and India: understanding how socio-contextual factors moderate the role of the state', *International Review of Education* 49: 153–76.

Romer, P.M. (1986). 'Increasing returns and long-run growth', *Journal of Political Economy* 94/5: 1002–37.

Romer, P.M. (1990). 'Endogenous technological change', *Journal of Political Economy* 98/5, Part 2: S71–S102.

Schultz, T. (1963). *The Economic Value of Education.* New York: Columbia University Press.

Schwab, K. and Sala-i-Martin, X. (2011). *The Global Competitiveness Report 2010–2011.* Cologny, Switzerland: World Economic Forum.

Schwab, K. and Sala-i-Martin, X. (2012). *The Global Competitiveness Report 2011–2012.* Cologny, Switzerland: World Economic Forum.

Schwab, K. and Sala-i-Martin, X. (2013). *The Global Competitiveness Report 2012–2013.* Cologny, Switzerland: World Economic Forum.

Schwab, K. and Sala-i-Martin, X. (2014). *The Global Competitiveness Report 2013–2014.* Cologny, Switzerland: World Economic Forum.

Schwab, K. and Sala-i-Martin, X. (2015). *The Global Competitiveness Report 2014–2015.* Cologny, Switzerland: World Economic Forum.

Schwartzman, S. (2015). 'Demand and policies for higher education', in S. Schwartzman, R. Pinheiro, and P. Pillay, (eds) *Higher Education in the BRICS Countries.* Dordrecht: Springer, 13–42.

Sen, A. (1999). *Development as Freedom.* New York: Anchor Books.

Silva, M.O., Kurlyandskaya, G., Andreeva, E., and Golovanova, N. (2009). *Intergovernmental Reforms in the Russian Federation: One Step Forward, Two Steps Back?* Washington, DC: World Bank.

Thomas, D. (1996). 'Education across generations in South Africa', *American Economic Review* 86/2: 330–4.

Thomas, V., Dailami, M., Dhareshwar, A., López, R., Kaufmann, D., Kishor, N. et al. (2000). *The Quality of Growth.* New York: World Bank and Oxford University Press.

Thompson, L.M. (2001). *A History of South Africa*. New Haven, CT: Yale University Press.

Todos Pela Educação (2017). *Anuário Brasileiro da Educação Básica 2017* [Brazilian Yearbook of Basic Education]. São Paulo: Editora Moderna.

Transparency International (2013). *Global Corruption Barometer 2013*. Available at www.transparency.org/research/gcb/overview, accessed 31 October 2018.

Tsang, M.C. (1996). 'Financial reform of basic education in China', *Economics of Education Review* 15/4: 423–44.

UNESCO (2014). *BRICS: Education for the Future*. Paris: UNESCO.

UNESCO (2017). *UIS.Stat* (Institute of Statistics). Available at http://data.uis.unesco.org/, accessed 31 October 2018.

van der Berg, S. (2007). 'Apartheid's enduring legacy: inequalities in Education 1', *Journal of African Economies* 16/5: 849–80.

Venkat, H. and Spaull, N. (2015). 'What do we know about primary teachers' mathematical content knowledge in South Africa? An analysis of SACMEQ 2007', *International Journal of Educational Development* 41: 121–30.

Wang, X., Luo, R., Zhang, L., and Rozelle, S. (2017). 'The education gap of China's migrant children and rural counterparts', *Journal of Development Studies* 53/11: 1–17.

Wjuniski, B.S. (2013). 'Education and development projects in Brazil (1932–2004): political economy perspective', *Revista de Economia Política* 33/1: 146–65.

World Bank. (2017). *World Bank Open Data. 2017*. Available at http://data.worldbank.org/, accessed 31 October 2018.

17 Early childhood and human development

Uruguay Crece Contigo

Giorgina Garibotto

Introduction

This chapter aims to relate the human development and capacities perspective to the Convention on the Rights of the Child on the understanding that these approaches complement each other when addressing early childhood public policy. In the first sections we focus on analysing both approaches and their contributions to early childhood. We also focus on presenting the situation in the country and region where the analysed case was applied.

Second, we present a case of early childhood policy whose design and implementation is based on both approaches. In the following sections we provide an account of the content of early childhood policy in Uruguay, in particular the case of *Uruguay Crece Contigo* [Uruguay Grows up with You]. We then present the results obtained through such policy.

Finally, by way of conclusion, we analyse the results obtained in the programme with the tools provided by the human development and capabilities approach and the rights approach.

Early childhood is human development

HUMAN DEVELOPMENT AS A CONCEPTUAL FRAMEWORK FOR EARLY CHILDHOOD POLICY

The human development approach, conceived by Amartya Sen, defines development as:

a process of expanding the real freedoms that people enjoy. In this approach, expansion of freedom is viewed as (1) the *primary end* and (2) the *principal means* of development. They can

Giorgina Garibotto, *Early childhood and human development: Uruguay Crece Contigo* In: *Handbook of BRICS and Emerging Economies*. Edited by: P.B. Anand, Shailaja Fennell, and Flavio Comim, Oxford University Press (2021). © Oxford University Press.
DOI: 10.1093/oso/9780198827535.003.0017

be called respectively the 'constitutive role' and the 'instrumental role' of freedom of development. The constitutive role of freedom relates to the importance of substantive freedom in enriching human life. The substantive freedoms include elementary capabilities like being able to avoid such deprivations as starvation, undernourishment, escapable morbidity and premature mortality, as well as the freedoms that are associated with being literate and numerate, enjoying political participation and uncensored speech and so on. Similarly, the creation of social opportunities, through such services as public education, health care, and the development of a free and energetic press, can contribute both to economic development and to significant reductions in mortality rates. Reduction of mortality rates, in turn, can help to reduce birth rates, reinforcing the influence of basic education—especially female literacy and schooling—on fertility behavior (Sen 2001).

Development is hence associated with the opportunities people have to live in decent conditions: the sooner people have access to these opportunities the more equality there will be among members of society. This is especially the case in generational inequality. This is how access to elementary capabilities, as stated by Sen, ensures the full development of children in a given society. Such development results in the welfare of children and in the economic development of the country.

The Convention on the Rights of the Child is also relevant in this case. Besides stating the need to ensure survival conditions, as does the human development approach, it includes the need to guarantee freedoms, rights of expression, and political rights.

The author further states that

> It is important to emphasize that this result, if vindicated by other empirical studies as well, would not show that life expectancy is not enhanced by the growth of GNP [gross national product] per head, but it would indicate that the connection tends to work particularly *through* public expenditure on health care, and *through* the success of poverty removal. The basic point is that the impact of economic growth depends much on how the fruits of economic growth are used (Sen 2001).

Some of the aspects which Nussbaum and Dixon (2012) mentions as essential to understand this approach from the children's rights perspective have to do with the human development approach as a tool to allow for participation. This is where the concept of progressive autonomy becomes especially relevant. From the perspective of progressive autonomy, children gradually acquire capabilities. Within the rights approach it is important to focus on these capabilities to begin to recognize the opportunities children have to gradually participate and choose freely.

From the legal perspective, some general principles of law related to childhood become especially relevant: the principles of non-discrimination, best interests of the child, progressive autonomy, and participation.

The Convention on the Rights of the Child enshrines children as rights bearers who will gradually acquire the capacity to exercise those rights. For as long as children cannot form their own opinions, their parents or guardians shall make decisions bearing in mind the best interests of the children, protecting their rights, and guaranteeing their full development.

The capabilities approach, as stated by Nussbaum and Dixon (2012), helps affirm the status of even very young people as rights bearers. In the case of children, the state must provide extensive forms of affirmative protection for individuals. This approach emphasizes the notion of long-term protection of such capabilities within the relevant social and historical context. From this perspective the focus is on the principle of 'each person as end'. In this analysis, focusing simply on economic growth is not enough: the focus should be on people's real opportunities. It is necessary to provide effective access to health, education, housing, etc., goods and services, and for people's capacity to fight for access to such goods, as well as the right to participate in decision-making processes. To this end, everyone should have a guaranteed minimum threshold for certain fundamental capabilities that enable them to function as necessary to take the action needed to exercise rights.

One of the most relevant debates in human development, and particularly in the capabilities approach, is which are these 'fundamental capabilities' that need to be guaranteed. This is still an ongoing debate in the literature, and becomes an even more complex subject in the case of children and adolescents. As already stated, as they gradually acquire their autonomy and decision-making capabilities, it is very difficult to build this list.

In 2004, Mario Biggeri made a list of capabilities specific to children and adolescents. This is a special list because, from the perspective of human development and the capabilities approach, it was built following a survey conducted among children and adolescents.

The main list of children's capabilities identified at that time was the following (Biggeri et al. 2004):

1. Life and physical health: being able to be born and to grow normally
2. Love and care: being able to love and be loved, to be cared for and protected*
3. Mental well-being
4. Physical integrity and safety: being protected from violence of any sort
5. Social relations: being able to be part of a social network and to give and receive social support*
6. Participation: participating and having free access to objective information and having a fair share of influence*
7. Education: being able to be educated
8. Freedom from economic and non-economic exploitation: being protected from all types of exploitation*
9. Shelter and environment: being able to be sheltered and to live in a safe and pleasant environment
10. Leisure activities: being able to engage in leisure activities
11. Respect: being able to be respected and treated with dignity
12. Religion and identity: being able to choose to live according to a religion or identity*
13. Time autonomy: being able to exercise autonomy in allocating one's time*
14. Mobility: being able to be mobile.*

* appropriate to the age and maturity of the child.

As can be seen in the above paragraphs, there seems to be a close connection between the capabilities approach and the Convention on the Rights of the Child. The list of capabilities mentioned by children and adolescents themselves has several points in common with the articles of the Convention on the Rights of the Child.

As can be seen in Table 17.1, almost all the capabilities defined in the survey conducted by Biggeri et al. (2004) have a counterpart article in the Convention on the Rights of the Child. It is only for mobility and time autonomy that an express counterpart is not found. The reference made to mobility is unclear, as it may include technical aid in the case of motor limitations or when having difficulty moving from one country to the other. In both cases, the convention cites specific instances, but does not label them as 'mobility' issues. Although time autonomy has no counterpart in the convention articles, it makes reference to the general principle of the law of progressive autonomy which is especially relevant for children and adolescents.

Additionally, the convention does not address social conventions in the same way as does the capabilities list. However, it does mention the need for state support on this issue.

An essential aspect to consider when analysing the convention is the role of the state as guarantor of the exercise of rights. As for the capabilities approach, it is people and their agency which play a key role.

As we try to analyse in depth the human development approach, especially the capabilities approach, to address early childhood issues, we must focus on who must: (a) have specific capacities to promote the access of children to equal opportunities; (b) promote the development of specific capacities in children.

Early childhood is especially relevant because children are still dependent at this stage in their lives. This means that the exercise of their rights is closely linked to their capacity to have parents or guardians that can defend such rights and enforce them. This is why we must remember children's capacities but also those of their caregivers. Therefore, the opinion and participation of these children's parents or guardians is essential for the children to have equal opportunities for development.

There seems to be total agreement and convergence in both approaches, i.e. human development and children's rights regarding the progressive autonomy of children. But who plays the role of transferring these capacities to children and how is this done?

The actions and benefits for the promotion of child development and the care of children are essentially the responsibility of their parents or legal guardians. In Latin American countries, where the welfare state is not fully developed, families that can afford it meet their needs by resorting to the market, paying for healthcare, education, etc.

So, what happens with families that cannot access these services in the market? Everyone seems to agree that it should be the state that must ensure that the population receives these benefits. From the perspective of the welfare state with universal vocation or even from neoliberal positions, there are people who need the services provided by the state as they cannot access them through the market.

Table 17.1 Comparison between children's capabilities described by Biggeri et al. and the articles of the Convention on the Rights of the Child

Capabilities	Rights
Life and physical health: being able to be born and to grow normally.	**Article 6** 1. States Parties recognize that every child has the inherent right to life. States Parties shall ensure to the maximum extent possible the survival and development of the child. **Article 7** 1. The child shall be registered immediately after birth and shall have the right from birth to a name, the right to acquire a nationality and, as far as possible, the right to know and be cared for by his or her parents. 2. States Parties shall ensure the implementation of these rights in accordance with their national law and their obligations under the relevant international instruments in this field, in particular where the child would otherwise be stateless. **Article 8** 1. States Parties undertake to respect the right of the child to preserve his or her identity, including nationality, name and family relations as recognized by law without unlawful interference. 2. Where a child is illegally deprived of some or all of the elements of his or her identity, States Parties shall provide appropriate assistance and protection, with a view to re-establishing speedily his or her identity.
Love and care: being able to love and be loved, to be cared for and protected.*	**Article 18** 1. States Parties shall use their best efforts to ensure recognition of the principle that both parents have common responsibilities for the upbringing and development of the child. Parents or, as the case may be, legal guardians, have the primary responsibility for the upbringing and development of the child. The best interests of the child will be their basic concern. 2. For the purpose of guaranteeing and promoting the rights set forth in the present Convention, States Parties shall render appropriate assistance to parents and legal guardians in the performance of their child-rearing responsibilities and shall ensure the development of institutions, facilities and services for the care of children. 3. States Parties shall take all appropriate measures to ensure that children of working parents have the right to benefit from child-care services and facilities for which they are eligible.
Mental well-being.	**Article 23** 1. States Parties recognize that a mentally or physically disabled child should enjoy a full and decent life, in conditions which ensure dignity, promote self-reliance and facilitate the child's active participation in the community. 2. States Parties recognize the right of the disabled child to special care and shall encourage and ensure the extension, subject to available resources, to the eligible child and those responsible for his or her care, of assistance for which application is made and which is appropriate to the child's condition and to the circumstances of the parents or others caring for the child. 3. Recognizing the special needs of a disabled child, assistance extended in accordance with paragraph 2 of the present article shall be provided free of charge, whenever possible, taking into account the financial resources of the parents or others caring for the child, and shall be designed to ensure that the disabled child has effective access to and receives education, training, health care services, rehabilitation services, preparation for employment and recreation opportunities in a manner conducive to the child's achieving the fullest possible social integration and individual development, including his or her cultural and spiritual development. 4. States Parties shall promote, in the spirit of international cooperation, the exchange of appropriate information in the field of preventive health care and of medical, psychological and functional treatment of disabled children, including dissemination of and access to information concerning methods of rehabilitation,

(*continued*)

Table 17.1 Continued

Capabilities	Rights
	education and vocational services, with the aim of enabling States Parties to improve their capabilities and skills and to widen their experience in these areas. In this regard, particular account shall be taken of the needs of developing countries.
Physical integrity and safety: being protected from violence of any sort.	**Article 19** 1. States Parties shall take all appropriate legislative, administrative, social and educational measures to protect the child from all forms of physical or mental violence, injury or abuse, neglect or negligent treatment, maltreatment or exploitation, including sexual abuse, while in the care of parent(s), legal guardian(s) or any other person who has the care of the child. 2. Such protective measures should, as appropriate, include effective procedures for the establishment of social programmes to provide necessary support for the child and for those who have the care of the child, as well as for other forms of prevention and for identification, reporting, referral, investigation, treatment and follow-up of instances of child maltreatment described heretofore, and, as appropriate, for judicial involvement.
Social relations: being able to be part of a social network and to give and receive social support.*	**Article 27** 1. States Parties recognize the right of every child to a standard of living adequate for the child's physical, mental, spiritual, moral and social development. 2. The parent(s) or others responsible for the child have the primary responsibility to secure, within their abilities and financial capacities, the conditions of living necessary for the child's development. 3. States Parties, in accordance with national conditions and within their means, shall take appropriate measures to assist parents and others responsible for the child to implement this right and shall in case of need provide material assistance and support programmes, particularly with regard to nutrition, clothing and housing. 4. States Parties shall take all appropriate measures to secure the recovery of maintenance for the child from the parents or other persons having financial responsibility for the child, both within the State Party and from abroad. In particular, where the person having financial responsibility for the child lives in a state different from that of the child, States Parties shall promote the accession to international agreements or the conclusion of such agreements, as well as the making of other appropriate arrangements.
Participation: participating and having free access to objective information and having a fair share of influence.*	**Article 12** 1. States Parties shall assure to the child who is capable of forming his or her own views the right to express those views freely in all matters affecting the child, the views of the child being given due weight in accordance with the age and maturity of the child. For this purpose, the child shall in particular be provided the opportunity to be heard in any judicial and administrative proceedings affecting the child, either directly, or through a representative or an appropriate body, in a manner consistent with the procedural rules of national law. **Article 13** 1. The child shall have the right to freedom of expression; this right shall include freedom to seek, receive and impart information and ideas of all kinds, regardless of frontiers, either orally, in writing or in print, in the form of art, or through any other media of the child's choice. 2. The exercise of this right may be subject to certain restrictions, but these shall only be such as are provided by law and are necessary: (a) For respect of the rights or reputations of others; or (b) For the protection of national security or of public order (ordre public), or of public health or morals.

Education: being able to be educated.	**Article 28** 1. States Parties recognize the right of the child to education, and with a view to achieving this right progressively and on the basis of equal opportunity, they shall, in particular: (a) Make primary education compulsory and available free to all; (b) Encourage the development of different forms of secondary education, including general and vocational education, make them available and accessible to every child, and take appropriate measures such as the introduction of free education and offering financial assistance in case of need; (c) Make higher education accessible to all on the basis of capacity by every appropriate means; (d) Make educational and vocational information and guidance available and accessible to all children; (e) Take measures to encourage regular attendance at schools and the reduction of drop-out rates. 2. States Parties shall take all appropriate measures to ensure that school discipline is administered in a manner consistent with the child's human dignity and in conformity with the present Convention. 3. States Parties shall promote and encourage international cooperation in matters relating to education, in particular with a view to contributing to the elimination of ignorance and illiteracy throughout the world and facilitating access to scientific and technical knowledge and modern teaching methods. In this regard, particular account shall be taken of the needs of developing countries.
Freedom from economic and non-economic exploitation: being protected from all types of exploitation.*	**Article 19** 1. States Parties shall take all appropriate legislative, administrative, social and educational measures to protect the child from all forms of physical or mental violence, injury or abuse, neglect or negligent treatment, maltreatment or exploitation, including sexual abuse, while in the care of parent(s), legal guardian(s) or any other person who has the care of the child. 2. Such protective measures should, as appropriate, include effective procedures for the establishment of social programmes to provide necessary support for the child and for those who have the care of the child, as well as for other forms of prevention and for identification, reporting, referral, investigation, treatment and follow-up of instances of child maltreatment described heretofore, and, as appropriate, for judicial involvement.
Shelter and environment: being able to be sheltered and to live in a safe and pleasant environment.	**Article 20** 1. A child temporarily or permanently deprived of his or her family environment, or in whose own best interests cannot be allowed to remain in that environment, shall be entitled to special protection and assistance provided by the state. 2. States Parties shall in accordance with their national laws ensure alternative care for such a child. 3. Such care could include, inter alia, foster placement, kafalah of Islamic law, adoption or if necessary placement in suitable institutions for the care of children. When considering solutions, due regard shall be paid to the desirability of continuity in a child's upbringing and to the child's ethnic, religious, cultural and linguistic background. **Article 21** States Parties that recognize and/or permit the system of adoption shall ensure that the best interests of the child shall be the paramount consideration and they shall: (a) Ensure that the adoption of a child is authorized only by competent authorities who determine, in accordance with applicable law and procedures and on the basis of all pertinent and reliable information, that the adoption is permissible in view of the child's status concerning parents, relatives and legal guardians and that, if required, the persons concerned have given their informed consent to the adoption on the basis of such counselling as may be necessary;

(*continued*)

Table 17.1 Continued

Capabilities	Rights
	(b) Recognize that inter-country adoption may be considered as an alternative means of child's care, if the child cannot be placed in a foster or an adoptive family or cannot in any suitable manner be cared for in the child's country of origin; (c) Ensure that the child concerned by inter-country adoption enjoys safeguards and standards equivalent to those existing in the case of national adoption; (d) Take all appropriate measures to ensure that, in inter-country adoption, the placement does not result in improper financial gain for those involved in it; (e) Promote, where appropriate, the objectives of the present article by concluding bilateral or multilateral arrangements or agreements, and endeavour, within this framework, to ensure that the placement of the child in another country is carried out by competent authorities or organs.
Leisure activities: being able to engage in leisure activities.	**Article 31** 1. States Parties recognize the right of the child to rest and leisure, to engage in play and recreational activities appropriate to the age of the child and to participate freely in cultural life and the arts. 2. States Parties shall respect and promote the right of the child to participate fully in cultural and artistic life and shall encourage the provision of appropriate and equal opportunities for cultural, artistic, recreational and leisure activity.
Respect: being able to be respected and treated with dignity.	**Article 39** States Parties shall take all appropriate measures to promote physical and psychological recovery and social reintegration of a child victim of: any form of neglect, exploitation, or abuse; torture or any other form of cruel, inhuman or degrading treatment or punishment; or armed conflicts. Such recovery and reintegration shall take place in an environment which fosters the health, self-respect and dignity of the child.
Religion and identity: being able to choose to live according to a religion or identity.*	**Article 14** 1. States Parties shall respect the right of the child to freedom of thought, conscience and religion. 2. States Parties shall respect the rights and duties of the parents and, when applicable, legal guardians, to provide direction to the child in the exercise of his or her right in a manner consistent with the evolving capacities of the child. 3. Freedom to manifest one's religion or beliefs may be subject only to such limitations as are prescribed by law and are necessary to protect public safety, order, health or morals, or the fundamental rights and freedoms of others.
Time autonomy: being able to exercise autonomy in allocating one's time.	There is not a specific counterpart article that relates to this aspect, as it has to do more with the general principle of law of progressive autonomy.
Mobility: being able to be mobile.*	

* Data are from the database accumulated since the beginning of the programme in September 2012 to 15 December 2014.

Source: Biggeri et al. 2004.

Why we need early childhood policy

THE RELEVANCE OF EARLY CHILDHOOD FOR DEVELOPMENT

Early childhood is defined as the period of a child's life from conception to age 5. It is in this period that the foundation is laid for all the later development of the child. While the first two years of life are crucial for the child's intellectual, emotional, physical/immunological, and social development, it is between the ages of 2 and 5 that the foundations for formal education and social skills are laid (Evans et al. 2000).

Early childhood is a 'short' and very dynamic period. Any disorder that might affect someone's health, nutrition, or development at this stage can cause problems that will extend over time.

Neurosciences have shown the importance of the care given to the child from gestation until the age of 3 Full and integrated care should be provided in the first eighteen months to enhance future development and prevent irreversible deficiencies. From birth and up to the age of 3, neuron connections (synapses) take place in the brain at high speed and efficiency levels, which will not be equalled in the rest of the child's life. In the first year of life, the brain doubles its size. At the age of 2, the child's brain has reached adult level, and at the age of 3 the existing synaptic connections in a child's brain (approximately 1,000 trillion) double the number of those in the adult brain (Mustard 2006).

From the beginning of the intrauterine life, first the foetus and then the child respond to exogenous stimuli coming from their surrounding environment. If these stimuli are unfavourable, such as lack of nutrients in the intrauterine life, certain genes are activated, making these individuals more prone, in their adult lives, to suffering from serious diseases called chronic non-communicable diseases such as diabetes, obesity, hypertension, arteriosclerosis, etc.

This accelerated development of the brain depends on genetics and on life experience, and is most marked at the foetus stage and in the first year of life. In this space of time there is a true 'moulding' of the child's genetic make-up from the stimuli in the surrounding environment. This process can have a positive effect as it enhances the child's development potential. Conversely, if the environment exposure is negative, it can have a debilitating effect. Adverse conditions during pregnancy and early childhood are related to (physical and emotional) health in adult life, a higher mortality rate, a conflictive social performance, and difficulties in school life (Landers et al. 2006). On the other hand, a positive experience can entail highly favourable effects on all these aspects. Proximity and attachment to caregivers, loving care, a harmonious and devoted environment, and play are all fundamental aspects when it comes to enhancing development in these first years of life. Nutrition, health, protection, the necessary care, and stimuli at this stage are the essential nutrients the brain needs to develop.

INVESTMENT IN EARLY CHILDHOOD POLICY

Investing in early childhood promotes the reduction of poverty and inequality. The success or failure of other social policies is conditioned to a great extent by childhood policies. Early childhood action that yields good results has major benefits on education, health, and social coexistence during adulthood, hence fully improving the social policy system. Finally, investing in early childhood is the best way to prevent poverty from spreading and to reverse social inequality by creating conditions that are equal for everyone from the beginning of life.

Heckman (2006), Nobel Prize winner in economics in 2000, showed in his work that investment in early stages of life has a very high rate of return, which is always greater than the investment made after early childhood.

EARLY CHILDHOOD IN THE LATIN AMERICAN PUBLIC AGENDA

> Nowadays in Latin American societies, certain population sectors excluded from specific areas of citizenship and from the exercise of some rights have started to demand a special place in national agendas. This is how women (from the gender perspective), communities of African and indigenous descent (from an ethnic-racial perspective) and children (in generational terms) are a few of the groups that have incorporated specific actions in protection systems.
>
> (Dagnino, 2008: 211)

These processes are accompanied by a new development model and new social demands (Esping-Andersen et al. 2002; Esping-Andersen and Palier 2010). These authors state that the idea is to go from remedy policies when social disadvantages accumulate, to preventive policies based on the logic of social investment. That is to say, what is done today to help these population sectors will bring about social well-being in the future.

From this perspective, early childhood policy is key, as it renders opportunities more equal for those children born in households with unequal income or characteristics from the beginning of life. This population is special because they cannot act on their own: they depend on the demands made by their representatives. This is the case especially in early childhood care, which was traditionally included within the private sphere of the family. With women massively entering the employment market, the demand for childhood benefits in the public sphere as a social demand appeared.

EARLY CHILDHOOD IN URUGUAY

Uruguay has always been one of the countries in Latin America with the lowest levels of income inequality. Furthermore, the country's income level exceeds that of most of these countries. However, a significant process of infantilization of poverty was detected several decades ago (Terra et al 1989). In Uruguay, intergenerational inequality has remained the same, even in times of economic growth. A number of public policies have been implemented to address this problem and overcome this inequality. The Equality Plan (2008), both in its structural components and from the Social Assistance and Integration Network, has made considerable progress towards the protection of families with children and adolescents living in poverty. A non-contributory family allowances system was created to support families with children and adolescents below the threshold defined through the Critical Deprivation Index [Índice de Carencias Críticas]. This index allows us to measure the needs of families in a multidimensional way. The coverage of initial education and education for 4- and 5-year-olds is now universal. Education for 1-, 2- and 3-year-olds has steadily expanded its coverage. It is through the National Integrated Health System that coverage and benefits have expanded (new vaccines, preventive check-ups, etc.) to pregnant women and children under 4 years of age.

However, there is still significant intergenerational inequality in the country. Although the percentage of people below the poverty line has decreased every year, there are twice as many poor households with children under age than any other as there are poor households in general. In 2013, the percentage of households with children under 6 years of age below the poverty line was 22.6 per cent, while the total percentage of poverty was just 11.5 per cent. Although there has been a significant increase in the number of social policies that have good effects, a 'hard core' of people remain without access to already existing social goods and services because of exclusion.

Regarding health indicators, despite the steady decrease in child mortality rates, the main causes remain unchanged, most of which could be potentially reduced. Preterm-related conditions are still the main cause of mortality in the neonatal period (0 to 28 days) (Giachetto 2010). Regarding post-neonatal mortality (28 days to 12 months old), the main problem is death at home (MSP 2010).

In 2012, 2.7 per cent of newborns had congenital syphilis according to the Perinatal Information System (the World Health Organization (WHO) states that a country should have a figure of 0.5/00 to be considered free of congenital syphilis).

Prematurity and low birthweight are high, even when compared to other similar countries in the region. The percentage of premature infants (born before week 37) was 9 per cent and the percentage of low-weight infants (less than 2,500g) was 8 per cent in 2012, according to data provided by Live Birth Certificates.

Early childhood anaemia poses several serious consequences that mainly affect growth and development. According to data obtained from the 2011 MSP/MIDES/RUANDI/UNICEF survey on eating practices, nutritional condition and anaemia, the global prevalence of anaemia among children aged between 6 months and 24 months is 31.5 per cent. No significant differences were detected between public and private sectors.

Regarding child nutrition, the data available (see Table 17.2) suggest that the country has even higher levels of chronic malnutrition. This is measured by relating the child's height to his/her age, which shows a deficient nutrition history that is reflected in a

Table 17.2 Summary of social and health indicators

Indicator	Percentage
Poverty among children under 6 (INE 2013)	22.60%
Aid to initial education—0 to 3 years of age (2011)	36%
Child mortality (2012)	9.3/00
Prematurity (2012)	9%
Low birth weight (2012)	8%
Newborns with connatal syphilis (2012)	2.70%
Childhood anaemia (6 to 23 months around the country) (MSP/MIDES/RUANDI/UNICEF 2011)	31.50%
Stunting in infants under 24 months of age (Bove and Cerruti 2011)	10.90%

Source: Author's work.

height that is lower than it should be for children of that age. According to the data collected by MSP/MIDES/RUANDI/UNICEF, the prevalence of stunting among children under 24 months in 2011 was 10.9 per cent.

Early childhood public policy in Uruguay

Uruguay has directed its efforts towards building a social protection matrix to address the social and economic inequalities exacerbated in the last decades of the twentieth century. Several structural reforms have been undertaken for this purpose, the most significant being the health reform, the tax reform, and the social reform.

The 2010–30 National Childhood and Adolescence Strategy (ENIA) was developed in 2008, when organizing the actions of the state based on an assessment of the situation and the singularities of the population. This strategy is the result of discussion among different social stakeholders, both governmental and non-governmental, in each of the departments in the country, including representatives from all political parties and academia.

During the strategy's implementation process, and based on the results of a continuous evaluation process, the government decided to strengthen those programmes and actions, targeting households with pregnant women and children under the age of 4.

Given the country's situation, the government has identified three challenges with regard to early childhood:

I. improving the quality of current universal benefits targeting early childhood and, at the same time, increasing coverage of key services for child development;
II. providing special support to those sectors of the population that remain in a situation of high socio-economic vulnerability, which in turn translates into harm and risks affecting childhood development;

III. improving conditions under which early childhood policies are implemented, through the establishment of a *Comprehensive Early Childhood Protection System* that ensures and guarantees improved development of all children in the country, from gestation to the age of four.

The first challenge is the support provided to those sectors of the population still living in poverty and socio-economic vulnerability, which in turn translates into harm or risks affecting childhood development.

It is worth noting that, notwithstanding the progress made in favour of poverty and extreme poverty reduction, there are still households in the country that require specialized and continuous support to promote their social integration.

A second challenge is to strengthen and streamline the process of improving the quality of the benefits and services targeting early childhood and to increase coverage of several key services for this population.

Coordination and synchronization are the key inputs needed to address this challenge, so as to prevent conflict among the services and benefits, and overlapping in their implementation and access.

Therefore, the third challenge is to build an *Early Childhood Protection System* that ensures and guarantees improved development of all children in the country, from gestation to the age of 4.

The system is conceived from a perspective of rights, equity, and social justice, so as to become a permanent and sustainable early childhood public policy. These elements support the notion that early childhood policies should be conceived as a single integrated system, highlighting the need for clearer and more effective governance.

Uruguay has a very important base of programmes and benefits that are implemented from different public institutions or through working agreements with public institutions or civil society organizations. Nevertheless, there is a clear need to strengthen inter-institutional coordination and enhance institutional design to allow for proper management of the system.

DESCRIPTION OF *URUGUAY CRECE CONTIGO*

The Office of the President of the Republic created the *Uruguay Crece Contigo* (UCC) Programme to address these challenges, with the aim of supporting the consolidation of a *Comprehensive Early Childhood Protection System* that ensures and guarantees improved development of all children in the country from gestation to the age of 4.

The programme was designed based on the implementation of four components: (i) family support and proximity work (see Table 17.3); (ii) universal coverage: social, education, and health actions (see Table 17.4); (iii) knowledge production (see Table 17.5); (iv) strengthening of institutional capabilities (see Table 17.6).

The design combines universal strategies with approaches that target the most underprivileged households, so as to empower the more vulnerable families to first, become aware of their rights and second, to have access to them. This allows for a differentiated treatment of those who have alternative opportunities.

Territorial deployment is a key feature of the programme. An office for inter-institutional coordination was set up in each department (decentralized government). UCC appointed an expert as regional facilitator to support the implementation of the programme and regional coordination efforts with the sectoral agencies involved (health, education, social development, etc.).

For the implementation of the Family Support and Proximity Work component, the UCC has, in addition, put together *proximity teams*, comprised of departmental supervisors whose role is to: (a) ensure the quality of the implementation of such components; (b) coordinate efforts with the remaining proximity teams of other initiatives in the health and social fields; (c) supervise the teams of experts of the component, who are in charge of a group of families in each territory of reference, for support and monitoring.

Family Support and Proximity Work

This is conducted through teams of 'proximity operators' who visit vulnerable households with pregnant women and/or children under the age of 4 to strengthen their capacities to develop good parenting practices, and therefore improve the health, nutrition, and child development conditions as well as their social inclusion.

Focusing on this aspect in particular, the programme has looked for a positive impact on the reduction of: (i) the prevalence of anaemia; (ii) the incidence of gestational syphilis; (iii) the incidence of children who have low height and weight for their age. In addition, it seeks to improve the quality of prenatal care and early pregnancy detection, enhance child development, and ensure access to existing social protection benefits.

In proximity support, the groups of experts, formed of a healthcare professional and a social services professional, work with families for a period of between six months and two years depending on the characteristics of the family (members and risks). To achieve the goals of the programme, during this period the work entails home visits with a socio-educational purpose, allowing families to increase their knowledge on early childhood care, but also to help them learn about the benefits and services available both to both children and to women—who are for the most part the caregivers in the lives of these boys and girls. Another core component of the programme is to escort family members when doing paperwork or collecting benefits. For example, helping schedule a doctor's appointment and going with the person to the healthcare centre.

These tasks serve different purposes: (a) facilitating access to benefits; (b) informing the families about these benefits and their rights; (c) working with the administrative staff to improve the quality of services, especially when dealing with families who are not familiar with the institutional culture and have difficulties in accessing such state services.

Universal Coverage: Social, Education, and Health Action

The programme develops lines of work with regard to social communication through awareness campaigns on the importance of early childhood and prenatal care, the promotion of a healthy lifestyle, and the education on parenting skills and child-rearing practices. Through this component, the UCC coordinates and supports the actions of the other agencies involved in early childhood care.

This component targets the entire population of children under the age of 4 in the country and their families. Given the characteristics of the country (second demographic transition in progress) and a tradition of public policy historically dependent on social security, in order to place the issue of early childhood in the public agenda it is necessary to take targeted actions to move away from inertia and conventionalism in the allocation of public resources.

Knowledge Production

Nationwide studies are conducted in order to have accurate and updated information on early childhood.

It is within this framework that there are efforts in place to put together an information system on early childhood by: (a) enhancing existing systems, so the country will have a comprehensive early childhood monitoring system (management dashboard); (b) promoting specific studies to keep the information on early childhood issues updated.

At present there are several agreements in force with different academic institutions that seek to promote research on subject matters considered a core priority for decision making. There is also close cooperation with the National Institute of Statistics for the design and implementation of nationwide surveys on early childhood.

Strengthening of Institutional Capacities

The aim is to contribute to the improvement of the quality of the services that support pregnant women and children under the age of 4.

As previously noted, there are several institutions in the country that provide early childhood services. The strengthening of institutional capacities entails, among other things, improving the quality of the services as well as coordinating the actions of the different institutions. This will be achieved by: (a) upgrading equipment; (b) training staff (administrative and technical); (c) coordinating actions.

RESULTS OF *URUGUAY CRECE CONTIGO* PER COMPONENT

Table 17.3 Family support and proximity work

COMMITMENTS. GOALS	Situation in December 2014
UCC proximity teams in all departments.	100% of departments implementing the UCC programme.
Family support for 10,000 pregnant women and/or children under the age of 4 throughout the country.	12,224 children under 4 years of age and pregnant women in 7,316 households being supported, where 34,160 people live.
Haemoglobin (hb) test performed on at least 80% of pregnant women and children under 4 from the families supported.	Hb screening done on 83% of the children. 90% of the pregnant women had their hb measured.
Child developmental screening performed on at least 80% of children under 4 from the families supported.	88% of children had the child developmental screening performed.
At least 70% of pregnant women had regular check-ups in accordance with current regulations after they began receiving UCC support.	65% of pregnant women had regular check-ups in accordance with current regulations after they began receiving UCC support. 58% of pregnant women had at least five check-ups.
At least 50% of children under 2 years of age improve their weight/age ratio by 0.5 in the Z-score and at least 30% of children under 4 improve their height/age ratio by 0.5 in the Z-score.	40% of children over 2 years of age improve their weight/age ratio by 0.5 in the Z-score (n=2122). 35% of children under 4 improve their height/age ratio by 0.5 in the Z-score (n=3156).
At least 20% reduction of childhood anaemia among the children.	85% of the children with anaemia at the start of the support process did not have the condition after the proximity work.
20% reduction in situations where child development is disrupted.	58% of children that showed disruption in their development at the beginning of the process were not in that situation at the end of the proximity work done by UCC.
At least 50% of families without the social benefits provided by the *Uruguay Social* card, the Nutritional Risk Basket provided by INDA and the civil identification office started to enjoy these benefits.	53% of families without the social benefits provided by the TUS card[†] started to have access to the card. The remaining ones are still being evaluated by MIDES. 66% of families without the Nutritional Risk Basket provided by INDA[$] started to receive the basket. 77% of pregnant women who did not have prenatal allowances[**] started to receive them. 81% of the households that did not receive allowances[††] on account of their children started to receive them. Percentage of children that do not attend a CAIF[††] dropped from 67% to 43%.

In the 2012–14 [*] period, this component organized groups of 188 operators that worked with 7,316 households where a total of 12,224 people were supported: 8,997 children under 4 years of age and 3,227 pregnant women. Work was done with at least 34,160 people in these households. The actions began in ten departments [†] and as of June 2013, they were extended to the whole country.

Notes: Data are from the database accumulated since the beginning of the programme from September 2012 to 15 December 2014.

[†] The following are the departments where the programme was implemented: Montevideo, Canelones, San José, Maldonado, Cerro Largo, Tacuarembó, Rivera, Artigas, Salto, Paysandú.

[†] Tarjeta Uruguay Social—with credit to buy food and basic household products.

[$] Instituto Nacional De Alimentación [National Food Institute].

[**] Non-contributory money transfer specifically for pregnant women.

[††] Non-contributory money transfer on account of children under 18 years of age in the households.

[††] Centros de Atención a la Infancia y la Familia [Infant and Family Care Centres]. Public initial education centres whose main users are children from low-income households.

Source: Author's work based on UCC Monitoring system (UNICEF 2014).

Table 17.4 Universal coverage: social, education, and health action

GOALS	Situation in December 2014
Universal delivery of 'educational support sets'.[§§]	Since 2013 we have been delivering 'Welcome sets' in all public and private maternity wards around the country: 56,890 sets as of December 2014.
Universal campaign to foster awareness raising and communication on the importance of early childhood. TV, radio, press, graphic material.	A universal campaign was launched in November/ December 2013 to foster awareness raising and communication on the importance of early childhood. Design of graphic material for all 19 departments to be delivered to all local institutions.

[§§] Educational material is delivered to all children around the country when they leave the maternity ward. It has one music CD, one storybook, one toy, one book on nutrition, one book on child-rearing guidelines, and one book of general recommendations. We also provide a focalized set to the families that participate in the proximity support component with warm clothes, eating utensils, crawling rugs, and practical cots.

Source: UNICEF 2014 Uruguay Crece Contigo (UCC) Annual Report.

Table 17.5 Knowledge production

GOALS	Situation in December 2014
National survey on health, nutrition, and child development	Implementation of the survey within the agreement with INE and Universidad de la República. Field work: 3,070 children surveyed.
External evaluation of the results of the programme	Being implemented since October 2013.
Consolidation of information systems	Actions are being coordinated with AGEV, MSP, MVOTMA, MEC, INAU, MIDES, BPS,[***] and INDA in order to improve each institution's information system so that the Early Childhood Management Dashboard can be implemented.

[***] AGEV (Management and evaluation Agency)
MVOTMA (minister of housing, urban development and environment)
MEC (Minister of education and culture)
INAU (Childhood and adolescence institute of Uruguay)
BPS (Bank of Social Protection of Uruguay)
(All are in their Spanish acronyms.)

Source: UNICEF 2014 Uruguay Crece Contigo (UCC) Annual Report.

Conclusion

It has been very difficult to convey in one chapter the arguments that link human development to human rights: tradition and theoretical development are very broad in both approaches. However, the key seems to lie in the existence of equal opportunities. Both paradigms seem to highlight the importance of analysing the difficulties different populations face in accessing minimum levels of well-being.

Additionally, the public policy approach provides a very interesting perspective regarding who should guarantee and implement actions that allow people access to

Table 17.6 Strengthening of institutional capacities

GOALS	Situation in December 2014
Technical support to review healthcare rules and criteria	Jointly with the MSP, we aim to review and unify healthcare criteria in all the maternities around the country, so as to guarantee quality service for everyone regardless of their socio-economic situation. The MSP published, promoted. and updated the guides for the prevention of anaemia throughout the country.
Technical support for the design of a common initial education programme for children between 0 and 6 years of age.	Agreement with the Early Childhood Advisory Board of Education created in the law of education and formed by MEC, ANEP, INAU, MSP, and SINTEP.‡‡‡ Common initial education programme for children between 0 and 6 years of age already agreed on.
30 people were hired to support pregnancy control	15 family doctors and 14 OB-GYN midwives hired in December 2013 working to provide public services in Montevideo and Canelones.
Equipment and infrastructure work in health centres and early childhood services.	Implementation of the telemedicine innovative project, which is the only alternative system to improve access to prenatal control ultrasounds. This is how the needs of pregnant women whose health is covered by ASSE‡‡‡ are met.

‡‡‡ ANEP (Public Education National Administration
SINTEP (Public education labor union)
‡‡‡ National Health Services Administration.

Source: UNICEF (2014) Uruguay Crece Contigo (UCC) Annual Report.

opportunities and how this should be done. In this sense, the role played by the state regarding individuals and their capacities is essential, even for the promotion of these capacities. Early childhood calls for interrelation between adult caregivers and the state, as they are the key participants that will determine equality of opportunities from the beginning of life in a given society. Therefore, the sooner opportunities become equal, the greater the chances children will have to fully develop on personal and social levels.

Finally, it has been an interesting challenge to conceptualize human development and rights in practice. This is to say, analysing the specific strategies that a state, the Uruguayan State in this case, has implemented so that families can have access to benefits and services and also acquire the necessary capacities so that they can demand their own rights.

According to the results shown, it seems possible to go from theory to practice, at least in the hard data that reflect the improvement of specific indicators related to health and access to benefits. The proximity family support approach allows families to directly participate in the construction of improvement and care strategies for the children themselves. However, there is still a long way to go regarding participation, and we still need to evaluate the capacity needed to maintain the abilities acquired through these processes in the long term.

Furthermore, early childhood as a population to be addressed by social policy poses specific challenges. In this sense, awareness raising and the production of specific knowledge are essential to making the specific needs of these generations visible. In terms of human development, the capacities acquired by these children from a very young age will lead to freedom.

ACKNOWLEDGEMENTS

The author gratefully acknowledges the support and encouragement of Dra. Cristina Lustemberg as Chief of Uruguay Crece Contigo (2012–15) and Mag. Florencia Cerruti and Ec. Nathalia Martínez for their technical assistance.

REFERENCES

Biggeri, M., Libanora, R., Mariani, S., and Menchini, L. (2004). 'Children establishing their capabilities: preliminary results of the survey during the first children's world congress on child labour'. Paper presented at the 4th International Conference on the Capability Approach, September, Pavia: University of Pavia.

Bove, M.I. and Cerruti, F. (2011). Encuesta Nacional sobre estado nutricional, prácticas de alimentación y anemia en niños menores de dos años usuarios de servicios de salud de los subsectores público y privado del Uruguay [National survey on the nutritional status, feeding practices and anemia in children below two year old who use the public and private health services of Uruguay]. Montevideo: MSP/MIDES/RUANDI/UNICEF. Available at www.unicef.org/uruguay/spanish/publications.html, accessed 18 February 2019.

Dagnino, E. (2008). 'Los significados de ciudadanía en América Latina' [Citizenship meanings in Latin America], in A. Chaparro, C. Galindo, and A.M. Sallenave (eds) *Estado, Democracia y Populismo en América Latina* [State, democracy and populism in Latin America]. Bogotá: Editorial Universidad del Rosario.

Esping-Andersen, G. and Palier, B. (2010). *Los Tres Grandes Retos del Estado de Bienestar* [Three lessons about the welfare state]. Ariel, Barcelona: Editorial Planeta.

Esping-Andersen, G., Gallie, D., Hemerijck, A., and Myles, J. (2002). *Why We Need a New Welfare State.* New York: Oxford University Press.

Evans, J., Myers, R., and Ilfeld, E. (2000). *Early Childhood Counts: A Programming Guide on Early Childhood Care for Development.* Washington, DC: World Bank.

Giachetto, G. (2010). 'Mortalidad infantil en Uruguay: una mirada crítica' [Child mortality in Uruguay: a critical review], Montevideo, Editorial, *Archivos de Pediatria del Uruguay* 81/3: 139–40.

Heckman, J.J. (2006). 'Skill formation and the economics of investing in disadvantaged children'. 30 June, vol 312. Science, www.sciencemag.org. Available at http://jenni.uchicago.edu/papers/Heckman_Science_v312_2006.pdf, accessed 1 November 2018.

INE (Instituto Nacional de Estadistica) (2013). *Uso del tiempo y trabajo no remunerado. Encuesta continua de hogares* [Use of time and unpaid work. Household survey]. Montevideo: INE.

Landers, C., Mercer, R., Molina, H., Eming Young, M. (2006). *Desarrollo integral en la infancia: una prioridad para la salud. manual de desarrollo temprano para profesionales de la salud*

[Comprehensive development in childhood: a priority for health. Early development manual for health professionals]. Geneva: PAHO/WHO.

MSP (Ministerio de Salud Pública) (2010). *Informe jornada por la vida de niños, niñas, adolescentes y jóvenes. Causas y estrategias para reducir la mortalidad. Comunicación y Salud* [Children, adolescents and young people's report. Causes and strategies to reduce mortality], pp. 1–6. Available at www.msp.gub.uy, accessed 5 November 2018.

MSP (Ministerio de Salud Pública), MIDES, RUANDI and UNICEF (2011). Available at www.unicef.org/uruguay/spanish/publications.html, accessed 1 March 2019.

Mustard, F. (2006). *Early Child Development and Experience-Based Brain Development: The Scientific Underpinnings of the Importance of Early Child Development in a Globalized World.* Falta Editorial. Washington, DC: Brookings Institution.

Nussbaum, M. and Dixon, R. (2012). 'Children's rights and a capabilities approach: the question of special priority'. University of Chicago, Public law and legal theory working papers No 384. Available at www.lawschool.cornell.edu/research/cornell-law-review/upload/Dixon-Nussbaum-final.pdf, accessed 5 November 2018.

Sen, Amartya (2001). *Development as Freedom,* 2nd edn. Oxford and New York: Oxford University Press.

Terra, J.P., Piedra Cueva, E., and Roba, O. (1989). *Creciendo en condiciones de riesgo: niños pobres del Uruguay* [Growing in risk: child poverty in Uruguay]. Montevideo, CLAEH, UNICEF.

UNICEF (2014) Uruguay Crece Contigo (UCC) Annual Report. Available at ww.unicef.org/about/annualreport/files/Uruguay_Annual_Report.pdf, accessed 1 March 2019.

18 Building world-class universities in BRICS and emerging economies

The Indian experience

C. Raj Kumar

Introduction

Administrative and procedural roadblocks have affected the aspirations of building world-class universities in a developing country such as India. Other challenges, such as funding, faculty appointments, and the absence of emphasis on research and innovation are just some of the challenges towards creating world-class universities in India. The urgent need for world-class universities in India especially, is highlighted by the meagre representation of just two Indian institutions across three different ranking systems spanning over five years (Table 18.1).

Given this general state of affairs, there is indeed an urgent need to understand and identify the requirements towards building world-class universities in India. This will have ramifications for the improvement of aspiring universities in Brazil, Russia, India, China, and South Africa (BRICS) and emerging economies.

Identification of these requirements will involve answering several questions, such as—Why does a developing country need a world-class university? What are the core elements required for a world-class university? What should India do to build world-class universities? This chapter will provide a survey of these central issues that need to be addressed for India to create a few world-class universities.

Reasons for the need of world-class universities in emerging economies

BRICS and emerging economies, especially those with a colonial past from Asia and Africa have traditionally witnessed an exodus of students and researchers seeking

C. Raj Kumar, *Building world-class universities in BRICS and emerging economies: The Indian experience* In: *Handbook of BRICS and Emerging Economies*. Edited by: P.B. Anand, Shailaja Fennell, and Flavio Comim, Oxford University Press (2021). © Oxford University Press.
DOI: 10.1093/oso/9780198827535.003.0018

Table 18.1 BRICS universities in world university rankings (top 200) from 2011 to 2015

	QS World University Rankings					Times Higher Education World University Rankings					Shanghai Jiao Tong University's—The Academic Ranking of World Universities (ARWU)				
Year	2015–16	2014–15	2013–14	2012–13	2011–12	2015–16	2014–15	2013–14	2012–13	2011–12	2015	2014	2013	2012	2011
Brazil	2	1	1	1	1	0	1	1	1	1	1	1	1	1	1
Russia	1	1	1	1	1	1	0	0	0	0	1	1	1	1	1
India	2	0	0	0	0	0	0	0	0	0	0	0	0	0	0
China	7	7	7	7	7	2	2	2	3	3	7	6	5	4	1
South Africa	1	1	1	1	1	1	1	1	1	1	0	0	0	0	0
Hong Kong	5	5	5	5	5	3	4	3	4	4	1	2	1	4	1
Japan	8	10	9	9	11	2	5	5	5	5	7	8	9	9	9
Singapore	2	2	2	2	2	2	2	2	2	2	2	2	1	1	1
Malaysia	1	1	1	1	1	0	0	0	0	0	0	0	0	0	0

Source: Compiled with data obtained from: *QS World University Rankings*, available at www.topuniversities.com/qs-world-university-rankings, accessed 18 May 2017; *Times Higher Education World University Rankings*, available at www.timeshighereducation.com/world-university-rankings, accessed 18 May 2017; *Academic Ranking of World Universities*, available at www.shanghairanking.com, accessed 18 May 2017.

opportunities in established universities outside their home country to develop their academic careers (Rajan and Wadhawan 2013). However, a culmination of democratic values, aspirations of citizens from these countries, and globalization have resulted in the need for world-class universities in BRICS and emerging economies.

DEMOCRATIZATION OF HIGHER EDUCATION

At the heart of the aspiration for creating world-class universities in BRICS and emerging economies is the long felt recognition that democratic values have shaped and contributed to the evolution of human civilization (Blessinger and Anchan 2015). The entrenchment of democratic values in these countries has resulted in the need for standards of higher education that act as a harbinger of ideas in sciences, engineering, medicine, social sciences, and humanities. It would be unfair to restrict the growth of these disciplines to a few developed countries of the world. It is this creation of knowledge, and establishing a culture of academic research in BRICS and emerging economies, which is the best advocate for the creation of world-class universities.

ASPIRATIONAL GOALS OF CITIZENS OF BRICS AND EMERGING ECONOMIES

As a result of democratization, students from BRICS and emerging economies are some of the most aspirational students. However, pursuing a world-class education from a university in the developed world is not within everyone's financial means (Varuni Khosla 2015). The creation of world-class universities in the BRICS and emerging economies will have to address this existing demand for a world-class university that caters to the intellectual curiosity of aspiring academicians.

There is a strong recognition that the pursuit of excellence in all its manifestations needs to be deeply embedded in the institutional imagination of universities. Access and equity have been central policy choices that were made in higher education in the past and will continue to shape the future of universities.

GLOBALIZATION

Another reason for BRICS and emerging economies to create world-class universities is the growing recognition of globalization and its impact on higher education. Increasing globalization, the transnational nature of student and faculty mobility, and the focus on interdisciplinary learning have influenced the idea of what world-class universities should be.

The vision for establishing world-class universities has indeed caught the imagination of educationists and policymakers around the world. Regardless of the inherent challenges associated with defining what constitutes a world-class university, the need for raising the standards of universities with a view to promoting excellence, fostering research through scholarship and publications, and providing opportunities for faculty and students to achieve their full potential remains the hallmark of all university education.

Elements required for a world-class university

The evolution of a world-class university according to a World Bank report (Salmi 2009: 7) requires the confluence of three basic criteria:

> (a) a high concentration of talent (faculty and students), (b) abundant resources to offer rich learning environment and to conduct advanced research, and (c) favorable governance features that encourage strategic vision, innovation, and flexibility and that enable institutions to make decisions and to manage resources without being encumbered by bureaucracy.

In the Indian context, the basic criteria for world-class universities may require the following to be deliberated upon by all stakeholders.

VISION

In emerging economies, it is imperative that the vision of a new university is designed to address the needs of the society.

World-class universities are built on the basis of a strong foundation that has an inspiring vision that aims to address the needs of a developing society. Generally these requirements of the society should be addressed in a broad based manner and should pursue the collective goals of the society.

Owing to the pluralistic nature of universities, universities are perhaps best suited to address the long-term goals and aspirations of a developing society. However, it is important to recognize that a boilerplate approach to the establishment of a new university will not be successful as each developing society may have its own unique set of needs.

In this context, Indian universities need to re-examine their founding vision on the basis of which they were established. It helps to articulate a vision of the university even after many years of its establishment, as the vision will direct the academic consciousness among the faculty, students, and staff towards fulfilling a set of goals and objectives. The vision of the university should be a farsighted one. This will promote learning and imagination among faculty and students of the university, while being fully conscious of the reality of its existing challenges.

Universities don't become world-class institutions as soon as they are created, but evolve to become world-class universities through long years of work pursued by the commitment and dedication of students, faculty, and staff. Even then, promoting excellence is an evolving project for world-class universities and that is why the vision of the university helps shape its present and future. Indian universities need to develop their vision with a view to becoming institutions of global excellence.

RESOURCES

In India, the question of funding is invariably linked to the role of the government and other regulatory authorities (Sharma and Thakur 2010: 143).

World-class universities around the world are established and developed through a great deal of commitment of resources. In India there is an urgent need for major reforms that can begin to address the crisis that prevails due to an acute shortage of funding and availability of resources. The Indian university landscape has a range of actors: state government-funded public universities, central government-funded public universities; state private universities, deemed universities, and many other colleges in the form of degree-awarding institutions (*Economic Times* 2006). The current cookie-cutter approach to allocation of funds and resources on the basis of classification of universities needs to be re-examined (Tilak 1995).

The present hierarchies of classifications for allocation of funds and resources have not been able to identify properly the true potential of Indian universities to become world-class institutions (UGC 2014). Every aspect of funding and resource allocation, including tuition fees, scholarships for students, infrastructure in universities, faculty salaries, library development, research funding including research infrastructure, endowments, philanthropy, and many other areas, needs a thorough re-examination.

In India, there is currently a lack of understanding and realization that the resources that are required to build world-class universities are substantial. Arguably, the state may not always be in a position to allocate precious resources to universities. It is in this context that there is a need for promoting private universities in India (FICCI 2011). Deterioration in the academic standards of public universities in India is due to a number of factors, including, but not limited to poor infrastructure at our university campuses, lack of motivation among faculty members to perform, inability of universities to create a research environment for faculty publications, absence of interdisciplinary programmes for the students, lack of innovation in curriculum and course design, inadequate compensation for faculty, and a bureaucratic and hierarchical governance structure that does not motivate faculty members to perform.

Unfortunately, in the Indian experience the establishment of private universities did not result in a substantial change in the quality of higher education. Rather, Indian private universities in general have been equated with all the problems of public universities. In addition to this, many private universities have often engaged in malpractices that have undermined the reputation of private university education. They have fostered a culture of mediocrity and dubiousness, both of which have led to adverse consequences for higher education. There is an urgent need for a paradigm shift in the availability of funding and resources. For instance, the public–private nature of a university should not be the criterion for allocation of resources to universities. Instead, allocation of resources should be based upon the merits of faculty, research capacities, and the future potential of universities.

ROLE OF GOVERNMENT AND REGULATORY BODIES

As briefly mentioned in the foregoing section, the roles of government and other regulatory bodies are inextricably linked to any question about most Indian universities. This relationship between the government/regulatory bodies and universities warrants serious examination.

At present, the role of government in the case of state universities is significant and the higher education department of a state government is minutely involved in every aspect from the creation of the university to granting of approvals and permissions that are essential for administering the university. Generally, a university in India can only be established by an act of the Indian Parliament or a State Legislative Assembly, which grants various appendages of the government to exercise control over these universities. This does pose serious problems for autonomous university governance.

There are elaborate procedures that are created and implemented by higher education departments within the state government that are involved in every aspect of institution building even before the creation of the university itself. While this is desirable, there is a need for recognizing that once the university is established, the role of government departments and agencies will have to undergo a significant change. Instead, the departments ought to become facilitators and should ensure the autonomy and independence of universities so that the institutions are able to grow on their own. The need for approvals and permissions from the higher education departments within the state government for starting new academic programmes or new disciplines should be dispensed with so that the internal governance mechanisms of universities are activated to work effectively.

In India, maintaining high academic standards in universities is a serious area of concern for the higher education policymakers and educationists (British Council India 2014: 12). Essentially, there is a continuing fear that in the absence of external checks and balances, universities will exercise powers in an arbitrary manner and offer courses and programmes that are devoid of academic content. This argument is problematic at different levels: first, it distrusts the university as an academic institution which is expected to act with a sense of responsibility; second, it creates an atmosphere of suspicion and animosity where the faculty members of the university who are expected to take critical decisions relating to the academic programmes are not in a position to drive the academic agenda; and third, it creates opportunities for vested interests and corruption at the level of government departments exercising such powers.

One of the better ways to deal with this problem is to make the process of establishing the university more rigorous and transparent. The necessary conditions that need to be fulfilled to create a university should reflect the highest academic standards, availability of qualified faculty members, and the necessary resources and objective measures to assess the bona fide intentions of the promoters of private universities. The government's role should be one of a facilitator and not that of a regulator. There is a need to empower departments, faculties, and internal governance mechanisms within Indian universities so that they are able to take responsibility and are duly accountable for their decisions. Steadily, the role of government departments in the decision making of the university should be negligible, if present at all. World-class universities are not developed through government departments exercising powers over institutions; they are nurtured only when faculty members, students, staff, and other stakeholders of the university are able to take decisions about the university in an independent and transparent manner.

Another significant challenge for the growth of Indian universities is the power and control exercised by regulatory bodies such as the University Grants Commission (UGC), Bar Council of India (BCI), Medical Council of India (MCI), All Indian Council for Technical Education (AICTE), and other similar bodies (Centre for Civil Society 2014). Although some degree of regulatory assessment and external accountability is essential towards ensuring the quality of education in universities and institutions of higher education, it is important to achieve the right balance between regulatory control and institutional autonomy that will encourage innovation and creativity. The current approach stifles innovation and creativity in the Indian university system where the regulatory bodies play a significant role in many aspects of university governance. Besides the more pivotal role that the regulatory bodies play in the inspection of universities to determine their suitability and worthiness for state funding, these bodies are also constantly involved in formulating policies that have a direct impact on the governance of universities. Given the fact that there are over 800 universities in India, there is little scope for any consultation whatsoever before any sets of rules or regulations are drafted by the regulatory bodies and are made applicable uniformly to all institutions.

As a result of the regulatory system, a good part of the time of vice-chancellors and registrars of Indian universities is devoted to ensuring that they are in compliance with these rules and regulations. Indian regulatory bodies tend to exercise enormous powers and they are also exercised in an arbitrary manner. Arbitrariness in the exercise of regulatory powers of higher education regulators has affected the public image and reputation of these bodies (Centre for Civil Society 2014: 21). Their role and responsibilities have been challenged, primarily because of the lack of trust in the ability of regulatory bodies to perform the tasks of a facilitator.

There is no doubt that there are serious instances of malpractice prevailing in the higher education sector. There are unscrupulous higher education providers who are engaged in illegal and unethical practices, which affect the interests of students. A larger problem is the practice of regulatory bodies to equate a general institutional culture of all universities and colleges in the same manner as they would have dysfunctional institutions. Not only does this effect the morale of good institutional endeavours, but also creates a cynical environment where innovation cannot occur. World-class universities need a free, liberal, and facilitative environment.

FACULTY

In any part of the world, one of the most important factors towards establishing a world-class university is retaining a strong academic faculty.

Outstanding faculty members who can make great substantive contributions to teaching and research create world-class universities. It is only by hiring and retaining inspiring teachers and rigorous researchers that we can hope to establish world-class universities in India. At its best, most Indian universities are largely teaching institutions (Venkatesha 2003). The focus of the academic agenda is to be engaged in teaching and faculty members tend to teach a significant number of hours in a week (UGC, 2010). This has undermined any possibility for faculty members to be engaged in research and publications. Indian aspirations to build world-class universities ought to focus on the hiring of faculty from India and internationally.

Globalization has created new opportunities for Indian academics allowing them to move around the world. In fact, many Indian graduates from universities in India seek higher education opportunities around the world and even if some of them choose to come into academia, they rarely decide to work in India. There are a number of reasons why Indian universities are not in a position to attract very bright graduates across disciplines to come into academia in India, but this situation is slightly changing with new opportunities (Bhattacharyya 2013).

Generally, Indian universities do not provide sufficient opportunities, both in terms of time and space, for pursuing research; there is also a serious lack of funds and other forms of resource for pursuing research and writing (Chetan 2013). This has to change. So long as we don't provide for research to be the central focus of higher education, at least in some of our premier universities, we will not be able to build world-class universities.

Universities are expected to be knowledge creating institutions. Knowledge cannot be created in the absence of scholars who are prepared to read, think, reflect, and write. The essence of a great university is its ability to influence change through research and the process of the discovery of truth leading to a rigorous analysis that creates knowledge and promotes innovation. This is true in the case of hard sciences, social sciences, and humanities. Indian universities need to recognize this aspect of university education for them to develop higher standards in their pursuit of excellence.

STUDENTS

Like any other part of the world, the creation of a world-class university also depends on students.

Students are at the heart of any university community. Great institutions have attained the status of world class because of their alumni achieving distinction in various walks of life. Indian universities have indeed produced great alumni who have made outstanding contributions in India and around the world.

In the recent past questions have been raised regarding the role of Indian universities themselves for shaping the education and learning process of students. Access to the premier universities in India continues to be the luxury of a privileged few who have most probably received sound, quality education in their high school and are better geared to do well in their examinations and standard tests which qualify them to be admitted into these universities. However, one fundamental aspect that needs to be carefully examined about Indian universities and students is the learning outcomes.

The existing framework of accountability of the university to the student needs to be revisited. Most Indian universities do not have a rudimentary form for students to be able to provide feedback on the teaching of the faculty. There are hardly any faculty development programmes in Indian universities with a view to enhancing the teaching abilities of the faculty. Students need to be given a holistic learning experience that will not only help them with acquiring substantive knowledge, but also develop their critical thinking skills, writing skills, and their ability to articulate effectively. The current paradigm of a significant number of students in Indian universities largely engaged in learning on their own has to change.

TEACHING AND RESEARCH

Teaching and research are key to pedagogic learning and primacy of knowledge in any university. Similarly in India, these two core areas are also essential towards the creation of a world-class university.

Ranking systems in general afford more weightage to universities that nurture research among their faculty members and students (Fowler 2014). Indian universities are facing the twin challenges of both teaching and research in their efforts to build institutions of excellence. There has been a serious shortage of faculty members in most Indian universities. Even the most prestigious institutions in the country are facing a crisis when it comes to faculty hiring. Furthermore, the research capacities of most Indian universities tend to be mediocre. This is due to lack of academic rigour for engaging in research resulting in publications among the faculty. The debate over teaching versus research is old and insipid. Indian universities will have to ensure that teaching and research go hand in hand and a lot still needs to be done to strike a balance between these equally important objectives.

A larger question that Indian universities need to address is about the importance of research and scholarship that can generate ideas for change. Research in every discipline, in the arts, humanities, sciences, and social sciences, can have a profound impact on our society and beyond. Indifference and complacency to research has led to the inability of universities in India to produce knowledge that can impact policy; that can produce innovation; that can provide solutions to social, economic, and political problems that affect India as a nation. Indian universities ought to become fertile avenues for the generation of ideas through research and publications. Rigorous research in all fields is critical to India, as it will be expected to respond to new problems for which old solutions and perspectives may not be helpful. Research produces knowledge that gives clarity on the basis of informed and deeper understanding of the issues involved.

INTERNATIONAL COLLABORATIONS

Indian universities have to carefully consider their policies for establishing global collaborations and activities that promote global interaction and provide for a global student experience. Collaboration with other universities and centres for education results in the creation of an internationally aware faculty and student body (Dhawan 2012). Unfortunately, not many Indian universities strive to collaborate with other universities from around the world.

Although it is useful to sign numerous memoranda of understanding (MoU) seldom do these translate into concrete forms of collaboration among partners leading to implementation of programmes for students and scholars. Universities, as a part of their internal governance mechanisms, should evolve policies that will guide them in establishing collaboration with other institutions. We need to innovate on programmes that enable direct interaction between foreign teachers and Indian students, and a true collaboration that provides for a rich student experience as opposed to collaboration that remains only on paper. One of the important areas in which global collaboration can revolutionize student experience is in the area of teaching and learning. Today's technologically advanced world provides scope for innovation in terms of promoting e-learning and virtual global classrooms based on meaningful international collaboration. Such methods can provide students with the benefit of interacting with academics and experts from around the world and benefit from their knowledge and pedagogical methodology.

If India needs to create world-class universities, our focus needs to be on providing an experience of transnational education to the students. This will expose them to emerging frontiers of knowledge and perspectives. It will also introduce them to new cultures and peoples and help them to appreciate diversity in an increasingly cosmopolitan world. Transnational education is no longer the luxury of the few, but will become a necessary aspect of educational and learning experiences around the world.

INTERNATIONAL RANKINGS

Establishing universities in India that are consistently awarded high rankings is an important goal that is worth pursuing. It is important that Indian universities work towards getting noticed in international rankings, as they are reliable indicators of success for a university. Every ranking strategy has its own methodology for awarding points, nonetheless they are comprehensive in their approach (Topuniversities.com n.d.).

The Times Higher Education World University Rankings has underscored the importance of research and publications for rankings. Rankings assess universities on the basis of the following criteria: teaching (30 per cent); research (30 per cent); citations (30 per cent); international outlook (7.5 per cent); and industry income (2.5 per cent) (Times Higher Education 2015). The QS World University Ranking's methodology adopted for rankings has reinforced the importance of research and publications for universities to be globally recognized as institutions of excellence. The weightage for the six indicators used for these rankings are as follows: academic reputation: 40 per cent; citation per faculty: 20 per cent; faculty–student ratio: 20 per cent; employer reputation: 10 per cent; international faculty ratio: 5 per cent; international student ratio: 5 per cent (Topuniversities.com n.d.). Academic reputation, which is the largest indicator, is based on the views and perspectives of fellow academics around the world with regard to universities that are producing the best research in their field of expertise. This essentially means that 60 per cent of the weightage for these rankings is based on the research contribution from universities.

ROLE OF THE PRIVATE SECTOR

As mentioned previously, in India there exists an institutional and general bias against private universities (Powar 2015). Alternatively, universities should be assessed on the basis of objective and determinable standards relating to the quality of teaching, faculty, research, and capacity building rather than on the sole criteria of the public or private status of the university.

It is important to note that some of the top universities in the world are private universities, such as Harvard, Yale, Stanford, and MIT, while some of the oldest and most reputed universities remain public, such as Oxford, Cambridge, and London. At one level, we are aspiring to increase the gross enrolment ratio (GER) in higher education so that a larger proportion of eligible students can come into the higher education system. At another level, we are facing the problem of mediocrity institutionalized across our universities with even postgraduate degree holders not getting suitable jobs for want of knowledge, expertise, and skills. Higher education in India cannot be reformed if we are not able to develop strong private universities that are truly non-profit, philanthropic, and committed to promoting academic freedom and institutional excellence.

The effort to promote private initiatives in higher education should go hand in hand with other equally committed efforts to strengthen and develop our public universities. Indian universities must re-examine their substantive role and contribution to promoting creativity and innovation. In the course of a quantitative leap resulting in the expansion of higher education in India, quality and excellence suffered significantly. Mediocrity has been institutionalized leading to a lack of creativity and innovation in our efforts to build world-class universities. The mere celebration of a few islands of excellence, mostly in the form of specialized single-discipline institutions, is not going to address the larger problem of lack of creativity and innovation. The quality of Indian universities has to be significantly enhanced and the best of global good practice needs to be brought into India, contextualizing it to our circumstances and context. We need to understand and appreciate the remarkable transformation in higher education that has taken place in countries in Asia, such as Japan, Singapore, South Korea, Taiwan, Hong Kong, and mainland China. The heart of this transformation in Asia is about creativity and innovation in curriculum, courses, programmes, teaching pedagogy, faculty recruitment, student admission and mobility, international collaboration, research, and publications.

A committee constituted by the Planning Commission and headed by the then Chief Mentor of Infosys, Naryan Murthy, submitted a report that focused on the role of the corporate sector in higher education. This committee acknowledged the importance of stronger private initiatives in the field of higher education and had recommended such groundbreaking measures as free land for 999 years, 300 per cent deduction in taxable income to companies for contributions towards boosting higher education, and ten-year multiple entry visas for foreign research scholars. It has also suggested that mandatory accreditation is essential for Indian universities. To promote greater accessibility of higher education to underprivileged people, the committee has recommended the establishment of a scholarship fund of Rs. 1,000 crores, while contributions made by the corporate sector will receive tax exemption.

Innovative solutions need to be found in addressing the challenges of higher education. Corporate philanthropy needs to be significantly promoted as the private wealth of India has not adequately contributed to the growth and development of not-for-profit higher education (Planning Commission 2012).

Policy recommendations

Indian universities need a transformational change for them to become relevant in the context of a globalized world. The past two decades have witnessed extraordinary changes in university systems around the world. The higher education system in India should consider the following reforms and policy initiatives.

First, there is an urgent need to recognize that not all universities need to be engaged in the same manner on different aspects of institution building. They need to be treated differently depending on the kind of contribution they are making. Indian universities should not be differentiated based on whether they are public or private; the categorization instead should be based on quality, performance, and contribution with more resources being made available for universities that are performing exceedingly well. We also need to recognize that not all universities in India should be considered research focused; instead they should be measured for their quality and excellence in a certain focus area, such as skills development or teaching.

Second, taking inspiration from the Project 5-100 initiative (Moscow Institute of Physics and Technology n.d.), India could similarly consider empowering fifty of its top universities in every possible manner to seek global excellence. For a similar project to be successfully implemented in India a clear mandate is required, along with funding and resources given to some of these universities identified to augment their capacities. The selection of these institutions and universities should be based on criteria such as institutional diversity, and the institutions' potential for achieving global excellence. For instance, ten central government universities, ten state government universities, ten private universities, ten deemed universities, and ten institutions of national importance could be considered for such an initiative. The diversity of institutions will enable India to build a strong capacity for establishing a few model institutions of excellence that can compete globally.

Third, the issue of regulatory reform has been at the heart of policy reforms in higher education. There is an urgent need to rework the regulatory framework (ICRIER 2006). Universities in India need to be made more autonomous; they need freedom, in every sense of the word, from both government and from regulatory bodies. The agenda of universities needs to be established by the faculty and students, keeping in mind the needs and aspirations of everyone in society.

Special education zones for world-class universities

The creation of special education zones (SEZs) in India would enable the establishment of world-class universities (*The Hindu* 2010).

The following could be some of the unique characteristics of these SEZs in India.

ESTABLISHMENT

Universities in these SEZs should be invited specifically with the main objective of building world-class universities in India. These universities could be both Indian as well as international universities; nonetheless standards of education should be comparable to the best in the world. Legislation from central government will help establish these universities on a pan-India basis. The legislation should provide a clear mandate that will ensure institutional autonomy.

REGULATION

Special Economic Zones are ecosystems where certain national and state laws are not applicable, with the aim of promoting economic development. SEZs in the context of education should aim to provide autonomy to the universities. For this purpose, the existing legal and regulatory framework needs to be reworked to permit autonomous universities in SEZs.

FUNDING

Funding and resources for the establishment of world-class universities in SEZs may be sourced from private donors and the international higher education sector. One of the important requirements for building world-class universities is the need for abundant resources and this may not come from the government as its priorities will inevitably be to expand opportunities in the higher education sector and create access to a large number of individuals. At present, the not-for-profit private sector in higher education has few or no incentives to contribute to the creation of universities in India.

The proposed SEZs in higher education need to develop a vision that will significantly attract the wealthiest individuals and corporations in India and around the world to establish world-class universities through individual and corporate philanthropy.

It is suggested that the prime minister of India and the human resource development minister are well suited to convene a brainstorming session for promoting the idea of SEZs in higher education with all stakeholders including educationists, parliamentarians, policymakers, philanthropists, institutions, and corporations. This could be the basis for creating the prime minister's task force on building world-class universities in India. This task force could be mandated to recommend all steps that involve the development of a vision, strategic plan, legal and regulatory processes, institutional mechanisms, policies, and guidelines that will enable the creation of SEZs in higher education.

The way forward

The Indian higher education system commanded awe and respect in the ancient world. Important seats of learning like Nalanda and Takshashila attracted the best students and academics from across the globe. Unfortunately, over a period of time, our higher education system lost its global competitiveness. This is exemplified by the fact that not many Indian higher education institutions feature in the annual world university rankings like the Times Higher Education World University Rankings or the QS World University Rankings.

This gradual decline in global competitiveness can be attributed to a multitude of factors. Let me list some of the more important concerns and the way these might be redressed.

First is the lack of incentives for research. The amount of funding that is currently available for research in Indian universities is meagre by global standards (Live Mint 2013). Apart from increasing the quantum of funds and promoting specific research on the state of the Indian higher education system itself, there is a need for significant reform in the overall policy and management framework for disbursing research grants.

For example, the existing framework to disburse grants is multilayered and complex, leading to inordinate delays, frustration, and loss of research focus among faculty members who are trying to secure these grants. A proactive regulatory mechanism set up by ministries like the Ministry of Human Resource Development (MHRD) can help mitigate these concerns.

Further, there is need to attract and retain faculty with good research skills. This will require a review of the current system of faculty recruitment, appraisal, assessment, promotions, and rewards based on performance as measured through research contributions and publications.

Second, we do not have world-class training programmes for academic administrators (Altbach 2010). High-quality education administration is one of the seriously ignored aspects of the Indian higher education system. As providers of relevant educational support services, academic administrators form the backbone of any educational institution, especially one that aspires to constantly improve the academic experience of its students and teachers.

Indeed, a world-class university requires world-class faculty supported by world-class administration. Unfortunately, there are no comprehensive training programmes for academic administrators in India to deal with different nuances of our higher education system.

Specifically, the lack of managerial training programmes for higher authorities in education administration has compromised the evolution of generic best practice in the sector. Institution building has suffered and creativity has been stifled as the Indian higher education system continues to be driven by individual persona and the charm of education administrators instead of adherence to sustainable and institution-driven quality assurance mechanisms and innovative processes.

Third, we need a more outward-looking approach. One of the strongest critiques of Indian higher education institutions is that they tend to get complacent with little success. Unique socio-political contexts cannot be used to justify the lack of sustained global competitiveness. There is need for a renaissance in our attitude towards higher education. There is also a need to understand and contextualize global best practice for Indian conditions, for instance, in course design and pedagogy.

Indeed, international collaboration in the form of student exchanges, faculty exchanges, joint teaching, joint research, joint conferences, joint publications, joint executive education programmes, summer and winter schools, and study-abroad programmes are ways to promote the global engagement of Indian higher education institutions (UGC 2013).

Indian universities must also explore greater collaboration with leading regional and global institutions, particularly in their own neighbourhoods and groupings such as the BRICS. Formalized frameworks between institutions can play an important role in deepening institutional partnerships. An example of such a framework is the Sonipat declaration on World-Class Universities in BRICS and Emerging Economies that was signed by representatives of universities located in various countries who met at the invitation of *Times Higher Education* (THE), O.P. Jindal Global University (JGU), and the International Institute for Higher Education Research and Capacity Building (IIHEd) on the occasion of the THE BRICS and Emerging Economies Universities Summit held in Sonipat and New Delhi in December 2015 (see Appendix).

Fourth, we have failed to appreciate interdisciplinarity in higher education. There is a dearth of courses and programmes in India that offer interdisciplinary perspectives. Considering the fact that most of our societal problems cannot be solved by experts from one single academic discipline, there is a need for better coordination and synergy between experts from different academic disciplines to find sustainable solutions to the challenging problems faced by our country.

This will make higher education relevant to both Indian and global society. Thus, specialized training in a particular academic discipline must be complemented by generic interdisciplinary courses. The government should play a proactive role in setting up and promoting universities offering interdisciplinary courses in India.

Fifth, we seem to have greater tolerance for mediocre institutional standards. A lot needs to be done by our institutions and regulators to restore transparency, coherence, and confidence in the higher education system. At the institutional level, a code of self-regulation and self-restraint has to be adopted. Institutions have to lead by example, not only by promoting best practice but also by curbing malpractices. Higher standards of data sharing and transparency have to be mandated at the policy level, along with empowering prospective and current students to compare institutions.

As rightly asserted by President Pranab Mukherjee, no country can aspire to become a sustainable superpower without becoming a knowledge powerhouse (Business Standard 2015). Although a few stand-alone institutes like the newly established International Institute for Higher Education Research and Capacity Building (IIHEd) at O.P. Jindal Global University can play an important role in this arena, there is a need for more such institutes in the higher education sector, which provide constructive thought–leadership, policy inputs, and subsequent action plans to implement them.

Indeed, there is a need to create a vibrant policy ecosystem on higher education in India. Only then can our higher education system be revitalized.

Conclusion

In the final analysis, the current state of Indian higher education requires urgent reformation that addresses several of the concern areas such as lack of research initiatives, bureaucratic control of institutions, and lack of funding, among others. Therefore, transformational change needs to take place at every level of policymaking, regulation, and governance in higher education if Indian universities are serious about seeking global excellence.

Appendix Sonipat Declaration

Sonipat Declaration on World-Class Universities in BRICS and Emerging Economies

We the representatives of higher educational institutions from around the globe, meeting at the invitation of the Times Higher Education (THE), O.P. Jindal Global University (JGU), and the International Institute for Higher Education Research and Capacity Building (IIHEd), on the occasion of the BRICS and Emerging Economies Universities Summit on the theme: 'Why Emerging Economies need World Class Universities' held in Sonipat (Haryana), National Capital Region of Delhi, India, 2–4 December 2015, declare the following principles to guide the creation and development of world-class universities within our countries.

PRINCIPLE 1. THE MISSION OF WORLD-CLASS UNIVERSITIES IS THE PURSUIT OF KNOWLEDGE AND PROMOTION OF INNOVATION

1.1. A world-class university is one that considers access to higher education to be a human right and a public good. It recognizes that the pursuit of knowledge for knowledge's sake is itself part of the academic enterprise and should always be valued. The objective of a world-class university is not only to produce a skilled workforce but also to prepare citizens to serve society and to understand and share human values. It is therefore incumbent on such universities to provide a liberal education, including the social sciences and humanities, so that students acquire, beyond professional preparation, the ability to think critically and to understand and appreciate their civilizational heritage and their role in a complex world.

1.2. Universities in the BRICS and emerging economies should encourage creative thought and value the diverse backgrounds of the different university stakeholders.

Universities should be free, open, and liberal spaces where the heritage of the past is transmitted to new generations, where critical thinking is stimulated, and where innovation is promoted.

PRINCIPLE 2. THE HIGHEST QUALITIES OF STUDENTS, FACULTY, AND STAFF MUST BE PROMOTED

2.1. Recruitment, selection, retention, and promotion of students, staff, and faculty should reflect a balanced commitment to both excellence and equity and not be distorted by ideological, political, or financial pressures.
2.2. Gender equality within the university environment should be a priority goal at the student, staff, and faculty levels.
2.3. Special efforts should be made to ensure the highest quality of teaching, based on how students learn, and, for that purpose, teaching staff should be motivated and trained to achieve excellence in teaching.

PRINCIPLE 3. RESEARCH SHOULD ADHERE TO THE HIGHEST STANDARDS

3.1. World-class universities in BRICS and emerging economies have a special challenge to promote and produce the highest-quality research at the undergraduate, graduate, and professional school levels.
3.2. It is essential that all who engage in such research adhere to the highest standards of academic honesty and integrity and, in particular, that they ensure that all ideas, data, findings, reasoning, conclusions, and recommendations that are not original be properly attributed by faculty and researchers in their scholarship and by students in all the work they submit.
3.3. Governments should not interfere with the autonomy and academic freedom of higher education institutions. Research excellence should be a priority of universities in BRICS and emerging economies in their pursuit of world-class status.

PRINCIPLE 4. UNIVERSITIES MUST BE PROVIDED APPROPRIATE RESOURCES TO ACHIEVE GREATNESS

4.1. Universities in BRICS and emerging economies cannot achieve greatness unless they have sufficient financial and human resources, which may be from public or private funding. Governments have a particular responsibility to provide adequate resources to higher education and to facilitate private support for universities while ensuring that private support does not interfere with the other principles in this declaration.

4.2. The role of philanthropy has been crucial historically in creating world-class universities and is beginning to provide the resources for quality education in BRICS and emerging economies. This trend should be encouraged in ways that maintain the independence of the institution while encouraging private contributions to the funding of higher education.
4.3. Access to higher education should be affordable. While it is also sometimes necessary for students to pay tuition and fees for higher education, the burden on students and their families should be limited and adequate financial support should be provided to qualified students with limited financial means through scholarships and loans.
4.4. Funding from industry may be a valuable source for research but must be administered so as to avoid any conflict of interest and interference with academic integrity and freedom. A conflict of interest policy should be made explicit and transparent by the university, which should require a conflict of interest statement by the researcher receiving such support.
4.5. Excellent facilities and technology constitute an essential element of the resources needed to achieve world-class status for universities in BRICS and emerging economies. Investment by governments and philanthropic entities in physical infrastructure should be strongly encouraged.

PRINCIPLE 5. GOVERNANCE OF UNIVERSITIES MUST PROVIDE AN ENVIRONMENT FOR FREE ENQUIRY AND CAREER DEVELOPMENT

5.1. As part of their effort to achieve world-class status, universities in BRICS and emerging economies must adhere to the highest standards of academic freedom, honesty, and integrity. Academic freedom requires that students, faculty, and other researchers have the freedom to teach and disseminate ideas and information, however inconvenient to university or state authorities, without fear of reprisals from university or state officials, including providing legal safeguards where appropriate.
5.2. While maintaining the above standards, universities may have a valuable role to play in informing government policy at the local and national levels to help governments address issues affecting public welfare.
5.3. Universities should adhere to the best global policies and practices in ensuring the well-being of their faculty members and students, both in terms of infrastructure as well as social support systems.

PRINCIPLE 6. UNIVERSITIES CAN ENHANCE THE QUALITY OF TEACHING AND RESEARCH THROUGH LOCAL AND GLOBAL CONNECTIONS

6.1. Part of building world-class universities is fostering local and international collaborations. Engagement with local communities through such activities as participatory action research and community outreach enhances the role and relevance of the university with local realities and in cultivating local knowledge and indigenous traditions.

6.2. In addition, universities should cultivate collaboration with institutions across the globe through joint teaching, faculty and student exchanges, joint research, seminars, training programmes and conferences, and joint publications.

The above principles are designed to guide universities in BRICS and emerging economies to advance towards world-class status. Ranking of universities may be a useful stimulus for improvement and in future should reflect achievements in relation to these principles.

ACKNOWLEDGEMENTS

I am grateful to my Research Associate, Srinjoy Sarkar, for his assistance in the editing of this chapter.

REFERENCES

Altbach, P.G. (2010). 'Training university administrators: Should management schools do it?'. *Center for International Higher Education Blog*, web log post 4 November. Available at www.insidehighered.com/blogs/the_world_view/training_university_administrators_should_management_schools_do_it, accessed November 2018.

Bhattacharyya, R. (2013). 'India lures young global faculty in international perspective of research, teaching', *Economic Times*, 8 November.

Blessinger, P. and Anchan, J.P. (2015). *Democratizing Higher Education: International Comparative Perspectives*. London: Routledge.

British Council India (2014). *Understanding India: The Future of Higher Education and Opportunities for International Cooperation*. Available at www.britishcouncil.org/education/ihe/knowledge-centre/national-policies/report-understanding-india, accessed 29 December 2018.

Business Standard (2015). '5 steps to revitalize India's higher education system', 1 December. Available at www.business-standard.com/article/pti-stories/most-indian-students-leave-uk-after-degree-117082401211_1.html, accessed 19 January 2020.

Centre for Civil Society (2014). 'Regulatory structure of higher education in India'. Available at https://mygov.in/sites/default/files/user_comments/research-regulatory-structure-of-higher-education-in-india.pdf, accessed 5 November 2018.

Chetan, P. (2013). 'Focus on R&D', *The New Indian Express*, 1 December.

Dhawan, H. (2012). 'UGC to let only top 500 foreign universities enter India', *Times of India*, 3 June.

Economic Times (2006). 'What are the different types of universities in India?', 1 May.

FICCI (Federation of Indian Chambers of Commerce & Industry) (2011). 'Private sector participation in Indian higher education'. Final report prepared by Ernst & Young.

Fowler, N. (2014). 'Rankings provide a more complete picture of worldwide research', *Elsevier*, 19 November. Available at www.elsevier.com/connect/rankings-provide-a-more-complete-picture-of-worldwide-research, accessed 5 November 2018.

The Hindu (2010). 'M.P. to setup special education zones', 8 July.

ICRIER (Indian Council for Research on International Economic Relations) (2006). 'Higher education in India: The need for change'. Prepared by Pawan Agarwal.

Live Mint (2013). 'Indian universities need financial strength', 3 October.

Moscow Institute of Physics and Technology (n.d.). 'About Project 5–100'. Available at https://mipt.ru/en/science/5top100/, accessed 5 November 2018.

Planning Commission (2012). 'Committee on corporate participation in higher education'. Report of NR Narayan Murthy Committee, p. 14.

Powar, K.B. (2015). 'India's private universities: Solutions or problems?', *International Higher Education* 81: 10.

Rajan, S.I. and Wadhawan, N. (2013). *Future Diasporas? International Student Migration from India to UK*. Ministry of Overseas Indian Affairs, Centre for Developmental Studies.

Salmi, J. (2009). *The Challenge of Establishing World Class Universities*. Washington, DC: World Bank. Available at http://siteresources.worldbank.org/EDUCATION/Resources/278200-1099079877269/547664-1099079956815/547670-1237305262556/WCU.pdf, accessed 8 January 2019.

Sharma, N. and Thakur, A.K. (2010). *Indian Higher Education and Tribals*. New Delhi: Deep & Deep Publications.

Tilak, J. (1995). 'Funding higher education in India', *Economic and Political Weekly* 30/9: 426–9.

Times Higher Education (2015). 'World university rankings 2015–16 methodology'. Available at www.timeshighereducation.com/news/ranking-methodology-2016, accessed 5 November 2018.

Topuniversities.com (n.d.). 'QS world university rankings: Methodology'. Available at www.topuniversities.com/university-rankings-articles/world-university-rankings/qs-world-university-rankings-methodology, accessed 5 November 2018.

UGC (University Grants Commission) (2010). 'Work load and code of ethics', June. Available at http://www.dauniv.ac.in/notices/UGCWorkloadandCodeEthicsRegulation.pdf, accessed 5 November 2018.

UGC (University Grants Commission) (2013). *Promotion and Maintenance of Standards of Academic Collaboration between India and Foreign Educational Institutions, UGC 2013*. Available at www.ugc.ac.in/pdfnews/9578034_English.pdf, accessed 5 November 2018.

UGC (University Grants Commission) (2014). *Guidelines for General Development Assistance to Central, State Universities and Institutions Deemed to be Universities during the XII Plan*. New Delhi: University Grants Commission. Available at www.ugc.ac.in/pdfnews/0423748_Guidelines-for-General-Development-Assistance-to-Universities.pdf, accessed 9 Janury 2019.

Varuni Khosla (2015). 'Around 3 lakh Indian students go abroad annually, 33% take property-backed loans', *Economic Times*, 28 August.

Venkatesha, M.G. (2003). 'Teaching vs research in Indian universities', *Current Science* 84/11: 1384.

19 Beyond cash transfers

The hijacking of social assistance

Kenia Parsons

Introduction

In September 2015, seventeen Sustainable Development Goals (SDGs) were agreed by world leaders at the UN Sustainable Development Summit in New York. These seventeen goals and 169 targets comprise the 2030 Agenda for Sustainable Development. These goals are a result of a three-year participatory process in which governments, businesses, civil society, and other stakeholders proposed ideas to renew their commitment to the transformational agenda that includes ending poverty and promoting a concerted global action towards economic growth, social inclusion, and environmental protection. According to the United Nations, since 1990, 700 million people were lifted out of extreme poverty, half the world's extreme poor (UN 2014: 5).

It has been argued that those of the world's extreme poor who exited poverty were the 'easy to assist' poor (Hulme and Shepherd 2003: 404), and that those who remain extremely poor are those who are 'hard to assist' or 'hard to reach'. These are people who face structural constraints limiting their chances of becoming less poor, such as low human capital, lack of public services or difficulty in accessing them, low wages, and persistent unemployment. Taking into account multidimensional aspects of poverty, some of these structural causes demand long-term investment (UNSRID 2010). The SDGs have this additional challenge in place.

Some advocate the focus on middle-income countries, since these are countries where 75 per cent of the world's poor live (Kanbur and Sumner 2012; Sumner 2012), half of them in India and China alone. The remaining quarter live in thirty-five low-income countries (Sumner 2012: 7). The world is, therefore, paying attention to middle-income countries, particularly BRICS, and their development strategies.

Although social protection[1] policies addressing income shortfalls and temporary poverty have traditionally been used in developed countries, developing countries,

[1] There are some differences in terminology. 'Social protection' is a 'set of public and private policies and programmes aimed at reducing and eliminating economic and social vulnerabilities to poverty and deprivation' (UNICEF 2012: 1). It encompasses social assistance, social insurance, and labour market interventions.

Kenia Parsons, *Beyond cash transfers: The hijacking of social assistance* In: *Handbook of BRICS and Emerging Economies*. Edited by: P.B. Anand, Shailaja Fennell, and Flavio Comim, Oxford University Press (2021). © Oxford University Press.
DOI: 10.1093/oso/9780198827535.003.0019

especially BRICS countries, have also introduced them, particularly in the form of social assistance, in the last two decades, with the aim of addressing poverty and vulnerability (ISSA 2013; UNSRID, 2010). Social protection has also become an important component in international development strategies; and along with economic growth and human development, it is now mainstreamed as a tool to address persistent poverty and its structural context (Shepherd 2011; UNSRID 2010).

A wave of cash transfers, both conditional and unconditional, has swept over developing countries, as a 'quiet revolution' of the Global South (Hanlon et al. 2010). This revolution has shifted the development paradigm towards providing transfers directly to poor households. Examples of those policies include the National Rural Employment Guarantee Scheme in India, the rights-based Child Support Grant in South Africa, the conditional cash transfer programme (BFP) [*bolsa família program*] in Brazil, and the minimum livelihood guarantee (*dibao*) in China.

This chapter argues that the use of cash transfers as a development strategy could divert attention away from social investments and social assistance interventions that address the structural causes of poverty. Cash transfers could crowd out other expenditures that are also important in the fight against extreme poverty, e.g. public social services (Hall 2006). Cash transfers without a long-term perspective reinforce the safety net model in a residual state. Meeting the demands of ageing populations, regional disparities, and unemployment, and raising people out of persistent and extreme poverty, requires long-term investment beyond what cash transfers offer.

The second section discusses social assistance within the discourses of major international development organizations, while the third analyses the rise in popularity of cash transfers. The fourth section analyses the *bolsa família* conditional cash transfer programme in the context of Brazilian social spending in the last decade. The fifth section concludes this chapter.

Changes in the development discourse

Debate about social assistance policies in international development has undergone substantial changes in the past decades, from the absence of discussion in the 1980s (Barrientos 2013b), to social protection as a key policy in the fight against poverty in the 2000s. It is worth exploring these changes further.

'Social assistance' is the direct transfer in cash or in kind to poor individuals or households, e.g. social pensions, public work programmes. UNICEF recognizes social support and care services as a form of social assistance.

The neoliberal era of the 1980s resulted in cuts in social spending in developing countries through the implementation of structural sdjustment loans (SALs). The harmful effects of SALs on social sectors (particularly education and health) were documented in a seminal UNICEF report (Cornia et al. 1987).

In the 1990s, while governments were addressing financial crises with austerity measures as part of the 'Washington Consensus', social movements became increasingly concerned about deteriorating social indicators and growing poverty. In 1995, governments taking part in the UN World Summit for Social Development in Copenhagen pledged their commitment to social and human development, including the protection of human rights, equality, and equity (UN 1995). In 1998, the World Bank started work on a Social Protection Sector Strategy Paper (Holzmann et al. 2003), which laid the foundations for what later became the social risk management (SRM) conceptual framework.

In 2000, governments signed the UN Millennium Declaration and agreed on the Millennium Development Goals (MDGs). Poverty reduction and its variety of forms beyond income poverty were placed at the forefront of the international development agenda. The goal of reducing poverty to half of the 1990 rate was an agreed international development objective. It is in this context that social protection, particularly social assistance, gains relevance as a means of addressing the pressing needs of those in poverty in developing countries. With Sustainable Development Goals (SDGs), social protection systems became an integral part of the fight against poverty, representing one of the targets of SDG 1: to end poverty in all its forms.

SOCIAL PROTECTION IN INTERNATIONAL DEVELOPMENT: SEVERAL APPROACHES

The years that followed saw the formulation of social protection strategies and a substantial increase in the use of social policy by national governments and international agencies, resulting in significant changes in the development discourse. Social protection, once understood as ineffective, expensive, and even harmful for economic growth, became increasingly important in the development agenda (Holzmann et al. 2003).

Several social protection papers, strategies, frameworks, and policy documents have been released by international organizations and donors since 2000 (ILO 2012; Solesbury 2003; UNSRID 2010; World Bank 2001). Although these all relate to social protection, they differ in their approach to poverty reduction strategies, even to the extent of taking opposing positions in the social protection debate, e.g. the World Bank and the United Nations Research Institute for Social Development/International Labour Organization (UNSRID)/ILO).

The World Bank's strategy paper (World Bank 2001) placed social protection under an SRM framework which targets those in greatest need. Social protection was both a 'safety net'[2] for those with severe needs facing high risks, and a 'springboard' helping them to take on activities of higher return. The key concept of the SRM framework was 'vulnerability' (Holzmann et al. 2003). With risk and vulnerability assessments, social protection could be designed for the protection of vulnerable groups at high risk (social assistance), the prevention of further destitution (social insurance), and the promotion of access to work (Deacon 2013). This strategy opened up space for selective government interventions targeted at the poor.

Another social protection strategy is the sustainable livelihoods framework (SLF), which arose out of discussions of sustainable rural livelihoods (Chambers and Conway 1991; Scoones 1998), and was adopted in policy circles around 2000 (Solesbury 2003). The framework places capability, equity, and social sustainability at the centre of the debate, and criticizes the growth orthodoxy that emphasizes employment, production, and income. Scoones (1998) links the sustainable rural livelihoods with a framework of livelihoods resources, institutions, strategies, and sustainable outcomes. The SLF was used by the Department for International Development (DFID), United Nations Development Programme (UNDP), Oxfam, and Care International (Solesbury 2003). However, it focuses on the local level and hence fails to engage with the macro-policies that are needed to support the changes proposed by the framework.

These debates in social protection culminated in the social protection floor initiative (SPF-I), one of nine UN initiatives to address the 2007–08 global financial crisis. The SPF-I is a coalition of UN bodies, international financial institutions, and development partners (bilateral donors, development banks, international NGOs), coordinated by the ILO and WHO (World Health Organization) (ILO 2012).

The 100th Session of the International Labour Conference in 2011 recognized the limitations of targeting and that universal social security coverage has social and economic benefits, and advised national governments to reach as many people as possible as soon as possible (ILO 2012: 15–16). The recommended social security strategy has two dimensions: horizontal, providing minimum levels of social protection; and vertical, gradually increasing levels of social insurance by extending the range of benefits and the extent of personal coverage.

In 2012, the ILO issued the social protection floors recommendation No. 202, which said that national social protection floors should comprise at least the following four social security guarantees (ILO 2012: 5):

a) access to essential health care, including maternity care;
b) basic income security for children, providing access to nutrition, education, care, and any other necessary goods and services;

[2] Safety nets 'may be defined as non-contributory transfer programmes targeted in some manner to the poor and those vulnerable to poverty and shocks. The terms welfare (especially in the United States) and social assistance (especially in Europe) are often used for the same concept' (World Bank 2009: 135).

c) basic income security for persons in active age who are unable to earn sufficient income, in particular in cases of sickness, unemployment, maternity, and disability;
d) basic income security for older persons.

The ILO documents recommend and reaffirm the message of universal social security as a human right, by stating that:

> Protection should be universal, based on social solidarity, aiming at social inclusion, including of persons in the informal economy. Such universal protection can be achieved progressively, including by setting targets and time frames. It should be based on the principles of non-discrimination, gender equality and responsiveness to special needs. Entitlements to benefits should be prescribed by national law, and should also be accompanied by efficient and accessible complaint and appeal procedures. The rights and dignity of people covered by social security guarantees should be respected. Benefits should be adequate and predictable (ILO 2012: 4).

The UNSRID (2010) report calls for a radical rethinking on the use of social protection policies to reduce poverty. The report criticizes the current approach to poverty reduction, arguing that it focuses on 'measuring things that people lack to the detriment of understanding why they lack them', and suggesting that poverty reduction is part of 'long-term processes of social, economic and political transformation' (2010: 2).

The report says that 'sustained progress in combating poverty requires effective states that are both developmental and redistributive' (6). It advocates a role for government in employment-centred structural changes and in promoting a social policy framework grounded in universal rights with limited conditionalities and targeting.

Social protection is important in the contemporary development agenda, but there are different ways of formulating social protection interventions, from the World Bank's approach of targeting the poor via social safety nets, to UNSRID's and ILO's rights-based approach using a framework of universal policies and redistributive state intervention.

CONTINUING THE RESIDUALIST ROLE OF THE STATE?

Although policy regimes are often a mix of both systems (Mkandawire 2005), these two approaches mirror Titmuss's (1974) conceptualization of types of welfare state. On the one hand, targeting social policies to the poor is a 'residual welfare model', where the state steps in temporarily to meet needs unmet by the market or the family. On the other hand, there is the universal approach, an 'institutional redistributive model' (IRM), where social policies are based on rights and needs, not on merits, conditionalities, ability to work, or earning capacity. Titmuss's model shows the differences between these two contrasting approaches that dominate contemporary debate on social protection.

The World Bank's 2001 document clearly stated that income redistribution must take second place to social protection programmes:

> Income redistribution is an important aspect of social risk management and social protection activities, *but unlike traditional social protection or the welfare state*, it is not necessarily the primary or only goal. In the social risk management framework, income redistribution is present as an equity objective linked to adverse risk and as an important outcome of good social protection programs. *The support of the critically poor is a main objective of social protection.* (World Bank 2001: 11, emphasis added)

Subsequent bank documents also place less emphasis on redistribution than do proponents of IRM. The bank's 2008 review of the 2001 strategy discussed the redistributive role of social protection in the context of the safety nets. Redistribution is to be achieved by transfers, with little attention paid to the state and regulatory policies that might influence the capacity of states to redistribute.

The second World Bank Social Protection and Labor Strategy (2012) focused on resilience (social insurance), equity (social assistance), and opportunity (access to work and human capital development). The bank continues to focus on social safety nets instead of entitlements, and on selective policies instead of universal provision.

In this strategy, the bank falls short of formally endorsing ILO's SPF-I (Deacon 2013), and moves away from social protection as a right. Deacon (2013) adds that the bank gives particular attention to the provider role of non-state actors (e.g. microcredit, social funds), and gives less emphasis to the beneficiaries' entitlements or the responsibilities of sources of finance. Nonetheless, the bank insists that its policy 'is broadly consistent with human rights-based approaches' (World Bank 2009: 8). It also says that the debate is undecided:

> Whether social risk management should happen through universal access and means-tested provisions or, more selectively, through conditionality is open for discussion, and policy choices should be evidence based (World Bank 2009: 8).

However, I would argue that whether or not policies accord with human rights very much depends on whether they are universal or selective. For example, targeted policies providing free access to education or health to the extreme poor would need regular adjustments to the means-testing to update the threshold of poverty, thus arbitrarily separating the included from the excluded; those who pay market rates for services from those who don't. With a human rights framework, there is no question of means-testing or capacity to pay, and hence no discrimination between groups or individuals. Within such a framework, targeted policies are the exception rather than the rule, justified when universal policies are not able to reach specific individuals. Selective policies, therefore, without a social protection system based on universal access and provision, are inconsistent with a rights-based framework.

UNSRID (2010) addresses the shortcomings of targeted poverty reduction policies, pointing out that targeted programmes not linked to universal access can increase exclusion and result in restricted access to services. When poverty is widespread, targeting might not result in much progress. Targeted policies also demand state capacity that might be absent in some developing countries.

Furthermore, strategies to curb poverty need not be directly related to poverty reduction (UNSRID 2010). Poverty specialists have shown that temporary residual strategies to fight severe and intergenerational poverty often do not address the multitude of needs of this particular type of poverty (CPRC 2005, 2008). These needs are structural and require long-term policy in a variety of forms, not only the provision of social protection, but also public services, collective assets, and a transformative legal framework that produces inclusive policies.

The World Bank's residual welfare model is in line with the historical neoliberal policy approach. Although the state is now acknowledged to be an important player, its role continues to be reduced by giving priority to market provision and using targeted interventions when the market fails. This is a compromise solution to meeting the needs of the most deprived while still retaining the structural adjustment framework. This approach to social protection ignores those issues of redress and redistribution belonging to the IRM with its framework of social solidarity and social inclusion.

Nonetheless, as the World Bank states '[i]t is no exaggeration to say that the new SRM framework effectively has become the reference point for the thinking about SP [Social Protection] in a development context' (Holzmann et al. 2003: 4–5) and cash transfers within the SRM framework have become a growing trend in developing countries, as the following section shows.

The emergence of cash transfers as a policy to fight poverty

The last few decades have seen a substantial increase in conditional cash transfer (CCT) initiatives, from Brazil and Mexico in the mid-1990s (Britto 2008), to twenty-seven countries in 2008 and fifty-two countries in 2013 (World Bank 2014: xiii). During this period, lending for safety nets grew in importance within the bank's SP and labour portfolio, rising from 23 per cent in 2002 to 42 per cent in 2007 (World Bank 2009: 8). In 2009, the bank released a review focused exclusively on CCTs, because of their overall positive impacts on poverty reduction (Fiszbein and Schady 2009).

Figure 19.1 illustrates the growing proportion of social safety nets in the bank's SP and labour portfolio from 1998 to 2010.

Cash transfers, both conditional and unconditional, are 'key modalities' of social safety nets, along with conditional or unconditional in-kind transfers, such as school lunch programmes and public works (World Bank 2014: 1). Figure 19.2 shows the increased spending on social safety nets by country.

It is important to note that there are many social services, such as nutrition, housing, social care, and family support, that the bank does not include in the social safety net. Figure 19.3 shows the boundaries between social assistance, social services, and social insurance. For the bank, social assistance is confined to the social safety net; for other

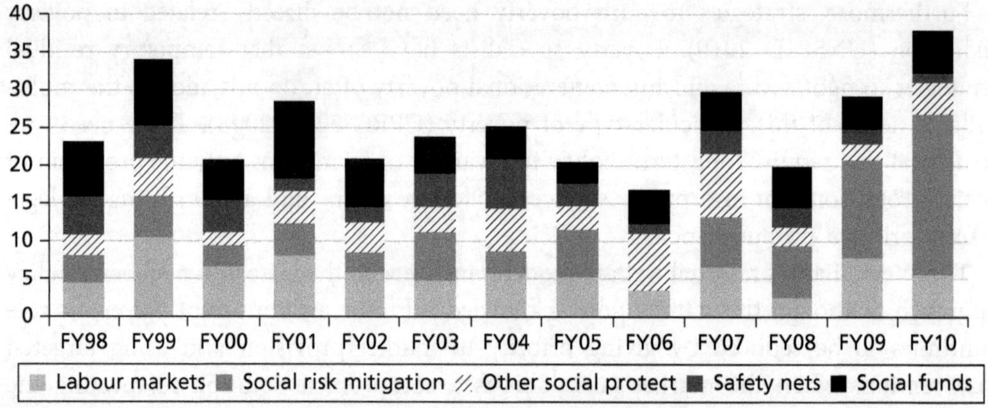

Figure 19.1 New World Bank commitments to social protection and labour, 1998–2011 (US$ million)

Source: Reproduced from World Bank (2012: 10).

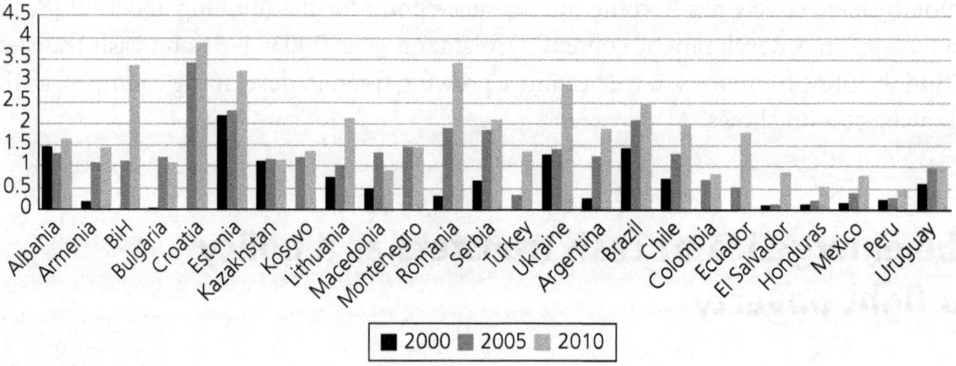

Figure 19.2 Growth of social safety net spending in Eastern Europe, Central Asia, and Latin America (% GDP)

Source: Reproduced from World Bank (2014: 21).

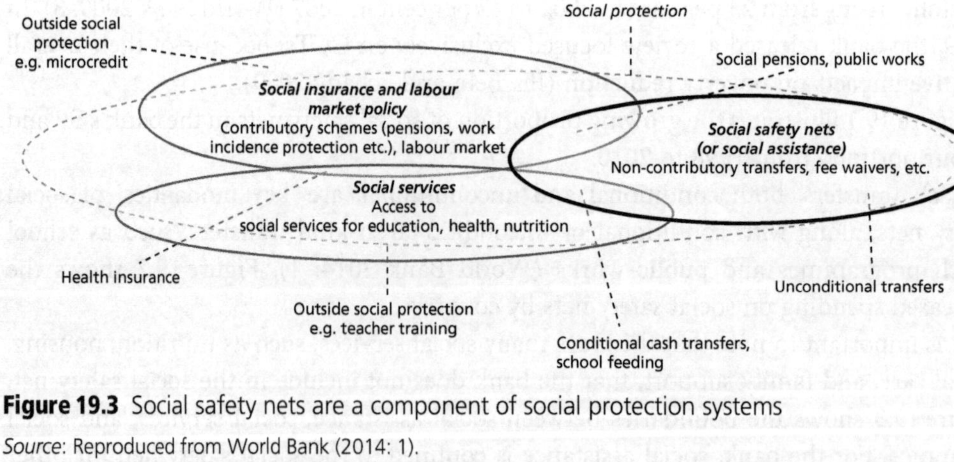

Figure 19.3 Social safety nets are a component of social protection systems

Source: Reproduced from World Bank (2014: 1).

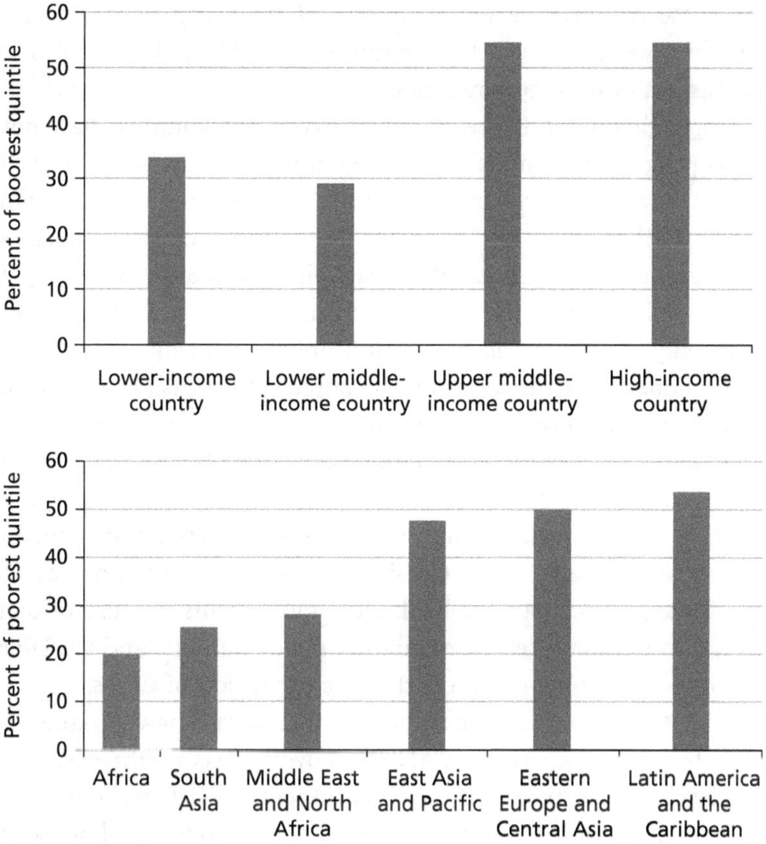

Figure 19.4 Coverage of the poorest quintile by region

Source: Reproduced from World Bank (2014: 5).

organizations, like UNICEF, social assistance also includes social welfare services (see note 1).

The bank's minimalist concept of social assistance has important implications for policy prescriptions and state participation. Confining social assistance to social safety nets restricts social assistance's scope, limiting state support to the temporary provision of cash or in-kind transfers. This reinforces the key message of this chapter: that cash transfers are 'hijacking' or taking precedence over other types of social assistance (e.g. social care services).[3] This reduces the possibility of the state to redress inequalities and to promote an adequate standard of living.

The bank recognizes some of the limitations. It acknowledges the issue of under-coverage in social safety net programmes, mainly in the poorest countries, as Figure 19.4

[3] The World Bank's State of Social Safety Nets report mentions 'social services' as part of 'other interventions' under 'social safety nets/social assistance'. The focus, nonetheless, continues to be placed on transfers, public works, school feeding instead of social services. Social services are restricted to 'transfers for caregivers' (World Bank 2018).

illustrates. In these countries, external sources of financing represent an important source for funding social safety net programmes (World Bank 2014: 17), reinforcing the temporary aspect of these programmes.

The bank's report highlights the reason for low coverage: countries have not scaled-up social safety net programmes and targeted programmes that are aimed at sections of the population, such as the old, orphans, and so forth. These findings support UNSRID's criticism (2010: 3) that, in countries where the majority of the population is poor, targeting programmes is unlikely to 'make significant inroads'. However, even where programmes are well scaled-up, like the BFP in Brazil, coverage for the lowest quintile is estimated to be only 53 per cent; in Mexico it is only 55 per cent (World Bank 2014: 4).

There are a number of explanations for the popularity of cash transfers, despite their limitations. First, they are low cost. The bank estimates that social safety nets average around 1.5 per cent of GDP worldwide (World Bank 2018: 16). Second, there is evidence that cash transfers have had positive impacts on household consumption, income poverty reduction, food consumption, school enrolment rates, and reduction of child labour (Fiszbein and Schady 2009; Grosh et al. 2008). In addition, as Hall (2015) highlights, CCTs appeal to both the bank and governments because of their political benefits, quick disbursements, easily monitored policy outputs, and available technical expertise. All of these factors played a part in the expansion of CCTs.

Thus, the increased use of social safety nets—either in cash or as in-kind transfers—as a targeted and temporary measure to address poverty, has dominated SP practice in international development in recent years. With these policies, responsibility for social assistance is individualized through the provision of cash to targeted households. Social assistance has become identified with social safety nets—a major underestimation of need. Other services, such as social work, social support, care services, and personalized social services, are rarely present in this debate. Although low-income countries might not have the resources for social support services, this is not the case for emerging economies like BRICS. Trying to reduce poverty through SRM does not address the multiple structural causes of poverty that require long-term intervention (Hall 2006, 2008). The challenge resides in how to address short-term needs with long-term structural transformation (Barrientos 2013b).

The restricted SRM view of social assistance incurs two consequences, which Titmuss (1987) had long warned us against:

(1) the dominance of the economic and the technocratic over the social in the approach to the problems of change
(2) trends towards the depersonalization of access to and the use of social welfare services. Both can lead to the abstraction of man from his social context; a theoretical attempt to isolate what cannot be isolated (1987: 255).

Addressing poverty and its multidimensional facets requires a combination of approaches and cash transfer is only one of them. It also involves a broader understanding of social assistance, which includes personalized social services and other social interventions that situate policies, institutions, and norms within the specific social context. A broader view of social policy that takes into account the interrelated effects of different policies is also required. Although it is a major achievement that SP is now more prevalent in the development discourse, social assistance in developing countries is still being framed in terms of the residual state.

The Brazilian case: cash transfers and social spending during Lula's and Dilma's administrations

SOCIAL ASSISTANCE IN BRAZIL: A HISTORICAL OVERVIEW

For most of Brazilian history,[4] calls for social assistance have been answered by communities, religious groups, and families. In 1974, the government created the *renda mensal vitalícia* (RMV) [lifelong monthly income] aimed at people with disabilities and those above 70 years of age who could not provide for themselves. However, the RMV required contributions and formal engagement in work for at least five years.[5]

It was only in 1988 that the Constitution brought together social assistance, social insurance, and health as the three pillars of the Brazilian social security system. The provision of a universal social minimum is based on human rights and citizenship principles, moving away from past social assistance practices guided by paternalism and clientelism (IPEA 2006).[6] The Constitution repackaged the RMV as a non-contributory cash transfer benefit, *benefício de prestação continuada* (BPC).

The Brazilian social security system is in its early stages. The Social Assistance Law (LOAS) [*Lei Orgânica da Assistência Social*][7] was approved in 1993, but was only implemented in 1996 (Delgado and Schwarzer 2000). Article 4 of the LOAS states the social assistance principles as: the primacy of social needs above economic profitability; the universality of social rights; receipt of benefits as a right; equal rights of access to quality services; citizens' dignity and autonomy; non-discrimination.

[4] In 2016, President Dilma Rousseff was impeached and the Vice-President Michel Temer came into power in a highly controversial succession and amid a deep recession in the Brazilian economy. Temer's focus was on fiscal stability and economic reforms, resulting in low popularity. One of the most controversial reforms is an austerity package to freeze spending for the next twenty years, known as 'New Fiscal Regime' or Consititutional Amendment No. 95. This includes freezing the spending on education and the social security system. The continuous economic recession, political instability, and corruption scandals set the background for the election of the far-right candidate Jair Bolsonaro in 2018. This chapter, however, does not analyse Temer's or Bolsonaro's administrations, but it provides a snapshot of the situation prior to Constitional Amendment No. 95.

[5] Law No. 6.179, 11/12/1974.

[6] Brazilian history is riddled with clientelist, sporadic, and temporary political practices aimed at influencing electoral outcomes. This practice is given the name of *assistencialismo*, and is often linked with social assistance and non-contributory temporary policies.

[7] Law No. 8.742, 07/08/1993.

Since then, the government has created the foundations for an SP network with the 2004 National Social Assistance Policy (PNAS) [*Política National de Assistência Social*], the Social Assistance Unified System (SUAS) [*Sistema Único de Assistência Social*], and the 2005 Basic Operational Norm of SUAS [*Norma Operacional Básica do SUAS*]. These efforts aim to reduce fragmentation of isolated policies (MDS 2009: 4).

However, there is a contradiction between the rights-based SP system of these initiatives and the 1988 Constitution on the one hand, and on the other, the economic imperative of minimal state intervention and maximum economic efficiency prescribed during the neoliberal era of the 1980s (da Silva et al. 2004). This contradiction is reflected in the different SP approaches, analysed in the second section, which resulted in a form of 'restricted universalization': public provision of services competing with private and non-governmental services, and attempts to provide universal benefits amid targeted benefits to the poor (IPEA 2006: 8).

Implementation of the 1988 Constitution allowed for a period of 'policy experimentation' (Fenwick 2013) and 'municipal activism' (Barrientos 2013a). In 1995, two cash transfers targeting low-income families and conditional on school attendance were introduced in the municipalities of Brasília and Campinas. These pilot initiatives were nationalized under the federal school grant [*bolsa escola*] in 2001.

The first federal CCT, the Child Labour Eradication Programme (PETI) [*Programa de Erradicação do Trabalho Infantil*] was introduced in 1996. It was targeted at children at risk of child labour and conditional on school attendance and attendance at health and social assistance services. Another two cash transfer programmes were created in 2001—the food grant [*bolsa alimentação*] and the gas grant [*auxílio gás*]. The food grant was targeted at pregnant women and mothers with children up to 11 months at nutritional risk, and it was conditional on health-related actions, like prenatal checks, vaccination, and nutritional follow-up. The gas grant was targeted at low-income families.

In 2003, the newly elected President Lula formally endorsed the 'fight against poverty' as one of his policy goals. President Lula created the food card [*cartão alimentação*] aimed at low-income families. Because these CCT programmes were all housed in different ministries, despite the fact that they served the same beneficiaries, President Lula also created the BFP, also in 2003. This is an umbrella programme to unify these cash transfer programmes into a single programme, under a single ministry—the newly created Ministry of Social Development (MDS)[8]—using a single registry [*cadastro*].[9]

The BFP is a non-contributory CCT programme, for families below an administrative poverty line (of which there are two: poverty and extreme poverty), on condition that they comply with education and health requirements. It is not an entitlement—it is dependent on budget availability, and it has a national quota of beneficiaries. The BFP

[8] The *Ministério do Desenvolvimento Social e Combate à Fome* [Ministry of Social Development and the Fight against Hunger].

[9] *Cadastro Único para Programas Sociais do Governo Federal* [Single Registry for Social Programmes of the Federal Government].

started with 3.6 million households in the first year of implementation, and had reached 11.1 million by 2006. In 2009, the number of places was increased to 13 million, which was reached in 2011. In 2017, the programme reached 13.3 million households (MDS 2017).

In 2014, the poverty line was R$154 (US$49)[10] per capita per month. In 2009, the BFP reached 22.2 per cent of the population (16.2 per cent of households), accounting for 9.5 per cent of their monthly household income. The average benefit transfer per beneficiary per month was R$21 in 2009 (US$6.70), and the programme cost 0.4 per cent of GDP (Soares 2012; Soares et al. 2010: 34).

Although small, the programme has had an impressive impact in Brazil. For the first time, people who had traditionally been left out of social protection—the able-bodied working-age poor with earnings insufficient to care for themselves or their children—were now included. Using the national household survey, Soares et al. (2010: 41, 7) showed that the BFP was responsible for a 16 per cent reduction in inequality between 1999 and 2009, and a 17 per cent reduction in poverty and a 40 per cent reduction in extreme poverty between 2003 and 2005. Thus, the Brazilian government continues the BFP, as it has achieved efficient results in reducing poverty and inequality at relatively low cost.

However, researchers caution that the BFP CCT strategy has reached its limit, as the rate of poverty decline has been slowing since 2007, to 5 per cent of urban poverty and 10 per cent of rural poverty (Rocha 2013: 173). Another important issue relates to the fundamental influence of the labour market in reducing poverty and inequality (Rocha 2013; Schwartzman 2006). Two-thirds of the six-percentage-point reduction in the Gini coefficient between 1997 and 2009 (0.599 to 0.538) is attributed to income from labour. In 2009, that income represented three-quarters of the family income (Rocha 2013: 152). Without continuing economic growth and stronger investment in social sectors, as demonstrated in the following sub-section, it is unlikely that the gains obtained by social policy will continue.

The BFP continues to be a key social assistance programme under President Dilma Rouseff. When she started her first term in 2011, she launched the Brazil without Misery Plan, aimed at overcoming extreme poverty through income guarantee programmes, access to services, labour market insertion, and other measures. The BFP is a constitutive part of this plan.

President Dilma has made some changes to the BFP. She increased the number of children who could receive the benefit from three to five per household, and she created another benefit linked to extremely poor families, called Benefit to Overcome Extreme Poverty. This benefit is calculated as the gap between household monthly income per capita and the extreme poverty line. The average benefit received by 13.8 million BFP households in July 2013 was R$120.19 (US$38.58).

[10] All dollar values are as of 30 July 2017.

President Dilma's changes with their targeted cash transfers fall within a residualist state framework in two ways. First, the BFP still doesn't use the language of entitlement or human rights; and the national cap means that there are 2–3.84 million households 'eligible but not beneficiaries' (Rocha 2011; Soares 2012). Furthermore, the programme continues to be perceived by Brazilian society (and beneficiaries) as a temporary measure to help the poor to 'lift themselves' whenever the market fails, i.e. the 'springboard' logic of safety nets. However, considering that the BFP transfer is only 9.5 per cent of household income, this is not sufficient to 'help' the poor 'lift themselves' out of poverty.

Second, giving priority to cash transfer social assistance policies deflects attention from other social spending needed to support families facing poverty.[11] This is what I turn to next.

SOCIAL SPENDING IN BRAZIL

The BFP has done much to fill a gap in social provision in Brazil by protecting vulnerable children (Camargo 2004) and the able-bodied, working-age poor. The political importance of the BFP as a social assistance programme during the labour party presidency terms (Hall 2008, 2013) brought the BFP to the forefront of social policy debates in Brazil. Figure 19.5 illustrates the increase in spending on this programme, and the continuous financial support over the years.

There is a clear policy priority for the allocation of the *social assistance* budget in Brazil in the last decade, favouring cash transfers instead of other social assistance policies. Figure 19.6 shows the importance of cash transfer programmes in the social assistance budget in 2014. Although most of the social assistance budget goes to SUAS, 92 per cent of SUAS is allocated to *Benefício de Prestação Continuada* (BPC—another cash transfer benefit), leaving only 8 per cent of the SUAS budget to support other social assistance services. The BPC and the BFP together represent 90 per cent of the overall social assistance budget, or R$61.6 billion (MPOG 2014).

Although the Social Assistance Law was passed in 1993, the institutions and policies that constitute the body of social assistance were only consolidated in the following decades. For example, SUAS was proposed on the occasion of the Fourth National Conference on Social Assistance in 2003; and major municipal-level service provision through the Social Assistance Reference Centres[12] was implemented by the MDS in the same year. It is remarkable that the Brazilian government was able to set the foundations for SUAS during this period, through the construction of centres, the attraction and

[11] President Temer's social reforms moved the Brazilian state even further towards a residualist model.

[12] Social Assistance Reference Centres [*Centro de Referência de Assistência Social*] aim to prevent social risks through the provision of basic social welfare support. Social Assistance Specialised Reference Centres [*Centro de Referência Especializada de Assistência Social*] work with individuals and families whose rights have already been violated.

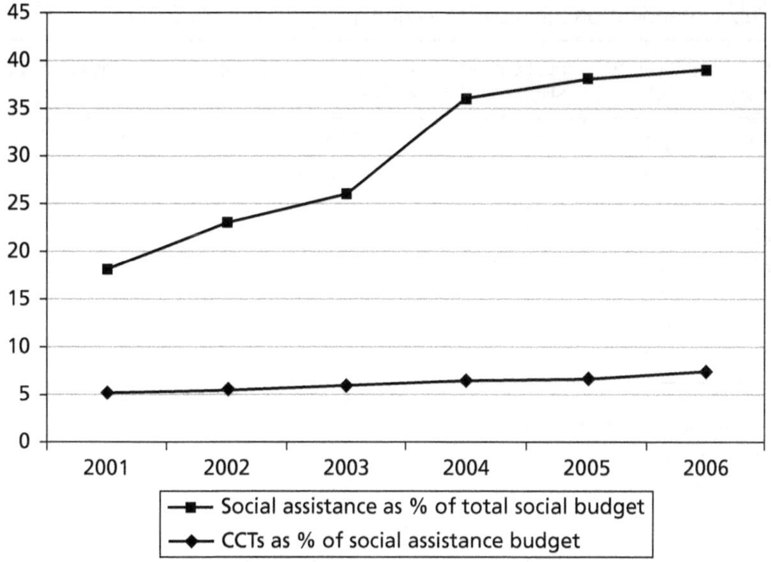

Figure 19.5 Trends in public spending on social assistance and CCTs, Brazil, 2001–06

Source: Reproduced from Hall (2008: 803).

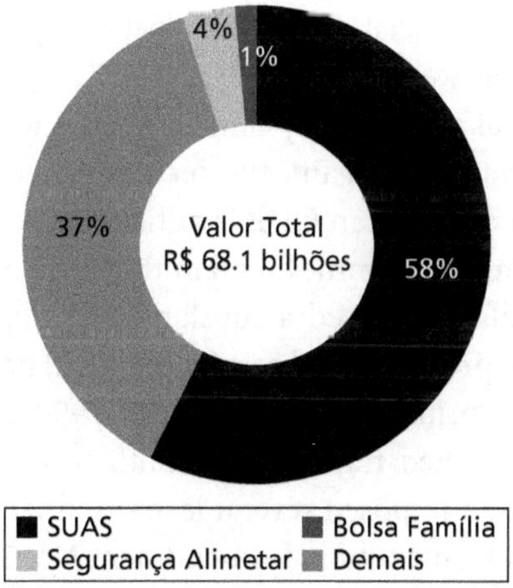

Figure 19.6 Social assistance budget, main areas, 2014

Note: Author's translation.

Source: Reproduced from MPOG (2014: 17).

training of qualified staff, and so forth, given the underinvestment in this initiative (INESC 2008; Mota 2007; Salvador 2010).

The services offered by Social Assistance Reference Centres are pivotal in the effort to build human capabilities and implement the citizenship rights enshrined in the Brazilian

Table 19.1 Public spending on main social security programmes (% GDP)

Year	Social insurance	BPC&RMV	Inpatient care (SUS)	Pensioners and people on leave	Cash transfers	Other	Total
2000	5.50	0.17	0.86	2.22	0.02	1.25	10.01
2001	5.73	0.20	0.87	2.19	0.07	1.41	10.48
2002	5.82	0.24	0.83	2.17	0.19	1.26	10.50
2003	6.27	0.27	0.78	1.96	0.23	1.15	10.65
2004	5.65	0.39	0.71	1.97	0.35	1.88	10.94
2005	6.63	0.43	0.70	1.93	0.33	1.16	11.18
2006	6.83	0.49	0.75	1.90	0.32	1.33	11.61
2007	6.94	0.53	0.80	1.96	0.36	1.32	11.91

Note: PBF is under the column heading 'Cash transfers'.
Source: Salvador (2010: 254).

Constitution. These services include family support, mediation, intervention, work with abused children, parenting programmes, disability support, community services, psychological services, and so forth. But SUAS can only guarantee rights if sufficient resources are allocated to build its infrastructure and promote its services (INESC 2008).

But how does this wave of cash transfers in social assistance relate to expenditures in other social investments? The social security budget comprises resources allocated to social insurance and health as well as social assistance. Table 19.1 shows the importance of cash transfers in the social assistance system compared to the main expenditures on other social security programmes. Again, the increasing percentage of cash transfers (BFP/BPC) as a proportion of Brazilian GDP is noticeable, whereas expenditures on the main health and other social programmes remain the same over time.

The 1988 Constitution also proposed a substantial change in *health* policy. It prescribed a right to health and provided the basis for a unified health system [*sistema unico de saúde*] (SUS), prioritizing primary health care.[13] In 1994, following fiscal adjustment policies the government detached funding for health from the social security budget (Piola et al. 2013), and instead imposed several levies to finance this gap.

It wasn't until 2000, with Constitutional Amendment No. 29 [*Emenda Constitucional No. 29 de 13 de setembro de 2000*], that funds for health were guaranteed. This amendment stated that 12 per cent of state and 15 per cent of local government revenues must be used for health. However, several loopholes allowed local governments to invest less than required and to invest in items not directly related to public services in health. This situation was addressed in 2012 by the *Lei Complementar No. 141*. This law

[13] Despite challenges, SUS has been highlighted by the World Bank and the WHO as a successful system, and a 'point of reference in the international health community'. Available at www.worldbank.org/en/news/opinion/2013/12/20/brazil-sus-unified-public-healthcare-system-new-study and www.who.int/bulletin/volumes/86/4/08-030408/en/, accessed 6 November 2018.

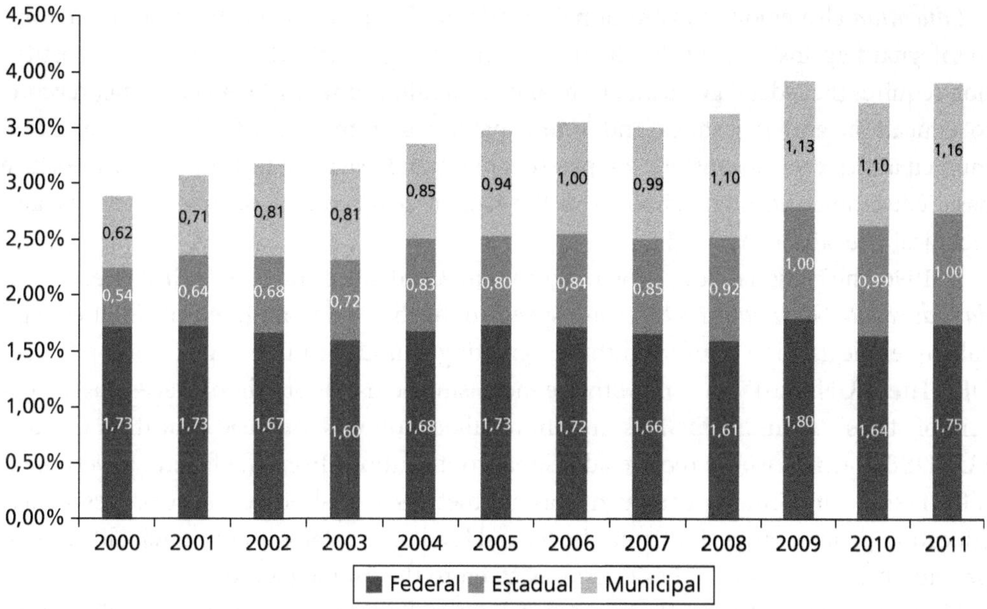

Figure 19.7 Public spending on health by government level, 2000–11 (% GDP)

Source: Reproduced from Piola et al. (2013: 16).

regulates health allocations, and specifies the minimum amounts to be reserved for health at the federal, state, and municipal levels, and what to do in cases where the minimum is not met. The federal allocation is based on the previous year's allocation plus the nominal variation of GDP (although allocations at the state and municipal levels are calculated differently) (Piola et al. 2013).

Figure 19.7 shows the changes in health expenditure from 2000 to 2011. During this decade, the health budget increased one percentage point (2.89 per cent to 3.91 per cent), a result of the increasing participation of states and municipalities in funding the budget. While the federal level remained practically the same, state funds increased from 0.54 per cent of GDP in 2000 to 1 per cent of GPD in 2011, and municipal funds increased from 0.6 per cent of GDP in 2000 to 1.16 per cent of GDP in 2011.

Even with the increased participation of state and local governments, the total percentage of financing in health is only around 4 per cent of GDP, while the OECD average was 8.9 per cent in 2013. The United Kingdom, a country with universal health systems like SUS, spends between 6 per cent and 7 per cent of its GDP on public health (OECD 2015).

Moreover, private healthcare spending is at around 4.7 per cent of GDP, outstripping the amount spent on public health (IPEA 2010: 74). However, private healthcare covered only about 40 million people in 2006 (or 21 per cent of the population), while SUS provides universal coverage to the majority of Brazilians (Vasconcelos 2006). In addition, private healthcare is subsidized by public funding through several personal and corporate tax breaks.

Education also enjoys constitutional mandatory budgetary allocations, as an attempt to safeguard against cuts in the Brazilian overall budget. Art. 212 of the 1988 Constitution requires the federal government to allocate a minimum of 18 per cent of tax revenue to education, and the states and municipalities a minimum of 25 per cent. Local municipalities are responsible for pre-schooling and basic education, states prioritize basic education and high school, and the federal government focuses on tertiary and technical education (Art. 211).

In 1996, the National Educational Norms and Guidelines law [*Lei de Diretrizes e Bases da Educação Nacional, 20/12/1996*] specified further roles and responsibilities, and subsequent legislation reinforced this by creating a fund for financing education (FUNDEF, later FUNDEB)[14] to cope with the increasing demand for school places. Eighty per cent of states' and municipalities' minimum allocation was for basic education through FUNDEB,[15] which would receive additional contributions from the federal government if the national minimum per student was not met. As in healthcare and social assistance, education policies saw a shift from the federal level to the states and municipalities, with priority in the provision of basic services given to the municipalities.

Figure 19.8 illustrates the changes in public spending on education from 1995 to 2009. During that time, public spending on education increased from 4.01 per cent to almost 5 per cent of GDP. However, it is important to note that there was no increase in the spending on education for a decade; it remained around 4 per cent from 1995 to 2005, only rising 1 per cent after that (IPEA 2011: 11).

Other initiatives created during this period include: financing tertiary education; providing public transport to school; and improving internet access. The government has also made an effort to expand access to education. In 1980, there were 2.4 million pre-school children, 24.1 million enrolled in primary education, 2.4 million in secondary education, and 585,000 in tertiary education. In 2009, these numbers reached 6.7 million pre-school children, 31.7 million in primary education, 8.3 million in secondary education, and, in 2008, five million tertiary students (IPEA 2010: 76). Thus, public spending on education during this period was not sufficient to address the increase in service demand, or the additional cost of new programmes.

The difficulty in seeking additional funding for education is demonstrated by the lack of agreement in Congress about the 2001–10 National Education Plan (PNE) (IPEA 2014). While the Ministry of Education proposed increasing public spending on education from 5 per cent to 7 per cent of GDP (although not the civil society benchmark of 10 per cent), the government decided instead to focus on the PNE for the next decade

[14] *Emenda Constitucional* No.14/1996, later regulated by Law No. 9.424/1996 created FUNDEF. *Emenda Constitucional* No.53/2006, later regulated by Law No.11.494/2007 created FUNDEB.

[15] Civil society participation in the financing debates was represented by the 'National Campaign for Rights to Education'. Started in 1999, the campaign is today a peak body that combines a network of more than 200 social movements, unions, student bodies, foundations, and non-governmental organizations (NGOs). It advocates for a quality public education within a human rights framework.

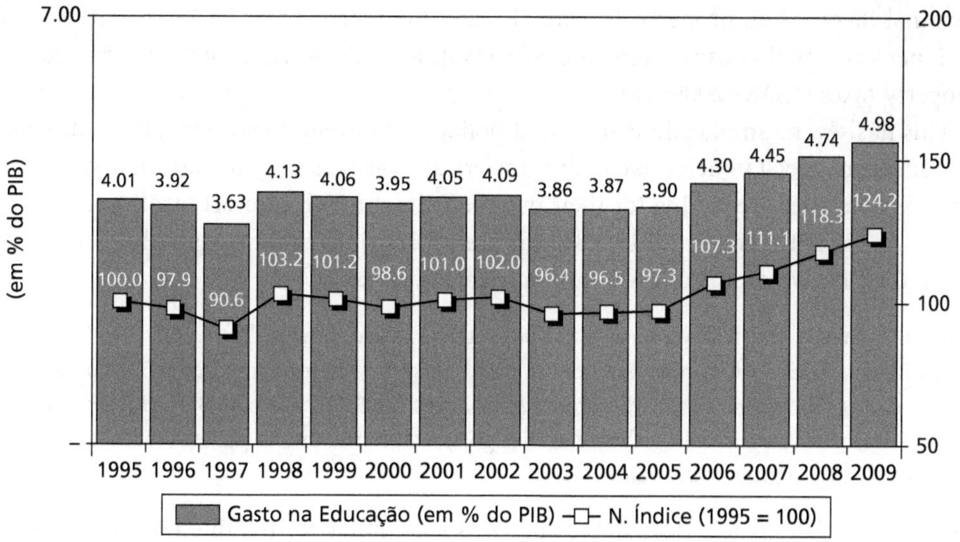

Figure 19.8 Public spending on education (% GDP) 1995–2009 (R$ billion)

Source: Reproduced from IPEA (2011: 11).

(2011–20). This plan included important changes to the education budget, which Congress approved on 3 June 2014.

Among those changes were twenty promising goals, one of which was a gradual increase of the percentage of GDP spent on education from 7 per cent in 2016 to 10 per cent in 2020 (MEC 2014). Other goals aimed to address challenges such as youth and adult education, illiteracy rates, and the quality of teaching and training. Most importantly, decisions on sources of funding, sharing of revenues, and collaboration between the federal government, the states, and the municipalities, are still to be regulated.

This analysis of trends in the Brazilian social budget places social assistance and cash transfers in a historical context. Cash transfers occupy an important place within the strategy of 'restricted universalization' with its tension between universal provision of services and targeted transfers for the poor, and between a human rights framework and a temporary safety net of residual SP.

The analysis of cash transfers should take into consideration the effects of the taxation system. This is of particular importance in Brazil, a country with high levels of market income inequality. A progressive taxation system combined with redistributive social policies would be able to compensate for some of this inequality. However, researchers indicate that the Brazilian system is regressive, lacks transparency, and inadequately finances the social investment areas that are a priority for long-term social welfare (CDES 2009; Salvador 2010; Silveira 2008).

For example, those whose earnings totalled two minimum wages in 2004 paid 48.8 per cent of their income in taxes, whereas those with incomes above thirty minimum wages paid only 26.3 per cent (CDES 2009: 21). This is because of the regressive effects of high levels of indirect taxes, which are not compensated for by progressive taxation on personal income and property. In 2005, Brazil's tax revenue was 33.8 per cent of GDP: 46.1 per cent of this came from indirect taxation and 24 per cent from income and property taxes (CDES 2009: 26).

This has several implications for social policy and development. First, the redistributive effects of social policies like cash transfers are weakened by the taxation system, as poor beneficiaries are paying for their own benefits through indirect taxation (Salvador 2010). As the IPEA report (2010: 93) indicates, this brings into question the 'generosity' and redistributive claims of the Brazilian social policy:

> After all, what is the real value of R$85.00 – the average receipt of the BF [BFP] transfer, according to MDS – when basic staples are highly taxed? When buying items like cooking gas (34% [of the price is due to taxes]), sugar (32.3%), eggs (20.6%), bread (16.8%), chicken (16.8%), rice (15.3%) and beans (15.3%), these families give back to the public purse something between 12% to 35% of the purchasing value?

As Lavinas (2007) has indicated, the current social policy for fighting poverty in Brazil, through cash transfers without other social investments, does not resolve the problem of inequality. I would also add that this model is inadequate for fighting long-term and structural poverty. Although social assistance in the form of cash transfers has reduced income poverty, using social policies as transformative tools to create more equal and fair societies also needs to focus on issues of social spending and redistribution in order to redress social injustices created by market mechanisms, institutions, and social norms.

Conclusion

The chapter reviewed the changes in international development debates and practices, in the use of social assistance policies as a mode of poverty reduction. It argued that there are contrasting approaches to SP, as well as contrasting understandings of social assistance policies, that tip the discussion either to a residualist or to a redistributional institutional state.

The chapter argues that the rise of cash transfers as a development strategy framed under a social safety net policy positions the debate in a residualist framework, limiting the scope as well as the understanding of social assistance policies. It also argues that cash transfers may be 'hijacking' or taking precedence over other types of social assistance policies, applicable in BRICS countries, in the fight against poverty as a long-term development goal.

As Mota (2007) cautions, it is a myth that social assistance is a central instrument for addressing social inequalities, replacing debates on structural inequalities and precarious labour markets. Despite that, social assistance has taken centre stage in policies to lift the poor out of poverty, instead of being simply a mediator supporting policies and rights.

Governments should be wary of the effects of cash transfers, as they are not sufficient to address the multidimensionality of long-term structural extreme poverty. Providing a safety net through cash transfers, although an important first step may be crowding other social spending out of the fiscal space. Social assistance requires a much broader set of policies than safety nets, and development involves not only economic growth, but also transformative social policies that promote redistribution and social justice.

REFERENCES

Barrientos, A. (2013a). 'The rise of social assistance in Brazil', *Development and Change* 44/4: 887–910.

Barrientos, A. (2013b). *Social Assistance in Developing Countries*. Cambridge: Cambridge University Press.

Britto, T. (2008). 'The emergence and popularity of conditional cash transfers in Latin America', in A. Barrientos and D. Hulme (eds) *Social Protection for the Poor and the Poorest: Concepts, Policies and Politics*. Basingstoke: Palgrave Macmillan, 181–93.

Camargo, J.M. (2004). 'Política social no Brasil: prioridades erradas, incentivos perversos' [Social policy in Brazil: wrong priorities, perverse incentives], *São Paulo em Perspectiva* 18/2: 68–77.

CDES (Conselho de Desenvolvimento Econômico e Social) (2009). *Indicadores de equidade do Sistema Tributário Nacional—Relatório de Observação nº 1 Brasília* [Equity indicators of the National Tax System - Observation Report No. 1]. Brasília. DF: CDES.

Chambers, R. and Conway, G.R. (1991). *Sustainable Rural Livelihoods: Practical Concepts for the 21st Century*. Sussex: Institute of Development Studies.

Cornia, G.A., Jolly, R., and Stewart, F. (1987). *Adjustment with a Human Face: Protecting the Vulnerable and Promoting Growth*. Oxford: UNESCO.

CPRC (Chronic Poverty Research Centre) (2005). *The Chronic Poverty Report 2004–5*. Glasgow: Bell & Bain.

CPRC (Chronic Poverty Research Centre) (2008). *'Chronic Poverty Report 2008–9—Escaping Poverty Traps Summary'*. Northampton: Belmont Press.

da Silva, M.O., Yazbek, M.C., and Di Giovanni, G. (2004). *A política social Brasileira no Século XXI: A prevalência dos programas de transferência de renda* [Social Policy in Brazil during the 21st Century]. São Paulo: Cortez Editora.

Deacon, B. (2013). 'The social protection floor and global social governance: Towards policy synergy and cooperation between international organizations', *International Social Security Review* 66/3–4: 45–67.

Delgado, G. and Schwarzer, H. (2000). 'Evolução histórico-legal e formas de financiameno da previdência rural no Brasil' [Legal-historic evolution and forms of financing of rural social security in Brazi], in G. Delgado and J. C. Cardoso Jr (eds) *A Universalização de Direitos Sociais no Brasil: A Previdência Rural nos Anos 90* [The universalisation of social rights in Brazil: rural social security in the 1990s]. Brasília, DF: Instituto de Pesquisa Econômica Aplicada, 187–210.

Fenwick, T.B. (2013). 'Stuck between the past and the future: conditional cash transfer programme development and policy feedbacks in Brazil and Argentina', *Global Social Policy* 13/2: 144–67.

Fiszbein, A. and Schady, N. (2009). *Conditional Cash Transfers: Reducing Present and Future Poverty. Overview*. Washington, DC: World Bank.

Grosh, M., Del Ninno, C., Tesliuc, E., and Ouerghi, A. (2008). *For Protection and Promotion: The Design and Implementation of Effective Safety Nets*. Washington, DC: World Bank.

Hall, A. (2006). 'From Fome zero to Bolsa Família: social policies and poverty alleviation under Lula', *Journal of Latin American Studies* 38/4: 689–709.

Hall, A. (2008). 'Brazil's Bolsa Família: a double-edged sword?', *Development and Change*, 39/5: 799–822.

Hall, A. (2015). 'It takes two to tango: conditional cash transfers, social policy and the globalising role of the World Bank', in S. McBride, G. Boychuk, and R. Mahon (eds) *Social Policy and the Global Financial Crisis*. Vancouver, BC: UBC Press, 140–60.

Hanlon, J., Barrientos, A., and Hulme, D. (2010). *Just Give Money to the Poor*. Sterling, VA: Kumarian Press.

Holzmann, R., Sherburne-Benz, L., and Tesliuc, E. (2003). *Social Risk Management: The World Bank's Approach to Social Protection in a Globalizing World*. Washington, DC: World Bank.

Hulme, D. and Shepherd, A. (2003). 'Conceptualizing chronic poverty', *World Development* 31/3: 403–23.

ILO (International Labour Organization) (2012). *The Strategy of the International Labour Organization—Social Security for All: Building Social Protection Floors and Comprehensive Social Security Systems*. Geneva: ILO, 9789221267461.

INESC (Instituto de Estudos Socioeconômicos) (2008). *Orçamento, direitos e desigualdades: um olhar sobre a proposta orçamentária/2009* [Budget, Rights and Inequality]. Brasília, DF: INESC.

IPEA (Institute of Applied Economic Research) (2006). *Edição especial 13—Políticas sociais acompanhamento e análise* [Social policy bulletin: monitoring and analysis. Special Edition No 13]. Brasília, DF: Instituto de Pesquisa Econômica Aplicada.

IPEA (Institute of Applied Economic Research) (2010). *Perspectivas da política social no Brasil, Projeto Perspectivas do Desenvolvimento Brasileiro, Livro 8* [Social policy outlook in Brazil, Book No 8. Brazilian Development Outlook Project]. Brasília, DF: Instituto de Pesquisa Econômica Aplicada.

IPEA (Institute of Applied Economic Research) (2011). *Financiamento da educação: necessidades e possibilidades, Comunicado No. 124* [Financing education: needs and possibilities. Bulletin No 124]. Brasília, DF: Instituto de Pesquisa Econômica Aplicada.

IPEA (Institute of Applied Economic Research) (2014). 'Education', in *Políticas Sociais: Acompanhamento e Análise* [Social policies: monitoring and analysis]. Brasília, DF: Instituto de Pesquisa Econômica Aplicada.

ISSA (International Social Security Association) (2013). *Social Security Coverage Extension in the BRICS: A Comparative Study on the Extension of Coverage in Brazil, the Russian Federation, India, China and South Africa, 9789284361823*. Geneva: ISSA.

Kanbur, R. and Sumner, A. (2012). 'Poor countries or poor people? Development assistance and the new geography of global poverty', *Journal of International Development* 24/6: 686–95.

Lavinas, L. (2007). 'Gasto social no Brasil: programas de transferência de renda versus investimento social' [Social spending in Brazil: income transfer programs *versus* social investments], *Ciência & Saúde Coletiva* 12: 1463–76.

MDS (2009) (Ministry of Social Development). *Lei orgânica de assistência social—LOAS anotada* [Annotated Social Assistance Law (LOAS)]'. Brasília, DF: Ministério do Desenvolvimento Social e Combate à Fome.

MDS (Ministry of Social Development) (2017). *Bolsa Família pagará R$2.4 bilhões aos beneficiários no mês de maio* [Bolsa Família will pay R$2.4 billion to beneficiaries in May]. Brasília,

DF: MDS. Available at www.mds.gov.br/webarquivos/sala_de_imprensa/boletins/release/2017/maio/18052017_Release_Bolsa%20Fam%C3%ADlia%20pagar%C3%A1%20R$%202,4%20bilh%C3%B5es%20aos%20benefici%C3%A1rios%20no%20m%C3%AAs%20de%20maio.html, accessed 2 February 2009.

MEC (Ministry of Education) (2014). *Planejando a próxima década: conhecendo as 20 metas do Plano Nacional de Educação* [Planning the next decade: the twenty goals of the National Education Plan]. Brasília, DF: Ministério da Educação.

Mkandawire, T. (2005). *Targeting and Universalism in Poverty Reduction.* Geneva: United Nations Research Institute for Social Development, 1020–8208.

Mota, A.E. (2007). 'Serviço Social e Seguridade Social: uma agenda política recorrente e desafiante' [Social work and social security: a recurrent and challenging political agenda], *Revista em Pauta* 20: 127–40.

MPOG (Ministério do Planejamento, Orçamento e Gestão) (2014). *Projeto de Lei Orçamentária Anual PLOA 2014—Orçamento federal ao alcance de todos* [Annual Budget Law 2014 – Federal budget, providing access to all]. Brasília, DF: MPOG.

OECD (Organisation for Economic Co-operation and Development) (2015). *Focus on Health Spending—OECD Health Statistics 2015.* Paris: OECD.

Piola, S., Barreto de Paiva, A., Batista de Sá, E., and Mendes Santos Servo, L. (2013). *Financiamento público da saúde: uma história à procura de rumo* [Public health financing: history in search of direction]. Rio de Janeiro: Instituto de Pesquisa Econômica Aplicada.

Rocha, S. (2011). 'O programa Bolsa Família Evolução e efeitos sobre a pobreza' [The Brazilian Bolsa-Familia Program: evolution and impacts on poverty], *Economia e Sociedade* 20/1: 113–39.

Rocha, S. (2013). *Transferências de Renda no Brasil–O Fim da Pobreza?* [Cash transfers in Brazil – the end of poverty?]. São Paulo: Elsevier Editora.

Salvador, E. (2010). *Fundo público e seguridade social no Brasil* [Public fund and social security in Brazil]. São Paulo: Editora Cortez.

Schwartzman, S. (2006). *Redução da desigualdade, da pobreza, e os programas de transferência de renda (versão 3)* [Inequality and poverty reduction and cash transfer programs]. Rio de Janeiro: Instituto de Estudos do Trabalho e Sociedade.

Scoones, I. (1998). *Sustainable Rural Livelihoods: A Framework for Analysis.* Brighton: Institute of Development Studies.

Shepherd, A. (2011). *Tackling Chronic Poverty: The Policy Implications of Research on Chronic Poverty and Poverty Dynamics.* Manchester: Chronic Poverty Research Centre.

Silveira, F.G. (2008). *Tributação, previdência e assistência sociais: impactos distributivos* [Taxes, social security and social assistance: redistributive impacts]. Brasília, DF: Tesouro Nacional.

Soares, S. (2012). *Bolsa Família, its Design, its Impacts and Possibilities for the Future, 89.* Brasília, DF: International Policy Centre for Inclusive Growth.

Soares, S., Ferreira de Souza, P.H., Osório, R.G., and Gaiger Silveira, F. (2010). 'Os impactos do benefício do programa Bolsa Família sobre a desigualdade e a pobreza' [Impacts of the Bolsa Família Program on poverty and inequality], in J.A. de Castro and L. Modesto (eds) *Bolsa Família 2003–2010: avanços e desafios—Vol 2.* Brasília, DF: Instituto de Pesquisa Econômica Aplicada.

Solesbury, W. (2003). *Sustainable Livelihoods: A Case Study of the Evolution of DFID Policy London.* London: Overseas Development Institute.

Sumner, A. (2012). *Where do the World's Poor Live? A New Update.* Brighton: Institute of Development Studies.

Titmuss, R.M. (1974). *Social Policy - An Introduction*. London: George Allen and Unwin.

Titmuss, R.M. (1987). *The Philosophy of Welfare. Selected Writings of Richard M. Titmuss*. London: George Allen and Unwin.

UN (United Nations) (1995). *World Summit for Social Development—Copenhagen Declaration on Social Development—Part C*. New York: United Nations. Available at www.un.org/esa/socdev/wssd/text-version/, accessed 6 November 2018.

UN (United Nations) (2014). *The Road to Dignity by 2030: Ending Poverty, Transforming All Lives and Protecting the Planet—Synthesis Report of the Secretary-General on the post-2015 Sustainable Development Agenda—Report A/69/700*. New York: United Nations.

UNICEF (United Nations Children's Fund) (2012). *Integrated Social Protection Systems Enhancing Equity for Children*. New York: UNICEF.

UNSRID (United Nations Research Institute for Social Development) (2010). *Combating Poverty and Inequality: Structural Change, Social Policy and Politics*. Geneva: UNSRID.

Vasconcelos, L. (2006). 'Planos de saúde - Um setor em desequilíbrio' [Health plans - an imbalanced sector], *Revista Desafios do Desenvolvimento* 3/23: 22–8.

World Bank (2001). *Social Protection Sector Strategy: From Safety Net to Springboard*. Washington, DC: World Bank.

World Bank (2009). *Social Protection and Labor at the World Bank, 2000–2008*. Washington, DC: World Bank.

World Bank (2012). *The World Bank 2012–2022 Social Protection and Labor Strategy: Resilience, Equity, and Opportunity*. Washington, DC: World Bank.

World Bank (2014). *The State of Social Safety Nets*. Washington, DC: World Bank.

World Bank (2018). *The State of Social Safety Nets 2018*. Washington, DC: World Bank. doi:10.1596/978-1-4648-1254-5. License: Creative Commons Attribution CC BY 3.0 IGO.

20 Mexico's Progresa-Oportunidades-Prospera programme and the rise of social assistance in Latin America

Miguel Niño-Zarazúa

Introduction

At the turn of the century, social assistance emerged as a new paradigm that has shifted the antipoverty policy agenda in Mexico and Latin America, from conventional approaches to food aid and subsidies to regular, reliable, and predictable forms of institutional assistance. This new paradigm, described elsewhere as a 'quiet revolution' (Barrientos and Hulme 2008), is currently reaching nearly 900 people worldwide, 25 per cent of whom live in Latin America and the Caribbean (see Table 20.2). This means that social assistance has become one (if not the most) important policy instrument against extreme poverty and vulnerability at the present time. The shift in policy thinking reflects an emerging consensus that eradicating poverty requires economic growth, basic service provision, and social protection. It also reflects a shift in the conventional wisdom on the nature and causes of poverty, moving from poverty as a lack of income to notions of poverty as a multidimensional phenomenon.

The International Labour Organization (ILO) divides the notion of social protection into three general categories: social insurance; labour market regulation; and social assistance. *Social insurance* includes contributory schemes designed to protect workers against life-course and work-related contingencies. *Labour market regulations* are legal frameworks aimed at ensuring minimum standards for employment and safeguarding workers' rights. *Social assistance* includes tax-financed, and also donor-funded, policy instruments designed to address poverty and vulnerability (ILO 2001). In this chapter, I focus on social assistance, as it represents the most important innovation to social protection systems in Latin America, and in the developing world more generally, over

Miguel Niño-Zarazúa, *Mexico's Progresa-Oportunidades-Prospera programme and the rise of social assistance in Latin America* In: *Handbook of BRICS and Emerging Economies.* Edited by: P.B. Anand, Shailaja Fennell, and Flavio Comim, Oxford University Press (2021).
DOI: 10.1093/oso/9780198827535.003.0020

the last two decades. In particular, I focus on one of the earliest and most studied programmes in the developing world: Mexico's Progresa (later renamed as Oportunidades during the conservative government of Vicente Fox, and more recently as Prospera under the Presidency of Enrique Peña Nieto). In the chapter, the programme, hereafter referred to as 'POP', is identified for having been revolutionary in at least four important respects.

First, the programme embraced, by design, a multidimensional approach to poverty. It links income transfers with simultaneous interventions in health, education, and nutrition, placing a strong emphasis on tackling the intergenerational transmission mechanisms of poverty through human capital investment. The programme requires parents sending their children to school and attending periodical health check-ups in exchange for income transfers that support expenditures on schooling, health, and nutrition. The 'human development' approach to social assistance has expanded rapidly in Latin America and beyond, with over thirty countries with large-scale programmes in place (Fiszbein and Schady 2009). Barrientos et al. (2010) also report a number of pilot schemes emerging particularly in the sub-Saharan African region, with pilot projects already introduced in Kenya, Malawi, Ghana, and Zambia; and at implementation stage in Nigeria, Liberia, Uganda, and Tanzania.

Second, one of the most distinctive features of POP is its focus on the poor. This is in clear contrast to generalized food subsidies and other targeted interventions that dominated the antipoverty agenda in the past, and which were regarded as being highly regressive, and plagued with inclusion errors that benefited the non-poor (Levy 2006). Third, POP followed a complex and statistically based system of identification and selection of beneficiaries at the household level, with the specific objectives of improving the efficacy of policy outreach and preventing discretionary manipulation associated with opportunistic political behaviour and clientelism, as occurred with previous antipoverty policies. That would ensure, it was assumed, that public resources distributed through the programme would be directed to those in most need. Fourth, but not least, POP included an independent impact evaluation protocol that included the academic research community both nationally and internationally. That helped not only in improving the programme's effectiveness over time, but also in strengthening its legitimacy across different political factions and constituencies (Skoufias 2005).

These four elements are found at different levels in transfer programmes that have adopted the human development approach of POP. The scale, coverage, transfer size, regularity of transfers, and the duration and timing of support can also be associated with broader political and economic factors, and well-grounded theoretical principles underpinning the design and implementation of the programme. In the remainder of this chapter I discuss these broader issues. The next section discusses the political and economic conditions that preceded the emergence of POP, and which help explain the shift in the antipoverty policy agenda in Mexico. The third section discusses the principles and design features that characterize this type of policy intervention, while the fourth section analyses institutional design features, and the fifth section reviews the existing evidence on the social impact of POP and other social assistance programmes in Latin America. The last section concludes with a brief discussion on the key policy lessons.

Shifting the antipoverty policy agenda in Mexico: the emergence of Progresa-Oportunidades-Prospera

Mexico's POP was launched in August 1997, two years after the country experienced one of the most difficult political and economic crises in more than five decades. In January 1994, the uprising of the Zapatista Army for National Liberation in the southern state of Chiapas coincided with a series of events, notably the assassination of the presidential candidate of the ruling Institutional Revolutionary Party (PRI) in March that year. These events generated great political uncertainty and contributed to triggering the Peso crisis of December 1994 (Gil-Diaz and Carstens 1996). The setback of 7 per cent in real GDP in 1995 had a devastating impact on household welfare. To illustrate, the headcount index associated with a food-based poverty line soared from 21.2 per cent just before the crisis to 37.4 per cent in 1996.[1]

In the aftermath of the crisis, the incoming Zedillo administration (1994–2000) was faced with limited capacity to assist the poor, for two important reasons: on the one hand, severe budgetary restrictions resulting from the slowdown of the economy and austerity measures meant that the government had very little room for manoeuvre to increase social spending; on the other hand, most antipoverty policies at the time consisted of generalized and targeted food and in-kind subsidies that reached just a fraction of the poor. Indeed, more than 75 per cent of the total budget for subsidized food consumption was allocated in urban areas, despite the fact that nearly 60 per cent of the poor lived in rural communities. That meant that a large percentage of the income transfer distributed through food subsidies was captured by the non-poor (Levy 2006). As a result, temporary measures adopted to offset the impact of the crisis had very limited poverty reducing effects.

The other major social policy available, the National Solidarity Programme (Pronasol)—a matching grant programme for financing small and medium-sized infrastructure and social projects, introduced by President Salinas de Gortari to compensate for the adverse

[1] Two additional poverty lines have been used in Mexico: A *capabilities-based* poverty line that includes, as well as the food-based basket, other expenditure items such as healthcare, education, clothing, housing, and public transport. If adopting that poverty threshold, the headcount index increased from 30 per cent in 1994 to 47 per cent in 1996. The third poverty line is *asset-based,* and results from adding to the food-based basket the mean value of non-food expenditure of households belonging to the lowest 10th percentile. When this poverty line is adopted, the poverty incidence rises from 52.4 per cent prior to the crisis to 69 per cent in 1996. For more details, see Secretaria De Desarrollo Social (2002).

effects associated with the rapid market liberalization and structural change of the 1980s—lost legitimacy, as it was heavily criticized for its political manipulation by the ruling PRI during the presidential election of 1994 (Molinar Horcasitas and Weldon 1994).[2]

POLITICAL CONSIDERATIONS

Political manipulation in the distribution of social spending in Mexico had been more of a norm than an exception, particularly in the absence of clear and effective transparency and accountability rules. Practices of this sort have also been reported from other incumbent governments in Latin America but also industrialized countries. For example, Schady (2000) finds that during Alberto Fujimori's administration, an increased expenditure of Peru's social fund Foncodes was given to provinces where his party had received support in previous elections. Gibson and Calvo (2000) show that Carlos Menem's government in Argentina manipulated social spending to gain support at Congress for introducing economic reforms. Dahlberg and Johansson (2002) also find strong evidence of a skewed distribution of municipality grants towards regions with large proportions of swing voters during the Swedish 1998 election.

Political clientelism in Mexico was exacerbated by a one-party autocratic regime that under the PRI dominated the political system for over seventy years (1929–2000). The country, however, as the rest of the Latin American region, witnessed important political shifts in the late 1990s and early 2000s, towards more competitive and democratic systems. Changes in political competition also meant that governments had stronger incentives to become more proactive in instituting antipoverty policies that appealed to the constituencies. The 'politicization' of poverty intensified in the late 1990s and led to the introduction of POP under more transparent operational rules.

Indeed, in a context of rapid democratization and increasing political competition, the Zedillo administration decided to reform the rules of antipoverty policy to improve the transparency and efficiency of those systems (Escobar Latapi 2002). In particular the government began a process of decentralization that culminated in a new law (Law of Fiscal Coordination), in which funding decisions on public infrastructure such as schools, health clinics, and rural roads were taken at state and municipality level and allocated on non-discretionary principles, on the basis of a statistically based poverty index (Somuano et al. 2006). These reforms, in addition to the introduction of POP, signalled a major shift in antipoverty policy thinking in Mexico. In particular, a major change in policy was the focus on households rather than on communities. POP aimed, by design, at promoting a direct relationship between the federal government and the

[2] Studies have found strong correlations between allocation of Pronasol funds and political outcomes. Overall, evidence suggests that Pronasol was used to mobilize PRI's electoral machinery to gain support from both core and swing constituencies. For further discussion, see Dion (2000).

recipient households, while explicitly limiting the involvement of local governments and civil society organizations. This had the objective of preventing the reproduction of corporatist, authoritarian, and clientelist practices that peasants' cooperatives, rural workers' unions, and community associations have shown in the past (Dagnino et al. 2006; Levy and Rodríguez 2004). And although some private intermediaries were involved at the beginning of the operation of the programme, from 2002 onwards, the entire operation was under the management of a federal coordinating agency without the participation of any civil organization. At the same time, civil society organizations showed no particular interest in overseeing or taking part in the programme, as there were no economic incentives and/or means to cover fees, commissions, and other administration costs. They left most activities to the federal coordinating agency (Hevia de la Jara 2008).

The democratization process in Mexico, and the fall of authoritarian regimes in Latin America also coincided with a series of market-oriented economic reforms, following the Washington Consensus that aimed to open the Latin American economies to the international capital markets (Pastor and Wise 1999; Filipovich et al. 2018). The social costs of such economic reforms led to social mobilization and increasing public pressure that placed the issue of raising poverty at the centre of policy debates and political agendas (Teichman 2008). By the early 2000s, several Left and Centre-left candidates had been elected to office in Argentina, Brazil, Bolivia, Chile, Ecuador, Nicaragua, Paraguay, Peru, and Uruguay, and with them, social assistance became a central antipoverty strategy in the region (Grugel and Riggirozzi 2012).

To a certain degree, Left governments were expected to prioritize the antipoverty agenda through inter alia, the expansion of social assistance, partly because of their more socially progressive political manifestos (Barrientos 2013). However, it is important to note that not only Left and Centre-left governments were active in adopting antipoverty agendas. Other countries including Colombia, Guatemala, and Mexico voted Centre-right governments into office and also expanded their antipoverty social assistance institutions. In Mexico, the political relevance of POP became evident after the incoming conservative Fox administration decided to keep the programme, and even expand it to become not only a programme operating in rural communities, but also to include urban towns and cities. This decision triggered a significant expansion of POP in terms of coverage and allocated budget (see Figure 20.1). Political incentives under a more competitive political environment, together with the fact that the National Action Party (PAN) to which Vicente Fox belonged had strongholds in urban areas, explains the consolidation of POP throughout the conservative regimes of Fox (2000–06) and Calderon (2006–12).[3]

[3] For a discussion on the electoral incentives that POP generated to the incumbents during the 2000 political transition in Mexico, see Filipovich et al. (forthcoming).

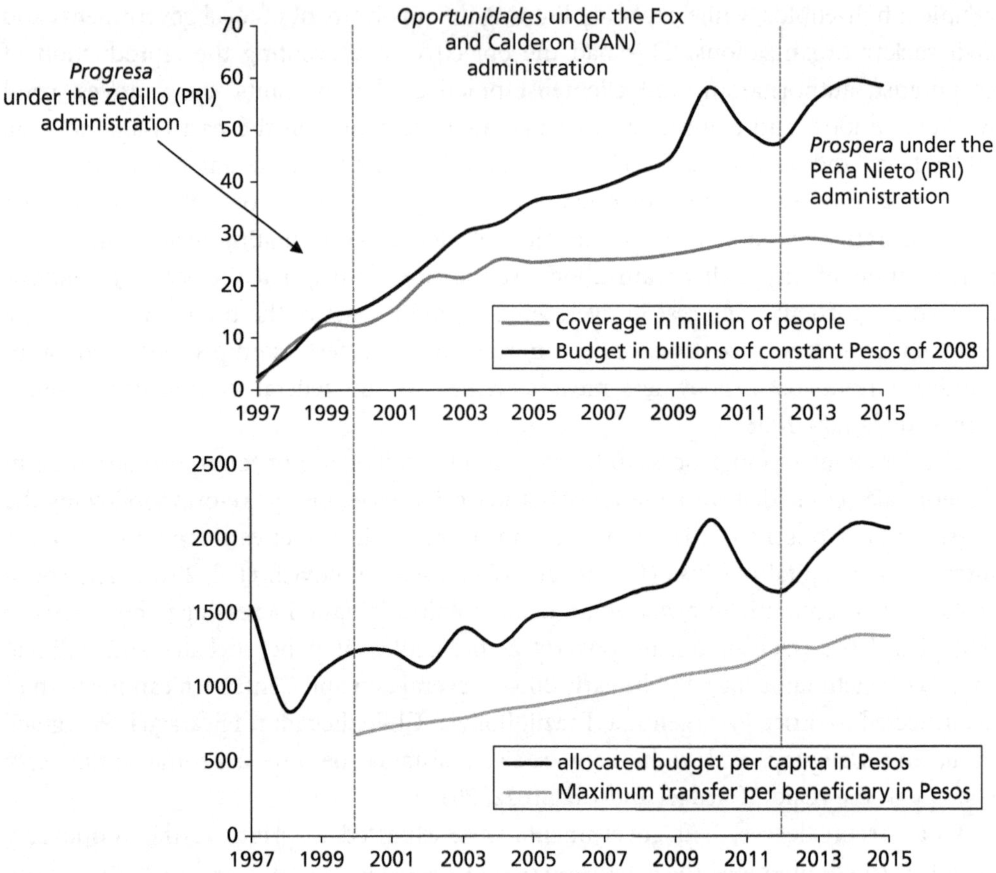

Figure 20.1 Political regimes and the evolution of Progresa-Oportunidades-Prospera

Source: Author, based on the Social Assistance Politics and Institutions (SAPI) database (UNU-WIDER 2018).

FINANCING ISSUES

Financing has emerged as a key constraint in discussions on extending social assistance, particularly in low-income countries. Tax revenues are a major source for financing social assistance. In low- and lower middle-income countries, taxes represent about 80 per cent of government revenues, followed by revenues from property income, sales of goods and services, international aid, and property income (IMF 2009). Low-income countries in particular face heavy constraints on their capacity to improve tax collection effort. These constraints are associated with the structure of the economy and the limited administrative capacity of revenue authorities (Barrientos and Niño-Zarazúa 2011).

Budgetary considerations have contributed to making the global coverage of social assistance largely skewed towards middle-income countries. The mean spending on social assistance in Latin America is in the order of 1 per cent of GDP, although that proportion is conditional on the size of the economy, the efficiency of tax collection systems, and the scale and scope of the interventions. So while upper middle-income countries, such as Colombia, Chile, Mexico, Peru, and Uruguay, spend less than 1 per cent of GDP on social assistance, lower middle-income countries, such as Bolivia and Honduras, allocate more than 2 per cent of GDP (Grosh et al. 2008). In particular, POP absorbs just a fraction of Mexico's GDP, about 0.3 per cent, and that proportion is expected to diminish under positive economic growth and a sustained reduction in poverty.

It is worth noting that POP gradually replaced previous food subsidies that were ineffective in reaching out to the poor. That was a key policy decision during the Zedillo administration, as the introduction of POP on top of food subsidies would have simply been unfeasible under conditions of limited fiscal resources in the aftermath of the Peso crisis. Levy (2006) has pointed out the importance of the presidential leadership in phasing out food subsidies that had been in place for over two decades. The substitution of social policies helped the incumbent government at the time to avoid additional pressures on the federal budget.

However, expansion of POP as well as other social assistance programmes in Latin America throughout the 2000s would have been difficult to observe without the favourable macroeconomic conditions and the fiscal space that high international commodity prices generated (Teichman 2008). Indeed, natural resources have been an important source of government revenue in the region (see Figure 20.2). In Mexico, as well as in the region, natural resource rents averaged about 6.5 per cent of GDP, although for countries such as Bolivia, Chile, Ecuador, and Venezuela, exports of crude oil and minerals represented more than 10 per cent of GDP (Mainwaring and Pérez-Liñán 2014). Despite the recent fall in international commodity prices, government spending on social assistance has remained largely unaffected in Mexico and in most Latin American countries, partly due to the counter cyclical nature of social assistance (see Barrientos and Niño-Zarazúa 2011 for a discussion), but also because of the high political cost that a reduction in coverage or transfers size would imply for incumbent governments.

Another important aspect of POP was its domestic roots, in terms of design, and financing sources, although the international community, via the Inter-American Development Bank and the World Bank, supported the expansion of the programme financially and with technical assistance, especially after the political transition of 2000.[4] Most importantly though was the role of the international community in disseminating the experience of POP and replicating similar models across the developing world.

[4] In 2002, the Inter-American Development Bank agreed a US$1 billion loan to Progresa-Oportunidades, the largest loan ever made by the bank to a poverty reduction programme, and in 2005 the loan was renewed for US$1.2 billion for another four years (Levy 2006). In January 2010, the government announced an expansion of Progresa-Oportunidades to cover an additional 600,000 low-income households, primarily in urban areas. However, as the budgetary capacity of the Mexican government had been severely constrained as a result of the global financial crisis, the expansion of the programme was financed with public borrowing: a US$1.5 billion fixed-spread loan from the World Bank and a US$600 million loan from the Inter-American Development Bank (see Barrientos and Niño-Zarazúa 2011).

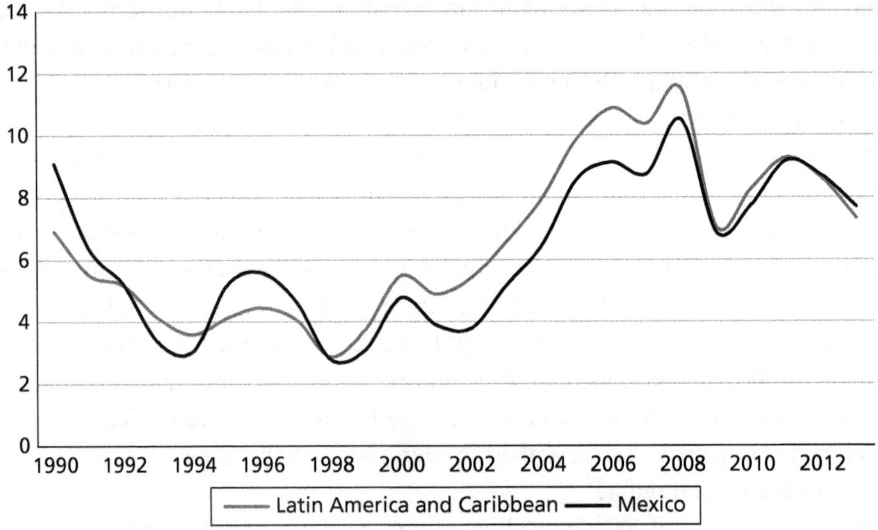

Figure 20.2 Total natural resources rents as % GDP in Mexico and Latin America

Source: World Development Indicators (World Bank 2016).

Overall, the economic crisis of 1994–95, coupled with a number of factors—notably a process of rapid democratization and political competition, a reallocation of budgetary resources from regressive subsidies to pro-poor social spending in the initial phase of the programme, and then favourable macroeconomic conditions in the first decade of the 2000s—laid down conditions for the introduction and later expansion of POP. In the following section, I briefly discuss the principles and objectives underpinning the programme, whereas in the fourth section attention is paid to relevant institutional design features.

Principles and programme objectives

Mexico's POP, as do many other human development programmes in Latin America, combines income transfers—also referred to in the literature as conditional cash transfers or CCTs—with preferential access to health or education services. The programme is centrally run by a federal agency that identifies and selects programme beneficiaries (see following section). That agency also coordinates payments, monitoring systems, and service delivery with ministries and agencies at federal and state level. Thus, while the federal government is responsible for making payments and coordinating policy, state governments are in charge of the direct provision of health and education services. Human development programmes explicitly aim at both reducing extreme poverty and promoting investment in human capital, particularly among children. These two policy objectives are linked to co-responsibilities that require parents to send their children to school and attend periodic health check-ups.

TARGETING EXTREME POVERTY

The first policy objective, i.e. reducing extreme poverty, is a distinctive feature of POP and other social assistance programmes in Latin America. Unlike food subsidies and other development interventions in the past, these programmes aim at protecting basic levels of consumption of the poor and most vulnerable. There is an important political economy dimension associated with social assistance focusing on the extremely poor. Shared perceptions and values about causes of extreme deprivation can play a role in persuading political constituencies to support policy interventions that assist the poor (Barrientos and Neff 2010). This was actually what happened in Mexico. A general consensus about the urgent need to tackle the rising poverty observed in the years after the Peso crisis of 2005, together with emerging evidence pointing at significant impact from Progresa (see penultimate section of this chapter), persuaded the incoming conservative Fox administration to keep, and subsequently expand the programme to urban areas. Similarly, in Brazil, President Lula signed a law in 2004 that introduced the notion of universal basic income for all; however, due to budgetary constraints, it was decided that the focus of *Bolsa Família* would be on the poorest first, as they were the most urgently in need of support.

The judgement about assisting the poorest with social assistance has a strong foundation in principles of social justice. Welfare economics suggests that policies focusing on the poorest are welfare-enhancing. This means that an additional unit of income transferred to the poorest would produce a greater benefit than the same additional unit of income transferred to the rich. As Rabin (2000: 1281) has pointed out: 'a dollar that helps us avoid poverty is more valuable than a dollar that helps us become very rich'. The effectiveness of social assistance programmes in reaching out to the poor is largely contingent on the methods for identification and selection of the intended beneficiaries (Rawls 1971).

FACILITATING HUMAN CAPITAL INVESTMENT

The second policy objective of POP, i.e. promoting investments in human capital, was based on strong theoretical principles and empirical evidence showing that the formation of human capital, through improvements in education, health, and nutrition, plays a central role in enhancing people's capacity to produce, interact with their peers, and integrate in society. On the contrary, poor nutrition, poor health, and limited schooling are associated with low labour productivity, low incomes, and 'vicious cycles' of poverty. In low-income countries, 43 per cent of children under age 5 are underweight and the prevalence of malnutrition is often two to three times higher among the poorest income quintile (Wagstaff and Watanabe 2000). There is also systematic evidence that poor households are less likely to be in a position to support their children's education (World Bank 2006; Masino and Niño-Zarazúa 2018). Children who do not have the opportunity to complete their basic education are also likely to face a lifetime of poverty (Hoddinott and Quisumbing 2003).

Social assistance programmes are critical in that context, as they can relax households' budget constraints while encouraging human capital investment. Indeed, empirical evidence shows that human development programmes in Latin America have allowed poor households to increase the quantity and quality of food they consume. They also seem to have facilitated intra-household time reallocation, so that their children can go to school (see penultimate section). More schooling and better health and nutrition for children can translate into greater future productivity, higher economic development, and social mobility. The complementarities between nutrition, health, and education, and the spillover effects and positive externalities emerging in labour and credit markets, are key to understanding the expansion of social assistance, in terms of scale and global coverage, with a human development focus.

But while design features, particularly the so-called conditionalities, have dominated the discussion surrounding human development programmes in Latin America, issues of coverage, scale and transfer size, regularity, and duration of support are of much greater significance. The theoretical principles underpinning conditionalities in social assistance rely on the assumption that under situations of extreme deprivation, households heavily discount children's future consumption on healthcare and education. In those contexts, conditionalities are expected to price up the underestimated value of service utilization and, therefore, have a greater impact on household welfare than unconditional transfers. However, the evidence on this is inconclusive. While conditions are reported to increase service utilization more than unconditional transfers in Latin America (see e.g. Bourguignon et al. 2003; de Brauw and Hoddinott 2008; Schady and Araujo 2006), other studies show that unconditional transfers can also have a positive impact on household welfare (Duflo 2000; UNICEF 2000). Few controlled experimental studies are currently being conducted to compare the effects of conditional and unconditional transfers, and they may provide further evidence on this particular subject. The marginal costs and benefits of enforcing conditionalities are not fully known either, and more empirical work is needed in this area. Nonetheless, the idea of households' co-responsibilities in tackling poverty have played an important role in gaining public support to expand social assistance, particularly at early stages of institutional development of pioneer programmes such as POP, as rigorous impact evaluations were not available at the time. In the following section, I discuss the features that characterize the institutional design of POP.

Institutional design

The effectiveness of POP has been largely contingent on the methods adopted for the identification and selection of beneficiaries. The programme developed complex systems of identification and selection, with the specific objective of improving the efficacy of policy outreach and avoiding its politicization, as occurred in the past with other social policies. These systems involve the geographic selection of poor areas using census-based marginality index, categorical criteria to identify poor households using socio-economic survey and census data, and proxy-means tests to select beneficiaries.[5]

Budget restrictions made it necessary for the Mexican government to roll out the programme gradually. In 1997, Progresa was introduced in rural areas, in selected regions, and only in localities with school and health infrastructure, as its multidimensional approach to poverty required the provision of public services. About 300,000 households living in 6,344 rural communities received support. The programme focused on rural localities first, as a large percentage of households in poverty lived in rural localities. By 2000, before the presidential elections of July 2000, the roll-out phase of the programme was completed, reaching nearly 2.5 million households living in 53,232 communities (see Table 20.1).

However, by focusing exclusively on rural areas, Progresa was de facto excluding the urban poor who remained disqualified from receiving support simply for not having lived in the selected geographical settings. At the same time, the requirement that communities possessed the necessary public infrastructure excluded remote rural areas with poor infrastructure. The human development focus of the programme also militated against the inclusion of households without children. These induced 'exclusion errors', in addition to electoral incentives, are key to understanding why the Fox administration decided to keep and then expand the programme to urban areas, and in 2003 also include other vulnerable groups, such as people in old age.[6]

By June 2015, POP had covered more than 6.1 million households (28 million people), meaning that around one-fifth of the population in Mexico received support from the programme. More than 70 per cent of beneficiaries are regarded as extremely poor. The rapid expansion of the programme coincided with a steep rise in global coverage of social assistance in Latin America. The share of the population covered by transfer programmes in Latin America varies from country to country, from just a fraction of those in poverty covered by Paraguay's Red de Protección y Promoción Social, to nearly 40 per cent of households covered by Ecuador's Bono de Desarrollo Humano. All in all, different types of transfers reach nearly 165 million poor people in Latin America (see Table 20.2), making social assistance the most important policy instrument against extreme deprivation in the region at the present time. Remarkably, POP and other programmes in Latin America have made a significant contribution to tackling poverty and severe deficits in well-being (see following section). Several factors seem to contribute to the poverty effectiveness of social assistance, but especially important are transfer size, regularity of transfers, and duration of support.

[5] This section borrows from the discussion in Barrientos and Niño-Zarazúa (2011: s. 3).
[6] For a detailed discussion, see Skoufias (2005).

Table 20.1 Coverage and scale of Progresa-Oportunidades-Prospera

Year	Name	Coverage millions of people	Coverage millions of households	Coverage % of total population	Budget billions of constant pesos, 2008	Budget per capita pesos	Government and type of regime
1997	Progresa	1.6	0.3	1.66	2.52	1,553	Zedillo (PRI)—Centre
1998	Progresa	8.6	1.6	8.65	7.31	848	Zedillo (PRI)—Centre
1999	Progresa	12.5	2.3	12.30	13.74	1,104	Zedillo (PRI)—Centre
2000	Progresa	12.4	2.5	12.04	15.45	1,247	Zedillo (PRI)—Centre
2001	Oportunidades	15.6	3.1	14.95	19.41	1,246	Fox (PAN) Centre-right
2002	Oportunidades	21.6	4.2	20.48	24.70	1,142	Fox (PAN) Centre-right
2003	Oportunidades	21.6	4.2	20.23	30.28	1,400	Fox (PAN) Centre-right
2004	Oportunidades	25.0	5.0	23.09	32.09	1,283	Fox (PAN) Centre-right
2005	Oportunidades	24.5	5.0	22.32	36.23	1,479	Fox (PAN) Centre-right
2006	Oportunidades	25.0	5.0	22.45	37.33	1,493	Fox (PAN) Centre-right
2007	Oportunidades	25.0	5.0	22.10	39.01	1,560	Calderon (PAN) Centre-right
2008	Oportunidades	25.2	5.0	21.96	41.73	1,653	Calderon (PAN) Centre-right
2009	Oportunidades	26.0	5.2	22.30	45.16	1,734	Calderon (PAN) Centre-right
2010	Oportunidades	27.2	5.6	22.97	58.04	2,130	Calderon (PAN) Centre-right
2011	Oportunidades	28.6	5.8	23.72	50.58	1,771	Calderon (PAN) Centre-right
2012	Oportunidades	28.6	5.8	23.46	47.22	1,649	Calderon (PAN) Centre-right
2013	Prospera	29.0	5.9	23.45	55.39	1,909	Peña Nieto (PRI) Centre
2014	Prospera	28.2	6.1	22.49	59.33	2,104	Peña Nieto (PRI) Centre
2015	Prospera	28.2	6.1	22.19	58.50	2,075	Peña Nieto (PRI) Centre

Source: Author, based on Social Assistance Politics and Institutions (SAPI) database (UNU-WIDER 2018).

Table 20.2 Coverage of social assistance in Latin America and the Caribbean by type of programme

Programme title	Country	Type	Number of beneficiaries (millions)	Income group[1]	Poverty focus[2]
Bolsa Família (absorbed Bolsa Escola in 2003 and Child Labour Eradication in 2006)	Brazil	Income transfer plus	53.9	Upper middle income	High
Progresa-Oportunidades-Prospera (POP)	Mexico	Income transfer plus	28.1	Upper middle income	High
Beneficio de Prestaçao Continuada	Brazil	Pure income	10	Upper middle income	High
Renta Dignidad	Bolivia	Pure income	9.5	Lower middle income	High
Prêvidencia Rural	Brazil	Pure income	5.8	Upper middle income	Categorical
Red Unidos	Colombia	Income transfer plus	4.8	Upper middle income	High
Mas Familias en Acción	Colombia	Income transfer plus	4.6	Upper middle income	High
Mi Bono Seguro (replaced Mi Familia Progresa)	Guatemala	Income transfer plus	4.2	Lower middle income	High
Programa de Apoyo Alimentario (PAL)	Mexico	Income transfer plus	4.13	Upper middle income	High
Programa Familias para la inclusión social (replaced by Asignacion Universal por Hijo)	Argentina	Income transfer plus	3.5	Upper middle income	High
Pensiones Asistenciales — became Pensiones Solidarias 2009	Chile	Pure income	3.5	Upper middle income	Moderate
Programa de Atención a Jornaleros Agrícolas (PAJA)	Mexico	Public works	3.25	Upper middle income	High
Programa Juntos	Peru	Income transfer plus	3.2	Upper middle income	High
Bono Vida Mejor	Honduras	Income transfer plus	3	Lower middle income	High
70 y mas	Mexico	Pure income	3	Upper middle income	Categorical
Bono de Desarrollo Humano (Bono Solidario)	Ecuador	Income transfer plus	2.8	Lower middle income	High
Programa Solidaridad	Dominican Republic	Income transfer plus	2.3	Upper middle income	High
Bono Juancito Pinto	Bolivia	Pure income	2	Lower middle income	High
Programme of Advancement through Health and Education	Jamaica	Income transfer plus	1.59	Upper middle income	High
Pensiones para Adultos Mayores	Ecuador	Pure income	1.3	Lower middle income	Moderate
Pensiones Asistenciales	Argentina	Pure income	1.2	Upper middle income	Moderate
Bono Madre Niño and Bono Juana Azurduy de Padilla	Bolivia	Pure Income	1.2	Lower middle income	High

(continued)

Table 20.2 Continued

Programme title	Country	Type	Number of beneficiaries (millions)	Income group[1]	Poverty focus[2]
Colombia Mayor	Colombia	Pure income	1.2	Upper middle income	Moderate
Chile Solidario (replaced by Ingreso Etico Familiar)	Chile	Integrated antipoverty	1.1	Upper middle income	High
Pensiones Solidarias	Chile	Pure income	1	Upper middle income	Moderate
PRAF II	Honduras	Income transfer plus	0.85	Lower middle income	High
Tekopora/PROPAIS II	Paraguay	Income transfer plus	0.6	Lower middle income	High
Asignaciones Familiares	Uruguay	Pure income	0.6	Upper middle income	Categorical
Plan de Equidad (replaced Plan de Atención Nacional a la Emergencia Social)	Uruguay	Integrated antipoverty	0.6	Upper middle income	High
Momunidades Solidarias Rurales (before Red Solidaria)	El Salvador	Income transfer plus	0.4	Lower middle income	High
Pension 65	Peru	Pure income	0.4	Upper middle income	Moderate
Red de Oportunidades	Panama	Income transfer plus	0.32	Upper middle income	High
Avancemos	Costa Rica	Income transfer plus	0.17	Upper middle income	High
Target Conditional Cash Transfer Programme (TCCTP)	Trinidad and Tobago	Income transfer plus	0.16	High income	High
Ti Manman Cheri	Haiti	Income transfer plus	0.1	Low income	High
100 a los 70	Panama	Pure income	0.1	Upper middle income	High
Pensiones Alimentarias para Adultos Mayores	Paraguay	Pure income	0.1	Lower middle income	Moderate
Programa de Pensiones No-Contributivas por Vejez o Invalidez	Uruguay	Pure income	0.1	Upper middle income	Moderate
Régimen No Contributivo de Pensiones por Monto Básico	Costa Rica	Pure income	0.091	Upper middle income	High
Red de Protección y Promoción Social	Paraguay	Income transfer plus	0.05	Lower middle income	High
Pension Basica Universal	El Salvador	Pure income	0.02	Lower middle income	Moderate
Total Latin America and the Caribbean			164.831		
TOTAL developing world			900		

[1] This column classifies countries by income groups according to 2009 gross national income (GNI) per capita, calculated using the World Bank Atlas method. The groups are: low income, US$995 or less; lower middle income, US$996–3,945; upper middle income, US$3,946–12,195; and high income, US$12,196 or more.

[2] Poverty focus has three categories: high if targeted on extreme poverty or poverty; moderate if covering some of the non-poor; categorical covering poor and non-poor.

Source: Author, based on Social Assistance Politics and Institutions (SAPI) database UNU-WIDER 2018).

TRANSFER SIZE

Transfer size is connected with programme objectives and the principles underpinning programme design choices. Among human development programmes in Latin America, the generosity of transfers varies considerably. Measured as a percentage of household income, transfers range from 6 per cent in Brazil to nearly 20 per cent in Mexico (Grosh et al. 2008). Transfer size can be important in determining the poverty effectiveness of social assistance programmes. Larger transfers are likely to have greater effects on poverty reduction, but with limits. The results from some studies suggest that *ceteris paribus* the marginal social return to transfer size—in terms of increasing schooling, improving nutritional and health status, or reducing poverty—may become lower in high levels of transfers (see e.g. Bourguignon et al. 2003; Filmer and Schady 2009). There is an important gender dimension worth noting here. First, income transfers are given to mothers under the explicit assumption that women are more effective agents of social change, given that they are found to be more committed than men to the well-being of their children (Dwyer and Bruce 1988; Gómez-Hermosillo 2005). Second, the size of the educational grant for girls increases with school progression. This is with the explicit objective of providing incentives to keep girls at school to reduce gender inequalities at secondary and higher education.

REGULARITY AND DURATION

Regular, predictable, and reliable income transfers provide a minimum level of security that is essential for consumption smoothing and medium- and longer-term investment decisions. Empirical evidence suggests that regular transfers can relax credit constraints. In Brazil, the regularity of Prêvidencia Social Rural, which was introduced to cover informal workers, has enabled pensioners to access bank loans, as the membership to the programme seems to have reduced screening and other informational costs to lenders (Schwarzer 2000). Similar effects are reported from Bolivia (Martinez 2007), where a large percentage of beneficiaries of social pensions have invested part of their transfer in small-scale enterprises, livestock, and productive assets to support their households. In that context, social transfers are a critical element for protecting the poor and vulnerable.

As regards transfer duration, there is no rule of thumb to guide policy, as the optimal length of assistance may be contingent on the targeted population and the socio-economic context. Households facing extreme poverty are more likely to require a longer time frame of support to tackle accumulated deficits in productive capacity and basic capability. Human development programmes in Latin America provide support to the poorest families for a period long enough to build human capital among beneficiary children. POP, for example, makes payments in cash every two months, at distribution points or via savings accounts, and for periods that can last for several years until children graduate from high school.[7] The timing of policy is also important here. Nutritional and health interventions in early life are significant determinants for improving the productive capacity of people in adulthood. This connects to the issue of breaking the intergenerational transmissions of poverty and the factors that make poverty persist over time. In fact, there is limited knowledge on how POP and other transfer programmes should respond to the dynamics of poverty. (Villa and Niño-Zarazúa 2018) find that only 10.7 per cent of urban households and 11.6 per cent of rural households that were poor and recipients of POP in 2002 could have been 'graduated' from the programme ten years later. The real value of transfers is important too, as inflationary pressures can erode the purchasing power of transfers and undermine their effectiveness. In the next section, I briefly review the impact evidence emerging from POP and other transfer programmes in Latin America.

Impact evaluation of POP and other social assistance programmes in Latin America

The rigorous and independent evaluation protocol of POP has been one of its hallmarks. It marked a precedent to the general practice that characterized previous antipoverty policies in Mexico—and in most developing countries. Indeed, until the introduction of POP, social spending was hardly subjected to rigorous evaluations, meaning that governments lacked reliable information to assess whether programmes worked, and to take decisions to improve policy effectiveness. The decision to incorporate an experimental design to the impact evaluation protocol—opened to public scrutiny—also meant that impact results could be treated as reliable and detached from political manipulation. Indeed, impact studies played an important role in making the case to sustain POP during the political transition of 2000. The evaluation protocol also set a precedent in Mexico to assess social policy, and prompted other countries to adopt similar impact evaluation policies.

In the remainder of this section, I briefly discuss the impact evidence from POP and other social assistance programmes in Latin America. I pay attention to the effects on human capital and poverty, as these are two key policy objectives.[8] The first sub-section reviews impact studies on nutrition; the second presents evidence on health; the third reviews evidence on schooling; and the fourth discusses the impact on poverty. These sub-sections cannot review the available evidence in a systematic way but, instead, aim at

[7] In 2003, Progresa-Oportunidades, together with a Bansefi and a network of savings and credit cooperatives and microfinance institutions, began a programme to distribute payments through electronic savings accounts in nearly 1,800 branches that the network has across the country. By 2010, half a million households had received Oportunidades through debit cards. For a detailed discussion, see Masino and Niño-Zarazúa (2018).

[8] For a detailed review of the impact of social assistance programmes, see ILO (2010).

outlining general findings associated with these well-being dimensions. By and large, the focus is on quantitative studies, as their methodology facilitates a comparative discussion across countries and programmes.

IMPACT ON NUTRITION

Nutrition plays a central role in enhancing human development. A well-balanced diet is the foundation for healthy living and a central input for labour productivity. Good nutrition is especially important for young children, as critical cognitive development takes place at an early age (see Alderman et al. 2006; Glewwe and King 2001). Child (mal)nutrition is normally measured with the use of anthropometric data. Weight for age provides insights into the short-term impact of improved nutrition, whereas height for age provides information on the long-term effects of improved nutrition. Height for age is particularly informative as regards the longer-term impact of social transfers, as studies have consistently found that height deficits originating in early life are associated with limited cognitive development (Hoddinott and Kinsey 2001), and low future earning capacity (Thomas and Strauss 1997).

Evaluation studies of POP find that children exposed to the programme gained one centimetre in height for age compared to a control group, two years after the start of the programmes. The gain was 0.65cm six years after the start of the programme (Neufeld et al. 2005). In Ecuador, households receiving support from Bono de Desarrollo Humano had a 25 per cent increase in food expenditure, which was linked to improvements in nutritional status (Ponce and Bedi 2010). In Colombia, a substantial increase in intake of protein-rich foods and vegetables was reported as a result of participation in Familias en Acción (Attanasio 2003). Changes in consumption especially benefited small children: 12-month-old boys grew 0.44cm more than similar children who did not benefit from the transfer. A more recent review of the literature (Manley et al. 2013) concludes that transfer programmes on average have positive effects on height-for-age measures, although the size of the effect is small. Most disadvantaged areas and girls seem to benefit more from transfer programmes.

IMPACT ON HEALTH

By design, human development programmes in Latin America have the objective of improving access to, and utilization of, health services as a direct means of improving the health status of programme beneficiaries. Overall, programmes appear to have met their objectives. An evaluation of Colombia's Familias en Acción reports a rise in the percentage of children under twenty-four months attending healthcare check-ups (Attanasio et al. 2005). Improved utilization of healthcare facilities directly affects morbidity rates. The proportion of children affected by diarrhoea declined from 32 per cent to 22 per cent among children under 24 months, and from 21.3 per cent to 10.4 per cent among older children.

Similar improvements in healthcare utilization have been reported from Mexico, Chile, and Nicaragua. In Mexico, POP is reported to have doubled the per capita healthcare visits in rural communities A study of Chile Solidario reports that preventative health care among children living in rural areas improved in the order of 4 to 6 percentage points (Galasso 2006). In Nicaragua, Red de Protección Social was associated with an 18 per cent increase in immunization among children aged 12–23 months (Maluccio and Flores 2004). In-time immunizations can play a significant role in reducing illness and premature deaths among toddlers. In Mexico, a study reports a 12 per cent lower incidence of illness among children receiving support from POP vis-à-vis a corresponding control group (Skoufias 2005). A recent systematic review of the literature on health impacts, predominantly from programmes operating in Latin America, found that transfer programmes, together with relative well-functioning health systems, are effective policies in improving child health by addressing constraints to healthcare accessibility, maternal malnutrition, morbidity risks, and immunization coverage (Owusu-Addo and Cross 2014).

IMPACT ON SCHOOLING

The design of POP has been shaped by the knowledge that reducing poverty requires effective policy instruments to improve schooling among the poor. Studies have found a strong correlation between the programme and several education-related outcomes, including higher school enrolment rates, less grade repetition, better grade progression, lower dropout rates, and higher school re-entry rates among dropouts. The impact was especially notable in rural areas, where the number of children entering the first grade of secondary school rose by 85 per cent and second grade by 47 per cent (Molyneux 2007); dropout rates decreased by 24 per cent, with a corresponding rise in completion rates of 23 per cent for rural secondary schools (Skoufias and di Maro 2005). These results predict an increase in children's future permanent earnings by about 8 per cent when they reach adulthood (see Freije et al. 2006).

In middle-income countries, where enrolment in primary education is nearly universal, the impact of social assistance has been more significant on secondary education (see e.g. Attanasio et al. 2005; Cardoso and Portela Souza 2003; Schady and Araujo 2006). The extent to which these changes translate into improvements in knowledge and reduction in intergenerational transmissions of poverty is, however, more difficult to confirm at present. Schooling is a necessary, but not sufficient, condition to ensure that beneficiary children reach the labour markets with improved educational attainment levels. The quality of education and the functioning of domestic labour markets are also important.

IMPACT ON POVERTY AND INEQUALITY

A key objective of social assistance in Latin America is to reduce poverty. There is a large literature assessing the poverty reduction effectiveness of these programmes. The findings from these studies cover social transfers of different typology and operating in different settings. In Mexico, an evaluation of POP showed a small reduction in the poverty headcount ratio—in the order of 10 per cent after two years of programme implementation; however, a large reduction in the poverty gap and the squared poverty gap[9] was reported with reductions in the order of 30 per cent and 45 per cent, respectively (Hoddinott et al. 2000; Skoufias 2005). This is confirmed by more recent studies which find greater impact on the poverty gap and poverty severity than on the headcount index (see e.g. Cortés et al. 2007). At the national level, the programme is reported to have reduced about 1 per cent in terms of the food-based poverty line, while in rural areas, the poverty impact has been between two to three times greater than the one observed nationwide. Many other impact studies conducted in Latin America consistently confirm the positive impact of social assistance on poverty and food security.[10]

More recently, and amid the global financial crisis, some critics have questioned the effectiveness of POP in addressing poverty. Between 2006 and 2008, the headcount index that measures the food-based poverty incidence increased from 13.8 per cent to 18.2 per cent, whereas the capability-based poverty incidence, which in addition to the food-based basket includes other expenditure items such as healthcare, education, clothing, housing, and public transport, increased from 20.7 per cent to 25.1 per cent. However, the setback in poverty reduction can be attributed to the level of systemic vulnerabilities that Mexico and other developing countries have faced against covariate shocks. In particular, the increase in international food prices, especially staples that averaged 43 per cent between March 2007 and March 2008 (FAO 2008) caused an annual growth in the food basket values of about 18 per cent in 2008. This had a significant negative income effect on households at the lowest income quintile. And with the global spread of the financial crisis, the net per capita income experienced a fall of nearly 13 per cent

[9] The poverty gap measures the mean distance below the poverty line or income threshold that separates the poor from the non-poor, as a proportion of the poverty line, where the mean is taken over the entire population, counting the non-poor as having zero poverty gap. In order words, the poverty gap is an indicator of poverty intensity, reflecting the amount of income that would be needed to bring the poor above the poverty line, i.e. to eliminate poverty. While the poverty gap measures the distance that separates the poor from the poverty line, the squared poverty gap measures the squared of that distance and can be seen as an indicator of poverty severity. The squared poverty gap takes inequality among the poor into account by giving more weight to the poorest.

[10] For the case of Brazil's Bolsa Família, see Lindert et al. (2007); for a discussion on Ecuador's Bono de Desarrollo Humano, see Ponce (2008); for a study of Colombia's Familias en Acción, see Attanasio et al. (2005); and for studies of social pensions in Chile, Argentina, Uruguay, and Bolivia, see Bertranou et al. (2002), and Bertranou and Grushka (2002).

between 2006 and 2008, with remittances and wages dropping by 29 per cent and 26 per cent, respectively (see Consejo Nacional de Evaluacion de la Politica de Desarrollo Social 2009). These figures are likely to have only partially captured the full extent of the impact of the financial crisis, as the GDP growth rate fell by -6 per cent in 2009.

It is worth noting here that the income contribution of POP to poor households increased by 20 per cent, which reflects the direct public intervention introduced in 2008 to address food insecurity in the country (Barrientos and Niño-Zarazúa 2011). Moreover, it is estimated that in the absence of POP and other social protection programmes in the country, the food-based headcount index would have increased by 13.5 per cent, which represents about 2.6 million additional people in extreme poverty, 2.2 million of whom would have lived in rural areas and 0.4 million in urban areas (Consejo Nacional de Evaluacion de la Politica de Desarrollo Social 2009). So although covariate shocks are at the root of the recent poverty increase in Mexico, poverty would have been much higher had POP not been in place.

There is often an expectation that social transfers could have effects beyond the reduction of poverty and contribute to reducing income inequality. Transfer programmes in industrialized countries are generally referred to as having effectively contributed to reducing income inequalities. But it is often forgotten that the coverage and size of these programmes are of a different order of magnitude from the ones operating in Latin America and other developing countries. Moreover, the Gini coefficient of industrialized nations is on average significantly lower than in Latin America. Nonetheless, and with a share of about 0.5 per cent of GDP in Brazil and Mexico, social transfer programmes are reported to have contributed to a 21 per cent reduction of income inequality, in relative terms (Soares et al. 2007). Other studies of Brazil's Bolsa Família (Lindert et al. 2007) and Beneficio de Prestaçao Continuada (Soares et al. 2006), also report contributions from these programmes in *relative* reductions in the Gini coefficient.

However, the distributional argument should not be mistaken. The contribution of these programmes to an *absolute* reduction in the aggregate Gini coefficient is marginal. In 2001, for instance, Brazil's, Mexico's, and Chile's Gini coefficients were in the order of 0.58, 0.51, and 0.55, respectively. By 2007, the Gini coefficient of these countries had reduced, marginally, to 0.55, 0.51, and 0.52, respectively (World Bank 2016). This is simply because the lowest deciles of income distribution receive a very small share of aggregate income. Nevertheless, as pointed out, evidence shows that these programmes can contribute to addressing inequality among the poor, via reductions in the poverty gap and the squared poverty gap.

All in all, the overview of impact studies presented in this section shows that social assistance makes a significant contribution to reducing poverty and facilitating human capital investment. The capacity of social assistance in improving well-being outcomes is, nonetheless, heterogeneous across programmes, target groups, and socio-economic environments. Design factors, programme objectives, and institutional, political, and financial considerations seem to play an important role in programme effectiveness.

Conclusion

Analysis of Mexico's POP and other social assistance programmes in Latin America shows that these programmes are effective in addressing poverty and severe deficits in well-being. They have led to an important shift in antipoverty policy thinking, moving from food aid and subsidies to reliable and predictable forms of assistance. Important policy lessons can be drawn from the presented discussion.

First, the emergence of social assistance reflects important advancements in the conventional wisdom on the causes of extreme poverty. Human development programmes have paid special attention to reducing extreme poverty and facilitating human capital investment. The latter is particularly relevant to tackling the intergenerational transmission mechanisms of persistent deprivation. Second, design features have relied on strong theoretical principles underpinning programmes' objectives. In particular, they justify the focus on the poor and the multidimensional approach to poverty. This is in clear contrast to food aid in-kind subsidies that dominated antipoverty interventions in the past.

Third, the success of POP and other transfer programmes in Latin America must be understood in a broader context. For Mexico, the harsh economic environment that preceded the introduction of POP, coupled with a democratic transition and increasing political competition, laid down the foundations for the introduction and then sustained expansion of the programme.

Fourth, well-designed systems of identification and selection of beneficiaries have set a precedent in several Latin American countries to prevent discretionary political manipulation that characterized past social policies. That has helped to generate political legitimacy and support across the political spectrum. The inclusion of rigorous impact evaluation protocols also meant that governments could test and improve programmes' effectiveness, while strengthening their legitimacy.

Fifth, limited financial resources also meant that the incumbent government had the political motivation to replace highly regressive and ineffective food and in-kind subsidies, and that political decisions prevented the government from incurring additional costs when POP was rolled out. Financing has emerged as a key constraint in extending social assistance in Latin America and developing countries as a whole. The fiscal space to sustain social assistance is conditional on size of economy, efficiency of tax collection systems, scale and scope of the interventions, but also external factors such as the international price of commodities.

For most countries in Latin America, public spending on social assistance has remained stable, largely because of the size and structure of most economies in the region, although the recent fall in international commodity prices has meant that lower middle-income countries face important challenges for the future financing of social assistance. The experience of Mexico's POP has shown that interaction between government, research community, bilaterals and multilaterals is paramount to advancing knowledge in the area of poverty to increase impact and improve policy and practice, while political conditions are as relevant as financial considerations.

REFERENCES

Alderman, H., Hoogeveen, H., and Rossi, M. (2006). 'Reducing child malnutrition in Tanzania: combined effects of income growth and program interventions', *Economics & Human Biology* 4: 1–23.

Attanasio, O. (2003). *Baseline Report on the Evaluation of 'Familias en Acción'*. London: Institute for Fiscal Studies.

Attanasio, O., Battistin, E., Fitzsimons, E., and Mesnard, A. (2005). 'How effective are conditional cash transfers?'. *Institute for Fiscal Studies Briefing Note No. 54.* London: Institute for Fiscal Studies.

Barrientos, A. (2013). *Social Assistance in Developing Countries.* Cambridge: Cambridge University Press.

Barrientos, A. and Hulme, D. (2008). 'Social Protection for the poor and poorest in developing countries: Reflections on a quiet revolution'. BWPI Working Paper No. 30. Manchester: Brooks World Poverty Institute, University of Manchester.

Barrientos, A. and Neff, D. (2010). 'Attitudes to chronic poverty in the "Global Village"', *Social Indicators Research* 100/1: 101–14.

Barrientos, A. and Niño-Zarazúa, M. (2011). 'Financing social protection for children in crisis contexts', *Development Policy Review* 29/5: 603–20.

Barrientos, A., Niño-Zarazúa, M., and Maitrot, M. (2010). *Social Assistance in Developing Countries Database* (version 5.0). Manchester: Chronic Poverty Research Centre.

Bertranou, F. and Grushka, C.O. (2002). *The Non-Contributory Pension Programme in Argentina: Assessing the Impact on Poverty Reduction.* Geneva: ILO.

Bertranou, F., Solorio, C., and Van Ginneken, W. (2002). *Pensiones no-contributivas y asistenciales* [Non-contributory and welfare pensions]. *Argentina, Brazil, Chile, Costa Rica y Uruguay.* Santiago: ILO.

Bourguignon, F., Ferreira F.H., and Leite, P.G. (2003). 'Conditional cash transfers, schooling and child labor: micro-simulating Brazil's Bolsa Escola program', *World Bank Economic Review* 17/2: 229–54.

Cardoso, E. and Portela Souza, A. (2003). *The Impacts of Cash Transfers on Child Labor and School Attendance in Brazil.* Sao Paolo: Department of Economics University of Sao Paolo.

Consejo Nacional De Evaluacion De La Politica De Desarrollo Social (2009). 'Reporta CONEVAL cifras de pobreza por Ingresos 2008' [Report CONEVAL poverty figures by income 2008], in Dirección de Información y Comunicación Social (ed.) *Comunicado de Prensa No. 006/09.* Mexico City.

Cortés, F., Banegas, I., and Solís, P. (2007). 'Pobres con oportunidades: Mexico 2002–2005' [Poor opportunities: Mexico 2002–2005], *Estudios Sociologicos* XXV: 3–40.

Dagnino, E., Olvera, A., and Panfichi, A. (2006). 'Introducción: Para otra lectura de la disputa por la construcción democrática en América Latina' [Introduction: Another reading of the democratic construction dispute in Latin America], in E. Dagnino, A. Olvera, and A. Panfichi (eds) *La Disputa por la Construcción Democrática en América Latina.* Mexico City: FCE, CIESAS, UV. Available at https://controlatugobierno.com/archivos/bibliografia/olveradisputa.pdf, accessed 14 March 2019.

Dahlberg, M. and Johansson, E. (2002). 'On the vote-purchasing behavior of incumbent governments', *American Political Science Review* 96/1: 27–40.

de Brauw, A. and Hoddinott, J. (2008). 'Must conditional cash transfer programs be conditioned to be effective? The impact of conditioning transfers on school enrollment in Mexico'. IFPRI Dicussion Paper No 005757. Washington, DC: International Food Policy Research Institute.

Dion, M. (2000). 'La economía política del gasto social: el Programa de Solidaridad de México, 1988–1994' [The Political Economy of Social Spending: Mexico's Solidaridad programme, 1984–1994], *Estudios Sociológicos* 18/53: 329–62.

Duflo, E. (2000). *Grandmothers and Granddaughters: Old Age Pension and Intra-Household Allocation in South Africa*. Cambridge, MA: National Bureau of Economic Research.

Dwyer, D. and Bruce, J. (eds) (1988). *A Home Divided: Women and Income in the Third World*. Standford, CA: Stanford University Press.

Escobar Latapi, A. (2002). 'The Progresa Programme and social change in rural Mexico', in L. Haagh, and C.T. Helø (eds) *Social Policy Reform and Market Governance in Latin America*. New York: Palgrave Macmillan, 219–41.

FAO (Food and Agriculture Organization) (2008). *Food Outlook, Global Market Analysis*. Rome: FAO.

Filipovich, D., Niño-Zarazúa, M., and Santillán Hernández, A. (2018). 'Campaign externalities, programmatic spending, and voting preferences in rural Mexico: the case of Progresa-Oportunidades-Prospera Programme'. WIDER Working Paper 2018/27. Helsinki: UNU-WIDER.

Filipovich, Dragan, Niño-Zarazúa, Miguel, and Santillán-Hernanez, Alma (forthcoming). 'Information externalities, programmatic spending and voting preferences. The case of Mexico's Progresa-Oportunidades-Prospera program', *European Journal of Political Economy*.

Filmer, D. and Schady, N. (2009). 'Are there diminishing returns to transfer size in conditional cash transfers?'. Policy Research Working Paper 4999. Washington, DC: World Bank.

Fiszbein, A. and Schady, N. (2009). 'Conditional cash transfers: reducing present and future poverty'. A World Bank Policy Research Report. Washington, DC: World Bank.

Freije, S., Bando, R., and Arce, F. (2006). 'Conditional transfers, labour supply, and poverty: Microsimulating Oportunidades', *Economía* 7/1: 73–124.

Galasso, E. (2006). *'With Their Effort and One Opportunity': Alleviating Extreme Poverty in Chile*. Washington, DC: World Bank, Development Research Group.

Gibson, E.L. and Calvo, E. (2000). 'Federalism and low-maintenance constituencies: territorial dimensions of economic reform in Argentina', *Studies in Comparative International Development* 35/3: 32–5.

Gil-Diaz, F. and Carstens, A. (1996). 'One year of solitude: some pilgrim tales about Mexico's 1994–1995 crisis', *American Economic Review* 86/2: 164–9.

Glewwe, P. and King, E.M. (2001). 'The impact of early childhood nutritional status on cognitive development: does the timing of malnutrition matter?' *World Bank Economic Review* 15/1: 81–113.

Gómez-Hermosillo, R. (2005). *Con oportunidades las mujeres mejoran sus condiciones de vida e incrementan su autonomía* [With *Oportunidades*, women improve their living conditions and increase their autonomy]. Mexico City: Coordinación Nacional del Programa de Desarrollo Humano Oportunidades.

Grosh, M., Del Ninno, C., Tesliuc, E., and Ouerghi, A. (2008). *For Protection and Promotion. The Design and Implementation of Effective Safety Nets.* Washington, DC: World Bank.

Grugel, J. and P. Riggirozzi (2012). 'Post-neoliberalism in Latin America: rebuilding and reclaiming the state after crisis', *Development and Change* 43(1): 1–21.

Hevia de la Jara, F. (2008). 'Between individual and collective action: citizen participation and public oversight in Mexico's Oportunidades programme', *IDS Bulletin* 38/6: 64–72.

Hoddinott, J. and Kinsey, B. (2001). 'Child health in the time of drought', *Oxford Bulletin of Economics and Statistics* 63/4: 409–36.

Hoddinott, J. and Quisumbing, A. (2003). 'Methods for microeconometric risk and vulnerability assessments'. Social Protection Discussion Paper Series No. 324. Washington, DC: World Bank.

Hoddinott, J., Skoufias, E., and Washburn, R. (2000). *The Impact of PROGRESA on Consumption: A Final Report.* Washington, DC: International Food Policy Research Institute (IFPRI).

ILO (International Labour Organization) (2001). *Social Security. A New Consensus.* Geneva: ILO.

ILO (International Labour Organization) (2010). *Effects of Non-Contributory Social Transfers in Developing Countries: A Compendium.* Geneva: ILO.

IMF (International Monetary Fund) (2009). *Government Finance Statistics Database.* Washington, DC: IMF.

Levy, S. (2006). *Progress against Poverty. Sustaining Mexico's POP Program.* Washington, DC: Brookings Institution Press.

Levy, S. and Rodríguez, E. (2004). 'El Programa de Educación, Salud y Alimentación, PROGRESA – Programa de desarrollo humano oportunidades' [PROGRESA, an education, health and nutrition programme – Oportunidades, a human development programme], in S. Levy (ed.) *Ensayos Sobre Desarrollo Económico y Social de México* [Essays on the economic and social development of Mexico]. Mexico City: Fondo de Cultura Económica, 181–379.

Lindert, K., Linder, A., Hobbs, J., and De La Brière, B. (2007). 'The nuts and bolts of Brazil's Bolsa Família program: Implementing conditional cash transfers in a decentralized context'. World Bank Social Protection Discussion Paper No. 0709. Washington, DC: World Bank.

Mainwaring, S. and Pérez-Liñán, A. (2014). *Democracies and Dictatorships in Latin America: Emergence, Survival, and Fall.* Cambridge: Cambridge University Press.

Maluccio, J.A. and Flores, R. (2004). *Impact Evaluation of a Conditional Cash Transfer Programmes: The Nicaraguan Red de Protección Social.* Washington, DC: IFPRI.

Manley, J., Gitter, S., and Slavchevska, V. (2013). 'How effective are cash transfers at improving nutritional status?', *World Development* 48: 133–55.

Martinez, S. (2007). 'Invertir el Bonosol para aliviar la pobreza: Retornos económicos en los hogares beneficiarios' [Bonosol as an invesrtment to alleviate poverty. economic returns of beneficiary households], in G. Aponte, L. C. Jemio, R. Laserna, S. Martinez, F. Molina, E. Schulze et al. (eds) La Inversión Prudente. Impacto del Bonosol Sobre la Familia, la Equidad Social y el Crecimiento Económico [Prudent investment. impact of Bonosol on the family, social equity and economic growth]. La Paz, Bolivia: Fundación Milenio, 109–28.

Masino, S. and Niño-Zarazúa, M. (2018). 'Improving financial inclusion through the delivery of Cash Transfer Programmes: the case of Mexico's Progresa-Oportunidades-Prospera Programme', *Journal of Development Studies.* Available at https://doi.org/10.1080/00220388.2018.1546845, accessed 14 March 2019.

Molinar Horcasitas, J. and Weldon, J.A. (eds) (1994). *Electoral Determinants and Consequences of National Solidarity*. San Diego, CA: University of California, Center for US-Mexican Studies, UCSD.

Molyneux, M. (2007). *Change and Continuity in Social Protection in Latin America: Mothers at the Service of the State? Programme on Gender and Development*. Geneva: United Nations Research Institute for Social Development (UNRISD).

Neufeld, L., Sotres Alvarez, D., Gertler, P., Tolentino Mayo, L., Jimenez Ruiz, J., Fernald, L.C. et al. (2005). 'Impacto de Oportunidades en el crecimiento y el estado de nutrición de niños en zonal rurales' [The impact of *Oportunidades* on nutrition and child development in rural areas], in B. Hernández Prado and M. Hernández Avila (eds) *Evaluación Externa de Impacto del Programa Oportunidades 2004: Alimentación* [External impact evaluation of the 2004 Oportunidades Program: food]. Cuernavaca, Mexico: Instituto Nacional de Salud Pública, 17–49.

Owusu-Addo, E. and Cross, R. (2014). 'The impact of conditional cash transfers on child health in low- and middle-income countries: a systematic review', *International Journal of Public Health* 59/4: 609–18.

Pastor, M. and Wise, C. (1999). 'The politics of second-generation reform', *Journal of Democracy* 10/3: 34–48.

Ponce, J. (2008). *Education Policy and Performance. Evaluating the Impact of Targeted Education Programs in Ecuador*. Maastricht: Shaker Publishing.

Ponce, J. and Bedi, A.S. (2010). 'The impact of a cash transfer program on cognitive achievement: The Bono de Desarrollo Humano of Ecuador', *Economics of Education Review* 29/1: 116–25.

Rabin, M. (2000). 'Risk aversion and expected-utility theory: a calibration theorem', *Econometrica* 65: 1281–92.

Rawls, J. (1971). *A Theory of Justice*. Cambridge, MA: Harvard University Press.

Schady, N. (2000). 'The political economy of expenditures by the Peruvian Social Fund (FONCODES), 1991–1995', *American Political Science Review* 94/2: 288–304.

Schady, N. and Araujo, M.C. (2006). *Cash Transfers, Conditions, School Enrolment, and Child Work: Evidence from a Randomized Experiment in Ecuador*. Washington, DC: World Bank.

Schwarzer, H. (2000). *Impactos socioeconômicos do sistema de aposentadorias rurais no Brazil—Evidências empíricas de un estudio de caso no estado de Pará* [Socioeconomic impacts of the rural pension system in Brazil. Empirical evidence from the state of Pará]. Rio de Janeiro: IPEA (Institute de Pesquisa Econômica Aplicada).

Secretaria De Desarrollo Social (2002). *Medición de la Pobreza. Variantes metodológicas y estimación preliminar* [Poverty measurement. Methods and preliminary estimates]. *Documentos de investigación*. Mexico City: Comité Técnico para la Medición de la Pobreza.

Skoufias, E. (2005). 'Progresa and its impacts on the welfare of rural households in Mexico'. Research Report. Washington, DC: International Food Policy Research Institute (IFPRI).

Skoufias, E. and Di Maro, V. (2005). *Conditional Cash Transfers, Adult Work Incentives and Current Poverty*. Washington, DC: World Bank.

Soares, F.V., Soares, S., Medeiros, M., and Osório, R.G. (2006). 'Cash transfer programmes in Brazil: impacts on inequality and poverty'. International Poverty Centre Working Paper. Brazil: International Poverty Centre.

Soares, S., Guerreiro Osório, R., Veras Soares, F., Medeiros, M., and Zepeda, E. (2007). 'Conditional cash transfers in Brazil, Chile and Mexico: impacts upon inequality'. International Poverty Centre Working Paper. Brazil: International Poverty Centre.

Somuano, M.F., Perez Yarahuan, G., Ortega, R., Zavaleta, D., Ponce, O., and Ibarra, J.F. (2006). *Analisis de la vinculation del gasto de programas sociales con variables electorales. Monitoreo de Programas Sociales en Contextos Electorales* [Analysis of the association between spending on social programs and electoral variables. Monitoring of social programs in electoral contexts]. Mexico, DF: El Colegio de Mexico.

Teichman, J. (2008). 'Redistributive conflict and social policy in Latin America', *World Development* 36/3: 446–60.

Thomas, D. and Strauss, J. (1997). 'Health and wages: evidence on men and women in urban Brazil', *Journal of Econometrics* 77/1: 159–85.

UNICEF (2000). *A League Table of Child Poverty in Rich Nations*. Innocenti Report Card No 1. Florence: UNICEF.

UNU-WIDER (2018). Social Assistance, Politics, and Institutions (SAPI) database. Helsinki: United Nations University World Institute for Development Economics Research (UNU-WIDER). Available at www.wider.unu.edu/project/sapi-social-assistance-politics-and-institutions-database, accessed 16 January 2019.

Villa, J.M. and Niño-Zarazúa, M. (2018). 'Poverty dynamics and graduation from conditional cash transfers: a transition model for Mexico's Progresa-Oportunidades-Prospera program', *Journal of Economic Inequality*. doi:10.1007/s10888-018-9399-5.

Wagstaff, A. and Watanabe, N. (2000). 'Socioeconomic inequalities in child malnutrition in the developing world'. Policy Research Working Paper 2434. Washington, DC: World Bank.

World Bank (2006). *World Development Report 2006: Equity and Development*. Washington, DC: World Bank.

World Bank (2016). *World Development Indicators*. Washington, DC: World Bank. Available at https://databank.worldbank.org/data/source/world-development-indicators, accessed 14 March 2019.

21 Minimum wages and inequality in Mexico

An example (not) to follow

Alice Krozer, Stefanie Garry, and Juan Carlos Moreno-Brid

Introduction

Mexico is a country full of contradictions: despite ranking fifteenth among the wealthiest countries in the world by GDP, more than half of its population continues to live below the poverty line. As the Mexican National Council on the Evaluation of Social Development Policy (CONEVAL) reports (CONEVAL 2015), this share is increasing: in 2014 more than 53.2 per cent of the population was poor, while in 2008 the figure was 49.0 per cent. At the other extreme, the country's richest man, Carlos Slim, in 2015 owned wealth equivalent to almost 6 per cent of the country's GDP—more than the federal government's average annual healthcare expenditure (Krozer 2016). His income over the last year corresponds to almost half a million (470,623) times the country's average income. At the same time, the family of a worker earning the official minimum wage of MXN $73.04 (less than US$5) per day remains below the country's national poverty line.

In the context of such extreme disparities, a passionate debate over increasing the minimum wage was sparked in 2014 by Miguel Ángel Mancera, then mayor of Mexico City. Although it has gained momentum in the public discourse over the past year, the campaign to raise the minimum wage at the national level was met with remarkable resistance from certain private sector actors.[1] Despite a nominal increase in the minimum wage in January 2016, related policy proposals to invoke deeper changes remain stuck in the legislature. This curious resistance is interesting for at least four reasons: For one, Mexico is currently the most (or second-to-most, depending on the indicator used) unequal country in the OECD (OCED 2015), and among the top 25 per cent of the most

[1] For instance Juan Pablo Castañon, President of the Mexican Employers' Confederation, Juan Manuel Chaparro, a member of the Mexican Chamber of Industry, Canacintra, but also Aristóteles Nuñez, Chief of the Mexican Taxation Authority (SAT for its initials in Spanish) (Krozer et al. 2015).

Alice Krozer, Stefanie Garry, and Juan Carlos Moreno-Brid, *Minimum wages and inequality in Mexico: An example (not) to follow* In: *Handbook of BRICS and Emerging Economies*. Edited by: P.B. Anand, Shailaja Fennell, and Flavio Comim, Oxford University Press (2021).

DOI: 10.1093/oso/9780198827535.003.0021

unequal countries in the world, yet it lacks any consistent policy to address its inequalities. However, while acknowledging the potential benefits for poverty reduction, the debate has rarely considered the impact minimum wages may have on income distribution.

Second, at the same time, Mexico's notoriously high levels of inequality are matched by infamously low levels of minimum wages. Mexico continues to be the only country in the region with a minimum wage below the poverty line. Since the 1980s the Mexican Federal Government's labour policy has pushed the country's minimum wage into sharp deterioration. For decades its amount has been far below the level of 'adequate remuneration to meet the normal material, social and cultural requirements of a head of household, and to provide for the compulsory education of their children' as required by Article 123 Ap.VI of the Mexican Constitution. In fact it is insufficient to even cover the basic food basket, not to mention the enlarged basket including non-food items such as shelter. The deterioration of the minimum wage went hand in hand with a reduction in the share of wages in national income and an increase in inequality. These features are particularly problematic upon recognition of Mexico's historically unequal income distribution.

The third surprising element to this resistance is its timing. Despite significant steps by other G20 countries, including Mexico's northern neighbour and longstanding role model with regard to economic policies, the United States, South American countries including Brazil, and many European Union members such as Germany and the United Kingdom to introduce or significantly increase minimum wages at both local and national levels, Mexico appears to be stuck with policies to only very marginally increase real wages. This trend across many advanced economies recognizes increases in minimum wages as an explicit anti-inequality policy, acknowledging an association between, or at least evidence of the effectiveness of the minimum wage as a tool to decrease inequality. Similar steps are also being taken across the Latin American region. As this chapter will demonstrate, across the majority of Latin American countries, the trend to increase minimum wages often occurs in combination with decreasing levels of income inequality.

A fourth remarkable facet of the Mexican discussion concerns the locus of resistance. The debate has triggered an unusual alliance of supporters and adversaries criss-crossing traditional institutional lines. On the one hand, the National Minimum Wage Commission (CONASAMI), and some large unions and employers' organizations staunchly oppose a significant increase in the minimum wage, while on the other side civil society representatives, academics, and senior bankers, among others are in support of a rise. Paradoxically in Mexico, partisan lines have been rather blurred on this issue.

An ample body of literature has discussed the role of labour income as a key determinant of household resiliency in Latin America (see ECLAC 2014). However, much of this research on the effects of minimum wages has focused on its impact on poverty, and poverty reduction. As such, in Mexico, the relationship between poverty and the insufficient capacity of the minimum wage to provide a decent standard of living has been clearly captured, yet the relationship between inequality and the minimum wage has not been fully explored. Overall, little attention has been focused on the precise relationship between the minimum wage, a key component of labour and household income for many workers in Latin America, and its relationship to inequality trends over recent decades.[2]

In light of these puzzles and research gaps, the purpose of this chapter is to examine the status and dynamics of the minimum wage in Mexico and its relation with income inequality from a Latin American comparative perspective. In this context, we are mostly interested in juxtaposing the Mexican experience with the cases of Brazil, Argentina, and Chile, as three countries of roughly comparable economic development in the region pursuing labour policies diametrically opposing those of Mexico. What might be the relationship between minimum wages and inequality in Mexico, and could the former play a role in improving the country's income distribution? Should other countries aim to emulate the Mexican road to exceptionality in this terrain? Or could Mexico instead learn from the diverging experience of other countries? These major issues in the minimum wage debate, as outlined above, will be explored in detail in the subsequent sections, in an attempt to better understand the correlation and potential links between persistent inequality and labour policy, with the aim of providing some recommendations to policymakers.

To that end, first a current picture of the status of inequalities in Mexico will be drawn (second section), followed by a brief outline of the historical development of the country's labour share of gross national income (third section). Subsequently, trends in the minimum wage in Mexico, including a discussion of the most recent developments in the debate will be presented, and compared to the performance of a number of relevant Latin American countries (fourth section). Thereafter, the role of productivity in the development of the minimum wage will be explored (fifth section); as will be shown, the often used argument that minimum wages should not rise due to lagging productivity does not hold for Mexico. Next, the cases of Brazil and Mexico will be scrutinized more closely to better understand the interactions between their respective minimum wages and levels of inequality (sixth section). The final section concludes with a brief outlook on the likely developments in the minimum wage discourse and proposes some steps to be taken to improve its perspective.

[2] Unfortunately not all data sources have information available up to the latest year. Depending on the source used, we are thus able to look at time series spanning between two and three decades, lying somewhere between the early 1980s to the mid-2010s. Due to diverging methodological decisions in their respective definitions of 'income', moreover, quoted results such as Gini coefficients or shares tend to diverge slightly across institutions.

Interpersonal income inequality in Mexico and Latin America

Many Latin American countries managed to achieve (sometimes significant) reductions in inequality in the 2000s,[3] prompting scholars to celebrate 'Latin America's inequality success story' (Lustig 2013), which was to end the growth of inequality in the region. However, since 2010 this decline has slowed markedly, and in a number of countries inequality levels now seem to be on the rise again (Gasparini et al. 2016).

This is especially acute for Mexico (and Honduras), where inequality as measured by the Gini coefficient has increased the most over the period from 2010 to 2014, at an annual rate of 0.4 points (see Figure 21.1). Inequality dynamics in Argentina, Brazil, and Chile, on the other hand, display the exact opposite pattern: while inequality was increasing in the 1990s (stagnating in Chile), all three countries have seen their levels improve in recent years (though at a slower pace than in the 2000s). Although its current Gini coefficient rank of 49 places the country within the middle ranks of the region (and ahead of Brazil and Chile), Latin America by itself remains one of the most unequal regions in the world, placing Mexico among the highest inequality countries on a global level. Moreover, Mexico's preoccupying trend of increasing inequality has it stand out even in a Latin American comparative perspective.

The extent of the country's persistent inequality is illustrated by a few stark numbers. For instance, the difference between average incomes in the top and bottom deciles of the

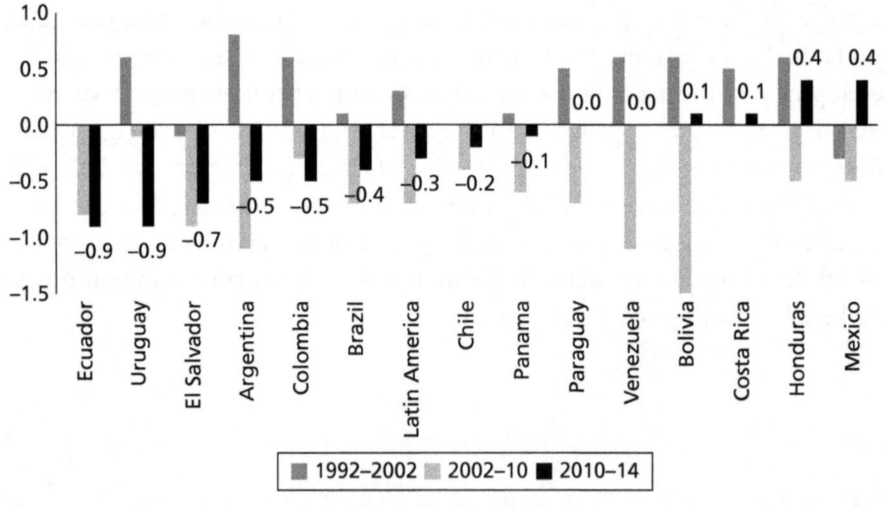

Figure 21.1 Annual changes in Gini coefficients, 1992–2014

Source: Authors' own elaboration based on Gasparini et al. (2016).

3 See, e.g. Lustig (2013), Lustig et al. (2012), and Lopez-Calva and Lustig (2010).

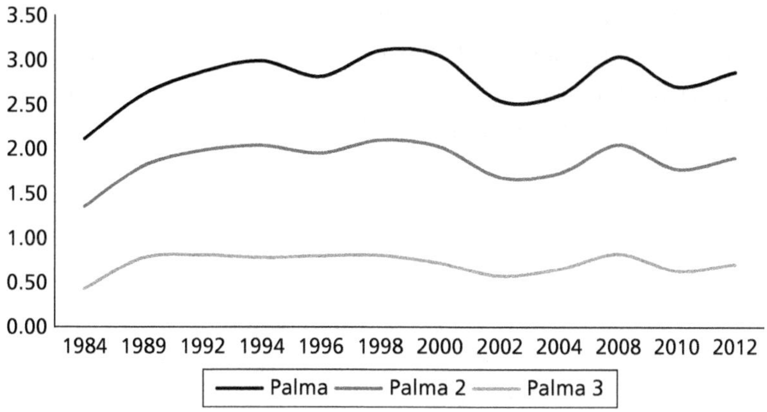

Figure 21.2 Mexico: Evolution of the Palma ratios, 1984–2012

Source: Authors' own elaboration based on data from LIS (2014).

Mexican population is almost 27-fold; a stark contrast in comparison to the average ratio of 10:1 that prevails in the OECD (OECD 2014). And the extremes of income distribution keep becoming more unequal: today the top 1 per cent of Mexico's distribution has an average annual income forty-seven times that of the poorest 10 per cent (Del Castillo Negrete Rovira 2012), while the share of total income the richest 1 per cent commands is estimated at 21 per cent—the highest in the OECD (Esquivel 2015).

To properly estimate inequality though, two additional technical aspects need to be considered. First, as has been well explored in the literature, household survey data on which these estimates are based consistently underestimate the true level of inequality (Lakner and Milanovic 2013). Latest estimates accounting for the under-reporting of top incomes in household survey data have shown that inequality in Mexico, rather than displaying a decreasing trend, has been rising over recent decades.[4] Additionally, it may be much higher than currently measured by the Gini coefficient (Esquivel 2015).

Second, by way of its construction, the Gini coefficient cannot account as explicitly for changes in the extremes of distribution. Yet, as Esquivel (2015) explains, the dichotomous events of per capita income growth and stagnating poverty levels in Mexico over recent years can only be explained if growth occurs at the top of the distribution. To account for this observation, Figure 21.2 depicts the evolution of Mexico's income distribution as measured by the Palma ratios, which divide the top income shares by the bottom income share to gauge developments specifically in the extremes of the distribution.[5] Even given the underestimations of household survey data, it can be appreciated that the underlying

[4] Unfortunately, most data sources have yet to adjust their figures to these more realistic levels, forcing the authors to work with the currently available unadjusted numbers throughout this chapter.

[5] The Palma ratio measures the share of total income held by the top 10 per cent of the income distribution relative to that of the bottom 40 per cent; the Palma v. 2 divides the share of the top 5 per cent over that of the bottom 40 per cent, and Palma v. 3. uses the top 1 per cent over the bottom 40 per cent. For more information on the original Palma ratio see Palma (2006, 2011), Cobham and Sumner (2013), and Krozer (2015) for its derivatives Palma v.

trend at the very top of the distribution drives the overall pattern of inequality, i.e. the tendencies displayed by the Palma v. 3 (top 1 per cent income share over bottom 40 per cent income share) are mimicked and consecutively amplified by the Palma v. 2 (top 5 per cent) and v. 1 (top 10 per cent), respectively. Whether we compare the top 10 per cent, top 5 per cent, or top 1 per cent share to that of the bottom 40 per cent, inequality in Mexico remains higher today than three decades ago, and has at no point since come to approach its 1984 level.

How do these tendencies in the overall income distribution differ from the dynamics of its individual components: labour, capital, and transfer incomes when we disaggregate disposable income? It is particularly the income from labour that we are interested in in this context, not only because wages, like few other sources of income, tend to be associated with 'worthiness' in a society organized around remunerated labour, but mainly because people continue to receive most of their income from wages: if the bottom decile in which there are numerous cases of de-saving is excluded, labour income per decile on average amounts to over 76 per cent (in some years close to 100 per cent for some groups) of total income, compared to transfer income reaching 20 per cent. The exception is the bottom decile, where transfers are important (over 60 per cent of income in 2010, the latest available data year, up from just over 20 per cent in 1984). Meanwhile, capital returns lie between 0.6 and 1.5 per cent up to the 9th decile (rising to 7.5 per cent only when the top 1 per cent is considered), showing that even at considerably high levels of income distribution, the largest income source remains labour income. This importance of wages in total income explains why the overall household disposable income distribution resembles that of labour income, as Table 21.1 shows.

In Table 21.1, we explore the evolution of disposable income, as well as the functional distribution of income, i.e. the trends in the shares of its key components: (i) labour remunerations; (ii) returns and profits accruing to capital; (iii) transfers received.

Table 21.1 Income shares and Palmas in Mexico, 1984 and 2010

2010	Bottom 40%	Top 10%	Top 5%	Palma v. 1	Palma v. 2
Disposable income	13.3	31.2	20.2	2.346	1.519
Labour income	10.5	32.4	20.9	3.086	1.990
Capital income	7.6	52.5	39.1	6.908	5.145
Transfer income	26.5	24.4	15.1	0.921	0.570
1984	**Bottom 40%**	**Top 10%**	**Top 5%**	**Palma v. 1**	**Palma v. 2**
Disposable income	13.5	30.8	18.6	2.281	1.378
Labour income	13	30.6	18.1	2.354	1.392
Capital income	6.8	52.6	40.8	7.735	6.000
Transfer income	22.3	22.8	14.3	1.022	0.641

Source: Krozer et al. (2015) based on data from LIS (2014).

The distribution of disposable income in 2010, although slightly more unequal than in 1984, is not markedly different compared to a quarter century earlier. However, this aggregation masks important divergence across income components. Unsurprisingly, considering the unequal distribution of wealth, the distribution of capital incomes is vastly more unequal than that of labour income, which again is more unequal than that of transfers. Despite a slight decrease in Palma ratios for transfers and capital income in 2010 compared to 1984, and the frequent attribution of much of the 2000s inequality decline to decreases in labour income inequality,[6] the preoccupying trend observable in Table 21.1 is that the distribution of labour income is considerably more concentrated at the very top now than it was twenty-five years ago, both in terms of the Palma and its derivative Palma v. 2, at the expense of the bottom deciles' shares.

However, not only is labour income more unequal now than it was three decades ago; the bottom decile, which allegedly benefited most from the transfer programmes implemented since the 1990s, has actually seen its share of total income deteriorate continuously since the mid-1980s. In 2010 disposable income for this group declined to just 0.8 per cent of the nation's total income, according to LIS data (LIS 2014). Accounting for the importance of wages in overall income for most of the population, and the consistently low unemployment in Mexico (below 5 per cent), this means that wages must increase faster at the top than at the bottom, further exacerbating inequality. The increasing share of labour earnings that accrue to the top end of the income distribution in Table 21.2, where simultaneously the poor struggle to remain afloat with ever smaller shares of the total income pie, testifies to this development.

All of the above would be less critical if a progressive system of redistribution were in place that could ameliorate the impact of labour income concentration. However, in redistributive terms, the combined effects of overall fiscal policy, i.e. both tax and transfer policies, in Mexico are virtually zero. Tax policy in Mexico fails to have any significant influence on income redistribution (Wang and Caminada 2011). Although many OECD countries have high pre-tax income inequalities as well, they manage to almost halve

Table 21.2 Gini indices of primary and disposable income, and fiscal redistribution

Country	Year	Gini primary income	Gini disposable income	Absolute fiscal redistribution	Relative fiscal redistribution %
Brazil	2006	0.570	0.486	0.084	15
Mexico	2004	0.476	0.458	0.018	4
The Netherlands	2004	0.459	0.263	0.196	43

Source: Authors' own elaboration based on data from Wang and Caminada (2011).

6 Campos-Vázquez et al. (2012: 3), 'the decline in labour income inequality was by far the most important proximate determinant of the observed decline in overall inequality.'

their Gini coefficients in the post-tax income distribution, as the example of the Netherlands in Table 21.2 shows.

Critically, Mexico's redistributive capacities seem to have declined considerably since the 1960s, to the extent that during the last two decades, on average they have been unable to reduce the country's Gini vis-à-vis its pre-tax levels (Krozer and Moreno-Brid 2014). Moreover, the progressive impact from pre- to post-tax and transfer distribution remains below 1 per cent for all but the highest decile, where it reaches 1.6 per cent—although if the top 5 per cent are considered instead, this difference shrinks to 1.1 per cent again (0.9 per cent for the bottom decile).

Considering the country's low, and compared to earlier decades, decreasing redistributive capacities paired with the polarization in the distribution of labour income, the wage distribution becomes even more decisive in determining households' final disposable incomes. Before looking more closely at the minimum wage as determinant of the lower boundary of the (formal) wage distribution, we will briefly consider how the totality of incomes in the economy, i.e. the labour share, has fared in Mexico, both from a comparative regional perspective and over time. This will show that not only are incomes distributed more unequally now than three decades ago, the overall amount of wages compared to capital as proportion of GDP has also significantly decreased since the early 1980s.

Labour share and minimum wage in Mexico and Latin America

In 2012, the share of wages in Mexican GDP had fallen to about 27 per cent from over 38 per cent in the early 1980s. This long-term trend of a decreasing labour share of total income coincides with the increasing inequality trends in Mexico described in the previous section. As Figure 21.3 shows, especially during the last decade, the evolution of the Gini coefficient and the labour share seem to exactly mirror each other, i.e. when the labour share decreased, inequality increased (and vice versa).

How does this development fit into the regional dynamics experienced in Latin America over this period? Placing Mexico within a broader comparative context, as in Figure 21.4, generates two key messages: first, the labour share of income in Mexico is significantly below the share in other large Latin American economies throughout the two decades for which data are available—twice as small as Brazil's, for instance. Second, and in contrast to Brazil, Chile, and Argentina, particularly over the recent decade, Mexico has shown a disturbing tendency to reduce its share of labour income as a percentage of GDP.

The increase in the labour share in Brazil, Chile, and Argentina over recent years, on the other hand, in all cases follows an increase in their respective minimum wages. As Figure 21.4 shows, Mexico is also the only country among these four major Latin

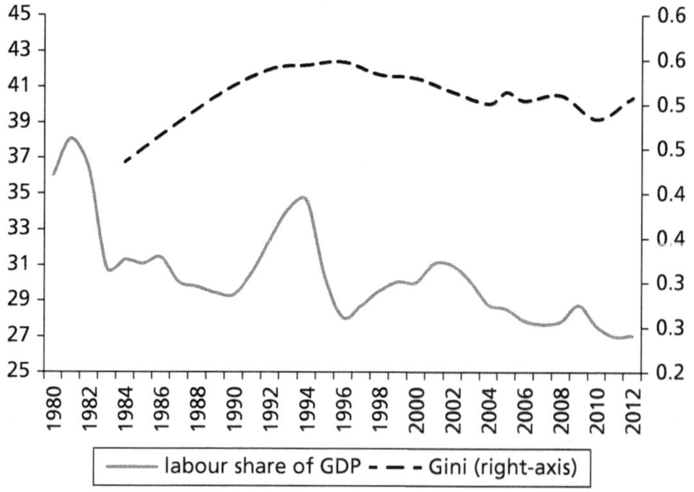

Figure 21.3 Mexico: labour share of GDP and Gini coefficient, 1980–2012

Source: Authors' own elaboration based on Samaniego (2014) and data from CEPALSTAT (2016).

American economies that has not seen a substantial increase in its minimum wage in recent years. Instead, real minimum wages plummeted in the early 1990s, and have continued to stagnate, albeit at a somewhat slower pace, since 1995. This trajectory makes Mexico an exception in the regional context of increasing minimum wages.

Partly as a result of a more interventionist policy approach, but also as a consequence of stronger labour markets, many countries in Latin America expanded labour policies in the 2000s (Gasparini et al. 2016). A particularly strong contrast between the virtually flat minimum wages in the 1990s and the strong rise in the 2000s can be observed for the case of Argentina, one of the countries with more ambitious active labour market policies in the 2000s. By helping to increase the earnings of low-income workers, the increasing real value of the minimum wage in these countries contributed to the reduction in earnings inequality (Bosch and Manacorda 2010; Maurizio 2014; Maurizio and Vazquez 2016).

Likewise, in Brazil, raising the minimum wage—in combination with improvements in labour protection through measures such as formalizing jobs, and government investment policies for the creation of jobs—led to a positive impact on income distribution (ILO 2013). Brazil has even accelerated its two-decade-old revaluation strategy of minimum wages over the past five years. In a counter-cyclical manner, the strategy to boost domestic consumption saw regular adjustments of the minimum wage level to rates matching inflation plus GDP growth. This improved inequality levels 'from below' by increasing gains for those at the bottom of the income distribution (Krozer 2016). This policy effort contrasts sharply with the case of Mexico, where minimum wage levels lie below the poverty line, with a real-term value that is 70 per cent below its 1980 level (Krozer et al. 2015).

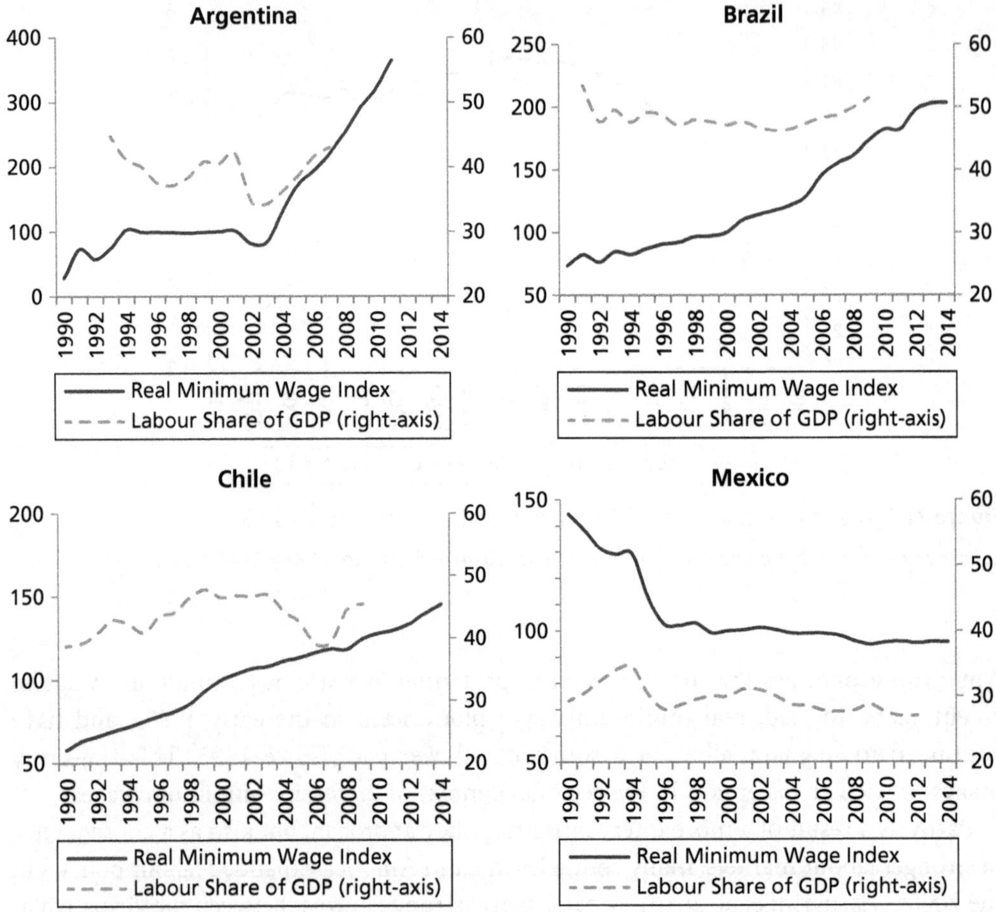

Figure 21.4 Selected Latin American economies: evolution of the real monthly minimum wage index and the labour share of GDP, 1990–2014

Source: Authors' own elaboration based on data from Abeles and Vega (2014) and CEPALSTAT (2016).

But Mexican exceptionality does not stop here. It also holds a unique status when considering the actual minimum wage level in the country. In Figure 21.5, only Nicaragua seems to be able to compete with Mexico in terms of the lowest regional monthly real minimum wage level in 2010 US$. Brazil, Chile, and Argentina on the other hand, have levels up to more than seven times Mexico's. In 2013, its salary was equivalent to US$112.2, slightly exceeded by that of Nicaragua (US$117.5) and Bolivia (US$117.5), and equivalent to 40 per cent of the minimum wage in Guatemala or Honduras, whose per capita GDP is well below that of Mexico.

To get a better picture of the disparate experiences of countries such as Brazil on the one hand, which have seen their rising minimum wage levels accompany continuously decreasing inequality levels, and Mexico with its stagnated minimum wage level paired with increasing inequality on the other hand, let us take a closer look at the recent history of the minimum wage in Mexico.

Figure 21.5 Monthly real minimum wage and the labour share of GDP, selected Latin American countries 2010

Note: Labour share of GDP refers to 2010 or the most recent year available in the data set (Nicaragua refers to 2004; Argentina and Paraguay refer to 2007; and Brazil, Chile, and Colombia refer to 2009).

Source: Authors' own elaboration based on data from ILO (2016) and CEPALSTAT (2016).

The recent history of minimum wages in Mexico and Latin America

In May 2014, indignation over the low level of the Mexican minimum wage, putting it in flagrant violation of the Mexican Constitution, exploded. The call to correct this unacceptable situation by the Governor of Mexico City sparked a national debate among journalists, academics, entrepreneurs, workers' and employers' representatives, and senior officers of the federal and local governments, the CONASAMI, the central bank, SAT, the Ministries of Finance and of Labour, and even the president. The ensuing debate led to the consensus that the minimum wage needs to be put on a sustainable path of growth in real terms so that it reaches its constitutionally mandated level.

Throughout the past half century, evolution of the minimum wage in Mexico has followed three distinct stages. During the first stage, from the 1950s to the second half of the 1970s, the minimum wage quadrupled in real terms. This rise occurred while the Mexican economy experienced its golden age when real GDP expanded at an average annual rate of 6 per cent and preserved low levels of inflation. The increase in the real minimum wage lost strength from the balance of payments crisis that Mexico experienced in 1976. In fact, during the oil boom years the minimum wage lagged slightly due to inflation. Later, when the oil boom collapsed in 1981–82, the stabilization policies adopted to manage this crisis launched a phase of sharp deterioration in the minimum wage. Indeed, as part of efforts to contain inflation, government policy was set to manage the adjustment of the minimum wage to below the increase in consumer prices. Depreciation of the exchange rate, decline of trade unions' influence in a context of a weakened labour market due to reduced economic activity, and government's concern to correct public finances and lower inflation led to a sharp deterioration in the minimum wage.

In the late 1980s—after the lost decade—productive activity in the country began to recover and inflation started to stabilize at a low level. But the minimum wage policy continued to be used as an anti-inflationary policy, and did not fulfil its original mission in the labour market to ensure income protection. As already shown, this coincided with deteriorating income distribution levels. Instead of placing it at a dignified level CONASAMI, with its formal decrees on nominal increases in the minimum wage in the country sanctioned insufficient adjustments for inflation that led to recurrent falls in value in real terms. By 1995 the minimum wage had lost 66 per cent of its purchasing power against its value fifteen years prior, as Figure 21.6 shows.

The following third phase in the evolution of the minimum wage, which lasts until today, is characterized by a further downward pattern in real terms, although the rate of decline has slowed, and the fall in real purchasing power appears to have stabilized in recent years. However, this policy, followed for nearly forty years by CONASAMI, or more precisely by the Ministry for Taxation and Public Debt (SHCP) as the institution to which it answers, has failed to follow through on the minimum wage's mission to protect citizens' rights established by the Constitution of 1917, and has had a serious detrimental effect on citizens' purchasing power. This systematic deterioration has for some time set the minimum wage as one of the lowest in dollar terms in Latin America and influenced the average wage in Mexico to remain among the lowest across countries. Incidentally, the national statistics institute INEGI (2015) reported a 3.2 per cent decrease in real

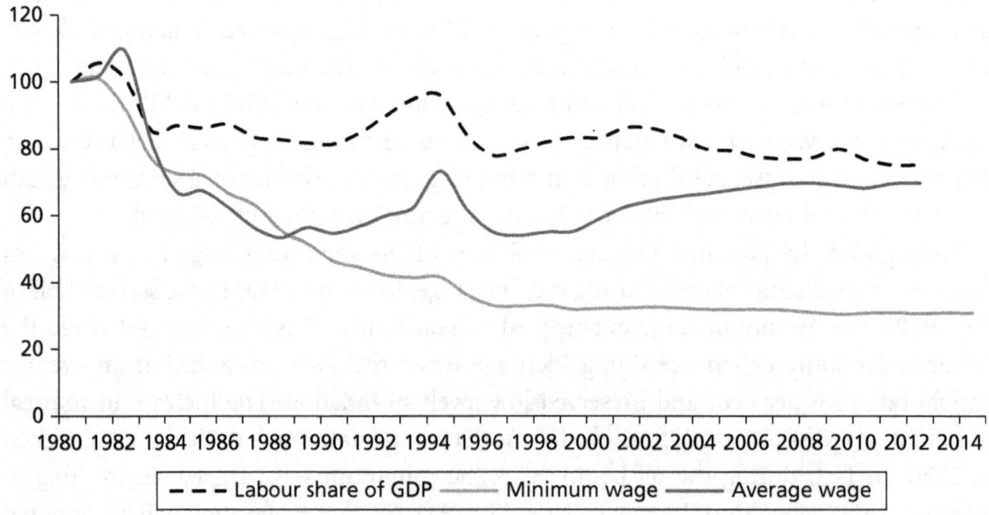

Figure 21.6 Mexico: indices of the labour share of GDP, the minimum wage, and the average wage, 1980–2014

Source: Authors' own elaboration based on Samaniego (2014) and data from CEPALSTAT (2016).

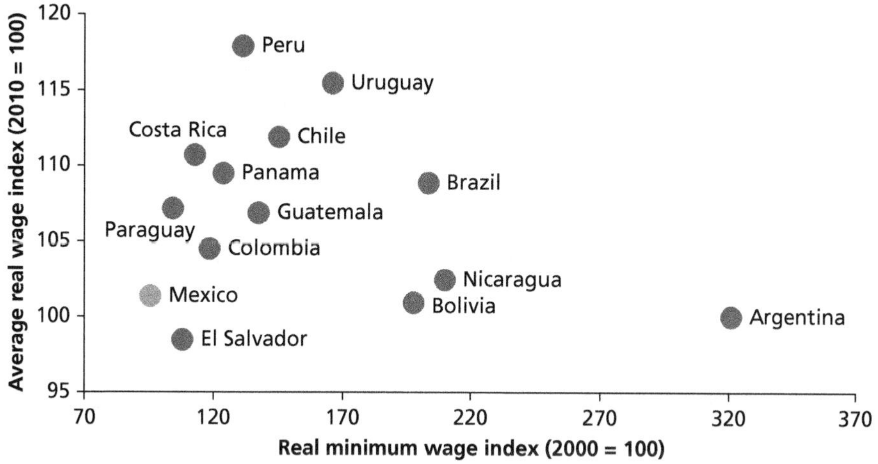

Figure 21.7 Real minimum wage and average real wage indices in selected Latin American countries, 2014

Note: Data for Argentina refer to 2010.
Source: CEPALSTAT (2016).

average wages over the period from 2012 to 2014. In fact, among those countries in the region with more recent comparative and reliable statistical information on the monthly minimum wage, Mexico now ranks last on both real minimum and average wage accounts, as illustrated in Figure 21.7.

How can low minimum wages translate into a compressed average wage? While the relationship between minimum and average wages is complex, Maloney and Mendez (2004) show that the minimum wage has an impact on wage setting far beyond those usually contemplated at the bottom end of the formal income distribution, showing effects both higher up in wage distribution and in the unregulated or 'informal' sector. As Fairris et al. (2008) find, instead of merely setting a lower bound on the wages of formal sector workers, minimum wages serve as a norm for wage setting more generally throughout the Mexican economy. This translation mechanism, or lighthouse effect, is of crucial importance in a context like Mexico, where nearly 60 per cent of workers have informal jobs (ILO 2014). The authors also show that wages are commonly set at multiples of the minimum wage, and that changes in minimum wages influence wage changes across the occupational distribution, thus also affecting average wage levels. These findings have them conclude that 'declining real minimum wages and stabilization programs that strengthened the link between wage levels, wage changes, and minimum wages, might account for a portion of the growing wage inequality in Mexico over the period of the late 1980s and early 1990s' (Fairris et al. 2008). We will return to this conjecture, but let us first take a brief look at how Mexico's minimum wage developments over time compare to those of other countries in its region.

As evidenced by Figure 21.8, evolution of the minimum wage in Mexico contrasts with the experience of, for instance, Brazil and Argentina. Both countries have seen a

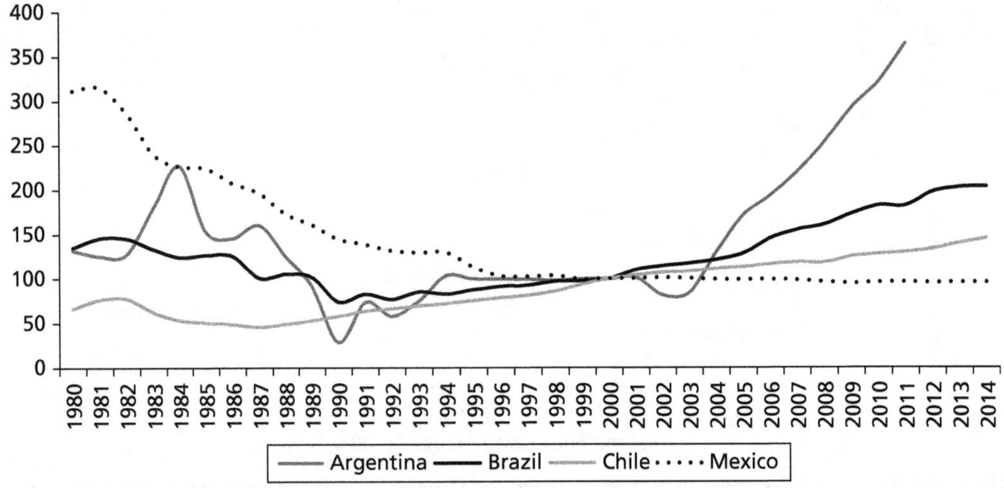

Figure 21.8 Real minimum wages in selected Latin American countries, 1980–2014

Source: CEPALSTAT (2016).

consistent increase in their minimum wages over the past decades, over and above inflation adjustments. They have followed a policy of explicit minimum wage appreciation, often directly targeting inequality.

This strong growth in Argentina and Brazil in recent years is explained by the rise to power of governments committed to more inclusive development agendas. This commitment led them to use various instruments of economic and social policy to better distribute the benefits of growth in output to their citizens. On the one hand, they ceased to consider the minimum wage as a mere accessory to anti-inflationary policy, and on the other hand they restored its functions as an instrument of labour policy (Marinakis and Velasco 2006). In contrast, the Mexican policy of minimum wage containment perhaps reflects the fact that social inclusion and equality, despite a shift in the ruling party of the president, still were not priorities of economic strategy. This containment was needed to support the reduction in inflation and limit government spending on benefits, pensions, and other expenses related to the minimum wage. Beyond the often expressed concerns about inflationary pressures created by allegedly 'artificial' and 'arbitrary' increases in minimum wages, for instance by Finance Minister Luis Videgaray,[7] a 1999 paper by Agustín Carstens, the current governor of the Mexican central bank and former minister of taxation and public debt, explicitly recognizes the practice of setting minimum wages according to budgetary requirements.[8] At the same time, the

[7] See for instance Milenio Digital (2014).

[8] The document reads on p. 17: 'Since 1996, all the monetary programs that Banco de México has implemented are fundamentally based on [...] [a] yearly annual inflation objective. This objective is established jointly by the Federal Government and the Banco de México, and it is perceived as the result of a concerted effort to coordinate fiscal and monetary policies. Based on such objective the fiscal and monetary policies are designed and it also *helps for the determination of the minimum wage*' (Carstens and Werner 1999, emphasis added).

lag served to compress labour costs via prices rather than via productivity, a competitive advantage of the inclusion of Mexico in the global economy.

The minimum wage and productivity in Mexico and Latin America

It has often been argued by analysts and officials alike that the low level of minimum wage in Mexico is correlated with the development or performance of labour productivity. Having examined the trends in inequalities and wages separately above, we can now test this claim, proceeding to a brief analysis of the relationship between the minimum wage and the evolution of labour productivity in Mexico and other countries in the region.

As documented above, the minimum wage in Mexico is the lowest in Latin America by any measure: in current prices, constant dollars, or in terms of purchasing power parity. Also its relative level compared to GDP per capita is very low and decreasing—as opposed to the Argentinean, Chilean, and Brazilian cases (see Figure 21.9). Mexico's 15 per cent of per capita GDP is the lowest ratio in most of Latin America and far from the 30 per cent for Brazil and Chile and about 50 per cent for Peru, Colombia, and Costa Rica. Its amount is 19 per cent of the average national wage, also one of the lowest percentages in the region. In one of the latest editions of its Global Wage Report, the ILO (2015) stressed that in Mexico 'the minimum wage is below market levels, even more so for unskilled workers'. In addition, according to ECLAC (2014), 'Mexico is the only country where at the end of the previous decade the value of the minimum wage was less than the per capita poverty threshold.'

The debate in Mexico related to the relative position of the minimum wage as compared to the rest of Latin America has placed a great deal of emphasis on the dependency that the minimum wage has—or should have—on productivity. This argument gave hope that at least Mexico's comparatively poor minimum wage performance in the region had good reason. However, this is not the case. The ILO's (2013) Key Indicators of the Labour Market (KILM) show that for more than twenty years average labour productivity in Mexico—measured in constant US$—has been and continues to be among the highest in Latin America. In 2012 it was the second highest, only 3 per cent lower than in Chile, and far ahead of Brazil (60 per cent). Furthermore, labour productivity was more than double that of the average of the rest of the region (see Figure 21.10).

While both variables have performed poorly in recent decades, the evolution of labour productivity and the real minimum wage in Mexico are not closely correlated, but rather contrasting. Indeed, at the regional level Mexico has displayed some of the highest levels of labour productivity for years. Its minimum wage, however, is the lowest in Latin America. During 1998–2013 when productivity rose 15 per cent, the real minimum wage remained stagnant. In 2013 labour productivity was 4.5 per cent above and the minimum wages 30 per cent below their 1990 levels. If the real minimum wage in recent

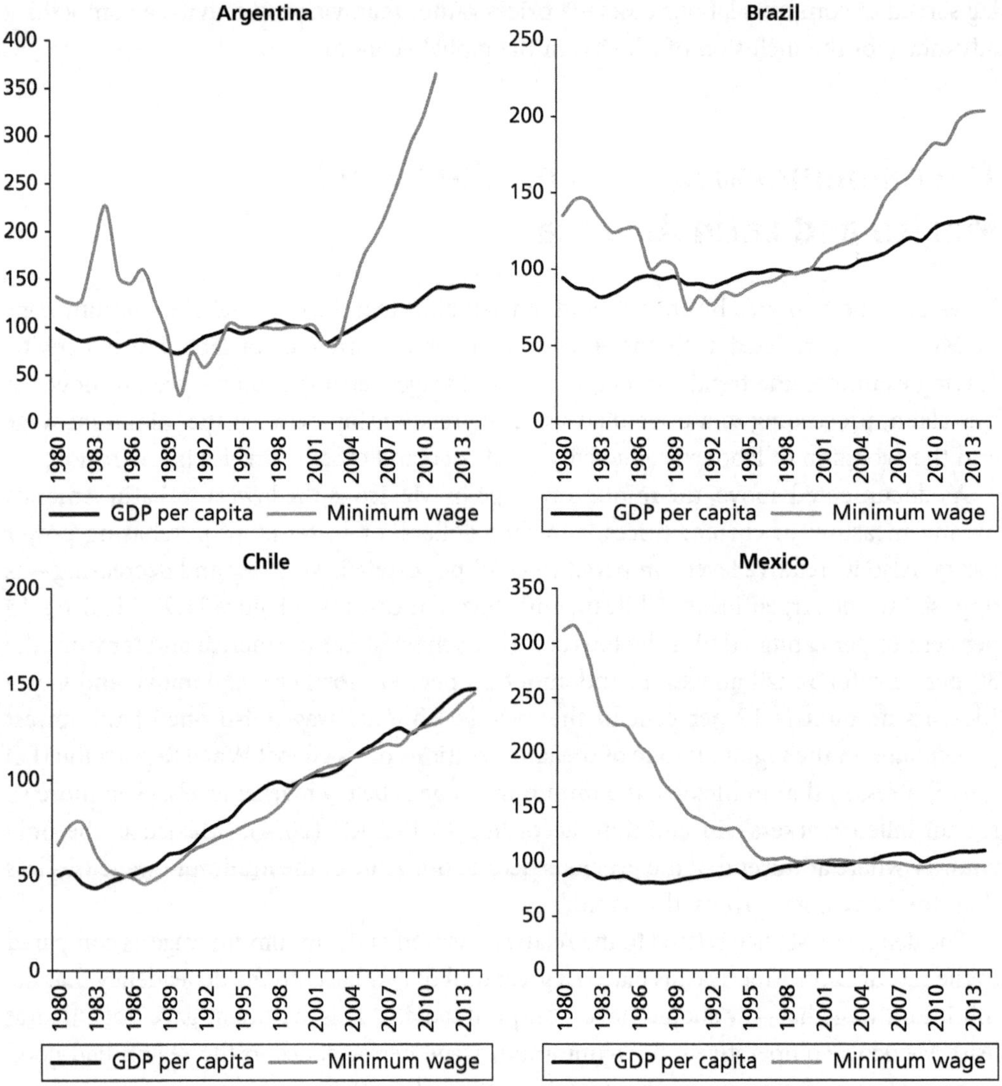

Figure 21.9 Evolution of the real minimum wage and GDP per capita in selected Latin American economies, 1980–2013

Source: Authors' own elaboration based on CEPALSTAT (2016) and World Development Indicators (World Bank 2016).

years had grown at the same rate as labour productivity, its level today would be 50 per cent greater, at about MXN$100 a day.

In sum, in those periods in Mexico's recent experience in which labour productivity has fallen, the real minimum wage has plummeted even more sharply. And during phases in which labour productivity has risen, the benefit is null or hardly reflected in the minimum wage in real terms.

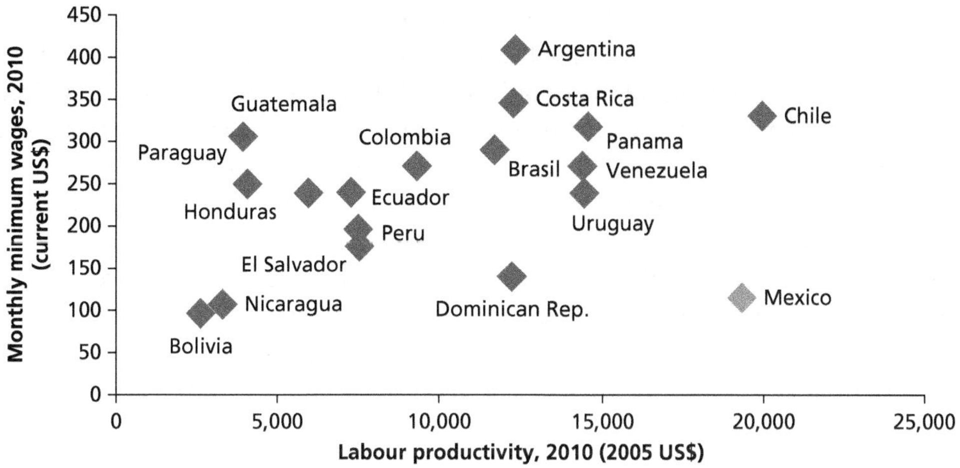

Figure 21.10 Minimum wage and labour productivity in selected Latin American countries, 2010

Note: Productivity data for Argentina refer to 2006, the last year available in the source.

Source: ILO and Key Indicators of the Labor Market (ILO 2013).

Interactions between inequality dynamics and minimum wage: lessons from Mexico and Brazil

Although Mexico has been historically unequal, the current distribution is by no means an outcome of a force of nature or a necessary consequence of its colonial legacy. There have been periods towards greater equality in Mexico, for instance prior to 1976, when the relationship between productivity growth and wage growth in manufacturing was relatively stable (Palma 2011). Their subsequent delinking under trade liberalization meant that increasing export competitiveness had little effect on living standards (Palma 2011). In fact, by the end of the 1990s, the average wage was only just recovering to its 1976 level, although productivity had increased by about 80 per cent in the meantime; in the same period, the real minimum wage fell by 80 per cent, and the share of wages and salaries in GDP fell from 40 per cent to 18.9 per cent. Profit margins greatly increased—with the result that, as Figure 21.2 showed, the distribution of labour income is even more unequal today than in the early 1980s.

At the same time, wage and productivity developments in the country coincided with the loss of labour income share of the bottom two income deciles, as outlined above. Instead of addressing this problem directly via concerted labour policies, successive Mexican governments have opted to mitigate the impact of increasing inequality almost exclusively through targeted social programmes. Created to compensate the poor population for their lack of sufficient labour income, these programmes include *Prospera* (formerly *Oportunidades*), a pioneer conditional cash transfer programme to poor households in return for obligatory schooling and health checks, as well as other programmes to benefit the elderly, akin to non-contributory pension schemes such as 'Seventy and More' and the Universal Elderly Pension in Mexico City. As indirect targets, they include the improvement of income distribution; their primary and direct focus remains on poverty reduction however. These programmes do have a progressive, albeit small, influence on income distribution. However, their partial success seems to have managed to distract from the disaster of the wage share declines at the lower bound evidenced above.

This contrasts strongly with the case of Brazil, which also features large-scale social redistribution programmes, such as *Bolsa Família* and rural pension schemes, but additionally pursues explicitly progressive minimum wage policies, and has seen its inequality decline considerably over recent years. As Figure 21.11 shows, in the four

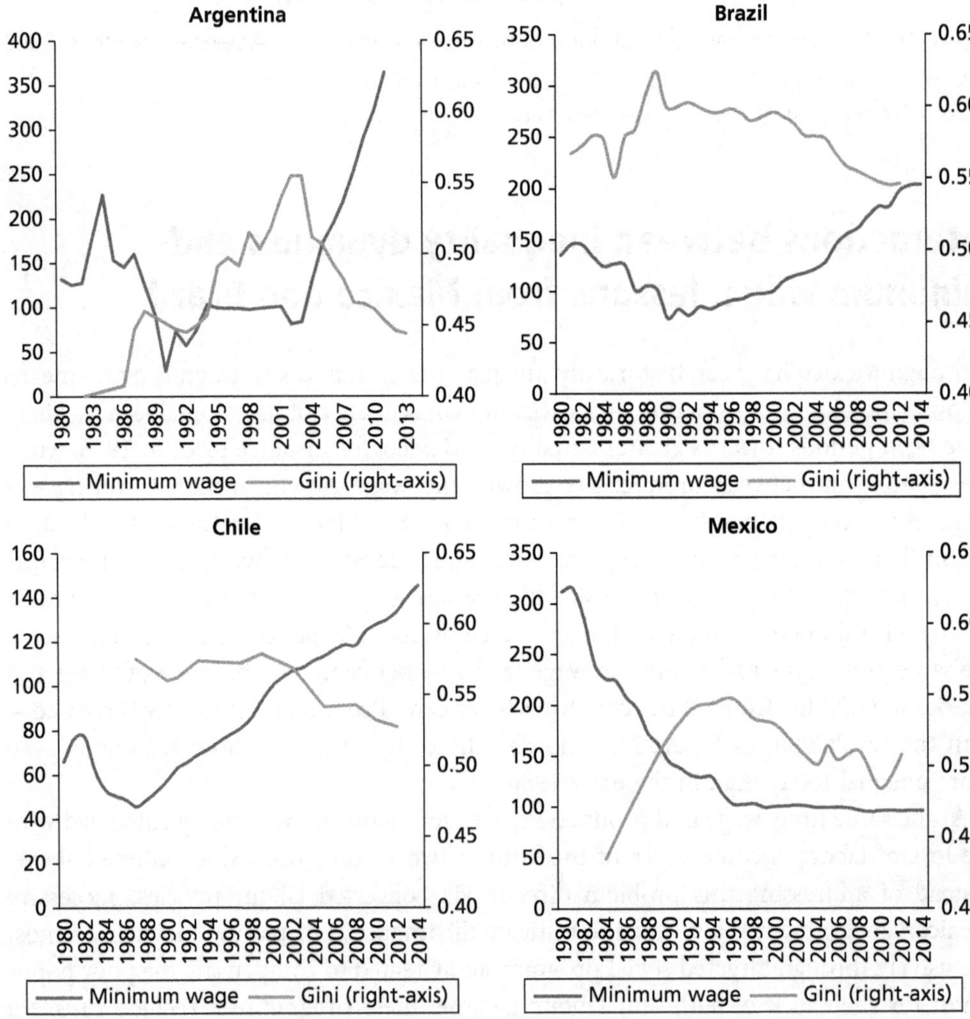

Figure 21.11 Selected countries: real minimum wage and Gini coefficients, 1980–2014

Source: Authors' own elaboration based on CEPALSTAT (2016) and SEDLAC (2016).

countries Argentina, Brazil, Chile, and Mexico, the Gini coefficient and minimum wages tend to be negatively correlated. While in Argentina, Brazil, and Chile the fast rise of the latter juxtaposes a fall in inequality levels, the Mexican case shows stagnating wages and, after some erratic developments in the Gini, a rebound in inequality levels. Rather than with productivity, it seems, minimum wages correlate with inequality in these countries.

Conclusion

Our analysis shows that Mexico continues to face high and recently increasing inequality levels. Moreover, the country still lacks a clear strategy to address its persistent inequalities, in terms of both functional and interpersonal inequalities, woefully neglecting one of the most promising tools to improve income distribution: minimum wages. In this sense, the Mexican case differs markedly from those of other countries in the region, such as Argentina, Brazil, or Chile, all of which have successfully implemented labour policies, particularly raising minimum wages, to decrease inequality. In our view, this makes Mexico an exemplary case for further study of the (negative) relationship between minimum wage and inequality, though not necessarily an example to follow for other countries aiming to decrease their inequalities.

While the causal mechanisms underlying the correlation between minimum wages and inequality trends are not explicitly explored in this chapter and will have to be addressed in future research, our analysis shows that, contrary to an often-held view in Mexico, a rise in labour productivity and international competitiveness by itself will automatically guarantee neither a significant and persistent rise in the real minimum wage, nor a consistent decline in inequality levels. It is not reasonable to expect such outcomes in the future without significant reform of the minimum wage policy; considering recent trends in the distribution of its wages, preoccupying levels of inequality in Mexico will not decrease substantially or sustainably if the increase in its labour inequality is not explicitly addressed. A new policy, then, needs to consider the country's unequal income distribution, rather than be strictly oriented towards achieving a fiscal balance and increased competitiveness, as has so far been the case in Mexico. It will require a shift away from the government's exclusive objective of inflation targeting, and instead focus on designing economic policy so as to transfer the benefits of labour productivity and competitiveness to minimum wage workers.

An initial administrative step in this direction was to delink the minimum wage from multiple transactions far outside the scope of the world of work—a role as reference point that it has played for years. Examples of these transactions include fines, certain payments of mortgages, and financial operations as well as budget allocations to political parties. After nearly two years of discussions, finally by late November 2015 both legislative chambers approved a reform to end such linkage practices. This step, though important, can only be the starting point to recover the salience of minimum wages. In an attempt to reinstall the minimum wage as a meaningful labour policy to counter not only poverty but also income inequalities, besides de-indexing the minimum wage as a unit of account transactions outside the labour market, its rate would have to be raised significantly so that it at least covers the cost of the national basic food basket, in line with constitutional requirements and social objectives of more equal distributions. This would simultaneously improve the country's poverty and its inequality levels.

After all, the debate over better national minimum wages goes beyond being a purely technical issue. It is a political one, in a political economy that reflects the weight of equality in the society we want and we can build. It touches the heart of the different perspectives that actors have on factorial distribution, its determinants, and its relationship with the pace of economic expansion. This glaring issue in the agenda of civil rights and respect for the Constitution that should govern the design of macroeconomic policy, and its evolution, showcases the political decision to ignore the acute social problems of the most vulnerable workers. In practice Mexico's Federal Government and Legislature had blocked or frozen efforts to ensure the formal separation of the minimum wage from other variables outside the labour market that are tied to its levels for nearly two years. Reversing this opposition is the first necessary step to setting the minimum wage on a recovery journey. Ultimately, improving the well-being of its citizens beyond a mere minimum (wage) level and towards a dignified remuneration requires a commitment to a development strategy in which equality and economic growth are not seen as antagonistic or as sequential objectives, and where gains in productivity, rather than being skimmed by the very top, are shared across distribution.

ACKNOWLEDGEMENTS

The opinions expressed herein are those of the authors and do not necessarily reflect those of the United Nations.

Parts of this chapter update and extend the analyses presented in Moreno-Brid et al. (2014) and Krozer et al. (2015).

The authors would like to dedicate this text to the memory of Giulio Regeni.

REFERENCES

Abeles, M., Amarante, V., and Vega, D. (2014). 'The earnings share of total income in Latin America, 1990–2010'. *CEPAL Review* 114.

Bosch, M. and Manacorda, M. (2010). 'Minimum wages and earning inequality in urban Mexico', *American Economic Journal: Applied Economics* 2/4: 128–48.

Campos-Vázquez, R., Esquivel, G., and Lustig, N. (2012). 'The rise and fall of income inequality in Mexico, 1989–2010'. ECINEQ WP 2012-267. Available at www.ecineq.org/milano/WP/ECINEQ2012-267.pdf, accessed 12 November 2018.

Carstens, A.G. and Werner, A.M. (1999). 'Mexico's monetary policy framework under a floating exchange rate regime'. Available at www.imf.org/external/pubs/ft/seminar/2000/targets/carstens.pdf, accessed 14 November 2018.

CEPALSTAT (2016). Database. Available at http://estadisticas.cepal.org/cepalstat/WEB_CEPALSTAT/Portada.asp, accessed 30 May 2016.

Cobham, A. and Sumner, A. (2013). 'Is it all about the tails? The Palma measure of income inequality'. Centre for Global Development Working Paper No. 343. London: Centre for Global Development.

CONEVAL (2015). 'CONEVAL informa de los resultados de la medición de pobreza 2014' [CONEVAL reports the results of the poverty measurement 2014]. Available at www.eluniversal.com.mx/articulo/nacion/sociedad/2015/07/24/crece-pobreza-en-mexico-hay-dos-millones-mas-coneval, accessed 12 November, 2018.

Del Castillo Negrete Rovira, M. (2012). 'La distribución del ingreso en México' [Distribution of income in Mexico], *Este País*, 1 April 2012, No. 252.

ECLAC (Economic Commission for Latin America and the Caribbean) (2014). *Pactos para la igualdad. Hacia un futuro sostenible* [Covenants for equality. Towards a sustainable future]. Santiago de Chile: ECLAC.

Esquivel, G. (2015). *Desigualdad Extrema en México: Concentración del Poder Económico y Político* [Extreme inequality in Mexico: concentration of economic and political power]. Mexico: Oxfam. Available at www.cambialasreglas.org/pdf/desigualdadextrema_informe.pdf, accessed 30 May 2016.

Fairris, D., Popli, G., and Zepeda, E. (2008). 'Minimum wages and the wage structure in Mexico', *Review of Social Economy* 66/2: 181–208.

Gasparini, L., Cruces, G., and Tornarolli, L. (2016). 'Chronicle of a deceleration foretold: income inequality in Latin America in the 2010s'. CEDLAS Documento de Trabajo Nro. 198. Buenos Aires: CEDLAS.

ILO (International Labour Organization) (2013). *Global Wage Report 2012/2013*. Available at www.ilo.org/wcmsp5/groups/public/@ dgreports/@dcomm/@publ/documents/publication/wcms_194843.pdf, accessed 15 March 2019.

ILO (International Labour Organization) (2014). 'Informal employment in Mexico: current situation, policies and challenges. Notes on formalization. Regional Office for Latin America and the Caribbean'. Available at www.ilo.org/wcmsp5/groups/public/%97americas/%97ro lima/documents/publication/wcms_245889.pdf, accessed 15 March 2019.

ILO (International Labour Organization) (2016). *Global Wage Report Collection*. Available at www.ilo.org/ilostat, accessed 13 November 2018.

INEGI (National Institute of Statistics and Geography) (2015). Available at www.inegi.org.mx/saladeprensa/boletines/2015/especiales/especiales2015_07_3.pdf, accessed 13 November 2018.

Informador.mx (2014). 'Incremento a salario mínimo aumentaría inflación: Carstens' [Increase in minimum wage would increase inflation: Carstens] 7 August 2014. Available at www.informador.com.mx/economia/2014/542491/6/incremento-a-salario-minimo-aumentaria-inflacion-carstens.htm, accessed 13 November 2018.

Krozer, A. (2015). 'The inequality we want. How much is too much?' WIDER Working Paper 2015/015. Helsinki: UNU-WIDER.

Krozer, A. (2016). 'for richer…or poorer? The capture of growth and politics in emerging economies'. *Oxfam International*, January 2016.

Krozer, A. and Moreno-Brid, J.C. (2014). 'Inequality in Mexico', *World Economics Association* 4/5: 4.

Krozer, A., Moreno-Brid, J.C., and Badan, J.C.R. (2015). 'Inequality and minimum wages: not even talking, much less walking in Mexico', *Investigacion Económica* 74/293, 3–26.

Lakner, C., and Milanovic, B. (2013). 'Global income distribution: from the fall of the Berlin Wall to the Great Recession'. Policy Research Working Paper No. 6719. Washington, DC: World Bank.

LIS (2014). Dataset created from LISSY. Available at www.lisdatacenter.org/, accessed 13 November 2018.

Lopez-Calva, L.F. and Lustig, N. (eds) (2010). *Declining Inequality in Latin America: A Decade of Progress?* Washington, DC: Brookings Institution Press and United Nations Development Programme.

Lustig, N. (2013). 'Latin America's inequality success story'. *Current History*, pp. 64–9. Available at www.noralustig.org/wp-content/uploads/2014/11/Current-History_Latin-America%E2%80%99s-Inequality-Success-Story.pdf, accessed 13 November 2018.

Lustig, N., López-Calva, L.F., and Ortiz-Juárez, E. (2012). 'Declining inequality in Latin America in the 2000s: the cases of Argentina, Brazil, and Mexico'. Policy Research Working Paper No. WPS 6248. Washington, DC: World Bank.

Maloney, W. and Mendez, J.N. (2004). 'Measuring the impact of minimum wages. Evidence from Latin America', in J. Heckman and C. Pagés (eds) *Law and Employment: Lessons from Latin American and the Caribbean*. Chicago, IL: University of Chicago Press, 109–30.

Marinakis, A. and Velasco, J.J. (2006). *¿Para qué sirve el salario mínimo?* [What is the purpose of the minimum wage?]. OIT. Geneva: United Nations.

Maurizio, R. (2014). *El impacto distributivo del salario mínimo en la Argentina, el Brasil, Chile y el Uruguay* [The distributive impact of the minimum wage in Argentina, Brazil, Chile and Uruguay]. CEPAL-Serie Políticas Sociales No.194. Santiago: CEPAL.

Maurizio, R. and G. Vazquez. (2016). 'Impactos distributivos del salario mínimo en América Latina. Los casos de la Argentina, Brasil, Chile y Uruguay' [Distributive impact of the minimum wage in Latin America: the case of Argentina, Brazil, Chile and Uruguay], *Revista Internacional del Trabajo* 135/1: 105–42.

Milenio Digital (2014). 'Debate sobre salario mínimo debe ser serio: Videgaray' [Debate on minimum wage should be serious: Videgaray], Milenio.com. 12 August. Available at www.milenio.com/politica/salario_minimo-aumento_salario_minimo-apoya_gobienro_aumento_salario-Luis_Videgaray_0_352764937.html, accessed 13 November 2018.

OECD (Organisation for Economic Co-operation and Development) (2014). 'Focus on top incomes and taxation in OECD countries: Was the crisis a game changer?'. Available at www.oecd.org/els/soc/OECD2014-FocusOnTopIncomes.pdf, accessed 14 November 2018.

OECD (Organisation for Economic Co-operation and Development) (2015). Better Life Index. *OECD Database*. Available at www.oecdbetterlifeindex.org/#/22101111101, accessed 30 May 2016.

Palma, J.G. (2006). 'Globalizing inequality: "Centrifugal" and "Centripetal" forces at work'. DESA Working Paper No. 35. New York: United Nations.

Palma, J.G. (2011). 'Homogeneous middles vs. heterogeneous tails, and the end of the "inverted-u": the share of the rich is what it's all about', *Development and Change* 42/1: 87–153.

Samaniego, N. (2014). 'Salario en México' presentación no publicada. Nuevo Curso de Desarrollo ['Salary in Mexico', unpublished presentation. New Development Course], *Economia Unam* 11/33: 78–93.

SEDLAC (Socio-Economic Database for Latin America and the Caribbean (2016). CEDLAS and the World Bank Database. Available at http://sedlac.econo.unlp.edu.ar/eng/statistics.php, accessed 30 May 2016.

Wang, C. and Caminada, K. (2011). 'Disentangling income inequality and the redistributive effect of social transfers and taxes in 36 LIS countries'. Leiden Department of Economics Research Memorandum #2011.02.

World Development Indicators (2016). Database. Available at http://data.worldbank.org/data-catalog/world-development-indicators, accessed 30 May 2016.

22 The illegal trade in organs and poverty in India

A comparative analysis with Brazil and China

Saradamoyee Chatterjee

Introduction

In the past two decades, world income inequality has risen. Inequitable distribution of resources between and within countries has resulted in greater economic polarization of the population of the world (Wade 2004; Singh 2013). Evidence suggests that the increasing wealth of developing economic powerhouses such as Brazil, India, and China has not resulted in any noteworthy social and economic equality (Jha 2002; Basu 2009; Clementi and Schettino 2013; Singh 2013). With 38 per cent of the world's population, China and India strongly influence the world's trend in poverty and inequality (Wade 2004). Economic reforms in India have largely favoured the rich, middle-income, and better-skilled than low-income and poorly skilled people, such as small or displaced farmers and farm owners. Over the years, therefore, not only has income inequality, but also expenditure inequality (purchasing power parity) widened (Bardhan 2007; Singh 2013). The World Bank estimates that 76 per cent of the population in India and 36 per cent in China live on less than US$2 per day. People living in poverty in India suffer from a lack of proper education and skills and are less likely to participate actively in the consumer-oriented job market and enjoy the supposed prosperity of globalization (Haub 2012).

A characteristic consumer-oriented market economy has the potential to convert anything into a marketable product and stimulate a hierarchical-based society driven by individual wealth and purchasing capacity. This market-driven divide in a society manifests the inequalities to a greater degree, reflecting a clear demarcation between affluence and poverty. The commodification of body or body parts is an expression of the endemic poverty, social inequality, and marginalization of a certain proportion of people in the financially less prosperous developing countries such as Brazil, India, and China. It is a result of the limited choices available to poor people to lift themselves from a colossal financial crisis, or in certain cases (such as in China, discussed in the fifth section) simply due to being powerless to protect themselves from this commercialization.

Saradamoyee Chatterjee, *The illegal trade in organs and poverty in India: A comparative analysis with Brazil and China* In: *Handbook of BRICS and Emerging Economies.* Edited by: P.B. Anand, Shailaja Fennell, and Flavio Comim, Oxford University Press (2021). © Oxford University Press.
DOI: 10.1093/oso/9780198827535.003.0022

The organ trade, Nagral (1995) suggests, is a powerful presentation of this social inequality and deprivation in our society. It is a display of some of the effects of global capitalism in present society that tends to convert everything into a commodity. The wide discrepancy between an organ donor's compensation and the ultimate market value of the organ (a kidney can be bought from a donor for US$1,000–US$3,000, and can be sold for up to US$40,000) shows the impact of a competitive, profit-focused market economy encouraged by globalization (Hudson 2008).

Time and time again the demerits and merits of the trade are discussed in national and international forums of different countries. The modus operandi of the trade, the contributing factors, the impact on the donor and recipients have been extensively studied. Questions are raised on ethical issues concerning the trade. Providing an overview of these issues, the main objective of this chapter is to discuss the illegal trade of organs as an expression of sustained poverty in India, China, and Brazil with a detailed focus on India.

The chapter is organized as follows: the second section discusses the global emergence of the organ trade; the third section is a detailed discussion of the illegal trade in organs in India; the fourth section discusses the illegal trade in organs in Brazil; the fifth section discusses the same in China; the sixth section draws a comparison between the illegal trade in organs in India, China, and Brazil, while the seventh section analyses the ethical issues related to the trade. Section 8 concludes.

The global emergence of the illegal trade in organs

A significant rise in malfunctioning metabolic conditions such as diabetes and hypertension has resulted in increased incidents of chronic kidney diseases (CKD) around the world. Around 10 per cent of CRF (chronic renal failure) patients are estimated to reach the advanced stage, i.e. end-stage renal disease (ESRD) (Aggarwal 2005). For a patient with ESRD, organ transplantation is critical for survival. Live related donor transplantation was the more prevalent mode of practice in the initial stages of organ transplantation due to a better survival percentage of patients. The success rate of deceased donor transplantation was not encouraging. Gradually, the advancement of surgical techniques and the discovery of better anti-rejection drugs such as cyclosporine in the 1970s opened the door for successful live unrelated and deceased donor transplantation. This discovery reduced the complete dependency on live related donors and expanded the scope of organ availability from live unrelated donors and deceased donors. In the following years, deceased donor transplantation became more popular in developed countries as it curtailed the risk of subjecting a living healthy individual to a major surgical procedure and the potential post-operative complications. On the contrary, the transplant programme in countries with financial limitations such as India and China continued to rely on live organ donors. The waiting list is a lot longer and the gap between demand and supply of organs is wider, while the lack of suitable legislation and infrastructure prevented the growth of deceased donor transplantation in these countries (Chugh and Jha 1996, 2000).

Therefore, since the 1980s, although the advancement in medical technology increased the potential for a variety of transplantations worldwide, a scarcity of organs remained a recurrent universal problem and affected many ESRD patients' lives. This chronic shortage of organs has paved the way for a lucrative global black market for purchased organs, mainly kidneys (due to their availability as a spare part in the human body). The availability of donors is a key factor in this trade and people struck by intense poverty served as regular donors in this trade. Scheper-Hughes (2003) projected the direction in which the kidney travels; the trajectory of kidneys in the world is usually from south to north, from east to west, from poorer to more affluent bodies, from black and brown bodies to white ones, and from female to male, or from poor, low-status men to more affluent men. Specifically, the worldwide shortage of organs has encouraged the sale of organs very conspicuously in India and stimulated the use of organs from executed prisoners in China. Thus in the early 1990s residents of Gulf States such as Kuwait, Saudi Arabia, Bahrain, Oman, and United Arab Emirates and other Asian countries (e.g. Malaysia, Singapore) frequently travelled to India to obtain a kidney. Residents of Taiwan, Hong Kong, and Korea went to China (Rothman et al. 1997).

Globally, every year, a million people develop ESRD, but only a fraction of those receive any kind of renal replacement therapy, and even fewer receive kidney transplants (Garwood 2007). The result is that CKD is associated with approximately 735,000 global annual deaths (Lozano et al. 2012). According to a recent estimate, 10 per cent of the 63,000 annual kidney transplants in the world involved payment to a non-related donor of a different nationality. This shows the international aspect of the organ trade, which is illegal in many countries (Garwood 2007). The trade in organs is not only illegal in most countries it is also against the principles of the World Health Organization (WHO). Guiding Principle 5 of WHO on human cell, tissue, and organ transplantation states that 'Cells, tissues and organs should only be donated freely, without any monetary payment or other reward of monetary value.' The principle explains that paid donation is likely to take unfair advantage of the poorest and most vulnerable groups, undermining altruistic donation, and leading to profiteering and human trafficking. Such payment conveys the idea that some persons lack dignity, that they are mere objects to be used by others (WHO 2010). According to the Declaration of Istanbul (2008), the illegal organ trade is an undesirable consequence of the global shortage of organs for transplantation.

Poverty and the global scarcity of organs, however, are not the only compelling factors for the commercialization of organs. Organ transplantation, being ranked as one of the most expensive medical procedures, is a financially rewarding practice. Disparities in the regulatory policies and in the cost of healthcare in most countries helped to promote 'transplant tourism', which in certain circumstances becomes synonymous with the organ trade. 'Transplant tourism' is a highly profitable and growing industry and has both legal and illegal dimensions. Transplant tourism is not illegal, if a related donor and recipient belonging to a country devoid of transplantation facilities travel to another country with such facilities for a transplant. Transplant tourism would be considered illegal and synonymous with the organ trade if patients travel from one country to another to furtively undergo transplant with purchased organs, mostly from poor donors in the destination country. Then commerciality i.e. the financial transaction becomes the central aspect of these transplants instead of the well-being of donors and recipients (Budiani-Saberi and Delmonico 2008).

A class of organ brokers or middlemen who are part of a bigger organized crime syndicate has emerged to facilitate financial transactions and drive this illicit organ trade with the single motive of economic gain. The international movement of potential recipients is also often arranged or facilitated by these intermediaries and healthcare providers who arrange the travel and recruit donors. Several websites offer all-inclusive 'transplant packages'—the price of a renal transplant package ranges from US$70,000 to US$160,000 (Shimazono 2007). Scheper-Hughes (2003) maintains that transplant tourism has become an asset to the medical economies of poorer countries including India, China, and Russia. In addition to India, China, and Russia, the organ trade is now prevalent in several other countries such as Brazil, Pakistan, the Philippines, Turkey, Egypt, South Africa, Moldova, and Romania and has manifested itself in different ways, depending upon the healthcare facilities, regulatory mechanisms, and socio-economic conditions of those countries (Scheper-Hughes 2003; Budiani-Saberi and Delmonico 2008).

The illegal trade in organs in India

HISTORY

In India, renal transplantation became a successful endeavour in the 1970s. The following decade witnessed mastering the surgical techniques and producing immunosuppressant drugs for achieving better survival rates in transplantations (Shroff 2009). Between the 1980s and 1994, there was a sharp rise in kidney transplants in India. Medical tourism, increased chances of survival from transplant, and an unlimited source of donors from economically weaker sections brought potential buyers of organs to India from several parts of the world. India became the 'hub' of the organ trade during that period (Acharya 1994). The high profitability of the trade created pockets of kidney supply or 'kidney zones' in the country. A large number of people deeply entrenched in poverty and indebtedness inhabited these pockets. A few of them had initially sold their kidneys and lured others with the small fortune they had earned to do the same. Later, these people would function as middlemen of a larger network, of doctors or transplant centres. Two such areas in Tamil Nadu became famous for their large supply of kidney donors. It was estimated that out of 580 transplants done in a transplant institute in that area between 1987 and 1995, 400 unrelated donors came from these two areas. People in these two areas were part of the unorganized workforce of a power loom factory, where poverty and indebtedness were very high. The factory owners lent money to these workers at high interest rates to keep them in bondage and tied to the factory. Workers sold their kidneys on average for US$393 to US$472 to relieve themselves from debt. However, they soon reverted to debt again in addition to a reduced capacity to work (*Frontline* 1997). Such pockets of kidney supply were not uncommon in other parts of the country.

These types of unscrupulous trading continued unabated until 1994, during which a successful legal market in organ trading developed in India. However, various ethical issues emerged in this active organ market such as uninformed, fraudulent kidney transplantations in which people were unaware that a kidney transplant procedure had even taken place or donors were deceived with monetary compensation. These issues compelled the Government of India (GOI) to pass legislation prohibiting the donation of organs for commercial gain. GOI passed the Transplantation of Human Organs (THO) Act in 1994, which allowed donation only from a dead person or a living close relative, including a spouse or a living unrelated donor who wanted to donate 'by reason of affection or attachment to the recipient'. The Act was a milestone in the history of organ transplantation in India as it defined and certified brain-stem death, permitted the removal of organs from a deceased person, and directed the taking of appropriate steps in the preservation of organs.

THO Act 1994 notwithstanding, the trade in organs continued. Rapid progress in the rate of organ failure ensured acceleration in the demand for organs against a dismally low supply. The organ donation count is only 0.8 per million people (pmp) in India (Sinha 2010). The transplant programme in India pre- and post- the THO Act relied primarily on live organ donors, whether related or unrelated. In this scenario, the licit and altruistic supply of organs which is primarily from family donors could not keep up with the rising demand, and, therefore, the emergence of an illegal trade in human organs in India became a reality. The pockets of kidney supply were no longer an open market for organ trade but became underground operative centres for the criminal networks once they learned to manipulate the law. For example, in the two areas of organ trade in Tamil Nadu mentioned earlier, immediately after the Act was enforced, fear of the law drove brokers out of the business and forced many hospitals to withdraw from active involvement in the trade. However, there were reports of reactivation of the trade soon afterward as brokers/middlemen became conversant in taking advantage of loopholes in the law (*Frontline* 1997). Section 9(3) of the THO Act, which permitted an unrelated person to donate an organ out of affection or attachment was manipulated by these middlemen to project a large number of transplants from unrelated donors out of affection in spite of the law. Further, as Section 9(1) allowed donation only from a 'near relative' this had indirectly led to marriage for the purpose of kidney donation. The Act was criticized for these limitations, particularly for its inability to reduce the organ trade.

Anand et al. (2015) estimate that a large gap exists in India between individuals with ESRD and those receiving renal replacement therapy, with over 90 per cent likely to die without ever accessing therapy. Due to the paucity of funds and infrastructure, and laxity at policy level, India is far from successful in establishing an active deceased donation programme all over the country. Deceased donor transplantation is at a rudimentary stage and performed in only a few states. The THO Act 1994 was also criticized for being unsuccessful in establishing a central deceased donation programme. GOI amended the Act in 2011 to reduce its limitations. Amendments included an increased level of punishment for the perpetrators of the organ trade, an expanded scope of organ donation from 'near relatives' by including grandparents and grandchildren, and directives to establish appropriate infrastructure to improve the deceased donation programme in India (Ministry of Law 2011).

Thus, on the one hand, there is a high demand for organs for transplantation against an inadequate supply and a weak law and regulatory authorities to control the illegalities of the organ trade. On the other hand, there is a vast section of the population living in poverty and debt vulnerable to being tricked by middlemen into selling kidneys at a nominal price. All these factors compounded the existence of the illegal trade in organs in India for decades. The following section discusses a few recent incidents from the organ trade in India.

INCIDENTS OF ILLEGAL TRADE IN ORGANS IN INDIA

Post-THO Act 1994, there were numerous incidents of organ trade reported by the media. It is beyond the scope of this chapter to discuss them all. A few recent incidents are highlighted here. In 2003, in Punjab, poor migrant labourers from neighbouring states became the victims of an organized network of the organ trade. Without any post-operative care, several labourers died. An estimated 1.5 billion rupees (US$30,348,400) changed hands between people involved in the trade (doctors, middlemen, and donors), but the donors were paid only a fraction (Kumar 2003). The incident which caught national and international attention took place in 2008. In that year, the police uncovered an illegal network of kidney transplantation in Gurgaon (a business centre close to the capital of India, New Delhi) from poor Indian labourers (sometimes against their wishes) primarily to foreign patients. The network had been in operation for almost a decade. It was estimated that there had been transplantation of as many as 500 kidneys. The doctor concerned and his accomplices were sentenced to seven years imprisonment by the court after they were charged with running illegal kidney transplantations (Robinson 2008). Although not of this scale, there were other reported incidents of illegal organ trade from Gujarat (*Times of India* 2007), Assam (PTI 2008), Kolkata (Times of India 2010), Kerala (*Times of India* 2013), and Andhra Pradesh (*Times of India* 2013).

ORGAN SALE IN INDIA: AN AFTER-EFFECT OF POVERTY AND DEBT?

A few earlier research studies—focused on India—discussed the circumstances driving people to sell organs and the impact on their economic life post-organ sale. Most of the studies linked organ sale with poverty and debt.

Cohen (2003) studied thirty commercial kidney donors in a slum of Chennai, India, and his findings echoed a common theme of poverty and debt. He argued that organ sale could rarely be for the purposes of future investment. The decision to sell a kidney is an outcome of a situation of severe indebtedness, driven by the urgency to settle a high-interest debt to local moneylenders. Cohen's study showed a very poor credit habit in the life of these people. There is complete absence of a formal banking system, citing reasons such as illiteracy or poor literacy to understand banking procedures. For any urgent financial need, these people depend on moneylenders who charge high interest rates. These moneylenders have a domineering presence in the lives of poverty-ridden slum dwellers. Therefore, most of the money from organ donation is spent to pay off debts incurred from moneylenders, followed by husbands' and children's expenses such as education, marriage, medical costs, and legal fees; and in some cases, men drank the savings. Therefore, conditions of indebtedness do not disappear. Expenditure soon exceeded income from the organ sale and it did not take very long for all of the thirty donors in Cohen's study to be back in debt. Cohen concluded that poor people sell a kidney to remove debt from their lives, but soon they are in debt again.

Cohen also discussed the gender imbalance in commercial kidney sales. Women were the predominant organ sellers, particularly in urban areas. It was the women who in most cases chose to bear the scar of the operation as they believed that surgery would weaken men's bodies and they would not have enough strength to work and earn money. Ironically, several women who were interviewed in the study were working post-surgery.

Scheper-Hughes (2003) studied organ trade in twelve countries including India, Brazil, and China. Her findings emphasized the debt theory. She argued that the kidney trade represents the poor person's ultimate indemnity against hunger, debt, and penury. Selling the kidney is their last resort. The dominance of women as organ sellers was also prominent in her study. She argued that women rarely receive a purchased organ anywhere in the world. In addition, she also discussed the negative impacts of selling a kidney. Commercial kidney donors are likely to experience chronic pain, ill-health, unemployment, reduced income, serious depression and a sense of worthlessness, family problems, and social isolation.

One of the largest studies on the organ trade in India was by Goyal et al. (2002). They studied the economic and health consequences of the organ trade on the 305 commercial kidney donors in Chennai. Their study reiterated the debt theory. Of the participants, 96 per cent sold their kidneys to pay off debts. Food and household expenses, rent, marriage expenses, and medical expenses were the most common sources of these debts. Therefore, most of the money received from kidney donation was spent on debts, followed by food and clothing or marriage expenses. The remainder was kept as future investment.

However, similar to Cohen's (2003) study, in this study also it was evident that selling a kidney did not make any significant impact on the financial situation of those donors. Their poverty did not diminish, rather their family income actually declined by one-third post-kidney donation. Most of the participants were still in debt and living below the poverty line at the time of the study. The gender difference in kidney donation was also prominent in the study. The majority of the sellers were women. Female kidney donors, rather than their husbands—around 30 per cent—chose to sell their kidney because husbands are the breadwinners in the family. Two women were coerced by their husbands to sell their kidney. About 86 per cent of participants experienced deterioration in their health status after kidney donation.

Haagen (2005) analysed the organ trade in India from a human rights discourse (HRD) and inequality poverty discourse (IPD). He argued about the lack of optimum choices among poor people to raise money in a situation of severe financial crisis, which then becomes the major motivation to selling a kidney. Selling an organ is, therefore, a last, and not a preferred option, but constitutes a much-needed option for raising money.

Carney (2011) linked the illegal trade in organs with poverty induced by natural disasters. He argued that following losses of livelihood in natural disasters, poverty in a region escalates and triggers an illegal organ trade. This became evident after the 2004 Indian Ocean tsunami. Due to the tsunami, fishermen lost their livelihoods; government aid being of little help, the affected area in Chennai developed the reputation of being a major hub for kidney trafficking. Similar to earlier studies, in this study also women were found to be the prominent donors. Women in almost every house in that area resorted to selling kidneys. The organ brokers in this 'Tsunami Nagar' (a poor refugee camp for tsunami survivors) took advantage of the most financially difficult time for these women. The brokers were mostly from the same area and quoted a price as high as US$3,000, but paid these women only a fraction. In addition, these women hardly received any post-operative care and suffered from different ailments after the transplantation.

Further, the author would cite here two case studies of commercial kidney donors (females), interviewed as a part of a research study on the illegal trade in organs in India.[1] Findings from the case studies are briefly discussed here to reinforce the fact that it is poverty in India which drives people to sell organs. The names of the two women are changed to maintain confidentiality. Both the women, Tamanna (37 years) (Box 22.1) and Sudha (52 years) (Box 22.2) sold kidneys to relieve their families from severe financial crisis. They were barely literate women, who earned a nominal wage to support their families.

BOX 22.1 INTERVIEW WITH TAMANNA

The family income of Tamanna was poor and they would often turn to the village moneylender for a loan to meet daily expenses. Inability to pay back the moneylender put her husband's life at risk. She saved her husband's life by selling her kidney and repaying the moneylender. She was never paid the full compensation money as promised or given any post-operative care. Half of the amount of compensation she received was quickly spent and the family was again in a state of financial crisis.

[1] The case studies are part of a study conducted by the author under a research project 'Illicit Trade of Organs Research Programme' (ITORP) of the Von Hügel Institute, University of Cambridge.

Tammana sold her kidney in 2007 when, in addition to the money owed to the moneylender, the family also needed a substantial amount of money for their daughter's impending marriage. Post-transplant, she experienced reduced physical capacity to undertake any strenuous work. 'I sometimes fear for my life and regret selling my kidney' Tamanna added.

Sudha's was also another story of commercial kidney donation driven by severe personal financial crisis.

BOX 22.2 INTERVIEW WITH SUDHA

Sudha sold her kidney to prevent her family of six (including four children) becoming homeless. Sudha's husband was a daily wage labourer and she was a vegetable vendor. Unable to pay rent from their meagre earnings, the family was on the verge of being homeless. She sold her kidney thus saving the family from this catastrophe. She received only half the amount of the promised compensation, which was insignificant in bringing any substantial change to her poor financial condition.

Sudha sold her kidney in 1988 when India had an active legal market for organs. She said, 'At that time many people were selling a kidney to earn money and I also got carried away in that trend.' Notably, similar to Sudha, deception in payment of compensation was also experienced by a few other commercial donors in her village. According to her, sixteen other people from her village never received their full compensation. Except the fact that she owned a house to live in, which she purchased with the compensation money from the organ sale, her financial condition remained the same. Sudha completely disapproves of organ sale.

The illegal trade in organs in Brazil

Brazil has a centralized organ procurement, allocation, and sharing system. The public health system finances more than 95 per cent of the transplants performed, in addition to the essential immunosuppressive drugs required post-transplantation to reduce the risk of organ rejection. From the year 2002 to 2013, there was a gradual increase in the number of transplants in Brazil. In the year 2002, 2,983 kidney transplants were performed in Brazil, in which 1,800 were from living donors and 1,183 were from deceased donors. The country has attained second position in the world in absolute numbers of kidney transplants (Medina-Pestina et al. 2004). In 2013, against a demand of 11,445 transplants, 5,433 kidney transplants were performed of which 1,373 were from living donors and 4,060 were from deceased donors. In total from 2003 to 2013, 64,639 transplants were performed (Brazilian Transplant Registry 2013). Brazil, with a 13.2 donation pmp (IRODaT 2013) has an impressive organ donation count among developing countries.

THE PRESUMED CONSENT LAW FOR ORGAN DONATION IN BRAZIL

Since 1998, organ donation in Brazil has been regulated under 'Presumed Organ Donor Law' (PODL). The law made it mandatory for every citizen in Brazil to donate organs unless a documented will stated otherwise. The major purpose of the law was to increase organ donation, simplify the organ donation process, and reduce organ trafficking. The law, however, was criticized for its 'mandatory' clause, as critics preferred a voluntary donation instead of an obligatory one. Most importantly, the law annulled the role of the family to object to a deceased donation in cases where the deceased did not have the opportunity to oppose organ donation before death. However, the law was amended later to allow family members to opt out against deceased donation, where the deceased did not have the opportunity to do so (Bailey 1999). According to the law, buying and selling human organs is a crime punishable by up to eight years in prison. In the case of the death of the 'donor', the sentence can reach twenty years. A person who sells his or her own organs also faces a sentence of three to eight years behind bars (Osava 2004).

Scheper-Hughes (2000) argues that the existence of an organ trade in Brazil could be traced back to the military regime of the 1970s. During that time, adults and children from the socially and politically marginalized classes were kidnapped for bodies, organs, and tissues. The organ trade in that era was widespread and also 'quasi-legal'. Surgeons were ordered to fulfil their quota of quality organs and were somewhat granted immunity from the police. The transplant teams in hospitals were desperate for organs and would fill quotas through illegal measures. Doctors and transplant teams would meet their quotas of organs by inducing symptoms of brain death in seriously ill patients. Those patients would usually belong to socially marginalized classes bereft of any means of fighting their case. The transplant team of a hospital would be escorted by military police while transporting the organs in an ambulance from one region to another. These reports of organ stealing became public after the democratization process began in Brazil and human rights report such as *Nunca Mas* (never again) came out.

THE MISTAKEN PERCEPTION OF ORGAN HARVESTING FROM KIDNAPPED CHILDREN

Banerjee and Duflo (2011), analysing the lives of the poor observed that the poor often lack critical pieces of information and believe things that are not true. An incident in Brazil in the 1980s showed a similarity to this observation. During that time, rumours of child kidnapping and body stealing disturbed the favelas of north-east Brazil. The suspected cases of child kidnapping and body stealing by 'medical agents' from the United States and Japan, who were said to be seeking a fresh supply of human organs for transplant surgeries in the 'first world' circulated widely in those areas. However, the rumour seemed to be the result of confusion generated among poor and semi-literate people in those areas between markets for children for international adoption with markets for organs of those children for transplant. These people, who were tricked or intimidated into surrendering their babies for domestic and/or international adoption, imagined that their children were taken away for transplant surgery (Scheper-Hughes 2000).

Further, in 1997, a case in Sao Paolo raised questions about medical practices and the possible existence of an organ trade in Brazil. A woman filed a complaint of removal of one of her kidneys on the pretext of operating on an ovarian cyst. The absence of the kidney was discovered by her family doctor in the follow-up examination. Surgeons in the hospital denied any malpractice and confirmed the necessity of the operation citing as the reason that the kidney was embedded in the large ovarian cyst, which is almost an improbable medical possibility—such incidents made common people and the poor perceive the presumed consent law of Brazil with suspicion. They feared that the law would victimize them into inducing untimely brain death and the organs would eventually feed the rich population. The law is believed to be against the welfare of the poor. Even the waiting list for transplants is believed to favour the rich. Wealthy patients with strong political and social connections could move up the list pushing patients without resources to the bottom. Furthermore, Scheper-Hughes (2000) discussed that even if not an obvious form of organ trade, a covert trade of organs through 'compensated gifting' also takes place in some cases. In compensated gifting, the organ is bartered from willing donors in exchange for a gift.

POVERTY AND THE ILLEGAL TRADE IN ORGANS IN BRAZIL

Around 4.6 per cent of the population in Brazil lives on fewer than US$2 per day (World Bank 2014). The percentage is a lot lower than in India and China. However, there are recent cases similar to India, which re-established the theory of poverty and organ trade in Brazil. According to a report in the *New York Times*, in 2004, a large network of organ trade exposed the international scale of the illicit trade in organs. The network of this trade was widespread and involved at least three countries, namely Brazil, South Africa, and Israel. An organ broker in Israel was engaged in the illicit trade with his operatives in Brazil and South Africa. In one case (see Box 22.3), the organ broker operating from Israel brought together a poor donor from Recife, Brazil, and a recipient from Brooklyn to undergo kidney transplantation in Durban, South Africa.

BOX 22.3 THE CASE OF DONOR ALBERTY JOSÉ DA SILVA

For Alberty José da Silva, a poor donor from Recife, Brazil, selling his kidney to earn a large sum of money seemed an opportunity of a lifetime. The prospective recipient, a woman (48 years of age) from Brooklyn had been on dialysis for fifteen years. Her health was constantly deteriorating and her other organs such as heart and lungs were also becoming affected. The kidney transplant was her only path to survival. She was aware of the illegal nature and ethics of transplantation. However, her long years of suffering made her overlook the legalities and take the risk of seeking an organ from the international market. The transplant was performed at a hospital in Durban, South Africa. Alberty José da Silva in exchange for his kidney received US$6,000 from the middlemen. It was not known by him that his deed of paid kidney donation was illegal.

There are several other poor men like Mr da Silva who migrated to slums from Brazil's parched north-eastern backland and sold their organs. About 100 men aged 20 to 40 in the slum of Recife agreed to sell kidneys through the middlemen of this network. Some were ultimately denied the opportunity either due to the negative matching of blood groups or signs of poor health or drug use. It is estimated that eventually about sixty men donated organs through this network in South Africa. The compensation (US$6,000–US$10,000) offered by the middlemen appeared very lucrative to them as the minimum wage in the area was a meagre US$80 per month. With poverty offering a renewable source of poor donors in Recife, the Israeli network was also considering moving their operations to hospitals in Recife and other nearby cities. In an effort to swell their earnings further, the network was also considering extending the market for other vital organs. The network was eventually dismantled by the police (Rohter 2004).

The illegal trade in organs in China

China has been under international scrutiny for some time due to the alleged practice of extracting organs from executed prisoners and selling them to politically well-connected Chinese officials and foreign patients. Some of the major reports which disclosed startling and disturbing facts about China's organ market were from Human Rights Watch/Asia (Scheper-Hughes 2000; Fan 2014), Laogai Research Foundation (Scheper-Hughes 2000; Carney 2011), and the Matas and Kilgour Report (Matas and Kilgour 2006; Carney 2011; Fan 2014).

CHINA—HARVESTING ORGANS FROM EXECUTED PRISONERS?

The Ministry of Health in China confirms that there are 1.5 million people waiting for an organ transplant but only 10,000 legally approved transplants take place (Phillips 2012). There is no organized system of organ donation in China and traditional Chinese custom discourages organ donation. Custom directs Chinese to be buried or cremated intact after death. At least 98 per cent of the transplants are from unrelated donors. In the case of renal transplants, only 0.6 per cent are from living related donors. The government endeavoured to fill the gap by harvesting organs from executed prisoners (Matas and Kilgour 2006). For more than two decades, China had been procuring organs from prisoners on death row, whose executions are sometimes expedited for harvesting their organs (Fan 2014). The practice was authorized in 1984 under 'Temporary Rules Concerning the Utilisation of Corpses or Organs from the Corpses of Executed Criminals'. However, in the absence of clear legal parameters and enforcement measures, the law has been used to the advantage of procuring organs from prisoners in abusive conditions by the Chinese government and selling them to foreign buyers (Hemphill 2007).

The foreign patients are mostly from Asia, for example Hong Kong, Taiwan, Singapore, and other Asian countries which will pay as much as US$30,000 for an organ. Organs were allegedly taken from some 2,000 executed prisoners each year. The actual figure though is difficult to estimate due to the secrecy maintained by the Chinese government. The rising profit from this market and the prospect of a replenished source of organs provided China the incentive to expand the list of capital crimes which also included non-violent crimes. The practice is internationally condemned but continued unabated at least until 2014 (Sharif et al. 2014). A Bellagio Task Force[2] member has made five research trips to China since 1995 to investigate organ harvesting in Chinese prisons. In a trip in 1997, he was accompanied by a Japanese organ broker. All of this broker's patients returned to Japan with a new kidney believed to have been procured from executed prisoners. China denied these allegations and did not allow any independent investigation into these executions or a review of the transplant medical records. A human rights activist, Harry Wu of the Laogai Research Foundation, viewed the practice as a gross violation of human rights. He described a case in which two kidneys were removed from a living anaesthetized prisoner late in the night who was executed the following morning. The brain death in this case followed rather than preceded the harvesting of his organs (Scheper-Hughes 2000).

In 2006, Matas and Kilgour, two Canadian attorneys, compiled a report on the organ market on China. The report was the result of a series of telephone interviews by Chinese informants with doctors in hospitals, officials in detention centres and courts, and other witnesses under the guise of a potential organ buyer. The report presented thirty-three pieces of evidence to prove that China regularly harvested organs from executed prisoners without their consent. The report discussed that due to the prevalence of this practice, the waiting period for organ transplants in China was very short in comparison to other countries in the world. The hospital websites boldly advertised the short waiting period for all organs in return for a big payment. Their report particularly investigated organ harvesting from Falun Gong religious practitioners who were declared political nonconformists by the Chinese government in the 1990s. The evidence in the report pointed towards regular organ harvesting from living Falun Gong practitioners who were believed to be executed after successful tissue matching. After execution, the bodies were immediately cremated to eliminate any proof of the operation. These organs were sold and transplanted for a huge profit. Over the years a large number of Falun Gong practitioners have gone missing in Chinese prisons (Matas and Kilgour 2006; Carney 2011; Fan 2014). These reports attracted criticism from human rights activists, transplant specialists, and doctors from several parts of the world including China and compromised China's image while it was striving to emerge as a superpower in the world.

[2] This is a task force composed of transplant surgeons, organ procurement specialists, human rights activists, and social scientists who met at the Rockefeller Conference Center at Bellagio, Italy, to examine the ethical, social, and medical ramifications of the organ trade (Rothman et al. 1997).

CHINA'S ANTI-ORGAN TRAFFICKING LAW

As a counter-response to these criticisms, in 2006 China enacted 'Provisions on the Administration of Entry and Exit of Cadavers and Treatment of Cadavers' legislation, which prohibits organs from exiting Chinese territory (organ trafficking) without government authorization. In the new Act, however, there are no provisions to regulate organ procurement procedures including organ procurement from deceased prisoners, or preventing the abuse of prisoners for organ removal. Therefore, critics and human rights groups are sceptical about the efficacy of the law in bringing any changes to China's organ procurement practice (Hemphill 2007).

In addition to the reports of organ procurement from executed prisoners, individual incidents of illegal organ trade in China also attracted national and international attention. One of these incidents in 2012 took the world by surprise. A 17-year-old boy sold his kidney to purchase an iPad and iPhone. Four traffickers, an anaesthesiologist, a surgeon, a medical assistant, and two nurses were detained in connection with the incident. The boy's kidney was sold for nearly six times the amount of the compensation he was paid. The boy, however, suffered renal failure after the surgery. Prior to that in 2011, a forced selling of a kidney by a 25-year-old migrant worker at a registered hospital caused public outrage. Organ traffickers in connivance with hospital staff members managed to extract a kidney from the migrant worker (Fan 2014). In 2012, another nationwide network of illegal organ trade was dismantled by the police. Approximately 127 organ suppliers were rescued. Potential donors were recruited online and were kept in secret confinement prior to the transplant. Some transplants were also conducted by force (Phillips 2012).

POVERTY AND THE ILLEGAL TRADE IN ORGANS IN CHINA

The case (see Box 22.4) which emphasizes the link between poverty and organ sale occurred in 2014.

BOX 22.4 A CASE OF ILLEGAL ORGAN TRADE IN CHINA

In 2014, members of a highly organized network of organ traffickers paid impoverished Chinese villagers up to £2,500 per kidney. These live donors were recruited online. Kidneys from these donors reached the recipients—spread across the country—in boxes labelled 'seafood' and the recipients paid five to six times more for each kidney. It was estimated that members of the network had earned a profit of £150,000 from this illicit trade.

Network members were initially engaged exclusively in the trade of organs from brain-dead patients. Mounting profits from the trade pushed them also towards live donors. The network hired a ward in a private hospital to carry out the transplants. All twelve members of this network were eventually arrested and sentenced to between three and twelve years (Newton 2014).

These incidents of the illegal trade in organs either through government-sponsored trade from executed prisoners or the trade with impoverished live donors involving individual criminal networks have set up a feeling of mistrust in China's medical and legal system. The common people are inclined to believe that for any specialized medical care including organ transplant, high-ranking officials with strong political connections would be favoured. If these officials were in need of organs they would turn to prisons to 'hunt' for inmates with matching blood and tissue type in procuring organs. For an ordinary citizen, there would be a long wait for an eventual transplant (Fan 2014).

Comparative analysis of the illegal trade in organs in India, China, and Brazil

The previous narratives were concerned with different aspects of the illegal organ trade such as the history, magnitude, dominant contributory factors, and different studies or reports related to the trade in the three countries. The most common factor that led to the emergence of the trade in these three countries is the scarcity of organs for transplantation. Mastering the surgical techniques of transplantation was a prerequisite. One of the most dominant factors which helped the trade to be sustained is the endemic poverty in these countries. Other factors that had an impact on the nature and magnitude of the trade varied. Brazil has a dark history of organ harvesting from socio-political marginalized classes during the military regime of the 1970s. Currently, with an impressive organ donation count among developing countries (certainly a lot better than India and China), a relatively accessible quality healthcare for all and stringent regulatory laws have managed to substantially reduce organ shortage and increase the number of transplantations over the years. Brazil's presumed consent law is primarily responsible for sustaining the commendable organ donation count. All these factors are instrumental in preventing a frequent large-scale illegal trade in organs in the country.

The most important aspect of the illegal organ trade in China is the organ harvesting from executed prisoners including religious minorities (Falun Gong). The magnitude of this trade is difficult to estimate due to the lack of substantial scientific evidence and political secrecy.

In comparison, there are numerous studies on the illegal trade of organs in India. In addition to the common factors listed above, there are a few other factors such as low organ donation count, absence of a central deceased donation programme, loopholes in the law, and weak regulatory mechanisms to control the trade, all of which have driven trade in the country. One of the most dominant factors which sustained the trade in India is the availability of a large number of people living in poverty, keen to sell organs in a situation of severe financial crisis. As a result, there are several reported incidents of organ trade in India involving poor people selling their organs to overcome financial crisis. Not in the same magnitude as India, but a few poverty-induced incidents of organ trade in Brazil (such as that of Recife) and in China have come into the public eye in recent times. The inhabitants of Recife and the impoverished villagers in China represented the unaddressed vulnerabilities induced by poverty such as was found among poor organ sellers in India.

A few other factors related to poverty such as debt and faulty credit habits were also found to be common among these commercial kidney donors. Banerjee and Duflo (2011) analysed the economic life of the poor and these factors in detail. Although the book is not specifically related to the organ trade, these are some of the omnipresent factors in a poor person's life which ultimately lead to a risk of taking action such as organ sale (in the long run the action is counterproductive both economically and physically). They argued that risk is a central fact of life for the poor who are either employed as casual labour or run a small business without any assurance of regular employment or income. On current income, they can barely manage or are unable to manage their daily living expenses, borrowing money from different sources. Thus, the poor, due to various compelling factors, are unable to reap any benefit from current income to secure a better future. They are unable to build a safety net to which they can turn in situations of financial crisis. They get poorer and poorer over time, getting entangled in a 'poverty trap'. A one-time intervention to break this trap by aid or infusion of money does not permanently change the dismal economic situation of the poor or prevent the poor from regressing again to poverty. Commercial organ donors can be imagined to be in such a 'poverty trap' due to their poor, irregular income and debt accumulated over the years. They attempt to free themselves from the trap by selling a kidney. However, this one-time infusion of money does not bring any drastic long-term change in their economic situation. They spend the money within a short period and plunge into a situation of financial crisis again. Further, Banerjee and Duflo also discussed the absence of a formal banking system in the lives of the poor and a more or less permanent existence of exploitative moneylenders and traders in their lives who charge high interest rates. They favoured the concept of small loans in the form of microfinance with a low-profit motive as more effective and less overbearing measures for the poor with which to face financial crises.

Islam and Gasper (2017) argued that the main motive behind a kidney sale is financial gain in situations of poverty and/or debt peonage and the necessity to support family. Constraining socio-economic power systems and inadequacy of material and social resources to secure a sustainable livelihood and manage daily lives led to the decision to sell a kidney. They further linked the decision to sell an organ with a few pre-existing sellers' capability gaps (linked to Amartya Sen's capability approach). This approach views capabilities and their formation as conditional on multidimensional relationships of structure and agency, and deal systematically with how social circumstances influence the lives of individuals. Sen's approach focuses on individuals' capabilities: their freedom to achieve what they value achieving. Sen's concept of human freedom relies on two other concepts—'functioning' and 'capabilities' (Sen 1999). Functioning refers to multiple diverse aspects of life that people value pursuing or want to be, while capability refers to a person's or group's freedom to achieve valuable functioning. The functioning that organ sellers valued was perceived as achievable by selling one's own kidney. Islam and Gasper (2017) studied organ sellers of another developing country, Bangladesh, and found that of valued functioning, repaying debt to microcredit non-governmental organizations (NGOs) and moneylenders was most prominent.

India outlawed the organ trade in 1994, China in 2006, and Brazil made organ sale a punishable offence in 1998. However, the vulnerabilities induced by poverty, the lack of safety nets, and the escalating demand for organs have never ceased to exist. Therefore, the trade in organs has continued. Trade in organs has negatively affected the 'trust' of the common man in the healthcare systems of the respective countries. They feel that in the waiting list for transplantation, the rich (who can afford to purchase an organ) will be favoured and for the poor, it will be a long delay and sometimes a lifelong wait.

Ethical dimension of the illegal trade in organs

'An exchange becomes "noxious" and ethically flawed if it fails to respect the equal value of persons engaged in it', as Islam and Gasper (2017) argued. Organ sale is one such exchange, in which one person's individual preferences, goals, and ends are subordinated to another person's wealth and power and established higher status (Islam and Gasper 2017). One of the principles of the Declaration of Istanbul (2008) prohibited organ trafficking and stated that organ trafficking violates the principles of equity, justice, and respect for human dignity. It is a consequence of globalization and the resulting privatization of healthcare, which exploits poverty-stricken individuals for their organs (Hudson 2008). It is a link, Cohen (2003) proposed, in a system of debt peonage reinforced by neoliberal structural adjustment.

Scheper-Hughes (2003) and Phadke and Anand (2002) in line with the Declaration of Istanbul (2008), argued that the organ trade is a practice against the notion of human dignity and integrity as it commercializes human body parts. The trade can lead to harmful physical and psychological consequences akin to other social evils such as child labour and forced sex work. Scheper-Hughes (2003), Acharya (1994), and Hudson (2008) discussed the potentially harmful physical consequences for donors. These donors are generally young and are at long-term health risk in the growing situation of diabetes and hypertension in the world. Moreover, as they come from the strata of society where their health and nutrition are already compromised due to economic limitation, removal of organs from them is likely to further impair their health and functional capacity. The risk of post-operative infections in these donors is also high, as they are less likely to receive any follow-up care post-transplantation. These health complications frequently perpetuate the indebted state from which those donors were expecting to free themselves in the first place.

Islam and Gasper (2017) discussed in their study on commercial kidney donors of Bangladesh that most poor sellers are unaware of the function of a kidney, but are tempted to sell one due to the fraudulent claim of the buyers that it is a 'safe', 'profitable', and 'noble' act. However, many sellers do not receive the full, promised compensation.

In some cases, the health of the recipients is also at risk because many of these commercial organ donors are not properly investigated for transmissible diseases like hepatitis, AIDS, malaria, and others which cause additional health risks to the recipients of these organs (Acharya 1994).

Phadke and Anand (2002) discussed ethical issues related to the organ trade in India. They argued that in a society like India, which has strong family ties and places a high value on gift giving and resource sharing, trading a body part is not ethically appropriate. The trade challenges the intrinsic values of a healthy society such as altruism, benevolence, compassion, and empathy on which the society flourishes. Moreover, the availability of paid donors impedes the success of transplantation with living related donors. The paid donors provide an appropriate alternative to the families to purchase an organ instead of donating. Besides, when the motive of donation is purely altruistic, the physical and psychological recovery of the patient is much better as the donor makes an informed decision with a clear understanding of the risks and benefits and receives post-operative care; the notion of altruistic giving provides a psychological boost to the donor. Further organ trade has led to a lack of trust in the healthcare system and also slowed down the evolvement of the deceased donation programme in the country.

The two case studies from India, Tamanna (Box 22.1) and Sudha (Box 22.2) equally supported the ethical arguments discussed above. The case studies showed the economically coercive circumstances the two women faced in selling their organs, never ultimately truly benefiting from the organ sale. Poverty, indebtedness, and most importantly the lack of opportunities to earn a viable income to support the family were crucial factors behind their organ sale. However, both of them (also sixteen other such donors as revealed by Sudha) never received any post-operative care and the full compensation money as promised. Therefore, deception is a key negative factor in such transactions. Moreover, the little money they received did not lead to any long-term benefit. They spent the money in haste to repay debts and fulfil other essential needs of the family and were back in the 'poverty trap' again. This time they had too little to invest to get out of that trap, not even another kidney.

Conclusion

A convergence of various factors, such as the global scarcity of organs, medical inventions for a better survival ratio in organ transplantations (specifically live, unrelated transplantations), economic disparity within and among the countries, and disparity in the policies and cost of healthcare between the countries leading to transplant tourism contributed to the emergence of the illegal trade of organs in the world. In this chapter, the organ trade prevailing in three countries—Brazil, India, and China—was discussed with a major focus on India. Poverty as a dominant reinforcing factor in the organ trade propelled a major part of the discussion. Evidence from all three countries (particularly from India) suggested that endemic poverty is one of the determining factors behind the survival of the trade for decades. These poor donors are perpetually in a 'poverty trap' and in the face of a massive financial crisis, are vulnerable to opportunities to commercially donate organs to raise the required money. That was the only choice, the last resort they perceived to have had in that situation of crisis. Although in China the illegal trade of organs mainly involved harvesting organs from executed prisoners, all except a few incidents related to poverty. The magnitude of the trade is minimal in Brazil among the three countries. However, the prevailing social inequality, organ trade, and lack of trust in the healthcare system appeared to be a few common characteristics of these three countries. Due to social inequalities, people distrust institutions and this affects the overall process of organ donation and escalates the organ trade.

The decision to sell an organ is linked to the concept of the capabilities approach and functioning. Repaying debt was prioritized most among the valued functioning by organ sellers, achieved by selling an organ. Ethically, the organ trade is condemned in most parts of the world as the trade victimizes the poor and marginalized sections of a population. The donor is deceived in monetary compensation in a substantial number of cases; they are at the risk of post-operative infections and the money received does not result in a permanent change in the economic conditions of the poor. Finally, as many of these donors already live in a compromised health situation, the recipients of organs from these donors are also at the risk of life-threatening infections such as HIV and Hepatitis B.

ACKNOWLEDGEMENTS

I wish to thank Dr Flavio Comim for providing me with the opportunity to contribute this chapter. I would also like to thank Professor John Loughlin, former Director of the Von Hügel Institute (VHI) and Dr Frank Madsen, coordinator of ITORP, for giving me the opportunity to conduct this study. However, the opinions, findings, and conclusions expressed in this chapter are those of the author and do not necessarily reflect the views of VHI.

REFERENCES

Acharya, V.N. (1994). 'Status of renal transplantation in India', *Renal Transplantation* 40/3: 158–61.

Aggarwal S. (2005). 'Chronic kidney disease and its prevention in India', *Kidney International* 68: S41–S45

Anand, S., Shivashankar, R., Ali, M.K., Kondal, D., Binukumar, B., Montez-Rath, M.E. et al. (2015). 'Prevalence of chronic kidney disease in two major Indian cities and projections for associated cardiovascular disease', *Kidney International* 88/1: 178–85.

Bailey, E. (1999). 'Should the State have rights to your organs? Dissecting Brazil's Mandatory Organ Donation Law', *The University of Miami Inter-American Law Review* 30/3: 707–26.

Banerjee, A.V. and Duflo, E. (2011). *Poor Economics: A Radical Rethinking of the Way to Fight Global Poverty*. Gurgaon: Random House India.

Bardhan, P. (2007). 'Poverty and inequality in China and India. Elusive link with globalisation', *Economic and Political Weekly*. 42/38: 3849–52.

Basu, S.R. (2009). 'Comparing China and India: Is the dividend of economic reforms polarized?', *The European Journal of Comparative Economics* 6/1: 57–99.

Brazilian Transplant Registry (2013). 'Organ transplantation in Brazil'. Available at www.abto.org.br/abtov03_ingles/Upload/file/BrazilianTransplantationRegistry/rbt-ing-parc.pdf, accessed 15 November 2018.

Budiani-Saberi, D.A. and Delmonico, F.L. (2008). 'Organ trafficking and transplant tourism: a commentary on the global realities', *American Journal of Transplantation* 8/5: 925–29.

Carney, S. (2011). *The Red Market*. Gurgaon: Hachette Book Publishing India

Chugh, K.S. and Jha, V. (1996). 'Commerce in transplantation in third world countries', *Kidney International* 49/5: 1181–86.

Chugh, K.S. and Jha, V. (2000). 'Problems and outcomes of living unrelated donor transplants in the developing countries', *Kidney International* 57/74: 1523–1755.

Clementi, F. and Schettino, F. (2013). *Income Polarization in Brazil, 2001–2011: A Distributional Analysis Using PNAD Data*. Rio de Janeiro: AIEAA (Italian Association for Agricultural and Applied Economics) Conference, Parma, 6–7 June. Available at www.unigramsci.it/site/assets/files/1206/ecopol1415-sche-lez7.pdf, accessed 15 November 2018.

Cohen, L. (2003). 'Where it hurts: Indian material for an ethics of organ transplantation', *Zygon* 38/3: 663–68.

Declaration of Istanbul. (2008). Available at www.declarationofistanbul.org/about-the-declaration/structure-and-content, accessed 15 November 2018.

Fan, J. (2014). 'Can China stop organ trafficking?', *The New Yorker*, 10 January. Available at www.newyorker.com/news/news-desk/can-china-stop-organ-trafficking, accessed 15 November 2018.

Frontline (1997). 'One-kidney communities', 13–26 December, 14/25. Available at www.frontline.in/static/html/fl1425/14250730.htm, accessed 15 November 2018.

Garwood, P. (2007). 'Dilemma over live-donor transplantation'. *Bulletin of the World Health Organization* 85/1: 5–6.

Goyal, M., Mehta, R., Schneiderman, L., and Sehgal, A. (2002). 'Economic and health consequences of selling a kidney in India', *Journal of American Medical Association* 288/13: 1589–93.

Haagen, M. (2005). *Indian Organ Trade: From the Perspective of Weak Cultural Relativism*. Centre for East and South-East Asian Studies, South Asia Track. Available at http://lup.lub.lu.se/luur/download?func=downloadFile&recordOId=1331422&fileOId=1331423, accessed 19 January 2019.

Haub, C. (2012). 'The BRIC countries'. Population Reference Bureau. Available at www.prb.org/Publications/Articles/2012/brazil-russia-india-china.aspx, accessed 15 November 2018.

Hemphill, J.E. (2007). 'China's practice of procuring organs from executed prisoners: human rights groups must narrowly tailor their criticism and endorse the Chinese constitution to end abuses', *Pacific Rim Law and Policy Journal* 16/2: 431.

Hudson, K.A. (2008). 'Globalization and the black market organ trade: when even a kidney can't pay the bills', *Disability Studies Quarterly* 28/4: 11.

IRODaT (International Registry in Organ Donation and Transplantation) (2013). Available at www.irodat.org, accessed 15 November 2018.

Islam, M.S. and Gasper, D. (2017). 'Kidney sales: how far do sellers exercise reasoned freedom? Cases from Bangladesh', in M. Deveaux and V. Panitch (eds) *Exploitation: From Practice to Theory*. London: Rowman and Littlefield, 195–220.

Jha, R. (2002). 'Reducing poverty and inequality in India: Has liberalization helped?'. Available at https://ccep.crawford.anu.edu.au/acde/publications/publish/papers/wp2002/wp-econ-2002-04.pdf, accessed 15 November 2018.

Kumar, S. (2003). 'Police uncover large scale organ trafficking in Punjab', *British Medical Journal* 326/7382: 180.

Lozano, R., Naghavi, M., Foreman, K., Lim, S., Shibuya, K., Aboyans, V. et al. (2012). 'Global and regional mortality from 235 causes of death for 20 age groups in 1990 and 2010: a systematic analysis for the global burden of disease study', *The Lancet* 380/9859: 2095–128.

Matas, D. and Kilgour, D. (2006). 'Report into allegations of organ harvesting of Falun Gong practitioners in China'. Available at http://organharvestinvestigation.net, accessed 15 November 2018.

Medina-Pestina, J.O., Vaz, M.S., Park, S.I., Garcia, V.D., Abbud-Filho, M., and de Holanda Campos, H. (2004). 'Organ transplantation in Brazil in the year 2002', *Transplantation Proceedings* 4/36: 799–801.

Ministry of Law, Justice and Company Affairs (Legislative Department) (2011). 'The transplantation of human organs (amendment act), 2011'. New Delhi. Available at https://mohfw.gov.in/acts-rules-and-standards-health-sector/acts/transplantation-human-organs-acts-and-rules, accessed 21 January 2019.

Nagral, S. (1995). 'Ethics of organ transplantation', *Indian Journal of Medical Ethics* 3/2: 18–23.

Newton, J. (2014). 'Organ trafficking gang who paid impoverished villagers £2,500 a kidney and transported them around in boxes labelled "seafood" are jailed', *Mail Online*. Available at www.dailymail.co.uk/news/article-2722979/Organ-trafficking-gang-paid-impoverished-Chinese-villagers-2-500-kidney-transported-boxes-labelled-seafood-jailed.html, accessed 15 November 2018.

Osava, M. (2004). 'Brazil: poor sell organs to trans-atlantic trafficking ring', *Inter Press Service News Agency*, 23 February. Available at www.ipsnews.net/2004/02/brazil-poor-sell-organs-to-trans-atlantic-trafficking-ring/, accessed 15 November 2018.

Phadke, K.D. and Anandh, U. (2002). 'Ethics of paid organ donation', *Pediatric Nephrology* 17/5: 309–11.

Phillips, T. (2012). 'Chinese organ trafficking ring dismantled', *The Telegraph*, 5 August. Available at www.telegraph.co.uk/news/worldnews/asia/china/9453357/Chinese-organ-trafficking-ring-dismantled.html, accessed 15 November 2018.

PTI (Press Trust of India) (2008). 'Human organ trade racket busted in Assam', *The Times of India*, 8 August. Available at http://timesofindia.indiatimes.com/india/Human-organ-trade-racket-busted-in-Assam/articleshow/3342438.cms, accessed 15 November 2018.

Robinson, S. (2008). 'India's black market organ scandal', *Time World*, 1 February.

Rohter, L. (2004). 'The organ trade: a global black market; tracking the sale of a kidney on a path of poverty and hope', *New York Times*, 23 May.

Rothman, D.J., Rose, E., Awaya, T., Cohen, B., Daar, A., Dzemeshkevich, S.L. et al. (1997). 'The Bellagio Task Force report on transplantation, bodily integrity, and the international traffic in organs', *Transplantation Proceedings* 29/6: 2739–45.

Scheper-Hughes, N. (2000). 'The global traffic in human organs', *Current Anthropology* 41/2: 191–224.

Scheper-Hughes, N. (2003). 'Keeping an eye on the global traffic in human organs', *The Lancet* 361/9369: 1645–48.

Sen, A.K. (1999). *Development as Freedom*. Oxford: Oxford University Press.

Sharif, A., Fiatarone Singh, M., Trey, T., and Lavee, J. (2014). 'Organ procurement from executed prisoners in China', *American Journal of Transplantation* 14/10: 2246–52.

Shimazono, Y. (2007). 'The state of the international organ trade: a provisional picture based on integration of available information', *Bulletin of the World Health Organization* 85/12: 955–62.

Shroff, S. (2009). 'Legal and ethical aspects of organ donation and transplantation', *Indian Journal of Urology* 25/3: 348–55.

Singh, L. (2013). 'Globalisation and poverty in India', *Voice of Research* 1/4: 47–50.

Sinha, K. (2010). 'Drive to right India's organ donation record', *The Times of India*, 27 November. Available at https://timesofindia.indiatimes.com/india/Drive-to-right-Indias-organ-donation-record/articleshow/7001940.cms, accessed 15 November 2018.

Times of India (2007). 'Gujarat in organ trade', 19 January. Available at http://timesofindia.indiatimes.com/city/ahmedabad/Gujarat-in-organ-trade/articleshow/1320081.cms, accessed 15 November 2018.

Times of India (2010). 'Kidney racket kingpin's first victim: himself'. Available at https://timesofindia.indiatimes.com/city/kolkata/Kidney-racket-kingpins-first-victim-Himself/articleshow/6488823.cms, accessed 21 January 2019.

Times of India (2013). 'Kidney racket returns to haunt Palnadu region', 15 February. Available at http://timesofindia.indiatimes.com/city/hyderabad/Kidney-racket-returns-to-haunt-Palnadu-region/articleshow/18507433.cms, accessed 15 November 2018.

Wade, R.H. (2004). 'Is globalization reducing poverty and inequality?', *World Development* 32/4: 567–89.

WHO (World Health Organization) (2010). 'WHO guiding principles on human cell, tissue and organ transplantation'. Available at www.who.int/transplantation/Guiding_PrinciplesTransplantation_WHA63.22en.pdf?ua=1, accessed 15 November 2018.

World Bank (2014). 'Poverty and equity data'. Available at http://povertydata.worldbank.org/poverty/region/LAC, accessed 15 March 2019.

Part IV

Inequality and Political Economies

23 Demography and roots of gender inequality in BRICS

Prabir C. Bhattacharya and Vibhor Saxena

Introduction

All BRICS countries suffer from gender inequality in many different dimensions. The purpose of this chapter is to highlight some of these inequalities. Three of the BRICS countries—India, China, and Russia—have highly skewed sex ratios and these have major social and economic consequences.

Demography

The human sex ratio, which is usually defined in terms of the number of males per 100 females, varies greatly between countries and regions. The biological norm is for the sex ratio at birth (SRB) to be about 105 more or less everywhere—meaning just over 51 per cent of births are boys and just under 49 per cent are girls. But with equal care and feeding, females experience lower mortality. It is therefore not surprising that the sex ratio of the population as a whole in the West and in many other regions leans in favour of women. In the UK this ratio is 99; in the US, 97; and in the EU, 96. In sub-Saharan Africa, where life expectancy at birth is relatively low for both sexes, the ratio is 99. In Russia, Ukraine, and some former Eastern Bloc countries, it is among the lowest in the world: 86 for both Russia and Ukraine.

RUSSIA'S 'MISSING MEN'

There are other countries—notably China and India—where the ratio is abnormally high: the ratio is 106 in both countries. Yet even in India and China, there are now more elderly women than men. The sex ratio among over-65s is 90 in India and 91 in China. By comparison, it is 76 for the UK and 75 for the US. For Russia this ratio seems astonishingly low: only 45. This, coupled with the fact that the overall sex ratio is also

Prabir C. Bhattacharya and Vibhor Saxena, *Demography and roots of gender inequality in BRICS* In: *Handbook of BRICS and Emerging Economies.* Edited by: P.B. Anand, Shailaja Fennell, and Flavio Comim, Oxford University Press (2021). © Oxford University Press.
DOI: 10.1093/oso/9780198827535.003.0023

quite low in Russia, while the sex ratios at birth and for childhood years are in line with the standard norms, leads one to wonder if the survival of men in Russia has not been particularly difficult. The difference in life expectancy at birth between males and females in Russia—a difference of thirteen years in favour of females—is the highest of any country in the world today. There would clearly appear to be a problem of 'missing men' in Russia (the reverse of the missing women problem in India and China).[1]

Since 1992, Russia's population has declined by 7 million from 149 million to 142 million. This decline is linked to high mortality rates and a sudden sharp decline in fertility. After the collapse of communism, the fertility rate plunged from 2.2 births per woman in 1987 to 1.17 in 1991 (the replacement level of fertility is 2.1). It has since recovered to around 1.3, but that is still among the lowest in the world. At the same time, the death rate went in the opposite direction. In 1991–92 it overtook the birth rate and since then Russia has recorded nearly 13 million more deaths than births.

This upsurge in mortality has been disproportionately concentrated among men and women of working age, particularly men. For men in their thirties and forties, Russia's death rate today is roughly twice what it was forty years ago. It has been estimated that if Russia had maintained the hardly-exacting survival rates of the years just before the collapse of communism, there would have been 6.6 million fewer deaths between 1992 and 2006 (4.9 million of them men).

While there have been rapid increases in HIV/AIDS infections and tuberculosis in Russia, the main causes of this mortality upsurge are deaths from heart disease and 'external causes' such as injuries, homicide, and suicide. Alcohol is the common denominator. Russian men in particular tend to consume hard spirits and to drink in binges.

It has been estimated that an average male adult drinks a bottle of vodka per week (or the equivalent). Russians have always drunk vodka, but the psychological stress following the collapse of communism would appear to have played an important role in recent times. One is tempted to say that a large number of Russians have lost the will to live and are simply drinking themselves to death.

But why have men of working age suffered more than women? It has been suggested that the gender order that developed during the Soviet era made men virtually redundant within the typical Russian household, especially in urban areas. It served the perceived needs of the state by expecting women to combine roles as workers, mothers, and household managers; while men's far more limited role involved serving as soldiers, workers, and managers.

Soviet society was 'matrifocal' with everyday family life relying 'heavily on cross-generational help and caregiving relations, taking place mostly between women', and men estranged from most family spheres. The respect men commanded within the household depended mainly on their role as primary breadwinners. Once that role came under threat or disappeared at the end of the Soviet era, they had no other roles

[1] For a discussion of the 'missing women' problem in India and China, see, among others, Sen (1990); Coale (1991); Klasen (1994). See also discussions in this chapter.

or support network to fall back on. Since vodka drinking had always been part of traditional Russian male culture, it was the obvious culturally appropriate way for men to cope with their hardships.

Apart from the effects of alcoholism on worker productivity, the danger here is that if dying young is common, it affects people's economic decisions. They will be less likely to spend years acquiring training and education to benefit their future. Companies become less likely to invest in their workforces. People are less likely to save for their futures, which can become a drain on the state in years to come. Also, activities where men may have comparative advantage may be adversely affected if there is a shortage of men in relevant age groups.

THE INDIA–CHINA COMPARISON

Be that as it may, men are not dying in larger numbers than women in Russia because of any deliberate discrimination against them. In India and China, by contrast, the culture of discrimination against females has been mainly responsible for the sex ratio imbalances. Both countries have a problem with sex-selective abortions and higher rates of female child mortality (see, among others, Cai and Lavely 2003; Bhattacharyya 2006; Kulkarni 2007). It has been estimated that if India had the normal SRB of 105 and the same mortality differentials by sex as in the West, then there would have been 9.8 million more girls in the age group birth to 14 years of age in 2001 (Kulkarni 2007). Of this, 3.78 million (38 per cent) is attributed to excess female mortality and the rest, 6.07 million, to a higher than normal SRB. This works out at 3.5 per cent of the female population in this age group. An estimate of 'missing girls' in China for the cohorts born in the period 1980–2000 puts the figure at 4.1 per cent of girls for the period as a whole, while in the late 1990s, the figure rose to over 8 per cent, a figure much higher than that seen in India (Cai and Lavely 2003).

It has been estimated that there will be 30 to 40 million more men than women of marriageable age in China and India by 2020 as a result of sex-selective abortions. Many young men will face difficulties in finding brides. The possible consequences of a large number of men remaining unmarried have attracted a great deal of attention in both academic and popular discussions in recent years. It has been argued that this marriage squeeze will result in socially disruptive behaviour among men unable to find brides, that there will be an increase in violence against women (including kidnapping and trafficking of women), a rise in sexually transmitted diseases, and an increase in mental health problems.

In this context it is well to remember that the excess female child mortality in China and India in the past meant that there must always have been a shortage of brides in their age groups for young men in these countries. In India, the marriage system evolved such that husbands are usually older than their wives. In China, there is evidence to suggest that a shortage of females was a pervasive feature of the Qing dynasty (1644–1912) and the republican period (see, among others, Lee et al. 1994; Skinner 1997). Under the Qing dynasty 'about 10 per cent of men probably never married' (Smith 1994). There have also been other societies where many men never married. In Ireland, for example, in the late nineteenth and the early twentieth centuries, late marriage was quite common and a considerable proportion never married at all. Also, in the West today the proportion of men over 40 years of age who have never married has been rising. In the USA, for example, while in 1970, 4.9 per cent of men in the age group 40–44 years had never married, in 2008, the figure was 16.9 per cent (US Census Bureau 2010). It is also well to remember that many of the ills attributed to gender imbalance in China could also be explained by the massive migration of males from rural to urban areas.

Life expectancy at birth for both males and females has been increasing in both India and China. The gains for females have been much greater than for males in the past few years, and overall female life expectancy now exceeds male life expectancy in both countries by about four years. In India, in the early years of the twentieth century, overall life expectancy was around twenty years. By 1961, this had risen to 41.3 years (41.9 for males, 40.6 for females). There was an increase to 61.9 years by 2000 (61 for males, 62.7 years for females). The figures for 2009 show life expectancy at 69.89 years, with that for males being 67.46 years of age and for females at 72.61 years of age. China's record here has been better than India's. Average life expectancy in the 1964–82 intercensal period was sixty years (males 59 and females 61.4 years of age) and improved to nearly seventy years in the period 1990–2000 (males 69.7 and females 72.8 years of age). Since then it has risen further, with gains for females being higher than for males. The 2009 figures are: 71.61 years for males and 75.5 years of age for females. This increase in female life expectancy is tilting the sex ratio away from its male bias.

But why is there the preference for sons in China and India? At the heart is thought to be the patrilineal kinship system. Lineage of the family is continued only through sons, and daughters are typically excluded from inheritance rights. In societies where social security provisions for old age are absent or minimal, sons are expected to support their parents, and sons provide the best assurance of security in parents' old age. By contrast, married daughters become members of their husband's families with little or no obligation towards their natal families. Marriages tend to be patrilocal (meaning that married couples live near the husband's family) or virilocal (married couples reside with the husband's parents). The parents of married sons, therefore, have the additional help of their daughters-in-law for farming and related activities. Equally, it becomes extremely difficult for married daughters to have equal rights vis-a-vis the settled male members of their new families. In South Asia, the practice of dowry adds to the financial burden of having daughters. Further, given the patrilineal inheritance system, a mother without a son will lose her husband's assets on his death. Overlaying all of these is the stipulation in both Hinduism and Confucian tradition that certain death rites can be performed only by sons.

In India, the practice of dowry would appear to have been of great significance in the Indian context. It is reportedly one of the main reasons for son preference in the country.

The practice involves the giving of money, jewellery, and other durable goods by a bride's family to a groom's family. The amounts can be huge, constituting several years of household income of the bride's family, and often indebting them severely. The 'social justification' for this practice has been in terms of it being the 'last expense' that a girl's family must bear before she becomes the 'responsibility' of her husband's family and also in terms of compensating the daughter for her exclusion from inheritance rights (though, of course, the 'dowry gifts' never accrue to the daughter; instead, they accrue to the husband and his family). In reality, the practice is more like a groom purchase—in general, the more educated and the wealthier the groom, the higher the dowry demanded. The practice, which at one time used to be confined mainly to North India and among the upper castes, has now become widespread across India, despite the government enacting legislation banning the practice. The Dowry Prohibition Act of 1961, subsequently strengthened through amendments in 1984 and 1986, banned the practice. The law, however, has been impotent in the face of widespread acceptance of the practice by society. There has also been dowry inflation in recent years as economic prosperity has fuelled an increase in 'consumerism'. Indeed, in the early years of the availability of sex-determination tests, they were marketed with slogans such as: 'Spend Rs. 500 now, save Rs. 50,000 later.'

What have been the economic effects of skewed sex ratios in India and China? It has been argued that about of half of the increase in the China savings rate over the last twenty-five years could be attributed to the rise in SRBs: households with sons need to save more to attract brides in the highly competitive market (Wei and Zhang 2011). In India, however, the dowry gifts given in the form of jewellery often get hoarded and may indeed have detrimental effects on the economy.

What is the future of sex ratio evolution in these countries? There are now signs that in those states in India which have had the highest SRBs—Punjab and Haryana, in particular—SRBs have begun to decline. However, this has to be set against the fact that the sex ratio of the population in the age group 'birth to six years' has seen an increase in some of the other states which previously had lower SRBs (see Paper 1, provisional population totals [Government of India 2011]). In China, SRB did decline appreciably during 2000–05 in several regions such as in the contiguous provinces of Guangdong, Hainan, and Guangxi in the south-eastern part of the country. In some other areas, the SRB is simply stagnating.

BRAZIL AND SOUTH AFRICA

In contrast to the other three BRICS nations, Brazil and South Africa do not have the problem of skewed sex ratios (cf. Figures 23.1 and 23.2). In relation to Figure 23.1, Russia's high sex ratio from the 1950s to 2000s is to be explained in terms of the excess male deaths that occurred during the Second World War. In relation to Figure 23.2, it will be noted that South Africa had a sudden surge in the number of male children to

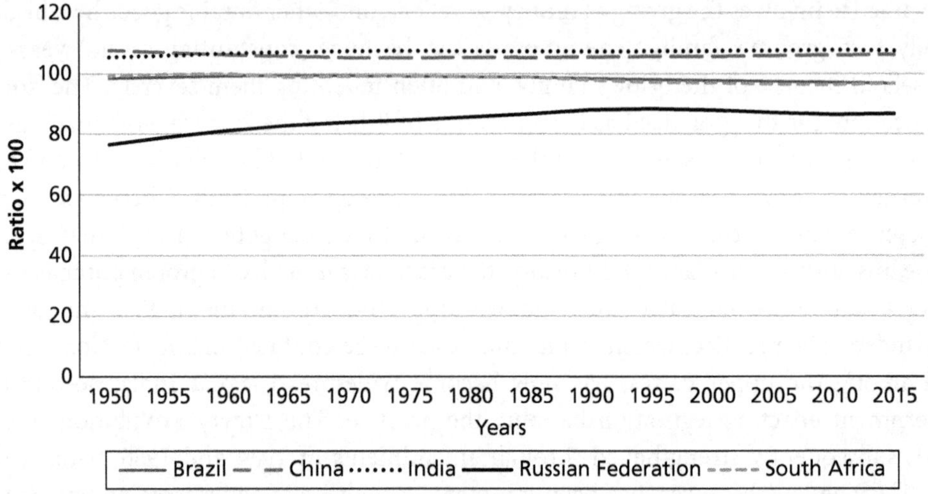

Figure 23.1 Male to female sex ratios, BRICS, 1950–2015

Source: United Nations Population Division (UN 2015).

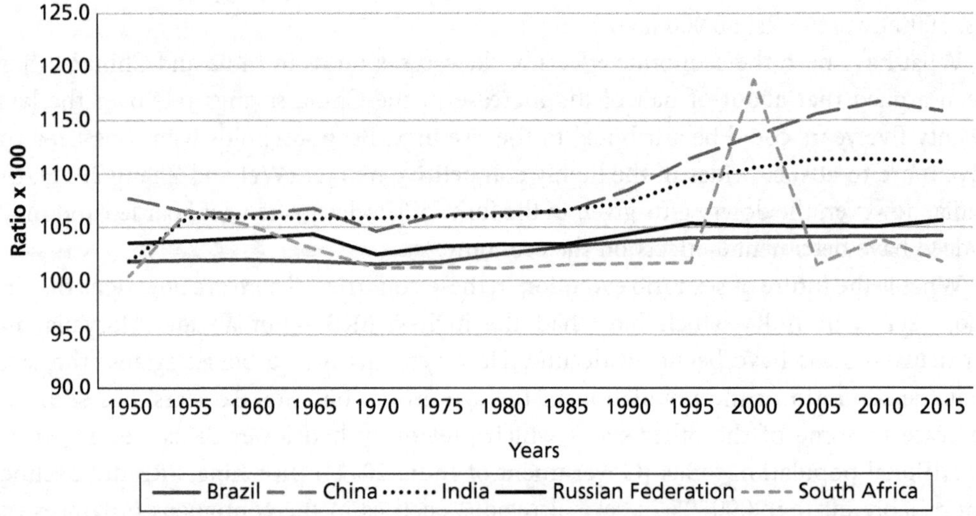

Figure 23.2 Male to female sex ratios (0–4 age group), BRICS, 1950–2015

Source: United Nations Population Division (UN 2015).

female children in the age group of 0–4 years after the end of apartheid, but this ratio has since returned to normal.

In Latin America, including in Brazil, the Catholic Church with its anti-abortion stance has an important influence on people's lives. In South Africa, as in most of sub-Saharan Africa, a woman's role as income earner has been a fabric of society. Further, in Brazil, South Africa, and Russia, marriages are not patrilocal or virilocal; inheritance rights as embedded in culture also differ substantially in these countries as compared to those in India and China.

On these grounds, one would expect the bias against women to be more pronounced in India and China than in the other three BRICS nations. Further, in China, given the one-party rule, it is possible for the state to intervene more directly to improve the status of women if it so wishes, as indeed it did so effectively at the onset of communist rule. When the communists came to power in 1949, they enacted a series of laws that supported freedom of marriage, equal pay, equal benefits, and equal educational opportunities for women, and most demographers agree that these policies helped to bring down sharply the practice of female infanticide in the 1960s. The economic reforms that began in the late 1970s changed the landscape. However, while under the market system bias against women in the labour market reappeared, there are recent signs of changes. Changes in India, by contrast, have been slow and India, therefore, continues to display the greatest bias against women among the BRICS countries.

Women's agency

In this section, we look at some of the usual indicators of gender inequality. These too bring out the particular problems faced by women in India. Table 23.1 presents the proportion of population engaged in economic activity in each of the BRICS countries. India and South Africa have the lowest proportion of population in the workforce. Statistics on male and female labour force participation rates in these countries are presented in Tables 23.2 and 23.3, respectively, and it is immediately seen that the female labour force participation rate has been consistently and abysmally low in India. (For comparison, labour force participation rates for males and females in the OECD countries as a group, and for the USA and UK separately are presented in Table 23.4). By contrast, China has had a female labour force participation rate that has been consistently high. Brazil, too, has shown a consistently rising trend in its female labour force participation rate.

Table 23.1 Proportion of economically active population in BRICS

	1990	1995	2000	2005	2010	2013
Brazil	64.6	69.2	68.2	70.2	70	69.8
China	78.9	78.6	77.1	73.2	70.7	71.3
India	60.9	60.5	59.1	60.8	55.4	54.2
Russia	67.2	60.5	60.7	61.9	63	63.7
South Africa	53.5	55.1	56.8	54.1	51.3	52.1

Source: World Bank (ILO estimates) (World Bank 2018).

Table 23.2 Male labour force participation

	1990	1995	2000	2005	2010	2013
Brazil	85.4	84.8	82.1	82.1	81.1	80.8
China	84.8	84.8	84.8	84.8	84.8	84.8
India	85.1	84.0	82.8	83.3	80.8	79.9
Russia	76.3	69.9	68.4	68.7	70.8	71.7
South Africa	68.2	66.2	64.5	62.2	59.9	60.5

Source: World Bank (ILO estimates) (World Bank 2018).

Table 23.3 Female labour force participation

	1990	1995	2000	2005	2010	2013
Brazil	44.6	54.2	54.9	58.9	59.4	59.4
China	72.7	72.2	70.7	66.5	63.5	63.9
India	34.8	35.4	33.9	36.9	28.6	27
Russia	59.6	52.7	54.1	56.2	56.4	57.1
South Africa	39.4	44.5	49.6	46.5	43.5	44.5

Source: World Bank (ILO estimates) (World Bank 2018).

Table 23.4 Labour force participation rates in OECD, USA, and UK

	OECD		USA		UK	
	Male	Female	Male	Female	Male	Female
1990	82.2	58.1	85.6	67.8	88.3	67.3
1995	81.2	58.1	84.3	69.7	84.7	67.1
2000	80.9	59.1	83.9	70.7	84.1	68.9
2005	80.2	60.3	81.8	69.2	83.1	69.6
2010	79.7	61.8	79.6	68.4	82.5	70.2
2013	79.6	62.6	78.7	67.2	82.9	71.6

Source: OECD 2019.

Female labour force participation rate is an important indicator of women's autonomy and it is clear that much remains to be done in these dimensions in India and South Africa, particularly so in India. Similarly, female literacy—another indicator of women's autonomy—remains a particular problem in India (Table 23.5).

One way of empowering women would, of course, be for them to have a greater say in the political process. Table 23.6 presents data on the proportion of seats held by women in national parliaments. In the case of India, although the statistics are not particularly impressive, they show an improvement over time. South Africa has been a star performer

Table 23.5 Literacy rates in BRICS

Country Name	Total Literacy	Male	Female
Brazil	92.6	92.2	92.9
China	96.4	98.2	94.5
India	71.2	81.3	60.6
Russian Federation	99.7	99.7	99.6
South Africa	94.3	95.5	93.1

Source: World Factbook (CIA annual).

Table 23.6 Proportion of seats held by women in national parliaments (%)

	1990	1998	2001	2003	2005	2010	2014
Brazil	5.3	6.6	6.8	8.6	8.6	8.6	9.9
China	21.3	21.8	21.8	20.2	20.3	21.3	23.4
India	5.0	8.1	8.8	8.8	8.3	10.8	11.4
Russian Federation	15.6	10.2	7.6	7.6	9.8	14.0	13.6
South Africa	2.8	28.8	29.8	29.8	32.8	44.5	41.5
OECD members	12.1	16.4	17.9	19.7	20.8	23.4	27.0
United States	6.6	11.7	14.0	14.3	15.2	16.8	19.3

Note: Data are presented for the years where information is available for all regions.
Source: World Bank (IPU estimates) (World Bank 2019).

here. At the time of apartheid women formed only 2.8 per cent of representatives in parliament; today, the figure is over 40 per cent.

However, it is important to mention that among BRICS, Russia is the only country which has no official policy of quotas for females in the political sphere. These quotas, whether at the national or sub-national level, have been proven statistically beneficial for gender equality and also for the other social indicators (Bratton and Ray 2002; Chattopadhyay and Duflo 2004).

Conclusion

Gender inequality continues to be a problem in BRICS as in most other countries. Within BRICS, India—given the extent of gender inequality in that country—probably has most to gain by reducing such inequality. Equally, Russia—given the extent of excess male mortality in the working-age group in that country—stands to gain most by changing the gender order that estranges men from most family spheres.

ACKNOWLEDGEMENTS

Part of the material in this chapter is adapted from the corresponding author's previous work in this area.

REFERENCES

Bhattacharyya, S.C. (2006). 'Energy access problem of the poor in India: is rural electrification a remedy?', *Energy Policy* 34/18: 3387–97. doi:10.1016/j.enpol.2005.08.026.

Bratton, K.A. and Ray, L.P. (2002). 'Descriptive representation, policy outcomes, and municipal day-care coverage in Norway', *American Journal of Political Science* 46/2: 428–37. doi:10.2307/3088386.

Cai, Y. and Lavely, W. (2003). 'China's missing girls: numerical estimates and effects on population growth', *China Review* 3/2: 13–29. https://doi.org/10.1017/S0268416012000240.

Chattopadhyay, R. and Duflo, E. (2004). 'Women as policy makers: evidence from a randomized policy experiment in India', *Econometrica* 72/5: 1409–43. doi:10.1111/j.1468–0262.2004.00539.x.

CIA (Central Intelligence Agency) (annual). *Library Publications, The World Factbook*, Field Listing: Literacy(%). Available at www.cia.gov/library/publications/the-world-factbook/fields/2103.html, accessed 14 January 2019.

Coale, A.J. (1991). 'Excess female mortality and the balance of the sexes in the population: an estimate of the number of "missing females"', *Population and Development Review* 17/3: 517–23. doi:10.2307/1971953.

Government of India (2011). 'Paper 1, provisional population totals'. New Delhi. Available at http://censusindia.gov.in/2011-prov-results/prov_results_paper1_india.html, accessed 16 November 2018.

Klasen, S. (1994). '"Missing women" reconsidered', *World Development* 22/7: 1061–71. doi:10.1016/0305-750X(94)90148-1.

Kulkarni, P.M. (2007). 'Estimation of missing girls at birth and juvenile ages in India'. New Delhi. Available at www.unfpa.org/sites/default/files/resource-pdf/UNFPA_Publication-39767.pdf, accessed 16 November 2018.

Lee, J., Feng, W., and Campbell, C. (1994). 'Infant and child mortality among the Qing Nobility: implications for two types of positive check', *Population Studies* 48/3: 395–411. doi: 10.1080/0032472031000147936.

OECD (Organisation for Economic Co-operation and Development (2019). *Labour Force Participation Rate (Indicator).* doi: 10.1787/8a801325-en.

Sen, A. (1990). 'More than 100 million women are missing', *The New York Review of Books*, 20 December. Available at www.nybooks.com/articles/1990/12/20/more-than-100-million-women-are-missing/, accessed 16 November 2018.

Skinner, G.W. (1997). 'Family systems and demographic processes', in D.I. Kertzer and T. Earl (eds) *Anthropological Demography: Toward a New Synthesis*. Chicago, IL: University of Chicago Press, 53–95.

Smith, R.J. (1994). *China's Cultural Heritage: The Qing Dynasty, 1644–1912*, 2nd edn. Boulder, CO: Westview Press.

United Nations (2015). *Department of Economic and Social Affairs, Population Division (2015). World Population Prospects: The 2015 Revision*. Geneva: United Nations.

US Census Bureau (2010). *Statistical Abstract of the United States: 2010*. Available at www.census.gov/library/publications/2009/compendia/statab/129ed.html, accessed 16 November 2018.

Wei, S.-J. and Zhang, X. (2011). 'The competitive saving motive: evidence from rising sex ratios and savings rates in China', *Journal of Political Economy* 119/3: 511–64. doi: 10.1086/660887.

World Bank (2018). *World Development Indicators, Labor Force Participation Rate*, total (modeled ILO estimate). Available at https://data.worldbank.org/indicator/SL.TLF.CACT.ZS, accessed 14 January 2019.

World Bank (2019). *World Development Indicators, Proportion of Seats Held by Women in National Parliaments (%)*, (Inter-Parliamentary Union estimates). Available at https://data.worldbank.org/indicator/SG.GEN.PARL.ZS, accessed 14 January 2019.

24 Equality of opportunity in Brazil and India

An Empirical Exercise for the Period 1993–2013

Sabino da Silva Porto Jr, Bernardo Frederes Krämer Alcalde, and Izete Pengo Bagolin

Introduction

Comparing the path and stages of development of different countries has been one of the ways to measure and rank—quantitatively and qualitatively—economic progress and well-being, as well as contribute to furthering the debate over and proposition of new analytical tools. Brazil and India are comparable in a number of aspects; their development paths have been studied by several researchers and according to Ravallion (2009), both countries still have much to teach one another. At first, it might be suggested that Brazil and India find themselves at the same stage of development; however, their paths and the effects of their public policies have not always yielded equivalent results.

It is important to remember that studies from the early 1990s suggested that Brazil would keep on its path of concentrated growth, and at that time it was feared that India would follow suit (Drèze and Sen 1995). The most recent studies show that in the post-reform period of the 1990s and early 2000s, India behaved as expected, having met with relatively more success in terms of economic growth, while Brazil reversed its trajectory and became more efficient in the process of converting growth into development. Thus it is that India seems to have followed in the steps of the old Brazil of the 1960s and 1970s.

It is undeniable that both countries have undergone changes and improvements. However, when these changes are analysed and disaggregated under the lens of conceptually more demanding theoretical approaches such as equality of opportunity, the path towards true development seems not to have actually yet begun. Under this same prism, advancement in terms of justice, equality, and well-being require deeper, more consistent transformation. In view of the foregoing, is it still pertinent to question what such advancements really mean in terms of opportunity equality? How do the millions of Indians and Brazilians live? Have similar advancements in access to education, healthcare, and other facilities taken place?

Sabino da Silva Porto Jr, Bernardo Frederes Krämer Alcalde, and Izete Pengo Bagolin, *Equality of opportunity in Brazil and India: An empirical exercise for the period 1993–2013* In: *Handbook of BRICS and Emerging Economies.* Edited by: P.B. Anand, Shailaja Fennell, and Flavio Comim, Oxford University Press (2021).
DOI: 10.1093/oso/9780198827535.003.0024

The purpose of this chapter is to assess inequality in educational opportunity for Brazil and India by using a non-parametric measure as proposed by Yalonetzky (2010), which calculates the degree of association between different Pearson–Cramer distributions. Further, this chapter features a brief introduction to the debate over Roemer's (1998) theory of equality of opportunity and over morally unacceptable well-being inequalities.

The chapter is divided as follows: in addition to the aforementioned introduction, the second section presents a review of recent literature on the performance of Brazilian and Indian economies. The third section focuses on some aspects of the theory of equality of opportunity. The fourth and fifth sections feature the methodology and database used and the main results found in measuring inequality of educational opportunity in those two countries.

Literature review

This section is purposed to substantiate the interpretation of results and provide the reader with a synthesis of the main policies, economical facts, and transformations, as well as their effects on the economy and life conditions of the Brazilian and Indian populations. The analysed period was marked by significant changes with heterogeneous consequences.

India is currently under economic policies introduced with the reform that began in 1991. This period has been marked by an opening up of the economy and a reduction of state participation in it. Such measures completely altered the direction of economic policies. India distanced itself from the state-centred model it had historically followed and became highly integrated into the world economy (Kotwal et al. 2011). According to the authors, the main changes consisted of commercial liberalization by means of the reduction of tariffs, control over the market, and barriers to the entrance of new enterprises.

According to Basu and Miroshnik (2013), the reform period promoted gains in the services sector, especially in information technology, and losses in other sectors, especially agriculture, industry, and mining. According to the authors the policies adopted and the economic growth are the consequence of bubbles generated by the entry of foreign resources and are unsustainable in the long term.

From Das's (2006) perspective, instead of growing with the assistance of the state India is growing in spite of the state. The country's good results are due to entrepreneurship, which has been at the centre of the current model's history of success. Although the state has undergone a few changes, these changes are not yet sufficient to promote social protection and egalitarian development.

The economic growth rate in India was approximately 5 per cent per year during the reform period. In that period, based on the official line, poverty plummeted from 42 per cent in 1981 to 24 per cent in 2005. The Gini index, in turn, rose from 0.31 in 1990 to 0.33 in 2005 (Ravallion 2009). According to Desai et al. (2010), regional inequalities are not new in the country and, despite that, recent economic changes have deepened them even further.

Das (2006) highlights that India grew 6 per cent between 1980 and 2003, and 7.5 per cent between 2002 and 2006. Between the last decade of the twentieth century and the first decade of the twenty-first century, the middle class quadrupled and 1 per cent of the poor rose above the poverty line. Population growth decreased from 2.2 per cent to 1.7 per cent per year. Additionally, according to the author, the growth strategy adopted by India differs from that of the rest of Asia. India focuses on intensive technology services aimed at the domestic market.

Drèze and Sen (2013) admit the benefits and advancements that the current model has brought to India's progress. They question, however, the country's ability to convert such high achievements in terms of economic success into inclusive or fair development. According to the authors, besides not going through comprehensive, integrating development, the country faces negligence and silence on the part of public authorities and the media. As a result, many of the flaws and much of the exclusion are not being countered in the current model.

Among the various challenges India must face, Drèze and Sen (2013) highlight disparities among Indians of different origins as well as governmental and organizational flaws. The authors offer as examples of such challenges the problems that the country has been facing in the energy sector and in the most varied aspects of its infrastructure.

What distinguishes India's post-reform model of growth, according to Kotwal et al. (2011), is the existence of a qualified labour force; the country's entrepreneurial ability to take advantage of monopoly break-ups, in addition to its ability to use technologies available to the rest of the world; and the improvement in communications. The authors highlight that those factors are a positive legacy from the previous model.

Another distinctive factor was its focus on services, which made the Indian model different from others in the region. Several authors admit, however, that the agricultural sector has not benefited.

Considering education policies, according to Drèze and Sen (2013) 'it is hard to think of a more urgent challenge that India faces today than the reshaping of school education to achieve universal coverage with good-quality education for the children of India'. Such a statement is based on the challenges and gaps that India's education system still faces despite the government's investment in infrastructure and coverage that had been made.

From 1986 onwards, India has significantly heightened its attention to the education system. According to De et al. (2011), the turning point was the 1986 National Policy for Education (NPE), which stressed the need for universal enrolment, universal retention, and substantial improvements in the quality of education. In its first stage, the old existing programmes, such as Non-Formal Education (NFE), were revised and new programmes, such as Operation Blackboard (OB), the Mahila Samakhya programme, and the District Primary Education Programme (DPEP), were launched. Most of the new ones were multi-stage programmes. In Box 24.1 there is a summarized presentation of the three main programmes.

BOX 24.1 MULTI-STAGE EDUCATIONAL PROGRAMMES IMPLEMENTED IN INDIA FROM 1986 ONWARDS

Operation Blackboard, DPEP, and SSA

Operation Blackboard (OB) came out of the 1986 National Policy for Education (NPE). It was set up in 1987–88 to improve facilities in primary schools with the aim of boosting retention. The provisions under OB were:

- a building with at least two reasonably large all-weather rooms, and separate toilet facilities for boys and girls;
- at least two teachers in every school, as far as possible one of them a woman;
- essential teaching materials (e.g. blackboards, maps, charts, toys).

In 1992, the scope of OB was enlarged to include three classrooms for the primary stage and three teachers; it was also extended to the upper primary stage.

The DPEP was a major initiative aimed at universalizing primary education. It was begun in 1994 in forty-two districts in seven states and then expanded over later phases to 272 districts in eighteen states. Its major aims included:

- providing access to primary education for all children;
- reducing primary dropout rates to fewer than 10 percent;
- increasing learning achievement of primary school students by at least 25 per cent over measured baseline levels, and ensuring basic literacy and numeracy competencies;
- reducing gender and social gaps in enrolment, dropout rates, and learning achievements to fewer than 5 per cent.

Sarva Shiksha Abhiyan

Sarva Shiksha Abhiyan (SSA) was launched in 2001 to universalize elementary education by community ownership of the school system, in a mission mode. The objectives of SSA include:

- all children in school, Education Guarantee Centre, Alternate School, or 'Back-to-School' camp by 2003;
- all children completing five years of primary schooling by 2007;
- all children completing eight years of elementary schooling by 2010;
- bridging all gender and social category gaps at primary stage by 2007 and at elementary education level by 2010;
- universal retention by 2010.

SSA was launched in 2001–02. It retained most of the DPEP goals, extended coverage to all districts in the country, and shifted the DPEP target of universalizing primary education to that of universalizing elementary education. SSA was envisaged to bring all existing schemes in the area of elementary education into one.

Source: Probe Revisited: A Report on Elementary Education in India (De et al. 2011).

According to Drèze and Sen (2013), in recent years India has managed to address many aspects that were previously neglected. The Right to Education Act, 2010, and the all-India Srava Shiksha Abhiyan campaign for universal education had a positive and significant impact on the efforts to expand and improve school facilities (appropriate rooms, presence of toilets, textbooks, uniforms, meals). Such efforts resulted in a steady increase in school enrolment for both girls and boys. India's education system was very heterogeneous and unequal between regions. The campaign results were particularly rapid for the disadvantaged communities where enrolment rates and school amenities were much lower.

However, improvements in facilities and enrolment have not yet been converted into better results in terms of achievement. Drèze and Sen (2013) say that 'functioning of the schools remains seriously—perhaps even disastrously—deficient'. Such a statement is based on evidence that children's and teachers' absenteeism is very high in Indian schools. According to De et al. (2011), more than one-third of pupils were absent on a regular school day in the last survey. The report also identified that around 12 per cent of schools had only one appointed teacher and many had no head teacher. The rate of teachers arriving late, departing early, not showing up, or not effectively teaching, is also high.

Such a scenario results in low achievement by Indian children in standard tests. For example, in PISA Plus, conducted in 2009, India stands at the bottom of the seventy-four countries included in the test. And the tests conducted in 2006 for the PROBE report found that half the pupils in Classes 4 and 5 could not perform single-digit multiplication, or a simple division by 5. About two-thirds in the same classes could not measure the length of a pencil with a ruler.

As regards Brazil, at the beginning of the analysed period, the Brazilian economy was characterized by the transition from a long phase of high inflation and failed stabilization plans to one of efforts, as from 1994, to achieve economic stability. All efforts and measures adopted in the latter phase came to be known as Plano Real. During the initial phase of this period, economic policies centred on three aspects, or stages: fiscal adjustment; creation of a stable value standard; and establishment of rules for issuing and backing the new currency (Giambiagi et al. 2005; Versiani 2011). The greatest obstacles, or pressure elements, sprang from the inflationary pressure resulting from the country's economic overheating and inflationary memory. Moreover, following that, the country had to face the effects of the Mexican crisis, the decrease of international reserves, and foreign exchange challenges.

As a result of such factors, in the first four years of the Fernando Henrique Cardoso administration (1995–98), themes of stabilization, fiscal recovery, and regaining credibility dominated the country's agenda. The year 1998 was especially marked by an unfavourable foreign scenario, a foreign exchange crisis, and negotiations with the International Monetary Fund (IMF). GDP growth during those four years was 2.6 per cent, and inflation 9.4 per cent (Giambiagi et al. 2005).

Fernando Henrique Cardoso's second term (1999–2002) was marked by a change in the foreign exchange regime and adoption of the inflation goals regime. Foreign trust was regained, and 1999 and 2000 were years of optimism and resumed growth. In 2001, though, the country faced on the domestic scene a crisis in the energy sector, and on the foreign scene the effects of the Argentine crisis and of the 9/11 tragedy, which impacted world markets.

In addition to economic policies focused on stabilization, state recovery, and the foreign scene, according to Giambiagi (2005), the country underwent important reforms, which can be summarized as: privatization; end of the monopoly of state-owned companies in the oil and telecommunications sectors; changes in the treatment of foreign capital; sanitation of the financial system; a partial reform of social security; renegotiation of state debts; approval of the Fiscal Responsibility Act; and the creation of several regulating agencies for public utility services.

In spite of challenges in the area of the economy, a number of social policies were created or expanded during those eight years. Among them, the following might be highlighted: the expansion of measures provided in the social security law—which came to ensure a minimal wage for the elderly and disabled; creation of the Bolsa Escola, Bolsa Renda, and Bolsa Alimentação programmes; establishment of liquified petroleum gas (LPG) assistance; and the creation of a programme to eradicate child labour.

The 1994–2013 decades can be characterized by significant advancement in the realization of the right to education for all, guaranteed by the 1988 Federal Constitution. In 1996, the Directives and Bases Act [Lei de diretrizes e bases, LDB; Lei n.º 9334, 10/12/1996] was an important landmark in the pursuit of universalized access and definition of guidelines to improve education in Brazil. Moreover, the public budget dedicated to education was continuously increased throughout the period, reaching 17.2 per cent of total public expenditure in 2013 (OECD 2015).

However, Brazil's indicators and, above all, per capita expenditure on children are still quite unsatisfactory. Thus, in 2013, according to data from Instituto Nacional de Estudos e Pesquisas Educacionais (INEP), only 23.2 per cent of children aged 0–3 had access to day care in Brazil. An even more concerning result: among individuals in the 25–64 age range, 54 per cent had a below-high-school level of education and only 14 per cent had access to higher education. 'A Brazilian individual in the 80th percentile of income distribution has six times more chance of studying at university than a Brazilian individual in the 20th percentile of income distribution' (Azevedo and Salgado 2012: 99).

Also, in spite of successive improvements in the distribution of and access to education for the youngest age cohorts, there is a picture of low general educational mobility in Brazil. As stressed by Reis and Ramos (2011: 178): 'Workers with educated parents have a much higher level of education than that of individuals with little-educated parents.'

In this period, Brazil succeeded in promoting the universalization of access to elementary education and significantly increasing school attendance at all levels, thus meeting the goals outlined in the 2007 Plano de Desenvolvimento Educacional (Curi and Mezezes-Filho 2013). The population's average length of time in education rose from 4.9 years in 2000 to 8 years in 2013. According to Lorel (2008), the country achieved an elevated reduction of educational inequalities as measured by the educational Gini index, but still features great regional differences as regards the formation of human capital.

In addition, the country features low high-school coverage—only 51 per cent of youth aged 15–17 according to Pesquisa Nacional por Amostra de Domicílios (PNAD) data (Tavares et al. 2014). There remains an acute condition of age/grade dispersion in classrooms, which negatively impacts individual proficiency (Machado et al. 2013). Many schools in the São Paulo metropolitan area and in most Brazilian metropolises are located in violent communities with a high reported crime index, which ends up negatively impacting youth's school performance (Gama and Scorzafave 2013; Teixeira and Kassouf 2015).

Brazil's performance in PISA is still quite mediocre, occupying the fifty-eighth position among sixty-five countries, which indicates serious problems with the country's quality of education. That is an aspect that affects public and private schools, and all of the country's regions. There is progress in the sense that each successive age cohort features a higher education level and lower internal inequality than the previous cohort. However, in Brazil, 'very few people over thirty years old are still at school'. School facilities still present serious dysfunctionalities, and there is unequal resource distribution within cities and between urban and rural schools in Brazil.

Education takes on pivotal importance in Brazil, as it is one of the main sources of inequality in the distribution of income and well-being (Fernandes and Menezes-Filho 2012; Medeiros and Galvão 2015). In a reality where one more year of education earns high income, where education alone accounts for over 87.8 per cent of wages, and where 64.7 per cent of the population spends fewer than seven years at school (Lorel, 2008), there still is much to do to promote real opportunity equality in Brazil.

Equality of opportunity

In his essays on equality of opportunity, Roemer (1998, 2012) elegantly and meticulously features his view on how to promote equality of opportunity in a society. In essence, Roemer (1998) proposes some form of compensation for those who live their lives under adverse circumstances which are not the result of responsible, free, autonomous choice. The list of circumstances[1] is quite broad, and defining which of them are relevant and should have their effects mitigated is not a simple task. Yet, references to the following circumstances are recurrent in the literature: ethnicity, education of the parents, gender, place of birth, amount of books in the home, family background, etc.

The goal of a social policy, in such a context, is to promote compensation in society, so that individuals in disadvantaged situations would have equal conditions to be able to live a satisfying life in terms of achievements and, in adult life, would be able to compete for advantages in conditions equal to those of other individuals in society. Since Roemer's view is discriminatory—not meritocratic, in the sense defended in Lucas (1995)—to him, 'the purpose of an equal-opportunity policy is to level the playing field' (Roemer 1998: 4).

In short, the emphasis of an equal-opportunity policy should not be on promoting an equal allocation of resources, because equality of resources would not promote an adequate standard of justice, on principle. In the case of access to education, such

[1] In this aspect, and in many others, Roemer (1998) converges with Amartya Sen's (1999) view in defending that the choice of relevant circumstances in democracy involves continuous public reason.

equal allocation of resources is crucial, because as stated by Roemer (1998: 55), 'children come in different types, with respect to their ability or propensity to transform educational resources into future economic productivity'. Thus, children with greater difficulty and disadvantaged living circumstances should receive proportionally more resources than others. The only morally acceptable inequality is that which comes from differences in regards to deliberate acts and an individual's autonomous, responsible choice as to exercising a given 'degree of effort'.[2]

In several passages, however, Roemer (1998, 2012) recognizes that it is not his goal to define the scope and volume of resources allocated to promote equality of opportunity. He also admits that his view on equality of opportunity does not seek to define the extent to which a society should allocate resources so as to repair opportunity inequalities. Those two tasks—where to intervene to promote justice and to what extent—would only be feasible, according to Roemer (1998: 3), from the selection of a distributive justice theory and by means of public debate in a free, democratic society. Fleurbaey (2012: 212) explicitly states that point: 'His [Roemer's] approach is not really a formal embodiment of the philosophical theory of justice.'

Roemer's goal would be a more pragmatic one, in the sense of proposing 'an algorithm that would enable the public official who defines public policies to design compensatory policies capable of promoting equality of opportunity' (Roemer 1998: 2). Public policies would be discriminatory[3]—not egalitarian—as to resource distribution, because they would imply transferring relatively more resources to the group of individuals suffering disadvantage, as observed within the field of circumstances defined by society. Therefore, inequalities caused by factors not directly related to choice, to the individual's will, and to responsibilities, and directly or indirectly influenced by their personal circumstances are not fair distributions. The opportunity space, 'equal well-being for equal responsibility', is the most suitable for an ethical evaluation of outcome distribution among adult individuals. 'The equal-opportunity ethic wants to eliminate inequalities due to "circumstances" and not inequalities due to "effort" characteristics' (Fleurbaey 2012: 202).

Most empirical strategies use that definition of Roemer, for instance, Barros et al. (2009) and Yalonetzky (2009, 2010). However, we will also comment on Fleurbaey's (2008) similar concept, which points to the neutralization of circumstances as an alternate way to promote equality of opportunity. If a society could effectively neutralize circumstances, it would present an equal distribution of free opportunities for all the people who make it up. Such neutralization may be interpreted in at least two ways.

[2] Some authors also consider luck as a random outcome-defining component; see Lefranc et al. (2008). The average effort expenditure would also be influenced by circumstances, so it would not be possible to adequately separate them. In addition, there is a heroic assumption that the level and degree of the expended effort are observable. One way to deal with such limitations is to admit that the notion of effort includes relevant factors—the most relevant in order to assess the distribution of opportunities being the degree of effort expended—and assume that it is possible to measure effort expenditure (Roemer 1998).

[3] Another necessary discussion would be the distinction between responsibility and accountability, and between desert and merit, both important to Roemer's view on equality of opportunity.

In the first interpretation, neutralization occurs if an individual's circumstances do not affect his or her performance in the pursuit of outcomes he/she deems worth obtaining. For instance, children who went to public schools and were born in a favela in Rio de Janeiro should, in adult life, have equal conditions to perform satisfactorily in the labour market when compared to middle-class children who were born in traditional neighbourhoods and went to private schools, provided control is maintained over all other circumstances.

The other interpretation of circumstance neutralization would be to consider it as a situation in which factors related to an individual's degree of responsibility (such as the degree of effort expended, using Roemer's (1998) concept) would be the only factors used as criteria to assess the existing distribution of outcomes or well-being among different groups of individuals in society. A different compensation for different groups of individuals in different circumstances would neutralize the impact of circumstances on the life that an individual wishes to have.

That concept of equality of opportunity is crucial to the empirical strategy adopted in Yalonetzky (2010). An example related to the distribution of access to education illustrates that importance. There would be a neutralization of circumstances related to access to education if both public and private schools had the same level of quality and functionality, which would neutralize, for the effect of realizing 'functionings' in education, adverse circumstances such as one's having been born in a low-income household whose parents' educational background is low, living on the outskirts of Rio de Janeiro or Delhi.

The direct empirical implication of Fleurbaey's (2008) concept relates to the manner of measuring the level of inequality of opportunity existing in a given society. The goal, then, would be to compare the observed level of outcomes achieved by individuals of the same type—individuals having identical circumstances—respecting a situation of circumstance neutralization for that specific sample. Therefore, the observed level of difference among the group is compared to the average distribution in that society; that difference, roughly, would be the prevalent level of opportunity inequality. We would thus assess how distant the observed outcome distribution in each type is from a situation of circumstance neutralization in the analysed sample. Such a strategy is endogenous, because the empirical exercise consists of comparing the observed distribution to the average distribution for the whole sample.

The Pearson–Cramer opportunity inequality index proposed by Yalonetzky (2010) uses that strategy as well as following Roemer's (1998) definition. Moreover, that index also allows for multidimensionally measuring inequality of opportunity as to outcomes and circumstances. Now there is a possibility of measuring and comparing the joint distribution of variable outcomes by type or by different groups of individuals. That represents an improvement on the indices that analyse dissimilarities in isolated variables, such as the degree of inequality in access to services assessed by the Barros et al. (2009) index.

It is understood that building up empirical evidence of opportunity inequality into some relevant functioning is fundamental, whether to stimulate public debate over injustices observed in the performance of functionings important to a dignified, happy life, or to aid in understanding poverty pitfalls which affect some social groups in Brazil and India.

Methodology—Cramer–Pearson dissimilarity index

Most indices that measure inequality of opportunity are based on Roemer's definition of equality of opportunity: 'Equality of opportunity is achieved if and only if the conditional distributions of outcomes/advantages are equal across circumstances sets' (Roemer 1998: 8). Accordingly, the distribution of resources in an economy must be such that it allows all the people who expend the same levels of effort or dedication, that is, who have the same degree of responsibility, to receive equal levels of well-being.

The Cramer–Pearson dissimilarity index, initially proposed by Yalonetzky (2010)[4] to measure educational inequality in society, can be considered a general case of the inequality index proposed by Barros et al. (2009), the Human Opportunity Index (HOI). Both are measured from the distribution of relative frequencies to the analysed variables, and therefore deal with probability. However, HOI analyses the dissimilarity of only one dichotomous variable at a time. The use of relative frequencies in dissimilarity indices additionally allows for the analysis of joint or multinomial distributions of several outcomes of the same type and by type.

Consider a society with a population of N individuals who have different life circumstances. Circumstances are factors that influence outcomes achievable by individuals in adulthood and in regards over which they have no control, autonomy, or responsibility (e.g. average education of parents, gender, talent, or ability of the individual, and so on). Some individuals, however, are similar regarding a set of circumstances; therefore, it is possible to divide this society into groups or types (T) of individuals with identical circumstances, being $T < N$. Any circumstance can also be partitioned into a number of categories (e.g. parents that completed secondary or primary school, etc.). The combination of all categories and circumstances defines a space of types for a given population.

Adult individuals, belonging to different types, can achieve the outcomes or advantages that they pursue or value. Hence, we can characterize a space of outcomes $A \in O$ where O is the global set of outcomes. Each outcome can also be divided into a set of k different categories (e.g. the outcome 'school quality' can be subdivided into the categories public schools or private schools). From this simplified framework of society we compare the relative and absolute frequencies of people who belong to a given type and realize a given level of well-being or realization in a given functioning. According to Roemer (1998), we find the distribution of probabilities of outcomes inside the types

[4] Due to similarities with Pearson's homogeneity of distributions statistics test and a mathematic conclusion by Cramer, the index is known as the Cramer–Pearson index. See also Yalonetzky and Azadullah (2010).

(inequality related to the degree of expended effort) and the distribution of probability of outcomes between the types (inequality related to circumstances).

Formally, we can now calculate the mean results obtained by type T:

$$p_a^* = \frac{\sum_{t=1}^{T} N_a^t}{\sum_{t=1}^{T} N^t}$$

p_a^* = Weighted averge of the group-specific probabilities for outcome a.

N_a = The absolute frequency of people in a society attaining outcome a.

N^t = Absolute frequency of people being of type t in a society.

$\mathrm{N}_{\mathrm{a}}^{\mathrm{t}}$ = Absoltute frequency of people being of type t in a society an attaining a combination [k = a] of oucomes.

A = Space of outcomes

Where:

$$\mathrm{N} = \sum_{t=1}^{T} \sum_{a=1}^{A} \mathrm{N}_{\mathrm{a}}^{\mathrm{t}}$$

The Pearson–Cramer education opportunity inequality index is, as pointed out by Yalonetzky (2010) a statistic that aims at capturing the disproportionality between the types for a given distribution of outcomes or advantages. The central idea, then, is to measure the degree of dissimilarity between the relative frequencies of the outcomes achieved by a given type and the average outcomes achieved in society. The average of dissimilarities in this index is sensitive to the difference between the probability of achieving a given advantage conditional on belonging to a given type or specific group (p_k^t) and the aggregate average probability of achieving a given outcome or advantage (p_α^*). This dissimilarity is formally defined[5] by:

$$d_{(p_\alpha^t, p_\alpha^*)} = \left|\frac{p_\alpha^t - p_\alpha^*}{p_\alpha^*}\right|^\beta \ \forall \beta \in \mathrm{N}_{++}$$

Last, the Pearson–Cramer dissimilarity index consists of the function dissimilarity divided by the maximum reachable value by the dissimilarity function[6] and for a $\beta = 2$:

$$ID^{PC} = \frac{d_{T,A}^2}{d_{T,A,max}^2} = \sum_{t=1}^{T} \sum_{\alpha=1}^{A} \frac{N^t}{\sum_{k=1}^{T} N^k} \cdot \frac{(p_\alpha^t - p_\alpha^*)}{min\{T-1, A-1\} p_\alpha^*}$$

This index is a dissimilarity indicator based directly on the standard statistics test used for multinomial distributions homogeneity analysis. This statistics test is well aligned to

[5] This is an alternative notation but, in essence, this is the original index by Yalonetzky (2010).

[6] See Cramer (1946) for the final configuration.

the family of Pearson's tests. The zero value indicates homogeneity of types and, as a consequence, equality of opportunity. The maximum value, nonetheless, depends not only on the size of the population. In the Pearson–Cramer index, the maximum inequality value is equal to 1 and indicates that there is a complete or absolute correlation between the circumstances and results (Azadullah and Yalonetzky 2010: 11).

This statistics' intuition is obtained from the analysis of a contingency table, since it regards a multinomial distribution of outcomes conditioned to types. The index can also be calculated only for a result (k =1), which turns it essentially similar to the Barros et al.'s (2009) HOI—though at the same time, conclusions obtained here can differ between the two indices. It is a multidimensional opportunity inequality index (see Yalonetzky 2010: 16).

DATA SET AND OUTCOMES FOR EDUCATIONAL INEQUALITY OF OPPORTUNITY IN BRAZIL

The empirical exercise performed here uses data from PNAD, the main data set of results by family in Brazil. The aim is to estimate the index of educational dissimilarity by age for the circumstances gender and ethnicity, using level of education categories as a result variable. The population is divided into two types by gender (men and women) and by ethnicity (white and non-white). The indexes were estimated in isolation for each type, only by regions inside the country, and for the years 1993–2013. The age groups were divided in the following manner: Young—age 15 to 21; Adult—age 22 to 31; Adult—age 32 to 41; Adult—age 42 to 51; and Adult—over 62 years of age.

Figure 24.1 shows medium Brazilian education in 2013 by age groups; on average, the young are more educated. The mean level of education observed for Brazil, when measured

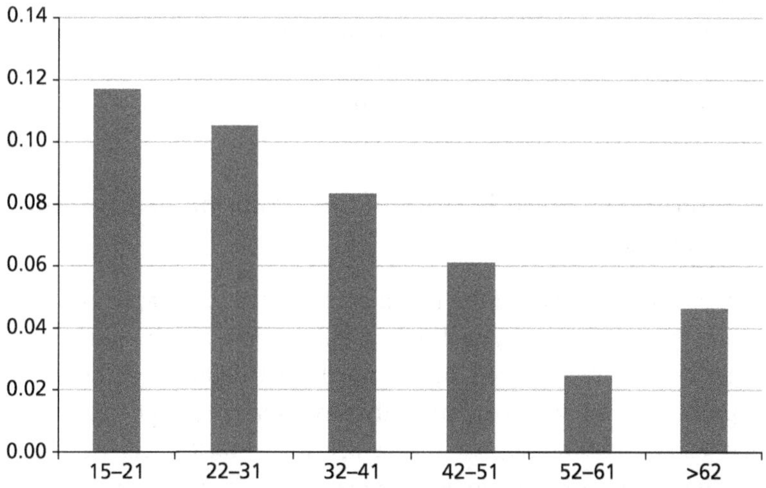

Figure 24.1 Average education by years of study and by age cohort in Brazil, 2013

Source: Elaborated by the authors.

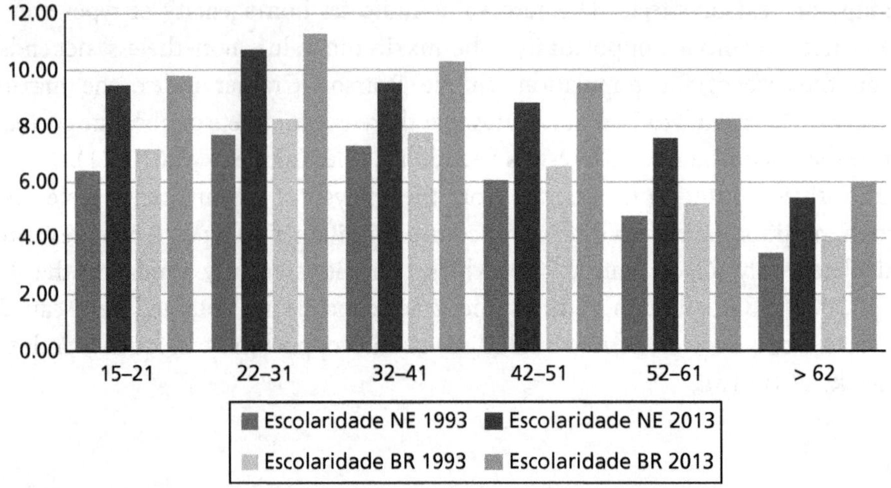

Figure 24.2 Average education by age cohort: Brazil and north-east (1993 and 2013)

Source: Elaborated by the authors

by years of schooling, has risen monotonically for all the analysed period, which can be observed on the graph in Figure 24.2. We see that the mean growth rate of medium schooling of the young is higher than that of the older groups. However, Brazil still presents a low level of mean schooling—9.2 years for the 2013 PNAD data. The age group with higher levels of education is the one composed of young adults aged from 22 to 31. Schooling in the older groups is significantly lower than the mean observed in the period.

The mean number of years of study has risen for all the groups, regarding Brazil as well as the north-east region. We can highlight two details. One, the variation rate for the north-east age group from 32 to 41 was lower by 2 percentage points than the variation level for Brazil as a whole. Yet, the north-east youth from age group 15 to 21 have augmented their schooling in levels much higher than the country mean—32.8 per cent against 26 per cent for Brazil. Mean education is not a good measure of functioning, because it does not indicate the quality of the education offered, but these numbers on years of study show a convergence of the north-east with the rest of the country.

A Brief Descriptive Statistical History of the Evolution of Education in Brazil in 1993–2013

In 1993, average schooling years of the Brazilian population was approximately 6.62. For the same period, the highest average schooling was observed in the southern region, 7.11 years, while the lowest average was in the north-east region, a little below six years. Under the aspect of gender, it was observed that women had a slight advantage over men as to average years of schooling. In the centre-west, north, and north-east regions, average schooling years for women was higher than those for men, whereas in the south-east and south regions the opposite occurred.

Taking into consideration only the oldest age cohorts, it is observed that in any region, men had more education than women; a reality that is inverted as one advances towards the youngest cohorts. The reason why average schooling years of men surpasses that of women in the south and south-east is due to the fact that such inversion occurred later in those regions.

When it comes to ethnicity, the differences are more pronounced than those observed between genders. The schooling of whites surpasses that of non-whites by almost two years: 7.45 and 5.62 years respectively. That fact is repeated in all regions, being more acute in the north-east and less pronounced in the north and centre-west.

By observing the evolution of the difference in schooling years between ethnic groups along age ranges, one can perceive that, although no surpassing takes place, the difference between whites and non-whites decreases in all regions towards the youngest generations.

In 2013, the average schooling years of Brazilians had leaped to 7.97, a difference of 1.36 years. In addition, all regions experienced such elevation, the highest increase being observed for the north-east (24 per cent), which nevertheless remained the region with the lowest average schooling years. On the other extreme, the average in the south-east is 8.37 years.

From the perspective of ethnicity, the difference in schooling years remains favourable to whites. However, from 1993 to 2013, a drop in inequality was observed for all regions. The north-east recorded the most marked reduction, a drop of 1.18 years in the difference in schooling years between whites and non-whites. Even so, it is also in the north-east that non-whites have the lowest number of schooling years. In the centre-west, the highest number of schooling years of non-whites is observed as 7.72, whereas in the north is found the lowest inequality between both groups.

Estimated Indices and Results

In the empirical exercises performed, we estimated the Pearson–Cramer index (non-type population invariance (non-TPI) and TPI) for each year; for the five regions of the country; for Brazil as a whole; and for all age groups. In general, for the gender circumstances we observe that there was a persistent rise in inequality between the younger samples. The non-TPI index rose by 21 per cent—an impressive rate—between 1993 and 2013. The proportionally higher rise in schooling years of women in relation to men in the period might be mainly responsible for this rising inequality—see Figure 24.3.

Figure 24.4 presents the estimated indexes for Brazil in the initial and final periods of the sample. There is a clear change in the pattern of behaviour of gender educational inequality in Brazil.

In 1993, differences between gender inequalities in schooling years were not statistically significant between the extreme age groups, young and old (see Figures 24.4 and 24.5). In 1993, educational inequality was higher between men and women in the older

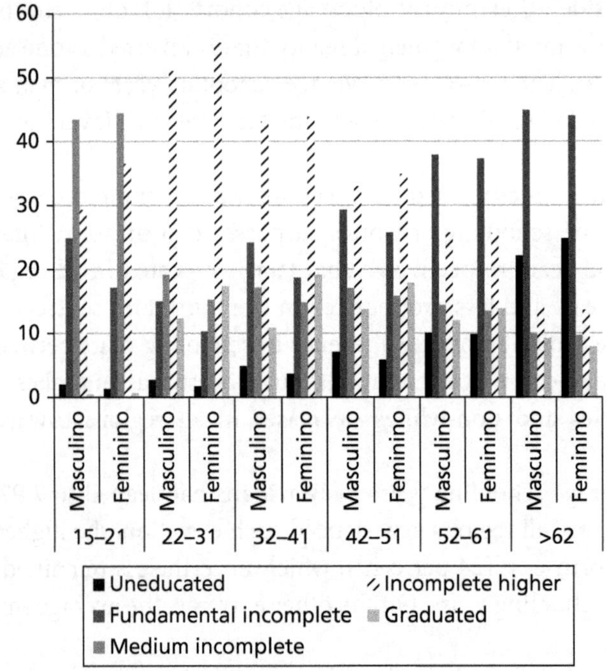

Figure 24.3 Distribution of educational attainment by gender and cohorts Brazil 2015

Source: Elaborated by the authors.

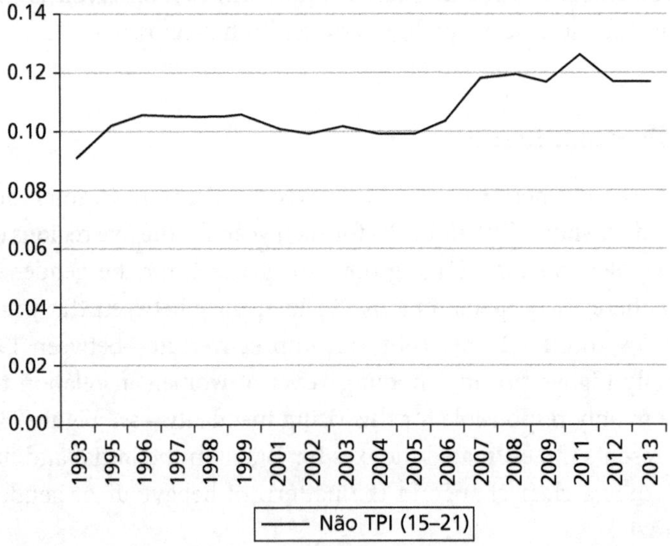

Figure 24.4 Dissimilarity index non-TPI by gender for young cohort Brazil 1993–2013

Source: Elaborated by the authors.

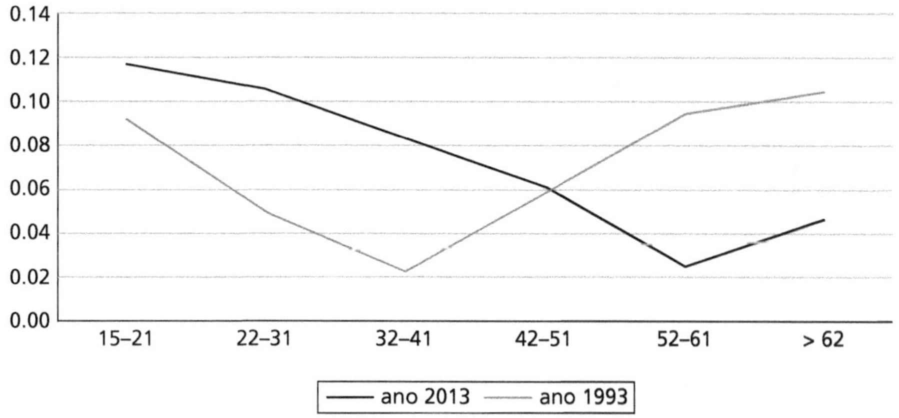

Figure 24.5 Dissimilarity index non-TPI by age cohort and gender circumstances Brazil 1993–2013

Source: Elaborated by the authors.

Table 24.1 TPI dissimilarity index by gender and age: regions of Brazil (2013)

Age group	Middle-west	Northeast	North	Southeast	South	Brazil	Deviation
15–21	0.103	0.142	0.102	0.104	0.137	0.117	0.020
22–31	0.119	0.120	0.102	0.097	0.109	0.105	0.010
32–41	0.087	0.092	0.125	0.068	0.087	0.083	0.021
42–51	0.094	0.075	0.101	0.044	0.065	0.061	0.023
52–61	0.028	0.043	0.042	0.031	0.035	0.025	0.007
>62	0.025	0.035	0.013	0.087	0.058	0.047	0.029

Source: Elaborated by the authors.

age group. The lowest inequality level is observed in the intermediate age group (32–41), where both men and women had low education levels.

The behaviour of the education dissimilarity index estimated for 2013 is practically an inverted image of 1993 (Table 24.1). There is a continuous rise of gender inequality in education towards the younger groups' ages, and the lowest inequality levels are found among the elderly (52–61 years of age). The difference between inequalities estimated between young and old is significant and elevated. Between the young, gender inequality has risen and remains high for the result 'years of schooling' in Brazil (Figure 24.6).

The behaviour of educational and gender inequality in the north-east region of Brazil, the relatively poorest region for most social indicators, has presented similar behaviour to that of Brazil as a whole: a small difference and lower inequality in the initial period, 1993, higher inequality between the young, and continuous rise in educational gender inequality towards the younger (see Figure 24.4). The figure shows that the north-east region presents (in 2013) the highest gender inequality in education among

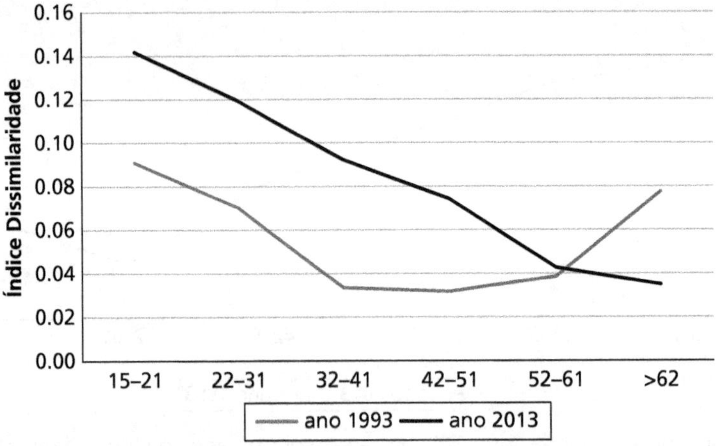

Figure 24.6 Educational dissimilarity index by gender and age group by the Brazilian north-east 1993 and 2013

Source: Elaborated by the authors.

Table 24.2 Schooling difference between whites and non-whites (PNAD 2013)

Age Group	Middle-west	North-east	North	South-east	South	Brazil	Maximum
15–21	0.75	0.67	0.52	0.79	1.02	0.80	1.02
22–31	1.35	1.09	1.22	1.60	1.65	1.45	1.65
32–41	1.68	1.29	1.32	1.83	2.06	1.72	2.06
42–51	1.73	1.37	1.46	2.05	1.82	1.80	2.05
52–61	2.41	1.79	1.70	2.43	1.94	2.14	2.43
62–	1.73	2.13	1.61	2.14	2.26	2.16	2.26

Source: Elaborated by the authors.

all regions in Brazil. Again, the relatively higher expansion of access to education for women is one of the facts that can explain this dynamic.

Table 24.2 summarizes the difference in years of schooling between whites and non-whites in Brazil in 2013 and for all regions. In every observed case, whites present a higher level of schooling than non-whites. That is a compelling indicator of the existence of inequality of educational opportunity due to ethnicity circumstances in Brazil.

The biggest difference is found among the young in the southern region where, on average, white youngsters possess one schooling year more than non-whites. In the other regions, this difference favourable to the whites is also found; however, all are lower than the mean difference observed for the young group in Brazil. For the older age groups, this schooling difference is even bigger and more unequal in the whole country.

Educational inequality for the race circumstance in Brazil, nevertheless, when evaluated by the Pearson–Cramer dissimilarity index, has been falling systematically in the

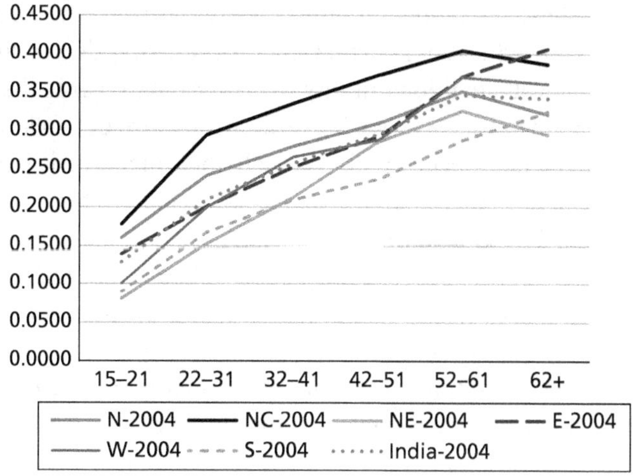

Figure 24.7 Non-TPI dissimilarity index—India

Source: Elaborated by the authors.

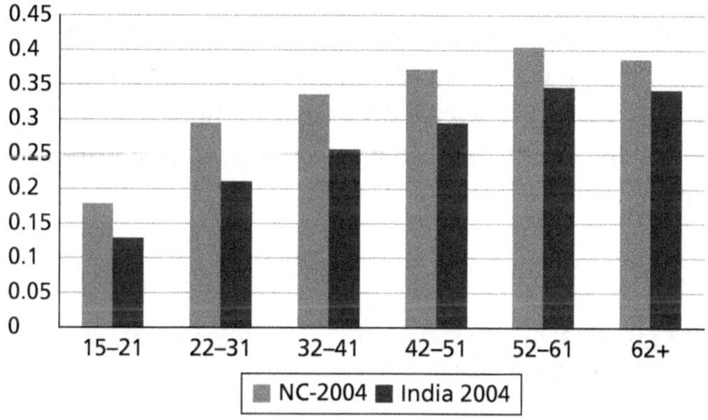

Figure 24.8 Dissimilarity index—India and north-central region NC

Source: Elaborated by the authors.

period 1993–2013 in virtually all regions of Brazil. The only exception is the southern region of the country, where, in the same period, educational inequality between whites and non-whites has risen.

Results for India

We used data for India on the level of education by age cohort, by gender, and by region. Such data were obtained from the National Sample Survey (NSS) database for six regions of India. These regions are divided as follows: Northern Zonal Council; North-Central Zonal Council; North-Eastern Zonal Council; Eastern Zonal Council; Western Zonal Council; Southern Zonal Council. Our goal is to estimate the index of educational dissimilarity by age cohort for gender circumstance. Unfortunately, we have not found ethnicity-specific data on educational achievement; therefore, due to limitation of the available data, we only evaluated dissimilarity by gender. As regards the level of education, data on the NSS database are available according to the following categories: uneducated, below elementary, below high, below higher, higher. Also due to limitation of the available data, we only estimated the dissimilarity indices for India for the period 1983–2004 (see Figures 24.7 and 24.8).

We initially compared average schooling in Brazil and in India, as featured in Table 24.3. On average, according to UNDP's (2010) Human Development Report data, Brazil's adult population presents 7.21 years of schooling. In the 1980s that average was only 2.6 years. The variation rate for years of schooling in the 1980–2013 period in Brazil was 68.3 per cent. That rate is considered to be very low, and Brazil occupies the 79th position in the Human Development Index (HDI) education ranking. Results for India are even more modest: in 2013 an adult Indian had, on average, only 4.41 years of schooling, and the variation rate in the period was only 59.9 per cent. It is not surprising that India is placed 135th in the HDI education ranking.

The graph in Figure 24.9 summarizes the main results found for gender-related opportunity inequality when evaluated by the Pearson–Cramer index. There is a monotonous reduction of dissimilarity towards the youngest age cohorts, which is a sign that gender difference in education is much smaller today among young people in India. The graph in Figure 24.10 also corroborates the inferring of a monotonous drop in dissimilarity indices over the years.

Table 24.3 Average years of schooling for adults, Brazil and India (HDI)—1980–2013

Year	Brazil	India
1980	2.6	1.9
1985	3.2	2.4
1990	3.8	3.0
2000	5.6	3.6
2005	6.6	4.0
2006	6.7	4.1
2007	6.8	4.2
2008	6.9	4.2
2009	7.1	4.3
2010	7.2	4.4
2011	7.2	4.4
2012	7.2	4.4
2013	7.2	4.4

Source: UNDP 2010.

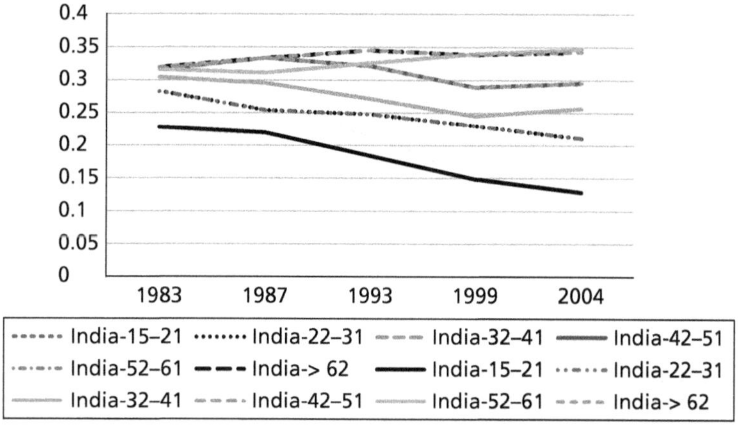

Figure 24.9 Non-TPI dissimilarity index—India by gender circumstances

Source: Elaborated by the authors.

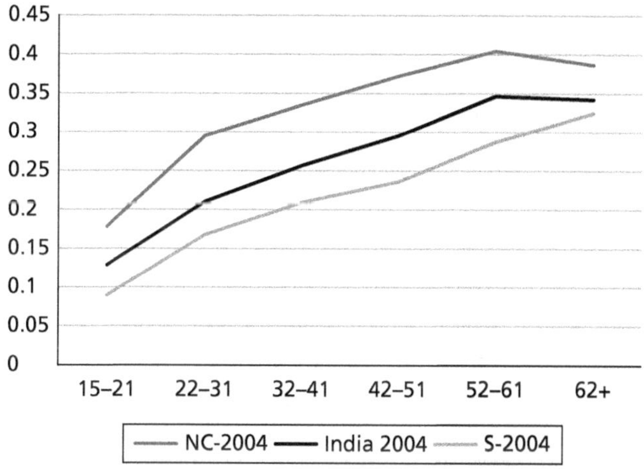

Figure 24.10 Dissimilarity index—India and regions

Source: Elaborated by the authors.

However, there is significant regional variation in the behaviour of the inequality of educational opportunity between genders. Table 24.3 and Figures 24.9 and 24.10 illustrate that difference. The north-central Zonal Council region presents the highest indices in India. The indices estimated for that region are higher than the average indices estimated for India as a whole. The negative variation rate in that region only occurs for the youngest cohorts, in rates lower than the variation for the whole country in the 1983–2004 period. The graph in Figure 24.11 features the indices of the north-central Zonal Council region for the years 1983 and 2004. As of 2013, when compared to the initial period, there has been a noticeable improvement in the sense of reduction in dissimilarity indices for the youngest and an increase in dissimilarity among the oldest cohorts in 2013 (Table 24.4).

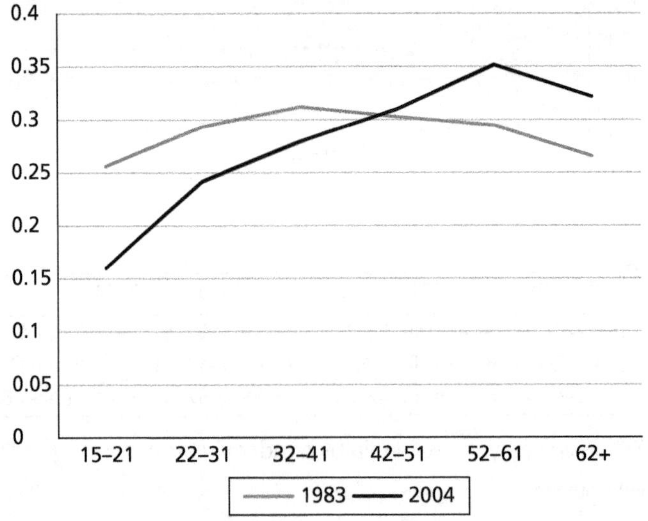

Figure 24.11 Non-TPI dissimilarity index India—northern Zonal Council

Source: Elaborated by the authors.

Table 24.4 Dissimilarity indices estimated for India and north-central region—1983–2004

Cohort	North-central 1983	North-central 2004	% variation NC	India 1983	India 2004	% variation India
15–21	0.3210	0.1783	–44.44	0.228	0.129	–43.41
22–31	0.3588	0.2948	–17.84	0.283	0.211	-25.48
32–41	0.3364	0.3355	–0.28	0.304	0.257	–15.51
42–51	0.3269	0.3721	13.83	0.316	0.295	-6.62
52–61	0.3175	0.4044	27.36	0.316	0.346	9.66
62 +	0.3238	0.3866	19.39	0.319	0.342	7.26

Source: Elaborated by the authors.

Finally, the Southern Zonal Council (S) is the region that presents the lowest indices of gender-related dissimilarity in India in 2004. Figure 24.12 illustrates this point, as it contrasts indices estimated for the most equal region, the least equal region, and India as a whole. The dissimilarity curve of S region in 2004 is more negatively inclined and, also in level, less unequal than that of other regions—and the country itself—in 2004, the last year for which we were able to estimate inequality of opportunity.

Conclusion

The notion of separating inequalities due to factors beyond an individual's control or autonomy (circumstances) from inequalities due to characteristics for which the individual can and must be held accountable (effort), and of deeming unfair and morally

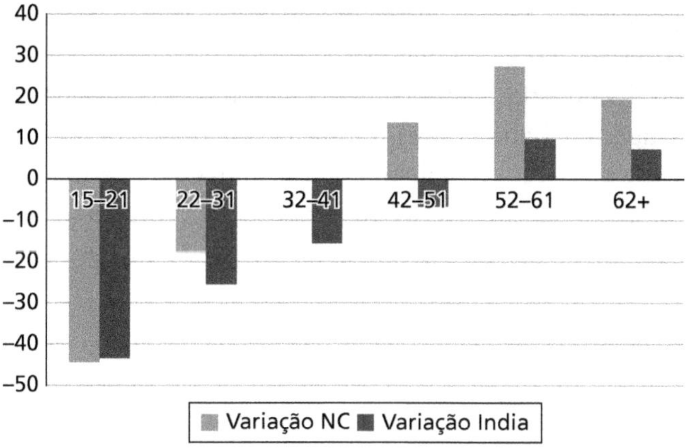

Figure 24.12 Variation % rate of dissimilarity index—India and north-central region

Source: Elaborated by the authors.

unacceptable those of the first kind is fundamental to the approximation of a concept of distributive justice; it belongs to a long tradition of political philosophy, beginning with John Rawls (1971) and Amartya Sen (1985, 1999). Nevertheless, several issues remain open or, at the very least, controversial. Elizabeth Anderson (1999: 287–337), for instance, is strongly critical of what she calls 'luck egalitarianism'.

The purpose of this chapter, however, was to analyse the trajectory of two countries from the vantage point of the opportunity equality measurement of the education outcome, over time and for various age cohorts. Once again, the empirical literature in this area offers no consensus, and many relevant issues remain open. Further, the choice of circumstances (in our case, gender and ethnicity for Brazil, gender only for India) was an arbitrary choice suited to the availability of data. There are limitations in the number of circumstances analysed and the difficulty in measuring effort, despite Roemer's (1998) ingenious proposal of evaluating the degree of effort based on individual outcomes in the outcome distribution of the type to which an individual belongs. Therefore, such limitations should be taken into account in an analysis of the results herein. We have found that there is inequality of opportunity for the circumstances of gender and ethnicity in contemporary Brazil in spite of the country's clear advancement towards greater opportunity equality among the youngest. We have found a similar result as to gender-related inequality in India. The data also suggest a less intense reduction in education opportunity inequality among Indians of the youngest age cohorts.

Analysing a broader set of circumstances, and doing so using complementary parametric and non-parametric methodologies, would be a natural sequence to this research. In addition, the outcomes which serve as means of assessing the degree of effort exerted by individuals—pivotal in distinguishing fair and unfair inequalities—might be closer to the notion of functionings and follow Sen's model of capabilities, a goal that has been pursued lately with relative success in the deprivation and poverty multidimensional evaluation literature.

The analysed period was marked by significant changes in educational policies. Both Brazil and India invested in the expansion of access with a view to the universalization of basic education. Both countries, however, still need to face the challenges of improving quality and reducing spatial and between-group inequalities.

For the period in which it is possible to draw a comparison between Brazil and India, both countries featured advancements in terms of aggregated offer of educational opportunities. Aggregated advancements in Brazil were greater, but the results for India suggest a larger reduction in gender-related inequality.

ACKNOWLEDGEMENTS

We hereby record our thanks to Coordenação de Aperfeiçoamento de Pessoal de Nível Superior (CAPES) for Prof. Sabino da Silva Porto Jr's post-doctorate fellowship.

REFERENCES

Anderson, Elizabeth S. (1999). 'What is the point of Equality?', *Ethics* 109/2: 287–337.

Asadullah, N. and Yalonetzky, G. (2010). 'Inequality of educational opportunity in India: changes over time and across states'. IZA Discussion Papers, n. 5146. Bonn: Institute of Labor Economics (IZA).

Azevedo, E.M. and Salgado, P. (2012). 'Universidade pública deve ser grátis para quem pode pagar?' [Should public universities be free of charge for those able to pay?], *Revista Brasileira de Economia* [Brazilian review of economy] 66/1: 99–116.

Barros, R.P.D., Barros, R.P., Ferreira, F.H.G., Veja, J.R.M., Chanduvi, J.S., Franco, M. de C., et al. (2009). *Measuring Inequality of Opportunity in Latin America and the Caribbean*. Washington, DC: World Bank.

Basu, D. and Miroshnik, V. (2013). 'A critical analysis of the structural adjustments and economic reform in India', *India Quarterly* 69/2: 159–77.

Cramer, H. (1946). *Mathematical Methods for Statistics*. Princeton, NJ: Princeton University Press.

Curi, A.Z. and Menezes-Filho, N.A. (2013). 'Mensalidade escolar, background familiar e os resultados do Exame Nacional do Ensino Médio [School fees, family background and performance in the National exams] (ENEM)', *Pesquisa e Planejamento Econômico* 43/2: 223–54.

Das, G. (2006). 'The India model'. Foreign Affairs. 85/4 (July–August): 2.

De, Anuradha, Khera, Reetika, Samson, Meera, and Shiva Kumar, A.K. (2011). *Probe Revisited: A Report on Elementary Education in India*. Oxford: OUP Catalogue, Oxford University Press.

Desai, S., Dubey, A., Joshi, B., Sen, M., Shiriff, A., and Vanneman, R. (2010). *Human Development in India: Challenges for a Society in Transition*. New Delhi: Oxford University Press.

Drèze, J.P. and Sen, A.K. (1995). *India: Economic Development and Social Opportunity*. Oxford: Oxford University Press.

Drèze, J. and Sen A. (2013). *An Uncertain Glory: India and Its Contradictions*. Princeton, NJ: Princeton University Press.

Fernandes, R. and Menezes-Filho, N. (2012). 'Educação, salários e a alocação de trabalhadores entre tarefas: teoria e evidências para o Brasil' [Education, wages and the allocation of workers between tasks: theory and evidence for Brazil], *Pesquisa e Planejamento Econômico* [Research and Economic Planning] 42/3: 311–28.

Fleurbaey, M. (2008). *Fairness, Responsibility and Welfare*. Oxford: Oxford University Press.

Fleurbaey, M. (2012). 'Equal opportunity, reward and respect for preferences: reply to Roemer'. *Economics and Philosophy* 28/Special issue 02: 201–16.

Gama, V.A. and Scorzafave, L.G. (2013). 'Os efeitos da criminalidade sobre a proficiência escolar no ensino fundamental no município de São Paulo' [The effects of crime on school proficiency in elementary school in the city of São Paulo], *Pesquisa e Planejamento Econômico* [Research and Economic Planning] 43/3.

Giambiagi, F., Villela, A., De Castro, L.B., and Hermann, J. (2005). *Economia Brasileira Contemporânea* [Contemporary Brazilian economy]. Rio de Janeiro: Elsevier.

Kotwal, A., Ramaswami, B., and Wadhwa, W. (2011). 'Economic liberalization and Indian economic growth: what's the evidence?', *Journal of Economic Literature* 49/4: 1152–99.

Lefranc, A., Pistolesi, N., and Trannoy, A. (2008). 'Inequality of opportunities vs. inequality of outcomes: are Western societies all alike?', *Review of Income and Wealth* 54/4: 513–43.

Lorel, B. (2008). 'Assessing Brazilian educational inequalities', *Revista Brasileira de Economia* 62/1: 31–56.

Lucas, J.R. (1995). *Responsibility*. Oxford: Clarendon Press.

Machado, D.C., Firpo, S., and Gonzaga, G. (2013). 'A relação entre proficiência e dispersão de idade na sala de aula: a influência do nível de qualificação do professor' [The relationship between proficiency and age dispersion in the classroom: the influence of the level of teacher qualification], *Pesquisa e Planejamento Econômico* 43/3: 419–45.

Medeiros, M. and Galvão, J.C. (2015). 'Educação e o rendimento dos ricos no Brasil' [Education and income of the rich in Brazil]. Texto para Discussão, No. 2080. Brazil: Institute for Applied Economic Research (IPEA).

OECD (Organisation for Economic Co-operation and Development) (2015). *Indicators. Education at a Glance 2015*. Paris: OECD publishing. Available at www.keepeek.com/Digital-Asset-Management/oecd/education/education-at-a-glance-2015_eag-2015-en#page3, accessed 16 November 2018.

Ravallion, M. (2009). 'A comparative perspective on poverty reduction in Brazil, China and India', *World Bank Research Observer* 26/1: 71–104.

Rawls, J. (1971). *A Theory of Justice*. Cambridge, MA: Harvard University Press.

Reis, M.C. and Ramos, L. (2011). 'Escolaridade dos pais, desempenho no mercado de trabalho e desigualdade de rendimentos' [Parental schooling, labor market performance, and income inequality], *Revista Brasileira de Economia* [Brazilian Journal of Economics] 65/2: 177–205.

Roemer, J. (1998). *Equality of Opportunity*. Cambridge, MA: Harvard University Press.

Roemer, J.E. (2012). 'On several approaches to equality of opportunity', *Economics and Philosophy* 28/Special issue 02: 165–200.

Sen, A. (1985). *Commodities and Capabilities*. Amsterdam: North-Holland.

Sen, A. (1999). *Development as Freedom*. Oxford: Oxford University Press.

Tavares, Priscila, Lobbuque, A., et al. (2014). 'Uma análise dos fatores associados à frequência ao Ensino médio na educação de jovens e adultos (EJA) no Brasil', [An analysis of the factors associated with attendance at secondary education in youth and adult education (EJA) in Brazil] *Pesquisa e Planejamento Econômico* [Research and Economic Planning] 44/1: 7–35.

Teixeira, E.C. and Kassouf, A.L. (2015). 'Impacto da violência nas escolas paulistas sobre o desempenho acadêmico dos alunos' [Impact of violence in schools in São Paulo on the academic performance of students, *Economia Aplicada* [Applied Economics]] 19/2: 221–40.

UNDP (United Nations Development Programme) (2010). *Human Development Report. The Real Wealth of Nations: Pathways to Human Development*, 20th Anniversary edn. New York: UNDP.

Versiani, F.R. (2011). 'A Economia Brasileira nas últimas décadas' [The Brazilian economy in recent decades]. Available at https://introducaoaeconomia.files.wordpress.com/2011/11/a-economia-brasileira-nas-c3baltimas-dc3a9cadas-final-15-11.pdf, accessed 17 April 2015.

Yalonetzky, G. (2009). 'Comparing economic mobility with heterogeneity indices: an application to education in Peru'. OPHI Working Papers N0. 33. Oxford: OPHI.

Yalonetzky, G. (2010). 'A dissimilarity index of multidimensional inequality of opportunity (revised and updated)'. OPHI Working Papers No. 39. Oxford: OPHI.

Yalonetzky, G. and Azadullah, N. (2010). 'Inequality of educational opportunity in India: changes over time and across states'. IZA Discussion Papers, No. 5146. Bonn: IZA.

25 Women, law, and collective action

Examining negotiations to claim gender rights in China and India

Shailaja Fennell

Introduction

The primary focus of the development policies of BRICS countries has been to achieve the same significant rates of economic growth that they consequently achieved in the last two decades of the twentieth century; yet gender equality did not always follow as a corollary. Economic growth may indeed fail to generate social development and can exacerbate gender inequality (Seguino 2000). The OECD database had indicated that there were large variations in labour force participation rates for women among BRICS in 2012, with China having 70 per cent of women employed (almost on a par with the United Kingdom), followed by Russia with 68 per cent of women (aged 12–64 years), Brazil with 60 per cent of women, South Africa with just under half of women, while India had just 27 per cent of women employed (OECD 2014).

The recent focus on designing policy to ensure the achievement of gender equality has resulted in attention being directed at ensuring legal provision for gender equality in both economic and social spheres (ILO 2017). Any legislation introduced to bring about gender equality faces the challenge of ensuring that existing gender norms, arising from a process of social construction, are not able to discriminate against individuals. The subordination that arises due to persistently unequal power relations that operate within communities and households is a consequence of the operation of these gendered social norms. These powerful social norms regarding what is deemed appropriate behaviour for men and women in society are also the driver for aggressive, even unprovoked force by members located within communities (Fennell 2009).

This chapter examines how women negotiate dominant social norms regarding what is deemed appropriate behaviour for them, both as participants in the labour force as well as contributors to the household. The existence of social norms modifies the amenability of the legislative process to introduce laws to ensure gender equality in the

Shailaja Fennell, *Women, law, and collective action: Examining negotiations to claim gender rights in China and India* In: *Handbook of BRICS and Emerging Economies.* Edited by: P.B. Anand, Shailaja Fennell, and Flavio Comim, Oxford University Press (2021).
DOI: 10.1093/oso/9780198827535.003.0025

various spheres of life, be they social or economic. Using an institutional lens facilitates the identification of those mechanisms that make it easier to legislate for gender equality. The focus is on understanding why there is greater likelihood of successful legislation in those sectors of society where there is a preponderance of women, using this institutional approach to examine the methods for achieving gender equality. This permits an analysis of the choices and costs that face women when deciding how to access laws, and deliberate on whether the chosen route of access should be through the household sphere with a focus on family matters and intimate relations or through the labour market with a focus on matters regarding employment and wage discrimination.

Addressing the role of women as productive members of the household only became standard practice in the 1990s, with the revision of Gary Becker's standard work, which posited that women chose to stay at home because they realized that they—rather than their prospective husbands, who were better skilled at earning income in the labour market—were more efficient as homemakers. This simple model of comparative advantage was based on the assumption that it was the aim of individual members in the family to generate the maximum outcome for the household. This assumption promotes the notion that there is little cause for conflict among members of a household, and that there is a seeming complementarity between the roles of men and women. The predominantly male labour market is therefore regarded to be the result of a cooperative decision achieved by a sorting process that ensures that an 'economically rational' team of husband and wife maximize their joint preferences.[1] The New Home Economics (NHE) provides additional dimensionality that helps to understand household decision making by explaining that marriage reduces costs, and that the reassigning of duties between married men and women increases gains from specialization.

In the context of this model it is important to consider the economic rationale that might explain why there is an upward trend in the labour participation rate of women in the labour market in high-income (OECD) countries. The answer appears to lie in the trade-off between the rising wages for women and later and fewer births in these marriages (Goldin 2006), and this points to changes in household decisions regarding the number of children in relation to the opportunities to work in the labour market. It seems that what this model has identified is the ability of a household to work as a Coasean firm that is based on a contractual set of obligations (Fennell 2009). While this is indeed an advance on regarding the household as a consensual or patriarchal unit, there still needs to be work done to learn how to model household situations where these negotiations do not take place.

There are situations where contestation between household members may not result in agreed forms of labour allocation. It might be appropriate to regard rights and duties

[1] *A Treatise on the Family* was written by Becker in 1981 and used economic analysis, particularly the importance of bargaining and cooperation, to understand how a household maximizes returns. His work was highly influential and new institutional analysis in the relation to household bargaining models, in turn, gave rise to the New Household Economics.

as specific instruments that are contractually binding, but presence of an asymmetry of information between parties can result in hierarchies of power that do not bode well for mutually advantageous interactions (Lundberg and Pollak 1996). While marital promises, and resulting rights and duties, are not dissimilar to those of commercial contracts, everything within the context of marriage is not voluntary. Such a situation might arise where a younger family member questions the decision made by an older family member as this goes against the nature of power in a family hierarchy, e.g. a younger son objecting to a family decision to deny him funds for a choice of art as a subject of study, or a younger daughter being denied the right to marry while an elder sister remains unmarried. In these situations, the decision of the young person to disregard the family decision would result in the unacceptable possibility of a Paretian sub-optimal solution. This could result in unilateral actions being taken by those situated advantageously in the hierarchy. This might even result in the use of violence as penalty for oppositional behaviour of subordinate household members as it is not deemed appropriate in these contexts.

Identity economics and institutions: thinking through collective action problems

Akerlof and Kranton highlight the importance of identity in understanding individual behaviour in economics. They point out that identity can be based on individuals' perception of themselves, or on other's perception of them, or on a third party's ability to influence their identity, and on the individual's desire to achieve/acquire certain characteristics. Such identities should not be regarded as matters that merely relate to the social sphere, for they are central to how individuals are regarded in the labour market and they fundamentally influence an individual's economic behaviour (Akerlof and Kranton 2000). For example, the extent to which an individual finds a match, between his/her own beliefs and preferences with a firm's style of management and strategic approach to its business, is emerging as a key factor in the individual's decision on choice of employer. The deciding factor for an individual, in choosing between working for a company or as an external and independent player in the market, is not based on any difference in the costs of operating within both structures, but on the ability to share a common identity (Akerlof and Kranton 2005).

The importance of individual rationality as the primary basis for decision making can now be discussed alongside the importance of a common group identity as a basis for decision making. Furthermore, the key to understanding individual behaviour appears to lie in the interaction between the group and the individual (Fennell 2009). This particular tendency to use group identity to identify the suitability of institutions for employment or other forms of productive contractual relationship indicates that individuals possess the ability to internalize social norms. This feature of human behaviour has been identified as having a corresponding match with tendencies that individuals display in the field of collective action. In that situation humans are faced with the predicament of finding a common interest that might create a sustained basis for subscribing to the membership of a group interested in ensuring the provision of the same public good (Ferguson 2013). The predilection of humans to try and overcome collective action problems (CAPs) often works better if there is already a stable membership signed up to by a particular group. In such circumstances, the focus can be solely on resolving a second order CAP of the necessary selective incentives needed to ensure that the group is active in pursuing the realization of its desired public good.

The distinction in orders of collective action was first discussed by Mancur Olson in his classic, *The Logic of Collective Action*, and it has come back into prominence with the recognition that identity is one such form of membership subscription that could convert a large-scale first order CAP into a more specified order of CAP (Ferguson 2013: 48–54). The value of expanding the domain of study in the field of identity and economics into an exploration of orders of CAP is that it permits us to examine the costs and benefits associated with forming a group (first order CAP) and working within a group (second order CAP). There was an early distinction made by Olson between the incentives of signing up (with or without a subscription) to the features associated with achieving first order CAP conditions, and the awarding of official positions such as secretary and treasurer (which he termed selective incentives) as a second order CAP. This chapter is making the case that it is important to think of what decisions organizations make regarding selection of a strategy to further their goals as a more advanced version of a second order CAP problem. The assigning of official positions is, in this new formulation, a first stage in a larger process of discussions among officers about their strategic approach to achieve their agreed goal. In the case of women's organizations this would be in relation to the most effective way of achieving gender equality.

An examination of this process from viewing such organizations from the outside would proceed by identifying the particular causes within the field of gender equality with which they associate themselves. The process of selecting these causes is important to these organizations for two separate reasons: (a) that they are the closest to their internal understanding of what aspects of gender equality they wish to achieve; and (b) how likely they are to attract more potential members to support their cause.

The affinity of individuals to choose organizations with which they can identify can be fruitfully used to show why both households in the social sphere and labour employment in the economic sphere can be preferred sites for identity alignment. This does not imply that the individuals are making an explicit or conscious choice when they acknowledge that particular social groups, such as gender, are their preferred form of affiliation. It could be that the individual is simply fitting in with dominant norms—so in communities where it is predominantly the case that young women do not take up formal employment after marriage this social norm is adhered to by new brides coming into that community. This kind of behaviour is in contrast to the situation where objecting to the imposition of gendered social norms forces women into the position of victims. The enforcement of sanctions can result in the infliction of gendered violence on women, and in extreme cases this can result in strictures against the victims themselves, such as enforced marriage of rape victims to perpetrators of these acts in some communities (Baxi 2014).

The study of such dominant social norms, in both social and the economic spheres can provide a valuable opportunity to examine how women and women's groups identify the most effective methods of negotiating access to gender rights and thereby achieving gender equality. An institutional framing of such a process of accessing gender rights permits us to link the prominence of social norms regarding appropriate gender behaviour to methods used by advocacy groups to overturn gender discrimination through demanding legal remedy.

The decision to take a case to court depends on a person's position with regard to their family, community, and the state.

Women's organizations and collective action

Feminist scholars have made the case that women's organizations are powerful vehicles for achieving gender equality. Their power resides in the use of group action that is an effective way of pushing for social change (Cook et al. 2002). The success of group action lies in its ability to bring together a large number of individuals who share a singular objective, i.e. overcoming the CAP. The importance of collective action in ensuring legal change to advance the rights of women can also ensure measurable improvements, so that it has a decided impact of improved gender equality data (an instrumental value). It can also have the consequence of increasing women's self-esteem, thereby adding to their sense of identity (an intrinsic value) (Evans and Nambiar 2013). The role of collective action in achieving gender equality provides an important starting point for understanding the pathways to achieving gender equality. It is also helpful to take note of how gender equality is approached in different countries, by examining the formulations and spaces that are most advantageous for achieving it.

It is also pertinent to dwell on how introducing the possibility of different formulations of collective action and group action affects the earlier feminist propositions regarding gender rights. The universalist position on gender rights regards it as crucial that women's rights should not fall prey to accommodating cultural relativism (Nussbaum 1999). The focus in this perspective is on women's commonalities and their humanity (Bunch 2001; Okin 1999). The ability of collective action to succeed in ensuring new legislation to remedy gender injustice does not necessarily have the ability to change gendered social norms that often discriminate against women in local communities. Undertaking comparative studies of how women's organizations have worked in different countries to ensure that they can advance women's rights in the household and in labour markets is a valuable way of comprehending the most effective avenues for reducing discrimination and violence against women (Vanegas and Pruitt 2009).

The study of social movements uses the conceptual analysis of frame resonance to analyse how women's organizations can relate their own expressed demands to those of national and global agendas and thereby increase the chance of success for a particular form of collective action (McAdam et al. 1996). The ability of an organization to relate to larger national and international concerns thereby makes their demands more amenable to being accepted and supported. This alignment is based on a cognitive process that works with existing social norms, using this form of 'frame resonance' to amplify the acceptability of the group demands (Oliver and Johnston 2000). The framing approach to understanding the relative effectiveness of a range of women's organizations is helpful in providing a mapping from international gender agendas to national campaigns. There is clearly a very significant role played by international agendas—particularly of the universality of human rights—that has influenced national gender agendas. On the other hand, it is also crucial to recognize the influential role played by locally driven agendas for gender equality that have been taken up and turned into dynamic social movements in developing countries.

This chapter makes the case that there is a critical need to evaluate the role of such locally informed and dynamically garnered women's movements in developing countries. These movements often have a distinctive and different history from that of internationally driven agendas as they emerge from a closer and more intimate understanding of the prevailing gender norms in local and sub-national contexts. This generates an internal understanding of the formulation and manifestation of gender norms in these organizations and results in their being more accessible to women who live and work in local contexts far away from the national and international gaze.

It is this key feature that draws women to these organizations, as they feel a kindred spirit among existing women members, and often there are strong linguistic affinities as well as similar community contexts. This is the reason that there might be a preference to identify with an existing gender organization that is already drawing on commonalities at the level of local community, particularly intersecting features such as young mothers or linguistic particularities. It is these group features that attract women rather than their own individually ascribed identities.

Where there are dominant gender norms, an individual might choose to use their primary alignment within a gender grouping, such as married women, thereby drawing on a second order CAP configuration. This would mean that women's organizations that are working to improve the personal rights of women in the household and community, as in the case of domestic violence, become the immediate vehicle for the pursuit of legal remedy in this area. If instead it is the case that employment in the labour market is the dominant form of women's identification with a group identity, then women's organizations that are concerned with matters of workplace discrimination such as sexual harassment or unfair dismissal would be the vehicle to take up the cause.

National policy and opportunities for negotiating gender equality in China and India

Economic development has been typically driven by the need to develop an industrial policy that ensures a stable economic growth rate, and this is regarded as a sufficient condition for ensuring better lives for its urbanization labour force.[2] The gender relations that were forged within this process designated as 'modern economic growth' clearly signalled that women would move out of the social sphere into the economic sphere, typically through being employed in the modern labour market and contributing to a rise in GDP. The changing sectoral composition of employment and production has also resulted in subsequent changes in the law to ensure the legal provision of safeguards for labour, of which gender equality has become an increasing requirement to ensure the increased participation of women in the labour force (OECD 2014). The process of industralization in the emerging economies, who have been 'latecomers' to development, to use the Gerschenkronian turn of phrase, have also required that BRICS countries address the need for introducing labour laws that ban gender discrimination and sexual harassment in the work place, and this has been significant in reducing the gender gap in OECD countries (ILO 2017). There has also been a demand for legal provision to cover the responsibility of care that constitutes a core part of personal responsibilities within the household sphere. The provision of financial support to permit women, and men, to undertake caring responsibilities in the family has been a major achievement of international agendas for gender equality, such as the UN programmes for Women in Development, and Gender and Development in the decades of the 1970s and 1980s (Goetz 1998). It has also been bolstered by feminist thinking in the politics of care, which underlines the dangers of focusing solely on the contribution of individuals as employees in the labour market without accounting for the costs of employment on those who are left to look after family members—children, the disabled, and the elderly (Folbre 2002). There is a further dimension of gendered norms which arises from the presence of patriarchal thinking, that regards women as repositories of community honour, so that the law does not recognize the gender discrimination imposed on women (Okin 2004). The historical processes that have constructed the national and local contexts within which gender relations are played out indicate the need for subversive forms of resistance by which women can, as a group, challenge the prevalent patriarchal norms (Kapur and Cossman 1996).

[2] The positive consequences of industrialization through migration flows from rural to urban locations as set out in the Lewis model (Lewis 1954) are a key characteristic associated with a successful industrial policy. This feature is the consequence of the increased productivity of the urban industrial population that results in a rising share of output and labour force, with a growing income share of the rising urban population and ensures changing sectoral composition in GDP, which Kuznets famously termed 'modern economic growth' (Kuznets 1966).

The opposition that feminist frameworks provide to patriarchal models of the household designs and deploys intricate methods, using both individual rights as well as group identity claims to negotiate improved gender relations. The 'implicit contracts' that emerge from such negotiation can chart different pathways in individual countries, as a result of distinct ideological, historical, and religious considerations.

The UN's demand, since the Declaration of Economic and Social Rights in 1945, was for recognition of women and children as distinct individuals, who must be respected as full human beings in their own right. Claims for human rights have often been opposed by developing countries, as these demands are deemed to be a specific form of western cultural imperialism that consequently disregards the role of patriarchal norms in imposing group restrictions on all women and enforcing sanctions, even violent actions, in the case of inappropriate behaviour on the part of any women in the community.[3] The identification of specific forms of patriarchal norms in individual countries has resulted in a move from regarding a single pathway as the most effective way to achieve gender equality. Instead, it is replaced by regarding the process of achieving gender equality requiring the use of second order CAP solutions, rather than individual rights that emerge from a first order CAP solution. This shift to regarding gendered identity as set out by social norms in both the household and labour market as the most appropriate starting point in devising negotiating strategies, be these through subversive or collaborative processes, provides a novel approach to achieving gender equality.

Legislation against gender discrimination such as sexual harassment at work or domestic violence in the household is intended to prevent unfair, even discriminatory, treatment of individuals on account of their gender. Where gender relations are mediated by powerful social norms that operate in the community, this law works in a contradictory manner as it does not give women individual rights bur rather it imposes prescribed behaviour on all their women members. This contradiction to what the law intended is on account of prevalent gender hierarchies demanding that individual women adhere closely to the designated and very specific forms of group identity set out for women's conduct in the community. For example, a labour law that demands women be given employment could be interpreted as a need for segregation of women in the workplace specified by designated female traits such as 'nimble fingers' and in the case of the household this specification might be constructed around womanly 'virtue' or 'sacrifice' (Elvin 1984).

These local constructions result in the gendered identity of women being defined by locally constructed social norms and it follows that the characteristics will vary across different geographies and histories. The location-specific gendered identification of women would indicate that the manner in which women and women's groups negotiate for gender equality will also differ. Talpade Mohanty's deconstruction of the notion of a singular category of women replaces it with a differentiated identity by social markers.

[3] Okin 1989 provides a valuable analysis of the difficulties that universal categories face in the context of different cultural understandings regarding how to legislate for gender rights.

> The assumption, of women as an already constituted and coherent group with identical interests and desires, regardless of class, ethnic or racial location, [which] implies a notion of gender or sexual difference, even patriarchy, can be applied universally and cross-culturally. Mohanty 1988: 64

Local social norms impose constraints on individual members in a community in relation to personal choices regarding modes of dress or forms of address. The consequences of unseemly behaviour triggers the threat of sanctions against women and these are meted out in both the labour market and the household. The nation state has the sole authority to regulate human behaviour, and by promulgating new gender legislation it can also control and reorder gender relations (Connell 1987). The state has the greatest interest in managing groups within its national borders (Hensman 2004) and consequently it can be argued that there will be a greater readiness to engage with demands for gender equality, when they are made by gender groups that are significant in size and status.

Figures 25.1 and 25.2 provide data on the presence and absence of legislation with regard to domestic violence, an indication of gender inequality in the household sphere; and sexual harassment, an indication of gender inequality in the labour market, in 2014. The data indicate that countries at the bottom of the G20 ladder such as Saudi Arabia in relation to female labour participation and female autonomy do not have legislation in either sphere. China has laws against sexual harassment but did not have approved

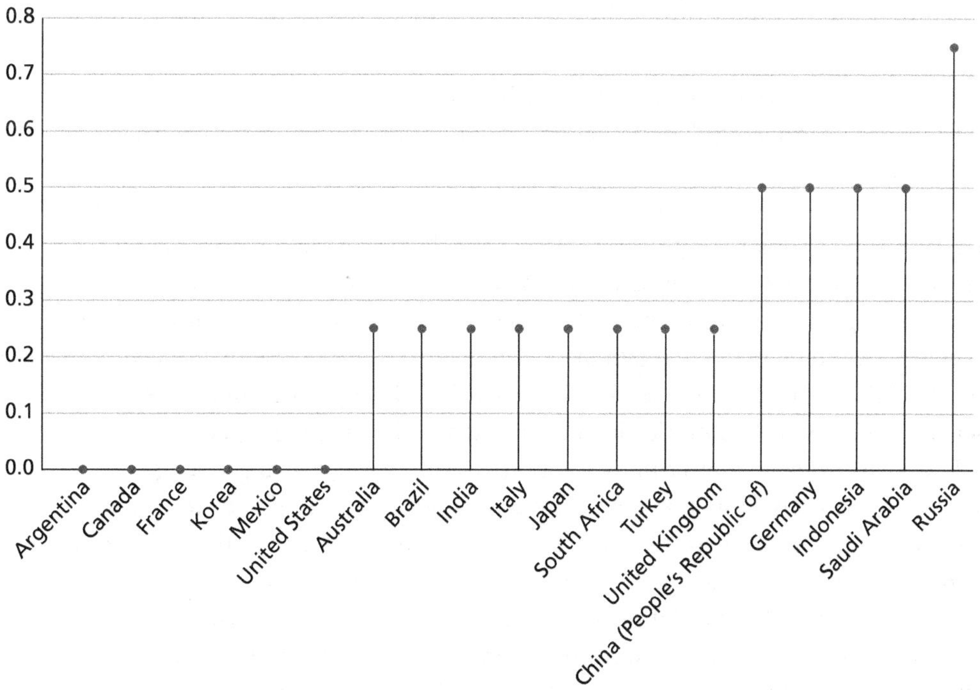

Figure 25.1 Indicator of legislation on domestic violence

Source: Author's work generated from OECD (2018).

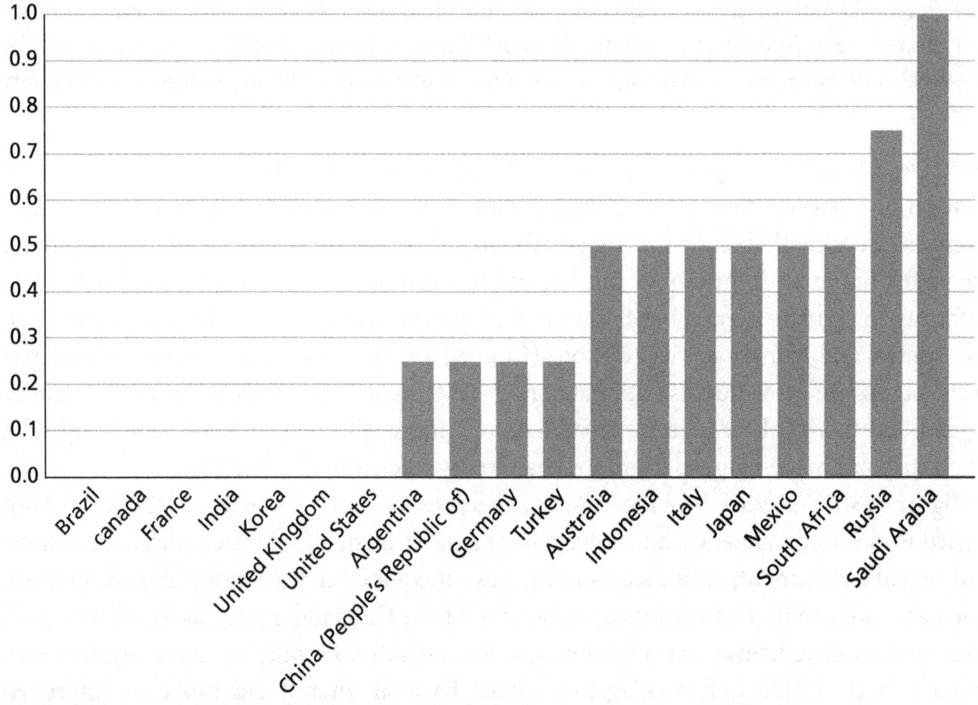

Figure 25.2 Indicator of legislation on sexual harassment

Source: Author's work generated from OECD (2018).

legislation on domestic violence until 2016. India has laws on domestic violence but did not have formal legislation against sexual harassment in the workplace until the end of 2013.

It could be argued that acquiescence of the state to the demands for gender legislation is a strategic 'Olsonian' response: going for the 'biggest bang for its buck' and giving a decided preference for gender demands made by the largest womens' organizations. As women are primarily located in the household in India (nearly two-thirds of women of working age) compared to women in the labour market in China (70 per cent) a second order CAP is required in the labour force which will drive the nation state to accede to demands for laws on domestic violence in India and sexual harassment in India.

It follows that gender discrimination inflicted on local specified gender groups that are neither numerically large nor politically powerful would be difficult to dismantle. The need for legislation in these cases might not be easily negotiated with the state. It might be necessary in these situations to develop an institutional pathway that requires more prolonged forms of contestation that can then be effectively harnessed by women's groups in China and India. The contestation may vary, ranging from covert individual acts of resistance to overt group mobilization—from everyday acts of resistance to the setting up of a women's shelter. For instance, contestation can occur over how women's actions in the household are perceived, or over what constitutes appropriate treatment of women in the workplace. This could be the case of a woman in rural conservative communities, such as that of Bhanwari Devi, or a worker on a women's development project in Rajasthan. Bhanwari Devi was raped in 1992 by dominant male members of the locality to punish her for launching a formal objection to the proposed marriage of a one-year-old child in accordance with local gender norms. This horrendous event led women's groups to file a public interest litigation that led to the Supreme Court drawing up the Vishaka guidelines in 1997, to deal with sexual harassment cases in India (Mehta Sood 2006). An equally shocking act of violence that took place in the household sphere in China was the case of Li Honxia who was 29 years old, and was murdered by her husband. Li was a victim of repeated acts of violence inflicted by her husband, and was strangled by him while recovering in hospital after a miscarriage in February 2016.[4] The news made the national headlines as the event occurred just a few weeks before the promulgation of a national law against domestic violence.

It could be argued that these violent incidents should be dismissed as outliers, that they are atypical in the light of the prominence of women in positions of power and fame; for instance, the case of heads of state in South Asia, such as Indira Gandhi in India and Benazir Bhutto in Pakistan, and Chinese sportswomen who have been outperforming Chinese sportsmen achieving more gold medals in every Olympics since 1998. To do so, and suggest that extreme acts of violence against women are anomalous would be a gross misrepresentation. The symbolism of successful women in public office and elite sports events does not have any impact on what is expected of women in the confines of their communities or their workplace. Within these spaces, far removed from the rarefied public gaze of high politics and international sports events, gendered norms continue to dominate, and the pathway to gender equality is not easy.

It is the inordinate power wielded by these norms that makes it impossible for women to act as sole individuals and why negotiation to change norms is best effected by drawing on the group identity of women, permitting the resolution of a second order CAP. Furthermore, to ensure that there is visible contestation that cannot be dismissed as rogue action, collection action groups such as women's organizations and their use of innovative legal actions such as public interest litigations to overturn existing practices of sanctions to control women are necessary in overcoming prevailing forms of gender discrimination.

The promulgation of gender laws in China and India

As legal systems have a tendency to enact labour laws in response to demands made by the predominant group of workers in a sector, this would imply that in male-dominated

[4] http://www.chicagotribune.com/news/nationworld/ct-china-domestic-abuse-20160502-story.html, accessed 19 January 2019.

spheres of work, such as the industrial sector, there would be no reason to recognize the contribution made by women nor the sexual harassment that they might face in such male-dominated spheres. Equally in the household sphere, where forms of violence are perpetrated by men through sanctions to punish women who do display unbecoming behaviour, there would be no laws prohibiting such actions. This might appear contradictory, as women are far more numerous in carrying out household activities, yet as they are not visible in the important areas of household decision making such as with regard to finance and assets the laws favour men in relation to matters of property (Okin 2004). This tacitly privileges male interests by not recognizing the different ways in which the law treats men and women, the different ways in which women and men face abuses of rights, or the different outcomes of seeking justice for men and women on account of gender hierarchies in the family and society (Irving 2008). The institutional rule-making process that can work to deny women access to their rights can result in women being unable to get legal redress in relation to the violence they experience in the family and community.

Duara (2017) draws our attention to the importance of the distinction between the formal and substantive notions of gender equality. The formal notion can be regarded as emphasizing equality as 'equality as consistency' as set out in identifying discrimination (Fredman 2016). The implication of this principle is that a gender equality law would treat women as though they were men, i.e. a 'gender neutral legal order'. The substantive notion has a deeper understanding of difference, and builds on the need to distinguish likeness from unlikeness. Within this notion, equality can only be achieved by locating how an individual is situated within a hierarchy, and if two people are not in the same position in a given hierarchy, then they can only be treated equally if the remedy ensures that they are treated fairly in relation to others like themselves.

Substantive equality is a complex notion, and it is suggested that it can be investigated along four dimensions: the redistributive dimension to examine disadvantage; the recognition dimension to identify prejudice and violence; the participatory dimension to locate exclusionary/inclusionary processes; and the transformative dimension to explore the accommodation of difference (Fredman 2016: 10). The possibility provided by a dimensional approach is that it permits us to create a multidimensional structure that can trace how individuals are located by others through a series of social constructions.

While Fredman and Okin address the pivotal matter of equality from the point of view of providing direct remedy to an individual experiencing gender discrimination or gendered violence, or what could be termed as the resolution of a first order problem, it is important to understand how the matter of equal treatment can be interpreted in relation to second order problems. In the case of a CAP type second order problem, the matter of equal treatment requires us to ascertain how existing gender norms impact among individual behaviour through their power to impose sanctions on 'inappropriate actions' played out in social, economic, and legal spheres. An improved understanding of the implications of such mechanisms of control for individuals who have been identified

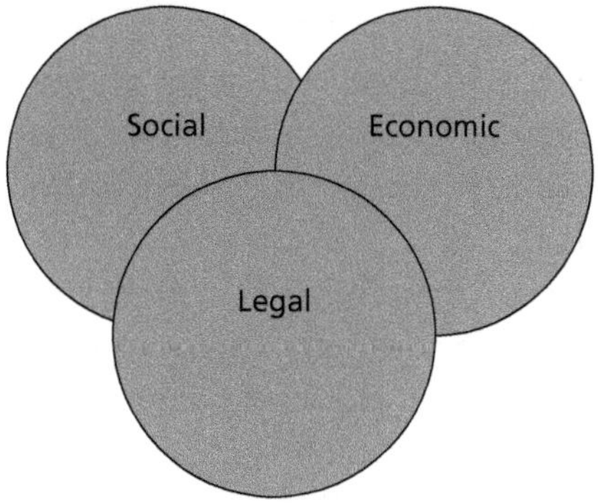

Figure 25.3 Overlapping norms across economic, social, and legal spheres

Source: Author's compilation.

by social markers such as gender or race, is an important intellectual device for understanding how these structural impositions control and constrain. Ensuring equal treatment would mean working to loosen, even undo, these constraints imposed on women who are themselves accused of violating norms and therefore deserving of the sanctions meted out against them—so that a woman is regarded as having invited sexual attention by being present in a public place, or that her inability to perform a household chore requires her to be physically or sexually attacked.

The achievement of gender equality, therefore, requires us to understand how women acquired the ability to ensure social, economic, and legal spheres, and this might be more likely to occur through a device to utilize a second order CAP approach, to change gendered norms. Figure 25.3 provides us with a pictorial representation of these overlapping spheres and a dominant norm might appear in any of these spheres, as well as in the intersections between spheres. An example of such an intersection is when women who have previously been largely visible in the household begin to enter the world of work, and they are regarded as either 'weak' or 'sexually promiscuous' because they are now cast in the role of having transgressed traditional norm boundaries when they move from the household sphere to that of the labour market. Another example is when women have worked in occupations alongside men, and yet their rights to maternity-related benefits are regarded as an excessive cost rather than a legal duty of the firm. In both cases it is the dominant norm, constructed around male characteristics, that proscribes behaviour. Furthermore, it employs the mechanism of guilt so that the responsibility is not of providing legal remedy to a group but places the onus on the individual to show that they were not unseemly in their behaviour.

Programmes that bring together economic, social, and legal spheres permit explicit recognition of the ability of gender norms to operate when women attempt to move from one sphere to another, and are a form of using the notion of substantive equality to move towards gender equality. As Fredman points out, the recognition aspect is crucial for addressing the role that prejudice and violence play in perpetuating gender inequality. For instance, when more women enter the world of work and there is an explicit mechanism for identifying how gender norms might be dismantled; there is a reduction in the gender gap and this is associated with faster economic growth (OECD 2014). Equally, data indicate that in the domestic sphere the greater the share of household income controlled by women the greater the spending that benefits children in the household (World Bank 2012).

Furthermore, when women are marginalized in the economic, social, or legal spheres, empowerment mechanisms can be effectively introduced through creating community-based decision making that adopts an inclusionary approach, which is another dimension of substantial equality. This local institution is important as it can target marginalized women effectively, and it is for this reason that it is crucial to be able to identify the role of women's organizations in the negotiation and contestation processes to achieve gender equality in each country.

THE PATH TO GENDER EQUALITY

The earliest gender laws in China, those of gender equality and of the equal rights of men and women to employment, were promulgated in the early 1950s. This was among the earliest actions of the Peoples Republic of China (PRC) government to support the right of women to work outside the home and was often identified as an important basis on which to treat men and women equally within both the public and private spheres (Zheng 2013). The early mobilization of the state and civil society ensured that gender equality had been further advanced by more recent laws, after the adoption of the new constitution in 1982. The revised constitution set out the principle that gender equality is important in political, economic, social, and cultural spheres, and highlighted that it was of the utmost importance that gender equality in the family be upheld.

The Indian Constitution, adopted in 1949 guaranteed equality to all persons who were resident in India. Article 15 prohibits discrimination on gender grounds. On the other hand, the substantial equality dimension of identifying discrimination was only valid in relation to state actions, and there was no constitutional protection against discrimination by private individuals or organizations This equality guarantee is available to all persons within India but it is a limited guarantee that is available only in cases of abuse by the state (Sankaran and Madhav 2011).

The Indian Constitution, on the other hand, retained the provision of religious personal law to account for the different religious groups that were residing in India. This decision was taken despite earlier discussions in the political sphere about the need for a uniform civil code (UCC), in the aftermath of the violence that had been witnessed in India during its Partition (Nussbaum 2001). The continuing debate around UCC has resulted in waves of campaigning by civil society over the past four decades, with a range of women's organizations, both those supporting and those opposing a UCC, coming out in force on the suitability of taking women's rights outside the realm of religious law (Solanki 2011). Such a code would regard it as possible for women to have personal rights regarding family matters, which would fall outside the domain of religious law. By recognizing that family courts should not necessarily regard an individual's right to marriage and divorce within the norms set out by religious law, the debate on UCC shows the challenge of regarding women as a collective entity, or second order form, that has the right to decide whether it should use the route of religious affiliation to access equal treatment or whether the state should create a law (in this case UCC) that lays down the requirement that equal treatment must be for individual women irrespective of the social norms that operate in their own religious spheres. The ability to identify the very different results obtained by thinking through first and second order problems when addressing the matter of equal treatment has significant implications for legislation for achieving gender equality.

DOMESTIC VIOLENCE

India signed the Convention on the Elimination of all Forms of Discrimination against Women (CEDAW) in 1980 and ratified it on 9 July 1993, with two declarations. These declarations dealt with India's stated obligations to eliminate cultural stereotypes constructed around the role of women (Mehra 2013). This was a fundamentally important inclusion as it directly addresses the structural impediments imposed on women by dominant gender norms.

The rise in the phenomenon of dowry deaths, where young women were murdered by their husbands, often assisted by the husband's family and after long periods of abuse, routinely followed persistent and increasingly violent demands for a larger dowry from the young woman and her family and shook the national capital and other large cities in the 1980s. The outrage felt by citizens was channelled by women's organizations who went on to play a leading part in the national campaign against dowry (Gandhi and Shah 1992). This led to a series of anti-dowry laws in response to the spate of public protests, and the restricting of family law through providing remedy to victims and families of dowry-related violence (Kumar 1993). The legal penalties permit a reconstituted remedy to gender violence that reduces gender discrimination by assigning guilt to victims' husbands and their families and thereby reducing the power of gender norms that are caused by intersections between social and economic inequalities. Dowry payments required as part of social norms acquired increasing economic importance with growing commercialization and globalization (Greenberg 2003).

The Indian judiciary has taken the lead in writing the United Nations International CEDAW principles into the legislation; the greatest challenge has been to rework the costs and sanctions associated with existing gender norms. The ability of legal discourse and practice in changing gender norms is critical in this process of changing the onus of guilt from the victim to the perpetrator (Baxi 2014).

In 1980, China ratified the CEDAW principles and went on to promulgate the Law on the Protection of Rights and Interests of Women (LPWRI) which was adopted in 1992 as part of China's obligations under CEDAW. There were no further changes to China's gender laws to specifically increase the protection of women for a decade until the All China Women's Federation (ACWF)—a national women's association which is part of the official political institutional structure—took up a campaign in response to a rising spate of horrific crimes in relation to violence against women. The ACWF provided extensive input to support the National Working Committee on Children and Women (NWCCW) under the State Council to draft the State Party report (Attané 2014). Drafting of these reports was facilitated by the previous advocacy work undertaken by the ACWF, through the forming of the Anti-Domestic Violence Network in 1998. The network has since become an important mechanism by which to conduct research on gender norms and stereotypes used in the judicial system.[5]

It was the volume of analysis and report writing undertaken by the ACWF on the subject of domestic violence that was largely responsible for the positive results for the Chinese government passing amendments to the LPWRI in August 2005. The change in the law was announced at the time of the tenth year commemoration of the 1995 Fourth World Conference on Women (de Silva de Alwis 2010). The introduction of a mechanism by ACWF for reviewing the reality of how gender laws have been implemented in communities in different provinces in China has been a major contributory factor to the amendment to the law. Their use of the anti-domestic violence network to develop a method of data collection from Chinese provinces has been very effective in this regard. The presentation of such evidence was an important catalyst for the promulgation of a new Domestic Violence Law in March 2016, that not only recognizes the impact of domestic violence on the lives of Chinese women, but also sets out explicit procedures for prevention measures as well as physical protection orders for victims, based for the first time on a clear definition of domestic violence.

EMPLOYMENT LAW

With the opening up of the Chinese economy in the post-1978 reform period, China promulgated LPWRI in 1992. There is a particularly notable innovation that permits a favourable intersection between the social and the economic, by making explicit provision for the protection of women during pregnancy and maternity leave. The law was explicit in providing equal rights for women and men in all walks of life, and the remedies for gender inequality are closely aligned with the principle of equal treatment. The recognition and redistributive aspects of substantive equality are clearly addressed with the right provided for the initiation of legal proceedings against concerned government departments of other organizations. There is, however, one feature of gender

[5] Interviews conducted with ACWF officials in Beijing and Shanghai in June 2016.

discrimination that continues, due to the fact that there is a social norm to regard types of employment variously designated as better suited to men or women.

The ACWF has been active in supporting demand for revisions in employment law resulting in an amendment in 2005 and the introduction of the Employment Promotion Law in 2007. The primary reason spelt out by the ACWF for its strong support for improving the employment rights of women is because they regard it as the most effective route in creating a positive spillover from legislation in the economic sphere to dealing with the widely prevalent incidents of domestic violence in households across China.[6]

While the Vishaka guidelines did set in motion a move to address gender discrimination in the workplace in India it was regarded as inadequate by a majority of Indian women's organizations (Mehra 2013). There was particular concern that the ability to place the onus of guilt on the perpetrator of sexual harassment in the public sphere was difficult to achieve. Matters came to a sudden and publicly explosive juncture with the case of the brutal gang rape and murder of a young woman in Delhi in 2012. The case of Nirbhaya resulted in national outrage and a concerted campaign to reform the law and resulted in the Criminal Law (Amendment) Act in 2013 that redefined sexual harassment to take into account acts of stalking, voyeurism, and unwanted sexual attention.

The explosion of public rage and the outcry against sexual harassment as a result of the sexual violence inflicted on a young woman in India resulted in heated public discussion as well as legal advocacy on the need to recognize that women are regarded as lesser citizens (Sunder Rajan 2003), mainly on account of their being largely absent from the public sphere. This results in a predilection among official agencies—both the police and sometimes the courts themselves—to fall into the trap of regarding women as the guilty party for being in places that are 'ill-suited' and undertaking actions that are 'unseemly'. It follows that their complaints against sexual harassment are not readily recognized as true accounts, and their actions are more often than not deemed malicious or outright false accusations (Kapur 2013).[7] The privileging of the dominant construction of patriarchal gender norms in Indian communities has been an insurmountable challenge that women's organizations have had to confront. It has been inordinately difficult for women's organizations to contest these gendered norms and in the face of this harsh opposition such organizations might do better if they change their strategies to ones that use a negotiatory approach to accommodating gender norms. It is essential that approaches to gender equality are willing to recognize the necessity for locally driven approaches to gender norms, and that these organizations might indeed be more effective and valued because they are built on local practice. This significant feature is

[6] Interviews with national and provincial members of the ACWF in July 2016.

[7] An additional problem that is evident in both countries is the far lower level of protection for women working in the informal sector. As there is an inordinately high proportion of women compared to men working in this sector in both China and India this constitutes another area of institutionalized gender discrimination in the legal system that works to perpetuate unfair social norms.

of notable value for expounding why comparative studies in gender equality should not begin with the consideration that developing countries must necessarily have a lower measure of gender equality than more economically developed economies. These studies should be built on a baseline understanding that there are principles that must be agreed upon for achieving gender equality, rather than a predetermined version of what constitutes a model of economic development.

The principle of substantive equality is very valuable in this regard as it recognizes that patterns of disadvantage and oppression exist in society and requires policymakers, lawmakers, and the government to take inequality of circumstances into account when formulating law or policy. Substantive equality requires that the roots of inequality be identified, and that mechanisms be put in place for removing the barriers associated with the individual or group's 'special characteristics', rather than securing an equal result. It examines the impact of law within its surrounding social context to make sure that laws and policies promote full participation in society by everyone, regardless of personal characteristics or group membership, thus enabling the state to make special provision for women and children. It is through provisions such as these that job reservation and special provision for women are made possible.

The impact of public interest litigation and legal aid on negotiating strategies

The introduction of the mechanism of public interest litigation (PIL) has been revolutionary in permitting group action to access the courts. This feature was far more commonly used in the context of developing countries than in the case of high-income countries in the first decades of its use in the 1970s. In the legal texts group actions around class and public interests are very frequently clubbed together. While it is indeed true that particular groups in the labour market or located in communities have suffered due to discrimination, it would be inappropriate to place them in the same category as there is a distinction between the context of the labour market and that of the household. The former context would require use of arguments relating to labour legislation and the latter to those relating to marriage and divorce. It is precisely because of this important distinction that it is vital to investigate the overwhelming importance of PILs with regard to promoting gender equality in many developing countries.

India spearheaded the use of PIL in the 1980s to provide an alternative route to bringing justice to those who were socially and spatially distant from the law. The inordinate importance of providing the marginalized with the opportunity to demand their rights from the state was couched in the language of democracy rather than that of human rights. This was not incidental but strategically intentional as it placed the onus squarely on national government to ensure that the fundamental rights enshrined in the constitution were made available to the ordinary citizen. The enshrining of human rights within the language of democracy was crucial to ensuring that the judiciary was called upon to do its duty in protecting the rights of all citizens, and that an organization as petitioner in the case was therefore in a non-adversarial position vis-à-vis the state (Mehta Sood 2006). The ability to gain redressal for the marginalized and subjugated through the legal instrument of PIL also provides the possibility of significantly increasing the visibility of the identified crime. In the case of gender crimes, this permits a very public discussion of the gender norms that are associated with the perpetration of the crime. This public discussion can itself be the catalyst for changing the contours of what is publicly regarded as permissible and also change the definition of what is unseemly in relation to gendered behaviour (Narrain and Tiruvengadam 2013).

It has been argued that PIL is a particularly suitable instrument for representing the group interests of women, as they have not historically been politically mobilized in India (Mehta Sood 2008). In the absence of any electoral support or other public advancement of women's rights, PIL provides a novel and very visible pathway to gain support for women's rights and to advance gender equality. Since the Vishakha case, the judiciary has become an important institution for the advancement of gender rights, and is regarded as the vanguard for bringing the voices of the oppressed and unacknowledged across India (Fennell 2009). The development of PIL is therefore of critical importance to the advancement of gender justice in India, and despite India being a country with many very severe gender disparities the arguments for substantive equality have become more audible and have led to far better visibility of gender disparities than might otherwise be expected given the widespread evidence of gender discrimination.

In the case of China, the active use of PIL to advance the rights of women has taken off in the last two decades. The ACWF has made a particular effort to link the use of PIL to the provision of legal aid for particularly disadvantaged groups of women—those in distant rural locations and the case of migrant women. This resulted in amendments being made to the LWPRI in 2005, to recognize the right of women's organizations in filing a complaint on behalf of victims (de Silva de Alwis 2010). The difficulties faced by women who are not in the formal labour market, such as those in the domestic economy and working on individual agricultural contracts with the local state (Gao and Fennell 2017) and the challenges that migrant women have in the face of marital breakdowns and family disputes are the most common challenges that are reported to the ACWF.

Over the last two years, there has been an active movement in the creation of legal aid cells in provincial chapters of ACWF, and this is the result of vigorous lobbying of the central ACWF within Central Party organizations.[8] These actions resulted in the introduction of clauses in the domestic violence bill of 2016, to permit legal aid to be part of

[8] These details emerged in discussions with officers of the ACWF Shanghai and Beijing chapters. This is part of the research being conducted by the Centre of Development Studies in conjunction with the Thailand Institute of Justice, on Gender Justice in Asia.

the these moves to explicitly bring in the role of women's watchdog organizations to monitor and report on women's rights. These provide a more institutionally aligned public space where women are accorded the right to make claims against discrimination or other forms of structural or personal violence.

While PIL has been used by both countries it is also clear that the approaches adopted by women's organizations in India and China are distinctively different. The alacrity with which Indian women's groups chose to use the most public platform to deliberate gender norms is the result of strategic deliberation to bring the world of gendered household and community norms into public scrutiny. This set of decisions, which permits a large cross-section of society to discuss and contest the predominant gender norms, can result in a shift in what is regarded as acceptable and sanctionable behaviour. This strategy has the impact of linking the inflicting of violence in acts of domestic abuse to more widely understood forms of coercion and bodily harm, such as the use of the term 'battering' in relation to the effect of domestic violence (Weiner 2003). In the case of the ACWF, the explicit intention of the introduction of remedy for domestic violence through raising the matter through the avenue of women's rights in the labour market is a case of working within the public debate that is more commonplace in the PRC, i.e. that of making the case that addressing the need for sanctions against sexual harassment should also be taken into the private sphere. This resulted in a far quicker leveraging of gender rights in relation to domestic violence as it shows the discrepancy between what the law has deemed acceptable in the formal labour market and the household. The ability to work with the state in both these countries and through the institution of women's organizations shows the exceptional value of choosing a different route for achieving gender equality, one that does not focus on the individual or on demanding universal human rights framing. The explicit choice of a negotiatory strategy that allows women's organizations to contest the nature of gender norms but not to simultaneously confront or antagonize the state is feasible through PILs, and explains why the pathway to achieve gender equality in India is different from that in China.

Negotiating gender equality through changing social norms

The negotiation of gender equality through changing gender norms is a strategy that is adopted by each country as it traverses its own development trajectory. The OECD Social Institutions and Gender Inequality (SIGI) indicators show that there is a wide variation in the extent to which gender equality has been achieved in different countries.[9]

[9] The OECD's SIGI database has been developed in close conjunction with the research methodology developed by Professor Stefan Klassen, a leading expert on the conceptualization and measurement of gender gaps.

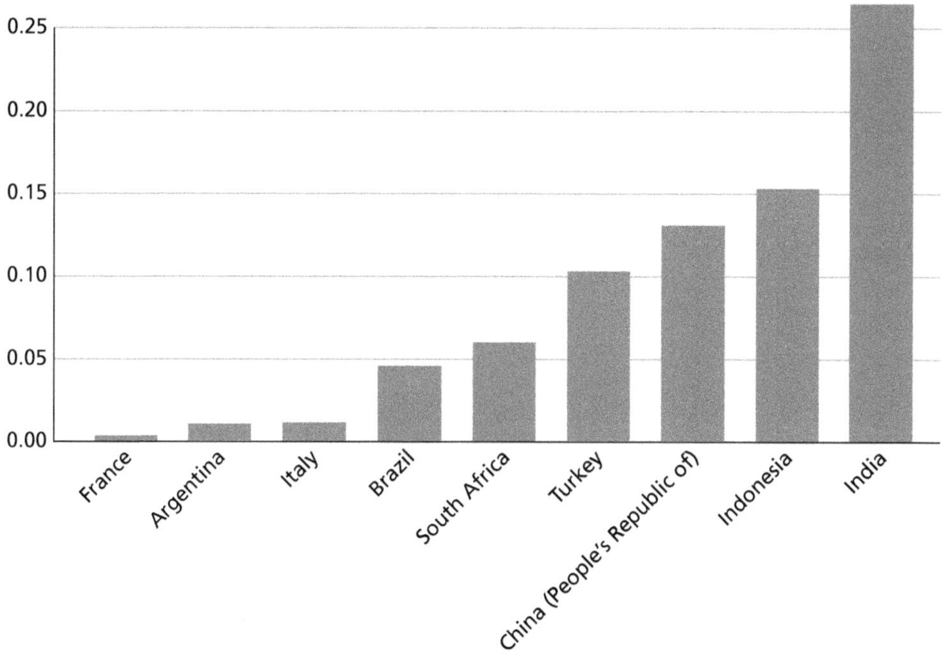

Figure 25.4 Social institutions and gender

Source: Author's work generated from OECD (2018).

SIGI is a measure of discrimination against women in a range of social institutions that intersect various spheres and ages: discriminatory family code; restricted physical integrity; son bias; restricted resources and assets; and restricted civil liberties. The index presents scores from 0 to 1, with 0 indicating no discrimination and 1 indicating a high level of discrimination.

Figure 25.4 shows the position of countries in relation to the total SIGI index, and that India has the highest level of gender discrimination, with China slightly less extreme in its treatment of women, while the best of the BRICS countries is Russia. However, if there is a breakdown of the components of SIGI, and focus is on the discriminatory family code, the discriminatory family code sub-index is constructed around the following variables: early marriage: percentage of women married between 15 and 19 years of age; parental authority after divorce: on whether women and men have equal rights with regard to legal guardianship in the context of divorce; and legal age of marriage: whether women and men have the same legal minimum age of marriage. The value of 0 implies that the law guarantees the same rights, while 1 implies that the same rights do not apply. In this regard, Figure 25.5 shows that while India remains the least equal, South Africa emerges as approaching gender equality, with Russia appearing to be far more equal than Brazil. Furthermore, there does not appear to be a direct correlation between levels of per

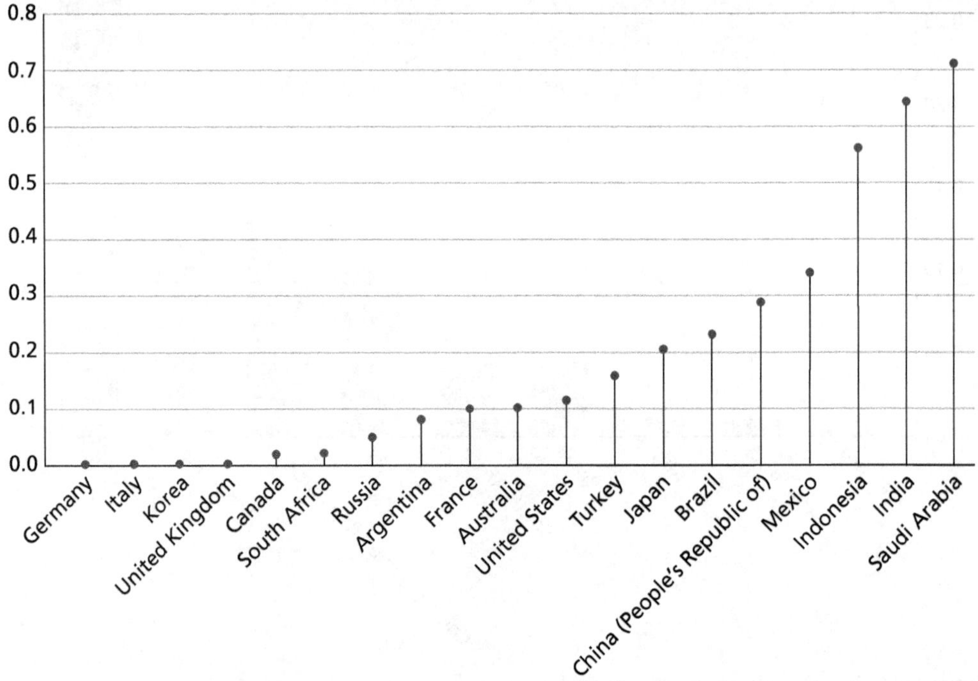

Figure 25.5 Discriminatory family code and gender

Source: Author's work generated from OECD (2018).

capita GDP and gender equality, for Japan falls just below Brazil in terms of inequality, and the United States and France both appear as having unequal treatment of men and women with regard to these criteria.

It is clear that social norms continue to play a role with regard to considerations of gender equality and it is difficult to ensure substantive equality despite adherence to the UN declaration of human rights. It is now evident that women's organizations in each of the BRICS countries have encountered strong gendered norms and it is important to understand the strategic decisions taken in each country to take forward the pursuit of gender equality. The cases of India and China show that the most effective way to ensure remedy to gender discrimination is to work within the sectors where there is the greatest relative preponderance of women. It is the critical mass provided by the large numbers of women in these sectors, be that within the community and household or within formal factory employment in the labour market that ensures that the demands of women's organizations are heard in the public sphere. It is particularly important that women's organizations strategize to ensure that they are able to use their campaigns, and even their legal demands, to ensure that there is public discussion of gender norms that can facilitate an erosion of their hegemony in the future.

Conclusion

Social norms are a basis for violence against women and often the consequences of these acts do not result in legal action.[10] It is often regarded to be the case that contestations against these gender norms are of crucial importance to shift the geographical locus of researching gender relations. There has been widespread understanding that such contestation plays a key role in understanding how development policy and practice from the Global North can become translated into national and local contexts (Wilson 2015). This gives rise to the possibility that local constructions of social norms can become a basis for new opportunities to transform gendered relations to locally forged forms of resistance. In contradistinction, it is also possible that national and sub-national women's organizations have considerable ability to address gender discrimination both in the labour market and household spheres. Their particular expertise is in using existing forms of women's lives and work to raise the possibility of engaging with prevalent social norms. Women in these communities, who are identified by a specific group identity, may choose to cling on even more strongly to their ways of doing/being, and use this group identity to solve a second order CAP. In this way, small and conservative communities with strong social norms can find ways to circumvent the immediate threat of violence. This is an important consideration as it moves away from a singular focus on an individualized notion of gender identity to addressing the important role of social norms in creating and maintaining gendered power. There could be future implications of this innovative approach for a more effective procedure for accessing gender equality for women in other national contexts.

The framework that we have adopted uses the lens of social norms to identify the mechanisms by which control and negotiation function in a community. This permits an analysis of the choices and costs that face women when deciding how to access the laws of the land regarding family matters relating to marriage, caring, and divorce, as well as labour market matters regarding employment and wage discrimination. The approach has been valuable in showing that gendered relations impose unwritten rules on its members; the difficulty that women face in choosing to break away from the household hierarchy of power cannot be understood without explicit recognition of the importance accorded to familial and community norms.

Furthermore, we have been able to show that regarding gender equality as an achievement that emerges as a solution to a first order CAP has resulted in failure more often than success. Regarding group identity as an important framing device for turning the achievement of new avenues for negotiation and contestation has been helpful in identifying new pathways that women can traverse in familial and employment contexts. The costs and

[10] See Paula England for an analysis of the consequences of regarding men and women as equal in the marketplace, while accepting the difference logics of altruism and selfishness in the household and market respectively. England in Ferber and Nelson (eds) *Beyond Economic Man* Chicago, IL: Chicago University Press, 2003 [1993]).

sanctions associated with a second order CAP are not associated with individual choice but rather with community norms. Consequently, in a context where it is no longer deemed to be 'masculine' or 'honourable' to inflict violence on women in the community, there is a new and very negative social weight associated with such actions and by association against all community members who might behave in this manner. In contrast with the individual choices that beset first order CAP situations, focus is on the individual shifting, thus creating a trade-off between income earning activities undertaken in the labour market, and the much larger number of unpaid hours expended by women in the family to effect a better personal equation with other household members.

As the case for the provision of laws relating to sexual harassment and domestic violence seems to be ordered as a relative priority in relation to the relative size as well as the political importance of the gender group, it would appear that smaller and less powerful gender groups might need longer periods of negotiation, as well as outbursts of contestation, to be able to change the costs and sanctions associated with unseemly behaviour. It is therefore particularly important that in cases where there is a smaller and therefore less visible gender group, costs and sanctions are mediated through the group identity, such as grandmothers in the household context or key workers in the workplace to change the costs associated with a particular social norm that perpetuates gender discrimination. This approach also has the ability to bring in explicitly cultural norms, and these can be used to leverage the negotiation underway by women's groups ensuring that there is wider public consensus on the need to change patriarchal social norms.

REFERENCES

Akerlof, G. and Kranton, R. (2000). 'Economics and identity', *Quarterly Journal of Economics* 115/3: 715–53.

Akerlof, G. and Kranton, R. (2005). 'Identity and the economics of organizations', *Journal of Economic Perspectives* 19/1: 9–32.

Attané, I. (2014). 'Being a woman in China today: a demography of gender', *China Perspectives* 2: 1–12.

Baxi, P. (2014). 'Sexual violence and its discontents', *Annual Review of Anthropology* 43: 139–54.

Bunch, C. (2001). 'Women's human rights: the challenges of global feminism and diversity', in Marianne DeKoven (ed.) *Feminist Locations: Global and Local, Theory and Practice in the Twenty-First Century*. New Brunswick, NJ: Rutgers University Press.

Connell, R. (1987). *Gender and Power: Society, the Person and Sexual Politics*. Stanford, CA: Stanford University Press.

Cook, S., Kabeer, N., and Suwannarat, G. (2002). *Social Protection in Asia*. New Delhi: Har-Anand Publications.

de Silva de Alwis, R. (2010). 'Opportunities and challenges for gender-based legal reform in China', *East Asia Law Review* 5: 197–302.

Duara, J. (2017). *Gender Justice and Proportionality in India: Comparative Perspectives*. London: Routledge.

Elvin, Mark (1984). Female virtue and the state in China', *Past & Present* 104/1: 111–52.

Evans, A. and Nambiar, D. (2013). 'Collective action and women's agency: a background paper, women's voice, agency and participation'. Research Series, 2013, no. 4. Washington, DC: World Bank.

Fennell, S. (2009). *Rules, Rubrics and Riches: The Interrelations between Legal Reform and International Development.* Abingdon: Routledge-Cavendish.

Ferguson, W.D. (2013). *Collective Action and Exchange: A Game Theoretic Approach to Contemporary Political Economy.* Stanford, CA: Stanford University Press.

Folbre, N. (2002). *The Invisible Heart: Economics and Family Values.* New York: New Press.

Fredman, S. (2016). 'Emerging from the shadows: substantive equality and Article 14 of the European Convention on Human Rights', *Human Rights Law Review* 16/2: 273–301. Available at DOI: https://dx.doi.org/10.1093/hrlr/ngw001, accessed 8 July 2019.

Gandhi, N. and Shah, N. (1992). *The Issues at Stake: Theory and Practice in the Contemporary Women's Movement in India.* New Delhi: Kali for Women.

Gao, Y. and Fennell, S. (2017). 'The role of Tunqin Guanxi in building rural resilience in North China: a case from Qinggang', *China Quarterly* 229/March: 44–63.

Goetz, A.M. (ed.) (1998). *Getting Institutions Right for Women in Development.* London: Zed.

Goldin, C. (2006). 'The quiet revolution that transformed women's employment, education and family', *American Economic Review* 96/2: 1–21.

Greenberg, J. (2003). 'Criminalizing dowry deaths: the Indian experience', *Journal of Gender, Social Policy & the Law* 11/2: 801–45.

Hensman, R. (2004). 'Globalisation, women and work: what are we talking about?', *Economic and Political Weekly* 39/10: 1030–34.

ILO (International Labour Organization) (2017). *World Employment and Social Outlook: Trends for Women Report.* Geneva: ILO.

Irving, H. (2008). *Gender and the Constitution: Equity and Agency in Comparative Constitutional Design.* Cambridge: Cambridge University Press.

Kapur, R. (2013). 'Gender, sovereignty, and the rise of a sexual security regime in international law and postcolonial India', *Melbourne Journal of International Law* 14/2: 1–26.

Kapur, R. and Cossman, B. (1996). *Subversive Sites: Feminist Engagements with Law in India.* New Delhi: Sage.

Kumar, R. (1993). *The History of Doing: An Illustrated Account of Movements for Women's Rights and Feminism in India, 1800–1990.* New Delhi: Kali for Women.

Kuznets, Simon (1966). *Modern Economic Growth: Rate, Structure and Spread.* New Haven, CT: Yale University Press.

Lewis, W. Arthur (1954). 'Economic development with unlimited supplies of labor', *Manchester School of Economic and Social Studies* 22: 139–91.

Lundberg, S. and Pollak, R. (1996). 'Bargaining and distribution in marriage', *Journal of Economic Perspectives* 10/4: 139–58.

McAdam, D., McCarthy, J.D., and Zald, M.N. (1996). *Comparative Perspectives on Social Movements: Public Opportunities, Mobilizing Structures, and Cultural Framings.* Cambridge: Cambridge University Press.

Mehra, M. (2013). 'India's CEDAW story', in A. Hellum and H. Aasen (eds) *Women's Human Rights: CEDAW in International, Regional and National Laws.* Cambridge: Cambridge University Press, chap. 13.

Mehta Sood, A. (2006). *Litigating Reproductive Rights: Using Public Interest Litigation and International Law to Promote Gender Justice in India.* New York: Centre for Reproductive Rights.

Mehta Sood, A. (2008). 'Gender justice through public interest litigation: case studies from India', *Vanderbilt Journal of Transnational Law* 41: 833.

Mohanty, C.T. (1988). 'Under Western eyes: feminist scholarship and colonial discourses', *Feminist Review* 30: 61–88.

Narrain, A. and Thiruvengadam, A.K. (2013). 'Social justice lawyering and the meaning of Indian constitutionalism: a case study of the alternative law forum', *Wisconsin International Law Journal* 31/3: 525.

Nussbaum, M. (1999). *Women and Development: The Capabilities Approach.* Cambridge: Cambridge University Press.

Nussbaum, M. (2001). 'India: implementing sex equality through law', *Chicago Journal of International Law* 2/1: 35–58.

OECD (Organisation for Co-operation and Development) (2014). 'Achieving stronger growth by promoting a more gender balanced agenda'. Report prepared for the G20 Labour and Employment Ministerial Meeting, Melbourne, Australia, 10–11 September.

OECD (Organisation for Co-operation and Development) (2018). *Gender Data Portal.* Available at www.oecd.org/gender/data/, accessed 27 December 2019.

Okin, S.M. (1989). *Gender, Justice and Family.* New York: Basic Books.

Okin, S.M. (1999). *Is Multiculturalism Bad for Women?* Princeton, NJ: Princeton University Press.

Okin, S.M. (2004). 'Gender, justice and gender: an unfinished debate', *Fordham Law Revue* 72/5: 1537. Available at http://ir.lawnet.fordham.edu/flr/vol72/iss5/9, accessed 8 July 2019.

Oliver, Pamela E. and Johnston, Hank (2000). 'What a good idea! Ideologies and frames in social movement research', *Mobilization: An International Quarterly* 4: 37–54.

Sankaran, K. and Madhav, R. (2011). 'Gender equality and social dialogue in India'. Working Paper 1. Geneva: International Labour Organization.

Seguino, S. (2000). 'Gender inequality and economic growth: a cross-country analysis', *World Development* 28/7: 1211–30.

Solanki, G. (2011). *Adjudication in Religious Family Laws: Cultural Accommodation, Legal Pluralism, and Gender Equality in India*. Studies in Law and Society. Cambridge: Cambridge University Press.

Sunder Rajan, R. (2003). *The Scandal of the State: Women, Law, and Citizenship in Postcolonial India*. Durham, NC: Duke University Press.

Vanegas, N. and Pruitt, L. (2009). 'CEDAW and rural development: empowering women with law from the top down, activism from the bottom up', *University of Baltimore Law Review* 41/2: 263–320.

Weiner, M. (2003). 'The potential and challenge of transnational litigation for feminists concerned about domestic violence here and abroad', *American University Journal of Gender, Social Policy and the Law* 11/2: 749–800.

Wilson, K. (2015). 'Towards a radical re-appropriation: gender, development and neoliberal feminism', *Development and Change* 46/4: 803–32. Available at http://onlinelibrary.wiley.com/doi/10.1111/dech.12176/abstract, accessed 8 July 2019.

World Bank (2012). *World Development Report: Gender Equality and Development*. Washington, DC: World Bank.

Zheng, Y. (2013). *China: Governance and Development*. Singapore: World Scientific.

26 Violence and BRICS

Lucy McMahon

Introduction

The rapid economic growth that gave rise to the categorization of the BRICS countries was described by OECD as 'a structural change of historical significance', in which 'the world's economic centre of gravity has moved towards the East and South' (Kiely 2015: 10; Ghosh 2016: 276). The direction and significance of this change is unclear, and the rationality of grouping these countries together at all remains disputable. As the chapters in this book demonstrate, it is the diversity in the BRICS countries' different approaches to—for example—health, education, and political organization that makes their development stories collectively interesting. Together BRICS put an end to any (already dubious) assumption that 'development' forms one linear path in which political, social, and economic goals are homogenous (Chang 2003: 84). In so doing, they open wide questions about what 'development', 'progress', and 'growth' really mean.

This chapter takes on one of these questions in its exploration of violence[1] in the development stories of the BRICS countries. The fact that such a powerful grouping together of countries occurs because of just one development indicator reveals the hierarchy of priorities in current international development discourse. After criticism that the millennium development goals (MDGs) overlooked violence, the fourth of the twelve goals proposed by the High Level Panel on the Post 2015 Development Agenda is to 'build peace'. This is combined with 'good governance', which seems to merge two quite separate although equally vague projects. In her analysis of how violence prevention could be incorporated into the post-2015 agenda for the Overseas Development Institute, Lisa Denney argues that 'negative peace' is a crucial factor for 'development' (2013). Denney claims that while there are strong correlations between insecurity (or the 'absence of negative peace') and development, there are few such correlations between positive peace and development. By positive peace she means the kind of anti-violence

[1] The chapter uses the definition of violence from the World Health Organization, as: 'the intentional use of physical force or power, threatened or actual, against oneself, another person, or against a group or community, that either results in or has a high likelihood of resulting in injury, death, psychological harm, maldevelopment or deprivation' (WHO 2019: 4).

Lucy McMahon, *Violence and BRICS* In: *Handbook of BRICS and Emerging Economies.* Edited by: P.B. Anand, Shailaja Fennell, and Flavio Comim, Oxford University Press (2021). © Oxford University Press.
DOI: 10.1093/oso/9780198827535.003.0026

suggestions proposed for post-2015 by Saferworld and Save the Children, including 'violence reduction... against women and girls, constructive resolution of societal divisions, political freedoms, access to social services and resources' (2013: 6). She draws from a range of empirical evidence to argue that such policies have negligible effects on economic growth, even if they are 'laudable aspiration[s]' (2013: 7). Despite the vague distinctions between what would really constitute 'negative' as opposed to 'positive' peace, the argument laid out is clear: the only types of violence prevention that have a significant role in the post-2015 agenda are those that are instrumental to economic growth.

Violence could equally be used as an indicator of 'how well' a country is doing, or of its geopolitical significance. What, indeed, would 'development' look like if reducing violence were seen as a conceptual and practical priority over increasing growth? Rather than assuming that violence may pose a threat to economic growth, in this chapter I highlight the kinds of violence that appear to be *essential in order for current patterns of economic growth to continue.* The chapter therefore questions whether the goals that Denney dismisses as 'laudable aspirations' would in fact be threats to business as normal, which provides a more convincing reason for their relegation to a lower importance.

Since the scale of this exploration massively exceeds the scope of a single chapter, I use brief case studies as a way of illustrating just a few different dimensions through which economic growth and violence interact. The intention is to open up broader questions and discussion about development, and not to make claims about the nature of BRICS in general, nor each country individually. The chapter looks at suicides in the Special Economic Zones (SEZ) in China, practices of imprisonment in Russia and South Africa, the police pacification projects in Brazil, and sexual violence in India. All of the case studies are important elements of the development story in each country. However, my selection of each type of violence is not based on a claim of its magnitude or special importance for any particular country. If my selection reflects anything it is simply the publicity bias given to these cases in the English-language 'international' media. I am not in any way presuming that this publicity has any automatic correlation to severity, or that severity can be measured at all.

Our ability to measure 'how bad' violence is, or to compare countries is anyway obstructed by the fact that statistics on violence are notoriously unreliable. Some forms of violence lend themselves better to statistical measurement than others, which have no automatic relationship with the extent to which they affect people's lives. For example, rape goes overwhelmingly unreported, homicide statistics rarely include police 'disappearances', while slavery statistics do not include forced labour in prison (Belser et al. 2005: 10; Ellsberg and Heise 2005: 18; Zdun 2011: 189). A subjective conception of what kinds of violence matters will invariably filter any attempt we make to understand violence using statistics. This means that it is difficult to approach violence through some kind of 'indicator' or development goal, because within current thinking, it is likely to demand highly limited and numerical ways of measuring success and failure.

Another problem with using measurements of violence, or insecurity, in the post-2015 agenda is that we risk falling into the same trap as the trickle-down theory of economic growth, where increased profits for some are believed to translate into improved economic well-being for all. The equivalent 'trickle-down' theory of security leads to situations where the apparent 'security' of one group involves the mass incarceration or political exclusion of another. I am concerned that a focus only on a 'negative peace' in the 2015 development agenda justifies security for some at the expense of insecurity for others; a theme that recurs through the case studies in this chapter.[2]

At the end of the chapter I very briefly mention the considerable work already being done against violence in the BRICS countries. All five countries stand out for the diversity of creative and peaceful ways of confronting violence. The chapter calls for a nuanced approach to violence in the post-2015 agenda that is mindful of the complexities of its relationship with economic growth.

Factory suicides in China

《我就那样站着入睡》
'I Fall Asleep, Just Standing Like That'

眼前的纸张微微发黄
The paper before my eyes fades yellow
我用钢笔在上面凿下深浅不一的黑
With a steel pen I chisel on it uneven black
里面盛满打工的词汇
Full of working words
车间，流水线，机台，上岗证，加班，薪水…
Workshop, assembly line, machine, work card, overtime, wages…
我被它们治得服服贴贴
They've trained me to become docile
我不会呐喊，不会反抗
Don't know how to shout or rebel
不会控诉，不会埋怨
How to complain or denounce
只默默地承受着疲惫
Only how to silently suffer exhaustion
驻足时光之初
When I first set foot in this place

[2] While violence constitutes a form of insecurity, an absence of violence is not quite the same as security. If my house is about to be repossessed or I lose my job, I will feel insecure without necessarily also experiencing violence. Economic insecurity can be managed in a way to avoid violence, for example through rent controls, social housing, job creation, and unemployment benefit.

> 我只盼望每月十号那张灰色的薪资单
> I hoped only for that grey payslip on the tenth of each month
> 赐我以迟到的安慰
> To grant me some belated solace
> 为此我必须磨去棱角，磨去语言
> For this I had to grind away my corners, grind away my words
> 拒绝旷工，拒绝病假，拒绝事假
> Refuse to skip work, refuse sick leave, refuse leave for private reasons
> 拒绝迟到，拒绝早退
> Refuse to be late, refuse to leave early
> 流水线旁我站立如铁，双手如飞
> By the assembly line I stood straight like iron, hands like flight,
> 多少白天，多少黑夜
> How many days, how many nights
> 我就那样，站着入睡
> Did I – just like that – standing fall asleep?
> Xu Lizhi (许立志)—20 August 2011. (Lizhi and Nao 2014, trans. Helena Laughton)

Xu Lizhi was a 24-year-old poet and worker at a Foxconn factory in Shenzhen when he took his own life in September 2014. Migrant worker suicides in Foxconn and other factories in China have continued apace since the much publicized eighteen attempts at Foxconn in 2010 (Ngai and Chan 2012; Lizhi and Nao 2014). Now all Foxconn factories are surrounded by nets, incorporating the suicidal nature of the work into the very fabric and appearance of the buildings (Johnson 2011). Chan claims that the Foxconn suicides represent 'a phenomenon that has no precedent in China's industrial history' and it has drawn attention from national and international researchers and human rights groups (2013: 1).

Although China accounts for 22 per cent of the world's suicides, per capita the suicide rate in China is not comparatively high (Zhang et al. 2014: 1). Indeed the suicide rate has statistically decreased. During the 1990s the country had one of the highest rates in the world, mostly attributable to suicides of young rural women facing extreme and inescapable family pressures (*The Economist* 2014). A study for *The Lancet* in 2002 estimated that the suicide rate for young women in China was 37.8 per 100,000 in 1995–99, which declined to just over three per 100,000 in 2011 (Phillips et al. 2002). The fall in suicides has been attributed to rapid economic growth and expanded migration and work opportunities for women (*The Economist* 2014; Zhang et al. 2014). Chan explains how 'left behind children' whose parents migrated to cities from the 1980s onwards now join their parents in the Special Economic Zones where China's export orientated development allows multinationals to take advantage of low-tax, low-cost land, and relaxed labour laws (Chan 2013: 87). As Foxconn claimed, suicide at its factories is below the national rate of twenty-three per 100,000 people (Chan 2013: 85). This chapter does not intend to single out factory suicides as any worse than other suicides in China and elsewhere, or than other forms of violence. The aim is rather to illuminate the dependency of China's industrial model—and that of the multinational corporations operating in the country—on what can only be termed extreme violence against workers.

Research into conditions in the factories has been carried out by undercover reporters for Chinese newspaper *Southern Weekend* and by Hong Kong-based labour rights group Students and Scholars Against Corporate Misbehavior (SACOM). Academic work has included Ngai and Chan's factory surveys and 1,736 questionnaires filled in in 2010 and 2011 by Foxconn workers in nine cities (2012). The problems identified are not so much with the written laws but rather that employees regularly work longer hours than stipulated by the company's code of conduct, Chinese law, and the laws of the multinational buyers.

Chinese Labour Law permits a maximum of thirty-six hours per month overtime; for Foxconn workers this figure is closer to eighty (Ngai and Chan 2012: 407). The SACOM study found that workers at Foxconn worked thirteen days straight, twelve hours a day. Ngan and Chen report that workers have to sign written agreements for overtime or they risk being fired, and their questionnaires showed that over 80 per cent of respondents had less than four days of rest each month. Foxconn is certainly not the only offender, and similar research by the National Labour Committee[3] (NLC) uncovered similar conditions at the KYE Systems factory in Dongguan which makes Microsoft hardware. The NLC reports that Microsoft, like other well-known multinationals benefits from local companies' disregard for labour laws while maintaining its commitment to codes of conduct (Kernaghan 2014). KYE workers are instructed not to reveal the levels of overtime they work when Microsoft inspects the factories and to report that they are 'very satisfied' with working conditions. However, quotas imposed by multinationals mean that local factories have to rely on overtime to meet their demands. As one worker reported, 'On the bulletin board in our workshop, the actual assigned production goal is always higher than what we expect. Our team just broke the record and finished 15,000 pieces! Today the goal becomes 18,000 pieces. They are trying to kill us!' (Kernaghan 2014: 5). Managers time workers' fastest possible times for assembly and set this as an expected quota. The fastest times rely on workers not wearing gloves, not going to the bathroom, nor eating.

Foxconn is not some kind of barbaric outlier but rather is seen by many as 'one of the top places to work', with one worker reporting that 'In terms of infrastructure, Foxconn is by far the best factory in China' (Johnson 2011). Ngai and Chan note that Foxconn represents a new form of economic organization in China which has changed from guaranteed lifetime state employment to reliance on migrant labourers working for international firms with severe suppression of wages, labour protection, and labour organizing (2012: 388). This is encouraged by the state, with township governments recruiting workers for free for Foxconn in Chengdu. Government officials are given Foxconn recruitment targets as part of their job requirements and are encouraged to recruit people for 'student internships' which is a way in which Foxconn can pay sub-minimum wages to people who also do not qualify for government-run social insurance (Ngai and Chan 2012: 391). Ngai and Chan also call attention to the way in which

[3] Now the Institute for Global Labour and Human Rights.

Foxconn's policies are not just purely 'economic' but form part of a new ethical praxis peppered with quotations by Terry Gou, Foxconn's founder (2012: 396). To gain a promotion in Foxconn some of the test questions involve citing *Gou's Quotations* from memory, which include 'Growth, thy name is suffering', 'Value efficiency every minute, every second', 'Achieve goals, otherwise the sun will no longer rise', and 'Heart to heart, Foxconn and I grow together' (2012: 398). To be a successful Foxconn worker does not just involve working fast but also working with the right kind of spirit. This involves being keen, terrified of mistakes, and highly competitive. At the beginning of the day management asks all workers 'How are you?' and workers must respond shouting 'Good! Very good! Very, very good!'(2012: 397). If a worker is too slow or makes a mistake, at the end of the day they must read a statement of self-criticism loudly in front of all workers (2012: 397).

Foxconn is not the only company to embrace a code of ethics that justifies the demands that it places on workers. In response to the suicide of an 18-year-old girl who worked cleaning mobile phone cases at the Wangxin factory in Shenzhen, the vice-president of the factory claimed that the factory denied responsibility for the fact that 'kids born after the 90s are mentally too weak' (IGLHR 2011). Wenqing Wang, General Manager of Beijing IRTOUCH Systems Co. made an address about the ideal culture among workers in the Shenzhen SEZ. He asserted that material incentive must be subordinated to emotional and spiritual incentives towards 'self-respect, self-love and self-improvement' (IGLHR 2011). A worker with such 'corporate values' will have 'high spirits' to pursue the individual values that meet the company's demand. According to Tina Yu, at Foxconn induction managers tell stories of Bill Gates and Steve Jobs to inspire workers (Chan 2013: 87). Terry Gou's personal assistant, who was made chairwoman of a phony union in the factories, commented publically that 'suicide is foolish, irresponsible and meaningless and should be avoided' (Heffernan 2013). After the suicides, the company required all applicants to complete a psychological test, blaming suicides on 'weak capability to handle personal problems' and 'fragile spirits' (Chan 2013: 92).

This feeling of weakness—or inferiority to machines—has led workers to claim they feel like 'just a speck of dust in the workshop' (Ngai and Chan 2012: 401). This is accentuated by the lack of division between working and living space. At the KYE factory, one worker told the NLC, 'It seems like we live only to work. We do not work to live. We do not live a life, only work' (Hull and Sorrell 2010). This alienation of workers also takes social forms. Zheng Ding Technology, which makes circuit boards for Apple, Amazon, and other companies, encourages their workers to confess to their own and spy on each others' mistakes (Kernaghan 2014: 13). At Foxconn, workers are set against each other for competitive production bonuses. One worker reported that 'My new friends, whom I met during the training, were all placed in different positions... I consider this arrangement as a way of preempting workers from "making trouble" (闹事). This is why Foxconn workers are free to jump from buildings but not to "make trouble"' (Ngai and Chan 2012: 403).

These stories complicate Zhang et al.'s argument that 'With the better living standards and more freedom in migration (going to the cities to work), there have been more opportunities for the rural young women who used to be confined to the traditional family environment with social and psychological oppressions in the countryside' (Zhang et al. 2014: 566). Women face disproportionate discrimination in factories; a study by the Sunflower Women Workers Centre in Gunagzhou conducted a survey of female factory workers, and 70 per cent reported some form of workplace sexual harassment (Larson 2013). For the Dongguan KYE Systems factory workers, the majority of whom are young women, a report by the NLC reveals widespread sexual harassment (Eaton 2010). After the Foxconn suicides, hours were reduced to sixty or fewer per week, but China Labour Watch reports that employees are required to complete the same amount of work as before (Culpan and James 2012). A new movement known as '354' was initiated in which three workers got paid for four people's salary—but had to do the equivalent of five people's labour (Kernaghan 2014: 9). The intense diligence, discipline, and hierarchies associated with factory work are part of a 'successful' development model with an acutely painful reality. As the poetry of Xu Lizhi asserts, suicide statistics are a way in which workers are making this reality visible through the little freedom accorded to them.

Imprisonment in Russia and South Africa

This section looks at the economic arguments that justify the violence of prison. The prison is a classic case of a 'security' institution in which the security of some is explicitly violated for the sake of what might be argued to be a broader 'national' security; whether this is security from violence or from economic instability—which, as argued in the Introduction, tends to be increasingly conflated.

Imprisonment is a violence carried out by the state against prisoners. The motivation for this in some cases is to reduce other forms of violence, as in the imprisonment of murderers. However, the majority of prisoners in the world are there for non-violent crimes, a large percentage of these are 'victimless' as in the cases of drug-related or immigration offences, and another large percentage of people in prison are still technically 'innocent', awaiting trial (Walmsley 2013: 1; Allen 2015: 2, 14). The imprisonment of people invariably leads to other forms of violence: violence among prisoners, attacks by prison guards and intelligence agencies, and violence in communities as released prisoners return with post-traumatic stress disorder (PTSD) and increased connections with or debts to violent crime (Samara 2003: 279).

There is a general consensus that imprisonment does not work as a means of reducing crime or insecurity, and that in many cases it makes things worse (Davis 2003: 12). At the pan-African Seminar on Prison Conditions in Africa at Kampala in 1996, more than forty African countries adopted the Kampala Declaration which stated that the 'over-use of imprisonment does not serve the interests of justice, nor does it protect the public, nor is it a good use of scarce public resources' (Nathan 2003: 7). In their *Ready to Govern* statement in 1992, the African National Congress (ANC) declared that 'Apartheid's overcrowded and authoritarian jails are crime factories which dehumanise their inmates, feeding a culture of violence and despair. The ANC asserts that adequate resources must be made available for the humane accommodation, education, training and job placement of convicts. Failure to do so will only lead to expenditure on an ever increasing number of new jails' (*Ready to Govern*, 1992 cited in Samara 2003: 291).

Pallot suggests that a study of the relationship between the state and the prison system brings out a fundamental conflict between the modernist and structuralist schools of development (Pallot 2015: 685). In the modernist school it is presumed that the more a state develops towards a market-based liberal democracy the less punitive and more rehabilitative its punishment regime has to be. The structuralist school claims that the prison and security system is in fact inseparable from the development of the modern state and that the failure of the prison system to prevent crime is irrelevant to its reason for existence. In light of the failure of prisons to reduce crime and violence, this chapter looks at what else is served by the prevalence—indeed the rapid increase—of the use of the prison in Russia and in South Africa over the periods in which both countries experienced rapid growth.

RUSSIA

In 2013, Masha Alyokhina and Nadya Tolokonnikova of Pussy Riot drew the world's attention to prison conditions in Russia, which is still second only to the USA in its incarceration rates. After serving nearly two years in Russian jails and prison colonies the women set up an organization for reporting prison conditions *MediaZona* and a parallel organization to support prisoner victims of human rights abuses *Zona Prava.* Alyokhina claims that prisoners in Russia are being 'turned into slaves' (Walker 2013). Tatyana Gavrilova, who spent sixteen years in Russian jails and penal colonies, testified about her experiences to MediaZona. The report reveals practices of frequent beatings, confessions under torture, withdrawal of food and heat, forced injection of illegal drugs such as sulfozinum as a punishment (found to cause severe muscle pain), and the use of other prisoners to assault inmates seen by the guards to be a problem (Klimova 2014). An investigation by the Russian newspaper *Novaya Gazeta* estimated that 3,907 people died in Russian prisons in 2012, which is three times the proportion who die in US prisons which are globally notorious for violence, torture, and suicide (Gordienko and Fitzpatrick 2013). This section looks at the ways in which the violence of imprisonment fits inside Russia's contemporary political and economic strategy.

In the Soviet Union, prison labour was profit making and played a central role in the Soviet economy (Christie 2004: 57). Pallot argues that the Gulag was in fact 'a system of forced labour disguised as a penitentiary system' (Pallot 2012: 7). Prisoners constructed the White Sea Baltic Canal, the Moscow Volga Canal, the Baikal-Amur railway, and many other Siberian industrial ventures (Library of Congress 2010). Soviet prisons tended to be located in remote regions which depended on the prisons for employment (Moran et al. 2011).

Today the prisons remain roughly in the same locations, but the 1990s change in national economic planning meant the migration of industry to parts of the world where labour was cheaper even than that of prisoners. Most people sent to prison are still sent to penal colonies or 'koloniyas', where they are forced to work for wages from which the prison deducts the costs of their subsistence. In the early post-Soviet period the labour of prisoners was the only thing that kept many prisons functioning and their inmates alive (Moran et al. 2011: 716). This is a classic neoliberal technique in which people are made responsible for their own survival through underpaid labour in terrible conditions; in which, as Laura Piacentini states, prisoners are 'involved in the administration of their own punishment' (*The Economist* 2013).

Prisons in Russia also reflect other dimensions of the country's political and economic structure. Russian neoliberalism is famous for being fast, lethal, and dramatically inegalitarian (Stuckler and Basu 2013). Putin's rise to power was partly attributable to his opposition to this International Monetary Fund (IMF) and 'Western-' imposed market neoliberalism; but in the end he preserved Yeltsin's pro-market strategies and maintained reliance on private corporations (Rutland 2013: 336). He also strengthened the particular way in which privatization had occurred in Russia which was the accumulation of private wealth in the hands of a very few (often state-connected) oligarchs (Rutland 2013: 348). Stephen White argues that the increase in imprisonment in post-Soviet Russia is deeply connected to the country's reliance on finance capital in its economic development (Rutland 2008: xi). Finance capital does not necessarily increase employment in a country or develop local industries, and it tends to concentrate in a small number of cities and benefit a small number of individuals, meaning that divides between rich and poor, city and countryside, are vast. The coexistence of extravagance and poverty fuels the demand by the rich for punitive approaches to poverty, and also seems to have fuelled crime, with rates rising steadily since 1991 (Schröder 2008: 20).

The Russian political and economic model—as in many other countries—also favours the development of individual cities as 'showcases' to attract international investment and mega events (Golubchikov 2010: 627). Golubchikov shows how in Russia this was justified by a neoconservative argument that socialism's focus on equality led to a misallocation of resources across the country and needed to be reversed through 'polarised' development in a limited number of 'growth locomotives' such as Moscow or St Petersburg (2010: 633). This focus on certain cities as growth epicentres at the expense of the rest of the country is reflected in the geographies of imprisonment. Prisons still provide an important if not the only source of employment in some areas—Pallot claims that they prevent 'the total destitution of places which have suffered badly since Russia's adoption of the market' (2007: 19). Prisons therefore constitute 'inferior public goods' in that they provide stable labour for remote communities. Pallot argues that post-Soviet interest in maintaining the prisons in remote locations comes also from the perspective of the cities from which many of the inmates come, who are 'able to displace deviancy to the peripheries' and away from these global showcase cities (2007: 19).

Although Putin's presidency has seen a fall in the numbers of prisoners, with the release of minor criminals and moves to replace prison with other schemes such as tagging, authoritarianism has grown in the country with severe consequences for prisoners (Danks 2009: 225). This may in part be due to the fact that many of the political elites are former security service employees, including Putin himself. White argues that the security service is seen by some as the 'very core of the postcommunist regime', and its staff, who at times are so powerful as to constitute a 'state within a state' are 'orientated primarily towards security categories and not towards principles such as democracy' (2008: x). After Chechen separatists killed 300 children and adults in a school in Beslan, North Osseria, Putin took advantage of a climate of fear to implement a hard-line response not just to Chechen terrorism but also other crimes. According to Danks, the Beslan tragedy has been used as an excuse to crack down on other opposition to Putin and the government which particularly affected Muslim citizens (Danks 2009: 226). Repressive measures include the detention and beating of a thousand men in the city of Blagoveshchensk by police in December 2004, sanctioned in a secret Ministry of the Interior document that advocated the use of extreme force and the establishment of detention or 'filtration' camps in the case of political protest. These already existed in Chechnia but are now being used elsewhere in Russia (Danks 2009: 227).

Pallot argues that the current penitentiary system retains the same kind of 'culture of punishment' of the Soviet regime, particularly the reliance on collective labour and hierarchies of prisoners used to organize and punish the workers, promote competition, and also act as informants (2012: 2). Prisons are partly run by 'prison servants' who can operate outside the law unpunished in their control over other prisoners (Ponomarev 2007). In this respect the Russian prison shares much with the Chinese factories discussed in the previous section. The parallels are clear in this report by Larisa who was imprisoned in a colony in Ivanovo:

> In our colony, there a sewing factory was set up, we sew uniforms for the police... Officially we worked 8 hours a day, but in practice on the average it was 16... the women who are already in for a second time or more as a rule are single, and have no one to help them. Therefore, many of them work to exhaustion, just to earn a kopeck... If you work poorly, you are punished, if you work well, you are not allowed out on early release. 'It's too bad to lose ones like that,' says the warden. (Cited in Gordienko and Fitzpatrick 2013)

Larisa's report demonstrates how people are still kept in prisons for the value of their labour power, as under Soviet rule. Moran et al. (2011) claim that penal collectivism in Russia's new economic system has shifted its goal, although not its practices, towards a more individualist 'responsibilisation' strategy in which prisoners are made to feel responsible both for their crimes and for their rehabilitation through forced labour

(2011: 716). Prisons demand that their inmates be economically self-sufficient through gruelling labour undertaken under conditions of authoritarian oppression. Ponomarev argues that the system of control established over Russian prisons is 'analogous only to totalitarian systems' with widespread torture used to break inmates psychologically as well as obtain confessions (2007). Prison labour in Russia can be seen then as a microcosm of neoliberal labour conditions under Putin at the harshest end of the economic spectrum.

SOUTH AFRICA

In South Africa the connection between neoliberal economic strategy and imprisonment is even starker because money is made much more directly *off* the prison system through prison privatization. While there is a threat of this practice in Russia through the introduction of public–private partnerships, it is not yet on the government's agenda (Piacentini 2012: 133; RAPSI 2013).

Like Russia, South Africa also saw a rapid change in economic policy over the 1980s and 1990s that served to perpetuate some of the political structures of apartheid-era security policy. The ANC switched quickly from advocating an 'intense ideological struggle against neoliberalism' in their 1994 Reconstruction and Development Programme (RDP) to the 1996 Growth, Employment, and Redistribution (GEAR) strategy. This switch towards business and market-led growth coincided with changes in criminal justice policy, away from the progressive ideals of early post-apartheid plans (Gordon 2001: 57). As Samara writes:

> Emergent in South Africa is a discourse and practice of safety and security that takes as its starting point and conclusion that crime is the greatest obstacle the country faces in its transition, displacing an alternative rationale that explains crime as an expression of the shortcomings of the transition thus far. (2003: 281)

This discourse is used to justify apartheid-like approaches to crime in which 'criminals' are separated from citizens as an enemy that needs to be combated (Samara 2003). Changes included tightening bail requirements that prevent almost all possibility of pre-trial release, harsher minimum sentences, and a consequent massive expansion of the prison population to over 400 per cent over capacity (Gordon 2001: 61). These policies are very expensive, with an increase of 456 per cent in spending for the Departments of Safety and Security, Justice, and Correctional Services between 1990 and 1999, with no statistical evidence to show any resulting improvement. The failures of these policies in terms of preventing crime have only seemed to lead for stronger calls for the same policies to be intensified (Gordon 2001: 24).

It is a commonly noted paradox of neoliberalism that calls for a 'shrinking' state to coexist with the massive expansion of state spending on security (see Wacquant 2010). Just as with the case of Brazil (see next section), this kind of spending is justified as a strategy to attract investment and counter the image of economic instability created by high crime rates. It could be said to constitute a striving for what Denney would call 'negative peace'. Yet Gordon notes that 'crime reduction would be equally likely to generate foreign confidence whether achieved through a "get tough" strategy or through policies that emphasized development as crime prevention' (2001: 63). She suggests that South Africa opted for the more punitive approach in order to conform to a US neoliberal political and economic model with the presumption that perhaps aid and investment would favour a more 'American' punitive style (2001: 63).

Another justification for the American model is that it has shown that 'getting tough' on crime has economic benefits (for some) on its own terms. Copying the US is not just about copying a particular culture of punishment but also a strategy of capital accumulation through crime as a business interest. As noted by the Corrections Corporation of America (CCA), prisons are 'an industry with positive investment characteristics' as they thrive off recessions because of the 'potential of accelerated growth in inmate populations following the recession' (Galbraith 2012). The CCA also asserts that prison populations are likely to grow with the US population, and importantly with the growing number of immigration-related imprisonments. Prison companies directly profit then from poverty, forced migration, and increased community violence.

In a report on women in prisons across the world, Sudbury writes that the way in which private prisons prioritize low staffing ratios, employ low-paid non-unionized staff, and make budget cuts wherever possible contributes to increasing levels of prisoner abuse, and this is covered up when companies expand their projects to other countries (2005). The expansion of US prison corporations to South Africa is a way of maintaining profits even where domestic practices are threatened by human rights groups, while the expansion of the 'war on drugs' agenda in the Vienna Convention has meant that signed up member states have pledged to use incarceration in place of medical or social solutions to drug crimes (Sudbury 2005: 81).

The argument for private prisons is that a government can quickly commission the building of prisons without having up-front capital costs, so it is seen as a fast solution to South Africa's catastrophic overcrowding problems. It is also a subcontracting of the responsibility for—and control over—prisoners' welfare from the state to private companies. Mangaung Correctional Centre was South Africa's first public–private prison, branded by its owner G4S as 'world class' despite the plethora of human rights abuses that are increasingly emerging (Sambrook 2013). The Wits Justice Project uncovered data that showed that sixty-two Mangaung inmates were kept in solitary confinement for up to three years. Prisoners reported receiving electric shock treatment as punishment and were forcibly injected with the anti-psychotic drugs Clopixol Depot, Risperdal, Etomine, and Modecate which are associated with memory loss, muscle rigidity, and strokes (Hopkins 2013; Private Corrections Working Group 2017). Former wardens recall the sounds of inmates screaming in a supposedly soundproofed 'dark room' where electroshocks were practised. According to a former G4S employee in a BBC report, these electroshocks were justified because: 'we are understaffed and we are expected to bring out the results and also to instil fear on the inmates... sometimes you go and shock them individually in a segregation unit just to make sure they could be afraid of us.' He asserted that the management were happy with this practice: 'we stripped them naked and we throw with water so the electricity can work nicely... Again and again... He can tell the truth but if that's not the truth that I want, I will shock him until he tells the truth that I want even if it's a lie' (Hopkins 2013; Sambrook 2013). These abuses have been termed 'unavoidable accidents' by Andy Baker of G4S (Sambrook 2013).

There is no evidence that private prisons even bring the economic benefits they promise; indeed their track record across the world seems to be considerably worse for the state than public provision (see Nathan 2003). Group 4 failed to meet the conditions for having its contract renewed for its Altcourse prison in north-west England due to the cells being 'unfit for use' and inadequate staffing (Nathan 2003: 15). Their shareholders then pocketed an extra £10 million profit to that which was initially agreed on by the government (Nathan 2003: 16). Apart from G4S, other US multinationals Wackenhut Corrections Corporation and Group 4 Falck are expanding their operations in Africa. South African contracts made these companies more than ZAR3 billion over twenty-five years. Nathan showed that the privatization of prisons in some cases has made social and economic conditions worse, for example in the freezing of thousands of public sector jobs in order to allocate money to the new private prisons and a special task team to monitor them. This task team found that the companies and banks involved in prison privatization were overcharging the government, while at the same time Frikkie Venter, Managing Director of Group 4 in South Africa, claims that his prison plays a fundamental role in boosting the area's economy (Nathan 2003: 8).

In October 2013, the Congress of South African Trade Unions made a statement against the firing of 300 Police and Prisons Civil Rights Union (POPCRU) members for staging a strike. They state that the use of private companies to run prisons is part of a neoliberal discourse of 'security', and claim that:

> Security, in this context, does not imply security for everyone, but rather, when one looks at the major clients of G4S Security (banks, governments, corporations etc.) it becomes evident that when G4S says it is 'Securing your World', as the company slogan goes, it is referring to a world of exploitation, repression, occupation and racism. (COSATU 2013)

Private prisons provide an economic incentive to increase the prison population for profit. This can be seen in a new version of the profit-making Russian Gulag. Instead of prisoners' labour making money, it is the prison buildings and services that are now the assets.

Practices of imprisonment in South Africa are part of a larger 'war on crime' in which private companies play a significant role. Other dimensions of this 'war' that feed the prison industrial complex include the Cape Town Partnership, which is a public–private venture founded in 1999 to reduce crime in the city. Their main activities are the mass arrest of street children for 'loitering' who are then imprisoned for indefinite periods before trial in the notorious Pollsmoor prison where Mandela was once incarcerated (Samara 2003: 279). The next section turns to similar relationships between policing tactics and profit in Brazil.

Pacification in Brazil

The 'Police Pacification Units' (UPPs) of Rio de Janeiro are a strategy devised to reduce the levels of drug-related violence in the city's favelas.[4] UPPs involve an initial military invasion of a favela, with a weapons amnesty and gun battles until the police manage to take control of the streets. After this, BOPE (Special Police Operations Batallion) stay in the area for a few months until the UPP forces take over (Cano et al. 2014). The final stage is supposed to be the implementation of 'UPP social' (now called Rio+Social) where new services such as libraries and transport links are installed in the favela.

UPP is a highly controversial 'anti-violence' strategy, and provides another example of the ways in which security and economic policy are interrelated. The project has had some statistical successes, with a marked decrease in armed battles, lower mortality rates, and a shift in practices of drug trafficking away from armed control of territory (Cano et al. 2014). Improvements were most dramatic to begin with; killings by police declined from 1,330 in 2007 to 561 in 2011 (Muggah 2012). Opinion surveys showed 87 per cent of residents in the city centre favela of Santa Marta and 93 per cent of residents in the West Zone area of Cidade de Deus approved of pacification (Werling 2014: 6). A 2012 report by Freeman, based on interviews in seven favelas noted that residents felt that on balance the UPP had improved things, due to the end of conflict between rival gangs, the end of armed trafficker patrols, and a greater freedom of movement. Interviewees in the study also noted that the UPP were much less corrupt and violent than the ordinary police (2012: 104).

However, UPP has also received strong criticism for continuing high levels of police killings, and for the absence or paucity of any social or educational projects associated with the strategy (Paz and Livingstone 2014). Deaths by police include the beating and choking to death of Paulo Roberto Santos, an 18-year-old in Manguinhos in 2013, and the shooting of Caio Moraes and 60-year-old Antônio França in Complexo de Alemão (Soares and Livingstone 2013; Paz and Livingstone 2014). At the height of the 2013 nationwide protests (for, among other things, more public spending and against police violence), on 24 June, BOPE initiated an operation in the northern region of Complexo do Alemão, that killed ten people, left dozens injured, and left the whole favela without electricity for thirty-six hours in an operation that BOPE's commanding officer claimed he didn't even know about (Clarke 2013). Then, on 14 July 2013 Amarildo da Souza, a 43-year-old father and bricklayer was taken to the police station in Rocinha for questioning. He was tortured and later murdered. Although deaths in police custody are

[4] Self-built communities—known originally as *cortiços*—have existed in Rio since at least 1897, and were typically excluded from the infrastructure developments elsewhere in the city. Around 24 per cent of Rio's population (1.5 million people) lives in one of the 1,000 favelas (*Catalytic Communities* 2015a). Although nowadays most favela houses are made of brick, concrete, or reinforced steel, 30 per cent of Rio's population is still not connected to a formal sanitation system—a statistic which includes people in non-favela neighbourhoods too. The main distinction between favela and non-favela areas is the name, and long-standing prejudices about particular areas (*Catalytic Communities* 2015b).

common (Amnesty International 2015), in this case the residents of Rocinha organized a huge protest to draw attention to his disappearance, closing down the Lagoa-Barra highway—the main thoroughfare towards the prestigious Barra de Tijuca. The campaign was taken up by communities across the country and the slogan 'Where is Amarildo?' gained international prominence.

Despite their role in uniting sections of a highly divided city (see Zibechi 2013; McMahon 2017), protests against the death toll in favelas did little to combat levels of violence in the lead up to the World Cup and the Olympics. In April 2014, officers from UPP murdered DG, a local dancer and activist in Pavão-Pavãozinho through kicking him to death, and in response to two further shootings—of the 27-year-old Edilson Santos and a 12-year-old boy, the community staged a huge protest on 24 April, which ended with baton violence and tear gas (Hilderbrand 2014). In the weeks before the World Cup, 2,000 extra police were stationed on the streets, an 8-year-old was shot in the head in Morro dos Macacos, and 19-year-old Jonatan de Oliveira Lima was killed by UPP in Manguinhos (Clarke 2014). That same week, an Amnesty International study revealed that 80 per cent of Brazilians believed that they would be tortured if detained by police (Clarke 2014). There was then a notable increase in deaths during police operations in the run-up to the World Cup and Olympic Games (Aranda-Comer and Olivieri 2015; Barber 2016). In 2016, police killed at least 920 people in Rio, and the community reporter McNamara claims that 2017 is easily on course to beat that number (2017).

In a study of UPP officers in 2014 by the Center for Studies on Public Security and Citizenship (CeSEC), 46 per cent of officers thought that the majority of residents had negative feelings towards them, including fear, suspicion, and anger, while 15.5 per cent of officers claimed they were opposed to the UPP project entirely (Werling 2014: 7). Residents report repeated stop and searches with no criteria, the invasion of houses without a search warrant, and open random abuse of young people (Paz and Livingstone 2014). Critiques of UPP have likened it to a war against favela residents, with Vera Malaguti Batista, researcher and General Secretary of the Rio Institute of Criminology, claiming that the project is one of occupation, and of 'territory to be conquered' (Waldron 2014). Indeed, as Cano et al. argue, many favela residents oppose the term 'pacification' on the grounds that it implies that the violence was between favela residents, while they perceived the police to be the main perpetrators (2014).

There has also been a marked rise in non-lethal violence over the past few years (Freeman 2012: 105; Cano et al. 2014). In the CeSec study, UPP officers identified key deficiencies in training in using non-lethal arms and dealing with domestic violence. Reported rapes increased by 24 per cent between 2011 and 2012 in Rio with an average of 416 women reporting rape every month (Ortiz 2013).[5] Sexual violence is also associated

[5] A study by Rio de Janeiro's Institute of Public Security (IPEA) has shown that this statistic represents about 10 per cent of all rapes, with 90 per cent left unreported (Rocha and Cardoso 2014). The recorded increase is at least partly due to a change in the law in 2009 which broadened the definition of rape and

directly with the police; in 2015, a woman reported that she was raped by BOPE officers on her way back from a party, after she had approached them to find out the safest way home after a shoot-out in Rocinha; on the same night other police were accused of sexual violence in the Morro da Coroa area (Viva Favela 2015).

In 2017 a public meeting was held at the Rio Public Defenders Office between residents of the Complexo do Alemão area and the police. Residents called the meeting specifically to protest the way in which UPP were (illegally) taking over people's houses as bases. At the meeting, the resident Cleonice Madalena reported:

> They kicked an elderly couple out of their house violently, peed on a resident's television, stole a child's yoghurt while pointing a gun at her and saying 'If you don't shut up, I'll make you shut you up'. I'm not defending criminals, but no drug dealer has ever thrown people out of their houses like this. (Cited in Fenizola 2017)

Residents also argue that the laws under traffickers were more efficient in dealing with non-lethal crime than are the police (Freeman 2012: 105; Cano et al. 2014).

When analysing the relationship between UPPs and violence, I suggest that it is important to see the policy within the changing political context of the country. The policy was initiated under the right-wing Brazilian Democratic Movement Party in Rio (PMDB). It was supported by former President Dilma Rousseff of the Workers' Party (PT) as a way of 'respecting' residents, with her proviso that it needs to be 'more than a police force' and must involve the 'UPP Social' projects intended to combat social exclusion and deprivation of residents (UPP RJ 2013). Gestures towards progressive and inclusive politics are also evident in the then Security Secretary José Mariano Beltrame's claims that UPP 'is not only a security project, it is a state policy of valorising life and generating hope for the people of Rio', while Coronel Frederico Caldas, coordinator of UPPs claims that 'the UPP symbolises all the appreciation that we have to have for human life' (UPP RJ 2015).

The clash between such claims and the experiences of residents come partly from the fact that the so-called 'pacification' is led by precisely the institution held most responsible for violence. In his critical history of the UPPs in Rio, Ashcroft writes: 'There was simply no way the same police institution which killed 1,330 people in Rio in 2007 could suddenly, drastically, transform its philosophy and expect citizens to instantly accept this reincarnation' (2014). UPP can be seen as part of a wider strategy of militarization and an ever increasing shift from public spending on welfare to policing. In December 2014, the Rio's Human Rights Commission released a report that showed that more people had disappeared or been killed under Brazilian democracy than under military dictatorship

encouraged reporting, and—according to sociologist Jacqueline Pitanguy the presence of UPPs—making it safer for women living in favelas to report (ONU Mulheres and CEPIA 2011: 53). However, Pitanguy also suggests that the increase in reported rapes may reflect an increasing threat to masculine identity due to unemployment together with increased commodification of women's bodies (Pitanguy 2014). There is as yet insufficient research in the area of sexual violence in Rio to draw any conclusions (reflecting research funding priorities).

(Gonzalez 2014). Despite the fact that the UN Committee on Torture and Human Rights has recommended that Brazil eliminate its military police category, the government of Rio has gone in the opposite direction, expanding its military cadet programme while the federal government allocated funding for 10,000 riot troops across the country in 2014 (Sweet 2014: 63).

As for public spending in areas other than 'security', a favela is labelled as 'pacified' whether or not the 'UPP social' (a form of what Denney would refer to as 'positive peace') has been implemented (Werling 2014: 2). Six hundred telephone surveys in seven UPP controlled communities identified an urgent need for health services and schools (Werling 2014: 7).The prioritization of security over community development is symbolically represented in the way that the UPP bases often take over school and sports grounds (Fenizola 2017). In Alemão, for example, the new space occupied by UPP was a social centre used previously for sport, courses, and capoeira[6] (Fenizola 2017).

Another way of understanding the disconnect between the words of policymakers and practice is to question the homogenization implied in the words 'the people of Rio' and 'human life' in Beltrame and Caldas's comments above. It is unclear within the policy whether UPPs are intended for the security of those living in the favela, or for the city as a whole. Werling draws attention to the huge discrepancy in security across the city of Rio; homicide rates vary from 84 to 4.7 per 100,000 people across different areas (2014: 2). An interest in 'city wide' security is not, therefore, the same as an interest in all people's security. The peripheral areas of Niteroi and Marica had a 46 per cent rise in violent deaths between 2010 and 2011, and one of the perceived outcomes of the UPP installation in central favelas is that neighbourhoods outside of the city have been taken by trafficking gangs (Mesker 2014: 146).

This geography of violence also flags up the role of UPPs in Rio's project to brand itself as a global city, safe for tourists and investors. Marques argues that Rio's federal, state, and municipal governments have as their central aim the project of making Rio into a 'global city' in which sporting mega events are prioritized above other goals in order to attract private investment (2011). In Rio's report from the International Olympic Committee, the lowest score was in safety and security with the report citing chronic problems of violence (IOC 2008). Mega events are known for allowing city governments to act in the name of 'security' with projects which prioritize the safety of international visitors over that of the safety of city residents, for example slum clearance or zero tolerance policing (Steinbrink 2014). Walbert questions whether the UPP is really there for the communities or whether it is part of a mega event branding strategy that will not last after the games (Freeman 2012: 121). The majority of UPPs are in the areas closest to the stadiums and Olympic locations, as well as being in the most desirable real estate (Cano et al. 2014). Part of the motivation for this comes direct from the demands of FIFA and the IOC; in South Africa a FIFA delegate explicitly told the government that 'A

[6] An Afro-Brazilian martial art.

billion television viewers don't want to see shacks and poverty on this scale' (cited in Freeman 2012).

Apart from the militarization, these mega event projects have also led to widespread evictions, casting further doubt on the idea that favela policy is created with the interests of residents in mind. In December 2015, the Popular Committee on the World Cup and Olympics released the report: 'Rio 2016 Olympics: the exclusion games', which documented the evictions of 22,059 families between 2009 and 2015, and 2,486 more families in threat of eviction due to the (then) forthcoming Olympics (Robertson 2015). A study by Azevedo the same year found that the pre-Olympic administrations evicted more people between 2009 and 2015 than any other administration in history (Azevedo 2015). Infrastructure changes associated with the games also entailed doubling (and for some quadrupling) the time it takes to get from the northern suburbs to the centre of the city (Lindolfo 2014).

The UPP site claims the programme 'has as its objective the permanent retaking of the communities dominated by drug trafficking' (UPP RJ 2015). This claim is highly ambiguous because it leaves it unclear as to *whom* the communities are being 'retaken' for. A central goal is for UPPs to facilitate private sector 'entry' into the favelas, with Mesker, for example claiming that for UPPs to be truly successful they require the 'investment and the buy-in of the private sector' (2014: 152). Private companies heavily subsidized UPP projects and benefited from increased access to favela markets (Cano et al. 2014). A 2009 cable from the US Consulate in Rio released by Wikileaks read: 'There are... significant economic interests at stake, with some analysts estimating Rio de Janeiro's economy would grow by 38 billion Brazilian Reals (US$21 billion) should favelas be reincorporated into mainstream society and markets' (Halais 2013).

Most evidence suggests that this private sector investment in the favelas, together with gentrification, has been to the detriment of the economic, cultural, and social well-being of favela residents. An investigation by Rio on Watch showed that the switch from gang controlled to formal private sector controlled electricity has led to blackouts, electrical fires, poor or a total absence of service, and soaring prices compounded by serious (illegal) irregularities in billing techniques by the company Light Serviços de Eletricidade S.A. ('Light') (Parkin 2014). Freeman highlighted the case of a bricklayer living in the Santa Marta Favela who was sent a bill of R$575 (GBP144) for a single month of lighting just three lightbulbs (2012: 118). Globo reported that Light was set to increase profits from R$3.2 million a year to R$24 million as a result of these practices in Rocinha alone, while Thiago Firmino, an activist and film-maker from the Santa Marta Favela, asserts that such price rises are tantamount to '\' of residents (Leite 2011; Firmino 2013). On 25 June 2013, 2,000 protesters from the Rocinha and Vidigal favelas came to the South Zone in opposition both to the UPP and to the installation of the new privately managed cable car system, demanding instead basic sanitation, health, and education (Crumpler and Steiker-Ginzberg 2013).[7]

[7] Other neighbourhood days of protest included 2 July which saw 5,000 people demonstrating in Complexo do Alemao in response to the BOPE murders, protesting against the violence but also calling

Changes in Brazil's government since the impeachment of Dilma and the installation of Michel Temer have affected the extent to which communities benefit from the relationship between private sector and state, a further recent complication. The shift in government has led to a further withdrawal of state funding for social projects and a prioritization of corporate interests in economic policymaking (Sens 2017).

Freeman's concluding remarks on UPP are damning, and strongly recall POPCRU's statement for South Africa's prisons noted in the previous section. 'Instead of being a security strategy for the whole city, the UPP initiative is a security strategy dictated by the needs of the games, construction companies, real estate interests and those who see favelas as potential markets' (2012: 121).

A popular consensus is therefore that UPPs do not reduce—indeed in some cases they perpetuate—lethal violence, and that the benefits of 'pacification' are for an economic system that is not based on the interests of residents. Since the end of the Olympics, such opinions are gaining weight as UPP itself is facing funding cuts, with its planned expansion stalled (Barber 2016). Since 2016 there have been reports of an increase in armed conflict even in those favelas considered to be 'model' pacified communities (Barber 2016).

Throughout the history of UPPs, residents have mobilized in multiple ways to direct state policies and funding in a better direction, and to report and denounce police violence (Barber 2016). There is considerable evidence to suggest that these initiatives go much further than UPPs have managed in bringing communities together and breaking down cultures of impunity. For example, the founder of the blog, FavelaDaRocinha said that the unity between Rocinha and Vidigal shown in the 2013 protests against the UPP and the cable car was 'emotional . . . this hasn't happened in my lifetime or in my parents' life time', due to patterns of unequal investment and competing drug factions (Crumpler and Steiker-Ginzberg 2013). Other community initiatives include the app, Nós por Nós (Us for Us), used to report and investigate police violence created by the Rio de Janeiro Youth Forum (Mastrigt and Reist 2016). It is beyond the scope of this chapter to evaluate further these initiatives but it is worth noting that alternatives to the UPP abound in Rio, despite the ever more difficult economic and political context for community organizations (Sens 2017).

Sexual violence in India

The publicity given to the gang rape of Jyoti Singh in Delhi in 2012 brought international attention to both sexual violence and the feminist movement in India. This attention led Finance Minister Arun Jaitley to complain that 'One small incident of rape in Delhi —

for 'health and education' (Clarke 2013). Later in the month, residents from Horto, Vila Autodromo, and Santa Marta favelas demonstrated against evictions and violence, and actions included an occupation of the steps of the Finance Ministry (Pela Moradia 2013; Stacey 2013).

advertised world-over is enough to cost us billions of dollars in terms of lower tourism' (*The Times of India* 2014). In a reflection of the differential importance given to violence in different areas of Rio in the third section, this comment is enough to make clear how sexual violence is seen differently depending on its impact on a country's economy.

This section, as in the others, does not claim that sexual violence is particularly worse in India than in any other country; the unreliability of statistics on sexual violence make it almost impossible to make any kind of claims of that nature. Instead, it draws from the work of Indian feminists to outline three ways in which rape is made acceptable and even attractive in India's economic and political order. These ways are paralleled in most countries across the world; India is certainly no exceptional case.

The first is the way in which Indian economic policy has evolved; not only without regard for women's freedom and safety but with an active reliance on women's (and others') oppression. In her analysis of domestic violence in India, Armstrong cites the view of the All India Democratic Women's Association (AIDWA) that

> to see domestic violence only in terms of a man–woman relationship or non-relationship would be to miss out the essence of the problem, which is the institutionalized nature of female second class citizenship as . . . a part of the system as it exists in India today, but also . . . a necessity for (India's) further development. (Cited in Armstrong 2004: 49)

In 1991, the Indian government entered into a new agreement with the IMF, which imposed stringent conditions on its economic policy. These included cutting private and public spending and led to considerable casualization of the labour force and rural unemployment (Sarker 2014). As Bannerjea writes, 'Women are rigorously socialised to work uncomplainingly, under patriarchal control, at any allotted task however dull, laborious, physically harmful or badly paid it may be' (cited in Gupta 2005: 108). While the economic system became more and more dependent on passive and desperate women workers, the government made sweeping cuts to services that protected women from violent households and to campaigning groups (Gupta 2005).

Feminist commentators on the Delhi rape case in India emphasize the interconnectedness of sexual violence and India's economic reliance on women's subordination. Shiva argues that 'we are living in a very violent economic order to which war has become essential—war against the earth, war against women's bodies, war against local economies and war against democracy' (2013). She asks: 'could there be a connection between the growth of violent, undemocratically imposed, unfair economic policies and the intensification and brutality of crimes against women?' In her research for the National Commission of Women she found that changes to food, water, and agriculture were directly linked by women across the country to their increased experiences of sexual violence largely as a result of being made economic and ecological refugees. She also highlights the 'brutal' culture of the slums that the Delhi rapists came from into which refugees from the countryside are rapidly having to move and points to a 250 per cent rise in rapes since India's economy was made 'more open' (2013).

Another way in which the economic and political order affects sexual violence is through the funding and promotion of violence against women in cases where they are somehow identified as being 'outside' Indian citizenship. Roy (2012) highlights common practices of rape by agents of the state in positions of power, particularly by soldiers and police in Kashmir, Jharkhand, and Chattishgarh. On Jyoti's case she claims that 'We are having an unexceptional reaction to an event that isn't exceptional' and that 'we're not looking for laws. There *are* laws but when the police themselves go and burn down villages and gang rape women . . . ' She points to the case of Irom Sharmila who has been on hunger strike for fourteen years against the police raping of women and other violence committed as a result of the Special Powers Act in Manipur (Roy 2012). In another response to Jyoti's case, Shiva notes the extreme sexual torture experienced by Soni Soni when she was arbitrarily arrested for links to the Naxals. Soni Soni herself outlines the deep inequalities surrounding sexual violence perpetration: 'There are days when my children have nothing to eat. I don't have a job today while Ankit Garg, who has been accused of brutalizing me, has been awarded with the president's Police Medal of Gallantry' (cited in Sur 2014). In a similar argument, Gopal points to the election of Narendra Modi in Gujarat who was in control when religious violence saw the mass rape of Muslim women, and to the multiple sexual violence charges against other politicians in Gujarat as demonstrative of the elite acceptance of violence against (at least some) women (2012).

Kabeer connects this acceptance of police violence against women considered to be an 'enemy within' with a general acceptance of violence by men in higher castes or in higher positions of power against women from 'lower' castes or tribal groups (2014). In her thesis on women's movements in India, Maheshwari documents this widespread acceptance and outlines how the organization Mahila Mandal, among others, works towards making what is seen as 'routine' violence against Dalit women recognized as rape and as illegal. She also shows how this violence has only appeared to increase with the increasing inequality of the 1990s (2011).

The third way in which neoliberal economic policies are associated with rape is through the commodification of women's bodies in the economy and the endorsement of this by high-level politicians. Gupta questions what motivated Ram Singh and the other rapists in the case of Jyoti: 'Were Ram Singh and his cohort simply claiming a masculinity as promoted by their role models in politics, business and the media?' She points to the public use of pornography (in the Legislative Assembly) by Bharatiya Janta Party Members in Karnataka, while other members of the same party are filmed paying women to dance for them during functions, and to the report in former Prime Minister P.V. Narsimha Rao's biography that Congress leaders paid women for sex during working committee sessions (Gupta 2013). Desai argues that the normalization of rape as desirable is a trope used in the rapidly expanding pornography market in the country, and this has a dangerous impact on the ways in which sex work is approached by clients (2012). In a similar vein, Kabeer asserts that it is the interaction between the institutionalized economic and political inequality and 'the new global culture of consumerism and its relentless sexualisation of women's bodies' that produces rape culture (2014).

The case studies in this chapter have highlighted a number of different ways in which economic development, while potentially alleviating or improving lives is also complicit in violence. Some of the responses to the Delhi rape case in India are examples of resistance to violence that may be helpful in the determination of this agenda. The mass protests against sexual violence were notable for the participation of men, and particularly young men. Most protests were met with tear gas and police violence, and Shiva argues that this led to a widespread realization among men and women that 'the government, which should be protecting people, the state which should be protecting people, is afraid of people' (2013). She suggests that this realization broke down some of the social and gender divides between protesters and that Jyoti's case in many ways led 'each person to see their own story in her life and death', pointing to the commonly expressed sentiment among protesters that 'That girl could have been any one of us.' I suggest that Shiva's reflections point to an issue that is at the core of the challenge of combatting violence: how to create security policy that does not rely on an acceptance of some lives being more valuable than others; a security policy that does not depend on the sacrifice of those people least likely to complain, or—perhaps most commonly—those least important for economic growth.

Conclusion

In all of the cases outlined above, an economic policy that only survives through the perpetuation of inequality works through different specific ways in which nations divide people. In the case of China, factory labour conditions build on the glorification of dangerously hard work, competitive hierarchies, and the social isolation produced by migration. In Russia the notorious geographic economic inequality and 'strong state' militarism bolsters practices of imprisonment. In South Africa the state support of US multinational prison corporations benefits from a fear of crime that draws from the legacies of apartheid. In Brazil, the pressures from FIFA and the IOC to make a city around the needs of tourists and multinational investors combine with policing cultures sustained from the dictatorship. And in India the exclusion of people seen as 'less than' citizens, either for reasons of caste or (presumed) political affiliation make the reliance by neoliberal economic policy on the oppression of women much easier. These issues are not exclusive to BRICS—in fact, they form a crucial part of the global development story.

It is important to end this piece, however, by noting that for each of the above stories, there is another story of resistance to violence. Workers in Foxconn factories are constantly engaged in ways of resisting the extremities of management violence through collective resistance, including collective slowdowns, small-scale strikes, and sabotage, sometimes gaining small-scale managerial concessions (Ngai and Chan 2012: 398).

Indeed, Elfstrom and Kuruvilla report that Chinese workers are increasingly using the more assertive tactic of the strike to protest working conditions, with the support of the 2008 Labour Contract Law (2014: 461). Russia's prison system was brought to the world's notice by the linking of feminism and political freedom to prisoners' rights by Pussy Riot; but this built on a long tradition of human rights campaigning which is still growing today with bloggers linked to Zona Pravo and other organizations such as the For Human Rights Movement (see Agora n.d.; Gorst 2017). Protests against the authoritarianism of FIFA in both South Africa and Brazil provoked a massive public analysis of unequal government spending in each country (Freeman 2012; Sweet 2014). The anti-rape movement in India has brought unprecedented attention to the ways in which caste, economic vulnerability, and gender intersect not just in India but across the world (Bakshi 2017). These parallel stories articulate compelling, insistent, and credible alternatives for a post-2015 development agenda.

REFERENCES

Agora (n.d.). Agora International Human Rights Group. Available at http://en.agora.legal/, accessed 19 November 2018.

Allen, R. (2015). 'Global prison trends'. Penal Reform International. Available at www.penalreform.org/wp-content/uploads/2015/04/PRI-Prisons-global-trends-report-LR.pdf, accessed 19 November 2018.

Amnesty International (2015). 'Brazil: "Trigger happy" military police kill hundreds as Rio prepares for Olympic countdown'. Amnesty International. Available at www.amnesty.org/en/latest/news/2015/08/brazil-trigger-happy-military-police-kill-hundreds-as-rio-prepares-for-olympic-countdown/, accessed 19 November 2018.

Aranda-Comer, B. and Olivieri, F. (2015). 'Segregration [*sic.*], vigilantism & protest: Responses to Rio's beach robberies', *RioOnWatch*, 9 October. Available at www.rioonwatch.org/?p=24622, accessed 19 November 2018.

Armstrong, E. (2004). 'Globalization from below: AIDWA, foreign funding, and gendering anti-violence campaigns', *Journal of Developing Societies* 20/1–2: 39–55. Available at https://doi.org/10.1177/0169796X04048302, accessed 26 November 2018.

Ashcroft, P. (2014). 'History of Rio de Janeiro's military police Part 4: pacifying police units', *RioOnWatch*, 1 May. Available at www.rioonwatch.org/?p=14728, accessed 19 November 2018.

Azevedo, L. (2015). 'SMH 2016: Remoções no Rio de Janeiro Olímpico' [Shaking my head 2016: Evictions at the Rio de Janeiro Olympics] Mórula Editorial. Available at www.travessa.com.br/smh-2016-remocoes-no-rio-janeiro-olimpico/artigo/d5272a77-ac8f-4385-a6b1-0f8ea60d2053, accessed 19 November 2018.

Bakshi, G. (2017). 'The "Nirbhaya" movement: an Indian feminist revolution', *GnovisJournal*, 2 May. Available at www.gnovisjournal.org/2017/05/02/the-nirbhaya-movement-an-indian-feminist-revolution/, accessed 19 November 2018.

Barber, M. (2016). 'Funding shortage and increased violence amounts to UPP crisis', *RioOnWatch*, 28 April. Available at www.rioonwatch.org/?p=28108, accessed 28 November 2018.

Belser, P., de Cock, M., and Mehran, F. (2005). 'ILO minimum estimate of forced labour in the world'. International Labour Office, Geneva: International Labour Organization. Available at http://digitalcommons.ilr.cornell.edu/cgi/viewcontent.cgi?article=1006&context=nondiscrim, accessed 19 November 2018.

Cano, I., Borges, D., and Ribeiro, E. (2014). 'Os donos do morro: uma avaliação exploratória do impacto das Unidades de Polícia Pacificadora (UPPs) no Rio de Janeiro' [The owners of the hill: an exploratory assessment of the impact of the Pacifying Police Units (UPPs) in Rio de Janeiro]. Rio de Janeiro: Fundação Heinrich Böll, Laboratório de Análise da Violência—(LAV-UERJ), Fórum Brasileiro de Segurança Pública e Corporação Andina de Fomento (CAF). Available at https://br.boell.org/pt-br/2014/10/23/os-donos-do-morro-uma-avaliacao-exploratoria-do-impacto-das-unidades-de-policia, accessed 19 November 2018.

Catalytic Communities (2015a). 'Rio favela facts'. Available at http://catcomm.org/favela-facts/, accessed 19 November 2018.

Catalytic Communities (2015b). 'Why we should call them favelas'. Available at www.rioonwatch.org/?page_id=15162, accessed 19 November, 2018.

Chan, J. (2013). 'A suicide survivor: the life of a Chinese worker', *New Technology, Work and Employment* 28/2: 84–99. Available at https://doi.org/10.1111/ntwe.12007, accessed 19 November 2018.

Chang, H.-J. (2003). *Rethinking Development Economics*. London: Anthem Press.

Christie, N. (2004). *A Suitable Amount of Crime*. London: Psychology Press.

Clarke, F. (2013). 'Rocinha and Vidigal unite in protest', *RioOnWatch*, 29 June. Available at www.rioonwatch.org/?p=9924, accessed 19 November, 2018.

Clarke, F. (2014). 'UPP security crisis as World Cup approaches', *RioOnWatch*, 17 May. Available at www.rioonwatch.org/?p=15423, accessed 19 November 2018.

COSATU (2013). 'COSATU statement on the privatization of prisons'. Available at www.cosatu.org.za/docs/pr/2013/pr1007.html, accessed 19 November 2018.

Crumpler, C.A. and Steiker-Ginzberg, K. (2013, October 17). 'Favela residents join teachers day protest', *RioOnWatch*, 17 October. Available at www.rioonwatch.org/?p=11711, accessed 19 November 2018.

Culpan, T. and James, S. (2012). 'Apple supplier labor changes shifts focus to Microsoft, Samsung'. Available at www.globallabourrights.org/press/apple-supplier-labor-changes-shifts-focus-to-microsoft-samsung, accessesd 23 January 2019.

Danks, C. (2009). *Politics Russia*, 1st edn. Harlow and New York: Routledge.

Davis, A.Y. (2003). *Are Prisons Obsolete?* New York: Seven Stories Press.

Denney, L. (2013). 'Consulting the evidence: how conflict and violence can best be included in the post-2015 development agenda'. Overseas Development Institute (ODI). Available at www.odi.org/publications/7622-conflict-violence-post-2015, accessed 19 November 2018.

Desai, D. (2012). 'One-third of Gujarat MLAs face criminal cases, including rape', *The Hindu*, 25 December. Available at www.thehindu.com/news/national/other-states/onethird-of-gujarat-mlas-face-criminal-cases-including-rape/article4235994.ece, accessed 19 November 2018.

Eaton, N. (2010). 'Labor group: Chinese teens "like prisoners" in Microsoft tech factory – The Microsoft Blog', 13 April. Available at http://blog.seattlepi.com/microsoft/2010/04/13/labor-group-chinese-teens-like-prisoners-in-microsoft-tech-factory/, accessed 23 January 2019.

The Economist (2013). 'Slave labour and criminal cultures', 19 October. Available at www.economist.com/news/europe/21588130-russias-prison-colonies-resemble-old-soviet-camps-slave-labour-and-criminal-cultures, accessed 21 November 2018.

The Economist (2014). 'Back from the edge', 28 June. Available at www.economist.com/news/china/21605942-first-two-articles-chinas-suicide-rate-looks-effect-urbanisation-back, accessed 19 November 2018.

Elfstrom, M. and Kuruvilla, S. (2014). 'The changing nature of labor unrest in China'. *ILR Review* 67/2: 453–80. Available at https://doi.org/10.1177/001979391406700207, accessed 19 November 2018.

Ellsberg, M. and Heise, L. (2005). *Researching Violence against Women: A Practical Guide for Researchers and Activists*'. Washington, DC: World Health Organization, PATH.

Fenizola, L. (2017). 'Alemão residents show their strength during public meeting on police occupation', *RioOnWatch*, 2 May. Available at www.rioonwatch.org/?p=36228, accessed 19 November 2018.

Firmino, Thiago (2013). Histórias da Pacificação – Descaso da Light (2013). Available at www.youtube.com/watch?v=JuaXRHBMhqs&feature=youtube_gdata_player, accessed 19 November 2018.

Freeman, J. (2012). 'Neoliberal accumulation strategies and the visible hand of police pacification in Rio de Janeiro', *Revista de Estudos Universitários* 38/1: 95–126.

Galbraith, R. (2012). 'Private prisons – the best investment in America?', *RT*, 20 March. Available at http://rt.com/usa/private-america-cca-prison-050/, accessed 19 November 2018.

Ghosh, J. (2016). 'Indian capitalism in the global context', in N. Yokokawa, K. Yagi, H. Uemura, and R. Westra (eds) *The Rejuvenation of Political Economy*, 1st edn., 276–99. London and New York: Routledge.

Golubchikov, O. (2010). 'World-city-entrepreneurialism: globalist imaginaries, neoliberal geographies, and the production of new St Petersburg', *Environment and Planning A* 42/3: 626–43. Available at https://doi.org/10.1068/a39367, accessed 19 November 2018.

Gonzalez, E. (2014). 'Rio's human rights commission launches 2014 report', *RioOnWatch*, 16 December. Available at www.rioonwatch.org/?p=19591, accessed 19 November 2018.

Gopal, P. (2012). 'After the death of the Delhi rape victim, the fight for women's rights must go on', *The Guardian*, 31 December. Available at www.theguardian.com/commentisfree/2012/dec/31/delhi-rape-sexual-violence-india, accessed 19 November 2018.

Gordienko, I. and Fitzpatrick, C.A. (2013). 'Torture by filth: prison reforms which never took place', *The Interpreter*, 8 October. Available at www.interpretermag.com/torture-by-filth-prison-reforms-which-never-took-place/, accessed 19 November 2018.

Gordon, D.R. (2001). 'Side by side: neoliberalism and crime control in post-apartheid South Africa', *Social Justice* 28/3(85): 57–67.

Gorst, I. (2017). 'Russia's prisons under spotlight as activist goes missing in system', *The Irish Times*, 4 January. Available at www.irishtimes.com/news/world/europe/russia-s-prisons-under-spotlight-as-activist-goes-missing-in-system-1.2925443, accessed 19 November 2018.

Gupta, E.K.R. (2005). *Liberalisation and Globalisation of Indian Economy*. New Delhi: Atlantic.

Gupta, R. (2013). 'India: examining the motivation for rape', *Open Democracy*, 8 January. Available at www.opendemocracy.net/5050/ruchira-gupta/india-examining-motivation-for-rape, accessed 19 November 2018.

Halais, F. (2013). 'Pacifying Rio: what's behind Latin America's most talked about security operation', *Open Democracy*, 12 March. Available at www.opendemocracy.net/opensecurity/flavie-halais/pacifying-rio-whats-behind-latin-americas-most-talked-about-security-oper, accessed 19 November 2018.

Heffernan, M. (2013). 'What happened after the Foxconn suicides', *CBS News*, 7 August. Available at www.cbsnews.com/news/what-happened-after-the-foxconn-suicides/, accessed 19 November 2018.

Hilderbrand, R. (2014). 'UPP violence in Pavão-Pavãozinho/Cantagalo comes to a head following death of dancer DG', *RioOnWatch*, 26 April. Available at www.rioonwatch.org/?p=14686, accessed 19 November 2018.

Hopkins, R. (2013). 'G4S-run prison in South Africa investigated over abuse claims', *The Guardian*, 28 October. Available at www.theguardian.com/world/2013/oct/28/g4s-run-prison-south-africa-investigation, accessed 19 November 2018.

Hull, L. and Sorrell, L. (2010). 'The image Microsoft doesn't want you to see: too tired to stay awake, the Chinese workers earning just 34p an hour', *MailOnline*, 18 April. Available at www.dailymail.co.uk/news/article-1266643/Microsofts-Chinese-workforce-tired-stay-awake.html, accessed 19 November 2018.

IGLHR (Institute for Global Labour and Human Rights) (2011). '19-year-old jumps to her death at China cell-phone factory', *Global Labour Rights*. Available at www.globallabourrights.org/alerts/19-year-old-jumps-to-her-death-at-china-cell-phone-factory, accessed 23 January 2019.

IOC (International Olympic Committee) (2008). '2016 working group report'. Report by the IOC Candidature Acceptance Working Group, International Olympic Committee. Available at www.olympic.org/Documents/Reports/EN/en_report_1317.pdf, accessed 19 November 2018.

Johnson, J. (2011). '1 million workers. 90 million iPhones. 17 suicides. Who's to blame?', *Wired*, 28 February. Available at www.wired.com/2011/02/ff_joelinchina/all/, accessed 21 November 2018.

Kabeer, N. (2014). 'Grief and rage in India: making violence against women history?'. Available at www.opendemocracy.net/5050/naila-kabeer/grief-and-rage-in-india-making-violence-against-women-history, accessed 21 November 2018.

Kernaghan, C. (2014). 'Exhaustion has no limit at Apple supplier in China'. Available at www.globallabourrights.org/reports/document/1412-IGLHR-China-AppleZhenDingTech.pdf, accessed 23 Janury 2019.

Kiely, R. (2015). 'The rise of the South: rising BRICs, declining US?', in *The BRICs, US 'Decline' and Global Transformations*, 9–32. London: Palgrave Macmillan. Available at https://doi.org/10.1057/9781137499974_2, accessed 23 January 2019.

Klimova, M. (2014). '"Violence breeds violence": one woman's story of 16 years inside a Russian jail', *The Guardian*, 4 December. Available at www.theguardian.com/world/2014/dec/04/-sp-russia-prison-tatyana-gavrilova-pussy-riot, accessed 21 November 2018.

Larson, C. (2013). 'China's female factory workers face widespread sexual harassment', *Bloomberg Businessweek*, 10 December. Retrieved from www.christina-larson.com/chinas-female-factory-workers-face-widespread-sexual-harassment/, accessed 21 November 2018.

Leite, R. (2011). 'Rocinha descobre o preço da regularização' [Rocinha discovers the price of regularisation], *O Globo*, 26 November. Available at http://oglobo.globo.com/rio/rocinha-descobre-preco-da-regularizacao-3331304, accessed 21 November 2018.

Library of Congress (2010). 'The gulag'. Available at www.loc.gov/exhibits/archives/gula.html, accessed 21 November 2018.

Lindolfo, B. (2014). 'É devagar, devagarinho...' [It is slow, very slow], *Maré de Noticias*, May. Available at http://redesdamare.org.br/wp-content/uploads/2014/05/Ed-53-PARASITE1.pdf, accessed 21 November 2018.

Lizhi, X. and Nao. (2014). 'The poetry and brief life of a Foxconn worker: Xu Lizhi (1990–2014)', *libcom.org*, 29 October. Available at http://libcom.org/blog/xulizhi-foxconn-suicide-poetry, accessed 21 November 2018.

McMahon, L. (2017). '"Ungrievable labour" and "unruly" politics: NGOs, workers' rights, and the 2013–2014 protests in Brazil', in S. Lazar and A. Alexander (eds) *Where are the Unions? Workers and Social Movements in Latin America, the Middle East and Europe*. Zed Books, 167–86.

McNamara, B. (2017). 'War on who? Discussion of drug enforcement highlights key problems in current policies', *RioOnWatch*, 15 June. Available at www.rioonwatch.org/?p=36898, accessed 21 November 2018.

Maheshwari, N. (2011). *Politics of Funding, Philanthropy & Women's Rights Movements in India: An Ethnography*. New York: University at Buffalo.

Marques, G. (2011). 'Pão e Circo: Copa, Olimpíadas, movimentos sociais e cidade de exceção – Comitê popular da copa e das Olimpíadas do Rio de Janeiro' [Bread and Circus: The World Cup, the Olympics, Social movements and City of Exception – the Popular Committee of the World Cup and the Olympics in Rio de Janeiro]. Available at http://rio.portalpopulardacopa.org.br/?p=110, accessed 8 February 2019.

Mastrigt, J. van and Reist, S. (2016). 'Youth forum launches "Nós por Nós" application to denounce police violence', *RioOnWatch*, 24 March. Available at www.rioonwatch.org/?p=27670, accessed 21 November 2018.

Mesker, E. (2014). 'Community policing of Rio's Favelas: state-led development or market-oriented intervention?', in J.N. Pieterse and A. Cardoso *Brazil Emerging: Inequality and Emancipation*. London: Routledge, 138–53.

Moran, D., Pallot, J., and Piacentini, L. (2011). 'The geography of crime and punishment in the Russian Federation', *Eurasian Geography and Economics* 52/1: 79–104. Available at https://doi.org/10.2747/1539-7216.52.1.79, accessed 21 November 2018.

Muggah, R. (2012). 'Counterinsurgency in Rio de Janeiro'. Available at www.seguridadenbarrios.cl/delito_violencia_policias/rmuggah.pdf, accessed 5 August 2019.

Nathan, S. (2003). 'Prison privatisation: the international experience and recent developments in Africa'. Paper presented at the OSF-SA Seminar on Prison Privatisation, August, Cape Town. Available at http://posa.org.au/wp-content/uploads/2010/08/Prison_Privatisation_South-Africa.pdf, accessed 21 November 2018.

Ngai, P. and Chan, J. (2012). 'Global capital, the state, and Chinese workers', *Modern China* 38/4: 383–410. Available at https://doi.org/10.1177/0097700412447164, accessed 23 January 2019.

ONU Mulheres and CEPIA (2011). *O progresso das mulheres no Brazil 2003–2010*. Rio de Janeiro: ONU Mulheres and CEPIA. Available at http://onumulheres.org.br/wp-content/themes/vibecom_onu/pdfs/progresso.pdf, accessed 21 November 2018.

Ortiz, F. (2013). 'Rape in Brazil still an invisible crime', *Inter Press Service News Agency*, 24 June. Available at www.ipsnews.net/2013/06/rape-in-brazil-still-an-invisible-crime/, accessed 21 November 2018.

Pallot, J. (2007). '"Gde muzh, tarn zhena" [Where the husband is, so is the wife]: space and gender in post-soviet patterns of penalty', *Environment and Planning A* 39/3: 570–89. Available at https://doi.org/10.1068/a39138, accessed 21 November 2018.

Pallot, J. (2012). 'The gulag as the crucible of Russia's 21st-century system of punishment'. Paper presented at the conference Gulag Unbound: Remembering Soviet Forced Labour, June, University of Cambridge. Available at https://s3-eu-west-1.amazonaws.com/esrc-files/.../6OPjOZ6p60eorV-empCZwg.pdf, accessed 23 January 2019.

Pallot, J. (2015). 'The gulag as the crucible of Russia's 21st-century system of punishment', *Kritika* 16/3: 681.

Parkin, B. (2014). 'Light's abusive billing and questionable service in UPP favelas', *RioOnWatch*, 2 April. Available at www.rioonwatch.org/?p=14223, accessed 21 November 2018.

Paz, V. and Livingstone, C. (2014). 'The favela where I live is bleeding', *RioOnWatch*, 27 October. Available at www.rioonwatch.org/?p=18578, accessed 21 November 2018.

Pela Moradia (2013). 'Moradores das comunidades do Horto, Vila Autódromo e do Movimento Nacional de Luta pela Moradia fazem vigília contra às remoções' [Residents of the communities of Horto, Vila Autódromo and the National Movement for Struggle for Housing watch over evictions]. Available at. https://pelamoradia.wordpress.com/2013/07/17/moradores-das-comunidades-do-horto-vila-autodromo-e-do-movimento-nacional-de-luta-pela-moradia-fazem-vigila-contra-as-remocoes-rj/, accessed 22 July 2019.

Phillips, M.R., Li, X., and Zhang, Y. (2002). 'Suicide rates in China, 1995–99', *The Lancet* 359/9309: 835–40. Available at https://doi.org/10.1016/S0140-6736(02)07954-0, accessed 21 November 2018.

Piacentini, L. (2012). *Surviving Russian Prisons*. London: Routledge.

Pitanguy, J. (2014). 'Uma violência invisível. Entrevista especial com Jacqueline Pitanguy', *Instituto Humanitas Unisinos*, 19 August. Available at www.ihu.unisinos.br/entrevistas/534396-uma-violencia-invisivel-entrevista-especial-com-jacqueline-pitanguy, accessed 21 November 2018.

Ponomarev, L. (2007). 'Revival of the GULAG? Putin's penitentiary system'. Available at https://open.bu.edu/handle/2144/3648, accessed 21 November 2018.

Private Corrections Working Group (2017). 'Group 4 rap sheet'. Available at www.privateci.org/rap_group4.html, accessed 21 November 2018.

RAPSI (Russian Legal Information Agency) (2013). 'Russia does not consider option of private prisons – official', *RAPSI*, 13 March. Available at http://rapsinews.com/news/20130313/266700552.html, accessed 21 November 2018.

Rio on Watch (2018). "Timeline: Vila Autodromo, Story of Resistance" Available at: www.rioonwatch.org/?page_id=28610;

Robertson, C. (2015). 'Popular committee launches final human rights violations dossier ahead of Rio 2016 "Exclusion Games"', *RioOnWatch*, 10 December. Available at www.rioonwatch.org/?p=25747, accessed 21 November 2018.

Rocha, I. and Cardoso, N. (2014). 'Brazil has half a million rapes per year – one per minute. And only 10 are reported', *Compromiso Atitude* 06/06/2014. Available at www.compromissoeatitude.org.br/brasil-tem-meio-milhao-de-estupros-por-ano-um-por-minuto-e-apenas-10-sao-denunciados-puc-rio-06062014/, accessed 3 May 2019.

Roy, A. (2012). 'Arundhati Roy speaks about the rape culture in India', 22 December. Available at www.youtube.com/watch?v=4uQobrC002M, accessed 21 November 2018.

Rutland, Peter (2008). 'Putin's economic record: is the oil boom sustainable?'. Europe Asia Studies, 60/6: 1057–78. doi:10.1080/09668130802180975.

Rutland, P. (2013). 'Neoliberalism and the Russian transition', *Review of International Political Economy* 20/2: 332–62. Available at https://doi.org/10.1080/09692290.2012.727844, accessed 21 November 2018.

Samara, T.R. (2003). 'State security in transition: the war on crime in post apartheid South Africa', *Social Identities* 9/2: 277–312. Available at https://doi.org/10.1080/1350463032000101605, accessed 21 November 2018.

Sambrook, C. (2013). 'G4S: A tale of two troubled prisons', *OpenDemocracy*, 7 October. Available at www.opendemocracy.net/shinealight/clare-sambrook/g4s-tale-of-two-troubled-prisons, accessed 21 November 2018.

Sarker, K. (2014). 'Neoliberal state, austerity, and workers' resistance in India', *Interface: A Journal on Social Movements* 6/1: 416–40.

Schröder, H.-H. (2008). 'What kind of political regime does Russia have?', in S. White (ed.) *Politics and the Ruling Group in Putin's Russia*. Springer, 1–26.

Sens, E. (2017). 'After passing austerity amendment, what's next for public education in Rio de Janeiro?', *RioOnWatch*, 13 February. Available at www.rioonwatch.org/?p=34903, accessed 21 November 2018.

Shiva, V. (2013). 'Vandana Shiva on Int'l Women's Day: "Capitalist patriarchy has aggravated violence against women"', *Democracy Now*, 8 March. Available at www.democracynow.org/2013/3/8/vandana_shiva_on_intl_womens_day, accessed 21 November 2018.

Soares, F. and Livingstone, C. (2013). 'Protest in Manguinhos denounces serious violations on International Human Rights Day', *RioOnWatch*, 14 December. Available at www.rioonwatch.org/?p=12947, 21 November 2018.

Stacey, Laura (2013). 'Santa Marta Protests: real Estate and Commodity Prices, Evictions and Jeep Tours'. Available at www.rioonwatch.org/?p=10367, accessed 21 July 2019.

Steinbrink, M. (2014). 'Festifavelisation: mega-events, slums and strategic city-staging – the example of Rio de Janeiro', *Die Erde—Journal of the Geographical Society of Berlin* 144/2: 129–45.

Stuckler, D. and Basu, S. (2013). *The Body Economic: Why Austerity Kills*. New York: Basic Books.

Sudbury, J. (2005). *Global Lockdown: Race, Gender, and the Prison-industrial Complex*. London: Psychology Press.

Sur, Priyali (2014). 'The long and lonely fight: Q&A with Indian tribal rights activist Soni Sori', Women's Media Centre July 29 2014. Available at www.womensmediacenter.com/women-under-siege/the-long-and-lonely-fight-qa-with-indian-tribal-rights-activist-soni-sori, accessed 8 July 2019.

Sweet, C. (2014). 'Brasil despertó más fuerte? Poder, protesta y política en 2013' [Did Brazil wake up stronger? Power, protest and politics in 2013], *Revista de Ciencia Política (Santiago)* 34/1: 59–78. Available at https://doi.org/10.4067/S0718-090X2014000100003, accessed 21 November 2018.

The Times of India (2014). '"Small incident of rape": Finance minister Arun Jaitley clarifies after uproar over remark', 22 August. Available at http://timesofindia.indiatimes.com/india/Small-incident-of-rape-Finance-minister-Arun-Jaitley-clarifies-after-uproar-over-remark/articleshow/40668391.cms, accessed 21 November 2018.

UPP RJ (Police Pacification Units, Rio de Janeiro) (2013). 'Dilma visita Rocinha e anuncia investimento de 2,6 bilhões' [Dilma visits Rocinha and announces 2.6 billion investment], 14 June. Available at www.upprj.com/index.php/acontece/acontece-selecionado/dilma-visita-rocinha-e-anuncia-investimento-de-26-bilhoes-para-obras/Rocinha, accessed 26 November 2018.

UPP RJ (Police Pacification Units, Rio de Janeiro) (2015). 'O que é?' [What is it?], 9 December. Available at www.upprj.com/index.php/o_que_e_upp, accessed 26 November 2018.

Viva Favela (2015). '"Quero que isso acabe", diz mulher estuprada na Rocinha' ['I want this to stop', said woman who was raped in Rocinha. Available at www.youtube.com/results?search_type=search_videos&search_query=Viva+Favela+%282015%29.+%E2%80%98%E2%80%9CQuero+que+isso+acabe%E2%80%9D%2C+diz+mulher+estuprada+na+Rocinha%E2%80%99+%5B%E2%80%98I+want+this+to+stop%E2%80%99%2C+said+woman+who+was+raped+in+Rocinha.+&search_sort=relevance&search_category=0&page=, accessed 8 July 2019.

Wacquant, L. (2010). 'Crafting the neoliberal state: workfare, prisonfare, and social insecurity', *Sociological Forum* 25/2: 197–220. Available at https://onlinelibrary.wiley.com/doi/abs/10.1111/j.1573-7861.2010.01173.x, accessed 8 February 2019.

Waldron, I. (2014). 'Debate reflects on Rio's pacifying police units', *RioOnWatch*, 22 November. Available at www.rioonwatch.org/?p=19287, accessed 26 November 2018.

Walker, A.N.S. (2013, December 23). 'Freed Pussy Riot members say prison was time of "endless humiliations"', *The Guardian*, 23 December. Available at www.theguardian.com/world/2013/dec/23/freed-pussy-riot-amnesty-prison-putin-humiliation, accessed 26 November 2018.

Walmsley, R. (2013). *World Prison Population List*, 10th edn. International Centre for Prison Studies. London: Birkbeck University. Available at www.aidsdatahub.org/sites/default/files/publication/World_prison_population_list_10th_edition_2013.pdf, accessed 26 November 2018.

Werling, E. (2014). 'Rio's pacification: paradigm shift or paradigm maintenance? Discussion Paper No. 11, Ottawa, IL: Humanitarian Action in Situations other than War. Available at www.hasow.org/uploads/trabalhos/131/doc/331172740.pdf, accessed 23 Janury 2019.

White, S. (2008). *Politics and the Ruling Group in Putin's Russia*. New York: Springer.

WHO (World Health Organization) (2019). *Definition and Typology of Violence*. Geneva: WHO.

Zdun, S. (2011). 'Difficulties measuring and controlling homicide in Rio de Janeiro', *International Journal of Conflict and Violence* 5/1: 198–9.

Zhang, J., Sun, L., Liu, Y., and Zhang, J. (2014). 'The change in suicide rates between 2002 and 2011 in China', *Suicide and Life-Threatening Behavior* 44/5: 560–8. Available at https://doi.org/10.1111/sltb.12090, accessed 26 November 2018.

Zibechi, R. (2013). 'Autonomy in Brazil: Below and behind the June uprising', *Occupy Wall Street*. Available at http://occupywallstreet.net/story/autonomy-brazil-below-and-behind-june-uprising, accessed 26 November 2018.

27 Inequality and crime in Latin America

Catalina Droppelmann Roepke and Nicolás Trajtenberg

Introduction

In the field of criminology 'social inequality has long been theorized to be associated with crime' (Matsueda and Grigoryeva 2014: 2). This issue has been extensively studied and empirical research has shown that income inequality and low socio-economic status are positively associated with crime perpetration and victimization (Fajnzylber et al. 1998; van Wilsem 2004; Soares and Naritomi 2010), and even with bullying (Elgar et al. 2009; Elgar et al. 2013), and with child and adolescent antisocial behaviour (Piotrowska et al. 2015). However, some scholars have been more cautious regarding this association, arguing that inequality is neither a necessary nor a sufficient causal condition for the occurrence of crime. For example Felson (1994) has argued that this association exemplifies the 'pestilence fallacy' under which criminologists tend to assume that a social evil such as crime must be caused by other social evils such as inequality. Other scholars remind us of the two-way causal relationship between both phenomena. While it cannot be rejected that some individuals will react with crime and violence to social exclusion from goods and opportunities, violence has also a negative causal impact on economic and human development, poverty, and inequality (Rubio 1997; Blackwell and Duarte 2011; Enamorado et al. 2014; Jaitman 2016).

Latin America constitutes a particularly interesting case study in which to analyse the association between crime and inequality. Simultaneously, it is considered to be one of the most unequal and violent regions on the planet. Therefore, it might be tempting to conclude that inequality must play a major role in the explanation of this region's high levels of crime and violence. While this possibility cannot be rejected, the overall goal of this chapter is to analyse and discuss this complex relationship focusing not only on (i) how inequality might explain crime and violence, but also on (ii) how criminal justice institutions stigmatize, label, and reproduce social inequalities and social exclusion.

The chapter is organized into two sections. In the first section we describe inequality and crime in Latin America, we briefly present the main theoretical arguments that make sense of this association and we review the empirical evidence in the region and its main

Catalina Droppelmann Roepke and Nicolás Trajtenberg, *Inequality and crime in Latin America* In: *Handbook of BRICS and Emerging Economies.* Edited by: P.B. Anand, Shailaja Fennell, and Flavio Comim, Oxford University Press (2021).
DOI: 10.1093/oso/9780198827535.003.0027

weaknesses. The second section discusses the consequences of crime policies on inequality and social exclusion. It starts by describing the factors that have been involved in the ways in which crime has been managed in Latin America. Then we discuss how prisons in the region not only segregate the most vulnerable individuals from society, but also how social exclusion is reproduced through their degrading conditions and practices. Finally, we make some concluding remarks and discuss possibilities for future research.

The role of inequality in the explanation of crime

LATIN AMERICA: AN UNEQUAL AND VIOLENT REGION

Despite Latin America's economic boom in the past decade with robust levels of GDP growth over 5 per cent—particularly in the period between 2003 and 2012 (Moreno-Brid and Garry 2016)—and considerable improvements in health, employment, education, poverty, and inequality reduction (Lustig et al. 2011; CEPAL 2014; UNDP 2014), it still remains one of the most unequal regions on the planet. Inequality in Latin America is even worse than in sub-Saharan Africa, revealing a persistent pattern with the highest appropriation of income from the top decile in relation to the lowest decile (Boyer 2016).

While property and violent crime are diminishing in the whole world including both high- and low-income countries (Pinker 2011; Eisner 2014; Farrell et al. 2014; Tonry 2014), one of the few regions where this trend is not taking place is in Latin America (Malby 2010; Eisner 2014; Vilalta, 2015).[1] At present, Latin America is considered one of the most violent regions in the world in terms of the high incidence of crime, the variety of forms of violence, and its persistence (Imbusch et al. 2011; UNODC 2014). Robberies have tripled in the last three decades, and more than half of the countries of the region have epidemic levels of violence (homicide rates higher than 10 per one hundred thousand inhabitants) according to World Health Organization (WHO) standards (UNDP 2014). According to the Homicide Monitor of the Igarapé Institute (2015) 'fourteen of the twenty most murderous countries in the planet are in Latin America and the Caribbean, and one third of the world homicides take place in Latin America and the Caribbean home to just 8% of global population'. However, violence is not homogenously distributed in the region: homicides are more prominent in Central American and Caribbean countries, together with Mexico, Venezuela, and Colombia where drug and gun trafficking routes are more relevant (Solis and Torre 2016). Ironically, most of the scientific research on crime and violence and prevention of violence has been carried out in the developed nations and only 10 per cent is located in low- and middle-income societies, despite the fact that they concentrate on more than four-fifths of violent deaths, as is shown in Figure 27.1 (Krisch et al. 2015).

[1] However, in recent years some countries in the region such as Colombia, Guatemala, El Salvador, and Costa Rica have experienced stabilization and even some decrease (UNDP 2014).

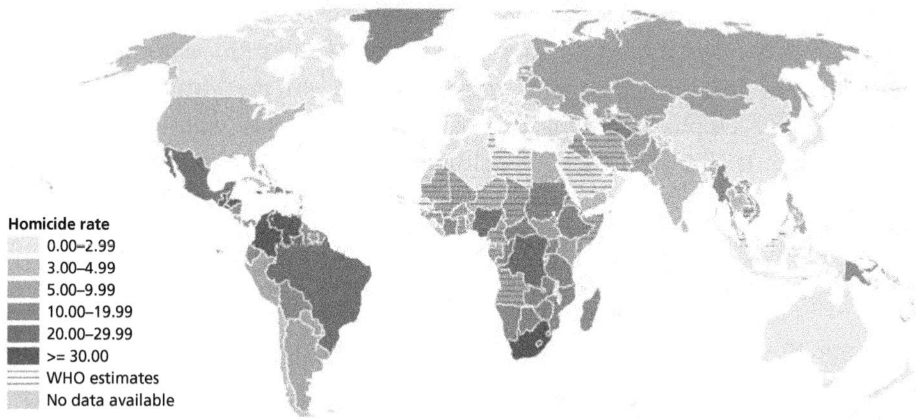

Figure 27.1 Homicide rates, by country or territory (2012 or latest year)
Source: UNODC (2011).

MAIN THEORETICAL APPROACHES ON INEQUALITY AND CRIME

Economic theory suggests that offenders compare the expected economic returns of crime with the certainty and severity of penal punishment and the opportunity costs of crime in relation to legitimate employment (Becker 1968; Mocan et al. 2005). Higher levels of inequality between the rich and poor affect the poor's net gains and thus encourage their involvement in criminal activities. The higher is inequality the greater the chances are for individuals at the bottom of the society to obtain additional returns through crimes, particularly through victimization of wealthy individuals (Kang 2016). Yet income inequality might involve an improvement in measures and technologies of self-protection (CCTV, private security, etc.) implemented by the wealthiest citizens and potential victims, increasing the likelihood of arrest and punishment, and thus favouring the victimization of the poorest citizens (Demombynes and Ozler 2005; Kang 2016). According to Whitworth (2013), the association between inequality and crime at the local or neighbourhood level provides a link between economic theory, routine activities theory, and rational choice theory. In areas characterized by high inequality, the proximity between poor and rich encourages crime through the convergence of motivated offenders, suitable targets, and lack of effective guardians as predicted by routine activities theory (Cohen and Felson 1979; Felson and Boba 2010). Likewise, rational choice theory shows that offending is characterized by a more bounded rationality limited by habitual non-criminal activities, local knowledge, and the opportunities available in environments characterized by social exclusion and lack of legitimate opportunities (Clarke and Cornish 1986).

From a sociological perspective, Merton's (1938) *Strain Theory* argues that the main cause of crime is the structural divergence between society's valued cultural goals (e.g. wealth, prestige, etc.) and the scarce legitimate social means to achieve them. Offenders are individuals that belong to lower socio-economic strata and while they learn these cultural goals, they reject the legitimate means as unrealistic and use criminal means to obtain them. *The institutional anomie theory* focuses on the structural/macro-level making a stronger emphasis on the criminogenic role of the cultural sphere of the American dream. It is argued that the cultural shared aspirations of material success have a pervasive effect on criminality, promoting the predominance of the economic sphere over other social institutions such as the family, the political system, the education system, and religion. As a result of this economic colonization, social institutions' capacity to limit and control criminal and deviant behaviours is severely weakened (Messner and Rosenfeld 2006). At a more micro-level, Agnew (2001) extended the strain model and suggested that apart from the above mentioned failure to obtain economic goals, there are two additional strains that can lead young people to crime such as the loss of valued stimuli (e.g. sickness, death of relatives) and the presence of negative valued stimuli (e.g. physical abuse). These three types of strain can frequently be experienced in disadvantaged areas, and are more likely to lead to crime when they have higher magnitude, are evaluated as unfair, and are associated with negative emotions of anger and frustration.

In recent years, criminologists have focused attention on the role of the *legitimacy* of societies in citizens' rule compliance and involvement in crime (Tankebe and Liebling 2013). Lack of legitimacy of the state is one of the main causal mechanisms that connects inequality and crime. Crime and violence has risen in societies where inequality is coupled with the perception that there is no rule of law, public institutions are unfair and biased, and where economic success is unrelated to hard effort and merit (Chamlin and Cochran 2006; Nivette and Eisner 2012). According to Arsenio and Gold (2006), where children suffer toxic experiences which include being raised in unequal, unfair, and hostile environments, such experiences can have undermined their moral development, their capacity for emotional reciprocity, and concern for others, promoting a cynical view of society where violence is viewed as a more efficient means of achieving goals.

EMPIRICAL EVIDENCE IN LATIN AMERICA

Most of the empirical research of the causal mechanisms of the aforementioned criminological theories has been conducted in the United States and some countries in Western Europe. Despite Latin America's high levels of crime and violence, there is little research of these causal links between inequality and crime. Evidence regarding the relationship between inequality (routinely using the Gini index as proxy)[2] and crime in

[2] Whenever this is not the case we will specify the measure used.

Latin America has come mostly from three types of macro-level studies:[3] a first group of five comparative studies involving different Latin American countries; a second group of nineteen national case studies; and finally, a small group of studies that evaluated the impact of conditional cash transfer (CCT) programmes.

Regarding *comparative studies*, Londoño and Guerrero (1998) used fixed effect regressions on homicides with seventeen Latin American countries between 1970 and 1995 and showed that inequality was a significant predictor of the increase in levels of violence and lethal violence, controlling by other risk factors such as education, economic development, and poverty. Another study from the World Bank (Fajnzylber et al. 1998) uses the United Nations World Crime Survey data set for a similar period (1970–94) to explain the national homicide and robbery rates. Cross-sectional and fixed effects analysis showed that inequality (measured as Gini index and as the percentage of the national income received by the lowest quintile of a country's income) was significantly associated with property crime but not with violent crimes, controlling by urbanization, education, GNP per capita, police levels, and conviction rates. In one of the few cases where victimization data were used in a comparative study (the 'Latinobarometer', a public opinion survey covering seventeen Latin American countries, for the period 1996–98)[4] a positive association was found between victimization rates and inequality (together with size of cities and high population growth). Results of regression models with country and year fixed effects showed that individuals from middle-class and rich households were more likely to suffer property crime victimization. However, additional analysis showed that in the more unequal societies the burden of crime suffered by the wealthiest citizens decreased (Gaviria and Pagés 2002).

Camara and Salama (2004) estimated a regression of homicide rates using panel data from ten Latin American countries for a more recent period of time between 1995 and 2000. They combined data sets from the United Nations, WHO, the Economic Commission for Latin America, the World Bank, and the Brazilian Center of Crime Juncture. Inequality (measured as the level of participation of the 10 per cent richest sector of the society in the national income) was also found to be significantly associated with homicides, controlling for urbanization rates, efficacy of the repressive system, economic development, and education. Soares and Naritomi (2010) compared Argentina, Brazil, Chile, Colombia, Costa Rica, Mexico, and Venezuela with two of the most developed countries in the world: one with low crime rates (Japan) and the other with high crime rates (US); an Eastern country with levels of development akin to Latin America societies (South Korea); a European country with common Latin cultural roots (Spain); and two countries with different cultural roots, one with low crime rates (Sweden) and one with high crime rates (Russia). The analysis showed that one of the main differences between

[3] Some have argued that the effect of inequality on crime is spurious, and ceases to be statistically significant once proxies of poverty are included (Pare and Felson, 2014). However, this was not the case and most of the studies in Latin America included poverty as a covariate of the econometric models.

[4] This study added data from national victimization surveys from Colombia, El Salvador, and Peru.

Latin American countries and the comparison countries to explain their higher levels of crime and violence was their high levels of inequality, which provide incentives for people to engage in criminal activities.[5] However, in the most recent comparative study inequality turned out to have no explanatory role. Rivera (2016) estimated time series cross-sectional models of homicide rates using panel data from nineteen Latin American countries for the period between 1980 and 2010 using data sets from the United Nations Crime Trend Surveys, the World Bank, and the Standardized World Income Inequality Database. Unexpectedly, there was no support for a positive association between inequality and homicides, controlling for growth, unemployment, use of repression by police, judicial system capacity, education attainment, level of urbanization, and the proportion of youth population.

In the last two decades there have been a great number of Latin American studies focused on the *national level*. Most of these studies are based on panel data with some level of aggregation (usually state or municipality level), using time series and regression models, and mainly conducted in Brazil, Uruguay, Argentina, Chile, Peru, Colombia, and Mexico.

Almost all of the twenty reviewed studies show that inequality is among the relevant explanatory predictors of crime. Only four studies from Brazil (dos Santos 2009), Chile (Núñez et al. 2003),[6] Uruguay (Borraz and Gonzalez 2010), and Peru (Obando and Ruiz 2007) reveal that inequality was not significantly associated with different measures of crime that included property crimes, crime against persons, and general indices of crime.

Seven studies mostly from Brazil (Fajnzylber and de Araujo Jr 2001; Mendonça 2002; Cerqueira and Lobão 2004; Oliveira 2005; Cerqueira 2014), but also from Argentina (Spinelli et al. 2008) and Mexico (Ramírez 2014) provide evidence that inequality is a significant predictor of homicides, controlling for other socio-economic, demographic, and deterrence variables. Particularly interesting is Cano and Santos's (2001) study in Brazil that shows that the relationship between inequality and homicides is ambiguous and highly dependent on the level of aggregation of the unit analysis. There was additional evidence for the role of inequality as a predictor of non-lethal violent crimes such as burglaries in Uruguay (Campanella 2008),[7] property crimes in Chile (Garcia 1995) and Argentina (Chambouleyron and Willington 1998),[8] and thefts in Peru (Mendoza 2015). A study conducted in Uruguay found that inequality was a significant predictor of property crimes such as thefts, burglary, and damage, but also found that the

[5] Other relevant factors found by Soares and Naritomi are: poor economic performance; a large proportion of youth population, particularly belonging to unstructured families from low socio-economic strata; and less efficient criminal justice institutions.

[6] Núñez et al. (2003) used as inequality measures both the Gini index and the ratio of income of the highest to lowest quintile.

[7] Campanella (2008) also operationalized inequality as the ratio of income of the highest to lowest quintile.

[8] In this study inequality was measured using the ratio between the number of illiterates and the number of persons that completed the third level of education.

econometric models poorly fitted the data when crime against persons such as homicides, injuries, or sexual crimes were included (Aboal et al. 2007). However, in Argentina Cerro and Rodriguez (2016) found that although inequality was a significant predictor of crime against persons, it was not the case with property crimes. Finally, only three studies from Argentina (Cerro and Rodriguez 2016), Uruguay (Aboal et al. 2007), and Colombia (Bourguignon et al. 2003a) found that inequality was a significant predictor of global indices of crime.

There is some research focused on evaluating the impact of CCT programmes in Latin America that provides indirect additional support for the association between crime and social exclusion or low socio-economic status. Some studies have shown these types of programmes have interesting income effects[9] thus reducing crime. For example, the *Familias en Accion* programme from Bogota had significant effect on property crimes, but not on homicides (Camacho and Mejía 2013); the *Bolsa Família* from Sao Paulo also showed robust and significant effect on crimes, mainly associated with property crimes; but there was also some effect on violent crimes and drug-related crimes (Chioda et al. 2015); in Argentina, two CCT programmes, *Social Help* and *Unemployed Heads of Household Program*, also showed significant effects particularly diminishing property crimes; but while the first was not effective in reducing property crimes that involved violence, the second showed significant effects also on robberies, aggravated assaults, and larceny, but not on murders (Freira 2014; Meloni 2014). One exception is the programme *Ingreso Ciudadano* from Uruguay, which not only lacked any positive outcome, but in fact showed a perverse effect: an increase in property crime (Borraz and Munyo 2014).[10]

PROBLEMS WITH LATIN AMERICAN STUDIES

Overall, studies show there is a link between inequality and crime in Latin America. However, there is a series of problems that weakens the empirical evidence for the inequality-crime hypothesis.

The first problem is the lack of consistency in the relationship of inequality–crime across studies. As mentioned, some studies show that inequality plays no role in the explanation of crime, and in particular inequality seems to be a less robust predictor for those studies that are used as a dependent variable of property crime or global indices of crime. Some of these inconsistencies might be due to differences in crime reporting and recording across Latin American nations (Soares 2004). Inconsistencies are also

[9] The impact on crime and violence of these programmes sometimes involves mechanisms that are less directly associated with the economic condition of families such as *incapacitation effects* associated with an inability to commit illegal activities due to being in educative centres, or *interaction effects* where absence of crime is associated with change of peer groups and family routines.

[10] According to the authors, when welfare transferences are not delivered through debit cards, there is an increase in the amount of money available on the streets, and thus, the opportunity for illegal and criminal activities which can outperform the expected *income effect* of CCT programmes (Wright et al. 2017).

associated with the type of independent variable used. Bourguignon and colleagues' (2003a) study provides an illustrative example that shows how inequality's effects on crime strongly depended on the type of measure used:[11] while it was significant when using Gini coefficients, it had almost no significant effect when using the Atkinson index.

A second issue is the problematic validity and reliability of official crime data sets used by these studies. There is an important problem of measurement error and underestimation of crime which is due to: the type of crime and victims' differential willingness to report; criminal justice and health agencies' institutional reporting practices; and the multiple heterogeneity of these practices between agencies (Thornberry and Krohn, 2000; Goudriaan et al. 2004; Young, 2004; Maguire 2008). This problem is even more serious in Latin America given the limitations, lack of resources, poor functioning and management of information, weak transparency, and lack of legitimacy of criminal justice institutions (Dammert et al. 2010; Guerrero et al. 2012; Corbacho et al. 2014). Most of the studies use intentional homicide rates as dependent variables since they are one of the most available and effectively recorded crimes (Malby 2010). Not only is this methodological decision problematic since many of the criminological theories and hypothesis were originally devised for property crime and general deviance, rather than for lethal violence, but also homicide rates are not short of problems and particularly in Latin America where data sets can exclude or include lethal violent events depending on the legal framework; information systems use different counting rules for the aggregation of homicides; and many criminal justice agencies lack the organization and resources to have adequate management of the coding of criminal records and fail to update many deaths (Ribeiro et al. 2015; see also Cano 2000; dos Santos and Kassouf 2008). One way of avoiding some of these problems is to combine criminal justice and public health sources (Malby 2010). However, while comparative studies and some national studies from Brazil (e.g. Mendonça 2002; dos Santos 2009; Cerqueira 2014) include health statistics, most of the research in crime in Latina America is based on law-enforcement data. Yet even health sources are not without problems, and particularly in areas where violence is epidemic and health services lack resources and are overwhelmed and unable to produce quality information, excluding lethal violence events in health statistics, such as civilians' deaths in confrontations with the police (Ribeiro et al. 2015; see also Borges et al. 2013).

A third problem of this body of research mainly based on macro-level data is that it provides weak or incomplete empirical tests of what are the underlying causal mechanisms behind the association between inequality and crime. Most of these studies are conducted under the economic approach and yet it is impossible to determine which is the predominant mechanism: a rational one associated with the disutility related to the relative deprivation suffered; or an irrational one associated with social capital and

[11] More generally, some authors have called into question the explanatory role of inequality by showing the relevance of the type of methodological design: while the inequality–crime association is usually supported by cross-sectional data sets, this is not the case in longitudinal data sets (Brush 2007; Eisner 2015).

community characteristics, or cultural subcultures/street codes. There is a need to develop more micro-level studies based on alternative sources of data such as victimization or self-report surveys that allow one to evaluate more of the different causal mechanisms involved in the association between inequality and crime.[12] Some recent micro-level research in Latin America includes empirical evidence of the criminogenic role of strains (Vera et al, 2012; Chouhy et al. 2014), criminal peers and social learning processes (Olate et al. 2012; Chouhy et al. 2014), social bonds with parents and family structure (Curto et al. 2011; Moral de la Rubia and Ortiz Morales 2011), and processes of school exclusion (Olate et al. 2012). However, none of these studies empirically addresses the association of these mechanisms with inequality and social exclusion.

The consequences of crime policies on inequalities and social exclusion

In the previous section we discussed how Latin American inequalities might be involved in the rise of crime. In this section, we analyse the way in which crime has been managed through punitive policing and penal practices, and its role in the reproduction and exacerbation of the existing levels of inequalities and social exclusion in Latin America. Although several factors have been involved in the ways in which it has been tried to manage crime, two main issues dominate the scholarly discussion: the politicization of crime management (Pratt 2007; Müller 2012) and the neoliberal governance of marginality (Garland 1985, 2001; Beckett and Western 2001; Reiner 2007; Wacquant 2010).

PENAL AND WELFARE REGIMES IN LATIN AMERICA

Latin America is the region of the world where people feel less safe (GALLUP 2016). In thirteen out of eighteen countries, crime is the major public concern (Latinobarómetro 2015) and people feel extremely vulnerable because of the lack of trust in the police, in the judiciary, and the excessive levels of impunity. More than 47 per cent believe that the police are corrupt and more than 39 per cent do not trust the judiciary (Transparency International 2015). While in Organisation for Economic Co-operation and Development (OECD) countries the impunity rate for homicides is 35 per cent, in countries such as Mexico it reaches 76 per cent (Zepeda and Jimenez 2016), and in Brazil 75 per cent (Beato 2012). These issues have strongly influenced public opinion demands for punitive

[12] Apart from the causal mechanisms mentioned in the theoretical section, an illustrative example is drug trafficking networks, although they have a key role in the explanation of the increase in violence and crime in Latin America (e.g. Gaviria 2000; Solis and Torre 2016) and they are associated with processes of social exclusion and inequality, they are visibly absent in most of the aforementioned quantitative studies of Latin America (but see Camara and Salama 2004; Cerqueira 2014).

intervention: more than half of citizens think that the best solutions to decrease crime are increasing the presence of police forces on the streets and implementing harsher penalties (Latinobarómetro 2015). Politicians have latched onto *tough-on-crime* policies, because they are straightforward, visible, and popular (Swanson 2013), shifting their responsibility from providing social welfare towards the provision of protection against crime (Beckett and Sasson 2004). Electoral campaigns have been strongly based on this rhetoric, promoting the decrease of the age of criminal responsibility; the implementation of anti-gang measures; the introduction of new laws to criminalize behaviours and lengthen sentences; greater police autonomy and discretion; and the use of armed forces to combat crime (Ungar 2007; Müller 2012; Basombrio and Dammert 2013).

Several scholars have argued that penal and social welfare approaches are both components of a single policy regime to regulate social marginality and crime (Rushe and Kircheimer 1984; Garland 1985, 2001; Beckett and Western 2001). Integrative welfare regimes consider crime as partly caused by society, and thus social protection, rehabilitation, and reintegration are adequate measures to decrease deviant behaviour (Garland 1985). On the contrary, it is argued that in neoliberal regimes crime is viewed as a purposive behaviour, due to free choice, which must be deterred, increasing the costs of offending through harsh punishment and retribution (Reiner 2007). Some scholars have stated that this is the case for Latin American countries, which embraced different degrees of neoliberalism during the 1980s that strongly imprinted their punitive crime policies (Hojman 2004; Goldstein 2008; Wacquant 2009; Müller 2012; Swanson 2013). However, some authors have challenged the association between neoliberal regimes and punitive criminal policies, showing that they oversimplify the processes of punitive convergence and ignore relevant counter-examples among some market-oriented societies in Europe (O'Malley 1992; Zedner, 2002; Lacey 2008; Loader 2009). An interesting case in Latin America is Uruguay. Although Uruguay has been governed by a left coalition of political parties (Encuentro Progresista) during the last decade, the last years have been characterized by a conservative shift that embraced penal populism which involved a security-oriented discourse that promotes governance through crime, a consolidation of the privatization of security, the introduction of harsher penalties, and the increased presence and relevance of the police (Paternain 2014; Vernazza 2015).

Leaving aside the causes behind the Latin American approach towards crime, the idea that crime can be controlled through tough, smart, and cost-efficient solutions has been the paradigm, focusing mainly on the importation of practices developed in non-Latin American countries without adequate cultural adaptation. Moreover, as a mixed legacy of colonialism, authoritarian regimes, and cultures of extra-legal violence, the policies of crime control have been characterized by practices that easily violate the rule of law and in which human rights are marginal issues (Aguirre 2007; Koonings and Krujit 2007).

Although it has not been systematically documented, the importation of *tough-on-crime* policies has had several consequences reproducing marginality in Latin America (Hojman 2004; Müller 2012; Basombria and Dammert 2013; UNDP 2014). Perhaps the most popular measure has been *zero-tolerance policing*—a set of policing strategies based on strong law enforcement against minor crimes and incivilities, under the belief that social disorder paves the road to serious crimes because of decreased levels of informal social control (Kelling and Coles 1998). Following the apparent success of these measures in New York during the 1990s,[13] countries such as Mexico, Guatemala, Venezuela, Argentina, Brazil, Salvador, and Honduras have imported and implemented them in different degrees. Nonetheless, given the high levels of inequality and police corruption in several countries, these policies have mainly targeted the poor and thus have expanded social exclusion (Swanson 2013). Under the slogan of recuperation of public spaces, street children and homeless people have been removed from the streets, increasing the prevailing urban segregation that already existed in several cities of the region (Caldeira 2000; Jüttersonke et al. 2009; Muggah 2012). The strongest impact has been suffered by more than 27 million youth in Latin America who relied on informal economic survival practices (i.e. car cleaners, street vendors, shoeshiners, among others), which have been criminalized by these policies (Pansters and Castillo Berthier 2007; ILO 2015). These practices have also impacted working-class citizens, through what has been called *victims' responsibilisation* (O'Malley 1992; Garland 2001), in which citizens have progressively taken responsibility for the protection against crime that governments cannot provide. This is evidenced by the expansion of the private security industry, which has increased more than 10 per cent since 1980, with private guards outnumbering police officers in several Latin American countries (Ungar 2007; UNDP 2014). Nevertheless, the greatest harm has been observed in the rise of imprisonment rates over the past fifteen years. The following discussion shows how prisons in Latin America not only concentrate on the most vulnerable individuals from society, but also how social exclusion is reproduced through their degrading conditions and practices.

IMPRISONMENT AND SOCIAL EXCLUSION IN LATIN AMERICA

The imprisonment rate in Central America has increased 80 per cent and in South America 145 per cent in the past fifteen years (Figure 27.2). Only two countries (Guatemala and Bolivia) are below the world prison population rate and three countries (El Salvador, Belize, and Panama) are among the twenty countries with the highest prison population rates of the world (World Prison Brief 2016).

Although appalling prison conditions are stagnating and even deteriorating due to high levels of overpopulation, there have been only marginal reforms, and prisons continue concentrating and perpetuating social marginality all over Latin America.

The concentration of disadvantaged individuals in prisons cannot only be explained by the differential in criminal propensities (Pettit and Sykes 2017). Evidence suggests that law enforcement and penal practices such as policing strategies, access to justice, prosecution,

[13] However, for critical reviews that challenge the apparent success of the zero-tolerance policies in the US see Bowling (1999), Greene (1999) and Levitt (2004).

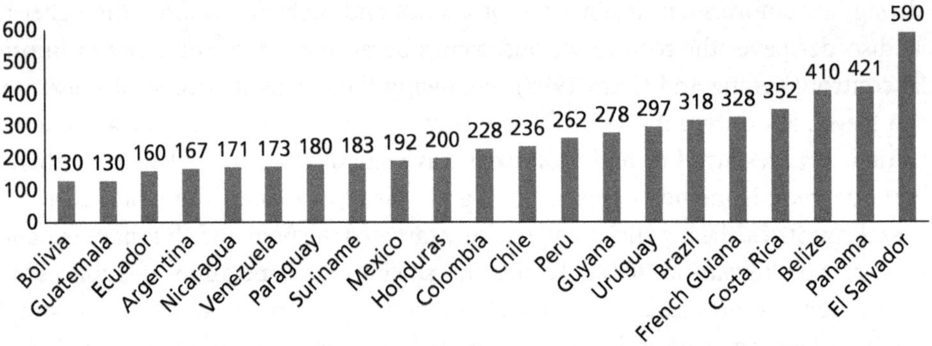

Figure 27.2 Prison population rates in Latin America

Source: World Prison Brief (2016).

and sentencing guidelines strongly affect imprisonment rates and intensify social exclusion (Tonry 1995; Mauer 2006; Western 2006; National Research Council 2014).

Studies conducted in Anglo-Saxon countries have shown that there is direct racial discrimination in sentencing outcomes; being of indigenous, black, and Latino status is a significant predictor of the likelihood of imprisonment (Kansal 2005; Steen et al. 2005; Snowball and Weatherburn 2006; Tonry 2011). Although in Latin America research is scarce, several studies conducted in Brazil have shown that racial inequalities play a crucial role in the process of criminalization (Ribeiro 1995; Human Rights Watch 1997; Mitchell and Wood 1998). A study conducted in Sao Paulo showed that although blacks and whites committed violent crimes in equal proportions, blacks were more harassed by the police, have poorer criminal defence (most of them relied on legal aid or public defence), and have higher probabilities of being convicted (Adorno 1995). Moreover, black minorities are disproportionally targeted by police through stop-and-frisk practices, and more subjected to body search than whites (Ramos and Musumeci 2005). They also receive harsher treatment and are more likely to be killed by police in confrontations inside and outside the favelas (Cano 2010).

Access to justice is a crucial procedural right for people accused or suspected of crimes in order to get access to a fair trial and fostering transparency. Although the total number of judges sitting in courts does not necessarily ensure the efficacy of the system, it certainly makes the criminal procedure fairer and strongly affects the amount of time that individuals spend on pre-trial detention without a judge determining the lawfulness of the arrest (UNODC 2014). Latin American countries show great disparities in this regard: while in countries such as Costa Rica there is a rate of twenty-six judges per 100,000 inhabitants, in Ecuador and Guatemala the rate is only one (Alertamerica, 2016).[14]

Legal aid is a key factor to avoid unfair legal procedures and miscarriages of justice. Although several Latin-American countries provide free legal aid for people who cannot afford it, this is not a consistent practice and in countries such as Bolivia, only 3 per cent

[14] Own elaboration of data from Alertamerica 2016.

of the municipalities are served by a public defender (IACHR 2007). In Guatemala, while the rate of prosecutors is ten per 100,000 inhabitants, the rate of public defenders is only one (Binder et al, 2015). In 2013, the National Commission for the Development of Indigenous People (CDI 2015) Mexico stated that around 80 per cent of the indigenous prison population were incarcerated without due process. The great majority did not understand Spanish and did not have access to a specialized public defender that spoke their language during the trial. In 2014, 1,693 of them were freed from Mexican prisons after being found innocent of the crimes of which they were accused. Lack of legal aid is also strongly related to the probability of pre-trial detention. This is especially relevant considering that there are several procedural rules in Latin American countries that strongly contribute to the excessive and arbitrary use of this measure. For example, in countries such as Brazil, Argentina, and Mexico pre-trial detention can be decided without judicial supervision and it is also mandatory for certain types of crimes (Open Society 2014; Binder et al. 2015). Almost half of the prison population in Latin America is composed of pre-trial detainees. However, there is considerable heterogeneity across the region: the percentage ranges from 12 per cent in Nicaragua to 69 per cent in Bolivia (World Prison Brief 2016). In Brazil, a study conducted in Rio de Janeiro that assessed the impact of legal aid on pre-trial detention showed that two-thirds of the individuals in the study were illegally detained; and that the individuals assisted by a public defender were less likely to obtain pre-trial freedom than the ones assisted by private lawyers (Lemgruber and Fernandes 2011).

Even if countries provide free legal aid, the criminal justice process involves other formal costs, such as the payment of bails, fines, and bribes that poor people cannot afford. Indeed, between 2006 and 2010, 13 per cent of the individuals sent to prison in Chile related to people who failed to pay a fine (Muñoz and Welsh 2012). It is not unusual that bribes are implicated in legal procedures in Latin America. In Venezuela, Peru, Mexico, and Bolivia, more than 30 per cent of the people declared that they had paid a bribe to the judiciary. Regarding police corruption the situation is even worse in countries such as Bolivia and Mexico, where more than half of the people have paid a bribe to a police officer (Transparency International 2013).

Finally, as was mentioned above, prosecution strategies and sentencing guidelines often target the most marginalized groups of society. A stunning example has been the implementation of what has been called the 'Mano Dura' approach to tackle gang activities (Maras) in Central America. In 2003, Honduras introduced an anti-gang law and in El Salvador the penal code was reformed to facilitate the prosecution of gang members and youths suspected of being part of the Maras (Cruz 2011). These reforms allowed police to arrest individuals based on arbitrary information, such as dress codes and tattoos, without due process (Rodgers et al. 2009). In 2004, 95 per cent of the 20,000 juveniles who were arrested under this scheme in El Salvador were released because the Supreme Court declared that the Anti-Maras Act was unconstitutional, violating human rights, and performing violent repression over juveniles (Savenije and van der Borgh 2014).

Table 27.1 Prison population versus general population—social exclusion rates in Chile

	Prison population rate (%)	General population rate (%)
Incomplete education	86	46
Access to health security	68	97
Homelessness	2	0.1
Has voted in at least one political election	20	49

Source: Own elaboration based on Fundación Paz Ciudadana (2016).

PRISONS CONCENTRATE AND PERPETUATE SOCIAL EXCLUSION

Although there is no comprehensive evidence regarding the socio-economic composition of prisons in Latin America (Müller 2012), few existing studies confirm the intuition that they concentrate on poor and marginalized individuals (IACHR 2011; Amnesty International 2014; CNDH 2014; HRW 2015). Based on a representative survey conducted in Chilean prisons, Fundación Paz Ciudadana (2016) compared prison population and general population rates according to several social exclusion dimensions. Table 27.1 shows that the prison population had less access to education, health, and housing than the general population and has voted fewer times in political elections due to previous imprisonment.

Imprisonment could be seen as an opportunity to compensate, through programmes and interventions, pre-existing inmates' disadvantages (Wakefield and Uggen 2010). Nevertheless, this is not the case in Latin America, where most countries invest less than 1 per cent of the corrections budget in rehabilitative interventions (Dammert and Zuñiga 2008). Brassiolo (2014) used data from a survey conducted in prisons in Argentina, Brazil, El Salvador, and Peru, and showed that only one-third of the inmates had access to education, recreation, or work during imprisonment. The above, together with degrading prison conditions deepens pre-existing social segregation and perpetuates inequality (Garland 2001) as is now discussed.

Unequal Access to Services

Several prisons in Latin America do not provide access to basic services, leaving individuals in a vulnerable position in comparison with the general population (IACHR 2011; FIO 2014). In Guatemala, 93 per cent of prisons do not provide access to potable water (Alertamerica 2016),[15] in Brazil around 50 per cent of prisons do not provide beds (FIO 2014), and in most countries of the region prison food is inadequate to maintain health and diet (IACHR 2011). As Figure 27.3 shows, prisons in the region

[15] Own elaboration of data from Alertamerica 2016.

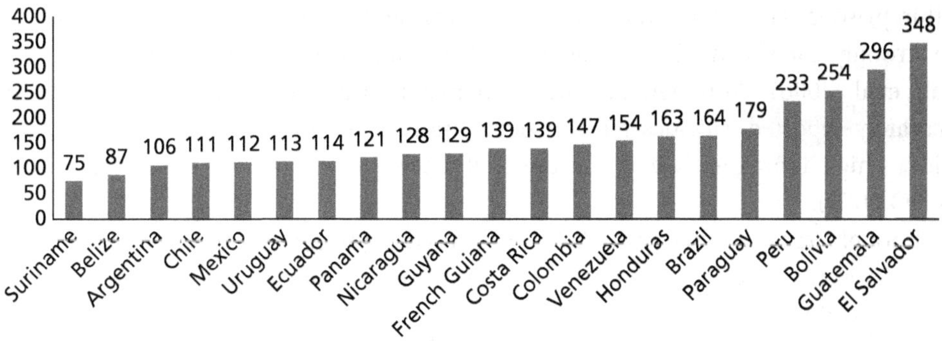

Figure 27.3 Prison occupancy levels (%) based on official capacity

Source: World Prison Brief (2016).

are also severely affected by overpopulation, many of them exceeding the critical level of 120 per cent, with only Belize and Suriname working within their capacity.

In several Brazilian prisons individuals do not have a space bigger than a square metre in which to live and in one of Rio de Janeiro's prisons, several inmates have to sleep standing tied against the walls because of the lack of space (IACHR 2011). These precarious living conditions together with malnutrition and lack of access to medical services have resulted in a high prevalence of health diseases. In European prisons, the prevalence of tuberculosis is estimated to be up to seventeen times higher than in the general population (Aerts et al. 2006). In the case of Pernambuco Brazil, this is even worse; with HIV prevalence forty-two times higher and tuberculosis prevalence 100 times higher than the general population (HRW 2015). Although it varies among countries, between 20 per cent and 50 per cent of the prisoners in Latin America do not have access to medical services (UNDP 2014). In countries with precarious prison systems such as Panama, most inmates do not have access to medical services at all, with an availability of five doctors to cover twelve prisons (Dammert and Zuñiga 2008).

Mental disorders are significantly more frequent among prisoners than among the general population and these differences tend to be higher in low-/middle-income countries than in high-income countries (Fazel and Seewald 2012). Although evidence from Latin American prisons has confirmed the above (Pondé et al. 2011; Mundt et al. 2013; Andreoli et al. 2014), the provision of mental health treatment in prisons is very scarce. Almanzar et al. (2015) estimated that while countries such as Sweden and the United States have fourteen forensic beds per 100,000 inhabitants, South America has 1.6 and Central America has only 0.5. Moreover, they observed from a selection of nine Latin American countries[16] that only one (Mexico) had psychiatric forensic services

[16] The countries selected were: Salvador, Costa Rica, Panama, Uruguay, Brazil, Dominican Republic, Peru, Mexico, and Argentina.

within prisons. This situation is extremely worrying if we consider that mental disorders are strongly correlated with suicide and self-harm among prisoners (Shaw et al. 2004; Pratt et al. 2006). Although in Latin America imprisonment suicides rates are not accurately reported, suicides tend to occur more often in prison than outside, being twice as high among individuals on pre-trial detention than among convicted prisoners (WHO 2000).

Although female imprisonment has increased significantly in the past ten years,[17] prisons are still male oriented institutions and women suffer strong discrimination in a system that does not consider their gender particularities. The lack of medical assistance mainly affects women, since they have a higher incidence of mental disorders and sexually transmitted diseases (Strazza et al. 2007). In the case of Belize, it was observed that while 13 per cent of the women in prison suffered from sexually transmitted diseases, only 4 per cent of males did so (Dammert and Zuñiga 2008). In Bolivia, there is only one gynaecologist for the entire female prison population of the country (FIO 2014). One of the main problems among women prisoners is the fragmentation of their family bonds. Although more than 80 per cent of women in Latin American prisons have children, fewer than 8 per cent of them live with their children in prison (UNDP 2014). Women not only have less access to education and training programmes than men, but also the skills they learn in prison are mainly recreational, strongly biased by gender stereotypes, and failing to provide them with any financial gain (Cárdenas 2010). Unlike men, women must meet several conditions to get access to conjugal visits in Latin American prisons. In several countries they have to prove that they are married or have children with their partner and they are obliged to use a contraceptive method (Bascary 2008). In some prisons in Mexico, the visits can be denied simply because the prison personnel determine that the relationship is not convenient for the inmate (Azaola and Bergman 2003). Prisoner prostitution is a common practice in several Latin American prisons (CEJIL 2007; CDI 2015). In Paraguay, the prison of Tacumbú runs an illegal prostitution business that operates during family visits, making monthly gains for the prison of more than US$50,000 (CEJIL 2007).

Inequalities within Prisons

Prison culture and dynamics also reproduce the social hierarchies that prevail in unequal societies (Müller 2012). In Latin America prisoners have unequal access to services within prisons due to corruption and lack of control (IACHR 2011). In Peru, 76 per cent of prisoners perceive prison authorities as corrupted with regard to granting access to benefits, visits, and classification (Defensoría del Pueblo Bolivia 2013). Institutional abuse and violence have been also documented, with more than 70 per cent of prisoners in Chile and Argentina arguing that they have been beaten by prison staff (UNDP 2014). The

[17] Between 2000 and 2014 the female prison population increased four times in Guatemala and Brazil, eight times in Salvador, and three times in Colombia (World Prison Brief 2016).

Inter-American Commission on Human Rights (IACHR 2011) observed that in Paraguay, female inmates are victims of sexual abuse from the prison's guards in exchange for food and personal hygiene products.

Perhaps the most astonishing example occurring in countries such as Guatemala, Bolivia, Colombia, Mexico, Brazil, Salvador, and Honduras are self-ruled prisons, in which authorities are unable to exercise control, offering minimal or only perimetral surveillance and marginal living supplies (IACHR, 2011; Arrarás and Bello-Pardo 2014). For instance in Mexico 58 per cent of prisons are ruled by the inmates (CNDH 2014) and in Guatemala, inmates are in charge of the prison's discipline, implementing sanctions that range from indefinite solitary confinement to beatings that may result in death (IACHR 2011). Inequalities are enormous in these prisons. Inmates are segregated by income, with poor prisoners living in degrading conditions, while the powerful enjoy privileges such as daily visits, air conditioning, and satellite TV, among others (Estefania 2009; IACHR, 2011). Prisoners administer all the services, such as accommodation, food, health, and visits. Usually they also perform the activities that are carried out by prison officers, such as protection against violence, discipline, and turnkey and clerk duties (Darke 2013). Under these regimes, prisoners have to pay a monthly rent to get access to a place to sleep. Although the price varies, in Brazil it costs around US$570 (HRW 2015) and in San Pedro's Bolivian prison luxury cells can cost US$1,500 while basic ones (four square metres) cost around US$10 per month (Estefania 2009). A study conducted in Mexico showed that families spend between US$55 and US$280 per month supporting a relative in prison (Pérez 2015). One of the most emblematic examples of self-ruled prisons is San Pedro prison in Bolivia. This prison, originally designed to hold 250 inmates is now occupied by more than 1,300 prisoners, their families, and children (Estefania 2009). Inmates have freedom of movement within the prison and they engage in economic interchange with the outside, running restaurants, bars, mini markets, and a hotel for visits. In 2013 the government announced that San Pedro was going to be closed after the sexual abuse and subsequent pregnancy of a 13-year-old girl who was living there with her father.

Social Exclusion beyond Prison Walls

The removal of individuals from the community through incarceration affects their social capital and social bonds (Hagan and Wheaton 1993; Wakefield and Uggen 2010; Raphael 2011). A survey conducted in Chilean prisons showed that 69 per cent of inmates lost a close relationship during imprisonment (Fundación Paz Ciudadana 2016). Incarceration also removes inmates from the important social networks that might assist them in finding work, while simultaneously strengthening their ties to others with similarly dismal prospects, perpetuating violence and crime (Hagan and Wheaton 1993). In Guatemala it was observed that 80 per cent of the country's extortion crimes were developed from inside prisons (CIEN 2014). It has been argued that in El

Salvador, the mass imprisonment of Maras's members was a key factor contributing to their escalation from gang-related activities to organized crime (Santamaría 2013).

Imprisonment does not only perpetuate and exacerbate inequalities among individuals who are incarcerated; it also affects their families and the communities where they belong. In poor neighbourhoods where incarceration rates are particularly high, every individual has had a direct or a vicarious experience with imprisonment that shapes their socialization process and daily lives (Garland 2001; Fagan 2004; Harding et al. 2013). In a survey conducted in Mexico 41 per cent of inmates' relatives argued that they lost their jobs, 30 per cent that they stopped bringing their children to school, and 18 per cent that they had to move residence because of the imprisonment of their relatives.

Children of imprisoned parents are also strongly affected: evidence suggests that they foster greater developmental problems, levels of aggression, antisocial behaviour, mental diseases (Murray et al. 2009; Wildeman 2010), and deep financial struggles (Lopoo and Western 2005; Comfort 2007; Geller et al. 2009). A study conducted in Chile with a representative sample of females in prisons showed that 70 per cent of their children end up living without the father after their mothers' imprisonment, with 38 per cent of them staying in a more vulnerable familial environment than before (Valenzuela et al. 2012). Although the United Nations Standard Minimum Rules for the Treatment of Prisoners (UNODC 2015) state that children who stay with their mothers in prison must have access to day care and they should not be treated as prisoners, the situation in Latin American prisons significantly differs from these standards. In Mexico in 2014 there were approximately 410 children living inside prisons with their mothers, some of them until the age of 12 (CNDH 2015) with no access to education at all. In Bolivia, in 2012 there were more than 1,400 children living in prisons with their mothers (Defensoría del Pueblo Bolivia 2013) with only two nurseries available for the whole country (CEJIL 2007). Several cases of abuse have been observed in these prisons, such as the fact that children have to stay with their mothers when they are sent to solitary confinement (CEJIL 2007). In Argentina, until 2006, the fact that a child was born in prison was stated on their birth certificate, further reproducing stigma and social exclusion beyond prison walls (CEJIL 2006).

Conclusion

In criminological studies inequality is believed to be one of the main macro-level predictors of crime and violence. Latin America is one of the most unequal and violent regions of the world. However, what is the nature of this relationship? Empirical evidence reviewed in this chapter shows that inequality tends to be significantly associated with crime across different types of studies and countries from Latin America. However, support for the inequality–crime association must be seen with caution for various reasons. First, inequality is not consistently associated with crime, and particularly when studies aim at explaining property crime or global indices of crime. Additionally, there is some evidence that the association might be less robust and contingent depending on how inequality is measured. A second problem is the weak validity and reliability of official data sets used in most of these studies. Methodological shortcomings that usually characterize official data sets are aggravated in Latin America by the scarcity of resources, poor functioning, and weak legitimacy of criminal justice and health institutions that produce and manage crime data. Finally, most of the research is based on macro-level studies and therefore provides weak empirical tests of the underlying causal mechanisms operating under the association between inequality and crime; in particular there is scarce evaluation of the most relevant mechanisms emphasized by sociological theories. Is violence in Latin America the product of high levels of inequality coupled with singular structural strains that simultaneously produce cultural inclusion and structural exclusion? What is the role of the progressive weakening of social control institutions like the family, the political system, or the education system? Is this violence reinforced in contexts where citizens perceive state and public institutions as weak, untrustworthy, and corrupt? These are the key questions that must be answered to properly understand the link between inequality and crime in Latin America.

Therefore, there is a need to develop a wider research agenda in Latin America that combines the already existent macro-level research based on official data with longitudinal micro-level studies based on self-reported and victimization data. These studies should test the explanatory relevance of inequality and its relationship with meaningful theoretical constructs such as strain, institutional anomie, and perception of legitimacy and inequality among others in order to evaluate their moderator or mediator role in the link between inequality and crime. In particular, the estimation of multilevel models will help produce a better evaluation of effects associated with neighbourhoods' structural disadvantages that might be moderating the link between inequality and crime. Micro-level studies also provide the opportunity not only to measure more accurately the intensity and duration of individuals' relative lack of resources, the frequency and seriousness of individuals' involvement with crime (Tittle and Meier 1990; Wright et al. 1999; Jarjoura et al. 2002), but also to evaluate empirically alternative measures of poverty, inequality, and socio-economic status. For example Agnew and colleagues (2008) showed how individuals get involved in crime not due to their poverty, or their low socio-economic status, but rather because they suffer several economic problems that generate negative emotions, affect their physical well-being and lifestyle, and therefore are more difficult to ignore and cope with without resorting to crime.

Additionally, we also need more research that provides empirical evidence about the perverse effects of criminal justice institutions. Indeed, as was discussed in the second section of this chapter, when analysing the link between crime and inequality we cannot be limited by exploring only how income inequality might cause crime, we also have to look at the role that policing and penal practices play in the reproduction and exacerbation of existing levels of inequalities and social exclusion in Latin America. Using the prison system as a case study, it was shown how prison culture, conditions, and, in some cases, the absolute absence of the state perpetuates the extreme levels of social exclusion of inmates, their families, and the communities to which they return. It was also pointed out that the concentration of disadvantaged people in prisons cannot simply be explained by the fact that this group of individuals are the ones who commit most of the crimes. Policing strategies, prosecution, and sentencing guidelines very frequently discriminate against them and evidence suggests that there is an unequal access to justice, affecting mostly racial minorities and the poor.

The foregoing provides evidence that prison reform is an imperative in Latin America. A suitable starting point would be the implementation of independent prison inspectorate strategies that accurately monitor prison conditions and generate comparable information. Nevertheless, although fourteen Latin American countries have ratified the United Nations Optional Protocol to the Convention against Torture and Other Cruel, Inhuman or Degrading Treatment or Punishment (OPCAT) almost nothing has been done and accurate information regarding prison conditions remains extremely scarce. A research agenda must be carried out that considers crime prevention and penal practices as a continuum and informs the development of a solid and comprehensive regional strategy to decrease crime. This research must be oriented first at the macro-level in order to explore the link between penal and welfare policies in Latin American states and test the empirical validity of the 'punitive convergence hypothesis'. Finally, micro-level longitudinal studies are needed to follow cohorts of individuals throughout the crime prevention and penal continuum in order to accurately establish the effects these policies have on vulnerable and excluded populations.

REFERENCES

Aboal, D., Lorenzo, F., and Perera, M. (2007). *Crimen y Violencia en Uruguay*. Montevideo. Available at www.cinve.org.uy/wpcontent/uploads/2013/01/Crimen_AboalLorenzoPerera.pdf, accessed 16 August 2017.

Adorno, S. (1995). 'Discriminação racial e justiça criminal em São Paulo' [Racial discrimination and criminal justice in Sao Paulo], *Novos Estudos* 43: 45–63.

Aerts, A. Hauer, B., Wanlin, M., and Veen, J. (2006). 'Tuberculosis and tuberculosis control in European prisons', *International Journal of Tuberculosis and Lung Disease* 10: 1215–23.

Agnew, R. (2001). 'Building on the foundation of general strain theory: specifying the types of strain most likely to lead to crime and delinquency'. *Journal of Research in Crime and Delinquency* 38: 319–61.

Agnew, R., Matthews, S., Bucher, J., Welcher, A., and Keyes, C. (2008). 'Socioeconomic status, economic problems and delinquency', *Youth Society* 40/2: 159–81.

Aguirre, C. (2007). 'Prisons and prisoners in modernising Latin America (1800–1940)', in F. Dikötter and I. Brown (eds) *Cultures of Confinement. A History of the Prison in Africa, Asia, and Latin America*. Ithaca, NY: Cornell University Press, 14–54.

Alertamerica (2016). OAS Hemispheric Security Observatory. Available at www.oas.org/dsp/observatorio/database/indicators.aspx?lang=en, accessed 16 August 2017.

Almanzar, S., Katz, C.L., and Harry, B. (2015). 'Treatment of mentally ill offenders in nine developing Latin American countries', *Journal of the American Academy of Psychiatry and the Law* 43: 340–9.

Amnesty International. (2014). 'Key human rights concerns'. Available at www.amnesty.org/en/countries/americas/bolivia/report-bolivia/, accessed 16 August 2017.

Andreoli, S., dos Santos, M., Quintana, M., Silva Ribeiro, W., Luiz Blay, S., Vernet, J., and Mari, J. (2014). 'Prevalence of mental disorders among prisoners in the state of Sao Paulo, Brazil. *PLoS ONE* 9: e88836.

Arrarás, A. and Bello-Pardo, E. (2014). 'Inventando Caminos: cannabis regulation in Uruguay', in R. Zepeda and J. D. Rosen (eds) *Cooperation and Drug Policies in the Americas: Trends in the Twenty-first Century*. Lanham, MD: Lexington, 173–97.

Arsenio, W.F. and Gold, J. (2006). 'The effects of social injustice and inequality on children's moral judgments and behavior: towards a theoretical model', *Cognitive Development* 21/4: 388–400.

Azaola, E. and Bergman, M. (2003). *El Sistema Penitenciario Mexicano*. Center for U.S.-Mexican Studies, Universidad de California. Available at http://escholarship.org/uc/item/18w2r3h7, accessed 16 August 2017.

Bascary, L. (2008). 'Informe sobre violencia contra mujeres privadas de la libertad en Argentina' [Report about violence against women in prisons in Argentina], in *CLADEM Violencia contra las Mujeres Privadas de la Libertad* [Violence against women in prisons in Argentina]. *Sistematización Regional. Argentina, Brasil, Chile, Colombia, Paraguay y Uruguay. Informe de investigación*. Available at www.cladem.org/images/pdfs/publicaciones/regionales/violencia/estudio-mujeres-privadas-libertad.pdf, accessed 16 August 2017.

Basombrio, C. and Dammert, L. (2013). *Seguridad y populismo punitivo en America Latina* [Safety and popular punishment in Latin America]. Washington, DC: Woodrow Wilson Center Update on the Americas. Available at www.wilsoncenter.org/sites/default/files/Seguridad%20y%20Populismo%20Punitivo%20en%20America%20Latina.pdf, accessed 16 August 2017.

Beato, Claudio (2012). *Crimes y Cidades*. UFMG: Belo Horizonte.

Becker, G.S. (1968). 'Crime and punishment: an economic approach', *Journal of Political Economy* 76/2: 169.

Beckett, K. and Sasson, T. (2004). *The Politics of Injustice: Crime and Punishment in America*, 2nd edn. London: Sage.

Beckett, K. and Western, B. (2001). 'Governing social marginality', in D. Garland (ed.) *Mass Imprisonment: Social Causes and Consequences*. London: Sage, 35–50.

Binder, A., Cape, E., and Namoradze, Z. (2015). *Defensa penal efectiva en América Latina*. Bogotá, Colombia: Ediciones Andropos.

Blackwell, A. and Duarte, P. (2011). 'Violence, crime, and social exclusion', in OEA (ed.) *Inequality and Social Exclusion in the Americas*, 111–34.

Borges, D. Miranda, D., Duarte, T., Novaes, F., Ettel, F., Guimaraes, K., et al., (2013). 'Mortes violentas no Brasil: uma análise do fluxo de informações' [Violent deaths in Brazil: an analysis of the flow of information], in I. Figueiredo, C. Neme, and C. Lima (eds) *Pensando a Segurança Pública - Homicídios no Brasil: Registro e Fluxo de Informações* [Thinking about public security – homicides in Brazil: register and flow of information]. Brasilia, 329–409.

Borraz, F. and Gonzalez, N. (2010). 'Determinantes económicos y sociodemográficos de la delincuencia en Uruguay' [Economic and sociodemographic determinants of delinquency in Uruguay], *Bienestar y Politica Social* 6/2: 47–77.

Borraz, F. and Munyo, I. (2014). 'Conditional cash transfers and crime: higher income but also better loot'. Working paper Montevideo: Centro de Economıa, Sociedad y Empresa del IEEM, Universidad de Montevideo.

Bourguignon, F., Núñez, J. and Sánchez, F. (2003a). 'A structural model of crime and inequality in Colombia', *Journal of the European Economic Association* 1/2–3: 440–9.

Bowling, B. (1999). 'The rise and fall of New York murder: zero tolerance or crack's decline?', *British Journal of Criminology* 39/4: 531–54.

Boyer, R. (2016). 'A world of contrasted but interdependent inequality regimes: the Latin America paradox', *Review of Political Economy* 28/1: 1–22.

Brassiolo, P. (2014). 'The impact of incarceration on crime in Latin America'. Unpublished manuscript.

Brush, J. (2007). 'Does income inequality lead to more crime? A comparison of cross-sectional and time-series analyses of United States counties', *Economics Letters* 96/2: 264–8.

Caldeira, T. (2000). *City of Walls: Crime, Segregation and Citizenship in São Paulo*. Berkeley, CA: University of California Press.

Camacho, A. and Mejía, D. (2013). 'Las externalidades de los programas de transferencias condicionadas sobre el crimen: El caso de Familias en Acción en Bogotá' [Negative externalities on crime of the Conditional Transference Programms The case of families in action in Bogotá]. BID Working Paper # IDB-WP-406IDB-WP-406. Washington, DC. Available at http://services.iadb.org/wmsfiles/products/Publications/37722842.pdf, accessed 16 August 2017.

Camara, M. and Salama, P. (2004). Homicidios en America del Sur: los pobres son peligrosos? [Homicides in South America: are the poor dangerous?] *Revista de Economia Institucional* 6/10: 159–81.

Campanella, J. (2008). 'Una aproximación económica a los determinantes del delito en Montevideo en el período 1986–2005' [An economic perspective on the determinants of crime in Montevideo in the period 1986–2005], in R. Paternain and R. Sanseviero (eds) *Violencia, Inseguridad y Miedos en Uruguay. ¿Qué tienen para decir las Ciencias Sociales?* [*Violence, insecurity and fears in Uruguay: what can social sciences say?*]. Montevideo, Uruguay: Friedrich Ebert Stiftung.

Cano, I. (2000). 'Registros Criminais da Polícia no Rio de Janeiro: problemas de validade e Confiabilidade' [Police criminal records in Rio de Janeiro: problems of validity and reliability], in D. Cerqueira, J. Lemgruber, and L. Musumeci (eds) *Forum de Debates – Criminalidade, violência e segurança pública: uma discussão sobre as bases de dados e questões metodológicas I* [Forum of Debates – Criminality, violence and public safety: a discussion of the data sets and methodological questions]. Rio de Janeiro: Ipea/CESEC–UCAM, 111–21.

Cano, I. (2010). 'Racial bias in police use of lethal force in Brazil', *Police Practice and Research* 11/1: 31–43.

Cano, I. and Santo, W. (2001). *Violência letal, renda e desigualdade social no Brasil* [Lethal violence, income and inequality in Brazil]. Rio de Janeiro: 7letras. Available at www.7letras.com.br/violencia-letal-renda-e-desigualdade-social-no-brasil.html, accessed 16 August 2017.

Cárdenas, A. (2010). *Mujeres y cárcel: diagnóstico de las necesidades de grupos vulnerables en prisión* [Women and gaols: diagnosing the needs of vulnerable groups in prison]. Santiago: Universidad Diego Portales-ICSO. Available at www.icso.cl/wp-content/uploads/2011/03/

Proyecto-Grupos-Vulnerables-CPF-GIZ-MINJU-ICSO-versión-final-para-página-web-Diciembre-2011.pdf, accessed 16 August 2017.

CDI (2015). Comisión Nacional para el Desarrollo de los Pueblos Indígenas. Available at www.gob.mx/cdi/#648, accessed 16 August 2017.

CEJIL (Center for Justice and International Law) (2006). Mujeres Privadas de Libertad. Informe Regional: Argentina, Bolivia, Chile, Paraguay y Uruguay. Available at https://cejil.org/es/mujeres-privadas-libertad-informe-regional-argentina-bolivia-chile-paraguay-y-uruguay, accessed 23 July 2019.

CEJIL (Center for Justice and International Law) (2007). *Women in Prison*. Regional Report: Argentina, Bolivia, Chile, Paraguay, Uruguay. Available at https://viejaweb.cejil.org/sites/default/files/women_in_prison.pdf, accessed 16 August 2017.

CEPAL (United Nations Economic Commission for Latin America and the Caribbean) (2014). *Pactos para la igualdad: hacia un futuro sostenible* [Covenants for equality: there was a sustainable future]. Santiago de Chile: CEPAL.

Cerqueira, D. (2014). *Causas e consequencias do crime no Brasil* [Causes and consequences of crime in Brazil]. Pontifícia Universidade Católica do Rio de Janeiro (PUC). Available at https://bibliotecafea.com/novas-aquisicoes/causas-e-consequencias-do-crime-no-brasil/, accessed 16 August 2017.

Cerqueira, D. and Lobão, W. (2004). 'Criminalidade, ambiente socioeconômico e polícia: desafios para os governos' [Criminality, socio-economic environment and police: challenges for governments], *RAP* 38/3: 371–99.

Cerro, A.M. and Rodriguez, A.R. (2016). 'Características del delito en las provincias argentinas' [Characteristics of crime in provinces of Argentina], in A. M. Cerro and O. Meloni (eds) *Investigaciones sobre Economia de la Delincuencia en Argentina* [Economic research of crime in Argentina]. Buenos Aires: Dunken Editorial, 11–38.

Chambouleyron, A. and Willington, M. (1998). 'Crimen y Castigo en la Argentina: un enfoque empírico' [Crime and punishment in Argentina: an empirical approach], *Anales de la XXXII Reunión Anual de la Asociación Argentina de Economía Política*, 21/85: 1–15.

Chamlin, M.B. and Cochran, J.K. (2006.) 'Economic inequality, legitimacy, and cross-national homicide rates'. *Homicide Studies* 10/4: 231–52.

Chioda, L., De Mello, J.M.P., and Soares, R.R. (2015). 'Spillovers from conditional cash transfer programs: Bolsa Família and crime in Brazil', *Economics of Education Review* 54: 306–20.

Chouhy, C., Cullen, F.T., and Unnever, J.D. (2014). 'Mean streets revisited: assessing the generality of rival criminological theories', *Victims & Offenders* (January 2015): 1–26.

CIEN (Centro de Investigaciones Económicas Nacionales [Center for National Economic Research]) (2014). *Cárceles hacinadas ¿problema de pocos o de todos?* [Overcrowded prisons – a single or multiple problem?] Available at www.cien.org.gt/index.php/carceles-hacinadas-problema-de-pocos-o-de-todos/, accessed 16 August 2017.

Clarke, R. and Cornish, D.B. (1986). *The Reasoning Criminal*. Piscataway, NJ: Transaction Publishers.

CNDH (Comisión Nacional de los Derechos Humanos) (2014). Diagnóstico Nacional de Supervisión Penitenciaria. Available at www.cndh.org.mx/sites/all/doc/sistemas/DNSP/DNSP_2014.pdf, accessed 16 August 2017.

CNDH (Comisión Nacional de los Derechos Humanos) (2015). Diagnóstico Nacional de Supervisión Penitenciaria. Available at www.cndh.org.mx/sites/all/doc/sistemas/DNSP/DNSP_2015.pdf, accessed 16 August 2017.

Cohen, L.E. and Felson, M. (1979). 'Social change and crime rate trends: a routine activity approach', *American Sociological Review* 44/4: 588.

Comfort, M. (2007). 'Punishment beyond the legal offender'. *Annual Review of Law in the Social Sciences* 3: 271–96.

Corbacho, A., Philipp, J., and Ruiz-Vega, M. (2014). 'Crime and erosion of trust: evidence for Latin America', *World Development* 70: 400–15. Available at http://dx.doi.org/10.1016/j.worlddev.2014.04.013, accessed 16 August 2017.

Cruz, J.M. (2011). 'Government responses and the dark side of gang suppression in Central America', in T. C. Bruneau, L. Dammert, and E. Skinner (eds) *Maras: Gang Violence and Security in Central America,* Austin, TX: University of Texas Press, 137–58.

Curto, B., Silvestre, C., Nascimento, R., Murray, J., and Bordin, I. (2011). 'Environmental factors associated with adolescent antisocial behavior in a poor urban community in Brazil', *Social Psychiatry and Psychiatric Epidemiology* 46/12: 1221–31.

Dammert, L. and Zuñiga, L. (2008). *La Cárcel: problemas y desafíos para las Américas* [Gaol: Problems and challenges for the Americas]. Santiago: *Flacso Chile y OEA*. Available at www.flacsochile.org/publicaciones/la-carcel-problemas-y-desafios-para-las-americas/, accessed 16 August 2017.

Dammert, L., Salazar, F., Montt, C., and González, P. (2010). *Crimen e inseguridad: indicadores para las Américas* [Crime and insecurity: indicators for the Americas]. Santiago: *FLACSO-Chile/Banco Interamericano de Desarrollo (BID).* Available at www.vanderbilt.edu/lapop/news/FLACSO_on_crime.pdf, accessed 16 August 2017.

Darke, S. (2013). 'Inmate governance in Brazilian prisons', *Howard Journal of Criminal Justice* 52/3: 272–84.

Defensoría del Pueblo Bolivia (2013). 'Informe sobre el ejercicio de los derechos humanos en el Estado Plurinacional de Bolivia' [Human Rights report in the State of Bolivia]. Available at www.defensoria.gob.bo/archivos/INFORME_SOBRE_DDHH_2013_06121012.pdf, accessed 16 August 2017.

Demombynes, G. and Ozler, B. (2005). 'Crime and local inequality in South Africa', *Journal of Development Economics* 76/2: 265–92.

dos Santos, M. (2009). 'Dinâmica temporal da criminalidade: Mais evidências sobre o "efeito inércia" nas taxas de crimes letais nos estados brasileiros' [Temporal dynamics of crime: more evidence regarding the "efeito inercia" in lethal crime rates in Brazilian states], *Revista Economia*. Available at http://raceadmv3.nuca.ie.ufrj.br/BuscaRace/Docs/mjsantos3.pdf, accessed 16 August 2017.

dos Santos, M. and Kassouf, A.L. (2008). 'Estudos Econômicos das Causas da Criminalidade no Brasil: Evidências e Controvérsias' [Economic studies of the causes of criminality in Brazil: evidence and controversy], *Revista Economia* 9: 343–72.

Eisner, M. (2014). 'Reducing homicide by 50% in 30 years. Universal mechanisms and evidence-based public policy'. Paper presented at WHO and University of Cambridge Global Violence Reduction Conference, Cambridge.

Eisner, M. (2015). *Como reducir los homicidios en un 50% en los proximos 30 anios* [How to reduce homicide by 50 per cent in the next 30 years]. Instituto Igarapé. Retrieved from https://

igarape.org.br/en/como-reducir-los-homicidios-en-un-50-en-los-proximos-30-anos/, accessed 21 October 2016.

Elgar, F., Craig, W., Boyce, W., Morgan, A., and Vella-Zarb, R. (2009). 'Income inequality and school bullying: multilevel study of adolescents in 37 countries', *Journal of Adolescent Health* 45/4: 351–9.

Elgar, F., Picket, K., Picket, W., Craig, W., Molcho, M., and Hurrelmann, M. (2013). 'School bullying, homicide and income inequality: a cross-national pooled time series analysis', *International Journal of Public Health* 58/2: 237–45.

Enamorado, T., Lopez-Calva, L.F., and Rodriguez-Castelon, C. (2014). 'Crime and growth convergence: evidence from Mexico', *Economics Letters* 125/1: 9–13.

Estefania, R. (2009). 'Photo journal: inside a Bolivian Jail'. *BBC News*. Available at http://news.bbc.co.uk/1/shared/spl/hi/picture_gallery/06/americas_inside_a_bolivian_jail/html/1.stm, accessed 16 August 2017.

Fagan, J. (2004.) 'Crime, law, and the community dynamics of incarceration in New York City', in M. Tonry (ed.) *The Future of Imprisonment in the 21st Century*. New York: Oxford University Press, 27–61.

Fajnzylber, P. and Araujo, A.F. Jr (2001). 'Violencia e criminalidade', in M. B. Lisboa and N. A. Menezes (eds) *Microeconomia e Sociedade no Brasil.* Rio de Janeiro: FGV EPGE, 333–94.

Fajnzylber, P., Lederman, D., and Loayza, N. (1998). *Determinants of Crime Rates in Latin America and the World: An Empirical Assessment.* World Bank Latin American and Caribbean studies viewpoints. Washington, DC: World Bank. Available at http://documents.worldbank.org/curated/en/198251468752978462/Determinants-of-crime-rates-in-Latin-America-and-the-world-an-empirical-assessment, accessed 16 August 2017.

Farrell, G., Tilley, N., and Tseloni, A. (2014). 'Why the crime drop?', *Crime and Justice: A Review of Research* 43/1: 421–90.

Fazel, S. and Seewald, K. (2012). 'Severe mental illness in 33588 prisoners worldwide: systematic review and meta-regression analysis', *British Journal Psychiatry* 200: 364–73.

Felson, M. (1994). 'Crime and everyday life: insight and implications for society'. Available at www.ncjrs.gov/App/abstractdb/AbstractDBDetails.aspx?id=157562, accessed 16 August 2017.

Felson, M. and Boba, R. (2010). *Crime and Everyday Life.* London: SAGE.

FIO (La Federación Iberoamericana del Ombudsman) (2014). *Sistema penitenciario Iberoamericano* [The prison system in Latin America], Vol. 2. Available at www.portalfio.org/recursos/revista-2-de-2014-en-portugues/, accessed 22 July 2019.

Freira, M.L. (2014). 'La ayuda social disminuye los delitos?' [Does social assistance reduce crime?], in A. M. Cerro and O. Meloni (eds) *Investigaciones sobre Economia de la Delincuencia en Argentina* [Research into the crime economy in Argentina]. Buenos Aires: Fundación Paz Ciudadana, 73–109.

Fundación Paz Ciudadana (2016). *Estudio sobre los niveles de exclusión social en personas privadas de libertad* [Study of the levels of social exclusion in people deprived of their liberty]. Available at www.pazciudadana.cl/wp-content/uploads/2016/02/exclusion-social-final-3.pdf, accessed 16 August 2017.

GALLUP (2016). *Global Law and Order Report.* Available at www.gallup.com/services/193631/gallup-global-law-order-2016-report.aspx?ays=tl9XrFePBQvrGd7pGYpnn1.CnFZwy4q8YIvyOgPFtmMbsKZvEJTw.uUpWEF7EA1-3SF3JpodwtQGZRnju1de6G108njj08d0G4oGPn79657o5MfTRggvpf8bQd27ktbBiSA4UL3BC4ZZmgC9KIREEwaa, accessed 16 August 2017.

Garcia, R. (1995). 'Participacion en actividades ilegales: evidencia empirica del robo en el caso Chileno' [Participation in illegal activities: empirical evidence of burglary in the case of Chile]. Tesis de Economía: Pontificia Universidad Catolica de Chile.

Garland, D. (1985). *Punishment and Welfare: A History of Penal Strategies*. Aldershot: Wower.

Garland, D. (ed.) (2001). *Mass Imprisonment: Social Causes and Consequences*. London: Sage.

Gaviria, A. (2000). 'Increasing returns and the evolution of violent crime: the case of Colombia', *Journal of Development Economics* 61/1: 1–25.

Gaviria, A. and Pagés, C. (2002). 'Patterns of crime victimization in Latin American cities', *Journal of Development Economics* 67/1: 181–203.

Geller, A., Garfinkel, I., Cooper, C.E., and Mincy, R.B. (2009). 'Parental incarceration and child wellbeing: implications for urban families', *Social Science Quarterly* 90/5: 1186–202.

Goldstein, Daniel M. (2008). 'Flexible justice: neoliberal violence and "self-help" security in Bolivia', in D. Pratten and A. Sen (eds) *Global Vigilantes*. New York: Columbia University Press, 239–66.

Goudriaan, H., Lynch, J.P., and Nieuwbeerta, P. (2004). 'Reporting to the police in Western nations: a theoretical analysis of the effects of social context', *Justice Quarterly* 21/4: 933–69.

Greene, J.A. (1999). 'Zero tolerance: a case study of police policies and practices in New York City', *Crime & Delinquency* 45/2: 171–87.

Guerrero Valasco, R., Gutiérrez Martínez, M.I., Fandiño-Losada, A., and Cardona, S. (2012). 'Sistema de indicadores comparables de convivencia y seguridad ciudadana: un consenso de países' [Comparable system of indicators of coexistence and public safety: a consensus of countries], *Revista Panamericana de Salud Pública* 31/3: 253–9.

Hagan, J. and Wheaton, B. (1993). 'The search for adolescent role exits and the transition to adulthood', *Social Forces* 71/4: 955–80.

Harding, David J., Morenoff, Jeffrey D., and Herbert, Claire W. (2013). 'Home is hard to find: neighborhoods, institutions, and the residential trajectories of returning prisoners', *ANNALS of the American Academy of Political and Social Science* 647: 214–36.

Hojman, D.E. (2004). 'Inequality, unemployment and crime in Latin American cities', *Crime, Law & Social Change* 41: 33–51.

HRW (Human Rights Watch) (1997). 'Police brutality in Urban Brazil'. Available at www.hrw.org/reports/1997/brazil/, accessed 16 August 2017.

HRW (Human Rights Watch) (2015). *Human Rights Watch World Report 2015*. Available at www.hrw.org/world-report/2015, accessed 16 August 2017.

IACHR (Inter-American Commission on Human Rights) (2007). *Access to Justice and Social Inclusion: The Road towards Strengthening Democracy in Bolivia*. Available at http://cidh.org/pdf%20files/BOLIVIA.07.ENG.pdf, accessed 16 August 2017.

IACHR (Inter-American Commission on Human Rights) (2011). *Report on the Human Rights of Persons Deprived of Liberty in the Americas*. Available at www.oas.org/en/iachr/pdl/docs/pdf/PPL2011eng.pdf, accessed 16 August 2017.

Igarapé Institute (2015). Homicide Monitor. Available at https://homicide.igarape.org.br, accessed 16 August 2017.

ILO (International Labour Organization) (2015). *World Employment and Social Outlook-Trends 2015*. Available at www.ilo.org/global/research/global-reports/weso/2015/WCMS_337069/lang–en/index.htm, accessed 16 August 2017.

Imbusch, P., Misse, M., and Carrión, F. (2011). 'Violence research in Latin America and the Caribbean: a literature review', *International Journal of Conflict and Violence* 5: 87–154.

Jaitman, L. (2016). *Los costos del crimen y la violencia en America Latina y el Caribe* [Costs of crime and violence in Latin America and Caribe]. New York: Banco Interamericano de Desarrollo.

Jarjoura, G., Tripplet, R., and Brinker, G. (2002). 'Growing up poor: examining the link between persistent childhood poverty and delinquency', *Journal of Quantitative Criminology* 18(2): 159–87.

Jüttersonke, Ol., Muggah, R., and Rodgers, D. (2009). 'Gangs, urban violence, and security interventions in Central America', *Security Dialogue* 40/4–5: 373–97.

Kang, S. (2016). 'Inequality and crime revisited: effects of local inequality and economic segregation on crime', *Journal of Population Economics* 29/2: 593–626.

Kansal, T. (2005). 'Racial disparity in sentencing: a review of the literature'. The Sentencing Project. Washington, DC. Available at www.opensocietyfoundations.org/sites/default/files/disparity.pdf, accessed 16 August 2017.

Kelling, G. and Coles, C. (1998). *Fixing Broken Windows: Restoring Order and Reducing Crime in Our Communities*. New York: Free Press.

Koonings, K. and Kruijt, D. (2007). *Fractured Cities: Social Exclusion, Urban Violence and Contested Spaces in Latin America*. London: Zed Books.

Krisch, M., Eisner, M., Mikton, C., and Butchart, A. (2015). 'Global strategies to reduce violence by 50% in 30 years: findings from the WHO and University of Cambridge Global Violence Reduction Conference 2014, University of Cambridge.

Lacey, N. (2008). *The Prisoners' Dilemma: Political Economy and Punishment in Contemporary Democracies*. Cambridge: Cambridge University Press.

Latinobarómetro. (2015). Informe Latinobarómetro 2015. Available at www.latinobarometro.org/latNewsShow.jsp, accessed 16 August 2017.

Lemgruber, J. and Fernandes, M.A. (2011). *Impacto da assistência jurídica a presos provisórios: um experimento na cidade do Rio de Janeiro* [Impact of legal assistance on short term prisoners: an experiment in the city of Rio de Janeiro]. Rio de Janeiro: ARP/CESeC. Available at www.ucamcesec.com.br/wp-content//uploads/2011/09/PresosProvisorios_final.pdf, accessed 16 August 2017.

Levitt, S.D. (2004). 'Understanding why crime fell in the 1990s: four factors that explain the decline and six that do not', *Journal of Economic Perspectives* 18/1: 163–90.

Loader, I. (2009). 'Ice cream and incarceration on appetites for security and punishment', *Punishment & Society* 11/2: 241–57.

Londoño, J.L. and Guerrero, R. (1998). *Violencia en América Latina Epidemiología y Costos* [Violence in Latin America: epidemiology and costs]. Washington, DC: Interamerican Development Bank. Available at www.utp.edu.co/~porlapaz/docs/violencia/pxp2.pdf, accessed 23 July 2019.

Lopoo, L.M. and Western, B. (2005). 'Incarceration and the formation and stability of marital unions', *Journal of Marriage and the Family* 67/3: 721–34.

Lustig, N.C., Lopez-Calva, L.F., and Ortiz-Juarez, E. (2011). 'The decline in inequality in Latin America: how much, since when and why', *SSRN Electronic Journal* April/i: 1–22. Available at www.ssrn.com/abstract=2113476, accessed 16 August 2017.

Maguire, M. (2008). 'Crime statistics', *The Oxford Handbook of Criminology*. Oxford: Oxford University Press.

Malby, S. (2010). 'Homicide', in S. Harrendorf, M. Heiskanen, and S. Malby (eds) *International Statistics on Crime and Justice*. Helsinki: European Institute for Crime Prevention and Control, 7–20.

Matsueda, R.L. and Grigoryeva, M.S. (2014). 'Social inequality, crime, and deviance', in *Handbook of the Social Psychology of Inequity*, 1–52.

Mauer, M. (2006). *Race to Incarcerate*. New York: The New Press.

Meloni, O. (2014). 'Does poverty relief spending reduce crime? Evidence from Argentina', *International Review of Law and Economics* 39: 28–38. Available at http://dx.doi.org/10.1016/j.irle.2014.05.002, accessed 16 August 2017.

Mendonça, M.J.C. (2002). 'Violência e Criminalidade no Brasil: uma abordagem empírica e teórica' [Violence and criminality in Brazil: an empirical and theoretical approach], *Brazilian Journal of Business Economics* 2/1: 33–49.

Mendoza, J.L. (2015). 'Determinantes de la violencia urbana en Lima Metropolitana y Callao: Casos de delitos contra el patrimonio' [Determinants of urban violence in metropolitan Lima and Callao: cases of crimes against property], *Pensamiento Critico* 20/1: 75–96.

Merton, R.K. (1938). 'Social structure and anomie', *American Sociological Review* 3: 672.

Messner, S.F. and Rosenfeld, R. (2006). 'The present and future of institutional-anomie theory', in *Taking Stock: The Status of Criminological Theory*, 127–48. Available at http://ezp-prod1.hul.harvard.edu/login?url=http://search.ebscohost.com/login.aspx?direct=true&db=psyh&AN=2006-22890-004&site=ehost-live&scope=site, accessed 16 August 2017.

Mitchell, M.J. and Wood, C.H. (1998). 'Ironies of citizenship: skin color, police brutality and the challenge to democracy in Brazil', *Social Forces* 77: 1001–20.

Mocan, H.N., Billups, S.C., and Overland, J. (2005). 'A dynamic model of differential human capital and criminal activity', *Economica* 72/288: 655–81.

Moral de La Rubia, J. and Ortiz Morales, H. (2011). 'Un modelo predictivo de conducta disocial por análisis de senderos' [A predictive model of antisocial behavior by trail analysis], *Portada de Anuario de Psicología Jurídica* 21: 27–40. Available at www.copmadrid.org/webcopm/resource.do?recurso=7000&numero=2011060215285476500, accessed 16 August 2017.

Moreno-Brid, J.C. and Garry, S. (2016). Economic performance in Latin America in the 2000s: recession, recovery, and resilience? *Oxford Development Studies*. Available at http://dx.doi.org/10.1080/13600818.2015, accessed 16 August 2017.

Muggah, R. (2012). *Researching the Urban Dilemma: Urbanization, Poverty and Violence*. Ottawa: IDRC. Available at www.idrc.ca/sites/default/files/sp/Images/Researching-the-Urban-Dilemma-Baseline-study.pdf, accessed 16 August 2017.

Müller, M. (2012). 'The rise of the penal state in Latin America', *Contemporary Justice Review: Issues in Criminal, Social, and Restorative Justice* 15/1: 57–76.

Mundt, A., Alvarado, R., Fritsch, R., Poblete, C., Villagra, C., et al. (2013). 'Prevalence rates of mental disorders in Chilean prisons', *PLoS ONE* 8/7: e69109.

Muñoz, N. and Welsh, G. (2012). *La pena de multa en Chile y su efecto en la población penal*. [Punishment by fine in Chile and its effect on the prison population]. Report n. 25. Santiago: Fundación Paz Ciudadana. Available at www.pazciudadana.cl/wp-content/uploads/2012/01/conceptos-25-la-pena-de-multa-en-chile.pdf, accessed 16 August 2017.

Murray, J., Farrington, D.P., Sekol, I., and Olsen, R. (2009). *Systematic Review of the Effects of Parental Imprisonment on Child Antisocial Behavior and Mental Health, 1960–2008*. ICPSR31704-v1. Ann Arbor, MI: Inter-University Consortium for Political and Social Research.

National Research Council (2014). *The Growth of Incarceration in the United States: Exploring Causes and Consequences*. Washington, DC: National Academies Press.

Nivette, A.E. and Eisner, M. (2012). 'Do legitimate polities have fewer homicides? A cross-national analysis', *Homicide Studies* 17/1: 3–26.

Núñez, J. Rivera, J., Villavicencio, X., and Molina, O. (2003). 'Determinantes socioeconomicos y demograficos del crimen en Chile. Evidencia desde un panel de datos de las regiones Chilenas' [Socio economic and demographic determinants of crime in Chile. empirical evidence from a panel data set from the regions of Chile], *Estudios de Economia* 30/1: 55–85.

Obando, N. and Ruiz, C. (2007). *Determinantes Socio Economicos de la Delincuencia: una primera aproximacion al problema a nivel provincial* [Socio economic determinants of delinquency: a first aproximation of the problem at a provincial level]. Final report. Lima: CIES (Consorcio de Investigación Económica y Social).

Olate, R., Salas-Wright, C., and Vaughn, M.G. (2012). 'Predictors of violence and delinquency among high risk youth and youth gang members in San Salvador, El Salvador', *International Social Work* 55/3: 383–401.

Oliveira, C.A. (2005). 'Criminalidade e o tamanho das cidades brasileiras: um enfoque da economia do crime' [Crime and city size in Brazil: a crime economics approach], *Anais do XXXIII Encontro Nacional de Economia* [Proceedings of the 33rd Brazilian Economics]: 1–23.

O'Malley, P. (1992). 'Risk, power and crime prevention', *Economy and Society* 21: 252–75.

Open Society Justice Initiative (2014). 'Presumption of guilt the global overuse of pretrial detention'. Available at www.opensocietyfoundations.org/sites/default/files/presumption-guilt-09032014.pdf, accessed 16 August 2017.

Pansters, W. and Castillo Berthier, H. (2007). 'Mexico city', in K. Koonings and D. Kruijt (eds) *Fractured Cities. Social Exclusion, Urban Violence and Contested Spaces in Latin America* London: Zed Books, 36–56.

Pare, P.P. and Felson, R. (2014). 'Income inequality, poverty and crime across nations', *British Journal of Sociology* 65/3: 434–58.

Paternain, R. (2014). 'Políticas de seguridad en el Uruguay: desafíos para los gobiernos de izquierda' [Safety policies in Uruguay: challenges for left wing governments], *Cuestiones de Sociología* 10. Available at www.cuestionessociologia.fahce.unlp.edu.ar/article/view/CSn10a04/6026, accessed 16 August 2017.

Pérez, C (2015). *Las mujeres invisibles: Los costos de la prisión y los efectos indirectos en las mujeres* [Invisible women: the costs of prisons and the indirect effect on women]. Washington, DC: Interamerican Development Bank. Available at https://publications.iadb.org/bitstream/handle/11319/7235/ICS_DP_Las%20_mujeres_invisibles.pdf, accessed 16 August 2017.

Pettit, B. and Sykes, B. (2017). 'Incarceration'. The Stanford Center on Poverty and Inequality. Available at http://inequality.stanford.edu/sites/default/files/Pathways_SOTU_2017_incarceration.pdf, accessed 16 August 2017.

Pinker, S. (2011). *The Better Angels of our Nature*. New York: Viking.

Piotrowska, P., Stride, C., Croft, S., and Rowe, R. (2015). 'Socioeconomic status and antisocial behaviour among children and adolescents: a systematic review and meta-analysis', *Clinical Psychology Review* 35: 47–55.

Pondé, M., Freire, A., and Mendonca, M. (2011). 'The prevalence of mental disorders in prisoners in the city of Salvador, Bahia, Brazil'. *Journal of Forensic Science* 56: 679–82.

Pratt, D., Piper, M., Appleby, L., Webb, R., and Shaw, J. (2006). 'Suicide in recently released prisoners: a population-based cohort study', *Lancet* 368/9530: 119–23.

Pratt, J. (2007). *Penal Populism*. Oxford: Routledge.

Ramírez, L. (2014). 'Crimen y Economia: Analisis de la Tasa de Homicidio en Mexico a partir de variables economicas (2000, 2005, 2010)' [Crime and the economy: analysis of the homicide rates in Mexico based on economic variables] (2000, 2005, 2010), *Estudios Sociologicos* XXXII/ 96: 505–40.

Ramos, S. and Musumeci, L. (2005). 'Elemento suspeito: abordagem policial e discriminação na cidade do Rio de Janeiro' [Suspended aspects: police approach and discrimination in the city of Rio de Janeiro], *Civilização Brasileira* 229–81.

Raphael, S. (2011). 'Incarceration and Prisoner Reentry in the United States', *The ANNALS of the American Academy of Political and Social Science* 635/1; 192–215.

Reiner, R. (2007). *Law and Order*. Cambridge: Polity.

Ribeiro, C.A. (1995). *Cor e Criminalidade. Estudo e Análise da Justiça no Rio de Janeiro (1900–1930)* [Skin colour and criminality. Study and analysis of justice in Rio de Janeiro (1900–1930)]. Rio de Janeiro: Editora UFRJ.

Ribeiro, E., Borges, D., and Cano, I. (2015). *Calidad de los Datos de Homicidio en America Latina* [Quality of homicide data in Latin America]. Final report. Rio de Janeiro: LAV, Rio de Janeiro State University.

Rivera, M. (2016). 'The sources of social violence in Latin America: an empirical analysis of homicide rates, 1980–2010', *Journal of Peace Research* 53/1: 84–99.

Rodgers, D., Muggah, R., and Stevenson, C. (2009). 'Gangs of Central America: causes, costs, and interventions'. Small Arms Survey, Occasional Paper 23. Geneva: Small Arms Survey. Available at www.smallarmssurvey.org/fileadmin/docs/B-Occasional-papers/SAS-OP23-Gangs-Central-America.pdf, accessed 16 August 2017.

Rubio, P.M. (1997). 'Los costos de la violencia en América Latina' [The costs of violence in Latin America], *World* 3: 1–27. Available at www.ops.org.bo/textocompleto/ivi27768.pdf, accessed 16 August 2017.

Rusche, G. and Kirchheimer, O. (1984). *Pena y estructura social*. Bogotá: Temis.

Santamaría, G. (2013). 'La difusión y contención del crimen organizado en la subregión México-Centroamérica' [The dissemination and containment of organized crime in the Mexico-Central America sub-region], en Eric Olson y Juan Carlos Garzón (eds) *The Criminal Diaspora: The Spread of Transnational Organized Crime and How to Contain its Expansion*. Washington, DC: Woodrow Wilson Center.

Savenije, W. and van der Borgh, C. (2014). 'De-securitising and re-securitising gang policies: the Funes Government and gangs in El Salvador', *Journal of Latin American Studies* 47/01: 1–28.

Shaw, J., Baker, D., Hunt, I.M., Moloney, A., and Appleby, L. (2004). 'Suicide by prisoners: national clinical survey', *British Journal of Psychiatry* 184/MAR: 263–7.

Snowball, L. and Weatherburn, D. (2006). *Indigenous Over-Representation in Prison: The Role of Offender Characteristics*. Sydney, NSW: NSW Bureau of Crime Statistics and Research. Available at www.bocsar.nsw.gov.au/Documents/CJB/cjb99.pdf, accessed 16 August 2017.

Soares, R. (2004). 'Development, crime and punishment: accounting for the international differences in crime rates', *Journal of Development Economics* 73/1: 155–84.

Soares, R. and Naritomi, J. (2010). 'Understanding high crime rates in Latin America: the role of social and policy factors', in Di Tella, Rafael, Edwards, S., and Schargrodsky, E. (eds) *The Economics of Crime: Lessons for and from Latin America*. Chicago, IL: University of Chicago Press, 19–55.

Solis, J.M. and Torre, V. (2016). 'Demócratas pero Violentos: Una Aproximación a las Variables Estructurales para Entender la Inseguridad en América Latina' [Democrats but violent: an approach to structural variables to understand insecurity in Latin America], *Revista Mexicana de Análisis Político y Administración Pública* IV/I: 29–62.

Spinelli, H., Macías, G., and Darraidou, V. (2008). 'Procesos macroeconómicos y homicidios. Un estudio ecológico en los partidos del Gran Buenos Aires (Argentina) entre los años 1989 y 2006' [Macroeconomic processes and homicides. An ecological study in Greater Buenos Aires (Argentina) between 1989 and 2006], *Salud Colectiva* 4/3: 283–99.

Steen S., Engen R.L., and Gainey R.R. (2005). 'Images of danger and culpability: racial stereotyping, case processing, and criminal sentences', *Criminology* 43/2: 435–67.

Strazza, L., Massad, E., Azebedo, R., and Carvalho, H. (2007). 'Estudo de comportamento associado à infecção pelo HIV e HCV em detentas de um presídio de São Paulo, Brasil' [Study of behavior associated with HIV and HCV infection in prison inmates of São Paulo, Brazil], *Cad. Saúde Pública* 23/1: 197–205.

Swanson, K. (2013). 'Zero tolerance in Latin America: punitive paradox in urban policy mobilities', *Urban Geography* 34/7: 972–88.

Tankebe, J. and Liebling, A. (2013). *Legitimacy and Criminal Justice. An International Exploration*. Oxford: Oxford University Press.

Thornberry, T. and Krohn, M. (2000). 'The self-report method for measuring delinquency and crime', in *Measurement and Analysis of Crime and Justice*. Rockville, MD: National Institute of Justice, 33–83.

Tittle, C. and Meier, R. (1990). 'Specifying the SES/delinquency relationship', *Criminology* 28/2: 271–99.

Tonry, M. (1995). *Malign Neglect: Race, Crime, and Punishment in America*. Oxford: Oxford University Press.

Tonry, M. (2011). *Punishing Race*. New York: Oxford University Press.

Tonry, M. (2014). 'Why crime rates are falling throughout the western world', *Crime and Justice* 43/1: 1–63.

Transparency International (2013). Corruption Perception INDEX 2013. Available at www.transparency.org, accessed 16 August 2017.

Transparency International (2015). Corruption Perception INDEX 2015. Available at www.transparency.org, accessed 16 August 2017.

UNDP (UN Development Programme) (2014). 'Citizen security with a human face: evidence and proposals for Latin America'. Available at http://hdr.undp.org/sites/default/files/citizen_security_with_a_human_face_-executivesummary.pdf, accessed 16 August 2017.

Ungar, M. (2007). 'The privatization of citizen security in Latin America: from elite guards to neighborhood vigilantes', *Social Justice* 34: 20–37.

UNODC (UN Office on Drugs and Crime) (2011). *Global Study on Homicide*. Geneva: UNODC. Available at www.ncbi.nlm.nih.gov/pubmed/22057928, accessed February 2016.

UNODC (UN Office on Drugs and Crime) (2014). *UNODC Global Study on Homicide 2013*. Geneva: UNODC. Available at www.unodc.org/documents/data-andanalysis/statistics/GSH2013/2014_GLOBAL_HOMICIDE_BOOK_web.pdf, accessed February 2016.

UNODC (UN Office on Drugs and Crime (2015). *Standard Minimum Rules for the Treatment of Prisoners*. Geneva: UNODC. Available at www.unodc.org/pdf/criminal_justice/UN_Standard_Minimum_Rules_for_the_Treatment_of_Prisoners.pdf, accessed 16 August 2017.

Valenzuela, E., Marcazollo, X., Stuven, A.M., Larroulet, P., and Simonetti, E. (2012). *Impacto social de la prisión femenina en Chile. Propuestas para Chile, Políticas Públicas* [Social impact of female prison in Chile. Proposals for Chile, Public Policies], Pontificia Universidad Católica de Chile'. Available at http://politicaspublicas.uc.cl/wp-content/uploads/2015/02/propuestas-para-chile-2012-capitulo-ix.pdf, accessed 16 August 2017.

van Wilsem, J. (2004). 'Criminal victimization in cross-national perspective: an analysis of rates of theft, violence and vandalism across 27 countries', *European Journal of Criminology* 1/1: 89–109.

Vera, J.Á., Bautista, G., Ramírez, M., and Yáñez, A.I. (2012). 'Relación entre anomia social, alienación y conducta antisocial en jóvenes infractores mexicanos', [Relationship between social anomy, alienation and antisocial behavior in young Mexican offenders], *Revista Latinoamericana en Ciencias Sociales, Niñez y Juventud* 10/2: 943–55.

Vernazza, L. (2015). 'El dilema de las politicas de seguridad en los gobiernos de izquierda. Uruguay 2005–2014' [The dilemma of security policies in left governments. Uruguay 2005–2014]. MPhil thesis en Desarrollo Humano, FLACSO, Buenos Aires, Argentina, 73–7.

Vilalta, C. (2015). *Tendencias y proyecciones globales en la violencia homicida: 2000 a 2030. Notas de Homicidios 2 del Instituto Igarapé* [Global tendencies and projections of lethal violence: 2000–2030. Notes of homicides 2 from Igarapé Institute], Rio de Janeiro. Available at https://igarape.org.br/wp-content/uploads/2016/04/Homicide-Dispatch_2_ES-22-04-16.pdf, accessed February 2016.

Wacquant, L. (2009). *Prisons of Poverty*. Minneapolis, MN: University of Minnesota Press.

Wacquant, L. (2010). *Castigar a los pobres* [Punishing the poor]. Barcelona: Gedisa.

Wakefield, S. and Uggen, C. (2010). 'Incarceration and stratification', *Annual Review of Sociology* 36: 387–406.

Western, Bruce (2006). *Punishment and Inequality in America*. New York: Russell Sage Foundation.

Whitworth, A. (2013). 'Local inequality and crime: exploring how variation in the scale of inequality measures affects relationships between inequality and crime', *Urban Studies* 50/4: 725–41.

WHO (World Health Organization) (2000). *Preventing Suicide: A Resource for Prison Officers*. Geneva: WHO Mental and Behavioural Disorders Team. Available at https://apps.who.int/iris/handle/10665/66725, accessed 22 July 2019.

Wildeman, C. (2010). 'Paternal incarceration and children's physically aggressive behaviors: evidence from the Fragile Families and Child Wellbeing Study', *Social Forces* 89/1: 285–310.

World Prison Brief (2016). Available at www.prisonstudies.org, accessed 16 August 2017.

Wright, B.R., Caspi, A., Moffitt, T.E., Miech, R.A., and Silva, P.A. (1999). 'Reconsidering the relationship between SES and delinquency: causation but not correlation'. *Criminology* 37: 175–94.

Wright, R., Tekin, E., Topalli, V., McClellan, C., Dickinson, T., and Rosenfeld,R. (2017). 'Less cash, less crime: evidence from the Electronic Benefit Transfer Program', *Journal of Law and Economics* 60/2: 361–83.

Young, J. (2004). 'Voodoo criminology and the numbers game', in J. Ferrell, K. Hayward, W. Morrison, and M. Presdee (eds) Cultural Criminology Unleashed. London: Glass House Press, 1–26.

Zedner, L. (2002). 'Dangers of dystopia in penal theory', *Oxford Journal of Legal Studies* 22: 341–61.

Zepeda, R. and Jimenez, P. (2016). 'Impunidad frente al homicidio doloso en México, Impunidad Cero' [Impunity against intentional homicide in Mexico, zero impunity]. Available at www.impunidadcero.org/articulo.php?id=20&t=impunidad-frente-al-homicidio-doloso-en-mexico, accessed 16 August 2017.

28 Political economy of inequality in Chile: historical institutions, taxation, and elite power

Javier González

The owners of Chile are ourselves, the owners of capital and of the soil:
the rest is masses who can be influenced and sold;
they do not matter either as opinion or as prestige.

Eduardo Matte, Member of Chilean Elite, 1892

Introduction

Chile has usually been considered a development success story within the Latin American region for its consolidated democracy, social stability, and sustained economic growth. In 2010, Chile became the first South American country to join the Organisation for Economic Cooperation and Development (OECD); in 2012, the World Bank classified it for the first time as a 'high-income' country, achieving the highest GDP (PPP) per capita in the region (World Bank 2015).

Despite these achievements, Chile seems to manifest two important paradoxes: first, behind its general façade of progress and prosperity, it hides a much more complex reality characterized by inequality and social injustice; second, over the last decades, Chile has embodied a unique case of high levels of inequality combined with relatively low levels of social conflict. The latter have only come to emerge since 2011.

What are the underlying roots of inequality in Chile? Why does an important part of Chilean society seem to be at ease with such high levels of social injustice?[1] This chapter attempts to provide a conceptual framework and key clues for answering these important questions. The chapter is organized in four parts: the first provides a brief account of the

[1] Since 2011, part of Chilean society has actively mobilized; since 2017, a new left-wing coalition, which strongly critiques the current state of affairs, was created (Frente Amplio). Finally, in October 2019, Chile experienced the largest social crisis and public demonstrations in decades. This chapter was written in 2017 and updated in October 2019, before being published in 2020. Thus, at the time of its completion, it is still too soon to assess its impact in the long term.

Javier González, *Political economy of inequality in Chile: historical institutions, taxation, and elite power* In: *Handbook of BRICS and Emerging Economies.* Edited by: P.B. Anand, Shailaja Fennell, and Flavio Comim, Oxford University Press (2021).
DOI: 10.1093/oso/9780198827535.003.0028

levels of inequality of outcomes and opportunity in Chile; the second section critically analyses a variety of myths usually used to justify high levels of inequality, while also presenting an institutional analysis framework to aid better understanding of inequality in Chile; the third discusses drivers of institutional change and the role of different dimensions of power in the configuration and maintenance of unequal institutions and low levels of social conflict; the fourth and final part briefly summarizes the discussion.

Chile: a case study of extreme social inequality

Chile represents an extreme case of inequality worldwide. Its income distribution ranks as the eighteenth most unequal among 154 countries for which comparable data are available (World Bank 2017). In 2015, its Gini coefficient reached 0.48 (CEPAL 2017). This level is similar to the Latin American average—which, as a region, is ranked as the most unequal in the world (de Ferranti et al. 2004; Lustig 2015).

These elevated levels of income inequality are not a recent phenomenon, but one that has characterized Chilean society since its origins. Although historical data are scarce, recent research efforts have allowed estimating income Gini coefficients that extend as far as the second half of the nineteenth century (Rodriguez Weber 2017).

As Figure 28.1 shows, despite medium run variations (in some cases important ones, such as the egalitarian gains experienced between 1933 and 1973), income inequality has steadily fluctuated between 0.5 and 0.6 Gini coefficient points over the last 160 years.

From this perspective, although it is a fact that the levels of inequality have decreased in the last 25 years from 0.52 Gini points in 1990 to 0.48 in 2015 (UNDP 2017), this 'medium-term' trend should not encourage excessive degrees of triumphalism. Indeed,

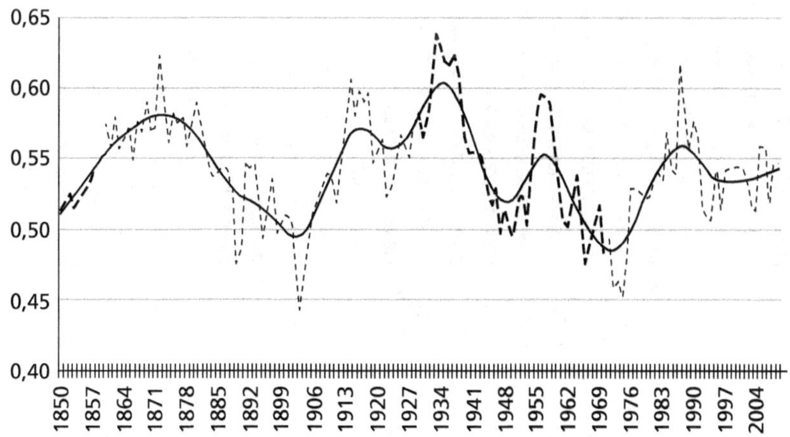

Figure 28.1 Historical evolution of personal income distribution in Chile: Gini coefficient 1850–2009

Source: Rodriguez Weber (2017).

inequality levels in Chile are still exceptionally high by any world standard, and are still located within the country's historical bounds.

There is no doubt that economic growth experienced in the last two decades has contributed to increase the quality of life of those at the bottom of the income distribution. Poverty rates have fallen from 68 per cent in 1990 to 11.7 per cent in 2015 (UNDP 2017). Nevertheless, national income has historically been—and continues to be—largely captured by those in the top 1 per cent of the distribution: the local elites.

Indeed, Lopez et al. (2013) estimate the proportion of GDP accrued by individuals in the top 1 per cent of income distribution during the 2005–10 period, observing that the richest percentile successfully captured 21.1 per cent of GDP. This proportion reaches 30.5 per cent when capital gains are properly included.

When comparing Lopez et al.'s (2013) estimates with the latest comparable data made available for several countries in the World Top Incomes Database (2015), as shown in Figure 28.2, it may be concluded that the Chilean case represents a unique case of income concentration.

The Chilean elite is capable of capturing 19 per cent more income, in relative terms, than its peers in the United States and even 252 per cent more than those in Denmark.

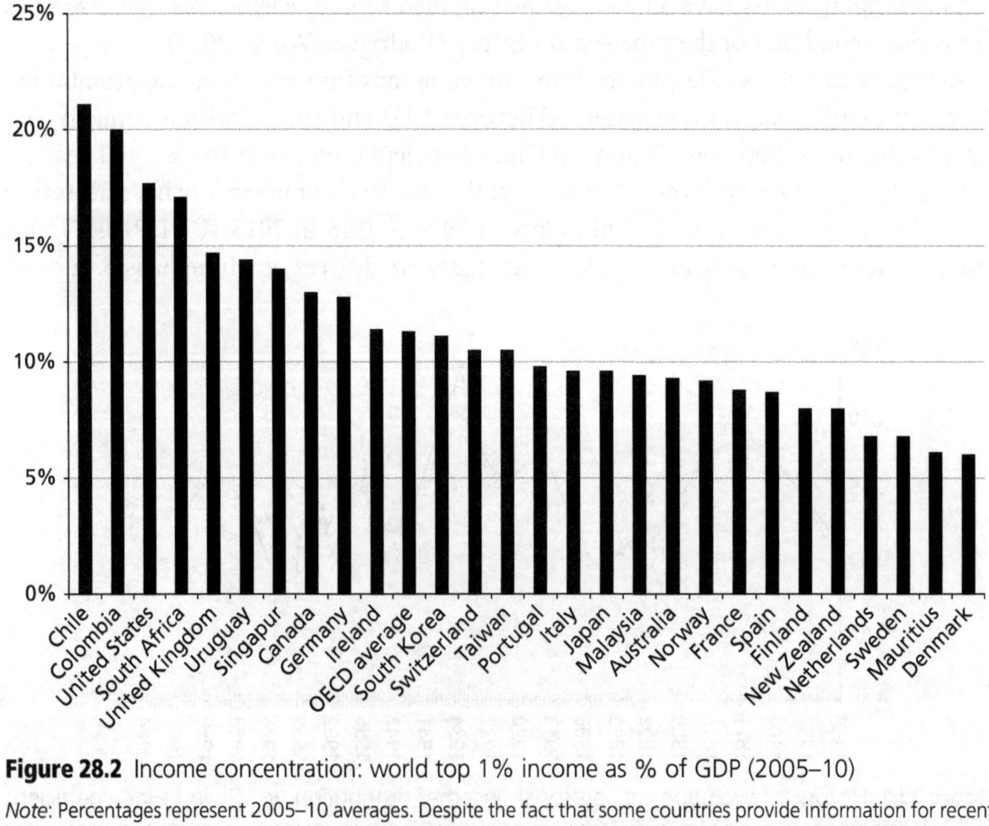

Figure 28.2 Income concentration: world top 1% income as % of GDP (2005–10)

Note: Percentages represent 2005–10 averages. Despite the fact that some countries provide information for recent years, the period 2005–10 is used in order to analyse a comparable interval considering data availability for most countries in the sample.

Source: Author's elaboration, based on the World Top Incomes Database (2015) and Lopez et al. (2013).

When compared with the average, Chilean elites accrue 87 per cent more income as a percentage of GDP than the average of those other countries in the sample. In conclusion, Chile's income concentration at the top of the distribution is the highest, considering those countries for which comparable data are available.

Some may argue that the high levels of income concentration observed in Chile could be explained by its lower stage of development. Nevertheless, if current Chilean concentration rates are compared with the historical concentration rates observed in OECD countries, i.e. when both shared a similar level of development (in terms of GDP per capita), the opposite conclusion is reached: Chile seems to be comparatively even more unequal than OECD countries, when these had Chile's current GDP per capita.

In fact, Figure 28.3 presents the level of income concentration at the top 1 per cent when OECD countries had a similar GDP per capita (PPP) to Chile's in 2013 – the year

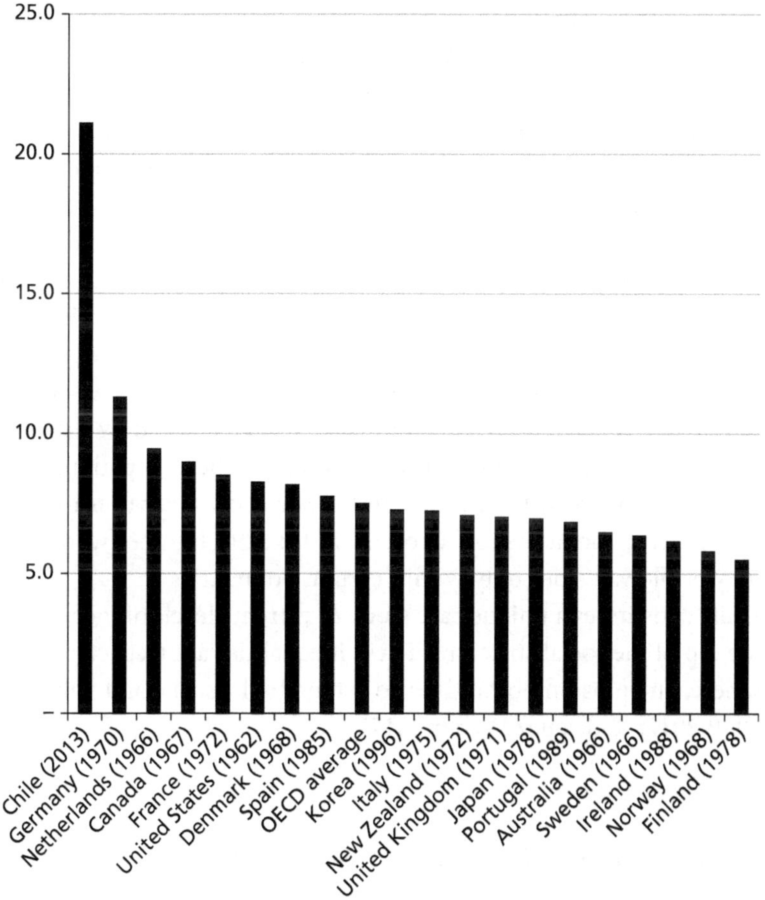

Figure 28.3 Top 1 % incomes when OECD countries had GDP per capita similar to Chile in 2013

Note: Years in which each country had the same GDP per capita (PPP), at constant prices 2005, are shown in parentheses. OECD average excludes Chile. Figures for the Netherlands, Norway, Sweden, and United States are based on author's estimates of GDP per capita (PPP), at constant prices.

Source: Author's calculations based on the World Top Incomes Database (2015) and Lopez et al. (2013).

after Chile officially became a high-income country, according to the World Bank classification. As this exercise shows, while Chile's elite accrued over 20 per cent of GDP, the elites of OECD countries were only able to capture 7.5 per cent of GDP, when they all had a similar GDP per capita (PPP) to Chile's in 2013. Therefore, it would seem that it is not a problem linked to Chile's development stage.

The extreme concentration in the upper tail of the distribution should be a matter of serious concern, as it is a key determinant of the overall distribution. Palma (2011) presents robust evidence showing that income inequality derives basically from a struggle between the top and bottom tails of the income distribution. He reveals the existence of two contradictory forces that constitute a common characteristic of distribution around the world: on the one hand, a centripetal force operating to create a uniform pattern across countries, where 50 per cent of the population, the one located between the 5th and 9th income deciles, obtains half of national incomes; on the other, a centrifugal force, which explains inequality differences observed between countries. These differences are the result of distribution struggles between the richest decile (10th) and the four poorest (1st to 4th deciles). The asymmetric power relations between these segments determine how the remaining 50 per cent of national income is distributed. Therefore, the welfare of the bottom and upper classes is intimately intertwined.

Not only is the inequality of outcomes stark, but the inequality of opportunities as well. This should be expected, since international evidence shows that countries with high levels of income inequality tend to have lower intergenerational income mobility (Corak, 2013). Indeed, estimates show that Chile has lower levels of income mobility than several developing and developed countries, for which data is available (Nuñez and Risco, 2004; Corak, 2013). Similarly, Torche (2005) studies the levels of social mobility in Chile concluding that the pattern of class mobility is 'characterised by a strong barrier to mobility to and from the professional class at the top of the occupational structure but much higher fluidity between the middle and lower classes, a pattern consistent with high income concentration at the top' (Torche, 2014: 629). In other words, intergenerational mobility is allowed—but only within certain boundaries.

In sum, Chile constitutes a unique case study of extreme levels of inequality and social rigidity at the top of the social structure. These inequalities are restricted not only to the economic sphere, but, most importantly, also extend to the social and political spheres of society (UNDP 2017; Rodriguez Weber 2017).

Justifications of inequality in society: myths meet reality

There are four main types of explanation provided by the economic discipline to justify high levels of inequality: the first argues that inequality is necessary for economic development; the second argues that it is a normal and predictable consequence of development; the third emphasizes its inevitability due to the existence of forces beyond human control (e.g. globalization and skill-biased technological change); the fourth explanation highlights the importance of historical paths and underlying institutions. This latter argument may be separated in two sub-explanations: path dependency and institutional change-based explanations. This section explores the explanatory power of each one of these hypotheses in light of recent comparative evidence.

GROWTH-PRECONDITION MYTH: INEQUALITY IS NECESSARY FOR ECONOMIC DEVELOPMENT

Classical and several neoclassical economists have believed that inequality is necessary to generate incentives, stimulate investment, and promote economic growth. Supporters of this view tend to argue that Chile's high levels of inequality have been necessary to sustain high economic growth rates. In fact, when Friedrich Hayek visited Chile in the 1980s he declared in an interview:

> As I have argued on other occasions, if redistribution were equal there would be less to redistribute as it is precisely the inequality of income which allows the current levels of production. (Reality 1981, cited in Cristi 2000: 23–58)

This line of thought is not new: it may be tracked back through the history of economic thought. Classical economists, such as David Ricardo (1817), divided society into three main social classes (landlords, capitalists, and workers). According to his view, income concentration in the hands of the capitalists fostered economic growth, as they would reinvest their profits and put them to good use in productive activities. Keeping profit rates high was the key mechanism for promoting the process of capital accumulation. In fact, rising wages, which had the effect of reducing profit rates, constituted a threat to economic growth (Ricardo, 1817; Kaldor, 1955). Moreover, landlords and workers would tend to spend their income, due to their higher marginal propensity to consume, making no contribution to capital accumulation (Chang, 2011). From this perspective, transferring income to the working class would only reduce economic growth.

Neoclassical economists, such as Okun (1975), reformulated the classical paradigm by arguing for the existence of a trade-off between efficiency and equality: reducing inequality could only be achieved at a large cost in terms of efficiency. Accordingly, Friedman and Friedman (1980: 136–7) argued that it was 'important to recognise how much we benefit from the very unfairness we deplore'. Following this line, International Financial Institutions (such as the IMF and the World Bank) tried, in the context of the so-called Washington Consensus, to legitimate inequality as a socially beneficial phenomenon which created the right incentives and rewarded individuals for their effort, risk-taking, creativity, and entrepreneurship. This view has changed in recent years (cf. Berg and Ostry 2011).

Indeed, both classical and neoclassical approaches are flawed for several reasons. First, historical evidence disproves these theoretical hypotheses. For example, during the three golden decades that followed the Second World War, developed countries experienced substantial improvements in the distribution of income, matched by elevated growth rates (Piketty 2014). Similarly, the increased income concentration that has been observed in developed nations since the 1980s, especially at the top 1 per cent of incomes, has been accompanied by lower growth rates (Chang 2011). Moreover, recent comparative evidence using large panel data shows that high inequality is bad for growth. In fact, Alesina and Rodrik (1994) have found that higher levels of income and land inequality tend to be associated with lower economic growth rates. Similarly, Cornia (2004), analysing data for more than seventy countries, finds that economic growth rates tend to be hindered when inequality reaches a certain threshold (Gini coefficient above 0.45). Finally, Berg and Ostry (2011), using large panel data of countries, demonstrate that countries with high levels of inequality are unable to sustain long periods of high economic growth. In conclusion, high inequality affects not only the rate of growth, but also its sustainability over time.

Second, capitalists do not necessarily have a compulsion towards investment and innovation, especially in Latin America. Palma (2011) shows that private investment—as a percentage of the income share of the top decile in the extremely unequal Latin America—is less than half of what is observed in more egalitarian East Asian countries. Latin American capitalists, despite their elevated share in total income, do not seem to be pulling the wagon of investment and growth.

Third, high inequality may create the problem of insufficient demand and macroeconomic instability. Karl Marx argued that excessive income concentration at the top of the social structure, to the detriment of the middle and working class, would tend to engender an economic crisis due to a lack of effective demand and inability to realize surplus value (Kaldor 1955; Harvey 2010). Also, since high-income individuals tend to have a higher marginal propensity to save (Dynan et al. 2004), some economists argue that the higher current levels of inequality are promoting aggregate demand insufficiencies, lower economic growth rates, and macroeconomic instability (Stiglitz 2012).

Fourth, and most importantly, high inequality and the resulting disproportionate empowerment of the economic elites enables these high-net-worth individuals to accumulate power to distort political and economic institutions (laws, regulations, government policies, etc.), giving way to monopolistic and rent-seeking behaviour that negatively affects economic growth (Frank, 1971; Knight 1992; Acemoglu and Robinson 2012; Stiglitz 2012).

Fifth, high levels of inequality negatively impact human capital formation, as has been evidenced in the case of Latin America in general, and Chile in particular (Engerman et al. 2009). Evidence shows that in the presence of credit constraints, high levels of inequality prevent a portion of the population from making optimal human capital investment decisions and therefore is detrimental to human capital formation and economic growth (Galor 2012). Moreover, a high level of concentration at the top of the income distribution usually allows elites to opt-out of public education and enrol in exclusive private schools. Consequently, elites have less incentive to pay taxes to fund public education, hindering the long-run development and quality of this education sector. Moreover, some authors argue that, in the context of high levels of inequality, privileged individuals are able to lobby against redistributive policies, such as schooling, hindering human capital investment and economic development (Saint Paul and Verdier 1996; Benabou 2000, 2002).

Finally, evidence also shows that high inequality is not only bad for economic growth, but also for society as a whole (not only those at the bottom). It leads to increasing levels of crime, health problems, education inequality, social cohesion, and erosion of trust and democracy (Boix 2003; Acemoglu and Robinson 2006; Wilkinson and Pickett 2009). As Wilkinson and Pickett (2009: 28) conclude, 'at almost any income level, it's better to live in a more equal place'.

PREDICTABILITY MYTH: INEQUALITY LEVELS ARE FIXED OR FOLLOW AN EXPECTED PATTERN AS A CONSEQUENCE OF THE ECONOMIC DEVELOPMENT PROCESS

Distributional concerns were essential for classical economists working in the nineteenth century. Ricardo (1817: 5) argues that 'to determine the laws which regulate this distribution (rents, profits and wages), is the principal problem in Political Economy'. Nevertheless, this problem was mostly neglected during the twentieth century by the discipline of economics (Milanovic 2011). The main reason may probably be found in the works of Vilfredo Pareto and Simon Kuznets.

Analysing limited data from the late nineteenth century, Pareto (1906 [2006]) argues that the distribution of income in different European countries follows an almost inevitable pattern, which could be translated into a universal rule: the '80/20 law'. That is, the richest 20 per cent of the population owned 80 per cent of wealth, independent of the institutional framework in place in each country. Pareto thus argued that inequality was fixed in time and place. Elites could circulate, they could rotate, but inequality among groups would be preserved as old classes were overthrown and new ones took their place. Inequality was an unshakable natural fact of social life.

This changed later with the famous work of Kuznets (1955: 26), who argued, with very limited available data,[2] that there was a certain pattern relating the distribution of income to the economic development process of a country. Contrary to Pareto's law,

[2] According to Kuznets (1955: 26), his paper was '5 per cent empirical information and 95 per cent in speculation, some of it possibly tainted by wishful thinking'.

inequality was not fixed in time; however, it would seem to follow a common pattern—an inverted 'U'—in relation to the country's developmental stage. In Kuznets (1955: 18) own words: 'One might thus assume a long swing in the inequality characterizing the secular income structure: widening in the early phases of economic growth when the transition from the pre-industrial to the industrial civilization was most rapid; becoming stabilized for a while; and then narrowing in the later phases'. Moreover, Kuznets (1955: 20) argued that 'the long swing in income inequality must be viewed as part of a wider process of economic growth'. In other words, inequality was mainly determined by the economic pathway of each country (beyond the impact of other social and political factors). According to this author, on the one hand, the main underlying factors negatively affecting the distribution of income were related to the higher marginal propensity to save of upper-income groups, and the process of urbanization and industrialization (related to inter- and intra-sector income differences). On the other hand, the counteracting factors positively reducing income inequalities were related to expected modernization factors, such as the increasing weight of incomes from the service sector which depended on human capital and talent (as opposed to the relevance of capital gains during the industrialization phases), and the increasing social and economic dynamism due to entrepreneurship and the rapid creation of new industries. Beyond economic factors, Kuznets also recognized the relevance of the political and social pressure promoted by lower-income groups. This pressure accumulated during the initial phases of the economic development process and then, in the later phases, was used to mobilize 'legislative interference and political decisions' that affected the income share of privileged groups, as the country moved towards higher economic levels (Kuznets 1955: 9). However, under Kuznets's perspective, social and political pressures were rather predictable outcomes of economic progress (normal dynamics of a 'free economic society'). Moreover, although he recognized that the 'legislative interferences' resulting from political tensions played a role during the downward phase of Kuznets's inverted U, he did not see them as the ultimate drivers of inequality reduction (Kuznets 1955: 18–19).[3]

This theory had a harmful impact on policymakers and neoclassical economists. On the one hand, it suggested that inequality should not constitute an urgent matter of concern for policymakers, since inequality would tend to diminish in the long-run as the development process picks up. On the other hand, neoclassical economists have usually used this argument to dismiss the importance of devoting time and effort to understanding the underlying forces of the distribution of income. In Lucas's (2004) own

[3] Kuznets (1955: 18–19) stated that 'if there is some evidence for assuming this long swing in relative inequality in the distribution of income before direct taxes and excluding free benefits from government, there is surely a stronger case for assuming a long swing in inequality of income net of direct taxes and including government benefits. Progressivity of income taxes and, indeed, their very importance characterize only the more recent phases of development of the presently developed countries; in narrowing income inequality they must have accentuated the downward phase of the long swing'. In other words, policy changes supported and accentuated the downward phase of the curve, but did not cause it.

words, 'of the tendencies that are harmful to sound economics, the most seductive, and in my opinion the most poisonous, is to focus on questions of distribution'.

However, Kuznets's thesis has been discredited due to the substantial increase in the quality and quantity of longitudinal data available (Bruno et al. 1998; Ferreira and Ravallion, 2009; Piketty 2014), showing that there is no deterministic relation between levels of economic development and income distribution across countries. As Piketty (2014: 14–15) argues, 'the theory of the Kuznets curve was a product of the Cold War . . . the magical Kuznets curve theory was formulated in large part for the wrong reasons, and its empirical underpinnings were extremely fragile'. The evidence shown by Piketty debunks the inevitability of declining inequalities in wealthy countries, and demonstrates how easily egalitarian gains may be reversed. Similarly, Rodriguez Weber (2017) convincingly show that, in the case of Chile, inequality has not followed a predetermined pattern. In fact, for example, the egalitarian gains obtained between the mid-1930s and early 1970s were rapidly reversed between the mid-1970s and 1980s. Moreover, it must also be pointed out that the inequality decline (the downward slope) that Kuznets observed in his study occurred when developed countries were much poorer than emerging countries, such as Chile, are today. Thus, if inequality was predictably bounded to decrease with development, as observed in Europe after the 1940s, it should have strongly decreased several decades ago in Chile—a trend only observed since the 2000s.

Indeed, examining the evolution of inequality in Chile during the last 160 years, the data demonstrate no clear relation between levels of development and inequality (as shown in Figure 28.1). As a result, today we know that patterns of inequality are neither fixed (à la Pareto) nor follow a predetermined trajectory (à la Kuznets).

INEVITABILITY MYTH: INEQUALITY IS A PHENOMENON CAUSED BY FORCES BEYOND HUMAN CONTROL

One of the main explanations often used to justify the increasingly high levels of inequality is based on the 'skill-biased technological change' hypothesis (Berman et al. 1998; Katz and Autor 1999; Blau and Kahn 2009). According to this view, technological change has revolutionized the global economy—and with it, the type of job requirements and workers needed to function adequately in this new scenario. Technology requires skilled workers who know how to operate new machines and computers in the workplace. By contrast, technological change would tend to substitute unskilled workers who perform routine manual and non-manual tasks (Autor et al. 2003). As a result of this skill-biased technological change, relative demand for skilled workers has strongly increased relative to unskilled workers, driving skill premia and education returns upwards (Blau and Kahn 2009). Consequently, this wage gap between skilled and unskilled workers would be the main source of wage inequality. Since technological change is a phenomenon beyond the direct control of society and government, it is argued that inequality cannot be constrained.

Historical empirical evidence shows that technological progress does not need to breed higher levels of inequality, however. Skill premia are driven by the interaction between relative (skilled/unskilled) labour demand and supply. While technological change mainly affects the demand side, its final impact on skill premia and wage inequality is nevertheless determined by what happens on the supply side. For example, as Goldin and Katz (2008) demonstrate, during the decades that followed the Second World War, the US government enacted vital legislation and committed substantial public funds to promote higher education participation. This public support radically increased the number of college graduates, which allowed outpacing the relative increase of demand for skilled labour. As a result, skills premia decreased and wage inequality declined until around 1980, when the supply of graduates started to slow down (Goldin and Katz 2008). Similarly, Sapelli (2011) analyses income distribution trends in Chile by age cohorts, and finds a decline among those cohorts born after the late 1950s due to the expansion of average education and the reduction of education attainment dispersion among individuals.

Other and new inevitability myths and sentiments arise as globalization produces radical transformations in local economies and geographies, promoted by the deregulated global financial capital sector, which creates new forms—visible and invisible—of expulsion of individuals from a sustainable society (Sassen 2014). These forms of expulsions are happening as a consequence of, among others, the shrinking of the economies due to the monopolization of knowledge and technologies by a global elite (with the resulting increase in unemployment); the exclusion of small farmers due to global land markets, which expel communities from their territories; the pervasive financialization of the economy; and the biodegradation of the environment, due to new technologies in several sectors, e.g. the mining sector. However, once again, none of these occur in the void. In fact, according to Sassen (2014: 2), 'these expulsions are made. The instruments for this making range from elementary policies to complex institutions, systems, and techniques that require specialized knowledge and intricate organizational formats'. As a result, they may and can be regulated and controlled with new and proper mechanisms. The problem is that many times regulations and mechanisms do not exist or they need to go beyond national boundaries, and thus global coordinating bodies to regulate multinational corporations are needed.

To be sure, technological change and globalization should not unequivocally translate into higher levels of inequality. It is how society responds to them that matters. Education, labour, tax, and social policies are key determinants of the primary and secondary distribution of income. Markets do not function in the void; they are embedded in social institutions (Polanyi 1944).

TOWARDS A COMPREHENSIVE CONCEPTUAL FRAMEWORK: THE KEY ROLE OF PATH DEPENDENCY AND INSTITUTIONS

As discussed, the manner in which societies have explained and justified inequality has changed throughout human history. Although neoclassical economists have tended to disregard the central role of institutions, it has not been the case in other disciplines. Indeed, the preponderance of institutionally driven theories may be tracked across social sciences and humanities, all seeking to understand the origins of inequality among individuals.[4]

In the field of political philosophy, Jean Jacques Rousseau (1755) argued that men were in essence equal, challenging the Aristotelian theory of natural inequalities which had been widely accepted for two millennia. According to Rousseau, inequality arose from private property and men's propensity to constantly seek ways of distinguishing themselves from others. Inequality persisted over time because the powerful and rich were able to shape institutions to protect their interests. As a result of this view, inequality may be seen as a phenomenon that is both socially structured and structural: the former because inequality arises from unequal social interactions and relations of power, i.e. it is not a natural fact of life; the latter because these asymmetries are translated and solidified in institutions, which embody and reproduce the very same asymmetries that gave them birth. Such is the importance accrued to institutions in political philosophy that they constitute not only the main cause of the origins of inequality but also of injustice. In Rawls's (1971: 102) own words, 'the natural distribution is neither just nor unjust; nor is it unjust that persons are born into society at some particular positions. These are simply natural facts. What is just and unjust is the way that institutions deal with these facts'.

Institutions have also played a central role in founding sociological theories. On the one hand, Marx (1976 [1867]) claimed that private property (which allowed the control of means of production) and the division of labour were key elements engendering exploitation and alienation of the proletariat by the capitalist class. Although for Marx it was the economic base that shaped cultural, social, and political institutions (the superstructure), the latter also played a vital role in reinforcing inequalities. Most importantly, this account assumes that capitalists control the state in order to shape laws and regulations, allowing them to protect their class interests and become the de facto *ruling class* (Wright 2005; Keister and Southgate 2012).

Weber (1922 [1978]) views inequality and social stratification as a process arising from power struggles occurring in the economic, social, and political sphere of society. For him, economic class, status, and parties were the main (overlapping) elements

[4] An important exception is Aristotle, who argues that men are naturally unequal, and thus the inequalities observed in society are only a mere reflection of essential differences. It is simply a matter of justice and proportional equality that those of supposed natural superiority should receive higher social benefits.

through which social classes emerged in modernity and social competition for power was exercised. Power, in turn, proved vital in influencing bureaucracies, which distribute authority and shape social life (Keister and Southgate 2012; Wright 2005).

Other sociologists have also highlighted the role of norms in the creation of inequality among men. Dahrendorf (1968) argues that the source of inequality is found in formal and informal norms, and the sanctions and rewards that are attached to them. Norms create social stratification, a rank order of social status, because they distinguish between those who comply and those who deviate from the socially expected norm of behaviour. This perspective contributes to a better understanding of inequality generating processes that go well beyond the economic sphere. Discriminatory practices tend to emerge as a result of the imposition of strict social norms that fix expected canons of behaviour, setting out what ought to be valued and permitted, and what ought to be despised, restricted, and/or excluded.

Finally, new institutional economists have also appended a fundamental role to institutions when explaining the roots of inequality. According to this approach, institutions can be understood as 'the rules of the game in a society' (North 1990: 3). These rules, laws, and regulations, both formal and informal, not only determine the incentives, transaction costs, and levels of uncertainty affecting the exchange and resource allocation in a market economy, but also the definition of property rights and therefore, income distribution, social rights, status, and power in society. In sum, the prevailing institutions in a country affect its economic growth, but also predominantly determine those who benefit from it (Knight 1992).

Acemoglu and Robinson (2012: 84) argue that 'the fundamental problem is that there will be dispute and conflict over economic institutions. Different institutions have different consequences for the prosperity of a nation, how that prosperity is distributed, and who has power'. Studying the historical development paths of different countries, these authors suggest the existence of two types of institutions, depending on their long-run effect on growth and distribution of resources. On the one hand, 'Inclusive Institutions' are those that promote the wide and fair participation of all members of society in contributing to the economy and the benefits resulting from it; on the other, 'Extractive Institutions' are only designed to obtain and transfer wealth from vulnerable groups (the poorest and weakest) to the elites (the richest and most powerful). In light of this, it is possible to state that the underlying causes of the differences among men in a given society are found in its institutions.

North and Thomas (1973: 2) have argued that factors such as innovation, economies of scale, education, and capital accumulation 'are not causes of growth; *they are growth.*' In the same spirit, this dissertation will argue that low education attainment, precarious wages, and social exclusion are *inequality*. In order to understand the real *causes* of inequality, one must study the underlying key social, economic, and political institutions in a society: its political constitution, level and progressivity of the tax system, prevailing welfare regime, bargaining power of labour unions and other labour market regulations (e.g. minimum wage), and the structure of the educational system, among others.

When, in a country like Chile, the richest 1 per cent of the population—its elite—is able to appropriate 30.5 per cent of all goods and services produced every year, there would seem to be a serious problem with the institutional framework, at least from a distributional perspective. This explains the persistence and increasing power of social movements since 2011, demanding profound changes in the economic, social, and political spheres.

In the next sub-sections, this chapter provides examples of key institutions that have played an important role in the creation and maintenance of high levels of inequality in Chile. First, it will briefly review some key institutional historical roots of inequality that characterized the colonial and post-colonial periods. Second, it will analyse the main features of a key contemporary institution—that is, the Chilean tax system—and its implications for secondary income distribution.

The Origin of Social Inequalities: Path Dependency and the Relevance of History

Although there is a considerable degree of agreement regarding the importance and impact of historical institutions over the current levels of economic development and inequality in Latin America, there is much discussion about the underlying causes explaining their specific formation (Bértola 2011).[5]

Dependendist economists have stressed the key role of international imperialist powers in driving and structuring the world capitalist system, resulting in economic structures in peripheral nations that are instrumental in the subordination of Latin America and its disadvantageous insertion into international trade (Baran 1968; Frank 1971). In Frank's (1972: 19–20) own words:

> Dependence is the result of the historical development and contemporary structure of world capitalism, to which Latin America is subordinated, and the economic, political, social, and cultural policies generated by the resulting class structure, especially by the class interests of the dominant bourgeoisie. It is important to understand, therefore, that through-out the historical process, dependence is not simply an 'external' relation between Latin America and its world capitalist metropolis but equally an 'internal', indeed, integral, condition of Latin American society itself.

The resulting asymmetric trade relations between countries in the periphery and the centre would be among the key underlying factors that fuel inequality in the former nations. In fact, as explained in Kay (1989: 146) when discussing Marini's (1973) perspective:

> The circuit of capital in dependent countries differs from that of the centre countries. In dependent countries the two key elements of the capital cycle – the production and circulation

[5] Some recent researchers have currently questioned the relevance of colonial institutions (see Williamson 2010; Lindert and Williamson 2016).

of commodities – are separated as a result of the periphery being linked to the centre through the over-exploitation of labour. Production in the Third World countries does not rely on internal capacity for consumption but depends on exports to the developed countries. Wages are kept low in the dependent countries because the workers' consumption is not required for the realization of the commodities . . . In the dominant countries, meanwhile, the two phases of the circulation of capital are completed internally.

Structuralist economists, while also highlighting the inadequate integration to the world economy, put a stronger focus on industrialization and innovation policies, and the role of the developmentalist state (Prebisch 1950). In fact, according to ECLAC (2019), 'recognising the asymmetric dynamic of innovation and job creation between the centre and the periphery and within the peripheral structure is key to understanding why the heterogeneity and extreme inequality characteristic of our region persist'.

Alternatively, in order to understand the specific formation of Latin American institutions and their impact on current inequality levels, some researchers have focused on cultural or geographical differences between different regions (Landes 1999), while others, such as new institutional economists, have taken into account the characteristics of the colonial power involved (Coatsworth 2008), the natural factor endowments (Engerman and Sokoloff 1997), or the vital risks and diseases to which colonizers were exposed (Acemoglu and Robinson 2012).

Despite this open debate, most researchers studying the historical trajectory of Latin American countries highlight the relevance of colonial institutions in shaping the current distribution of social outcomes: 'The contemporary situation cannot be understood without recognizing that extreme inequality emerged soon after the Europeans began to colonize the Americas half millennium ago, and has been reflected in the institutions they put in place' (Sokoloff and Robinson 2004: 109–12). Moreover, the same authors highlight the biases built into the institutional arrangements by the local elites: 'The fundamental reason for the persistence of extreme inequality appears to have been the continued pattern of institutional change that favoured the interests of the elite and provided the bulk of the population with only limited access to economic opportunities.'

Indeed, research shows that the Latin American roots of inequality may be found in underlying colonial institutional arrangements pervading the economic, social, and political sphere. Bértola (2011: 46) argues that Latin American inequality 'was at a high level by the end of the colonial period, and that this kind of inequality can hardly be estimated merely in terms of a Gini-coefficient. What really matters is the kind of social and power relations underlying economic life and the distributional and technological dynamics they involved'. In fact, this author argues that a continent 'with 25 per cent of slaves and 60 per cent of rural indigenous population deprived from private property, civil rights, education and political participation, as it was the case of colonial Latin America, can hardly be considered equitable' (Bértola and Williamson 2016: 20).

The inegalitarian institutions imposed during the colonial period might be observed in all spheres of social, economic, and political life. In the social sphere, the exploitation of the indigenous population was made possible by the establishment of 'Encomiendas',[6] which gave Spaniards 'legitimate' control over indigenous labour and the possibility of implementing schemes of forced labour, exploitation, and systematic appropriation of economic surplus (Frank 1971; Salazar 2003). Moreover, there were periods in Chile during which slavery of the Mapuches was allowed by the colonial power, as a punishment for their rebellion against the Crown. Additionally, as in the rest of Latin America and the Caribbean, there were also African slaves in Chile—although fewer in number compared to other latitudes. For example, the black and mulato population in Chile, at the beginning of the nineteenth century, was around 10,000 to 12,000, of which approximately half were slaves. This condition was partially abolished in 1811, with the declaration that any newborn descendant of slaves would be free, and then finally and completely abolished (including adult slaves) in 1823 (Feliú 1973). These institutions, such as the Encomienda and slavery, produced a clear stratification of society based on ethnic origin and skin colour.

In the economic sphere, land concentration was a result of conquest, expulsion of indigenous people, unequal distribution of royal grants of land, and other various illegitimate methods of land acquisition, such as falsification of entitlements (Frank 1971). The initial advantage given to the Encomenderos (who had access to forced labour) allowed them to rapidly accumulate wealth and acquire large portions of land, which in turn gave them access to further privileges. As Frank (1971: 47) maintains: 'Owners of land often became indistinguishable from owners of monopoly rights in international or domestic commerce, mining licences, means of transports, loan capital, civil and religious office, and other sources of privilege.'

These colonial institutions had an immense impact on the pattern of wealth concentration and distribution of property rights, even after independence. Land concentration persisted in Latin America during the post-colonial era, which contrasted with the situation in North America. In fact, at the dawn of the twentieth century while the percentage of males who owned land in the United States and Canada was 75 per cent and 87 per cent respectively, in Latin American countries—such as Mexico and Argentina—this proportion only reached 2.4 per cent and well below 30 per cent respectively in most provinces (Engerman and Sokoloff 2002).

In addition to the Latin American trend, land distribution in Chile was also shaped in the late nineteenth century by the state occupation and appropriation of the southern territories, which were previously occupied by the Mapuche communities. These lands were redistributed and mainly granted to the local elite and European immigrants using dubious mechanisms and criteria that hindered indigenous groups.

Moreover, land concentration gave the local elite an advantage over the rest of the population to exploit new business opportunities. For example, large landowners in Chile had a privileged access to loan and credit. In the 1850s, large landowners faced

[6] This institution was developed in the colonial period. It entailed a right provided by the Spanish Crown to 'protect' and 'evangelice' natives in exchange for their (compulsory) labour.

interest rates of 6 per cent in the incipient financial market, while those for workers were as high as 24 per cent (Rodriguez Weber 2017). This of course had a pivotal effect on the reproduction of inequalities.

In the political sphere, access to positions of power in the colonial administrative bureaucracies was racially stratified (Williamson 2009). But, once again, political exclusion persisted even after countries gained independence. Bértola (2011: 42) argues that 'Constitutions were designed to extend rights to the broad mass of the population, but ultimately they were limited and constrained by underlying forces, and in the end they gave political rights only to the white elites.' Conservatives and liberals, to the detriment of radicals, heavily determined the constitutional orders established after independence in most Latin American republics. As a result, due to 'their distrust of majority rule, they [*the conservative-liberal elite*] discouraged rather than promoted political participation, majoritarian assemblies, and popular debates' (Gargarella 2010: 228).

Laws governing franchise tended to be restrictive. For example, in 1869 in Chile, wealth and literacy requirements had to be met in order to vote (Sokoloff and Robinson 2004).[7] This had a great impact on political participation. In 1869, only 1.6 per cent of the Chilean population voted (Engerman et al. 2000). Moreover, ballots were not entirely secret in Chile until 1958, thus allowing landowners to threaten and control the voting preferences of their workers in rural areas. In fact, after 1958, the proportion of right-wing (conservative) voters dramatically declined in rural areas where patron–client relationships were more prevalent (Baland and Robinson 2008).

The exclusion of the majority from political participation allowed the elite to easily control the Chilean state, turning its monopoly of violence against those threatening their interests. This was especially clear during the late nineteenth and early twentieth centuries. During that period, the power of the state was misused to obscurely distribute large territories that had recently been taken from the Mapuche indigenous communities in the south of the country, and brutally control and suppress the incipient labour movements demanding better working conditions. Indeed, the killing of Iquique in 1907, when the Chilean army massacred hundreds of protesters and their families, constitutes a dark moment in history (Rodriguez Weber 2017).

Since its independence, the truncated and low level of political participation in Chile has had an important impact on the provision of public goods. The case of education is paramount. The limited and biased political participation avoided the early expansion of education services, which would have benefited a large portion of the population (Sokoloff and Robinson 2004). This probably demonstrates the capacity of conservatives to block progressive reforms, since these would have required increasing the tax burden,

[7] It must be said that this is not a situation exclusive to Chile. In fact, this type of barrier existed in other countries, such as the United States. According to Chang (2002: 73), 'universal male suffrage was introduced in 1870, but reversed between 1890 and 1908 through the disenfranchisement of the blacks in the Southern states. It was only restored in 1965'.

which—in the context of an unequal society—would have been borne disproportionally by the local elites. In fact, the expansion of education experienced in the nineteenth century in Chile, although slow, may likely be better explained by the economic boom (which generated extra revenues and demanded skilled workers) and as part of a state policy intended to attract European migrants at the end of that century (Engerman et al. 2009).

The existence of stark levels of social and racial discrimination and exploitation, land and income concentration, weak political participation, and inadequate levels of provision of public goods in the colonial and post-colonial periods no doubt created the basis of an unequal and extremely hierarchical social structure that has endured to the present day. This situation has been verified by several studies investigating intergenerational income mobility looking at surname groupings in the long run. For example Clark (2014) analyses the Chilean case following the income trajectories since 1853 of individuals sharing the same surnames. Historically, since the level of indigenous ancestry and social class tend to be inversely correlated (Cruz-Coke and Moreno 1994), social groups are created differentiating them in terms of their location within an indigenous/European ancestry continuum. Clark finds high levels of long-run social rigidity. Individuals whose surnames match those of the 1850s elite/substantial landowners (e.g. Basques, French, Germans, Italians) tend to have, 150 years later, levels of income that are substantially higher than the average income of their birth-cohort. In fact, at the upper end of the social ladder, current descendants of 1850s extra-substantial landowners, French and Germans have incomes that are 71 per cent, 51 per cent and 56 per cent higher, respectively, than the cohort average. At the lower end of the ladder, Mapuche descendants receive incomes that are 25 per cent lower than the average. These results are consistent with other studies researching social stratification and labour market discrimination in Chile. Nuñez and Gutiérrez (2004) find that there is a 30 per cent to 35 per cent wage differential among professionals from different social classes (measured by last name of employee and other socio-economic variables), even after all other productivity-related factors are taken into account.

In sum, it is clear that the series of 'extractive' and unfair social, economic, and political institutions put first in place by colonial powers and then consolidated in the newly independent nations by the conservative local elites, allowed privileged groups to benefit disproportionally from the developmental process, and to constantly distort and reshape property rights to their own advantage, setting the long-run foundations of an unequal and divided society.

Current Institutions Are the Main Responsibility of Distributional Outcomes: The Case of Tax Policy in Chile

Historical institutions (colonial and post-colonial in the case of Chile) are important for understanding the roots of social asymmetries. Nevertheless, they cannot provide a full account. Path dependency must not be confused with historical determinism. Comparative evidence provides a series of examples demonstrating that conscious collective social and political decisions can be made regarding the levels of inequality that a society is willing to accept. Moreover, recent experience shows that collective choices can in fact reduce inequality in the short run. The construction of social democratic welfare states in many post-Second World War Western European countries and the consequent reduction of inequality constitute an emblematic example of how a collective can use the public apparatus as a powerful equalizing device.

Contrary to the latter example, social choices and political struggles may also give rise to unequal and unfair institutional frameworks. Thus, institutions such as labour market policies (including unions), macroeconomic policies, taxation, and welfare and social policies (education, health, pensions, etc.) are critical in determining levels of inequality in a society.

In the next sub-section, the main characteristics of the Chilean tax system are examined as a case study of a current key institution that has been deficiently designed (perhaps intentionally), hindering the capacity of the state and its ability to reduce inequality.

This analysis is made taking 2013 as a year of reference due to extensive comparable data availability. Also, this period is not affected by President Bachelet's 2014 tax reform, the gradual implementation and impact of which will only be possible to assess in the medium and long term. As a result, the prevailing tax regime up until 2013 better explains the inequality levels observed in Figure 28.2 (average income concentration in 2005–10), and thus constitutes an adequate focus for this study.

Tax policy in Chile: collecting without discomforting the local elite. Chile's tax policy is inadequate to properly finance the consolidation of a welfare state capable of ensuring social rights and reducing inequality. A rigorous institutional analysis of the Chilean tax system reveals that it has three main weaknesses: (1) the level of tax revenues is low as a percentage of GDP; (2) it promotes a low level of progressivity; (3) it has a low redistributive capacity.

(a) Low level of revenues as percentage of GDP. Chile, as most Latin American countries, is characterized by a low level of tax revenues. Figure 28.4 presents the levels of total tax revenues as percentage of GDP in OECD countries. In 2013, the level of tax revenues in Chile reached 19.9 per cent of its GDP, which is 40 per cent lower than the OECD average (33.7 per cent), and well below highly egalitarian countries such as Sweden (42.9 per cent), Norway (39.9 per cent), and Denmark (45.9 per cent).

A common argument used by those who oppose increasing the role and weight of the state in the economy is that Chile (and other developing countries in similar stages of development) cannot afford to increase taxes because it would mean a high burden for the economy. It is argued that raising taxes beyond the current level would eventually jeopardize economic growth rates and the competitiveness of the economy. Current high-income economies, the argument goes, can have high levels of taxes because they have reached a higher stage of development. In other words, it is a luxury only rich countries can afford. Developing countries are thus condemned to fiscal austerity and weak states until they catch up with developed countries.

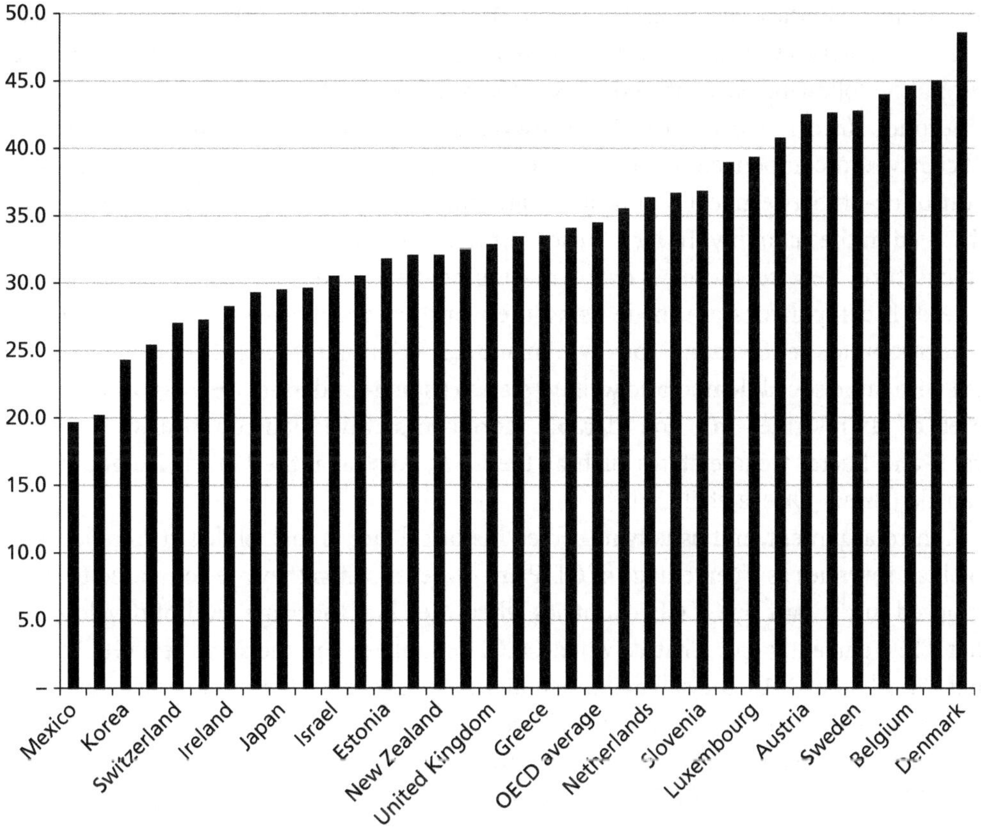

Figure 28.4 Total tax revenues as % of GDP (2013)

Note: OECD average excludes Chile.
Source: Author's elaboration based on OECD (2019).

Three counter-arguments must be made in order to debunk the above myth. First, historical evidence shows that taxes do not necessarily harm economic growth. In fact, there is no clear relation between taxes and growth rates. Among several reasons, this is due to the fact that the impact of taxes on growth depends not only on the level of taxes, but also on the quantity and quality (productive vs non-productive) public expenditure and investments carried out with the collected taxes. In the case of tax cuts, the key factor determining its impact relates to how this tax cut is funded. For example, tax cuts that are not financed by a reduction in public spending can generate public deficits that end up increasing interest rates and thus reducing investment (Gale and Orszag 2005). As a result, it would seem unsurprising that the relation between level of taxes and economic growth is unclear and difficult to determine. Indeed, several studies confirm that the correlation between the levels of taxes and the long-run economic growth rates is negligible or non-existent (e.g. for the United States see: Feldstein and Elmendorf 1989; Stokey and Rebelo 1995; Gale and Potter 2002; Hungerford 2012. For international comparative studies, see Mendoza et al. 1997; Piketty et al. 2011). In some cases, researchers have even observed that higher taxes are followed by higher growth rates during the following years after the tax reform (Huang 2012).

Second, historical evidence also shows that taxes do not necessarily hinder the efficiency and competiveness of the economy. Comparative data show that there is no clear trade-off between levels of taxation and the degrees of competitiveness/innovation observed in the economy. In fact, those countries with higher levels of tax revenues and expenditure are also those who are most innovative and competitive in the world. Indeed, if comparisons are made using the world competitiveness index, it is possible to corroborate that Sweden, Norway, Finland, and Denmark—countries usually identified with large social democratic welfare states (Esping-Andersen 1990) and the highest levels of tax revenues—are considerably more competitive than countries with smaller states and liberal welfare states such as the USA, Australia, the United Kingdom, and Canada (Bravo-Ortega et al. 2012).

A third argument, and usually neglected historical fact, is that Chile's current levels of total tax revenues as a percentage of GDP are low even when they are compared to those achieved in the past by OECD countries when they had the same level of development that Chile currently has. That is, when OECD countries had the same real GDP (PPP) that Chile had in 2013, they all had much higher levels of total tax revenues (Figure 28.5).

In fact, while Chile's tax revenues represented 19.9 per cent of GDP in 2013, they constituted an average of 30.1 per cent among the rest of the OECD countries when each had Chile's current GDP (PPP). This historical comparison allows an appreciation of the 'relative institutional lag' of Chile's tax system, even when development levels are taken into account. This illustrates that taxation is not something determined by an economy's developmental stage, but by political struggles and social choices regarding the levels of inequality that are defined as acceptable, legitimate, and just in each society. In light of this, it seems clear that Chile is restricting its policy space and limiting the redistributive capacity of its state far more than did OECD countries in their own time.

Three main factors explain the relative tax revenue gap between Chile and the OECD average: the lower levels of income taxes, social security contributions (especially those of employers), and property taxes (OECD 2019).

Indeed, in 2013, taxes on income, profits, and capital gains accounted on average for 11.1 per cent of GDP among OECD countries. Nevertheless, that same year, this tax component represented a proportion 38 per cent lower in Chile (6.9 per cent of GDP). This was brought about in several ways.

First, tax expenditure (deductions, exemptions, credits, etc.) in Chile is considerable, especially when considering that it is highly regressive in its composition (Jorrat 2013).[8] In fact, in 2011 tax expenditures accounted for 4.79 per cent of GDP in Chile, while in Germany (2004), Korea (2006), the Netherlands (2006), Spain (2008), and the

[8] Seventy-five per cent of tax expenditure in Chile is related to income taxes.

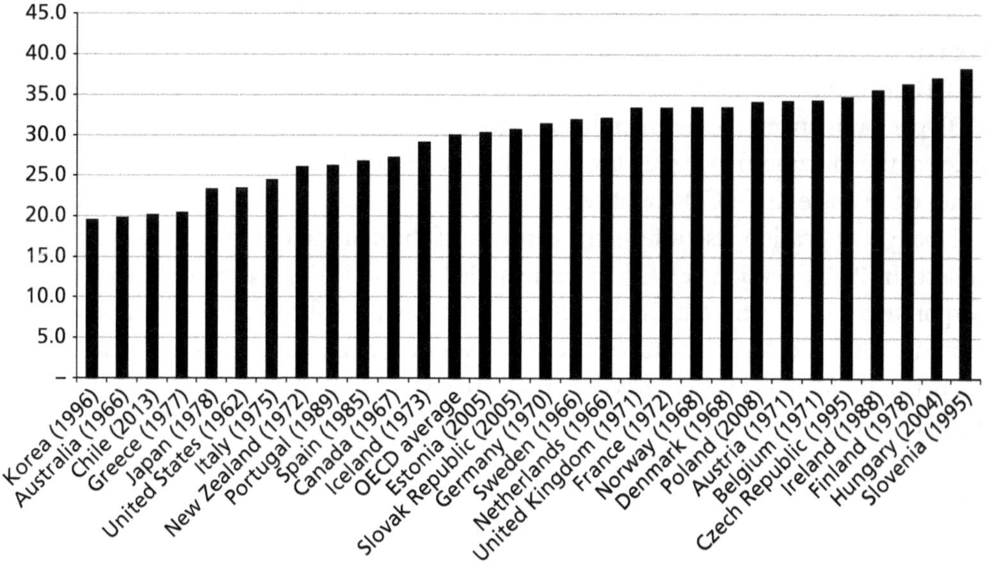

Figure 28.5 Total tax revenues as % GDP: year in which all countries had GDP per capita similar to Chile (2013)

Note: Years in which each country had the same GDP per capita (PPP), at constant prices 2005, are shown in parentheses. OECD average excludes Chile. Figures for the Netherlands, Norway, Sweden, and United States are based on author's estimates of GDP per capita (PPP), at constant prices. Tax revenue data for United States is based on year 1965 (1962 not available); Iceland based on year 1975 (1973 not available).

Source: Author's calculations based on OECD (2019).

United States (2008), it reached 0.74, 2.48, 2.0, 4.55, and 5.97 per cent, respectively (OECD 2010).[9]

Second, in Chile, the lowest threshold of income at which personal taxes begin to be required is comparably high. In 2010, all incomes below the average GDP per capita were exempt from paying taxes. This threshold is much more generous (higher) than the normal situation in OECD countries, where personal taxes are paid when incomes surpass 0.24 times the GDP per capita. Even when compared to middle-income countries, Chile's exemption threshold is 54 per cent higher (Corbacho et al. 2013).

Third, the level of income from which the top marginal personal income tax rate is applied is extremely high from a comparative perspective. In fact, in 2010, the top marginal tax rate in Chile affected individuals that had incomes higher than or equal to 11.2 times the nation's GDP per capita. In contrast, in OECD countries, on average, this marginal tax rate already comes into action when personal income levels reach as little as 2.4 times their GDP per capita. Even when compared to other middle-income countries, Chile's threshold for activating top income marginal taxes is 73 per cent higher (Corbacho et al. 2013).

[9] Moreover, in 2018 Chile had nearly 200 tax expenditure provisions, which was above the number for the median OECD country, with available information in 2018 (Redonda and Neubig 2018).

As a result of the previous point, the income distance between the minimum marginal tax rate and the maximum marginal tax rate is much larger than the one observed in OECD countries. In 2013, an individual in Chile had to transit 10 times the national GDP per capita from the moment he/she started being taxed to the moment he/she was taxed at the maximum marginal tax rate. This income distance was only approximately 2 times on average in OECD countries.

Finally, tax evasion also affects the capacity of the state to obtain the taxes it aims to collect. In 2009, evasion related to value-added taxes (VAT) reached 18 per cent and corporate taxes 34 per cent. Jorrat (2013) estimates that, for every evasion percentage point in VAT and corporate taxes, the state experiences a loss of revenues equivalent to 0.1 per cent and 0.05 per cent of GDP, respectively. In other words, the Chilean state has a total revenue loss of 3.5 per cent of GDP every year due to tax evasion. In order to assess this figure from a comparative perspective, Buehn and Schneider (2012) provide cross-country tax evasion estimates which demonstrate that tax evasion in Chile is significant. In fact, according to their estimate, while tax evasion in thirty-eight OECD countries in 2009 represented 2.5 per cent of GDP on average, in Chile it reached 3.4 per cent (similar to Jorrat's (2013) estimates). In conclusion, Chile suffers a tax evasion rate which is 36 per cent higher than its OECD peers.

(b) Low tax progressiveness. Any well-designed tax system should aim not only to collect the right amount of taxes, but also to do so in a progressive manner. From this perspective also, the Chilean system is deficient. Its low level of progressiveness is due to several reasons. First, the composition of tax revenues is heavily skewed towards regressive indirect taxes that affect middle and lower social classes the most, such as value-added taxes (VAT). For example, in 2013 VAT taxes represented 20.1 per cent of total tax revenues in the average OECD country; in the same year, this component represented 40.8 per cent of Chilean total tax revenues (OECD 2019).[10] This compares unfavourably to other countries such as Germany (19 per cent), Korea (17 per cent), the Netherlands (17.8 per cent), Spain (17.8 per cent), and the United Kingdom (20.8 per cent). It is even higher than other Latin American countries with similar GDP per capita in 2013 such as Argentina (23.9 per cent), Panama (16.6 per cent), and Uruguay (30.4 per cent) (OECD 2019).

Another factor relates to corporate and personal income tax rates, which are particularly low in Chile as compared to OECD countries. In fact, in 2013, while corporate tax rates were, on average, 25.4 per cent in OECD countries, in Chile they were 20 per cent (Figure 28.6).[11]

[10] It must be noted that the excessive weight of this kind of taxation is mainly the result of lower total revenues, which increases its relative weight. That is, in terms of percentage of GDP, it is not higher that the OECD average.

[11] It might be argued that, in practice, Chile has a corporate tax rate of 0 per cent, since it has a 100 per cent integrated system wherein corporate taxes constitute a credit for personal income taxes. This was partially modified in the 2014 tax reform.

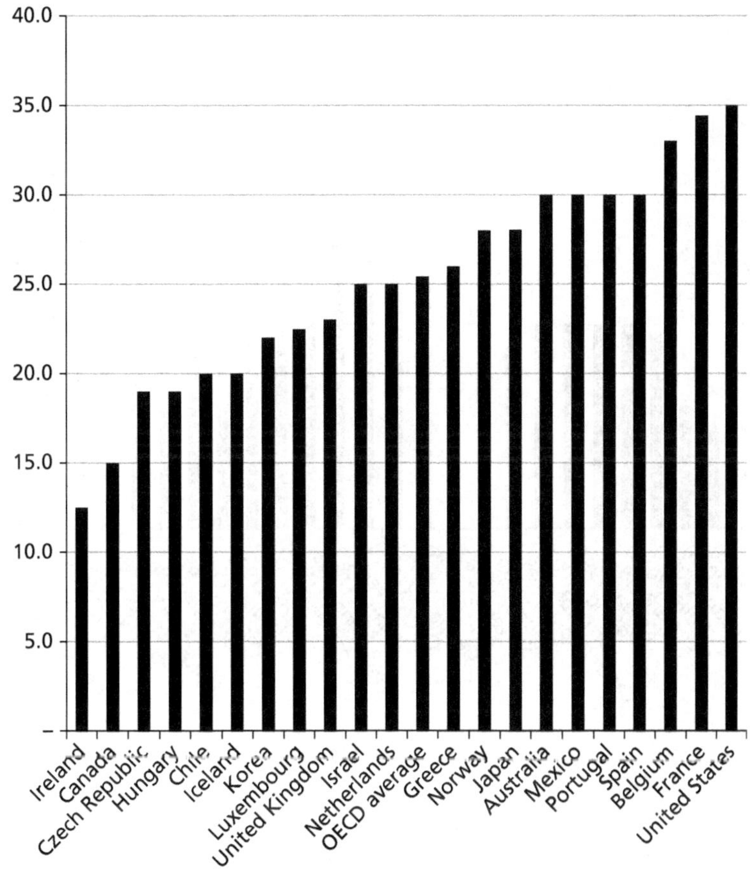

Figure 28.6 Corporate tax rates (2013)

Note: OECD average excludes Chile.
Source: Author's elaboration, based on OECD (2019).

Similarly, top marginal personal income tax rates are lower in Chile than the current international standard. While in 2013, top marginal tax rates reached an average of 43.5 per cent among OECD countries, it stood at 40 per cent in Chile (and was lowered to 35 per cent as a result of the 2014 tax reform). Although this difference seems rather small (3.5 percentage points in 2013), it transforms into a substantial gap when we repeat the exercise of measuring the level of top marginal tax rates when OECD countries had a similar level of development (GDP per capita (PPP)) to Chile in 2013. As shown in Figure 28.7, OECD countries used to have top tax rates around 57 per cent, on average—that is, 17 percentage points higher than the 2013 Chilean tax rates (and 23 percentage points higher than the rate prevailing after 2014 tax reform).

Once again, this historical comparison allows the debunking of the myth that Chile, due to its development stage, should not increase its top tax rates because it would have a negative effect on investment and economic growth. Defenders of this myth argue that

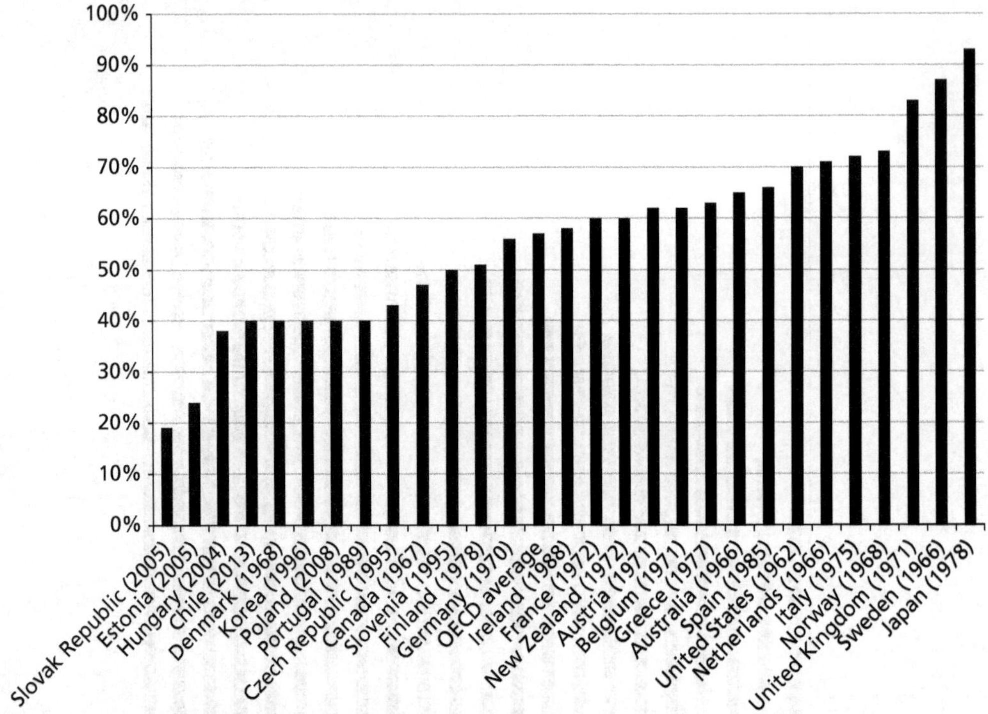

Figure 28.7 Top marginal personal income tax rates: year in which all countries had GDP per capita similar to Chile (2013)

Note: Years in which each country had the same GDP per capita (PPP), at constant prices 2005, are shown in parentheses. OECD average excludes Chile. Figures for the Netherlands, Norway, Sweden, and United States are based on author's estimates of GDP per capita (PPP), at constant prices. The OECD has only provided top marginal personal income tax rates since 1975. Thus, countries that reached the level of GDP per capita (PPP) of Chile (2013) before that date are assigned the 1975 tax rate.

Source: Author's calculations based on World Tax Database, Office of Tax Policy Research (1975–1999); (OECD 2019).

only developed countries can bear the luxury of taxing the rich in society; if Chile did so, the argument goes, it would negatively affect incentives, frighten away investors, and create a burden for capital accumulation and growth. These arguments do not seem to be based on historical data.

Leading economies such as the United States, United Kingdom, Germany, and France are useful to illustrate this point. As shown in Figure 28.8, all of them sustained top income tax rates well above 50 per cent for several decades in the twentieth century, even when they had lower income per capita than does Chile currently. Moreover, these decades coincided with decades of high economic growth, the so-called golden age of capitalism.

A detailed analysis of Figure 28.8 shows that the UK and US kept top tax rates at 70 per cent or above for more than four decades, between the mid-1930s and beginning of

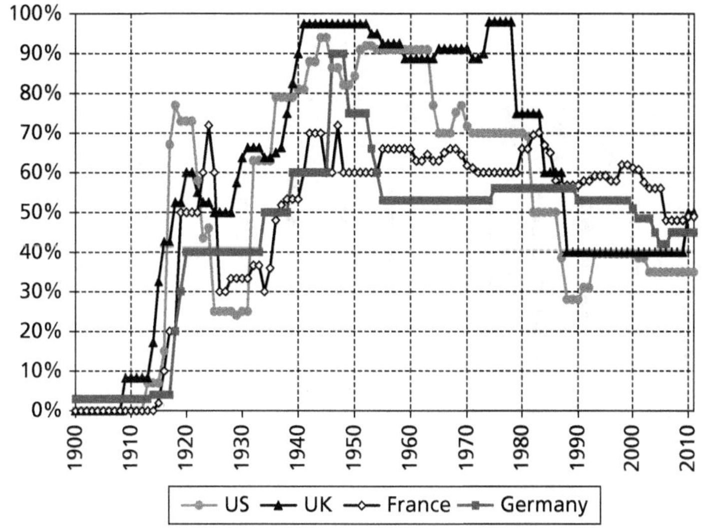

Figure 28.8 Historical top marginal income tax rates (1900–2010)

Source: Piketty and Saez (2012).

the 1980s. Moreover, after the Second World War, they both had several periods in which rates were 90 per cent or higher.

The most important lesson provided by these countries is that the high level of top marginal income tax rates certainly did not prevent them from leading the world economy (especially in the case of the United States), although it did provide them with one of the most egalitarian periods of their history.

(c) Low redistributive capacity. The deficiencies of the Chilean tax system may also be corroborated by looking at its redistributive capacity. That is, in relation to its ability to reduce income inequality after taxes are collected and government transfers are made. As Figure 28.9 and many other studies (e.g. Goñi et al. 2011) demonstrate, the progressiveness of the Chilean taxation and social protection system is insignificant. The state's intervention leaves the distribution of income practically unaltered. For example, in 2013 in Chile while the distribution of income resulting from the labour market (primary distribution) was 0.50 Gini points, that which prevailed after taxes and transfers (secondary distribution) was 0.47 – in other words, only a 0.03 point difference. This is quite a unique case for OECD standards since in general most OECD countries are able to reduce inequality substantially through government intervention. For example, in 2013, the OECD countries shown in Figure 28.9 were able to reduce 0.18 Gini points on average—that is, six times more than Chile.

Using Esping-Andersen's (1990) classification of welfare regimes, Figure 28.9 confirms that social democratic welfare states (prevailing, for example, in Norway, Denmark, Finland, Belgium, and Sweden) tend to have greater levels of final distributional

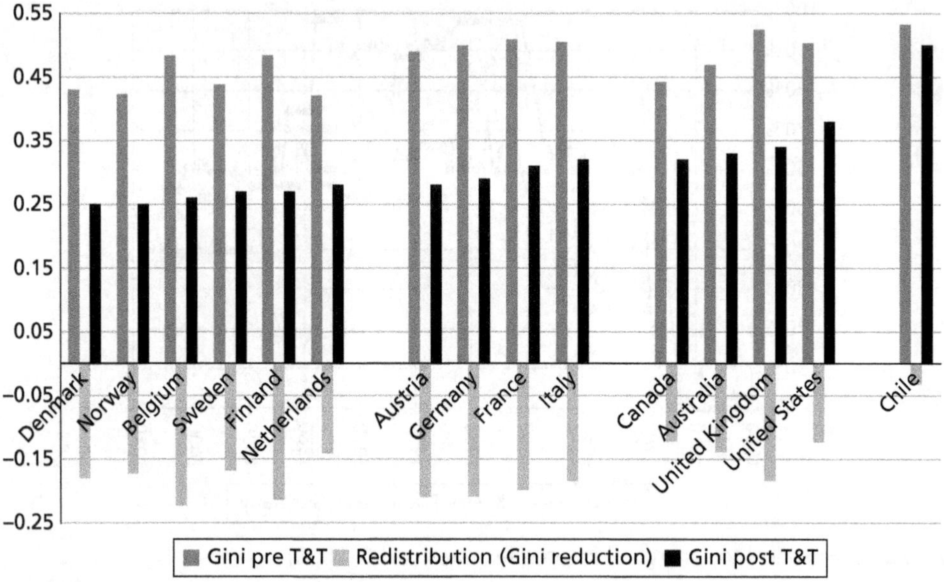

Figure 28.9 Pre/post taxes and transfers Gini (2013)

Note: For each country, 2010–11 averages are presented.
Source: Author's elaboration, based on OECD (2019).

equality. Conservatives are less egalitarian, but are also able to reduce income gaps considerably through taxes and redistribution. The regimes of liberal welfare states are the least egalitarian and have the smallest capacity to redistribute. Nevertheless, Chile's case is anomalous, resisting comparison even with the most liberal regimes, such as that which prevails in the United States. In conclusion, the Chilean state stands out for its inefficacy to alter the country's socio-economic reality.

Institutional change: drivers and the role of power

The elevated levels of inequality observed in Chile give rise to several questions. Why are institutional frameworks that sustain social injustices not modified? Why, despite alarming disparities, does social conflict seem to be moderate?[12] A better understanding of the drivers behind institutional persistence and change is warranted, and this section therefore briefly explores some tentative answers.

Although there is no single theoretical consensus of institutional emergence and change among researchers, most of them may be classified by three main

[12] Recent social movements since 2011 seem to constitute a new trend, although it is still too early to assess the persistence and long-term impact of this phenomenon.

approaches: utilitarian–functionalist, cultural–sociological, and powerful–distributional (Thelen 2003).

The utilitarian–functionalist approach explains the emergence and change of institutions in terms of their functionality and capacity to solve collective action problems (Thelen 2003). Their relevance rests on their capacity to reduce uncertainty and transaction costs, and promote exchange. As a result, the main driver for change is efficiency gains (maximization of aggregate welfare). From this viewpoint, institutions emerge and evolve as a result of: (1) unintended interactions among actors seeking to reduce transaction costs; (2) competitive selection processes of institutions (resembling a Darwinian approach, in which the most efficient persist); and/or (3) intended design of rational utility-maximizing individuals (Groenewegen et al. 2010). This approach seems unconvincing, and inadequately explains why countries fall into the trap of inefficient institutions. If institutional change is efficiency driven, inadequate institutions should be replaced within a reasonable time frame—yet this has not happened (at least not in the Chilean case). In fact although high levels of inequality have impeded an open and efficient use of talents and hindered economic development in Chile, numerous unequal/inefficient institutions have persisted. As a result, it is possible to question (at least in part) the explanatory power of this approach, on the basis of its inappropriateness as an explanation of the persistence of unequal institutions.

The cultural–sociological approach perceives institutions as embodying shared cultural scripts and beliefs regarding how the world works (Thelen 2003). As Scott and Meyer (1994: 234) argue, institutions correspond to the 'construction over time of a social definition of reality such that certain ways of action are taken for granted as the "right" if not the only way to do things'. Despite its importance, the cultural–sociological approach seems to be more relevant for explaining persistence rather than institutional change in the short and medium term. In fact, in the Chilean case, this account would seem to inadequately explain the sudden, radical, and most significant structural changes (neoliberal reforms) experienced in the modern history of the country after 1973 (under the Pinochet dictatorship, which in fact had a significant impact on inequality levels). This does not mean that cultural scripts are not relevant to consolidate changes that may be driven by power struggles in the first place; in fact, as Thelen (2003: 217) argues, 'it turns out that in many cases changes in power relations hold the key to creating the openings in which new scripts (or scripts previously only in the margins . . .) can become more central'. Thus, this approach may prove to be most useful in combination with the powerful–distributional approach.

The powerful–distributional approach (and the extensive historical evidence that supports it) shows that institutions emerge and change as a result of conflict, asymmetric power relations, and imbalances between different social groups, with each one fighting for their own benefits (Thelen 2003). Institutions are shaped by those who have greater ability to impose their terms, those with more political and economic power—in other words, the richest 1 per cent of the population that is able to influence the institutional design and the definition of property rights affecting the regulation and functioning of diverse spheres of society. As Knight (1992: 20) puts it, 'institutional development is a contest among actors to establish rules which structure outcomes to those equilibria most favourable for them'. If we apply this approach to our case study, it certainly sheds light regarding the previously discussed deficiencies and 'relative institutional lags' of the Chilean tax system. These defects would not be the result of efficiency-driven decisions, but the outcome of power struggles among classes, which have most certainly allowed the Chilean elite to limit taxation and block recent reforms in this sphere. In fact, this is exemplified by the 2014 tax reform (one of the most important in decades), when, after several negotiations (and despite the explicit political commitment of President Bachelet to promote a progressive tax reform), the top income marginal tax rate was reduced from 40 per cent to 35 per cent.

Within this power-based approach, it is also important to realize that power is not only exercised by domestic elites, but also by international actors. As the historic analysis of the Chilean economy reveals, foreign interest groups have played a considerable role shaping national policies, domestic structures, and property rights (especially those linked to the exploitation of natural resources and creation of monopolies) for their own benefit,[13] in accordance with Chile's subordinate integration and status within the world economic system (Frank 1971).

In order to fully reveal the explanatory capacity of powerful–distributional approaches, it becomes paramount to gain a better understanding of the concept of power and the way it is exercised. Indeed, power is a complex concept.[14] For Hobbes, it entailed a conception of cause and effect, described as an 'agent' acting on a passive 'patient' (Ball 1987). This conception influenced Weber, who defined power as 'the probability that one actor in a social relationship will . . . carry out his own will' (Weber 1922 [1978]: 53). It is important to note that, in this case, the agent is able to carry out his 'will' even when others, who are affected by it, oppose it. This conception might be applicable to the use of coercion and brute physical power over an opponent, as well as other forms of exercising power in the context of democratic political systems. In fact, the capacity of a government or political actor to carry out its will and promote its objectives through an open and deliberative democratic process is considered the observable or 'one-dimensional' account of power (decision-making facet developed by Dahl). The latter might be distinguished from the 'two-dimensional' expression of power that includes the possibility of exercising power in a more veiled and unobservable manner through 'closed door negotiations' (agenda-setting facet developed by Bachrach and Baratz). As Ball (1987: 398) exemplifies:

> [one actor] C might exercise power by controlling the agenda, thereby limiting the discussion, debate, and decision-making to 'safe' issues which do not threaten C's interests. Or C might be

[13] Mainly Spanish in the sixteenth and seventeenth centuries, British in the eighteenth and nineteenth centuries, and American in the twentieth century.

[14] This discussion draws on Ball (1987), which elaborates a lucid synthesis of the different conceptions of power.

able to take advantage of biases built into the political system that tend to favour C's interest over R's. Or R, anticipating defeat and/or reprisal, might be unwilling to challenge C on a particular issue.

In other words, the fact that we are not able to observe R challenging C (and losing) or C explicitly exercising power over R (and prevailing), does not mean that power relations are not operating.

The implicit key assumption made by both previous accounts of power, which is challenged by the 'three-dimensional' approach (developed by Lukes), is that actor R (the one resisting and/or being affected by C's will) is aware and knows which are his (R's) real interests. Indeed, in accordance with Marxist theory, if R is not aware or able to know what his real interests are, or has an incorrect understanding of them, then his potential agreement with C's views might not be in his 'real' interest, but only apparent based on his mistaken views (false consciousness). As Ball (1987: 399) argues, 'the most effective way in which C can exercise power over R is to shape R's very beliefs about what is and is not in R's interest'. This way, conflict is minimized and C's power made invisible—despite being strongly exercised.

These different manners of interpreting and analysing power seem most useful and pertinent in understanding the Chilean case and the ability of its elite to exercise its economic and political power to shape the local 'rules of the game'. Indeed, there is evidence showing that the structural institutional transformations that Chile has experienced since the neoliberal reforms (promoted from 1973 onwards) were in many cases driven by the intention of the elites to advance their own interests, reversing the egalitarian gains achieved in previous decades (Monckeberg 2015).

Chile's recent history shows how all dimensions of power have unfolded in a rather sequential manner. The coercive dimension of power was clearly exercised by the conservative local and international forces determined to eradicate the Marxist threat and its progressive reforms from Latin America during the second half of the twentieth century. In fact, in 1973, the democratically elected socialist government led by Salvador Allende was overthrown by the armed forces (directly supported by the CIA), putting an end to its agenda of structural economic and social reforms. As Pinochet's dictatorship unfolded, civil rights were violated, political rights suppressed, and social rights reduced to a minimum. Real social spending declined, poverty increased, and inequality escalated. Chile quickly changed from being the second most equal country in Latin America in the early 1970s, to the second most unequal in the 1990s (Garreton 2013). Simultaneously, the economic elites benefited from increasing deregulation and (in many cases corrupt) privatization of public enterprises and services that allowed them to accumulate even larger shares of national income and wealth (Monckeberg 2015).

The hidden sphere of power (two-dimensional account) started being heavily exercised by the right-wing parties and economic elites once the country transitioned towards democracy in 1990. The Political Constitution of Chile, which had been designed and imposed in 1980 during the Pinochet dictatorship, now played a key role in democracy, structuring the political playing field through the electoral system, designated senators, and undemocratic voting schemes (Garreton 2013). The electoral system that favoured the elections of right-wing candidates, together with undemocratic rules that allowed introducing representatives of the armed forces into the parliament as designated senators,[15] allowed the conservatives and the armed forces to be over-represented in the Congress.

Moreover, the constitution established undemocratic voting schemes to approve or change organic laws,[16] which required a 'qualified quorum', i.e. from 4/7 up to 2/3 of votes from members of parliament. Thus, although in theory Chile recovered its democracy in 1990, in practice the conservatives maintained disproportionate power and control over the legislative process thanks to the 'hidden' provisions established in the 1980 constitution. Any important legislative change would therefore require confidential negotiations and the consent of the minority right-wing coalition. As result, the democratic popular expression, participation, and will of the Chilean majority were suppressed and institutionally restricted. In fact, economic and political elites now not only had the power of shaping institutions, but also of obstructing their reform, increasing the 'transition costs' involved in the process (Khan 1995). As Jaime Guzman, one of Pinochet's top collaborators and key intellectual authors of the 1980 constitution, once commented:

> The Constitution must ensure that if the opponents come to rule, they may be constrained to follow a not so different plan of action than the one we would aspire, because – allow the metaphor – the range of alternatives that the playing field imposes upon the players is limited enough to make the contrary extremely difficult.[17]

Finally, the power of the conservative elites was exercised in Chile in a subtle manner (à la Lukes) by acting on society's values, perceptions of inequality, and the criteria it uses to judge and legitimize injustices. In fact, it would normally be expected that the existence of high levels of inequality, such as those in Chile, would give rise to social conflict and political mobilization of middle and lower social classes for redistributive policies (as anticipated, for example, by the median voter theorem (Meltzer and Richard 1981)). Nevertheless, social discontent and demand for redistributive policies have been quite moderate in Chile for more than two decades (1990–2010). Social conflict has only started to build up since the 2011 social movement, which progressively contested a series of neoliberal policies inherited from the Pinochet era. In this context, how can we explain this paradox of general social peace and rampant inequality?[18]

[15] In fact, Pinochet himself became a designated senator after stepping down from power.

[16] Organic laws are those special laws that address issues 'protected by the constitution' and therefore require more than a majority of votes (at least 4/7 of total congressmen) in order to be modified.

[17] Author's translation.

[18] The social crisis which started in 2019 could reflect the fact that this paradox could be coming to an end, and that a social movement demanding more equality is emerging. In other words, individuals might be increasing their awareness and consciousness regarding social injustices in Chile. Indeed, a lower rate of

One hypothesis is that neoliberal policies enforced since the Pinochet era affected not only formal institutions, but also the criteria by which they are judged. As argued by Wegener (2000: 75), 'the stability of a society, the absence of anomie, of normlessness, or even revolt, depends on a conception of justice that, if it is accepted by its members, provides legitimacy to the social institutions and the state'. In fact, the egalitarian ideologies and discourses promoted during the 1960s and early 1970s in Chile, stressing collective values, equality, the state, social rights, and redistribution of income, seem to have been partly substituted after 1973 by neoliberal and individualist ideologies. These emphasized individualistic values, freedom, markets, private property, meritocracy, equality of opportunity, and the eradication of poverty. Inequality, as an object of analysis, was intentionally removed from public discourse and national debate (Garreton 2013). It would thus be the conscious or unconscious adoption of the neoliberal ideology by the majority of the Chilean population, which explains the legitimacy of higher levels of inequality and resulting social stability (Gomez 2012).

Interestingly, Gomez (2012) argues that one of the main supporters of the neoliberal ideology has been not solely the elite, but also the middle class. This class has embraced the individualistic and meritocratic discourse and the inequalities it creates, because it helps to distinguish it from the lower classes. Whereas universal social rights and public provision, for example in education, tend to eliminate social differences, a dualistic public–private model of provision of education, such as the one existing in Chile, creates profound differences between the lower classes, which send their children to under-financed free public schools, and the middle class which enrols their youngsters in fee-charging private, subsidized schools (González 2017). These types of mechanisms not only create a sense of distinction, but also allow the latter to secure access to better positions in the labour market and thus reproduce social inequalities (Bourdieu and Passeron 1964 [1979]; Bourdieu and Passeron 1990).

The cultural acceptance of neoliberalism by the Chilean middle classes, which saw the shrinking of the state and experienced the removal of universal social benefits, seems consistent and a consequence of an intended inferiorization process promoted by the elites and social media to implicitly devalue those who receive social assistance from the state, as failed individuals who lack effort, entrepreneurial skills, and talent to succeed in a market society (as the one promoted since 1973 onwards). In this context, a part of the Chilean middle class seems to have embraced the 'Chilean dream' (local version of the American dream), where effort and responsibility are rewarded in the labour market, and social rights as a communitarian ideal are substituted for the right to compete in the market, demonstrating that anyone can reach the 'top of the hill' if they are honest, talented, and hardworking. Jock Young (1999: 22), analysing the American society (one

economic growth, high levels of household debts, scandals involving collusion between firms, low-quality social services, and insufficient levels of democratic representation could be among the factors explaining the recent social demonstrations.

upheld by local neoliberal elites as the model society to be followed), discusses a similar perspective:

> In the American Dream the ideal is equality of opportunity: all get a chance to compete in the meritocratic race, but it is the winners who get the prizes and the losers who naturally do not. And losers fail because of individual qualities, it is their fault that they have lost (see Merton 1938). The notion of citizenship has, therefore, a strong stress on legal and political equality and much less on social equality. It is a cocktail glass society where social and cultural focus is on the successful and where winners, more and more, take all (see Frank and Cook 1996). In a way, then, social citizenship is something to be earned by hard work and forthrightness ('the American way'): it is not a right of citizenship.

From an empirical perspective, Castillo (2011) studying public opinion surveys in Chile, shows the importance of ideology in legitimizing inequality. As shown in his study, individuals' ideology has a statistically significant effect over the wage gap size judged as 'just'. In fact, those individuals who believe in individualistic values tend to legitimize higher wage gaps than those who support egalitarian values. Whereas egalitarians tend to demand redistributive policies and create social dissensus, individualists tend to justify and legitimate larger inequalities, thus contributing to the legitimation and justification of those inequalities. As a result, as proposed by Castillo (2011), it is not difficult to accept the hypothesis that the neoliberal policies imposed in the Pinochet era promoted individualistic values in the population, and thus provided the cultural and ideological grounds for the acceptance and legitimation of higher levels of inequality. This may well explain the apparent paradox of high inequality and (aside from specific social movements) general social consent.

Additionally, it may be argued that societies that are exposed to higher levels of inequality tend to be more permissive of high inequality in the long run. In fact, Castillo (2012), studying the Chilean case, confirms the hypothesis that 'perceived' levels of inequality have an important effect over the size of wage gaps that are considered 'just' by society. Reality acts as a cornerstone upon which normative judgements are built—that is, those who perceive higher levels of inequality are also those justifying higher levels of it. Perhaps Alexis de Tocqueville (1835: II.13) was correct to point out that:

> When inequality of conditions is the common law of society, the most marked inequalities do not strike the eye; when everything is nearly on the same level, the slightest are marked enough to hurt it. Hence the desire of equality always becomes more insatiable in proportion as equality is more complete.

Conclusion

Chile represents a complex case study of economic growth and general social consent, combined with persistent extreme levels of inequality. Economic growth has reduced absolute poverty rates, but inequality has persisted unchallenged.

Although classical and neoclassical economists have tried to justify inequality as being necessary for capital accumulation and growth, recent datasets show that inequality hampers economic development. Moreover, contrary to most dominant theories, inequality is not inevitable (fixed in time and space), nor does it follow a predictable path determined by the country's stage of development. Although technological change and globalization constitute important challenges, comparative evidence shows that it is how countries (and the institutions they put in place) react to globalization and technological change that determines their final impact in the distribution of income. As a result, we argue that it is how institutions are shaped and who they serve that really matter. Market forces are of course relevant, but they should operate embedded within institutional frameworks that limit their possible outcomes.

Investigating Chile's underlying institutions is key to understanding the profound roots of inequality, with both historical and current institutions playing an important role. Nevertheless, although historical institutions are important for providing a better understanding of the role of path dependencies, it is current institutions that must be scrutinized and reformed in order to ensure desired levels of equality and social justice. This has not proven to be an easy task, especially because institutions are usually the product of social struggles that reflect and reproduce asymmetries of power in society. It is in fact the consistent facilitation of an extreme concentration of economic and political power among the Chilean elite that allows this group not only to accrue a highly uneven portion of society's fruits, but also to 'convince' by coercion and/or persuasion that the unfair final distribution of outcomes is actually just and beneficial to all.

REFERENCES

Acemoglu, D. and Robinson, J.A. (2006). *Economic Origins of Dictatorship and Democracy*. Cambridge: Cambridge University Press.

Acemoglu, D. and Robinson, J.A. (2012). *Why Nations Fail: The Origins of Power, Prosperity, and Poverty*. New York: Crown.

Alesina, A. and Rodrik, D. (1994). 'Distributive politics and economic growth', *Quarterly Journal of Economics* 109/2: 465–90.

Autor, David H., Levy, Frank, and Murnane, Richard J. (2003). 'The skill content of recent technological change: an empirical exploration', *Quarterly Journal of Economics* 118/4: 1279–333.

Baland, J.M. and Robinson, J. (2008). 'Land and power: theory and evidence from Chile', *American Economic Review* 98/5: 1737–65.

Ball, T. (1987). 'Power, in D. Miller (ed.) *The Blackwell Encyclopedia of Political Thought*. Oxford: Basil Blackwell.

Baran, P. (1968). *The Political Economy of Growth*. New York: Monthly Review Press.

Benabou, R. (2000). 'Unequal societies: income distribution and the social contract', *American Economic Review* 90/1: 96–129.

Benabou, R. (2002). 'Tax and education policy in a heterogeneous-agent economy: what levels of redistribution maximize growth and efficiency?' *Econometrica* 70/2: 481–517.

Berg, A. and Ostry, J. (2011). 'Inequality and unsustainable growth: two sides of the same coin?', IMF Staff Discussion Note 11/08. Washington, DC: International Monetary Fund.

Berman, E., Bound, J., and Machin, S.J. (1998). 'Implications of skill-biased technological change: international evidence', *Quarterly Journal of Economics* 113/3: 1245–79.

Bértola L. (2011). 'Institutions and the historical roots of Latin American divergence', in J. A. Ocampo and J. Ross (eds) *The Oxford Handbook of Latin American Economics*. Oxford: Oxford University Press.

Bértola, L. and Williamson, J. G. (eds) (2016). *The Fracture: Past and Present of the Search for Social Equity in Latin America*. Mexico: Fondo de Cultura Económica.

Blau, F. and Kahn, L. (2009). 'Inequality and earnings distribution', in W. Salverda, B. Nolan, and T. Smeeding (eds), *The Oxford Handbook of Economic Inequality*. Oxford: Oxford University Press.

Boix, C. (2003). *Democracy and Redistribution*. Cambridge: Cambridge University Press.

Bourdieu, P. and Passeron, J.C. (1964 [1979]). *The Inheritors: French Students and Their Relation to Culture*. Chicago, IL: University of Chicago Press.

Bourdieu, P. and Passeron, J.C. (1990). *Reproduction in Education, Society and Culture*. London: Sage Publications.

Bravo-Ortega, C., Cea, C., Hojman, D., and Landerretche, O. (2012). Algunas Correlaciones Incómodas: Carga Tributaria y Bienestar Social en Chile y la OCDE [Some uncomfortable correlations: tax burden and social welfare in Chile and the OECD]. TIPS, Trabajo de Investigación en Políticas Públicas [Public Policy Research Working Paper], May, No. 11.

Bruno, M., Ravallion, M., and Squire, L. (1998). 'Equity and growth in developing countries: old and new perspectives on the policy issues,' in Vito Tanzi and Ke-young Chu (eds) *Income Distribution and High-Quality Growth*. Cambridge, MA: MIT Press.

Buehn, A. and Schneider, F. (2012). 'Size and development of tax evasion in 38 OECD countries: What do we (not) know?'. Working Paper No. 4004. Munich: CESifo.

Castillo, J.C. (2011). 'Legitimacy of inequality in a highly unequal context: evidence from the Chilean case', *Social Justice Research* 24: 314–40.

Castillo, J.C. (2012). 'Is inequality becoming just? Changes in public opinion about economic distribution in Chile', *Bulletin of Latin American Research* 31/1: 1–18.

CEPAL (United Nations Economic Commission for Latin America and the Caribbean) (2017). *Social Panorama of Latin America 2016. Economic Commission for Latin America and the Caribbean*. Santiago: United Nations.

Chang, H.-J. (2002). *Kicking Away the Ladder: Developmental Strategy in Historical Perspective*. London: Anthem Press.

Chang, H.-J. (2011). *23 Things They Don't Tell You about Capitalism*. New York: Bloomsbury Press.

Clark, G. (2014). *The Son also Rises: Surnames and the History of Social Mobility*. Princeton, NJ: Princeton University Press.

Coatsworth, J. (2008). 'Inequality, institutions and economic growth in Latin America', *Journal of Latin American Studies* 40: 545–69.

Corak, M. (2013). 'Inequality from generation to generation: the United States in comparison', in Robert Rycroft (ed.) *The Economics of Inequality, Poverty, and Discrimination in the 21st Century*. Santa Barbara, CA: ABC-CLIO.

Corbacho, A., Fretes Cibils, V., and Lora, E. (2013). *Recaudar no Basta: Los impuestos como instrumento de desarrollo* [Collecting is not enough: taxes as an instrument of development]. Washington, DC: Banco Interamericano de Desarrollo.

Cornia, G.A. (ed.) (2004). *Inequality, Growth, and Poverty in an Era of Liberalization and Globalization*. Oxford: Oxford University Press.

Cristi, R. (2000). *El pensamiento político de Jaime Guzmán* [Political thoughts of Jaime Guzmán]. Santiago: LOM Ediciones.

Cruz-Coke, R. and Moreno, R. (1994). 'Genetic epidemiology of single-gene defects in Chile', *Journal of Medical Genetics* 31/9: 702–6.

Dahrendorf, R. (1968). *Essays in the Theory of Society*. Stanford CA: Stanford University Press.

de Ferranti, D., Perry, G., Ferreira, F., and Walton, M. (2004). *Inequality in Latin America: Breaking with History?* Washington, DC: World Bank.

de Tocqueville, Alexis (1835). *De la démocratie en Amérique II* [Democracy in America]. Chicago, IL.

Dynan, K., Skinner, J., and Zeldes, S. (2004). 'Do the rich save more?' *Journal of Political Economy* 112/2: 397–444.

ECLAC (United Nations Economic Commission for Latin America and the Caribbean) (2019). 'Raúl Prebisch and the challenges of development of the XXI century'. Biblioguías—Biblioteca de la CEPAL. Available at https://biblioguias.cepal.org/prebisch_en/XXIcentury/structural-heterogeneity, accessed 4 November 2019.

Engerman, S. and Sokoloff, K. (1997). 'Factor endowments, institutions and differential paths of growth among New World economies: a view from economic historians of the United States', in S. Haber (ed.) *How Latin America Fell Behind*. Stanford, CA: Stanford University Press.

Engerman, S. and Sokoloff, K. (2002). 'Factor endowments, inequality, and paths of development among new world economies', *Economia* 3/1 (Fall): 41–88.

Engerman, S., Haber, S., and Sokoloff, K. (2000). 'Inequality, institutions, and differential paths of growth among New World economies', in C. Menard (ed.) *Institutions, Contracts and Organization*. Cheltenham: Edward Elgar.

Engerman, S., Mariscal, E., and Sokoloff, K. (2009). 'The evolution of schooling institutions in the Americas, 1800–1925', in D. Eltis, F. Lewis, and K. Sokoloff (eds) *Human Capital and Institutions: A Long Run View*. New York: Cambridge University Press, 93–142.

Esping-Andersen, G. (1990). *The Three Worlds of Welfare Capitalism*. Princeton, NJ: Princeton University Press.

Feldstein, M. and Elmendorf, D. (1989). 'Budget deficits, tax incentives, and inflation: a surprising lesson from the 1983–1984 recovery', in Lawrence H. Summers (ed.) *Tax Policy and the Economy (3)*. Cambridge: National Bureau of Economic Research.

Feliú, G. (1973). *La Abolición de la Esclavitud en Chile* [Abolition of slavery in Chile]. Santiago: Editorial Universitaria.

Ferreira, F. and Ravallion, M. (2009). 'Poverty and inequality: the global context', in W. Salverda, B. Nolan, and T. Smeeding (eds) *The Oxford Handbook of Economic Inequality*. Oxford: Oxford University Press.

Frank, A.G. (1971). *Capitalism and Underdevelopment in Latin America*. London: Pelican Books.

Frank, A.G. (1972). 'Economic dependence, class structure, and underdevelopment policy', in J. D. Cockcroft, A.G. Frank, and D.L. Johnson (eds) *Dependence and Underdevelopment: Latin America's Political Economy*. New York: Doubleday.

Friedman, M. and Friedman, R. (1980). *Free to Choose: a Personal Statement*. San Diego, CA: Harvest.

Gale, W.G. and Orszag P. (2005). 'Deficits, interest rates, and the user cost of capital: reconsidering the effects of tax cuts on investment', *National Tax Journal* 58/3: 409–26.

Gale, W.G. and Potter, S. (2002). An economic evaluation of the Economic Growth and Tax Relief Reconciliation Act. *National Tax Journal* 55/1: 133–86.

Galor, O. (2012). 'Inequality, human capital formation and the process of development'. IZA Discussion Paper No. 6328. Bonn: IZA.

Gargarella, R. (2010). *The Legal Foundations of Inequality: Constitutionalism in the Americas, 1776–1860*. Cambridge: Cambridge University Press.

Garreton, M.A. (2013). *Neoliberalismo Corregido y Progresismo Limitado: los gobiernos de la Concertación en Chile* [Corrected neoliberalism and limited progressism: the governments of the Concertación in Chile], *1990–2010*. Santiago: Editorial ARCIS.

Goldin, C. and Katz, L.F. (2008). *The Race between Education and Technology*. Cambridge, MA: Harvard University Press.

Gomez, J.C. (2012). 'Estado, dominación, hegemonía y crisis política en la sociedad neoliberal, Chile 1973–2012' [State, domination, hegemony and political crisis in neoliberal society, Chile 1973–2012], in Mabel Thwaites Rey (ed.) *El Estado en América Latina: Continuidades y Rupturas* [The State in Latin America: Continuities and Ruptures]. Santiago: Editorial Arcis.

Goñi, E., López, H., and Servén, L. (2011). 'Fiscal redistribution and income inequality in Latin America', *World Development* 39/9: 1558–69.

González, J. (2017). 'Putting social rights at risk: assessing the impact of education market reforms in Chile', in B.S. Ndimande and C. Lubienski (eds) *Privatization and the Education of Marginalized Children: Policies, Impacts and Global lessons*. London: Routledge.

Groenewegen, J., Spithoven, A., and van den Berg, A. (2010). *Institutional Economics: An Introduction*. London: Palgrave Macmillan.

Harvey, D. (2010). *The Enigma of Capital and the Crises of Capitalism*. New York: Oxford University Press.

Huang, C. (2012). *Recent Studies Find Raising Taxes on High-Income Households Would Not Harm the Economy: Policy Should Be Included in Balanced Deficit-Reduction Effort*. Washington, DC: Center on Budget and Policy Priorities.

Hungerford, T. (2012). *Taxes and the Economy: An Economic Analysis of the Top Tax Rate since 1945*. Washington, DC: Congressional Research Service.

Jorrat, M. (2013). 'Gastos tributarios y evasión tributaria en Chile: evaluación y propuestas' [Tax expenditures and tax evasion in Chile: evaluation and proposals], in J.P. Arellano and V. Corbo (eds) *Tributación para el desarrollo. Estudios para la reforma del sistema chileno* [Taxation for development. Studies for the reform of the Chilean system]. Santiago: Uqbar Editores.

Kaldor, N. (1955). 'Alternative theories of distribution', *The Review of Economic Studies* 23/2 (1955–1956): 83–100.

Katz, L.F. and Autor, D.H. (1999). 'Changes in the wage structure and earnings inequality', in O. Ashenfelter and D. Card (eds) *Handbook of Labor Economics, vol. IIIA*. Amsterdam: North-Holland, 1463–555.

Kay, C. (1989). *Latin American Theories of Development and Underdevelopment*. London: Routledge.

Keister, L. and Southgate, D. (2012). *Inequality: A Contemporary Approach to Race, Class, and Gender*. Cambridge: Cambridge University Press.

Khan, M. (1995). 'State failure in weak states: a critique of the new institutionalist explanations', in J. Harriss, J. Hunter, and C. Lewis (eds) *The New Institutional Economics and Third World Development*. London: Routledge.

Knight, J. (1992). *Institutions and Social Conflict*. Cambridge: Cambridge University Press.

Kuznets, S. (1955). 'Economic growth and income inequalities'. *American Economic Review* 45/1: 1–28.

Landes, D. (1999). *On the Origins of the Wealth and Poverty of Nations*. New York: W. W. Norton.

Lindert, P. and Williamson, J. (2016). *Unequal Gains. American Growth and Inequality since 1700*. Princeton, NJ: Princeton University Press.

López, R., Figueroa, E., and Gutiérrez, P. (2013). 'La "parte del león": nuevas estimaciones de la participación de los súper ricos en el ingreso de Chile' [The "lion's share": new estimates of the super rich's contribution to Chile's income]. Serie Documentos de Trabajo No 379. Santiago: Departamento de Economía, Universidad de Chile.

Lucas, R. (2004). 'The Industrial Revolution: Past and Future', *The Region* 18(1).

Lustig, N. (2015). 'Most unequal on earth', *Finance & Development* 52/3. Washington, DC: International Monetary Fund.

Marini, R. M. (1973). *Dialéctica de la dependencia* [Dependency dialectics]. Mexico: Era.

Marx, K. (1976 [1867]). *Capital, Vol. I*. London: Penguin.

Meltzer, A. and Richard, S. (1981). 'A rational theory of the size of government', *Journal of Political Economy* 89/5: 914–27.

Mendoza, E., Milesi-Ferretti, G., and Asea, P. (1997). 'On the ineffectiveness of tax policy in altering long-run growth: Harberger's superneutrality conjecture', *Journal of Public Economics* 66/1: 99–126.

Milanovic, B. (2011). *The Haves and Have-nots*. New York: Basic Books.

Monckeberg, M.O. (2015). *El Saqueo de los Grupos Económicos al Estado Chileno* [The looting of economic groups from the Chilean State]. Santiago: Debolsillo.

North, D.C. (1990). *Institutions, Institutional Change and Economic Performance*. Cambridge: Cambridge University Press.

North, D. and Thomas, R. (1973). *The Rise of the Western World: A New Economic History*. New York: Cambridge University Press.

Núñez, J. and Gutiérrez, R. (2004). 'Class discrimination and meritocracy in the labor market: the case of Chile', *Estudios de Economía* 31/2: 113–32.

Núñez, J. and Risco, C. (2004). 'Movilidad Intergeneracional del Ingreso en un País en Desarrollo: El Caso de Chile'. Documento de Trabajo No. 210. Santiago: Departamento de Economía, Universidad de Chile.

OECD (Organisation for Economic Co-operation and Development) (2010). *Tax Expenditure in OECD Countries*. Paris: OECD.

OECD (Organisation for Economic Co-operation and Development) (2019). OECD.Stat: OECD Revenue Statistics/Comparative tables. Available at http://stats.oecd.org/Index.aspx?DataSetCode=REV, accessed 22 June 2015.

Okun, A. (1975). *Equality and Efficiency: The Big Trade-off*. Washington, DC: Brookings Institution Press.

Palma, J.G. (2011). 'Homogeneous middles vs. heterogeneous tails, and the end of the "Inverted-U": the share of the rich is what it's all about', *Development and Change* 42/1: 87–153.

Pareto, V. (1906 [2006]). *Manuale di Economia Politica*, edited by A. Montesano, A. Zanni, and L. Bruni, Milan, EGEA—Università Bocconi Editores.

Piketty, T. (2014). *Capital in the Twenty-First Century*. Cambridge, MA: Belknap, Harvard University Press.

Piketty, T. and Saez, E. (2012). 'Optimal labor income taxation'. NBER Working Paper Series, No. 18521. Cambridge, MA: National Bureau of Economic Research.

Piketty, T., Saez, E., and Stantcheva, S. (2011). 'Optimal taxation of top labor incomes: a tale of three elasticities.' Working Paper 17,616. Cambridge, MA: National Bureau of Economic Research.

Polanyi, K. (1944). *The Great Transformation*. New York: Farrar & Rinehart.

Prebisch, R. (1950). *The Economic Development of Latin America and its Main Problems*. New York: United Nations.

Rawls, J. (1971). *A Theory of Justice*. Cambridge MA: Harvard University Press.

Redonda, A. and Neubig, T. (2018). 'Assessing Tax Expenditure Reporting in G20 and OECD Economies'. Discussion Note 2018/3, Zurich, Switzerland: The Council on Economic Policies (CEP).

Ricardo, D. (1817). *On the Principles of Political Economy and Taxation*, 3rd edn. London: John Murray.

Rodriguez Weber, J. (2017). *Desarrollo y Desigualdad en Chile, 1850–2009: Historia de su economía política* [Development and inequality in Chile, 1850–2009: history of its political economy]. Colección Sociedad y Cultura. Santiago: Ediciones de la Dirección de Bibliotecas, Archivos y Museos (DIBAM).

Rousseau, J.J. (1755). *Discourse on the Origin and Foundations of Inequality among Men*. Oxford: Oxford University Press.

Saint Paul, G. and Verdier, T. (1996). 'Inequality, redistribution and growth: a challenge to the conventional political economy approach', *European Economic Review* 3/40: 719–28.

Salazar, G. (2003). *History of the Capitalist Accumulation in Chile*. Santiago: Lom ediciones.

Sapelli, C. (2011). *Chile: ¿Más equitativo?: una mirada distinta a la distribución del ingreso, la movilidad social y la pobreza en Chile* [Chile: more equitable?: A different perspective towards income distribution, social mobility and poverty in Chile]. Santiago: Ediciones UC.

Sassen, S. (2014). *Expulsions: Brutality and Complexity in the Global Economy*. Cambridge, MA: Harvard University Press.

Scott, W. Richard and Meyer, John W. (1994). *Institutional Environments and Organizations: Structural Complexity and Individualism*. Thousand Oaks, CA: Sage.

Sokoloff K. and Robinson, J. (2004). 'Historical roots of Latin American inequality', in *The World Bank, Latin America and the Caribbean: Breaking with History?* Washington, DC: World Bank.

Stiglitz, J. (2012). *The Price of Inequality*. London: Penguin Books.

Stokey, N. and Rebelo, S. (1995). 'Growth effects of flat-rate taxes', *Journal of Political Economy* 103/3: 519–50.

Thelen, K. (2003). 'How institutions evolve: insights from comparative historical analysis', in James Mahoney and Dietrich Ruschemeyer (eds) *Comparative Historical Analysis in the Social Sciences*. New York: Cambridge University Press.

Torche F. (2005). 'Unequal but fluid: social mobility in Chile in comparative perspective', *American Sociological Review* 70: 422–50.

Torche, F. (2014). 'Intergenerational mobility and inequality: the Latin American case', *Annual Review of Sociology* 40: 619–42.

UNDP (United Nations Development Programme) (2017). *Desiguales. Orígenes, cambios y desafíos de la brecha social en Chile. Programa de Naciones Unidas para el Desarrollo* [Unequal. Origins, changes, and challenges of the social gap in Chile]. Santiago: UNDP.

Weber, M. (1922 [1978]. *Economy and Society*. Berkeley, CA: University of California Press.

Wegener, B. (2000). 'Political culture and post-communist transition – a social justice approach: introduction', *Social Justice Research* 13/2: 75–82.

Wilkinson, R. and Pickett, K. (2009). *The Spirit Level: Why Equality is Better for Everyone*. London: Penguin Books.

Williamson, E. (2009). *The Penguin History of Latin America*. London: Penguin Books.

Williamson, J. (2010). 'Five centuries of Latin American inequality', *Journal of Iberian and Latin American Economic History* 28/2.

World Bank (2015). World Bank org website. Available at https://datahelpdesk.worldbank.org/knowledgebase/articles/906519-world-bank-country-and-lending-groups, accessed 11 January 2020.

World Bank (2017). *World Development Indicators*. Available at http://wdi.worldbank.org/table/1.3#, accessed 28 August 2017.

World Tax Database, Office of Tax Policy Research (1975–1999). Available at www.wtdb.org/index.html, accessed 16 July 2002.

World Top Incomes Database (2015). Available at https://wid.world/, accessed 11 January 2020.

Wright, E.O. (ed.) (2005). *Approaches to Class Analysis*. Cambridge: Cambridge University Press.

Young, J. (1999). *The Exclusive Society*. London: Sage.

29 Development and inequality in the African lions

David Potts

Introduction

This chapter investigates data for seven sub-Saharan African economies and analyses the dynamics of growth and inequality over the period 1995 to 2014. Data derived from World Development Indicators are used to investigate changes in the incomes of different groups and the extent to which economic growth has improved the incomes of the poor and impacted on the levels of inequality. Some specific factors are considered as possible explanations for variations in the extent to which growth has benefited the poor, in particular the possibility that agriculture-led growth may be pro-poor and mineral led growth may be pro-rich. There are considerable variations in the experiences of different countries in relation to the extent to which growth has improved the position of the poor. In all cases except one the incomes of the poorest have improved over the periods for which data on distribution are available. However, in all cases there is some evidence that inequality has tended to increase.

The origin of the term 'African lions' can be traced back to the earlier term of 'Asian tigers', originally referring to the fast growing economies of Hong Kong, South Korea, Taiwan, and Singapore but later extended to include a number of other Asian economies experiencing rapid industrialization and growth such as Thailand and Indonesia in the period 1988–96. In those countries the share of manufacturing in GDP rose to more than 25 per cent and real GDP per capita grew at about 8 per cent and 6 per cent respectively per annum. In Thailand the share of manufacturing in GDP increased more or less continuously from the 1960s until 2010 but is now declining slowly. In Indonesia a similar process of increasing relative importance of manufacturing occurred until 2001 followed by a slow decline. In both cases the relative importance of agriculture has declined steadily and the proportion of people living in the urban areas has increased, reaching more than 50 per cent in both cases.

The experience of success in Asia raised the question as to why similar progress was apparently not being observed in Africa. The McKinsey Global Institute published a report (MGI 2010) referring to 'Lions on the Move' suggesting that a similar experience *has* been occurring in a number of African economies. A very different interpretation is provided by Taylor (2014: 156) who argues that

David Potts, *Development and inequality in the African lions* In: *Handbook of BRICS and Emerging Economies.* Edited by: P.B. Anand, Shailaja Fennell, and Flavio Comim, Oxford University Press (2021).
DOI: 10.1093/oso/9780198827535.003.0029

the story of Africa rising is just that: a story. In this tale, where growth for growth's sake is cast as a manifestation of development and progress, the agenda of industrialization and moving Africa up the global production chain has been abandoned. Instead, analysis has been hypnotized by growth rates, often channelled through poor reporting desperate to compensate for previous—and equally poor—overly negative reporting.

An alternative and perhaps more balanced perspective is that

> despite significant advances in terms of macroeconomic stability, it is evident that the structure of the African region's growth remains of concern . . . lack of complexity in production, underpinned by constraints in infrastructure, a poor regulatory and governance framework, and high unit labor costs serve to reinforce challenges to growth, development, and employment generation strategies. (Bhorat and Tarp 2016: 1)

Rodrik (2014: 14–15) also urges caution arguing that 'Much of the recent performance seems to be due to temporary boosts: an advantageous external context and making up of lost ground after a long period of economic decline' and 'If African countries do achieve growth rates substantially higher than what I have surmised, they will do so pursuing a growth model that is different from earlier miracles based on industrialization.' The most recent McKinsey Global Institute report (MGI 2016) points to a slowdown in growth from 2010 to 2015 but argues that 'in an aging world, Africa has the advantage of a young and growing population . . . and, so far, job creation is outpacing growth in the labor force'. The 2016 Least Developed Counties Report (UNCTAD 2016) signalled that the 'apparent resilience to the international economic and financial crisis, economic growth in the least developed countries (LDCs) has declined steeply since 2012, reaching a low of 3.6 per cent in 2015' (2016: 18). It appears that some of the optimism about sustaining the economic growth achieved by some of the poorest countries in the first decade of the twenty-first century is wavering. Important factors in the more cautious assessment of prospects include falling commodity prices, difficulties in tax collection, and declining aid inflows.

Greater caution about the prospects of the 'African lions' relates in part to the perspectives of the developed Western countries that provide most of the aid Africa receives. However, the relative importance of aid from Development Assistance Committee (DAC) countries is declining and the relative importance of private investment, and both private investment and aid from non-DAC sources, particularly China, are increasing (Moss 2011: 237–8). Private investment from India and South Africa (Lawrence 2010: 36; Paul 2014: 183–95) is also increasingly important. The 'lions' therefore have more options available in terms of sources of inward investment and this may have implications for their range of policy choices. In particular Chinese investors have been claimed to be indifferent to governance measures in terms of property rights and the rule of law (Chen et al. 2016).

Part of the problem with generalizing about the African growth experience is that there are very different circumstances facing different countries. One of the most important factors is the effect of prolonged conflict which has caused considerable

Table 29.1 Index of real GDP per capita (1995=100.0)

Country	1995	2000	2005	2010	2015
Zambia	100.0	104.4	124.0	162.8	181.0
Ghana	100.0	110.0	123.8	149.3	191.3
Tanzania	100.0	108.7	133.9	154.0	183.1
Uganda	100.0	115.2	134.9	168.1	185.9
Mozambique	100.0	150.2	198.8	247.1	301.8
Rwanda	100.0	120.0	152.9	199.4	248.5
Ethiopia	100.0	107.6	127.4	186.9	265.8

Source: Author's estimate based on data from World Development Indicators 2017 (World Bank various years).

disruption to many but not all African countries. This chapter refers to the experience of seven African countries[1] that have all experienced levels of economic growth that have comfortably exceeded population growth over the last twenty years (Table 29.1). These countries have also experienced relative political stability over the same period and, while they may have been affected to some extent by conflicts in neighbouring countries, they have experienced relatively peaceful conditions internally. They are all medium-sized countries in terms of population (more than 10 million and fewer than 100 million). Overall average annual per capita income growth over the entire period ranged from 3.0 per cent (Zambia) to 5.7 per cent (Mozambique). The highest overall economic growth was experienced by the three initially poorest countries in order of poverty, Mozambique, Ethiopia, and Rwanda. The other four economies have experienced fairly similar patterns of overall growth.

Structural change

The process of economic development generally involves significant structural change. We would normally expect that the relative importance of agriculture would decline and that the population would become more urbanized. If the experience of the Asian tigers were to be repeated in sub-Saharan Africa we would also expect the relative importance of manufacturing to increase initially before a later fall as the service sector expands. Has this been the case in the seven selected countries?

Agriculture has declined as a proportion of GDP in all seven countries and this proportion is now below 50 per cent in all cases (Table 29.2). However, the relative importance of agriculture and the speed of its relative decline has varied considerably. In the case of Zambia, minerals have contributed a significant proportion of GDP for a long

[1] The countries selected were Ethiopia, Ghana, Mozambique, Rwanda, Tanzania, Uganda, and Ethiopia. They have been listed in order of 1995 per capita income in all tables.

Table 29.2 Structural change (% of GDP, period averages)

Country	Sector	1995–99 %	2000–04 %	2005–09 %	2010–14 %
Zambia	Agriculture	17.1	17.6	13.8	10.0
	Industry	34.1	27.0	32.8	34.9
	—manufacturing	*11.8*	*10.9*	*9.8*	*8.2*
	Services	48.8	55.4	53.4	55.9
Ghana	Agriculture	41.4	39.9	33.3	25.2
	Industry	27.7	27.9	22.1	26.3
	—manufacturing	*10.3*	*9.7%*	*10.1%*	*10.0%*
	Services	30.9	32.1	44.6	48.5
Tanzania	Agriculture	42.0	32.9	30.7	32.2
	Industry	16.5	20.9	21.3	23.7
	—manufacturing	*8.3*	*9.0*	*7.6*	*7.3*
	Services	41.5	46.2	48.0	44.2
Uganda	Agriculture	43.4	26.6	25.4	27.5
	Industry	17.2	23.2	25.0	21.4
	—manufacturing	*8.4*	*7.4*	*8.1*	*10.5*
	Services	39.4	50.2	49.6	51.2
Mozambique	Agriculture	32.1	24.4	27.6	27.5
	Industry	18.4	22.0	20.7	19.3
	—manufacturing	*14.0*	*16.4*	*14.4*	*10.4*
	Services	49.5	53.6	51.7	53.2
Rwanda	Agriculture	44.0	37.3	35.9	33.0
	Industry	17.2	13.7	12.1	14.2
	—manufacturing	*10.2*	*11.5*	*12.0*	*11.2*
	Services	38.8	49.0	52.0	52.8
Ethiopia	Agriculture	53.6	43.5	46.6	44.8
	Industry	11.7	13.3	11.8	11.5
	—manufacturing	*5.2*	*5.5*	*7.8*	*5.6*
	Services	34.6	43.2	41.6	43.7

Source: Author's estimate based on data from World Development Indicators 2017 (World Bank various years).

time and agriculture already contributed less than 40 per cent of GDP before the start year of the period under consideration (1995). The share of services in the economy of Mozambique was already relatively high in 1995 and that of agriculture relatively low (33.7 per cent).

The relative importance of industry has been fairly stable in most countries although it has increased in Tanzania and also increased in Uganda before falling in the most recent period. However, the overall category of industry includes a number of activities including mining, which is particularly important in Zambia and Ghana and more recently in Mozambique, Tanzania, and Uganda. The relative importance of the manufacturing sub-sector has either remained stable or in some cases declined. It is only in Uganda that the relative importance of manufacturing has increased. A major difference between the growth pattern of the African lions and the Asian tigers is that manufacturing has not been the main engine of growth.

The relative importance of the service sector has tended to increase, particularly in Rwanda, Ghana, and Uganda. The service sector takes up more than 50 per cent of GDP in Mozambique, Rwanda, Uganda, and Zambia, suggesting that the transition to a service-based economy has taken place without substantial industrialization. This has implications for poverty reduction since the industrial sector is not absorbing enough of the migrants from rural areas into employment and many of the jobs available in the formal service sector require skills that such migrants may not have.

Employment and urbanization

Economic structural change and population movement have implications for the major sources of employment. As expected there has been a general decline in the relative importance of agricultural employment in most cases, but the extent of change varies considerably. The proportion of employment in agriculture in Zambia and Uganda does not appear to have fallen at all and the falls in Rwanda and Ethiopia have not been substantial. On the other hand there seems to have been significant structural change in Tanzania with a shift from agriculture to industry and services. A similar shift appears to have taken place in Ghana more recently, although the relative importance of agriculture was already lower at the start of the period under consideration.

Economic structural change is related to urbanization since a shift away from agriculture is likely to imply greater urbanization. All the countries considered are urbanizing but from quite different starting points and also at different rates. The most urbanized countries at the start of the period were Ghana, Zambia, and Mozambique. Urbanization in Ghana has continued at a relatively rapid rate and more than 50 per cent of Ghana's population is now urban. This is reflected in the employment structure. In Zambia the proportion of the population living in urban areas actually declined at one stage and over the whole period under consideration this proportion only rose from 37 per cent to 41 per cent. The experience of Mozambique has been similar with the urban population rising from 27.5 per cent to just over 32 per cent. Urbanization has also been slow in Ethiopia and Uganda, but in Tanzania and Rwanda urbanization is taking place at a much faster rate.

An important implication of the data presented in Tables 29.2 and 29.3 is that the gap between rural and urban incomes is widening, partly because of a failure to generate enough jobs in the manufacturing sector. An indicator of this phenomenon can be derived by comparing the trends in the contribution of agriculture to GDP and the percentage of the population living in rural areas. The percentage of the population living in rural areas has declined far more slowly than the percentage contribution of agriculture to GDP. In the most extreme case of Zambia, the proportion of the population living in the rural areas has declined by about 5 per cent while the contribution of agriculture to GDP has declined by over 40 per cent. Such changes have implications for poverty and inequality since the majority of the population of six of the seven countries live in rural areas. Even in Ghana the rural population is still nearly half of the

Table 29.3 Employment by sector (% of total) and urban population (% of total)

Country	Sector	1995–99	2000–04	2005–09	2010–14
Zambia	Agriculture	70.0	71.6	71.8	
	Industry	7.0	5.8	7.3	
	Services	23.0	22.6	20.8	
	Urban population	36.2	35.4	37.5	39.6
Ghana	Agriculture	55.0		57.2	43.1
	Industry	14.0		13.6	14.9
	Services	31.1		29.1	42.0
	Urban population	41.7	45.3	48.7	52.1
Tanzania	Agriculture		81.6	71.9	66.9
	Industry		0 3.2	0 4.6	0 6.4
	Services		15.2	23.5	26.6
	Urban population	21.2	23.2	26.1	29.5
Uganda	Agriculture		67.1	72.8	71.9
	Industry		7.1	5.9	4.4
	Services		22.8	21.3	20.2
	Urban population	11.8	12.3	13.6	15.1
Mozambique	Agriculture		80.5		
	Industry		3.4		
	Services		16.1		
	Urban population	28.3	29.5	30.4	31.4
Rwanda	Agriculture			78.8	75.3
	Industry			0 3.8	0 6.7
	Services			16.4	16.2
	Urban population	12.2	16.7	21.1	25.9
Ethiopia	Agriculture			75.3	72.7
	Industry			0 6.7	0 7.4
	Services			16.2	19.9
	Urban population	14.2	15.1	16.2	18.2

Note: Some figures are averages for more than one year and not all of the source data totalled 100%.

Source: Author's estimates based on data from World Development Indicators 2017 (World Bank various years).

population so any strategies to reduce poverty must pay attention to the livelihoods of the rural population as well as to employment generation in the urban areas.

Export structure

There are significant differences in the pattern of export structure both over time and between countries (see Table 29.4). Ethiopia's exports have remained predominantly agriculture based with very little change over time. Uganda's exports have also remained predominantly agricultural but there has been a significant increase in the importance of manufacturing. This has also occurred in Tanzania, but the importance of minerals has also increased and agricultural products now take up less than half of Tanzania's total exports. Similar trends in mineral exports can be observed in Ghana and Rwanda, but manufacturing exports remain relatively low in Rwanda, while in Ghana the relative

Table 29.4 Export structure (% of total, period averages)

Country		1995–99 %	2000–04 %	2005–09 %	2010–14 %
Zambia	AG	10.4%	16.7%	10.4%	10.0%
	MAN	12.0%	12.9%	7.4%	11.2%
	MIN	77.6%	70.4%	82.2%	78.8%
Ghana	AG	70.3%	65.4%	67.2%	42.5%
	MAN	14.7%	15.2%	25.6%	14.9%
	MIN	14.9%	19.4%	7.1%	42.7%
Tanzania	AG	82.9%	74.0%	58.3%	47.8%
	MAN	15.7%	16.7%	22.7%	24.5%
	MIN	1.5%	9.3%	19.1%	27.7%
Uganda	AG	90.1%	86.6%	73.7%	67.0%
	MAN	8.6%	7.4%	21.6%	28.4%
	MIN	1.3%	6.0%	4.6%	4.6%
Mozambique	AG	77.2%	31.4%	19.9%	21.4%
	MAN	13.0%	6.9%	7.3%	10.7%
	MIN	9.8%	61.7%	72.8%	67.9%
Rwanda	AG	83.3%	49.8%	59.7%	48.9%
	MAN	6.1%	12.0%	6.7%	8.9%
	MIN	10.6%	38.3%	33.7%	42.2%
Ethiopia	AG	89.8%	88.0%	90.5%	89.1%
	MAN	8.6%	10.6%	8.3%	8.9%
	MIN	1.6%	1.4%	1.2%	2.0%

Notes: AG = Agricultural raw materials and food; MAN = Manufactures; MIN = Ores, metals, and fuels.

Source: Author's estimate based on data from World Development Indicators 2017 (World Bank various years).

importance of manufacturing exports increased in 2005–09 and then fell back to previous levels. The relative importance of mineral exports increased dramatically for Mozambique from 2000 onwards with a corresponding fall in the relative importance of agriculture. Mineral exports have dominated the export pattern of Zambia throughout the period under study.

Human development, poverty, and inequality

At first glance the data in Table 29.1 might suggest strong evidence of development success and pro-poor growth, but this ignores the nature of the growth and the internal distribution of growth in the countries covered. Has growth delivered human development and has the income growth experienced trickled down to the poor? A broader measure of development can be obtained from the Human Development Index (HDI), which includes life expectancy and years of education as indicators of welfare (Table 29.5). The HDI shows a steady improvement for all seven countries but in

Table 29.5 Human Development Index (HDI) and Inequality Adjusted HDI (IAHDI)

Country	1995	2000	2005	2010	2015	
	HDI	HDI	HDI	HDI	HDI	IAHDI
Zambia	0.405	0.424	0.479	0.543	0.579	0.373
Ghana	0.473	0.485	0.510	0.554	0.579	0.391
Tanzania	0.368	0.391	0.446	0.498	0.531	0.396
Uganda	0.320	0.396	0.434	0.477	0.493	0.341
Mozambique	0.230	0.298	0.353	0.397	0.418	0.280
Rwanda	0.230	0.332	0.404	0.464	0.498	0.339
Ethiopia	n.a.	0.283	0.346	0.411	0.448	0.330

Source: Human Development Report (UNDP 2016).

percentage terms the greatest improvements since 2000 were experienced by Rwanda and Mozambique. This is even more pronounced if the comparison is made with 1995 although the initial low values in 1995 were clearly influenced by the process recovery from serious internal conflict. The least progress was experienced by Ghana and Uganda.

One of the disadvantages of the HDI is that it does not take direct account of inequality. UNDP has constructed an inequality adjusted HDI (IAHDI) in which the HDI values are adjusted downwards to take account of inequality. When this factor is taken into account the IAHDI values are much more evenly spread, which suggests that the largest part of overall economic growth tends to accrue to those with the highest incomes. However, the effects are not uniform for all countries and the rank ordering changes with Tanzania achieving the highest IAHDI and the values for the mineral exporting countries of Zambia, Ghana, and Mozambique falling significantly.

Another way of assessing the distributive impact of growth is to consider the growth in the per capita incomes of people in different cohorts. This can only be deduced for years where household expenditure survey data allow measurement of the incomes of specific deciles of the population. These surveys are not available for the same years for each country and, in the case of Ghana, the most recent available data are for 2006.

The nearest indication of the comparative relative position of the poorest groups can be obtained by providing available data for each country in a period of two to three years (Table 29.6). These data suggest that, in all countries except Ghana and Zambia, the per capita incomes of the poorest 10 per cent have increased quite significantly. However, the per capita income values of the poorest are quite similar for all the countries investigated despite the fact that the overall per capita incomes of the different countries vary considerably, confirming the impression gained from the IAHDI. Ghana and Zambia are the two countries with the highest overall GDP per capita values but show the least improvement in the incomes of the poor. Only Ethiopia and Tanzania appear to have exhibited pro-poor growth and even in Tanzania, while the per capita income of the poorest 10 per cent has increased at the same rate as the richest 10 per cent, the incomes

Table 29.6 Real GDP per capita of the poorest 10% and poorest 40% (US$ constant 2011 prices PPP)

Country		1995–96	1998–00	2002	2004–06	2007–09	2010–12
Zambia	10%	99.3	89.9	147.5	89.9		135.4
	40%	259.2	243.6	373.5	235.2		346.2
Ghana	10%		95.8		95.3		
	40%		173.6		189.8		
Tanzania	10%		94.3			114.8	160.9
	40%		159.0			195.8	241.0
Uganda	10%	70.1	64.2	69.4	78.4	91.3	102.6
	40%	171.9	163.0	172.6	194.8	233.0	261.1
Mozambique	10%	49.1		66.8		82.2	
	40%	87.0		117.5		155.6	
Rwanda	10%		44.8		49.3		77.4
	40%		79.1		90.8		125.2
Ethiopia	10%	32.9	51.0		60.6		75.5
	40%	51.6	74.1		83.5		122.5

Source: Author's estimate based on data from World Development Indicators 2017 (World Bank various years).

of the poorest 40 per cent have grown more slowly. The overall picture suggests that there is some difficulty in translating economic growth into a significant impact on poverty reduction, especially in the mineral rich countries of Ghana, Mozambique, and Zambia. In Zambia in particular, the proportion of rural population to total population has only declined from 63.8 per cent (1995–09) to 60.4 per cent (2010–04), but the proportion of GDP attributed to agriculture has fallen from 17.1 per cent to 10 per cent. This implies that the average income of the rural population has fallen from about 27 per cent of the national average to 17 per cent.[2]

Estimates of income growth and the per capita incomes of specific groups do not measure the incidence of poverty directly. An alternative indicator is the poverty headcount measure applied in terms of moderate and extreme poverty (US$3.10 and US$1.90 per day respectively). Table 29.7 shows the poverty headcount data for the same countries. The data are generally consistent with the conclusions from Table 29.6. For five of the countries considered there has been a clear but slow reduction in the incidence of both moderate and extreme poverty. The most significant declines in extreme poverty have occurred in Ethiopia and Tanzania followed by Uganda, Rwanda, and Mozambique. Some improvement has also been experienced in Ghana but there are insufficient observations to derive clear conclusions, although national data do indicate that a similar reduction in poverty rates to those experienced between 1998 and 2005 occurred

[2] These figures make the very crude assumption that the incomes of households in rural areas are only derived from agriculture but it provides some explanation for the failure of Zambian growth to significantly reduce poverty.

Table 29.7 Percentage of the population in poverty at US$1.90 and US$3.10 per day

Country		1995–96	1998–2000	2002	2004–06	2007–09	2010–12
Zambia	$1.90	41.7	42.1	49.4	60.5		64.4
	$3.10	63.3	64.3	75.1	76.9		78.9
Ghana	$1.90	33.9			25.2		
	$3.10	60.5			49.0		
Tanzania	$1.90		84.7			52.7	46.6
	$3.10		95.3			77.9	76.1
Uganda	$1.90	59.6	64.1	62.2	53.2	41.5	34.6
	$3.10	83.4	84.6	82.5	76.3	69.4	65.0
Mozambique	$1.90	85.4		80.4		68.7	
	$3.10	94.0		92.0		87.5	
Rwanda	$1.90		77.0		68.0		60.3
	$3.10		89.7		84.1		80.7
Ethiopia	$1.90	66.4	55.4		36.3		33.5
	$3.10	86.4	87.1		76.2		71.3

Source: Author's estimate based on data from World Development Indicators 2017 (World Bank various years).

between 2005 and 2012. However, it appears that, in Zambia, the overall incidence of both extreme and moderate poverty has actually worsened.

The apparent contradiction between the increase in the overall incidence of poverty in Zambia and the improvement of the income levels of the bottom 10 per cent can be explained by income changes within the lowest income groups, in particular the steadily increasing overall proportion of the population falling in World Bank categories that include households with per capita incomes below both categories. The real growth in the incomes of the third quintile in Zambia was lowest of all, suggesting a greater polarization in the distribution of income between the relatively rich and the relatively poor. Such changes can be identified using measures of inequality such as the Gini coefficient and the Kuznets ratio (Table 29.8).[3] It is clear that Zambia has been the country with greatest overall inequality and the level of inequality has worsened in the last decade. Rwanda also has a very unequal income distribution which worsened between 2000 and 2005. This explains the relatively modest reduction in poverty given the country's strong growth performance. A similar situation applies to Mozambique although inequality is lower.

Inequality in Tanzania and Uganda has not changed very much. Inequality worsened in the late 1990s, possibly as a consequence of economic liberalization measures, but it has since improved. Meanwhile Ethiopia experienced a substantial decrease in inequality in the late 1990s but this has since been partially reversed, although the level of inequality remains the lowest of all the countries included in the study.

[3] The Gini coefficient measures the ratio of the area of inequality defined by the Lorenz curve to the area defined by a line of equality. The higher the Gini coefficient the higher the level of inequality. The Kuznets ratio measures the ratio of the incomes of the richest 20 per cent to the poorest 40 per cent.

Table 29.8 Indicators of inequality (Gini coefficient and Kuznets ratio)

Country		1995–96	1998–2000	2002–2004	2004–06	2007–09	2010–12
Zambia	Gini	48.33	49.13	42.06	54.29		55.62
	Kuznets	4.19	4.36	2.99	5.66		5.78
Ghana	Gini	40.07			42.77		
	Kuznets	2.87			3.21		
Tanzania	Gini		37.3			40.28	37.78
	Kuznets		2.47			2.79	2.48
Uganda	Gini	39.04	43.0	45.17	42.94	44.2	41.01
	Kuznets	2.64	3.12	3.38	3.13	3.26	3.06
Mozambique	Gini	44.41		47.04		45.58	
	Kuznets	3.31		3.64		3.50	
Rwanda	Gini		48.55		52.04		51.34
	Kuznets		3.91		4.58		4.33
Ethiopia	Gini	44.56	29.98		29.81		33.17
	Kuznets	3.18	1.76		1.75		2.02

Source: Author's estimate based on data from World Development Indicators 2017 (World Bank various years).

Two of the three most agricultural economies (Ethiopia and Tanzania) have relatively low levels of inequality but the third (Rwanda) does not. The mineral exporting economies of Ghana, Mozambique, and Zambia show some of the highest levels of inequality and the increasing relative importance of minerals in Ghana has corresponded with rising inequality. Overall there are sufficient variations in the data to suggest that policy options do exist to deliver more pro-poor growth, but the conclusions are limited by data availability due to the time intervals between the conduct of surveys, particularly in the case of Ghana for which the most recent indicators of poverty and inequality that are comparable to the other countries relate to 2005. However, data for Ghana based on national poverty lines suggest a 24 per cent reduction in poverty between 2005 and 2012. This change was caused by a combination of 13–15 per cent reductions in the rural and urban poverty rates and the effects of migration from the relatively poor rural areas to the relatively affluent urban areas.

Aid dependence

All seven countries have received significant inflows of foreign aid (Table 29.9). In all cases except Zambia the absolute value of aid has tended to increase but, in all cases, the percentage of gross national income (GNI) coming from aid has declined. In this sense all the countries included in this study have become less aid dependent. The decline in the relative importance of aid has been greatest in those countries with the highest per capita incomes (Ghana and Zambia). This suggests both that the targeting of aid appears to be in line with stated aid objectives in relation to poverty reduction and that the perception that aid increases the dependency of recipient countries is not supported by

Table 29.9 Net overseas development assistance (US$ million constant 2013 prices and % of GNI, period averages)

Country		1995–99	2000–04	2005–09	2010–14
Zambia	Total	1176	1169	1328	1016
	% of GNI	23.9	18.7	10.2	4.3
Ghana	Total	838	1179	1396	1559
	% of GNI	8.9	13.1	6.5	4.1
Tanzania	Total	1370	2023	2505	2885
	% of GNI	12.8	12.8	10.3	7.5
Uganda	Total	1040	1329	1729	1662
	% of GNI	11.8	14.5	13.2	7.3
Mozambique	Total	1425	1938	1908	2121
	% of GNI	26.1	25.7	19.3	15.4
Rwanda	Total	617	525	811	1066
	% of GNI	27.7	20.3	19.7	15.7
Ethiopia	Total	1038	1848	2955	3549
	% of GNI	9.0	15.2	13.2	8.9

Source: Author's estimate based on data from World Development Indicators 2017 (World Bank various years).

the overall evidence. Aid dependence may have been an issue in some places at some times but it is not getting worse. However, the two most aid dependent countries (Mozambique and Rwanda) have the highest levels of inequality apart from Zambia. Aid dependence may be falling and aid may have contributed to poverty reduction but there is no evidence to suggest that it has had a significant impact on inequality. It could be argued that aid inflows have had a positive impact on poverty reduction but the policy conditions that were attached, particularly in the 1990s, may have contributed to the rising trends in inequality.

Official aid from the traditional donors may have declined in relative importance but, in many cases, the gap has been filled by other sources, particularly the BRICs countries, the largest source being China. Alternative external sources of funds are increasingly available, particularly for infrastructure. They can be associated with varying types and levels of concessionality and conditionality and are not always described as 'aid', but they have allowed greater space for policy choice with varying consequences for overall development and governance issues.

Conclusion

Available empirical evidence suggests that robust economic growth has occurred in a number of sub-Saharan African economies. This has coincided with a decline in the relative importance of agriculture and an increase in the proportion of the population living in urban areas. As expected, the relative importance of agriculture has declined and the relative importance of services has increased in most cases except Mozambique where it was already high at the start of the period covered. The relative importance of industry has increased in some cases but much of it is associated with mineral extraction and this has not led to a significant increase in the relative importance of manufacturing.

Economic growth has resulted in significant improvements in the standard of living of the poor in most cases. The per capita income of the poorest groups has increased in all seven countries observed except Zambia for which data are inconclusive. The proportion of the population living below the US$1.90 and US$3.10 per day poverty lines has fallen in all countries except Zambia for which this proportion has increased. The extent of the decline in poverty rates has been greatest in Ethiopia and Tanzania.

However, the economic growth has resulted in increasing inequality in most of the countries considered in this study. Ethiopia has the lowest level of inequality but this has started to increase in the last five years. Only in Tanzania and Uganda has there been relatively little change in indicators of inequality.

All seven countries have received substantial aid inflows but all seven have become less dependent on aid, particularly the countries with the highest per capita incomes. This suggests that targeting of aid is relatively effective and that it is making some contribution to poverty reduction.

The structure of exports has changed significantly in most countries. Agriculture is no longer the leading export sector in three countries and only contributes more than 50 per cent of exports in Uganda and Ethiopia. It is only in Ethiopia that it has maintained its traditional importance. It is no coincidence that the relative importance of agriculture in Ethiopia is combined with the lowest level of inequality. The relative importance of mineral production appears to be associated with higher levels of inequality, particularly in Zambia and Mozambique. An important question for mineral exporting countries is how to ensure that national mineral wealth is used to support pro-poor investment. In the absence of such measures the already high levels of inequality experienced in most countries will only increase.

Overall it can be argued that the basis for sustained economic growth in the African lions has been established, but it is critically dependent on outside influences, particularly inflows of both aid and foreign direct investment (FDI) and the terms of trade for the products that they export. The extent to which this growth will deliver significant poverty reduction in all cases depends on how well both internal and external resources are used and therefore on the internal policy environment and the extent to which this reflects the needs of the poor. In view of the observed tendency for decreases in the relative importance of agriculture to exacerbate income differentials, some pro-poor policy interventions are required to redress the balance.

REFERENCES

Bhorat, H. and Tarp, F. (2016). *Africa's Lions: Growth Traps and Opportunities for Six African Economies*. Washington, DC: Brookings Institution Press.

Chen, W., Dollar, D., and Tang, H. (2016). 'Why is China investing in Africa? Evidence from the firm level', *World Bank Economic Review* 32/3: 610–32. Available at https//doi: 10.1093/wber/lhw049, accessed 4 October 2018.

Lawrence, P. (2010). 'The African tragedy: international and national roots', in V. Padayachee (ed.) *The Political Economy of Africa*. London: Routledge, 19–38.

MGI (McKinsey Global Institute) (2010). *Lions on the Move: The Progress and Potential of African Economies*. MGI.

MGI (McKinsey Global Institute) (2016). *Lions on the Move II: Realizing the Potential of African Economies*. MGI.

Moss, T. (2011). *African Development*, 2nd edn. Boulder, CO: Lynne Rienner.

Paul, A. (2014). 'Indian foreign direct investment: a way to Africa', *Procedia—Social and Behavioral Sciences* 157: 183–95.

Rodrik, D. (2014). 'An African growth miracle?'. NBER Working Papers 20188. Cambridge, MA: National Bureau of Economic Research.

Taylor, I. (2014). 'Is Africa rising?', *Brown Journal of World Affairs* 21/1: 143.

UNCTAD (United Nations Conference on Trade and Development) (2016). *The Least Developed Countries Report 2016*. New York: United Nations.

UNDP (United Nations Development Programme) (2016). *Human Development Report 2016: Human Development for Everyone*. New York: United Nations. Available at http://hdr.undp.org/en/data#, accessed 27 November 2018.

World Bank (various years). *World Development Indicators*. Washington, DC: World Bank.

Part V
Sustainable Development Issues

30 Happiness in BRICS

Tadashi Hirai

Introduction

Since the late twentieth century, happiness has been investigated for well-being assessment particularly in relation to economic development in the school of 'economics of happiness' or 'happiness economics'. This paradigm shift can be seen as a revival, given that happiness had been treated directly in evaluating well-being in the past (e.g. utilitarianism, Greek philosophy). Under the dominance of the neoclassical economic theory, however, happiness is treated indirectly, on the assumption that it is to be enhanced automatically together with economic growth. Against this assumption, it has been argued that economic growth does not necessarily increase happiness, known as the Easterlin Paradox. By now, the significance of happiness in well-being assessments has become worldwide. For example, the World Happiness Report has been published since 2012, which helps, together with other UN publications such as the Human Development Report, to attack the single-minded economic development policy promoted by the Bretton Woods institutions. Concurrently, the International Day of Happiness was established in the General Assembly and has since been celebrated every year around the world.

In this context, the investigation of happiness seems particularly relevant to BRICS not only because as with developed nations economic growth tends to be underscored at the risk of other important aspects of our living, but also because its impact on happiness would be represented more revealingly in its transition. As much as economic growth does not move together with happiness, it is essential to examine how happiness has been affected in the emerging economies. As will be seen, however, the research on this issue has been rather limited across countries (except for the recent boom of publications in China). Given this, it is important to comprehensively review the past publications on happiness in BRICS and to establish whether any lessons can be found among them. Although each country has unique features and determinants of happiness, some commonality will be found in the similar stages of economic development. More broadly, some convergence will also be found between the determinants of happiness over time (subjective assessments) and the requirements typically set for a good living (objective assessments).

The structure of this chapter is as follows. First, the concept of happiness will be reviewed and classified in order to examine the relevance of the type of happiness to the way of assessment. Next, the determinants of happiness will be examined by reviewing

Tadashi Hirai, *Happiness in BRICS* In: *Handbook of BRICS and Emerging Economies.* Edited by: P.B. Anand, Shailaja Fennell, and Flavio Comim, Oxford University Press (2021).
DOI: 10.1093/oso/9780198827535.003.0030

past publications on happiness in each BRICS country. Finally, both weaker and stronger claims will be addressed: a weaker claim is that some lessons will be able to be shared for happiness in face of emerging economies; and a stronger claim is that happiness would be better evaluated through both subjective and objective lenses.

Realm of happiness and its way of assessment

Generally, the term 'happiness' tends to be used interchangeably across different debates. For example, all happiness, well-being, life satisfaction, utility, and welfare have been very much used in the same way in the field of economics as Easterlin (2005), van Praag (2005), and Frey (2008) argue. This tendency is, to a lesser extent, also applied to the field of psychology, as Diener et al. (2004) point out. All in all, happiness has not been defined, at least in practice, in a uniformed way. To make the best of the happiness research for public policies, however, it seems important to review the concept of happiness and to clarify what type of happiness is at issue for discussion.

The interchangeable interpretation of happiness seems to be caused mainly by its generic nature. In order to avoid confusion, it is imperative to take the distinction between each element into account within the umbrella terminology, rather than using them interchangeably or focusing on either of them while excluding others. In this respect, Nussbaum indicates the ambiguity inherent in psychological questions and advocates the necessity of the conceptual clarification which is worth quoting at length:

> Since the psychologists who work with this question ('Taking all things together, how satisfied are you with your life as a whole these days?') do not notice this ambiguity (between feelings and judgment), they do nothing to sort things out, so we do not really know which question their subjects are answering. Probably some are answering one question, some the other. What would be needed to progress would be conceptual work to separate the feeling-conception from the judgment-conception, and then a set of questions designed to tease apart those distinct notions. (Nussbaum 2008: S87, parentheses added)

It is true that the feeling conception could not be clearly separated from the judgement conception, given that reasons are affected by emotions and vice versa. However, some clarification has been developed.

MENTAL STATES—THE PURE HAPPINESS THEORY

According to Brülde (2007a, 2007b), happiness could at least have the following conceptions: (1) the pure affective view (including hedonism); (2) the pure cognitive view; (3) the hybrid view (composing both affective and cognitive components).

On the one hand, happiness is commonly interpreted as affective. For example, it is seen as equivalent to a balance between positive affect and negative affect (Bradburn

1969), a temporal integral of instant utility or simply pleasure (Kahneman et al. 1997, 2004; Kahneman 1999; Layard 2005).[1] Here, happiness is seen as a single quantitative thing without any qualitative or normative substance, as clearly stated: '. . . no good feeling is bad in itself – it can only be bad because of its consequences' (Layard 2005). In this regard, Layard goes further, accusing John Stuart Mill of believing that happiness varies both in quantity and quality: he was right in his intuition about the true sources of lasting happiness, but wrong to argue that some types of happiness are intrinsically better than others. Relevant to this viewpoint but more systematically, Kahneman et al. (1997) propose a concept of 'experienced utility', an instant utility to measure hedonic and affective experience more accurately by immediate reports of current subjective experience, as opposed to 'decision utility' which is vulnerable to cognitive judgement. Not clearly but supposedly, Bruni and Porta (2005) also see it as affective by defining it as a part of subjective well-being which is completed with life satisfaction.

On the other hand, happiness is interpreted as cognitive. In this view, to be happy is to evaluate one's life based on one's own values and often referred to as life satisfaction (e.g. Haybron 2007).[2] This view is typically found in most motivation researchers, among which are the social cognitive theory in Bandura (1986, 1997), the general control theory in Carver and Scheier (1981), and the goal setting theory in Locke and Latham (1990). Their common argument is that happiness (psychological health) would follow as long as one evaluates that adequate progress is being made towards goals based on one's own values. According to Deci and Ryan (2000), these theories treat motivation as a unitary concept, variable only in amount rather than kind. It implies that the cognitive view is similar to the affective view in terms of the focus on quantity rather than quality. This category can also be shared by van Praag and Ferrer-i-Carbonell (2004), who define happiness as satisfaction in nine dimensions (health, job, finance, housing, leisure, environment, social life, marriage, politics) so as to quantify happiness.

More comprehensively, the hybrid view is advocated by many such as Headey and Wearing (1992), Diener (1994), Veenhoven (1996, 2000, 2005), Argyle (2002), Diener et al. (2004), Nettle (2005), and Hirata (2008), and often regarded as equivalent to subjective well-being (e.g. Headey and Wearing 1992; Diener 1994; Nettle 2005). Indeed, Diener et al. (2004) think of it as an umbrella term, although stressing on the affective side. Similarly, recognizing happiness as a generic term which consists of both affective (we estimate how well we feel generally) and cognitive (we compare life as it is with a perceived standard of how life should be) information, Veenhoven (1996, 2000, 2005) maintains that happiness be primarily based on the affective level and that cognitive information be only secondary, and thus not calculated by comparing life as it is to standards of how life should be but rather inferred from how well one feels generally. The

[1] Elsewhere, Kahneman implies happiness in a cognitive sense (e.g. Nickerson et al. 2003), as Bruni (2008) points out.

[2] In contrast, Brülde (2007a, 2007b) categorizes life satisfaction into the hybrid view which will be explained in the next paragraph.

reasons for prioritizing the affective side are both constitutive and practical: while it is constitutive given that the affective orientation capacity precedes the development of cognition in evolution (Veenhoven 2000, 2005), it is practical to the extent that overall judgement of life satisfaction would be possible by affective information rather than cognitive information which requires calculation based on the comparison among multiple dimensions in life (Veenhoven 2000). Consequently, he goes further to argue, in favour of affective information, that happiness is sometimes distorted by cognitive information in a short run but corrected in a long run. In contrast, Nettle (2005) and Hirata (2008) stress the cognitive aspect: while Nettle views happiness as judgements about the balance of feelings, Hirata similarly regards it as always a judgement where some sort of cognitive judgement (e.g. reflection, approval) must precede the affective side even though the latter need not, but can, be involved.

Overall, all the conceptions of happiness described here depend solely on mental states and the conception has been named as the 'pure happiness theory' by Brülde (2007a, 2007b) in order to highlight the importance of a group of theories of well-being that depend on the state of affairs. In the pure happiness theory (the cognitive view in particular), it is sufficient that one *believes* that one's life is going the way one wants, whereas it is essential to other theories of well-being (which require the state of affairs) that one's life is *actually* going the way one wants.

STATE OF AFFAIRS—MODIFIED VERSION OF THE PURE HAPPINESS THEORY OR EUDAIMONIA

To make happiness more relevant to a characterization of well-being or a good life, the hybrid view of the pure happiness theory has been modified, not only by stressing the cognitive side (e.g. Nettle 2005; Hirata 2008) but also by trying to go beyond mental states and covering the state of affairs to the extent that one is required to be autonomous and informed of the circumstances of their own and others while adhering to subjective assessments. Among these are 'authentic happiness' by Sumner (1996) and Seligman (2002), and 'prudential happiness' by Haybron (2000).

One step further, following Aristotle, happiness can be interpreted as eudaimonic.[3] This view builds on some criteria for a good life, which is distinct from a modified version of the hybrid view (e.g. Sumner 1996; Haybron 2000; Seligman 2002) in terms of requiring objective/public assessments in addition to subjective/individual assessments. Among which are the 'ideal happiness' by Tatarkiewicz (1976) and the 'real happiness'

[3] A eudaimonic side of happiness has been acknowledged by some psychologists but not developed further. For example, Veenhoven refrains from explicating it to avoid confusion (Veenhoven 2000, 2007), while Diener simply distinguishes happiness which encompasses the judgement of experts (i.e. an additional requirement of virtues) (Diener et al. 2004) from subjective well-being defined as individual's own assessments of one's life (Diener 1994), ending up focusing on the investigation of the latter.

by Nussbaum (2008). A main feature of this type of happiness is the very requirement of external goods. It differs from virtue which cares for the goods of the soul only independently of the existence of other goods. In this sense, virtue is necessary but not sufficient for this type of happiness (Annas 1993); and happiness, unlike virtue, certainly requires freedoms from external impediment by means of the equipment with external goods (Engstrom 1996). In other words, eudaimonia concerns not only what is under the agent's control (the goods of the soul) but also what is not (external goods including the goods of the body) from the perspective of morality (Annas 1993) and distributive justice (Nussbaum 2008). In contrast, virtue seems to correspond to the modified version of the pure happiness theory which insists on the necessity of adjusting subjective/individual assessments based on mental states by taking the state of affairs into account but not on the necessity of external goods required for a good living in objective/public assessments in view of morality and justice. The bottom line is that eudaimonia is more comprehensive than the modified version of the pure happiness theory in a private sphere, to the extent that the distribution of external goods is required to be justified in a public sphere.

Unlike those who prioritize the affective side in the hybrid view of the pure happiness theory (e.g. Diener 1994; Veenhoven 2000, 2005), those who are categorized here regard the affective side (pleasure) not as primary but as a by-product of fulfilment which leads to eudaimonia. For example, Franklin (2010) views that pleasure is considered as only incidental to eudaimonia and not the cause of it. More decisively, Nussbaum (2005) argues that some pleasures are ethically bad in that those closely associated with bad activities do not lead to eudaimonia. To the extent that pleasure is often seen as a fallible indicator of healthy living and wellness (e.g. Ryff and Singer 1998; Ryan and Deci 2001), those who support this view recognize the difference in quality, instead of seeing it as a single thing which varies only in quantity in terms of intensity and duration (e.g. Kahneman 1999; Layard 2005). Nonetheless, they think it essential as a motivational tool for human activities towards eudaimonia. For example, Franklin (2010) advocates that the affective side (e.g. desire, emotion) is not rational but is the source of energy that powers our actions when being combined with reason. Similarly, Nussbaum (2008) argues, in normative thinking, that emotions express correct evaluation and spur to good action.

HAPPINESS—SUBJECTIVE AND OBJECTIVE

Unlike the current tendency to regard happiness as mental states (the pure happiness theory regardless of being modified or not), a eudaimonic view of happiness has a long historical root. According to Tatarkiewicz, this view ('an idea which seems strange to us now' [Tatarkiewicz 1976: 33]) had pervaded as a mainstream over two thousand years before the influence of Bentham in the period of the Enlightenment. Given this historical perspective, together with some overlap (reviewed in the previous sub-section), a comprehensive reflection of happiness seems to be a natural direction rather than an exclusive view of either of them.

Indeed, no single theory can reflect the whole story of the discussions about happiness and well-being, as implied by Parfit when arguing that: 'What is good for someone is neither just what Hedonists claim, nor just what is claimed by Objective List Theorists. We might believe that if we had *either* of these, *without the other*, what we had would have little or no value' (Parfit 1984: 502, emphasis in original). Similarly, Griffin goes further to discredit the significance of the dichotomy: 'the distinction between objective and subjective . . . does not mark an especially crucial distinction. It would be better if these terms . . . were put into retirement. But if they are not, if the question "Subjective or objective?" is pressed, then the answer has to be "Both"' (Griffin 1986: 33). This naturally implies the necessity of both subjective and objective assessments and also the impossibility of distinguishing between happiness and well-being.

Now, let us briefly consider the problem of adaptive preferences because it is a justification of objectivity together with subjectivity in well-being evaluations. The problem is eloquently argued in the following lines by Sen:

> A person who has had a life of misfortune, with very little opportunities, and rather little hope, may be more easily reconciled to deprivations than others reared in more fortunate and affluent circumstances. The metric of happiness may, therefore, distort the extent of deprivation, in a specific and biased way. The hopeless beggar, the precarious landless labourer, the dominated housewife, the hardened unemployed or the over-exhausted coolie may all take pleasures in small mercies, and manage to suppress intense suffering for the necessity of continuing survival, but it would be ethically deeply mistaken to attach a correspondingly small value to the loss of their well-being because of this survival strategy. The same problem arises with the other interpretation of utility, namely, desire-fulfilment, since the hopelessly deprived lack the courage to desire much, and their deprivations are muted and deadened in the scale of desire-fulfilment. (Sen 1987: 45–6)

Simply put, the problem here is the malleability of subjective views, personal preferences, values, and evaluations. This point is also expressed by Griffin who is a supporter of the objective list theories: 'Our desires are shaped by our expectations, which are shaped by our circumstances. Any injustice in the last infects the first' (Griffin 1986: 44). The indispensable appeal of objective assessments is the requirement of morality and justice from a political perspective. This problem has been indeed acknowledged by those who support the modified version of the pure happiness theory while being in favour of subjective assessments (e.g. Sumner 1996; Brülde 2007b; Chekola 2007). To address it, Sumner, in particular, breaks an impasse on the issue of 'autonomy':

> In that case, the obvious remedy is to correct for the conditions under which their expectations about themselves came to be formed. The problem is . . . that they have never had the opportunity

to form their own values at all. They do not lack enlightenment, or insight into the Platonic form of the good; they lack autonomy. (Sumner 1996: 166)[4]

However, it is not clear how the values skewed by deprived conditions can be adjusted only by being autonomous. On the one hand, such values cannot be adjusted in deprived conditions even if autonomy is secured precisely because of being deprived; on the other hand, such values are difficult to adjust once developed in non-autonomous circumstances.[5] Consequently, Griffin voices his stance of rejecting autonomy: 'considerations of autonomy are, on reflection, no recommendation of it' (Griffin 1986: 11). In a similar but more nuanced manner, Nussbaum demonstrates an objection to the simple application of autonomy: 'If one cares about autonomy, then one must care about the rest of the form of life that supports it and the material conditions that enable one to live that form of life' (Nussbaum 1992: 225). Autonomy is surely important, but it does not automatically lead the skewed values to be fixed in an always justifiable manner. In order to make autonomy work, values ought to be formed by the needs required to be human. Thus, it seems that a certain level of objective criteria is needed to deal with adaptive preferences.[6]

To be fair, Sumner (1996) accepts the possibility of generating a list of standard human goods despite individual differences, while insisting that well-being is assessed subjectively by individuals on the basis of how well their life is going. In turn, Griffin (1986) also acknowledges the importance of subjectivity (desire) to make the objective theories more flexible and sensitive, while stressing the strengths of the needs account in view of morality and advocating that well-being is the level to which basic needs are met. With both in mind some compromise can be found from subjective to objective accounts (e.g. Sumner) and also vice versa (e.g. Griffin) for a comprehensive well-being assessment.

The realm of happiness and its way of assessment can be illustrated in the following diagram which represents eight patterns described in the subsidiary table (Figure 30.1).[7]

The pure happiness theory consists of both affective and cognitive spheres which are assessed individually and so subjectively. It is also true of the modified version of the

[4] His remedy is also followed by Chekola 2007 and Brülde 2007b. However, it seems that Brülde accepts the necessity of objective assessments to greater extent by proposing the possibility of objectively predetermined life domains.

[5] In this regard, self-determination theory (SDT) demonstrates that those who are raised in a non-autonomous environment tend to prioritize extrinsic values over intrinsic values, which does not help autonomy to be cultivated in a justifiable way (e.g. Kasser et al. 1995).

[6] Note here that the objective criteria in this case do not follow perfectionism, as human needs surely include 'practical reason' which allows us to reconsider what needs would be necessary for the standards of well-being and thus offers us the possibility of revising objective criteria of needs.

[7] A similar analysis has been made by Nettle (2005) by categorizing happiness into three types: momentary feelings (joy, pleasure), judgements about feelings (satisfaction), and quality of life (flourishing). Instead of drawing on the convergence among them, however, he regards three types of happiness as hierarchical (from momentary feeling as level one to quality of life as level three) and deals with the first two levels (i.e. the pure happiness theory) while excluding the third level to protect individual judgements from the tyranny of experts and thus avoid moralizing happiness.

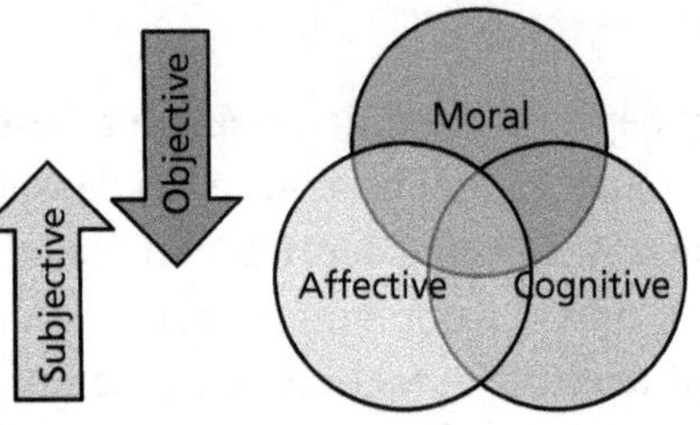

E	A	C	Description
o	×	×	Morality disharmonised
o	o	×	Physiological goals pursued
o	×	o	Other-regarding goals pursued
o	o	o	Eudaimonia pursued
×	o	o	Self-regarding goals pursued
×	o	×	Affection biased
×	×	o	Cognition biased
×	×	×	Happiness not pursued

Figure 30.1 Realm of happiness and its way of assessment

Source: Hirai (2017).

pure happiness theory with the cognitive sphere more stressed. In contrast, the moral sphere differs in the requirement of objective assessments in view of justice formed in public. The ultimate happiness would therefore be a sphere where the pure happiness theory (affection and cognition) converges with morality, namely where individual assessments of one's own life correspond to public assessments of human flourishing. This characterizes eudaimonia and can be a possible direction of the happiness research for public policies.

Determinants of happiness in BRICS

In order to browse the happiness research in BRICS with a special focus on the influence from economic development, the online search engine 'EconLit' was used. Searching the keywords of 'happiness' and the name of each country without setting up any search limits (i.e. Boolean search mode, open date, all publication types, all geographic regions), it has been found that the number of publications varies enormously from four in Brazil to sixty-one in China.[8] In order to investigate the characterization of happiness in each country, they were further filtered to pick up those that focus on the determinants particular to each country. Consequently, those that deal with the determinants of happiness either too broadly or too narrowly have been removed (e.g. philosophical argument which can be applied to many other countries, happiness of a specific population type such as investors and patients).[9]

[8] Accessed April 2015.

[9] The publication written in other than English has been also excluded because of the lack of author's reading ability, but it seems not to much affect the investigation given that the number of publications excluded for this reason counts two in China, one in Russia, and none in Brazil, India, or South Africa.

BRAZIL

Happiness research in Brazil has not gone into high gear yet. The total publication count is only four so far, with the first one published in 2009. Apart from an article on the significance of property rights for happiness, the remaining three address the impact of aspirations for public safety and health/ethical norms on happiness.

On the one hand, making a comparative study between Brazil and the US, Cavalcanti et al. (2009) find that policy towards improvements in public safety has a stronger effect on happiness in Brazil than the US. On the other hand, Graham (2011) points out that the overall health satisfaction in Brazil is the lowest among the Latin American and Caribbean countries, which implies the health norms in Brazil are the highest given similar objective conditions across the region. Moreover, James (2011) compares the effect of ethical norms (e.g. inappropriately claiming government benefits, cheating on taxes) on happiness in Brazil, the US, Canada, and Mexico, and finds that it is highest in Brazil (nearly twice as large as in the US and nearly three times stronger than in Canada). With all the three researches considered, it can be said that all the aspirations for public safety, health, and ethical norms are high in Brazil compared not only with neighbouring countries (Latin America and the Caribbean countries) but also developed countries (US and Canada). These findings reveal that the phenomenon of adaptive preferences cannot be confirmed in Brazil given the actual living conditions.

RUSSIA

The search engine hit sixteen publications, with a particular concentration in 2001 when the *Journal of Happiness Studies* had a special issue focusing on happiness in Russia. As a result of filtering further for the purposes of this research, nine publications have been found relevant. An overall theme here is the relation between happiness and the transition that Russia has faced, as expected in the preface to the special issue of the *Journal of Happiness Studies* (Veenhoven 2001a). Generally, the transition in Russia has had a negative effect on happiness (Veenhoven 2001b). More concretely, the arguments can be categorized into the following three topics: (1) income level; (2) unemployment and mobility; (3) economic insecurity. Interestingly, these topics have been investigated chronologically in the literature.

Starting with the first point, a positive effect of income level has been found by Saris (2001), Saris and Andreenkova (2001), Schyns (2001), and Graham and Pettinato (2002). In addition, Graham and Pettinato (2002) discover that this effect outweighs the effect of educational level (as is the case in Latin American countries). Referring to the phenomenon of the Easterlin Paradox, it can be interpreted that Russia at the beginning of the transition had not reached the point where income and happiness do not move together.

This point is indeed connected to the second point, namely unemployment. Surprisingly, unemployment has an insignificant effect on happiness in Russia (unlike in the US and Europe) (Graham and Pettinato 2002) and even has a positive effect (Eggers et al. 2006). The first finding is justified by the view that it is not unemployment in itself but fear of losing a job that negatively affects happiness, while the second finding by the view that the positive effect of unemployment is caused by revising standards downwards in face of peers suffering in a troubled economy. With both in mind it seems that mobility (accompanied with being out of employment) has been regarded as promising and that its effect is stronger than that of losing a job. Related to this, Graham (2005) finds a positive effect of self-employment in Russia similar to the US but unlike Latin America. Given that Latin America has the same result in terms of the positive effect of income which outweighs the effect of educational level (Graham and Pettinato 2002), a possible interpretation would be either that the positive effect of income and mobility in transition is strong enough to overcome the negative effect of the risks accompanying self-employment in Russia unlike in Latin America, or that a more stable social structure has been offered in Russia than in Latin America (or both). The latter view is supported by the finding that minorities are happier than other groups in Russia unlike in Latin America (Graham 2005) and the US (Graham et al. 2004). Given that Russia has a positive effect of both self-employment and minorities on happiness whereas the US has a positive effect of self-employment but a negative effect of minorities, and Latin America has a negative effect of both, the social structure in Russia could be judged at this stage of the transition as a good mixture between communism and capitalism.

More recently, Linz and Semykina (2010) examined the effect of economic insecurity, an inherent characteristic of the transition from a planned economy to a market-oriented economy, and found it to be negative. Comparing this negative effect with the positive effects found earlier, it seems that people are affected positively because of income and mobility up to the halfway point of transition but turn to be affected negatively as economic insecurity grows over time. It reinforces the view that the effect of income and mobility is strong enough to cancel out the negative effect of others accompanied with transition but it does not last long unless economic insecurity is to be overcome.

INDIA

Although seventeen publications were found by the search, most of them are either about philosophical argument which can be applied to many other countries or about happiness of a specific population type (e.g. patients, employees, consumers). Furthermore, two out of the remaining three publications deal with either the international comparison of happiness including India or the empirical relevance of mental health to happiness which can be generalized in other countries. As a result, only one article has remained relevant for this research.

Fontaine and Yamada (2014) investigate the relation between the caste system and happiness and discover not only that the caste comparison has a negative effect in general but also that the between-caste comparison has a stronger negative effect than the within-caste comparison. This finding is particularly important in addressing the issue of stratification uniquely embedded in India's social structure and justifies the effort to tackle horizontal inequality prior to vertical inequality.

CHINA

Happiness research in China seems particularly popular, standing out with the hit of sixty-one publications. After excluding those irrelevant for the purpose of this chapter (e.g. philosophical argument, happiness of a special population type such as investors, marrieds, and the elderly), forty-one have remained, which have been further filtered to remove publications whose arguments can be generalized in other countries (e.g. positive effect of consumption, social harmony, fair reward, and public investment for transformation on the one hand; negative effect of inflation, pollution, inequality, and loneliness on the other). Consequently, twenty-four publications have been found relevant for investigation. Overall, they are concerned with economic transition with some reference to migration, which can be categorized into the following four topics: (1) aspirations and expectations (with a particular focus on income);[10] (2) insecurity and inequality; (3) education; (4) cultural values.

Starting with aspirations and expectations, both Gao and Smyth (2011) and Frijters et al. (2012) find that income expectations are particularly optimistic among migrants and have a positive effect on their current levels of happiness. This finding has been found also among rural women whose husbands have migrated (Liang et al. 2014).[11] In contrast, Knight et al. (2009) demonstrate that migration overall negatively affects happiness because of aspirations set by their wrong reference groups (i.e. false expectations); this has been investigated in a series of their successive works. For example, comparing migrants in the urban area with those remaining in the rural area, Knight and Gunatilaka (2010a) reveal that migrants tend to have false expectations about their urban conditions and themselves in future, while Knight et al. (2009) analyse that rural people are happy confining their reference groups to the village. More generally, Knight and

[10] In sociology, aspiration is often distinguished from expectation in the sense that the former refers to idealistic goals while the latter refers to realistic appraisals (Morgan 2006). Although this distinction has not been made clearly in the happiness research, it is interesting to note that in the literature expectation tends to be accompanied with adjectives (e.g. false, optimistic) unlike aspiration.

[11] In this regard, Zhang (2013) demonstrates that inflation does not have a significant effect among migrants in China, whereas Chen et al. (2014) find a negative effect of inflation on happiness among the poor population in particular. The reason for the difference would be that the former targets migrants exclusively (whose aspirations are higher) while the latter targets a wider range of samples (whose aspirations are lower).

Gunatilaka (2010b, 2011) illustrate that rural people are indeed happier than urban people, including migrants.

Second, the relevance of insecurity to happiness is examined by Knight and Gunatilaka (2010b, 2011), Knight (2012), and Liang and Wang (2014), with all proving negative. In this context, von Kleist (2010) modifies the utility function of migrants in China by featuring the relation of the positivity of the income effect to the negativity of this insecurity effect together with the status effect (closely related to the specification of reference groups as argued above). Moreover, Knight (2012) analyses that social instability is caused partly by income inequality which cannot be justified by productivity or effort, while Knight and Gunatilaka (2010b) find that income inequality in itself has a positive effect on happiness. In this regard, Jiang et al. (2012) go further in separating income-related inequality from identity-related inequality and reveal that the latter negatively affects happiness but the former (after controlling identity) positively affects happiness. These findings imply that the positive effect of income-related inequality is counterbalanced by the negative effect of identity-related inequality (including inequality which cannot be justified by productivity or effort) and that the former is stronger than the latter at the early stage of economic transition but getting weaker over time. To solve the problem, Liang and Wang (2014) propose the significance of enhancing social security systems through education, medical access, and employment.

Third, with regard to the effect of education on happiness, two opposite views have been articulated. On the one hand, Knight et al. (2010) examine the determinants of happiness in the rural area and find that education has a positive effect on happiness (together with income and health). More broadly, Lam and Liu (2014) compare the effect of education on happiness between China and the US and reveal that education (similar to income and non-agricultural work) is positively affected in China unlike in the US in which there is no systematic difference in happiness across education groups. On the other hand, Cheung and Leung (2004) discover that the effect of education in higher class positions is negative (together with ownership) unlike in other countries. In a more nuanced manner, Knight et al. (2009) point out the indirect effect of education on happiness and interpret this result as a sign of raising aspirations (falsifying expectations) by widening reference groups. Note here that the findings between Knight et al. (2009) and Knight et al. (2010) are controversial although both focus on rural areas in China using the same data. A possible interpretation would be that the positive effect of education on happiness is counterbalanced by the negative effect of frustration caused by unfulfilled raised aspirations.

Finally, the influence of cultural values has also been examined in the context of the economic transition in China. On the one hand, it has been acknowledged that happiness is oriented more socially (e.g. role obligation, dialectical balance) for the Chinese whereas it is more individually oriented (e.g. individual choice, personal accountability, explicit pursuit) for Western counterparts (Lu and Gilmour 2004; Roets et al. 2012), and that the importance of collectivity in China (as well as in other East Asian countries) has been viewed from the perspective of the Confucian culture where an interpersonal relationship is more important than the amount of knowledge and wealth (Shin and Inoguchi 2009). Facing the current economic development in collaboration with these cultural features, Shu and Zhu (2009) evaluate that a majority of Chinese have experienced a higher quality of life than those in some more prosperous countries without them. On the other hand, against these optimistic views, Steele and Lynch (2013) point out that individualistic factors are becoming more important than collectivist factors in China over time. For cxample, Chen (2012) demonstrates that a main factor of the positive effect of education is monetary in China in contrast to other East Asian countries where the main factor is non-monetary (such as more extensive social networks and greater involvement with the wider world). This point seems to correspond partly to the finding by Oshio et al. (2011) that individual income is more significant in China whereas family income is more significant in Japan and South Korea. In this context, Li and Raine (2014) reveal that Chinese life satisfaction has declined over the past two decades despite tremendous economic and social progress. These findings demonstrate that their happiness has been affected positively with the growth of the market economy while affected negatively in the transformation of traditional cultural values.

SOUTH AFRICA

Out of sixteen publications found by the search, six remained after removing those irrelevant for this research (e.g. general argument applicable universally such as a positive effect of family functioning and public services on happiness on the one hand and a negative effect of crime on the other) and research papers published later in a book or a referred journal. All but Kim-Prieto and Eid (2004) are concerned with how the socio-political transition affects social stratification deriving from apartheid in South Africa, and can be categorized into two topics: democracy and education.[12]

Regarding the impact of democracy on happiness in South Africa, a series of researches have been conducted by Møller over time. First, Møller (1996) highlights that, contrary to the trend in the era of apartheid, black South Africans marked higher levels of happiness and satisfaction than white counterparts, right after the introduction of democratic election. Later, Møller (2001) demonstrated that the past tendency came back soon afterwards and thus that social divides in subjective well-being including happiness and satisfaction had remained between them despite some improvements in their objective living conditions. More recently, Møller (2013) carried out follow-up research to reflect the influence of the successful hosting of the World Cup in 2010, and

[12] Comparing the five sub-Sahara African countries, Kim-Prieto and Eid (2004) find that South Africans regard positive emotions (joy, affect, pride, contentment) as more desirable (similar to Zimbabweans; unlike Ghanaians) and negative emotions (anger, fear, sadness, guilt) as less desirable (similar to Zimbabweans and Nigerians; unlike Ghanaians and Tanzanians).

confirmed that there still remain huge disparities in subjective well-being (together with material well-being) although the highest levels of subjective well-being were observed in the overall population following the first democratic election.

With regard to education, Powdthavee (2007) discloses that, unlike more developed countries, this has a negative effect in South Africa—regardless of race before the abolition of apartheid—and interprets this result to mean that income levels do not meet the high aspiration levels associated with a high educational level. In contrast, Ebrahim et al. (2013) find the effect of education to be positive and further reveal that women are less satisfied and blacks are least satisfied. A possible interpretation from these findings would be that social structure in South Africa has been improved recently in terms of mobility with higher education but not yet in terms of gender and ethnicity.

Lessons learned

TREND OF PUBLICATIONS

As seen at the beginning of the fourth section, the number of publications on happiness varies enormously across the BRICS nations: four in Brazil, sixteen in Russia, seventeen in India, sixty-one in China, and sixteen in South Africa. Another finding is the difference in the trend of publications over time (Figure 30.2).

Among the five countries, the publication was found first in Russia (1994), followed by China (1995), South Africa (1996), and India (1997). Although the first publications in Russia, China, and India have not been covered because they do not deal with the characteristics of happiness in each country and thus are not relevant for the purpose of this chapter, the article published first in South Africa has been covered because it addresses the influence of the abolition of apartheid on happiness. Another interesting point is a sharp rise in Russia in 2001. It results from the special issue of the *Journal of Happiness Studies* which aims to investigate the effect of transition on happiness. Indeed, the special issue contributes to six out of seven publications of the year. Besides, a recent boom in publications in China is outstanding. It has had a steady increase since 2005 and reaches thirteen publications in 2014. It worth noting that twelve out of sixty-one publications have been written by John Knight, an Oxford economist, together with his colleagues. From a different angle, the small number of publications on happiness in other nations would be surprising, particularly in Brazil with the first one only in 2009. Overall, publications started only after the mid-1990s, and only up to three publications have been produced each year across the nations except Russia in 2001 and China since 2007.

Obviously, BRICS stands for an association of five major emerging economies. It means that they have faced similar experiences at the stage of economic development, while keeping unique socio-cultural differences. It would be thus worthwhile if some

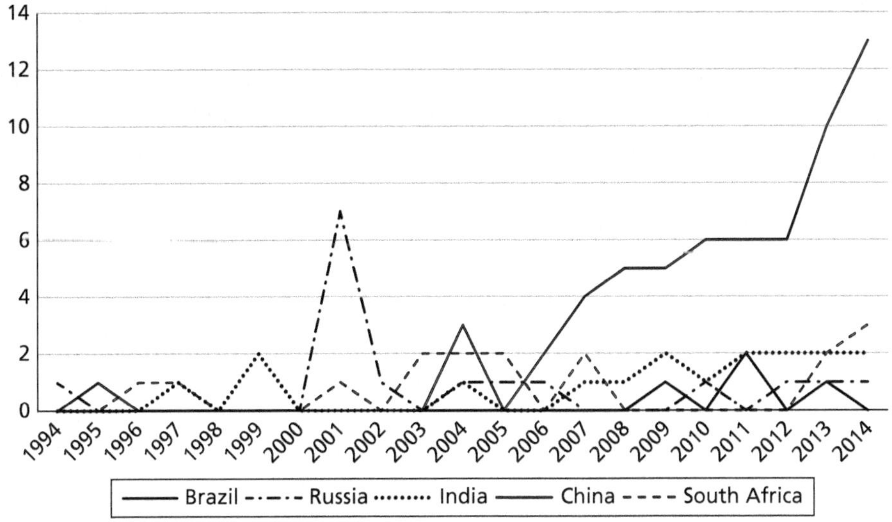

Figure 30.2 Trend of publications on happiness across BRICS

Source: Author's own elaboration.

commonality could be found and examined for the determinants of happiness across these countries, all the more given the limited range of research on happiness in BRICS.

LESSONS FROM RUSSIA AND CHINA: ECONOMIC TRANSITION

The effect of economic transition on happiness investigated centrally in Russia and China is significant, and it is applicable to the other BRICS nations, as economic transition always accompanies emerging economies. A main finding here is the relevance of income (both actual level and aspirational) on the one hand and insecurity on happiness on the other. In both countries, the positive effect of income has been confirmed, to the extent that it surpasses the negative effects of unemployment, inflation, and identity-oriented inequality (not income inequality in itself). In other words, these 'undesirable' factors can be ignored or even seen as promising in terms of mobility in emerging economies. All in all, it has been found that income and happiness move together because of both actual improvement and aspiration for better living conditions at least at the early stage of economic transition. It seems, however, not to continue for long. The positive effect of income is soon cancelled out by the negative effect of prolonged insecurity caused by the lack of social security systems. This negative effect is strengthened by the shift in reference groups, which leads to false expectations prevailing in transitional societies, among migrants in particular. The decline of happiness in the process of economic transition, therefore, signals the necessity of a social safety net through education, health, and employment regardless of their temporal effects.

LESSONS FROM INDIA AND SOUTH AFRICA: SOCIAL STRATIFICATION

The cases of India and South Africa call attention to the grave effects of social stratification. Social grouping is certainly a human characteristic and affects the level of happiness by comparing oneself with those who are in similar circumstances (i.e. reference groups). However, as reviewed in the fourth section, this relative concept has been based unjustifiably on caste in India and ethnicity in South Africa. It is unjustifiable in the sense that the classification is not based on one's merits and efforts but rather on existent authoritative power, and thus should not be left intact simply as a human characteristic. This negative effect could be counterbalanced or even surpassed by the positive effects of rising aspiration in the process of emerging economies, but the situation would not be sustainable. Although social stratification examined here is of particular cases of caste system and apartheid, it would also be applicable to the other BRICS nations stricken with inequality standing in particular social groups (i.e. identity-oriented inequality). To surmount such unjustified social grouping and inequality caused by it, a democratic structure is essential. Indeed, both India and South Africa have adopted democratic systems, at least formally, to construct a sound socio-political structure, which helps the vulnerable to have an opportunity to raise their own voices, although the quality of democracy remains to be improved.

LESSONS FROM BRAZIL: ASPIRATIONS AND NORMS IN RELATION TO LIVING CONDITIONS

The case of Brazil illustrates how aspirations and norms are affected by living conditions in the areas of public safety, health, and ethics. Empirical studies show that Brazilians hold the highest levels in all the aspirations for public safety, health, and ethical norms among the samples (Americans, Canadians, and Mexicans on the one hand and the Latin American and Caribbean peoples on the other). These results seem to contradict Brazil's lower or similar levels than/with them in each objective condition (e.g. prevalence of violation, accessibility to hospitals, spread of corruption). They imply that people's aspirations and norms are not fully affected by their circumstances. In this sense, the problem of adaptive preferences is detectable to some extent, if not perfectly, and it demonstrates that subjective assessments are not always unreliable.

HAPPINESS THROUGH BOTH SUBJECTIVE AND OBJECTIVE LENSES

Going back to the realm of happiness and its way of assessment discussed at the beginning, all the researches covered in this chapter deal with conceptions of happiness in the pure happiness theory (either affective, cognitive, or hybrid view) assessed individually. At the same time, however, all determinants of happiness identified (e.g.

income, security, equality) are commonly regarded as important and thus can be assessed publicly for a good living or eudaimonia. As the above lessons have shown, the problem of adaptive preferences can be detected to some extent, but it would not always be the case. Subjective assessments are to this extent not perfect and thus need to be compensated by objective assessments in view of morality and justice: in the case of economic transition, 'false expectations' based on subjective assessments need to be adjusted by securing a social safety net assessed objectively; in the case of social stratification, while the vulnerable could disclose their unjustifiable conditions subjectively in democratic systems, the quality of democracy needs to be enhanced in more justifiable ways based on objective criteria.

In turn, objective assessments also need to be compensated by subjective assessments. In order to reflect how the determinants (set up in public) are actually appreciated by each person, individual assessments are inevitable. Indeed, it seems awkward to evaluate someone as happy or flourishing simply based on one's living conditions. It is particularly true of the phenomenon of the Easterlin Paradox in which one can increase happiness together with income growth only to some degree. This paradox can be reflected partly by the lack of other determinants of happiness (e.g. safety, equality) but not fully unless being investigated by asking people directly about their living. Likewise, both positive and negative effects of education on happiness reviewed earlier support the significance of subjective assessments together with objective ones.

Conclusion

Happiness ultimately requires both individual and public spheres. It is only in the realm where both spheres converge that we can lead a good life over time and across people. This chapter has dealt with happiness in BRICS, but this claim can be applied more extensively.

ACKNOWLEDGEMENTS

I am very grateful for Ana Rosa Soares's comments on the first draft of this chapter.

REFERENCES

Annas, J. (1993). *The Morality of Happiness.* Oxford: Oxford University Press.

Argyle, M. (2002). *The Psychology of Happiness.* New York: Routledge.

Bandura, A. (1986). *Social Foundations of Thought and Action: A Social Cognitive Theory.* Englewood Cliffs, NJ: Prentice Hall.

Bandura, A. (1997). *Self-Efficacy: The Exercise of Control.* New York: Freeman.

Bradburn, N.M. (1969). *The Structure of Psychological Well-Being.* Chicago, IL: Aldine.

Brülde, B. (2007a). 'Happiness and the good life: introduction and conceptual framework', *Journal of Happiness Studies* 8/1: 1–14.

Brülde, B. (2007b). 'Happiness theories of the good life', *Journal of Happiness Studies* 8/1: 15–49.

Bruni, L. (2008). 'Back to Aristotle? Happiness, eudaimonia, and relational goods', in L. Bruni, F. Comim, and M. Pugno (eds) *Capabilities and Happiness*. Oxford: Oxford University Press, 114–39.

Bruni, L. and Porta, P.L. (2005). 'Introduction', in L. Bruni and P. L. Porta (eds) *Economics and Happiness: Framing the Analysis*. Oxford: Oxford University Press, 1–28.

Carver, C. and Scheier, M. (1981). *Attention and Self-Regulation: A Control-Theory Approach to Human Behavior*. New York: Springer-Verlag.

Cavalcanti, T.V.V., Guimaraes, J.F., and Nogueira, J.R. (2009). 'Is Brazil the land of happiness? A comparative study using a sample with economics students from UFPE and Purdue', *Brazilian Review of Econometrics* 29/1: 17–35.

Chekola, M. (2007). 'Happiness, rationality, autonomy and the good life', *Journal of Happiness Studies* 8/1: 51–78.

Chen, W.-C. (2012). 'How education enhances happiness: comparison of mediating factors in four East Asian countries', *Social Indicators Research* 106/1: 117–31.

Chen, Y., Li, T., Shi, Y., and Zhou, Y. (2014). 'Welfare costs of inflation: evidence from China', *Social Indicators Research* 119/3: 1195–218.

Cheung, C.-K. and Leung, K.-K. (2004). 'Forming life satisfaction among different social groups during the modernization of China', *Journal of Happiness Studies* 5/1: 23–56.

Deci, E.L. and Ryan, R.M. (2000). 'The "what" and "why" of goal pursuits: human needs and the self-determination of behavior', *Psychological Inquiry* 11/4: 227–68.

Diener, E. (1994). 'Assessing subjective well-being: progress and opportunities', *Social Indicators Research* 31/2: 103–57.

Diener, E., Scollon, C.N., and Lucas, R.E. (2004). 'The evolving concept of subjective well-being: the multifaceted nature of happiness', *Advances in Cell Aging and Gerontology* 15: 187–219.

Easterlin, R. (2005). 'Building a better theory of well-being', in L. Bruni and P.L. Porta (eds) *Economics and Happiness: Framing the Analysis*. Oxford: Oxford University Press, 29–64.

Ebrahim, A., Botha, F., and Snowball, J. (2013). 'Determinants of life satisfaction among race groups in South Africa', *Development Southern Africa* 30/2: 168–85.

Eggers, A., Gaddy, C., and Graham, C. (2006). 'Well-being and unemployment in Russia in the 1990s: can society's suffering be individuals' solace?', *Journal of Socio-Economics* 35/2: 209–42.

Engstrom, S.P. (1996). 'Happiness and the highest good in Aristotle and Kant', in S.P. Engstrom and J. Whiting (eds) *Aristotle, Kant, and the Stoics: Rethinking Happiness and Duty*. Cambridge: Cambridge University Press 102–38.

Fontaine, X. and Yamada, K. (2014). 'Caste comparisons in India: evidence from subjective well-being data', *World Development* 64: 407–19.

Franklin, S.S. (2010). *The Psychology of Happiness: A Good Human Life*. Cambridge: Cambridge University Press.

Frey, B.S. (2008). *Happiness: A Revolution in Economics*. Cambridge, MA and London: MIT Press.

Frijters, P., Liu, A.Y.C., and Meng, X. (2012). 'Are optimistic expectations keeping the Chinese happy?', *Journal of Economic Behavior and Organization* 81/1: 159–71.

Gao, W. and Smyth, R. (2011). 'What keeps China's migrant workers going? Expectations and happiness among China's floating population', *Journal of the Asia Pacific Economy* 16/2: 163–82.

Graham, C. (2005). 'Insights on development from the economics of happiness', *World Bank Research Observer* 20/2: 201–31.

Graham, C. (2011). 'The economics of happiness and health policy: how health norms vary across cohorts in Latin America', in D. Cotlear (ed.) *Population Aging: Is Latin America Ready?* Washington, DC: World Bank, 191–210.

Graham, C. and Pettinato, S. (2002). *Happiness and Hardship: Opportunity and Insecurity in New Market Economies*. Washington, DC: Brookings Institution Press.

Graham, C., Eggers, A., and Sukhtankar, S. (2004). 'Does happiness pay? An exploration based on panel data from Russia', *Journal of Economic Behavior and Organization* 55/3: 319–42.

Griffin, J. (1986). *Well-being: Its Meaning, Measurement and Moral Importance*. Oxford: Clarendon.

Haybron, D. (2000). 'Two philosophical problems in the study of happiness', *Journal of Happiness Studies* 1/2: 207–25.

Haybron, D. (2007). 'Life satisfaction, ethical reflection, and the science of happiness', *Journal of Happiness Studies* 8/1: 99–138.

Headey, B. and Wearing, A. (1992). *Understanding Happiness: A Theory of Subjective Well-Being*. Melbourne, VIC: Longman Cheshire.

Hirai, T. (2017). *The Creation of the Human Development Approach*. Basingstoke: Palgrave Macmillan.

Hirata, J. (2008). 'The division of labor between the capability and the happiness perspectives', in L. Bruni, F. Comim, and M. Pugno (eds) *Capabilities and Happiness*. Oxford: Oxford University Press, 160–86.

James, H.S. (2011). 'Is the just man a happy man? An empirical study of the relationship between ethics and subjective well-being', *Kyklos* 64/2: 193–212.

Jiang, S., Lu, M., and Sato, H. (2012). 'Identity, inequality, and happiness: evidence from urban China', *World Development* 40/6: 1190–200.

Kahneman, D. (1999). 'Objective happiness', in D. Kahneman, E. Diener, and N. Schwarz (eds) *Well-Being: The Foundations of Hedonic Psychology*. New York: Russell Sage Foundation, 3–25.

Kahneman, D., Wakker, P.P., and Sarin, R. (1997). 'Back to Bentham? Explorations of experienced utility', *Quarterly Journal of Economics* 112/2. 375–405.

Kahneman, D., Krueger, A.B., Schkade, D.A., Schwartz, N., and Stone, A.A. (2004). 'A survey method for characterizing daily life experience: the Day Reconstruction Method', *Science* 306/5702: 1776–80.

Kasser, T., Ryan, R.M., Zax, M., and Sameroff, A.J. (1995). 'The relations of maternal and social environments to late adolescents' materialistic and prosocial values', *Developmental Psychology* 31/6: 907–14.

Kim-Prieto, C. and Eid, M. (2004). 'Norms for experiencing emotions in sub-Saharan Africa', *Journal of Happiness Studies* 5/3: 241–68.

Knight, J. (2012). 'The economic causes and consequences of social instability in China'. Working Papers 619. Oxford: University of Oxford, Department of Economics.

Knight, J. and Gunatilaka, R. (2010a). 'Great expectation? The subjective well-being of rural-urban migrants in China', *World Development* 38/1: 113–24.

Knight, J. and Gunatilaka, R. (2010b). 'The rural–urban divide in China: income but not happiness?', *Journal of Development Studies* 46/3: 506–34.

Knight, J. and Gunatilaka, R. (2011). 'Does economic growth raise happiness in China?', *Oxford Development Studies* 39/1: 1–24.

Knight, J., Song, L., and Gunatilaka, R. (2009). 'Subjective well-being and its determinants in rural China', *China Economic Review* 20/4: 635–49.

Knight, J., Shi, L., and Quheng, D. (2010). 'Education and the poverty trap in rural China: closing the trap', *Oxford Development Studies* 38/1: 1–24.

Lam, K.-C.J. and Liu, P.-W. (2014). 'Socio-economic inequalities in happiness in China and U.S.', *Social Indicators Research* 116/2: 509–33.

Layard, R. (2005). *Happiness from a New Science*. London: Allen Lane.

Li, J. and Raine, J.W. (2014). 'The time trend of life satisfaction in China', *Social Indicators Research* 116/2: 409–27.

Liang, H., Tang, Y., and Huo, X. (2014). 'Liushou women's happiness and its influencing factors in rural China', *Social Indicators Research* 117/3: 907–18.

Liang, Y. and Wang, P. (2014). 'Influence of prudential value on the subjective well-being of Chinese urban-rural residents', *Social Indicators Research* 118/3: 1249–67.

Linz, S. J. and Semykina, A. (2010). 'Perceptions of economic insecurity: Evidence from Russia', *Economic Systems* 34/4: 357–85.

Locke, E.A. and Latham, G.P. (1990). *A Theory of Goal Setting and Task Performance*. Englewood Cliffs, NJ: Prentice Hall.

Lu, L. and Gilmour, R. (2004). 'Culture and conceptions of happiness: individual oriented and social oriented SWB', *Journal of Happiness Studies* 5/3: 269–91.

Møller, V. (1996). 'Household satisfaction: past, present and future perspectives', *Development Southern Africa* 13/2: 237–54.

Møller, V. (2001). 'Happiness trends under democracy: where will the new South African set-level come to rest?', *Journal of Happiness Studies* 2/1: 33–53.

Møller, V. (2013). 'South African quality of life trends over three decades, 1980–2010', *Social Indicators Research* 113/3: 915–40.

Morgan, S.L. (2006). 'Expectations and aspirations', in G. Ritzer (ed.) *The Blackwell Encyclopedia of Sociology*. Oxford: Blackwell, 1528–31.

Nettle, D. (2005). *Happiness: The Science behind Your Smile*. Oxford: Oxford University Press.

Nickerson, C., Schwarz, N., Diener, E., and Kahneman, D. (2003). 'Zeroing in on the dark side of the American Dream: a closer look at the negative consequences of the goal for financial success', *Psychological Science* 14/6: 531–6.

Nussbaum, M. (1992). 'Human functioning and social justice', *Political Theory* 20/2: 202–46.

Nussbaum, M. (2005). 'Mill between Aristotle and Bentham', in L. Bruni and P. L. Porta (eds) *Economics and Happiness: Framing the Analysis*. Oxford: Oxford University Press, 170–83.

Nussbaum, M. (2008). 'Who is the happy warrior? Philosophy poses questions to psychology', *Journal of Legal Studies* 37/S2: S81–S113.

Oshio, T., Nozaki, K., and Kobayashi, M. (2011). 'Relative income and happiness in Asia: evidence from nationwide surveys in China, Japan, and Korea', *Social Indicators Research* 104/3: 351–67.

Parfit, D. (1984). *Reasons and Persons*. Oxford: Clarendon.

Powdthavee, N. (2007). 'Happiness and the standard of living: the case of South Africa', in L. Bruni and P. L. Porta (eds) *Handbook on the Economics of Happiness*. Cheltenham: Edward Elgar, 447–86.

Roets, A., Schwartz, B., and Guan, Y. (2012). 'The tyranny of choice: a cross-cultural investigation of maximizing-satisficing effects on well-being', *Judgment and Decision Making* 7/6: 689–704.
Ryan, R.M. and Deci, E.L. (2001). 'On happiness and human potentials: a review of research on hedonic and eudaimonic well-being', *Annual Review of Psychology* 52/1: 141–66.
Ryff, C.D. and Singer, B. (1998). 'The contours of positive human health', *Psychological Inquiry* 9/1: 1–28.
Saris, W.E. (2001). 'What influences subjective well-being in Russia?', *Journal of Happiness Studies* 2/2: 137–46.
Saris, W.E. and Andreenkova, A. (2001). 'Following changes in living conditions and happiness in post-communist Russia: the Russet Panel', *Journal of Happiness Studies* 2/2: 95–109.
Schyns, P. (2001). 'Income and satisfaction in Russia', *Journal of Happiness Studies* 2/2: 173–204.
Seligman, M.E.P. (2002). *Authentic Happiness: Using the New Positive Psychology to Realize Your Potential for Deep Fulfillment*. London: Nicholas Brealey.
Sen, A. (1987). *On Ethics and Economics*. Oxford: Basil Blackwell.
Shin, D.C. and Inoguchi, T. (2009). 'Avowed happiness in Confucian Asia: ascertaining its distribution, patterns, and sources', *Social Indicators Research* 92/2: 405–27.
Shu, X. and Zhu, Y. (2009). 'The quality of life in China', *Social Indicators Research* 92/2: 191–225.
Steele, L.G. and Lynch, S.M. (2013). 'The pursuit of happiness in China: individualism, collectivism, and subjective well-being during China's economic and social transformation', *Social Indicators Research* 114/2: 441–51.
Sumner, L.W. (1996). *Welfare, Happiness, and Ethics*. Oxford: Clarendon.
Tatarkiewicz, W. (1976). *Analysis of Happiness*. The Hague: M. Nijhoff; Warszawa: PWN/Polish Scientific Publishers.
van Praag, B.M.S. (2005). 'The connection between old and new approaches to financial satisfaction', in L. Bruni and P. L. Porta (eds) *Economics and Happiness: Framing the Analysis*. Oxford: Oxford University Press, 196–222.
van Praag, B.M.S. and Ferrer-i-Carbonell, A. (2004). *Happiness Quantified: A Satisfaction Calculus Approach*. Oxford: Oxford University Press.
Veenhoven, R. (1996). 'Happy life expectancy: a comprehensive measure of quality-of-life in nations', *Social Indicators Research* 39/1: 1–58.
Veenhoven, R. (2000). 'The four qualities of life: ordering concepts and measures of the good life', *Journal of Happiness Studies* 1/1: 1–39.
Veenhoven, R. (2001a). 'Preface', *Journal of Happiness Studies* 2/2: 93–4.
Veenhoven, R. (2001b). 'Are the Russians as unhappy as they say they are? Comparability of self-reports across nations', *Journal of Happiness Studies* 2/2: 111–36.
Veenhoven, R. (2005). 'Happiness in hardship', in L. Bruni, L. and P. L. Porta (eds) *Economics and Happiness: Framing the Analysis*. Oxford: Oxford University Press, 243–66.
Veenhoven, R. (2007). 'Subjective measures of well-being', in M. McGillivray (ed.) *Human Well-Being: Concept and Measurement*. Basingstoke: Palgrave Macmillan, 214–39.
von Kleist, K. (2010). 'Migrant happiness in China', *Journal of Chinese Economic and Business Studies* 8/2: 157–66.
Zhang, S. (2013). 'The effect of inflation on domestic migrant worker households in China', *Journal of Reviews on Global Economics* 2/2: 416–32.

31 Urban economic development

Franklin Obeng-Odoom

Introduction

This chapter focuses on an African emerging economy. Ghana's national economic transformation has been widely celebrated. In the Economic Community of West African States, its economy is second only to Nigeria's, contributing 10.3 per cent of the subregion's GDP (Alagidede et al. 2013). Between 2000 and 2011, Ghana's national GDP grew by 700 per cent (Ahadzie 2016). As an oil frontier, Ghana is often cited as a prime example of how best to combine a windfall with strong democratic institutions and economic growth in Africa (Heilbrunn 2014). Even among emerging economies more broadly, Ghana is highly regarded, occupying seventieth place in the 2015 league table on ease of doing business—twenty places higher than China (World Bank 2014). Ghana's national economy has been widely praised for its role in this economic transformation.

But what about the role of the country's cities? Typically, the contribution by cities in Ghana to the country's transformation is typically seen as negative, or non-existent to negligible, at best. Urban development is so much associated with the many well-known trawls of inadequacies—of transport, housing, land, water, employment, and so on (see a summary in Obeng-Odoom 2009)—of urbanity that it is commonly claimed that crippling poverty in the countryside is what drives Ghana's urbanization (Yeboah et al. 2013a, 2013b); not urban economic development. Indeed, the country's *National Urban Policy* (Government of Ghana 2012) suggests that urban economies in Ghana are so weak that they are disarticulated from the vibrant macroeconomic conditions. 'It [the urban economy]', the policy notes, 'continually fails to generate enough industrial development and growth; it fails to induce and advance adequate development and growth of the urban hinterland; and it has a large struggling informal component that receives little institutional credit support. The urban economy also generates limited, inadequate employment for a rapidly growing urban population' (Government of Ghana 2012: 16). This characterization is quite common for cities in Africa which *The State of Africa Cities* reports mostly brand as rural poverty-driven settlements (for reviews of such reports, see Obeng-Odoom 2010a, 2013c, 2014b). None of these claims, however, is based on a systemic analysis of the contribution cities in Ghana have made to the country's economic transformation.

Franklin Obeng-Odoom, *Urban economic development* In: *Handbook of BRICS and Emerging Economies.* Edited by: P.B. Anand, Shailaja Fennell, and Flavio Comim, Oxford University Press (2021).
DOI: 10.1093/oso/9780198827535.003.0031

This chapter, on the other hand, seeks to provide a more careful analysis of the existing statistical and historical evidence by examining a range of interlinked processes, namely: (a) the nature of urbanization and national development in the country in historical context; (b) the correlation between urbanization and national economic development; (c) trends in rural poverty; (d) actually existing motives for rural–urban migration; (e) trends and the nature of these in Ghana's urban economies. It uses a spatial political economy methodology (see for example Stilwell and Primrose 2010) which (a) places primary emphasis on urban, regional, and spatial distribution in the analysis of the national economy; (b) simultaneously probes questions about urban efficiency, equity, quality of jobs, and sustainability; (c) contests the common theoretical and methodological bases of orthodox economics; (d) critically engages with neoliberal policies which draw inspiration from the politics of mainstream economics theory. From this perspective, this chapter argues that most urban residents are either born in cities or are attracted to them from the countryside; but urbanization cannot be explained as 'poverty driven', especially when rural poverty in the country has been falling and the urban economies of many cities are thriving. There is some notable rural–urban migration, but this is driven by a concatenation of complex *institutional* factors and wider system changes such as climate variability and the privatization of the commons, rather than the rational–utility maximizing of individuals' calculations. While urban centres tend to be quite small in size, cities have simultaneously contributed to, and benefited from, national economic development. Indeed, even Ghana's nascent oil has been shaped and constrained by its cities.

To highlight the contribution of cities, however, is not to accept that urban development in Ghana has attained what in mainstream urban economics is known as 'spatial equilibrium', the idea that urban development under capitalism produces harmonious cities where everyone benefits. Poverty has declined and there is some evidence that even informal and precarious work may be on the decline. However, there is growing inequality within cities, between the national capital and the regional capitals, and between cities and rural areas (Dickson, 1993; Obeng-Odoom, 2013a). There is a small, almost negligible middle class, a large stratum of people who are not statistically poor but possess only very low incomes, while there is much evidence of growing and actual concentration of wealth perceived in the hands of a few. In turn, the rich have developed excruciating fear of what the 'others' may do to them, a fear that underpins the flight to seek refuge in gated housing and walls of affluence under the watch of private security. The 'victory' of the rich, then, is pyric.

With a symbiotic relationship between cities and national development, this argument implies that planning the future of national development in the country will need to pay close attention to making cities inclusive by placing more emphasis on the systematic reduction of inequalities, and focusing more on growth with structural change that enhances the quality of the environment, improves the quality of jobs, and provides a more balanced spatial and regional development. Doing so will require a careful rebalancing of the institutions of the state, market, and society. Oil will be instrumental in ways that are distinct from what is established in the literature (Obeng-Odoom 2015a): first as 'fuel' for funding the social programme and second through the spatial distribution of oil projects.

To develop this argument, the rest of the chapter is divided into three sections. The second section examines the relationship between cities and national development, seeking to show the contribution that cities have made to national development in Ghana in the first decade of the millennium. The third section extends this analysis to 2010 and beyond, highlighting the development and role of Ghana's oil industry, while the fourth section looks at the future of Ghana's economy and how more effective socio-spatial policymaking can contribute to it.

Cities and national development

The view that grinding poverty in rural areas in Ghana is what has pushed rural residents to move to cities is unfounded. As shown in Table 31.1, rural poverty in Ghana has been falling since the late 1990s.

Also inaccurate is the view that rural poverty has urbanized. The country's urban poverty has sharply declined from 27.7 per cent in 1991/92 to 10.8 per cent in 2005/06 (GSS 2007). While there is a push from rural areas to cities, it is neither the result of individual rational calculations about the bonanza in cities nor is it about rural economic stasis. Ten years of ethnographic work by Ghanaian sociologist, Vivian Amantana (2012), shows that the push is partly related to weak rural economies, partly to grinding poverty, but particularly related to a range of institutional challenges. The breakdown of kinship fosterage, as well as the persistence of cultural expectations of both sons (to take care of the family in the absence of the father) and daughters (to provide homemaking items such as cooking utensils) and the disintegration of the family (through death, divorce, or abandonment) combine to push children to migrate into the streets and remain there. More recent evidence (Tsikata and Yaro 2014) shows that socio-ecological crises, including the loss of land to transnational corporations and continuing colonial national development work to push people into cities.

The pull factors are not merely about expectations, however, as is typically argued in mainstream urban economics (Todaro and Smith 2006). Rather, the decision to migrate

Table 31.1 Rural poverty in Ghana, 1991–2013

Severity of poverty	1991/92	1998/99	2005/06	2012/13
Poverty incidence	63.6	49.5	39.2*	37.9
Extreme poverty incidence	47.2	34.6	23.4	15

Note: * GSS entered 43.7 per cent in its 2014 report (2014: 11).
Source: GSS (2007: 9, 2014: 11–12).

Table 31.2 The urban situation in Ghana, 1960–2010

	1960	1970	1984	2000	2010
Tier 1	>100,000				
No. of cities	2	2	4	8	12
% urban population	34.6	33.3	37.6	45.0	46.5
Tier 2	50,000–99,999				
No. of cities	1	4	6	9	16
% urban population	4.9	10.3	8.8	7.3	8.2
Tier 3	20,000–49,999				
No. of cities	5	17	24	42	63
% urban population	12.1	18.6	17.0	14.9	14.7
Tier 4	10,000–19,999				
No. of cities	23	29	42	90	140
% urban population	21.3	15.3	14.8	14.8	15.0
Tier 5	5,000–9,999				
No. of cities	60	83	127	215	288
% urban population	27.0	22.4	21.7	18.0	15.6
All					
No. of urban settlements	91	135	203	364	519
% urban population	23.1	29.5	33.1	43.8	50.9

Source: Adapted from Yeboah et al. (2013b).

is based on actual evidence of others returning to the rural areas as mostly better-off than they were when they lived in the country. Also, interviews with migrants show that they assess their conditions as substantially improved (in the sense that at least they get some work to do and often are able to save) and much better than they were in their origin of migration (Amantana 2012). Cities in Ghana, then, are major economic magnets. It is in this context that growing urbanization—as shown in Table 31.2—can be understood.

Table 31.2 shows that not only is the share of the population in urban areas increasing but also the number of urban settlements is on the rise, increasing from 91 when the first full census was conducted to 519 when the last census was conducted in 2010—an increase of 470.3 per cent. In addition, the share of urban population is now greater than the rural share of the national population and the number of tiers 1- and 2-type cities (typically called big cities in Ghana) is also on the rise. The majority of these urban areas are in the southern part of Ghana where much of the country's population lives (Otiso and Owusu 2008). About 34 per cent of Ghana's urban population lives in the cities of Accra and Kumasi (DESA 2006). Accra is the national capital and largest city in Ghana (Grant and Yankson 2002), while Kumasi is the second largest city and is the home of the king of the Ashanti Kingdom (Korboe and Tipple 1995; Adarkwa, 2011). Other big cities include Cape Coast, which was the national capital of Ghana until 1877 (Agyei-Mensah

2006), and the Sekondi-Takoradi twin-cities of Ghana (Busia 1950), which is now the hub of much of Ghana's oil industry (Obeng-Odoom 2014a).

Most of these cities are quite vibrant. Cape Coast is an example (Agyei-Mensah 2006). It is known for fishing-related activities, but it has also been able to market its historical sites in such a way that tourists troop to the city to look at its castles and forts. Its educational facilities are another asset. Many from around the country will go to its prestigious high schools. The University of Cape Coast is the premier supplier of university-trained teachers and it has attracted many who want to be trained as teachers. Accra is the powerhouse of the urban system in Ghana (Grant 2009). With new shopping malls, vibrant real estate development, and construction activities, its recorded sector's singular contribution of more than 10 per cent to the country's GDP is suspected to be conservative, particularly because the majority of its economic activities are in the informal economy and unrecorded (Obeng-Odoom 2011a). Accra is reputed for its Odawna electronics clusters. These clusters are small and dominated by only small-scale enterprises employing a maximum of twenty workers—by world standards, that is—but they perform similarly important economic functions such as labour and technology sharing as well as information sharing (McDade and Malecki 1997). Kumasi too has industrial clusters such as those in Suame Magazine (electronics cluster) and Anloga (wood cluster), both of which are quite vibrant (McDade and Malecki 1997). So, in the cities in Ghana, there is much evidence of both localization and urbanization economies. Indeed, in spite of the vast informality of the urban economy, there is much knowledge production and incubation in that urban economy space, including university-educated and professionally mentored valuation, and real estate workers (Obeng-Odoom and Ameyaw 2014). As shown in recent research (Adaawen and Owusu 2013), this economic vibrancy itself has contributed to the reduction of poverty in rural areas through remittances sent from cities to the countryside.

The increases in per capita income in Ghana that eventually culminated in the emerging economy status are matched with growing urbanization in the country. Correlation analysis conducted by Franklin Obeng-Odoom (2010a) shows a fairly strong correlation between the time series of observations on the percentage of population that is urban and GDP per capita in Ghana. Obeng-Odoom's (2010a) attempt also showed that the relationship has a Pearson Correlation Coefficient of 0.83 and a coefficient of Determination (R-squared) value of 0.69. In order to test for possible errors in the computation, a test of significance was carried out which returned a P-value of 0.001, suggesting that the result is statistically significant (i.e. $P < 0.05$). This positive statistical correlation is not surprising, given the general tendency for both urbanization and GDP per capita to rise over time. But there is the need for some circumspection in interpretation here because, even though urbanization correlates positively with GDP/capita, the two do not perfectly grow in tandem.

Looked at on a year-by-year basis, there are clearly exceptional episodes. Apart from the years 1970, 1974, 1978, and 1984, when the rate of GDP growth per capita exceeded the rate of urbanization, for all other years from 1960 to 2005 the rate of urbanization was higher than the rate of GDP per capita growth (Obeng-Odoom 2010a). However, it is pertinent to note that, in Ghana, the official rate of GDP per capita growth *is* bigger than actually recorded because about 51 per cent of production goes unrecorded in the informal sector (Obeng-Odoom, 2013a). Further evidence comes from the results of a correlation analysis between the share of industrial contribution to GDP and the percentage of the population that is urban. Obeng-Odoom's work shows that there is an R-value of 0.69 and an R-squared value of 0.48 for these variables. Since the test of significance yields a P-value of 0.00009, both the R-value and R-squared values are statistically significant. Thus we can conclude that increased economic development (proxied by industrialization) is correlated with increased urbanization (Obeng-Odoom 2010a).

The other side of this process is the relative decline in the importance of agriculture in the overall economy. The correlation between urbanization and the agricultural share of GDP is, not surprisingly, negative. The correlation coefficient is −0.78 with a P-value of 0.00005 (Obeng-Odoom 2010a). This negative correlation between urbanization and agriculture is consistent with the view that, with greater economic development and increased employment opportunities in cities, there is increased rural–urban migration. This scenario was evidently the case during the 1960s when economic boom in the Ghanaian economy drew migrants from rural areas and countries like Nigeria to Ghanaian cities (Afolayan 1988). It is not that there is no agriculture in cities: indeed urban agriculture is an important feature of the urban livelihoods strategy of many urban residents (Obeng-Odoom 2010a). However, unlike a rural economy which is predominantly based on agriculture, the urban economy is substantially more diversified into secondary activities such as mining production and tertiary activities such as banking and education services.

Obeng-Odoom's correlation analysis also shows that a higher literacy rate, proxied by the primary school gross enrolment ratio, is also positively correlated with urbanization. The R-squared value is 0.67, and the test of significance (0.01) suggests that the result is statistically significant. Higher literacy rates tend to go hand in hand with higher urbanization and the agglomeration of humans itself also provides much learning. Cities in Ghana provide most of the schools in the country and, hence, cities attract education migrants. Cities also provide more avenues for employment that requires more advanced and specialized education. There is much rural–urban migration for educational (both formal and informal) and employment purposes (Konadu-Agyemang 2001). This, however, does not imply that the cities destroy the countryside through 'urban bias'. Instead, there is much symbiotic relationship between urban and rural development. For instance, returning migrants have been found to make a large contribution to the rural economy; some keep farms in rural areas to support themselves in cities but also to invest in some of these farms (Obosu-Mensah 1999, 2002).

Evidence shows that Ghanaian cities have been key to shaping national development. They have contributed to the process of change and have simultaneously mediated the transformation, giving it particular characteristics. This role has become even more amplified since Ghana became an emerging oil economy in 2010, the same year that Ghana was declared an 'emerging economy' by the World Bank.

Oil, spatial, and national development

The contribution of the oil industry to national economic growth has been quite substantial, as shown in Table 31.3.

More recent figures by the Ministry of Finance and Economic Planning (2016 budget appendix 2A) shows that oil contributes about 10 per cent to the nation's GDP, making Ghana a petro-state (Heilbrunn 2014). The national contribution of oil is not restricted to GDP, but the power of oil can underwrite the Ghanaian state's requests for loans aimed at national development. Indeed, the oil industry has led to the creation of new property rights both on land and in the sea created because of oil production (Chalfin 2015).

It is cities that have provided the space for production, distribution, and consumption to support these national processes. Cities have provided infrastructure, accommodation, and office and other workspace for international and national oil companies to function and to enable local oil service companies to operate. Nearly all major oil companies are headquartered in cities. The Jubilee Partners, as the leading oil producers in Ghana are called, are headquartered or concentrated in cities such as Accra and Takoradi. Similarly, companies that are registered with the Enterprise Development Centre mostly operate from, and originate in, cities (Ablo 2012, 2015 Ablo and Overå 2015). Of the jobs that have been created in the upstream sector of the oil industry, most are for Ghanaians and most are located in cities (see Table 31.4). The multiplier for such jobs extends to the household and extended families (Ablo 2012, 2015), but they are *concentrated* in cities (Obeng-Odoom 2014a).

Whether construction-related jobs such as those in the road sector are mostly captured by Ghanaians is, however, contestable. As much road building and other construction activities are carried out by Chinese companies who typically employ Chinese labour (Obeng-Odoom 2015b; 2016b), any celebration about 'success' in local

Table 31.3 Growth indices in Ghana, 2009–13

Year	2009	2010	2011	2012	2013
Per capita GDP (US$)	1,103.5	1,284.7	1,605.7	1,602.8	1,838.3
Growth rate of GDP at constant 2006 prices (with oil)	4.0	8.0	15.0	8.8	7.1
Growth rate of GDP at constant 2006 prices (without oil)	n/a	7.6	8.2	8.6	6.7
Percentage of GDP	n/a	0.4	6.8	n/a	8.2

Note: n/a = not available.

Source: (GSS 2014 (for rows 1–3); Owusu 2014).

Table 31.4 Employment in the oil industry in Ghana

	Employment	Registered companies	Monetary value
Total	7,000	474	
Ghanaians (national)	5,589	321 (all Ghanaians) 46 (joint)	US$1,149,806,724.45*
Ghana (urban)	Over 70 per cent	Over 80 per cent	Over 90 per cent

Note: * Between 2010 and Q3 of 2015.
Source: Adapted from Addae-Mensah (2015).

content has to be measured. Nevertheless, it is true that with the totality of jobs created in and about the oil industry *together with* the expansion of economic growth and public sector programmes, the unemployment rate in the country has been declining. Between 1992/95 and 2006/08, the urban unemployment rate fell by 45 per cent (Obeng-Odoom 2013a: 69–70). Between 2010 and 2012, during which time the economy had come under the influence of the oil industry, the national unemployment rate fell from 5.8 per cent to 3 per cent in 2012 (Alagidede et al. 2013). With the increase in the number of jobs created in the oil sector concentrated in cities where related multiplier effects have also been identified (Obeng Odoom 2014a: tab 32.4; Ablo 2015 tab 32.4; Ablo and Overå 2015), the urban unemployment rate is expected to decline even more noticeably although the number of jobs created in the oil industry has been much smaller than expected, especially by the youth (see, for example Darkwah 2013); and the livelihoods of others have been destroyed by the industry especially in towns and peri-urban areas (Adusah-Karikari 2015).

The contract sums are also spent mostly in cities, with much less being spent in the countryside. Research on Sekondi-Takoradi (Obeng-Odoom 2014a) and the countryside (Hilson 2014) return quite different conclusions, with those studying cities showing the vibrant activities therein while research on settlements such as Cape Three Points (Boohene and Peprah 2011), Atuobo, and Axim (Adusah-Karikari 2015), respectively a rural settlement, a town, and a smaller city, shows negligible or no spatial transformation. In turn, Cape Three Points where the biggest oilfields are located has no substantial direct engagement with the international oil companies whose influence can be seen in urban centres.

Urban centres possess the facilities and processes to attract, and at least attempt, to retain some of the investment related to oil. It is such features that distinguish cities from other settlements. Thus, in her influential book *The Economy of Cities,* Jane Jacobs (1969: 262), the American urbanist, defined a city as 'a settlement that consistently generates its growth from its own local economy'. Cities also provide many advantages or urbanization economies such as the sharing of labour which help them to retain investment in the city.

Table 31.5 Regional distribution of ABFA-funded projects, 2011–13

Region	Share of ABFA-funded projects	Poverty incidence
Western Region	27	20.9
Ashanti	15	14.8
Eastern	14	21.7
Greater Accra	14	5.6
Volta	10	33.8
Brong Ahafo	7	27.9
Central	4	18.8
Northern	4	50.4
Upper East	4	44.4
Upper West	1	70.7

Source: PIAC 2014.

In contrast, in towns and settlements closest to the rigs but which do not have these urbanization economies, there is hardly any substantial capture of oil activities save admiring the lights on the rigs from a distance. From that vantage point, it is tempting to call the oil industry an enclave (Hilson 2014), but it is perhaps better to call it spatially concentrated. While the capture of oil activities in cities can be said to be a measure of the vibrancy of those cities, global and national institutional policies have reinforced this pattern of uneven development. The distribution of oil revenue funded projects is one example of institutional complicity.

As Table 31.5 shows, there is not much balance in the distribution of projects. It is intuitive that any related multipliers are likely to be similarly unbalanced. While this distribution is inconsistent with the Petroleum Law which insists on regional balance in the distribution of projects, even if the projects were evenly distributed, the chances of regional balance would still be slim. As the column on poverty incidence (Col. 3) shows, regions in Ghana have dramatically different levels of poverty. Starting from an uneven playing field, mere even distribution will at least maintain the starting levels of inequality. Indeed, based on the notion of 'circular and cumulative causation' developed by Swedish institutional economist Gunnar Myrdal (1944, 1957), it is more likely that inequalities are likely to be accentuated. A cycle of inequality intensifies over time as the initial level of inequality cumulatively increases after every round or spell of inequality. Similar issues apply to inequality within regions, within cities, and between cities as well as between rural areas and cities.

In 1987, the extent of income inequality, as measured by the Gini coefficient, in Ghana was 0.38. It has consistently increased since then: to 0.42 in 1998 and 0.55 in 2007. Also, whereas the richest 10 per cent of the population controlled 29.5 per cent of income in Ghana in 1998, the share of income of the richest 10 per cent had increased to 32.8 per cent by 2007 (Vanderpuye-Orgle 2002; UNDP 2009). By 2008 the share of the population who perceived that they were 'better' or 'much better' off than others stood at 38 per cent, more than those who felt they were worse off (31 per cent), or those who did not perceive any inequality (26 per cent). Currently, 36 per cent of the general population feel that their conditions are 'much better' or 'better' than others, while 32 per cent feel that their conditions are 'worse' or 'much worse' than others. These figures suggest that some 68 per cent of the population perceive inequality. Since 2008, the share of population who feel that they are worse off than others has increased slightly from 31 to 32 per cent, while those who feel that they are better off than others have declined from 38 to 36 per cent. Generally, the perception that inequality is pervasive has not improved since 2008 (CDD 2012). While the Gini figures are national rather than urban or spatial more broadly, economists in Ghana have established that spatial inequalities account for some 80 per cent of national inequality in Ghana (cited in Owusu and Boatemah 2014: 215). So, the Gini figures are as much a reflection of the urban and spatial inequalities as they are of national inequalities. This growing inequality shows that the classic claim by orthodox economists (e.g. Kuznets 1955) that inequality diminishes with per capita income is inapplicable to the case in Ghana—a more realistic explanation is needed.

The nature of growth in Ghana is a key explanation for the growing levels of inequality in the country. Anchored on private capital that is mobile in a highly globalized or globalizing context (Grant 2009), this growth relies on the private accumulation of capital to expand the economy. Yet the private sector companies are usually small scale, the work in that sector is insecure and non-unionized, and the wages are typically low. For comparable work, the public service can pay 1.9 times higher than the private employer (Obeng-Odoom 2013a). Of all the reported suicide cases in Ghana between 2006 and 2008, 56.1 per cent were related to insecure employment and conditions that threatened financial stability as well as persistent health problems, and deviant or criminal behaviour (Adinkrah 2012). More recently, *The Lancet Psychiatry* has published a longitudinal study (Nordt et al. 2015), which shows that the risk of unemployment increased the chances of committing suicide. Even more definitive diffusing private employment, then, can be a pact for suicide.

The owners of private enterprises, however, earn significantly more, typically three to four times higher than workers' earnings in a valuation company, for example (Obeng-Odoom and Ameyaw 2011). While informal economies have declined over the years from 74.1 in 1999/2000, they still constituted around half (47.7) of urban jobs at the last count (2006/08). Conditions here are harsh and are consistently made so by private capital and the state (Obeng-Odoom 2011b) and even if some have better conditions than in some private sector work (Obeng-Odoom 2013a), many more work under very harsh conditions with no employment benefit, overtime, holidays, or breaks.

Following colonial urban development in which the spaces most able to guarantee profit dictated the direction of investment, the private sector also invests mainly in already well-endowed regions and cities. The inequalities between regional capitals and the rest of the urban system are strongly driven by this dynamic. A third feature of the private sector-based paradigm which sustains inequality is the emphasis on the enclosure and commodification of land for business and private uses. Although the creation of private property rights in Ghana's mostly customary land tenure system has been advocated by economists who claim that doing so reduces transaction costs, encourages investment in land, and provides a good exchange for technology transfer through foreign investment, the commodification process has led to much displacement of many urban residents who have lost their land to private investors seeking to invest in residential, office, and commercial real estate in urban centres (Obeng-Odoom 2013a).

Large-scale estate developers, on the other hand, have benefited considerably from the privatization of land and the subsequent capture of rent, from speculation but also public investment in urban infrastructure generally. In cities such as Sekondi-Takoradi, Accra, and Kumasi, landlords who have not necessarily made major upgrades to their rental properties are able to leverage on urban-wide public investment to impose exorbitant rents and arbitrarily review them upwards in clear contravention of housing laws such as the Rent Act 1963 (Obeng-Odoom 2011c, 2013a, 2014a). In turn, low-income renters have been forced to spend substantially more of their income on renting—in an environment with declining public sector investment in housing. Private landlords and property owners, especially, have gained much wealth from speculating on the trends in landed property investment. Such speculation, in turn, has hurt non-speculators who have typically been evicted from their housing or have found it much harder to find appropriate accommodation.

The public sector has also played its part in fuelling growing inequalities in the country, but for reasons related to the new public management ideas introduced in the civil service as part of the neoliberal agenda which commenced in the 1980s. Prior to the implementation of the neoliberal agenda, the ratio of the salary of a senior to that of a junior civil servant was less than 2:1 but by 1991 the ratio had increased to 10:1, slightly short of the 13:1 that was the ratio recommended by the government's overseas consultants on reforms in the civil service, who claimed, in line with the neoliberal theory, that inequality is an incentive for hard work and creative ideas (Ayee 2001: 13). Between 1986 and 1991, salaries for senior civil servants rose about 33 per cent, but medium-salaried workers got only a 4 per cent raise, while minimum-waged workers experienced an average decline of 15 per cent of their salaries (Kraus 1991: 32). Between 1992 and 1999, the mean income of the richest 10 per cent of workers increased by 600 per cent, while the mean income of the poorest 10 per cent increased by only 38 per cent, suggesting that the ratio of the average income of workers in the top decile to the average income of workers in the bottom decile was 150:1 (Trades Union Congress of Ghana 2004: 19–20).

More fundamentally, there are systemic factors that sustain and worsen this state of inequality. One such factor is the recurrent power crisis (Obeng-Odoom 2015b). While much has been said about how this crisis could erode the gains from poverty, the differentiated coping and adaptation strategies of diverse social classes suggest that it is inequality that is more likely to be worsened: the rich, not the poor, are likely to get substitute generators. The cost of a power crisis can better be shouldered by the rich than the poor, with the incidence of damage likely to be less for the rich who are better able to diversify their assets and move them around.

This evidence of economic inequality is troubling. Contrary to the neoliberal claim that inequality is necessary for economic growth and long-term transformation of economies (World Bank 2009), inequality can have adverse growth effects (Birdsall et al. 1994). International evidence shows that inequality reduces reported levels of human happiness (Stilwell and Jordan 2004). A study (Fosu 2009) focusing on inequality and poverty reduction in sub-Saharan Africa has shown that inequality slows down poverty reduction. That was evidently how inequality choked off growth and poverty reduction in Accra where the share of the population under the poverty line increased from 4.4 per cent to 10.6 per cent between 1998/99 and 2005/06 (GSS 2007: 8–9), although overall urban poverty declined. There is evidence that inequality is at the root of fear of crime (Obeng-Odoom et al. 2014) which contributes to the development of gated housing, reliant on private security.

Our cities; our nation; our future

Cities, then, have contributed substantially to raising the status of Ghana as an emerging economy; but cities have also been a major impediment for inclusive spatial and national development. What requires further analysis is how to strengthen the contribution of cities to national development and the future of Ghanaian society and minimize or eliminate the systemic inequalities and their drivers. The existing scholarly and policy recommendations fall short of this aspiration.

For instance, while the country's *National Urban Policy Framework* (Government of Ghana 2012) has a long list of what is necessary, underpinning all the demands is a particular vision of economic growth: growth led by the private sector and through the use of private credit facilities. The growth-centric nature of Ghana's, indeed national urban policies in Africa, has been well-established in the literature (Okeke 2014; Turok 2015). What has not been clarified is that it is a particular type of growth that is emphasized in the National Urban Policy (NUP), one that is implicitly Solow-type or endogenous, at best. From this perspective, the emphasis is on physical capital and some human capital, combined with the formalization of the informal economy under private finance. Together, it is assumed that there will be income convergence and sustainable development with better growth—without placing specific emphasis on inequality, the quality of jobs, and ecological imperatives (see details of this growth theory in Obeng-Odoom 2016a). As the previous sections have shown, however, this model of growth is highly problematic. Growth powered by private sector-led jobs tends to be poorly distributed, the jobs are poorly paid, and labour exploited. There is much displacement arising from privatizing nature's commons in the form of land use and stewardship and, through speculation and the capture of public investment, wealth becomes concentrated in the hands of private landlords and property developers. Added to these, neoliberalism in the public sector and in the distribution of public goods has been skewed towards richer areas of society. So, in spite of its best intentions, the NUP does not offer a sustainable path from 'our cities' to 'our nation and our future'.

A second set of options was canvassed by the National Development Planning Commission (NDPC) which tried to develop a forty-year development plan for example by aggregating the best ideas from the manifestos of all political parties in the country into *the* national plan. To make sure that there is no deviation from this plan, advocates demand that such a plan is written into the national constitution. Yet, political party manifestos are hardly a good starting point for developing a national policy because, as one study showed (Obeng-Odoom 2010b), almost without exception political parties demonstrate a rather superficial understanding of the nature of the urban challenge, often reduced to a simplistic view about beautiful cities or affordability matters which are disarticulated from the conditions of labour. So any national policy based on political manifestos is likely to face major problems and is unlikely to be an effective response to the challenge of linking cities to national and future ecological transformation.

A modified approach is to devise an ideology-less plan, entrench it in the national constitution, and ask politicians to design *strategies* for meeting the plan (Gyampo 2016). This revised model is foregrounded on claims about the finitude of ideological differences the world over and hence what matters is not ideology but universal goods such as 'development'; it is the strategies that separate political parties. In this sense, two things are needed (Byrne 2015): the plan must be binding and comprehensive (defined as covering economic, social, and environmental roles). Yet, the question of development is extremely complex; not as straightforward as advocates suggest. Should development be about human or physical capital? Should it be growth-based or in need of fundamental changes? There are even those who talk of 'post-development'. What, if at all, should be the relationship between development and post-development, underdevelopment, and un-development? Even within development, there are substantial *ideological* differences. The New Patriotic Party (NPP) and the National Democratic Congress (NDC) have strikingly similar ideologies in *essence*, but the Convention People's Party (CPP) has a clearly different ideological orientation on development (Obeng-Odoom 2010b). So, while this approach is much more plausible, particularly because it has the potential to make political parties collaborative, it is founded on contestable assumptions.

The NDPC itself is following the procedures for making plans (see detailed discussion in Gyampo (2016) of how this process works), with broad consultation as a key part of the process. Notably, it is seeking to engage people directly to ascertain their aspirations. In doing so, neither can past lessons from previous plans be totally ignored, even if the plans have run their course. Previous plans produced by this same methodology have, especially in the twenty-first century, led to one vision: growth. This was cast differently—*Ghana Poverty Reduction Strategy 1: An Agenda for Growth and Prosperity (2003–2005); Growth and Poverty Reduction 2 (2006–2009); and Ghana Shared Growth and Development Agenda* (2010–2013); but in essence it was a particular growth vision wedded to private sector leadership that was articulated. Indeed, since the onset of the neoliberal agenda, such development plans have captured the mood of the vision, sometimes with 'poverty' or 'prosperity' seeking to broaden these plans (Obeng-Odoom 2013b: 62–74). The recent work by Kwasi Dartey-Baah et al. (2015) makes a worthwhile point of asking that the target be based on national needs not on global goals such as the Sustainable Development Goals (SDGs), a point which is beginning to be strongly emphasized by Charles Gore (2015), a critic of mainstream international goal-setting. Yet, Dartey-Baah and others seek support for a local orthodoxy in the sense that local revision is based on widening the number of contributors by including more private entities to subscribe to the national development vision—growth—through corporate social responsibility (CSR) in what is called a 'win-win situation' (see e.g. Dartey-Baah et al. 2015: 89). 'A review of spatial planning in Ghana's socio-economic development trajectory' by Fuseini and Kemp (2015) clearly shows that, without explicitly incorporating spatial planning in national development, huge inequalities result. In this sense, the development of a National Urban Policy that explicitly places planning emphasis on cities and spatial development is useful. Indeed, a policy of this nature has the potential to unite spatial and sustainable development for example through land use planning. Yet, as Fuseini and Kemp (2015) note, development of the policy itself is not a sufficient condition for wider transformation because of logistical constraints, implementation challenges, human resource capacity, as well as problems of scale, resources, and plan coherence *within* a global or globalizing society with conflicting and contradictory agendas of the world development agencies, former colonizers, and current imperial pressures. Looking from this perspective, scaling up the plan, resourcing planning agencies, and wider institutional transformation as well as integrating it with the ongoing effort to develop a national development plan for the next forty years can be a useful strategy.

Conclusion

However, as this chapter has shown, even more limiting in a fundamental way are assumptions about the relationship between cities and national development, the NUPs, and indeed, all other post-1980 plans' avowed commitment to economic growth of the orthodox order; characteristic neglect of growing socio-economic inequalities captured in and strongly shaped by spatial inequalities; and the socio-spatial separatist analyses of the environment. Most of these features are derivative from the inequality cancer, so making inequality *the* direct emphasis in the next forty years could help to focus attention more tightly on returning lands to the commons, providing stronger social protection, including public housing, and strengthening public sector jobs creation processes. Similarly, prioritizing the environment in the focus on growth such that interest is not just in the industrial cluster in Odawna, but also about socio-ecological transformation. The *approach* is to be centred on inequality first and foremost. If growth is to be part of the mix of policies, it has to be growth with structural change; with a greater role for the public sector, and a more tightly embedded market within the society–environment milieu in which the reduction of inequality is front and centre. The state can use the location of oil investment and the rents from the oil industry to link spatial development to inclusive social and national development and change (see Anand (2014) and Obeng-Odoom (2015b) for details of this strategy) that will more strongly rely on cities both as drivers and obstacles of growth and change; of inclusive socio-economic and ecological transformation for 'our future'. In short, Ghana neither needs just another plan nor wants a new planning vision. Instead, what Ghana needs is a plan for a new development paradigm.

REFERENCES

Ablo, A.D. (2012). 'Manning the rigs: a study of offshore employment in Ghana's oil industry'. MPhil thesis submitted to the Department of Geography, University of Bergen, Norway.

Ablo, A.D. (2015). 'Local content and participation in Ghana's oil and gas industry: can enterprise development make a difference?', *Extractive Industries and Society* 2/2: 320–7.

Ablo, A.D. and Overå, R. (2015). 'Networks, trust and capital mobilisation: challenges of embedded local entrepreneurial strategies in Ghana's oil and gas industry', *Journal of Modern African Studies* 53/3: 391–413.

Adaawen, S.A. and Owusu, B. (2013). 'North–south migration and remittances in Ghana', *African Review of Economics and Finance* 5/1: 29–45.

Adarkwa K.K. (2011). *Future of the Tree: Towards Growth and Development of Kumasi*. Kumasi: University Printing Press.

Addae-Mensah, I. (2015). 'Status and national policy of local content'. Paper presented at the Ghana Academy of Arts and Sciences, November, Accra.

Adinkrah, M. (2012). 'Better dead than dishonored: masculinity and male suicidal behavior in contemporary Ghana', *Social Science and Medicine* 74/4: 474–81.

Adusah-Karikari, J. (2015). 'Black gold in Ghana: changing livelihoods for women in communities affected by oil production', *The Extractive Industries and Society* 2/1: 24–32.

Afolayan, A. (1988). 'Immigration and expulsion of ECOWAS aliens in Nigeria', *International Migration Review* 22/1: 4–27.

Agyei-Mensah, S. (2006). 'Marketing its colonial heritage: a new lease of life for Cape Coast, Ghana?', *International Journal of Urban and Regional Research* 30/3: 705–16.

Ahadzie, D. (2016). 'The economic, technological and structural demands of the construction industry in emerging markets south of the Sahara: a case study of Ghana', in T.R. Abdulai, F. Obeng-Odoom, E. Ochieng E, and V. Maliene (eds) *Real Estate, Construction and Economic Development in Emerging Market Economies*. London: Routledge, 146–73.

Alagidede, P., Baah-Boateng, W., and Nketiah-Amponsah, E. (2013). 'The Ghanaian economy: an overview', *Ghanaian Journal of Economics* 1/1: 4–34.

Amantana, V. (2012). *A Sociological Study of Street Children in Ghana: Victims of Kinship Breakdown and Rural-Urban Migration*. Lewiston, NY: The Edwin Mellen Press.

Anand, P.B. (2014). 'Extractive economies and sustainable development: An analysis of infrastructure, health and social development'. Paper presented to the United Nations Development Programme and government of Brazil on 'Dialogue on the extractive sector and sustainable development – Enhancing public-private-community cooperation in the context of the post-2015 agenda', 3–5 December, Brasilia, Brazil.

Ayee, J. (2001). 'Civil service reform in Ghana: a case study of contemporary reform problems in Ghana', *African Journal of Political Science* 6/1: 1–41.

Birdsall, N., Ross, D., and Sabot, R. (1994). 'Inequality and growth reconsidered'. Paper for the Annual Meetings of the American Economics Association, 3–4 January, Boston, MA.

Boohene, R. and Peprah, J.A. (2011). 'Women, livelihood and oil and gas discovery in Ghana: an exploratory study of Cape Three Points and surrounding communities', *Journal of Sustainable Development* 4/3: 185–95.

Busia, A. (1950). *Report on a Social Survey of Sekondi-Takoradi.* London: Crown Agents for the Colonies for the Gold Coast Government.

Byrne, R. (2015). 'Binding national development plan to ensure continuity?', *Ghana Business and Finance* 054: 10–12.

CDD (Centre for Democratic Development) Ghana (2012). *Economic and Social Conditions of Ghanaians: What the Afrobarometer Survey Says.* Accra: CDD.

Chalfin, B. (2015). 'Governing offshore oil: mapping maritime political space in Ghana and the Western Gulf of Guinea', *The South Atlantic Quarterly* 114/1: 101–18.

Darkwah, K.A. (2013). 'Keeping hope alive: an analysis of training opportunities for Ghanaian youth in the emerging oil and gas industry in Ghana', *International Development Planning Review* 35/2: 119–34.

Dartey-Baah, K., Amponsah-Tawiah, K., and Agbeibor, V. (2015). 'Corporate social responsibility in Ghana's national development', *Africa Today* 62/2: 70–93.

DESA (Department of Economic and Social Affairs) (2006). *World Urbanization Prospects, 2005 Revision.* New York: United Nations.

Dickson, K. (1993). 'What role may one expect of the regional capitals of Ghana in the country's development?', *The Future of Our Cities: Proceedings of the Ghana Academy of Arts and Sciences* 28: 13–30.

Fosu, A. (2009). 'Inequality and the impact of growth on poverty: comparative evidence for sub-Saharan Africa', *Journal of Development Studies* 45/5 726–45.

Fuseini, I. and Kemp, J. (2015). 'A review of spatial planning in Ghana's socio-economic development trajectory: a sustainable development perspective', *Land Use Policy* 47: 309–20.

Gore, C. (2015). 'The post-2015 moment: towards sustainable development goals and a new development paradigm', *Journal of International Development* 27/6: 717–32.

Government of Ghana (2012). *National Urban Policy Framework.* Accra: Ministry of Local Government and Rural Development.

Grant, R. (2009). *Globalizing City: Urban and Economic Transformation of Accra, Ghana.* New York: Syracuse University Press.

Grant, R. and Yankson, P. (2002). 'City profile Accra', *Cities* 20/1: 65–74.

GSS (Ghana Statistical Service) (2007). *Pattern and Trends of Poverty in Ghana 1991-2006.* Accra: Ghana Statistical Service.

GSS (Ghana Statistical Service) (2014). *The Ghana Living Standards Survey, Round 6: Poverty Profile in Ghana.* Accra: Ghana Statistical Service.

Gyampo, R. (2016). 'Dealing with winner-takes-all politics in Ghana: the case for national development planning', *IEA Governance Newsletter* 20/1: 11.

Heilbrunn, J.R. (2014). *Oil, Democracy, and Development in Africa*. New York: Cambridge University Press.

Hilson, A.E. (2014). 'Resource enclavity and corporate social responsibility in sub-Saharan Africa: the case of oil production in Ghana'. DPhil thesis in Management, Birmingham: University of Aston.

Jacobs, J. (1969). *The Economy of Cities*. London: Jonathan Cape.

Konadu-Agyemang, K. (2001). *The Political Economy of Housing and Urban Development in Africa: Ghana's Experience from Colonial Times to 1998*. London: Praeger.

Korboe, D. and Tipple, G. (1995). 'City profile Kumasi', *Cities* 12/4: 267–74.

Kraus, J. (1991). 'The struggle over structural adjustment in Ghana', *Africa Today* 38/4: 19–37.

Kuznets, S. (1955). 'Economic growth and income inequality', *The American Economic Review* 45/1: 1–28.

McDade, B.E. and Malecki, E.J. (1997). 'Entrepreneurial networking: industrial estates in Ghana', *Tijdschrift voor Economische en Sociale Geografie* 88/3: 262–72.

Myrdal, G. (1944). *An American Dilemma: The Negro Problem and Modern Democracy*. New York: Harper and Brothers.

Myrdal, G. (1957). *Economic Theory and Underdeveloped Regions*. London: Methuen, University Paperbacks.

Nordt, C., Wanke, I., Seifritz, E., and Kawohl, W. (2015). 'Modelling suicide and unemployment: a longitudinal analysis covering 63 countries, 2000–11', *The Lancet Psychiatry* 2/3: 239–45.

Obeng-Odoom, F. (2009). 'The future of our cities', *Cities*, 26/1: 49–53.

Obeng-Odoom, F. (2010a). 'Abnormal urbanisation in Africa: a dissenting view', *African Geographical Review* 29/2: 13–40.

Obeng-Odoom, F. (2010b). 'An urban twist to politics in Ghana', *Habitat International* 34/4: 392–99.

Obeng-Odoom, F. (2011a). 'Developing Accra for all? The story behind Africa's largest millennium city', *Development* 54/3: 384–92.

Obeng-Odoom, F. (2011b). 'The informal sector in Ghana under siege', *Journal of Developing Societies* 27/3–4: 355–92.

Obeng-Odoom, F. (2011c). 'Real estate agents in Ghana: a suitable case for regulation?', *Regional Studies* 45/3: 403–16.

Obeng-Odoom, F. (2013a). *Governance for Pro-Poor Urban Development: Lessons from Ghana*. London: Routledge.

Obeng-Odoom, F. (2013b). 'Managing land for the common good? Evidence from a community development project at Agona, Ghana', *Journal of Pro-Poor Growth* 1/1: 29–46.

Obeng-Odoom, F. (2013c). 'The state of African cities 2010: governance, inequality, and urban land markets', *Cities* 31: 425–29.

Obeng-Odoom, F. (2014a). *Oiling the Urban Economy: Land, Labour, Capital, and the State in Sekondi-Takoradi, Ghana*. London: Routledge. Available at www.taylorandfrancis.com/books/details/9780415744096/, accessed 20 March 2019.

Obeng-Odoom, F. (2014b). 'The state of African cities', *Journal of Asian and African Studies* 51/4: 389–97. Available at https://doi.org/10.1177/0021909614547604, accessed 21 August 2019.

Obeng-Odoom, F. (2015a). 'Oil rent, policy, and social development: lessons from the Ghana controversy'. United Nations Research Institute for Social Development (UNRISD) Research Paper 2. Geneva: United Nations.

Obeng-Odoom, F. (2015b). 'Global political economy and frontier economies in Africa: implications from the oil and gas industry in Ghana', *Energy Research and Social Science* 10: 41–56.

Obeng-Odoom, F. (2016a). *Reconstructing Urban Economics: Towards a Political Economy of the Built Environment*. London: Zed.

Obeng-Odoom F. (2016b). 'Oil, construction, and economic development', in R. Abdulai, F. Obeng-Odoom, E. Ochieng, and V. Maliene (eds) *Real Estate, Construction and Economic Development in Emerging Market Economies*. London: Routledge, 19–36.

Obeng-Odoom, F. and Ameyaw, S. (2011). 'The state of surveying in Africa: a Ghanaian perspective', *Property Management* 29/3: 262–84.

Obeng-Odoom, F. and Ameyaw, S. (2014). 'A new informal economy in Africa: case study of Ghana', *African Journal of Science, Technology, Innovation and Development* 6/3: 10–20.

Obeng-Odoom, F., Elhadary, Y.A., and Jang, H.S. (2014). 'Living behind the wall and socio-economic implications for those outside the wall: gated communities in Malaysia and Ghana', *Journal of Asian and African Studies* 49/5: 544–58.

Obosu-Mensah, K. (1999). *Food Production in Urban Areas: A Study of Urban Agriculture in Accra, Ghana*. Aldershot: Ashgate.

Obosu-Mensah, K. (2002). 'Changes in official attitudes towards urban agriculture in Accra', *African Studies Quarterly* 6/3: 19–32.

Okeke, I.N. (2014). 'Towards a new growth path in Africa: a study of national urban policy responses to urbanisation'. Working Paper, South African Cities Network, Available at www.sacities.net/wp-content/uploads/2014/09/2014-08_sacn_national_urban_policy_in_africa_working_paper.pdf, accessed 19 April 2019.

Otiso, K. and Owusu, G. (2008). 'Comparative Urbanization in Ghana and Kenya', *GeoJournal* 71/2–3: 143–57.

Owusu, A.Y. (2014). 'The dimensions of oil discovery in Ghana: what can it do for the economy and the people?', in E. Aryeetey, R.D. Osei, and P. Quartey (eds) *Managing Ghana's Oil Boom for Structural Transformation*. Accra: Sub-Saharan Publishers and ISSER, 225–53.

Owusu, G. and Boatemah, H.B. (2014). 'Oil and the Western region: implications for regional and local development', in E. Aryeetey, R.D. Osei, and P. Quartey P (eds) *Managing Ghana's Oil Boom for Structural Transformation*. Accra: Sub-Saharan Publishers and ISSER, 196–224.

PIAC (Public Interest and Accountability Committee) (2014). *Report on Management of Petroleum Revenues for 2013*. Accra: PIAC.

Stilwell, F. and Jordan, K. (2004). 'The political economy of land: putting Henry George in his place', *Journal of Australian Political Economy* 54: 119–34.

Stilwell, F. and Primrose, D. (2010). 'Economic stimulus and restructuring: infrastructure, green jobs and spatial impacts', *Urban Policy and Research* 28/1: 5–25.

Todaro, M. and Smith, S. (2006). *Economic Development*. London: Pearson Addison Wesley.

Trades Union Congress of Ghana (2004). 'Incomes in Ghana'. A policy research paper submitted to the Global Policy Network, São Paolo.

Tsikata, D. and Yaro, J.A. (2014). 'When a good business model is not enough: land transactions and gendered livelihood prospects in rural Ghana', *Feminist Economics* 20/1: 202–26.

Turok, I. (2015). 'Turning the tide? The emergence of national urban policies in Africa', *Journal of Contemporary African Studies* 33/3: 348–69.

UNDP (United Nations Development Programme) (2009). *Human Development Report 2009. Overcoming Barriers: Human Mobility and Development.* New York: UNDP.

Vanderpuye-Orgle, J. (2002). 'Spatial inequality and polarisation in Ghana, 1987–1999'. Paper presented at ISSER/Cornell Universities Conference, 'Ghana at the half century', 18–20 July, Accra 18–20.

World Bank (2009). *World Development Report 2009: Reshaping Economic Geography.* Washington, DC: World Bank.

World Bank (2014). *Doing Business 2015: Going Beyond Efficiency.* Washington, DC: World Bank.

Yeboah, I.E.A., Codjoe, S.N.A., and Maingi, J.K. (2013a). 'Producing an urban system for the spatial development of Ghana: lessons for sub-Saharan Africa', *African Geographical Review.* Available at doi:10.1080/19376812.2013.776893, accessed 10 December 2018.

Yeboah, I.E.A., Codjoe, S.N.A., and Maingi, J.K. (2013b). 'Emerging urban system demographic trends: informing Ghana's national urban policy and lessons for sub-Saharan Africa', *Africa Today* 60/1: 98–124.

32 Institutional change in the oil industry

China vs Russia

Nikolay Kolev and Yue Xu

Introduction

China and Russia are the two largest emerging economies that have experienced tremendous institutional changes. Both have been shifting from the old centrally planned to the new market-oriented economic system (Smallbone and Welter 2012). In China, the shift was triggered by the Third Plenum of the Eleventh Communist Party Central Committee in 1978 with the promulgation of the 'Open-Door' policy. In Russia, the shift started with radical changes in its economic and political structure following the collapse of the USSR in 1991.

Although China and Russia are geographically close, and share close political and economic links, the two countries have adopted their own approaches to economic development. After three decades, China emerges as a global manufacturer and is increasingly relying on imported oil to sustain its fast growth. In comparison, Russia emerges as a fast developing economy mainly based on its natural resources, especially the production and export of oil. Apparently, the development of the oil industry is strategically important for both nations.

Anecdote suggests that China has always been active in building institutional change in the oil industry in order to improve the competitiveness of its domestic oil companies. In the process of institutional change quite a number of new institutions have been created such as the State-owned Assets Supervision and Administration Commission (SASAC), and the National Development and Reform Commission (NDRC). In comparison, the Russian side shows a different picture. Institutional change occurred in conjunction with political and economic turbulence. This started in the 1990s when Russia promoted liberalization and privatization under President Yeltsin. Shortly afterwards, during the mid-1990s the Russian economy experienced hyperinflation and in 1998 financially collapsed. Then, in 2000 Vladimir Putin became president. With support from a majority in Parliament, President Putin was able to implement his ideas and initiated administrative reform. In the interests of this research, questions

Nikolay Kolev and Yue Xu, *Institutional change in the oil industry: China vs Russia* In: *Handbook of BRICS and Emerging Economies*. Edited by: P.B. Anand, Shailaja Fennell, and Flavio Comim, Oxford University Press (2021). © Oxford University Press.
DOI: 10.1093/oso/9780198827535.003.0032

arise: *What institutional changes have been made by both countries in their oil industries, and how to understand their differences?*

The rest of this chapter is organized as follows. First, we review theoretical arguments regarding both the antecedents and processes of institutional changes. This is followed by our explanation on why a comparative approach is necessary and important. We then present the evolution of institutional changes in both China and Russia respectively. We also discuss the key similarities and differences that emerged from our secondary data. Finally, we conclude the chapter with our view on the direction of future research.

Theoretical background

ANTECEDENTS OF INSTITUTIONAL CHANGES

North (1990: 3) provides perhaps the most-cited definition of institutions. According to him, institutions 'are the rules of the game of a society', or, more formally, are the humanly devised constraints that structure human interaction. In consequence they structure incentives in human exchange, whether political, social, or economic. According to North (1990: 4) institutions can be formal such as 'rules that human beings devise' and informal such as 'conventions and code of behaviour'. Scott (2013) suggests three institutional pillars: regulative, normative, and cultural-cognitive as specific institution constructs. First, the regulative institutions are constituted by formal rules such as laws, regulations, and political power, which guide actions through coercion and treatment of formal sanction by the state. Second, normative institutions refer to actions that organizations ought to take such as commercial behaviour and conventions, which guide action through morality, acceptability, and ethics norms (Scott 2013). Normative institutions comprise both values and norms. Third, the cultural-cognitive pillar refers to the rules that constitute the nature of reality and the frames through which meaning is made (Scott 2013).

Although institutions are relatively resistant to change (Jepperson 1991) they are not static (Weaver and Rockman 1993). Institutional change may stem from changes in the character and content of formal and informal institutions or their relevant enforcement mechanisms (North 1990). Scott (2013) also acknowledges that although institutions do provide stability and order, they also undergo changes, either incrementally and/or revolutionarily. Below we explore empirically observations of why institutions may change.

Some argue that institutions change because the three pillars of institutions do not evolve in the same way. Scott (2013) suggests that when the three institutional pillars are aligned, the strength of their combined force can be significant. However, institutions evolve and are not static. North (1990: 6) stresses that while the change in formal institutions may occur overnight, informal institutions need time and are 'much more impervious to deliberate policies'. Similarly Hoffman (1999) addresses the fact that changes in regulative institutions are not necessarily accompanied by changes in the other two pillars, especially in the early stages of institutional change. In situations where the three pillars are not aligned they provide resources that different actors can employ for different ends (Strang and Sine 2002), hence conditions for institutional change are provided (Dacin et al. 2002).

Other studies address the fact that institutional changes are mainly triggered by external factors. Exogenous drivers can be technological evolution, changes in preferences (may create new markets), new information, and evolution in related games (Aoki 2001). Exogenous shocks disrupt established institutional logics and structures 'by motivating search process[es] that create awareness of flaws in the current arrangement and increase the salience of the alternatives' (Sine and David 2003: 202). Economists maintain that institutional flaws increase transaction costs due to the way that resources are allocated or cause the loss of new market opportunities (Brousseau et al. 2011). Consequently, exogenous shocks trigger the need to create a 'branching point' where institutional change takes place (Gourevitch 1986).

However, the emphasis on external shocks 'underestimates both intra- and inter-institutional dynamics and source of change' (March and Olsen 2008: 168). North (1990) claims that—for change in formal institutions in particular—the impetus of institutional changes may come from exogenous or endogenous parameter changes. Greif and Laitin (2004: 639) go further and argue that 'institutions can change due to endogenous processes, exogenous shocks, and combinations of both'. For example, in addition to technological change as exogenous, depletion of resources over time may relate to endogenous drivers (Ostrom 2009). Furthermore, Scott (2013: 58) acknowledges the influence of external shocks, such as wars and financial crises, but he indicates that 'much of the impetus for change occurs through endogenous processes, involving conflicts and contradictions between institutional elements'.

In fact, institutional change requires endogenous drivers, such as: characteristics of both political context and target institutions, and the presence of certain types of changing agents (Mahoney and Thelen 2009). For example, institutional change can stem from changes in principal-agent relationships. Typically, modifications of their relationship are needed when principals face extensive agency loss (Heritier 2007). Furthermore, Greif and Laitin (2004) argue that central to endogenous institutional changes are the dynamics of self-enforcing belief and its associated behaviour. They stressed that institutional change has endogenous character when a change in beliefs is observed, because the associated behaviour is no longer self-enforcing, resulting in individuals acting in a way that does not reproduce associated beliefs.

Beyond the argument of internal and external reasons for institutional changes, Oliver (1992) offers a structured approach suggesting institutional changes or deinstitutionalization are caused by functional, political, and social pressures. Functional pressure arises from perceived problems in performance or perceived utility associated with institutionalized practices. They can often be associated with broad environmental changes.

Political pressure stems from shifts in the interest and underlying power distributions in existing institutional arrangements. As stressed by Lawrence (1999), power is also a driver of institutional change, as powerful actors can shape the institutional environment depending on their particular interests. Social sources of institutional change can be those that might hinder the continuation of a practice such as changes in laws or social expectations (Dacin et al. 2002).

Finally, studies on ideology seem to provide another overarching proposition on the reason for institutional change. As an important aspect of cognitive institutions, the concept of ideology deserves further explanation here. North (1981: 48–9) views ideology as 'intellectual effort to rationalize the behavioural pattern of individuals and groups' or 'an economizing device in which individuals come to terms with their environment and are provided with a "world view" so that the decision-making process is simplified'. Later, he abandons the term ideology and replaces it with 'belief systems', because ideology connotes the Marxist notion of false or incorrect beliefs (North 1999). Seliger (1976: 11) sees ideology as 'sets of ideas by which men posit, explain and justify ends and means of organized social action, and specifically political action, irrespective of whether such action aims to preserve, amend, uproot or rebuild a given social order'. An obvious issue stands out in this definition which concerns the relationship between politics/ideology and institutional change. Gerring (1997: 967) shares some similar concerns. He argues that it is impossible to study ideology as a purely ideational phenomenon, as we are more concerned with what political stakeholders do than what they say. Tan (2005) asserts that ideology influences the direction of institutional change, as well as the likelihood that interest groups will succeed in their efforts. Similarly, Krug and Hendrischke (2008) argue that ideology plays a role by selectively opting for certain policies in the ongoing process of institutional building. Scott (2013: 68) goes further and stresses that 'shared assumptions and ideologies define preferred political and economic systems at national and transnational level'.

PROCESSES OF INSTITUTIONAL CHANGE

Pierson (1996) has emphasized that institutional design is likely to contain some unanswered and dysfunctional elements that need to be addressed through institutional changes. The question of how institutions may undergo change remains under-explored (Scott 2013).

Sociologists view institutional change as a process of institutionalization and deinstitutionalization. They also tend to view institutional change in a functionalist way—institutions have to address changes in the field and adapt to those changes. This approach suggests a passive reaction of institutions to changes in the field. This passive approach is challenged by the fact that some institutional organizations can be proactive and inclined to change institutions (Pfeffer and Salancik 1978; Oliver 1991). Peters

(2011) comments that such a proactive approach can be common in public institutions because of their capacity to manipulate their field.

Historical institutionalism tends to look at institutional change mainly in two more or less similar ways: the punctuated equilibrium (Krasner 1984) way, or 'critical juncture' way (Collier and Collier 1991). The former admits that while most of the time institutions are in equilibrium, they could be changed. In Krasner's words equilibrium may be punctuated in times of 'rapid bursts of institutional change followed by long periods of stasis' (1984: 242). The latter emphasizes that institutional change occurs when a number of significant drivers break up institutional inertia.

Regarding the pace of institutional change, one side of the argument claims that institutional change tends to be incremental. This is mainly because institutional changes comprise 'marginal adjustments to the complex of rules, norms and enforcement that constitute the institutional framework' (North 1990: 83). Because institutional change takes time, how current changes may occur can be significantly affected by existing institutions, hence are path-dependent. Williamson (2000: 598) argues that major changes in the rules of the game occur slowly taking decades or centuries; this is because 'cumulative change of a progressive kind is very difficult to orchestrate' unless 'rare windows of opportunity' occur that enable broad reform to be pursued.

By contrast, another side of the argument suggests that under certain conditions, institutional changes follow abrupt processes. For example North (2003: 4) accepts the view that on only rare occasions might abrupt institutional change occur. Institutional change can take place 'abruptly, in dramatic episodes that present large discontinuities with former patterns' (Dacin et al. 2002). Moreover, institutional change often involves short and turbulent periods of deliberate institutional change and experimentation (Aoki 2001). Key events, also known as disruptive events (Hoffman 1999), critical junctures (Hall and Taylor 1996), and jolts (Meyer, 1982), have a major impact on the process of institutional development in certain contexts.

Scholars try to understand conditions in which incremental or abrupt institutional change may occur. For example, Mahoney and Thelen (2009: 14) argue that incremental change emerges in 'the gaps or soft spots between the rule and its interpretation or the rule and its enforcement'. In other words, incremental changes occur when glitches occur in mechanisms of institutional reproduction. Kingston and Caballero (2009) argue that evolutionary theories tend to neglect the role of the political process in institutional change. Institutional change is introduced 'through process of reform . . . explicitly mandated or endorsed by governments' (Hall and Thelen 2009: 20). In line with this argument, political scientists (Thelen 1999; Streeck and Thelen 2005; Mahoney and Thelen 2009) emphasize the role of the political character in incremental institutional change, indicating that abrupt change involves deliberate acts by political actors.

The relationships between the old and new rules in institutional change are concerned. For example, Mahoney and Thelen (2009: 15–17) delineate four modes of institutional change taking into account the possible relationships between new and existing rules. As shown in Table 32.1, each mode represents a part or the whole process of institutional

Table 32.1 Modes of gradual change

	Displacement	Layering	Drift	Conversion
Removal of old rules	Yes	No	No	No
Neglect of old rules	-	No	Yes	No
Changed impact/enactment of old rules	-	No	Yes	Yes
Introduction of new rules	Yes	Yes	No	No

Source: Mahoney and Thelen (2009: 16).

Table 32.2 Types of institutional change: processes and results

Process of change	Result of change	
	Continuity	Discontinuity
Incremental	Reproduction by adaptation	Gradual transformation
Abrupt	Survival and return	Breakdown and replacement

Source: Streeck and Thelen (2005: 9).

change. The *displacement* mode refers the removal of existing rules and the introduction of new ones. It often resembles abrupt and rapid changes that entail a radical shift, but also may emerge in a gradual way, with the introduction of new institutions, which compete with old ones. The *layering* mode means the introduction of new rules on top of or alongside existing rules. These rules are not entirely new, but rather represent amendments, revisions, or additions of existing ones. The *drift* mode refers to the changed impact of existing rules due to changes in the environment. While rules formally stay the same, their impact has changed because of a shift in external conditions. The *conversion* mode considers the changed enactment of existing rules due to their strategic redeployment. In this mode the rules are the same, but the redeployment institutions are converted to new goals, function, or purpose.

Despite whether the focus is on incremental or abrupt changes, as stressed by Streeck and Thelen (2005: 8), 'we must avoid being caught in a conceptual schema that provides only for either incremental change supporting institutional continuity through reproductive adaptation, or disruptive change causing institutional breakdown and innovation and thereby resulting in discontinuity'. Therefore, in order to tackle this limitation, they distinguish between the process of change (incremental or abrupt), and results of change (continuity or discontinuity) as shown in Table 32.2. The model acknowledges that abrupt changes may result in discontinuity through breakdown and replacement of existing institutions. It also emphasizes that incremental changes we observed may result in 'dramatic institutional reconfiguration beneath the surface of apparent stability or adaptive self-reproduction' (Streeck and Thelen 2005: 8).

Apparently, in the process of institutional change timing and sequence have an important place. In the words of Pierson (2011: 54) 'we want to know not just what, but when'. Time is explained as the dimension that links together separate social events in highly consecutive ways. Where one event proceeds before another, this will result in different outcomes than if the sequence order is reversed. The sequence of past events influences outcomes and trajectories. Therefore, institutional change may be triggered by a sequence of events, impact of an event on a long-term trend, or a combination of trends, rather than by a single event.

Method

Case study method: This study employs a case study method, especially the narrative approach to answering the research question. Eisenhardt (1989) suggests that inductive research is particularly useful when the research area is relatively less known, and the research is interested in theory building. In addition, we adopt a comparative approach which enables a broader exploration of research questions and theoretical elaboration (Eisenhardt and Graebner 2007). This approach is particularly important for augmenting the external validity of our findings and for reducing observers' bias (Voss et al. 2002). First, we trace institutional changes that occurred in individual cases. Then we look at the similarities and differences based on cross-case analysis. This process allows us to identify patterns that emerged regarding the antecedents and processes of institutional change.

Case selection: The selected case studies include the oil industries of two emerging economies, namely, Russia and China. China and Russia are geographically close, and share close political and economic links from the past. They are both partners (e.g. energy industry) and competitors (e.g. geopolitically). We select the oil industry given this industry is regarded as strategically crucial by both nations. In addition, both countries are among the most important players in the world oil market. According to the US Energy Information Administration (EIA 2014b), Russia was the second largest net oil exporter in 2013, while China is the second largest oil importer in the world. More importantly, both countries have experienced comparable periods in their development, most notably from centrally planned to market-oriented economies. This background provides rich contexts for institutional change to facilitate our theoretical building.

Data collection: We explicitly focus on development of the oil industry since 1978 in China, and since 1991 in Russia, when market-oriented reforms in both countries were triggered by policies. We are inspired by the argument from North (1991: 97) that 'history is largely a story of institutional evolution, in which the historical performance of economies can only be understood as a part of a sequential story'. Accordingly, our data collection focuses on key institutional changes that have remarkably changed the industry over decades. Institutional change in emerging economies can be seen as a process with distinct stages characterized by different degrees of the maturity and stability of the new institutions (Kostova et al. 2008). Since the oil industry is highly regulated and populated with government agencies our data collection focuses on regulative institutions and institutional changes.

Case study data are drawn from various documents including (1) official documents, legislation, governmental websites; (2) public media such as: *The Economist*, *Reuters*, *Bloomberg*, the *Financial Times*, *Izvestia*, *Kommersant*, *Vedomosti*, *China Daily*, *Xinhua*, etc.; (3) business and industry analysis reports (e.g. EIA, BP Statistics), think-tanks (e.g. Brookings, Chatham House, Valdai Club, Carnegie Russia, National Bureau of Asian Research [NBR]), and country study reports, as well as national oil companies' (NOCs) annual reports and website information; (4) international organization reports (e.g. Organisation for Economic Cooperation and Development (OECD), UN Conference on Trade and Development (UNCTAD), World Bank); (5) academic research published in books, conference papers, existing doctoral theses, and journal articles.

Analysis method: In order to examine the process of institutional change, we pursue a process analysis method (Mohr 1982). Pierson and Skocpol (2002: 698) suggest that researching institutions 'usually means to analyse processes over a substantial stretch of years, maybe even many decades or centuries'. In addition, 'patterns in events is . . . key to developing "process" theory' (Langley 1999: 962). Therefore, we keep a chronological flow of intuitional changes in order to gain a better grasp of the key events and processes that led to specific consequences (Poole et al. 2000; Jain and Sharma 2013). Major events are put into two categories: one for background events, and the other for oil-industry-specific events. Process analysis helps us to follow timing and sequence of the evolution and to understand the roles and influence of actors in that sequence. It helps not only to look at various levels of decision making across which institutional change occurs, but also highlight the types of actors (such as rule designers and rule implementers) involved in the process (Heritier 2007).

Single case findings

INSTITUTIONAL CHANGES IN CHINA'S OIL INDUSTRY (1978–PRESENT)

Stage One (1978–92)

The Third Plenum in 1978 brought China under the leadership of President Deng Xiaoping. Since then, economic reform based on the 'open-door' policy started. This is a key event that triggered the beginning of stage one for the case of China in our study. Prior to the 1970s the country had not formed a coherent energy policy. Although China promoted a self-reliance model in developing its economy, the shortcomings of this approach had already been realized. Therefore for the first time—between 1979 and 1983—the State Science and Technology Commission (SSTC) provided a series of national energy symposia to outline potential energy constraints, and the actions that the country should take.

In the 1970s, the oil industry in China was a key contributor to foreign earnings for the country, and the Ministry of Petroleum Industry (MPI) has 'exerted enormous influence over the entire economy', especially when oil prices increased (Lieberthal and Oksenberg 1988: 85). From the mid-1970s through the 1980s, MPI 'pioneered the policies of importing foreign technology and equipment, exporting natural resources, and forming joint ventures' (Lieberthal and Oksenberg 1988: 85). However, towards the end of the 1970s China's petroleum production stagnated.

The government was determined to establish a proper institutional structure in order to facilitate oil production, as it seems MPI did not have sufficient capacity to handle institutional changes alone. In addition it aimed to: introduce competition, economic efficiency, and a wider share of ownership; subject state-owned enterprises (SOEs) to market discipline; develop a domestic capital market; enhance tax revenues to the state; and reduce government expenses (Naughton 1995; Lewis 2007). Therefore, in 1982 and 1983, some of MPI's responsibilities were transferred to two newly-formed NOCs: China National Offshore Oil Corporation (CNOOC) with a focus on offshore activities, and China National Petrochemical Corporation (Sinopec) focused on downstream activities. As can be seen, the two NOCs did not cover the onshore upstream sector. In order to increase the autonomy of onshore oil and gas fields (upstream enterprises) vis-à-vis the MPI, the State Economic Commission (SEC) played a particularly proactive role by advancing the idea of creating a national petroleum corporation (Lieberthal and Oksenberg 1988).

In 1988, the China National Petroleum Corporation (CNPC) was established and became responsible for managing onshore oil reserves, exploration, and production. In fact, CNPC replaced the MPI and acquired its administrative power over the onshore sector and inherited its staff and organizational culture. Central government tried for the first time to remove government control over oil production (Yang et al. 1995). We can clearly see institutional change in terms of the new organizational form (NOC replaced the ministry), as well as changes towards specialization as each NOC focused on a particular segment of the value chain.

Stage Two (1993–2002)

In 1993, China became a net oil importer for the first time, a key event delineating stage two. This was immediately recognized as a disaster by the Chinese government, pushing the government to modernize the oil industry urgently (Yergin 2011). As a result, the Ministry of Energy was abolished in 1993 due to the lack of institutional capacity to coordinate production.

In 1994, the Corporation Law permitted SOEs to be established as independent entities, although still owned by the state. From 1998 SOEs were forced to become more commercially oriented in their operations (Meidan et al. 2009). In the meantime, government tried to reduce interventions in the governance of NOCs. At that time, the industry was dominated by CNPC (in charge of exploration and production) and Sinopec (in charge of refining and distribution). They play dual roles acting simultaneously as both a government body and a commercial entity (Andrews-Speed et al. 2000).

At this stage we observed gradual institutional changes. For example, several institutional changes aiming to improve the efficiency and competitiveness of NOCs were implemented. Also, after vertical integration the operations of CNPC and Sinopec started to cover both the upstream and downstream of the industry. CNPC became responsible for the North China market, while Sinopec was responsible for the South China market. NOCs were under pressure to increase their competitiveness after China's accession to the World Trade Organization (WTO) in 2001 (EIA 2001). At this stage the government was actively encouraging the three NOCs to list domestically and abroad in order to become globally competitive (Jiang 2012).

Stage Three (2003–11)

In 2003 SASAC and NDRC were created. SASAC provided an institutional vehicle for managing SOEs in the pursuit of national interests (Brødsgaard 2012). SASAC became 'the world's largest controlling shareholder' (*The Economist* 2012). In the oil sector, SASAC has responsibility for supervising NOCs, approving their development plan and strategy, and the appointment of senior managers. At the same time the very top leaders of NOCs are directly appointed by the Organization Department of the Chinese Communist Party (CPC). Therefore, we can say that NOCs are also ideologically committed to the CPC.

NDRC became 'the most important government agency involved in energy policy' (Downs 2004: 25). Under the NDRC the Energy Bureau was created in an attempt to centralize the control for 'formulating and implementing a more overarching energy policy' over the energy sector (Meidan et al. 2009: 596). It is interesting to note that these institutional functions were lower than CNPC and Sinopec ministry-level status.

China's dependence on an external oil supply had further increased at this stage. In order to enhance its energy security and buffer geopolitical issues, building the Strategic Petroleum Reserve became necessary. At this stage, the government continued its effort to improve NOCs' competitiveness and has tried to dilute NOCs' monopolies. With such an aim in mind, in 2004 CNPC and Sinopec were authorized to operate offshore (a territory exclusively occupied by CNOOC), while CNOOC was permitted to operate onshore. Despite efforts towards demonopolization, this step actually further fortified NOCs' status as key agents in the industry.

In 2008 the Energy Bureau was replaced by the National Energy Administration (NEA). Although NEA has more political clout than its predecessor, it has limited authority to coordinate the interests of different players in the energy sector. Brødsgaard (2012: 630) comments that 'there were a number of ministries and agencies that did not always share the same interests or pursue the same policies'. Despite few reforms in institutional structure, NOCs continued to influence the oil industry significantly. New government agencies such as the Energy Bureau and NEA had lower administrative status than NOCs. In reality this means that NOC need not comply with their supervisors. This stage evidenced a complex bureaucratic structure in the industry.

The problem was recognized and in 2010, the National Energy Commission (NEC) was established as a 'super-ministry' to consolidate energy polices among different players under the State Council (EIA 2014a). NEC's key functions were to create energy development plans, review energy security, and coordinate international cooperation.

Stage Four (2012–present)

In 2012 China became the world's largest net importer of oil after the US (Blas 2013). In the same year *China's Energy Policy 2012* was announced. The policy aims to encourage the participation of private capital in the exploration and development of hydrocarbons, and network pipeline construction. Soon after this policy, in January 2013 the State Council released the Twelfth Five-Year Energy Development Plan. The plan addresses several energy problems such as: increasing international competition for energy resources; tight energy security; and a need for further reforms in the energy industry as institutional challenges became increasingly apparent.

Despite all the effort to create a market-oriented industrial structure, China's oil market is characterized by 'having excessive market power, leading to accusations of weak capital controls, inefficiency, and rent-seeking' (Andrews-Speed et al. 2014). Therefore, institutional change aims to create a mixed-ownership economy which allows 'non-state capital to participate in investment projects . . . in areas such as oil' (Xinhua 2014). As a result of this institutional change, for example, Sinopec announced its intention to sell 30 per cent of business in downstream for US$17.5 billion to domestic and foreign investors (Aldred 2014). In addition, given the fact that in February 2014 more than 80 per cent of oil and gas pipelines in China were owned and operated by CNPC, NEA published a document that pushed the operators of oil and gas pipelines to open up the domestic pipeline network to third parties. Shortly after, CNPC announced that it would open up its pipeline network. This movement, according to CNPC's chairman Zhou Jiping, 'will increase the efficiency of the industry as specified under the central government's guidance on energy reform' (Du 2014).

INSTITUTIONAL CHANGES IN RUSSIA'S OIL INDUSTRY (1991–PRESENT)

Stage One (1991–99)

The collapse of the USSR challenged both institutional and organizational structures with radical changes in the oil industry in Russia (Locatelli and Rossiaud 2011: 5588). First, the former Soviet Ministry of Oil was dissolved in 1992 and replaced by

Rosneftegaz Corporation, a voluntary association among domestic oil companies. In 1993 Rosneft was established by the government as an SOE on the basis of Rosneftegaz.

In February 1992 the transformation of the oil industry continued with the introduction of the Subsoil Law. The law stressed that oil sector activities can be performed under licence. This law shifts a centrally planned coordination mechanism to a contract-based coordination one (Kornai 1992). The Subsoil Law also stated that subsoil resources are state property. According to the Constitution of the Russian Federation, natural resources were part of the joint jurisdiction of the federal government and regional authorities. In other words, the allocation of licences for exploration and production was based on a joint decision between both authorities.

A key institutional act in this period was the change in the ownership structure of the domestic oil companies. In November 1992, the presidential decree declared the privatization of the oil industry. As an effect, three vertically integrated companies emerged: Lukoil, Surgutneftegas, and Yukos. However, despite the aimed privatization, the government did not give up its control over the oil industry. For example, top managers of the vertically integrated companies were appointed by the federal government or authorized by its institutions. By doing so, the state retains control over these enterprises.

In April of 1995, a presidential decree further consolidated the vertical integration of the largest oil companies. In September, the presidential decree declared 'loans for shares' auctions. The decree aimed to temporarily transfer shares in oil companies to financial institutions, in return for loans provided to the federal budget. However, the government refused to buy these shares back, because of a worsened budget deficit. Thus, large oil companies became privately controlled. After privatization the state-owned companies' share of oil production dropped from 81 per cent in 1994 to 13 per cent in 2003. The only area of the industry the state retained control over was in pipeline networks. Transneft stock is kept under federal ownership, and was also barred from being transferred to investors. According to Ahrend and Tompson (2006: 19) retaining state ownership over the pipeline network can be seen as 'an important check on the power of the oil companies'.

Stage Two (2000–09)

At the end of the last period, the new Prime Minister, Yevgeny Primakov, aimed to re-establish state control over the oil industry by the promotion of an NOC (Henderson 2012). Soon after, Vladimir Putin became the main political figure. At the start of his tenure, privatization continued. The creation of TNK-BP was the most notable example. However, Putin was 'looking to find a way of counterbalancing the influence of the oligarch group and of reasserting the control of the state' (Henderson 2012: 6). Moreover, as highlighted by Poussenkova (2013) state intervention in the economy was 'first and foremost in the oil and gas sector'.

In 2003, four private companies (Lukoil, Yukos, TNK-BP, and Surgutneftegaz) dominated the oil industry. In order to change that, state intervention in the oil industry culminated in October 2003 and led to the Yukos Affair—the head of Yukos was arrested on charges of tax evasion, fraud, and embezzlement, and jailed in 2005. According to *The Economist* (2004) his arrest was 'a prelude to snatching much of Russia's energy industry from its present owners, either to put it back into state hands or to hand it to people more loyal to President Vladimir Putin'. In December 2004, Rosneft bought Yukos's assets. The purchase confirmed Rosneft as a national champion (*The Economist* 2014). In 2006, Rosneft was listed in London and Moscow and became the biggest listing in Russian history to date, by raising US$10.7 billion (Rosneft 2014). The partial rationale behind the initial public offering (IPO) was to obtain cash to pay off a big debt. Another rationale for Rosneft to enter the stock market was that Russian institutions can 'legitimise their tactics and their hold on the assets' bought from Yukos (*The Economist* 2006).

In 2008, the Strategic Investment Law (SIL) and amendments to the existing Subsoil Law were adopted. The new legislation stated that the development of deposits that are of federal significance become strategically important activity for Russia. Hence, it can be said that the changes in legislation broke up with the previous model of joint jurisdiction between federal and regional authorities. These changes reaffirmed the superiority of the federal state over regional authorities.

The SIL confirmed that only Russian state-owned companies (the state holds more than 50 per cent of their voting shares) can participate in the development of offshore deposits. Foreign private companies that wish to acquire more than a 10 per cent stake in a Russian entity involved in such activities must first receive approval from a special commission chaired by the Russian prime minister. The new law positioned companies like Rosneft in a privileged position, because private companies' access to resources was restricted (Locatelli and Rossiaud 2012).

In November 2009, the Energy Strategy up to year 2030 was presented. The strategy aims to make two Russian companies world top ten energy companies and world top ten companies. At this stage Gazprom has already been one of the largest corporations in the world. Therefore, the strategy clearly wishes to maintain the role of Rosneft as a national champion and to promote it into a world-leading oil company. It should be noted that at stage two, institutional changes pointed to the emergence of Rosneft as a key state agent in the industry.

Stage Three (2010–present)

Two privatization plans on state property were announced by the federal government in 2010 and 2013. The rationale was to partially privatize SOEs, while keeping the government's controlling stake in them. In regard to the oil sector, reduction of the state share in Rosneft, Transneft, and Zarubezhneft is envisaged. It should be stressed that despite the course towards privatization, the share of SOEs in Russia's oil production increased from 13 per cent in 2003 to 40 per cent in 2011.

In 2012, the Commission for Strategic Development of the Fuel and Energy Sector and Environmental Security (CSDFESES) headed by the president was created. The commission aimed to coordinate the work of the different authorities and organizations in developing the energy sector. It also has significant financial and regulative clout over the tariff, tax, and price policy of oil and its products. The commission is an important institutional change, because the president challenged government control and gained direct influence over key energy industry dimensions.

In March 2012 President Dmitry Medvedev ordered that all government officials had to step down from boards of SOEs within three years (*Russia Today* 2014). This has resulted in several key directors/government officials such as Igor Sechin, deputy prime minister, leaving the board of Rosneft. However, 'it does not necessarily signify a more independent decision making by SOEs, neither does it promise a more transparent business environment' (Shadrina 2013: 19).

In 2012 President Putin signed a decree which included Rosneft on the list of strategic enterprises in the Russian Federation. Effectively this act put Rosneft under Putin's control. He also signed a decree regarding the privatization of state-owned energy companies. A few weeks later in June 2012, Putin announced that energy companies would not be sold because of the current market conditions.

In September 2014, the owner of Bashneft, one of the largest private oil companies was arrested and accused of money laundering during 2005–09 when Bashneft was purchased. In December 2014, Bashneft was nationalized. Somewhat contradictory to the privatization plans at the start of this period we actually also observed a clear trend towards nationalization.

In December 2014, the Russian authorities issued an order on partial privatization of Rosneft. It stated that as much as 19.5 per cent of Rosneft stock capital would be sold. The president of Rosneft highlighted that privatization would be open to Russian, as well as foreign investors. The final institutional initiative at stage three occurred a few weeks later in December 2014, when the Russian Prime Minister, Dmitry Medvedev, ordered civil servants to return to SOEs' boards of directors. This was necessary because the government aimed to tighten control over their activities (*Russia Today* 2014).

Cross-case analysis and discussion

Following the single case study, we compared both the antecedents and processes of institutional change between China and Russia. Several key differences emerge and are discussed as follows.

The influence of ideology: We observe the influence of communist ideology via the intervention of the Communist Party in making institutional change. We find that in China, the Communist Party has encompassed direct intervention in institutional changes via governmental agencies through all stages of the development of the industry.

Andrews-Speed et al. (2014) commented that energy strategies in China are set within a prevailing paradigm which values the leadership of the Communist Party. In comparison, the influence of the Communist Party in Russia is only more obvious at the early stage which focused on deregulation for industrial restructuring. Partly because of the collapse of the USSR in the early 1990s, since then the Communist Party has been struggling to generate influence at institutional functions. Thus, the influence of ideology diverges between the two cases.

> *Pattern 1: In China's case, institutional change maintains a communist ideology via direct intervention by the Communist Party. In comparison in Russia, institutional change promotes a capitalism ideology with rapidly decreasing intervention and control by the Community Party.*

The concern of state ownership: We find that in China state ownership of the domestic oil companies has been maintained after various institutional changes. Despite the fact that the three largest NOCs were listed domestically and abroad during 2000–01 the Chinese government still holds majority ownership in these companies. Energy security has become seriously concerned since 1993 when China became a net oil importer; the share of imported oil of total oil consumption has increased from 30 per cent in 2000 to about 57 per cent in 2014. For example, in 2006 SASAC highlighted the state-owned character of key economic industries such as the oil industry. In comparison, institutional change has dramatically changed the ownership of domestic oil companies in Russia. Between 1992 and 1995 large domestic oil companies became vertically integrated and privately controlled. Only since President Putin came to power in 2003 has the state increased its ownership control. The acquisition of Yukos's assets shows the determination of Russia to make Rosneft a national champion (*The Economist* 2014). Thus far, we see institutional changes are different in terms of shaping state control of domestic oil companies.

> *Pattern 2: In China's case, institutional change consistently tries to maintain state ownership of its domestic oil companies. In comparison in Russia, institutional change aims to privatize its domestic oil companies with indirect government control.*

The influence of domestic oil companies: We find that domestic oil companies in China have more influence on institutional change. For example, in order to encourage oil production in 1982 and 1983, CNOOC was even assigned supervision roles for offshore production. Sinopec also took responsibility to supervise downstream production. Similarly, in 1988, CNPC was not only assigned responsibility for managing upstream production, but also allowed to take over the administration power of MPI. Today we can see CNPC retains its administrative power in North China and Sinopec in South China, while both hold ministerial rank. Unlike China, domestic oil companies in Russia hardly act as state agents to influence institutional change. Perhaps Transneft (pipeline operator) was the only exception. Rosneft was empowered to act as the agent of the

Russian government 'for establishing a semblance of order in the chaotic post-Soviet industry' (Henderson 2012: 4). In 1995, Rosneft was transformed into a joint stock company and started losing its direct influence on institutional change. Due to state ownership in its privatization, Rosneft became a quasi-intermediary between the private sector oil companies and the state authorities regulating the oil industry (Henderson 2012: 10). Our finding shows domestic oil companies have different degrees of influence on institutional change between the two case countries.

> *Pattern 3: In China's case, NOCs act as the key state agent with relatively strong influence on institutional change. In comparison in Russia, domestic oil companies are hardly empowered to act as state agents to influence institutional change.*

The concern of competition: We find that institutional change in China's case followed a gradualism for stimulating industrial competition. Over years, the three NOCs dominate the domestic supply market. CNPC, Sinopec, and CNOOC are in charge of upstream, downstream, or offshore parts of the industry respectively. Only since 2012 has the State Council encouraged the entry of private companies into the industry to increase competition. For example, CNPC (through PetroChina) decided to divest 50 per cent of its pipeline stake to Trans-Asia Pipeline Co. in 2015 (Guo 2015) to encourage a gradual entry and the growth of other companies. In comparison, Russia has been active in promoting competition by creating several vertically integrated companies to compete in both domestic and global markets (Lane and Seifulmulukov 1999). In mid-1990 there were already thirteen vertically integrated oil companies in Russia. Competition in downstream also became severe among private commercial companies (Lane and Seifulmulukov 1999). It was only from the mid-2000s that companies with state ownership such as Rosneft, Gazprom Neft, and Surgutneftegaz became actively involved in competition with private companies such as Lukoil, TNK-BP, and Bashneft. In 2009, the SIL started influencing competition, as it limited the development of strategic resources to SOEs. Thus, we see the two case countries have followed different institutional approaches to influence intensity of the competition.

> *Pattern 4: In China's case, institutional change aims for gradually stimulating competition in the domestic market. In comparison in Russia, institutional change aims for injecting high competition intensity.*

Bureaucracy in institutional change: We find that institutional change in China tends to engage more complicated functions of different institutions. Kong (2009) comments that the complexity may result in bureaucracy as institutions are both vertically and horizontally structured. For example, after the dissolution of the Ministry of Energy in 1992, several government bodies were responsible for the energy industry at the same time. These heterogeneous actors shared overlapping institutional functions, consequently creating confusion (Child et al. 2007). In contrast, Russia seems to have created fewer institutional functions although this does not mean bureaucracy and confusion are less present than in the case of China. For example, Alekperov (2011) suggests that during 1991–92, the Ministry of Fuel and Energy adopted many contradictory and unjustified polices. Despite this, given the oil industry is such a crucial industry for its economy, Russia cannot afford to have any lack of institutional functions at the ministry level. Thus, it seems that a more organized design of institutional functions is found in Russia's case.

Pattern 5: In China's case, institutional change occurs with more bureaucratic functions engaged. In comparison in Russia, institutional change seems to occur with fewer bureaucratic functions engaged.

Conclusion

This study explores antecedents and processes of institutional change in the oil industry in China and Russia. Both countries have shared similarities in their past and present. They had undergone rapid economic development since market-driven reforms were initiated at the end of the 1970s in China, and the early 1990s in Russia. We were intrigued to explore what institutional changes have occurred in the oil industries in both Russia and China to understand differences in institutional change.

We find five main differences in both antecedence and processes of institutional change. First, one main difference between the two cases is the influence of ideology. In China's case, institutional change maintains a communist ideology whereas in Russia, we observed abrupt changes in the course towards capitalism. Second, we find different rationales in terms of maintaining state ownership. In China's case, institutional change in every stage has tried to maintain state ownership of its domestic oil companies. In comparison in Russia, institutional change aims for privatizing its domestic oil companies with indirect government control. Although President Putin heads towards increased state control, private companies are relatively more dominating in the oil industry landscape. Third, the role of domestic oil companies in creating institutional change is different. In China's case, NOCs are the key state agent with relatively strong influence on institutional change. Government agencies do not exercise significant control over NOCs. In comparison in Russia, domestic oil companies are hardly ever empowered to act as state agents to influence institutional change. Only since 2006 has Rosneft received partial status in such a direction. The fourth main difference is competition in the industry. In China's case, institutional change aims for gradually stimulating competition in the domestic market. In comparison in Russia, since the very beginning, high competition intensity was laid down. Fifth, one important part of our findings regards the level of bureaucracy in institutional change. In China's case, institutional change occurs with more bureaucratic functions engaged, which is evidenced by the engagement of various agencies with different and conflicting responsibilities. In comparison, in Russia institutional change seems to occur with fewer bureaucratic functions engaged although this does not mean its institutional system is more efficient.

Our findings aim to inform policymakers particularly in other emerging economies that may have just started their path towards similar development. One key limitation of this research concerns access to data. We believe that access to interviews with participants in the aforementioned events (e.g. policymakers, company executives, industry insiders) would enrich findings and contributions. At the same time this represents a potential research direction. We also start this exploration based on the two largest emerging economies. Future studies may include other emerging countries to enrich theoretical debate in this field.

REFERENCES

Ahrend, R. and Tompson, W. (2006). 'Realising the oil supply potential of the CIS: the impact of institutions and policies'. OECD Economics Department Working Papers 484. Paris: OECD.

Aldred, S. (2014). 'Sinopec sells $17.5 billion stake in retail unit to investors', *Reuters*, 14 September. Available at www.reuters.com/article/2014/09/14/us-china-sinopec-idUSKBN0H90JS20140914, accessed 5 October 2018.

Alekperov, V. (2011). *Oil of Russia: Past, Present & Future*. Minneapolis, MN: East View Press.

Andrews-Speed, P., Dow, S., and Gao, Z. (2000). 'The ongoing reforms to China's government and state sector: the case of the energy industry', *Journal of Contemporary China* 9/23: 5–20.

Andrews-Speed, P., Herberg, M., Li, Z., and Shobert, B. (2014). 'China's energy crossroads: forging a new energy and environmental balance', in NBR (ed.), *NBR Special Report #47*. Available at www.nbr.org/publications/specialreport/pdf/Free/011715/SR47_China.pdf, accessed 29 January 2015.

Aoki, M. (2001). *Toward a Comparative Institutional Analysis*. Comparative Institutional Analysis Series. Cambridge, MA and London: MIT Press.

Blas, J. (2013). 'China becomes world's top oil importer', *Financial Times*, 4 March. Available at www.ft.com/content/d33b5104-84a1-11e2-aaf1-00144feabdc0, accessed 23 January 2020.

Brødsgaard, K.E. (2012). 'Politics and business group formation in China: the party in control?', *China Quarterly* 211: 624–48.

Brousseau, E., Garrouste, P., and Raynaud, E. (2011). 'Institutional changes: alternative theories and consequences for institutional design', *Journal of Economic Behavior & Organization* 79/1–2: 3–19.

Child, J., Lu, Y., and Tsai, T. (2007). 'Institutional entrepreneurship in building an environmental protection system for the People's Republic of China', *Organization Studies* 28/7: 1013–34.

Collier, R.B. and Collier, D. (1991). *Shaping the Political Arena: Critical Junctures, the Labor Movement, and Regime Dynamics in Latin America*. Princeton, NJ: Princeton University Press.

Dacin, M.T., Goodstein, J., and Scott, W.R. (2002). 'Institutional theory and institutional change: introduction to the special research forum', *Academy of Management Journal* 45/1: 43–56.

Downs, E.S. (2004). 'The Chinese energy security debate', *China Quarterly* 177: 21–41.

Du, J. (2014). 'CNPC moves to open pipeline facilities', *China Daily*, 30 June. Available at http://usa.chinadaily.com.cn/epaper/2014-06/30/content_17626883.htm, accessed 5 October 2018.

The Economist (2004). 'Russian oil companies: that sinking feeling', 3 June. Available at www.economist.com/node/2735910, accessed 5 October 2018.

The Economist (2006). 'Russian oil: thou shalt not steal', 25 May. Available at www.economist.com/node/6975839?zid=298&ah=0bc99f9da8f185b2964b6cef412227be, accessed 5 October 2018.

The Economist (2012). 'A choice of models', 21 January. Available at www.economist.com/node/21542924, accessed 5 October 2018.

The Economist (2014). 'Rosneft: Arctic chill', 2 August. Available at www.economist.com/news/business/21610239-sanctions-will-thwart-rosnefts-ambitions-join-ranks-oils-superpowers-arctic-chill, accessed 5 October 2018.

EIA (Energy Information Administration) (2001). *China Country Energy Analysis.* Washington, DC: Department of Energy, EIA.

EIA (Energy Information Administration) (2014a). *China.* Washington, DC: Department of Energy, EIA. Available at www.eia.gov/countries/cab.cfm?fips=CH, accessed 5 October 2018.

EIA (Energy Information Administration) (2014b). *Russia.* Washington, DC: Department of Energy, EIA. Available at www.eia.gov/countries/cab.cfm?fips=RS, accessed 5 October 2018.

Eisenhardt, K.M. (1989). 'Building theories from case study research', *Academy of Management Review* 14/4: 532–50.

Eisenhardt, K.M. and Graebner, M.E. (2007). 'Theory building from cases: opportunities and challenges', *Academy of Management Journal* 50/1: 25–32.

Gerring, J. (1997). 'Ideology: a definitional analysis'. *Political Research Quarterly* 50/4: 957.

Gourevitch, P. (1986). *Politics in Hard Times: Comparative Responses to International Economic Crises.* Ithaca, NY: Cornell University Press.

Greif, A. and Laitin, D. (2004). 'A theory of endogenous institutional change', *American Political Science Review* 98/04: 633–52.

Guo, A. (2015). 'PetroChina's $2.4 billion sale mixes profits with overhaul', *Bloomberg Business*, 25 November 25. Available at www.bloomberg.com/news/articles/2015-11-25/petrochina-plans-2-4-billion-sale-in-profit-drive-amid-reforms, accessed 5 October 2018.

Hall, P.A. and Taylor, R.C.R. (1996). 'Political science and the three new institutionalisms', *Political Studies* 44/5: 936–57.

Hall, P.A. and Thelen, K. (2009). 'Institutional change in varieties of capitalism', *Socio-Economic Review* 7/1: 7–34.

Henderson, J. (2012). 'Rosneft—on the road to global NOC status?'. Working Paper: WPM 44. Oxford Institute for Energy Studies. Available at www.oxfordenergy.org/wpcms/wp-content/uploads/2012/01/WPM_44.pdf, accessed 5 October 2018.

Heritier, A. (2007). *Explaining Institutional Change in Europe.* Oxford: Oxford University Press.

Hoffman, A.J. (1999). 'Institutional evolution and change: environmentalism and the U.S. chemical industry', *Academy of Management Journal* 42/4: 351–71.

Jain, S. and Sharma, D. (2013). 'Institutional logic migration and industry evolution in emerging economies: the case of telephony in India', *Strategic Entrepreneurship Journal* 7/3: 252–71.

Jepperson, R. (1991). 'Institutions, institutional effects, and institutionalism', in W.W.P.P.J. DiMaggio (ed.) *The New Institutionalism in Organizational Analysis.* Chicago, IL: University of Chicago Press, 143–63.

Jiang, B. (2012). 'China National Petroleum Corporation (CNPC): a balancing act between enterprise and government', in D.G. Victor, D.R. Hults, and M.C. Thurber (eds) *Oil and*

Governance: State-Owned Enterprises and the World Energy Supply. Cambridge and New York: Cambridge University Press, 379–417.

Kingston, C. and Caballero, G. (2009). 'Comparing theories of institutional change', *Journal of Institutional Economics* 5/2: 151–80.

Kong, B. (2009). 'China's energy decision-making: becoming more like the United States?', *Journal of Contemporary China* 18/62: 789–812.

Kornai, J. (1992). *The Socialist System: The Political Economy of Communism*. Oxford: Oxford University Press.

Kostova, T., Roth, K., and Dacin, T. (2008). 'Institutional theory in the study of multinational corporations: a critique and new directions', *Academy of Management Review* 33/4: 994–1006.

Krasner, S.D. (1984). 'Approaches to the state: alternative conceptions and historical dynamics', *Comparative Politics* 16/2: 223–46.

Krug, B. and Hendrischke, H. (2008). 'Framing China: transformation and institutional change through co-evolution', *Management and Organization Review* 4/1: 81–108.

Lane, D. and Seifulmulukov, I. (1999). 'Structure and ownership', in D. Lane (ed.) *The Political Economy of Russian Oil*. Lanham, MD: Rowman & Littlefield.

Langley, A. (1999). 'Strategies for theorizing from process data', *Academy of Management Review* 24/4: 691–710.

Lawrence, T.B. (1999). 'Institutional strategy', *Journal of Management* 25/2: 161–87.

Lewis, S. (2007). 'Chinese NOCs and world energy markets, CNPC, Sinopec and CNOOC', Rice University: Houston: James A. Baker III Institute of Public Policy. Available at http://bakerinstitute.org/files/3896/, accessed 5 October 2018.

Lieberthal, K. and Oksenberg, M. (1988). *Policy Making in China: Leaders, Structures, and Processes*. Princeton, NJ: Princeton University Press.

Locatelli, C. and Rossiaud, S. (2011). 'A neoinstitutionalist interpretation of the changes in the Russian oil model', *Energy Policy* 39/9: 5588–97.

Locatelli, C. and Rossiaud, S. (2012). 'Russia, institutionalism and the effect on oil and gas investments'. Polinares Working Paper No. 45. Available at www.polinares.eu/docs/d3-1/polinares_wp3_case1.pdf, accessed 8 April 2019.

Mahoney, J. and Thelen, K. (2009). *A Theory of Gradual Institutional Change: Explaining Institutional Change*. Cambridge: Cambridge University Press.

March, J.G. and Olsen, J.P. (2008). *Elaborating the 'New Institutionalism'*. Oxford: Oxford University Press.

Meidan, M., Andrews-Speed, P., and Xin, M. (2009). 'Shaping China's energy policy: actors and processes', *Journal of Contemporary China* 18/61: 591–616.

Meyer, A.D. (1982). 'Adapting to environmental jolts', *Administrative Science Quarterly* 27/4: 515–37.

Mohr, L.B. (1982). *Explaining Organizational Behavior*. San Francisco, CA and London: Jossey-Bass.

Naughton, B. (1995). *Growing Out of the Plan: Chinese Economic Reform, 1978–1993*. Cambridge: Cambridge University Press.

North, D.C. (1981). *Structure and Change in Economic History*. New York: W.W. Norton.

North, D.C. (1990). *Institutions, Institutional Change and Economic Performance*. Cambridge: Cambridge University Press.

North, D.C. (1991). 'Institutions', *Journal of Economic Perspectives* 5/1: 97–112.

North, D.C. (1999). 'Response to Geddes and Keohane [Douglass C. North and institutional change in contemporary developing countries][Ideology and professionalism in international institutions: insights from the work of Douglass C. North]', in J.E. Alt, M. Levi, and E. Ostrom (eds) *Competition and Cooperation: Conversations with Nobelists About Economics and Political Science*. New York: Russell Sage Foundation, 247–52.

North, D.C. (2003). *Understanding the Process of Economic Change, Institutional Barriers to Economic Change: Cases Considered*. Arlington, VA: Mercatus Center, George Mason University.

Oliver, C. (1991). 'Strategic responses to institutional processes', *Academy of Management Review* 16/1: 145–79.

Oliver, C. (1992). 'The antecedents of deinstitutionalization', *Organization Studies* 13/4: 563–88.

Ostrom, E. (2009). *Understanding Institutional Diversity*. Princeton, NJ: Princeton University Press.

Peters, B.G. (2011). *Institutional Theory in Political Science: The New Institutionalism*. London: Bloomsbury.

Pfeffer, J. and Salancik, G.R. (1978). *The External Control of Organizations: A Resource Dependence Perspective*. New York: Harper & Row.

Pierson, P. (1996). 'The path to European integration: a historical institutionalist analysis', *Comparative Political Studies* 29/2: 123–63.

Pierson, P. (2011). *Politics in Time: History, Institutions, and Social Analysis*. Princeton, NJ: Princeton University Press.

Pierson, P. and Skocpol, T. (2002). 'Historical institutionalism in contemporary political science', in K. Ira and V.M. Helen (eds) *Political Science: State of the Discipline*. New York: W.W. Norton, 693–721.

Poole, M., Van de Ven, A., Dooley, K., and Holmes, M. (2000). *Organizational Change and Innovation Processes: Theory and Methods for Research*. Oxford: Oxford University Press.

Poussenkova, N. (2013). 'Russia's Eastern energy policy: a Chinese puzzle for Rosneft'. Institut français des relations internationales (IFRI). Available at http://ifri.org/downloads/ifrirnv70poussenkovarosneftengapril2013.pdf, accessed 10 August 2014.

Rosneft (2014). 'IPO'. Rosneft: Investors. Available at www.rosneft.com/Investors/structure/IPO/, accessed 10 December 2014.

Russia Today (2014). 'Medvedev seeks civil servants' return to state corporation boards'. *Russia Today*, 26 December. Available at http://rt.com/politics/217751-medvedev-russian-state-corporations-management/#.VLGTQvWxXng, accessed 5 October 2018.

Scott, W.R. (2013). *Institutions and Organizations: Ideas, Interests, and Identities*. Thousand Oaks, CA: SAGE Publications.

Seliger, M. (1976). *Ideology and Politics*. Crow's Nest, NSW: Allen & Unwin.

Shadrina, E. (2013). *Russia's State Capitalism and Energy Geopolitics of Northeast Asia*. University of Turku. 1/2013 Electronic Publications of Pan-European Institute. Available at www.utu.fi/sites/default/files/media/drupal/PEI%20Pub%20Shadrina%201_2013.pdf, accessed 9 April 2019.

Sine, W.D. and David, R.J. (2003). 'Environmental jolts, institutional change, and the creation of entrepreneurial opportunity in the US electric power industry', *Research Policy* 32/2: 185–207.

Smallbone, D. and Welter, F. (2012). 'Entrepreneurship and institutional change in transition economies: the Commonwealth of Independent States, Central and Eastern Europe and China compared', *Entrepreneurship and Regional Development* 24/3–4: 215–33.

Strang, D. and Sine, W.D. (2002). 'Inter-organizational institutions', in J. Baum (ed.) *Companion to Organizations*. Oxford: Blackwell, 497–519.

Streeck, W. and Thelen, K.A. (2005). *Beyond Continuity: Institutional Change in Advanced Political Economies*. Oxford: Oxford University Press.

Tan, E.S. (2005). 'Ideology, interest groups, and institutional change: the case of the British prohibition of wages in kind', *Journal of Institutional Economics* 1/02: 175–91.

Thelen, K. (1999). 'Historical institutionalism in comparative politics', *Annual Review of Political Science* 2/1: 369–404.

Voss, C., Tsikriktsis, N., and Frohlich, M. (2002). 'Case research in operations management', *International Journal of Operations & Production Management* 22/2: 195–219.

Weaver, R.K. and Rockman, B.A. (1993). *Do Institutions Matter? Government Capabilities in the United States and Abroad*. Washington, DC: Brookings Institution.

Williamson, O.E. (2000). 'The new institutional economics: taking stock, looking ahead', *Journal of Economic Literature* 38/3: 595.

Xinhua (2014). 'China to allow private capital into more state projecs', *Xinhua*, 5 March. Available at http://news.xinhuanet.com/english/special/2014-03/05/c_133161964.htm, accessed 30 January 2015.

Yang, F., Duan, N., Huan, J., Levine, M., Martin, N., Sinton, J. et al. (1995). 'A review of China's energy policy'. Lawrence Berkeley National Laboratory Report LBL-35336, Berkeley. Available at http://live.belfercenter.org/files/zhao.pdf, accessed 20 January 2015.

Yergin, D. (2011). *The Quest: Energy, Security, and the Remaking of the Modern World*. London and New York: Penguin Group.

33 Russia's green development

Olga Ulybina

Introduction

DEFINING 'GREEN'

Environmental sustainability is a foundation of the current development agenda (UN 2015). Green investment and green growth are frequent items on the international agenda (UNEP 2011; OECD 2015; G20 Leaders Communique 2016). Policymakers have come up with ever new buzzwords to label the environmentally friendly and prosperous world that we all want to live in: sustainability, green economy, eco-business, green growth, etc. (OECD 2011; UNEP 2011; World Bank 2011). Despite a variety of possible meanings (Schmalensee 2012), these terms essentially refer to the to-be-built world of 'reduced environmental risks and ecological scarcities', a 'low-carbon, resource efficient, and socially inclusive' economy (UNEP 2011: 16). To ensure this, investment needs to incorporate environmental criteria and be 'supported by targeted public expenditure, policy reforms and regulation changes' (UNEP 2011: 16) to stimulate 'innovative sources of growth' and 'more sustainable consumption patterns' (OECD 2012: 3). In addition to traditional environmental policies, the green agenda has come to focus on 'economic policy and many fiscal and regulatory interventions that are not normally associated with a "green" agenda' (OECD 2011: 10), such as efficiency, technological innovation, increasing resilience to environmental and economic shocks, green jobs, and so on (OECD 2012). The social aspect of development is framed as 'inclusive green growth', i.e. growth strategies which 'maximise benefits for, and minimise costs to, the poor and most vulnerable' and avoid policies 'with irreversible negative impacts' (World Bank 2012: xi). However, the overall tilt in high-level policy discussions remains towards economics, the affordability of green growth, and policy instruments aimed at fixing market failures, internalizing externalities, assigning property rights, and improving governance (World Bank 2012). Measuring progress towards a green and inclusive economy is seen in terms of economic transformation and the shift of investments, growth of environmentally friendly goods and services, resource efficiency, and meeting the basic needs of the poor and strengthening human capital (UNEP 2012). Another aspect of 'green' which, although discussed widely in the literature, has not attracted equal attention in international policy forums and has not gained a priority place in reform packages is environmental justice (Schlosberg 2007;

Olga Ulybina, *Russia's green development* In: *Handbook of BRICS and Emerging Economies.* Edited by: P.B. Anand, Shailaja Fennell, and Flavio Comim, Oxford University Press (2021). © Oxford University Press.
DOI: 10.1093/oso/9780198827535.003.0033

Walker 2012). Environmental justice is 'the fair treatment and meaningful involvement of all people . . . with respect to the development, implementation, and enforcement of environmental laws, regulations, and policies', 'when everyone enjoys the same degree of protection from environmental and health hazards and equal access to the decision-making process to have a healthy environment' (US Environmental Protection Agency 2014). Environmental justice is a broad and a multifaceted concept, which encompasses not only equity in the distribution of environmental benefits and risks, but also recognition of social diversity, human capabilities, and participation in political processes which affect environmental policy (Williams and Mawdsley 2006; Schlosberg 2007). What relevance do these debates have for Russia and its development towards being a 'greener' country?

WHAT DOES 'GREEN' MEAN FOR RUSSIA?

The Constitution of the Russian Federation guarantees the right to a clean and safe natural environment [право на благоприятную окружающую среду] (Constitution 1993: Article 42). Since the fall of the USSR, concepts of sustainable and green development have been included in the official discourse and the Russian government has adopted a number of strategic policy documents designed to help address global issues of climate change, the deficit of natural resources, and environmental protection (Framework 1996; Ecological doctrine 2002; Climate doctrine 2009; Energy strategy 2009; Water strategy 2009; Framework 2011). The goals of Russian environmental policy for the period until 2030 include creating a safe natural environment, minimizing the negative impacts of economic activity on the environment, conservation and rehabilitation of disturbed ecosystems, alleviating the legacy of pollution and environmental damage of the past, balancing the economic and ecological needs of society, developing a resource-efficient economy, and ensuring stakeholder participation in environmentally relevant decision making (Fundamental principles 2012). Russia has officially endorsed a large number of international environmental agreements and engaged in international partnerships. In 2014, a comprehensive environmental work plan was endorsed between the United Nations Environment Programme and the Russian Federation (UNEP 2014). The plan covers over thirty joint projects, including the promotion of ecologically safe technologies and green standards, and improved regulation of waste, water, and chemicals management.

At the same time, the stance of the Russian government towards green development remains pragmatic: Russia does not tend to support climate or eco-standards initiatives where these may restrict industrial development, trade, or political projects. A good example of this is the Sochi Olympics in 2014. The Sochi Games were carried out in a specially protected natural area with the richest biodiversity in Russia, and the ecological damage to the local wildlife and ecosystems has not been compensated (WWF 2014). Non-governmental organizations (NGOs) repeatedly reported cases of neglect of environmental issues at Sochi's construction sites, as well as the persecution of environmental activists (e.g. Gazaryan and Shevchenko 2013). Furthermore, 'under the pretext of Olympic needs, the nature conservation legislation was significantly weakened, especially parts concerning protected nature areas and environmental assessment of construction projects' (WWF 2014).

The Ministry of Natural Resources has focused on three priority areas: alleviating the past ecological damage, reducing the current negative environmental impact, and biodiversity conservation. As a result of government inspection, 340 large sites with about 400 million tonnes of polluting waste have been identified, mostly in the Urals, Siberia, and the Far East. Pilot projects have been launched to eliminate the most risky sites in the Arctic, Baikal region, and central Russia. Over the past decade, international competition and the need for industrial modernization have driven various developments associated with environmental improvement. In 2014, the principle of 'best available technologies' was introduced into law (see amendments to the law On Environmental protection 2002).

Despite these changes and the increase in Russian GDP over the last decade, the key indicators of polluting emissions and waste production remain on the whole at the same level (MNR 2013b). Sanctioned waste disposal sites occupy a territory of about four million hectares, and the area of illegal dumping sites exceeds that officially allocated (MNR 2013a).

So, is Russia going green? What policy shifts and indicators are key to evaluating the 'greening' process? This chapter provides an overview of the environmental situation in Russia since the fall of the USSR, to explore the progress made towards a greener society. We analyse the recent development of green policies and practices in Russia, and the impact thereof on the everyday lives of the population. Laws, statistics, and case studies for several key sectors are discussed: environmental pollution (nuclear, air, water and soil, forests, the Arctic), as well as developments in the energy sector, including climate change and energy efficiency. We discuss the situation around public environmental control, the role of public participation, and civil society in environmental governance. We look at the 'greening' process through the lens of the rule of law, civil rights, and environmental justice. The chapter concludes with a discussion of policy shifts that are required to ensure progress towards a greener society.

Environmental pollution

According to the Russian government's own figures, about 15 per cent of the territory is in a critical condition, and about 1 million people live in areas of ecological crisis (Putin 2013a). None of the Russian regions can be referred to as ecologically safe and about 70 per cent of the Russian population live in ecologically unsafe conditions. According to the World Health Organization (WHO), over 490,000 people die annually from ecologically dependent diseases in Russia, which is ten times higher than deaths from car accidents. Ecological factors account for one-third of diseases among under 19-year-olds, and 20-25 per cent of diseases across all populations (MNR 2013a). A particularly urgent ecological issue, due to its direct negative impact on quality of life, is environmental remedial action to clean up and decontaminate large areas of industrially polluted territory. By late 2012, Russia had accumulated about 90 billion tonnes of waste, resulting from past economic activities (Putin 2013b). Some particularly sensitive sites received support from international bodies and partner countries to help with environmental protection and decontamination, but this has been largely restricted to certain nuclear sites, and the level of support has been reducing in recent years. We will discuss major areas of environmental problems in Russia, and the impact of pollution on the lives of people living in affected areas.

NUCLEAR

Russia has inherited a particularly difficult legacy from the Soviet Union in the nuclear sphere. While the nuclear accident at Chernobyl, in present day Ukraine, is the best-known nuclear disaster from the Soviet era, it was not the only major accident and several continue to cause severe environmental pollution today. For example, the 1957 accident at the Mayak nuclear facility near Kyshtym in the Urals is the third most severe nuclear disaster in world history, after the disasters at Chernobyl and Fukushima. Despite being responsible for a long series of nuclear accidents, the Mayak facility, considered strategically important, is still operational and reprocessing spent nuclear fuel. About 10,000 people still live within the contaminated area, along the Techa River, which has been used for decades as a dumping site for liquid radioactive waste from the Mayak. Despite local community attempts to draw attention of the local government to their plight, the residents have not been relocated (Greenpeace Russia 2013). This shows that the constitutional right to a safe environment is poorly respected not only in terms of current levels of pollution and standard of living but also in terms of the recognition of the ecological and health damage.

A similar case is the 1956 Totskoye nuclear exercise in Orenburg oblast. As part of the exercise, between 45,000 and 60,000 soldiers were deliberately exposed to radiation, and the many victims among local civilians were never counted. Although the exercise became publicly known in the 1990s, the state has not recognized its responsibility for the health and environmental consequences. The civilian population who were exposed to radiation are denied any support or compensation from the state, and official information about the extent of nuclear pollution is missing (Greenpeace Russia 2014a).

Russian law secures citizens' rights to obtain accurate and timely information about the environmental situation and factors which affect their health (Fundamentals 2011). However, the realization of this right in practice is rather difficult. Since 2011, the Human Rights Ombudsman has been trying to obtain official information about two powerful radioactive thermoelectric generators, which had allegedly been 'lost' in the

Pacific Ocean off Sakhalin Island. Over the past few years, local communities and NGOs have repeatedly but unsuccessfully contacted various authorities requesting information about the location and potential recycling of these generators. In 2011, the Ombudsman reported on this case to the President of the Russian Federation, after which the Ministry of Natural Resources and Environment was instructed to include the search and rescue of the generators in the Federal programme 'Environmental safety of Russia in 2012–2020'. However, this programme does not include the clean-up of nuclear pollution. Therefore, the Ministry of Natural Resources suggested to the nuclear agency Rosatom to include this task in their federal programme 'Securing nuclear and radioactive safety in 2016–2020 and until 2025'. As of 2013, the Ombudsman still did not have any information regarding who would deal with—and when—the sunken generators or inform the local population about potential health risks (Lukin 2014).

Russia, however, is also one of the main countries researching fourth-generation nuclear power stations and is at the forefront of innovation in the nuclear industry. This includes for example the floating nuclear power reactor, the Akademic Lomosov, currently under construction (Conant 2013). Russia has the only operational fourth-generation power station, the BN-800 sodium-cooled fast reactor at Beloyarsk, which is designed to run from weapons-grade plutonium. This should enable Russia to reduce its large stockpiles of weapons-grade nuclear material, and reduce the amount of stored nuclear waste in future (Conant 2013). Despite such technological achievements, progress is made mainly in commercial areas, whereas on the whole the situation in the nuclear sector remains alarming.

AIR POLLUTION

Air pollution became a major problem in the Soviet Union following the country's rapid industrialization. From 1948, the USSR's Ministry of Health established over 140 indicators of maximum permissible concentrations (MPCs) for atmospheric pollutants (Mote 1975), which although very stringent, were not enforced (Mote 1975). In 1988, the Soviet total emissions were about 79 per cent of those of the USA; however, Soviet emissions were 1.5 times higher when calculated per unit of GNP (Shahgedanova and Burt 1994). One particularly problematic area was airborne particulates where emissions in the USSR in the late 1980s were 2.6 times greater than in the USA, mainly due to the use of solid fuel sources (Shahgedanova and Burt 1994). Fines for breaching regulations were not imposed consistently, and penalties for violations were low (Mote 1975). As a result, industrial towns and surrounding areas were under significant ecological pressure, and various toxic compounds and metals abundantly present in the air led to significant deterioration of the health and demographic structure of local populations (Revich 1992).

The fall of the USSR and consequent economic decline meant reduced industrial and transport activities, leading to a significant decline in air pollution in Russia in the early

1990s. The improvement in air quality was, however, offset by the increased number of automobile vehicles, the increased relative importance of heavy and energy intensive industries, a lack of investment in the ageing capital assets, and inefficient energy provision in the late 1990s (OECD 1999; Cherp et al. 2003).

Over the last fifteen years, the Russian government has passed new laws, such as Federal law No 96 (1999) 'On the protection of atmospheric air', and has adopted new air quality standards, detailed emission permits, and air pollution charges, as well as special air protection zones (OECD 1999). The government set a target of reducing the number of cities and towns with high and very high levels of air pollution by at least a factor of five by 2020, and reducing the number of people living in unfavourable ecological conditions by at least a factor of four (Framework 2008). There is, however, little evidence of positive changes in this area (MNR 2013b). Indeed, between 2007 and 2011, average annual concentration of nitrous oxide decreased by 11 per cent, benzo [a]pyrene by 17 per cent, airborne particulates, nitrogen dioxide, and carbon dioxide by 5-6 per cent (MNR 2013b). Reductions in nitrous oxide and CO2 may be attributed to improvements in the transport sector where there have been large improvements in emissions driven by international changes in engine design. At the same time, the concentration of sulphur dioxide—mainly produced by mining refineries—and formaldehyde remains largely the same (MNR 2013b), indicating the slow technological upgrading of large industrial polluters. The biggest single source of air pollution is the Norilsk Nickel Mining company operating in the Arctic, which contributes about 10 per cent of the total emissions from stationary sources (MNR 2013b). The level of pollution of individual industrial companies is still not independently monitored in Russia.

A standard practice among Russian oil companies is gas flaring, which causes about 400,000 tonnes of polluting emissions annually and is responsible for 12 per cent of overall pollution in Russia (Kirillov 2013b). Recently, major oil companies, mainly driven by market forces have started to increase their utilization of associated gas. However, so far only two companies (Surgutneftegas and Tatneft) have reached the target of 95 per cent utilization (Kirillov 2013b).

Over half the urban population in Russia lives in conditions where air pollution exceeds MPCs (OECD 2013). The extent of air control remains limited, and the current levels of air pollution still pose a serious risk to public health and the environment. The main sources of atmospheric pollution, as in the Soviet Union, are companies in the energy and metallurgy sectors.

WATER POLLUTION AND GROUND POLLUTION

The quality of water remains 'unsatisfactory' in Russia: across the country; 36 per cent of surface sources and 16 per cent of underground sources of drinking water did not comply with sanitary norms in 2011 (MNR 2013b: 14). The main reason for poor water quality has been an intensive exploitation of water resources over a long period of time. The poor quality of centrally supplied drinking water is also due to high wear and tear of water supplying facilities, the amortization of which in some regions reaches 70 per cent (MNR 2013b: 15).

Waste water, polluted with toxic and hazardous substances, has a significant negative impact on water resources. A major reason for this is the inability to secure an appropriate level of waste water purification due to insufficient capacity or ineffective use of existing facilities. In 2011, the share of polluted waste water in the total volume of waste water was 33 per cent (MNR 2013b: 42). The main actors responsible for polluted waste water are companies producing and distributing electricity, gas, and water (55 per cent), as well as processing industries (19 per cent) (MNR 2013b: 42).

A major problem is oil spills from poorly maintained pipelines, which are estimated at 4.5 million tonnes a year and make Russia the 'world leader' in this area (Greenpeace Russia 2014d). The accident-free lifetime of oil pipes is between ten and twenty years, however, companies focus on profitability and replace as few as 1.5 per cent of their pipes a year (Greenpeace Russia 2014d). Over the last ten years, there has been no decrease in the number of leaks (Greenpeace Russia 2014d). Oil companies are not required to report statistics regarding the extent of oil spills, and the state has no reliable data on the extent of the related environmental damage. Greenpeace Russia uses satellite monitoring to oversee oil spills, while the government only intends to start doing so. Existing legislation and the relationships between authorities and companies allow oil companies to conceal oil spills and ignore their responsibility to reclaim the affected land (Chuprov and Terentyev 2014); in fact some recent legal changes lowered environmental standards for the industry (Greenpeace Russia 2014d).

Russia has a large number of regulations concerning water and ground quality standards, many inherited from the Soviet Union. There are, for instance, around 1,300 defined maximum allowable concentrations of pollutant chemicals for drinking water (OECD 2006). However, these concentrations represent ideal levels which are not widely met throughout Russia (OECD 2006). Existing legislation fails to ensure safe water and ground quality. For example, as a result of recent legal amendments, since 2015 large companies have had to build their own waste treatment facilities, set norms for their waste emissions, and be responsible for their water pollution (On water supply 2011). Until now, companies were legally considered 'waste water-free', and it was the city waste treatment facilities that were supposed to ensure water purification. At the same time, the city received payments from companies but was unable to supply clean water: facilities were built to deal with household waste and were not designed to cope with specific pollutants emitted by industries. This results in excessively high levels of heavy metals, phenols, and mercury in the rivers (Greenpeace Russia 2014c). Unfortunately, the new law is unlikely to solve this problem because it only concerns companies that produce more than 200 cubic meters of waste water per day, and a large number of industrial polluters will not be covered by the law.

The most famous example of problematic public policy in water management is perhaps the story of Lake Baikal, the world's deepest lake. For decades, the lake was polluted by the Baikal pulp-and-paper plant (MNR 2012). Although the detrimental impact had been known for a long time, the plant continued to operate because it was the main employer and tax payer for the 14,000-strong town. In 2010, the Russian government even exempted it from pollution rules. Eventually, the plant was shut down in 2013.

An example of poor law enforcement and the passive reaction of authorities to urgent ecological problems, whereby even local decisions and their implementation take an inadequately long time, is the serious water and ground pollution caused by the 'Russian Chrome 1915' company in the Urals. The company has at least a decade-long history of polluting the local river and ground with the toxic and carcinogenic hexavalent chromium. Despite complaints from the local population and multiple checks carried out by the regional prosecutor's office, which rebuked the company for violating the environmental legislation, the situation did not improve. Eventually, after Greenpeace spent a year investigating the extent of pollution, complaining to the general prosecutor's office and other public bodies, the company was forced to pay a fine, although it was neither prevented from continuing operations nor forced to instal the necessary equipment in order to reduce the pollution (Greenpeace Russia 2014b). An effective monitoring system needs to be created, and developing cooperation between authorities, civil society, and the public seems necessary in order to ensure that environmental standards are actually enforced in practice.

FORESTS

Russia is home to roughly 20 per cent of all the world's forests (FAO 2012: viii), including a large share of the world's untouched forest (Potapov et al. 2008), which makes Russian forests particularly important to the planet's overall carbon budget and biodiversity. As in Soviet times, all forest land in Russia is owned by the state, and only 15 per cent of forest land is leased (Verbatim record 2013). The current situation in the forest sector is critical and deteriorating. As a result of destructive logging techniques over the Soviet and post-Soviet years, most economically valuable and accessible forests are now depleted, while forest regeneration has decreased and is under 25 per cent (Verbatim record 2013).

The Russian government passed a major federal reform in 2006 aimed at decentralizing forest management and encouraging private investment in the sector. This overhauled the state leasing system in favour of auctions and reduced state control of the forest such as the forest guard (Hitchcock 2010). These reforms were opposed by many working in the sector who felt it would lead to greater exploitation of the forest. The state forest monitoring and control have weakened, and illegal logging has been on the rise (Verbatim record 2013). Over the last decade, the average area of forest fires increased by a factor of 1.6 (Verbatim record 2013), which environmental groups blame in part on the changes made by the 2006 reform (see for example Kuzminov 2010). Overall, public policy remains rather rigid in that it regards forests predominantly as an abundant and underused economic resource.

The relatively large expanse of forests means that issues of forest degradation and habitat protection do not resound strongly with the Russian population. The only notable recent forest-related protest occurred at the Khimki Forest outside Moscow between 2007 and 2011. This protest aimed to preserve a legally protected old-growth forest, which was to be partly logged in order to build a motorway. Despite international attention, the protest was unable to prevent the construction.

Environmental NGOs work together with timber companies and authorities to improve awareness of the degradation of Russian forests, and promote the ideas of responsible forest management and sustained yield forestry (Ulybina 2014). However, their efforts to change the paradigm of Russian forestry remain severely hindered by the inert state policy and weak public involvement in forestry issues (Ulybina and Fennell 2013).

THE ARCTIC

The Artic environment, being most affected by climate change and particularly vulnerable to industrial exploitation, has seen increased international interest over recent decades. Roughly one-fifth of Russian territory lies within the Arctic Circle and the two largest cities north of the Arctic Circle are in Russia. Russia is responsible for large-scale pollution in Arctic waters. Recently, Russia has declared it a priority to ensure ecological safety in the Arctic (e.g. Fundamentals 2008; Strategy 2013). Pilot projects aimed at alleviating the accumulated environmental damage have been carried out in the Arctic. Over 17,000 tonnes of waste have been cleared from the Franz Josef Archipelago over the last two years, and over 80 hectares of land reclaimed. Similar work has been carried out on the archipelago Novaya Zemlya, where nuclear waste was dumped during the Soviet period. Two new national parks and a new strict reserve are expected to be set up in the Arctic zone (Framework 2011). Since 2011, Russia has participated in the Global Environment Facility's Arctic Agenda 2020 Programme, which aims to address the environmental challenges of ongoing Arctic exploration and development.

At the same time, the state policy towards the Arctic largely carries on from Soviet times, seeing it as an area that can be extensively exploited for its mineral wealth (Strategy 2013). Russian and international oil companies are targeting the large oil and gas reserves beneath the Arctic Ocean. In 2014, the Prirazlomnoye oil field was opened using the first ice-resistant oil platform. The area of the oil field, off the coast of the Novaya Zemlya islands is only ice free for around 110 days per year. Environmental groups, such as Greenpeace, argue that oil spills in such remote areas will be particularly damaging due to the fragility of the ecosystems and the difficulty of cleaning up oil in the harsh Arctic conditions. Greenpeace protestors were arrested when they tried to board the platform, leading to an international appeal for their release.

Furthermore, because the major Siberian rivers, such as the Ob and the Lena, drain into the Arctic Ocean, pollution from chemical and mining operations along the rivers drains into the Arctic waters. Possibly the worst ecological hotspot in the Arctic remains the mining and smelting company Norilsk Nickel, whose emissions suppressed vegetation over 7.5 million hectares and caused 600,000 hectares of forest mortality over the territory. The company does not comply with maximum permissible emissions limits, and because of its strategic importance, special emissions limits were set for the company (Kirillov 2013a).

Overall, lax state controls over the ongoing industrial pollution, along with increasing exploitation of Arctic natural resources once again indicates the priority of non-environmental goals in public policy.

Corporate environmental responsibility

While the Russian state does not guarantee effective environmental control, global competition and market forces have caused companies to take a greater interest in environmental matters. In particular, in order to raise funds in the global financial market, Russian companies are forced to pay more attention to their environmental practices. About 1,000–2,000 companies in Russia are now certified to ISO 14001:2004, an environmental management standard which is part of an international voluntary certification system (ISD 2012: 42). The number of private companies reporting on their sustainability strategies and policies has increased (KPMG 2012; Thurner and Proskuryakova 2014). More than fifty Russian companies joined the United Nations Global Compact initiative (ISD 2012: 43), thus manifesting their adherence to environmental principles derived from the Rio Declaration on Environment and Development.

However, systematic evidence about corporate environmental performance is lacking. For example, the first ratings of environmental responsibility of oil and gas companies in Russia were only prepared by the World Wide Fund for Nature (WWF) Russia and the Creon Energy consulting group at the end of 2014. NGOs, particularly Greenpeace and WWF, are working to improve public awareness about the operations of large companies and prevent them from avoiding their environmental responsibilities. For example, a 2012 WWF report analysed recent environmental practices of the oil and gas giant Gazprom. The report showed that a number of Gazprom's projects did not comply with best international practices or were even carried out with violations of Russian environmental legislation (Knizhnikov and Rogozhin 2012). The company was shown to generally fail to implement a consistent environmental policy. While individual subsidiaries engage in cooperation with NGOs and work on solving their ecological problems, the company as a whole does not function to the same corporate social responsibility (CSR) standards (Knizhnikov and Rogozhin 2012).

Unfortunately, NGOs' capacities are limited and there is still no source in Russia which can provide objective, up-to-date, and comparative information about the environmental responsibility of companies and the extent of their environmental impact.

Climate change and energy policy

Russia is a signatory to the original Kyoto protocol for reducing greenhouse gases (ghg), and Russia's ratification in 2004 allowed the treaty to come into effect. Russia was one of the major beneficiaries of the way the Kyoto protocol was drawn up. Because 1990 was used as the baseline year, Russia had a large reserve of unused carbon allowance due to large reductions in industrial output following the fall of the USSR. Between 1998 and 2010, Russian GDP grew by 86 per cent, whereas the ghg emissions grew by only 12 per cent (Bashmakov 2011), which is explained by both an increase in energy efficiency and an increased share of non-industrial sectors in the economy (MNR 2013b: 10). The dominant role continues to be played by the energy sector, which was responsible for over 80 per cent of total emissions in 2010 (MNR 2013b: 10). Russia is now the fifth largest emitter of ghg accounting for a little under 6 per cent of total emissions (EDGAR 2013). Notably, emissions are around 12 tonnes per year per capita, which means Russian economic output is more emission intensive than that of most countries (EDGAR 2013).

In 2013, Russia adopted a domestic ghg emissions target of (maximum) 75 per cent of the 1990 level by 2020. The longer-term target is 100–105 per cent of the 1990 level by 2030 (Energy Strategy 2009). Achieving these targets would require a number of changes, including technological improvements. However, fundamentally, the 2020 target indicates that Russia is most likely to choose an economically viable development mode, essentially meaning 'business-as-usual' (Kokorin and Korppoo 2014). Significantly lower levels of ghg emissions would require carbon regulation and increasing the price of carbon. Progress in this direction is slow: Russia's climate policy is primarily shaped by economic interests and aims first at energy efficiency and the introduction of new technologies, rather than emission reductions (Kokorin and Korppoo 2014: 14–15). Russia announced it would not sign up to an extension of the Kyoto protocol which would extend its initial scope from 2012 to 2020.

ENERGY POLICY

The energy sector dominates the Russian economy and has done so for many decades, with oil and gas responsible for more than half of Russia's exports, and the dependence of the federal budget on oil and gas revenues remaining very high (Accounts Chamber 2014). In order to reduce its own dependence on oil and gas, Russia has recently increased the capacity of existing nuclear power stations, which supply 16 per cent of the country's electricity, and is currently building ten new stations with another thirty-one being in a preparatory phase, in addition to twenty reactors confirmed or planned for export construction (World Nuclear Association 2013).

The main source of renewable energy in Russia is hydroelectric, predominantly from very large hydroelectric plants built by the USSR on Siberian rivers. The plants are often used in conjunction with large industrial sites and, while providing low pollution electricity, they are often criticized by environmental groups for the destruction of untouched habitats by flooding to create lakes for the hydroelectric plants. Due to the abundance of oil and gas and the historic tendency of the USSR to favour large industrial projects, such as the building of hydroelectric dams, more small-scale localized renewable energy sources are not well developed in Russia. The Russian government's energy plans predict an increase in renewable non-hydroelectric energy to 4.5 per cent of energy production by 2020 (Energy strategy 2009). The plans include expanding the current geothermal energy production in the Far East, building test plants for biofuels, and tidal energy generation, as well as reviving the small-scale hydro plants. Electricity generating wind turbines exist in remote rural areas where there is no connection to the main energy grid, and provide only 12MW of power as of 2010. Larger wind energy projects are planned, for example at Yeisk near the Sea of Azov. Very little solar power is currently generated but large-scale plants are planned with auctions being held for building over 100MW capacity solar farms.

To this end the Russian government declared the priority of energy efficiency and technological innovation and introduced ambitious energy policies (IEA 2014). However, the Russian economy remains largely inefficient: Russia's current energy inefficiency is equal to the annual primary energy consumption of France (Sargsyan and Gorbatenko 2008). Energy intensity, even though between 2000 and 2008 it has been steadily decreasing by about 4 per cent annually (ISD 2012: 30), is more than twice the world average and the highest among BRICS countries (IEA 2014). The recent increase in energy efficiency is largely due to improved technology and changes in the structure of the economy (Voigt et al. 2014).

Public environmental control: civil society, public participation, and civil rights

CIVIL SOCIETY

Despite limited political opportunities, various forms of environmental activism developed in the USSR (Yanitsky 2012). The green movement started in 1924, when the All-Russian Society for Nature Protection was founded, which had over 32 million members in the Soviet period. In the late Soviet period, the Socio-Ecological Union, an all-union umbrella environmental organization united about 200 local groups of eco-activists across the country, and the word 'ecology' entered wide public discourse (Yanitsky 2012). International contacts became more frequent, and the two leading international environmental organizations WWF and Greenpeace started working in Russia.

Simple statistics show the abundance of civil society, where 'millions of citizens are involved in volunteering' (ISD 2012: 39), however, the environmental movement has never been strong historically, nor is it in the modern Russia (Josephson et al. 2013: 300). Recently, Russian authorities have introduced a number of restrictive laws against civil society, harassed political activists, and unlawfully interfered in the work of environmental NGOs (Human Rights Watch 2013). According to Stoecker and Shakirova (2014: 8), 'Activities such as investigative reporting can be a dangerous endeavor.' The powerlessness of environmental civil society vis-à-vis political and business interests is regularly testified to by NGOs. WWF Russia was initially involved in the Sochi Olympic Games, trying to ensure protection of environmentally important sites. However, 'the construction companies and organizing committee' engagement with NGOs and other agencies became increasingly insupportable', and the seemingly successful regular meetings with the organizers did not result in any changes on the ground. This led to WWF and Greenpeace withdrawing from the environmental consultation of Sochi Olympics in 2010 (WWF 2014).

An important feature of the Russian environmental movement is its strong politicization and its historic shift 'from nature protection to politics' and 'the defence of local populations and their basic human rights' (Yanitsky 2012). 'Today it is practically impossible to separate ecological demands from social and political ones' (Yanitsky 2012: 937). The modern Russian environmental movement is not only about energy efficiency, compensation for health and ecological damage, and 'a struggle against . . . the currently dominant world-view—the resource paradigm of Russian society' (Yanitsky 2012: 937)—to a great extent, it is about a fight for equal political representation, respect for basic rights, and justice. It is important to take into account this crucial aspect of the 'greening' process in Russia when evaluating progress towards sustainability.

PUBLIC PARTICIPATION

Russian law provides for various forms of public participation in environmental governance. 'Official websites of public authorities contain drafts of laws. Citizens can send their suggestions or amendments to law' (ISD 2012: 39). The institutions of public hearings [публичные слушания[and [общественные слушания], public discussion [общественные обсуждения], public participation in environmental impact assessment, as well as everyone's right to environmental information are secured by various laws (for example, Constitution 1993; On Environmental Impact Assessment 1995; On Environmental Protection 2002; Urban Planning Code 2004; Forest Code 2006).

Despite the wide legal basis stipulating public participation in environmental decision making in Russia, citizens encounter many problems when trying to realize their rights. The mechanisms of participation are not always clear and often there are no regulations explaining how public opinion should be taken into account (Popravko 2013). Besides, most existing mechanisms of public participation are top-down, whereby a state body initiates a public consultation concerning a particular project where this is legally required. Since 2013, citizens have had an opportunity to initiate discussion of certain issues (About consideration 2013). Nevertheless, public discussion of federal laws is rare; the decision about the extent of public involvement rests with public officials, and citizens' rights to participation is realized selectively.

To improve public access to environmental information, the minister of ecology has promised to create a modern system of environmental monitoring across Russia by 2020. At the same time, Russia has still not ratified the Aarhus Convention on Access to Information, Public Participation in Decision-Making, and Access to Justice in Environmental Matters. Neither has the Espoo Convention on Environmental Impact Assessment in a Transboundary Context been ratified. Ratification of both conventions is included in government plans (Plan of realisation 2012). The development of public participation in environmentally important decisions is being pushed by eco-policies of international institutions (such as the European Bank for Reconstruction and Development [EBRD] and the World Bank) and international corporate reporting standards and management frameworks, such as Equator Principles.

Public policies are changing, even if slowly. However, in addition to legal and enforcement problems, there are other hindrances to public participation. Although environmental issues are of concern to the wider population (Yanitsky et al. 2013: 168), this concern is 'not linked to action or priority' (Crotty and Hall 2012). People tend to be naturally more concerned with socio-economic problems (Yanitsky et al. 2013: 169), which is aggravated by the often poor visibility of environmental pollution; and insufficient efforts of government and mass media to ensure information transparency and promote environmental sustainability. First, Russia is very unevenly populated, with about two-thirds of its 140 million people living in the European part of the country, while most of the oil, gas, and water resources are in Siberia. Given that many environmental accidents happen in low-populated areas where resource extraction takes place, they often remain unnoticed by the general population. Public attention often focuses on more visible problems of urban development, loss of green areas in cities related to infrastructure projects, etc. (Davydova 2014). Second, the post-Soviet environmental movement has been decentralized and regionalized, without a unified agenda for eco-activists: 'In the vast and ecologically diversified territory of Russia, each region has its priority issues' (Yanitsky 2012: 933). Third, the role of major mass media remains very modest in promoting environmental thinking or translating the voice of the people on environmental issues: 'The mass media discuss climate change, natural disasters and technological catastrophes, but only inform readers of the immediate consequences of such events, rather than analysing them' (Yanitsky et al. 2013: 168–9). Therefore, for Russia to go green, environmentally friendly law will need to be complemented by more investigative mass media and a more environmentally concerned and socially active population.

CIVIL RIGHTS

Despite the fact that the people of Russia have a constitutional right to a safe and clean natural environment, environmental issues are rarely perceived by Russian society in terms of 'citizens' rights' or 'state's responsibilities' (Lukin 2013). Examples of civic ecological activity where citizens 'demanded for their right to a safe natural environment to be respected', such as in the case of Khimki forest (2007-11), do exist but are exceptions rather than the rule (Lukin 2013).

'Most violations of environmental law in Russia take place due to the banal lack of enforcement rather than regulatory complexity or flaws' (Lukin 2013). The annual reports of the Human Rights Ombudsman provide ample examples of such violations at the national and regional level. People have to live in high-noise zones around airports, in dangerous proximity to industrial sites, or potentially highly polluted areas. Importantly, as is noted in the ombudsman's reports, ecological problems do not necessarily require high-cost solutions. Poor law enforcement is often caused by 'the irresponsibility of concrete state bodies and their individual officials' (Lukin 2014). The population is often a victim of bureaucratic red tape, with various authorities reluctant to solve problems and instead trying to shift responsibility onto each other. For example, in 2007, residents of two housing blocks in Tambov oblast contacted the Human Rights Ombudsman to help them relocate outside the industrial zone. According to sanitary norms, their houses should have been located at least 500 metres away from the factory; however these norms were violated and people lived in immediate proximity to the industrial facility. The ombudsman sent requests to the head of the municipal administration and the regional head of Rospotrebnadzor (the Federal Service for Surveillance on Consumer Rights Protection and Human Well-being). Rospotrebnadzor did not deny that the houses were built in violation of sanitary norms, however, its only action was to send a suggestion to local authorities to relocate the residents. In 2009, the residents filed a lawsuit in a regional court, which ordered the factory to relocate the residents outside the industrial zone. The factory asked the court to postpone execution of the judgement. As a result, the decision of the court was not enforced until 2011, when the factory eventually compensated the residents to help them purchase new housing (Lukin 2012).

Neither is the citizens' right to timely and accurate information about their natural environment effectively realized. For example, regional authorities are responsible for informing the local population about air quality. However, in reality, citizens may face various difficulties in accessing this information. In 2012, a citizen of Chelyabinsk oblast contacted the Human Rights Ombudsman and complained about air pollution in their town Karabash which has a copper smelting plant and high levels of pollution. Local authorities are legally obliged to arrange monitoring of the air quality, however,

Karabash did not have a municipal air controlling point, and the population did not have reliable information about the level of pollution. As a result of the ombudsman's request, an automated air monitoring point was arranged at the plant's expense. This however did not resolve the problem of information access. In order for air pollution data to be located on the website of the regional centre for environmental control, the plant that installed the monitoring points had to obtain a licence. At the same time, legally, the plant could not be forced to obtain the licence because there was no official list of organizations whose owners had to monitor air quality in the region. Eventually, the ombudsman was reassured by the regional authorities that some air quality data would be provided on the official website of the municipal administration (Lukin 2013).

For Russia to go green, there needs to be a significant shift in state–society relationships, whereby citizens fight for their basic rights, and the state respects their rights and the rule of law. So far, there is little evidence of such changes and the current political arrangements in Russia do not provide a clear path towards doing so.

Environmental justice

There is a striking contrast between the law, which generally provides for various forms of public participation in environmental governance, and the reality of widespread public exclusion from environmental decision making, essentially the non-existent practice of citizens defending their environmental rights in courts, and environmental crimes of public and commercial organizations perceived as 'nothing-we-can-do-about-it' and naturally de-prioritized by economic problems. Not dissimilar to Soviet reality, the now formally independent business and bureaucracy are often 'amalgamated' and 'form "a state within the state", beginning to exist independently from the rest of society' (Yanitsky 2012: 933). It is now officially admitted that the realization of citizens' right to a safe environment is strongly affected by power inequality: 'the stronger and the more powerful is the owner of the ecologically hazardous site, the more difficult it is to make them cooperate' (Lukin 2014). The latter is closely related to the poorly realized civil right to judicial protection. In Russia, human rights and freedoms are poorly realized at different stages of state–society relationships. Legal acts are often passed and abolished in haste, without due consideration of public opinion. Realization of the constitutional right to judicial protection is particularly difficult. The current system of justice does not guarantee the right to argue on equal terms with the state in an independent court. It is not uncommon for public bodies to consider the very recourse of an individual to a court as something unlawful. The judges rarely protect rights and freedoms of citizens which have been violated by state bodies. Court decisions are poorly enforced, particularly where individuals are expecting compensation from the federal budget (for example see annual reports of the Human Rights Ombudsman). Therefore, a full and accurate account of environmental policy changes and the 'greening' process requires not only analysis of environment-related court cases, related judicial practices, resulting court orders and their execution, but also an in-depth look at practices which have not become part of official statistics but illustrate the state of environmental justice: (informal) power relations between citizens, courts, businesses, and officials concerning environmental issues; environmental crimes committed by public bodies and officials; court cases which-did-not-happen; and environmental decisions made without due consideration of public opinion.

Conclusion

Over the last three decades, Russia has in many ways opened up to global influences, acknowledged ecological problems, and taken many steps towards a greener society. Energy efficiency has improved and industrial pollution decreased. Major companies are increasingly engaging in environmental reporting and have started moving to international environmental standards. These changes are largely due to two factors: (1) international availability of more efficient and cleaner technologies; (2) pressure from the international community (through capital markets or consumer demands).

However, there are good reasons to be sceptical about the extent of Russia's green progress. The Russian economy continues to be based on cheap internal energy supplies and strongly dependent on gas and oil exports, as well as mining and other polluting heavy industries. Since the fall of the USSR, there have been no drastic changes in environmental protection, legacy ecological damage has not been alleviated, and Russia continues to be 'colonized' by waste. The role of the Russian government, while of paramount importance, remains not unambiguous: whereas the government has officially declared priority of an innovation-driven, environmentally safe, and resource-efficient development, its policies remain largely shaped by economic and political goals. Authorities often protect large polluting companies, bureaucracy and political elites lack incentives to address environmental issues, and public policy enforcement remains ineffective. The Russian state still has not recognized its responsibility for various environmental problems, neither compensated nor cleaned up, and despite the constitutional right for a safe environment, the population of Russia continues to die from environmentally determined, preventable diseases.

The social environmental movement has also been rather weak, with little media discussion of ecological problems while socio-economic issues generally dominate the public agenda. There is little evidence to suggest that there has been any improvement in public environmental control: public participation in environmental decision making continues to be essentially non-existent, and environmental NGOs—although some of them are relatively successful in affecting public and corporate policies—have limited capacities. The effectiveness of international environmental treaties and international organizations is also questionable. Major hindrances to Russia's green development lie in political and economic inertia, as well as ineffective or selective law enforcement.

Understanding the extent of Russia's green progress is impossible without looking at recent developments through the lens of civil rights and environmental justice. Importantly, in the Russian context, environmental justice is not just about poor and minority populations. Nor is it merely a problem of 'urban versus rural'—geographically uneven distribution of environmental parameters and communities' unequal proximity to potentially hazardous sites. First and foremost, it is about poor respect for environmental rights for the whole population. Everyone in Russia, irrespective of their personal income, education, and social background runs the risk of being exposed to negative or even irreversible environmental impacts, while lacking the resources or power to defend their rights against the environmental polluter, be it a local private company, a major state monopoly, or a public agency. In this sense, Russia has so far failed to become a noticeably greener society. Environmental inequalities and injustice continue to be manifested through contrasting powers of on one side, business, political, or bureaucratic interests, and on the other side, the wider population with their interest in environmental protection, health, and well-being. As an individual, one is often deprived of one's rights for accurate environmental information, meaningful participation in environmental decision making, and access to justice. These problems are deeply entrenched in the nature of state-society relationships, and 'green' development in this sense requires a radical reform of the Russian state with its system of justice.

Crucially, there remain many unknowns about the extent of Russia's 'green' progress. Objective, accurate, and comparable data about companies' practices are missing, as well as various statistics characterizing changes in the environmental justice system and practice, the rule of (environmental) law, and the quality of public administration. Important statistics are mostly either not widely discussed or not available, for example: the number of environmental complaints filed, responded to, acted upon (and with what outcomes); the average time lag between public complaints, authorities' actions, or enforcement of legal decisions; 'environmental damage' court cases against the state or private companies; how often the courts refuse to hear environmental cases; the number and nature of environmental crimes committed by state and private companies, as well as by federal and regional authorities. The state also remains secretive about past environmental disasters.

The available fragmentary evidence from various official sources and media shows a rather grim picture. Although Russian society today has more opportunities to realize their rights compared to the Soviet period, these opportunities are still very limited compared to international standards and practices. The notion of 'green' implying humanity and respect for a citizen is still largely missing from the environmental agenda. Instead, one promotes its—politically more convenient—substitutes, such as 'technology', 'innovation', and 'investment'. The latter is possibly also the most important lesson learned for international 'green' policies. The situation in Russia is not that dissimilar to some other BRICS countries (e.g. for India see Williams and Mawdsley 2006), which highlights the need to review the 'green' policies in the national context, potentially leading to different policy priorities in the West and the 'rest'.

REFERENCES

About consideration of public initiatives, sent by citizens of the Russian Federation by means of the Internet-resource 'Rossiyskaya obshhestvennaya initsiativa' [Russian public initiative] (2013). Presidential decree No. 183. Moscow: Kremlin. Available at http://kremlin.ru/acts/bank/36853, accessed 10 April, 2019.

Accounts Chamber of the Russian Federation (2014). *Report of the Accounts Chamber of the Russian Federation on the Federal Law Draft about Federal Budget for 2015 and the Planning Period 2016–2017*. Moscow: Russian Federation.

Bashmakov, I. (2011). *Energy Efficiency in Russia: Policy, Achievements and Paradoxes*. Centre for Effective Energy Use (CENEF). Institute of World Economy and International Relations, Russian Academy of Science. Moscow: CENEF.

Cherp, A., Kopteva, I., and Mnatsakanian, R. (2003). 'Economic transition and environmental sustainability: effects of economic restructuring on air pollution in the Russian Federation', *Journal of Environmental Management* 68/2: 141–51.

Chuprov, V.A. and Terentyev, F.F. (2014). *Oil Pollution: Problems and Possible Solutions*. Moscow: Greenpeace Russia.

Climate doctrine (2009). 'The climate doctrine of the Russian Federation'. Presidential decree N 861-рп from 17 December 2009. Moscow: Kremlin. Available at www.president.kremlin.ru/news/6365, accessed 30.09.2019.

Conant, E. (2013). 'Russia's new empire: nuclear power', *Scientific American* 309/4: 88–93.

Constitution (1993). *The Constitution of the Russian Federation*. Moscow: Rossiyskaya gazeta. Available at www.constitution.ru/, accessed 30 September 2019.

Crotty, J. and Hall, S.M. (2012). 'Environmental awareness and sustainable development in the Russian Federation', *Sustainable Development* 22/5: 311–20. Available at doi:10.1002/sd.1542, accessed 12 December 2018.

Davydova A. (2014). *Ecological Results of the Year in Russia: 2013*. Available at https://bellona.ru/2014/01/16/ekologicheskie-itogi-goda-v-rossii-2013/, accessed 30 September 2019.

Ecological doctrine (2002). 'The ecological doctrine of the Russian Federation'. Government decree N 1225-р from 31 August 2002. Moscow: Collection of Laws of the Russian Federation.

EDGAR (Electronic Data Gathering, Analysis, and Retrieval) (2013). *Trends in Global CO2 Emissions*. Available at http://edgar.jrc.ec.europa.eu/news_docs/pbl-2013-trends-in-global-co2-emissions-2013-report-1148.pdf, accessed 5 October 2018.

Energy strategy (2009). 'The energy strategy of Russia for the period until 2030'. Government decree N 1715-р from 13 November 2009. Moscow.

FAO (Food and Agriculture Organization of the UN) (2012). *The Russian Federation Forest Sector: Outlook Study to 2030*. Rome: FAO. Available at www.fao.org/3/i3020e/i3020e00.pdf, accessed 27 September 2019.

Forest Code of the Russian Federation (2006). 'Federal law N 200'. Moscow. Available at https://rg.ru/2006/12/08/lesnoy-kodeks-dok.html, accessed 30 September 2019.

Framework (1996). 'The framework for the transition of the Russian Federation to sustainable development'. Presidential decree N 440 from 1 April 1996. Moscow. Available at http://kremlin.ru/acts/bank/9120, accessed 30 September 2019.

Framework (2008). 'The framework for the long-term socio-economic development of the Russian Federation for the period until 2020'. Government decree N 1662-p from 17 November 2008. Moscow. Available at http://government.ru/info/6217/, accessed 30 September 2019.

Framework (2011). 'The framework for developing a system of specially protected natural areas of federal importance for the period until 2020'. Government decree N 2322-p from 22 December 2011. Moscow. Available at http://government.ru/docs/4281/, accessed 30 September 2019.

Fundamental principles (2012). 'The fundamental principles of the state policy for ecological development of the Russian Federation for the period until 2030'. Presidential decree from 30 April 2012. Moscow. Available at http://kremlin.ru/events/president/news/15177, accessed 30 September 2019.

Fundamentals (2008). 'The fundamentals of the state policy of the Russian Federation in the Arctic for the period until 2020 and beyond'. Presidential decree N Пр-1969 from 18 September 2008. Moscow. Available at http://government.ru/info/18359/, accessed 30 September 2019.

Fundamentals (2011). 'The fundamentals of health care of the citizens of the Russian Federation'. Federal law No. 323. Moscow. Available at www.rosminzdrav.ru/documents/7025-federalnyy-zakon-ot-21-noyabrya-2011-g-323-fz-ob-osnovah-o, accessed 30 September 2019.

G20 Leaders Communique (2016). Available at www.consilium.europa.eu/en/meetings/international-summit/2016/09/Leaders-CommuniqueHangzhouSummit-final_pdf/, accessed 21 March 2017.

Gazaryan, S. and Shevchenko, D. (2013). *Sochi-2014: Independent Environmental Report.* Environmental Watch of North Caucasus. Available at http://ewnc.org/files/sochi/Doklad-Sochi-2014_EWNC-Eng.pdf, accessed 5 October 2018.

Greenpeace Russia (2013). '60 years beside the radioactive river is enough!'. Available at www.greenpeace.org/russia/en/news/24-04-13-Action-Chelyabinsk/, accessed 5 October 2018.

Greenpeace Russia (2014a). 'Greenpeace calls on the government to protect the rights of the victims of the nuclear testing at the Totskoye testing site'. Available at www.greenpeace.org/russia/ru/news/2014/12-09-2014-TotskRelis/, accessed 5 October 2018.

Greenpeace Russia (2014b). 'Russian chrome: A million for waste'. Available at www.greenpeace.org/russia/ru/news/2014/10-09-russlii-hrom-oshtrafovan-million-rublei/, accessed 5 October 2018.

Greenpeace Russia (2014c). 'Russian companies will have to build their own waste treatment facilities'. Available at www.greenpeace.org/russia/ru/news/2014/01-10-zavodi-obyazhut-ochustnie-sooruzheniya/, accessed 5 October 2018.

Greenpeace Russia (2014d). 'A brief overview of the oil spill problem in Russia'. Available at www.greenpeace.org/russia/Global/russia/report/Arctic-oil/GPRussia_Oil_spills_briefing_ENG.pdf, accessed 5 October 2018.

Hitchcock, E. (2010). 'The 2006 forest code of the Russian federation: an evaluation of environmental legislation in Russia', *Australian Slavonic and East European Studies* 24/1–2: 19–39.

Human Rights Watch (2013). 'Laws of attrition' [Available at www.hrw.org/reports/2013/04/24/laws-attrition, accessed 12 December 2018]: 'Crackdown on Russia's civil society after Putin's return to the presidency'. Available at www.hrw.org/reports/2013/04/24/laws-attrition, accessed 5 October 2018.

IEA (International Energy Agency) (2014). *Russia 2014: Energy Policies beyond IEA Countries.* Paris: IEA Publications.

ISD (Institute of Sustainable Development) (2012). *Report on Realising the Principles of Sustainable Development in the Russian Federation. The Russian View on a New Paradigm of Sustainable Development. Preparing for RIO+20.* Moscow: ISD, Civic Chamber of the Russian Federation.

Josephson, P., Dronin, N., Mnatsakanian, R., Cherp, A., Efremenko, D., and Larin, V. (2013). *An Environmental History of Russia* (Studies in Environment and History). Cambridge: Cambridge University Press.

Kirillov, V.V. (2013a). Securing the State Environmental Control within the Arctic Zone. Report of the Head of Rosprirodnadzor. Available at rpn.gov.ru/sites/all/files/documents/doklady/doklad_arktika_itog_19.11.13.docx, accessed 5 October 2018.

Kirillov, V.V. (2013b). *Poleznoe ispolzovanie poputnogo neftyanogo gaza v Rossiyskoy Federatsii.* [Useful utilization of associated petroleum gas in the Russian Federation]. Report of the Head of Rosprirodnadzor. Available at rpn.gov.ru/sites/all/files/documents/doklady/doklad_png_itogovyy, accessed 5 October 2018.

Knizhnikov, A. and Rogozhin, A. (2012). *Gazprom: One Group, Two Standards.* Moscow: WWF.

Kokorin A. and Korppoo, A. (2014). *Russia's Greenhouse Gas Target 2020.* Friedrich Ebert Stiftung. Available at https://library.fes.de/pdf-files/id-moe/10632.pdf, accessed 30 September 2019.

KPMG ((2012). *Reporting of Russian Companies on Sustainable Development.* Moscow: KPMG Russia

Kuzminov, I. (2010). 'Results of state initiatives for reforming the Russian forest legislation in 2006–2009', *Ustoychivoe Lesopolzovanie* 3/25: 28–33.

Lukin, V. (2012). *Report of the Human Rights Ombudsman in the Russian Federation for 2011.* Moscow. Available at http://old.ombudsmanrf.org/doklady, accessed 30 September 2019.

Lukin, V. (2013). *Report of the Human Rights Ombudsman in the Russian Federation for 2012.* Moscow. Available at http://old.ombudsmanrf.org/doklady, accessed 30 September 2019.

Lukin, V. (2014). *Report of the Human Rights Ombudsman in the Russian Federation for 2013.* Moscow. Available at http://old.ombudsmanrf.org/doklady, accessed 30 September 2019.

MNR (Ministry of Natural Resources and Environment) (2012). *About the State of the Lake Baikal and its Protection Measures in 2011.* Moscow: MNR of the Russian Federation.

MNR (Ministry of Natural Resources and Environment) (2013a). *The Resolution of the IV All-Russian Environmental Congress.* Available at www.mnr.gov.ru/docs/ofitsialnye_dokumenty/131936/?special_version=Y, accessed 30 September 2019.

MNR (Ministry of Natural Resources and Environment) (2013b). *On the State of Environment and Environmental Protection in the Russian Federation in 2011.* Moscow: MNR.

Mote, V.L. (1975). 'Air resource management in Soviet Russia'. *Proceedings of the American Philosophical Society* 119/3: 201–13.

OECD (Organisation for Economic Co-operation and Development) (1999). *OECD Environmental Performance Review: Russian Federation.* Available at www.oecd.org/env/country-reviews/2452793.pdf, accessed 5 October 2018.

OECD (Organisation for Economic Co-operation and Development) (2006). *Environmental Policy and Regulation in Russia.* Available at www.oecd.org/env/outreach/38118149.pdf, accessed 5 October 2018.

OECD (Organisation for Economic Co-operation and Development) (2011). *Towards Green Growth*. Available at www.oecd.org/greengrowth/towardsgreengrowth.htm, accessed 5 October 2018.

OECD (Organisation for Economic Co-operation and Development) (2012). *Incorporating Green Growth and Sustainable Development Policies into Structural Reforms Agenda*. Available at www.oecd.org/g20/topics/energy-environment-green-growth/G20_report_on_GG_and_SD_final.pdf, accessed 5 October 2018.

OECD (Organisation for Economic Co-operation and Development) (2013). *Russia Modernising the Economy*. Available at www.oecd.org/russia/Russia-Modernising-the-Economy-EN.pdf, accessed 5 October 2018.

OECD (Organisation for Economic Co-operation and Development) (2015). *Towards Green Growth? Tracking Progress*. Available at https://issuu.com/oecd.publishing/docs/brochure_-_final__en_issuu?e=3055080/13241151, accessed 5 October 2018.

On Environmental Impact Assessment (1995). Federal law N 174. Moscow.

On Environmental Protection (2002). Federal law N 7. Moscow.

On the Protection of Atmospheric Air (1999). Federal law N 96. Moscow.

On Water Supply (2011). 'On water supply and waste water disposal'. Federal law N 416. Moscow.

Plan of Realisation of the Foundations of State Environmental Development Policy of the Russian Federation for the period until 2030 (2012). Government decree N 2423-p. Moscow.

Popravko, N.B. (2013). *Legal Analysis of Public Participation in Decision Making*. St Petersburg: Bellona.

Potapov, P., Yaroshenko, A., Turubanova, S., Dubinin, M., Laestadius, L., Thies, C., et al. (2008). 'Mapping the world's intact forest landscapes by remote sensing', *Ecology and Society* 13/2: 51. Available at www.ecologyandsociety.org/vol13/iss2/art51/, accessed 30 September 2019.

Revich, A. (1992). 'Atmospheric air pollution and the health of the population in some industrial cities of Russia', *Public Health Reviews* 19/1–4: 83–91.

Putin, V. (2013a). 'Security Council session. verbatim records'. Available at www.kremlin.ru/news/19655, accessed 5 October 2018.

Putin, V. (2013b). 'Press release'. Moscow. Available at www.kremlin.ru/news/17869, accessed 5 October 2018.

Revich, B.A. (1992). 'Atmospheric air pollution and the health of the population in some industrial cities of Russia', *Public Health Revue* 19/1–4: 83–91.

Sargsyan, G. and Gorbatenko, Y. (2008). *Energy Efficiency in Russia: Untapped Reserves*. Washington, DC: World Bank. Available at http://documents.worldbank.org/curated/en/573971468107682519/Energy-efficiency-in-Russia-untapped-reserves, accessed 5 October 2018.

Schlosberg, D. (2007). *Defining Environmental Justice: Theories, Movements, and Nature*. New York: Oxford University Press.

Schmalensee, R. (2012). 'From "Green Growth" to sound policies: an overview', *Energy Economics 34* Supplement 1: S2–S6.

Shahgedanova, M. and Burt, T.P. (1994). 'New data on air pollution in the former USSR', *Global Environmental Change* 4/3: 201–27.

Stoecker S. and Shakirova, R. (2014). 'Envisaging environmental crime in Russia: past and present realities', in Sally Stoecker and Ramziya Shakirova (eds) *Environmental Crime and Corruption in Russia: Federal and Regional Perspectives*. London: Routledge, 7–19.

Strategy (2013). 'The strategy for the development of the Arctic Zone of the Russian Federation and ensuring the national security for the period until 2020'. Moscow.

Thurner, T. and Proskuryakova, L.N. (2014). 'Out of the cold – the rising importance of environmental management in the corporate governance of Russian oil and gas producers', *Business Strategy and the Environment* 23/5: 318–32.

Ulybina, O. (2014).' Interaction, cooperation and governance in the Russian forest sector', *Journal of Rural Studies* 34: 246–53.

Ulybina, O. and Fennell, S. (2013). 'Forest certification in Russia: challenges of institutional development', *Ecological Economics* 95: 178–87.

UN (United Nations) (2015). 'Transforming our world: the 2030 agenda for sustainable development'. Resolution adopted by the General Assembly on 25 September 2015. Available at https://sustainabledevelopment.un.org/post2015/transformingourworld, accessed 27 September 2019.

UNEP (UN Environment Programme) (2011). *Towards a Green Economy: Pathways to Sustainable Development and Poverty Eradication.* Available at www.unep.org/greeneconomy, accessed 22 November 2014.

UNEP (UN Environment Programme) (2012). 'Green economy: indicators'. Briefing paper. Geneva. Available at www.unep.org/greeneconomy/Portals/88/GE_INDICATORS%20final.pdf, accessed 22 November 2014.

UNEP (UN Environment Programme) (2014). 'UNEP-Russia work plan'. Press release. Available at www.unenvironment.org/news-and-stories/press-release/russia-and-unep-sign-agreement-strengthen-partnership, accessed 30 September 2019.

Urban Planning Code of the Russian Federation (2004). Federal law N 190. Moscow.

US Environmental Protection Agency (2014). Available at www.epa.gov/oecaerth/environmentaljustice/index.html, accessed 28 November 2014.

Verbatim record (2013). 'Verbatim record of the meeting of the Presidium of the State Council "About increasing the efficiency of the forest sector of the Russian Federation"'. Moscow. Available at http://news.kremlin.ru/news/17876, accessed 5 October 2018.

Voigt, S., De Cian, E., Schymura, M., and Verdolini, E. (2014). 'Energy intensity developments in 40 major economies: structural change or technology improvement?', *Energy Economics* 41: 47–62.

Walker, G. (2012). *Environmental Justice: Concepts, Evidence, and Politics.* Abingdon: Routledge.

Water strategy (2009). 'The water strategy of the Russian Federation for the period until 2020'. Government decree N 1235-p from 27 August 2009. Moscow.

Williams, G. and Mawdsley, E. (2006). 'Postcolonial environmental justice: government and governance in India', *Geoforum* 37/5: 660–70.

World Bank (2011). *Moving to a Green Growth Approach to Development.* Washington, DC: World Bank Communications. Available at http://web.worldbank.org/WBSITE/EXTERNAL/TOPICS/EXTSDNET/0,contentMDK:22865936~menuPK:64885113~pagePK:7278667~piPK:64911824~theSitePK:5929282,00.html, accessed 5 October 2018.

World Bank (2012). *Inclusive Green Growth: The Pathway to Sustainable Development.* Washington, DC: World Bank.

World Nuclear Association (2013). Available at www.world-nuclear.org/information-library/country-profiles/countries-o-s/russia-nuclear-power.aspx, accessed 30 September 2019.

WWF (World Wide Fund for Nature) (2014). 'Mistakes of Sochi-2014'. Position paper. Moscow. Available at www.wwf.ru/about/positions/sochi2014/eng, accessed 28 November 2014.

Yanitsky, O. (2012). 'From nature protection to politics: the Russian environmental movement 1960–2010', *Environmental Politics* 21/6: 922–40.

Yanitsky O., Porfiriev, B., and Tishkov, A. (2013). 'The state of social sciences on climate change and global environmental change in Russia', in *World Social Science Report, 2013*. Paris: UNESCO, ISSU, 166–74.

34 Indigenous communities, ICT, and rural development

Case studies in Tanzania and Sarawak, Malaysia

Terry van Gevelt

Introduction

The majority of rural development literature focuses on relatively homogenous ethno-linguistic communities based in peri-urban and middle rural areas. This literature has borne much fruit and there has been much progress in understanding what is required to catalyse rural development in these areas (Chambers 2013). At the same time, despite increased awareness through, for example, the 2007 United Nations Declaration on the Rights of Indigenous Peoples, there remains a lack of policy-relevant research focusing on indigenous communities and rural development (van Gevelt et al. 2017). This is especially pressing given that indigenous communities in BRICS and emerging economies are by and large the targets of government modernization policies that tend to lead to unsuccessful outcomes as they often clash with the values and preferences of indigenous communities (Curry 2003).

This chapter contributes to the nascent literature on indigenous communities and rural development. Specifically, this chapter focuses on the role that information and communications technology (ICT) can play in the rural development process for indigenous communities. Indeed, it is suggested that carefully executed ICT projects have the potential to alter the vector of economic distance for remote indigenous communities thereby both strengthening and expanding the set of economic activities undertaken. This is achieved through first conceptualizing the relationship between indigenous communities and rural development using the Thunen model. This is followed by the careful study of three different case studies in Tanzania and Sarawak, Malaysia. The first case study examines a community radio station in the Maasai village of Terrat in Tanzania. The second focuses on a telecentre in the Kelabit village of Bario in Sarawak, Malaysia. The final case study looks at how ICT has been used to augment traditional botanical knowledge in the Penan village of Long Lamai in Sarawak, Malaysia.

Terry van Gevelt, *Indigenous communities, ICT, and rural development: Case studies in Tanzania and Sarawak, Malaysia* In: *Handbook of BRICS and Emerging Economies.* Edited by: P.B. Anand, Shailaja Fennell, and Flavio Comim, Oxford University Press (2021).
DOI: 10.1093/oso/9780198827535.003.0034

Indigenous communities, ICT, and rural development

The relationship between indigenous communities and rural development can be conceptualized using the Thunen model. The Thunen model is able to explain the economic activities of rural communities at a particular time through a vector of economic distance. Usefully, the Thunen model is also able to explain the ways in which innovations are able to alter this vector of economic distance. In the original application of the Thunen model in nineteenth-century Germany, it was the introduction of a national railroad network that altered the vector of economic distance. While not detracting from the fundamental importance of physical capital and the impact that, for example good roads can have on the rural development trajectories of indigenous communities, there has been much discussion on the impact that ICT can have on rural development in remote communities (e.g. Unwin 2009).

The Thunen model is illustrated in Figure 34.1. In the Thunen model, rurality can be understood as remoteness from an urban centre and is therefore measurable along a vector of economic distance (Hite 1997). Moving outwards from an urban centre in concentric rings, the Thunen model shows that there are degrees of rurality. The first ring refers to rural areas that are located relatively close geographically to the urban centre. These are rural areas that are often considered peri-urban. Moving further out, the second concentric ring captures what can be conceptualized as middle rural areas. The final ring represents remote rural areas (Wiggins and Proctor 2001).

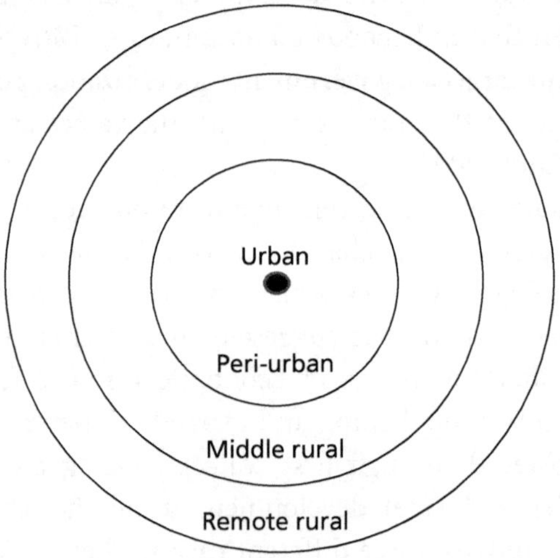

Peri-urban	Middle rural	Remote rural
High value commercial farming	Commercial farming	Subsistence farming
Employment in urban centre	Rural industry	Tourism
Rural industry	Tourism	

Figure 34.1 Thunen model and typically associated economic activities

Source: Author's work.

The Thunen model suggests that there is an economic disadvantage of distance that increases the further away rural communities are from urban centres. This economic disadvantage manifests itself through limiting the available set of stylized economic activities. For peri-urban areas the set of economic activities tends to include high-value commercial farming, employment in urban centres, and rural industry. For middle rural areas, the set of activities includes commercial farming, light rural industry, and tourism. Remote rural areas—the most economically disadvantaged by distance—tend to be limited to subsistence farming and tourism (Hite 1997; Wiggins and Proctor 2001).

There is an argument to be made that rural development literature has been dominated by a focus on peri-urban and middle rural areas. This is understandable given that the typical economic activities amenable to peri-urban and middle rural areas lend themselves well to rural development initiatives. A reading of the literature finds that this area of rural development is well enough developed that there is a general consensus that rural development in the peri-urban and middle rural areas can be achieved through an integrated approach consisting of investment in physical infrastructure, extension services and business support programmes, education, and health care. The exact mode of investment and implementation differs according to institutional capacity and context; however it is generally agreed that the approach must be mediated through champions at all governance levels to achieve maximum impact (see, for example van Gevelt 2014).

There is, however, no similar consensus on approaches to rural development in remote rural areas. This can be attributed to two main factors. First, the economic distance from urban centres means that remote rural areas are traditionally characterized by a limited set of economic opportunities. Second, in many developing countries a significant proportion of the communities that constitute remote rural areas are indigenous. Unlike more ethnically homogenous rural communities, indigenous communities tend to operate under a pluralistic institutional structure that sees interaction between traditional and state institutions. The addition of this complicated interaction variable complicates rural development initiatives and has the potential to result in unintended and suboptimal outcomes (Larcom et al. 2016).

Despite the lack of attention paid by rural development literature to indigenous communities, the field of ICT for Development (ICT4D) has devoted a sizeable amount of research on the role that ICT can play in improving the socio-economic outcomes of indigenous communities around the world through both empowering communities to find a balance between the consolidation of their traditions and culture and outside influences, and reducing the economic disadvantage of distance. A broad term, ICT consists of devices ranging from radio and telephones to computers and the internet. Its proponents argue that this range of devices has the ability to benefit remote rural communities through the provision of education (eLearning), health (telemedicine/mHealth), employment opportunities (eCommerce), and a range of governance services (eGovernance) (Unwin 2009; Holmes and van Gevelt 2015; Yeo 2015).

In terms of the Thunen model, ICT can be conceptualized as an innovation with the potential to alter the vector of economic distance for remote communities both directly, through eCommerce, and indirectly through eLearning, mHealth, and eGovernance. In turn, this can both strengthen existing economic activities and lead to the creation of a new set of feasible economic activities for remote rural communities.

Methods and materials

The case studies used in this chapter were selected on the basis of discussions emanating from panels on ICT and rural development at two international workshops on rural development held in Arusha, Tanzania, in June 2014 and Kuching, Malaysia, in February 2015. After engaging in a preliminary desk-based literature review regarding the three field sites, data were collected over the period June 2014 to November 2015 through site visits, focus group discussions, and semi-structured interviews. Site visits included visits to households, community facilities, schools, small businesses, community radio stations, telecentres, and utilities. Semi-structured interviews were undertaken with thirty key informants. Consistent with the qualitative approach of our study, we used a snowball sampling procedure to identify the thirty key informants interviewed. These included village leadership, village-based business owners, community service providers, household heads and spouses, as well as academics with a track record of collaborative research in the communities. Focus groups and workshop discussions were undertaken in each of the three community halls, and focused on the role of ICT in community development. Our survey of the literature consisted of reviewing related anthropology, history, and political economy peer-reviewed literature and the grey literature on the Maasai communities in northern Tanzania and on the Kelabit and Penan communities in Borneo.

Results

CASE STUDY 1: OROKONEREI COMMUNITY RADIO—TERRAT, TANZANIA

Located in the Manyara region of Tanzania, the Maasai village of Terrat is a thriving hub of economic and social activity that caters to approximately 1,252 households residing in the village and in hamlets within a day's walk. Despite its remoteness, located approximately 90km from the nearest city, Arusha, and only accessible through unpaved roads, Terrat impresses due to households having access to reliable and affordable renewable electricity generated through a community-owned off-grid utility, a pioneering and award-winning dairy processing industry, and the presence of an exciting cluster of small shops, hairdressers, and tea rooms. Although it is difficult to see today, the transformation of Terrat from a struggling Maasai settlement to an exemplar in rural development for many of the Maasai community in Tanzania can be traced largely back to the transformative impact of a community-level radio station: the Orkonerei Radio Service FM.

Beginning in the 1980s, the Maasai in Tanzania faced significant challenges to their traditional pastoralist way of life due to, among other reasons: land-grabs fuelled by investors eager to take advantage of the natural value of the plains by using the land for agriculture, biofuels, and tourism; more frequent and severe droughts; and an increased incidence of cattle epidemics (Nelson et al. 2012; Ykhanbai et al. 2014). In order to sustain their livelihoods, a significant number of young Maasai men turned to mining, petty trading, and agriculture or migrated to urban centres. In villages like Terrat (see Figure 34.2), this facilitated the introduction of a cash economy and introduced other elements of 'city-life' to the Maasai. Within the community of Terrat these changes sparked debate. Some argued that the cash economy and modernism were signs of progress and development. Others argued that these changes threatened the survival of the Maasai people and their culture (Jallov and Lwanga-Ntale 2007).

In response to this, twenty-one of Terrat's inhabitants joined together and in 1991 founded the Institute for Orkonerei Pastoralists Advancement (IOPA). A limited company with membership open to the Maasai community, IOPA can be effectively thought

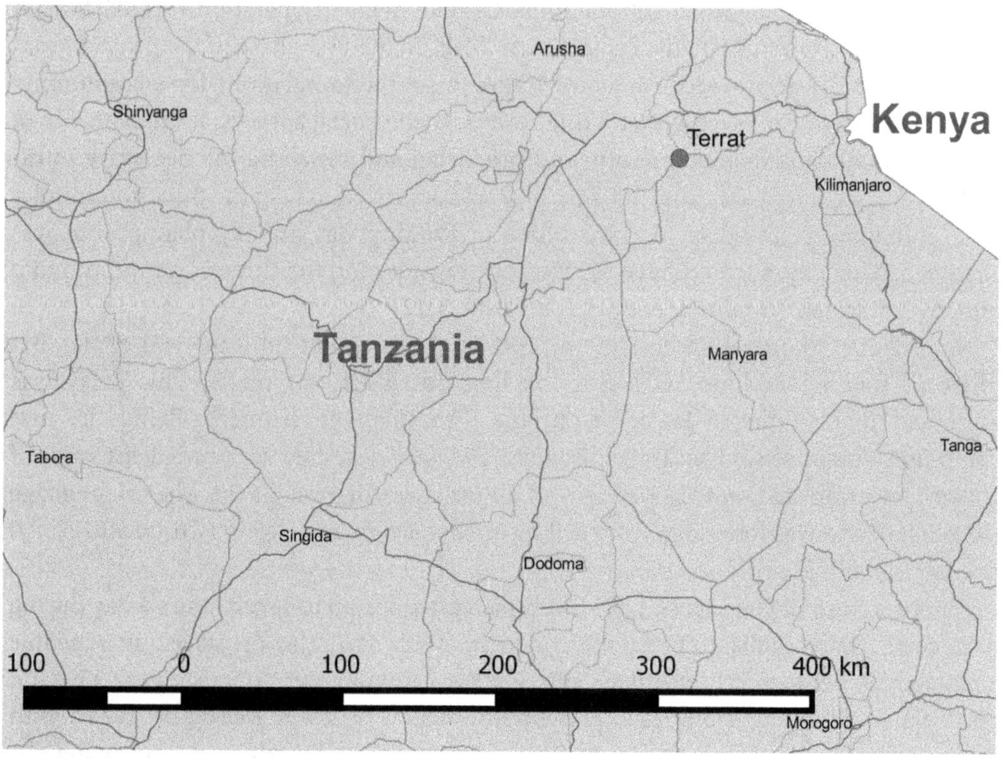

Figure 34.2 Terrat

Source: Author's work.

of as a service-oriented non-governmental organization (NGO) with the objective of bringing about positive social, economic, and cultural transformation to the Maasai in Tanzania through creating an informed pastoralist community. Initially, IOPA concentrated its resources on tackling the land-grabs facing the Manyara region of Tanzania. Through raising awareness in Terrat about the indigenous land rights of the Maasai, IOPA proceeded to file a number of court cases against the Tanzanian government with the Tanzanian High Court ruling in favour of IOPA in a landmark ruling. The success of IOPA in addressing Maasai land rights inspired IOPA to help the community in and around Terrat adapt to changing environmental conditions through a pastoral livelihood programme and vocational training. These activities took place at a community centre located in Terrat and, as a result, were limited to a subset of the community who were able to overcome geographic and time barriers to attend sessions. It quickly became apparent to the founding members of IOPA that they would need a different means of communication to have a wider impact on the Maasai community, both within Terrat and in the wider Manyara region (Jallov and Lwanga-Ntale 2007).

Radio was seen as an ideal medium by IOPA, especially with over 80 per cent of Terrat's residents being illiterate in the 1990s. The timing was fortuitous, with the international donor community seeing community radio initiatives as a means towards reducing poverty in Africa. IOPA was selected as one of three community-based organizations in the Swedish International Development Cooperation (SIDA) funded East African Community Media Project (EACMP). In the first phase of the project, from 1996 to 2002, SIDA provided funds for IOPA to set the foundations for a community radio station. This involved undertaking technical and social surveys, writing a code of conduct, mobilizing the community, and procuring and installing the necessary infrastructure. A second phase, from 2002 to 2007 was approved to help the three community radio initiatives consolidate. A third phase of funding was initially planned but was cancelled. This phase would have focused on transitioning the three community radio initiatives into self-sustaining entities (da Costa 2012).

Named the Orkonerei Radio Station (ORS) FM, it was not until the end of the first phase of funding in June 2002 that the first broadcast was made. This delay was attributed to obtaining a licence from the Tanzanian government. Being the first community radio station in Tanzania, ORS FM was restricted to a broadcast ratio of 100km, ensuring that only 10 per cent of all broadcasting was in the Maasai language (Kimaasai), and was forbidden from selling airtime for financial gain (Conrad 2011; Ali and Conrad 2015).

Run by a team of volunteers, ORS FM broadcasted for up to seven hours a day during its second phase (2002–07). As illustrated in Table 34.1, the broadcasting schedule consisted of news (local, regional, and global), programmes to raise awareness on particular health, education, legal, and environmental issues. A weekly broadcast with callers calling in for legal advice, as well as a broadcast focusing on improving the efficiency of managing livestock was also included in the programming. This was complemented by music (both Maasai and other genres) and greeting slots, where

Table 34.1 ORS FM broadcasting schedule during the second phase (2002–07) of SIDA funding

	15:00	16:00	17:00	18:00	19:00	20:00	21:00	22:00
Mo.	-	News	Health	Greetings	Greetings	News	Music	-
Tues.	Music	Music	Education	News	-	News	Discussion	Discussion
Wed.	Music	Advice	Advice	Environment	Greetings	News	News	Music
Thurs.	Music	News	Health	Greetings	Livestock	News	Discussion	Discussion
Fri.	-	Music	News	Sports	Greetings	Greetings	Music	Music
Sat.	-	Women	Sports	Sports	Guest	News	Music	Music
Sun.	-	Christian	News	News	Christian	Greetings	Music	Music

Source: Based on Kariongi as cited in Jallov and Lwanga-Ntale 2007.

individuals phone in and announce greetings to others in the Maasai community. Particularly noteworthy was a discussion programme titled 'through the eyes of women' that brought out female perspectives on issues in the traditionally patriarchal Maasai community. Contrary to the Tanzanian government's requirements, a significant proportion of programming was broadcast in Kimaasai rather than the national language, Kiswhaili (Jallov and Lwanga-Ntale 2007).

ORS FM is credited as having had a transformational impact on Terrat and the wider Maasai community. These impacts can broadly be disaggregated into three categories: consolidation of the Maasai identity; improvements in health, education, and income; and improved governance and political participation (Jallov and Lwanga-Ntale 2007; Conrad 2011).

Increasing interaction with the outside world had led to debate among the community regarding the identity and future of the Maasai. By providing a forum for people in Terrat and the wider Maasai community to communicate, ORS FM helped preserve elements of Maasai culture and traditions, especially the continued use of the Kimaasai language. At the same time, debates and discussions on topics such as women's rights led to positive changes in a typically patriarchal society. Public awareness broadcasts are credited by residents of Terrat as having improved health and educational outcomes, particularly among women and children. At the same time, broadcasts aimed at managing livestock are purported to have led to significant efficiency gains. Last, ORS FM has provided a medium for residents of Terrat and nearby areas to engage in the political process and ensure improved governance at the local, regional, and national levels. A tangible outcome of this is the negotiation of a successful payment for an ecosystem services agreement negotiated by the residents of Terrat with a consortium of tourism companies (Nelson et al. 2009; Ykhanbai et al. 2014).

Perhaps ORS FM's most significant impact, however, was indirect and unintended. Soon after commencing its first broadcast, ORS FM struggled with high fuel costs with over 40 litres of diesel per day required to power the generator for its seven-hour broadcast day. The high cost of diesel led IOPA to begin negotiations with the Tanzania

Electric Supply Company and the Ministry of Energy and Minerals for an extension of the electricity grid to Terrat. A feasibility study was undertaken and extension of the electricity grid was seen as prohibitively expensive at an estimated cost of US$340,000 (Batchelor et al. 2005). With the assistance of the Dutch Foundation Stichting Het Groene Woudt (SHGW),[1] IOPA established a community-level electricity utility. Technical expertise brought in by SHGW highlighted the potential for Terrat to make use of jatropha, a locally grown crop, as biofuel. A second-hand biodiesel generator along with jatropha processing machinery was brought in and provided the electricity for ORS FM.

Proving vastly cheaper than diesel generators, IOPA's community electricity utility not only allowed ORS FM to consolidate its seven-hour broadcast day, but allowed it to increase its hours of broadcasting to fifteen hours a day. The transformational nature of affordable electricity was not lost on IOPA, with the positive example at ORS FM leading to the purchase of two additional biodiesel generators taking the total generation capacity to 300kW. Today, the generators are operational from 06:30 to 23:30 daily and provide electricity to 189 households, schools, a health centre, churches, eight boreholes, dairy processing facilities, and small businesses, such as shops, bars, hairdressers, tea rooms, carpenters, and welders.

Arguably most impressive is the development of Terrat's dairy processing industry. This was the result of IOPA and SHGW examining potential livelihood strategies given access to affordable electricity and the main resources available to the community: milk and livestock. IOPA undertook an internal study to quantify the supply of milk during the rainy season—when milk is usually available in abundant quantities—and found that much of this surplus milk was being wasted. Processing milk into higher value-added dairy products, such as yoghurts, ghee, and cheese, was seen as a feasible strategy. Investment in dairy processing facilities, as well as the training of women, was funded by SHGW. Today, between 1,000 and 2,000 litres of milk per day are processed and the finished products are sold both locally and in cities all over Tanzania and the East African region.[2]

Despite its direct and indirect impact on the Maasai people in Terrat and its surrounding area, ORS FM has been at a crossroads since 2007. Due to the failure of SIDA's third period of funding to arise, insufficient provision was made towards achieving self-sufficiency and scale. In order to survive, ORS FM increased its broadcast range to beyond a radius of 300km and now sells airtime for advertisements. It has also actively sought funding partnerships with UNESCO, Johns Hopkins University, and a range of NGOs. This has brought ORS FM into conflict with the Tanzanian government and results in an annual fine for violating the community radio station broadcasting

[1] Stichting Het Groene Woudt is a Dutch family foundation with the mission of economically improving the livelihoods of marginal farmers in East Africa, India, and Indonesia.

[2] In 2014, Terrat's Gouda variety of cheese was recognized with an award of excellence from the Tanzanian Dairy Board.

agreement. Discussions within the community continue regarding how to safeguard the future of ORS FM. This is likely to result in the reinvention of ORS FM as a business entity. There is debate about this as, although ORS FM will be able to operate commercially, many in the community feel they will lose ownership over ORS FM and that the many benefits of ORS FM will eventually taper out (Conrad 2011).

CASE STUDY 2: EBARIO TELECENTRE—BARIO, SARAWAK

Hemmed in by mountain ranges on the east and west, Bario is considered the traditional homeland of the Kelabit people. One of the smallest groups of Sarawak's twenty-five ethnolinguistic groups, the Kelabit number approximately 6,000 in total of whom 4,500 now live in urban towns and cities. With roughly one thousand Kelabit within a day's walk, Bario serves as the Kelabit Highland's commercial and administrative centre (Amster 2006; Harris 2009, 2012). Consisting of nine hamlets, Bario is reachable from the nearest city only by nineteen-seater de Havilland Twin Otter aircraft operated by the Malaysian Airlines Rural Air Service or by a twelve-hour four-wheel-drive journey on unsealed logging roads (Cheuk et al. 2012).

Little was known about the Kelabit until the British Army based their guerilla operations against the Japanese in Bario during the Second World War and used Bario as one of their main staging sites during the Indonesia-Malaysia confrontation (1962–66). Subsequently, however, anthropologists have compiled a sizeable literature on Bario. According to Bala (2008), the Kelabit intrinsically embody a desire for progress and their interactions with the forces of modernity and development have very much reflected this.

Today, the local economy of Bario is dominated by agriculture and tourism. Bario is endowed with fertile agricultural land and produces renowned rice, salt, and pineapples. Its geographic remoteness, however, limits the market size for agricultural products with the vast majority of produce consumed and sold locally. Tourism has contributed to the Bario economy since 1985, when the first foreign tourist is recorded as coming to Bario (Jiwan et al. 2006). Tourists take advantage of Bario's access to large areas of primary rainforest. Trails through the rainforest range from a couple of hours to twelve days and allow tourists to experience Borneo's rich biodiversity[3] first hand (Rodger 2005).

The Kelabit desire for progress has seen the people of Bario embrace education since construction of the first school in the Highlands in 1946. A desire to continue education, along with the economic opportunities offered in urban areas, has resulted in a steady stream of outmigration from the Kelabit Highlands since the 1960s (Lee and Bahrin 1993; Amster 2006). On the whole, these migrants have performed disproportionately well with many Kelabit having achieved high-ranking jobs in industry and government

[3] This includes bioluminescent fungi, at least forty-two varieties of wild orchids, and the famous rafflesia.

(Amster and Lindquist 2005). This outmigration was accompanied by a need to maintain communication between the Kelabit in Bario and their kin in urban centres. At the same time, an indirect effect of outmigration has been the desire to improve the socio-economic condition of Bario, both for the remaining residents and as a means to offer the youth an alternative livelihood to migration to urban centres. According to Amster and Lindquist (2005), this is important given that a small segment of young Kelabit men do not find urban life satisfying and choose to return to Bario.

Prior to the eBario telecentre, communication between Bario and the Kelabit in urban areas was through a radio service centre. Calls were made via very high frequency radio services. Use of this technology, even with subsidies, was considered expensive by residents in Bario and the process arduous. This process consisted of waiting to book a call with an operator, who then placed a booking through a telephone operator based in Peninsular Malaysia. Provided the call did not drop, the operator would then connect the line (Harris et al. 2001; Tarawe and Harris 2009). Although Bario benefited from federal and state infrastructure (e.g. schools, health clinics, an airstrip), Bario's geographic remoteness (see Figure 34.3) made it difficult to improve the socio-economic condition due to the transportation costs associated with exporting agricultural goods and the high transaction costs involved in bringing tourists to Bario (Rodger 2005).

Working together with the community at Bario, researchers from the Universiti Malaysia Sarawak (UNIMAS) implemented eBario: a state-of-the-art telecentre to connect Bario with the wider world and improve socio-economic development. Community buy-in into the telecentre was established through the creation of steering and management committees. These consisted of the Paramount Chief, as well as village headmen and representatives from women, youth, and the church. All major decisions rested on the judgement of the steering committee, while the management committee was given responsibility for the operation of the telecentre. This process allowed UNIMAS' researchers to customize the services provided by the telecentre to the characteristics of Bario and its residents (Yeo 2015).

The eBario telecentre was sited on the commercial strip of Bario, nearby cafes, restaurants, shops, and government administration buildings. To access the internet, in 2002 very small aperture terminals (VSATs) were installed and connected to ten computers. The signal was then routed via satellite to a hub station in the closest city, Miri. In addition, satellite public telephones were set up at the telecentre using the same dial-way. As Bario did not have twenty-four-hour access to reliable electricity, the eBario telecentre was initially powered by a diesel generator. The difficulty in obtaining a steady supply of diesel and the cost of diesel, however, prompted the research team to power the system through an innovative solar-diesel hybrid system. In 2006, the eBario telecentre was handed over to the community (Cheuk et al. 2012; Yeo et al. 2011).

The eBario telecentre has been transformational for Bario. Qualitative evaluations by Tarawe and Harris (2009) and Cheuk et al. (2012) found that the most significant tangible impact was the result of increased connectivity. Specifically, a cross section of Bario's population (including the Paramount Chief, lodge operators, a local nature guide,

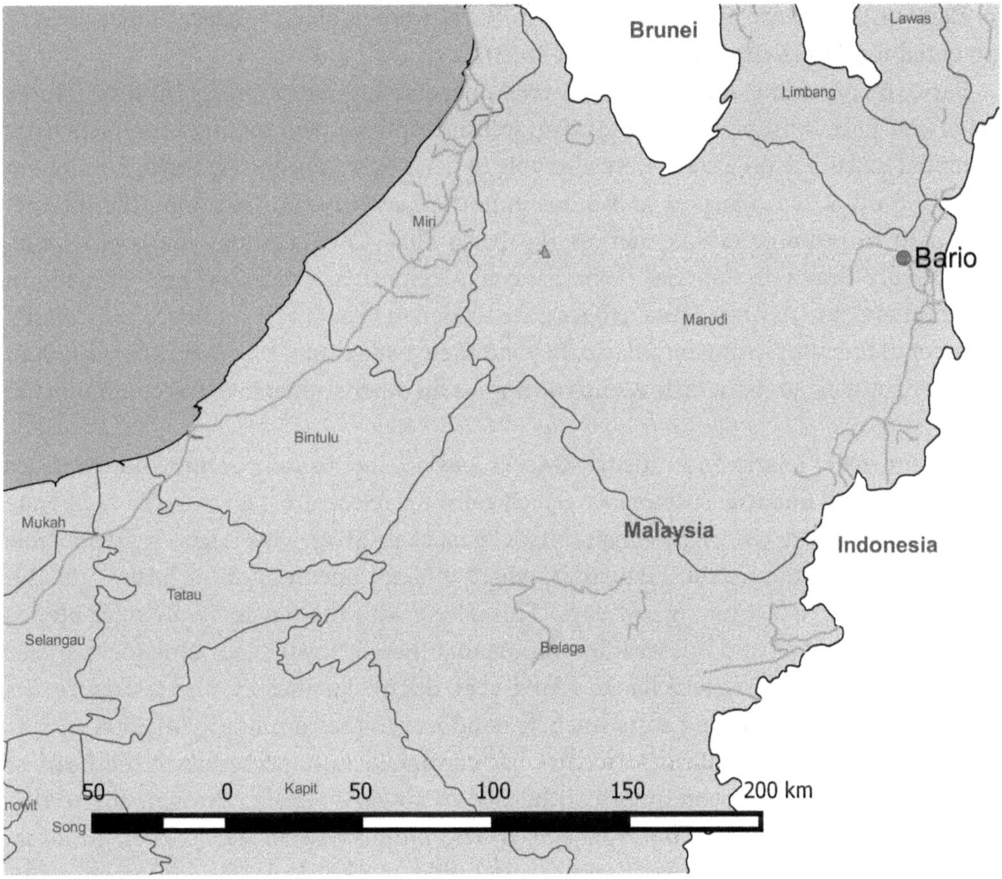

Figure 34.3 Bario

Source: Author's work.

a cafe operator, and a business woman) stated that eBario brought the world to Bario and put Bario on the global map through access to the internet. More concretely, this translated into being able to communicate with relatives in urban areas through email or satellite public phones—a marked improvement over the previous radio-telephone services and a significant reduction in the transaction costs of tourism.

Bario has experienced a steady trickle of tourists since 1985. With hospitality being a way of life among the Kelabit, the first tourists stayed for free at the home of the Paramount Chief. This continued until the Paramount Chief's son realized that it was acceptable to charge remuneration for lodging and put a 'guest house' sign on the front of the house. Over the years, a handful of other guest houses opened up to cater for tourists. Home stays in Bario operate an all-inclusive service that includes not only accommodation and meals, but also guides for treks in the forest. The flow of tourists, however, was severely limited due to high transaction costs with the tourists coming to Bario having to enquire through specialized travel agencies in Sarawak's main cities. Information was incredibly limited and it was difficult to make contact with home stays in Bario. At the same time, home stays in Bario were unable to market themselves to potential tourists (Rodger 2005; Harris 2012).

Bario, by providing access to the internet, benefited home stays significantly. Home stays were able to list on Sarawak tourism websites and respond to direct enquiries from potential tourists. Home stays were also able to liaise over appropriate times for pick-up and drop-off at Bario airport and other important services. Furthermore, the internet was used to promote events such as the Bario Slow Cook Festival—an event which successfully draws in tourists from Sarawak, Peninsular Malaysia, and abroad. In addition to home stay operators, guides have tended to benefit as a result of the increased number of tourists flowing into Bario. Beyond these two groups, however, Rodger (2005) argues that there has been little economic impact on other segments of the community at Bario.

The impact of eBario on tourism, however, has not met its full potential due to issues of technical and financial sustainably. Specifically, the telecentre has struggled to operate continuously due to electricity constraints (Cheuk et al. 2012). This is largely attributable to the climate in the Kelabit Highlands, where it is not uncommon for heavy rain and cloudy weather to last for several days. This, along with the sensitivity of solar photo-voltaic panels to wet and hot weather, means that there is insufficient time for the solar PV panels to charge battery banks (Anyi et al. 2010). Financially, the telecentre has struggled to cover operating costs since its handover to the community in 2006.

Now since 2016, the eBario telecentre has continued to stand proud in the heart of Bario. According to the community, it has led to tangible benefits through connecting Bario to the wider world. The expansion of telecommunication networks in Sarawak, however, means that Bario's residents are now able to use mobile phones to communicate both by phone and through the internet on affordable data plans. Bario's needs have changed and, to a large degree, the telecentre has accomplished its goals. According to Tarawe and Harris (2009) and Cheuk et al. (2012), many of Bario's residents believe the telecentre should continue to play a role, but that it must be reinvented to address today's needs.

CASE STUDY 3: AUGMENTING TRADITIONAL BOTANICAL KNOWLEDGE WITH ICT—LONG LAMAI, SARAWAK

Long Lamai is a remote Penan village located in the Baram river basin of Sarawak, Malaysia. It is only reachable through a combination of twin otter aircraft, four-wheel drive over logging roads, and a 90-minute boat ride through river rapids. The village has limited access to electricity through a 12kW run-of-river mini-hydro plant. There is not enough capacity for all households to be connected to the mini-hydro plant at the best of times. In the dry season, there is limited electricity from the mini-hydro plant and what electricity is available is used for public infrastructure, such as worship services at the

Borneo Evangelical Mission Church. Some households run small six-horse power diesel generators, but cannot afford to run generators for long. There is no proper water supply, and a limited telecommunication service, with a very weak signal from one telecommunication provider available from only certain spots in the village. As part of an initiative to replicate eBario in Sarawak, a telecentre stands at the centre of the village. It is regarded as transformational by the community due to the ability to communicate with the outside world through access to the internet and has led to the development of a very nascent ecotourism industry (van Gevelt et al. 2017).

With its 500 inhabitants, Long Lamai is one of the largest Penan settlements (see Figure 34.4) in Borneo (Zaman et al. 2013). Long Lamai was only permanently settled approximately fifty years ago, when many of Sarawak's Penan moved from a nomadic forest-dweller livelihood to a settled or semi-nomadic livelihood. As of 2010, national records suggest that of Sarawak's estimated 16,281 Penan people, 77 per cent were settled permanently, 20 per cent were semi-nomadic, and the remaining 3 per cent still lived nomadic livelihoods (Lyndon et al. 2013). All Penan settlements, however, still depend on the forest for a wide range of non-timber forest products that provide, among other uses, food, medicine, and construction material (Donovan and Puri 2004; Siew et al. 2013).

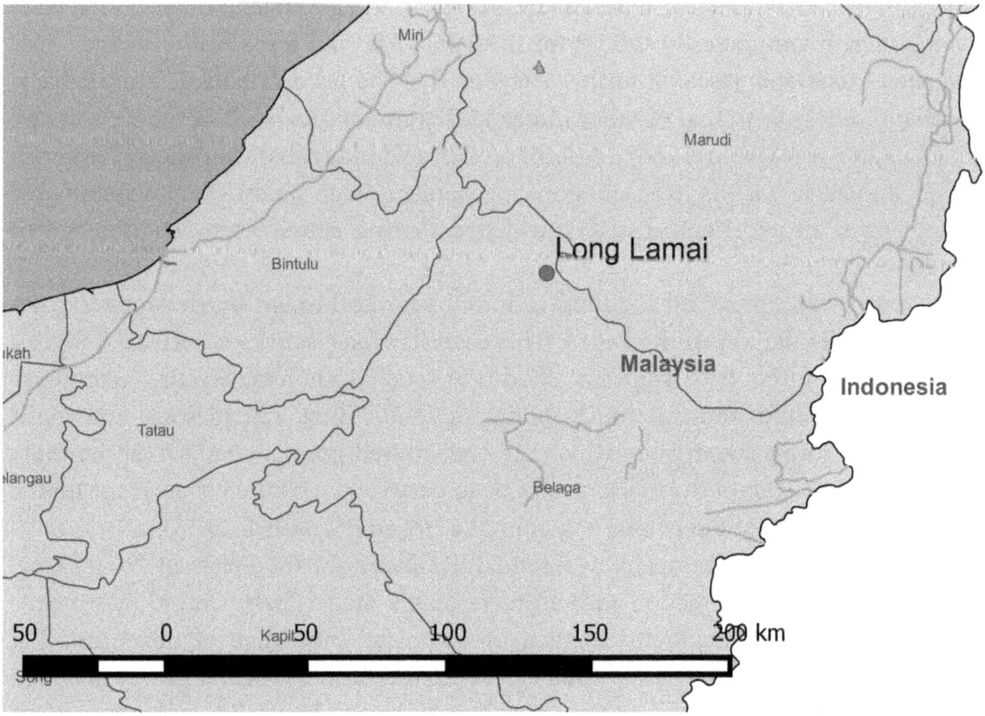

Figure 34.4 Long Lamai

Source: Author's work.

Table 34.2 Non-timber forest products known by the Penan, classified by use value

Use value	Number of species
Food and potable water	201
Construction and tools	321
Medicinal use	90
Cultural use	6

Source: Based on Koizumi and Momose (2007: 456).

Today, the main livelihood in Long Lamai is subsistence farming with three households engaging in the home stay business for a small number of tourists every year. Like the Kelabit in Bario, the Penan in Long Lamai face challenges to their traditional way of life as a result of settling and due to Malaysia's rapid economic development. This has manifested itself most significantly in increased migration of the youth due to few economic opportunities beyond farming and the allure of urban life. This migration and the disenchantment of the youth with traditional Penan lifestyles have contributed to the loss of indigenous knowledge (Brosius 2006).

Originally forest nomads, the Penan possess an intimate botanic knowledge of the forest and its non-timber forest products. This is illustrated in Table 34.2, with the Penan having catalogued at least 201 different species for food and potable water, 321 species for construction and tools, 90 species for medicinal use, and 6 species for cultural use. Detailed ethnobotanic research further suggests that the Penan's botanic knowledge is unique and differs from that of other indigenous communities, such as the Kelabit and Iban (Koizumi and Momose 2007). Another relatively unique characteristic of the Penan botanic knowledge is its transmission mechanism, with knowledge disseminated through *Toro*: an experience-based knowledge sharing activity between generations (Zaman et al. 2013).

Toro can be conceptualized as a journey into the forest through which younger males learn from elders the way of the Penan. This consists of key activities, such as: finding a location in the forest with sufficient food and water resources; erecting temporary accommodation; and foraging and hunting for food. These activities are embedded with values of forest stewardship which are transmitted generationally. The centrality of *Toro* and knowledge of the forest cannot be understated, with the Penan adage that 'if you do not know about the plants, you are not a Penan' (Siew et al. 2013).

The transition from a nomadic to a settled livelihood for the Penan at Long Lamai combined with more interaction with an increasingly modernized Sarawak has threatened *Toro*: the transmission mechanism of botanical knowledge of the forest. For example, Zaman et al. (2013) report that elders in Long Lamai are increasingly reluctant to transmit indigenous knowledge to a youth that prefers to find solutions from modern science and is increasingly likely to migrate to towns and cities. The impact of these changes on *Toro* means that without intervention this knowledge is likely to be lost completely (Koizumi and Momose 2007). Working with researchers from the University of Malaysia, Sarawak (UNIMAS), during the installation of the telecentre, elders at Long Lamai enquired about the potential for ICTs to assist in preserving their traditional knowledge through documentation. Discussion with four elders and four youths that were selected by the community led to the development of eToro (Siew et al. 2013).

eToro is an open source software tool that has been customized to record picture, textual, audio, and video data, as well as GPS coordinates. It has been created in a manner faithful to *Toro* and is designed as a tool through which elders and youth can venture into the forest and document botanical knowledge. This consists of three documentation activities: collection and documentation of data *in situ*, verification of the data at community meetings; and storing the data on an external hard disk drive. eToro is under the custodianship of a dedicated community-appointed manager. Access to the data is restricted, with only the manager afforded full access. Community elders are able to view all data, while the youth are unable to access data concerning the cultural value of plants in the database. Other users (e.g. botanists) are only able to use the software's search function and browse pictures of plants (Siew et al. 2013; Zaman et al. 2013).

In addition to cataloguing the Penan's botanical knowledge, eToro has encouraged the community at Long Lamai to look at how to harness their indigenous knowledge to improve their socio-economic well-being. Two activities being discussed within the community are using their indigenous knowledge to attract a niche market of ecotourists, and non-timber forest product (NTFP) commercialization. Despite the telecentre providing the means to market Long Lamai as a tourist attraction, it is difficult for Long Lamai to attract tourists in the same way that Bario can, given its relative geographical remoteness and the lack of transportation infrastructure in place. Realizing this, the community at Long Lamai believe that marketing the intimate relationship that the Penan have with the forest can help target a niche sector of tourists. Given that eToro contains picture, audio, and video data, the community is discussing whether selective use of this data can help market and differentiate Long Lamai as a unique tourist destination in Sarawak.

The second activity being discussed as a result of eToro is NTFP commercialization. Widely acknowledged as having the potential to provide economic benefits to remote communities, NTFP commercialization can prove to be a lucrative and ecologically sustainable economic activity if the high transaction costs characteristic of a thin market structure are addressed (van Gevelt 2014). This will require the identification of demand for niche market products and the development of a profitable value chain. Given Long Lamai's geographical remoteness and its high transportation costs, the community is investigating the potential of distilling aromatic NTFPs for potential sale in the luxury hospitality industry.

The example of eToro has shown how indigenous knowledge of NTFP products can be augmented through ICT. The success behind eToro arguably rests on two factors. The first factor was its ability to successfully draw in the youth of Long Lamai through the incentive of using modern technology in a novel way. The second factor was that eToro operates within the community's protocols governing traditional knowledge (Zaman et al. 2013). This is all the more important given the possibility of third parties' exploitation of indigenous botanical knowledge. Lastly, eToro has encouraged the community to explore ways in which their indigenous botanical knowledge can lead to socio-economic benefits.

Conclusion

Indigenous communities in BRICS and emerging economies face the twin challenges of balancing outside influences with the consolidation of traditional organizational structure and culture and a limited set of economic activities due to the disadvantage of economic distance. This contributes to their status as some of the most marginalized communities in the developing world (Eversole 2005). Our case studies of the Maasai community of Terrat in Tanzania, and the Kelabit of Bario and the Penan of Long Lamai, both in Sarawak, Malaysia, show how ICTs have the potential to alter the vector of economic distance for remote indigenous communities, thereby both strengthening and expanding the set of economic activities undertaken.

In Terrat, the community radio station Orkonerei Radio Station FM directly impacted the Maasai community by consolidating the Maasai identity, improving health, education, and income levels, and through facilitating improved governance and political participation. Indirectly, the community radio station led to the introduction of renewable electricity in Terrat and the establishment of dairy processing facilities and small businesses. In Bario, the eBario telecentre increased connectivity by improving communication with relatives in urban areas and reducing the transaction costs associated with tourism. Meanwhile, the eToro project in Long Lamai has helped catalogue and pass on the Penan's traditional botanical knowledge to the next generation. Furthermore, eToro has encouraged the community to explore how their indigenous botanical knowledge can contribute to tourism and NTFP commercialization—two economic activities that can result in socio-economic benefits for the Penan community.

The three examples, however, caution us from seeing ICT as a silver bullet for indigenous communities in BRICS and emerging economies. Specifically, we see the continued importance of physical infrastructure, financial sustainability, and market development. Starting with physical infrastructure, both the Orkonerei Radio Station FM in Terrat and the eBario telecentre in Bario were constrained by the high price of diesel in order to generate the necessary electricity required. In both cases, novel decentralized generation technologies were implemented through partnerships with external actors to address this. In the case of Bario, however, the innovative solar-diesel hybrid system continued to struggle to power the telecentre due to the climate in the Kelabit Highlands.

Both the community radio station in Terrat and the telecentre in Bario have struggled to be financially sustainable when external support was scaled back. This is not uncommon in ICT4D literature and is usually attributed to a top-down approach that was supply-led and not demand-driven (Unwin 2009). The argument espoused by this view is that demand-driven ICT initiatives will be financially self-sufficient due to the willingness of community beneficiaries to pay for the service. The examples of Terrat and Bario, however, question this viewpoint and suggest that ICT initiatives such as community radio and telecentres exhibit many public good characteristics and, as a result, will struggle to be financially self-sufficient without external support.

Last, the case study of eToro shows us that although ICT can help raise awareness about new value-adding economic activities, acting on these activities will often require significant market development. For example, in the case of NTFP commercialization connecting producers and consumers is often difficult due to niche market demand, difficulty supplying a sufficient quantity of high-quality products to meet demand due to the low density of production, yield variation due to climatic and ecological conditions, and the often rapid perishability of NTFPs. As a result, state and non-state institutions are often required to structure a supply chain to connect producers and consumers and an appropriate regulatory framework (Belcher et al. 2005; Wynberg and Laird 2007).

ACKNOWLEDGEMENTS

I am grateful to Alvin Yeo Wee, Tayyab Safdar, Claudia Canales Holzeis, Tariq Zaman, Garen Jengan, Roger Harris, Martin Kariongi, Steven Kariongi, and the communities of Terrat, Bario, and Long Lamai for their help during data collection. I am also thankful to Meredith Thomas for assisting in the generation of maps. Data collection for this article was undertaken as part of the Cambridge Malaysian Education and Development Trust's (CMEDT) Smart Villages Initiative and was funded through grant number 0096 from the Templeton World Charity Foundation (TWCF). The opinions expressed in this chapter are those of the author and do not necessarily reflect the views of CMEDT and TWCF.

REFERENCES

Ali, C. and Conrad, D. (2015). 'A community of communities? Emerging dynamics in the community media paradigm', *Global Media and Communication* 11/1: 3–23.

Amster, M. (2006). 'Narrating the border: perspectives from the Kelabit Highlands of Borneo', in A. Horstmann and R.L. Wadley (eds) *Centering the Margin: Agency and Narrative in Southeast Asian Borderlands*. New York: Berghahn Books, 207–27.

Amster, M. and Lindquist, J. (2005). 'Frontiers, sovereignty, and marital tactics: comparisons from the Borneo Highlands and the Indonesia–Malaysia–Singapore growth triangle', *Asia Pacific Journal of Anthropology* 6/1: 1–17.

Anyi, M., Kirke, B., and Ali, S. (2010). 'Remote community electrification in Sarawak, Malaysia', *Renewable Energy* 35/7: 1609–13.

Bala, P. (2008). *Desire for Progress: The Kelabit Experience with Information Community Technologies (ICTs) for Rural Development in Sarawak, East Malaysia*. Cambridge: Cambridge University Library.

Batchelor, S., Scott, N., and Eastwick, G. (2005). 'Community television for the poor – a scoping study'. Gamos Ltd and DfID, 1–90.

Belcher, B., Ruíz-Pérez, M., and Achdiawan, R. (2005). 'Global patterns and trends in the use and management of commercial NTFPs: implications for livelihoods and conservation', *World Development* 33/9: 1435–52.

Brosius, J. (2006). 'What counts as local knowledge in global environmental assessments and conventions?', in W. Reid, F. Berkes, T. Wilbanks, and D. Capistrano (eds) *Bridging Scales and Knowledge Systems: Concepts and Applications in Ecosystem Assessment*. Washington, DC: Island Press, 129–44.

Chambers, R. (2013). *Rural Development: Putting the Last First*. London: Routledge.

Cheuk, S., Atang, A., and Lo, M.C. (2012). 'Community attitudes towards the telecentre in Bario, Borneo Malaysia: 14 years on', *International Journal of Innovation, Management and Technology* 3/6: 682–7.

Conrad, D. (2011). 'Lost in the shadows of the radio tower: a return to the roots of community radio ownership in Kenya, Uganda and Tanzania'. PhD thesis. Centre for International Studies of Ohio University, 1–176.

Curry, G. (2003). 'Moving beyond postdevelopment: facilitating indigenous alternatives for "development"'. *Economic Geography* 79/4: 405–23.

da Costa, P. (2012). 'The growing pains of community radio in Africa: emerging lessons towards sustainability', *Nordicom Review* 33: 135–48.

Donovan, D. and Puri, R. (2004). 'Learning from traditional knowledge of non-timber forest products: Penan Benalui and the autecology of *Aquilaria* in Indonesian Borneo', *Ecology and Society* 9/3: 3.

Eversole, R. (2005). 'Overview – patterns of indigenous disadvantage worldwide', in R. Eversole, J. McNeish, and A. Cimadamore (eds) *Indigenous Peoples and Poverty: An International Perspective*. London: Zen Books, 1–321.

Harris, R. (2009). 'Tourism in Bario, Sarawak, Malaysia: a case study of pro-poor community-based tourism integrated into community development', *Asia Pacific Journal of Tourism Research* 14/2: 125–35.

Harris, R. (2012). 'Research partnerships to support rural communities in Malaysia with information and communication technologies', in J. Lazar (ed.) *Managing IT/Community Partnerships in the 21st Century*. London: IDEA Group Publishing, 247–70.

Harris, R., Bala, P., Songan, P., Lien, E.K.G., and Trang, T. (2001). 'Challenges and opportunities in introducing information and communication technologies to the Kelabit community of North Central Borneo', *New Media and Society* 3/3: 270–95.

Hite, J. (1997). 'The Thunen Model and the new economic geography as a paradigm for rural development policy', *Review of Agricultural Economics* 19/2: 230–40.

Holmes, J. and van Gevelt, T. (2015). 'Energy for development: the concept', in R.B. Heap (ed.) *Smart Villages: New Thinking for Off-Grid Communities Worldwide*. Cambridge: Banson, 13–20.

Jallov, B. and Lwanga-Ntale, C. (2007). 'Impact assessment of East African Community Media Project 2000–2006: Report from Orkonerei Radio Service (ORS) in Tanzania and selected communities'. SIDA Department for Democracy and Social Development, 1–52.

Jiwan, D., Chai, P., Teo, G.K., and Jiwan, M. (2006). 'Integrated highland development in Bario, Sarawak, Malaysia: an overview'. Paper presented at the International symposium towards sustainable livelihoods and ecosystems in mountainous regions, May, Chiang Mai University and the World Agroforestry Centre: Chiang Mai, 1–5.

Koizumi, M. and Momose, K. (2007). 'Penan Benalui wild-plant use, classification and nomenclature', *Current Anthropology* 48/3: 454–9.

Larcom, S., van Gevelt, T., and Zabala, A. (2016). 'Precolonial institutions and deforestation in Africa', *Land Use Policy* 51: 150–61.

Lee, B. and Bahrin, T. (1993). 'The Bario exodus: a conception of Sarawak urbanization', *Borneo Review* 4/2: 113–27.

Lyndon, N., Er, A., Sivapalan, S., Ali, H., Rosniza, A., Azima, M. et al. (2013). 'The world-view of Penan community on quality of life', *Asian Social Science* 9/14: 98–105.

Nelson, F., Foley, C., Foley, L., Leposo, A., Loure, E., Peterson, D. et al. (2009). 'Payments for ecosystem services as a framework for community-based conservation in Northern Tanzania', *Conservation Biology* 24/1: 78–85.

Nelson, F., Sulle, E., and Lekaita, E. (2012). 'Land grabbing and political transformation in Tanzania'. Paper presented at the Land Deals Politics Initiative Conference, October, Ithaca, NY: Cornell University, 1–24.

Rodger, C. (2005). 'A case study of ecotourism in the Kelabit Highlands: is it sustainable?' PhD thesis. Centre for East and South-East Asian Studies at Lund University, Available at https://lup.lub.lu.se/luur/download?func=downloadFile&recordOId=1331402&fileOId=1331403, accessed 5 August 2019.

Siew, S.T., Yeo, A., and Zaman, T. (2013). 'Participatory action research in software development: indigenous knowledge management systems case study', in M. Kurosu (ed.) *Human-Computer Interaction*. Berlin: Springer-Verlag, 470–9.

Tarawe, J. and Harris, R. (2009). 'Stories from eBario', in E. Alampay (ed.) *Living the Information Society in Asia*. Singapore: Institute of Southeast Asian Studies, 109–29.

Unwin, T. (2009). 'Development agendas and the place of ICTs', in T. Unwin (ed.) *Information and Communication Technology for Development*. Cambridge: Cambridge University Press, 7–38.

van Gevelt, T. (2014). 'Rural electrification and development in South Korea', *Energy for Sustainable Development* 23: 179–87.

van Gevelt, T., Canales Holzeis, C., George, F., and Zaman, T. (2017). 'Indigenous community preferences for electricity services: evidence from a choice experiment in Sarawak, Malaysia', *Energy Policy* 108: 102–10.

Wiggins, S. and Proctor, S. (2001). 'How special are rural areas? The economic implications of location for rural development', *Development Policy Review* 19/4: 427–36.

Wynberg, R. and Laird, S. (2007). 'Less is often more: governance of a non-timber forest product, marula (*Sclerocarya birrea subsp. caffra*) in Southern Africa', *International Forestry Review* 9/1: 475–90.

Yeo, A. (2015). *Leveraging Research and Innovation in ICTs for Socio-Economic Development in Malaysia*. Sarawak: UNIMAS,

Yeo, A., Hasiz, F., Zaman, T., Songan, P., and Hamid, K. (2011). 'Telecentre replication initiative in Borneo Malaysia, the CoERI experience', *Electronic Journal on Information Systems in Developing Countries* 50/3: 1–15.

Ykhanbai, H., Garg, R., Singh, A., Moikio, S., Beyene, C.E., Roe, D. et al. (2014). 'Conservation and "land grabbing" in Rangelands: part of the problem or part of the solution?'. Report from the International Land Coalition Secretariat at IFAD, Rome, 1–44. Available at www.landcoalition.org/en/resources/conservation-and-land-grabbing-rangelands-part-problem-or-part-solution-0, accessed 5 August 2019.

Zaman, T., Yeo, A., and Kulathuramaiyer, N. (2013). 'Augmenting indigenous knowledge management with information and communication technology', *International Journal of Services Technology and Management* 19/1–3: 137–48.

35 Emerging food and nutrition security challenges in Central Asia—implications for BRICS and emerging economies

Suresh Chandra Babu and Kamiljon Akramov

Introduction

There is a consensus that the economic development strategies of countries in Central Asia need to be revisited keeping the region's relationship with BRICS (Brazil, Russia, India, China, and South Africa) countries and other emerging economies in mind. Such reconsideration of policies and strategies has received wide policy attention among the leaders of Central Asian countries. Yet few serious efforts have been made to take stock of the issues, constraints, and challenges in various sub-sectors of these economies. In the last two decades, the Central Asia region has gone through several transitions in institutional structure and governance, each with varying impacts on and consequences for economic development, particularly in the context of the agricultural sector (Kazbekov and Qureshi 2011; Mogilevskii and Akramov 2014). It has been well recognized that agriculture plays a critical role in rural poverty reduction, employment, economic growth, and food security. Deterioration in the quality of diet consumed results in widespread malnutrition, leading to rapid increases in overweight, obesity, stunting, and chronic diseases as seen in Central Asia (Pinstrup-Andersen 2017). To utilize agriculture as an engine for increased food and nutrition security and reduced poverty, the agricultural sector and its institutions must be transformed to increase production and productivity.

Since independence, the five countries including Kazakhstan, Kyrgyzstan, Tajikistan, Turkmenistan, and Uzbekistan, have made considerable progress towards increasing domestic food production. In the last decade, Central Asia experienced significant agricultural and economic growth as well as improvements in household welfare (Peyrouse 2009). Yet food and nutrition insecurity persist among the most vulnerable groups (Babu et al. 2010). The region continues to be threatened by major geopolitical

Suresh Chandra Babu and Kamiljon Akramov, *Emerging food and nutrition security challenges in Central Asia—implications for BRICS and emerging economies* In: *Handbook of BRICS and Emerging Economies.* Edited by: P.B. Anand, Shailaja Fennell, and Flavio Comim, Oxford University Press (2021).
DOI: 10.1093/oso/9780198827535.003.0035

and socio-economic challenges including volatile food prices, low yields, limited investments in agriculture, climate change, and institutional constraints (Meyers et al. 2012). Although policy reforms have formed a major approach of intervention in these countries over several decades, the process of policy and institutional reforms has been slow due to limited capacity and evidence for policy planning (Babu and Tashmatov 2000; Pinstrup-Andersen et al. 2016). The lack of information on the effects of different policy alternatives has inhibited the development and implementation of appropriate food, agriculture, and nutrition policies.

This chapter will identify the critical issues and challenges facing Central Asian countries for attaining short-term and long-term food and nutrition security for all in the context of the technological, institutional, and policy reforms that have been undertaken by these countries and in the context of their relationship with BRICS and other emerging economies.

We review the basic structure of the Central Asian economies in relation to food and nutrition security in the second section, while the third section reviews food security and nutrition security challenges in the context of emerging global challenges. The fourth section discusses the possible impact of BRICS economies—Russia and China in particular—on Central Asian food and nutrition security, and the fifth section concludes with the identification of critical knowledge and research gaps.

Basic economic structure and food and nutrition security indicators

Agricultural development and food security in Central Asia have important implications for the agricultural and economic development of BRICS countries as well as the neighbouring emerging economies of Eastern Europe. Regional development in Central Asia is heavily reliant on the agricultural sector which has a key role to play in poverty reduction, employment, and sustainable development. However, in order for agriculture to play a leading role in development the sector must be transformed. In this section, we review the basic economic structures of the countries in Central Asia and present select food and nutrition security indicators to illustrate how food and nutrition security and poverty are skewed in the region.

Despite distinct economic differences, the countries in Central Asia share a common reliance on agriculture as a critical source of regional employment and foreign exchange (Goletti and Chabot 2000; Peyrouse 2009). Table 35.1 provides basic agricultural economic indicators in Central Asia. On average, nearly 60 per cent of the rural population lives in a rural area, illustrating their heavy dependence on the agricultural sector for economic livelihood. Countries in the Central Asia region exhibit a wide range of levels in per capita income indicating differences in the underlying factors contributing to

Table 35.1 Central Asia—basic indicators in 2015

	Per capita GDP (US$)	Employment in agriculture (%)	Rural population (%)	Poverty headcount ratio at national poverty lines (%)
Kazakhstan	10,510	18.0	46.8	2.7
Kyrgyzstan	1,121	29.3	64.3	32.1
Tajikistan	919	64.9	73.2	31.3
Turkmenistan	6,433	48.4 (2007 est.)	50.0	-
Uzbekistan	2,138	27.7	63.6	14.1 (2013 est.)

Source: *World Development Indicators 2007, 2013, 2017* (World Bank 2017); *Key Indicators for Asia and Pacific 2016* (Asian Development Bank 2016).

Table 35.2 Agriculture as % GDP, 2009–16

	2009	2010	2011	2012	2013	2014	2015	2016
Kazakhstan	6.4	4.8	5.5	4.7	4.9	4.7	5.0	4.8
Kyrgyzstan	21.1	19.4	18.6	19.2	17.0	17.1	15.9	14.9
Tajikistan	20.9	22.1	27.2	26.6	27.4	27.2	25.0	-
Turkmenistan	12.3	14.5	8.9	8.5	8.5	8.5	-	-
Uzbekistan	20.6	19.8	19.5	19.2	19.0	18.8	18.2	17.6
Average	16.3	16.1	15.9	15.6	15.4	15.3	. . .	. . .

Source: Asian Development Bank: *Key Indicators for Asia and Pacific 2016* (Asian Development Bank 2016).

income levels and economic growth. The per capita income was highest in Kazakhstan in 2015 (US$10,510) which is roughly equivalent to middle-income countries such as Hungary (US$12,365), Poland (US$12,566), and Croatia (US$11,580). In Central Asian countries, excluding Kazakhstan (18 per cent), agriculture constitutes at least one-quarter of employment, and over half in Tajikistan. This implies that of those households in rural areas, over half of the total population in the region are directly or indirectly dependent on agriculture.

Table 35.2 illustrates the trends in agriculture as a percentage of total gross domestic product (GDP) from 2009 to 2016. While the share of agriculture declined in Kazakhstan and Turkmenistan due to a rising energy sector, agriculture made up a significant share of GDP in Kyrgyzstan, Tajikistan, and Uzbekistan.

Achieving food and nutrition security requires addressing a multitude of challenges in Central Asian countries both individually and as a region. In 2000, Pandya-Lorch identified the following emerging global food security issues as critical to agricultural development in Central Asia:

- volatile cereal prices
- growing water scarcity
- declining soil fertility

- escalating concerns about food safety
- weather fluctuations and climate change
- conflicts and food security
- trade liberalization issues.

Fifteen years later, the challenges listed above remain relevant to achieving food and nutrition security in Central Asia. Lack of significant improvement in many of these areas furthers the need for action at the country and regional levels. In this chapter, we take a closer look at the current challenges facing food and nutrition security in Central Asia.

Food prices continue to be volatile and the recent food price crisis beginning in 2007 indicated that Central Asia, while isolated geographically, is vulnerable to food security issues arising from fluctuations in global food systems. This vulnerability highlights the need for regional cooperation to improve the trade of food commodities in the region. Water use efficiency remains very low across and within countries in the Central Asia region. To address the increase in demand for water, both for domestic and agricultural use, policy reforms are required to incentivize the effective and responsible use of water. If concerns regarding water usage are not addressed, we could see a significant decline in agricultural production and regional food security. Fertilizer production and distribution in the Central Asian republics is particularly important in the production of cotton. As fertilizers become expensive the cost of production increases which over time leads to low soil fertility. Due to continued production and the low availability of organic sources of fertilizers such as green manure and animal manure, the soil continues to be deprived of needed nutrients.

Due to changes in income in the region, demand for processed and prepared foods has been increasing. Similarly, concerns about food safety have been increasing as well. Climate changes have already started to impact agricultural production and food security across the globe, particularly in Central Asia. To address these changes, adaptive policies and practices should be introduced in the region to protect the well-being of farmers, particularly smallholders who are the most vulnerable to fluctuations in agricultural production (Christmann and Aw-Hassan 2010). Conflicts in Central Asia and the surrounding countries impact food and nutrition security in the region through their effects on food availability and prices. Geopolitical and security concerns in the regions surrounding Central Asia have increased in recent years, enhancing the need for more resilient agricultural systems. Finally, a substantial portion of the food trade in Central Asia is within neighbouring countries, requiring a regional rather than national approach. Agricultural and food trade in Central Asia has a significant impact on food security in these countries, requiring increased policy attention from all Central Asian country governments (Mogilevskii and Akramov 2014).

After the fall of the Soviet Union, countries in this region shifted their primary efforts to focus on becoming self-sufficient in food production. This was partially due to the collapse of trade and necessary infrastructure, a regional failure. This emphasis on self-sufficiency has had implications for the sustainability and environmental effects of food systems. Second, due to the land-locked geography of the region, trade within and around the countries is difficult and remains restricted. Next, although the shared structure of communal farms is typical of the Soviet Union dissolution after independence, the policies dictating what farmers could produce continued. This system has had many negative consequences including decreased soil fertility. Food production in the region is also restricted by the failure of irrigation systems, lack of improved technologies, and limited access to inputs such as fertilizer. Policies have kept the price of staple commodities such as wheat artificially low, making production not profitable for farmers. In addition, the degradation of natural resources from improper farm management has had devastating effects on the health of the now salt-encrusted Aral Sea, having major implications on food security.

The lack of support from institutions for advancement of farming has contributed greatly to the low levels of food security in this region. The needs of farmers are not currently met by research and extension institutions, as these institutions have suffered for the last twenty years, leading to weak coordination and limited linkages to farmers. Finally, the low capacity for designing evidence-based policies is a major challenge to food security in the region. It is crucial to increase this capacity since evidence-based decision making is more likely to be successful in achieving targets when compared to decisions based solely on ideological reasons (Pinstrup-Andersen et al. 2016). Food policy research is an important source of the evidence needed for sound policymaking. Limited individual, organizational, and system capacities at the national and regional levels have led to the ineffective development and implementation of policies including those related to food pricing, market, and input delivery systems. While some countries have attempted to implement land reform policies to enable better food production, for the most part these efforts have had limited success.

Underlying all the above challenges is the cross-cutting issue of regional security. Security concerns include both internal unrest as well as regional geopolitical challenges. Central Asia's proximity to the Middle East means that external threats have major implications for policy design. These security and stability concerns have diverted attention and resources from the goal of long-term food security. To increase policy and research attention to food security and production issues, this chapter will take stock of what policies and institutional innovations are currently addressing these challenges. This research will provide insights to enable policy changes to increase long-term food security across the region.

Central Asia in the global economy and implications for food and nutrition security

Despite key differences in the economies of Central Asia, the countries all share a common reliance on agriculture as a key source of employment and foreign exchange.

This section will review challenges facing agricultural development and inhibiting countries in the region from attaining food security. Central Asia is situated between three of the BRICS countries (Russia, India, and China) and is surrounded by several other emerging economies such as those in Eastern Europe. Although regional development has made some progress in the last decade, much more still needs to be done to achieve food and nutrition security.

The transformation of the traditional agricultural sector into a modern system of agriculture has been demonstrated as an engine of growth and a catalyst for overall economic development (Timmer 2014). Agricultural transformation is the process by which individual farms shift from highly diversified, subsistence-oriented production towards more specialized, market-oriented production. Advancing the transformation of the agricultural sector of Central Asia requires the transformation of its constituent sub-sectors as well as concerted efforts from governments to remove existing barriers that constrain agricultural productivity (Akramov 2011). Further, the transformation of each sub-sector requires highly capacitated and well-functioning organizations and institutions from the national level down to the farm level.

Following independence from the Soviet Union, Central Asian countries faced a high degree of uncertainty in meeting the food and nutrition security needs of their populations. At the same time, the challenges of mistrust and the lack of a common platform to discuss their food and agricultural problems confounded the welfare challenges that their populations faced. While the food and nutrition security situation has improved since independence, there is still a concern that without continuous improvement in technological, institutional, and policy innovations there could be backsliding from the progress already achieved. And there is a need to take stock of the issues, challenges, and constraints in making further progress in the context also of emerging global issues. Table 35.3 illustrates the diversity of the current status of food security in Central Asian countries.

Table 35.3 Selected food security indicators (2014–16); latest available data

	Average dietary energy supply adequacy (%)	Food imports/ total merchandize exports (%)	Per capita food production variability	Depth of food deficit (kcal/ capita/day)	Prevalence of undernourishment
Kazakhstan	137	3	64.8	18	<5
Kyrgyz Republic	122	25	5.9	40	6.0
Tajikistan	97	34	3.4	250	33.2
Turkmenistan	129	3	13.6	22	<5
Uzbekistan	122	7	5.4	29	<5
Average	121.4	14.4	-	71.8	-

Source: *World Development Indicators 2007, 2013, 2017* (World Bank 2017); *Key Indicators for Asia and Pacific 2016* (Asian Development Bank 2016).

REGIONAL TRADE—EXPORTS

Agricultural production is a key source of exports for the Central Asia region (Mogilevskii and Akramov 2014). In the past two decades, these countries have undergone major changes in trade patterns and policies. Since 2000, agriculture has been growing at a slower rate than other economic sectors except in Tajikistan. Subsequently, the agricultural sector is losing its position as a central economic sector (Mogilevskii and Akramov 2014). Figure 35.1 shows the declining share of agriculture in the national income comparing the Soviet era, the transition era, and recent years. Prior to independence, agriculture made up roughly one-third of GDP in every Central Asian country. However, in Kazakhstan this share has dropped below 5 per cent.

In recent years, agricultural production has become a relatively less important source of income and livelihood for a majority of the rural population in Central Asia (Mogilevskii and Akramov 2014; Pomfret 2014). This can be partially attributed to the increasing importance of remittances from labour migrants, which are replacing agricultural revenues in some rural households. Regional and global importance has become an important source of food and agricultural imports, and recent data show a significant increase in the ratio of imports to domestic outputs of agricultural commodities (Mogilevskii and Akramov 2014; Pomfret 2014). Three of the four countries above depend on imports of wheat, the main staple crop in Central Asia. Throughout the region, agricultural exports have become relatively less important as energy exports (e.g. oil and natural gas) generate more foreign exchange. As found by Mogilevskii and Akramov (2014), Central Asian agricultural exports are concentrated on a few crops. The data reveal that in Kazakhstan, Tajikistan, and Uzbekistan wheat or cotton make up more than half of agricultural exports. Fruit, vegetables, and processed foods are also becoming important sources of export earnings.

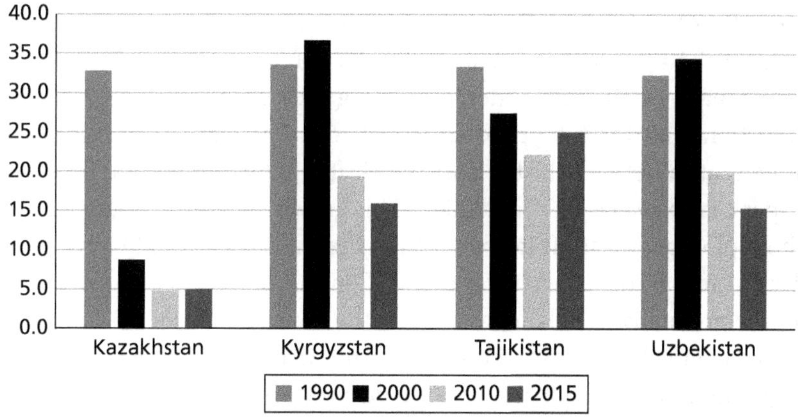

Figure 35.1 Role of agriculture in Central Asia economies

Source: *World Development Indicators 2007, 2013, 2017* (World Bank 2017).

In terms of geography, neighbouring countries are important destinations for agricultural trade with Central Asian countries. Russia, China, and the European Union are key trade partners for Central Asia, particularly in the food trade. While Russia is an important trade partner for both exports and imports, China and Europe are significant export partners for the region. While exports from Central Asia to China are primarily made up of cotton from Uzbekistan, exports to Europe primarily consist of grain and oil seeds from Kazakhstan in addition to cotton from all countries (Mogilevskii and Akramov 2014; Pomfret 2014). As a result of increasing living standards across Central Asia, the demand for processed food imports from Europe has grown significantly in recent years. Agricultural trade with Russia varies significantly across countries. For example, Kazakhstan is one of the largest importers of prepared food from Russia. Primary exports from Kyrgyzstan, Tajikistan, and Uzbekistan to Russia are made up of fruit, vegetables, and cotton.

Due to its remoteness from major international ports, Central Asia faces several challenges in the food trade. High transportation costs and lengthy transit times lead to higher domestic food prices, therefore limiting access to food and increasing food insecurity (Akramov 2011). Increasing regional cooperation and trade could increase the availability of food and make it more accessible to the rural poor. To do so would require that governments reduce trade tariffs and other restrictions that limit the movement of goods within and around the Central Asia region.

PRODUCTION/PRODUCTIVITY—CROPS AND LIVESTOCK

The differential changes in the distribution of land following the collapse of the Soviet Union led to dramatic changes in the structure of agricultural production in Central Asia, and these have varied among farm types (Lerman and Sedik 2009). While the share of production in agricultural enterprises declined substantially from 40 per cent in 1997 to less than 10 per cent in 2007, the production share of household plots remained relatively stable at 60 per cent (Lerman and Sedik 2009). The newly formed category of peasant farms made up the remainder, increasing their share from approximately 3 per cent to almost one-third of total production between 1997 and 2007. Lerman and Sedik (2009) found that in both Tajikistan and Uzbekistan total agricultural production grew to over 70 per cent between 1997 and 2007. This growth can be attributed to production on household plots and peasant farms through the transition to individual farmers after independence, and is observed throughout Central Asia. This transition led to an increase in the productivity of land, as seen by the increase in production as agricultural land remained relatively constant. Individual farms across the region have been shown to consistently achieve much higher levels of land productivity (Lerman and Sedik 2009). Agricultural productivity gains are a key contributor to the agricultural transformation (Timmer 2014).

Although there has been some effort to shift agricultural production from commercial to food crops in an effort to increase food and nutrition security, more intensive agricultural research is needed to understand the suitability of food crops in particular contexts (Babu and Djalalov 2006). This research could be used to inform and set research priorities as well as to allocate resources such as land more effectively.

NATURAL RESOURCES

Climate Change

Agriculture is among the most climate-sensitive of all economic sectors. Although agriculture constitutes a decreasing share of the economies of Central Asia, the sector continues to be critical for rural poverty reduction, employment, economic growth, and food security (Sutton et al. 2009). The commonly devastating effects of climate change are often most immediately felt by smallholders, who depend most on agriculture for their livelihoods. Climate change will most likely cause the greatest agricultural losses in the drier, warmer areas of the south where a majority of the population is concentrated. Climate change is also expected to have a significant impact on livestock production, due to decreased water access and lower feed and fodder crops (Sutton et al. 2009). The variations in average temperatures will also alter the growth and reproductive patterns of livestock. In recent years, Central Asia has experienced effects such as more extreme temperatures, erratic precipitation, and more frequent droughts. However, local awareness and action on climate change mitigation and adaptation in the region lags behind. To ensure the viability and competitiveness of agriculture and forestry and sustain rural livelihoods, it is critical to consider the impacts of climate change on the natural resources availability for agricultural production in Central Asia and implement appropriate adaptive measures (Sutton et al. 2009). Technological adaptation options for agriculture range from small-scale measures (e.g. changing timing of planting and harvesting) to large-scale systematic efforts (e.g. installation of drip irrigation facilities) (Sutton et al. 2009).

Reforms intended to enhance the management of natural resources in response to climatic changes have been largely unsuccessful and have had negative impact on the agricultural sector. Due to a limited natural resource base, increasing the output of food crop production without degrading the existing natural resource base has become a critical challenge. Any increases in production have mainly come from increases in output from land already under production (Babu and Djalalov 2006). The diversification of crops and agricultural activities is another key adaptation measure. Diversification can decrease farmers' vulnerability to climate shocks. Small farms are better positioned to diversify their production than large mono-cropped commercial farms (Sutton et al. 2009). Highly diversified farms are more resilient to climate and economic shocks, and these tend to be small but commercially oriented family farms.

For this reason, the role of small farms may become increasingly important in the agricultural economy, particularly in the face of climate risk. The development of capacity at the farm level allows for knowledge-based farming and responsive farming so that farmers can use weather forecasts to inform their production decisions (Sutton et al. 2009). Policies that encourage the use of modern agricultural technologies and practices should be implemented.

Soil (Erosion, Nutrients)

Soil degradation in Central Asia has been caused primarily by faulty irrigation patterns and increased application of fertilizer. In terms of adaptation for climate change, conservation or minimum tillage can reduce CO2 emissions from the soil, while the use of organic matter to protect field surfaces helps prevent the loss of soil moisture, therefore more effectively using water resources (Sutton et al. 2009).

Water

The countries of Central Asia have some of the largest irrigation schemes in the world, particularly to support the production of wheat and cotton. The average rainfall in these countries is 200–600 mm and evapotranspiration rates exceed 1,000 mm, which indicates that additional irrigation is necessary for sustainable crop production. Agriculture provides up to 25 per cent of GDP of these countries as illustrated by previous figures, with more than 22 million people directly or indirectly depending on irrigated agriculture (World Bank 2003). Due to climate changes, rainfall patterns in the region are becoming more erratic. The Amu Darya and Syr Darya rivers are the main sources of irrigation in the region. However, in recent years these rivers have much less water flow, leading to an uncertainty surrounding the availability of water. This uncertainty has led to water disputes that confront countries throughout the region. These disputes have the potential to disrupt agriculture and food production in the future if they are not resolved.

Following the transition era, public expenditure on agriculture significantly decreased across the region. This led to a noticeable deterioration in rural infrastructure and the availability of agricultural services. This deterioration is particularly evident in the irrigation network which was built to serve large farms and does not suit the needs of small family farms (Akramov 2011). Although some efforts have been made to revive the irrigation systems in Central Asia, the infrastructure continues to be dilapidated. During the Soviet era, the Ministry of Melioration and Water Resources had its own research institutes which studied aspects of irrigation. Following the end of the Soviet era, on-farm irrigation became a major challenge, particularly for small farms. In response, many republics replaced their production brigades with Water Use Associations (WUAs) which were formed under the ministries of agriculture. In Kyrgyzstan, WUAs took over the operation and maintenance of irrigation systems. Central government passed a law to ensure that WUAs were participatory organizations and funding was set aside for intensive capacity development programmes through designated WUA support units at the central, provincial, and district levels. Under the Water Productivity Improvement project in Tajikistan, the WUA support unit in the Osh Province provides its own extension activities to WUA members. These efforts complement those of the agricultural extension agents by providing training specifically focused on the efficient use of water in agricultural production (Kazbekov and Qureshi 2011). Institutional innovations such as WUAs have shown some progress; however these have not been fully evaluated to ensure their sustainable implementation.

Land

Agricultural land is at the centre of the reform agenda in any transition country and land reforms and farm restructuring continue to be critical components of the region's ongoing transition towards a market-oriented agricultural sector. The central goal of land reforms in transition economies is to increase the income and livelihoods of the large rural populations. During the Soviet era, agriculture was characterized by the coexistence of two farm structures: large collective and state farms (e.g. farm or agricultural enterprises) and subsistence-oriented household plots (Lerman and Sedik 2008). This dual structure embodied the formal commercial and 'private' (mostly informal) farm sectors respectively. Prior to independence, Soviet agriculture was dominated by the large state farmers, who controlled over 90 per cent of agricultural land (Lerman and Sedik 2008). The Agricultural Knowledge and Innovation Systems were designed primarily to 'assist large, public sector, collective farms in meeting pre-determined production targets for individual crop and livestock commodities' (Sutton et al. 2009). The disintegration of the traditional Soviet agricultural system, with its rigidly planned input supply, and planned purchases of outputs at fixed prices, led to a dramatic fall in agricultural production after 1991 throughout the post-Soviet countries (Deshpande 2006). Land reformation processes in Central Asia essentially created a new category of 'peasant farms' which were larger and more commercially oriented than the household plots found pre-independence (Lerman and Sedik 2008). Under the current structure, household and peasant farms are classified as family farms. On the other hand, former agriculture enterprises are referred to as corporate farms. The privatization of agricultural land along with the restructuring of formerly state-owned farms into family farms has the potential to create competition and stronger agricultural enterprises (Deshpande 2006).

Governments of the five Central Asian countries have had varied land policy responses to the fall in agricultural production. The principle aim of land reform in Tajikistan was to reallocate state-owned agricultural land among producers through the land use rights mechanism. The common goal of the many land reforms implemented in Tajikistan has been to achieve higher production levels through the efficient use of agricultural land. Reform legislation beginning in 1992, such as the Law of Land Reform (1992), established the right of every citizen to form an independent peasant (*dehkan*) farm and established the right of every member of a farm enterprise to share in non-land assets such as agricultural outputs. Land titling and registration was introduced through the Land Use Planning Law (2001) following the 'freedom to farm' principle. However, although an updated law was passed in 2008, the legislation still includes provisions that allow the government to interfere with cropping and production decisions, restricting the property rights of farmers (Lerman and Sedik 2008).

Land reform measures in Tajikistan brought agricultural production back to pre-transition levels by 2007, particularly within household plots. This growth has been driven almost entirely by the expansion of arable land accessible for household plots and *dehkan* farms (Lerman and Sedik 2008). Although land reform in Tajikistan has led to some significant achievements, these have been far fewer than in other Central Asian countries (Lerman and Sedik 2008). This is partly because central government has continued to maintain administrative control over farm decision making. In addition, the government has not considered the longer-term needs and goals of agriculture, rural development, and natural resource management. This has inhibited land reform from playing its full role in agricultural development.

In Uzbekistan, farms were under long-term land lease agreements. However, the state had a quota system for the cultivation of the dominant crops (e.g. wheat and cotton) and the fixed prices for these crops remained (Kazbekov and Qureshi 2011). In Kyrgyzstan, small farms were put under private ownership and producers had the freedom to farm (Kazbekov and Qureshi 2011).

INSTITUTIONAL REFORMS

Agricultural institutions play an important role in the rural economy. Following independence, the institutions in and around the agricultural sector underwent several structural reforms. These reforms were implemented to improve the productivity and efficiency of collective-farm-based agriculture in the region (Akramov 2011). The agricultural sector, like most others, experienced major upheaval, decline in output, and a lack of government investment for support (Sutton et al. 2009).

Markets

In addition to land reforms, creating an efficient system of markets is essential and beneficial to both producers and consumers. Following the break-up of the Soviet Union, the five Central Asian countries have aimed to liberalize their market systems. While the reduction of state control over agriculture was meant to benefit farmers, this caused disruptions in the food system by decreasing small farmers' access to credit and other inputs (Babu and Djalalov 2006). The agricultural sector has undergone a reorientation of cash crop to cereal production (Goletti and Chabot 2000). Agriculture is a crucial and growing source of foreign exchange across Central Asia.

Agricultural Research and Extension

The most salient features of the Soviet agricultural research system for Central Asia included its organized, fully funded, and overcapitalized system (Morgounov and Zuidema 2001). Across the region, there has been limited emphasis on agricultural research and investment. However, the development and application of modern agricultural technologies and practices could help to increase yields to support regional food and nutrition security. Many technologies being developed have the potential not only to increase farm productivity but also to reduce the environmental and resource costs sometimes associated with agricultural production (Meyers et al. 2012). However, increasing agricultural productivity by increasing yields will not be possible without increased investment in agricultural research. The management of agricultural research within a country, and within the Central Asia region as a whole, determines its impact as well as the uptake of agricultural technologies (Meyers et al. 2012). Despite high rates of return on agricultural investment, agriculture appears to be under persistent under-investment across the region. Recently, there has been renewed interest among countries in the region to support agricultural research and education to meet agricultural development goals (CACAARI 2009).

The major agricultural research institutions in the Soviet Union were part of the USSR's Ministry of Agriculture under the Agro-Industrial Committee which governed the All-Union Academy of Agricultural Sciences (VASKHNIL) (Kazbekov and Qureshi 2011). Both those research institutes specialized in a technical topic or regional focus. For example, the Central Asian branch was based in Tashkent, Uzbekistan. However, following independence the organization of these research institutions deteriorated. In Kazakhstan, all the existing research institutions were united to form the National Academic Center of Agricultural Research (NACAR) which became part of the Ministry of Sciences. Following a change in management structure, the strategic plans of institutions within NACAR are mandated by headquarters. Research programmes are implemented by regional research institutes which are encouraged to provide private or semi-private consultations and to provide extension services and training (Morgounov and Zuidema 2001).

All the countries in the region have reformed their agricultural research systems in different ways, with varying success. In Kyrgyzstan, the government reformed the agricultural research system to strengthen linkages between research and education. Formerly housed in the Ministry of Agriculture and Water Resources (MAWR), the new Kyrgyz Agrarian Academy is the major agricultural research and education institution in the country (Morgounov and Zuidema 2001). Uzbekistan consolidated its large regional research network into the Scientific Production Center of Agriculture (SPCA). Of the ten research programmes that SPCA is involved in, the top priority programmes include those focused on the development of technologies for efficient grain, cotton, and vegetable production (Morgounov and Zuidema 2001).

The economic transition of countries in Central Asia from centrally planned to market-oriented systems did not include the creation of agricultural extension systems (Kazbekov and Qureshi 2011). Prior to independence, the agricultural extension system was incorporated within the former *kolkhoz*, or cooperative agricultural enterprise, a system that was supported by the centralized state. Linkages between agricultural extension, research, and education were formed through specialized programmes within the ministries of agriculture and technical universities. Each *kolkhoz* had its own technical experts with specialized training that managed each large farm. Extension activities followed a commodity approach where efforts were focused on the technical, administrative, and commercial requirements for different crops (Kazbekov and Qureshi 2011).

However, this system deteriorated following independence, as each individual farmer was responsible for managing their own land, without any technical assistance. The linkages between research and agricultural practices are weak due to the lack of state support for extension (Bekchanov et al. 2009; Kazbekov and Qureshi 2011). The only extension efforts came from donors and were often not coordinated and came at too high a cost for most farmers. In addition, emerging or 'new' farmers have little to no agricultural experience, and require an immense amount of knowledge and technical advice as well as training in farm management. Presently, the only extension services available in Central Asia are project based. Many of the local extension activities are tied to non-governmental organizations (NGOs) with foreign funding. The efforts of these different initiatives are often small and duplicate the work of one another.

In Tajikistan, the main actors in the public sector involved in agricultural extension are the Ministry of Agriculture and the Ministry of Melioration and Water Resources. However, the Ministry of Agriculture has not invested in the creation of an agricultural extension system. The National Union of Dehkan Farms and Businessmen (UDFB) was established in 1996 (then as the Association of Dehkan Farms and Businessmen) as an independent, non-governmental social association. The UDFB aimed to support *dehkan* farmers by strengthening and coordinating farms and agro-entrepreneurs. However, the impact of this association has been limited by its lack of financial resources and poor management. There is a need to establish a comprehensive, sustainable, institutionally sound agricultural extension system in Tajikistan.

Although there is no single definition of 'agricultural extension', the service is meant to provide demand-based knowledge to rural men and women to enhance their capacity to undertake agricultural operations to improve productivity and livelihoods (Qamar 2002).

In Kyrgyzstan, for example, agricultural and rural advisory services are provided through a pluralistic system. Extension services are provided by several NGOs, public foundations, joint ventures, associations, cooperatives, financial credit organizations, and to a lesser extent, the private sector (Mirzabaev et al. 2009). The Ministry of Agriculture, Water Resources, and Processing Industry (MAWPRI) supports extension through policy, technical, and financial assistance to help farmers increase agricultural production. In the early 2000s, the government of Kyrgyzstan established a national rural advisory services network through financing and technical support from the World Bank, the International Fund for Agricultural Development, and the Swiss Development Corporation (Mirzabaev et al. 2009). This network, Rural Advisory Services (RAS), is an NGO that was created as part of the Kyrgyz-Swiss Agricultural Project (KSAP). RAS aims to increase agricultural production through the implementation of technical programmes in advisory services and dissemination of updated information through consultation and training (Bekchanov et al. 2009; Kazbekov and Qureshi 2011). The programme increases the capacity of Kyrgyz farmers through knowledge transfer via on-farm demonstrations and field trials. RAS is a decentralized organization which liaises with local governments and operates at the *oblast* and *rayon* levels. The role of the Kyrgyzstan government in the development and administration of agricultural extension services is increasing through the nationwide network that links farmers to six foundations operating at the district level. Although this programme has been well established, RAS has faced some challenges in implementing these activities due to several constraints. The Training and Extension System (TES) Center was founded in 1997 by Osh State University and the German Society for International Cooperation (GIZ). The focus of TES is on small farms with little resource endowment. TES provides contracts to contract field advisors to provide quality training and private advisory consultations to small farmers to enhance farmers' income derived from agriculture.

In Uzbekistan, the development of a national agricultural extension service has become a national concern. It has been observed that there is little incentive for extension among farmers producing state-ordered crops such as cotton and wheat. This is in contrast to those farmers involved in the production of fruit and vegetables, where the use of informal extension services is commonly used (Mirzabaev et al. 2009; Kazbekov and Qureshi 2011). The MAWR is responsible for providing technical advice to farmers to support the development of the agriculture and water sectors in the country. However, there is no dedicated institution for extension and advisory services. Therefore, technical advice is implicitly delivered through various public institutions and programmes such as universities, agricultural institutes, and scientific research institutes and centres. As opposed to Kyrgyzstan, there are no NGOs in Uzbekistan who are clearly focused on providing agricultural extension services. However, these organizations could play a key role in extension service delivery if the government were to develop a formal mechanism for extension (Qamar 2013).

Although each country's need for agricultural extension varies due to their diverse agro-ecological characteristics, the need for agricultural and rural advisory services to be revitalized in order to disseminate advanced information and technology is urgent. There is a need to develop an agricultural extension system that integrates the technical, financial, agronomic, and irrigation aspects of crop production in order to address the needs of farmers and reach development goals. In order to align agricultural extension services with national agricultural development priorities, a national framework is needed in each country (Bekchanov et al. 2009; Kazbekov and Qureshi 2011). A national policy framework could be used to ensure the political and financial commitment from the government and other stakeholders. Figure 35.2 presents the current organizational structure of the main actors involved in agricultural extension in Kyrgyzstan and provides an example of the type of extension system that could be formed in other countries in Central Asia.

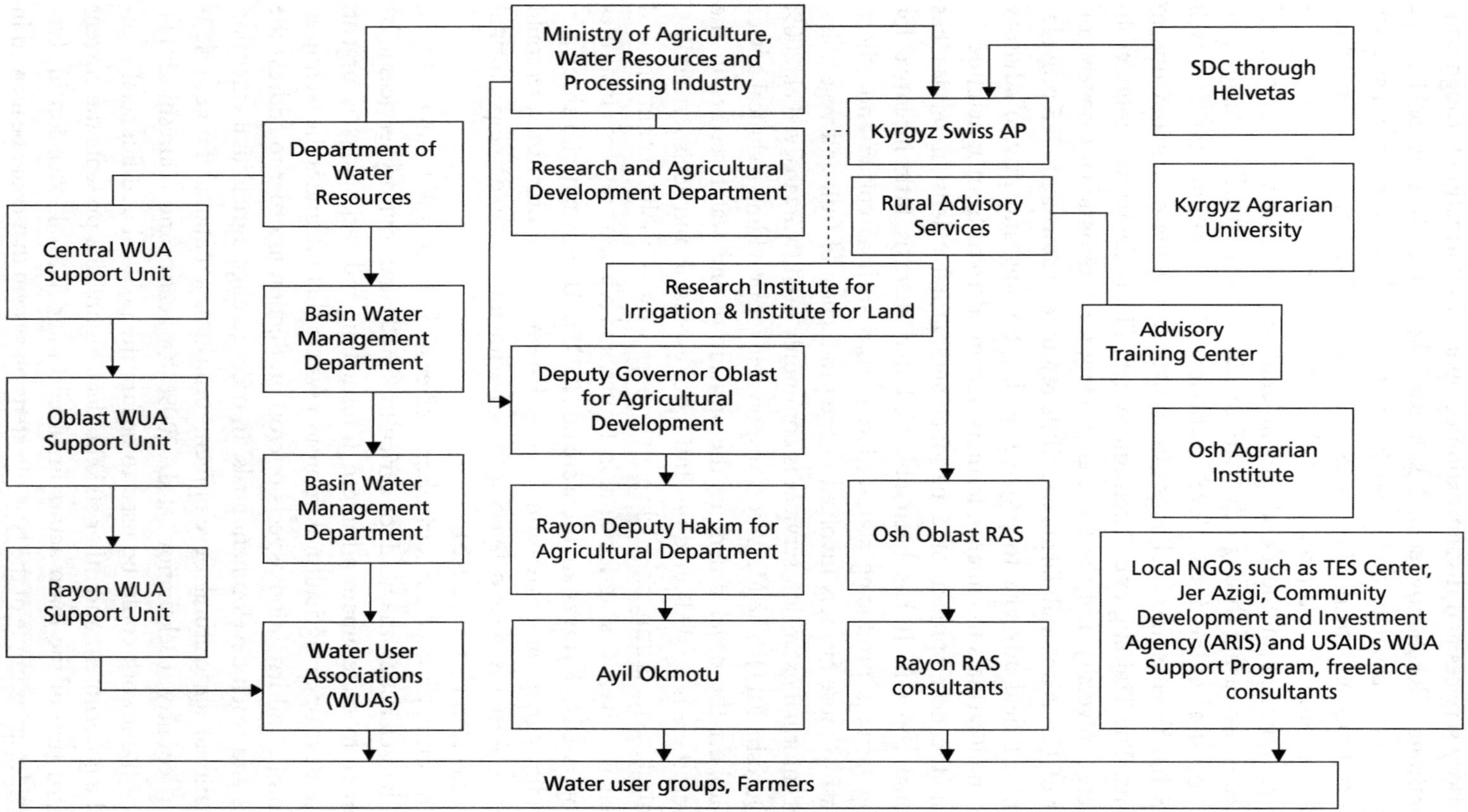

Figure 35.2 Existing agricultural extension systems in Kyrgyzstan (case from the Osh Province)

Notes: AP—agricultural program; RAS—rural advisory services; WUA—water user association.
Source: *World Development Indicators 2007, 2013, 2017* (World Bank 2017).

POLICY REFORMS

Since independence, agrarian reforms in Central Asia have included a reduction of government involvement in decision making, land reform, and farm reorganization, and the formation and strengthening of agricultural markets and institutions. These reforms are critical to supporting transformation of the agricultural sector to achieve food and nutrition security. The effectiveness of agriculture, food, and nutrition policies in Central Asian countries is key to the process of economic transition and institutional change in agricultural sectors (Cormier 2010). Policy reforms implemented in the agricultural sectors of Central Asia have had mixed results. For example, in 2002 the Government of Kazakhstan introduced an agricultural policy strategy, the National Program for Agricultural Production 2003–05. This programme increased the central agricultural budget from US$220 million in 2002 to US$407 million in 2005 (Cormier 2010). In addition, in 2003 the government initiated the Rural Development Program 2004–10 which allocated US$370 million to programmes that combat rural poverty. A majority of these programmes are implemented by state-owned enterprises such as KazAgroFinance. While these programmes illustrate the government's renewed focus on agriculture, challenges such as limited access to credit still face many small-scale agricultural producers (Cormier 2010).

Policy reforms should focus on reducing the cost of production through advanced production methods rather than increasing the amount of land under production (Babu and Djalalov 2006). Babu and Pinstrup-Andersen (2000) identified specific challenges for agricultural policy reforms in the Central Asia region. They include: stagnation in public investment in agriculture; market-driven growth relating to agro-processing and trade liberalization; institutional and capacity challenges in agriculture; agriculture-environment interaction relating to climate change and natural resource management; and the role of the rural non-farm sector.

Impact of BRICS economies—Russia and China on Central Asian food security

RUSSIA

Remittances from Russia have played an important role in the economic growth of the Central Asia region. However, the growth in global remittances will slow sharply this year due to weak economic growth in Europe and the slowdown of the Russian economy due to lower oil revenues and decreased trade. Central Asian countries have been hardest hit by this decline, due to their dependence on oil exports and/or on remittances from Russia. Roughly half of Tajikistan's total GDP is earned by remittances sent home by migrant workers, a source of revenue particularly vulnerable to the recent global recession (Babu et al. 2010). Excessive reliance on remittances intensified food and nutrition insecurity levels resulting in increased vulnerability of households in Tajikistan (Akramov and Shreedhar 2012).

Due to Kazakhstan's close economic relationship with Russia and its heavy dependency on oil exports (an estimated 69 per cent of exports in 2014), Kazakhstan has been the hardest hit in the region due to the global dip in oil prices (Economist Intelligence Unit 2015; Schenkkan 2015).

CHINA

China is a key trade partner for Central Asia, specifically as an export market. Central Asian exports to China primarily consist of cotton from Uzbekistan as it is estimated that one-third of Uzbek cotton exports go to China (Mogilevskii and Akramov 2014). Exports from China to Central Asia include meat, fruit, and prepared foods. With the planned agreement between Kyrgyzstan and Tajikistan through a customs union (CU), these countries may experience a decline in agri-food imports from China due to higher import tariffs. Both countries might also experience increases in agri-food exports to Kazakhstan and Russia due to the eventual elimination of customs borders for Kyrgyzstan. With the planned accession of Kyrgyzstan and Tajikistan to the CU, one can expect modest effects for these countries. These include a decline in agri-food imports from China and the EU due to higher import tariffs (Mogilevskii and Akramov 2014).

INDIA

Compared to other BRICS countries, Central Asia offers a relatively untapped market for Indian consumer goods. Exploring this market is crucial since Indian countries are constrained to choose between highly priced imported Western products and cheap but lower-quality Chinese manufactured goods. India's tea and pharmaceutical industries are already in the Central Asian market (Gulshan 2010). The most significant form of trade sought by India is in energy resources, particularly oil, natural gas, and hydroelectricity to provide for its energy security. In 2011 India was the fourth largest oil importer in the world, and the sixth largest liquid natural gas (LNG) importer with consumption growing at an annual rate of 10 per cent between 2001 and 2011. Since Kazakhstan has the eleventh highest oil reserves in the world, Turkmenistan, Kazakhstan, and Uzbekistan being rich in natural gas, and Tajikistan and Kyrgyzstan having large but relatively unexploited hydropower potential (CIA World Factbook 2011), establishment of this trade relationship could increase growth for these Central Asian countries (Lee and Gill 2015).

BRICS AND AGRICULTURAL DEVELOPMENT IN CENTRAL ASIA

The emergence of BRICS countries is reshaping the role of developing countries in the global economy, particularly concerning agricultural trade. BRICS countries have become new drivers of growth in developing countries such as those in Central Asia (IMF 2011). As the share of BRICS countries in world trade continues to rise, it is important to understand the effect of these countries on agricultural and food trades. The gravity model has become known as the workhorse of international trade analysis. This model has shown that growth in a BRICS country will lead to increased economic growth in the countries around it, as shown in its ability to explain Turkey's imports from BRICS countries (Dinçer 2014). This has important implications for Central Asia as it is located between three BRICS countries (Russia, China, and India). For this reason, it is important to open regional trade between the five countries in Central Asia to increase food and nutrition security. This would allow the countries to become more competitive by easing transport of the wide variety of agricultural commodities produced across the region. Increased regional trade would then allow the countries in Central Asia to tap into the surrounding markets of BRICS countries, leading to higher agricultural and economic growth. For example, India is a potential market for horticultural goods, particularly fruits and nuts. India currently imports most of its fruit, such as apples from Australia. However, removing barriers to trade in Central Asia would increase agricultural trade flows between these countries and the large South Asian market.

The five countries in Central Asia share relatively common problems of and approaches to agricultural productivity and food security. Technical cooperation, such as information sharing between agricultural researchers and policymakers, could help increase agricultural productivity in Central Asia through the sharing of advanced technologies and production practices. Exchanging technical assistance between these countries can help form collective responses to agricultural development challenges through the sharing of best practice.

To achieve long-term sustainable food security, Central Asian economies need to significantly improve both land and labour productivity in the agricultural sector. Transformation of the agricultural sector in Central Asia will directly drive poverty reduction by increasing agricultural productivity, thereby increasing farm incomes and reducing the prevalence of rural poverty. Indirectly, agricultural transformation and growth will reduce poverty through labour markets and reducing food prices.

Conclusion

In this chapter, we looked at the food and nutrition challenges faced by Central Asian economies in the context of the technological, institutional, and policy reforms implemented in these countries in the last twenty-five years and in the context of their interaction with BRICS and other emerging economies. While this chapter addresses selective challenges facing the food, agricultural, and natural resource sectors in Central Asia, it argues that to address these challenges, information and research gaps must be addressed, requiring increased capacity at the individual and institutional levels to set research and policy priorities. We categorize them in terms of knowledge gaps, research gaps, and the specific policy options.

The knowledge gaps that need to be addressed for speeding up agricultural transformation in the Central Asia region and thereby achieving food and nutrition security range from the individual capacity of farmers and farming communities to the policy-level evidence on what works and why. At the farmer level, increased information for the application of modern techniques coupled with the improved inputs needed would help in increasing the productivity of the farmers in the region. In this context, linking national research systems to contribute to context-specific technological innovations and connecting them with viable extension and rural advisory services are paramount needs. In addition, institutional innovation in the context of identifying domestic, regional, and global markets of food and agriculture are needed to support agricultural development. Existing institutions should be strengthened and reformed, and their roles redefined (Kazbekov and Qureshi 2011).

As most farmers in Central Asia have limited capacity for farm management, innovation that supports farmers' organizations would help to increase these skills and therefore increase the efficiency of agricultural production. All the countries have the necessary institutions to create an extension network (e.g. association of farmers in Tajikistan and Uzbekistan, or agricultural research and education coordination units in Kyrgyzstan, Tajikistan, and Uzbekistan) (Kazbekov and Qureshi 2011). However, capacity to organize and manage these large systems at the government level is lacking. To ensure ownership of the agricultural research and extension system, the state should play the role of mediator and facilitator for the proposed changes (Kazbekov and Qureshi 2011). This will require significant investment in the organizational and management capacity of the agricultural ministry. There is an urgent need for governments of Central Asia to align research priorities with national short- and long-term agricultural development goals. The strategy must consider future demand for agricultural research as reflected in emerging local and international markets and be conditioned by the optimal utilization of the human, financial, and physical resources available. Filling information and capacity gaps for food security research and analysis will enable governments to more clearly define agricultural research priorities.

Through Eurasian food policy case studies, Pinstrup-Andersen et al. (2016) provide an innovative mechanism to build the capacity of young students. By providing students with social entrepreneurial skills that are based on thematic knowledge of food policy and prompting debate of the pros and cons of various policy options, they make students the problem solvers thus resulting in a cadre of food policy professionals who can address real-world policy problems (Babu 2017).

It is recommended that countries in Central Asia increase agricultural expenditure (Babu et al. 2010). These investments could be put primarily towards the creation of sustainable, formal extension systems. This investment will help to achieve food and nutrition security in the region by increasing agricultural productivity and production through the application of modern technologies and practices. Similarly, it is recommended that governments of Central Asia strengthen the linkages between agricultural education, research, and extension. The effective design and implementation of climate change policies should take priority as fluctuations in rainfall and temperature threaten food production and security in the region. Policies and programmes that increase regional trade and remove restrictions should be put in place as a strategy for increased agricultural development. Policies that increase the effective management of land and natural resources should also be put in place. Capacity constraints greatly impede the ability of Central Asian governments to improve food security for the most vulnerable populations (Babu et al. 2010). Capacity strengthening in data collection and analysis, and policy design and implementation would greatly facilitate strategy development processes for enhancing food security in Central Asia.

REFERENCES

Akramov, K.T. (2011). 'International food prices, agricultural transformation, and food security in Central Asia', *Development in Practice* 24/4–5: 741–54.

Akramov, K.T. and Shreedhar, G. (2012). 'Economic development, external shocks, and food security in Tajikistan'. IFPRI Discussion Paper 01163. Washington, DC: International Food Policy Research Institute.

ADB (Asian Development Bank) (2016). *Key Indicators for Asia and Pacific 2016*. Available at www.adb.org/publications/key-indicators-asia-and-pacific-2016, accessed 20 August 2019.

Babu, S.C. (2017). 'Book review for food security in Eurasia: case studies'. *Food Security Journal* 9: 1133. Available at https://doi.org/10.1007/s12571-017-0723-x, accessed 20 August 2019.

Babu, S.C. and Djalalov, S. (eds) (2006). *Policy Reforms and Agriculture Development in Central Asia*. New York: Springer.

Babu, S.C. and Pinstrup-Andersen, P. (2000). 'Achieving food security in Central Asia: current challenges and policy research needs', *Food Policy* 25/6: 629–35.

Babu, S.C. and Tashmatov, A. (2000). 'Emerging issues and challenges for attaining food security in Central Asia', in S. Babu and A. Tashmatov (eds) *Food Policy Reforms in Central Asia: Setting the Research Priorities*. Washington, DC: International Food Policy Research Institute, 39–44.

Babu, S.C., Akramov, K.T., and Van Rheenen, T. (2010). 'Food security in Central Asia: past achievements and future challenges'. Presentation at the Central Asia Meeting, 3 February, Bishkek, Kyrgyzstan.

Bekchanov, M.B., Kan, E., and Lamers, J.P.A. (2009). 'Options of agricultural extension provision for rural development in Central Asia transition economies: the case of Uzbekistan'. Paper presented at 5th Annual Conference Proceedings for Sustainable Development, 14 May, Westminster International University, Tashkent.

CACAARI (Central Asia and the Caucasus Association of Agricultural Research Institutions) (2009). 'Key issues in agricultural research for development in Central Asia and the Caucasus'. Available at www.cacaari.org/filesarchive/reports/GCARD_CAC_Final_Report_En1.pdf, accessed 5 October 2018.

Christmann, S. and Aw-Hassan, A. (2010). 'New topics and high time pressure: climate change challenges agricultural research in Central Asia and the Caucasus'. Paper presented at Food Security and Climate Change in the Dry Areas: Proceedings of an International Conference, 1–4 February, Amman, Jordan.

CIA World Factbook (2011). 'Country comparison: oil—proved reserves', 1 January; See British Petroleum, *Statistical Review of World Energy*, June 2012: 20; Sarma (2010: 22). Available at www.cia.gov/library/publications/download/download-2011/, accessed 23 January 2020.

Cormier, K. (2010). 'Central Asia's changing agricultural sectors: a comparative analysis of transforming commercial practices', *Problems of Post-Communism* 57/6: 46–54.

Deshpande, R. (2006). 'Land reform and farm restructuring in Central Asia: progress and challenges ahead', in S.C. Babu and S. Djalalov (eds) *Policy Reforms and Agriculture Development in Central Asia*. New York: Springer, 131.

Dinçer, G. (2014). 'Turkey's rising imports from BRICS: a gravity model approach'. Paper presented at Proceedings of the New York State Economics Association 67th Annual Conference. 10–11 October, Siena College, Albany, NY. Available at https://nyseconomicsassociation.org/content/proceedings/2014/nysea_proceedings_2014.pdf, accessed 29 April 2019.

Economist Intelligence Unit (2015). 'Industries in 2015: The Economist Intelligence Unit's outlook for six key industry sectors for the year ahead'. Available at www.eiu.com/public/topical_report.aspx?campaignid=Industries2015, accessed 20 August 2019.

Goletti, F. and Chabot, P. (2000). 'Food policy research for improving the reform of agricultural input and output markets in Central Asia', in S. Babu and A. Tashmatov (eds) *Food Policy Reforms in Central Asia: Setting the Research Priorities*. Washington, DC: International Food Policy Research Institute, 45–69.

Gulshan, S. (2010). 'Regional economic linkages', in J. Nirmala (ed.) *Reconnecting India and Central Asia Emerging Security and Economic Dimensions*. Central Asia-Caucasus Institute & Silk Road Studies Program. Available at www.silkroadstudies.org/resources/pdf/Monographs/1004Joshi-VII-Linkages.pdf, accessed 29 April 2019.

IMF (International Monetary Fund) (2011). *New Growth Drivers for Low-Income Countries: The Role of BRICs*. Washington, DC: IMF.

Kazbekov, J. and Qureshi, A.S. (2011). 'Agricultural extension in Central Asia: existing strategies and future needs'. IWMI Working Paper 145. Colombo, Sri Lanka: International Water Management Institute.

Lee, L. and Gill, G. (2015). 'India, Central Asia and the Eurasian Union: a new ballgame?', *India Quarterly* 71/2: 110–25.

Lerman, Z. and Sedik, D.J. (2008). 'The economic effects of land reform in Central Asia: the case of Tajikistan'. Discussion Paper No. 16–08. Jerusalem: The Hebrew University of Jerusalem.

Lerman, Z. and Sedik, D.J. (2009). 'Sources of agricultural productivity growth in Central Asia'. Paper prepared for the AAEA and ACCI Joint Annual Meeting, 26–9 July, Milwaukee, WI.

Meyers, W.H., Ziolkowska, J.R., Tothova, M., and Goychuk, K. (2012). *Issues Affecting the Future of Agriculture and Food Security for Europe and Central Asia*. Policy Studies on Rural Transition No. 2012–3. Rome: Food and Agriculture Organization of the United Nations.

Mirzabaev A., Martius, C., Livinets, S., Nichterlein, K., and Apasov, R. (2009). *Assessment of Information and Communication Needs of Institutions and Stakeholders of the National Agricultural Research and Extension System of Kyrgyzstan*. Tashkent, Uzbekistan: International Center for Agricultural Research in the Dry Areas.

Mogilevskii, R. and Akramov, K. (2014). 'Trade in agricultural and food products in Central Asia'. Working Paper No. 27. Bishkek, Kyrgyzstan: University of Central Asia.

Morgounov, A. and Zuidema, L. (2001). *The Legacy of the Soviet Agricultural Research System for the Republics of Central Asia and the Caucuses*. Research Report No. 20. The Hague: International Service for National Agriculture Research (ISNAR).

Peyrouse, S. (2009). 'The multiple paradoxes of the agriculture issue in Central Asia'. EUCAM Working Paper No. 06. Brussels: Europe-Central Asia Monitoring.

Pinstrup-Andersen, P. (2017). *Suggested Priorities for Policy Research to Improve Food Security and Nutrition in Eurasia*. Washington, DC: The Eurasian Center for Food Security and the World Bank.

Pinstrup-Andersen, P., Shoba, S.A., Vasenev, I.I, Koshelev, V.M., and Sorkin, P.P. (eds) (2016). *Food Security in Eurasia: Case Studies*. Moscow: Eurasian Center for Food Security. (ISBN 978-5-9618-0077-7).

Pomfret, R. (2014). 'Trade costs and agricultural trade in Central Asia'. Discussion Paper No. 146. Halle Saale, Germany: Leibniz Institute of Agricultural Development in Transition Economies.

Qamar, M.K. (2002). 'Global trends in agricultural extension: challenges facing Asia and the Pacific Region'. Paper presented at the FAO Regional Expert Consultation on Agricultural Extension, Research-Extension-Farmer Interface and Technology Transfer, in Bangkok, 16–19 July, Thailand. Rome: Research, Extension, and Training Division. Sustainable Development Department, FAO.

Qamar, M.K. (2013). *Worldwide Extension Studies: Central Asia*. Lindau: Global Forum for Rural Advisory Services. Available at www.g-fras.org/en/world-wide-extension-study/97-world-wide-extension-study/asia/central-asia/328-uzbekistan.html, accessed 5 October 2018.

Schenkkan, N. (2015). 'Impact of the economic crisis in Russia on Central Asia', *Russian Analytical Digest* 165: 3–6.

Sutton, W.R., Block, R.I., and Srivastava, J. (2009). *Adaptation to Climate Change in Central Asia Agriculture*. Washington, DC: World Bank.

Timmer, P. (2014). *Food Security and Food Scarcity*. Philadelphia, PA: University of Pennsylvania Press.

World Bank (2003). *Irrigation in Central Asia: Social, Economic, and Environmental Considerations*. Washington, DC: World Bank.

World Bank (2017). *World Development Indicators 2007, 2013, 2017*. Washington, DC: World Bank. Available at http://databank.worldbank.org/data/views/variableSelection/selectvariables.aspx?source=world-development-indicators, accessed 5 October 2018.

Part VI
Governance Issues

36 Humane global governance—an area for the future where progress inches forward

Richard Jolly

Introduction

The failures and weaknesses of global governance in the twenty-first century 'should keep us awake at night'. Some even think that measures to strengthen global governance are yesterday's dream; all this in spite of the consequences of the 2008 global recession being worse than the Great Recession of the 1930s. The Covid19 pandemic should be a call for global governance reform.

Global governance

Proposals for strengthening global governance are overwhelmingly economic, focused on capturing the externalities lost in a world of global free markets, dominated by transnational corporations operating in a context where free movement of capital and finance overwhelms poorer and weaker countries and, indeed, often richer and stronger ones too. Yet efforts to strengthen global governance, even modest ones of strengthening regulation and ensuring greater coherence, fall by the wayside. Most of the actions and proposals in response to the 2008 global crisis were weak and short lived, though the stimulus measures agreed at the 2009 G20 meeting had positive effects, notably on raising economic growth rates in 2010, before the return to financial orthodoxy, austerity, and quantitative easing took centre stage.

In this context, calls for a broader approach to global governance may seem little more than whistling in the dark, so much so that many analysts hesitate even to suggest rethinking. A few however, like Richard Falk, David Held, and Rorden Wilkinson have put a brave foot forward and sketched what might be involved. Moreover the growing inadequacies and problems of the status quo—financial instabilities, surging migration, pandemics of Ebola and other transmissible diseases, cyber-insecurities, and a host of other problems which cross borders without respect to national sovereignty—suggest to

Richard Jolly, *Humane global governance—an area for the future where progress inches forward* In: *Handbook of BRICS and Emerging Economies*. Edited by: P.B. Anand, Shailaja Fennell, and Flavio Comim, Oxford University Press (2021).
DOI: 10.1093/oso/9780198827535.003.0036

the more optimistic analysts and leaders, that some limits to global laissez-faire may soon be rediscovered.

The purpose of this note is to suggest that the goal of economic efficiency and capturing externalities is too limited for the twenty-first century. As the world gets richer and economic growth reaches ever wider parts of the world, broader goals are required—sustainability in relation to climate change, stability in finance and financial flows, international measures to cope with the extremes of sovereign debts when they have become unpayable—and others. Equally important, and for many of us more so, are the goals of building a more humane world where hunger and malnutrition, lack of shelter and homelessness, children without education and basic health—and much else—evoke international help when needs exceed the capacities of poorer countries to provide for them. This could be a world of human rights, ensured on a universal basis.

Although still something of a dream, the international system has recognized this ambition in the form of the SDGs (Sustainable Development Goals), agreed by the UN's General Assembly in September 2015. These build on the Universal Declaration of Human Rights and much else debated and agreed internationally over the last seventy years. But this time, the goals have arisen through a widespread process of consultation and debate, involving virtually every country and many hundreds of non-government groups within them.

Some have already been inclined to dismiss the SDGs and the process behind them as impotent and irrelevant. This pessimistic view ignores the record of the Millennium Development Goals (MDGs) and the fifty or so global goals agreed by the UN between 1960 and 2000. The record of achievement of these goals was far from perfect but considerably better than many people seem to think—in terms of the number of countries that made substantial progress along the lines of the global goals and quantitatively fulfilled many of the original targets.

The role of international institutions focusing on human goals and supporting their achievement needs was also an important part of the record and needs to be recognized. The World Health Organization (WHO) in 1966 adopted a 10-year goal for the eradication of smallpox—achieved in 1977 and certified in 1980. At the cost of US $300 million, at the time equivalent to the cost of three fighter bombers, smallpox was eradicated. Smallpox had been a scourge of mankind almost since the beginning of time (more precisely since the population of urban centres reached sufficient size for interpersonal transmission to be self-sustaining) and in the 1960s was killing 2 million persons a year and disfiguring millions more. We hope that those wanting to weaken WHO take note of this history. Since the 1960s, the World Food Programme (WFP) has been providing food aid until it is now the world's largest humanitarian agency at the forefront of UN efforts to provide relief in emergency situations in many countries and development support in the form of school feeding and other programmes in many countries. All these are a form of humane global governance.

UNICEF, the UN Children's Fund has since its beginning in 1946 demonstrated a capacity for global leadership for children and for mobilizing country-by-country support for action to tackle the basic needs of children—reducing child mortality, improving child nutrition, raising school enrolments, and encouraging and supporting countries to develop the special services needed for children with special needs. This also can be seen as an example of humane global governance.

UNICEF experience can be used to explain more fully the links between global leadership and national and regional action, of the sort which is almost always involved in global governance. In 1978, UNICEF mobilized worldwide attention to the broader needs of children by declaring the Year of the Child and encouraging and supporting a wide range of activities, country by country. In 1982, UNICEF built on this by launching a child survival and development revolution, focused on expansion and universal coverage country by country of basic preventive health actions such as immunization, oral rehydration (to counteract the killing effects of diarrhoea), the encouragement of breastfeeding and supplementary feeding of children under 5 years, monitoring the growth of under-5s, and other such measures. There was worldwide expansion and some seventy countries achieved or exceeded the goal of 80 per cent coverage of immunization by 1990, with most other countries expanding immunization considerably. Supporting actions had also greatly increased. The result was a reduction in child deaths—by an estimated 3 million a year—25 million over 1980–95. Improvements have continued since, triggering other benefits, such as lowering birth rates as mothers and fathers can now anticipate children surviving to adulthood and being able to support their parents in older age.

It is important to stress that most of this action was by countries themselves, with support and encouragement from UNICEF (and WHO) but never with the international agencies either doing the work or even supporting financially more than a fraction of it. In this sense, it was humane global governance in action, with international action to set norms, encourage action, ensure coordination, assist monitoring, and provide global reporting and calls for further action.

Most of these global activities were brought together in the World Summit for Children held in the UN in 1990, which not only reviewed progress over the 1980s but set new goals for the 1990s. The World Summit was the first global summit ever held, attended by seventy-one heads of state or government, focused on assessing the needs and possibilities of children and to set future goals. Children are quintessentially a humane concern, raising issues far beyond economic and financial dimensions, important as the latter ones may be. And once the idea of holding a global summit for children had been demonstrated as a success, other global summits were organized: The Earth Summit in Rio (1992), the World Summit for Social Development in Copenhagen (1995), and the Millennium Summit in New York (2000).

A second point to emphasize is that UNICEF's role in humane global governance was and is far more than setting norms and goals, important as these are. At country level, UNICEF has helped countries prepare national plans of action (NPAs) for implementing the goals, usually based on a detailed situation analysis as the basis for five-year plans for children. The NPAs have identified national budgetary requirements as well as support needed from UNICEF and donors, though the latter are only a minor part of total needs.

The NPAs and country programmes were put to the UNICEF board for approval. These dimensions parallel those of the Bretton Woods institutions (BWI), though in the case of UNICEF were primarily human in focus, with the economic elements in support of human and social goals.

Many UN agencies now have something of this process—though in many respects UNICEF's is stronger and has been in place much longer—essentially since the 1970s. The key elements in UNICEF's institutional structure embody the following: a strong ethical and practical commitment to children throughout the organization, in accordance with international norms and the Convention on the Rights of the Child; a decentralized structure embodying localized authority which encourages country-focused initiatives led by UNICEF representatives in 150 developing countries and national committees in thirty-six developed countries; a long-standing record of creativity and pioneering innovation at country and regional levels as well as at headquarters; structures and procedures for learning from experience, from both countries and other organizations, including other parts of the UN; commitment to partnerships, especially with other groups and organizations working for children, though at the same time resisting formal integration or coordination under the leadership of others; a consistent focus on practical action and achieving results.

Perhaps less emphasized within the UN are procedures for appointment and promotion which have ensured that persons of competence and potential are in leadership positions, while indirectly ensuring balance at senior levels of impartiality between regions and nationalities without rigid quotas.

Although often not seen as such, these actions add up to humane global governance, defined as action towards human objectives and human rights. Even over the last three decades, when economic global governance has been driven and greatly extended by the major economic powers often with a focus on narrow economic objectives and the procedures and actions of the BWIs and the World Trade Organization (WTO), UNICEF, WHO, and WFP, other parts of the UN have continued with a more humane form of global governance.

Ironically, these forms of global action and humane governance have lost ground in the last decade or so to privately funded initiatives, for instance through the activities of GAVI (the Vaccine Alliance), GAIN (the Global Alliance for Improved Nutrition), and the Gates Foundation. Such activities have been better funded, often focused on specific objectives, and arguably sometimes more cost-effective. But by being private, they lack the legitimacy and universality of the UN and lack the country representation and coverage of the UN. These weaknesses could be mitigated if there were explicit commitments from the private groups to work within the frame of decisions taken within the UN and for these funds and donors to ensure more core support for the UN agencies.

Can such actions add up to a humanizing of global governance over the next half century? I would argue that this is both necessary and possible, providing the major powers and the electorates in their countries recognize the need for strengthening humane global governance. Just as within countries, a mixed economy is possible as a means of ensuring results which national markets by themselves alone cannot achieve, so internationally a mixed economy is needed, giving weight to human objectives in addition to objectives of economic efficiency and economic growth. Indeed, measures of sustainable development, equity within and between countries will require international and regional actions and support, institutional regulation, and monitoring as well as national measures.

Conclusion

These experiences can be seen as laying the foundations for humane global governance and demonstrating the possibilities for strengthening in the years ahead; but a core of priority actions are needed, such as:

1. strengthening a humane governance approach in all agencies of the UN, towards the goals of the SDGs, with priorities set by the country for international support for poverty reduction, greater equality, sustainability, and human rights;
2. achieving closer collaboration between the BWIs and the UN, with the former formally recognizing the need for human development and economic approaches which go beyond neoliberal orthodoxy;
3. prioritizing attention to peace-making, peace building, development, and institutional reconstruction in countries currently torn by conflict and civil war. The UN has considerable experience for such actions and a number of successes, but for which it needs sustained political and financial support;
4. improving UN effectiveness and accountability to encourage increases in core support for the mainstream UN funds and specialized agencies, working collaboratively towards country led support;
5. strengthening SDG monitoring, to broaden links with human development approaches and priorities, including human rights fulfilment, with attention to monitoring changes in urban–rural and regional inequalities;
6. ensuring that improved country-focused data and monitoring is channelled in real time to regional and global centres, thus making possible real time global monitoring and responsive global action and support.

The toll of the Covid19 pandemic could have been much worse without WHO efforts and information sharing. Elements of a humane global governance are visible but these need to be further nurtured and sustained through cooperation.

37 Governing a complex global financial system in the age of global instabilities and BRICS

Promoting global financial stability and growth with equity

Haider A. Khan*

Introduction

The main purpose of this chapter is to offer an evolutionary framework within a dynamic complex systems perspective for analysing the prospects for creating global and regional structures of financial governance that can promote stability, growth, and equity. The general theory and the model can be applied to the entire global system. However, the uneven development of this system is taken seriously. To this end, developments in Asia, Latin America, and BRICS receive special attention. Our analytical framework is erected against the background of recent financial crises, in order to present the most reasonable justification for the creation of both a modified Keynesian global financial architecture (KGFA) with similar Keynesian regional financial architectures (KRFAs) along with BRICS-like multi-regional financial architectures after the failures of global financial governance and global economic crises in the twenty-first century so far.

THE NEED FOR THE CREATION OF BRICS-LIKE MULTI-REGIONAL FINANCIAL ARCHITECTURES

Despite initial bafflement as the world economy was hit by the biggest financial crisis since the Great Depression, there is now broad agreement on the underlying causes of the first global financial crisis of the twenty-first century: banks and financial institutions indulged in excessive leverage and excessive risk-taking while regulators did not provide an adequate regulatory framework. In the US, the proximate causes also included the Fed policy under Alan Greenspan of supporting an artificial housing boom after the bursting of the stock market bubble through low interest rates and lax regulations in the housing

Haider A. Khan, *Governing a complex global financial system in the age of global instabilities and BRICs: Promoting global financial stability and growth with equity* In: *Handbook of BRICS and Emerging Economies.* Edited by: P.B. Anand, Shailaja Fennell, and Flavio Comim,
Oxford University Press (2021).
DOI: 10.1093/oso/9780198827535.003.0037

Table 37.1 Key features of Basel I and II

Key Features	Basel I	Basel II
Capital Adequacy Requirements (CAR)	Tier I Capital Requirements: Equity capital and disclosed reserves had to be held at 4% of risk weighted assets Tier II Capital Requirements: Miscellaneous debt held at 8%—Tier I holdings	Tier I & II requirements were not changed Assets of holding companies were included in requirements of banks Capital Reserves = 8% * Risk Weighted Assets + Operational Risk Reserves + Market Risk Reserves
Risk weighting	Categories of risk weights: 0%—included cash, sovereign debt held in domestic currency, OECD debt 20%—development bank debt, OECD bank debt, short term non-OECD debt 50%—mortgage debt 100%—private sector debt	Sovereign debt was weighted according to its credit rating Bank debt could be indexed to sovereign debt ratings or to their specific ratings Private corporate debt rated junk was weighted at 150% Home mortgages were risk-weighted at 35%; corporate mortgages 100%
Other features	Promoted the harmonizing of national regulations Allowed national regulatory specificities into capital requirements	Banks could choose between three approaches to risk weighting: Standardized Approach Internal Ratings (IRB) Approach Advanced IRB Approach Operational risk and market risk was separated from credit risk. Bank disclosures were made public. Regulators were given additional powers: Creating capital buffers requirements Intervene into internal risk modelling

Source: Documents of the Basel Committee on Banking Supervision, BIS. Available at https://www.bis.org/publ/bcbsca.htm, accessed 6 August 2019).

and financial sectors in particular. Through various channels, the crisis was transmitted to other sectors of the economy and to nations across the world, leading to significant human development impacts on the poor and vulnerable. As the 'Stiglitz Commission report' (the Report of the Commission of Experts of the President of the United Nations General Assembly on Reforms of the International Monetary and Financial System), among other sources, emphasizes, the deeper causes relate to historic reversal of post-depression checks and balances of national and global economic governance.

Against this backdrop, there have been many calls for change in the global financial and economic governance architecture that would lead to a more stable and less risky international financial system (see Table 37.1). For example, internationally, there is momentum around Basel III, a package of proposals to strengthen global capital and liquidity regulations. The United States government and various EU countries had introduced legislation aimed at reforming financial institutions under their jurisdiction.

Among the IFIs, the IMF has played a prominent role through several measures including the establishment of flexible credit lines, changes in conditions attached to emergency funding, and, more recently, in its interventions to support the Eurozone economies. At the same time, several regional arrangements, such as currency swap lines, have also been put in place. Whether global or regional mechanisms are more useful in preventing financial contagion and to what extent these complement each other, remain open questions.

Particularly in this changing context in a complex global economic system, it is significant that the leaders of BRICS countries (i.e. Brazil, the Russian Federation, India, China, and South Africa) approved in March 2013, during their meeting in Durban, the creation of a new Development Bank to finance investment in infrastructure and more sustainable development in BRICS and other emerging and developing countries. As the March 2013 Durban Summit Declaration and Action Plan states:

> In March 2012 we directed our Finance Ministers to examine the feasibility and viability of setting up a New Development Bank for mobilising resources for infrastructure and sustainable development projects in BRICS and other emerging economies and developing countries, to supplement the existing efforts of multilateral and regional financial institutions for global growth and development . . . We have agreed to establish the New Development Bank. The initial contribution to the Bank should be substantial and sufficient for the Bank to be effective in financing infrastructure (BRICS 2013: para 9).[1]

This chapter documents the nature and scope of these principal changes still evolving in the global economic governance system, and analyses their consequences for developing countries in particular. The role of BRICS initiatives is seen in this systemic context. While recognizing that the capitalization is still insufficient and modus operandi are not yet completely laid out, it can be argued that in a complex system, small initiatives can lead to large changes in the future in the entire system. But this is not foreordained. In a related way, this chapter also explores the important policy space for development issues by exploring analytically the conditions for their most effective responses. Without being exhaustive, the developments covered include:

- BASEL III reforms for more stringent capital requirements and their implications for the developing world in particular;
- the IMF's response to recent and emerging global economic and challenges, and the evolving nature of its role;
- the most appropriate role of regional arrangements in financial stabilization, based on experiences with such arrangements in this and prior episodes of crisis;

[1] See also E. Conway-Smith (2013). Developing nations to meet at the BRIC beach party in South Africa. *Global Post*. Available at www.globalpost.com/dispatch/news/regions/africa/south-africa/130323/developing-nations-meet-bric-summit-durban, accessed 7 October 2018.

Economic Times (2013). BRICS may agree on 100bn currency fund during G20 meeting. Available at https://economictimes.indiatimes.com/news/economy/finance/brics-may-agree-on-100-bn-currency-fund-during-g20-summit/articleshow/22182518.cms?from=mdr, accessed 8 August 2019.

Griffith-Jones, S. (2011). South–South financial cooperation. Background Paper No 2 to UNCTAD's *Least Developed Countries Report, 2011*. Available at https://pdfs.semanticscholar.org/c424/1dba72a86e0821aff712ebd3d3556fae4bab.pdf, accessed 7 October 2018.

- in particular the roles of regional financial arrangements in Asia and the BRICS facilities announced in July 2014 and analysed as parts of the emerging RFA structures that could lead to a more efficient and equitable financing for development.

The methodological approach adopted here is a type of *constructivist* and *evolutionary* analysis of our complex international economic system and political economy. The technical work on aspects of these dynamic complex adaptive economic systems (DCAES) has been discussed in Khan (2004, 2011) and Lin et al. (2008) among other sources. The institutions I discuss and the alternatives I propose here are all path dependent, but in a non-deterministic manner. Social practices based on collectively held ideas by both elite and non-elite groups can matter in crucial ways. However, given the structural aspects of global financial and economic systems and the conflicting ideas and norms, there are serious contradictions at all levels of the system. Recognition of such contradictions and conflicts at both ideational and material levels dialectically forms the 'critical' part of my constructivist adaptive complex systems approach (Khan 2004, 2006, 2011).[2]

In analysing the above in the context of developing countries (DCs) in particular, the following features of DCs are highlighted among others:

a. DCs have fewer resources for coping with financial crises, particularly one which is global in its scope.
b. Most DCs lack automatic stabilizers due to the embryonic nature of their fiscal and social protection systems.
c. They have limited borrowing ability in international financial markets and this limits their ability to pursue countercyclical policies.
d. These threats are often exacerbated by global financial market integration and free trade agreements (FTAs) and bilateral investment treaties (BITs). Many World Trade Organization (WTO) commitments also adversely affect DCs. International Monetary Fund (IMF) pro-cyclical structural adjustment policies can also constrict the policy space.

The social and political construction of global and regional financial arrangements also depends critically on a supporting structure of complementary institutional network (CIN), norms, ideas, and practices. Global financial architecture (GFA) and regional financial architecture (RFA) both depend on their respective CIN within a global system of nation states and international organizations. Given the real interdependence within the system, all actors have some stake in sustained growth and stability with equity. At the same time part of the complexity of the global financial system arises from various contradictions and asymmetries in the system itself. Thus the central argument of this

[2] At the same time corporate actors are legitimate under some conditions. In this my analysis is similar to Wendt's (1987, 1999) constructivist approach which does not contradict a deep and sophisticated version of Scientific Realism. Indeed, both Wendt and I build upon a scientific realist ontology avoiding narrow determinism. See also Khan (2003a, 2003b, 2008c), Best (2010), Blyth (2002), and Abdelal (2007).

chapter is that sustainable policies at the national level require a supporting network of GFA and RFAs that go some distance towards resolving the key issues arising from such contradictions and asymmetries. Appropriate national policies in their turn can contribute to the sustainability of the GFA and RFA. It can be shown that following an evolutionary theory of international financial institutions, two broad types of possible GFA can be identified.[3] In this chapter, following Khan (2002) the first is an *overarching type*, exemplified by the classical gold standard and the defunct Bretton Woods system. The second is a *hybrid form* that allows for the existence and co-evolution of some RFAs as well. The changing roles of the IMF and national economic policies can be examined within these two possible financial architectures under globalization. The ongoing politics of the re/construction of the IMF along a more functional and equitable line is and will remain complex and require a separate treatment that is beyond the scope of this chapter and therefore is not attempted here. However, the tentative steps taken towards regional cooperation in Asia since the Asian Financial Crisis (AFC) are discussed to illustrate the opportunities and challenges posed by the need to evolve towards a *hybrid* GFA. The opportunities and challenges arising from the current global crisis are analysed in this context.

In light of the above observations, in this chapter I will discuss the problems of creating and expanding national macroeconomic policy space and economic governance for developing countries in particular within a framework of overall GFAs and RFAs. The context of the recent global financial and economic crisis gives such an exercise an undeniable urgency. However, the theoretical approach towards a type of constructivist analysis which respects the structural complexities of a global real-financial economy with serious asymmetries, problems of managing risk and uncertainty, and uneven development may have broader applicability beyond the recent crisis. Whether state capacities exist for formulation and implementation of national economic policies may depend in large measure on the kind of GFA and RFA in existence at any point in time—with or without financial crises.

The structure of this chapter is as follows. In the second section, the proposed Basel III reforms and their implications for the developing world are discussed. Controlling portfolio capital flows particularly in the form of derivatives are an important dimension of preventive measures which can overlap with re-regulated banking but still go beyond this. For this reason, the third section takes up the Bank for International Settlements (BIS) proposals for better regulation of financial derivatives, including commodities futures, by moving away from OTC (over the counter) transactions towards organized exchanges in the context of developing countries' special needs. Important as the issues

[3] For specific models and arguments see those developed in Khan (2001, 2003, 2004, 2005, 2006) and Lin et al. (2008). Khan (2001, 2005) formalize various types of path dependence. In Khan (2003) a specific argument called "the extended panda's thumb" is advanced to urge the utilization of the existing IMF with some modifications in a new, hybrid GFA. See also Griffith-Jones et al. (2010), Eichengreen (1999; 2013a, 2013b), and Eichengreen and Dincer (2013).

in these two sections are, without a new and workable GFA, the prevention or even management of financial crises will very likely be impossible in particular for developing countries. Therefore, the remainder of the chapter up to the final section, Conclusion, concentrates on the problems of a new GFA and presents the case for a hybrid GFA.[4]

Basel III reforms with December 2017 finalization for more stringent capital requirements

IMPLICATIONS FOR THE DEVELOPING WORLD: LIMITATIONS AND NEED FOR HYBRID FINANCIAL ARCHITECTURE

The banking and finance world is now witnessing a transition from Basel I and II to Basel III. Drafted in 1988, the Basel I Accord was the first to set minimum capital requirements for international banks. The goal was to stop international banks from evading national regulators. Equity capital and published reserves from post-tax retained earnings (Tier I capital) were required to be equivalent to 8 per cent of risk-weighted assets. Tier 2 capital requirements (reserves to cover losses, subordinated debt holdings, gains from the potential sale of assets, etc.) were set at the same levels for Tier I capital. Much of the accord focused on delineating the appropriate risk weights for assets. Risk weights were drawn to privilege sovereign debt, public sector entities and long term claims on other banks. Mortgage and private sector debt were weighted much higher (50 per cent and 100 per cent respectively). The 1998 Accord allowed national supervisors to implement stronger/supplementary measures of capital adequacy for nationally chartered institutions.

Drafted in 2004, Basel II represented a significant revision of the 1988 Accord. It expanded the scope of the 1998 Accord to cover alternative approaches to a variety of topics. The goal of the accord was to promote the adoption of stronger risk management practices by the banking industry. The three pillars rationale (minimum capital requirements, supervisory review, and market discipline) was developed as a conceptual framework on the revision of the initial accord. While many of the key elements of the Basel I Accord were kept in place (general requirement for banks to hold capital equivalent to at least 8 per cent of risk-weighted assets, 1996 Market Risk Amendment, and the definition of eligible capital), a major change in the way risk was assessed was put into place. It allowed risk to be assessed under banks' own internal models, thus relying upon banks to largely self-monitor their own risk-taking strategies. National supervisors were to

[4] Khan (2004, 2006, 2011, 2013) presents arguments for investment and consumption demand-led growth with investment receiving priority in a Kaleckian model. See also the model of a complex financial economy in the appendix which is inspired by Kalecki's approach. An excellent recent argument for investment-led growth is presented in Cozzi and Griffith-Jones (2014).

buttress internal risk assessments by assuring minimum compliance to national standards. And banks were required to provide more public disclosures related to their capital positions. The Basel II framework was more risk sensitive than the 1998 Accord. Operational risk and market risk were separated from credit risk.

FURTHER EVOLUTION: GOING FROM BASEL II TO BASEL III

Under Basel III, banks will be required to hold more capital against their assets than under Basel I and II. Among other things, this will have the effect of decreasing the size of their balance sheets and their ability to leverage themselves. The minimum amount of equity, as a percentage of risk-weighted assets, will increase from 2 per cent to 4.5 per cent. There is also an additional 2.5 per cent buffer requirement, the so-called 'capital conservation buffer', bringing the total equity requirement to 7 per cent (Caruana 2010: 4). Total risk-adjusted capital requirements will remain unchanged at 8 per cent (Demirgüc-Kunt et al. 2010: 4). Deferred tax assets, mortgage servicing rights, and other obscure forms of capital are now not allowed to be used to boost capital levels. Deployment of capital and payment of dividends will be more constrained. In effect, banks will be required to triple core Tier I capital ratios from 2 per cent to 7 per cent to hold against potential losses. They have until 2019 to implement these requirements (Masters 2010a, 2010b).

There is also agreement on tough new liquidity rules. With the so-called *liquidity coverage ratio*, 'for the first time [that] Basel rules have specified a notional global target for liquidity needs' (Masters 2010a, 2010b). The rule would require banks to hold enough cash and sovereign debt to survive at least a month-long market crisis. Banks will have to hold reserves equal to 100 per cent of undrawn corporate borrowing lines. This could be potentially problematic for developing market banks in countries without liquid government bond markets. A second liquidity rule, the *net stable funding ratio*, would seek to reduce banks' dependence on short-term funding. Like much of the agreement, there is considerable delay over when banks have to begin formally observing the rules. For the new liquidity rules, banks have until 2015 to put them in place (Masters 2010a, 2010b).

Basel III imposes tougher requirements on the bonds that banks can count towards their regulatory capital. So-called hybrid securities which sit between equity and debt and were intended to act as a buffer to soak up unexpected losses must now include a mechanism (so-called 'bail-in' mechanism) for taking losses. This would allow them to be converted into equity or written off (Hughes and Masters 2011). This rule will have to be implemented domestically (through national regulatory laws) or individually (through each bond issue) by 2013. Hybrid forms of debt like this and preferred shares are used to bolster regulatory capital and are cheaper to issue than equity. However, Basel III will force the phasing out of these types of protected forms of debt.

The Basel Committee has also proposed a countercyclical buffer that could be imposed when aggregate credit growth is rapid enough to build up system-wide risk

(Caruana 2010: 5). The buffer would be as large as 2.5 per cent of risk-weighted assets and would be released on the judgement of domestic authorities to help absorb losses. Systemically important banks may also be asked to operate under more stringent rules. Capital surcharges, contingent capital, bail-in debt arrangements, and peer reviews are policies that could be employed under rules delineated for these kinds of institutions (Caruana 2010: 5). Basel III also embeds reciprocity into the operation of the agreement's countercyclical capital buffer:

> Consider the case of a country in the region receiving strong capital inflows and experiencing rapid credit growth and buoyant asset prices. Before Basel III, any tightening in capital required of locally incorporated banks would lead to the objection that foreign banks could lend to firms from offshore without being subject to the more rigorous capital requirements. With Basel III, however, internationally active banks would be required by their home regulators to calculate the countercyclical capital buffer add-on for exposures to the country whether booked in the local subsidiaries or offshore. (Caruana 2010: 5)

In 2008, the Basel Committee opened its membership to large emerging markets in the hope that a more globally relevant set of standards could be conceived (Taylor 2010). In some ways, developing countries *were able* to help shape a couple of the rules. New capital rules would have penalized countries which require international banks to take on local partners by requiring these banks to strip equity held by local partners from their Tier I capital totals. However, in July of 2010, a compromise was agreed upon to the benefit of these emerging economies (Masters 2010a, 2010b). (For key milestones of Basel III up to 2018, please see Appendix 1.)

However, Andrew Cornford is on the mark when he states:

> While the inclusion of the leverage ratio in Basel III is an attempt to strengthen the Basel capital framework, it only sets regulatory minima and is soft international law.[5]

CAPITAL ADEQUACY RATIOS AND DEVELOPING MARKETS

Stricter definitions on what constitutes core Tier I capital is of interest to developing market banks. Banks are going to have to hold much higher levels of common equity to satisfy their Tier I requirements (Caruana 2010: 4). Resilience and capability will be judged, then, by the soundness and depth of equity markets in developing countries. No doubt, domestic debt and equity markets must be strengthened to provide space for banks to raise fresh capital. Improving the quality and depth of debt and equity markets in developing countries will be quite a task, especially for countries who currently have very limited markets.

[5] See the Triple Crisis Blog, www.triplecrisis.com/ (accessed 7 October 2018) and also Cornford (2013) at the IDEAS site www.networkideas.org/news/jul2013/news19_Basel_III.htm (accessed 7 October 2018).

Boosting capital adequacy requirements may indeed lead to institutions being perceived as safer, lowering their costs of capital. Larger banks would benefit most by being able to issue debt more cheaply. Banks and corporate firms that are guaranteed through large banks will probably see their costs of issuing debt decrease. This will occur, because bonds issued by these institutions will be an attractive investment for firms wishing to purchase assets that are less risk-weighted.

The effects of higher capital adequacy ratios (CARs) on banks are nuanced and difficult to tease out. Simulations carried out on the effects of Basel II and increased capital adequacy ratios on the Brazilian and Mexican economies showed that GDP in each country would be adversely affected (Barrell and Gottschalk 2010). The analysis showed that a credit crunch would occur in each of these cases, and accompanied by an increase in lending rates. Although the Basel II reforms were never fully implemented, marginal changes in the nature of capital requirements will most likely not affect the results of the econometric analysis. If anything, tougher capital restrictions and more stringent ratios might affect GDP even more adversely.

From a different perspective econometric evidence by Ediz et al. (1998) showed that UK banks responded to regulatory pressures to add to their individual CARs not by lowering their risk or lending profile, but by actually increasing their capital provision. As a result, risky portfolios were complemented by raising new capital (Gottschalk and Sen 2010: 22). In the wake of Basel III then, it might be more difficult to tease out how even the developed country banks could respond to more stringent capital requirements. That the success of raising capital in equity markets was buoyed in 2010 can be noted here. As regards developing countries, banks in search of returns may therefore not shy away from ramping up lending and investment operations. Indeed, it is feasible that the total amount of credit to developing countries may continue to increase. More importantly, where and to whom will that credit go?

This result should be compared against the finding by Montgomery (2005) which indicated that since Basel I was implemented, international banks based out of Japan reduced their risk profile. This was, in part, caused by regulatory pressures from the Ministry of Finance (MoF) and the Bank of Japan (BoJ).

Econometric analysis on developing country banks showed that poorly capitalized banks reduced risk when under regulatory pressure (from Basel I and II regimes), as opposed to raising new capital (Gottschalk and Sen 2010: 23). More stringent CARs under Basel III will force poorly capitalized banks in developing countries to make difficult choices over how they will provision capital and furthermore, how they will dole out credit.

Banks in large developing markets have had to hold CARs higher than the 8 per cent minimum under Basel for some time now (Gottschalk and Sen 2010: 24). This is a result of domestic regulatory regimes which were more stringent than Basel I and II regimes and encouraged higher banking concentration in Brazil. Credit to the private sector declined, and holdings of sovereign securities went up significantly (Gottschalk and Sen 2010: 25). This is directly related to the risk-weighting formula imposed by earlier Basel regimes. The same effects have also been seen in India (Gottschalk and Sen 2010: 28–9). Increases in bank credit have notably lagged behind increases in deposits and holdings of sovereign debt by large Indian banks. Credit towards small and medium-size enterprises (SMEs) (as a percentage of total credit) fell by half between 2000 and 2007 (Gottschalk and Sen 2010: 29).

Towards a workable development-oriented global financial architecture with an enabling role for regional financial arrangements

A CONSTRUCTIVE EVOLUTIONARY THEORY OF GLOBAL FINANCIAL ACHITECTURE

It should be mentioned at the outset here that the constructive evolutionary theory (CET) of GFA developed here is an example of evolution within a dynamic complex adaptive economic system that operates globally. The dynamic instabilities in such a system can arise in both the real and the financial parts of the system, and in interactions between them. In my earlier work in the bounded rationality context using neuro-fuzzy models I was able to show the crucial role of social learning in order to avoid at least the possibility of deepening the crises if not entirely averting them. However, given the endogenous role of uncertainty and lack of coordination in a complex capitalist economy, crises cannot be completely averted. The pragmatic question is how to ensure that they are not deep crises.

Malthus, Sismondi, and Marx in the nineteenth century and Keynes and Kalecki in the twentieth century analysed some aspects of the possibilities of crisis without formalizing the complexity as such. Both Keynes and Kalecki presented models of aspects of endogenous crises from the real side. But these did not formalize complexity. Keynes had crucial insights about the fragile nature of a monetary economy and the role of uncertainty as opposed to insurable risk in making private and socially uncoordinated investment decisions crisis-prone, leading to periodic deficiencies in effective aggregate demand. Minsky pioneered modelling financial fragility and many of his followers have done the best work in advancing the modelling of financial fragility in a complex monetary economy.

In order to motivate empirically the discussion that follows, we can revisit some aspects of AFC before discussing the current reform moves within the IMF. In distinguishing among the countries that managed to survive the AFC and those that did not, John Williamson, one of the proponents of the 'Washington consensus' pointed out that whether or not these countries had liberalized their capital accounts could be construed as crucial; those that had not, survived.

All Asian crisis countries had accepted the IMF's Article VIII obligations, as evident from the historical documents. But as some (see for example, Bhagwati 1998) have pointed out, liberalizing trade and liberalizing the financial sector have different policy implications. In line with discussions in the previous section, theoretically, one should carefully distinguish the welfare impacts of financial market liberalization in an uneven world from such impacts in a smooth world of equals with information symmetry. Indeed, next to unevenness, the most critical element is the role and the presence of *asymmetric information*. In a financial market, gathering, selecting, using, and providing information are central to its proper functioning, yet it is precisely here that market failures from asymmetric information can arise.[6]

But the constructive evolutionary theory with appropriate attention to structure goes further than simply cataloguing moral hazard and adverse selection problems. On the *explanans* side are also *the asymmetries in the size, structure, and capabilities of the economies and polities*. These asymmetries constrain some polities—particularly the economically disadvantaged ones—from developing as quickly as possible in an equitable manner. The UNCTAD reports on the poorest underdeveloped countries point this out empirically (see UNCTAD 2002, 2003, 2007, 2011). The theoretical significance of these features of the real world is that no uniform set of rules can work for all the economies and polities in the world. *A fortiori*, it follows that for GFA and RFAs to serve these poor countries as well as the rich countries equally well, special provisions should be in place.

It may appear that only the least developed countries are a special case. But that is not the whole truth. The newly industrializing economies (NIEs), European social democracies, Japan, etc. each in its own way is also different. This poses the real theoretical challenge: how can we even attempt to theorize in the face of such diversity? The way out is through a consideration of the basic needs of the system and asking if these can be satisfied better under arrangements that are different from the old IMF and the Washington Consensus.

Further work by Barry Eichengreen and others[7] shows that it is possible to move beyond the post Bretton Woods and pre-(global) crisis situation. In contrast to the conservative Meltzer report after the AFC, all of these authors emphasize the need to strengthen the IMF in certain dimensions. However, not all of them recognize the crucial need also for the RFAs and the role they can play in creating an enabling environment for the state to implement beneficial economic policies. A CET theory of GFA recognizes the need for RFAs from both an *evolutionary* and a *structural* perspective. Given the lack of political resolve—a point made forcefully by Eichengreen among others—there is little chance of creating *institutional structures* in the manner of the 1944 Bretton Woods

[6] Stiglitz has been one of the pioneers of such an 'information theoretic' approach. For further analysis, see Stiglitz (1994).

[7] See in addition to Eichengreen (1999) cited earlier, Azis (1999); Khan (2004); Sachs et al. (1996); Sachs and Woo (2000); Summers (2000); Tobin and Ranis (1998); Yoshitomi and Ohno (1999).

agreement. The recent path of the world economy does not lead to this immediately. At the same time, the recent path does not lead only to neoliberalism. It is possible to both reform the IMF, as Eichengreen suggests, and create new RFAs to complement such reforms. Thus this theory leads to the question of identifying a spectrum of GFAs. Most important among these are those that combine the GFAs such as a reformed IMF with appropriate RFAs.

Formally, the heuristic argument presented above can be established via a careful consideration of *path dependence* during evolution of the GFA. In order to do this in a conceptually rigorous manner, the concept of *path dependence* itself has to be refined and formalized in a specific way. I have developed this idea elsewhere, and will only sketch the conceptual path to be followed (see Khan 2001, 2003). Briefly, there can be completely deterministic (CD), completely stochastic (CS), and partially deterministic (PD) characterizations of path dependence. Eschewing the formal apparatus of graph theory and neural network dynamics which can be used to describe these rigorously, we can simply say that in deterministic path dependence there is only one choice of path. Everything is as it should be, since there are no bifurcations at any point in history. In fact, we can make a stronger statement. At *no* point in history is there even a *possibility* of a bifurcation. Most people will see this as an extreme, and in the case of human institutional design, perhaps as an unrealistic case.

The purely stochastic case is all *random mutation*. Again, there is no way that conscious choice can play a role here either. Blind chance determines the outcome. The last type of path dependence, i.e. the PD variety leaves some room for evolution to be a result of at least some kinds of bounded rational human activities. In this case, a complex set of human activities including learning and improving policymaking capabilities can influence which network of paths are followed over time. While the number of available paths at any point in history may be large, they are never infinite. Therefore, combinatorial mathematics will in most cases show the existence of the most likely evolutionary outcome. However, the caveat that large, seemingly random fluctuations (e.g. a war) can throw off these calculations is always a (rare) possibility.

Fortunately, barring such events as wars, revolutions, complete meltdowns of financial systems, etc. there are not at present an unmanageably large number of outcomes that are possible for the GFA. In fact, if we are willing to assume a continuum with nothing but an overarching *global* architecture for international finance with regional impurities added as another type we have just two types of possible evolutionary outcomes for the institutional history of GFAs from a theoretical point of view.

The first type, which can be created at special evolutionary moments, can be called *overarching GFAs*. The gold standard under UK hegemony and Bretton Woods under the threats of a post-war depression, are two examples. Recent history does not support the hope that such events are about to happen again. Therefore, a second type of evolutionary path resulting in a hybrid form should be recognized. This is the hybrid coexistence of a GFA together with one or many RFAs. We can call this type a *hybrid GFA* for shorthand reference. Once again, Asia after the AFC is a good place to begin the analysis.

In the Asian case, as many have observed, financial sector liberalization followed the pre-AFC neoliberal GFA by default. There were some short-term gains from the policy, but ultimately it resulted in severe instability. More generally, as Kaminsky and Reinhart (1999), show, based on the episodes of seventy-six currency crises, of which twenty-six are also characterized by banking crises, financial sector liberalization can result in a boom–bust cycle by providing easy access to short-term financing. Proponents of liberalization suggested some sort of micro-sequencing in order to prevent such adverse consequences. With some variations, the most commonly suggested sequence was: improve the quality of regulations, make sure they are enforced, and then improve the supervisory mechanisms. Once the markets are liberalized, the level of banks' minimum capital requirements could then be brought closer to what the *Basel Accord* required.

As one author (Azis 2002c) who, of course, does not use the same terminology as developed here, nevertheless points out, there is a contradiction in this type of GFA arrangement.

But when the Asian crisis countries liberalized the financial sector in the 1980s, the aforementioned preconditions (assumptions) were not in place. Yet they were rushed to liberalize by the IFI. Ironically, when at the early stage the policy showed favourable impacts, e.g. higher economic growth and greater access to financial services, the international financial institutions (IFIs) applauded it. But when the crisis hit, the very same countries previously praised were swiftly placed into the category of those with misplaced development strategies. All of a sudden, nothing was right with these countries. When confronted with such an embarrassing contradiction, the international institutions are quick to claim that they actually *saw* the faults, and *had already reminded* governments about the existing flaws (e.g. weak banking system, unsustainable exchange rate system, and widespread corruption) (Azis 2002c: 3).

IMF recommendation during this period led to the increase in interest rates. Because of the common prescription under the GFA this occurred in all Asian crisis countries. Such high rates created more moral hazard and adverse selection problems, thus showing that the incentive system has indeed been altered, and led to the undertaking of bad risk by the banking sector.

In fact, the IMF did much worse—it prescribed the wrong medicine, a set of measures that worsened the impact of the AFC. This situation illustrates the danger of being in the grip of a (pseudo-) universalistic theory that simply cannot be applied in the real world of unevenness without serious distortions that may cause great harm. An alternative is to work with our type two hybrid combinations of GFA and RFAs. Again, Asia can be used as an illustration.

Prior to AFC, both the borrowing in short-term market and the increased flow of foreign capital occurred almost simultaneously in these countries. As the real exchange rate appreciated, competitiveness suffered, and vulnerability to sudden reversals of capital flows increased. It must be emphasized that these were systemic features that went largely unnoticed by the IMF or the private sector. As is well known, in a non-linear system the vulnerability to sudden shocks is a logical possibility. In the case of Asia, this became an empirical reality of nightmare proportions.

With most debtors being in the corporate sector during the AFC, the capacity to invest became severely constrained. The debt-deflation scenario became the reality because the price effects of depreciated exchange rates did not occur until much later, if at all. Hence, the initial currency crisis became first a more general financial crisis and then a full-blown economic crisis. In Indonesia it also became a social and political crisis.

The Asian crisis showed that the composition of capital flows matters. The fact that there were sudden reversals of capital flows during 1997 and 1998 led many to believe that most capital flows in the region were of the portfolio investment type. Reversals of such capital can strain the region's financial system sufficiently to cause or exacerbate its collapse (see for example, Rodrik and Velasco 1999). We now know that financial and balance-of-payments crises became interlinked precisely because of the existence of foreign currency-denominated liabilities (foreign debt) in the domestic financial system (see Krueger 2000). This hindsight can be used to develop RFAs in Asia, Latin America, and a few other regions and cross-regional BRICS facilities.

In Asia, a Washington Consensus policy mix of monetary tightening and fiscal restraints was imposed as part of IMF conditionalities. The experience during the Mexican crisis in 1995 had convinced the Fund that such a policy mix was appropriate for Asia as well, despite the fact that pre-crisis conditions in Asia were quite otherwise.[8] Another element emerged in Asia that was indeed new: the IMF suggested a rather radical and fundamental change in the countries' institutional structure.[9] In the event, neither set turned out to have been well-conceived.

The fund's insistence on severely tightening monetary policy by raising interest rates turned out to be an incorrect and counterproductive decision. Its arguments for remaking many institutions in Asia did not make evolutionary sense although all would agree that ending corruption, curtailing special business privileges, and imposing the practice of good governance, including good corporate governance, were good overall goals.[10] But quite apart from the well-known fact that this falls outside the fund's mandate, such adjustments at the time could result in further instability. In the words of Morris Goldstein, an ex-IMF staff member: 'both the scope and the depth of the Fund's conditions were excessive . . . They clearly strayed outside their area of expertise . . . If a nation is so plagued with problems that it needs to make 140 changes before it can borrow, then maybe the fund should not lend.' Although not a conscious advocate of the evolutionary theory advanced here, Goldstein's long experience and solid sense of institutional matters led him to the right conclusions in this matter.

[8] Tobin and Ranis (1998) were among those who believed that the IMF programmes in Asia were based on the Fund's experiences with Mexico in 1994.

[9] Azis (2002c) suggests: 'The experience with policy adjustments of this kind in Eastern Europe and the former Soviet Union (from communism to market economy) had inspired the Fund to do the same thing in Asia' (p. 7).

[10] See Khan (1999a, 1999b, 2001) on Asian corporate governance reform, and the sketch of an evolutionary theory.

TOWARDS A WORKABLE HYBRID GLOBAL FINANCIAL ARCHITECTURE: RFAS, THE IMF AND NATIONAL POLICY MANAGEMENT UNDER FRACTURED GLOBALIZATION

But how is the transition towards a hybrid GFA to be effected? What conceptual modifications are necessary to the way in which we have become accustomed to thinking under the present institutional order? The present and following sections are all intended to answer these questions. This section will consider steps taken by the IMF during the global crisis and some general issues and the possible formation of RFAs stemming from the AFC and the current crisis, while the following two sections will address more rigorously how the IMF needs to be modified and what such a modified IMF together with several RFAs could do. I achieve this strategically by discussing the counterfactual of what a hypothetical RFA in Asia could have done to handle the situation before, during, and after the AFC. This turns out to have broader applicability in twenty-first-century global crisis management. But in order to build fully the argument for a hybrid GFA, first the recent tentative but potentially important reformist IMF steps deserve consideration.

The IMF's Response to the Global Economic Crisis and its Evolving Role

The IMF's loss of stature after the Asian financial crisis. After the Asian financial crisis, the Fund lost much of its credibility with developing countries. As a result, the IMF's programme portfolio diminished significantly over much of the last decade. Prior to the most recent crisis, demand for the Fund's resources was at a historic low. Major borrowers had repaid their outstanding debt at the time of the most recent crisis, leading the Fund to contract its staff by around 15 per cent (Grabel 2010: 3; Kapur and Webb 2006; Thomas 2009). The Fund's loan portfolio shrank from US$105 billion to less than US$10 billion in the space of five years (2003–07) (Weisbrot et al. 2009).

Many have pointed to the Fund's continued insistence on using *ex ante* and *ex post* conditionality as a major reason as to why countries shied away from going to the institution for help. The historical use of conditionality within IMF programmes meant that developing countries had to acquiesce to dominant Western thinking on correct fiscal and monetary policy formulae. Embarrassment at having to ask the IMF for assistance during crises also played an important role in dissuading developing countries from ceding control over their fiscal and monetary policy over to the fund. Over the past decade or so, developing countries were able to resist relying upon the IMF, through:

- over-accumulation of reserves
- international private capital flows
- bilateral swap arrangements
- regional banks and financial arrangements
- South–South financial assistance.

Regaining Relevance

In December of 2008, the IMF was thrust into the global financial crisis through its Stand-By Arrangement with Iceland. The Fund package with Iceland totalled US$2.1 billion, with over US$800 million made available immediately for the country (Anderson 2008). IMF policy prescription was used to explicitly stem the fall of the Icelandic krona to ward off the potential of massive defaults in foreign denominated currency. Monetary and fiscal policy space was left largely open by the Fund. The IMF also provided assistance in restructuring the entire Icelandic banking and financial composition.

Since providing assistance to Iceland, the Fund has been very active in providing financial assistance to member states all over the globe. Notably, the global nature of crisis has meant the Fund is being seen in areas of the world (most especially Europe) for the first time in quite a while. With that said, the IMF's majority response to the crisis was built around a sharp increase in the amount of concessional lending to low- and middle-income countries.

Lending to low-income countries (LICs) during the crisis period was fourfold larger than historical levels (IMF 2009). In late 2009, concessional resources for LICs to meet projected demand were increased to nearly US$17 billion through 2014 (IMF 2009). Relief on interest payments by LICs to the IMF through 2011 were approved. Additionally, LICs now can access double the normal limits on annualized draw-outs from the Fund. The IMF approved a US$250 billion allocation of SDRs that will be distributed to all member countries of the Fund according to their quota levels. As such, more than US $18 billion will be available to LICs to augment their foreign exchange reserves to alleviate financing and balance of payments (BOP) constraints (IMF 2009).

In the wake of the global financial crisis the Fund did become relevant again. It is also trying to regain credibility in global financial governance—an effort that actually started with the AFC (Best 2010; Khan 2002c, 2004, 2006). It has served as a 'first responder' to financial crises in countries throughout the globe (Grabel 2010: 3). The restoration of the Fund to its 'proper place' in the international financial system was seen in its speedy response to the Icelandic crisis and from the boost it received from G20 nations. Indeed, the G20 meeting in April 2009 reaffirmed the Fund's mandate and provided new and large amounts of funding commitments (US$1.1 trillion for the crisis; US$750 billion through the IMF) to support the institution's efforts (Grabel 2010: 3). Even China and Brazil, notable critics of the Fund's governance policies, committed new resources and lending to the institution. These new commitments will facilitate greater interaction and sharing of resources between the IMF and regional development banks.

The G20 has backed the partial devolution of funding commitments from the IMF to regional development banks to allow resources to be available in a more timely fashion to countries in need. This kind of development speaks to a small, but growing, consensus that the IMF might be better served in the future to act as a central figure in a network of intergovernmental finance with regional development banks and institutions (Vols and Caliari 2010).

In 2009, the IMF also began issuing its own bonds to boost its available resources. Around US$90 billion of the US$500 billion in new resources for future IMF lending will come from BRICS countries and South Korea (Grabel 2010: 4). The development is important in two ways:

a. Lenders from emerging and developing markets can use their new lending capacity to exert greater influence over policies of the fund.
b. Buoyed by new commitments from BRICS reaffirms the central role the Fund will continue to play as a lender of last resort.

Changes in the IMF's Conditionality Regimes

In the wake of the global crisis, the IMF introduced a number of new financial programmes aimed at allowing countries to have more agency in delineating their loan/policy structures. The IMF has stated that these facilities 'will be more flexible and tailored to the increasing diversity' of member countries (IMF 2009). New instruments include:

- Extended Credit Facility—medium-term support and flexibility programme;
- Standby Credit Facility—addresses short-term and precautionary needs;
- Rapid Credit Facility—emergency support with limited conditionality;
- Flexible Credit Line—support for BOP pressures for countries with strong macroeconomic track records; no *ex post* conditionality (IMF 2010d);
- Precautionary Credit Line—lower standards of qualification than for the FCL; less *ex ante* qualifications, but stronger *ex post* conditionality.

Each facility and credit line has its own conditions, term structures, borrowing capacity, and availability. The IMF has strongly pushed to make its credit facilities more low-cost for member economies. Conditionality is being streamlined to 'focus on core objectives' (IMF 2009), and applies primarily to structural reforms. Conditionality is not supposed to affect countries' fiscal policies that directly target poverty alleviation, growth, and pro-poor spending. Programmes are now supposed to accommodate larger fiscal deficits, looser monetary policy, and increased inflation targets. Additionally, countries will not need to seek waivers for access to funds if reforms are not completed by a specific date.

In addition to paying lip service towards granting more policy autonomy to countries with IMF facilities, the Fund has softened its stance on capital controls and other macro-prudential measures (see, Ostry et al. 2010). The Fund and its sister organization the World Bank have indicated that the targeted and temporary use of capital controls can be an effective way for countries to defend themselves against exogenous financial shocks and preserve monetary policy space (Beattie 2010; Ostry et al. 2010). This is a far cry from the Fund's reaction to the controls put in place by Malaysia during the Asian financial crisis. As part of the Iceland's 2008 Stand-By Arrangement

(SBA), the IMF explicitly advocated the use of such controls (Anderson 2008). Nonetheless, one of the Fund's most recent papers on economic liberalization (Shah and Patnaik 2011) indicts the use of controls in India for their ineffectiveness in shielding the economy from exogenous shocks and their bias against small- and medium-sized private firms.

In reality, a close study of conditionality 'reforms' confirms that they are more ad hoc and piecemeal than might otherwise appear. Many of the recent studies of SBAs and other facilities negotiated during the crisis have shown that the IMF has continued to promote pro-cyclical macroeconomic policy targets or structural adjustments (Muchhala 2009; Solidar 2009; UNICEF 2010; Van Waeyenberge et al. 2010; Weisbrot et al. 2009). Questions have already arisen as to what fiscal programmes count as targeting 'poverty alleviation, growth and pro-poor spending'. Does the subsidizing of basic energy inputs for the poor (kerosene, heating oil, etc.) count under these spending exceptions? The evidence emanating from the IMF is mixed at best. Public outcries in Pakistan and the Kyrgyz Republic over the ending of energy input subsidies are important examples of how IMF policy prescription can directly lead to public unrest. In the midst of the crisis, the Hungarian government's public spat with the IMF over programme conditionality was especially notable, illustrating the unease within governments to work under the Fund's rules (Bryant 2010).

Governance Reforms at the IMF

The IMF has recently seen a change in the share of voting quotas. In November and December of 2010, IMF member countries agreed to an unprecedented doubling of quotas to SDR 476.8 billion (IMF 2010a). This doubling of quotas was complemented by changes in the quota shares among members. As a result, more than 6 per cent of quota shares will be shifted to 'emerging market and developing countries' and away from over-represented European countries. The shifting of shares will not impact the voting power of the Fund's poorest members. Starting from 2012, the Fund's ten largest contributors and quota shareholders have begun to more accurately reflect the countries' contributions to world GDP. The total shift in voting share to developing countries, when combined with the 2008 quota reform, is now about 5.3 per cent.

Changes to the IMF governance structure will also come via the Executive Board. The size of the board will remain at twenty-four members. However, advanced European countries will reduce their contribution to the board by two. Developing countries will up their contribution by the same amount. Further, from 2012, the Executive Board will consist only of elected Executive Directors, 'following entry into force of the proposed amendment of the Fund's Articles of Agreement, [and] end the category of appointed Executive Directors (currently the members with the five largest quotas appoint an Executive Director)' (IMF 2010c).

Supervisory Role in the World Economy

Key leaders at the Fund have acknowledged that the institution has not done a good enough job at understanding the effects of financial flows on the financial system, and in particular, the effects of flow velocity on contagion and crisis. While not a self-indictment per se, the Fund has been very vocal about the ways in which it can better serve the international financial system. Generally, the Fund has communicated that it must clarify its mandate and improve the role of the Fund in promoting global stability. On three issues in particular (cross-border research on capital flows, systemic changes in financial regulatory structure, taxes on flows), the Fund has focused a large amount of attention.

Fund Directors have noted that volatile capital flows played an important role in the transmission of shocks towards the depth of the current crisis. As it is the Fund's mandate to oversee international monetary stability, the institution acknowledges that it must strengthen its ability to 'advance in bilateral and multilateral surveillance and policy advice for member countries, based on extensive analytical work and taking into account country specific circumstances and relevant experiences' and 'develop a coherent Fund view and inform policy guidance on capital flows' (IMF 2011). The Fund has initiated work on *Cross-Cutting Themes from Recent Country Experiences with Capital Flows* as a starting point from which it can further elaborate its views on how to deal with cross-border flows. In particular, the Fund has highlighted the need for its research and surveillance to focus on the potential spillovers of capital flows and the implications for the international monetary system as a whole.

The Fund has been very vocal on the need for global policy cooperation in the international monetary and financial system (IMF 2010b). Directors at the Fund see it as necessary that, for the global recovery to accelerate, cooperation on financial regulatory architecture must be prioritized. The Fund is currently working hard with member states to guard against protectionist and mercantilist policy measures. In doing so, the Fund plans on delivering spillover reports for the world's major economies that assess the impact of domestic policies of systemic countries beyond their own borders (IMF 2010b). Part of this larger surveillance effort involves an enhanced understanding of macroeconomic and financial risks and their associated linkages. Similarly, the Fund has also produced research and policy proposals on the resolution of cross-border banking institutions (Hagan and Vinals 2010).

IMF directors have stressed the need for member states to develop a global financial safety net to protect against the threat of future shocks. Much of this discussion has centred around the ways in which such a safety net could be initiated. The Fund has been at the fore in assessing the potential regulatory and tax policies that could be used to develop such a safety net.

After losing much of its relevance after the Asian financial crisis, the IMF has suddenly become the most important financial and monetary institution in the world economy (save perhaps the Bank for International Settlements). Its loan portfolio has swelled to historic levels. New commitments from member states and direct borrowing by the Fund have meant that available resources are also at an all-time high. Dozens of countries from every continent on the globe currently have credit arrangements with the Fund. The Fund's geographic reach has put it in a unique position to monitor financial and economic developments. Critical research and surveillance by the Fund can help us better understand the linkages between financial flows and policies within and among member states. Greater voice has even been given towards the use of the Fund's SDR as future reserve currency.

Such importance and responsibility requires that the Fund seriously consider the weight of its continued use of conditionality on member states. No doubt the Fund is carefully considering the viability of its lending model along with the potential easing of terms and conditionality in its programmes. Recent quota and governance reforms indicate that the Fund is at least beginning the process of granting more agency to developing countries on the appropriateness of fiscal consolidation and tight monetary policy.

New South–South initiatives—BRICS

In this context, the July 2014 initiative by the BRICS group of countries to create a new financial facility for development is a noteworthy attempt. Although at a capitalization of US$100 billion it is far short of the actual needs, it is a good start in the right global direction. The key roles played by China and India from Asia together with Russia, Brazil, and South Africa can give it a multi-regional—indeed eventually a hybrid global–regional character emphasized in this analysis—dimension and capabilities.

Officially designated as the Contingent Reserve Arrangement (CRA), this fund is intended to serve as 'a self-managed contingent reserve arrangement to forestall short-term balance of payments pressures, provide mutual support and further strengthen financial stability'. Thus it is still in the nature of financing a temporary BOP disequilibrium. Therefore, the question of funding more medium- to long-term development projects needs to be put on the table. Perhaps parallel facilities can be set up for these purposes with longer time frames and more explicit developmental goals. In this context, Griffith-Jones's (2014) discussion of the BRICS development bank and future possibilities holds out hope for the future. Financing medium- to long-term development projects can be discussed in this context with a view to wider South–South cooperation.

As of July 2014, according to the treaty, China will contribute 41 per cent, Brazil, Russia, and India 18 per cent each, and South Africa 5 per cent. The CRA is to be governed by two boards. First, there is the *Governing Council* with five members, one each from the five BRICS countries. The next is the Standing Committee for operational matters. The Standing Committee will have five directors, one each from the five member countries. The Governing Council can only make all the fundamental decisions *by consensus*. This is an important difference in governance compared to that of the IMF. New countries can join the CRA if there is consensus. There is no effective veto power as in the IMF.

The Standing Committee will make executive and operational decisions—particularly decisions regarding seeking funding support. Providing parties will decide on funding requests based on simple and transparent majority voting. At present, according to Article 4, it appears that there are two kinds of financing instruments: (i) 'A liquidity instrument to provide support in response to short-term balance of payments pressures'; (ii) 'A precautionary instrument committing to provide support in light of potential short-term balance of payments pressures.' Again, the goals are short-term relief. There are specific details underlined in the text of the treaty regarding procedures and limits to funding.

It does not appear now that the CRA will fundamentally alter dependence on the IMF of developing countries; but it can lessen such dependence and through a combination of short-term BOP lending and other measures can help developing countries in increasing their policy spaces. But the CRA can only be seen as a start in the right direction. There is much more to be done. A good first step will be to hold an intellectual summit with committed experts from developing countries for a deep and serious discussion regarding future courses of action.[11]

As mentioned in the previous section, the BRICS development bank can serve in a complementary fashion the need for sustainable development finance. However, there are several issues to consider in making the bank an efficient instrument for sustainable development finance.

It must be emphasized that the scale of lending of the BRICS bank should be large enough to make an inter-sectoral impact (see the mathematical model in Appendix 2). As in all finance, the impact of the BRICS bank would be magnified through its capacity to leverage as well as through its ability to arrange for co-financing of projects with the relevant parts of private and public sectors. A related and important issue will be the quality of the loans made. Without careful and close monitoring and evaluation, there is a danger of a bad trade-off between the pace of growth of a portfolio of loans and the quality of loans. Thus, high quality of loans needs to be made an operational priority in order to maximize the development impact of the projects financed while minimizing the risk of default. In the neuro-fuzzy model developed and applied in Khan (2004) such monitoring and inductive learning is crucial.

Another related issue is the degree of financial 'sophistication' of the instruments used (Khan 2004: chs 8 and 9). As is well-known, the 'plain vanilla' loans can be made much faster than more complicated loan structures. Transactions involving equity take much longer (though they have desirable features, such as capturing part of the 'upside' if

[11] For details one can consult the text of the treaty. For an illuminating brief, please see Montes (2014), Initial Comments on BRICS Contingent Reserve Arrangement (CRA), The South Centre, Geneva, Switzerland July 17.

projects are very profitable). As a rule, the more complex the products, the longer they take to be designed and implemented. Here, complexity without proper regulation and oversight, as the first half of this chapter has been at pains to argue, can lead to crisis. Investing in an open, transparent, and concessionary manner in very poor countries through simple instruments will be the way to proceed—at least for a time while training of personnel and supervisory capabilities are developed both within the bank and in debtor countries.

The changing role of the IMF within a hybrid GFA and BRICs-type financing facilities

In this section I want to address what is perhaps the most important institutional and policy question that arises from the proposal for a hybrid GFA. What will be the role of the IMF, and how will this new role differ from its present or neoliberal role? As mentioned already, the handling of the AFC by the IMF had raised important issues of global governance. The Fund had been criticized by the left and the right, as well as the centre. The global financial crisis has elicited mixed but on the whole potentially constructive responses from the IMF. I have already alluded to some of the ways in which the IMF will need to change its ways if the hybrid form of GFA I am suggesting here is to become a viable option for institution building. Elsewhere (see Khan 2002c), I have pointed out the need for adhering to some basic principles as the IMF transforms itself consistent with a critical social constructivist approach. Chief among these principles are the principle of symmetry and the principle of burden-sharing. These are described briefly here:

1 *The principle of symmetry*, i.e. surplus and deficit countries should be treated equally; however, it was not realized in the past; nor is it likely to be realized in the near future. But there are various ways to pursue this as a goal even under the current set-up of the IMF. If serious efforts are made to follow this principle by a reformed IMF, that will be an important step towards a new and better GFA.
2 *The principle of burden-sharing*, i.e. during episodes of crisis management IMF will share the management burden with RFAs and through them also with the affected countries and their neighbours.

It should be borne in mind that in keeping with the critical constructivist argument developed so far both principles recognize the practical impossibility of the IMF being transformed into a global central bank in the near future. What the IMF cannot do now and will not be able to do in the foreseeable future is to follow Bagehot's dictum to lend freely against good collateral at a high interest rate in times of crisis. Unless SDRs become the commonly accepted and easily expandable means of settlement, this role will remain foreclosed. It is unlikely that the principal shareholders of the IMF will allow such a change to occur.[12] Also, compared to a national central bank dealing with a problematic domestic financial institution the IMF has a limited ability to force corrective action. Yet, there will clearly be a role for IMF lending, and the consequent moral hazard will need to be recognized. But just as the moral hazard from having firefighters ready to fight fires does not compel thoughtful communities to abolish fire stations, neither can the global community abolish the IMF or reduce its resources simply because there is a moral hazard problem associated with such institutions. The second principle above, the principle of burden-sharing with the RFAs, national governments, and the private sectors should go some distance towards both increasing the overall resources available, and mitigating the moral hazard.

While the Fund cannot now or even in the near future be expected to act as a global central banker, pressures for increasing the net supply and poor country allocations of SDR will have beneficial effects. Even if the increases are not significant in the short run, the tendency will keep alive the eventual goal of forming a global central bank, as Keynes had envisioned. More practically, putting pressure on the IMF to emit new SDRs in order to finance the stabilization of primary (and perhaps other) commodity prices will lead to benefits for both developing and developed countries in the intermediate run. Stabilization of these prices will help many developing countries avert BOP disasters. Furthermore, to the extent that the unusual price increases, such as the oil price increase in the 1970s, create general inflationary pressure such pressures can also be averted. A smooth international transactions pattern will also thus be consistent with domestic price stabilization.

In addition, the Fund can make a concerted effort to manage private creditors. Most important from the point of view of managing crises will be the incorporation of new provisions on loan contracts so that orderly workout procedures become feasible. The Fund can also lend into arrears as a means to provide debtor-in-possession financing. Such a provision, along with more direct measures vis-à-vis creditors, can help to bring creditors to the bargaining table during a crisis.

Such measures to manage creditors should also be complemented by increased surveillance of financial markets. Strengthening supervision is one aspect. Arriving at independent assessments of financial risk is another, related aspect of moving in this direction. However, it is important to realize that even after adopting this stance, the risk of crises will still remain. Not all crises can be foreseen, much less prevented. The best that can be done is to draw the countries, the private sector, and the RFAs together in an effort to strengthen the financial structures, including information gathering and processing capabilities. A cooperative structure where the Fund recognizes the need for hybridity will also help to reduce reaction time.

Reducing reaction time can help only if the policies undertaken cannot do much harm even if they are not successful in achieving their positive aim. The IMF has been correctly

[12] However, this should not be ruled out completely. Pressure for increased supply of SDRs will be beneficial in specific ways, as argued below.

criticized for suggesting a 'one-size-fits-all' policy package. Here again, a changed institutional structure with a more flexible IMF will mean a case-by-case approach where RFAs will play a significant role. National economic policies such as requiring borrowers to unwind positions in increasingly risky situations, curbing excessive foreign borrowing, limiting portfolio investment, cautionary policies towards derivatives and off-balance sheet items may need to be examined as serious policy options. Tobin tax, or individual country taxes of the Chilean variety should also be given serious consideration. The mantra of free capital movements together with the refrain that there is no alternative needs to be revised appropriately to incorporate the available tools that the Fund can help countries use to mitigate any risks arising from such capital movements.

It is not clear that the Fund can do much in instituting a more stable exchange rate regime. The pegged rate system, advocated by, among others, surprisingly the *Wall Street Journal*, will create one-way bets for speculators. Free floating, on the other hand, can lead to disasters when exchange rates collapse suddenly instead of finding a new stable equilibrium. Such perverse dynamics was observed during the AFC, particularly in the Indonesian case. The inability of Greece to use exchange rate policy during its own crisis shows how the EU and particularly the ECB may not be a model to emulate for creating future RFAs. Neither currency boards nor perfect flexibility can prevent vulnerable currencies from collapsing. Rather a managed float before any signs of crisis appear together with prudent management of the financial and real sectors would seem to be both pragmatic and feasible at this point. Strengthening the capacities of central banks will have better pay-off here than urging the IMF to twist the arms of the countries through conditionalities.

In Asia, in addition to the high interest rate standard recipe, the IMF seized the crisis as an opportunity to dismantle what remained of the particular mix of institutions that had historically evolved to create the so-called 'Asian Model of Development'. Widespread and massive bank closures, enterprise restructuring, opening up sectors to foreign ownership, tearing down labour institutions in the name of flexibility, and attacks on living standards seemed to be part of an overarching agenda. This type of radical restructuring under duress is not the way to apply the principles that are being advocated here.

In spite of widespread criticism from many quarters, the IMF still remains committed to capital account liberalization as *an ultimate* goal. The AFC and similar crises have merely given it pause to consider proper sequencing before liberalization. The critical constructive evolutionary theory developed here points to a more nuanced, less global approach. Some economies may be ready for capital account liberalization; others are not. The IMF needs to distinguish among them carefully, and not adopt capital account liberalization as a principle enshrined in its revised articles of agreement.

It goes without saying that proper sequencing, better monitoring and management of debt, greater transparency in both the government and private sector operations, and more effective regulation of domestic financial institutions are all desirable policy goals. Also desirable are domestic tax policies that do not encourage excessive reliance on short-term capital inflows. However, in a world of unevenness some countries may also require temporary capital controls through various means. The IMF, instead of taking a dogmatic approach that says 'no' to any form of capital control should set up facilities for examining the impacts of different alternatives. In doing so, it should also pay attention to the principle of symmetry so that the borrowing countries do not always and everywhere have to take the initiative. At the same time both capital inflows and outflows need to be controlled to some extent.

A reformed IMF together with RFAs could take leadership in providing the overall framework within which individual countries could pursue policies most advantageous from a systemic point of view. For example, the hybrid GFA could have a framework agreed to by IMF member countries so that when a crisis hits, lenders would be subject to credit standstills and orderly workouts. This would clearly force the creditors to shoulder some of the responsibility for the crisis. Such an arrangement will, in all likelihood, also reduce the need for large IMF loans. Another part of the new IMF responsibilities could be the collection of a global Tobin tax. Although no panacea, such a tax would almost certainly reduce returns to very short-term capital movements. A further consequence of a Tobin tax could be a somewhat more stable exchange rate system. Neither is adoption of a securities transactions tax a far-fetched idea. Even Lawrence Summers wrote academic articles before he joined the government advocating modest taxes on these transactions (see Summers and Summers 1989). As any international monetary economist knows, the 'impossible trinity' of international capital mobility, a fixed exchange rate system, and an independent monetary policy cannot all be pursued together although Mundell's carefully specified context for 'the assignment problem' and his solutions may be applicable in specific instances. Slowing down short-term capital movement need not prevent long-term capital from flowing across borders. However, fixed exchange rates must be given up if countries are still to pursue independent monetary policies. Thus, a return to the old IMF is neither necessary nor desirable. Transformation of the IMF into a handmaiden of the neoliberal agenda in the 1980s showed that something akin to a constructivist process was already at work in the post-Bretton Woods system IMF. Given sufficient political wisdom and will that process can be reversed towards creating a transformed IMF that can serve the cause of financial stability for global prosperity much better than it has done during the last decades of the twentieth century. This new IMF will adopt a more flexible approach towards national policies. It will recognize that in periods that seem to be leading towards a crisis there may need to be policy shifts such as a shift towards some types of capital controls. The present articles of the IMF actually allow some forms of capital controls when countries are in distress. Instead of dismantling, these provisions have to be made realistic and applicable whenever the financial system seems vulnerable. Thus flexibility and context-dependent policymaking will be key features of a hybrid system. To begin with, debt rescheduling, moderation in fiscal-monetary policy mix with an expansionary bias for most economies, and gradual restructuring of corporate sectors with strengthening of standards and corporate governance are steps that IMF can encourage economies to take without interfering directly with policymaking in specific countries.

Other measures that the IMF could allow or even encourage national governments to pursue might include requiring lending institutions to hold different levels of provisions for countries with different estimated levels of risk measured by such factors as state of the banking system and level of reserves relative to short-term debt. As many have observed, risk assessment by the credit rating agencies also leaves much to be desired and could be improved if the IMF provided some guidance and input. Another, more practical measure would be to impose different levels of taxation on earnings from overseas investments with different maturities. Although it will not be so sensitive to individual country risk it will nevertheless curb some of the tendencies towards short-termism. It should be mentioned that the Basel Committee regulations in effect during the AFC may have been a culprit in this respect. These regulations gave a lower weight to short-term foreign lending (20 per cent) for capital adequacy purposes than for loans with a maturity period of over one year (100 per cent). A new IMF could make such rules less biased by coordinating its guidelines with BIS, and being guided by a better theory than the one underlying the Washington consensus. Here some of the Basel III guidelines, if they check the currently systemic dysfunctional pro-cyclical tendencies can be helpful.

Conclusion

It is now clear from the available data that emerging and developing countries have the necessary savings and foreign exchange reserves in hard currencies and can finance a new development bank that could contribute to investment for sustainable development. In this context, it is encouraging that the leaders of the BRICS nations have committed to the creation of a new development bank for infrastructure and sustainable development. As our analysis makes clear, this bank would complement, not be a substitute for, existing financial institutions both in the public and private sector and thus contribute to development and financial stability as part of a multi-regional facility in a hybrid global financial architecture. No doubt such a BRICS facility will strengthen the voice of developing and emerging economies in the development finance architecture that is still evolving.

It is encouraging that BRICS leaders have also proposed the creation of other institutions such as the CRA among BRICS countries, which would provide official liquidity in times of need. The history of financial crises shows that they cannot be prevented once and for all in a globalized monetary economy with unpredictable ebbs and flows in capital movement. This history also shows that financial markets have short memories and limited long-term learning capacity. Thus there needs to be—within the limits of human fallibility—a well-designed set of institutions capable of dealing with tendencies towards financial instability and crisis. Thus both the steps following from the Chiang Mai initiative in Asia and the more recent BRICS CRA are wise responses by policymakers who wish to see and go further than the last crisis. A similar initiative in Latin America by widening and deepening the Bank of the South—Bancosur, founded in 2009—idea can further strengthen these moves in the right direction.

Furthermore, as the first BRICS summit hosted by the Russian Federation in Yekaterinburg in 2009 emphasized, there is a pressing need for the global economy to move away from too much dependence on the US dollar. Inter alia, the Yekaterinburg summit highlighted the lesson that is emphasized in this chapter regarding the problems created by dollar-denominated loans and assets. Both the Asian Financial Crisis of 1997–98 and the global financial crisis that began in 2007–08 point towards the need for a more rational global currency basket including an expanded role for SDRs. Most importantly, as this chapter highlights, such a world of multiple currencies and SDRs will need to have a transparent and democratic system of financial governance. Here technical economic arguments regarding efficiency and stability work in tandem with political and political/economic arguments regarding equity and democratic rights in a world of uneven development and opportunities.

Given the unevenness in the structure of the global economy, the developmental consequences of financial crises are particularly important to analyse when designing institutions to contain and manage such crises. In this chapter, particular attention has been given to the fact that the negative consequences for output growth, employment, income distribution, and poverty reduction are relatively more severe for the DCs and least developed countries (LDCs). This occurs at least in part because of the following characteristics, among others:

a. DCs and LDCs have fewer resources for coping with a financial crisis, particularly one which is global in its scope.
b. Most DCs and all LDCs lack automatic stabilizers due to the embryonic nature of their fiscal and social protection systems.
c. They have limited ability to borrow in international financial markets and this limits their ability to pursue countercyclical policies.
d. These threats are often exacerbated by global financial market integration and FTAs and BITs. Many WTO commitments also adversely affect DCs. IMF pro-cyclical structural adjustment policies can also constrict the policy space.

In areas such as the derivatives markets and portfolio capital flows, the shortfall in regulatory capacities for these countries can leave them vulnerable. Even in banking, the well-intentioned Basel regulations can either not be implemented, or worse; as this chapter illustrates, there are aspects of Basel II and Basel III that can harm the developmental processes. Thus a careful rethinking of these issues and further capacity building for DCs and LDCs will be necessary.

In light of the econometric estimates discussed earlier in this section, this chapter emphasizes the need for enhancing the ability of DCs and LDCs to use fiscal and monetary policy to support the growth of their economies. Because poor states are already fiscally constrained (whether through tax capacity, IMF/World Bank conditionality, economic shocks/hardships), Basel III further complicates the growth and poverty-reduction picture.

The analysis here leads to the conclusion that these states will need to become more reliant on each other to implement the reforms and support regional development initiatives. Failure to do so will then mean that these states will have to become more reliant on international technical expertise and resources which may or may not be forthcoming. This may be the time for multilateral agencies to devote significant resources towards building capacities in DCs and LDCs with the help of experts with combined technical and area specializations.

In this light, the fact that states have a full decade to delineate and implement a proper course is not as long a time horizon as first appears. Even if the banking sector is adequately reformed, the proper use of financial markets will also require an enabling global financial architecture and an overall reduction of systemic risk.

As an earlier paper (Khan 2009) showed, analysing the challenge of meeting the Millennium Development Goals (MDGs) which justifiably has high priority in both the UN and the affected countries presents us with the fact that some important gaps still remain.[13] In one way or another, these all involve problems of capacity building and cooperation among national, sub-national, and international actors both at the governmental and civil society levels. Related to this, the interests of those who live in rural areas or more remote regions and are disadvantaged for that reason would need greater representation. The combined disadvantages of gender, location, and ethnic identification raise particularly salient issues for widespread deliberation. Concrete step-by-step plans of action with identifiable outcomes need to be communicated clearly, and followed through properly. All these are made much more difficult if not impossible to achieve especially for LDCs during times of crisis and global contraction.

In times of crisis, there are well-meaning suggestions of radical institutional restructuring that fade away when the immediate crisis is over. Only a few farsighted or worrying types may still voice lingering concerns. Following this literature, but more importantly, the recent global crisis and the history of the AFC motivate my proposals for moving away from an *overarching type* of GFA—to use the terminology developed here.

Given the features of the real economic world, an evolutionary approach admits of multiple evolutionary equilibria, and a need for realistic institutional design that recognizes path dependence and the role of alternative theories and interpretations without the disabling and in most cases incorrect slogan that there is no alternative. Although social and political construction of new institutions and arrangements are difficult, except for rare circumstances, there is usually more than just one possibility. Real

[13] This applies particularly to those countries targeted to receive integrated package services (IPS).

struggles among competing ideas, norms, and politics at different levels are necessary aspects of the process of choosing among these possibilities. Such a critical constructivist approach applied to recent international financial and economic history leads to the identification of two broad categories of global financial architectures. The *hybrid* variety advocated here on the basis of both realism and systemic efficacy and equity will nevertheless involve much institution building that is always fraught with the danger of politics-gone-awry.

The dismantling of Chilean capital controls in 1998 is a case in point. In this particular instance, a balance of payments crisis prompted the loosening of capital controls instituted earlier (Agonsin 1998). It can be argued that the situation of policy and institutional reversal occurred because the interest groups favouring liberalization following a particular world view were strengthened. Such interests in Chile included at that time holders of foreign exchange, exporters, foreign creditors and investors, and the IMF and other international financial institutions. Thus the political problems of coalition building and ensuring the least cost cooperative outcome need attention. The limited achievements and remaining problems that can currently be seen from the Asian example discussed here should provide concrete motivation to think further about such problems of designing institutions in the real world.

Even under a far-from-complete RFA in Asia, the current global financial crisis has made the benefits of having an RFA structure obvious to the Asian central bankers and other players. All the surplus countries carry too much hard currency reserves which are costly. In particular the developmental opportunity costs from foregoing developmental projects are deemed to be quite high, as critics from China in particular stress. It is to be kept in mind that these foregone projects are not just in the reserve country, but in many DCs and LDCs outside the borders of Asian surplus economies. Thus the developmental opportunity costs of the current excess reserve-holding system are quite high indeed.

One way to assess the utility of an RFA for Asia is to raise a counterfactual question. From the policy perspective, it is interesting and important to know if the existence of an Asian RFA would have helped in any way during the AFC. The counterfactual question then asks: suppose there had existed an RFA for Asia during the AFC, how differently might it have responded to the crisis?

In contrast to the behaviour of the IMF, within the proposed hybrid GFA, had a regional financial architecture been present it could have done at least the following on the basis of applying an evolutionary theory of financial instabilities under globalization:

1. Through constant regional monitoring it would have sensed the danger ahead of time. Even a regional monitoring unit alone would have been able to do better than the IMF team in Asia.
2. Through constant formal and informal contact with officials in member governments and the private sector, it would have sized up the possible extent of the problem earlier and better than did the IMF.

3. Through prompt and early action it would have provided liquidity to the system, and punished bad management in coordinated measures with national governments.
4. It would have been able to start regional discussions about bankruptcy and work out procedures by keeping in close touch with the history and legal issues facing particular countries.
5. It would have been in a position to use both moral suasion and toughness to keep both regional creditors and debtors in line.

The fundamental requirement for this, however, was an actually existing RFA with enough liquidity and technical expertise. The Asian Development Bank provided considerable liquidity to Korea in particular, but did not even have a monitoring unit when the crisis broke out. Furthermore, the autonomy and integrity of any future RFA, in Asia and elsewhere are issues that need discussion. The relationship between the RFAs and the IMF also needs to be further specified. These are matters that are of necessity evolutionary by nature. In this chapter, I have tried to specify some principles that may help in selecting the more beneficial evolutionary path.

Once there is a fully fledged regional financial architecture for Asia, for instance, it could be a regional lender of last resort. It could also perform effective surveillance functions. In addition, it could promote financial and corporate restructuring that is necessary, but almost impossible for the IMF to do. Finally, in the event of a future global or regional crisis, a more timely response could come from such an RFA already in place. In addition to East Asia such useful RFAs could be constructed in South Asia, the MENA region, sub-Saharan Africa, and Latin America. In the EU, ironically, a deconstruction towards a more flexible RFA through a reform of the European Central Bank (ECB) and a construction of a more benign federalist revenue-sharing fiscal structure may be what is needed.

The critical constructivist argument developed so far points to the possibility of using our knowledge, interpretative flexibility within reasonable limits, and political skills and ingenuity to utilize existing institutions together with some new ones to achieve desirable goals of global financial governance. In the case of GFA, this argument strengthens the case for developing the hybrid variety. Using both the existing global institutions such as the IMF, albeit in a modified form, and building upon existing regional initiatives may offer a better chance of creating a beneficial makeshift hybrid GFA than the textbook type pie-in-the-sky schemes correctly dismissed by Eichengreen. However, Eichengreen does not consider the role of RFAs in his otherwise excellent analysis. One way to read the present chapter is to see it as filling this gap by using an evolutionary constructivist argument for a hybrid GFA. A set of realistic reforms of the IMF together with the formation of RFAs will offer the best chance for the global economy to achieve stability and prosperity with equity. The BRICS initiatives though small in scale are welcome moves as a multi-regional RFA within the hybrid GFA, and have the potential to move the complex global financial system in the direction of optimality under post-crisis conditions.

APPENDIX 1 BASEL III KEY MILESTONES

Capital Requirements

Table 37.2 Capital requirement milestones

Year	Milestone	Capital Requirements
2014	Minimum capital requirements	Start of the gradual phasing-in of the higher minimum capital requirements
2015	Minimum capital requirements	Higher minimum capital requirements are fully implemented
2016	Conservation buffer	Start of the gradual phasing-in of the conservation buffer
2019	Conservation buffer	The conservation buffer is fully implemented

Source: Author's work.

Table 37.3 Milestones by year and leverage ratios

Year	Milestone	Leverage ratio
2011	Supervisory monitoring	Develop templates to track the leverage ratio and the underlying components
2013	Parallel run I	The leverage ratio and its components will be tracked by supervisors but not disclosed and not mandatory
2015	Parallel run II	The leverage ratio and its components will be tracked and disclosed but not mandatory
2017	Final adjustments	Based on the results of the parallel run period, any final adjustments will be made to the leverage ratio
2018	Mandatory requirement	The leverage ratio will become a mandatory part of Basel III requirements

Source: Author's work.

Liquidity Requirements

Table 37.4 Milestones by liquidity requirements

Date	Milestone	Liquidity requirements
2011	Observation period	Developing templates and supervisory monitoring of the liquidity ratios
2015	Introduction of the LCR	Initial introduction of the LCR, with a requirement of 60 per cent. This will increase by ten percentage points each year until 2019
2018	Introduction of the NSFR	Introduction of the NSFR

Note: Liquidity coverage ratio.

Source: Author's work.

APPENDIX 2 A SIMPLE MODEL OF A COMPLEX FINANCIAL ECONOMY

Multiple Equilibria with Possibilities of Crisis

THE ROLE FOR BRICS-LIKE FINANCIAL FACILITIES

In order to give the reader some idea of the problem of formalizing global and regional complex financial cum real economic systems (GRFS and RRFS) we summarize here the basic structure of a 'simple' non-linear model embodying distinct financial architectures which can be applied to analyse the BRICS-like financial facilities. At any single point in time, the model can be presented as a Social Accounting Matrix (SAM) and flow-of-funds representation of the socio-economic system. We will indicate the first m sectors as real and the next n as financial. There are p households and q other institutions including global and regional governance institutions.

The key distinction here is the explicitly non-linear nature of the economy-wide functional relationships. The key theorem shows the existence of multiple equilibria. Some further considerations of complexity and increasing returns prospects for development show that multiple equilibria are indeed the 'natural' outcomes in such models. Thus, there would seem to be some role for domestic policy in guiding the national economy to a particular equilibrium among many. Likewise, such policy space in an RRFS within a GRFS can only be possible under some hybrid GFA of which BRICS-like multi-regional financial architecture can be an integral and desirable part.

The virtue of a global economy-wide approach to technology systems is the embodiment of various inter-sectoral linkages within and across regions. In an SAM, such linkages are mappings from one set of accounts to another. In terms of GRFS and RRFS, the production activities can be broken down into a production (sub-) system and a set of institutional innovative activities leading to the creation of BRICS-like multi-regional financial architectures.

Although the existence theorems for these global cum regional multi-sectoral models provide some structure for the equilibria as sequences of fixed points in the socio-economic structure with evolving technology systems, it is not specified a priori which equilibrium will be reached. The problem of equilibrium selection thus remains open and depends on global, regional, and national institutions. The idea behind a BRICS-like multi-regional financial architecture can now be stated somewhat more formally. It is to reach a sequence of equilibria for developing economies so that in the non-linear models of the entire economy the maximal fixed points that are attainable are in fact reached through a combination of market forces and policy manoeuvers over time. It should also be understood that path dependence would rule out certain equilibria in the future. Thus initial choices of projects and institutions can matter crucially at times. It has been argued in the chapter that BRICS-like multi-regional financial architectures matter precisely in this way.

The Model on a Lattice

Define X as a vector lattice over a subring M of the real field R. Let $x_{+} = \{x|x \in X, x \geq 0\}$

A non-linear mapping N is defined such that $N : X_{+} \rightarrow X_{+}, N_0 = 0$. Given a vector of exogenous variables d, the following non-linear mapping describes a simultaneous non-linear equations model of an economy, E

$$x = Nx + d \tag{1}$$

for a given $d \in X_{+}$.

This non-linear system represents a socio-economic system of the type described previously. In order to specify the model further, the following assumptions are necessary.

1. X is order complete
2. N is an isotone mapping
3. $\exists \hat{x} \in$ such that $\hat{x} \geq N\hat{x} + d$

In terms of the economics of the model, the non-linear mapping from the space of inputs to the space of outputs allows for non-constant returns to scale and technical progress over time. The three assumptions are minimally necessary for the existence of equilibrium. Assumption 3 in particular ensures that there is some level of output vector which can be produced given the technical production conditions and demand structure.

Existence of Multiple Equilibria:

Theorem: Under the assumptions 1–3, there exists $x^* \in X_{+}$ so that x^* is a solution of

$$x = Nx + d$$

Proof: Consider the interval $[0, x] = \{\hat{x}|\hat{x} \in X_{+}, 0 \leq \hat{x} \leq x\}$ where $\hat{x}$ is defined as in Assumption 3. Take a mapping F.

$$F : x \in X_{+} \rightarrow N_x + d$$

F is isotone and maps $[0, x]$ into itself.
Define a set $D \equiv \{x|x \in [0, x], x \geq Fx\}$.
By Assumption 3, D is non-empty.
We now show $x^* \equiv \inf D$ is a solution to $x = Nx + d$. $x^* \equiv \inf D$; therefore $x^* \leq x, \forall x \in D$. F is isotone; therefore $Fx^* \leq Fx \leq x$ for each $x \in D$ implying.
$Fx^* \leq x^*$
From Assumption (2) we have $F(Fx^*) \leq Fx^*$. Thus $Fx^* \in D$; hence $x^* \equiv \inf D \leq Fx^*$ so, $Fx^* \leq x^* \leq Fx^*$. Therefore $x^* = Fx^*$.

This is an application of Tarski's and Birkhoff's theorem. The key feature to note here is that the equilibrium is not necessarily unique. It should also be noted that under additional assumptions on space X and the mapping N the computation of a fixed point can be done by standard methods (e.g. Ortega and Rheinboldt).

MULTIPLE EQUILIBRIA ON BANACH SPACE

In this section the results for multiple equilibria are extended to functionals on Banach space. We can define the model again for monotone iterations, this time on a non-empty subset of an ordered Banach space X. The mapping $f : X \to X$ is called compact if it is continuous and if $f(x)$ is relatively compact. The map f is called completely continuous if f is continuous and maps bounded subsets of X into compact sets. Let X be a non-empty subset of some ordered set Y. A fixed point x of a map $N : X \to X$ is called minimal (maximal) if every fixed point y of N in X satisfies $x \leq y (y \leq x)$

Theorem: Let (E, P) be an ordered Banach space and let D be a subset of E.

Suppose that $f : D \to E$ is an increasing map which is compact on every order interval in D. If there exist $y, \hat{y} \in D$ with $y \leq \hat{y}$ such that $y \leq f(y)$ and $f(\hat{y}) \leq \hat{y}$, then f has a minimal fixed point x. Moreover, $x \leq y$ and $x = \lim F^k(y)$ That is, the minimal fixed point can be computed iteratively by means of the iteration scheme

$$\begin{aligned} x_0 &= y \\ x_{k+1} &= f(x_k) \quad k = 0, 1, 2.... \end{aligned}$$

Moreover, the sequence (x_k) is increasing.

Proof: Since f is increasing, the hypotheses imply that f maps the order interval $[\bar{y}, y]$ into itself. Consequently, the sequence (x_k) is well-defined and, since it is contained in $f[\bar{y}, y]$, it is relatively compact. Hence it has at least one limit point. By induction, it is easily seen that the sequence (x_k) is increasing. This implies that it has exactly one limit point $\bar{x}$ and that the whole sequence converges to $\bar{x}$. Since f is continuous, $\bar{x}$ is a fixed point of f. If x is an arbitrary fixed point in D such that $x \geq \bar{y}$, then, by replacing y by x in the above argument, it follows that $\bar{x} \leq x$. Hence $\bar{x}$ is the minimal fixed point of f in $(\bar{y} + P) \cap D$. It should be observed that we do not claim that there exists a minimal fixed point of f in D.

We can also show that if $F : x \in X_+ \to N_x + d$ is an intersecting compact map in a non-empty order interval $[x, \hat{x}]$ and $x \leq Fx$ and $F\hat{x} \leq \hat{x}$ then F has a minimal fixed point x^* and a maximal fixed point x^{**}. Moreover, $x^* = \lim F^k(x)$ and $x^{**} = \lim F^k(\hat{x})$. The first of the above sequences is increasing and the second is decreasing.

Complex Dynamics and Out-Of-Equilibrium Behaviour

As is well known, non-linear dynamic systems can display a wide range of dynamic behaviours. As Keynes perspicuously pointed out in the General Theory during the

Great Depression, the capitalist economies with complex financial systems are unstable but within limits. However, as we know, dissipative systems with a big enough perturbation can move to a new basin of attraction with much disorganization during transition. Also, even with bifurcations, we do not know for certain which path it will follow. Furthermore, catastrophic singularities are also possible.

My argument can now be summarized in terms of dissipative systems dynamics in a world of multiple equilibria none of which may be reached. Instead, a neoliberal global economy may simply go through cycles of instabilities. A large part of my argument, therefore, has been that the recent global crisis is an example of a large accumulated perturbation that has created instabilities giving us a foretaste of what may become a pattern in the twenty-first century unless a new flexible hybrid GFA with sufficient liquidity and enforcement power is constructed soon. The BRICS bank and financial facilities are moves that can possibly dampen further instabilities in the global financial system and help promote growth with equity particularly in the poorer countries in the global system. With the creation of enough BRICS-like multi-regional financial architectures after the failures and crises in the twenty-first century, the world will have a fighting chance to pursue appropriate capability-enhancing development strategies along with a deepening of civilized social democratic structures in the core countries.

ACKNOWLEDGEMENTS

I would like to thank Tanweer Akram, Ilene Grabel, Izumi Otomo, Derek Sarchet, Aaron Schneider, and the participants of my seminars at Korbel School, New Delhi, and Tokyo.

REFERENCES

Abdelal, Rawi (2007). *Capital Rules: The Construction of Global Finance.* Cambridge, MA: Harvard University Press.

Agonsin, M. (1998). 'Capital inflows and investment performance: Chile in the 1990s', in R. Ffrench-Davis and H. Reisen (eds) *Capital Inflows and Investment Performance: Lessons from Latin America.* Snatiago: University of Chile.

Anderson, C. (2008). 'Iceland gets help to recover from historic crisis', *IMF Survey Magazine*, 2 December. Available at www.imf.org/external/pubs/ft/survey/so/2008/int111908a.htm, accessed 7 October 2018.

Azis, I. J. (1999). *Do We Know the Real Causes of the Asian Crisis? Global Financial Turmoil and Reform: A United Nations Perspective.* Tokyo: United Nations University Press.

Azis, I.J. (2002c). 'Financial sector liberalization and the Asian financial crisis: the IFIs got it wrong twice'. Working Paper. Ithaca, NY: Cornell University.

Barrell, R. and Gottschalk, S. (2010). 'Capital adequacy requirements in emerging markets', in R. Gottschalk (ed.) *The Basel Capital Accords in Developing Countries: Challenges for Development Finance.* New York: Palgrave Macmillan.

Beattie, A. (2010). 'Rapid Global Trade Recovery Continues'. *Financial Times*, 1 March. Available at https://assets.publishing.service.gov.uk/media/57a08afbe5274a31e00008c2/Global-Financial-Crisis-Phase-2-Synthesis-Working-paper-316.pdf, accessed 24 January 2020.

Beattie, Alan. (2011). 'World Bank backs efforts to counter rapid inflows.' *Financial Times*, January 13. Available at www.ft.com/cms/s/0/ca0df71e-1e71-11e0-87d2-00144feab49a.html#axzz1BG96TMA0, accessed 24 January 2020.

Best, J. (2010). 'Bringing power back in: IMF's constructivist strategy in critical perspective', in R. Abdelal, M. Blyth, and C. Parsons (eds) *Constructing the International Economy*. Ithaca, NY: Cornell University Press.

Bhagwati, J. (1998). 'The capital myth', *Foreign Affairs*, May/June.

Blyth, M. (2002). *Great Transformations: Economic Ideas and Institutional Change in the Twentieth Century*. Cambridge: Cambridge University Press.

BRICS (2013). 'Fifth BRICS summit declaration and action plan'. Available at www.mea.gov.in/bilateral-documents.htm?dtl/21482/5th+BRICS+Summit++eThekwini+Declaration+and+Action+Plan, accessed 8 August 2019.

Bryant, C. (2010). 'Hungary PM rejects new IMF deal and austerity', *Financial Times*, 22 July. Available at www.ft.com/cms/s/0/bb43ff2c-95c2-11df-b5ad-00144feab49a.html#axzz1BG96TMA0, accessed 8 August 2019.

Caruana, J. (2010). 'Why Basel III matters for Latin American and Caribbean financial markets'. Financial Stability Institute, Bank for International Settlements. Available at www.bis.org/speeches/sp101125.pdf, accessed 7 October 2018.

Conway-Smith, E. (2013). 'Developing nations to meet at the BRIC beach party in South Africa', *Global Post*. Available at www.globalpost.com/dispatch/news/regions/africa/south-africa/130323/developing-nations-meet-bric-summit-durban, accessed 7 October 2018.

Cornford, A. (2013). 'More details from the Basel committee concerning the Basel III leverage ratio', IDEAS. Available at www.networkideas.org/news/jul2013/news19_Basel_III.htm, accessed 7 October 2018.

Cozzi, G. and Griffith-Jones, S. (2014). *Investment-Led Growth: A Solution to the European Crisis*. Greenwich: Foundation for Progressive Studies.

Demirgüc-Kunt, A., Detragiache, E., and Merrouche, O. (2010). *Bank Capital: Lessons from the Financial Crisis*, Washington, DC: IMF. Available at www.imf.org/external/pubs/cat/longres.cfm?sk=24494.0, accessed 7 October 2018.

Economic Times (2013). 'BRICS may agree on 100bn currency fund during G-20 meeting'. Available at https://economictimes.indiatimes.com/news/economy/finance/brics-may-agree-on-100-bn-currency-fund-during-g20-summit/articleshow/22182518.cms?from=mdr, accessed 8 August 2019.

Ediz, T., Michael, I., and Perraudin, W. (1998). 'The impact of capital requirements on UK bank behaviour', *Economic Policy Review*, October, 15–22.

Eichengreen, B. (1999). *Toward a New International Financial Architecture: A Practical Post-Asia Agenda*. Washington, DC: Institute for International Economics.

Eichengreen, B. (2013a). 'Currency war or international policy coordination?', *Journal of Policy Modeling*.

Eichengreen, B. (2013b). 'The Bretton Woods system', in R. Parker and R. Whaples (eds) *Routledge Handbook of Major Events in Economic History*. London: Routledge.

Eichengreen, B. and Dincer, N. (2013). 'The architecture and governance of financial supervision: sources and implications', *International Finance* 15/3: 309–25.

Gottschalk, S. (2010). 'Capital adequacy requirements in emerging markets', in R. Gottschalk (ed.) The Basel Capital Accords in Developing Countries: Challenges for Development Finance. New York: Palgrave Macmillan.

Grabel, I. (2010). 'Promising avenues, false starts and dead ends: global governance and development finance in the wake of the crisis'. PERI Working Paper Series, No. 241, November. Available at www.peri.umass.edu/fileadmin/pdf/working_papers/working_papers_201-250/WP241.pdf, accessed 7 October 2018.

Griffith-Jones, S. (2011). 'South–South financial cooperation'. Background Paper No. 2 to UNCTAD's Least Developed Countries Report, 2011. Available at https://pdfs.semanticscholar.org/c424/1dba72a86e0821aff712ebd3d3556fae4bab.pdf, accessed 7 October 2018.

Griffith-Jones, S. (2014). 'A BRICS development bank: a dream come true?'. Discussion Paper No. 215. Geneva: UNCTAD.

Griffith-Jones, S., Ocampo, J.A., and Stiglitz, J. (2010). *Time for a Visible Hand: Lessons from the 2008 World Financial Crisis*. Oxford: Oxford University Press.

Hagan, S. and Vinals, J. (2010). 'Resolution of cross-border banks – A proposed framework for enhanced coordination'. IMF Legal and Monetary and Capital Markets Departments, June 11. Available at www.imf.org/external/np/pp/eng/2010/061110.pdf, accessed 7 October 2018.

Hughes, J. and Masters, B. (2011). 'Basel hardens bank hybrid bond rules', *Financial Times*, 13 January. Available at www.ft.com/cms/s/0/4151fcaa-1f4c-11e0-8c1c-00144feab49a.html#axzz1BhSkwAMd, accessed 8 August 2019.

IMF (International Monetary Fund) (2009). 'The IMF response to the global crisis: Meeting the needs of low-income countries'. IMF Background Note. Washington, DC: Available at www.imf.org/external/np/lic/2009/072909.htm, accessed 7 October 2018.

IMF (International Monetary Fund) (2010a). 'IMF board of governors approves major quota and governance reforms', IMF Press Release, No. 10/477, December 16. Available at www.imf.org/external/np/sec/pr/2010/pr10477.htm, accessed 7 October 2018.

IMF (International Monetary Fund) (2010b). 'Global cooperation role takes center stage in new IMF work program', IMF Press Release, December 2. Available at www.imf.org/external/np/sec/pr/2010/pr10466.htm, accessed 7 October 2018

IMF (International Monetary Fund) (2010c). 'IMF executive board approves major overhaul of quotas and governance', IMF Press Release, No. 10/418, November 5. Available at www.imf.org/external/np/sec/pr/2010/pr10418.htm, accessed 7 October 2018.

IMF (International Monetary Fund) (2010d). 'The IMF's Flexible Credit Line (FCL)', IMF Factsheet, October 5. Available at www.imf.org/external/np/exr/facts/fcl.htm, accessed 7 October 2018.

IMF (International Monetary Fund) (2011). 'IMF financial activities update', IMF, 6 January. Available at www.imf.org/external/np/tre/activity/2011/010611.htm, accessed 7 October 2018.

Kaminsky, G.L. and Reinhart, C.M. (1999). 'The twin crises: the causes of banking and balance-of-payments problems', *American Economic Review* 89/3: 473–500.

Kapur, D. and Webb, R. (2006). 'Beyond the IMF'. Paper for G-24 Technical Group Meetings, March 2006. Available at https://g24.org/wp-content/uploads/2016/01/Session-1_2-7.pdf, accessed 8 August 2019.

Khan, H.A. (1999a). 'Corporate governance of family businesses in Asia: what's right and what's wrong?'. ADBI Paper No. 3, Tokyo.

Khan, H.A. (1999b). 'Corporate governance in Asia: Which road to take?'. Paper presented at 2nd high level symposium in ADBI, Tokyo.

Khan, H.A. (2001). 'A note on path dependence'. Unpublished manuscript.

Khan, H.A. (2002). 'The extended panda's thumb and a new global financial architecture: an evolutionary theory of the role of the IMF and regional financial architectures. University of Tokyo CIRJE Discussion paper No. 2002-CF-163.

Khan, H. (2003). The Mangled Miracle and the Alchemy of Finance, in EconPapers. Available at https://econpapers.repec.org/paper/tkyfseres/2003cf191.htm.

Khan, H.A. (2003a). 'Technology, modernity and development: creating social capabilities in a POLIS', in T. J. Misa, P. Brey, and A. Feenberg (eds) *Technology and Modernity: The Empirical Turn*. Cambridge MA: The MIT Press, 327–58.

Khan, H.A. (2003b). 'On paradigms, theories and models', *Problemas del Desarrollo* 34/134: 149–55.

Khan, H.A. (2004). *Global Markets and Financial Crisis: Towards a Theory for the 21st Century*. Basingstoke: Macmillan/Palgrave.

Khan, H.A (2005). 'Towards a new global financial architecture: the extended panda's thumb approach, Invited Distinguished Scholar Lecture at the Academy of International Business Southwest Meeting, Dallas, Texas', *Southwest Review of International Business Research* 16/1: 251–76.

Khan, H.A. (2006). 'Managing global risks and creating prosperity: the role of the IMF and regional financial architectures', in J. Nakagawa (ed.) *Managing Development: Globalization, Economic Restructuring and Social Policy*. Abingdon: Routledge, 17–41.

Khan, H.A. (2009). 'A theory of deep democracy in the age of postmodernism', in Readings in Law and Society Journal 1/): 1–22.

Khan, H.A. (2011). 'Analyzing the impact on financial crisis on developing countries'. Report submitted to the UNDP. New York: UNDP. Available at www.undp.org/content/undp/en/home/librarypage/poverty-reduction/the-financial-crisis-and-its-impact-on-developing-countries.html, accessed 24 January 2020.

Khan, H.A. (2013). 'Development strategies: lessons from South Korea, Thailand, Malaysia and Vietnam', in A. Fosu (ed.) *Lessons from Successful Development Strategies*. Oxford: Oxford University Press, all chaps.

Krueger, A.O. (2000). 'Conflicting demands on the international monetary fund', *American Economic Review* 90/2: 38–42.

Lin, C.-S., Khan, H.A., Chang, R.-Y., and Wang, Y.-C. (2008). 'A new approach to modeling early warning systems for financial crises', *Journal of International Money and Finance* 27/7: 1098–121.

Masters, B. (2010a). 'Basel III: emerging market banks get off lightly, for now', *Financial Times*, 13 September. Available at blogs.ft.com/beyond-brics/2010/09/13/basel-and-emerging-markets/, accessed 8 August 2019.

Masters, B. (2010b). 'Relief over delay to Basel liquidity rules', *Financial Times*, 13 September. Available at www.ft.com/cms/s/0/269cfa5c-bf13-11df-a789-00144feab49a.html#axzz1Bh SkwAMd, accessed 8 August 2019.

Montes, M.F. (2014). 'Initial comments on BRICS Contingent Reserve Arrangement (CRA)'. The South Centre, Geneva, Switzerland. July 17.

Montgomery, Heather (2005). 'The effect of the Basel Accord on bank portfolios in Japan', *Journal of the Japanese and International Economies* 19/1: 24–36.

Muchhala, B. (2009). 'The IMF's financial crisis loans: No change in conditionalities'. Third World Network. Available at www.twn.my/title2/ge/ge30.pdf, accessed 8 August 2019.

Ostry, J., Ghosh, A., Habermeier, K., Chamon, M., Qureshi, M., and Reinhardt, D. (2010). 'Capital inflows: the role of controls'. IMF Staff Position Note, SPN/10/04. Available at www.imf.org/external/pubs/ft/spn/2010/spn1004.pdf, accessed 7 October 2018.

Rodrik, Dani and Velasco, Andres (1999). *Short-Term Capital Flows*. Cambridge, MA: National Bureau of Economic Research.

Sachs, J.D. and Woo, W.T. (2000). 'Understanding the Asian financial crisis', in W. T. Woo, Jeffrey D. Sachs, and Klaus Schwab (eds), *The Asian Financial Crisis: Lessons for a Resilient Asia*. Cambridge, MA: The MIT Press.

Sachs, J.D., Tornell, A., and Velasco, A. (1996). 'Financial crises in emerging markets: the lessons from 1995', *Brookings Papers on Economic Activity* No 1. Available at www.brookings.edu/bpea-articles/financial-crises-in-emerging-markets-the-lessons-from-1995/, accessed 11 August 2019.

Shah, A. and Patnaik, I. (2011). 'India's Financial Globalisation'. (January 2011). IMF Working Papers, pp. 1–24, January. SSRN. Available at https://ssrn.com/abstract=1751417, accessed 8 August 2019.

Solidar (2009). 'Doing a decent job? IMF policies and decent work in times of crisis'. Available at www.eurodad.org/uploadedFiles/Whats_New/Reports/Doing%20a%20decent%20job.pdf, accessed 8 August 2019.

Stiglitz, J.E. (1994). 'The role of the state in financial markets'. Proceedings of the World Bank Conference on Development Economics 1993. Washington, DC: World Bank.

Stiglitz, J.E. (2010). *Freefall: America, Free Markets and the Sinking of the World Economy*. New York: W.W.Norton.

Summers, L.H. (2000). 'International financial crises: causes, prevention, and cures', *American Economic Review* 90/2: 1–16.

Summers, L.H. and Summers, V. (1989). 'When financial markets work too well: a cautious case for Securities Transactions Tax', *Journal of Financial Services Research* 3/December: 261–86.

Taylor, Michael (2010). 'Basel II fails the younger cousins', *Financial World*, October.

Thomas, L., Jr (2009). 'Known for tight spending, IMF may loosen reigns', *New York Times*, 5 April.

Tobin, J. and Ranis, G. (1998). 'The IMF's misplaced priorities: flawed funds'. *The New Republic*. Available at www.thenewrepublic.com/archive/0398/030998/tobin030998.html, accessed 8 August 2019.

Triple Crisis Blog. Available at www.triplecrisis.com/, accessed 7 October 2018.

UNCTAD (UN Conference on Trade and Development) (2002, 2003, 2007, 2011). *Reports on Least Developed Countries*. Geneva: UNCTAD.

UNICEF (2010). 'Prioritizing expenditures for a recovery with a human face: results from a rapid desk review of 86 recent IMF country reports'. Social and Economic Policy Working Brief.

Van Waeyenberge, E., Bargawi, H., and McKinley, T. (2010). 'Standing in the way of development? A critical survey of the IMF's crisis response in low-income countries'. Eurodad and

Third World Network. Available at http://eurodad.org/uploadedfiles/whats_new/reports/standing%20in%20the%20way%20of%20development(1).pdf, accessed 14 December 2018.

Vols, U. and Caliari, A. (eds) (2010). *Regional and Global Liquidity Arrangements*. Bonn: German Development Institute and the Center for Concern. Available at www.coc.org/node/6613, accessed 7 October 2018.

Weisbrot, M., Cordero, J., and Sandoval, L. (2009). 'Empowering the IMF: should reform be a requirement for increasing the fund's resources?'. Center for Economic and Policy Research: Issue Brief. Available at www.cepr.net, accessed 7 October 2018.

Wendt, A. (1987). 'The agent-structure problem in international relations theory', *International Organization* 41/3: 335–70.

Wendt, A. (1999). *Social Theory of International Politics*. Cambridge: Cambridge University Press.

Yoshitomi, M. and Ohno, K. (1999). 'Capital account crisis and credit contraction: towards a better management of systemic currency crisis'. Paper presented at ADB Annual Meeting, 29 April, Manila.

38 Governing dynamics of a changing global economic order

The case for emerging economies

Deepanshu Mohan

Introduction

A BRIEF BACKGROUND TO A CHANGING INSTITUTIONAL DYNAMICS

Since the Great Depression of the 1920s, the governing dynamics of the international financial system has warranted universally recognized mechanisms in forms of institutional oversight to guard and monitor the process of financial integration across developing[1] and developed nation states. Rivers of ink have been spilled over in studying the inception, organizational framework, and functioning of a few multilateral institutions that became fully operational only after the end of the Second World War. The governing principles in argument for a 'hard' rule-based multilateral approach to international economic governance back then (in the mid-1940s) included: (a) a need to reconstruct the war-torn economies of the developed world; (b) a need to establish surveillance measures at a global level in preventing catastrophic economic disasters; (c) a need to provide credible opportunities for developing countries to seek development assistance and credit for mitigating financial risks.

With this in view, the international monetary system was rebuilt in the 1940s (under the Bretton Woods (BW) arrangement) around institutions such as the International Monetary Fund (IMF) under an idea that any form of economic or political nationalism (evident in the 1930s) should be avoided (Bordo and James 2000). The World Bank was created from the same perspective, with the aim of financing the reconstruction and

[1] The author here uses the World Bank's conventional way of distinguishing between developing and developed economies based on their gross national product (GNP) per capita levels. The World Bank refers to low-income (GNP per capita of US$765 or less), middle-income countries (US$766–US$3035) as developing and high-income countries (US$9,386 or more) as 'industrial' or developed. This basis of classification used here is economic in nature and does not use any political, historical factors.

Deepanshu Mohan, *Governing dynamics of a changing global economic order: The case for emerging economies* In: *Handbook of BRICS and Emerging Economies.* Edited by: P.B. Anand, Shailaja Fennell, and Flavio Comim, Oxford University Press (2021). © Oxford University Press. DOI: 10.1093/oso/9780198827535.003.0038 development of member nations, primarily through the rebuilding of national infrastructures (Todaro and Smith 2009). The third institutional arrangement (in form of an agreement)—completing the original BW (Bretton Woods Committee 2015) arrangement—included the General Agreement on Tariffs and Trade (GATT). GATT in the early 1990s subsequently evolved into a more formal institution, as did the World Trade Organization (WTO), whose major objective has been to bring down tariff barriers and other restrictions to trade, by encouraging trade liberalization between all member countries.

It is important to highlight that from the beginning i.e. since the 1940s itself, the influence of the United States (discussed in the second section) remained decisive in designing the institutional architecture and the governing dynamics of these institutions, catering to a US backed global membership. The breakdown of the BW system and subsequently the dollar–gold fixed exchange parity system in 1971 led to a series of currency debt crises in developing countries across Latin America, etc. at a time when institutions like the IMF and World Bank became development financiers and crisis managers for the emerging world (Mohan et al. 2013).

The financial disintegration caused as a result of economic shocks (since the 1970s) allowed the more developed economies (for example the United States, Japan, Germany, Britain, France, Italy, and Canada) to work around the existing financial system by establishing *soft* multilateral arrangements such as the G7 (later, with the addition of Russia, the G8) (Kirton et al. 2010) that are non-binding, *sans* sanctions but can rapidly meet, manage, and coordinate decisions in addressing global economic and financial issues especially during emergencies. The United Nations Conference on Trade and Development (UNCTAD) back in the 1960s was similarly created to accommodate the economic problems faced by developing countries.

From the economic catastrophe caused later by the East Asian crises (during the late 1990s) affecting countries in East Asia (mainly Thailand, Indonesia, South Korea, Singapore, etc.), the crisis scenario then gave way to a more expansive *soft* multilateral arrangement, involving a group of states to call themselves the 'G20' (in 1999)—bringing together finance ministers and central bank governors of industrialized and emerging countries to discuss key issues in the global economy, including (since the financial crisis of 2008) the heads of government themselves.

Over the last two decades, with the growing importance of developing economies like China, India, South Africa, and Brazil, etc. it has become quite evident that the executive design of such 'hard' and 'soft' multilateral frameworks remains too narrow, thereby suffering from a lack of legitimacy (Buchanan and Keohane 2006). The problems faced in financially assisting most developing countries has surfaced largely due to weaker enforcement, monitoring, and evaluative mechanisms of policy decisions taken by multilateral institutions such as the IMF and WTO. A rich volume of literature offers country-based empirical insights on these issues, including the works of Jeffrey Sachs, Joseph Stiglitz, William Easterly, and Paul Krugman among others in recent decades.

During the last two decades, one has further witnessed a gradual transformation in the governing dynamics of the institutional architecture within the developing world, which now seems to be undertaking a more regionalized approach in the process of accumulating and disbursing financial capital for the growth of a group. We can call these nations the 'like-minded developing countries' (LMDCs).[2] These LMDCs include larger developing countries like India, China, Brazil, South Africa, etc. LMDCs today have started to enjoy an increasing role in the world economy and on political platforms which have resulted in a tectonic shift in the global power dynamics (discussed in the second section).

This chapter aims to provide a comprehensive narrative on the governing dynamics of a changing global economic order in an account that follows in three sections: the first section elaborates further on the legacy of the BW system through the older multilateral institutions and the issues related with them, and briefly comments on the role and influence of the United States in the functioning of 'hard' and 'soft' multilateral arrangements since the 1940s; the second section highlights the nature of the changing dynamics of global financial order in a contemporary context under the rise of LMDCs, particularly China and India, that have gained on the political and economic capital globally to establish new region-based institutional charters (like those of the Asian Infrastructure Investment Bank [AIIB]) aimed at representing the interests of an expanding developing world; the third section offers a more prescriptive institutional approach, highlighting the need for (re)defined collective action by existing multilateral institutions along with the rise of newer, more plurilateral and regional institutional groups such as AIIB—in financially developing economies facing different stages of economic development.

To add briefly to the discussion on *institution* designed development approaches—in the third section—I start with a short analysis on the economics of growth—an understanding of which remains vital for the effective design of financial lending policies from both the emerging and the existing multilateral/regional/plurilateral arrangements. The section introduces a threefold taxonomy approach (geography, institutions, integration) as used by Dani Rodrik (*c.*2003) to study processes of economic growth for developing countries, further building it into a fourfold taxonomy, geography, institutions, state, technology (GIST). This theoretically deducted, cross-disciplinary lens accompanied by a few focus goals can enable existing and newer institutions at a regional/multilateral level to cater to the best economic interests of developing member nations.

[2] As per the definition of LMDCs used by the United Nations Framework Convention on Climate Change (UNFCCC), 'The like minded group of developing countries (LMDC) is a group of developing countries who organize themselves as block negotiators in international organizations such as the United Nations and the World Trade Organization; they represent more than 50% of the world's population.' Available at http://unfccc.int/files/documentation/submissions_from_parties/adp/application/pdf/adp_lmdc_ws1_20140309.pdf, accessed 31 October 2018.

The Bretton Woods legacy and the weighted hegemonic influence of the United States

The global financial system—emerging from the end of the Second World War—sought to be different from previous hegemonic institutional frameworks (seen during the 1920s). The triumphant allied forces (particularly the United States, United Kingdom, and France) at the end of the Second World War realized the need for an institutional embodiment, able to provide high levels of financial coordination to face the challenge of reconstructing their war-torn economies. The new governance architecture born out of an international conference at Bretton Woods, New Hampshire, came into being in 1944.

In that spirit, the IMF, GATT (now known as the WTO), and the International Bank for Reconstruction and Development (later simply known as the World Bank) were created. The *IMF*'s primary purpose was to encourage international monetary cooperation among nations under some predefined rules of the game, and to provide short-term loans to member states facing temporary balance-of-payments difficulties under the IMF's conditionality prescriptions (Dicken 2011: 538).

The *World Bank*'s role in turn has evolved significantly since its inception. Overall, the institution's main role has been to facilitate development across member nations through capital investment. It was originally created more as a plurilateral set-up, to overcome capital market imperfections and to help in the reconstruction of post-war Europe.[3] By the late 1950s, with Europe reconstructed thanks to the success of the Marshall Plan, the World Bank, in a more multilateral stance, turned towards investment in poorer economies (Todaro and Smith 2009). The establishment of the International Development Association in 1960, to provide funds on concessional terms to the poorest countries (in gross per capita income terms), reflects this concern (Todaro and Smith 2009).

The third pertinent institutional agreement—originating under the BW system—was GATT, created in 1947 (now known as the WTO)[4]—laying the foundational basis for the world's trading regime. As per Capling and Trommer (2008), the purpose of the WTO was, and still is, to reduce the protectionism of national regulations and the uncertainty and unpredictability of international trade relations as well as to promote stability (Capling and Trommer 2008). In order to avoid the disastrous economic performance accompanying the protectionist measures and high tariffs of the 1920s and 1930s, some

[3] The World Bank's structure is similar to that of the IMF in terms of member governments (185) and voting power relying on annual contributions. Its primary purpose since its creation has been to promote economic growth and prosperity by providing funds for investment in projects that help raise productivity and output, with essential attention to poverty reduction.

[4] Two of the most important principles of the WTO are reciprocity and non-discrimination. The first is promoted as a political imperative where nations give tariff reductions to receive similar benefits from their partners. The second implies, for example, that any advantage, e.g. on tariffs granted to a contracting party, would immediately be accorded to all other contracting parties (this is known as a most favoured nation clause).

principles were designed to help governments undo the inefficient restrictions in trade caused by terms-of-trade externalities (Bagwell and Staiger 2000).

Two of the above institutions, i.e. the IMF and the World Bank, since their inception, had quite differentiated tasks; policies concentrating more on macroeconomic adjustments and microeconomic policies within member nations, respectively. Over the past four decades (particularly since the rise in frequency of oil shocks, and the rising frequency of financial crises from the 1970s), each of these institutions enacted policies that have not always been consistent with each other (see Cornia et al. 1987; Stewart 1991). When policies did intersect, any form of hardship inflicted upon poorer nations was further exacerbated.

As reflected in a paper by Todaro and Smith (2009) here:

> ... due to cuts in government services, rising unemployment, falling real wages, and the elimination of food subsidies ... Critics point out that the terms of conditionality [IMF requirement] associated with adjustment loans [World Bank conditions] are anti-developmental when they reverse or slow improvements in living conditions among the very poor. (Stewart 1991)

Moreover, the dynamics of these 'hard', rule-based, formal institutions (the IMF, World Bank, and WTO), have been shaped predominantly by power structures of a different world that existed in the late 1940s dominated then by Western nations, most notably by the United States and some larger Western European countries, reflecting their own priorities of that time. This consequently led to the eroding of faith in these institutional arrangements, particularly among developing member nations (since the 1990s) over the older BW economic governance architecture.

The key reasons explaining this eroding faith—as explained by Robert Wade (2011)—stem from the nature of (a) 'irrational one size fits all conditionality prescriptions' (imposed through structural adjustment programmes and the austerity measures by the World Bank and IMF) on developing member countries; (b) inadequate representation for developing economies in institutional governance decision-making mechanisms (like IMF); (c) perception of unfair treatment meted out to some emerging economies in organizations such as the WTO (in the case of agricultural subsidies), etc.

The conditionality requirement here, set by the IMF as a necessary prerequisite to receiving any form of disbursed financial assistance or aid, has often been criticized on several grounds. One such criticism pointed out by Bird (2009), was that the conditionality requirement was often used to implement orthodox short-term financial policies, leading to bad results for developing economies.

For instance, between 1982 and 1988, the IMF approach towards financial lending was tested in twenty-eight of the thirty-two nations of Latin America and the Caribbean (Dreher 2006). During that period, Latin America financed US$145 billion in debt payments but at a cost of economic stagnation, rising unemployment, and an overall decline in per capita income of 7 per cent. Countries adjusted but did not grow and the same situation prevailed in much of Africa (Todaro and Smith 2009: 681).[5]

[5] For a critique on *conditionality*, see Drazen (2002); Dreher (2006); Bird (2009).

William Easterly (2001), in his research on studying the impact of IMF and World Bank's structural adjustment programmes on financial lending policies since the late 1980s, argued this effect to be usually limited to a few highly visible macroeconomic indicators, such as the fiscal balance and devaluation (expenditure-reducing and expenditure-switching policies)[6] which may seem to more likely to affect the formal than the informal sector. Easterly (2001: 310) adds to this by saying:

> In economies growing under home-grown reform programs, where government ownership of the program creates stronger motivation for genuine change, the transformation of incentives is likely to be economy wide – stimulating both the informal and formal sectors. China in the 1990s is a good example of home-grown reform without adjustment lending, although it was open to advice from international financial institutions (IFIs). China reduced the percent living on less than $2 a day from 71 percent in 1990 to 50 percent in 1998. Chile 1987–1994 is another example of rapid reduction in poverty with an indigenous reform program and very little adjustment lending. Despite high inequality, the percent living on less than $2 a day in Chile fell from 31 in 1987 to 20 in 1994. El Salvador is an example of an economy going in the other direction, with economic expansion and intensive adjustment lending, but seeing poverty actually increase over this period.

Either way, the IMF's own role evolved from guardian of the BW 'adjustable peg' exchange rate system and financier of temporary accounts deficits for advanced economies to its present primary roles as development financier and crisis manager for the emerging world (Bordo and James 2000).

THE WEIGHTED INFLUENCE OF THE UNITED STATES

Robert Wade in a paper written in 2011 offers useful empirical insights into the level of influence commanded by the United States in governing the dynamics of IFIs. The United States' unique position since the 1940s, the size of its economy, its high average income, and its political and military power, among other factors, allowed it to ensure a form of 'hegemonic rule' over the international financial system. This phenomenon, according to Wade (2011), was probably reinforced by the ending of the original BW system in 1971.

The hegemonic influence of the United States can be analysed in terms of three periods as follows:

a) In the design and functioning of the BW institutions, particularly up until 1971:

From the outset the influence of the United States was decisive in the process of designing and implementing the policies of the BW financial institutions. John Maynard

[6] A documentary called *'Life and Debt'* brings this narration out while discussing the case of Jamaica from the impact of Washington Consensus-led structural adjustment programmes imposed by the IMF in exchange for short-term crisis financial assistance.

Keynes and Harry Dexter White—a senior US Treasury Department official—were instrumental in setting up the IMF and the World Bank (Wade 2011). As Wade (2011: 8) notes:

> The US exercised predominant power in the IMF and the World Bank – crystallized in its monopoly of the presidency of the Bank and the number two position at the Fund, and its veto over decisions requiring a super-majority, the only state with such power.

In a predominant position, the US enforced what Karl Polanyi calls 'embedded liberalism' on developing member nations. 'Embedded liberalism' denotes a compromise that member nations (particularly the developing countries) since the late 1940s made between safeguarding their domestic economic objectives, especially from a commitment to maintaining full employment, and an opening up of the domestic economy to allow for the restoration of international trade and investment. 'An acknowledgment of the legitimacy of governments giving priority to the pursuit of domestic economic objectives was also written into the rules of the game' (Ravenhill 2008).

This state of affairs gradually changed from the 1970s (discussed below), when the BW system broke down and the US untrammelled itself in terms of its monetary and fiscal policies with a lesser need to take into account other states' interests in designing its own economic policies. The state-led system was transformed into a market-led system and the position of the US was reinforced (Wade 2002).

b) In the period from 1971 to 2000:

The breakdown of the BW system in 1971, marked by the unilateral US decision to terminate the convertibility of the dollar to gold, turned the dollar into a 'fiat currency'[7] which was backed by nothing but the promise of the federal government (Slate 2011), giving United States the monetary freedom which the country was aiming for. The US dollar became the sole backing for currencies and a reserve currency for member states. While holding the sole rights to manage and issue the world's main reserve currency (i.e. US$), the United States was able to run current account deficits every year from 1992 until 2014).

The United States could take individual monetary decisions without further scrutiny, as reflected in the case of the Federal Reserve's decision to raise US rates in 1979 without assessing its impact on the rest of the world, especially Latin America, which was then heavily indebted to United States banks (Wade 2011). The US position, according to Robert Wade was reinforced by an ideological factor, since various circumstances during this period consolidated the pre-eminence of the capitalist market economy. The Reagan–Thatcher revolution, with the downsizing of government assets, massive

[7] Definition of a fiat currency: 'A Currency that a government has declared to be legal tender, but is not backed by a physical commodity. The value of fiat money is derived from the relationship between supply and demand rather than the value of the material that the money is made of. Historically, most currencies were based on physical commodities such as gold or silver, but fiat money is based solely on faith. Fiat is the Latin word for "it shall be"' (see Investopedia. Available at www.investopedia.com/terms/f/fiatmoney.asp#ixzz3oKn0PZoi, accessed 31 October 2018).

privatizations, and aggressive deregulation of the private sector; the collapse of the Soviet Union and Communism; and the Washington Consensus manifesto around a set of ten policy prescriptions[8] among other factors, all consolidated a strongly market-based approach with the US as the principal ideological reference (Mohan et al. 2013).

c) In the twenty-first century, with the rise of LMDCs:

The successive historic and institutional developments that reinforced and consolidated the market-based approach—with the US as its principal promoter and beneficiary—also created a more unstable environment while generating opportunities for some emerging economies. Successive financial crises in Latin America (1980s), Mexico (1994–95), East Asia (1997–98), Brazil, Russia, Turkey (1998–99), Argentina (2001–02), and the US (2008) are good examples of how complex it is to manage financial systems in a world of floating exchange rates and poorly regulated financial sectors.

As Reinhart and Rogoff (2008) observe, the number of years separating default episodes in the recent period (after 1945) indeed remained much lower (three years) than it was before (six years) (Reinhart and Roghoff 2011). Nevertheless, levels of financial instability have also been accompanied by, or have perhaps been the cause of bigger opportunities for developing economies.

Since the 1960s, some Asian economies—particularly Hong Kong, Taiwan, Singapore, South Korea, and more recently China—have managed to achieve and sustain high growth rates (further explained in the second section). This phenomenon, albeit not limited to East Asia, was found later in other latitudes, particularly in the cases of Brazil, Turkey, Indonesia, India, and Russia. Their growing weight, along with the increasing vulnerability of the US economy, gave rise to alterations in the international scenario that was later qualified as 'multipolar' (Mohan et al. 2013). However, greater 'multipolarity' doesn't necessarily translate into greater 'multilateralism'.

Robert Wade (2002) in this regard offers different criteria to assess the increase in multilateralism, through: (a) an entry of new states to apex governing forums (the expansion of the G8 to the G20); (b) an increase in the voting power of southern states ('developing' economies) in international organizations; and (c) new agreements on global issues subscribed to by many states of both the developed North and the developing South (Wade 2002).

The increase in multilateralism, whether as a consequence of a certain degree of multipolarity or not, had to deal with the hegemonic priorities. In the case of the US, as in any other possible hegemonic scenario, for most of the time this entailed a dilemma. On one hand, the US would wish to keep control over international organizations so that they promoted US foreign policy objectives. On the other hand, they however needed to structure and operate within these organizations in a way that maintained the

[8] The Washington Consensus reform package advocated for policies like fiscal discipline, reorientation of public expenditure, tax reform, interest rate liberalization, competitive exchange rates, trade liberalization, opening up to foreign investment, privatization, deregulation, and property rights.

organizations' appearance in accordance with the rules of the game, decided by the collective management of developed member nations.

With developing countries gaining an economic comparative advantage, gradually a growing discontent surfaced from the inadequacies of the decision-making process. As a result the US, particularly with the rise of China (over the last two decades), started losing its unique position.

The changing dynamics in the global economic order over the last few years has been surfaced with the formation of new intergovernmental institutions at a regional and plurilateral level which gradually seem now to be replacing the 'older', more US-dominated, global economic governance architecture. Also, any economic analysis speculating on the functioning of existing/new institutional arrangements while offering prophetic prescriptions on the future of the US and its influence in multilateral decision making (including in 'hard' financial institutions like IMF, WTO, World Bank) may fail to see the effects of a changing political landscape in times of an inward-protectionist leaning projection under a Donald Trump presidency and the roll-out of BREXIT and its impact on the European Union in the coming years.

THE SHIFTING WEIGHT OF GLOBAL ECONOMIC INFLUENCE TOWARDS CHINA

Entering 2017, the Chinese economy was witnessing its worst economic slowdown over the last three decades. China's economy, in 2015, grew at 6.9 per cent, its lowest growth performance in the last thirty years. In spite of being the second largest economy (after the United States), China seems to be now in a rebalancing act (since the recent devaluations of the Yuan) by undertaking structural economic reforms to push its source of growth towards the service sector at a time when growth in the manufacturing sector contracted for a fifth straight month (by the end of December 2015) (Gough 2016).

Having said that, at an aggregate level, during the last three decades China has established its economic supremacy through an export-led growth model accompanied by a rigorous state-directed investment plan to invest (bilaterally and multilaterally) within countries of Africa, East Asia, and the Asia-Pacific.

Y. Qian (2002) in his paper, 'How reform worked in China', explains the puzzle of the Chinese economic growth story which, despite the absence of many conventional institutions, such as rule of law and secured private property rights, has allowed a rapidly growing economy to achieve its goal of establishing itself as a global economic power.

> A series of institutional changes concerning the market, firms, and the government in the novel form of 'transitional institutions' which helped the Chinese economy improve its economic efficiency by unleashing the standard forces of incentives and competition on the one hand.
>
> (Qian 2002)

In the current context, with a foreign currency reserve pool of approximately US$3.50 trillion, China's success in establishing the AIIB (with more than fifty-seven founding members), and the inclusion of its currency (the Yuan) in IMF's special drawing rights (SDR) basket of reserve currencies, the weight of influence in shaping the governance architecture has gradually shifted towards China.

Moreover, instituting the AIIB under a Chinese dominated leadership has upturned itself into a diplomatic fiasco for the US (Eichengreen 2015). In spite of discouraging its allies from joining the AIIB, the current US administration has watched Britain leading a raft of Western European countries, followed by Australia and South Korea into just doing that. China will control a majority of the voting shares with 30 per cent of the total financial contribution in the AIIB capitalized at US$100 billion (Eichengreen 2015).

Even though India is one of the founding members of the AIIB and New Development Bank (NDB)—an initiative taken by BRICS—the Chinese share of investment in both these institutions remains the highest compared to any other country. In Asia too, a 'growing chorus of concern that China is building a sphere of influence in the region' can already be observed (Eichengreen 2015).

Looking at the larger picture, the creation of AIIB/NDB is now being seen as the start of 'an institutional competition for global economic governance'. For developing countries, which are in greater need of capital to finance a sustainable growth-led development plan, this competition between the old 'multilateral' financial order led by developed economies against a new more 'regionally' shaped financial order led by developing economies (like China, India, and others) looks like a good thing, for *two* reasons, as observed by Slaughter (2015):

First, developing member countries will now have more sources from which to seek financial lending without being circumscribed by the general conditionality requirements associated with loans from the World Bank/IMF. For example, Slaughter (2015) argues that a region like 'East Asia now is likely to get more of the roughly $8 trillion that the Asia Development Bank has estimated for the region to keep growing through 2020, in addition to receiving infrastructural loans through AIIB'.

Second, both developed and developing economies have since the 2008 financial crisis been facing 'a massive overhang of liquidity which has exacerbated debt levels'.[9] The establishment of regionally dedicated institutions like the AIIB and NDB can indubitably help in dealing with such problems associated with maintaining liquidity by ensuring 'target-based' financial assistance, especially for deficit investment areas like infrastructure and the energy sector within developing member economies.

The role for existing older multilateral institutions (World Bank, IMF) here can be to facilitate and guide the newer institutions in safeguarding such target-based financial lending practice by performing the role of 'knowledge banks'. Partaking of lessons and tools in effective monitoring and the evaluative measures involved with financial lending

[9] Albeit one may blame this on the unconventional nature of monetary and fiscal policies implemented in the advanced economies since the 2008 global financial crisis and the ongoing Eurozone crisis.

will be critical for developing economies in achieving long-term goals of increasing competitiveness and financial inclusion.

In addition to this, China's ambitious One Belt, One Road initiative aims to construct a Silk Road Economic Belt extending through Central Asia, and a Maritime Silk Road linking China with Southeast Asia, the Indian Ocean, the Middle East, and ultimately Europe.

As noted by Loesekrug et al. (2015: 10):

> The core of the 'One Belt, One Road' initiative lies in its strategic and geopolitical importance. China seeks to build a *cordon sanitaire* of regional stability. Its leadership firmly believes economic prosperity is the only way to maintain peace in its fragile neighbourhood, from volatile Central Asia via a fragmented Pakistan and war-torn Afghanistan to the terror belt in the Middle East and North Africa. The Chinese government has resisted the idea of labeling the 'belt and road' project as its own Marshall Plan, but the commonality of China's economic interests with the corridor nations and a sound infrastructure bond will be the best way to prevent regional conflicts. It's also a viable way to export China's model of development: the right to develop irrespective of political systems.

'New' dynamics of a changing global economic order

If we simply observe trends of some of the LMDCs (Brazil, India, China, Turkey, South Africa, etc.) over the last two decades across three critical macroeconomic parameters i.e. (a) GDP growth rates (1999–2015) (Table 38.1); (b) foreign direct investment (FDI): inward flows and stock, annual (1998–2014) (Table 38.2); (c) the net transfer in financial resources; it is easy to follow a shift in the thrust of financial power and economic dominance from the developed bloc of nations towards these large, developing countries within regions of South/East Asia, Latin America, Southern Africa, etc.

Larger developing economies like India in South Asia; mainland China, South Korea, and Taiwan in East Asia; Brazil, Mexico, and Chile in South America, etc. can be seen as drivers of higher, more consistent economic growth (Table 38.1)—as also mentioned in the Introduction to this handbook; maintaining favourable trade numbers these economies have also emerged as major recipients of FDI flows both from developed countries and those within the same region (Table 38.2). The level of financial integration ensured by a more fluid movement of capital flows holds critical importance for increasing the process of capital accumulation across these developing countries.

Albeit this transfer in financial power dominance doesn't come across as a new feature from the global movement of capital flows, in the last five years or so we have witnessed an increased political will among most of these countries to create formal institutional mechanisms in engaging gradually with each other under a more regionalized umbrella.

In its resolution 65/94 on 'The United Nations in global governance', the General Assembly also recognized the need for an 'inclusive, transparent and effective multilateral system to better address the urgent global challenges of today and reaffirmed the central role of the United Nations in ongoing efforts to find common solutions to such challenges' (United Nations 2015).

Table 38.1 GDP growth rate, 1999–2015

	2000	2001	2002	2003	2004	2005	2006	2007	2008	2009	2010	2011	2012	2013	2014	2015
High income: OECD	3.9	1.6	1.5	2.0	3.0	2.6	2.9	2.5	0.1	–3.5	2.8	1.6	1.2	1.1	1.7	2.0
Brazil	4.4	1.3	3.0	1.2	5.6	3.2	4.0	6.0	5.0	–0.2	7.6	3.9	1.8	2.7	0.1	–1.3
India	4.0	4.9	3.9	7.9	7.8	9.3	9.3	9.8	3.9	8.5	10.3	6.6	5.1	6.9	7.3	7.5
China	8.4	8.3	9.1	10.0	10.1	11.4	12.7	14.2	9.6	9.2	10.6	9.5	7.8	7.7	7.3	6.9
Russian Federation	10.0	5.1	4.8	7.3	7.2	6.4	8.2	8.5	5.2	–7.8	4.5	4.3	3.4	1.3	0.6	–3.8
United States	4.1	1.0	1.8	2.8	3.8	3.3	2.7	1.8	–0.3	–2.8	2.5	1.6	2.2	1.5	2.4	2.5
Thailand	4.5	3.4	6.1	7.2	6.3	4.2	5.0	5.4	1.7	–0.7	7.5	0.8	7.3	2.8	0.9	2.5
United Kingdom	3.8	2.8	2.5	3.3	2.5	3.0	2.7	2.6	–0.5	–4.2	1.5	2.0	1.2	2.2	2.9	2.4
Turkey	6.8	–5.7	6.2	5.3	9.4	8.4	6.9	4.7	0.7	–4.8	9.2	8.8	2.1	4.2	2.9	3.2
South Africa	4.2	2.7	3.7	2.9	4.6	5.3	5.6	5.4	3.2	–1.5	3.0	3.2	2.2	2.2	1.5	1.3

Note: GDP growth, constant 2010 US$.

Source: Author's calculations from Global Economic Prospects, World Bank Database. Available at https://datacatalog.worldbank.org/dataset/global-economic-prospects, accessed 18 February 2019.

Table 38.2 FDI: inward flows and stock, annual, 1998–2014 (US$ million)

Year/economy	1998	1999	2000	2001	2002	2003	2004	2005	2006	2007	2008	2009	2010	2011	2012	2013	2014
Argentina	7290.7	23988	10418	2166.1	2148.9	1652	4124.7	5265.3	5537.3	6473.2	9725.6	4017.2	11333	10840	15324	11301	6612
Bangladesh	576.46	309.12	578.64	354.47	335.47	350.25	460.4	845.26	792.48	666.36	1086.3	700.16	913.32	1136.4	1292.6	1599.1	1526.7
Brazil	28856	28578	32779	22475	16590	10144	18146	15066	18822	34585	45058	25949	48506	66660	65272	63996	62495
China	45463	40319	40715	46878	52743	53505	60630	72406	72715	83521	108312	95000	114734	123985	121080	123911	128500
Germany	24593	56076	198277	26402	53522	32377	10193	47449	55654	80212	8126.9	23805	65642	67515	20316	18193	1830.9
India	2633	2168	3588	5477.6	5629.7	4321.1	5777.8	7621.8	20328	25350	47102	35634	27417	36190	24196	28199	34417
Republic of Korea	5989.2	10726	11509	6522.3	5475.1	7010	13294	13643	9161.9	8826.9	11188	9021.9	9497.4	9773	9495.9	12767	9898.5
Netherlands	37277	41203	63855	51927	25038	32820	12452	39047	13978	119636	5776.5	38752	7184.5	24369	17655	32039	30253
Singapore	5958.7	18853	15515	17007	6157.2	17051	24390	18090	36924	47733	12201	23821	55076	48002	56659	64793	67523
South Africa	561.48	1503.2	887.34	6783.9	1569.2	733.67	798.03	6646.9	311.45	6538.1	9209.2	7502.1	3635.6	4242.9	4558.8	8300.1	5712.3
Sri Lanka	150	201	172.95	171.79	196.5	228.72	233	272	480	603.4	752.2	404	477.6	981.12	941.12	932.55	944.25
Thailand	7492	6106.4	3410.1	5073.2	3355.4	5222.3	5858.6	8066.6	9501.3	11359	8454.7	4854.4	9146.8	1194.7	9168.1	14016	12566
United Kingdom	74321	87979	121898	36935	21138	17033	61679	183822	148740	181661	93364	90591	58954	41803	59375	47675	72241
United States	174434	283376	314007	159461	74457	53146	135826	104773	237136	215952	306366	143604	198049	229862	169680	230768	92397

Source: Author's calculations from UNCTAD database. Available at https://unctadstat.unctad.org/EN, accessed 18 February 2019.

The AIIB as a regionally set up institution (headquartered in Beijing, China) seeks to do exactly this under the leadership of China (with the highest share of member contribution), welcomed by most in the developing world as a critical medium for sustainably financing the needs of developing countries during the twenty-first century. This view has also been endorsed by the IMF and World Bank.

In an age of increasing protectionism, under a Donald Trump-led US administration, AIIB presents a major opportunity for China to establish its supremacy both as a top regionalans global economic player through infrastructural lending to emerging economies. The purpose of the AIIB as per its Articles of Agreement (AIIB 2015: 3) is to:

> [F]oster sustainable economic development, create wealth and improve infrastructure connectivity in Asia by investing in infrastructure and other productive sectors; and promote regional cooperation and partnership in addressing development challenges by working in close collaboration with other multilateral and bilateral development institutions.

With the formation of regional/plurilateral institutional arrangements similar to those of the NDB by BRICS economies—AIIB is likely to allow for greater targeted financial investment for infrastructural development in LMDCs and for other plans necessary in achieving inclusive, developmental growth.

Towards a (re)defined institutional approach to developing economies

In this section, I briefly focus on the need to revisit some predefined approaches to growth (used by older IFIs) and focus goals for improving processes in financial lending for developing and transition economies. At the centre of an emerging alternative system of global economic governance, increasingly becoming more regional in nature, it is vital for developing member countries (in different stages of economic development) to work towards a redefined outlook on capably designing policies on financial credit allocation for member nations.

A (re-)defined economic governance architecture warrants to be sensitive in resolving endogenous (internal) problems faced by emerging economies due to the lack of (a) access to cheap financial credit; (b) creation of alternative employment opportunities; (c) rising debt and intra-regional disparities; (d) income inequalities; all of which are central to their financial development process.

FINANCING FOR A MORE ROBUST, INCLUSIVE GROWTH

The classical neoliberal approach to economic growth has often confused attainment of economic prosperity with greater economic openness through increased trade and investment per se, contributing to higher growth and per capita income making everyone 'better off' (Chang 2007). The focus on making everyone 'better off' in an economy rests more on increasing productivity levels across all lines of production and through greater capital accumulation (by domestic or foreign induced investment) in a developing economy. This as a uniform model prescription was followed by the older IFIs (the IMF, World Bank, etc.) in advising/designing financial lending policies for most late developing economies, seen particularly during the time of the Washington Consensus of the late 1980s.

However, lessons in economic history learnt from the study of economic crises (post-1970s) and the pattern of uneven growth in some of the late developing economies showcase that these models present half-baked truths at best. Economic openness through increased integration processes (trade, investment, less capital controls, etc.) does contribute well for the onset of higher economic growth over time by raising the per capita income for developing nations; however, to achieve a more robust, inclusive, and sustainable level of economic growth, a wider approach to growth economics acknowledging the necessity and role of the state needs to be well understood. Developing economic states as active stakeholders can not only create but manage market-created incentives while organically tapping into the potential of local *endogenous*[10] factors (see note).

GIST: A CROSS-DISCIPLINARY APPROACH TO THE ECONOMICS OF GROWTH

To shape our thinking about the economics of growth, Dani Rodrik's *In Search of Prosperity* (*c.*2003) helps us to distinguish between the 'proximate' and 'deep' determinants of growth According to Rodrik (*c.*2003):

> ... the growth of per capita output, can be expressed in terms of three proximate determinants: i) physical capital deepening ii) human capital accumulation and iii) productivity growth [Figure 38.1]. In the equation given [Figure 38.1], a as a constant represents the technical and allocative efficiency level for an economy which allows for studying the role of technology in measuring outcomes for capital accumulation. This efficiency level also reflects the optimum use of the resource endowments across varied economic activities. (Rodrik *c.*2003)

[10] The term endogenous growth, defined by Peter Howitt refers to a 'long run economic growth at a rate determined by forces that are internal to the economic system, particularly those forces governing the opportunities and incentives to create technological knowledge (like technology, institutions and integration processes (i.e. the role of public policy in trade, investment etc.))' Available at http://citeseerx.ist.psu.edu/viewdoc/download?doi=10.1.1.182.8496&rep=rep1&type=pdf, accessed 18 February 2019.

The term exogenous growth can be defined as 'the belief that economic growth arises due to influences outside the economy or company of interest. Exogenous growth assumes that economic prosperity is primarily determined by external rather than internal factors. According to this belief, given a fixed amount of labor and static technology, economic growth will cease at some point, as ongoing production reaches a state of equilibrium based on internal demand factors'. (Cited from Investopedia. Available at www.investopedia.com/terms/e/exogenous-growth.asp#ixzz3wAb7Vo8W, accessed 18 February 2019).

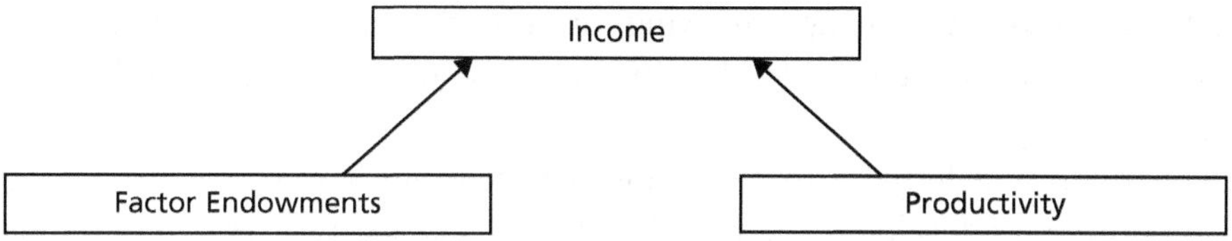

$$y = ak^{\alpha}(hl)^{1-\alpha}$$

Per capita growth = physical capital deepening + human capital accumulation + productivity growth

Figure 38.1 How economists think of income determination for measuring economic growth

Source: *In Search of Prosperity*, Rodrik (*c*.2003: 5).

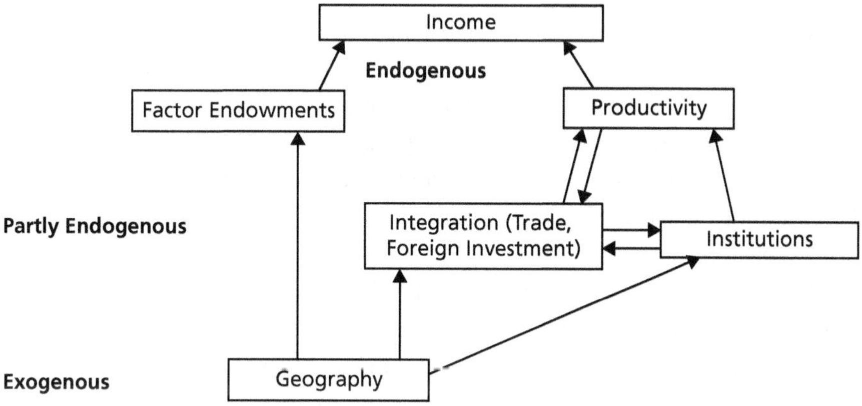

Figure 38.2 Growth economics in one page with a threefold taxonomy

Source: *In Search of Prosperity*, Rodrik (*c*.2003: 6).

In Rodrik's analysis on defining 'proximate determinants of growth with deeper determinants', he uses a threefold taxonomy (Figure 38.2) that adds to the final value of economic growth in an endogenous or exogenous way. As per this threefold taxonomy in Figure 38.2:

> *Geography* relates to the advantages and disadvantages posed by a country's physical location (latitude, proximity to navigable waters, climate, and so on). *Integration* relates to the market size, and the benefits (as well as costs) of participation in international trade in goods, services, capital, and possibly *labor* and *Institutions* refer to the quality of formal and informal sociopolitical arrangements ranging from the legal system to broader political institutions that play an important role in promoting or hindering economic performance. (Rodrik *c*.2003)

What remains missing in this taxonomy though is the defined role of the state[11] itself in shaping the path to higher growth through the design and implementation of effective

[11] Murray Rothbard (1978) defines a state through the eyes of some as 'an institution of social service; the apotheosis of society; an amiable, though often inefficient, organization for achieving social ends' and 'a necessary means for achieving the goals of mankind, a means to be ranged against the "private sector" and often winning in this competition of resources'.

policies as tools of economic change, allowing for an optimum use of resource/factor endowments (land, labour, capital, etc.) in generating income and producing the maximum production output.

Policies on reforming local institutions and safeguarding social security benefits (health, education, skills development, etc.) allowed the state to create equitable opportunities for distributing gains from production, trade, and foreign investment (received inwards) to all in a developing society.

The need therefore for emerging regional/plurilateral institutional arrangements is to widen their outlook towards targeting for growth among member nations (i.e. developing and transition economies) and incorporate the use of a fourfold taxonomy, in the form of the cross-disciplinary approach, GIST.

This theoretical cross-disciplinary macro-approach—breaking away from the old neoliberal economic methodology—can allow newer/existing multilateral/regional institutional arrangements to prioritize *first* reviewing the specific economic needs of a developing member country by studying its geography, nature of endogenous institutions, nature of the state, and level of technology; and *second*, providing short-/long-term financial lending in accordance with these endogenous features of a member economy for a more robust, inclusive growth.

The way for a GIST approach to work may involve a conscious measure by international institutions to station independent, local experts for conducting a GIST analysis and by empirically studying the member economy's *geography* (soil, climate, monsoon, proximity to the coast, geopolitical positioning, and explore comparative advantages for trade expansion); *the nature of the state* (democracy, federal polity vs centrally driven model, etc.); its local *institutions* (rule of law, private property rights, accountable frameworks, policies reforming labour rights, competition laws, and establish other rules of the game); and level of *technological readiness and capacity.*[12]

For example, in India, there is an enormous investment need from an institutional perspective (like AIIB), particularly in areas of physical infrastructure and financial inclusion for developing inclusive growth capacities (in areas of health care, education etc.). Both these goals can distinctly be identified for any form of loan assistance by AIIB, after developing a case profile for India studying the economy's own geography, nature of the state, its financial institutions, and the level of technological readiness present across the country. A list of focus indicators (defined in the next section) can be used that allow for effective monitoring and evaluation methods too in ensuring optimum utilization of loan assistance given for these areas.

[12] A definition from the Global Competitiveness Report (2013) can be aptly used in defining the meaning of technological readiness, which 'measures the agility with which an economy adopts existing technologies to enhance the productivity of its industries, with specific emphasis on its capacity to fully leverage information and communication technologies (ICTs) in daily activities and production processes for increased efficiency and enabling innovation for competitiveness'. Available at http://reports.weforum.org/global-competitiveness-report-2014-2015/methodology/, accessed 31 October 2018.

Similarly, for an economy like Mexico (*The Economist* 2015) too, a profile of its own based on the fourfold structure can highlight and can consequently address the issue of a large informal economy that usually curbs the level of prospective growth in an economy like Mexico. An impact evaluation done on the functioning of its private and public institutions can clearly bring out the economic scenario of how small, unregistered firms provide employment to most of the labour force, but are shunned by banks and anxious to remain below the taxman's radar, sapping the domestic economy.

FOCUS INDICATORS FOR INSTITUTIONS TO FINANCIALLY DEVELOP MEMBER ECONOMIES

For the fourfold theoretical approach to have a point, it is critical to highlight a set of composite focus goals that can help emerging institutional arrangements, both quantitatively and qualitatively, targeting areas for financial development within developing member nations. Any set of multivariate benchmark indicators for institutions should thus ideally focus at least *three* of these key goals:

a) Focus on *increasing competitiveness*—in a deeply integrated global financial system, a more competitive economy is likely to grow and develop faster over time. This is especially important for rising economies like India, Brazil, Turkey, South Africa, Indonesia, etc. The Global Competitiveness Index is quite useful in this regard, in identifying some key 'pillars'. A breakdown of these pillars is provided in the index under a list of sections defined as basic requirements, efficiency enhancers, and innovation builders for an economy to increase its overall competitiveness. The ranked performance of an economy as per the index score reflects a developing economy's competitiveness level at a regional level or an international level. Therefore, an index of such nature with revision (if required at a regional level) can significantly help in planning for the distribution of institutional finance based on an economy's stage of development and areas of focus to raise its level of productivity.

b) Investing in enabling *financial inclusion*—there is a proven demand for financial services at all levels of income, but for a variety of reasons the market has failed to meet those demands for poorer people, forcing many to rely on riskier and more expensive methods to borrow, save, and secure their assets. The financial inclusion process is critical for an economy to grow and develop sustainably. Measuring inclusion within economies can then help institutions channelize money for financial development accordingly.

In this case, the World Economic Forum's Global Financial Inclusion initiative over the last few years has engaged 'a variety of stakeholders—from financial services and telecommunications providers, to retail and consumer industries, local and international development institutions, civil-society organizations, regulators, policymakers, and academia in developing new collaborative models to promote improved and expanded access to financial services'. Available at https://globalfindex.worldbank.org/, accessed 8 February 2019.

The Global Financial Inclusion (*Global Findex*) database offers 'a measurement index maintained by the International Finance Cooperation (IFC) providing in-depth data showing how people save, borrow, make payments, and manage risk. Currently, it is the world's most comprehensive set of data providing consistent measures of people's use of financial services across economies and over time'. Available at https://globalfindex.worldbank.org/, accessed 18 February 2019. Channelling productive institutional credit requirements at a regional or plurilateral level in various economic sectors through institutions like AIIB or the New Development Bank (NDB) may help achieve greater financial inclusion under the guidance and monitoring of the IMF.

c) Investing in creating *trade opportunities by encouraging local business*: the Doing Business studies conducted annually by the World Bank group and other independent organizations offer a perspective on the 'ease in doing business' and report the performance of economies in ensuring promptness in business and property registration, enforcement of contracts, access to power, credit, etc. The role of new institutions could be significant in acknowledging this and through lines of credit, promote local business opportunities within the developing member economies.

Of course, aspects such as property registration, enforcement of contracts, tax reforms, etc. (mentioned in Doing Business studies) are circumscribed to a member country's own sovereign laws. The key here would be to allow investment through an external support of institutional framework in areas that assist in creating a more conducive business and investment climate. Institutions like the World Bank are already doing a lot in this regard in various member developing countries. With prior knowledge of an economy's weak areas (e.g. access to credit, enforcement of contracts, electricity, infrastructural capacity, etc.) institutions like the World Bank effectively play the role of a '*knowledge institution*'[13] in systematically sharing and exchanging their own experiences from financial lending practices gathered from varied impact evaluation studies. Newer institutions like AIIB can add to this by further enhancing financial capacities.

It is pertinent to mention that the role of developed countries, the older BW institutions (the World Bank, IMF) along with other pre-existing multilateral forums like the World Economic Forum, the International Bank for Reconstruction and Development (IBRD), the International Development Association (IDA, IFC, etc.) is equally important in encouraging developing member nations to financially develop in an inclusive, sustainable way. By using the incentive of the opportunity to trade with a larger group

[13] As per the World Bank's database, knowledge institutions or hubs are referred to as 'institutions or networks that enable countries to learn systematically by sharing and exchanging development experiences with domestic and international partners in order to accelerate development'. Available at https://collaboration.worldbank.org/content/sites/collaboration-for-development/en/groups/knowledge-hubs.html, accessed 18 February 2019.

of countries, the developed bloc can make reform politically appealing and credible for the developing or transition economy (Rajan and Zingales 2003).

For the process of crafting strong institutional foundations in developing economies that safeguard a robust rule of law, respect for private property rights needs to be cultured from developed countries; such institutional processes have allowed the flourishing of people's confidence in local ownership, private investment, innovation, multistakeholder partnerships, accompanied with an organized development through mutual accountability and transparency.

Conclusion

Starting from a brief description of the legacy of the BW era, this chapter has provided a bird's-eye view of the governing dynamics of global economic order since the 1940s up to 2015. An eroding faith in the (cap)abilities of the 'older' IFIs, i.e. IMF and World Bank, governed by the United States' weight of influence (discussed in the first section) has led to the proliferation of regional trade agreements and newer institutional arrangements such as the AIIB among the rising LMDCs.

While multilateral financial institutions like the World Bank and IMF have been circumscribed in their ability to finance investment in critical areas for most developing economies as argued in the third section, complementary regional institutions within Asia, Africa, and Latin America have now come up to meet the rising financial investment needs of regional member countries. The dynamics of this changing global economic order—under a shifting weight of influence from the US to China—raises fundamental questions on the approaches undertaken towards financially developing member economies in a more robust and sustainable manner which is deliberated in the third section.

GIST, as an endogenous theoretical framework accompanied with three sets of focus goals (competitiveness, financial inclusion, and trade expansion through local business development) is explained in this chapter, in argument for a (re-)defined approach, to let the emerging multilateral/regional institutional arrangements meet the growing economic needs of the developing world at an incremental level.

REFERENCES

AIIB (Asian Infrastructure Investment Bank) (2015). *Articles of Agreement*. Available at www.aiib.org/en/about-aiib/basic-documents/_download/articles-of-agreement/basic_document_english-bank_articles_of_agreement.pdf, accessed 31 October 2018.

Bagwell, K. and Staiger, R. (2000). 'GATT-Think'. NBER Working Paper No. 8005. Cambridge, MA: National Bureau of Economic Research.

Bird, G. (2009). 'Reforming IMF conditionality', *World Economics* 10/3: 81–104.

Bordo, M. and James, H. (2000). 'The International Monetary Fund: its present role in historical perspective'. NBER Working Paper, No. 7724. Available at www.nber.org/papers/w7724.pdf, accessed 31 October 2018.

Bretton Woods Committee (2015). 'About the Bretton Woods Institutions'. Available at www.brettonwoods.org/event/2015-05-19-0830/bretton-woods-committee-2015-annual-meeting, accessed 31 October 2018.

Buchanan, A. and Keohane, R. (2006). 'The legitimacy of global governance institutions', *Journal of Ethics & International Affairs* 20/4: 405–37. Available at www.brettonwoods.org/event/2015-05-19-0830/bretton-woods-committee-2015-annual-meeting, accessed 31 October 2018.

Capling, A. and Trommer, S. (2008). 'The evolution of the global trade regime', in J. Ravenhill (ed.) *Global Political Economy*, 2nd edn. Oxford: Oxford University Press, chap. 5.

Chang, H. (2007). *The Myth of Free Trade and the Secret History of Capitalism.* [Online]. London: Bloomsbury Press. Available at https://analepsis.files.wordpress.com/2011/08/ha-joon-chang-bad-samaritans.pdf, accessed 31 October 2018.

Cornia, G., Jolly, R., and Stewart, F. (1987). *Adjustment with a Human Face.* Oxford: Clarendon Press.

Dicken, P. (2011). *Global Shift – Mapping the Changing Contours of The World Economy.* London: Sage.

Drazen, A. (2002). 'Conditionality and ownership in IMF lending', *IMF Staff Papers* 49/Special Issue: 36–67.

Dreher, A. (2006). 'IMF and economic growth: the effects of programs, loans, and compliance with conditionality', *World Development* 34/5: 769–88.

Easterly, W. (2001). 'IMF and World Bank structural adjustment programs and poverty', in M. Dooley and J. Frankel (eds) *Managing Currency Crisis in Emerging Markets.* [Online]. Chicago, IL: University of Chicago Press. Available at www.nber.org/chapters/c9656.pdf, accessed 31 October 2018.

The Economist (2015). 'The two Mexicos', *The Economist.* [Online]. 15 October. Available at www.economist.com/news/leaders/21665027-its-combination-modernity-and-poverty-mexico-provides-lessons-all-emerging, accessed 31 October 2018.

Eichengreen, B. (2015). 'China the responsible stakeholder', *The Project Syndicate* [Online] 10 June. Available at www.project-syndicate.org/commentary/china-silk-road-aiib-policy-initiatives-by-barry-eichengreen-2015-06, accessed 31 October 2018.

Gough, N. (2016). 'China's Economy Ends 2015 at Slowest Pace in Years', *The New York Times* [Online] 2 January, p. 2. Available at www.nytimes.com/2016/01/19/business/international/china-gdp-economy.html, accessed 31 October 2018.

Kirton, J., Larionova, M., and Savona. P. (2010). 'Making global economic governance effective hard and soft law institutions in a crowded world'. *An International Journal of Policy. Administration and Institution* 25/1. Available at https://doi.org/10.1111/j.1468-0491.2011.01564.x, accessed 31 October 2018.

Loesekrug, A., Schaefer, M., and Shen, W. (2015). 'Why Europe can't afford to ignore China's new silk road'. The World Economic Forum Agenda. [Online]. 16 November. Available at https://agenda.weforum.org/2015/11/europe-china-new-silk-road/, accessed 31 October 2018.

Mohan, R., Debabrata Patra, M., and Kapur, M. (2013). 'The international monetary system: where are we and where do we need to go?' IMF Working Papers 13/224. Washington, DC: IMF.

Qian, Y. (2002). 'How reform worked in China', in D. Rodrik (ed.) (*c*.2003) *In Search of Prosperity*. [Online]. Princeton, NJ: Princeton University Press. Available at https://mitpress.mit.edu/books/how-reform-worked-china, accessed 31 October 2018.

Rajan, R. and Zingales, L. (2003). 'The road to prosperity: saving capitalism from capitalists', *Transition – the Newsletter about Reforming Economies* 14(7–9): 1–3.

Ravenhill, J. (2008). 'The study of global political economy', in J. Ravenhill (ed.) *Global Political Economy*, 2nd edn. Oxford: Oxford University Press, chap. 1.

Reinhart, C.M, and Rogoff, K.S. (2008). 'This time is different: a panoramic view of eight centuries of financial crises'. NBER Working Paper No. 13882. Cambridge, MA: NBER.

Reinhart, C.M. and Rogoff, K.S. (2011). 'From financial crisis to debt crisis', *American Economic Review* 101: 1676–706.

Rodrik, D. (ed.) (*c*.2003). *In Search of Prosperity*. [Online]. Princeton, NJ: Princeton University Press. Available at https://mitpress.mit.edu/books/how-reform-worked-china, accessed 31 October 2018.

Rothbard, M.N. (1978). 'Society without a state', *Nomos* 19: 191–207. Available at www.jstor.org/stable/24219047, accessed 2 March 2019.

Slate (2011). 'End the Fed? Actually, maybe not'. Available at www.slate.com/id/2284503/pagenum/all/, accessed 31 October 2018.

Slaughter, A. (2015). 'New-model development finance', *The Project Syndicate*. [Online]. 22 May. Available at www.project-syndicate.org/commentary/new-global-aid-model-by-anne-marie-slaughter-2015-05, accessed 31 October 2018.

Stewart, F. (1991). 'The many faces of adjustment', *World Development* 19/12: 1847–64.

Todaro, M.P. and Smith, S.C. (2009). *Economic Development*. London: Pearson Education.

United Nations (2015). Website –'Financing for development'. Available at www.un.org/esa/ffd/economicgovernance/, accessed 31 October 2018.

Wade, R. (2002). 'US hegemony and the World Bank: the fight over people and ideas', *Review of International Political Economy* 9/2: 215–43. Available at www.tandfonline.com/doi/pdf/10.1080/09692290110126092, accessed 31 October 2018.

Wade, R. (2011). 'Emerging world order? From multipolarity to multilateralism in the G20, the World Bank and the IMF'. *Politics & Society* 39/3. 1–20. [Online]. Available at http://pas.sagepub.com/content/39/3/347.full.pdf±html, accessed 31 October 2018.

39 United Nations? BRICS and international peacekeeping

Paul Jackson

Introduction

The BRICS countries have evolved during the last decade from a purely economic phenomenon into a set of global actors. The addition of South Africa to Brazil, India, China, and Russia brought a much smaller economy into the fold but a country that had extensive experience of international action as well as a strong regional hegemon. However, continuing this evolution by translating economic power into international influence is a complex process involving changing attitudes and behaviours.

The last decade has seen the emergence of BRICS as both a well-known phrase and also as a force in international affairs, while the countries themselves have consolidated their positions as very strong regional actors in their own right. BRICS take a lead at regional level both as individual actors but also in partnership with external international actors. Their role in global affairs has expanded to encompass a number of international issues, including important subgroups like BASIC (Brazil, South Africa, India, and China), which works on negotiation of climate change; and IBSA (India, Brazil, and South Africa), which works on promoting UN Security Council (UNSC) reform—effectively lobbying for inclusion alongside China and Russia. Collectively BRICS themselves are all involved in the reform of global financial institutions.

This active involvement in international affairs illustrates a broader desire and acknowledgement that BRICS see their own future as being deepening integration with the international system itself. However, this integration does not necessarily mean complete assimilation without any change and many of the BRICS advocate alternative ways of dealing with international issues that theoretically differentiate them from the Western international system. There are a number of reasons for this, not least that each of the BRICS seeks inclusion at the top table of international affairs and this cannot be achieved solely from their regional power bases. Yet within their regions, there are disputes over leadership and even China and Brazil face regional challenges or challenges from great powers from other regions.

All of the BRICS, with the possible exception of Russia, are now accepted as important global actors in their own right for the first time in their history. India's traditional power

Paul Jackson, *United Nations? BRICS and international peacekeeping* In: *Handbook of BRICS and Emerging Economies*.
Edited by: P.B. Anand, Shailaja Fennell, and Flavio Comim, Oxford University Press (2021). © Oxford University Press.
DOI: 10.1093/oso/9780198827535.003.0039

was largely confined to South Asia and to rivalry with China, despite a long history of UN peacekeeping participation, while China's power was also essentially regional and East Asian, but has spread with the Chinese diaspora and across the Pacific along with Japan and the US. Both South Africa and Brazil have short histories as regional powers in their own right with Brazil developing benign relationships across borders within its own region and South Africa, having had a long-term campaign of destabilization of hostile neighbours, now constructing similar benign relationships and taking on economic and political leadership.

BRICS have developed an economic strategy that can benefit from the world economy but the emergence of these countries as powerful political actors and the desire for inclusion as well as change within the global international system also brings responsibility. Heightened economic involvement with investment and alliances across the Global South also brings an economic interest in the traditional international concerns of security and stability. This chapter looks at this new set of responsibilities from the point of view of peacekeeping. All of the BRICS have become frequent participants in peacekeeping operations either through the UN or regionally, but not all of them view their role or their participation similarly. India, for example, has been a long-term contributor to UN peacekeeping, whereas Russia mainly contributes to regional operations and Brazil, South Africa, and China have recently increased their role within peacekeeping but for different reasons. The chapter will begin by looking at the history of peacekeeping by BRICS and then go on to look at the Responsibility to Protect (RTP) and the New Deal approaches. It will then look at the experience of Brazil as an example of some of the dilemmas faced by BRICS, concluding with an analysis of similarities and differences in approach.

The influence of BRICS on peacekeeping

BRICS have historically been less prominent in influencing international peace and security issues, largely because they have focused on their own internal development. However, their emergence onto the world stage has given them a direct interest in maintaining stability and playing a fuller part in the global security architecture. As an emerging group, they are very different, but they do share some common characteristics when it comes to security. In simple terms, Western powers have increased their willingness to intervene with a wide variety of actions, including force in some crises. However, BRICS have been far less willing to intervene and take the view that sovereignty and self-determination are paramount rather than acting as 'international police officers' (Richmond and Tellidis 2013). There is a suspicion, reflected in nervousness about broader participation in state-building for example, that intervention can be too often used by the West as a means to introduce international hegemony based on neoliberalism. BRICS share a publicly stated desire to counter this hegemony and to pursue an agenda that includes a more equitable sharing of international power and a more rules-based international order rather than a political alliance of neoliberal states.

In countering this hegemony, however, BRICS face a dilemma when it comes to the international security architecture. Most of them are outspoken about the need for fundamental reform of international security institutions, including the UN Security Council. However, both China and Russia are already permanent members of that council and are very cautious about reform. This may be a way of maintaining their own power, but there is a deeper reason that affects all of the BRICS. All of the BRICS have benefited from the current global economic order and they therefore have no interest in destabilizing that order. Too rapid reform of the global system would be a risk to the BRICS themselves and this produces a desire for evolutionary rather than revolutionary change (de Carvalho and de Coning 2013).

Given this, BRICS see peacekeeping as part of this broader question of both maintaining international stability, and also of enhancing their own positions as global players. In general BRICS prefer peacekeeping as part of stability rather than intervention as part of regime change. This has been relatively low on many of the BRICS agendas with the exception of high-profile interventions like Libya. The UN-authorized intervention in Libya in 2011 represents an interesting illustration of the dilemmas faced by BRICS. With some powers, including the UK, France, and the US openly arguing for regime change through international intervention, BRICS argued that regime change was the sole responsibility of those living in Libya and opposed any international intervention aimed at regime change from outside. The perception that the West manipulated the UN authorization in actually bringing about regime change led to an alteration in the international debate about the nature of international action and its level of intrusiveness (Takur 2013). The nature of this dispute over Libya cast a long shadow over the inability of the international community to deal with violence in Syria.

BRICS remain suspicious that future limited UN authorization may be expanded to overthrow domestic regimes and, as a consequence, they have all opposed any external military intervention in Syria. Brazil urged the UN to order an immediate arms embargo on Syria, Russia was supported by the BRICS in its proposals over chemical weapons, while China sent personnel to oversee their destruction. All of them support inclusive political dialogue and as early as 2011 India, Brazil, and South Africa issued a declaration calling for an end to the violence, blaming both sides and further calling for inclusive and transparent talks, offering to send their own envoy.

However, the 'non-interventionist' stance of BRICS is somewhat complicated by Russia's and China's own positions as Syria's main bilateral trade partners. In fact China is Syria's main importer and trade had surged to around US$2.5 billion in 2010 just before the violence, whereas the relationship with Russia is a long-term one with Russian defence industry contracts worth around US$4 billion, raising the possibility that prolonged conflict might actually be in Moscow's best interests (de Carvalho and de Coning 2013). Syrian President Assad has backed India over Kashmir and also supports Indian aspirations over a permanent seat in the Security Council; Brazil, also seeking a seat, has remained studiously non-aligned.

BRICS have presented their position on Syria as being one of mistrust following the Libyan intervention and are unwilling to trust the West with a limited mandate that can be extended into regime change. In February 2012 South Africa voted in favour of a resolution on Syria, but the South African permanent representative stated that:

> It is important that the Syrian people be allowed to decide their own fate including their future leadership. Fundamentally, no foreign or external parties should interfere in Syria as they engage in the critical decision making processes on the future of their country. Any solution must preserve the unity, sovereignty and territorial integrity of Syria. We were also satisfied that the final draft resolution was not aimed at imposing regime change in Syria, which would be against the purposes and principles of the Charter of the United Nations.
>
> (Permanent Mission of South Africa to the UN 2012)

These sentiments have been consistently backed up by the other BRICS who back the position that no one other than the nation itself can decide who governs.

In contrast to this position on military intervention, all of the BRICS have become positive about UN peacekeeping operations and have increased their participation over recent years. India has been a long-term contributor to UN peacekeeping missions and has been in the top three contributors for decades, as well as having a history as a provider of force commanders and senior officers. China is now the largest military and police contributor among the UN Security Council members and Russia has become a major contributor to operations—particularly in terms of aviation—and remains an important contributor to regional operations. Brazil has a long history, but has recently taken a leading role in Haiti and is active in several locations where there is a Lusophone dimension, including Guinea-Bissau and East Timor (Kenkel 2010a, 2010b; Abdenur and De Souza Neto 2014). South Africa, in keeping with its regional focus, has been a major contributor to peacekeeping in Africa and is usually within the top ten contributors to peacekeeping operations (Bellamy and Williams 2013).

The overall contributions do not tell the whole story and there are differences between BRICS in terms of what they contribute to missions. Despite its increase in numbers, China is also very cautious in terms of contributing combat troops partly because of its domestic emphasis on defence, but also because it has valuable logistical units that are in short supply, including engineering and medical units that are of value to the UN (Hirono and Lanteigne 2011; Richardson 2011). India has been deployed on Chapter VII of the UN Charter operations, which has been authorized to use force and has deployed troops, police, and other weaponry, including attack helicopters. Overall India has participated in forty of the UN's sixty-five peacekeeping operations, contributing more than 100,000 personnel (Vira 2011). Indian contributions have been important not just because of numbers but because India has been less risk-averse than some contributors, taking part in some of the more difficult second-order missions using its historical ability to undertake expeditionary actions. Indian peacekeeping troops are also part of a very small group of contingents that are willing to act kinetically, as they did in the UN Mission in Sierra Leone (UNAMSIL) in the early 2000s and in MONUSCO (the UN Organization Stabilization Mission in the Democratic Republic of the Congo [DRC]) more recently.

Brazil, however, has been far more reluctant to deploy more robust mandates, but has recently taken leadership in Haiti where its troops were effective in countering the urban environment of Port-au-Prince, joining a largely South American force within the UN Organization Stabilization Mission in Haiti (MINUSTAH) (Kenkel 2010b). In contrast, South Africa has, along with India, been far more willing to use force, for example contributing to an intervention brigade in the Eastern DRC and participating in a high number of African peacekeeping operations (IDS 2014).

Overall, it is partly accurate to say that BRICS broadly support the shift towards localized peacekeeping coupled with an emphasis on national decision making and respect for sovereignty (de Carvalho and de Coning 2013). This is, of course, in line with BRICS's desire to take national sovereignty as a core principle of intervention—or a brake on using intervention—but also because any support for international intervention without respect for national sovereignty could affect BRICS's own regional strategies. As de Carvalho and de Coning (2013) further point out, the BRICS approach is therefore partly aimed at transplanting international approaches across regions. As a result, China, for example, has opposed the idea of unified standards for peace-building, which may become an issue in any drive to include measurable outputs based on existing peace-building efforts in the post-2015 development debate, and could lead to approaches to indicators that allow for localized definitions (Saferworld 2012; IDS 2014).

This leads us into the actual difference that BRICS make in the international security and peace-building architecture. We will now go on to examine two areas where BRICS have been active: RTP and the New Deal.

UN peacekeeping and the responsibility to protect

All of the BRICS play, or have played, significant roles in the UN architecture. China and Russia are permanent members of the UN Security Sector, but other BRICS are frequently elected as non-permanent members. In 2011, for example all of the BRICS were on the Security Council and all of them—as noted above—provide significant numbers of troops and expertise to peacekeeping efforts, as well as political support. In addition, BRICS have been very supportive of the UN architecture, seeing it as a means of lessening the influence of 'Western' forms of intervention. In essence they have all become important players in the machinations of the UN system.

Each of the BRICS sees peacekeeping as an important part of engaging in this international framework and as a way of taking on international responsibilities. Brazil, for example, considers peacekeeping as part of the price it has to pay to be among the countries that make the rules (IDS 2014). India has always been an enthusiastic participant in peacekeeping, and China has become an increasingly significant contributor since the 1970s, when it refused to support any peacekeeping mission. At the same time, the addition of South Africa to BRICS added significant peacekeeping capabilities in a continent where there are a large number of UN operations. South African peacekeeping increased under the leadership of Thabo Mbeki and has continued, with South Africa seeing itself as having a strong regional leadership role. Russia is perhaps the least well known of the peacekeepers, but contributed more than US$20 million to peacekeeping efforts in Lebanon, Sudan, and Ivory Coast, as well as playing an important regional role, albeit complicated by Russia's own hegemonic ambitions.

The political issue for BRICS has been the balance of intervention and sovereignty in a peacekeeping landscape that has become increasingly unrelated to sovereign states and more concerned with civil wars, complex emergencies, and cross-border conflict. The doctrine of RTP introduced to allow international intervention in humanitarian crises does have problematic implications for a group that seeks to encourage national sovereignty and reduce blanket international liberal intervention. RTP was adopted by all member states in 2005 and stipulates that all countries have a responsibility to protect their own citizens from genocide, war crimes, ethnic cleansing, and crimes against humanity. The issue comes when the state cannot or will not assume this responsibility, or if the state itself becomes a perpetrator of those crimes—as both Libya and Syria have been by members of the UN. If the state is seen as perpetrator or incapable then the Security Council may authorize intervention as a last resort.

As noted above, BRICS have been reluctant to authorize the use of force in UN operations for a variety of reasons. The experience of the international intervention in Libya, when Western powers were accused by BRICS of taking a narrow mandate and broadening it out as regime change, has led to reluctance to support UN intervention in Syria. Note, however, that the criticism of Libya was essentially about NATO interpretation of RTP rather than the principle itself, and this has led to Brazil's suggestion of 'responsibility while protecting', denoting adherence to the principle of RTP while not sanctioning regime change.

A core issue here is that in order to fully accept the principles of RTP, BRICS will have to accept that human rights are more important than national sovereignty. This presents issues for those who perhaps have different interpretations of human rights and a desire to keep the international community out of domestic political or security issues. At the same time, BRICS are involved in a complicated balancing act. Too much non-cooperation with existing norms of RTP interventions could impede the possibility of UN Security Council reform as existing members of the council may begin to see new members from BRICS as making it less likely that the council could come to any future decision over security issues. This is further complicated by the increasing involvement of BRICS in the economic and political lives of regions where RTP is most likely to be invoked. Syria is a case in point, with China and Russia as important trading actors, India as an important importer of oil, and Brazil as a player more broadly in the region. All of which suggests that BRICS are perhaps less likely to oppose RTP interventions if they are in their own interests, but may make them less ideological about RTP and far more pragmatic in decision making about RTP approaches.

The New Deal and BRICS

The International Dialogue on Peacebuilding and Statebuilding has been an important focus of multilateral efforts to formulate coordinated approaches in fragile and conflict-affected states, and to act as a forum for discussion of why the existing machinery is failing. The dialogue includes the G7+ countries, representing nineteen conflict-affected states and was established in 2010 in Dili. The dialogue was instrumental in developing the New Deal for Engagement with Fragile States that established five peacebuilding and state-building goals: inclusive political settlements; access to security, justice, service delivery, and employment. The Organisation for Economic Co-operation and Development's Development Assisitance Committee (OECD-DAC) donors support the governments of fragile and conflict-affected states to meet those goals through adhering to a new set of commitments related to the management and provision of international aid. Aid recipient countries sign 'country compacts' with donor countries and engage in mutual confidence-building measures, including institutional reform and governance development with the aim of reaching those goals.

From the beginning the dialogue has made concerted efforts to include BRICS and to sign them up to the approach of the New Deal, but BRICS's response has been somewhat lukewarm in this regard in contrast to the OECD-DAC countries, which embrace the New Deal as being 'recognizably UN' in its approach. Perhaps because of this, both China and Brazil, for example, see the New Deal as being an OECD initiative designed to assimilate non-OECD countries into a Western international framework rather than allowing domestic or national sovereignty for those countries. At the same time, BRICS have rejected the definitions of 'failed' or 'fragile' states, and the associated approaches to constructing domestic political institutions, including accountability, democracy, and governance.

Clearly the domestic positions of some of the BRICS are influential in their rejection of the New Deal. China, Russia, and India are battling domestic insurgencies and are seeking to keep part of their own domestic agendas out of international discussions on fragility and conflict. Again, Syria is a good example of the complexity of the politics of the BRICS position and brings us back to the idea of BRICS not being purely ideological in their rejection of the New Deal, but acting in their own interests in taking a pragmatic approach as to when they intervene and when they don't. Having said all of that, there are areas where BRICS can engage in dialogue with the New Deal, not least changing the focus of peacekeeping, supporting regional approaches, and providing financial resources for reconstruction operations.

While BRICS have generally rejected the language and definitions of the New Deal, they have been closely involved in supporting regional peacebuilding approaches that draw on local/regional positions of local powers and sovereignty. It is important to note, however, that while BRICS generally adhere to non-interference in domestic politics, they have supported state-building (even if they do not refer to it as 'state-building') activities in local contexts, including Brazil in East Timor and South Africa in various parts of Africa, including the DRC. Despite this the main efforts of BRICS have overwhelmingly been in supporting domestic peace-building efforts, such as Chinese peacekeeping troops deploying in Mali alongside both the Economic Community of West African States (ECOWAS) and the African Union–UN Hybrid Operation in Darfur (UNAMID).

This is also seen as the desire of BRICS to enhance domestic economic development as an acceptable way to reduce the effects of post-conflict economic collapse. BRICS interventions here are governed by investment in infrastructure, education, and health, with Brazil's recent involvement in Mozambique dominated by agricultural support and technical training, studiously keeping away from trying to shape domestic political infrastructure.

Despite this, however, BRICS have been instrumental in supporting UN peacekeeping missions. For example, a number of Indian security experts hold senior positions in the UN Department of Peacekeeping Operations, and the centre for United Nations Peacekeeping in New Delhi has trained over 400 officers from more than seventy countries. Brazil has also assumed an important role in leading the peacekeeping component of MINUSTAH, while China's peacekeeping contributions to UN missions have also increased in recent years. The Chinese government has shown greater interest in funding and coordinating training facilities where Chinese peacekeeping contingents can work alongside other nationalities. This has been mirrored in the field with Chinese peacekeeping police and US troops jointly patrolling in Haiti, and the European Union and its member states intensifying cooperation with China in a number of 'soft' security-related fields, including joint exercises, planning, and educational exchanges. This also includes defence-related partnerships with the UK, France, and Germany and joint work with the EU in supporting the African Peace and Security Architecture (APSA). However, as Curtis (2013) suggests, rather than offering a clear alternative to Western approaches in the DRC, Chinese approaches have tended to reinforce stabilization, and development and both continued Chinese and Western involvement in the DRC are likely to lead to a continuation of long-term patterns of instability and conflict.

A distinct way of doing things? Brazil as a peacekeeper

Brazil is not a new peacekeeper. In fact, Brazil's engagement in UN peacekeeping operations goes back to 1956. Since then, Brazil has participated in forty-six of the sixty-five UN operations, deploying more than 11,500 personnel (Kenkel 2010b). However, until 2004 with Haiti, Brazilian contributions were largely symbolic and based in Lusophone countries. The recent changes in aid in general and peacekeeping in particular mirror clearly the desire of the Brazilian leadership (particularly Lula da Silva, but continued under Dilma Rousseff) to exercise a bigger global role.

In particular, Brazil reoriented its foreign policy towards a more international role in addition to its more traditional regional role under President Lula. A willingness to participate in UN operations, and to lead (MINUSTAH and UNIFIL [UN Interim Force in Lebanon]) was accompanied by calls for UN reform and a permanent seat on the UN Security Council. As such, Brazil does tread an interesting path between operating and legitimating an international structure and contesting that structure.

This has led to a certain ambivalence in Brazil's peacekeeping as, while the country has been regarded as one willing to play a distinctive role as a leader in civilian expertise, an advocate for the Global South, and a legitimate and regionally established authority opposed to Western-based military intervention agendas, the country has been accused of more traditional power roles rather than its normative approach, e.g. 'acting as an ally of the US in a controversial operation in Haiti'. At the same time, it is also true that while there has been a South American regional approach that has enhanced cooperation within MINUSTAH, there have been markedly differing domestic consequences of this intervention for the different countries involved (Braga 2010; Velázquez 2010; Moreno et al. 2012).

Brazil's peacekeeping history can be seen in three distinct phases: dictatorship (1964–85); 1985–2002; and post-Lula 2002 onwards. The dictatorship period was dominated by a distancing from multilateral forums and its limited (but frequent) participation in peacekeeping operations, accompanied by a stance of non-intervention in the internal affairs of countries.[1] The 1988 constitution lays down a clear break with authoritarianism and sets out an explicit set of international principles, including the promotion of human rights, non-intervention, self-determination, peaceful conflict resolution, diplomacy, and multilateralism. This was accompanied by Brazilian participation in many of the UN operations of this period including leadership of military observers in the UN Angola Verification Mission (UNAVEM), the United Nations Transitional Administration in East Timor (UNTAET), and the UN Operations in Mozambique (ONUMOZ)).

Despite this increase, the historical and regional stance (non-intervention is regarded as the main reason why Latin America has been so peaceful) favouring non-intervention meant that Brazil has been reluctant to get involved in Chapter VII operations, as opposed to Chapter VI authorizing only limited use of force—a stance that led Brazil, as a non-permanent member of the UNSC, to refuse interventions in Rwanda in 1994 and also initially in Haiti. In fact, Brazil's decision to join the International Force for East Timor (INTERFET) in 1999 and the UN Mission of Support to Timor-Leste (UNMISET) in 2002 signalled a change in direction away from non-intervention, which was significantly deepened with the country's participation in MINUSTAH. President Cardoso justified this decision in terms of the cultural and linguistic proximity

[1] There are always exceptions and during military rule Brazil joined an Organization of American States—a mandated mission endorsed by the US to oust the democratically elected President of the Dominican Republic, Juan Bosch, in 1965.

between Brazil and Timor-Leste and the fact that the hostile parties consented to these missions.

When Lula came to power in 2003 Brazil was involved in two UN operations, UNMA (UN Missions in Angola) and UNMISET. Between 2003 and 2010 the country participated in six of the eight UN missions established during that period, increasing the number of personnel deployed from 83 to 1,367, with a further increase in 2010 to around 2,200. The establishment of two training facilities for civilians and the military in peace operations—the army's Centro de Instrução de Operações de Paz (CIOpPAZ) in 2005 and the navy's Escola de Operações de Paz in 2008—further confirmed Brazil's increasing investment in peacekeeping operations. The 2008 National Defence Strategy further confirms this stance, emphasizing the need to promote armed forces training and participation in UN-led peacekeeping operations or regionally mandated missions.

As well as the depth of operations, the scope has also expanded beyond Lusophone countries, although the justification remains unusual. Lula himself justified Haitian involvement by invoking shared African roots, including cultural and ethnic history. In addition, justification was also related to a desire to take decisions rather than to just accept the decisions of northern powers, although Brazil was subsequently accused of just doing the US bidding given the difficulty of US forces engaging in Haiti. In fact this meant that the Brazilian mission led a Latin American operation involving significant cooperation across Latin American militaries and agencies.

In this way, Brazil was able to develop significant regional leadership as well as reaching out to the other BRICS. One of the interesting features of this was the introduction of the idea of 'non-indifference' as a counterweight to non-intervention and defined as 'active solidarity'. A clever device, this has been used to justify MINUSTAH and to ward off accusations of intervention, but also to provide a driver for wider international aid developments in Africa labelled as 'South–South cooperation', while deepening contacts in Africa in the light of international competition over mineral resources, consumer markets, and political support.

MINUSTAH was and remains contentious in some ways. Not only did it contravene the principle of non-intervention, but it was also seen as being complicit with US and French aims to usurp President Aristide. Brazil's justification was partly non-indifference, but also related to UN approval and a belief that intervention was requested by Haiti's authorities—and was therefore not unwarranted intervention. However, the rather surly reception by the Haitians should perhaps be contrasted with the Timorese who welcomed the Brazilian troops by dancing to Brazilian music and providing a warm welcome. At the same time, the Brazilian authorities clearly also looked on Haiti as a chance to improve their chances of gaining further credibility with the UN in their pursuit of a seat at the UNSC.

However, there are a number of important additional issues that come out of the Haitian experience:

1. The decision to join and lead MINUSTAH can also be connected to Brazil's military agenda, i.e. the prospect of training the national armed forces for future international and domestic deployments (particularly in Brazil's larger cities) and furthering the links between this agenda and that of the Ministry of Foreign Affairs. In essence, Haiti provided an excellent opportunity to develop skills in urban street fighting and to further modernize and professionalize the Brazilian military.
2. The Brazilian approach clearly linked security and development through the core idea of 'peace as social justice', whereby the Brazilian development approach recognizes that social and economic inequalities produce war and violence. This raises interesting questions regarding Brazil's domestic social and economic inequalities.
3. As a result, Brazil very explicitly strengthened the development mandates of peacekeeping operations under Lula, which reflects some international practice but also a very clear change from earlier, more 'technically-based' involvements and towards humanitarian assistance, state reconstruction, and long-term development programming. Given this, Brazil has clearly connected military participation to bilateral and regional development aid.
4. Despite the positive link established between security and development, the Lula government was also responsible for a record increase in arms sales to developing and conflict-ridden countries.[2]

When Dilma Rousseff took office in 2011 Brazil was engaged in eight peacekeeping missions. In general, the government has maintained its position and has expanded its role, contributing to UNFICYP (UN Peacekeeping Force in Cyprus) and UNIFIL (UN Interim Force in Lebanon), where Brazil became the only non-NATO country to lead the maritime operation to prevent arms smuggling along the coast (Abdenur 2016). In addition, Brazil also participates in UNISFA (UN Interim Security Force in Abyei, Sudan) and the short-lived UNSMIS (UN Supervision Mission in Syria). Brazil has very much continued the widening and deepening of Brazil's international role as exemplified by peacekeeping missions.

Brazil has also developed a policy of 'norm creation' towards its own participation in UN missions and has shown leadership following a series of critical debates surrounding the UN's doctrine of 'RTP'. Partly in response to this, Brazil developed an additional doctrine of 'Responsibility while Protecting' that lays down the standards of behaviour and principles of international law governing those who are intervening in order to effectively protect civilians.

[2] While the US was the main destination of the 187 per cent rise in arms sales observed during this period, countries like Yemen and Paraguay were among the top five targets of these flows. Data from the Norwegian Initiative on Small Arms Transfers (available at http://nisat.prio.org/, accessed 31 May 2019) indicate that in the first decade of the twenty-first century Brazil also sold small arms to South Africa, Angola, Botswana, Côte d'Ivoire, Egypt, Ghana, Kenya, Madagascar, Malawi, Mauritania, Morocco, Namibia, Nigeria, Pakistan, the Republic of Congo, Senegal, Uganda, and Zimbabwe.

The nature of Brazil's international dilemma

The post-war period in Brazil has largely been characterized by a normative commitment to non-intervention and respect for sovereignty. This has been accompanied by a respect for peaceful resolution of conflicts, development programming, and the non-use of force. In policy terms this has meant that Brazil has been able to act under Chapter VI, but not under Chapter VII.

However, the staged emergence of Brazil as an international actor in peacekeeping and development raises a number of questions about the dilemmas faced by it, not least the issues raised by its desire for an enhanced international role, an articulation of 'non-indifference', and its controversial involvement in military intervention in Haiti. Brazil's emergence as an international actor has been relatively graceful, but the country itself is straddling a series of dilemmas that it needs to resolve one way or another. In particular, Brazil has had a largely symbolic participation in many UN missions, but has recently developed leadership in missions closer to its own foreign policy objectives.

At the same time, it has also widened and deepened an international role that contains some degree of contradiction. Is Brazil an advocate for the Global South and endorsing a peace and development agenda, or merely facilitating the interests of traditional powers and a traditional vision of the world?

Brazil has also managed to enhance international responsibility through participation in political–institutional arrangements (the UN Peacekeeping Commission which Brazil chairs). At the same time, it has also been a regular member of discussions surrounding intervention in vulnerable states, an advocate of deepening relationships in South America, and has strengthened ties with developing countries outside its usual orbit.

In addition, participation in and leadership of peace operations has provided an opportunity for the Brazilian military to improve its own operational experience and skills, as well as improving defence cooperation within the region. In conclusion, therefore, the real question seems to be whether Brazil as a partner for northern donors like the UK is likely to provide a new way of doing things or whether it is a co-opted power inside the international system. So far, there is little evidence of a transformative impact of Brazil's 'distinct' way of doing things, or a gradual incorporation of Brazil into international networks of development and peace-building.

Drifting together, but apart?

Brazil's experience shows an evolving approach that drifts towards conformity with international norms and incorporation rather than deep transformational change. The position of Brazil, like other BRICS, is torn between its own interests as a power in its own right, its desire to set itself apart from the international system, but also the desire to be a powerful part of that same system. It remains to be seen how far incorporation can result in change in norms from within the system. China, as the main provider of peacekeeping troops on the Security Council, certainly sees peacekeeping as a means of gaining international legitimacy for itself as a major power, and India certainly sees its long history of participation in peacekeeping as being worthy of further recognition, particularly through acceptance of a seat on the Security Council.

Furthermore, India remains somewhat resentful of the attention that China receives in this area. This is not petty jealousy but a legacy of historical animosity between BRICS, particularly China, India, and Russia which not only share some common interests but also some rivalries. While China is frequently singled out as being one of the BRICS that is different, each one of the countries has its own agenda that might not amount to a coherent set of interests for the group as a whole. Do they pursue agendas because they are BRICS and 'BRICS' has some political meaning, or do they pursue agendas because they happen to be a group of countries that have the resources to act in a different way from many in the Global South?

There is, of course, the question of whether BRICS see the deconstruction of UN peacekeeping and the UN's issue with hegemony in this area as an opportunity to pursue their own agendas. An agenda that devolves peacekeeping to regional organizations is very much along the lines desired by BRICS. Indeed, the UN's desire to strengthen organizations like the Africa Union in this area has been supported by BRICS themselves, since a regional solution allows decisions more in line with sovereignty but also prevents the spread of peacekeeping approaches across regions.

Conclusion

BRICS at least partly see themselves as taking a view that counters the contemporary US hegemony. However, the great power aspect of this should not be overstated and for BRICS, the aim is as much about South–South cooperation to bring about southern development as it is about countering the West. The level of integration that exists within the world economy and the reliance of BRICS on the success of the world economy as a whole means that any action based on ideological rivalry is therefore constrained. There is thus a desire to reform but also a need to conform that creates pressure for BRICS.

Within this context, BRICS could be interpreted as a bloc that seeks to correct a perceived injustice within the world economy through rebalancing the system so that they can benefit from the same advantages as the West. Within this balance, BRICS seek to use the contemporary international architecture to improve their own positions relative to those who currently control it. Security and peacekeeping is critical to this in terms of constructing international credibility and gaining support for reform. This fits with the BRICS view that the proper operation of a rule-based system could ensure a more equitable solution for BRICS—evolution rather than revolution.

REFERENCES

Abdenur, A.E. (2016). 'Rising powers in stormy seas: Brazil and the UNIFIL maritime task force', *International Peacekeeping* 23/3: 389–415.

Abdenur, A.E. and De Souza Neto, D.M. (2014). 'Rising powers and the security–development nexus: Brazil's engagement with Guinea-Bissau', *Journal of Peacebuilding and Development* 9/2: 1–16.

Bellamy, A.lex J. and Paul D. Williams, P.D. (eds). (2013). *Providing Peacekeepers: The Politics, Challenges, and Future of United Nations Peacekeeping Contributions.* Oxford: Oxford University Press.

Braga, C.C.V. (2010). 'MINUSTAH and the security environment in Haiti: Brazil and South American cooperation in the field', *International Peacekeeping* 17/5: 711–22.

Curtis, D. (2013). 'China and the insecurity of development in the Democratic Republic of the Congo (DRC)', *International Peacekeeping* 20/5: 551–69.

de Carvalho, B. and de Coning, C. (2013). *Rising Powers and the Future of Peacekeeping and Peacebuilding.* Oslo: Norwegian Peacebuilding Resource Centre.

Hirono, Miwa and Lanteigne, Marc (2011). 'Introduction: China and UN Peacekeeping', *International Peacekeeping* 18/3: 243–56.

IDS (Institute of Development Studies) (2014). 'Beyond the new deal: global collaboration and peacebuilding with BRICS countries'. Policy Briefing, Issue 59, April.

Kenkel, K.M. (2010a). 'Stepping out of the shadow: South America and peace operations', *International Peacekeeping* 17/5: 584–97.

Kenkel, K.M. (2010b). 'South America's emerging power: Brazil as peacekeeper', *International Peacekeeping* 17/5: 644–61.

Moreno, M.F., Braga, C.C.V., and Gomes, M.S. (2012). 'Trapped between many worlds: a post-colonial perspective on the UN mission in Haiti (MINUSTAH)', *International Peacekeeping* 19/3: 377–92.

Permanent Mission of South Africa to the UN (2012). 'Statement by Ambassador Baso Sangqu in explaining the vote in the UN Security Council on the situation in Syria'. Available at www.southafrica-newyork.net/speeches_pmun/view_speech.php?speech=7659445, accessed 8 October 2018.

Richardson, Courtney J. (2011). 'A responsible power? China and the UN peacekeeping regime', *International Peacekeeping* 18/3: 286–97.

Richmond, Oliver O.P. and Tellidis, I. (2013). *The BRICS and International Peacebuilding And Statebuilding.* Oslo: NOREF. Available at http://bit.ly/WCvtHw, accessed 8 October 2018.

Saferworld (2012). 'Rising power and conflict: addressing conflict and violence from 2015'. Saferworld Issue Paper No. 3. 24 November. Available at www.saferworld.org.uk/resources/publications/1136-addressing-conflict-and-violence-from-2015-saferworld-issue-papers, accessed 31 May 2019.

Takur, R. (2013). 'R2P after Libya and Syria: engaging emerging powers', *Washington Quarterly* 36/2: 61–76.

Velázquez, A.C.S. (2010). 'Peacekeeping effects in South America: common experiences and divergent effects on civil–military relations', *International Peacekeeping* 17/5: 629–43.

Vira, V. (2011). 'India and UN peacekeeping: declining interest with grave implications', *Small Wars Journal.* Available at https://smallwarsjournal.com/jrnl/art/india-and-un-peacekeeping-declining-interest-with-grave-implications, accessed 8 August 2019.

40 Emerging powers coalitions

India and Brazil examined

Cassandra Sweet

Introduction

The ascendance of emerging economies was a driving narrative of global trade politics in the first decade of the twenty-first century. At a time when the United States and Europe convulsed in economic crises, key developing economies revelled in sustained economic growth. The popularized nomenclature for leading 'BRICS' economies obscured the unevenness and variation within this group, but between the period 2003 and 2013, expanding GDP was the norm for all: China (10.3 per cent), Russia (4.6 per cent), India (7.6 per cent), Brazil (3.7 per cent).[1] As of 2015, the combined GDP of these and other growing developing companies comprised about half of the world's economic activity.

For many, this changing global economic structure augured a reciprocal political shift: 'Clearly, the redistribution of economic weight on a global scale is beginning to manifest implications for global governance' (Stephen 2012). But another half-decade onwards, as we lurch towards the end of the twenty-first century's second decade, a re-evaluation of the tangible political power, efforts at coordination, and ultimately, the influence of emerging economies is due. Did the start of the 2000s mark a gain in political traction on developing countries' priorities in global trade negotiations? If the rise of newly emergent powers boded a new economic order, what gains were achieved? How can we understand the collaborative efforts and institutions the 'emerging powers' boom had left in its wake by the end of the twenty-first century's second decade?[2]

This chapter focuses on global trade governance at the multilateral and bilateral level. It looks to India and Brazil, two countries long regarded as key developing country 'protagonists' in World Trade Organization (WTO) trade debates. In the early 2000s, these countries were also at the helm of new trade and political blocs such as the G20 and the developing country alliance IBSA (India-Brazil-South Africa). The chapter follows a

[1] By way of comparison, over the same decade, the United States's GDP expanded the feeble rate of 1.7 per cent while the European Union's growth rate of 0.9 per cent indicated profound economic turmoil.

[2] For instance two countries at the centre of the so-called economic pivot are now facing international political and economic condemnation (Russia) or managing internal economic and political instabili

Cassandra Sweet, *Emerging powers coalitions: India and Brazil examined* In: *Handbook of BRICS and Emerging Economies*. Edited by: P.B. Anand, Shailaja Fennell, and Flavio Comim, Oxford University Press (2021). © Oxford University Press.
DOI: 10.1093/oso/9780198827535.003.0040

simple structure: the second section outlines recent scholarship on emerging powers and their ability to wield economic and political power in trade negotiations; the third section delves into the strategies pursued by India and Brazil in the Nairobi and Bali meetings, the latest rounds of WTO negotiations; the fourth section examines the roles of India and Brazil in pursing common global policies focusing on trade in generic medicines. The fifth section discusses the building of coalitions and shared interests, and the sixth brings together the chapter's conclusions.

Coalition building: joining together to achieving influence?

Such a waste of talent. He chose money over power, in this town a mistake nearly everyone makes. Money is the McMansion in Sarasota that starts falling apart after ten years, power is the old stone building that stands for centuries. I cannot respect someone who does not see the difference. Frances Underwood, in the Netflix series *House of Cards*

In the first decade of the twenty-first century, key emerging market countries rode a wave of prosperity. Commodity prices inflated state and private sector revenues, domestic output and exports surged, public sector surpluses became the norm. Some economists began to describe a 'new world order' in which key emerging powers would redefine trade patterns and the rules which oversaw their exchange. While their immediate rise was apparent, would these emerging giants secure more than fleeting wealth? Would their increased clout result in long-lasting power, or at the very least a higher level of midterm influence over global trade institutions?

Historically, the negotiating clout of developing countries at multilateral trade institutions has not been propitious. The Uruguay Round (UR) of WTO negotiations had a particularly bruising effect on emerging countries. Most of the concessions sought were not yielded; yet, industrialized countries achieved important liberalizations and maintained protection of key interests. What accounts for the poor returns experienced by developing countries? Political theorists have long understood the position of developing countries to be constrained by size, political power, and economic reach.[3] The limited bargaining power held by developing countries in international negotiation forums makes the existence of 'coalitions' particularly crucial for maximizing the effective diplomatic power.

Developing countries have to act in coalitions in order to gain sufficient leverage (or voice), because coalitions improve the quantitative and qualitative participation of members enhancing the organization's legitimacy. (Rolland 2007: 2)

[3] They also seem to have lost the ideational battle over liberalization. Once concessions were made and new institutions were implemented (Chorev 2007).

Coalitions form through temporary alliances united in the aim of shared activity or common purpose.[4] In her seminal book on coalition building among developing countries in the WTO, Amrita Narlikar distinguishes between two types of coalition, namely issue-based alliances (formed around concerns about a particular issue) and bloc-type coalitions (based on shared ideas on multiple concerns). The Narlikar model considers two possible hypotheses for the creation of coalitions: 'the defection hypothesis' and 'the collective gains hypothesis'. Under the defection hypothesis, the rationale for coalition formation is based on narrow individual interests; countries join a coalition first to establish their power, and then to better position themselves for purchase from outside parties. In this scenario, each member of the coalition is fearful of being isolated in an end game where they find themselves alone. This bleak, prisoner's dilemma-based interpretation of coalitions understands imminent collapse as generating a 'sucker's payoff' for those who stay. Three scenarios protect coalitions from this mindset: (a) countries will not cooperate in the first place if this logic becomes widespread; (b) opposing negotiations will not take the coalition seriously if it senses its members might fold; and (c) repeated defections by members will reduce the coalition's credibility. Instead, she argues that a more convincing rationale for coalition formation is captured by the concept of the 'stag hunt', where parties recognize that their collective interests are more likely to be achieved if they cooperate.

Narlikar suggests that blocs—particularly those with a large number of members—tend to pursue a strategy of obstruction rather than a positive negotiating agenda. Achieving diverse priorities and the interests of the bloc's participants often leads to the adoption of the largest common denominator of negative demands. While this may be effective in stalling negotiations and voicing the dissatisfaction of a large number of members, it does not lead to reorientation or regime change. Such groups also have a tendency to disaggregate (such as the G10 at Punta del Este and the Like-Minded Group at Doha), an unsurprising result given that the bloc is in practice unable to serve all the interests of its members, because of the lack of prioritization among often divergent interests. In principle, blocs with more homogeneous membership, negotiation priorities, and interests should be more successful. By contrast, Narlikar finds empirical evidence suggesting that issue-based bargaining works best for small and very specialized economies. The larger the issue and the more diverse the membership, the harder it is to maintain a coherent, united stance. In such situations, coalitions may be better used as a pool of research resources and a forum for exchanging ideas rather than as a direct negotiating tool. Overall, coalitions focused on specific issues seem more viable since members' individual agendas are more likely to be aligned with those of the coalition.

[4] 'Coalition' is usually defined as a group of players or decision makers who commit to coordinating their actions to achieve shared interests or common purpose.

Linked fates or lone tigers at the WTO?

A decade ago, the increasing economic clout of developing countries such as India and Brazil portended for many a shift in negotiations at global governance institutions. The collapse of the 2003 Cancun Ministerial meetings offered evidence that the ever-widening expansion of trade liberalization policies pursued by OECD countries in the 1990s would be adapted, mitigated, or altogether halted by new developing country 'protagonists'. From the failures of Cancun, the Doha Development Agenda (DDA) emerged as a new set of 'development attuned policies' attributed to coalitional politics and the 'new activism' of leading developing countries (Hurrell and Narlikar 2006a). The expectation was that increasing economic and political clout would enable new emerging global protagonists to push the rules governing trade integration policy towards measures facilitating more equitable and sustainable economic development. A decade on since the trade negotiation collapse at Cancun, has the promise of a procedural and policy outcome change been delivered at the WTO? This section addresses the latest rounds of global trade governance negotiations held at Bali in 2013 and issues that India and Brazil prioritized.

The WTO's negotiations during the late 1980s and early 1990s ushered in a number of important gains for industrialized countries through a global trade agreement. Trade liberalization expanded from regulation of goods to inclusion of intellectual property rights, services, and agriculture. Since the conclusion of the UR in 1996, the United States and other industrialized countries have been advocating for continued expansion of the measures established in Uruguay through a new trade facilitation (TF) agreement. These measures have been widely challenged by developing countries. India's central argument has been that before a protocol for a new TF can be established reform of agricultural subsidies within the Uruguay framework should be addressed.

One of the contradictions inherent in the UR negotiations was a series of 'exceptions' to trade liberalization in the Agreement on Agriculture (AoA).[5] These tools designated US and EU agricultural subsidies as non-distorting, 'Green Box' instruments, which included mechanisms supporting farmers' income, insurance, and anti-cyclical remedies.[6] They were considered by OECD countries to be 'non-distorting' in nature because they were categorized as income support rather than 'producer subsidies'.[7] Discussions during the UR on the mechanisms for support of these agricultural programmes did not include developing countries (Jawara and Kwa 2003). As a result, countries such as Brazil and India, Indonesia, Kenya, and Nigeria did not register Green Box subsidies in their

[5] These protocols are embedded in the so-called 1993 Blair House Agreement in which the US and EU set out a plan for the maintenance of domestic agricultural protections.

[6] The rulings of a 2010 WTO dispute panel suggest that actual trade-distorting subsidies paid by the US just for the year 2010 should be US$15 billion instead of the US$4 billion reported.

[7] Other exceptions to agricultural subsidy limits are the systems established in Amber Box and Blue Box rules. For more on these rules and their effects on agricultural exports in developing countries, see Wise (2013), Why the WTO Needs a 'Hypocrisy Clause'.

UR commitments. Although these countries have economies heavily skewed towards agricultural production and the large populations depending upon them, in the final UR agreement they were only allowed to maintain so-called 'de minimis support' up to 10 per cent of a crop's production.

In the wake of the UR agreement, developing countries widely in the main quietly questioned the trade governance systems. Their push back to the industrialized country's platform came to light in 2003, when together in a series of developing countries' coalitions the proposal for continued trade liberalization through TF was forced off the Doha agenda at the Cancun ministerial meeting.[8]

The Cancun victory proved to be pyric. By the end of the decade, negation of expanded TF measures reappeared and became the central focus of the WTO's ninth ministerial debates at Bali. Proposed TF measures included comprehensive market access agreement on issues including freedom of transit, import and exportation protocols, and publication of trade regulations. The central thrust is the expedition of trade and reduction in trading costs for exporters; micro regulations, addressing minor issues in trade policy. And yet the sum of these policies, including harmonization of border procedures, open and swift publication of trade laws and regulations, and quick review and release of goods at ports and in other areas of transit are viewed by OECD countries as crucial barriers to the expansion of trade.

In contrast to the Cancun negotiations, the Bali meeting and the proceedings leading up to the negotitations once again showcased division among developing countries. Neither did a common platform emerge in opposition to TF expansion, nor did a block form around interests that have been raised by developing countries since the last negotiating round on issues such as stockholding programmes for food security, duty-free and quota-free market access, and cotton subsidies by developed countries.

That the Bali meetings did not result in developing country interests gaining more negotiation leverage is especially curious given its direction by Brazilian diplomat Roberto Carvalho de Azevêdo who had recently assumed the position of Director-General of the WTO. As a leader from the developing world his arrival was anticipated as heralding a 'bridge' between industrialized and developing contingents. In practice, this bridge building effectively split developing countries' coalitions. In the months leading up to the Bali meetings, Azevêdo coordinated an understanding between the African Group, the Africa, Caribbean, and Pacific (ACP), and the LDCs (least developed countries), with the US and the EU over the TF text. This agreement effectively divided Cancun-established cross-regional developing country coalitions and solidified support for TF. The schism was especially isolating for India, which had arrived at the Bali

[8] Hurrell and Narlikar (2006b) argue that domestic policies in India and Brazil are ancillary to the formation of foreign negotiation techniques at the WTO and point to four 'planes' in which the trading behaviour of these countries has emerged: 'coalitions, insider activism, negotiation strategies, and transnational coalitions'.

conference in tepid agreement with some of the TF proposals but with a set of specific demands about the extension of rights on its public food stock programmes.

The role that India played in the Bali negotiations was focused principally on one issue: its food stock programmes. Six months in anticipation of the Bali meetings, India's Prime Minister, Manmohan Singh and his Commerce Minister, Anand Sharma, visited Washington where they articulated support for the TF without achieving a concession on the public stockholding programmes. They chose no conflict with the US at the same time that India's National Food Security Programme underwent significant expansion. In the final hours of the Bali negotiations, however, the Indian government raised a number of challenges to problems with the text. This was in part due to a public uproar spurred on regarding the programmes for food security once the draft of the text was circulated. The US strongly criticized India for this last-minute push to protect its food programme.[9] Isolated from other members of the G33 farming group, India pushed alone for a change to the food security issue. In the final hours, they secured a temporary four-year agreement until a permanent solution could be negotiated. This is an area in which many members of the G33 farm coalition have shared interests. Yet while the negotiation of the TF was highly contested during the same period (2011–13), attention to the AoA rules was repeatedly denied.[10]

The TF agreement that was secured at Bali comprised two sections: section one mandates a series of legally binding changes aimed at enhancing the ease of trade with developing and LDCs. Section two establishes a timetable for these changes and proposes a series of capacity-building instruments that may be offered by industrialized countries to facilitate the changes. The binding agreements are related to the TF.[11] Changes in agriculture including the controversial food security issues, tariff rate quota administration, and other instruments to facilitate exports from developing countries were relegated 'best endeavor' status. In short, industrialized countries secured the provisions to the benefit of their exports but developing countries did not.

By mid-2014, India chose not to ratify the Bali agreement, citing its disappointment in not having been able to secure an agreement on food stocks. Current WTO norms

[9] It should be noted that the US disburses approximately US$75 billion per year on its Supplemental Nutrition Assistance Program (SNAP), the main domestic food aid programme. Some estimates indicate that the programme's 47 million recipients received an average of 240 kg of grain totalling US$1,608 per year. Even before India's 2014 expansion of its food stocks programme, its programme reached more than ten times the number of recipients of US-targeted SNAP recipients; 475 million Indians receive food aid (58 kg per person), with a per capita cost of roughly US$27/year (Wise 2013). Why the WTO needs a 'Hypocrisy Clause'; Triple Crisis: Global Perspective on Finance, Development and Environment, is available at http://triplecrisis.com/why-the-wto-needs-a-hypocrisy-clause/, accessed 9 October 2018.

[10] For example, the first draft of the TF Agreement in 2011 included 800 brackets—an indicator of areas in which there is no agreement.

[11] The text reads: 'shall publish import procedures, duty rates, and classification/valuation rules; shall issue advance customs rulings where requested; shall provide administrative/judicial review of customs rulings; shall create infrastructure and procedures for expedited shipments of goods coming through air cargo [basically for American courier services]; shall establish procedures for pre-arrival processing; and shall allow authorised operators to move their goods on a fast track'.

restrict the value of food subsidies for non-exceptions to 10 per cent of total food grain production. Essentially India has proposed it be able to purchase food grains from its own farmers at the minimum support price and sell them to the poor at lower rates. India has been seen as a good potential partner for industrialized countries because it was believed to be an 'easy' negotiation partner given that languages and social contacts were shared because of a colonial connection; and the benefits of having an India cooperating would 'outweigh the costs' (Narlikar 2013).

One of the challenges for developing countries within the Bali agreement was that meeting the new TF commitments would likely require significant finance and technology upgrades. These obligations necessitated resource diversion towards legislative changes, human and capital investment, and physical infrastructure. This new implementation burden is addressed in Section 2 of the Bali Declaration, which states that support will be provided to developing countries for the implementation of these norms. At the same time that these commitments were made, developing countries did not secure any further concessions from developed countries regarding their subsidy programmes.[12] These policies comprise another area in which WTO is setting the norms and policies on domestic trade governance issues.[13]

How decisions were made on the non-binding aspects of the Bali agreement are also potent. These include issues of duty-free and quota-free market access, a services waiver, cotton, and preferential rules of origin for LDCs. Three players shaped the agreement: Nepal (the coordinator for LDCs), the US, and the director-general. This was interpreted by Indian media as a victory for India in the sense that its demands were met, and that 'India gains global leadership by getting a crucial poor-rich country imbalance corrected on a multilateral forum' (Mehra 2013).

Between the eighth and ninth ministerial meetings (2011–13) the thesis of 'emerging powers influence' was effectively buried. The US and its partners forced developing countries to accept the TF agreement but did not fulfil the principle of reciprocity. No commitments were achieved for agriculture and development, in particular the issue of public stockholding. Industrialized countries instead committed themselves to non-binding 'best endeavor outcomes', a declaration that they would do their best in areas that were of interest to developing countries.[14] The outcome of the Bali negotiations did not demonstrate a break with previous negotiations in global economic governance in its

[12] In 2005, the WTO committed itself to resolve the issue of the US's trade-distorting cotton subsidies 'in an expedited manner'. Eight years later, Africa's cotton producers are still waiting for US compliance. In Bali, the US has offered nothing on cotton, continuing the damage to some of the world's poorest farmers. Available at http://triplecrisis.com/why-the-wto-needs-a-hypocrisy-clause/#sthash.ujo3Bi5n.dpuf, accessed 9 October 2018.

[13] There are reports that Azevêdo, Director-General of WTO, was opposed to these actions in the case of Brazil, noting that they were merely measures to expand developed countries' interests.

[14] Specific examples of these accords settled at Bali include non-binding agreements granting preferential rules of origin on the export of manufactured goods by developing countries, duty-free and quota-free market access for LDCs, and the proposal for the creation of a mechanism to ensure differential treatment of products from poor countries.

outcome, nor does it suggest that India or Brazil is playing a pivotal role in their reshaping. Both the process and the product of the negotiations point to a replication of historic global governance patterns. Developing countries were either sidelined from key discussions or their interests were divided.

The process and outcome of the Bali negotiations suggest that the notion of a super-coalition emerging across developing countries has not been attainable. India's agreement and then subsequent rescindment has been broadly criticized outside of India by industrialized countries: 'This is not India against the West but against itself and the world, backing away from the terms of a deal it participated in designing as recently as December' (Ayeres 2014). Our assessment is that while India's influence during the Bali negotiations took the shape of an isolated power whose interests should be attended to, Brazil's position seemed to shift from that of a coalition builder among developing countries to a 'bridge builder' between industrialized and developing countries. Brazil has long been viewed as a stakeholder with an ability to communicate between the global development divide.[15] While India and Brazil insist that the ongoing Doha Round negotiations must be concluded to remove the disparity in agricultural trade rules tilted in favour of developed countries, they don't seem to agree on how to achieve it. Their differences were evident in the last ministerial conferences of the WTO. Both in Bali (2013) and Nairobi (2015), India and Brazil found their different positions on key issues difficult to reconcile.

Though the potential to be coalitional leaders and bridge builders was repeated in rhetoric at Bali and Nairobi conferences, Brazil and India instead appeared bound to national interests that put them at opposite ends of the spectrum (see Table 40.1).

Along with Australia and New Zealand, Brazil proposed and supported specific provisions relating to trade in perishable goods, the primary aim of which was swift movement and clearance. Meanwhile, India showed lukewarm reception regarding issues of TF. It was concerned about protecting its food programme and wanted to negotiate an agreement on food security issues.

The ability of Brazil and India to become partners in the Bali Round was effectively broken when Brazil accepted a maximum of 10 per cent subsidies for domestic agricultural production, in the face India's annual 30 per cent subsidies for production of rice and wheat. While India worked to create a special safeguard mechanism (SSM), Brazil aligned itself with the US, European Union, and Australia in disagreement with the proposal. Brazil and other countries effectively rejected a draft decision aimed at exempting programmes for supporting millions of resource-poor farmers from any subsidy limits. They argued that the draft ministerial decision for a permanent solution

[15] The idea of Brazil as a bridge-builder is at least 40 decades old: 'Of all the countries of the third world, Brazil is currently the country which has the most influence in international politics. This position depends, essentially, in its self-identification and impact on important countries in the first and third world' (Grabendoff 1979). La política exterior del Brasil, entre el premer y tercer mundo. Nueva Sociedad, 41, 108–19.

Table 40.1 Key trade interests of Brazil and India

Topic	Conference	Brazil	India
Doha Round negotiations	Bali, 2013 Nairobi, 2015	Current agricultural trade rules tilted in favour of developed countries-	
Internal agriculture subsidies	Bali, 2013	Restrict subsidies to 10%	Actually spends 30% of subsidies on production of rice and wheat
Commerce facilitation on perishable foods	Bali, 2013	Proposed and supported specific dispositions	Condition TF agreement on a settlement regarding the SSM
Special safeguard mechanism	Nairobi, 2015	Rejects proposal for exempting programmes for supporting resource-poor farmers	Claims for an effective SSM for supporting resource-poor farmers
Exports agriculture subsidies	Nairobi, 2015	Absolute priority; prohibits subsidies and establishes new rules and transparency requirements for state trading enterprises, non-emergency food aid, and credits, guarantees, and insurance for export	India uses subsidies for sugar exports, and calls for exceptions for certain products.Pending negotiation for state export companies

Source: Author's compilation.

being tabled by India along with its allies in the G33 farm coalition would distort global farm trade because of exemptions for such programmes from subsidy discipline.

Both emerging powers appear to be changing their global governance strategies on single-issue areas, leaving aside earlier attempts at multiple-issue cooperative bargaining platforms. India's focus on the food storage issue isolated it from wider calls for a more development-focused agenda. Brazil's division of developing countries and key role in securing an agreement for expanding TF without securing a reduction in industrialized countries' agricultural subsidies indicated that its role as a 'protagonist' is less clear-cut than that of an advocate for the interests of LDCs. Both these directions shed light on the fragility of the 'coalitional politics' which were so heralded at the beginning of the decade.

Mind the gap: the rhetoric of South–South trade politics and the limits of cooperation in the case of IBSA

The economic ascendency of developing powers combined with their disillusionment with the rules governing the international trading system around the turn of the century served to galvanize a new wave of trade cooperation institutions and political alliances.

One such example was the multilateral IBSA alliance forum, initiated in May 2004.[16] Early meetings of the first Trilateral Commission of the IBSA Dialogue Forum aimed to build cohesion across a number of areas for TF and development; yet reforming the rules of global trade governance was the first goal of the new coalition (Ministério das Relações Exteriores 2003).

From initial meetings in 2004, a set of IBSA institutions was born. The first was a Trilateral Joint Commission—a platform for the exchange of information and political cooperation. The second, the Trilateral Business Council (TBC), established two goals: to create an investment network for small, medium, and micro-enterprises; and to organize joint grievances at the WTO. A third evaluator branch established a commission to research the impact of global trade policies and trade imbalances among IBSA partners.[17]

This initial boom of institutional initiatives had met its first setbacks by the fourth ministerial conference. Challenges were both tangible and ideological in nature. Though member countries considered themselves the new emerging economic powers and shared a similar set of complaints regarding how multilateral institutions functioned, they found themselves at odds in both creating environments in which to promote South–South trade and evaluating the pace of their political and economic advances. The IBSA Business Forum was considered dormant by all parties and 'not working how the governments would like'.[18] As reported in the news, according to India's Minister Anand Sharma, the Business Forum had been dealing with issues of concern to all the nations but failed to harness the energies of states and entrepreneurs. A more sanguine view was held by Brazil's Mario Vilalva, then Director of the country's Trade Promotion Department. He argued that ideational politics were important: the mere formation of IBSA furthered a project of South–South economic integration:

> What is important in IBSA? The fact that you have created a group. The fact that you have begun to get together with people from that group. The fact that you have begun to meet with the authorities of that group. That fact that people have begun to write about the subject. The fact that people have begun to pay attention to the products that we are exporting. The fact that we signed an agreement of fixed preferential tariffs, still modest, but it will be expanded. All of this has added to the growing perception and the mobilization of the agents in each of the countries.
>
> (Vieira 2006)

The contrary visions of India and Brazil as to the progress that had been made at IBSA highlighted differences in agenda and the importance their states held in reshaping international cooperation mechanisms. These different views on the progress of IBSA

[16] Records from the first IBSA meeting are replete with complaints from foreign ministers from India, Brazil, and South Africa on the lack of predictable, rule-based, and transparent international trading systems and the need for leading developing countries to play a role in the reform of the WTO.

[17] The project was funded by the Swiss Agency for Development and Co-operation, to be undertaken by the Cuts Centre for International Trade Economics and Environment of India and the Institute for International Trade Negotiations of Brazil (Lourens 2005).

[18] Interview with Ambassador Mauro Vieira, IBSA Meeting, Rio de Janeiro, 26 March 2006.

were matched by contrasting opinions on a more primordial debate about the role of the state to facilitate trade. During meetings of the 2006 Trilateral Mission, South Africa voiced its scepticism on the viability of state-incentivized export promotion. Foreign Minister Zuma declared it a 'bit unusual' for endeavours in trade and investment to be driven by governments, adding that there was 'no precedence for the work we are undertaking'.[19] Brazil's former Foreign Minister Celso Amorim acknowledged state limits, citing the Brazilian political adage, 'we can make clouds, but we can't make the rain'.[20] Yet, Amorim vigorously defended the role of the state in trade promotion, consistent with a Brazilian *weltanschauung* of development policy. He cited Mercosul as a successful 'state project' which once was 'feared by the business class and now enjoys its ownership'.[21]

This Brazilian view of trade integration was perhaps no better captured by President 'Lula' da Silva, at his inauguration in January 2003, when he emphasized the importance of building a '*nova geografia comerical*' or a 'new trade geography' entailing economic partnership with countries of the Global South.[22] President da Silva pointedly pushed forth IBSA's cooperative efforts, grounded in ideological underpinnings that the new institution would not only further the South–South project but would reshape North–South relations:

> President Lula, he had this idea to launch this group of countries. He thought that there should be more interaction between emerging countries. There is a tendency in international commerce, that it always goes in the South-North, North-South flow, which is a legacy of ours—*herança nossa* from the colonial period... The alliance, in particular, with India, was part of realizing that [post-colonial] change.[23]

Breaking colonial trade legacies was echoed in India's calls for South–South cooperative efforts at IBSA:

> Sharing with other developing countries our capabilities, and assisting and cooperating with them in developing their own economies has been an integral part of Indian foreign policy from its very inception, much before the concepts of South–South cooperation and TC[24] became fashionable... South-South cooperation is the economic dimension of India's traditional political, moral and diplomatic support to the anti-colonial struggle. (Sikri 2003)

[19] Comments from South Africa's Minister Zuma, IBSA Meeting, Rio de Janeiro, 26 March 2006.

[20] The phrase was repeated by Brazilian interviews at Itamaraty, Brasilia.

[21] Amorim emphasized that more than 54 per cent of Brazil's exports were destined for developing country markets.

[22] Brazil's enthusiasm for diplomacy and institutional construction in Indo-Brazilian relations has been reciprocated in Indian foreign policy and planning. In a speech to the Indo-Brazilian Joint Business Meeting on 20 October 2003, Minister of Commerce and Industry Shri Vidyasagar Rao described Brazil as 'traditionally our major trading partner country in Latin America' and highlighted the Brazilian 'gesture' of having focused on India as one of the six countries (US, UK, Japan, Germany, China, and India) to which it would prioritize forging stronger trade and commercial ties (Rao 2003).

[23] Vieira 2006.

[24] Technical Cooperation among Developing Countries. India reported that in 2003, it allocated US$200 million towards technical cooperation with developing countries.

Brazil's foreign policy emphasis on building South–South cooperation dovetailed with Indian foreign policy across two levels.[25] The first was ideological; policies from both countries were grounded in a pro-South politics with roots in a shared history of anti-colonialism. The second was pragmatic. India, much like Brazil, sought to craft foreign and domestic policies that would facilitate its rise as a global economic power. Among Indian foreign economic policymakers, the Brazilian market was viewed as playing a critical role in increasing trade and investment with the Latin American region. Yet, even if the gap between the intention to fortify economic integration and coordination has persisted since it emerged at the fourth ministerial conference, the IBSA alliance has continued to serve as a collective forum for rejecting and evaluating work on global trade governance at the WTO.

> The Ministers expressed deep disappointment at the current impasse in the Doha Development Agenda (DDA) negotiations. They reiterated the need to conclude the Doha Round as soon as possible, building on the significant progress already achieved and on the careful balance of concessions negotiated since the launching of the Round in 2001 . . . The Ministers emphasized that 'plurilateral initiatives' go against the fundamental principles of transparency, inclusiveness, and multilateralism. These initiatives weaken the resolve of WTO Members to overcome the substantive gaps that exist among them and also fail to address the development deficit inherited from previous negotiating Rounds. (IBSA 2012)

IBSA was established to provide a counterbalance to the combined influence of OECD countries at multilateral institutions. Yet the lesson of the past decade is that even for emerging powers with comparatively high levels of influence, the recent negotiations have not fulfilled the promise. Brazil has worked diligently to expand its regional influence. While India has expanded its global trade networks and become, alongside China, a key investor in Africa (Taylor 2012), Brazil has had difficulty (Negri 2005) expanding into markets beyond that of a commodity supplier.

If India and Brazil have faced obstacles in maintaining and coordinating their influence across broad interest areas, some singular cases suggest the potential in their 'emerging power' status has been limited. Public health and generic pharmaceutical production has been a key area where India and Brazil have been advocates for each other and sustained the interest of developing countries. Brazil has taken more of a 'rights approach'. Its guarantee of providing access to HIV/AIDS patients has turned into a policy which it has expanded to other parts of the developing world. India has played a role in this as a key supplier of antiretrovirals (ARVs). In the rules that govern global

[25] Was Lula's clear articulation of a pro-South agenda a decisive break with the Cardoso administration? Burges 2005 argues that Lula's focus on developing countries did not represent a total break with his predecessor's policy, but a rhetorical shift towards 'the articulation of a psychologically transformative foreign policy agenda in the global South'. Interviews with policymakers at the helm of Itamaraty's Trade promotion reject this idea. 'Was this a break? Yes, Lula wasn't just about rhetoric, he wanted trade and investment, plain and simple. We were going to make our economies' destinities interlinked' (Vieira 2006).

trade evidence of this partnership was tested in the period 2008–09, when a series of conflicts arose regarding the rights of transport for generic medicines in the EU.

The conflict was ignited when Dutch officials detained a shipment of HIV/AIDS medicines produced by Aurobindo with a destination of Nigeria. The detainment of the ARVs, which were procured by the Clinton Foundation for distribution through a national UNITAID programme had direct impact on the treatment of people undergoing ARV treatment. Key international agencies concerned with the global trade of off-patent medicine condemned the practice and suggested it might set a troubling precedent:

> UNITAID is worried more generally about the trend that seems to have taken hold in recent months where generic medicines are stopped or confiscated while transiting through the Netherlands. Generic medicines are not counterfeit medicines. The Aurobindo abacavir tablets are legitimate products and there is no reason to raise concerns related to counterfeiting. (UNITAID 2009)

The questioned goods were in transit and not destined for a European market and were a part of five seizures (see Table 40.2).

The confiscation of Indian products at Dutch ports provoked a response by the Indian government at the WTO Council for Trade Related Intellectual Property Rights (TRIPS) meeting on the issue of public health. In March 2009 meetings, the Indian delegation described the seizure of Indian generics as 'developments which undermine the public health dimensions of TRIPS agreement'.[26] The delegation emphasized the global nature of the Dutch move, with implications for private and public sector actors and initiatives: 'Measures of this nature have an adverse systemic impact on legitimate trade of generic medicines, South–South commerce, national public health policies and the principle of universal access to medicines.' In concert with the Indian government, the Brazilian delegation submitted a legal intervention at the WTO TRIPS council. Delivered by then Ambassador Roberto Azevêdo, the Brazilian statement echoed the observation that the move by the Dutch government was systemic in nature,

Table 40.2 Seizures of Indian generics by the Dutch government

Date	Origin	Company	Product	Destination
15.10.08	India	Swift Laboratories Ltd	Clopidogrel Bilsulphate—API	Columbia
27.11.08	India	Cipla (Uni World Pharma Ltd, Dubai)	Olanzapine 10 mg tabs	Peru
27.11.08	India	Cipla Ltd, through Uni World Pharma Ltd Dubai	Rivastigmine 3 mg tabs	Peru
24.12.08	India	Dr Reddy's Laboratories Ltd, EMA	Losartan—API	Brazil

Source: Author's compilation.

[26] See the full intervention by India available at www.keionline.org/node/309, accessed 14 December 2018.

> We all know that the actions of the Dutch authorities are not in conformity with WTO disciplines in general nor with the flexibilities under the TRIPS Agreement. Nonetheless, these disciplines and flexibilities are under threat in other international fora, where some developed countries are attempting to adopt TRIPS-plus resolutions.[27]

The case of the seizure of Indian goods illustrates that despite the fact that the TRIPS agreement was perceived by developing countries to create a 'ceiling' for the upper limits of intellectual property rights, the contrary has occurred, with developed countries pushing for ever higher standards. (Grosse Ruse-Khan and Kur 2008)

> The general perception in international IP [intellectual property] regulation so far has been that above the prescribed minimum standards there is no ceiling or limit other than the sky. This construction results in a spiral movement – driven by bilateral agreements – towards ever-increasing levels of protection, and reducing the flexibilities and policy space left open under the TRIPS agreement. (Grosse Ruse-Khan and Kur 2008)

The outcomes of the seizure are clearly negative for Indian firms. Even if these particular shipments are released (and some of them have been), they create a level of uncertainty in international shipping for Indian products. This may provoke Indian firms to seek ports that do not run risk of seizure. It has especially negative implications for medium-size firms that may not have the access to legal services to defend their claims to transport. India's generic drugs have faced a slew of recent barriers in the global export of their products. The latest example is Kenya's Anti-Counterfeit Act, passed in December 2008. The legislation recognizes the intellectual property (IP) rights of pharmaceutical products recognized anywhere in the world, as opposed to in the country of import or export. The result is that the IP rights standards set in any other country may be enforced in Kenya, with the possible result of preventing the sale of a generic version of a drug that is not patented in Kenya. This is consistent with the efforts of developed countries at the World Intellectual Property Organization (WIPO), which would create a system in which patents in one country are recognized globally. In response, India and Brazil are planning to launch a complaint at the WTO.

In Brazil, the success of its publicly provided antiretroviral programme has become a device for engagement with other members of the Global South (Souza 2012). Brazil's ambassador to the WTO interpreted the seizures as part of a political and procedural challenge to the trade of medicine among developing countries: 'The risk of seizures meant generics producers in developing countries were avoiding shipping goods via Europe, driving up transport costs and so undermining the purpose of using cheap generics.'[28]

A confluence of commercial and public good interests has over the past decade pushed India and Brazil to the forefront in defending the rights of generics producers, exporters,

[27] See the Brazilian government's full statement, available at www.keionline.org/blogs/2009/03/04/brazilian-intervention-at-trips-council, accessed 14 December 2018.

[28] Henry J. Kaiser Family Foundation, 'India, Brazil Launch Trade Dispute against EU, Netherlands over Seizures of Generic Drugs, 13 May 2010. Available at http://kff.org/news-summary/india-brazil-launch-trade-dispute-against-eu-netherlands-over-seizures-of-generic-drugs/, accessed 9 October 2018.

and consumers. The seizure of off-patent medicines was resolved in 2011, via an agreement between the EU and India:

> the mere fact that medicines [were] in transit through EU territory, and that there is a patent title applicable to such medicines in EU territory, does not in itself constitute sufficient grounds for customs authorities in the EU to suspect the infringement of patent rights.
>
> (European Parliamentary Research Service 2014)

Sustaining a broad coalition through the G20, or pushing forth a multi-issue area alliance through IBSA has proven difficult. But a robust commitment to the issue area of access to medicine appears to be one where support by these emerging powers is more obdurate. This is a dispute that will likely arise in the future as the status of generic pharmaceuticals is challenged. The case of the collaborative resistance of India and Brazil to the EU confiscations and their ability to mobilize players in civil society and international organizations working on public health interest areas suggest this is an area where future political partnerships and strategies for protection of trade interests will emerge.

Discussion: building coalitions and shared interests in the Trump age

The strengthening of emerging economies and 'explosion' of South–South trade characterizing the early 2000s was heavily skewed towards a select number of countries and industries. If the first decades of the twenty-first century brought about a shift in the global political and economic paradigm, changes were distinctly uneven.[29] This chapter has focused on two leaders of South–South partnerships—India and Brazil—seeking to assess how and if cooperation manifested across multilateral, plurilateral, and bilateral issues. The context here was distinctly post-1990s and in the wake of new global frameworks for trade integration. As has been widely studied, the views and positions of developing countries were broadly disregarded at the WTO's foundational UR of negotiations from 1986 to 1994 (Jawara and Kwa 2003). The UR introduced a new international regime that was, in several key policy areas, adverse to the interests of Brazil and India.[30]

The first half of the 2000s witnessed a push back to these new regulations and the subsequent collapse of WTO negotiations, with Indian and Brazilian leaders many times

[29] Boston Consulting Group (BCG) has described an elite league of 'rapidly developing economies' which have become 'new global challengers', developing closer ties with one another, offering products in high-value segments, and facing off against northern multinationals which have traditionally dominated value-added industries such as pharmaceuticals, telecoms, shipping, IT, and consumer electronics (Boston Consulting Group 2007).

[30] Both assumed important policy costs: restrictions to national regulation of tariffs, implementation of IP rights, and limits on existing and future systems of agricultural subsidy.

at the helm. The scale and influence of 'rising powers' seemed to augur a logical and reciprocal shift in political power. But the real legacy of the post-2008 international economic crisis and the post-2017 neo-nationalist political switch is that the broad plan of 1990s harmonization has ground to a halt. In its wake, emerging powers struggled to forge an alternative path. What we can learn from this study is that most of the strategies for cooperation have fallen short: plurilateral initiatives such as IBSA have not resulted in concrete mechanisms for trade cooperation. The alliance forged through the G20 coalition was remarkably absent from recent WTO negotiations. In its place, India and Brazil pursued single-issue advances. Limited examples of synchronization of global trade interests, such as in India's and Brazil's rejection of limits on European restriction of generics transport do not appear to have spilled over or signified multiple areas of cooperation in trade and development policy.

The result is that by 2017 the gap between the rhetoric of South–South cooperation and the tangible advances in policy at the multilateral and bilateral levels had become ever more starkly evident. If the 'rise' of developing countries in the first two decades did not result in a political repositioning, how will the leaders of the Global South equilibrate their efforts in the face of the United States's hardened neoconservative isolationism under Trump and the deep fragmentation the European Union currently experiences? It seems particularly notable that in his first day of office, President Trump rescinded the United States' commitment to the Trans-Pacific Partnership (TPP) and signalled his move to policies of protectionism. As Martin Khor writes:

> With the demise of the TPP, its developing-country members regret the loss of their opportunity to gain greater access to the US market. But they are also spared from having to take on heavy obligations on investment, intellectual property, state-owned enterprises and other issues.
>
> (Khor 2017)

Conclusion

The withdrawal of the US from the policies of trade promotion will open the door to new opportunities for developing countries at the same time that it restricts others. Perhaps one of the most controversial areas for multilateral institutions will be seen at the WTO, where the US's purported intention to restrict trade with Mexico and China may go against the very rules it worked hard to establish in the 1990s.

India and Brazil, each facing its own domestic and regional challenges, will recalibrate their role in a context of collapsed liberalism. One possibility is that they find themselves more fragmented, with the divisions that blocked their coordination efforts at the WTO and in multilateral projects only exacerbated. Yet, in another scenario, it is possible that regional hegemons reassess their collaborative frameworks and strengthen them in the wake of the US's and EU's global retreat.

ACKNOWLEDGEMENTS

Research was financed by the author's FONDECYT Iniciación, Project N° 11140501, entitled 'The Political Economy of Innovation, Intellectual Property and Human Development in Latin America.' The study was also part of the work supported by the Millennium Nucleus for the 'Study of Stateness and Democracy in Latin America', Project N° NS100014. In addition, this project benefited from the financial and scholarly contributions of the Economic History and Cliometrics lab funding provided by Conicyt/Programa de Investigación Asociativa Project No. SOC1102. Andrea Neirot provided excellent research assistance. All the usual caveats apply.

REFERENCES

Ayres, A. (2014). 'India; Tough talk and the Bali trade facilitation agreement'. Council on Foreign Relations, July 29. Available at www.cfr.org/blog/india-tough-talk-and-bali-trade-facilitation-agreement, accessed 27 May 2019.

Boston Consulting Group (2007). *The 2008 BCG 100 New Global Challengers: How Top Companies from Rapidly Developing Economies Are Changing the World*. Boston, MA: BCG.

Burges, S. (2005). 'Auto-estima in Brazil: the rhetorical logic of Lula's South–South foreign policy', *International Journal* 60/4: 1133–51.

Chorev, N. (2007). *Remaking U.S. Trade Policy: From Protectionism to Globalization*. Ithaca, NY: Cornell University Press.

European Parliamentary Research Service (2014). 'Controversial issues in EU-India trade disputes at WTO level'. Briefing, 26 April. Available at https://epthinktank.eu/2014/05/06/controversial-issues-in-eu-india-trade-disputes-at-wto-level/, accessed 27 May 2019.

Grabendoff, W. (1979). 'La política exterior del Brasil, entre el premer y tercer mundo [Brazil's foreign policy between first and third worlds], *Nueva Sociedad* 41: 108–19.

Grosse Ruse-Khan, H. and Kur, A. (2008). 'Enough is enough – The notion of binding ceilings in international intellectual property protection'. Max Plank Institute for Intellectual Property, Competition & Tax Law Research Paper Series. Munich. Available at http://papers.ssrn.com/sol3/papers.cfm?abstract_id=1326429, accessed 9 October 2018.

Hurrell, A. and Narlikar, A. (2006a). 'The new politics of confrontation: developing countries at Cancun and beyond', *Global Society* 20/4: 415–33.

Hurrell, A. and Narlikar, A. (2006b). 'A new politics of confrontation? Brazil and India in multilateral trade negotiations', *Global Society* 20/4: 415–33.

IBSA (India-Brazil-South Africa) (2012). 'Declaração final do encontro ministerial India-Brazil-Africa dul Sul à margem do fórum ecônomico mundial [Final declaration of India-Brazil-Africa at South ministerial meeting on the fringes of the World Economic Forum]', *Resenha de Política Exterior do Brasil* 110: 77–9.

Jawara, F. and Kwa, A. (2003). *Behind the Scenes at the WTO*. London: Zed Books.

Khor, M. (2017). 'Shocks for developing countries from President Trump's first weeks', *Third World Resurgence* 317/318: 10–12.

Lourens, C. (2005). 'New effort to breathe life into SA-Brazil trade forum'. *Business Day*. Available at https://cuts-international.org/new-effort-to-breathe-life-into-sa-brazil-trade-forum/, accessed 19 December 2019.

Mehra, P. (2013). 'India's stand prevails in Bali', *The Hindu*, 7 December.

Ministério Das Relações Exteriores (2003). 'Declaração de Brasília'. Available at www.itamaraty.gov.br/pt-BR/politica-externa/mecanismos-inter-regionais/3673-forum-de-dialogo-india-brasil-e-africa-do-sul-ibas, accessed 18 January 2020.

Narlikar, A. (2013). 'India rising: responsible to whom?', *International Affairs* 89/3 595–614.

Negri, F. (2005). *O perfil dos exportadores industriais Brasileiros para a China* [A profile of Brazilian industrial exporters to China]. Rio de Janeiro: IPEA.

Rao, C.V. (2003). 'Indo Brazilian joint business meeting', in Commerce, FOICO (ed.) New Delhi. Available at www.ficci.com/, accessed 27 May 2019.

Rolland, S. (2007). 'Developing country coalitions at the WTO. In search of legal support', *Harvard International Law Journal* 48/2: 483–552.

Sikri, R. (2003). '13th session of the high level committee on the review of technical cooperation among developing countries', Additional Secretary, Ministry of External Affairs, New Delhi. New York. Available at www.belfercenter.org/publication/indias-foreign-policy, accessed 10 January 2020.

Souza, A.D.M.D. (2012). 'Saúde pública, patentes e atores não estatais: a política externa do Brasil ante a epidemia de aids [Public health, patents and non-state actors: Brazil's foreign policy in the face of the AIDS epidemic]'. *Política externa brasileira: As práticas da política e a política das práticas* [Brazilian foreign policy: the practices of politics and the politics of practices]. Rio de Janeiro: Editora FGV. Available at www.scielo.br/scielo.php?script=sci_nlinks&ref=000131&pid=S0102-85292013000100001000025&lng=pt, accessed 19 December 2019.

Stephen, M.D. (2012). 'Rising regional powers and international institutions: the foreign policy orientations of India, Brazil and South Africa', *Global Society* 26/3: 289–309.

Taylor, I.A.N. (2012). 'India's rise in Africa', *International Affairs* 88/4: 779–98.

UNITAID (2009). UNITAID statement on Dutch confiscation of medicines shipment. Available at http://lists.healthnet.org/archive/html/e-drug/2009-03/msg00020.html, accessed 19 December 2019.

Vieira, M. (2006). Interview, Director, Ministry of Foreign Relations, Trade Promotion Department, Palacio Itamaraty, Brasilia, 23 June 2006. Available at www.itamaraty.gov.br/en/perguntas-frequentes artigos/19384-itamaraty-and-the-foreign-service-careers, accessed 10 January 2020.

Wise, T. (2013). 'Why the WTO needs a "hypocrisy clause"'. Triple Crisis: Global Perspective on Finance, Development and Environment. Available at http://triplecrisis.com/why-the-wto-needs-a-hypocrisy-clause/, accessed 9 October 2018.

41 Economic, political, and social transformation in Brazil

A study in disorderly progress

Sunil Tankha

Introduction

Throughout its five-century existence, Brazil has been on a roller coaster of phases of rapid growth followed by an equal stagnation. Over the last two decades Brazil again emerged from economic doldrums into a period of enviable economic and social transformation, only to sink back into stagnation. Between 2002 and 2012, Brazil's economy grew by over 40 per cent but more importantly, over 20 million people left poverty and Brazil, notoriously unequal, became more egalitarian. The popular presses were until a few years ago filled with articles describing how more and more people were joining the middle classes at its lower end, how people were flying in airplanes for the first time in their lives, how the São Paulo upper classes were now finding it difficult to get maids (who were now commanding very decent wages), and how large infrastructure projects in the north-east of the country were finding it so difficult to get workers that they were forced to poach them from each other (see e.g. Barrionuevo 2011). Brazil's former President Lula da Silva—the son of poor sharecroppers from the north-east of the country who led the São Paulo industrial workers in courageous strikes against the military dictatorship and who became so popular that even Barack Obama half-enviously ribbed him in 2009 calling Lula 'the most popular politician on Earth'[1]—represented a country which appeared to be finally fulfilling the words of the émigré Austrian novelist and social commentator Stefan Zweig (1941): 'the country of the future'. But then economic growth stalled in 2012 and social cleavages have re-emerged in complicated forms. In 2013, protests against the government erupted throughout the country, led by established middle classes, traditional elites, and young professionals. By 2015, demands for the impeachment of President Dilma Roussef grew and some protestors were even calling for a military coup to remove her. In 2016, as the *Lava Jato*

[1] Available at www.youtube.com/watch?v=7vmuSZtiG4A, accessed 9 October 2018.

Sunil Tankha, *Economic, political, and social transformation in Brazil: A study indisorderly progress* In: *Handbook of BRICS and Emerging Economies.* Edited by: P.B. Anand, Shailaja Fennell, and Flavio Comim, Oxford University Press (2021). © Oxford University Press.
DOI: 10.1093/oso/9780198827535.003.0041

investigations began to unearth evidence of multi-billion dollar bribes being paid for public contracts, the Brazilian Congress finally voted to impeach her, putting an end to fourteen years of the Workers' Party (PT) administration.[2]

Given that Brazil does not suffer from any obvious handicaps—it has vast reserves of different natural resources, peaceful relations, and free trade agreements with all of its neighbours; a large and educated middle class; over two hundred years of independence to overcome colonial legacies—why is it still so erratic in its progress that one loses any sense of an orderly trajectory? To explore this question, we develop a narrative analysis of the historical record to explore Brazil's economic and social history since the founding of the First Republic in 1891 through to present times, paying particular attention to turning and tipping points. In so doing we find that strains of the current economic and political turmoil are themes that can be found throughout the twentieth century and that there are some clear parallels between the present and Brazil's recent past, especially during the Vargas years. We use this evidence to draw conclusions about the phases of evolution of national identify and social structure, which provide the 'tectonic plates' of contemporary Brazil in terms of which current debates and struggles around national economic and political strategy need to be understood.

We present our historical narrative analysis in the next three sections: the second section rapidly passes over the colonial and imperial centuries to set the stage for our enquiry. The third section discusses the social, economic, and political transformation of Brazil in the first phase of its republican history, and the fourth takes up from when the country re-democratized after two decades of military rule. The fifth section explains our main theme: the causes behind the alternation of disorder and progress in Brazil. The sixth section concludes.

Origins of the republic

Europeans discovered Brazil in 1500 when Pedro Álvarez Cabral, replicating Vasco da Gama's voyage to India, followed up on da Gama's reports of an unknown land mass to the west of his route. Swinging a little further out than the normal sea route (which generally took a lazy westward curve around the equator in order to take advantage of the prevailing winds) Cabral found and claimed the eastern protrusion of South America

[2] President Roussef was impeached despite the Lava Jato investigations not having found any evidence that she was personally involved in any corrupt act. The impeachment accusation against her was rather bland, charging that her administration misrepresented the state of federal finances in order to improve her re-election chances. Many observers feel that she was impeached because powerful members of the Brazilian Congress felt she was not stalling the Lavo Jato investigations which were beginning to implicate many of them.

for the Portuguese Crown. What the Portuguese found in their new territory was a stable though technologically unsophisticated post-Paleolithic civilization consisting of about a million indigenous peoples spread over two thousand tribes mostly speaking variations of the Tupi language (Ribeiro 1995). After brutally subjugating the native population, the Portuguese staved off French and Dutch incursions to have finally established dominance over their Brazilian territories by the middle of the seventeenth century.

As explained by Celso Furtado in his seminal work, *Economic Formation of Brazil*, over the next two centuries, first as a colony and then as an independent monarchy, Brazil made little progress in terms of transitioning to more sophisticated production and social structures. Its economy remained anchored to primary products—first Brazilwood dye, then sugar, followed by cotton, and finally coffee—which experienced periodic booms and extended slumps. In between there was a brief minerals boom when gold was discovered in the southeast in the eighteenth century but Brazil remained mostly a typical extractive plantation colony. There were hopes that independence from Portugal would lead to expanded economic opportunities but the independent Empire of Brazil, which lasted only during the lifetime of Pedro II, was a period of economic and political stalemate. The Brazilian population was divided into a small agricultural elite addicted to court distributed privileges, a large slave population that had few legal and no political rights, and a growing but generally frustrated urban and military class which was becoming increasingly inspired by positivist ideational influences (Nachman 1977; Amory 1999).

Positivism, with its emphasis on the scientific rational and by extension on social, political, and economic freedom, spoke more to the middle classes than the imperial court which had no privileges to confer to obtain the former's loyalty. A vocal group of positivists united against slavery, pushing through successive laws which curtailed slave practices, notably the Law of the Free Womb of 1871 which prohibited enslaving children born to slaves, until achieving total abolition in 1888.

Until the monarchy fell, however, economic modernization was paralysed by the small group of slave-owning elites whose interests were not symbiotic with industrialization. Indeed, they managed to thwart most industrial entrepreneurs including the Baron of Maua, a pioneer of modern industry in Brazil, who perspicaciously noted that the emperor liked none who was not beholden to him by privileges or who did not own slaves. Thus, by 1870, shortly before the monarchy fell, Brazil had a population of only 14.3 million, compared to the United States which had more than four times as many people. The difference is striking given that when Brazil had become independent in 1822, it had roughly half the population of the United States (4.6 million compared to 9.6 million). Moreover, the vast majority of the population was either mulatto (42 per cent) or African (28 per cent) and their economic interests were not just irrelevant but actively undermined (Bucciferro 2013). It was only after massive European immigration beginning in the 1870s that the demographic composition of the country changed and the stalemate was broken, which allowed the dismantling of the old regime and the establishment of a modern republic.

The United States of Brazil (1891–1988): economic modernization and authoritarian disorder

On the 15 November 1889, Marshal Deodoro da Fonseca marched against the monarchists, exiled the emperor and Brazil became a republic. The constitution Brazil adopted after the military deposed Pedro II took its inspiration from the United States (Love 2013). It pursued a liberal agenda, transferring more powers to the provinces—now renamed states—so that they, or at least their elites, could be free to pursue policies of local interest. Like the US Constitution, it established the president as the head of the state and enshrined the separation of church and state. As in the United States, voting privileges were restricted to men of property and education, and the vote was denied to native tribes, blacks, and women. Indeed, admiration for the United States ran so deep at the time that the country was named the United States of Brazil and its first flag was an imitation of the US Stars and Stripes. Eventually, the positivists asserted themselves and replaced it with the current Brazilian flag which features the motto *Ordem e Progresso* [Order and Progress] which is based on Comte's summary of the republican ideal: *L'amour pour principe et l'ordre pour base; le progrès pour but* [Love as the principle and order as the foundation; progress as the goal].

Political instability plagued the republic in its first decades. The overthrowing of the monarchy, which was weak, isolated, and obsolete, did not represent a definitive victory of one powerful interest group over another. The conservative rural agriculture elite had viewed the monarchy as a stabilizing buffer protecting its interests against reform pressures from the positivist republicans, but after Princess Isabel signed off on abolition on behalf of her father, the conservatives found little use to prop up the monarchy. After the monarchy fell, agricultural oligarchs of the economically dominant states of São Paulo and Minas Gerais manoeuvered quickly to take control of the national government, besting the positivists, the military, and the oligarchs of the south. In an accord that came to be known as 'coffee with milk' [*café com leite*] from the importance of coffee to the São Paulo economy (and of cattle and dairy in Minas), they agreed to alternate the presidency among themselves, thereby thwarting the military, other regional interests, and popular political will. Dissatisfaction of the military with this oligarchic system, led mainly by junior officers from the middle classes, remained a source of tension; and various revolts and attempted revolutions were a constant feature of the early republican period. In the 1920s, two major revolts—Copacabana in 1922 and Paulista in 1924—rocked Brazil's largest cities. However, it was not until President Washington Luis broke the *café com leite* accord in 1930 that the oligarchy was overthrown.

Dissolution of the accord is generally traced to the 1929 crash which drastically reduced global coffee demand and prices, and devastated the Brazilian economy as coffee represented over two-thirds of Brazilian exports. To bring about policies to compensate them for their losses, the São Paulo coffee elite attempted to get another Paulista elected to the presidency after the end of Washington Luis's term in 1930 and although their political manoeuverings initially managed to get Jose Prestes elected President with only the states of Minas Gerais, Pernambuco, and Rio Grande do Sul opposed, the schism between the São Paulo and Minas oligarchs and the economic and political instability exacerbated by the Great Depression in the United States allowed the military to depose Luis before Prestes could take the oath of office.

THE VARGAS INSPIRATION: THE STATE AS ENTREPRENEUR (1930–64)

Although the military junta was aiming to remain in power after the coup, Getúlio Vargas, the opposition presidential candidate supported by the new alliance of Minas and Rio Grande do Sul, mobilized popular demonstrations and swept into Rio de Janeiro to take over the presidency. A skilled politician, Vargas remained in the presidential palace for the next fifteen years, alternately playing democratic and military interests against each other. Exaggerating the threat of a communist takeover, he dissolved Congress in 1937 and overturned constitutional term limits. He also replaced almost all of the state governors with hand-picked military men and technocrats (Fausto 1999).

For some, Vargas's ascent to the presidency marked a fundamental shift in Brazil's political economy which had until then maintained a conservative and tenuous balance between rural elite interests and the modernizing positivists. Vargas's subversion of the constitution and centralization of Brazilian economic institutions under his office was politically possible because of his immense popularity with urban workers and the middle classes, which derived from his social and labour policies, characterized contemporarily by Lowenstein (1942) as 'progressive paternalism'. Even before he became president, when he was briefly the Minister of Economy under Washington Luis, Vargas had established a pension fund, Brazil's first, for employees of the federal government. After he became President, Vargas introduced a number of labour laws similar to those Franklin Delano Roosevelt was introducing in the United States. Surprisingly for a country only just beginning to industrialize heavily, Vargas's Consolidation of Labor Laws (CLT) was one of the most advanced systems of labour law in the world (Baer 1965).

For others, however, Vargas was politically astute enough to realize the limits of paternalistic populism and his labour laws accommodated oligarchs' interests by keeping their mostly rural labour outside the purview of the CLT. Instead, it was the growing state supported industrial sector which absorbed these sophisticated and progressive labour laws. Vargas accommodated oligarchic interests in other ways also, for example by instituting support policies for coffee which included buying up and burning coffee stocks.

In developing his economic and social policies, Vargas symbiotically channelled two formative forces of Brazilian modernization. In the economic sphere, Vargas reacted to the positivists' analyses of economic problems. At the turn of the century, positivists had already begun to lay the groundwork for shifting the economic discourse in the direction of state intervention arguing that foreign control over the commercialization of Brazilian products drained capital and that relying on foreigners for industrial imports stunted national development processes (Nachman 1977). As Serzedello Correa, a military officer and briefly President of the State of Parana after the revolution, had put it, 'about eighty five percent of the gains of commercial activity here does not belong to us and does not stay in the country'. Prioritizing industrial development, Vargas's administration began establishing large public sector enterprises in mining (e.g. the National Steel Company—CSN, and mining giant Company of the Rio Doce Valley—CVRD, and energy, e.g. the Hydroelectric Corporation of the São Francisco—CHESF). Vargas's entrepreneurial Brazilian state, which he managed to get enshrined in the country's 1934 Constitution, this time modelled after that of Germany, was an expression of an economic nationalism, a developmental ideology, and an economic theory. It intended to accelerate and internalize technological learning in order to create a robust and diversified domestic industrial base. It was also a very political vision, for it needed to channel the export earning of the traditional elites into a national development programme.

The other formative influence on Vargas's economic, political, and social policies can be traced to the massive Italian emigration to Brazil at the end of the nineteenth century. Attracted by a Brazilian government programme which paid for their passage, Italians began arriving by the millions headed initially for the coffee plantations of São Paulo; but given it was the explicit intent of the landowners to encourage excessive immigration as a means of keeping wages low, as soon as their obligatory annual contract at the coffee plantations would have expired, these immigrants would relocate to the city in search of better wages. By 1893, according to some estimates, Italians came to form about a third of the population of São Paulo city (Biondi 2010). A class identity also formed among immigrants. Rather than encounter an ethnic solidarity, Italian labourers found that their wealthier co-nationalists identified more with their rich Brazilian, Portuguese, and Spanish peers. In 1905, the Italo-Brazilian labour journal *Il Falegname* [the Carpenter] pointedly noted that Italian factory owners would employ without scruple Portuguese and mulatto workers in preference to Italians if the former were cheaper (Hall 2010). Over the next few decades, many of these immigrants, who had already been active in the anarchist and socialist labour movements in Italy, became active agents of political sensitization and organization among Brazilian immigrants as well as among the native labouring classes. As free men who brought with them some skills, suffered no sense of racial inferiority, and enjoyed a degree of social cohesion from their syndicalist experience in Italy, they quickly formed the core of the urban proletariat, at one stage composing almost the entire São Paulo industrial labour force. Vargas's state-led industrialization push provided a channel of social and economic betterment for these immigrants and their children, even though he consistently suppressed the more radical labour elements among them.

Even as he weakened political institutions to centralize power under himself in the *Estado Novo* that he established, Vargas oversaw the creation of the most important and durable institutions of Brazilian public and economic administration and in the process thoroughly transformed Brazil's economic structure and governance. Although the military forced Vargas to leave office after the end of the Second World War in 1945, he returned to the presidency following an overwhelming electoral victory in 1950. During his second tenure, which lasted until 1954, the BNDE (Banco Nacional de Desenvolvimento Econômico [National Economic Development Bank]), BNB (Bank of Northeast Brazil), CNPq (National Research Council), CNA (National Confederation of Agriculture & Livestock), Petrobrás, and Eletrobrás were all created to build the institutional and organizational capacity necessary to manage the process of massive and rapid state-led industrialization. All of these organizations still exist today and are among the most important pillars of Brazil's economic planning and industry.

Despite his popularity in 1950, Vargas's hold on power was tenuous because of the fragility of the post-war economy, which was buffeted by high inflation and balance-of-payments problems, many of these a legacy of the liberal economic policies of his predecessor, the military-backed Field Marshal Eurico Dutra. Rejecting Vargas's nationalist approach, Dutra had restored the earlier liberal regime of equality among national and foreign entities. To some extent, this was a response to high inflation, which the Dutra government hoped to counter by encouraging imports. These rose by 80 per cent while exports only rose 17 per cent (Ianni 1977), which then led to severe balance-of-payments problems. It should not be surprising then that when Vargas returned to power as a result of these failed policies, the military viewed his national developmentalist populism as an existential threat. Playing up allegations of corruption in his administration, the military aligned with his opponents and when Vargas was implicated in the attempted murder of a journalist who vigorously opposed him, the armed forces mobilized for another coup. Faced with this threat, on 23 August 1954 Vargas retired to his bedroom and shot himself through the heart.

Public response to Vargas's suicide ensured that his approach to managing the Brazilian economy—based on strong state entrepreneurship and import substitution industrialization—not only continued but picked up intensity. His successor, Juscelino Kubitschek, conducted an even more massive programme of economic transformation under central government control, establishing his *Plano de Metas* which intended to achieve fifty years of economic transformation in five years. Creating a hyper-planned economic institutional superstructure, the Brazilian state aimed for rapid progress in industrial transformation. Representing this order and progress, Brasilia, the new capital, was built, from scratch and in a forlorn vastness of scrubland in the middle of the country, in only forty-one months.

This frenetic pace of economic activity again resulted in a steep increase in public debt and in the already troubling rate of inflation. Kubitschek's successor, Janio Quadros, tried to deal with the growing crisis by slowing investment and on the one hand appealing to the US and the International Monetary Fund (IMF) for financing while on the other hand courting the Communist Bloc. Seven months into his presidency, he abruptly resigned. At that moment Vice-President João Goulart, an old Vargas confidant who was much more to the left of Quadros, had to rush back from China to take over the presidency before the military could depose him. A compromise which weakened the presidency and transferred powers to the Brazilian Congress persuaded the military to allow Quadros to become president but he managed to regain his powers through a plebiscite. Inflation and economic slowdown continued to plague Brazil while the United States, viewing Goulart as too leftist, rebuffed his attempts to renegotiate the national debt to keep him on a 'short leash' (Donnelly 1973). In these politically and economically tense times, Goulart passed decrees expropriating agricultural land for redistribution and nationalizing petroleum refineries. With the elites feeling economically threatened and other classes mostly ambivalent in the midst of the economic chaos, the armed forces, with the support and approval of the United States, overthrew Goulart on 1 April 1964 and set the basis for military rule over the next two decades.

EXHAUSTION OF THE ENTREPRENEURIAL STATE UNDER THE MILITARY (1964–85)

The economic and industrial policies of the early military government were contradictory to their official discourse. Economists associated with the military government were orthodox and adhered to the idea that for efficiency's sake public sector enterprises should imitate their private sector counterparts as much as possible. They argued, as would New Public Management proponents decades later, that public sector enterprises should be autonomous instead of subordinate to political authority (IPEA 2010). Paradoxically, rather than a withdrawal of the state during this period, there was an explosion in the size of the public sector. Public enterprises began to follow private sector logic and expanded into all potentially profitable areas, even to the extent of speculating on the stock market. Even though established public sector banks such as BNDE did not provide much financing to public sector enterprises, the latter had little trouble in expanding their operations since they had ample access to foreign private financing. With little supervision from ministries who exercised only nominal control over their areas of competence, these enterprises built up a stratospheric foreign debt. Dependence on foreign finance also introduced another pathology into the system: during times of economic stress, to overcome short-term balance of payments problems the government frequently compelled public enterprises to borrow, often excessively, in international markets but at the same time restrained the prices they could charge for their outputs, first to promote industrialization but then later to fight inflation. Thus the entrepreneurial state continued to yield strong and sustained economic growth in Brazil. Average annual growth rates between 1947 and 1979 were around 7.5 per cent while per capita income rose around 3 per cent annually. Only two countries—Finland and Japan—had higher rates of per capita income growth.

The logic of depending on heavy public sector investment to grow the economy—while at the same time suppressing the prices charged by public sector firms to fight inflation—became unsustainable after the macroeconomic shocks of the late 1970s and early 1980s. The military government initially gambled that it could grow out of trouble by initiating a massive debt-based investment programme in basic industries and infrastructure, but successive shocks from oil prices, interest rates, and emerging market lending left the government unable to service its debt, which had ballooned from US$6.2 billion in 1973 to US$91 billion in 1987.[3]

These shocks again transformed Brazil's political and economic landscape. During the military dictatorship, Brazilians had suffered through increasing political repression and social cleavages. In 1968, Institutional Act 5 was enacted in the face of increasing public protests and it suspended most constitutional rights and subordinated Congress to the military. Over the following years inflation eroded the purchasing power of the working class. On the basis of their infrastructure building and economic growth, the military could count on elite and conservative support but when the economy irreversibly stalled, the military government lost the support of the industrial classes and was compelled to relinquish political power. The intractability of Brazilian economic problems also began to make the idea of the entrepreneurial state obsolete. Squeezed between unremunerative prices and excessive debt, the Brazilian public sector came to be blamed both for its own financial insolvency and for Brazil's deficit problem. With Brazil's subsequent re-democratization, the policy windows opened for an economic project which would focus on reducing the scope and role of the state in the domestic economy.

The Federal Republic of Brazil (1988–present): the country of the future?

The transition to a civilian government in 1984 was a negotiated affair in which Brazil's generals agreed to transfer power to Tancredo Neves, a political moderate who, as leader of the officially sanctioned opposition party, had begun to oppose the military government only during its last years. However, Neves fell seriously ill on the day before he was to take the oath of office and passed away a few weeks later. Ironically, it was then Vice-President Jose Sarney, previously the leader of the military government's official party, who became Brazil's first post-military president. Thus, as before, the transfer of power from one centre of authority to another was relatively peaceful and partial. Incumbent elites ceded some political power, but did not lose their assets or their positions. Political and economic instability prevailed yet again.

[3] All data in this section were retrieved from the online data bank maintained by the Brazilian Institute for Applied Economic Research (IPEA). Available at ipeadata.gov.br, accessed 9 October 2018.

CONTINUING POLITICAL AND ECONOMIC DISORDER

The new Constitution drafted in 1988 finally provided for direct presidential elections. It also cemented political and human rights and, as decentralization was popular at the time, the constitution realigned powers between the centre and the states, guaranteeing the latter some measure of autonomy, especially in the form of financial and fiscal authority. Recognizing the tendency to legislative stalemate which existed in Brazil, the Constitution also strengthened the Office of the President by allowing the incumbent several legislative powers to break through congressional gridlock, principally the Provisional Measures clause which authorized the president to issue decrees. The Constitution also marked the transition in centre–state–society relations by changing the name of the country to the Federal Republic of Brazil [*Republica Federativa do Brazil*].

Rectifying Brazil's precarious economic situation proved more challenging than coming up with a new governance framework. Breaking the inherited cycle of deficit spending and inflation required telegraphing to the markets a fiscal and monetary discipline which the Sarney administration with its thin support was not well placed to do. More importantly it had no new ideas to combat inflation. It made three attempts to end inflation, all variations on a theme of indexing prices and changing currencies, but the results were poor. Sarney was succeeded in 1990 by Fernando Collor, who won Brazil's first direct presidential elections by marketing himself as an economic modernizer and a political outsider, though he himself was from one of the elite families of the north-east and his father had been both governor and senator in Alagoas. Promising radical market-friendly policies including privatization, Collor vowed to cut the privileges of overpaid public officials whom he derisively called maharajas. This message resonated with the Brazilian public; but before Collor could fully implement his economic agenda, he was charged with corruption in public procurement schemes and impeached in 1992. In any case, his programmes were not yielding results: Brazil continued to suffer high inflation rates (25 to 30 per cent a month), operational deficits (around 2.5 per cent of GDP), and a stagnant economy (real GDP declined about 1 per cent). Itamar Franco, Collor's Vice-President, took over after the impeachment. Brazil now lurched in the other direction as Franco was neither an economic modernizer nor enamoured of the market, and he reverted to indexing to control inflation. Again, these measures were ineffective and Franco was forced to appoint a political rival, Fernando Henrique Cardoso, as Finance Minister in May 1993.

ESTABLISHING ECONOMIC ORDER

When Cardoso took over as Finance Minister, Brazil was trapped in a vicious cycle of fiscal deficits, inflation, and high interest rates. Market scepticism over Brazil's ability to service its debt forced the government into ever-shortening terms of financing at very high interest rates, which increased the debt burden even more, further worsening

Brazil's fiscal balance and forcing the government to offer even higher interest rates (Amann and Baer 2003). It was widely believed that credibility of the reforms was the underlying problem because financial markets did not trust the government not to again inflate away its deficits. But Cardoso had access to a fundamentally different strategy from his predecessors. To break Brazil's inflationary cycle, he replicated a plan slightly modified from one Argentina had recently implemented successfully, which was to peg the value of the domestic currency to the US dollar and at the same time to float the currency. The legal commitment to the peg combined with the market as a mechanism for establishing the true value of the currency finally worked to end inflation.

The end to inflation delivered several and immediate benefits. Monetary stability reactivated investment and growth. Inequality also began to fall as price stability protected workers' real wage levels (Lustig et al. 2013). Success with the *Real Plan* propelled Cardoso to the presidency over the PT candidate Lula da Silva who according to contemporary opinion polls had been leading Cardoso by several points before the *Real Plan* had taken off.

The package of reforms associated with the *Real Plan* tackled and largely overcame weaknesses in Brazilian economic management institutions. Before the *Real Plan*, monetary and fiscal policies as well as the institutions which governed them were incompatible with what global finance and investment institutions were demanding. Cardoso strengthened the Brazilian Central Bank and made it more independent. He also pushed through Congress a Law of Fiscal Responsibility, which required state and municipal governments to balance their budgets. Together, these measures brought much-needed order to Brazilian public finances and managed finally to overcome Brazil's hyperinflationary cycle.

In addition to the *Real Plan*, the Cardoso administration pushed Brazil's extensive privatization programme, particularly of the electric power industry, presenting it as an effort to overcome public sector indiscipline and disorder which took the forms of soft-budget constraints, inflation-linked price controls, and undisciplined borrowing. While initially successful, Cardoso's privatization policies eventually became controversial and in no small measure contributed to the defeat of his party in the 2002 Brazilian presidential elections. An analysis of the *Real Plan* and privatization revealed that they were initially symbiotic but eventually cannibalized each other (Tankha 2009). In the symbiotic phase, the *Real Plan* provided the necessary monetary and economic stability which made the prospect of purchasing infrastructure assets attractive to foreign investors while the foreign exchange inflows through privatization helped increase the demand for *Reals* and thus maintain its value. In the cannibalizing phase, the *Real Plan* actually led to a large increase in Brazil's debt, which had been falling *before* the adoption of the *Real Plan*. To keep the *Real* from devaluing required maintaining foreign demand for the currency by paying very high rates of interest on debt titles and equally high returns on investment in privatized companies (which was achieved by allowing them to charge unsustainably high rates). The overvalued *Real* also cannibalized economic growth as the strong currency led to a fall in exports and a rise in imports. In 1995, Brazil's trade balance became negative for the first time in a decade, now making it more difficult to maintain demand for the *Real*. Cardoso nevertheless delayed the inevitable devaluation of the currency until he managed to get a constitutional amendment to allow him to serve a second term as president. After his re-election in 1998, the Brazilian Central Bank allowed the *Real* to float and the sharp fall in the currency then jeopardized many of the concessions contracts that had been signed with private infrastructure investors, who responded by freezing their investment programmes.

Cardoso's earlier reforms to balance the government's books and attract investors for Brazil's privatization programme, mainly by removing price controls on the output of state-owned enterprises such as in electric power, had enabled these companies to regain financial solvency and even become profitable (Tankha 2009). However, when privatization stalled after devaluation of the *Real* dampened investor interest and increased domestic opposition to his economic programme, the Cardoso administration remained opposed to allowing the remaining state-owned firms to ramp up their investment programmes to respond to the investment shortfalls which had accumulated during the long period of economic instability (Tankha 2009). As a result of underinvestment, the power sector continued to operate without any buffer capacity so that when a long drought dried up Brazil's hydropower reservoirs in 2001, the country was forced to implement a severe power rationing that lasted for almost a year. The rationing became emblematic of the failures of the second Cardoso administration's economic strategy and in the 2002 presidential elections, the PT made the most of these problems to defeat Jose Serra, Cardoso's anointed successor.

... AND PROGRESS

Discontentment with neoliberal policies in Latin America at the beginning of the twenty-first century, privatization in particular, reopened the windows for a more interventionist and entrepreneurial conceptualization of state responsibilities.[4] In Brazil, this approach was represented most coherently and consistently by the PT candidate, Lula da Silva, who thus finally came to power after being the unsuccessful run-off candidate in all of the country's post-military presidential elections (Amaral et al. 2008); but only after softening his approach towards domestic and global capital.

After an initially conservative start meant to reassure the markets, represented most clearly by his nomination of Henrique Mierelles, formerly President of BankBoston, to head the Brazilian Central Bank, the Lula administration reactivated state-led economic transformation efforts and terms such as the entrepreneurial state; and state capitalism returned to the mainstream political discourse. In 2004, the government adopted an Industrial, Technological and Foreign Trade Policy (PITCE) and also created two new

[4] For details on Latin American discontent with neoliberal policies, see Roberts (2007).

agencies—the Brazilian Industrial Development Agency (ABDI) and the National Industrial Development Council (CNDI)—to develop strategies for technological upgrading and increasing the competitiveness of higher-technology industries. In the same year Brazil began to again establish state-owned enterprises, such as Hemobras and the Energy Research Enterprise (in 2004), the Brazilian Communications Enterprise (in 2007), and National Center for Advanced Electronic Technology (in 2009). Public sector employment rose significantly, from about 370,000 workers in 2002 to 461,000 workers in 2009 (IPEA 2010).

On the surface there was a dramatic increase in investment made by federal public sector enterprises, which rose from R$29.7 billion in 2002 to R$71.5 billion in 2009 (IPEA 2010); but a closer look at these investments is necessary in order not to misinterpret the trend. Although the PT administration did create a new web of public sector firms in different segments of the economy, most of these involved relatively modest investment. The large majority of Brazil's public sector investments were made only by the Petrobrás companies, whose investments more than tripled over this period. This enormous increase was facilitated by increasing crude oil prices globally and the discovery of massive oil deposits in the pre-salt layer off the coast of Rio de Janeiro in 2006. With daily production already exceeding half a million barrels in 2014, this discovery substantially increased the Brazilian government's fiscal space. In all other sectors, the Lula administration oversaw *less* public sector investment than the Cardoso administration. For example, under Cardoso, Eletrobrás invested an average of R$4.8 billion annually, while under Lula it invested an average of R$3.9 billion (IPEA 2010). While the PT did create many government programmes to enhance the competitiveness of Brazilian industry, especially in technology-based arenas, those other efforts were insignificant in comparison to demand induced by Petrobrás.

Looking at the location of these investments is also revealing. In the second Lula administration, there was increasing decentralization of federal investments, with almost all regions receiving a greater percentage of total federal public sector enterprise investment. Investments that were national in character became proportionately fewer, falling from 30.3 per cent to 24.5 per cent of total investments between 2006 and 2009, but more revealingly, investment abroad fell much more, from 28.2 per cent to 16.3 per cent over the same period (IPEA 2010). This pattern of spending was in line with the PT administration's commitment to invest proportionately more in the poorer parts of the country, principally the north-east, which is also where a large segment of the PT's political support base was located (Bohn 2011).

Additional support for the PT's industrial policies came from the BNDES, which increased its disbursements rapidly, from fewer than R$50 billion in 2005 to almost R$200 billion in 2013.[5] BNDES had to continue playing a central role in Brazilian finance because of the underdeveloped and expensive private capital markets. Real

[5] For more details on BNDES's recent activities in support of developmentalism, see Hochstetler and Montero (2014).

interest rates in Brazil were consistently more than 30 per cent between 2005 and 2012. To put this in perspective, real interest rates in India were consistently below 10 per cent over the same period. Without BNDES support most investment would be economically unviable in Brazil. Not surprisingly, the bulk of BNDES loans went to a small group of large industrial concerns, partly because of economies in scale of managing a large portfolio and partly because these were the firms which had the most financing needs. In a similar manner, the expensive private capital markets also increased the importance of other government financial entities, such as PREVI (the public sector workers' pension fund) and Banco do Brasil, in financing private industrial investment in Brazil.

How did Brazil perform economically under the PT government before the slowdown caused by the fall in commodity prices in 2012?[6] Charting Brazil's purchasing power parity (PPP) GNI per capita against the global, Chinese, and Indian data reveal that Brazil's growth has been unremarkable over the last decade (see Figure 41.1). Only in 2008 and 2010, when commodity prices were at their peak, did Brazil grow noticeably faster than the rest of the world, and in most other years it made fewer gains. A few other charts tell the story in more detail. Exports as a percentage of GDP dropped from 16.4 per cent in 2004 to 12.6 per cent in 2013 (see Figure 41.2), which meant that the internal market was growing, reflecting increasing purchasing power especially among the poorer classes. Meanwhile, the global average, high-income countries, and India show a common and increasing trend of increasing export intensity. Of these high-tech exports, defined by the World Bank as 'products with high R&D intensity', Brazil's exports are so close to India's that one cannot tell the two countries apart in graphs (see Figure 41.3). In information and communications technology (ICT) exports, Brazil has been losing ground to India, which overtook it in 2009.

In agriculture, Brazil made strong gains. While the value added per worker was stagnant in India and China, it increased in Brazil from US$3,403 in 2004 to US$5,563 in 2013 (see Figure 41.4). Over this period, employment in agriculture fell from 21 per cent to 17 per cent of total employment, indicating increasing capital intensity and productivity in agriculture and also increased rural to urban migration (see Figure 41.4). Brazil's agriculture policies favoured industrial farming, especially in the far west of the country, often at the cost of family farming which actually provides most of the food consumed in the country. This reflects a continuing dichotomization in the agricultural production of the country which has persisted since early colonial times when sugar was Brazil's main export. Driving along the highways of the states of Mato Grosso and Mato Grosso do Sul, one sees vast stretches devoted to soya bean cultivation, each farm stretching for tens of kilometres and dotted with huge harvesters. Exports of soya bean (primarily to China to feed their growing pork consumption) more than doubled between 2002 and 2012, at the expense of even more deforestation in the Amazon

[6] Data retrieved in 2015 from the World Bank's online DataBank (World Bank 2015). Available at https://data.worldbank.org/, accessed 6 September 2019.

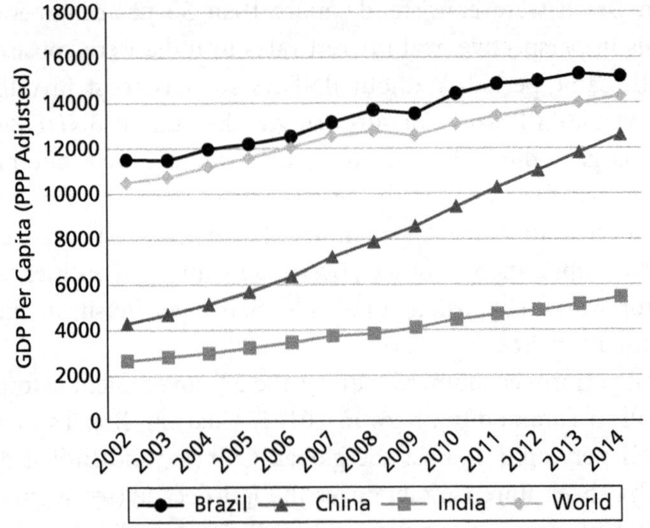

Figure 41.1 PPP-adjusted GNI per capita: Brazil, China, India, World (2002–14)

Source: Author's elaboration based on World Bank (2015).

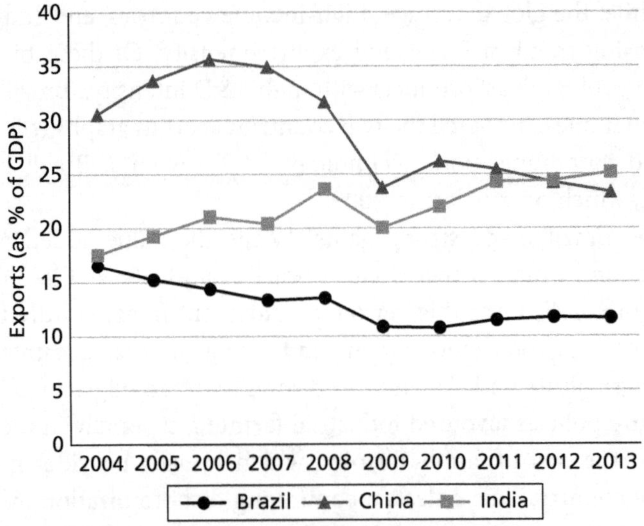

Figure 41.2 Exports (as % of GDP): Brazil, China, India (2004–13)

Source: Author's elaboration based on World Bank (2015).

(Brown-Lima et al. 2013). Export of other agricultural products increased similarly. For example, export of chicken more than doubled from 1.5 to 3 billion tons between 2002 and 2006. Meanwhile, other non-export areas of agriculture showed stagnating productivity and profits—another feature of the dichotomy that has characterized Brazilian agricultural productions since colonial years.

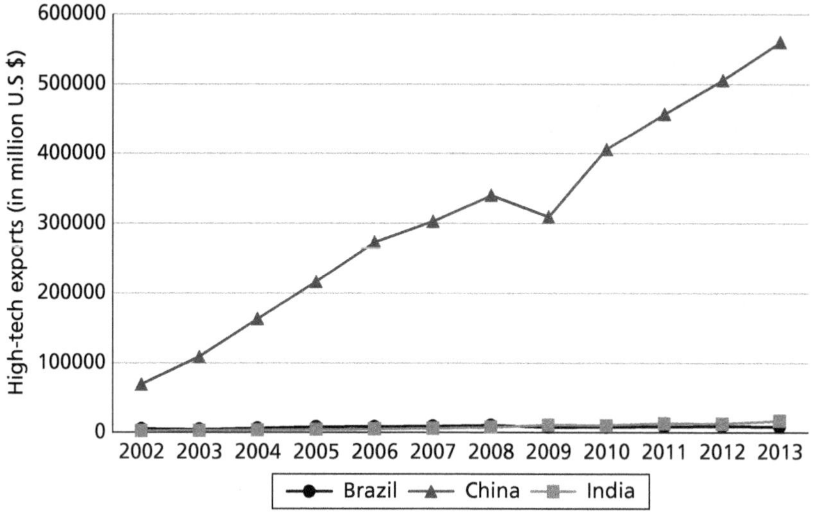

Figure 41.3 High-tech exports: Brazil, China, India (2002–13)

Source: Author's elaboration based on World Bank (2015).

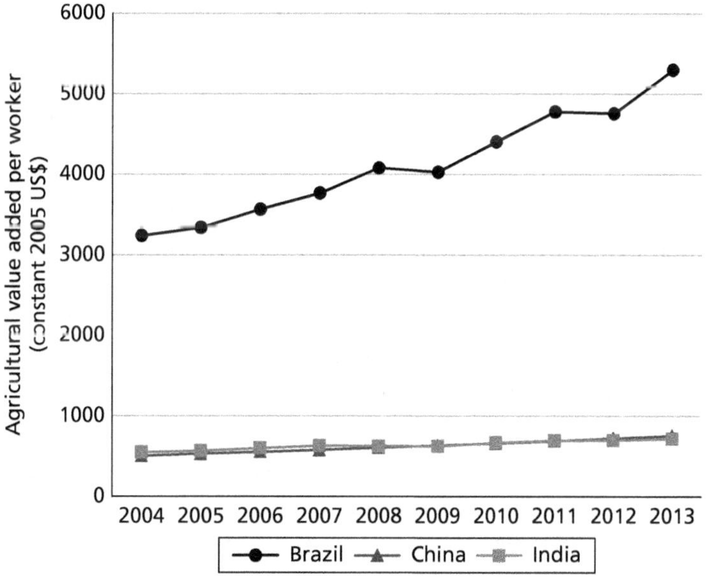

Figure 41.4 Agricultural employment and productivity: Brazil, China, India (2004–13)

Source: Author's elaboration based on World Bank (2015).

The biggest increase in exports, however, has been in the minerals sector—again driven by Chinese demand—which accounted for about a quarter of total exports.

This growth allowed the PT, perhaps unexpectedly, to reduce national debt which fell from 61.5 per cent of GDP in 2004 to 43.7 per cent in 2011 before rising to 49.7 per cent the following year. Meanwhile the costs for servicing overseas debt fell from almost

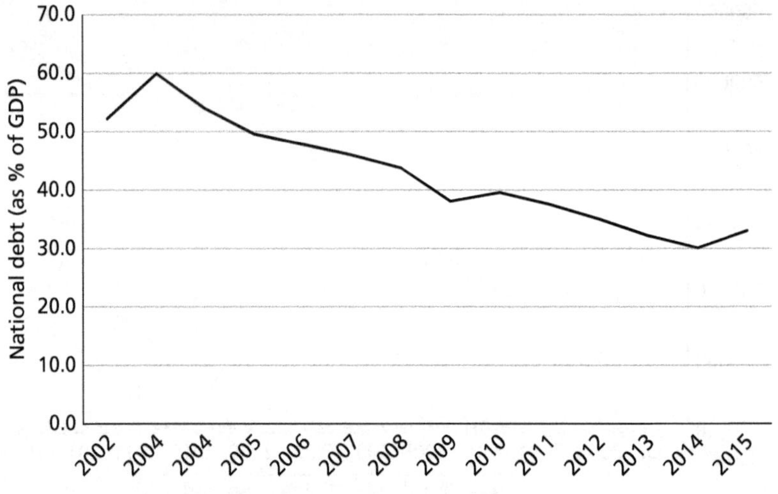

Figure 41.5 National debt (as % of GDP): Brazil 2002–15)

Source: Author's elaboration based on World Bank (2015).

50 per cent of export revenue in 2004 to only about 15 per cent in 2012. Brazil even paid off a year early the IMF loan it had taken out in 2002. This may seem paradoxical if one recalls that the fiscally responsible Cardoso administration presided over an *increase* in Brazil's national debt (see Figure 41.5), but is perfectly logical if one notes that fiscal health depends more on the state of the economy rather than on how conservative is government spending.

During this period, the PT administration oversaw prominent achievements in reducing poverty and inequality (see Figure 41.6). In 2004, 22.4 per cent of Brazil's population was below its nationally defined poverty line. By 2012, this had fallen to 9 per cent, meaning that over 20 million Brazilians had moved out of poverty. Over the same period, extreme poverty, defined in Brazil as living on less than R$70 a month, fell from 8.8 per cent to 3.6 per cent. Combined with a shift of federal investment to the north-east, key federal initiatives such as tripling the minimum wage between 2002 and 2013, and an extensive conditional cash transfer programme, the *Bolsa Família*, have been identified as being responsible for reducing poverty and inequality. Impressive as these gains have been, inequality persists, especially regionally with the north-east still substantially lagging behind the wealthier regions of the country (Barbosa 2010).

Federal spending was the key factor underlying the PT's industrial, economic, and social policies. For industrial policies, dependence on federal spending is now inevitable. World Trade Organization (WTO) rules permit much less protection and promotion of domestic industries, but one area where governments can actively discriminate in favour of domestic producers is in the case of public procurement. When the country is large and its public spending significant, this can make a substantial impact on the commercial prospects of domestic enterprises. Operationalizing this approach, the PT enacted a *Buy Brazil Act* in 2010, which allowed public procurement agencies to pay up to a 25 per cent

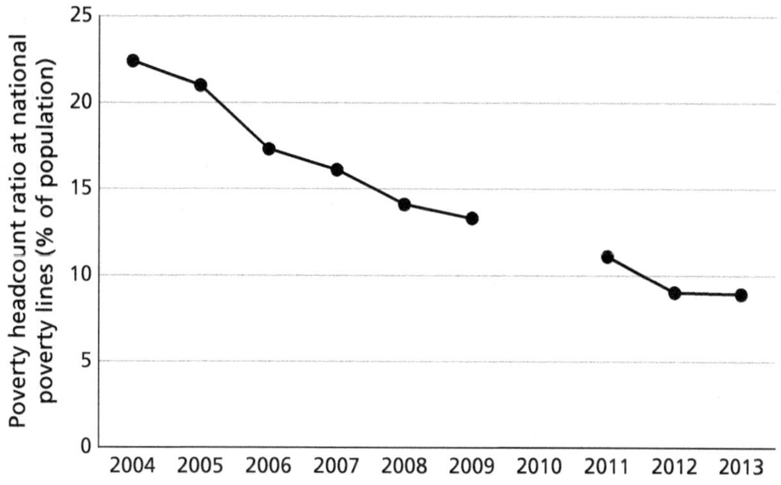

Figure 41.6 Poverty: Brazil (2004–13)

Source: Author's elaboration based on World Bank (2015).

premium for nationally produced goods and services. The impacts of Brazilian procurement policies were felt in a number of industries, including a hitherto moribund shipbuilding sector; here too most of the investment came through Petrobrás (Leahy and Pearson 2015; DuBois and Primo 2016).

As in the case of industrial policy, Brazil's poverty reduction achievement came on the back of massive government spending. Federal spending targeting infrastructure and social development was concentrated under the R$2 trillion plus Growth Acceleration Program. Meanwhile, the *Bolsa Família* disbursed almost R$25 billion annually to about 14 million families (or about a quarter of Brazil's population), on condition that they keep their children in school and take them to health clinics regularly. The shift of federal investment to the north-east of the country was a conscious break from the past when most investments were concentrated in the wealthier and more industrialized south-east. This helped the north-east grow faster than the rest of the country and reduced regional differences and alleviated poverty rates.

Against a backdrop of several successive years of high commodity prices, this level of federal spending appeared to be sustainable. The discovery of the pre-salt deposits funnelled additional billions to the government for development spending, and legislation passed in 2010 aimed to transfer half of pre-salt oil revenues to a fund to be used mostly for education but also for other social and environmental objectives. However, after the fall in commodity prices, itself partly a consequence of the global financial crisis, Brazil's public accounts began to deteriorate and made balancing the public accounts and inflation targeting more difficult to manage.

The share price of Petrobrás provides an interesting proxy of the fortunes of the Brazilian economy and also the PT administrations. Traded on the New York Stock Exchange, shares of Petrobrás were US$3 when Lula became President in 2003. Midway through his second term, the shares had increased steadily to reach US$70 in June 2008. By March 2015, they had dropped back down to US$5. While the share prices of all oil companies have fallen, the decline in the price of Petrobrás shares has been much greater and this reflects several trends that are pertinent to Brazil as a whole: (a) a decrease in global crude oil prices, which has reduced Brazil's fiscal space; (b) investor disillusionment with the government's management of the public sector, specifically the use of Petrobrás to serve industrial policy and inflation targeting goals; (c) a steady stream of revelations about the extent of corruption associated with the public sector. These created a negative feedback loop of macroeconomic management problems and governance shortcomings.

Meanwhile, life became increasingly expensive in Brazil's metropolitan cities with the prices of public as well as private services increasing rapidly.[7] In the middle of 2013, what began as a student movement for free bus passes in Porto Alegre erupted into a national movement against the government; but with so many disparate groups venting so many disparate grievances on the streets, the dissatisfaction did not immediately solidify into a coherent political movement against the PT (Saad Filho 2013). Nevertheless, the traditional elite and professional classes turned against the party and looked to both the right and the green left (to Marina Silva's Social Party of Brazil) for alternatives. While it did appear in the run-up to the presidential elections in 2014 that the PT might lose power, the advantages of incumbency, the superior organization of the party, and the support of Brazil's new lower middle classes and rural poor whose economic conditions had improved considerably under the PT, saw off the threat.

However, frustrations with the prospect of an even longer period of uninterrupted one-party rule during the fourth consecutive PT administration also mobilized elites and the urban professional segments of Brazilian society. When disorder on the streets was followed by revelations of pervasive corruption in the affairs of the state, especially related to Petrobrás, the political calculus for the PT's allies in the Brazilian Congress changed and they impeached Dilma Rousseff. Once more, an existing order battered by economic instability was replaced through a shift in alliances.

Explaining iterations of disorder and progress in Brazil

Spikes and depressions have been a consistent feature of Brazilian economic history. It started with Brazilwood dye, then sugar, cotton, gold, coffee, rubber, minerals, and now it is petroleum. Each of these sectors has boomed more than once in Brazilian economic history, each time creating in the country its own version of the Dutch disease. Notwithstanding these exaggerated cycles, there has been progress, first economic and more

[7] Inflation rates in Brazil have exceeded 6 per cent since 2013, and increased steadily since then to peak at over 10 per cent in 2016. Source: Brazilian Institute of Geography and Statistics (IBGE). Available at https://tradingeconomics.com/brazil/inflation-cpi, accessed 5 August 2019.

recently social. That the progress has not been smooth is surprising only because the difficulties of transitioning out of traditional sectors have often been underestimated. Brazil's economic development indeed continues to be driven by its enormous endowment of natural resources. Still, Brazil has managed to diversify its economy beyond its commodity sectors. How did this happen? We found that the periods of strong state-led industrial transformation did yield substantial and sustained economic growth in Brazil, even if the underlying basis of the economy remained vulnerable to bouts of volatility. In the fifty years between 1930 and 1980, Brazil was the fastest growing among the world's large economies. Periods where Brazil has grown slowly were those in which either liberal (1945–50) or neoliberal policies were followed (1996–2002) or when the country was forced into IMF structural adjustment programmes such as during the 'lost decade' of the 1980s. While this does raise questions about the efficacy of orthodox economic prescriptions, it is important for economic analysts to consider the fact that these prescriptions have been implemented often in response to and during times of economic crises.

However, we do not believe that Brazil's recurring problems are caused by wilfully following 'bad' heterodox or 'populist' economic policy. First, state entrepreneurship policies as practised episodically since Vargas have been thoroughly debated and there is no overwhelming empirical or theoretical consensus against them. These arguments were formalized by the dependency theorists at the Economic Commission for Latin America and the Caribbean (CEPAL) where Prebisch and his colleagues performed extensive statistical analyses to show that the fundamental weakness of Latin American economies was that they were dominated by primary goods exports which were both income and price inelastic (Prebisch 1950; Singer 1949).[8] The CEPAL dependency approach was not the only theoretical grounding for the import substitution policies underlying economic planning in Latin America and Brazil. A number of other development theories, including both balanced and unbalanced growth theories, all pointed to an interventionist approach to shifting the economy away from a Lewis-type economy via a big push (see, for example Nurkse 1953, Lewis 1954, Hirschman 1958). Brazil's economic strategies were also the operational epitome of Gerschenkron's later thesis that a late starter to industrialization needed an entrepreneurial and interventionist state to overcome underdeveloped and imperfect domestic markets, especially in capital (Gerschenkron 1962). These strategies had broad consensus in post-war development thinking.

Second, in Brazil, many of these policies were developed in close cooperation with the United States, most notably via the CMBEU (Mixed Commission Brazil United States)

[8] Being income inelastic, exports of primary products failed to rise proportionately with the rise in incomes in developing countries; being price inelastic, they failed also to rise with price reductions related to productivity improvements in Latin America. Thus, the only way to overcome the structural tendency towards deteriorating terms of trade was to industrialize and this required state intervention. Subsequent statistical analyses using different approaches and data sets have largely confirmed this hypothesis; see, for example Arezki et al. (2013), and Bloch and Sapsford (2000).

which was set up in 1951 to study and finance large infrastructure investments in Brazil and in particular led to the creation of the BNDE and the CANAMBRA (named for the three participating countries: Canada–America–Brazil consortium) which drew up a blueprint for Brazil's extensive hydroelectric industry; this today supplies over 80 per cent of Brazil's electricity (McCann Jr 1973). Finally, far from being a strategy followed exclusively by leftists or populists, state entrepreneurship has also been practised extensively by Brazil's military governments.

Rather, as the preceding sections have made clear, every generation in Brazil has rediscovered its own disorder and charted its own progress. Nevertheless, the disorder in Brazil is a moderate one. In this diverse and divided society, a critical mass of adherents has never coalesced around a single philosophy or movement. At the same time, neither have this division and diversity yielded strong fissiparous tendencies. Revolutionary movements have consequently never been strong in Brazil and the transitions between centres of power have been relatively bloodless. For this reason, Freyre (1957) has argued that Brazilian positivism was in fact rather conservative and not revolutionary in that it appealed to the Brazilians precisely because it called for change within a broadly acceptable and familiar framework. In any case, changes in power in Brazil have derived mostly from a shifting of alliances and this process of alliance formation and dissolution has happened outside of the formally established framework of rules and structures of institutions, leading to a persistent weakness in them. Incumbent elites, always small in number, have often lost their official positions of power but have always maintained their prestige and their core economic interests. Each new Brazil has therefore emerged into being burdened with a fairly unstable web of new accommodations. This accommodation is exemplified by the equestrian statue of Dom Pedro I that today stands in the middle of Praça Tiradentes, an important square in central Rio de Janiero: Tiradentes, whom the Brazilian Republicans mythologized as a national hero for organizing the *Inconfedência Mineira,* Brazil's first revolution against Portuguese colonization and the monarchy, had been executed under the orders of Pedro I's grandmother, Queen Maria I of Portugal.[9]

Since the beginning of the twentieth century, the fragility of this alliance has had a direct impact on economic policymaking, exacerbating Brazil's natural tendency of commodity-based cyclical growth. Indeed, it could be said that one of the Achilles heels of Brazilian economic planning is this need to accommodate a diversity of interests to secure political power—as it has repeatedly resulted in state spending being used heavily—not just in Keynesian ways during times when the economy was in the doldrums, but at precisely those times when commodity booms were filling the public coffers. Rather than countercyclical spending, the Brazilian state has repeatedly indulged in pro-cyclical spending, which has at first spurred inflation, and then—when the commodity boom has petered out—a harder landing with private spending

[9] For a detailed study of the *inconfidência mineira*, see Maxwell (2004).

and investment stalling; then public investment and spending, already at a high level, first accelerating to try and counter the crisis and then setting itself up for an even larger fall. Moreover, as state spending has occurred in times of plenty, discipline has been less strict. Cardoso and Faletto (1979) called this phenomenon 'developmentalist populism', which they described as a strategy of offering an industrialization programme which benefits a broad swathe of interests by new powers who wish to legitimize themselves. A prerequisite of this condition, according to Cardoso and Faletto, is that leading sectors of the country do not have a 'class unity' which, in a large and diverse country like Brazil is not unnaturally the case.

Under these conditions, when crises have hit, the tenuous political accommodation that has long been a staple requirement of Brazilian politics is lost and diverse interests again begin to jockey to position themselves to secure a new and better equilibrium for themselves. The old arrangements and regimes, the monarchy, the *café com leite* elite, Vargas (twice), and the military, having depleted themselves, were removed with little resistance or mass disturbance. Political disorder has in this manner influenced economic disorder which has then fed back into political disorder. The resulting inconsistency of economic policymaking in Brazil has led to a dissipation of the investments which the state made during boom times and an inability to maintain a consistent development trajectory.

The other Achilles' heel in Brazilian development is its long-underdeveloped capital market. Consider that even though the economies of Brazil and India are roughly of the same size, the São Paulo Stock Exchange has a market capitalization half that of the Bombay Stock Exchange and the number of companies listed in São Paulo is fewer than 500 while it is more than 5,000 in Bombay.[10] One of the reasons for this is that the economic class that most earned foreign exchange in Brazil through its exports had little interest in creating a diversified industrial enterprise (Furtado 1959). This is indeed one of the reasons that the state has had to intervene so directly in economic activities, for its power has been needed to channel export earnings into industrialization. The limited availabilities of domestic investment capital have led to three persistent problems in Brazil's economic trajectory: first, the reliance on foreign capital has meant that required rates of return for Brazilian investments are persistently high, which in turn hinders a diverse range of entrepreneurial opportunities; second, it has led to persistently higher foreign indebtedness, which is more difficult to manage politically and leaves the country vulnerable to foreign pressure in making economic policy; finally, this has required frequent state intervention in capital markets to subsidize favoured investments, which of course leads to the problems of selection bias in terms of investments and also an enormous concentration of decision-making power in state institutions such as the Ministry of Planning and BNDES.

[10] Source: Available at https://en.wikipedia.org/wiki/List_of_stock_exchanges, accessed 9 October 2018.

Achilles had two heels. Brazil perhaps has three and this last one is that the large majority of its population has descended from slaves. Whereas in the United States where the proportion of slaves or their descendants never reached more than 20 per cent, in Brazil much more than half of the population until the twentieth century was of African or mixed parentage and thus firmly denied political and economic rights. Not even Vargas, whose policies endeared him to the poor, paid any attention to the question of the Afro-Brazilians towards whom many in his administration were openly hostile (Viera 1976). Rectifying this long history of marginalization of such a large number of people will clearly cause internal stress.

Conclusion

According to most Brazilianists, the logic and patterns of human and natural exploitation established in the early colonial period have persisted well into modern times to create Brazil's contemporary economic, political, and social challenges. Transformation began accelerating only in the twentieth century but the processes in all three spheres are still substantially incomplete. The economy has diversified considerably, but its leading sectors remain primary products and the prices of commodities still determine the country's economic health. This has led to a situation where high commodity prices allow the government to invest heavily in other sectors for brief periods, and when these prices fall, the impact strongly reverberates throughout the economy. Capital is still very expensive in the country and this encourages the government to manipulate capital markets while dampening private entrepreneurial activity. Finally, inequality is being addressed but remains widespread, especially on a regional basis with the north-east of the country still lagging substantially. Clearly the socio-economic conflicts which pushed the country into a prolonged and oppressive military dictatorship in the 1960s have not been resolved fully. While all surfaces appear irregular when looked at very closely, Brazil's alternating periods of order and progress have been quite remarkable. We find Brazil's traditionally politically accommodating approaches have led to a less violent and disruptive history overall, but at the same time they have left economic, political, and social issues to simmer and resolve themselves quite slowly.

REFERENCES

Amann, E. and Baer, W. (2003). 'Anchors away: the costs and benefits of Brazil's devaluation', *World Development* 31/6: 1033–46.

Amaral, A., Kingstone, P., and Krieckhaus, J. (2008). 'The limits of economic reform in Brazil', in P. Kingston and T. Powers (eds) *Democratic Brazil Revisited.* Pittsburgh, PA: University of Pennsylvania Press, 137–60.

Amory, F. (1999). 'Euclides da Cunha and Brazilian positivism', *Luso-Brazilian Review* 36: 87–94.

Arezki, R., Hadri, K., Loungani, P., and Rao, Y. (2013). 'Testing the Prebisch-Singer hypothesis since 1650: evidence from panel techniques that allow for multiple breaks'. IMF Working Paper 13/180. Available at www.imf.org/external/pubs/ft/wp/2013/wp13180.pdf, accessed 9 October 2018.

Baer, W. (1965). *Industrialization and Economic Development in Brazil.* Homewood, IL: Richard D. Irwin.

Barbosa, A. (2010). *O Brasil Real: A disgualidade para além dos indicadores* [The real Brazil: inequality beyond the indicators]. São Paulo: Outras Expressões.

Barrionuevo, A. (2011). 'Upwardly mobile nannies move into the Brazilian middle class', *The New York Times*, 19 May.

Biondi, L. (2010). 'Imigrção Italiana e movimento operário em São Paulo: Um balanço historiográfico' [Italian immigration and the Industrial Workers' Movement in São Paulo], in M. Carneiro, F. Croci, and E. Franzina (eds) *Historia do Trabalho e Histórias de Imigração* [History of Labour and Histories of Immigration]. São Paulo: Editora da Universidade de São Paulo, 23–48.

Bloch, H. and Sapsford, D. (2000). 'Whither the terms of trade? An elaboration of the Prebsich-Singer hypothesis', *Cambridge Journal of Economics* 24/4: 461–81.

Bohn, S. (2011). 'Social policy and vote in Brazil: Bolsa Família and the shifts in Lula's electoral base', *Latin American Research Review* 46: 54–79.

Brown-Lima, C., Cooney, M., and Cleary, D. (2013). *An Overview of the Brazil-China SoybeanT-trade and its Strategic Implications for Conservation.* Arlington, VA: The Nature Conservancy, Latin American Region.

Bucciferro, J. (2013). 'A forced hand: natives, Africans, and the population of Brazil, 1545–1850', *Journal of Iberian and Latin American Economic History* 31/2: 285–317.

Cardoso, F. and Faletto, E. (1979). *Dependency and Development in Latin America.* Berkeley, CA: University of California Press.

Donnelly, J. (1973). 'External financing and short-term consequences of external debt servicing for Brazilian economic development, 1947–1968', *The Journal of Developing Areas* 7/3: 411–30.

DuBois, F. and Primo, M. (2016). 'State capitalism and clusters: the case of Brazilian shipbuilding', *International Journal of Emerging Markets* 11/2: 214–31.

Fausto, B. (1999). *A Concise History of Brazil.* New York: Cambridge University Press.

Freyre, G. (1957). *Ordem e Progresso* [Order and Progress]. São Paulo: Global Editora.

Furtado, C. (1959). *Formação Economica do Brasil* [The Economic Formation of Brazil]. Rio de Janeiro: Editora Fundo de Cultura.

Gerschenkron, A. (1962). *Economic Backwardness in Historical Perspective.* Cambridge, MA: Harvard University Press.

Hall, M. (2010). 'Entre a etnicidade e classe em São Paulo' [Between ethnicity and class in São Paulo], in M. Carneiro, F. Croci, and E. Franzina (eds) *Historia do Trabalho e Histórias de Imigração* [History of Labour and Histories of Immigration]. São Paulo: Editora da Universidade de São Paulo, 49–63.

Hirschman, A. (1958). *The Strategy of Economic Development.* New Haven, CT: Yale University Press.

Hochstetler, K. and Montero, A. (2014). 'The renewed developmental state: the National Development Bank and the Brazil model', *Journal of Development Studies* 49/11: 1484–899.

Ianni, O. (1977). *Estado e planejamento economico no Brasil (1930-1970)* [The State and Economic Planning in Brazil]. Rio de Janeiro: Civilização Brasileira.

IPEA (Instituto de Pesquisa Economica Aplicada) (2010). *Estado, Instituições e Democracia: Desenvolvimento* [The State, Institutions and Democracy: Development]. Brasília: IPEA.

Leahy, J. and Pearson, S. (2015). 'Rousseff's dream of Brazilian shipbuilding titan in deep water', *Financial Times*, 25 January.

Lewis, A. (1954). 'Economic development with unlimited supplies of labour', *Manchester School of Economic and Social Studies* 22/2: 139–91.

Love, J. (2013). 'The Brazilian federal state in the old republic (1889–1930): did regime change make a difference?', in M. Centero and A. Ferraro (eds) *State and Nation Making in Latin America and Spain: Republics of the Possible.* New York: Cambridge University Press.

Lowenstein, K. (1942). *Brazil under Vargas.* New York: Macmillan.

Lustig, N., Lopez-Calva, F., and Ortiz-Juarez, E. (2013). 'Declining inequality in Latin America in the 2000s: the cases of Argentina, Brazil, and Mexico', *World Development* 44: 129–41.

McCann, F. Jr (1973). *The Brazilian-American Alliance, 1937–1945.* Princeton, NJ: Princeton University Press.

Maxwell, K. (2004). *Conflicts and Conspiracies: Brazil and Portugal 1750–1808.* Abingdon: Routledge.

Nachman, R. (1977). 'Positivism, modernization, and the middle class in Brazil', *The Hispanic American Historical Review* 57/1: 1–23.

Nurkse, R. (1953). *Problems in Capital Formation in Underdeveloped Countries.* New York: Oxford University Press.

Prebisch, R. (1950). *The Economic Development of Latin America and its Principal Problems.* New York: United Nations.

Ribeiro, D. (1995). *O Povo Brasileiro* [The Brazilian People]. São Paulo: Companhia das Letras.

Roberts, K. (2007). 'Latin America's populist revival', *Sais Review* 27/1: 3–15.

Saad Filho, A. (2013). 'Mass protest under "Left neoliberalism": Brazil, June–July 2013', *Critical Sociology* 39/5: 657–69.

Singer, H. (1949). 'Post-war price relations between under-developed and industrialized countries'. UN document no E/CN, 1.

Tankha, S. (2009). 'Lost in translation: interpreting the failure of Brazilian electric power reforms', *Journal of Latin American Studies* 41/1: 59–90.

Viera, E. (1976). *Oliveira Vianna e O Estado Corporativo* [Oliveira Vianna and the Corporatist State]. São Paulo: Grijalbo.

World Bank (2015). World Bank DataBank. Available at http://databank.worldbank.org/data/home.aspx, accessed 9 October 2018.

Zweig, S. (1941). *Brasil, País do Futuro* [Brazil, the Country of the Future]. Rio de Janeiro: Editora Guanabara.

42 Reshaping Eurasia

Looking southwards?

Vsevolod Samokhvalov

Introduction

POST-SOVIET AND PAST-SOVIET REGIONALISMS

Two types of integration have been shaping the Eurasian continent for the past three decades. The first was described as post-Soviet integration or 'holding-together regionalism', which aimed at preserving the geo-economic unity and subjectivity of the Soviet economic complex (Libman and Vinokurov 2012). Even though this regionalism, according to Libman and Vinkurov, was initially prone to politicization, in the long run this politicization would decrease and participating states would engage in deeper forms of regional integration. The second approach did not attach special value to the Soviet geo-economic complex and sought speedy integration into the world economy and various regional economic complexes. The two approaches coexisted, and sometimes were pursued by the same policymakers, for a long period after and even before the collapse of the Soviet Union.

Tensions between various visions of Eurasian integration appeared even before the Soviet Union collapsed. On the one hand, Soviet leadership tried to maintain Soviet geo-economic unity through the creation of the Commonwealth of Independent States (CIS) with a free trade area and potentially common economic space. On the other hand, sometimes the same policymakers sought to create past-Soviet forms of Eurasian integration. In fact, the late Soviet leadership treated multilateral economic cooperation as an instrument to strengthen the Soviet economy. For example, Soviet leadership supported the idea put forward by Turkish President T. Ozal to create a free trade zone in the Black Sea area. Simultaneously Central Asian republics of the USSR ran negotiations on joining the Free Trade Agreement under the Organisation of Economic Cooperation, which had been created by Iran, Pakistan, and Turkey. After the collapse of the Soviet Union all republics of Central Asia and Azerbaijan decided in November 1992 to join the Organisation for Economic Development.

The vision of preserving post-Soviet links as the core of Eurasian integration was pursued by the leaders of four major central Soviet republics—Belarus, Kazakhstan,

Vsevolod Samokhvalov, *Reshaping Eurasia: Looking southwards?* In: *Handbook of BRICS and Emerging Economies.* Edited by: P.B. Anand, Shailaja Fennell, and Flavio Comim, Oxford University Press (2021). © Oxford University Press.
DOI: 10.1093/oso/9780198827535.003.0042

Russia, and Ukraine—which formalized the end of the Soviet Union as a geopolitical reality, but created the CIS as a form of loose economic cooperation. At the same time, some policymakers in these republics firmly believed that post-Soviet integration should pursue more ambitious goals. One of the most active promoters of post-Soviet Eurasianism was the President of Kazakhstan, Nursultan Nazarbaev, who first articulated a vision for new substantive integration in the entire former Soviet space. The Kazakh president was behind the Alma-Ata Declaration of 1991 which set a detailed agenda for further economic cooperation within the CIS. He also articulated early in 1995 a grand vision for a new Eurasian Union. Throughout the 1990s and into the early twenty-first century Kazakhstan was the steam engine of post-Soviet Eurasian integration.

Post-Soviet regionalism was not a coherent political programme, but rather a vision driven by various rationales. The first tension was between grand strategies to reunite the entire former Soviet space and smaller integration schemes within various subregions of vast Soviet territory. For example, Kazakhstan itself, while promoting integration within the entire CIS, also participated—together with Uzbekistan and Kyrgyzstan—in the creation of the first customs union in Central Asia in 1994 (Molchanov 2015: 4). The Belarus President, A. Lukashenko, while actively advocating grand post-Soviet economic integration in the 1990s, also actively promoted bilateral integration in the form of a Belarus–Russia Union State.

The second tension within post-Soviet integration was between intergovernmentalism and federalism. The federalist design was often pursued by Russia. For example, in the early 2000s President V. Putin tabled the idea that the Belarus–Russia Union State should move beyond common custom and defence space to deeper forms of political integration such as the election of a common parliament and a common currency. However, Belarus refused to support the project. Similar tensions could be identified in the Collective Security Treaty Organisation—the defence arm of post-Soviet integration. Finally, in 2011–15, Moscow sought to pursue political integration within the Eurasian Economic Union (EEU)[1] with the launch of a common parliament and currency. Kazakhstan, however, repeatedly rejected this idea. With all the tensions and failures, however, the general drive for some form of exclusive post-Soviet regionalism was more or less consistently maintained by three former Soviet republics—Belarus, Kazakhstan, and Russia. Two smaller former republics, whose economy and security depends on Russia—Armenia and Kyrgyzstan—joined later on.

When it comes to supporters of past Soviet integration one can identify two groups of former Soviet states. Those include six countries in three subregions of the former Soviet territory—Ukraine, Moldova in the West, Georgia and Azerbaijan in the Caucasus, and Uzbekistan and Turkmenistan in Central Asia. All these countries explicitly refused to join deeper forms of post-Soviet regionalism—the EEU. The first group—Georgia, Moldova, and Ukraine (GMU)—is often depicted as a group of states that are trying

[1] Armenia, Belarus, Kazakhstan, Kyrgyzstan, and Russia.

to escape the Russian sphere of influence by seeking closer association with the European Union (EU). The second group comprises Azerbaijan, Turkmenistan, and Uzbekistan (ATU)—which tend to be discarded as mostly inward-looking totalitarian regimes in pursuit of isolationist policies. Such interpretations do not entirely grasp the complexity of these countries' foreign policy and economic choices. In fact, the attitudes of these countries to post-Soviet economics and past-Soviet schemes vary and change over time. Therefore, a closer look into these groups and comparisons between them will provide a better understanding of the post- and past-Soviet dynamics in the Eurasian space. The chapter will then move to consider how the crisis in Ukraine and the launch of the Chinese One Belt, One Road (OBOR) project effected the core of post-Soviet integration—the EEU and its main players.

Not Escapers, but Pragmatists—Georgia, Moldova, and Ukraine

The geo-economic choice of this group of states is often depicted in zero-sum terms. Their decision to pursue further trade relations with the European Union was often described within the country as political, and even a civilizational choice between East (Russia) and West (Europe) (White and Feklyunina 2014; Fesenko 2015: 135). This dichotomy does not, however, depict all the complexity of these countries' policies. Even though pro-European rhetoric was used by some of the governments of these countries, in reality their economic choices, especially towards Russia, have remained quite balanced and pragmatic throughout the past twenty-five years. This commitment to pragmatism remained strong regardless of their foreign policy orientation, either pro-European or pro-Russian. Despite significant fluctuations in the rhetoric of local governments, security concerns and sometimes even dramatic deterioration of bilateral relations, these three states overall pursued pragmatist foreign policy trying not to disrupt economic interaction with Russia and did not abolish existing trade regimes.

This stability was the outcome of several counteracting factors. On the one hand, the strong wish of some pro-European forces to pursue closer relations with the EU was stalled by Europe's inability to integrate these countries. At that point in time, the EU was only prepared to offer quite a basic form of economic interaction—Partnership and Cooperation Agreements (PCAs) coupled with technical assistance (TACIS) and infrastructure projects (TRASECA). This lack of interest on the part of the EU drove countries of the region to remain on the two tracks of their foreign policy. All three countries joined the post-Soviet regional project, the CIS, with its main geo-economic symbol the CIS Free Trade Agreement (FTA) in 1994. Even though the 1994 FTA contained a number of exemptions and did not function in some cases, all three countries of GMU chose to sign a number of bilateral trade agreements and use non-conflictual means of dispute arbitration in most situations.

On the other hand, some attempts by 'pro-Russian forces' to deepen post-Soviet integration were blocked by internal opposition, over worries about the dubious background and political practices of 'pro-Russian' politicians. In the case of Ukraine, some attempts by pro-Russian elites to proceed with deeper post-Soviet integration (i.e. the Single Economic Space, 1998/2003) were undermined by broader popular protests against the authoritarian President L. Kuchma. In the case of Georgia, even the corrupt and allegedly 'pro-Russian' President E. Shevardnadze made an effort to integrate the country into the system of global economic governance by joining the World Trade Organization (WTO) in 2000 and politely declining any offers to join deeper forms of post-Soviet integration, e.g. the Common Economic Space (2003). At the same time, the Georgian leader promised to look for cooperative forms of interaction with the CES-4 (Common Economic Space countries)[2] and made an effort to maintain good relations with Moscow (Korrespondent.net 2003).

Similarly, Moldova was also concerned with the situation in its pro-Russian breakaway region of Transnistria and generally pro-Russian autonomous republic Gagauzia. For some time, pro-Russian leadership led by the Communist Party leader V. Voronin pursued a policy of neutrality and closer ties with the Russia–Belarus Union State. However, by 2003 strategic partnership with Russia had not resulted in any progress in resolving the Transnistrian conflict and also prevented the country from receiving international aid. As a result of these considerations, even the Communist Party of the Republic of Moldova in 2003 effectively adhered to the national common denominator free trade area with Russia and European integration (Shapovalova 2012: 60–1).

Overall, Eurasian pragmatists maintained normal working relations with other core countries of post-Soviet integration. For example, the Communist President of Moldova, V. Voronin, maintained effective relations with Belarus before and after the EU launched its Eastern Partnership. The pro-European coalition in Moldova also maintained positive relations with Belarus. Regular high-level meetings were held and a number of agreements signed of which sixty-four entered into force (Froltsov 2012: 2–8). As a sign of reciprocity, Belarus refused to recognize independence of the breakaway region of Transnistria. Similarly, Ukraine and Georgia maintained effective relations with Belarus and Kazakhstan. Even though the pro-Western Georgian President M. Saakashvili initially pursued an extremely neoliberal policy and the vision of democratization of post-Soviet space, his relations with Belarus eventually improved (Eurasianet 2007).

Tension between post-Soviet and European integration became stronger with Russia's actively promoting the EEU and the EU promising closer economic integration with countries of the Eastern Partnership (EaP). However, the response from local elites—despite their ideological differences—was similar: pragmatist balancing between Russia and the EU. Even though the new, allegedly 'pro-Russian' Georgian leadership had strong personal animosities with old 'pro-Western' President M. Saakashvili, it still

[2] Poland, Hungary, Czech Republic, and Slovakia.

pursued similar economic policies. Even though described as a 'Russia-backed oligarch' new Georgian Prime Minister B. Mirabishvili pursued policies of deeper economic cooperation with the EU trying at the same time not to antagonize Russia. Within this framework, Georgia signed an Association Agreement which stipulated a Deep Comprehensive Free Trade Area (AA/DCFTA) with the EU (Ellena 2015). But at the same time, Prime Minister B. Mirabishvili did not exclude the probability that Georgia would join the EEU (RFE/RL 2013) and discussed options of deepening relations with the EEU (Civil Georgia 2015).

Identical policies were simultaneously pursued by 'the most pro-Russian' President of Ukraine, V. Yanukovich, and the 'most pro-European government' of Moldova. Both governments sought to deepen trade relations with the EU and prepared to sign an AA/DCFTA. At the same time, Yanukovich made symmetric diplomatic moves towards Russia. For example Ukraine joined the new FTA within CIS (CISFTA), created by eight CIS states on 18 October 2011. Similarly to Ukraine, the pro-European government of Moldova signed an AA/DCFTA with the EU and at the same time acceded to the CISFTA. The pro-European coalition in Moldova also ratified the agreement in September 2012 (Ionesii 2013).

However, President V. Yanukovich stated explicitly that Ukraine would not accede to any forms of integration which would challenge its European association. He tried to avoid escalation of the conflict with the Eurasian Union by depoliticizing this issue. The question was sent to one of the respected Ukrainian businessmen and centrists, Petro Poroshenko, at the time Minister of Foreign Trade of Ukraine. Following a period of trade wars between Russia and Ukraine in early 2012, the Minister of Trade P. Poroshenko signed a Memorandum of Understanding (MoU) with the main decision-making body of the post-Soviet regional project—the Eurasian Commission. The main idea of the MoU was to create various mechanisms which would allow the removal of tariff—and non-tariff—barriers and avoid recourse to judicial mechanisms (Real Economy 2012).

It should be noted that alongside this pragmatism the three states tried to balance their dependence on trade with Russia. One of the objectives of their economic policies was China. As a result of this balancing move, China's growing presence and interest was similarly welcomed by all governments of Eurasian pragmatist states regardless of their orientations. Georgia most actively sought to diversify its economic relations and by 2015 achieved the turning point in its geo-economic position. By 2015, China's economic presence in Georgia had outweighed Russia's (Cecire 2015). With the launch of the Chinese regional infrastructure project for Eurasia—OBOR—Tbilisi did not miss the opportunity to integrate the country into its global transport infrastructure by building a new transport harbour on the Black Sea coast and a railroad through Georgia (Rinna 2015). At the time of writing the first cargo train from China had arrived at the Tbilisi railway hub (Fokht 2015). Even though there are some serious doubts as to sustainability of the project, this turn by Georgia demonstrates that the country is clearly looking for a third alternative to diversify its choices (Inozemtsev 2015).

Similarly, pro-Russian Ukrainian President V. Yanukovich tried to reduce Ukraine's dependence on Russian energy and markets. In particular, he sought to deepen relations with China. Three high-level visits were paid. Ukraine agreed to lease China 160,000 hectares of arable land in the Crimea and to start building a deep-water port in the peninsula which would become part of the Chinese OBOR project (Xinhua 2011; Izmirli 2014; LaRouchePac 2013). Similarly to Ukraine, the country sought to intensify its relations with China both under 'pro-Russian' President Voronin and under the pro-European coalition (Moldova.Org 2015). Similarly to Ukraine, Chisinau sought and achieved inclusion of the country into the Chinese OBOR project. In April 2015, the China Shipping Group, tasked to implement the Chinese government's OBOR strategy launched container shipping services through Giurgiulesti—Moldova's only port on the Danube River. This contract effectively linked the Great Silk Road to the European waterway infrastructure (Lakshmi 2015).

The quest of centrist pragmatist consensus did not change even after the Russian–Ukrainian conflict. Despite the negative consequences of the Russian–Ukrainian war and Ukraine's effective departure from the CIS, Kiev tried to stick to business as usual with Russia. Despite militant rhetoric coming from both capitals during 2014–18, the pro-European President of Ukraine P. Poroshenko effectively conducted similar pragmatist foreign policy aiming at (a) striking a balance between Russian and European choices and (b) broadening room for manoeuvre by bringing in the Chinese factor. In particular, both sides were reluctant to entirely cut off economic ties. The trade of coal, electricity, and other goods continued even with some disruptions to informal cross-border movement on the Ukrainian/Crimean demarcation line. The Ukrainian government agreed to continue trilateral negotiation to address Russia's concerns about EU–Ukraine DCFTA. Even though, at the time of writing, negotiations had been effectively stopped, it was formally the European Commission which made the move to finish the negotiations.

Similarly to his 'pro-Russian' predecessor, 'pro-Western' President Poroshenko seeks to further engage with China and deepen collaboration. The two leaders met in the framework of the Davos Economic Forum, and investments of yuan 15 billion were agreed. High-level commissions prepared top state visits (Gazeta-2000, 2015). After the annexation of Crimea, Beijing tried to transfer the old Crimea contracts to Russia, which now controlled the peninsula, but failed to reach an agreement (Popov and Skorobagatko 2015). As a result, Chinese companies committed to transfering economic and infrastructure projects from Crimea to mainland Ukraine (Liga News 2015). Despite all personal conflicts between current 'pro-Russian' Georgian leadership and radical 'anti-Russian' president Mikheil Saakashvili—who currently governs the Odessa region of Ukraine—both expressed keen interest in being included in the Chinese Silk Road (Centre for Transport Strategies 2015) and signed a series of agreements with Georgia, Azerbaijan, and Kazakhstan about the improvement of transport modalities (Trend 2016). This also demonstrates that regardless of their political preferences and ideologies non-ideological pragmatist consensus emerges among the elites of the shared Russian–European neighbourhood and the presence of China becomes an even more important factor, which will change regional configuration from a bilateral Russian–European stand-off to a more complex and trilateral great power interaction.

Not Isolationists, but non-Aligners—(Azerbaijan, Turkmenistan, Uzbekistan)

It might look as though members of the second group, energy rich countries of the Caucasus and Central Asia—Azerbaijan, Turkmenistan, and Uzbekistan—pursue isolationist foreign policy. Two of the countries of the group—Azerbaijan and Turkmenistan—made their commitment to non-alignment policy explicit or even a legal act. The concept of 'Finlandization' of Azerbaijan was used explicitly on various occasions (Valiyev 2010). Similarly Turkmen foreign policy pursued one of positive neutrality through the United Nations Security Council (UNSC) Resolution. Uzbekistan pursued a similar ideology of self-reliance (mustaqilik). The ideology was pervasive and penetrated all spheres of Uzbek life. Even though this type of domestic environment can facilitate extremely isolationist interaction with the external world, in reality the foreign policy behaviour of these countries was more responsive and creative.

Eurasian non-Aligners sought to maintain an optimal trade regime both with the CIS and other economic actors, but avoided any strong symbolic commitment; Azerbaijan and Turkmenistan refused to join the Free Trade Zone Agreement in 2011. Uzbekistan reluctantly joined two years later. All three countries declined invitations to establish special relations with the EEU. At the same time, the European Union remained at the level of a PCA. Turkmenistan under President Saparmurat Niazov demonstrated such a poor human rights record that EU member states refused to ratify the generic EU–Turkmenistan PCA. For the past twenty years, the two sides have had to use the Interim EU–Turkmen Trade Agreement as a framework for their relations. This shallow type of relationship allowed the countries to avoid any strong symbolic geopolitical dilemmas in relations with Russia.

Within this framework, Azerbaijan developed cooperation with the EU mostly in the sphere of transport and energy transit. In particular, Baku actively worked on the EU-funded TRACECA and INOGATE transport programmes. In 1997, Georgia and Azerbaijan tabled a proposal for revitalization of the Great Silk Road. But at the same time Azerbaijan maintained close cooperation with Russia in the energy field (Iftiyev 2010). However, Azerbaijan made it clear that any participation in deeper forms of post-Soviet integration would be unacceptable. Notably, the offer to join and, respectively, the polite refusal to participate in the EEU was expressed by Azeri President Ilham Aliyev during his meeting with Kazakh President Nursultan Nazarbayev (Izzet 2014). At the same time, 'taking into account the potential geopolitical problems that may arise from signing the agreement with the EU, Azerbaijan agreed only to limited cooperation [with the EU]. Instead of the Association Agreement and the Deep Comprehensive

Free Trade Area, the EU and Azerbaijan signed only an agreement on visa facilitation' (Ibrahimov 2013: 117).

In addition to potential external risks, significant liberalization of trade either with a customs union or the EU created serious internal risks. Removal of trade barriers, many of which are income for some specific 'political clans' in Azerbaijan, might create serious tensions within the increasingly oligarchic elites and jeopardize the legitimacy of the current leader (Guliyev 2012: 117–30). For similar reasons, closer relations with the EU did not offer many incentives, only risks. Azerbaijan was able to gradually increase its trade with the EU without association agreements. Currently, Azerbaijan's trade is mostly focused on the European Union (47.3 per cent). Trade exchange with Indonesia, Russia, Turkey, and the US follows, with about a 6 per cent share each (European Commission 2015a). Therefore, certain risks of signing a formal agreement with the EU would outweigh any potential benefits of such a move. But at the same time, Azerbaijan resisted some attempts by Russia to exert pressure through the increasingly insecure situation in Karabakh, and insisted on staying out of the EEU. Baku decided not to engage with further integration with Russia as it could provide further leverage for Russia's pressure against the elites.

The crisis in Ukraine and other major economic and political developments of the Russian–Ukrainian conflict of 2014–19 have prompted these countries to adopt a more positive attitude towards certain forms of past-Soviet integration. Falling energy prices, US rapprochement with Iran, and the arrival of shale oil made these countries less wealthy and prompted them to promote certain liberal economic reforms and seek engagement with the global economy. There were immediate repercussions on the politics and foreign economic activity of Azerbaijan (Broers 2015). President I. Aliev introduced a series of measures aiming at liberalization of business activities and import exchanges (Haqqin 2015). Moreover, arrests among the top security officers accused of interference with business activities seemed to send a strong signal to the traditional Azerbaijan elites about the changing policies (RFE/RL 2015). In this situation, the launch of the Chinese OBOR project became an important event echoing Azerbaijan's long-standing vision about the ancient Great Silk Road and its vision for infrastructure development. Azerbaijan's economic perspectives were explicitly linked to closer ties with the Great Silk Road Belt (Donnan 2015). Significant investment was made to upgrade capacity at the port of Baku on the Caspian Sea. Inaugurated personally by the Azeri president, the port became an important link between Central Asian and Caucasian parts of the Great Silk Road (Gasimli 2015).

Similarly Turkmenistan after its negative experience of energy cooperation with Russia showed strong interest in deepening interaction with China and later with Europe. Some efforts at diversification of the Turkmen gas exports were recorded in 2007–08 when the construction of the Central Asia–China gas pipeline started. Ever since then Russia's import of Turkmen gas gradually decreased from 40 bcm (2008) per annum to 8–10 bcm per annum (2009–14) while China was gradually overtaking Russia as the main consumer of Turkmen gas (Gurt 2015). This slow change was formalized with the high-level visit of the Chinese president to Central Asia in 2013. During the visit Turkmenistan and China signed a Joint Declaration on Establishing the Strategic Partnership. The two leaders attended a ceremony of opening the world's second largest gas field (Galkynysh) which highlighted the growing Chinese primacy in Turkmen gas exports. A number of high-level visits followed and twelve agreements on diplomacy, economy, energy, finance, education, culture, and sub-national cooperation were signed (Ministry of Foreign Affairs of the Chinese People's Republic 2015). Currently, China and Turkey outweigh the EEU as the destination of Turkmen exports (74.1 per cent). In the structure of Turkmen imports Turkey, China, UAE, and the US are gradually overtaking the countries of the EEU—51 per cent vs 13.4 per cent (CIA Factbook 2015). These data suggest that even though formerly Turkmenistan pursued a policy of neutrality and isolationism the country is gradually entering the Asian economy's international system of exchange.

In relations with Europe, the new Turkmen President G. Berdymukhammedov promised to make some concessions in the field of human rights, which resulted in the EU governments promising to ratify the EU–Turkmen PCA (Foreign and Commonwealth Office 2014). Soon after, the Turkmen president met the EU Commissioner on Energy, S. Šefčovič, on 1 May 2015. The same day Azerbaijan, Turkey, Turkmenistan, and the EU Energy Commissioner signed the Ashgabat Declaration expressing their intention whereby signatories agreed to link the Turkmen–Azeri Trans-Caspian pipeline to the EU sponsored Southern Gas Corridor, which would secure delivery of Turkmen gas to the EU (European Commission 2015b). The first meeting of the Ashgabat Declaration Enlarged Working Group (comprising the EU, Azerbaijan, Turkey, and Turkmenistan) at the level of deputy energy ministers took place in Brussels on 14 July 2015. Pursuing further diversification of energy exports, Turkmenistan completed a new pipeline, East–West, which will become part of the Trans-Caspian Southern Corridor link to Europe (Turkmenistan Zolotoi Vek 2015). In addition, it has started the construction of pipelines going southwards (TAPI [Turkmenistan-Afghanistan-Pakistan-India]), which was supported by Western institutions (Hasanov 2015). Furthermore Turkmenistan actively promotes the development of transport networks through the UN and other multilateral forums. In 2016 it will host the first world conference on international transport infrastructure (Ministry of Foreign Affairs of Turkmenistan 2014; CaToday.org 2015). The Turkish low-cost airline Pegasus was one of the few low-cost airlines which were allowed to launch flights to Ashgabat (Trend 2015a). All this demonstrates that despite their formal policy of neutrality or isolationism and non-adherence to the formal regional structure of the EEU, energy and transport links lead to de facto past-Soviet regionalization of these two countries.

In the case of Uzbekistan, the main motive behind its adherence to past-Soviet regionalization was a growing ideology of self-reliance (mustaqilik). Started as a cultural renaissance and de-Russification, this doctrine resulted in situations when Uzbekistan was prepared to break its economic and production ties with Russia regardless of the risks of deindustrialization (Teles Fazendeiro 2015). For example, Uzbekistan did not hesitate to sacrifice deeper collaboration with Russia in air industries and engage in short-term partnership with Washington even if it resulted in halting its own high-tech industry. The main modus operandi of the Tashkent attitude to post-Soviet integration was to stay in as long as it remained non-binding and shallow. Within this approach, Tashkent participated in a loose form of post-Soviet EEC and, after careful consideration, joined the multilateral agreement on the free trade area with the CIS. But it was always wary of deepening integration. After signing the agreement Uzbekistan made sure that it would not be obliged to apply national treatment to imports from the CIS (Gadimova 2014). Having made all necessary reservations, Uzbekistan in reality did not apply any trade barriers (Garkun 2015: 50). But when any discussion of further forms of integration was raised without proper consultation, Tashkent vigorously refused to participate in deeper formats of integration—a customs union and/or a Eurasian Economic Union.

At the same time, Uzbekistan got actively involved in alternative, past-Soviet forms of Eurasian integration. Tashkent expressed its keen interest in developing bilateral relations in China. Top-level official visits have taken place every year since 2004 when China allocated more than US$1 billion in grants to the Uzbek government (Molchanov 2015: 115). Official meetings of Uzbek and Chinese presidents in 2011, 2012, and 2014 resulted in the signing of the Declaration on Strategic Partnership agreement on expanding gas pipelines from Uzbekistan to China and thirty-one more documents between Uzbekistan and China (National Information Agency of Uzbekistan 2013). Within this logic Uzbekistan expressed its firm intention to participate in the development of the Chinese Great Silk Road project. This question was the subject of discussion of several meetings of an intergovernmental committee, launched as a part of the Chinese–Uzbek Strategic Partnership. It was the theme of the Third China–Central Asia Cooperation Forum held in June 2015 in Shandong Province (Xinhua 2015a). During the forum several logistic centres were opened jointly by Chinese and Central Asia representatives. The meeting of the Chinese–Uzbek Intergovernmental Committee was held within the framework of the forum. The two sides signed MoUs to strengthen cooperation in trade, investment, finance, and communications within the Silk Road Economic Belt framework (Xinhua 2015b, 2015c). Three gas pipelines were built to deliver Uzbek gas to various parts of China (Yaqing 2015).

The presence of Chinese companies in Uzbekistan has grown substantially over the past two years. Trade turnover rose from US$904 million (2007) to US$4.7 billion (2014) (Trend 2015b). Infrastructure projects implemented by the two sides aim to give China access to South Asia (National Information Agency of Uzbekistan 2013). In addition, Uzbekistan seeks to involve other Asian powers for further internationalization of their trade options. As a result, China and Turkey are gradually overtaking the EEU as the main destination of Uzbek exports (39.9 per cent vs 29.1 per cent). Increasing roles by other Asian partners confirms this trend (CIA Factbook 2015). Similarly in the structure of Uzbek imports China, South Korea, Turkey, Germany, and the US noticeably exceed the share of Russian-Kazakh imports (50.4 per cent vs 35.1 per cent). The fact that Tashkent and Ashgabat warmly welcomed South Korea's growing presence and infrastructure projects in the region demonstrates these countries' commitment to diversify its trade and transport orientation to broader past-Soviet Eurasian space (Fumagalli 2015).

Eurasian Economic Union: More Asian than Eurasian

Despite numerous declarations about partnership, relations between Russia and China have eventually entered a phase of strong competition. Over the past quarter of a century China sought to and seems to have succeeded in penetrating into the Eurasian core. Beijing exports high-tech products to Russia and imports mostly raw materials. Even in the arms trade, where Russia remains a high-tech exporter to China, Beijing works hard to reverse-engineer the military technologies it is purchasing. Pursuing its economic agenda for broader Eurasia, China tried hard to add an economic dimension to the activities of the Shanghai Cooperation Organisation. This Chinese effort was repeatedly blocked by Russia (Molchanov 2015: 120–33). So the Great Silk Road comes as a second Chinese attempt to implement its economic interest in post-Soviet Eurasia.

Even though China and Russia have repeatedly stated their intentions to ensure smooth interaction between the EEU and the Great Silk Road there are some indications that competitive logic prevails in this relationship. Russia's leadership in the project is limited. It did not become part of the Asia Infrastructure Investment Bank. Even though Belarus has benefited hugely and remains part of the EEU, it has always been seeking opportunities at the market outside of post-Soviet space. After a significant increase in trade with EEU countries and a decrease in trade with other countries, Minsk made an extra effort to return to a more balanced trade composition. In 2017, Belarus's trade with the countries of the EEU dropped by 5.1 per cent. Notably, Belarus tried to reduce imports from these countries which decreased by 10–12 per cent (Belstat 2017a). At the same time, economic exchanges with China have been growing dynamically over the past decade. After a comparative decline in 2015–16, President Lukashenko prioritized trade with other markets (Belstat 2017b; Interview at the Trade Chamber of Belarus 2017).[3] There were important symbolic moves made by Belarus. When the Chinese launched the Great Silk Road project Minsk officials straightforwardly asked for Belarus to be included in this project (Daly 2015). Belarus also turned to China when it came to such a symbolically important domain as provision of satellite services to Belarus (People's Daily Online 2016) and invited China to launch a big Techno Park in Belarus (Belta News Agency 2017).

Similarly, Kazakhstan, while having championed the concept, never subscribed to exclusive commitment to the EEU. It pursued a multi-vector foreign policy. In the framework of this policy, Astana prepared and signed an enhanced PCA with the

[3] Available at http://indonesia.mfa.gov.by/en/media/, accessed 30 November 2019.

EU. The volume of EU–Kazakh trade has bypassed Russian–Kazakh exchanges (Azernews 2017). Even though Russian–Kazakh trade turnover remains significantly higher than Kazakh–Chinese, trade has also been growing at similar rates and has more capacity for growth (Gatev and Diesen 2016). In terms of transit potential, the Chinese Silk Road Economic Belt, namely its Central Asian–Caspian connection, fits nicely with the Kazakh programme Nurly Zhol and has unbeatable value in comparison with any other alternatives (Rapoza 2017). Chinese development strategies, which seek to connect western and south-western Chinese provinces with Central Asian steppes as for example a logistic hub on the Kazakh–Chinese border in Khorgos—all these suggest that future economic exchanges and transit in Eurasia are likely to move southwards. This vision is clear in its infrastructure projects, which focuses on the direction of Western Europe–Western China (Ordabayev 2015). In the framework of this collaboration, China acquired stakes in a number of Kazakh state-owned enterprises. Most noticeable is probably China's acquisition of Kazakh KMG International—a state-owned energy company operation mostly in Central and Eastern Europe. With the acquisition of KMG International, China became the owner of network and storage capacities in Romania (Putz 2015).

One more significant piece of evidence is a number of infrastructure projects which seek to develop the north–south transport vector, the north–south axis through Turkmenistan continuing to the Islamic Republic of Iran. The most prominent example is the development of the north–south transnational rail link along the eastern shore of the Caspian Sea from Uzen (western Kazakhstan) via Gyzylgaya-Bereket-Etrek (Turkmenistan), which ends in Gorgan in the Islamic Republic of Iran (Rastogi and Arvis 2015). Similarly, the Chinese–Pakistani economic corridor seeks to unlock Central Asia for north–south exchanges. An important infrastructure project from China to Pakistan, Port Gwadar, is actively promoted by China (Thai 2017). This project has stirred the interest of India, Iran, and Afghanistan to redirect trade routes to the new Chabahar project, which is currently under construction (Mallet 2016). All these demonstrate that Central Asia will have several offers for potential transit routes and will most likely hedge its bets, which will lead to a further shift in Eurasian exchanges southwards.

Conclusion

The Eurasian continent is passing through its bifurcation point. Post-Soviet regionalism, which seeks to maintain a significant part of the former Soviet space as a single geo-economic unity, is under pressure from a new wave of past-Soviet regionalism. The events of the last two years, and the policies pursued by Russia, the EU, and China seem to lead to defragmentation of this space. Out of twelve former Soviet republics, which initially committed to exclusive post-Soviet integration, only five seem to stick to this commitment. The rest are gradually drifting away for various reasons. The departures take place in different forms.

The first group of countries of Eurasian pragmatists includes Georgia, Ukraine, and Moldova (GMU). Despite some rhetorical differences (pro-European or pro-Russian) the leaders of this group refused to join the Eurasian Union and pursued pragmatist policies of balancing between the post-Soviet and past-Soviet integration. The ideal arrangement for these countries was a DCFTA with the EU and bilateral free trade arrangements with the countries of the EEU agreed earlier. Even trade wars and the most dramatic events of the Ukrainian crisis did not change this pragmatist approach. However, the EEU (driven mostly by Russia in this case) does not accept such a compromise, which leads to effective exclusion of these countries from post-Soviet integration. The growing presence of China allows the countries of Eurasia to reframe the strategic dilemma 'Russia vs Europe' and effectively outbalance Russia's pressures and secure alternative trade options with other Asian and Eurasian partners. This fragmentation will apparently reveal itself in the coming years.

The second group of ATU states pursues policies which in fact lead to their radical distancing from post-Soviet regionalism. However, unlike the group of GMU countries, the absence of a strong alternative to post-Soviet regionalism made this move by the second group less symbolically painful for Russia and generated less tension and allows more space for manoeuvring and accommodation. As a result Azerbaijan, Turkmenistan, and Uzbekistan have effectively escaped post-Soviet Eurasia and have gradually entered a global trade complex through Asian (Chinese, Korean) or European trade complexes.

All of the above suggests that in the next decade the following major developments will take place in Eurasia. First, growing trade with Europe and China will gradually 'dissolve' the region, with various parts of it being integrated into the world economy through European and Asian geo-economic complexes. Second, from an entity that was mostly centred around Russia's vast territory and stretched from East to West, the former Soviet space gains new centres of gravity which 'pull' southwards. The Chinese OBOR project brings new transport infrastructure, which moves transit routes from Northern Eurasia southwards to Central Asia, Caucasus, Turkey, and then to Southern and Eastern Europe. Also, new transit routes from Central Asia move southwards redirecting Eurasian flows to new destinations. The West–East direction of transit also gains prominence challenging the traditional image of Eurasia as an entity stretching from the East to the West.

The Russian–Ukrainian conflict struck an additional blow to Eurasia. The Chinese approach of "nothing political, just business" generated strong advantages for China and undermined Russia's leadership even within the EEU. Kazakhstan and Belarus could not but be concerned with Russia's policy vis-à-vis another important former Soviet republic. Nor were they happy about Russia's 'sanction war' against the West and Turkey. During the crisis Belarus and Kazakhstan effectively refused to introduce any restrictive measures on Ukrainian, European, and Turkish imports. In fact Kazakhstan viewed Russia's sanction policies as an opportunity for its own development. In this regard, the Chinese business-like approach looks a much safer option than Russian geopoliticking, which puts yet another time bomb under the EEU.

For the time being, special personal relations between Russian President V. Putin and Chinese leader Xi Jinping and their shared strategic vision allow them to prevent this tension from degrading into conflict (Bin 2016: 267). But even this personal relationship cannot prevent a growing element of competition in Sino-Russian relations. The fact that Russia and China bargained hard for bringing their allies—India and Pakistan—as observers to the Shanghai Cooperation Organisation suggests that the escalation of competitive logic is emerging in the partnership. China is successfully competing with Russia in a number of traditionally sensitive areas, including high-tech trade and nuclear power plants.

This element of competition will probably become even stronger when the current generation of Russian and Chinese elites change. In any case, even though the two major players manage to avoid open conflict for primacy in Eurasia, the next twenty years will be featured politically by the emerging reconfiguration of Eurasia. Tension will grow between Russia-led institutions of regionalism and the objective processes of China-led regionalization. Russia's apparent decline, an increase in China's interests in the Russian Far East and Eastern Siberia, may lead to the deterioration in relations between these two major Eurasian powers, with a series of crises forthcoming along the new Great Silk Road.

REFERENCES

Azernews (2017). 'Kazakhstan's main trade partners: Russia, EU and China', 10 April. Available at www.azernews.az/region/111632.html, accessed 9 October 2018.

Belstat (2017a). 'Eksport i Import so stranami EEAS v ianvare-avguste 2017 goda' [Export and Import with EEC countries during January-August 2017], *Belarus Statistics Agency*. Available at www.belstat.gov.by/ofitsialnaya-statistika/makroekonomika-i-okruzhayushchaya-sreda/vneshnyaya-torgovlya_2/osnovnye-pokazateli-za-period-s-__-po-_____gody_10/eksport-i-import-so-stranami-eaes-v-2015-godu/, accessed 25 October 2017.

Belstat (2017b). 'Dannye o vneshnei torgovle Belarusi so stranami vne SNG v ianvare-avguste 2017 goda' [Data on foreign trade of Belarus with countries outside the CIS during January-August 2017], *Belarus Statistics Agency*. Available at www.belstat.gov.by/ofitsialnaya-statistika/makroekonomika-i-okruzhayushchaya-sreda/vneshnyaya-torgovlya_2/operativnye-dannye_5/eksport-import-s-otdelnymi-stranami, accessed 25 October 2017.

Belta News Agency (2017). 'Plans to implement Chinese trade city project in Belarus (2017)', 17 August. Available at http://eng.belta.by/economics/view/plans-to-implement-chinese-trade-city-project-in-belarus-104126-2017/, accessed 9 October 2018.

Bin, Y. (2016). 'The SCO, China and Eurasian integration', in P. Dutkievicz and R. Sakwa (eds) Eurasian *Integration View From Within*. London & New York: Routledge, 256–73.

Broers, L. (2015). 'Parliamentary election highlights Azerbaijan's change dilemma', *Chatham House Policy Brief*, 29 October. Available at www.chathamhouse.org/expert/comment/parliamentary-election-highlights-azerbaijan-s-change-dilemma#sthash.HB3P8DWr.dpuf, accessed 9 October 2018.

CaToday.org (2015). 'Ashgabat mozhet stati krupneishim mezhdunarodno-tranzitym tsenrom' [Ashgabat can become a major international transit hub], 30 December. Available at http://catoday.org/centrasia/24067-ashhabad-mozhet-stat-krupneyshim-mezhdunarodnym-transportno-tranzitnym-centrom.html, accessed 9 October 2018.

Cecire, M.T. (2015). 'China's growing presence in Georgia', *The Diplomat*, 2 May. Available at http://thediplomat.com/2015/05/chinas-growing-presence-in-georgia/, accessed 9 October 2018.

Centre for Transport Strategies (2015). 'Saakashvili promises to redirect "Silk Road through Ilyichevsk', 12 August. Available at http://en.cfts.org.ua/news/saakashvili_promises_to_redirect_silk_road_through_ilyichevsk, accessed 9 October 2018.

CIA (Central Intelligence Agency) Factbook (2015). *Turkmenistan Export and Import Partners*. Available at www.cia.gov/library/publications/the-world-factbook/geos/tx.html, accessed 30 November 2018.

Civil Georgia (2015). 'Belarus, Georgia pledge to deepen ties', 23 April. Available at www.civil.ge/eng/article.php?id=28213, accessed 12 December 2015.

Daly, J.C.K. (2015). 'China, Belarus deepens ties', *Eurasia Daily Monitor*, 12/164, 14 September. Available at http://goo.gl/xXoAI9, accessed 9 October 2018.

Donnan, S. (2015). 'Azerbaijan's economic promise is tied to Silk Road', *Financial Times*, 12 March. Available at www.ft.com/cms/s/0/b72375ee-be99-11e4-8036-00144feab7de.html#axzz3tBtbPtKu/, accessed 2 December 2015.

Ellena, M. (2015). 'Georgia's EU trade deal: more pain than gain?', 26 June. Available at http://www.eurasianet.org/node/74041, accessed 9 October 2018.

Eurasianet (2007). 'Odd bedfellows? Georgia, Belarus explore partnership', 7 April. Available at http://www.eurasianet.org, accessed 30 November 2019.

European Commission (2015a). 'Azerbaijan, trade with world', Directorate-General for Trade: Brussels, 20 October. Available at http://trade.ec.europa.eu/doclib/docs/2006/september/tradoc_113347.pdf, accessed 9 October 2018.

European Commission (2015b). 'Ashgabat declaration', 1 May. Available at https://ec.europa.eu/commission/2014-2019/sefcovic/announcements/ashgabat-declaration_en, accessed 9 October 2018.

Fesenko, V. (2015). 'Ukraine: between Europe and Eurasia', in P. Dutkiewicz and R. Sakwa (eds) *Eurasian Integration View from Within*. London & New York: Routledge, 126–49.

Fokht, E. (2015). 'Pervy poezd po velikomu "Shelkovomu puti" v obkhod Rossoii pribyl v Gruziu [The first train along the great 'Silk Road' bypassing Rossoii arrived in Georgia] 13 December. Available at www.rbc.ru/business/13/12/2015/566d50109a79472274a8feec?from=main, accessed 9 October 2018.

Foreign and Commonwealth Office (2014). 'EU–Turkmenistan relations'. Documents considered by the Committee on 17 December 2014. European Scrutiny Committee, London. Available at www.publications.parliament.uk/pa/cm201415/cmselect/cmeuleg/219-xxvi/21908.html, accessed 31 December 2015.

Froltsov, V.V. (2012). 'Belarus: a pragmatic approach toward Moldova', in M. Kisienkowski and W. Schreiber (eds) *Moldova: Arena of International Influences*. Plymouth, MD: Lexington Books.

Fumagalli, M. (2015). 'Growing inter-Asian connections: links, rivalries, and challenges in South Korean–Central Asian relations', *Journal of Eurasian Studies* 7/1. Available at https://doi.org/10.1016/j.euras.2015.10.004, accessed 26 June 2019.

Gadimova, N. (2014). 'Uzbekistan joins CIS free trade zone', *AzerNews*, 3 April. Available at www.azernews.az/region/65752.html, accessed 9 October 2018.

Garkun, G.V. (2015). 'Razvitie i deatelnosti sodruzhestva nezavisimyh gosudarstv v 2014-m godu' [Development and activities of the Commonwealth of Independent States in 2014]. Collection of Analytical Materials, Issue 3, Minsk: Executive Committee of the Commonwealth of Independent States, Department of Information and Analysis.

Gasimli, V. (2015). 'The new Baku international seaport: a nexus for the new Silk Road', *Eurasia Daily Monitor*, 2 October. Available at www.jamestown.org/programs/edm/single/?tx_ttnews[tt_news]=44442&cHash=7239541e890627e857bebc29ff6186eb#.Vl89YysXuBp, accessed 9 October 2018.

Gatev, I. and Diesen, G. (2016). 'Eurasian encounters: the Eurasian Economic Union and the Shanghai Cooperation Organisation', *European Politics and Society*. Available at DOI:10.1080/23745118.2016.1171364, accessed 9 October 2018.

Gazeta-2000 (2015). 'Posol Ukrainy v KNR Oleg Demin o visite Poroshenko v Kitai, sintez-gaze I vizovoi luposti' [Ambassador of Ukraine to PRC Oleg Demin about Poroshenko's visit to China: comments on synthetic gas and visa insanity], 1 December. Available at www.2000.ua/spectemy/2000-v-kitae/demin.htm, accessed 9 October 2018.

Guliyev, F. (2012). 'Political elites in Azerbaijan', in A. Heinrich and H. Pleines (eds) *Challenges of the Caspian Resource Boom. Domestic Elites and Policy-Making*. Houndmills: Palgrave Macmillan, 117–30.

Gurt, M. (2015). 'Turkmenistan says Russia's Gazprom has not paid for any gas this year', Reuters, 8 July. Available at http://uk.reuters.com/article/gas-turkmenistan-gazprom-idUKL8N0ZO30Q20150708, accessed 9 October 2018.

Haqqin (2015). 'Ilham Aliev likvidiroval monopoliu na import' [Ilham Aliev abolished monopoly on imports], 30 December. Available at http://haqqin.az/news/60358, accessed 9 October 2018.

Hasanov, H. (2015). 'Energy charter supports TAPI Project', *Trend*, 23 December. Available at http://en.trend.az/business/economy/2471960.html, accessed 9 October 2018.

Ibrahimov, R. (2013). *EU External Policies towards the Counties of South Caucasus: How Far it is from Realization*. Baku: CAM.

Iftiyev, E. (2010). 'Gazprom-SOCAR gas deal: Should Azerbaijan commit to a long-term contract?' *Today's Zaman*, 11 April. Available at www.turkishnews.com/en/content/2010/04/11/gazprom-socar-gas-deal-should-azerbaijan-commit-to-a-long-term-contract/, accessed 11 November 2019.

Ionesii, I. (2013). 'Zona de comerţ liber CIS – un accord modernizat' [CIS free trade area – a modernized agreement], Radio Europa Libera, 16 January. Available at www.europalibera.org/content/article/24825216.html, accessed 9 October 2018.

Inozemtsev, V. (2015). 'From China to Europe without Russia?', *Intersections*, 17 December. Available at http://intersectionproject.eu/article/economy/china-europe-without-russia#sthash.mrid3ulF.dpuf, accessed 9 October 2018.

Izmirli, I. (2014). 'Sale of Crimean land by Yanukovych: "Made in/for China"', *Eurasia Daily Monitor*, 6 February. Available at www.jamestown.org/single/?tx_ttnews[tt_news]=41930&no_cache=1#.VnQ2fysXvAE, accessed 9 October 2018.

Izzet, I. (2014). 'Azerbaijan has no intentions yet of joining the Eurasian Union', *Trend*, 11 June. Available at http://en.trend.az/azerbaijan/politics/2284020.html, accessed 9 October 2018.

Korrespondent.net (2003). 'Edinoevekonomicheskoevprostranstvo: reaktsia stran-sosedei' [Common economic space: response from neighbouring countries], 24 February. Available at http://korrespondent.net/business/65727-edinoe-ekonomicheskoe-prostranstvo-reakciya-stran-sosedej, accessed 9 October 2018.

Lakshmi, A. (2015). 'China shipping service to Moldova', *Maritime Professionals*, 27 June. Available at www.maritimeprofessional.com/news/china-shipping-service-moldova-273650, accessed 9 October 2018.

LaRouchePac (2013). 'Yanukovych in China signs agreements, invites Xi to Kiev, supports "Silk Road"', 6 December. Available at http://archive.larouchepac.com/node/29109, accessed 18 December 2015.

Libman, A. and Vinokurov, E. (2012). *Holding-Together Regionalism*. Basingstoke: Palgrave Macmillan.

Liga News (2015). 'Poroshenko priglasil premier-minister ipredsedatelia KNR posetitiUkrainu' [Poroshenko invited the Prime Minister and President of the PRC to visit Ukraine], 21 January. Available at http://censor.net.ua/photo_news/320992/poroshenko_priglasil_premerministra_i_predsedatelya_knr_posetit_ukrainu_foto, accessed 9 October 2018.

Mallet, V. (2016). 'India to bypass Pakistan on the road to Central Asia', *Financial Times*, 24 May. Available at www.ft.com/content/8510176c-2188-11e6-9d4d-c11776a5124d, accessed 1 January 2016.

Ministry of Foreign Affairs of the Chinese People's Republic (2015). 'China and Turkmenistan'. Available at www.fmprc.gov.cn/mfa_eng/wjb_663304/zzjg_663340/dozys_664276/gjlb_664280/3245_664372/, accessed 9 October 2018.

Ministry of Foreign Affairs of Turkmenistan (2014). 'Ashgabat declaration on the role of transport and transit corridors in ensuring international cooperation, stability and sustainable development', 4 September. Available at www.mfa.gov.tm/en/news-en/1962-ashgabat-declaration-on-the-role-of-transport-and-transit-corridors-in-ensuring-international-cooperation-stability-and- sustainable-development, accessed 30 November 2019.

Molchanov, M. (2015). *Eurasian Regionalisms and Russian Foreign Policy*. Aldershot: Ashgate Publishing.

Moldova.org (2015). 'Republica Moldova îşiintensificărelaţiileeconomice cu China' [Republic of Moldova intensifies economic relations with China], 12 March. Available at www.moldova.org/republica-moldova-isi-intensifica-relatiile-economice-cu-china/, accessed 9 October 2018.

National Information Agency of Uzbekistan (2013). 'Uzbekistan i Kitai: Novye Gorizonty strategicheskogo partnerstva' [Uzbekistan and China: New Horizons for a Strategic Partnership], 9 September. Available at http://uza.uz/ru/politics/uzbekistan-kitai-novye-gorizonty-strategicheskogo-partnerstva-09.09.2013–25180, accessed 9 October 2018.

Ordabayev, A. (2015). 'The geopolitics of transport corridors in Central Asia'. Working Paper, June 2015. The Institute of World Economics and Politics: Astana. Available at http://iwep.kz/files/attachments/article/2015-07-05/geopolitics_of_transport_corridors_in_central_asia.pdf, accessed 30 November 2019.

People's Daily Online (2016). 'China launches Belarus telecom satellite'. Available at http://en.people.cn/n3/2016/0116/c90000-9004713.html, accessed 9 October 2018.

Popov, E. and Skorobagatko, D. (2015). 'Chinese investment in Crimea is "political" backing for Russia', *Worldcrunch*, 6 May. Available at www.worldcrunch.com/world-affairs/chinese-investment-in-crimea-is-political-backing-for-russia/c1s15851/, accessed 9 October 2018.

Putz, C. (2015). 'China and Kazakhstan: roads, belts, paths, and steps', *The Diplomat*, 17 December. Available at http://thediplomat.com/2015/12/china-and-kazakhstan-roads-belts-paths-and-steps/, accessed 9 October 2018.

Rapoza, K. (2017). 'Kazakhstan bets big on China's Silk Road', *Forbes*. Available at https://www.forbes.com/sites/kenrapoza/2017/07/18/kazakhstan-bets-big-on-chinas-silk-road/#66f9c3ac5805, accessed 9 October 2018.

Rastogi, C. and Arvis, J.-F. (2015). *The Eurasian Connection Supply-Chain Efficiency along the Modern Silk Route through Central Asia*. Washington, DC: World Bank. Available at https://openknowledge.worldbank.org/bitstream/handle/10986/18779/888910PUB0Box300EPI199120\June122014.pdf, accessed 9 October 2018.

Real Economy (2012). Ukrainapidpysala Memorandum pro spivpratsiu z Evraziyskoyu Komissieyu' [Ukraine signed Memorandum of Cooperation with Eurasian Commission]. Available at http://real-economy.com.ua/news/21698.html, accessed 9 October 2018.

RFE/RL (2013). 'Interview: Georgian PM still aiming for EU, but doesn't rule out Eurasian Union', 9 September, Available at www.rferl.org/content/georgia-ivanishvili-interview/25100642.html, accessed 9 October 2018.

RFE/RL (2015). 'Azerbaijan arrests seven security officials', 2 December. Available at www.rferl.org/content/azerbaijan-arrests-seven-security-officials/27316464.html, accessed 9 October 2018.

Rinna, T. (2015). The South Caucasus and China's rising presence, *New Eastern Europe*, 3 December. Available at http://neweasterneurope.eu/old_site/articles-and-commentary/1811-the-south-caucasus-and-china-s-rising-presence, accessed 30 November 2019.

Shapovalova, N. (2012). 'The European Union: a privileged partnership with Moldova', in M. Kisienkowski and W. Schreiber (eds) *Moldova: Arena of International Influences*. Plymouth, MD: Lexington Books, 51–76.

Teles Fazendeiro, B. (2015). 'Uzbekistan's "spirit" of self-reliance and the logic of appropriateness: TAPOich and interaction with Russia', *Central Asian Survey* 34/4: 484–98.

Thai, M. (2017). 'Gwadar: A case of South–South cooperation'. *Cambridge Journal of Eurasian Studies*, 7 June. Available at www.veruscript.com/journals/cambridge-journal-of-eurasian-studies/gwadar-a-case-of-south-south-cooperation/, accessed 9 October 2018.

Trend (2015a). 'Turkish low-cost airline to start flights to Turkmenistan', 1 December. Available at http://en.trend.az/business/economy/2463419.html, accessed 2 December 2015.

Trend (2015b). 'China, Uzbekistan hail strategic partnership, eye co-op boost', 3 September. Available at http://en.trend.az/casia/uzbekistan/2429435.html, accessed 9 October 2018.

Trend (2016). 'Ukraine joining Trans-Caspian transportation route', 4 January, [Online]. Available at http://en.trend.az/azerbaijan/business/2477218.html, accessed 9 October 2018.

Turkmenistan Zolotoi Vek (2015). 'Gazoprovod "Vostok-Zapad" otkryvaet novye vozmozhnosti diversifikaciii eksporta uglevodorodov' [Gas pipeline opens up new opportunities on diversification of export hydrocarbons], 25 December. Available at www.turkmenistan.gov.tm/?id=10163, accessed 9 October 2018.

Valiyev, A. (2010). 'Finlandization or strategy of keeping the balance? Azerbaijan foreign policy since the Russia-Georgia war'. PONARS Eurasia Policy Memo No. 112. Available at www.ponarseurasia.org/sites/default/files/policy-memos-pdf/pepm_112.pdf, accessed 30 November 2019.

White, S. and Feklyunina, V. (2014). *Identity and Foreign Policy in Russia, Ukraine and Belarus*. Basingstoke: Palgrave Macmillan.

Xinhua (2011). 'Chinese president kicks off state visit to Ukraine', 18 June. Available at www.gov.cn/english/2011-06/18/content_1887470.htm, accessed 11 November 2019.

Xinhua (2015a). 'China, Central Asia seek cooperation on Silk Road economic belt', 16 June. Available at http://news.xinhuanet.com/english/2015-06/16/c_134331124_2.htm, accessed 9 October 2018.

Xinhua (2015b). 'China, Uzbekistan to strengthen cooperation under the Silk Road initiative', June 2015. Available at www.xinhuanet.com/english/2019-10/30/c_138516139.htm, accessed 30 November 2019.

Xinhua (2015c). 'China, Uzbekistan sign protocol for closer trade ties', China Daily, 16 June 2015. Available at www.chinadaily.com.cn/business/2015-06/16/content_21017520.htm, accessed 11 November 2019.

Yaqing, D. (2015). 'Advancing towards the West', *Bejing Review*, 29 July. Available at www.bjreview.com/Business/201509/t20150909_800037814.html, accessed 9 October 2018.

43 Turkey

Always at a crossroads, never quite there

Utku Teksoz

Introduction

Turkey is a country that is full of contradictions and still continues to do its soul-searching. It finds itself always at crossroads. Indeed, a simple Google search of the expression 'Turkey at crossroads' yields over two million results, and that is only scratching the surface. In a similar vein to the following quote, attributed to the eminent German art historian Karl Scheffler, it is '[...] condemned forever to becoming and never to being',[1] Turkey seems to be always on the road to somewhere. Viewed from the vantage point of an emerging market economy, it is on the road to becoming a developed economy. From a historical perspective, the Turkish Republic is built on the remnants of the Ottoman Empire, which until its demise controlled territories in three different continents. Turkey is still coming to terms with its imperial legacy on the road to finding its feet amid the challenging realpolitik in its region. From a demographic perspective, it is like a pressure cooker with 42.7 per cent of its population—over 32.5 million persons—under the age of 25 on the crossroads to either being able to be provided with jobs and security thereby turning this into a phase of demographic gift, or following a vicious cycle of unemployment and loss of social cohesion feeding off of one another.

From a strictly economic perspective, it is at a crossroads where it could break the middle-income trap and become a high-income country provided that the right socio-economic policies are implemented. In fact, Turkey's current leadership has set itself an ambitious goal to that effect, namely that of becoming one of the top ten economies in the world by 2023, the one hundredth anniversary of the foundation of the Turkish Republic.[2] In practice, this will require policies to ensure that per capita GDP more than doubles over its current level to reach the tune of US$25,000. Such an economic

[1] The analogy is drawn by the author to the case of Turkey from the original quote that referred to Berlin and read as follows 'Berlin ist eine Stadt, verdammt dazu, ewig zu warden, niemals zu sein' [Berlin is a city, doomed to become eternal, never to be]. Karl Scheffler, Berlin: Ein Stadtschiksaal (Sheffler 1915 [1910]).

[2] To mark this symbolic milestone of the centenary of the foundation of the Turkish Republic, the government formulated a vision to become one of the top ten economies in the world with a GDP of circa $2 trillion, population of 82 million, exports worth $500 billion and single digit inflation and interest rates. For

Utku Teksoz, *Turkey: Always at a crossroads, never quite there* In: *Handbook of BRICS and Emerging Economies*. Edited by: P.B. Anand, Shailaja Fennell, and Flavio Comim, Oxford University Press (2021).
DOI: 10.1093/oso/9780198827535.003.0043

performance would in fact allow Turkey to pack a much stronger punch in both regional and global affairs—economically and geopolitically. In the meantime, the country continues to stand at the crossroads trying to chart its path forward.

Indeed, where to classify the Turkish economy has often been a point of contention in international agreements. It is considered an upper middle-income developing country, and it is part of the somewhat elite and exclusive club of the group of twenty (G20), comprised of the world's twenty largest economies. While Turkey seems to be comfortable in its skin as an emerging market economy in the G20 context, it is considered a developed economy as far as negotiations in the context of the United Nations Framework Convention on Climate Change (UNFCCC) are concerned. In other words, it is included in Annex I parties to the convention among other developed countries with associated responsibilities. Turkey is also a founding member of the OECD as well as a member of a number of other international organizations, including the European Bank for Reconstruction and Development, Asian Infrastructure Investment Bank, African Development Bank, Asian Development Bank, etc.

Turkey is also part of a whole host of European Union (EU) institutions thanks to its EU Association Agreement. It is economically integrated to the EU through the customs union, and boasts strong historical, cultural, and sports ties to the continent. The CIA Factbook classifies Turkey as a developed country whereas the World Bank classifies it as an upper middle-income country. Within the United Nations, remarkably it does not belong to the Group of 77 and China, which includes most developing countries as well as those with similar income and prosperity levels to Turkey. By contrast, Turkey is part of the Western Europe and Others Group (WEOG)—a very loose coalition of fairly divergent economies. The UN Development Programme (UNDP) classifies Turkey as a high Human Development country, based on its Human Development Index (HDI) 2014, yet Freedom House takes into account other institutional factors, such as media and internet freedom, and classifies the country as partly free (Freedom House 2016). On the one hand, it has ambitions to play a much bigger economic and political role in its immediate region; on the other hand, it is trying to come to terms with the limits of its own power.[3] As was captured by the motto of its failed bid for organizing the 2000 Olympic Games—'Let's meet where the Continents meet'—the country is still trying to chart the best course for itself as a relatively stable country in a troubled region by synthesizing elements from the East and the West.

further details of Turkey's Strategic Vision 2023 Project 2008–2023, please see www.tsv2023.org/index.php/en/ (accessed 10 October 2018).

[3] An example of such a contradiction is the doctrine of zero-problems with neighbours, developed by the then Foreign Minister Ahmet Davutoglu and the shift in Turkey's foreign policy position that followed the Arab Spring.

Turkey in global economic governance—making sense of the acronyms

Former Goldman Sachs chief economist Jim O'Neill coined the term BRICS in an investment research paper published in 2001.[4] Ever since, there has been a quest among economists to identify the second generation BRICS, which led to an 'acronym salad': O'Neill and his team analysed up and coming emerging market countries based on a diverse set of criteria, such as macro stability, political maturity, trade openness, education quality, and favourable investment policies and came up with a set of eleven countries that they considered would become among the world's largest economies in the twenty-first century along with BRICS. The N11 brings together a diverse mix of advanced economies (South Korea), upper middle-income countries (Iran, Mexico, and Turkey), and lower middle-income countries (Bangladesh, Egypt, Indonesia, Nigeria, Pakistan, the Philippines, and Vietnam). The most economically prominent four of these countries, namely Mexico, Indonesia, South Korea, and Turkey, account for over 70 per cent of N11 GDP and are also grouped together under the acronym MIST. A slight variation of MIST that leaves out South Korea in favour of Nigeria is MINT—a term coined by Fidelity Investments in 2011 (Fraser 2011).

In 2009 the Economist Intelligence Unit contributed to the attempt to identify the successor of BRICS with the acronym CIVETS, standing for Colombia, Indonesia, Vietnam, Egypt, Turkey, and South Africa.[5] Their forecasts suggested that this group of countries would consistently grow on average by 4.5 per cent for the next twenty years, easily beating the G7 growth forecast for the same period and coming close to that of BRICS. Furthermore, these countries have a common set of strengths, such as favourable demographics thanks to large and young populations, diversified economic structures that are not commodity-dependent, and relatively sophisticated financial architectures, as well as a common set of challenges, such as high unemployment, corruption, and inequality.

Just like BRICS, MIKTA is also a subset of the G20 and consists of Mexico, Indonesia, South Korea, Turkey, and Australia. This grouping was created in New York in September 2013 in the margins of the General Debate of the 68th Session of the UN General Assembly. According to its own vision statement, the group consists of countries coming from diverse cultures and regions, yet sharing core values and similarities. They are all democracies with open economies with robust growth prospects. As part of the world's twenty largest economies, they account for close to 6 per cent of global GDP among themselves. MIKTA aims to constitute a cross-regional consultative platform that will play

[4] J. O'Neill (2001). 'Building better global economic BRICs'. Global Economics Paper No. 66. New York: Goldman Sachs & Co. Initially, the acronym referred only to Brazil, Russia, India, and China—all four countries being part of the G20. Starting from 2009 these countries began holding their own mini-summits ahead of G20 summits. South Africa was invited to join in 2010.

[5] Economist Intelligence Unit Global Forecasting Service (2010). 'Beyond the BRICs'. The acronym CIVETS was presented as an alternative to BRIC, hence the inclusion of South Africa in the former.

a bridging role between developed and developing countries to promote global governance reform and to seek pragmatic and innovative solutions to regional and global challenges.[6]

Turkey has also been active in regional diplomacy as a founding member of the organization of the Black Sea Economic Cooperation (BSEC), which was established as an outcome of the Istanbul Summit of 1992 with a Bosphorus statement signed by heads of states from eleven governments, namely Albania, Armenia, Azerbaijan, Bulgaria, Georgia, Greece, Moldova, Romania, Russia, Turkey, and Ukraine. Serbia joined later in 2004. The organization's headquarters is located in Istanbul and the BSEC aims to foster greater cooperation among its member states, especially with a focus on peace, stability, and prosperity, and programmes targeted towards the further development of small and medium enterprises (SMEs) and entrepreneurship across the region. Membership is not restricted only to countries that have a coastline on the Black Sea and the organization also welcomes observer nations from the EU and North Africa as well as the United States of America.

Last but not least, it is playing an ever more active role in international multilateral forums; it is host to a myriad of United Nations system organizations, including hosting the regional hub for the UN Development Programme (UNDP). Turkey has also hosted major UN conferences, including the Second United Nations Conference on Human Settlements (Habitat II) in 2006, and the Fourth United Nations Conference on Least Developed Countries (LDC-IV) in 2011, which led to the adoption of the Istanbul Programme of Action to be implemented for the next decade. In 2016, the country will be host to the first ever World Humanitarian Summit as well as hosting a mid-point review of the implementation of the Istanbul Programme of Action. Within the United Nations, Turkey has been stepping up its game to play an ever more visible role in mediation and in 2009–10 served as a rotating member of the UN Security Council. In line with the increasingly more visible role it is playing in the governance of international organizations, Turkey is among the winners of the International Monetary Fund's (IMF) 2010 quota and governance reforms and will see an over 30 per cent increase in its voting share on the IMF's board when reforms are finally implemented.

A historical perspective

A brief discussion on the economic history of Turkey is in order here to better contextualize Turkey's place in the global economy.[7] It is fair to say that Turkey became part of the Western camp for good in the decade of the 1950s when it joined NATO and established

[6] MIKTA Vision Statement, adopted in Seoul on 22 May 2015. Available at http://www.mikta.org/about/vision.php, accessed 10 October 2018.

[7] For a more detailed and longer-term analysis of the path that the Turkish economy has followed since the late nineteenth century until today as well as an accounting exercise that decomposes Turkish growth, please see the authoritative article by Altuğ et al. (2008).

strong ties with the United States under the Truman Doctrine and the Marshall Plan. Turkey maintained NATO's second largest army in terms of manpower and was also a Cold War outpost sharing borders with the Soviet Union as well as Iran, Iraq, and Syria. In the economic sphere, after a decade of experimentation with liberal policies during Prime Minister Adnan Menderes of the Democrat Party's term in office, Turkey moved to import substitution industrialization (ISI) during the 1960s and 1970s, which was fairly commonplace among developing countries until the 1980s. Such policies created their own dependencies; however, while Turkey succeeded in creating a vibrant internal market through ISI policies and heavy state protection of the manufacturing sector, its economy was never internationally competitive during these two decades with virtually no export markets of its own.

By contrast, the 1980s started with a military coup, where the military regime changed the fabric of the Turkish economy—for better or worse—towards one that aimed to be competitive in global markets. This approach also captured the mainstream economic thinking of these decades where a new round of globalization was gradually taking force. That, in turn, required withdrawal of the state from the manufacturing sector in favour of undertaking more infrastructure investments that would first unite the internal market and second make it possible to have a better reach and access to export markets. The state economic enterprises that were symbolic of the economic model of the previous two decades were to be rapidly privatized and protectionism was to end. The new era would be symbolized by low-cost and high-quality production of export goods as well as foreign direct investment (FDI) in the manufacturing sector. Ahmad (2003) argues that the policies of this decade resulted in a marked worsening of income distribution as wages had to be further depressed in order to be able to produce competitively in global markets. Accordingly, the share of wages in Turkey's GDP was halved from 36 per cent to 18 per cent between 1977 and 1987. While exports increased substantially from US$2.3 billion in 1979 to US$11.7 billion in 1988 with diversification of the export markets to include the Middle East often leading analysts to conclude that this was a decade of 'export miracle', a closer examination yields a somewhat different picture; part of the increase in exports to the Middle East was in fact attributable to the Iran–Iraq War (1980–88) that artificially increased the demand for Turkish goods. Another part is due to the rampant corruption that characterized this period where statistics included claims for the so-called 'phantom exports' [*hayali ihracat*] which was indeed no more than a scheme by the so-called exporters to collect export subsidies from the state. In short, the true value of exports is likely to have been overstated for this period. Nevertheless, this does not change the fact that during this decade the Turkish economy undertook structural transformation from inward-looking autarchic economic policies towards export orientation.

Another transformation that was happening quietly but surely during this decade was the change in nature of the Turkish middle class, pioneered by the so-called 'Anatolian Tigers' that benefited from the generous export subsidies handed out by the state. An economic power struggle between the established Republican elite of Istanbul and

Western Turkey and this new upstart class of Anatolian middle class ensued that was to put its marker on Turkish politics and society even to this day.[8]

With a transition from the military junta to the civilian rule in 1983 and a new constitution, the rest of the decade saw transformative and liberal policies implemented under the stewardship of Prime Minister Turgut Özal of the Motherland Party (ANAP). While this period was characterized by the aspirations of Turkey to become a regional superpower, a 'mini-USA' so to say—and Özal's rhetoric of fast-tracking Turkey's economic development, expressed in his own words as 'making the country skip an epoch'—in reality most of the export boom was built on shaky foundations, as mentioned above, and was financed by massive debt that continues to be the Achilles heel of the Turkish economy to this day.

The collapse of ISI policies in the late 1970s and the military coup that defined the transition of the 1980s to the neoliberal export-led growth model had one major shortcoming that is often shared with other emerging market economies: the transition in economic policies from ISI to an export-led growth model was not accompanied by a parallel transition in the role of the state 'from an inward-oriented developmentalist state to an outward-oriented competition state' (Öniş 2009).

In the absence of this type of an institutional innovation, the Turkish experience was characterized by the weakness of state capacity, which prevented the Turkish economy from reaching macroeconomic stability. For instance, the premature transition to full capital account openness in 1989 was undertaken in the absence of the requisite regulatory frameworks that would otherwise underpin macroeconomic and fiscal discipline. This in turn resulted in a volatile and lopsided pattern of development dependent on short-term capital flows that were easily reversible. The consequent crisis-prone nature of the Turkish economy led to three economic crises in the 1990s, with significant ramifications for income distribution, and eventually led to a shift of political power from the mainstream liberal parties to an upstart political party in the form of the Justice and Development Party (AKP).

Öniş (2009) characterizes the era that started in 1980s as the neoliberal era with three distinct phases. The first phase, described above, was by and large immune to economic crises. Yet, the second phase, roughly corresponding to the 1990s, reversed this with three economic crises, in 1994, 2000, and 2001, within a decade—an experience more reminiscent of the Latin American countries to which Turkey is often compared. The third phase of the neoliberal era came in the aftermath of the 2001 crisis, which was deeper and more severe than the previous one to the extent that it affected all segments of

[8] The former elite represented the secular ideology and world values on which the Turkish Republic was founded by Kemal Ataturk in 1923 whereas the latter elite was a more conservative and pious group, to which Ottoman values seem to have appealed more. Nowhere is this contradiction more apparent than in the acronyms of TUSIAD and MUSIAD, the Turkish Association of Industrialists and Businessmen, and the Independent Association of Industrialists and Businessmen, respectively. Yet, it is an open secret that the 'M' in MUSIAD actually represents 'Muslim'—wordplay that is probably meant to tease the traditional secular Turkish elite.

society in equal measure. In particular, weaknesses in the banking sector came to the fore, leading to a massive restructuring and a risk-averse approach to banking regulation. Unemployment rose massively by an additional one million people and bankruptcies among SMEs followed.

It was in fact this February 2001 crisis that had an even more transformative impact in the sense that it brought to the fore the public's deep disillusionment with all the mainstream political parties that had taken part in coalition governments of the 1990s. The end result of all of this was to pave the way for the rise of the AKP—a novel political force with Islamist roots combined with a moderate rhetoric and liberal economic tendencies. In fact, the electorate marginalized all the mainstream parties and handed out victory to the AKP in the early general elections of November 2002. This marked the beginning of the third phase of Turkey's neoliberal era, one that has seen fundamental economic and political transformations take place.

In the aftermath of the crisis, the coalition government was united in implementing a somewhat unusual response. They created a technocratic position in the government—that of a minister in charge of all powers over the economy and tasked with overseeing Turkey's economic recovery. Kemal Derviş, a highly respected and seasoned top-level economist from the World Bank, who had enjoyed an international career at the bank for more than three decades and had held senior management positions at the level of vice-president, occupied this position at such a critical time. At the time he became a minister, Mr Derviş was not a member of any political party. His international reputation as an experienced and competent crisis manager allowed him to reach across the aisle and bring the entire country behind an economic recovery programme. The presence of Mr Derviş at the helm also brought with it much needed credibility in the eyes of international financial institutions that made it possible for Turkey to secure the financial resources it needed to underpin its economic recovery as well as implementation of structural reforms under the IMF's auspices.[9]

While the actual period in which Kemal Derviş was in charge of the economy was fairly short-lived (March 2001 to August 2002) and the aforementioned elections brought the AKP to power in late 2002, the economic leadership of the AKP did not take any risks and implemented the Derviş programme to the letter, thereby overseeing the structural adjustment that nursed the Turkish economy back to health and subsequently to a period of strong economic performance that made Turkey one of the most attractive investment destinations among emerging markets. Although it would probably be an exaggeration to attribute all of these transformative policies to the AKP government, it must still be recognized that the period in which the AKP has been in power has brought about much needed stability and unity of purpose in government in a

[9] It is relatively rare to get an insight into the experiences and actions of senior government figures, especially regarding their roles in responding to crises. See Derviş (2005) for a first-hand narrative of his experience as the Minister in Charge of the Economy including the domestic and international challenges that he had to overcome to ensure recovery of the Turkish economy.

country which suffered from serious fatigue from short-lived coalition governments and their often incoherent social and economic policies. While counterfactual, it is reasonable to assume that political instability could have become the exception rather than the rule and the reform process could have proven much shorter-lived had it not been backed by a single party in power.

As of writing, the AKP government has been in power for a solid fourteen years and has won five successive general elections, namely in 2002, 2007, 2011, and the two elections in 2015.[10] It has elected two of its leaders, namely Abdullah Gul and Recep Tayyip Erdoğan, to the presidency—although mostly a ceremonial position, it is still the highest public office and yields veto power on crucial issues.[11] In spite of its conservative voting base, the AKP government has a strong reformist orientation insofar as both economic management and democratization processes are concerned. Among the major successes of AKP's period in power is the official launch of the EU accession process in late 2004 and the country's ability to weather the economic and financial crisis of 2008 without the help of an external anchor, such as an IMF Stand-By Arrangement (SBA).

Öniş (2009) characterizes this period as the third phase of the Turkish neoliberal experiment from a big picture perspective and refers to a US–EU–IMF triangle. From the vantage point of the United States, Turkey has been a key NATO ally situated in a key geostrategic location with substantial military muscle and economic opportunities thanks to its young population and strong industrial production base. If anything, the country's strategic importance, as a key US foreign policy ally between the Middle East and Europe, increased considerably in the aftermath of the 9/11 terror attacks on the World Trade Center, and continued with the unfolding of the Arab Spring and its consequences for the entire region.

To complete the triangle, the IMF structural adjustment programmes and the case for Turkish membership to the EU provided a double external anchor to policymakers providing them with the space to push through the conditionality involved in both processes. Öniş (2009) explains that these two anchors were intertwined in a fairly unique way: the reforms required to make progress with the Copenhagen criteria—the prerequisite for EU membership—would include measures to enhance Turkish democracy, human rights, and the rule of law. These reforms, in turn, would be key to securing a stable business environment—a key element of the post-Washington Consensus, and would eventually facilitate implementation of the economic and fiscal conditionality that was often associated with the IMF structural adjustment programmes of the era.

What is unique to the AKP, however, is the fact that the usual governmental fatigue that appears to set in after a given party wins successive elections is absent from the

[10] Two general elections were held in 2015. The first elections in June produced a hung parliament and a government could not be formed, which led to the second elections in November.

[11] Since this chapter was drafted, a tightly contested constitutional referendum took place in April 2017. The proposed amendments move Turkey's governance towards an executive presidential system. The broad implications of this referendum for the future of Turkish democracy are significant and a promising subject for future research.

equation as observed by Öniş (2013). The AKP, once seen as an outsider, has in fact proven to be much more durable and capable of adapting to changing circumstances than most of its predecessors, keeping a large portion of the electorate behind its programme. To go deeper into the analysis of the reasons for the party's success during this period goes beyond the scope of this chapter.[12] However, the AKP hegemony especially towards the end of the period under consideration has resulted in an unprecedented concentration of power and a subsequent weakening of checks and balances that are the *sine qua non* of democratic systems. Furthermore, the internal power struggle between various strands of the party that had hitherto worked in harmony to ensure the AKP's rise to power, an increasingly authoritarian and centralizing attitude of the incumbent government, and allegations of corruption against some senior government figures led to increasing polarization of Turkish society, which manifested itself, *inter alia*, in the Gezi Park protests that started in May 2013. The government's disproportionate reaction to the protesters and the media drew criticism in international circles. Moreover, in spite of some early progress in normalizing relations with the Kurdish minority under the AKP government, tensions have increased again since then.

Turkey came to the brink of disaster numerous times during its recent history and managed to walk away unscathed. Once again it is going through tough times with the simultaneous weakening of the soft power of external anchors like the EU, an ever more difficult external environment south of its borders with Syria, and a humanitarian crisis that has stretched its capacity to cope with the influx of an unprecedented number of displaced migrants and refugees within its borders. It may well be too early to draw lasting conclusions as to the direction that the country will go. Suffice it to say at this juncture that in keeping with the main theme of this chapter, Turkey is once again standing at a crossroads

Comparative macroeconomic analysis

Typically, comparative studies of the Turkish economy would pitch the country against Latin American developing countries using Argentina, Mexico, and Brazil as comparators. Given the scope of this chapter, the Turkish economy will be examined from the perspective of a near-BRICS country following the term coined by Öniş and Kutlay (2013). Taking into account the fact that Turkey is a G20 member, it is probably warranted to broaden the scope of the analysis by using the informal grouping of MIKTA as the relevant comparator, thanks to those countries' self-proclaimed shared values as well as shared strong macroeconomic fundamentals.

Table 43.1 shows the annual GDP growth as well as the per capita GDP in constant 2011 international US$ since 2000 for BRICS and MIKTA countries, respectively. Over

[12] For a comprehensive and critical analysis of this period, see Kirişçi (2009).

the decade and a half, BRICS clearly displayed a strong economic performance that allowed Russia to increase its GDP per capita by over 75 per cent with India more than doubling it and China raising it almost by 250 per cent—albeit from a relatively low base value. After a decade and a half of robust growth, China has become the world's second largest economy after the US in current US$, and is expected to overtake that of the United States by 2024.[13] Yet, China's development quest is simply just beginning since on a per capita GDP basis, it has only reached where Turkey stood in 2000. Although China's growth has been both robust and predictable with a very low variance over the period under consideration, recent headwinds faced by the Chinese economy have led to reduced growth prospects, which is a cause for broader concern given the interconnectedness of the global economy. For instance, the slowdown in Chinese industrial production coupled with the fall in commodity prices poses serious downside risks for many developing countries, especially those that are dependent on raw material exports. By contrast, growth in South Africa and Brazil has been more modest by BRICS standards during this period, yet these countries were already at or close to US$10,000 GDP per capita at the turn of the millennium.[14]

The picture is more nuanced among MIKTA countries, as covered by the lower panel of Table 43.1. Needless to say, the growth champion over the period is South Korea, which grew at a steady pace at around 4.4 per cent on average with a relatively low volatility. Thereby, Korean GDP per capita increased by over 60 per cent over the period from US$20,756 to US$33,629. By contrast, Mexico grew by 2.3 per cent on average over the same period and at the same time experienced more volatility, thus raising its GDP per capita by only around 10 per cent. At 3 per cent on average for the period, Australian growth was not much higher. Yet, it was a lot less volatile, which allowed Australia to comfortably raise its already high GDP per capita from US$35,244 to US$42,218, which amounts to a respectable 22.6 per cent increase over the period. Indonesian growth was equally stable over the same period yet at a higher average rate of 5.3 per cent. Hence, Indonesia saw its per capita GDP increase by over 70 per cent, from US$5,805 to US $10,033.

Against this backdrop, Turkey's growth performance since 2000 is a story of what-could-have-been. Taken as a whole, at 4.3 per cent its average growth rate was comparable to that of South Korea and was better than those of Mexico and Australia. Nevertheless, this average growth brought with it massive volatility. The variance of Turkish GDP growth for the period stood at 21.9 per cent and was by far the highest

[13] IHS Economics, Report on China, September 2014. Available at https://news.ihsmarkit.com/press-release/economics-country-risk/china-become-worlds-largest-economy-2024-reports-ihs-economics, accessed 4 December 2019. The report argues that the Chinese economy will likely rebalance towards domestic consumption and will also benefit from growth in the Asia-Pacific region.

[14] The World Bank Group uses the GNI per capita, calculated using the World Bank Atlas method, to determine the income groups. Accordingly, the cut-off for lower middle-income countries is a GNI per capita of $1,045, and that for upper middle-income countries is $4,125. Countries with a GNI per capita of $12,736 or more are classified as high-income economies.

Table 43.1 GDP growth and per capita GDP in BRICS and MIKTA countries 2000–14

	Country		2000	2001	2002	2003	2004	2005	2006	2007	2008	2009	2010	2011	2012	2013	2014
BRICS	**Brazil**	GDP growth (annual %)	4.38	1.28	3.07	1.22	5.66	3.15	4.00	6.01	5.02	(0.24)	7.57	3.92	1.76	2.74	0.14
		GDP per capita, PPP (constant 2011 international $)	11,377.08	11,352.55	11,531.53	11,508.48	11,997.31	12,219.96	12,560.79	13,171.07	13,691.19	13,524.75	14,408.73	14,830.90	14,951.81	15,222.32	15,109.83
	Russia	GDP growth (annual %)	10.00	5.09	4.74	7.30	7.18	6.38	8.15	8.54	5.25	(7.82)	4.50	4.26	3.41	1.34	0.64
		GDP per capita, PPP (constant 2011 international $)	13,172.73	13,902.33	14,628.95	15,767.64	16,967.29	18,118.14	19,659.64	21,374.13	22,505.72	20,739.33	21,663.64	22,569.81	23,299.19	23,561.37	23,292.91
	India	GDP growth (annual %)	3.84	4.82	3.80	7.86	7.92	9.28	9.26	9.80	3.89	8.48	10.26	6.64	5.08	6.90	7.29
		GDP per capita, PPP (constant 2011 international $)	2,521.34	2,597.59	2,651.13	2,812.62	2,986.82	3,213.06	3,457.06	3,739.27	3,828.35	4,094.46	4,452.93	4,685.86	4,861.06	5,131.83	5,438.62
	China	GDP growth (annual %)	8.43	8.30	9.09	10.02	10.08	11.35	12.69	14.19	9.62	9.23	10.63	9.48	7.75	7.68	7.27
		GDP per capita, PPP (constant 2011 international $)	3,678.16	3,954.56	4,285.26	4,685.36	5,126.90	5,675.45	6,359.95	7,224.91	7,879.72	8,564.59	9,429.50	10,274.49	11,016.99	11,805.09	12,599.18
	S. Africa	GDP growth (annual %)	4.20	2.70	3.70	2.95	4.55	5.28	5.59	5.36	3.19	(1.54)	3.04	3.21	2.22	2.21	1.52
		GDP per capita, PPP (constant 2011 international $)	9,926.85	9,988.36	10,213.19	10,382.02	10,715.34	11,132.77	11,597.13	12,051.84	12,263.09	11,902.85	12,086.92	12,290.89	12,374.53	12,454.19	12,446.37
MIKTA	**Mexico**	GDP growth (annual %)	5.30	(0.61)	0.13	1.42	4.30	3.03	4.94	3.22	1.38	(4.74)	5.20	3.92	4.04	1.39	2.23
		GDP per capita, PPP (constant 2011 international $)	14,845.00	14,552.57	14,386.99	14,412.82	14,841.81	15,084.28	15,597.76	15,850.79	15,813.26	14,825.51	15,359.38	15,729.64	16,136.28	16,140.66	16,284.15
	Indonesia	GDP growth (annual %)	4.92	3.64	4.50	4.78	5.03	5.69	5.50	6.35	6.01	4.63	6.22	6.17	6.03	5.58	5.02
		GDP per capita, PPP (constant 2011 international $)	5,805.81	5,935.75	6,119.48	6,326.48	6,556.64	6,838.42	7,119.90	7,472.81	7,819.07	8,074.50	8,465.30	8,870.28	9,282.71	9,674.61	10,033.48

S. Korea	GDP growth (annual %)	8.83	4.53	7.43	2.93	4.90	3.92	5.18	5.46	2.83	0.71	6.50	3.68	2.29	2.90	3.31
	GDP per capita, PPP (constant 2011 international $)	20,756.78	21,536.08	23,008.08	23,565.61	24,627.61	25,541.46	26,733.65	28,063.27	28,650.28	28,716.10	30,440.40	31,327.13	31,901.07	32,684.32	33,629.42
Turkey	GDP growth (annual %)	6.77	(5.70)	6.16	5.27	9.36	8.40	6.89	4.67	0.66	(4.83)	9.16	8.77	2.13	4.19	2.91
	GDP per capita, PPP (constant 2011 international $)	13,011.53	12,090.01	12,649.36	13,127.05	14,160.31	15,149.35	15,994.72	16,546.18	16,458.95	15,463.10	16,634.16	17,873.70	18,032.27	18,560.11	18,869.01
Australia	GDP growth (annual %)	3.87	1.93	3.86	3.07	4.15	3.21	2.98	3.76	3.71	1.82	2.02	2.38	3.63	2.44	2.50
	GDP per capita, PPP (constant 2011 international $)	35,244.50	35,443.37	36,363.74	37,020.73	38,112.44	38,818.84	39,391.34	40,617.01	41,286.82	41,180.55	41,363.22	41,763.12	42,540.97	42,829.72	43,218.52

Source: World Development Indicators (World Bank 2016).

among the entire BRICS+MIKTA group. Only the variance of Russian GDP growth came close at 18.4 per cent. Consequently, the Turkish per capita GDP grew by 45 per cent from US$13,011 in 2000 to US$18,869 in 2014. Needless to say, this is a respectable growth performance in a period that included two economic crises—the first induced domestically in 2001 and the second being the global finanicial crisis of 2008 that brought down the entire world economy. However, a close inspection of the trend seems to suggest that Turkish growth had been pro-cyclical.

Figure 43.1 plots the average growth of BRICS and MIKTA for the entire period. While the trends are broadly similar, it is worth noting that the MIKTA average fell below 1 per cent in 2001 due to a combination of the Mexican GDP shrinking by 0.61 per cent and the Turkish GDP shrinking by an alarming 5.7 per cent, whereas the average BRICS growth for that year was 4.4 per cent with none of the BRICS economies contracting. This deviation from the global trend was brought about in Turkey by agency factors rather than structural ones. In other words, it was by and large a political rather than an economic crisis. Turkish growth almost came to a screeching halt in 2008 well before those of the comparator countries since characteristically it is highly dependent on short- and long-term foreign capital flows; at least portfolio investments were quick in their flight to safety when confronted with the credit crunch of late 2007—a precursor of what was to follow. Consequently, the economy shrank by 4.8 per cent in 2009—much the same as the economy of Mexico. Yet, what followed is a remarkable

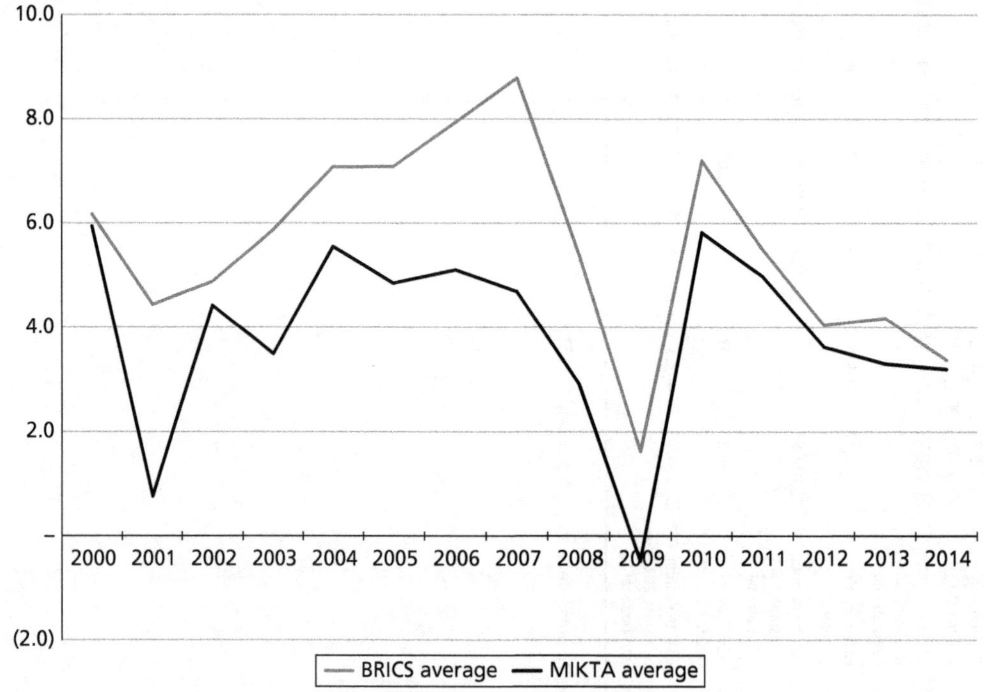

Figure 43.1 GDP growth: BRICS vs MIKTA (annual average, %)

Source: World Development Indicators (World Bank 2016).

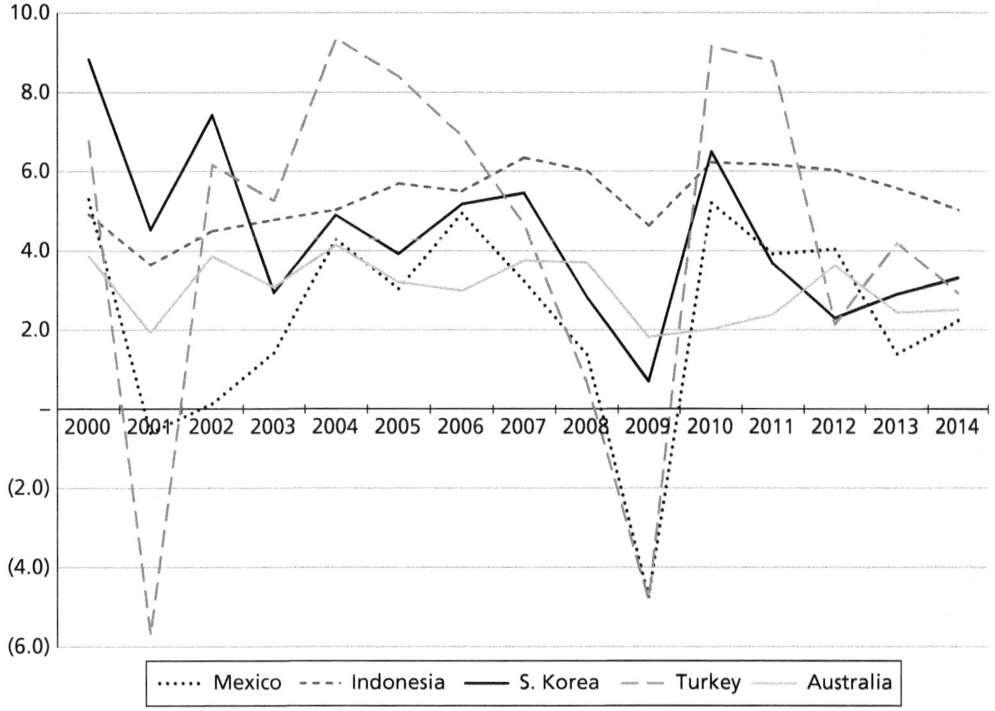

Figure 43.2 GDP Growth—MIKTA (annual, %)

Source: World Development Indicators (World Bank 2016).

pattern: the Turkish economy bounced back to post close to double-digit growth rates in 2010 and 2011, yet it has only grown by around 2 per cent to 4 per cent every year since then. Figure 43.2 plots the annual growth rate of the MIKTA economies since 2000. The Turkish economy follows a pro-cyclical trend during the entire period, yet its volatility appears to have been enhanced—most likely due to domestic factors in 2001 when it dipped way below any other comparator countries. Also worth noting is the fact that although Turkey and Mexico experienced a similar dip in the aftermath of the 2008 crisis, the Turkish economy did bounce back much faster in 2010, yet the volatility could not be reined in by policymakers.

Demographics plays a key role in the Turkish economy. Table 43.2 shows youth unemployment and total unemployment rates for the period under consideration. South Africa seems to be an outlier for the entire period not only among BRICS, but also taking the entire sample into consideration, with its average youth and total unemployment rates reaching almost 50 per cent and 25 per cent, respectively. Elsewhere, there are very few good examples of youth unemployment being addressed effectively. South Korea appears to be an exception as its youth and total unemployment rates average 3.0 per cent and 3.9 per cent, respectively, for the entire period. The Turkish economy has also followed the now familiar pattern of burgeoning youth

Table 43.2 The extent of unemployment and youth unemployment in BRICS and MIKTA countries 2000–14

			2000	2001	2002	2003	2004	2005	2006	2007	2008	2009	2010	2011	2012	2013	2014
BRICS	**Brazil**	Youth unemployment (% of total)	18.00	17.70	17.90	19.00	18.00	19.40	17.70	16.70	15.50	17.80	17.20	15.20	14.40	14.70	15.20
		Unemployment (% of total)	9.50	9.30	9.10	9.70	8.90	9.30	8.40	8.10	7.10	8.30	7.90	6.70	6.10	6.50	6.80
	Russia	Youth unemployment (% of total)	20.80	18.00	15.60	17.50	17.30	15.40	16.50	14.50	14.00	18.40	16.80	15.30	15.00	14.10	12.90
		Unemployment (% of total)	10.60	9.00	7.90	8.20	7.80	7.10	7.10	6.00	6.20	8.30	7.30	6.50	5.50	5.50	5.10
	India	Youth unemployment (% of total)	10.00	10.50	9.90	9.00	9.10	9.90	10.00	8.90	10.00	9.70	10.20	10.30	10.70	10.40	10.40
		Unemployment (% of total)	4.30	4.00	4.30	3.90	3.90	4.40	4.30	3.70	4.10	3.90	3.50	3.50	3.60	3.60	3.60
	China	Youth unemployment (% of total)	9.30	9.40	9.20	8.90	8.90	8.60	8.30	8.00	9.10	9.30	9.00	9.30	9.70	10.10	10.50
		Unemployment (% of total)	4.50	4.50	4.40	4.30	4.30	4.10	4.00	3.80	4.40	4.40	4.20	4.30	4.50	4.60	4.70
	S. Africa	Youth unemployment (% of total)	45.30	50.30	53.00	55.40	51.30	48.40	46.80	46.50	45.60	48.20	50.80	50.10	52.20	51.40	52.60
		Unemployment (% of total)	26.70	25.40	27.20	27.10	24.70	23.80	22.60	22.30	22.70	23.70	24.70	24.70	25.00	24.60	25.10
MIKTA	Mexico	Youth unemployment (% of total)	5.10	4.70	5.90	6.20	7.70	6.50	6.20	6.70	7.00	10.00	9.40	10.00	9.50	9.40	9.90
		Unemployment (% of total)	2.60	2.50	2.90	3.00	3.70	3.50	3.20	3.40	3.50	5.20	5.20	5.30	4.90	4.90	4.90

Indonesia	Youth unemployment (% of total)	18.10	22.50	26.30	26.40	28.60	32.70	30.90	25.60	23.50	22.50	25.00	21.40	20.30	21.80	21.80
	Unemployment (% of total)	6.10	8.10	9.10	9.50	9.90	11.20	10.30	9.10	8.40	7.90	7.10	6.60	6.10	6.30	6.20
S. Korea	Youth unemployment (% of total)	5.00	4.50	3.80	3.90	4.00	4.00	3.80	3.70	3.60	4.10	4.00	3.70	3.40	3.30	3.90
	Unemployment (% of total)	3.50	3.20	2.60	3.20	3.30	3.30	2.80	2.50	2.60	2.90	3.30	3.00	2.90	2.80	3.10
Turkey	Youth unemployment (% of total)	12.80	15.90	18.80	19.90	20.00	19.20	18.40	19.30	19.90	24.50	21.20	17.90	17.10	16.50	17.70
	Unemployment (% of total)	6.50	8.40	10.40	10.50	10.80	10.60	10.20	10.30	11.00	14.00	11.90	9.80	9.20	8.70	9.20
Australia	Youth unemployment (% of total)	12.10	13.60	12.90	11.90	11.40	10.60	10.00	9.30	8.70	11.50	11.40	11.40	11.70	12.20	13.10
	Unemployment (% of total)	6.30	6.80	6.40	5.90	5.40	5.00	4.80	4.40	4.20	5.60	5.20	5.10	5.20	5.70	6.00

Source: World Development Indicators (World Bank 2016).

unemployment alongside a secular rise in total unemployment. Demographics could support the fundamentals of the Turkish economy, or, if it is not actively managed, it could turn out to be a time bomb. As of 2013, out of a total population of 76.5 million people, some 42 per cent were at or below the age of 25. Among these, the 0–15 age group constituted over 26 per cent of the total population. For as long as this young population could be kept gainfully employed as they reach working age, this demographic gift could indeed unlock the potential of the Turkish economy. To that effect, Turkish policymakers could learn from the Korean experience and aim to emulate that for the domestic economy to the extent possible.

To the extent that this can be coupled with inclusive and targeted policies to bring the untapped potential of female labour into the market, the Turkish economy could benefit from a rapid growth streak for the foreseeable future. Figure 43.3 shows that there has been an implicit or explicit gender bias in the breakdown of unemployment trends since 2000. At the turn of the millennium, the Turkish economy had a lower rate of female unemployment than male unemployment, which appears to be the exception rather than the rule among BRICS and MIKTA economies. Not only has female unemployment shot up since then, but it also seems to have decoupled from the trend of male unemployment. To benefit most from the demographics, this issue should also be tackled through

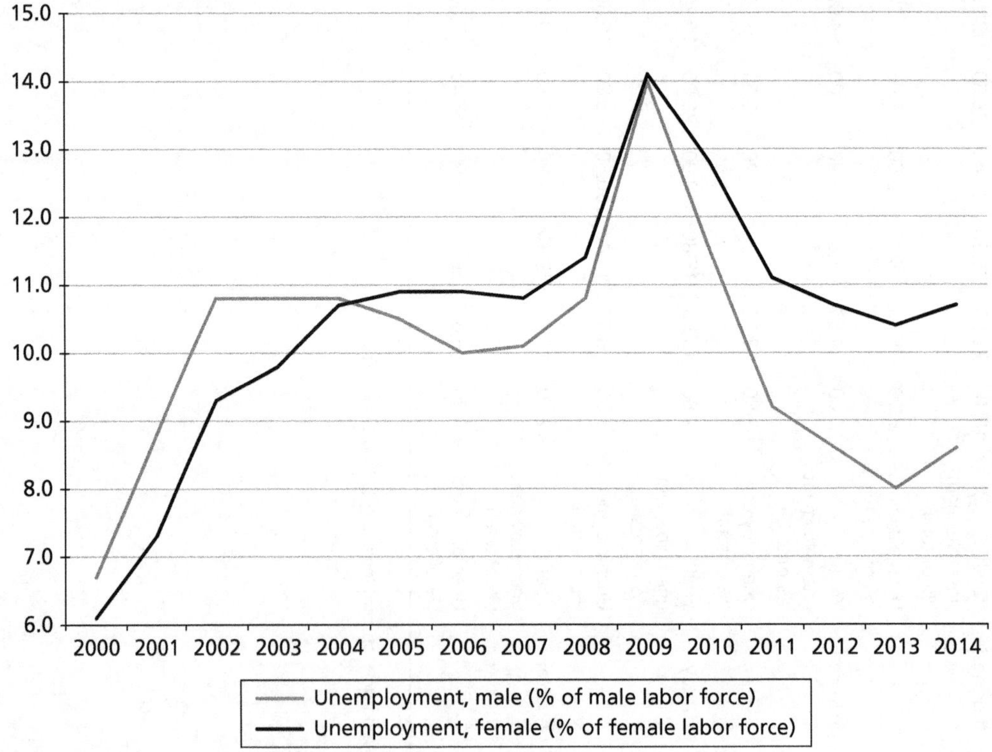

Figure 43.3 Turkey: male and female unemployment trends since 2000

Source: World Development Indicators (World Bank 2016).

inclusive labour market policies that would address both the labour force participation rate of females as well as unemployment among the female labour force.

In spite of the global trend of increasing relative importance of the services sector in advanced economies, Turkish exports continue to be dominated by output from the manufacturing sector. As seen in Figure 43.4a, the services that are exported amount to a negligible percentage of the total. The breakdown of these manufacturing exports as of 2014 is presented in Figure 43.4b, which shows textiles and apparel, motor vehicles, and basic metals as the leading categories. One potential problem with this structure of exports is that textiles and apparel production relies on the continued availability of cheap labour. While the demographic projections are likely to be supportive in the foreseeable future, competition from abroad in driving down these wage costs cannot be ruled out. Similarly, motor vehicle exports form a crucial lifeline for the Turkish economy. However, the Turkish automotive sector is dominated by foreign manufacturers, which produce under licence in Turkey in order to gain duty-free access to the EU market. Most of the design, innovation, and value added is done elsewhere. It is

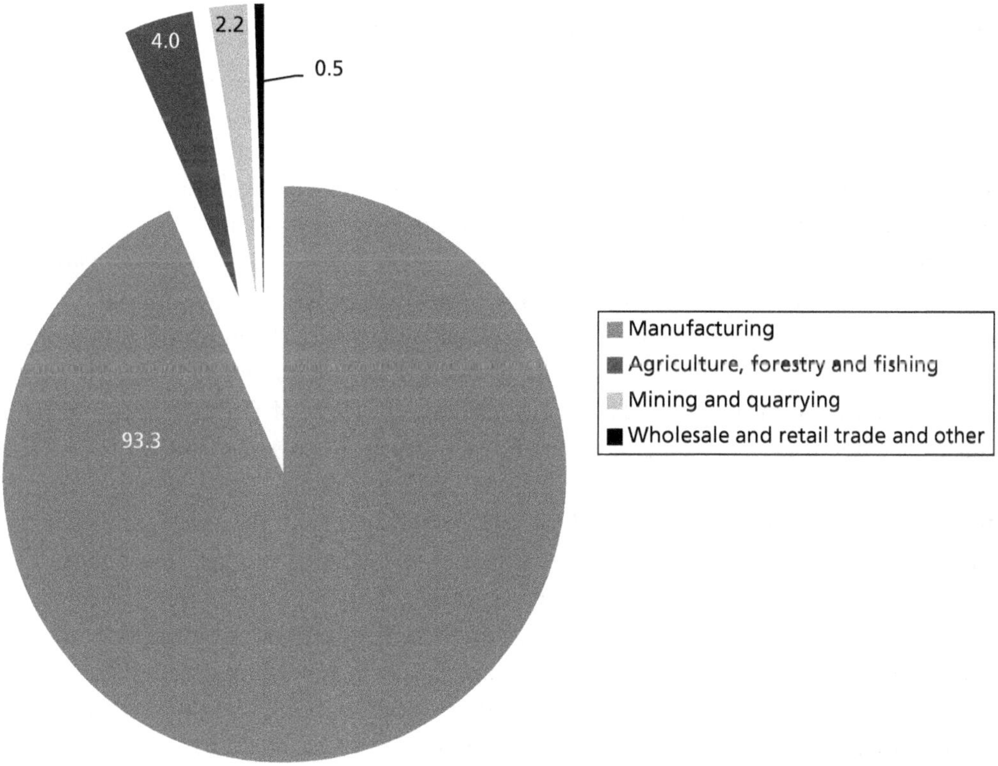

Figure 43.4a Breakdown of Turkish exports (%, 2014)

Source: TURKSTAT, Foreign Trade Statistics, November 2015. Available at www.aa.com.tr/en/economy/turkeys-exports-imports-rose-in-november-turkstat/716943, accessed 4 December 2019.

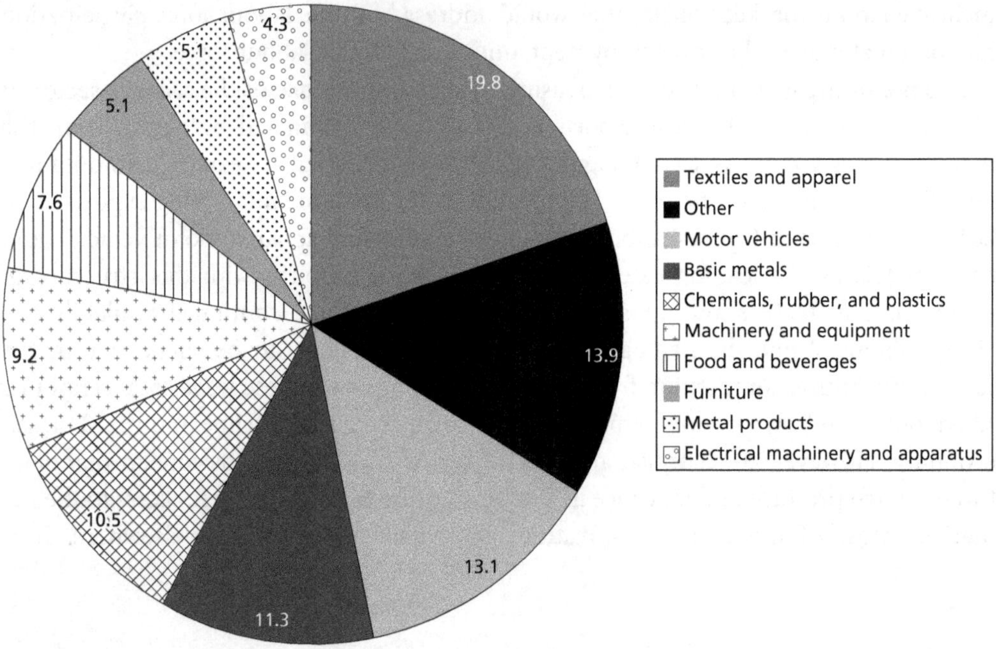

Figure 43.4b Breakdown of Turkish manufacturing exports (%, 2014)

Source: TURKSTAT, Foreign Trade Statistics, November 2015. Available at www.aa.com.tr/en/economy/turkeys-exports-imports-rose-in-november-turkstat/716943, accessed 4 December 2019.

somewhat ironic, therefore, that a country where the automotive sector plays such an important role has so far failed to generate a brand name of its own.

Öniş and Kutlay (2013) argue that in line with the relatively robust economic growth since the 2001 crisis, Ankara started implementing a more assertive foreign policy, especially with a view to style itself as a regional superpower. In line with this foreign policy, the Turkish economy also rapidly diversified its trade linkages and added new trading partners to the traditional ones. For instance, the share of Turkish exports to Asia more than doubled from 15 per cent to 35.3 per cent in the decade from 2002 to 2012 mainly owing to the rise of the Middle East as a trading partner. Over the same period, the share of Turkey's exports to the EU shrank from 56 per cent to 38 per cent in spite of the fact that the Customs Union Agreement with the EU was in effect throughout the entire period. According to the World Bank (2014), Turkey started exporting to some 137 countries, up from around ninety in 2000. Broadly speaking, the Turkish economy used to be over-reliant on the European business cycle in preceding decades. Thus, this was a welcome development to rebalance the export markets. However, this strong performance ran into headwinds with the turmoil in the Middle East and North Africa region brought about by the Arab Spring.

It must be said, however, that over the last decade and a half the Turkish economy not only increased the number of markets to which it exports, but also improved the quality of its export basket, moving away from labour-intensive goods towards capital-intensive ones with the relative importance of metals, machinery, and plastics increasing in the product mix. It must be remembered that at the beginning of the millennium, Turkish exports were still dominated by textile products. The period also saw an increase in Turkey's competitiveness in international markets as well as an increase in the quality of export products leading to a steady rise in the country's market share in global exports from 0.55 per cent to 0.82 per cent during the decade from 2002 to 2012.

Interestingly enough, the main driver of rising income in the Turkish economy over the last decade and a half has not been exports. World Bank (2014) points out that the ratio of exports to GDP rose from an average 20 per cent in 1998–2000 to only 23 per cent by 2009–11. By contrast, there was an 11-percentage point increase in India and 9-percentage point increase in China in the same period. While Turkey increased its product mix, it still appears to be specialized in mid-tech sectors, and has little or no comparative advantage in high-tech products with growth potential. In other words, Turkey needs to move upstream in global value chains, for which sizeable investment, especially greenfield FDI, as well as a total revamp of the skill set of its labour force will be required. Government has a role to play in creating a stable, secure, and investor-friendly business environment and in investing in technology, infrastructure, and education to unlock the innovative potential of the Turkish economy so that both SMEs and the service sector, which have both been lagging behind in their contributions to Turkey's exports and thereby its growth, could start to deliver.

In spite of its strong export performance, the Turkish economy is structurally dependent on imports. Figure 43.5 displays the Turkish trade balance which has always been in deficit during the period of analysis. Similarly, a proportion of imports covered by exports have been volatile, fluctuating between 50 per cent and 75 per cent since 2000, and currently stand at 60 per cent. Current account deficit has also been a major problem and a constant downside risk factor in the Turkish economy. From a comparative perspective, current account deficits seem to have been the rule rather than the exception for BRICS and MIKTA countries between 2005 and 2014, as shown in Table 43.3, with the notable exceptions of China, South Korea, and Russia. Indonesia started the period with a surplus and maintained it for much of the decade. Although it has recorded deficits for the last three years, its current account has on average been balanced. Brazil's current account was also in surplus in 2005, yet this pattern was reversed quickly and its current account was in deficit on average for the period examined. Turkey comes across as the outlier of this group: its current account has always been in deficit through the entire period of analysis. While Australia also seems to have struggled with controlling its current account since 2005, the magnitude of its problem seems to have shrunk in recent years. The exact opposite is true for Turkey. It has consistently been the current account deficit champion of the entire group since 2010, lending credibility to concerns of the sustainability of its current account.

Energy dependence is another structural weakness of the Turkish economy. Table 43.4 shows that the only country in the BRICS and MIKTA group whose energy imports as a percentage of its total energy use exceeds that of Turkey is South Korea. Interestingly

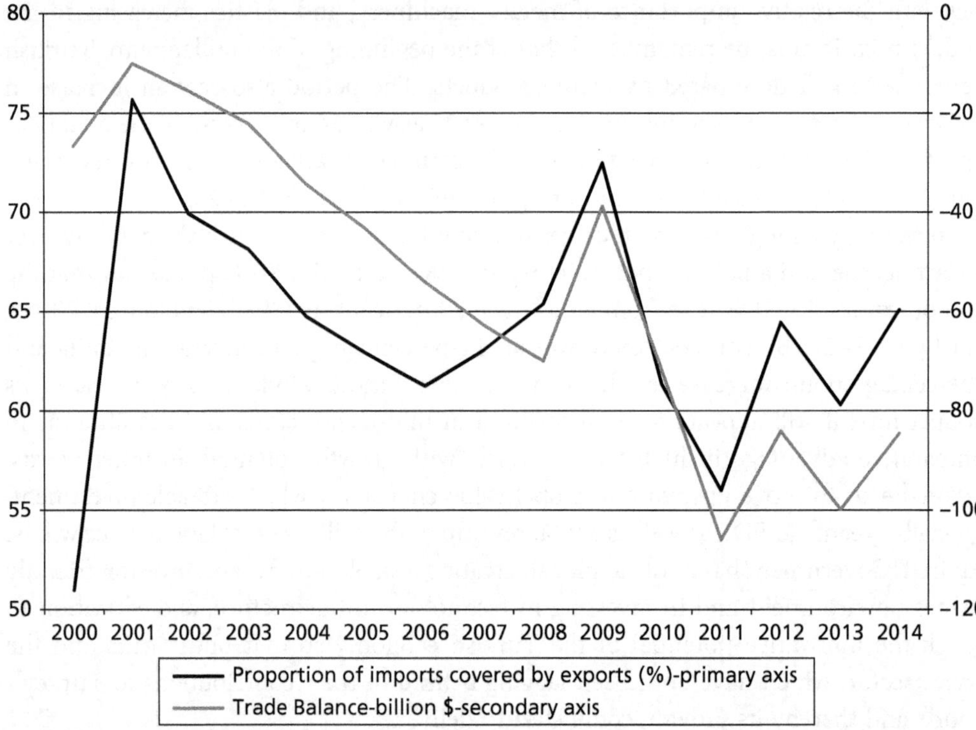

Figure 43.5 Turkish trade balance

Source: TURKSTAT, Foreign Trade Statistics, November 2015. Available at www.aa.com.tr/en/economy/turkeys-exports-imports-rose-in-november-turkstat/716943, accessed 4 December 2019.

Table 43.3 Current account balance (% of GDP)

	Country	2005	2006	2007	2008	2009	2010	2011	2012	2013	2014
BRICS	Brazil	1.6	1.2	0.1	-1.7	-1.5	-2.1	-2.0	-2.2	-3.4	-4.4
	Russia	11.0	9.3	5.6	6.3	4.1	4.4	5.1	3.5	1.7	3.1
	India	-1.2	-1.0	-0.7	-2.5	-1.9	-3.2	-3.4	-5.0	-2.6	-1.5
	China	5.8	8.5	10.0	9.2	4.8	3.9	1.8	2.5	1.9	n/a
	South Africa	-3.1	-4.4	-5.4	-5.7	-2.7	-1.5	-2.2	-5.0	-5.8	-5.5
MIKTA	Indonesia	0.1	3.0	2.4	0.0	2.0	0.7	0.2	-2.7	-3.2	-2.9
	Mexico	-1.0	-0.8	-1.4	-1.8	-0.9	-0.5	-1.1	-1.3	-2.4	-2.0
	Korea, Rep.	1.4	0.4	1.1	0.3	3.7	2.6	1.6	4.2	6.2	6.3
	Turkey	-4.4	-6.0	-5.8	-5.5	-2.0	-6.2	-9.7	-6.2	-7.9	-5.8
	Australia	-6.3	-6.1	-7.5	-4.9	-5.3	-3.9	-3.2	-4.4	-3.2	-2.8

Source: World Development Indicators (World Bank 2016).

Table 43.4 Renewable energy consumption (% of total final energy consumption)

		2000	2001	2002	2003	2004	2005	2006	2007	2008	2009	2010	2011	2012
BRICS	Brazil	42.8	41.5	43.0	45.3	45.4	46.3	46.9	47.4	47.3	49.1	47.0	45.5	43.6
	Russia	3.5	3.6	3.5	3.3	3.6	3.6	3.5	3.7	3.3	3.6	3.3	3.2	3.2
	India	52.4	52.6	51.4	51.7	50.5	49.4	48.0	46.9	45.0	41.8	40.6	39.9	39.0
	China	29.2	29.3	28.6	26.0	23.3	21.8	20.7	20.0	20.0	19.8	19.1	18.0	18.4
	S. Africa	18.5	19.1	18.4	17.6	17.3	16.9	17.0	15.9	16.3	16.6	16.9	17.1	16.9
MIKTA	Mexico	12.4	11.6	10.9	10.6	10.5	10.7	10.3	9.7	10.4	9.6	10.0	9.6	9.4
	Indonesia	45.2	43.9	44.3	42.7	41.4	41.4	40.0	40.0	40.2	39.1	37.8	38.5	37.1
	Korea, Rep.	0.7	0.7	0.7	0.8	0.8	0.9	0.9	1.0	1.0	1.2	1.3	1.3	1.6
	Turkey	17.3	18.1	17.5	16.3	16.8	15.3	14.3	12.5	12.4	13.4	14.4	12.8	12.8
	Australia	8.4	8.4	8.7	7.1	6.7	6.7	6.8	6.9	6.8	6.8	7.2	7.5	8.4

Source: World Development Indicators (World Bank 2016).

enough, while that percentage appears to have remained stable since 2000 in the Korean case, energy dependence seems to have become a more acute problem over time in the case of Turkey (66 per cent in 2000 vs 74 per cent in 2012).

As a way to break energy dependence, investment in sustainable energy is the path to the future. The Turkish economy is endowed with sufficient natural resources to venture into this field. While not among the leading economies in terms of the use of renewable energy in its overall energy mix, Turkey has, on average, maintained this ratio at around 15 per cent since 2000. While the latest available data show a tapering towards the end of the period, it is reasonable to expect the government to redouble its efforts to increase renewable energy use. This is not only a simple corollary of the international agreements, such as the UN's Agenda 2030 for Sustainable Development and the Paris Climate Change Deal to which Turkey was a signatory in 2015, but also strategic best practice for a country that imports most of its energy from a geopolitically turbulent region.

Remittances have played an important role as a stable and countercyclical source of capital flows for most emerging markets especially when other sources of external financing temporarily dried up during the 2008 financial crisis. According to a World Bank study analysing the behaviour of remittances vis-à-vis other capital flows during sudden stops, remittances to emerging markets increased by about 10 per cent whereas other capital inflows shrank by over 80 per cent at the height of the 2008 economic and financial crisis (World Bank 2015: chap. 4). As a result, remittances are likely to smooth out domestic consumption in the face of fluctuations in economic output and capital and FDI inflows.

While the argument concerning the countercyclical nature of remittances is broadly sensible for emerging markets, another phenomenon is worth noting regarding the Turkish experience. Scores of Turkish nationals emigrated to the then Western Germany during the 1960s and 1970s to respond to labour shortages while the German economy was going through an expansionary phase, referred to as *Wirtschaftswunder*, or economic miracle, owing to the rapid reconstruction and redevelopment phase of the economy in the post-Second World War period. An estimated 3 million Turks live in Germany today, with around 5 million Turkish emigrants in Europe. Their remittances have historically been an important and robust source of financial inflows to the Turkish economy especially during periods where other forms of capital inflows were more volatile, hence less predictable. The relative importance of remittances has since declined, however—a factor mostly attributed to the fact that Turkish emigrants, who initially expected to remain abroad temporarily, settled, often bringing their families with them, and sought to integrate into their host countries' economy, thereby gradually cutting their economic and financial ties to their home country.

Akkoyunlu (2012) provides a detailed analysis of Turkish remittances starting from the 1960s.[15] She argues that remittances have typically constituted an important part of

[15] The main tenet of her paper is to analyse the remittances from Turkish *Gastarbeiter* in Germany. When looking at this subset in isolation, she finds that the remittances have been more or less stable at around €1 billion per year, including through the 2008 financial crisis. Using an econometric model, she

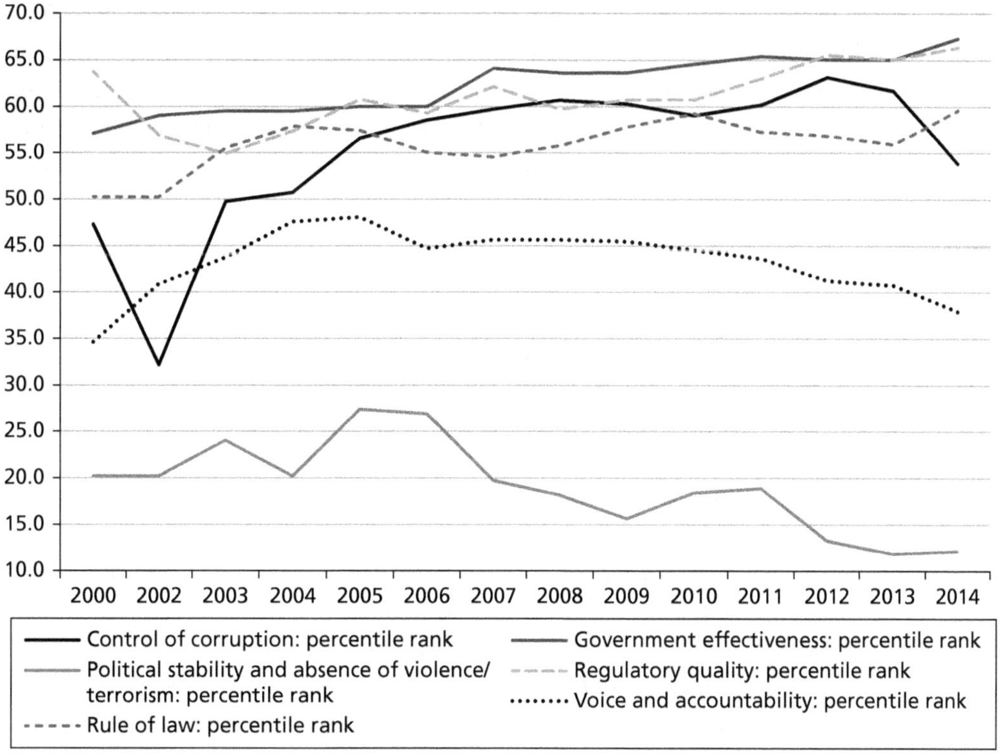

Figure 43.6 Remittances as % of GDP (selected countries)

Source: World Development Indicators (World Bank 2016).

the financial flows to Turkey and were not affected substantially by the economic crises of the 1970s and 1980s as well as that of 1994. Yet, this pattern appears to have changed with the 2001 crisis, prior to which remittances to Turkey had reached their peak. A more comprehensive analysis of remittance flows goes beyond the scope of this chapter. However, Figure 43.6 plots for a selected subset of BRICS+MIKTA economies the remittances as a percentage of GDP across time. As described above, the relative loss of importance of remittances is manifest in the Turkish case falling from 1.7 per cent of GDP at the beginning of the period of analysis down to 0.1 per cent at the end. By contrast, this ratio has increased from 2.7 per cent to 3.4 per cent in the case of India and from 1.1 per cent to 1.9 per cent in the case of Mexico for the same period.

Another non-trivial structural factor that is worth highlighting to ensure that our understanding of the Turkish economy is complete is the size of the informal economy. There is no hard and fast methodology to measure informality in an economy that would be immune to criticism. One of the most highly respected sources is Schneider et al.

forecasts that the ratio of Turkish workers' remittances to the GDP will remain roughly the same as the pre-crisis period.

(2010), which provides comparative figures for 162 economies over the period 1999 to 2007. Accordingly, the size of the informal economy in Turkey averaged at 31.3 per cent for the period, although it is worth mentioning that it came down slightly from 32.3 per cent in 1999 to 29.1 per cent in 2007. Schneider's estimates show that the size of the informal economy was structurally persistent in the Turkish case. Using an expenditure-based Pissarides-Weber approach, Davutyan (2008) presents a much lower estimate of around 21 per cent. Other estimates and methodologies vary widely; Öğünç and Yilmaz (2000) estimate the unofficial economy to be between 0 and 46 per cent of official GDP for 1960–98 using the money demand method. Ilgın (2002) finds the informal sector's size to fluctuate between 26 per cent and 184 per cent of official GDP based on tax collections data from the period 1985–2001. Another estimate, 5 per cent to 64 per cent of GDP comes from Us (2004), calculated using electricity usage data for the period 1997–2003. Besides academic sources, the Turkish Finance Ministry also presents an estimate of 30 per cent for 2004 based on an analysis of tax losses due to informality.

In short, the estimates presented above make it clear that the Turkish economy does in fact have a non-trivial informal economy. While this may provide an additional, yet largely unpredictable, buffer zone for adjustment during times of crisis, it is also associated with losses in tax revenues as well as difficulty in targeting socio-economic programmes from the perspective of the state. For instance, the key to understanding the true extent of the shortfalls in female labour participation rates and to designing policies to overcome the constraints lies with the ability of the state to design the right incentives for the actors operating in the shadow economy to regularize their activities and take part within the formal economy.

Institutional analysis

Measuring institutional characteristics of a country and aggregating a number of diverse governance indicators into a single number is a difficult and imprecise undertaking. Carrying out detailed case studies is a partial answer. Yet, in spite of all the caveats, case studies need to be complemented with data, at least to be able to carry out comparative analyses. Such data tend to come from either expert assessments or surveys. For instance, the World Bank publishes annual data on governance indicators, which are compiled as a *survey of surveys*.[16]

Table 43.5 presents these institutional factors for BRICS and MIKTA countries for 2014. Besides the score, the table also presents each country's percentile ranking indicator by indicator to help put these scores in perspective. First, we will take a look at these scores from a cross-sectional perspective. Second, we will also plot and discuss how Turkey ranked over time in each of these measures.

[16] Please see Kaufmann et al. (2010) for a discussion of the methodology.

Table 43.5 Governance Indicators—estimates and percentile ranks (BRICS and MIKTA, 2014)

	Brazil	Russia	India	China	S. Africa	Mexico	Indonesia	Korea, Rep	Turkey	Australia
Control of corruption	-0.4	-0.9	-0.5	-0.3	-0.1	-0.7	-0.6	0.5	-0.1	1.9
Percentile rank	*44.2*	*19.7*	*38.9*	*47.1*	*54.3*	*26.4*	*34.1*	*69.7*	*53.8*	*95.2*
Government effectiveness	-0.2	-0.1	-0.2	0.3	0.3	0.2	0.0	1.2	0.4	1.6
Percentile rank	*47.1*	*51.4*	*45.2*	*66.3*	*65.4*	*61.1*	*54.8*	*86.5*	*67.3*	*91.8*
Political stability and absence of violence/terrorism	0.0	-0.8	-1.0	-0.5	-0.1	-0.8	-0.4	0.2	-1.1	1.1
Percentile rank	*45.1*	*18.4*	*13.6*	*29.6*	*43.2*	*20.9*	*31.1*	*53.9*	*12.1*	*87.4*
Regulatory quality	-0.1	-0.4	-0.4	-0.3	0.3	0.4	-0.1	1.1	0.4	1.9
Percentile rank	*50.5*	*36.5*	*34.6*	*45.2*	*63.9*	*66.8*	*49.0*	*83.7*	*66.3*	*98.1*
Rule of law	-0.1	-0.7	-0.1	-0.3	0.2	-0.5	-0.3	1.0	0.0	1.9
Percentile rank	*55.3*	*26.4*	*54.3*	*42.8*	*63.9*	*38.0*	*41.8*	*80.8*	*59.6*	*96.2*
Voice and accountability	0.4	-1.0	0.4	-1.5	0.7	-0.1	0.1	0.7	-0.3	1.4
Percentile rank	*60.6*	*20.2*	*61.1*	*5.4*	*68.5*	*47.8*	*53.2*	*69.0*	*37.9*	*93.6*

Source: Worldwide Governance Indicators (World Bank 2019).

The World Bank's Worldwide Governance Indicators are scored on a range from -2.5 to 2.5 with positive scores being the desirable outcomes. Control of corruption appears to be a challenging institutional dimension, not only for Turkey, but also for most of the comparator countries. Of the ten countries examined, only Australia and South Korea have a positive score, the former ranking within the 95.2 percentile with a remarkable score of 1.9. While Turkey and South Africa score negatively (both at -0.1) for this indicator, they nevertheless rank well above the rest of their peers.[17] With -0.9, Russia scores the lowest in this category, being placed in the 19.7 percentile.

As for Government Effectiveness, Australia and South Korea once again turn out to be the champions—this time with a smaller distance among them. Turkey trails this group again with a score of 0.4 and a percentile rank of 67.3. Not far behind are China, South Africa, and Mexico—all scoring positively. Brazil, Russia, and India, on the other hand, fail to generate a positive score in this indicator.

Political Stability and Absence of Violence/Terrorism appears to be the soft belly of the Turkish economy. Indeed, with its score of -1.1, this is the indicator in which Turkey ranks the lowest among BRICS and MIKTA countries. With the exception of Australia and South Korea, all other comparator countries score negatively in this indicator. Australia and South Korea also lead the pack for Regulatory Quality. Mexico and Turkey, both scoring 0.4, follow this group with a small distance between them. South Africa also scores positively, with the rest of the group scoring below zero.

The Rule of Law indicator also follows the by now familiar pattern of Australia and South Korea ranking at the top, this time followed by South Africa and Turkey. With a score of an even zero, Turkey's percentile rank for this indicator is 59.6, which is superior to the rest of BRICS as well as Mexico and Indonesia. While the Voice and Accountability indicator follows the same pattern at the top, with its score of -0.3 and percentile rank of 37.9, Turkey lags far behind its peer group. In fact, only Russia and China rank lower than Turkey in this case, whereas Brazil, India, Indonesia, and South Africa all score positively.

In summary, the broad pattern among the BRICS/MIKTA group of countries as far as institutional aspects of their development is concerned is that Australia tops the charts in every indicator closely followed by South Korea. Turkey appears close to the top of the rest with the two exceptions noted above, namely Political Stability and Absence of Violence/Terrorism, and Voice and Accountability. Given that throughout the entire period of analysis, Turkey had a single party in power as well as regular elections, the former indicator appears to capture the rising incidence of terrorist attacks due to the tense geopolitical situation beyond Turkey's borders with Syria. As for the latter, it appears to be due to the tension between the incumbent government and the media.

[17] It is interesting to note in passing that there were several grand corruption allegations in 2015 in Turkey, which may not have been captured by the 2014 aggregate score. It is worth watching the future path of this indicator to see whether the perceptions thereof will impact on the aggregate data.

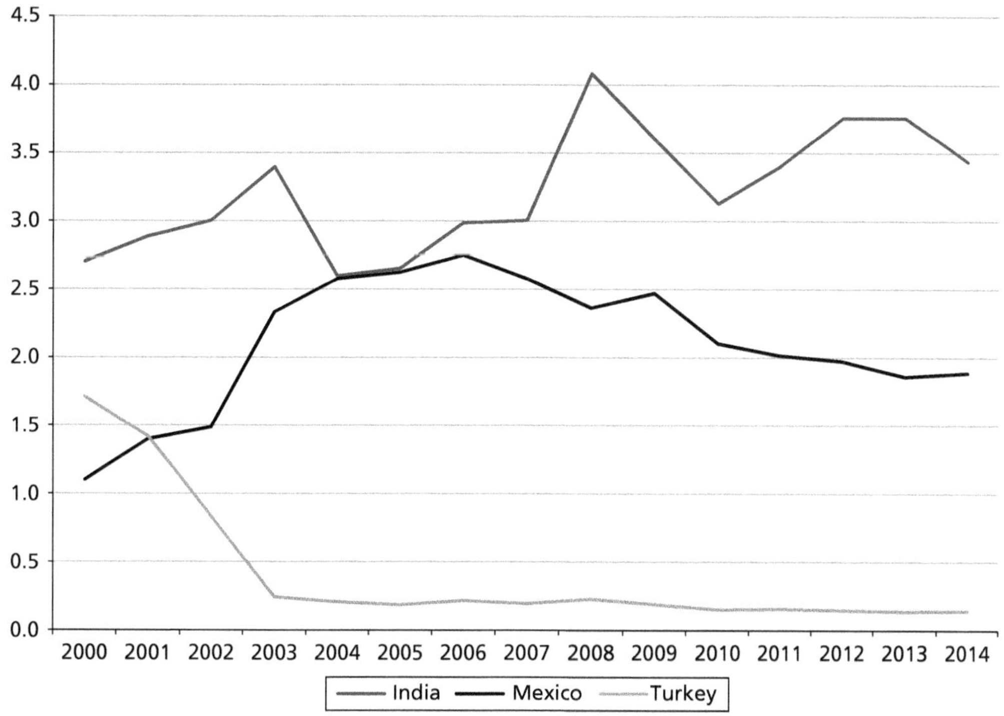

Figure 43.7 Turkey—governance trends 2000–14

Source: Worldwide Governance Indicators (World Bank 2019).

Figure 43.7 plots Turkey's percentile ranking in each of the aforementioned indicators over time in order to get a better insight into the path followed by Turkish institutions. A secular downward trend in the Political Stability and Absence of Violence/Terrorism indicator is evident. That said, Turkey ranked no higher than a percentile rank of 20 even at the beginning of the period of analysis. As for Voice and Accountability, a secular rise in Turkey's ranking in the early part of the decade of the 2000s seems to have been underpinned by the successes in Turkey–EU relations that led to the opening up of Turkey's EU accession process in December 2004. Progress seems to have plateaued around a 45 percentile rank for most of the rest of the decade before taking a nosedive from 2010 onwards, leaving Turkey only slightly better off compared to where it started.

From its nadir in 2002, Control of Corruption shows a persistent trend of improvement until 2012, leading to Turkey doubling its percentile rank over the decade. Yet, some of the gains seem to have been reversed in this case as well with the ranking falling from over a 60th percentile in 2012 to below 55th in 2014. In the three remaining aspects of governance, namely Regulatory Quality, Rule of Law, and Government Effectiveness, Turkey ends the period of analysis at a higher ranking than where it started, albeit by a small margin in some cases.

Table 43.6 Business environment—evidence from Enterprise Surveys

	Brazil (2009)	Russia (2012)	India (2014)	China (2012)	S. Africa (2007)	Mexico (2010)	Indonesia (2009)	S. Korea (2005)	Turkey (2013)
% of firms choosing the following as the biggest obstacle to their business:									
- access to finance	7.5	14.8	11.7	22.4	7.5	12.4	47.9	n/a	8.9
- business licensing and permits	0.6	4.5	2.1	0.2	2.9	9.0	3.3	n/a	2.0
- corruption	3.3	8.2	19.9	1.2	7.1	11.3	1.6	n/a	3.6
- courts	1.8	0.6	1.6	2.0	1.2	0.8	0.2	n/a	0.1
- customs and trade regulations	2.6	2.1	1.2	1.8	1.1	0.3	1.4	n/a	0.2
- labour regulations	7.4	0.5	4.9	1.9	5.6	3.3	1.3	n/a	1.5
- informal sector	12.4	7.0	12.2	19.6	4.9	16.0	13.7	n/a	20.2
- tax administration	6.7	1.9	3.7	4.2	0.1	1.4	0.4	n/a	1.9
- tax rates	33.5	36.1	12.9	15.1	1.6	14.3	1.3	n/a	37.4
Delays and red-tape: # of days it takes to . . .									
- clear direct exports through customs	16.4	5.6	5.8	7.6	4.5	7.0	2.3	7.2	6.2
- clear imports from customs	24.7	19.3	6.0	9.4	5.3	14.9	3.5	8.1	6.3
- obtain an operating license	79.7	56.3	17.8	27.5	36.2	54.0	21.1	n/a	39.7
Corruption, red-tape, and security of property rights:									
- Senior management time spent dealing with the requirements of government regulation (%)	14.2	14.7	1.9	0.9	6.0	13.6	1.6	0.1	19.0
- Bribery index (% of gift or informal payment requests during public transactions)	8.4	9.7	19.6	9.9	3.0	9.6	23.0	n/a	2.5
- Value of gift expected to secure a government contract (% of contract value)	0.4	2.5	0.2	0.2	1.7	4.5	1.8	0.2	0.6
- Percent of firms paying for security	72.6	65.4	52.3	66.0	76.4	42.8	23.5	n/a	58.2

Notes: Database: latest round of the survey available for each country. No surveys were conducted in Australia throughout the period of analysis.
Source: World Bank Enterprise Surveys. Available at https://databank.worldbank.org/reports.aspx?source=enterprise-surveys, accessed 4 December 2019.

Once again, Turkey seems to be at a crossroads from an institutional perspective. Institutions are hard to build and maintain. Furthermore, they change only gradually. Course correction is very difficult. For this reason alone, it is absolutely crucial that the trend should be in the right direction. Turkey has had significant gains over the period of analysis, yet the data show that some of these have been clawed back. Needless to say, good institutions do not grow overnight, and as economic history teaches us progress is not always linear (North 1990). What is beyond debate, however, is the fact that Turkey needs strong institutions and a system of checks and balances to ensure that its economic growth and development as well as its peace and security turn out to be sustainable. Hence, this particular crossroads seems to be a fundamental one that would underpin success in all other fields from the strictly macroeconomic to the social and environmental domains.

To give a better sense of the business environment in Turkey from the vantage point of businesses, Table 43.6 displays some evidence based on the World Bank's Enterprise Surveys. The benefit of presenting these surveys for comparative analytics is the fact that they have been implemented in all countries using the same methodology every three to four years. However, the downside of this is that not all the surveys are coming from the same year. Therefore, interpretation of Table 43.6 should be subject to that caveat. The Turkish survey was conducted in 2013 and is likely most comparable to the surveys conducted in Russia and China (2012) and India (2014) from a chronological perspective.

As for the Turkish enterprises, the main obstacles for their businesses in the order of their magnitude appear to be tax rates (37.4 per cent), the informal sector (20.2 per cent), and access to finance (8.9 per cent). The next biggest obstacle, that of corruption, gets mentioned as the main obstacle by only 3.6 per cent of the survey respondents. Tax rates and the informal sector both appear to be more serious obstacles in the case of Turkey than in any other comparators, whereas in access to finance and corruption obstacles Turkey seems to be doing better than the average. The percentage of firms identifying tax rates as the main obstacle to business is fairly similar in Brazil, Russia, and Turkey at 33.5 per cent, 36.1 per cent, and 37.4 per cent respectively. Access to finance, on the other hand, appears to be a bigger obstacle in Russia (14.8 per cent), India (11.7 per cent), China (22.4 per cent), Mexico (12.4 per cent), and Indonesia (47.9 per cent). Corruption also features as a main obstacle at a higher frequency in India (19.9 per cent), Mexico (11.3 per cent), and Russia (8.2 per cent).

Experience of import and export delays at customs appears not to be a major problem in the case of Turkey with the average number of days to clear customs below the average of the comparator countries. However, there is room for improvement in terms of cutting the red tape as evidenced by the fact that it took on the average 39.7 days to obtain an operating licence in Turkey according to the survey carried out in 2013. While this is just below average for the entire comparator group, it is worth pointing out that the waiting period was much shorter in India (17.8 days) and Indonesia (21.1 days) in particular. Furthermore, China and South Africa both seem to be doing better than Turkey in this measure.

The lowest panel of the table displays the statistics for corruption, red tape, and security of property rights. Turkish business executives are topping the list in terms of time spent dealing with the requirements of government regulations, spending close to 20 per cent of their time dealing with the red tape. This ratio is just short of 15 per cent in Russia and Brazil and of 14 per cent in Mexico. The bribery index relates to the frequency of bribes requested and the next row displays the value of these as a percentage of the value of the contract. With an incidence rate of only 2.5 per cent, Turkish businesses do not view requests for or size of bribes in public transactions as a major problem. Among the comparators, Indonesia tops the list in terms of frequency and value of bribes requested. In terms of the former, India, China, Russia, Mexico, and Brazil follow suit with South Africa falling in the same camp as Turkey. However, the percentage of firms paying for security is quite high all across the board. As for this indicator, at 58.2 per cent, Turkish firms find themselves just above the average of the comparator group. More than 70 per cent of firms in the South African and Brazilian samples confirm making security payments followed by China and Russia with both above 65 per cent and by India over 50 per cent. It is likely to see the results here intertwined with the relatively low incidence of corruption. It may well be that the incidence of corruption ceases to be a major problem owing to these security payments—a topic that is well worth researching further.

Turkey and the EU: a never-ending saga—the anchor that wasn't meant to be

Turkey had embarked on its long quest to be part of the Western club long before any of the countries in the recent waves of EU expansions were even remotely on that path. In fact, Turkey signed its Association Agreement with the European Economic Community (EEC)—the predecessor of the EUas of 1963. In 1980, it was asked to apply for full membership at the same time as Greece (Ahmad 2003). A series of myopic and feckless decisions by the then Prime Minister Süleyman Demirel, trying unsuccessfully to appease the conservative elements within his electorate, led Turkey to suspend the application, thus decoupling from the favourable arrangement with Greece for fast-tracking full membership. The rest is history: the following year, Greece joined the EEC and Turkey missed the boat—perhaps once and for all.

Turkey's later attempts failed to make up for this error and the seeming absence of a clear strategy and a vision to guide these efforts to completion also resulted in Turkey giving away its most important bargaining chip, i.e. duty-free access to its markets for the EU in 1996 without a clear commitment by the EU accompanied by a roadmap for Turkey's accession to full membership.

There has never been another country that waited so long for EU membership and lost its place in the queue to so many other countries, many of which were still in the process of transition to market economies and democracy. This was yet another example of Turkey being at the crossroads, yet failing to take control of its own destiny.

It took roughly another two decades until Turkey–EU relations gained momentum once more. The announcement of Turkey's candidacy to the EU came officially during the Helsinki Summit of December 1999, marking the official start of the latest stage of Turkey's quest to join the EU.

The role of external anchors in providing for reform rationale and momentum is well understood. In the case of Turkey's quest to join the EU, there has indeed been a golden age of reforms towards democratization and human rights during the first half of the first decade of the 2000s, which led to the official launch of the accession process in December 2004, yet lost momentum shortly thereafter. Initially, polls suggested a strong support for Turkey's EU accession among the public domestically. Yet, this was never complemented by an equally strong commitment by European public opinion, with 59 per cent of EU27 citizens against and 28 per cent for Turkey's accession.[18] Especially, the right-wing conservative governments in France and Germany did everything within their power to slow down the accession process short of officially calling it off by freezing chapters in progress or blocking the opening of new chapters. Some of the reasons for this sudden loss of momentum might therefore have to do with the perception within Turkey that the EU applied double standards to applicants, providing fast-track accession to Eastern European countries at a time when their democracies and market economies were still in transition, thereby allowing them to skip the queue ahead of Turkey in spite of the fact that the country had been seeking to join the EU for decades. Whatever the merits of this argument, these perceptions generated a deep-seated suspicion among the Turkish public that they would not be allowed to access the EU no matter what and the end result was reform fatigue and a disbelief in the possibility of the objective.[19]

Öniş (2013) provides further *ex-post factum* analysis as to why the EU lost its soft power on Turkey so dramatically over such a short period of time. Having gone through various rounds of structural adjustment programmes under IMF tutelage, the Turkish economy was in reasonably good shape entering the 2008 economic and financial crisis thanks in no small part to the restructuring of its own financial sector in the aftermath of the 2001 financial crisis. As a result, it was seen to have weathered the crisis better than most EU countries. The persistence of the euro area crisis further raised questions as to the value of EU membership since the core of the EU was seen to impose tough austerity packages on its periphery often penalizing the leaders of sovereign EU member

[18] European Commission (2006a), *Eurobarometer 66: Public Opinion in the European Union* and European Commission (2006b), *Special Eurobarometer: Attitudes towards European Union Enlargement.*

[19] In fact, EU leaders have also contributed to this problem by refusing to provide a firm deadline for Turkey's accession process to the Union—a date by which the country would either be in or out—thereby calling the accession process an open-ended one. Others, such as France and Austria, indicated that even if Turkey fulfils all of prerequisites for accession, such as the Maastricht criteria, they would still put the Turkish membership to the EU to a referendum, which would seemingly defeat the purpose of the entire accession process.

countries, who were acting under fresh mandates from their electorates to reject austerity measures, e.g. in the case of Greece. While on the one hand Turkey was questioning the fairness of this intra-EU process and growing its economic ties with the Middle East and North Africa thus breaking its longstanding dependence on trade with European economies, on the other hand the EU was in fire-fighting mode trying to stop its own economic crisis in its tracks, which left very little enthusiasm or policy space for further enlargement. Uğur (2010) looks at the same issue from the perspective of commitment credibility. Using a political economy model, the author shows that the open-ended accession negotiations lead to suboptimal equilibria whereby candidate countries fail to achieve the desired convergence for accession due to lack of sufficient reforms. This model explains the deterioration in Turkey–EU relations from a theoretical perspective owing to the fact that it is not possible to commit credibly to a prospect that is left open ended and recommends stronger commitments to ensure shocks and deadlocks to the process are overcome.

Since then, the pendulum has been swinging both ways. Losing patience with the stalemate with the EU in early 2013, Turkey's then Prime Minister Recep Tayyip Erdoğan expressed his wish to join the Shanghai Cooperation Council, whereas Jean-Claude Juncker, EU President since November 2014, made it clear that no further enlargement would take place over the next five years, indicating separately that Turkey was far away from EU membership as the country had turned its back on the EU democratic values and was not ready for membership.[20] More recently, geopolitics once again played a key role in revitalizing what once seemed to be a frozen relationship. In response to the humanitarian crisis in Syria and the resulting inflows of mass refugees and migrants to Turkey and Europe, a joint EU–Turkey Action Plan on Migration Management was adopted in November 2015. The plan foresees financial commitments by the EU towards Turkey, which at the time was hosting some 2 million Syrian refugees within its borders as well as the opening of a new chapter in accession negotiations, namely Chapter 17 (economic and monetary policies), agreements on a roadmap for visa liberalization between Turkey and the EU as well as structured and more frequent high-level dialogue, including twice yearly summits, to address issues of common concern.[21]

What the future will bring is uncertain and the road ahead will be bumpy. However, there is reason for cautious optimism that the tide might be turning once again as recent opinion polls in Turkey indicate that the percentage of those that believe that Turkey's EU membership would be good for the country increased from 40 per cent in 2013 to 53 per cent in 2014.[22]

[20] Juncker (2014), My Foreign Policy Objectives. Available at http://juncker.epp.eu/sites/default/files/attachments/nodes/en_03_fp.pdf (accessed 10 October 2018).

[21] European Commission 2015, Statement: Meeting of heads of state or government with Turkey - EU-Turkey statement, Brussels, 29 November 2015. Available at http://europa.eu/rapid/press-release_STATEMENT-15-6194_en.htm (accessed 10 October 2018).

[22] Transatlantic Trends, Key Findings Report 2013 and 2014. Available at http://trends.gmfus.org/transatlantic-trends/key-findings/6/, accessed 30 June 2019.

Conclusion

This chapter addresses some of the most salient macroeconomic challenges and opportunities facing Turkey in its quest to break the middle-income trap and become one of the top ten economies in the world by 2023. To put these opportunities and challenges in perspective, the chapter has explained the historical backdrop to illuminate some of the seemingly paradoxical choices and pathways Turkey has been following from the 1960s to date. Furthermore, a political economy framework is applied to identify institutional successes and failures of the Turkish economy with a view to highlight areas for further research.

Broadly speaking, the Turkish economy has weathered the 2008 economic and financial crisis reasonably well so far. Yet, weaknesses remain. Its over-reliance on current account deficits and external financing is a cause for concern. There are also other downside risks due to the slowdown of the Chinese economy and the fall in commodity prices, which once again fundamentally change the backdrop against which the Turkish economy needs to perform. Furthermore, the geopolitical situation beyond Turkey's borders also presents significant challenges ahead, and Turkey's foreign policy, in spite of all the initial goodwill, has fallen short of bringing about zero problems with neighbours.

In a comprehensive survey of the incumbent government's period in office, Öniş (2013) makes a broad observation that Turkey has mastered the procedural aspects of democracy, such as regular, free, and fair elections. Yet, this is only the beginning. The true challenge lies in transforming this procedural democracy into a substantive one that underpins a truly pluralistic political order similar to those that prevail in most advanced economies—the level to which the political elite in Turkey aspire to bring the country by 2023. There is still room for improvement here as captured by the institutional indicators that were presented in this chapter. Continuing with the economic, socio-political, and environmental reforms to harmonize with the EU will not only prevent a train-wreck in negotiations for full accession, but will also ensure that gains from Turkey's relatively strong growth performance throughout the period of analysis will become more sustainable and shared across a larger group of stakeholders with more equity.

An optimistic medium- to long-term scenario is entirely possible with the right domestic policy mix and a supportive external environment. While mutual suspicions still persist, the EU anchor still remains relevant for Turkey's path ahead. Its geopolitical and strategic importance at the crossroads between East and West will almost certainly ensure that Turkey will be at or close to the centre stage of the world economy and politics for the foreseeable future. The question is what Turkey will make of its opportunities and how it will overcome the challenges ahead. The overall conclusion of this chapter is that Turkey is once again at a crossroads—this time the choices it will make will have much broader ramifications across a sizeable geography ranging from Europe, the Middle East, and North Africa to Central Asia. From a broad historical perspective, every time it has found itself at a crossroads, Turkey has so far risen to the occasion and plotted its course quite sensibly. Therefore, there is plenty of reason for cautious optimism that it will continue to do so in the future.

ACKNOWLEDGEMENTS

The views and opinions expressed in this chapter are those of the author and do not in any way reflect the official policy or position of any institutions with which he has ever been affiliated.

REFERENCES

Ahmad, F. (2003). *Turkey: The Quest for Identity*. Oxford: Oneworld.

Akkoyunlu, Ş. (2012). 'Forecasting Turkish workers' remittances from Germany during the financial crisis', in I. Sirkeci, J.H. Cohen, and D. Ratha (eds) *Migration and Remittances during the Global Financial Crisis and beyond*. Washington, DC: IBRD, 273–88.

Altuğ, S., Filiztekin, A., and Pamuk, Ş. (2008). 'Sources of long-term economic growth for Turkey, 1880–2005', *European Review of Economic History* 12/3: 393–430.

Davutyan, N. (2008). 'Estimating the size of Turkey's informal sector: an expenditure-based approach', *Journal of Economic Policy Reform* 11/4: 261–71.

Derviş, K. (2005). 'Returning from the brink: Turkey's efforts at systemic change and structural reform', in T. Besley and R. Zagha (eds) *Development Challenges in the 1990s: Leading Policymakers Speak from Experience*. New York: Oxford University Press, 83–102.

Economist Intelligence Unit Global Forecasting Service (2010). 'Beyond the BRICs', EIU, 26 July. Available at http://gfs.eiu.com/Article.aspx?articleType=wif&articleId=242, accessed 10 October 2018.

European Commission (2006a). *Eurobarometer 66: Public Opinion in the European Union*. Brussels: European Commission.

European Commission (2006b). *Special Eurobarometer: Attitudes towards European Union Enlargement*. Brussels: European Commission.

European Commission (2015). Statement—'Meeting of heads of state or government with Turkey'. EU–Turkey statement, Brussels, 29 November. Available at http://europa.eu/rapid/press-release_STATEMENT-15-6194_en.htm, accessed 10 October 2018.

Fraser, I. (2011). 'Fidelity is confident its MINTs won't suck', *FinancePractitioner.com*, 10 May. Available at www.financepractitioner.com/blogs/ian-fraser/2011/05/10/fidelity-is-confident-its-mints-wont-suck-emerging-economies, accessed 30 June 2019.

Freedom House (2016). *Freedom in the World 2016: Anxious Dictators, Wavering Democracies: Global Freedom Under Pressure*. New York and Washington, DC: Freedom House.

Ilgın, Y. (2002). 'Kayıt Dışı Ekonomiyi Tahmin Yöntemleri ve Türkiye'de Durum' [Methods of estimating the size of the informal economy and the case of Turkey]. DPT Planlama Dergisi, Özel Sayı (in Turkish).

Juncker, J.C. (2014). 'My foreign policy objectives'. Available at http://juncker.epp.eu/sites/default/files/attachments/nodes/en_03_fp.pdf, accessed 10 October 2018.

Kaufmann, D., Kraay, A., and Mastruzzi, M. (2010). 'The worldwide governance indicators: methodology and analytical issues'. World Bank Policy Research Working Paper No. 5430. Washington, DC: IBRD.

Kirişçi, K. (2009). 'The transformation of Turkish foreign policy: the rise of the trading state', *New Perspectives on Turkey* 40: 29–57.

North, D.C. (1990). *Institutions, Institutional Change and Economic Performance.* Cambridge: Cambridge University Press.

Öğünç, F. and Yılmaz, G. (2000). 'Estimating the underground economy in Turkey'. Discussion paper. Ankara: Central Bank of the Republic of Turkey, Research Department.

O'Neill, J. (2001). 'Building better global economic BRICs'. Global Economics Paper, No. 66. New York: Goldman Sachs.

Öniş, Z. (2009). 'Beyond the 2001 financial crisis: the political economy of the new phase of neoliberal restructuring in Turkey', *Review of International Political Economy* 16/2: 409–32.

Öniş, Z. (2013). 'Sharing power: Turkey's democratization challenge in the age of the AKP hegemony', *Insight Turkey* 15/2: 103–22.

Öniş, Z. and Kutlay, M. (2013). 'Rising powers in a changing global order: the political economy of Turkey in the age of BRICS', *Third World Quarterly* 34/8: 1409–26.

Schneider, F., Buehn, A., and Montenegro, C.E. (2010). 'Shadow economies all over the world: new estimates for 162 countries from 1999 to 2007'. World Bank Policy Research Working Paper No. 5356. Washington, DC: IBRD.

Sheffler, Karl (1915 [1910]). *Berlin: ein Stadtschiksal* [Berlin – destiny of a city]. Frankfurt: Suhrkamp Verlag AG.

Transatlantic Trends (2013–14). Key Findings Report 2013 and 2014. Available at http://trends.gmfus.org/transatlantic-trends/key-findings/6/, accessed 30 June 2019.

Uğur, M. (2010). 'Open-ended membership prospect and commitment credibility: explaining the deadlock in EU–Turkey accession negotiations', *Journal of Common Market Studies* 48/4: 967–91.

Us, V. (2004). *Kayitdisi Ekonomi Tahmini Yöntem Önerisi: Turkiye Örneği, Turkiye Ekonomi Kurumu* [A proposal on estimating the size of an informal economy: the case of Turkey], 2004/17 (in Turkish). Ankara: Turkiye Ekonomi Kurumu.

World Bank (2014). *Country Economic Memorandum: Trading up to High Income.* Report No. 82307-TR. Washington, DC: IBRD.

World Bank (2015). *Global Economic Prospects: Having Fiscal Space and Using it.* Washington, DC: IBRD.

World Bank (2016). *World Development Indicators.* Washington, DC: World Bank. Available at https://datacatalog.worldbank.org/dataset/world-development-indicators, accessed 30 May 2019.

World Bank (2019). *Worldwide Governance Indicators (WGI).* Washington, DC: World Bank. Available at https://info.worldbank.org/governance/wgi/#home, accessed 4 December 2019.

Zürcher, E.J. (2004). *Turkey: A Modern History.* London: I.B. Tauris.

AUTHOR INDEX

Note: Tables are indicated by an italic '*t*' following the page number.

INDEX

Note: Tables and figures are indicated by an italic '*t*' and '*f*', respectively, following the page number.